COUNTRY LIVING

500
QUICK & EASY
DECORATING
PROJECTS & IDEAS

COUNTRY LIVING

500 QUICK & EASY DECORATING PROJECTS & IDEAS

From the Editors of COUNTRY LIVING Magazine

Text by Dominique DeVito

Hearst Books
A Division of Sterling Publishing Co., Inc.
New York

Library of Congress Cataloging-in-Publication Data
DeVito, Dominique C.
Country living: 500 sensational quick and easy decorating projects & ideas / Dominique C. DeVito.
p. cm.
Includes index.
ISBN-13: 978-1-58816-606-7
ISBN-10: 1-58816-606-6
1. Decoration and ornament, Rustic--Handbooks, manuals, etc. 2. Interior decoration--Handbooks, manuals, etc.
I. Country living (New York, N.Y.) II. Title. III. Title: 500 sensational quick and easy decorating projects & ideas.
NK1994.R87.D48 2007
747--dc22
2006027588

10 9 8 7 6 5 4 3 2 1

Published by Hearst Books
A Division of Sterling Publishing Co., Inc.
387 Park Avenue South, New York, NY 10016

Cover and interior design by 3+Co. (www.threeandco.com)
Jacket photographs: *front cover*, Jonn Coolidge; *spine*, Keith Scott Morton; *back cover right*, David Prince; *back cover left*, Tim Street-Porter

Country Living and Hearst Books are trademarks
of Hearst Communications, Inc.

www.countryliving.com

Distributed in Canada by Sterling Publishing
c/o Canadian Manda Group, 165 Dufferin Street
Toronto, Ontario, Canada M6K 3H6

Distributed in Australia by Capricorn Link (Australia) Pty. Ltd.
P.O. Box 704, Windsor, NSW 2756 Australia

Manufactured in China

ISBN 13: 978-1-58816-680-7
ISBN 10: 1-58816-680-5

Table of Contents

Introduction

Empty rooms are as intimidating to the would-be decorator as blank pages are to the would-be writer. Filling them in ways that give meaning can seem like an endless project—or it can become a means to discover things about yourself, your family, your lifestyle, and the things you love. Gleaned from the pages of *Country Living*, the ideas in this book are designed to make the adventure—the process—of decorating less daunting and more playful and inspiring. There are tips about color choices; how to work with textures, patterns, and styles when putting rooms together; organizing collectibles; turning found objects into functional or fanciful accessories; and much, much more. With 500 tips organized by rooms, you can beautify and personalize any area of your house.

—Nancy Mernit Soriano
Editor in Chief, *Country Living*

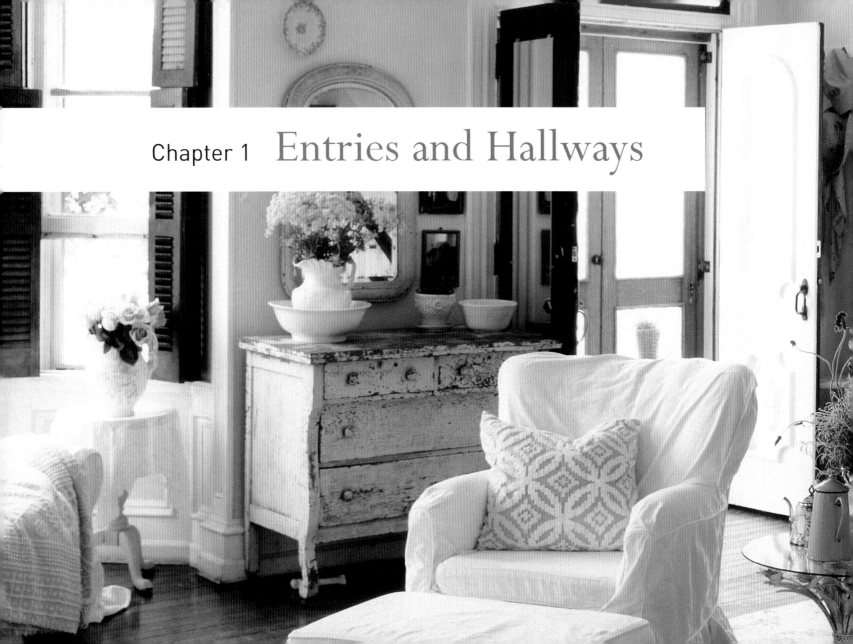

Chapter 1 Entries and Hallways

1

The calming influence of the color green is intensified in a collection of old vases and bottles that are artfully arranged on a simple shelf.

_

Entryways that serve as mudrooms need to be durable as well as functional. Using horseshoes as hooks adds a rustic touch to a space that's designed to be well used.

3

Bring the attention from room to room by repeating a trim color as a main color in a nearby room, or successively changing the tint of paints in adjacent spaces. A color-coordinated primary object like this desk adds to the perspective.

4
—

Decorative trim work adds
ornamentation that enhances
the character of a home. Here,
arches and columns create a
dramatic entryway.

5

Beat the winter blahs by nurturing an amaryllis. The dramatic flower, available in many colors, takes eight to twelve weeks to bloom, making it the perfect fall-to-winter transitional plant.

6

Transportable organization meets fun and fashion when colorful totes like these rattan bags are labeled and hung on a wall covered with gingham wallpaper.

7

Old clocks that no longer tell
the time make a graphic wall
arrangement when hung together.
Add charm by placing a rustic
table—with its original finish and
topped with a tin vase of daisies—
under the arrangement.

8

A contrasting trim like the pale blue that's around the front door here is all that's needed to help pop your curb appeal.

9

When you know pets are going to be climbing on the furniture, incorporate pet-friendly fabrics that are durable and machine washable.

10

Fresh hydrangeas in a white ceramic vase are a summertime must and add color and personality to a hallway featuring a dark, dramatic staircase with contrasting dark and white wood.

11

A basic bench can be accessorized in all kinds of ways, the most practical of which is with accent cushions and the seat-cushion fabric itself. Open compartments below offer storage for shoes, blankets, and whatever else can fit.

12

Custom-built cubbies with space for baskets and peg rails are perfect for storing umbrellas, bags, winter wear, and other items in mudrooms and entryways.

13

A gold-framed mirror echoes the honey-toned maple floors and complements the warm coloring of the "slip-proof" wool carpeting. The mirror enlarges the space and fills the empty wall.

14

Why buy new furniture when the next yard sale may land you a one-of-a-kind something that can make all the difference in a special spot? This cabinet's multiple panes make finding extra linens easy.

15

Customize fabric bouquets to complement your decor using remnants left over from crafting projects. A single contrasting color adds drama.

16

A seven-foot-long bench is the centerpiece of this entryway without taking up too much space. Instead of adding pillows, put flowers in old trophies used as vases on one end of the bench for a decorative touch.

17

The unique collection of wall hangings above the bench reflects the family's love of history and nature. The eclecticism of the selections is balanced by the color theme and by the stenciled backdrop.

18

A strong but soothing color in an entryway sets the mood for the whole house. Here, architectural details are painted white to create a sophisticated and welcoming foyer.

19

Quilts can be welcoming works of art when hung on large walls. Too pretty to stash away, they can also find their way onto balustrades, where they are especially complementary to wide-planked wood floors.

20

An eclectic collection of glass bottles can be displayed in rows according to size (or randomly) along window sills or stairway ledges.

21

For dog lovers, there's nothing like cast-iron doorstops resembling their favorite breeds to add whimsy and personality to a room.

22

Reflecting the light from the double front doors is the job of the multiple mirrors positioned along the stairwell.

23

A rich, saturated color makes an excellent foil to cherry-stained and white-painted wood. Hang a throw on the end of a banister for easy access on chilly evenings.

24

Throw something modern into the mix to shake things up. A white star light fixture does the job here, while unifying the passageway with the next room.

25

A rustic bench provides a spot for further organizing miscellaneous items that are left in entryways, such as antique quilts and an oversized picnic basket.

26

The gentle curves of this small wooden table and chair soften the rigid corner of the entryway where they have been placed.

27

A large bouquet of fresh and fragrant flowers in an entryway guarantees a cheerful and memorable greeting for everyone who enters the house.

28

Simplicity and style distinguish this cheery entrance. The green-themed bouquets pick up on the wall color, and a convenient stepping stool can be stored away under the decorative table.

29

Painting a wall a color that's reminiscent of new spring growth, showy summer shades, the luster of fall green apples, and the promise of greenery brings the outdoors in all year long.

30

Resist updating the imperfections of an old home. This well-used stair banister is original to the house and is part of its charm.

31

Express your creative color
sense in an entry- or hallway
with a chair painted a luscious
shade of pink and finished
with an espresso-colored seat.

32

Going bold with color works when the wood trim throughout the house is painted a high-gloss white, as it helps the colors pop. The intensity of the colors should be equal, and their hues should be incorporated from room to room.

33

The earth tones and white trim help pull the mango color from one room to the next, and draw the eye through this series of adjoining rooms.

34

An old milk jug painted a vibrant color by the front door in a foyer serves as a distinctive and practical repository for walking canes or umbrellas.

35

A floor that is functional yet fun is achieved in a small entryway by pairing checkerboard-patterned tiles and a bold throw rug.

36

A mirror in an entryway helps guests transition from outside to inside and can instantly make a small space seem larger.

37

If your passions are horses and riding, you can turn a collection of helmets, boots, and gloves into a display by arranging them with equine-themed art.

38

Red steps located right inside the front door pop against walls and trim painted stark white, and offer a warm welcome and a colorful passageway.

39

Create a bold, dramatic entryway with an eclectic mix of flea market and antique store finds, such as this character-filled cabinet and tarnished mirror.

40

Show off your collection of crafts where you think they will look best. These horses made of fabric scraps are right at home on a tweed-covered settee.

41

If you have the space—and the desire—you may want to consider having a mural painted in part of your house.

42

The large painted diamond pattern on the floor is reminiscent of a style popular in the mid-1800s and adds charm to this upstairs hallway.

Chapter 2   Kitchens

43

Foster a country look in the
kitchen with simple elements
like distinctive woodwork
(here, unpainted pine) and
marble counters.

44

Recessed shelving is a handy spot for displaying useful and visually appealing collectibles like creamers, pitchers, and dry-goods containers.

45

Get organized and add color and texture to the kitchen by storing cookware in baskets, like these wicker ones that complement the neutral earth tones around them.

46

Awaken an overlooked wall with a series of framed prints hung one over another on the thin wall space between two windows.

47

When you love something, let
it out. If red is your color, find
places for it, in all its variations,
in the rooms you like to spend the
most time in, like the kitchen.

48

Position colors and patterns so that your eyes travel around them. Here, the patterns on the bowls are slightly mirrored in the clock, and a small plate with similar colors keeps the composition from being static.

49

Clean lines, contrasting colors, and uncluttered surfaces give this kitchen a refreshing, inviting, and easy-to-live-in feel.

50

If you're looking to spruce up your kitchen, a couple of quick fixes that won't break the bank are finding new hardware for the cabinets and installing a new faucet for the sink.

51

Blue-and-white transferware arranged symmetrically in the corner of a breakfast nook stands out against cream-colored walls and picks up the blue in the fabric used on the seat covers and bench.

52

Pink appliances are the showpieces in this kitchen, where simple white cabinetry and a checkered linoleum floor offset the rosy hues and create a retro, cheery atmosphere.

53

Working with a common color theme, arrange plates of different sizes and patterns in descending order by size for a pretty focal point over a small table in the dining area of a kitchen.

54

White, vertically oriented tiles extending all the way up to a stainless steel range hood will bring a feeling of greater height to a kitchen.

55

One way to vary the walls is to use colored grout with white tiles. In this cozy country kitchen, a chocolate-colored grout creates a gingham effect.

56

Place a long narrow table in a kitchen with no defined eating nook. It puts diners in the middle of things and can serve as extra prep space in a pinch.

57

To house a large collection of cookbooks and keep them handy in the kitchen, construct custom shelves on either side of and above the refrigerator.

58

An antique dish rack makes a unique display piece while keeping pieces handy for use. Shelves below offer space for bowls and an eclectic collection of teapots and creamers.

59

A recessed area of the kitchen is painted a slightly warmer tone for visual interest and to further differentiate it from the rest of the room.

60

A kitchen chandelier becomes whimsical—and even practical— by hanging mismatched porcelain teacups from its branches.

61

Instead of an island, place a moveable, low-to-the-ground table in the middle of a kitchen to create a kid-friendly eating area.

62

A large armoire with shelves, hooks, and vertical compartments can be stocked with everything from pots and pans to cookbooks, trays, and utensils.

63

Cupboards are excellent showcases for kitchenware, plus arrangements of photographs and personal treasures. Leave the doors open for easy access and a decorative display.

64

Make the most of small spaces by using furniture that folds away. These chairs are transformed into art when put on display, especially when painted a bright color.

65

A simple wooden table can be painted a neutral color, such as white, and embellished with a stripe or a stenciled pattern around the outside.

66

The beauty and durability of a large pine table in the kitchen is paired with a practical stainless-steel top. The vintage porcelain sink and mismatched stools add to the charm of the room.

67

A top shelf provides additional storage and opportunity for displaying a collection—in this case, glasses. A towel rack below is convenient while drying dishes.

68

A plain table and pair of wingback chairs under a pendant lamp create a cozy nook in the kitchen for enjoying coffee or doing homework.

69

Just as no two guests are alike, your kitchen-table chairs needn't be, either. Mix and match to add comfort, informality, and individual style to your seating.

70

Help usher summer in by growing small pots of herbs in a sunny kitchen window in early spring. When the ground thaws, transplant your little garden outdoors.

71

The freestanding pie stand was once a staple of French country cooks. Today, it's being recast as a handsome decorative feature that can display a host of items.

72

Unaligned restaurant supply shelves keep canisters, teapots, teacups, and various kitchen accessories within easy reach while making the wall more interesting visually.

73

A distressed mantel hung in front of a kitchen window makes a unique shelf upon which to display vintage coffee servers, flowers, herbs, and other collectibles.

74

Sheer linens can be hemmed with fabric glue and secured with curtain pin hooks to hang from a rod over a window.

75

The tiling that serves as a short backsplash along the cabinetry near the sink is extended onto the adjoining wall to enhance its appearance and add texture.

76

Shelves of natural planks reflect the warm earth tones of the rest of the space while showing off a collection of white porcelain china.

77

The new stainless-steel dishwasher and range merge into the overall scheme of this kitchen, with its zinc-wrapped countertops.

78

Line the back of a kitchen eating area cabinet with vintage fabric or wallpaper to help a favorite collection stand out.

79

A witty way of introducing color is to put a white-based gingham check on the ceiling. This makes the color appear lighter than a solid hue.

80

For a festive and inspiring focal point, try a multihued backsplash that incorporates the color theme of the kitchen.

81

High-gloss acrylic applied to butcher block seals the wood, brings out its warmth, and helps the kitchen shine.

82

Here, the black backsplash and countertops are reflected in the checkerboard pattern on the floor. The mustard-colored walls bring out the white cabinets.

83

A round table promotes harmony and helps conversation flow over breakfast or lunch in the kitchen.

84

Enamel canisters can be arranged on a kitchen counter so short ones intermingle with tall ones for a less structured, more playful look.

85

Window-paned cabinets are a means of introducing more color to a kitchen. In this case, they showcase dinnerware and stemware in shades of green that are picked up in other pieces in the room.

86

A trio of shiny white pitchers employed as vases make lovely containers for cut or planted white tulips and create a fresh, springlike atmosphere in a charming country kitchen.

87

Mount hooks in a cabinet with glass doors to make the most of the space and create an eclectic display.

88

Once a theme is established—like green-hued glassware—finding additional pieces of it to display becomes a hobby that pays off in completing a look.

89

An antique Magic Chef 1000 Series oven from the 1930s is the stunning centerpiece of this retro-style kitchen.

90

What's more cheerful than a kitchen with candy-colored accents, including the table and chairs? All it takes is perseverance in shopping flea markets for the table and chairs, and the selection of paint colors to work with the rest of the room.

91

A painted floor can hide the faults of an otherwise dreary wood finish. To redo it, decide on a design; sand then prime the entire floor with the lighter color; draw the pattern on with water-soluble colored pencils and a ruler; apply the color; and finish with a sealant.

92

Clean lines and sleek, minimalist appliances dominate in this open and airy space, providing a sense of greater expansion.

93

In a pale-hued space, the addition of a few large, colorful items—like a vase filled with lemons and a vintage sign behind the stove—adds vitality.

94

An island with plenty of leg room and a cast of stools and chairs help bring people in to chat and share the day.

95

In this kitchen, the countertops are crafted of different materials to suit the work that's done there: marble for the cooking zone, stainless steel around the sink, and oiled walnut for the center island.

96

Simple, open shelves adorned
with vintage brackets become a
functional focal point in a kitchen,
and provide extra storage space.

97

In a kitchen, a simple metal bakery rack is the perfect place to display a colorful, eclectic collection of kitchenware piled high.

98

Two ways to add more space and convenience to a small kitchen: Install a countertop at the end of the room to create an eating area and prep zone, and put up a rack that has both a shelf and hooks for hanging pots.

99

A quirky set of prints can be mounted in fairly inexpensive frames and hung together to create an instant collection and point of interest.

100

Here, a panel of the basement door has been covered with chalkboard paint to give this small kitchen a big memo board to write on.

101

A bench with storage extends the seating area and provides a place to store bulk items like paper towels or bottled water.

102

Give a simple space an updated look with chrome-faced appliances and simple hardware for drawers and cabinets.

103

Break up a monochromatic palette and add comfort in a kitchen with a multicolored runner in front of the sink/stove/dishwasher area of the room.

104

Turn what might be a cramped and inefficient space at the end of a small kitchen into a delightful breakfast nook. Bring in elements that work together and make the best use of the space with a round table, seating bench with storage, and clean colors that open the space.

105

Modern stainless-steel appliances are given a furniture treatment in this rustic kitchen with planked walls and a beamed ceiling.

106

Warm, tan-colored walls unite the various shades of wood in this country kitchen. A unique touch is the frieze of dried maple leaves alternating with yellowed pages from a child's workbook above the cabinet.

107

The microwave has its own "house" on the wall, making it a handy but decorative feature.

108

The arched cherry-wood cupboard is both a place to stash everyday items and a display piece for collectibles.

109

A handcrafted island helps bring a woodsy feel to the kitchen, as do the faux vines circling the droplights overhead.

110

To vary the look of storage areas, some cabinets are open, some are screened pie safe–style, while others have beadboard doors.

111

Consider hanging a small ladder from the ceiling to function as a pot rack. Make sure the wood is sturdy enough to support the hardware and the cookware.

112

The rich, bold red of this shelving makes the collection of McCoy and Hall pottery it supports really stand out. Your current collections can tell you a lot about what colors you're drawn to. Use that knowledge to choose other colors when expanding the collection.

113

An informal dining area in a large kitchen is decorated in a primary color scheme, picking up strong blues, yellows, and reds. The tablecloth brings everything together.

114

Beadboard used as a kitchen backsplash adds a nice textural element in a cottage-style kitchen with white appliances and window shutters.

115

Vinyl tiles in the same color family as the cabinets and backsplash form a checkerboard on the kitchen floor and make for easy cleanup.

116

Pale blue walls are accented by pure white cupboards and trim. Open stainless-steel shelves complement the range and countertops.

117

Small tiles accentuate the mosaic pattern behind kitchen counters and make an interesting backsplash and visual point.

Chapter 3 Bathrooms

118

With some fresh herbs from a
farmers' market, create a personal
bouquet for the bath that will
perk up and refresh you or a guest
after a long, hot summer day.

119

Spruce up a metal dresser with a rust remover and paint to transform even inexpensive retro office or medical furniture into a showy and practical piece.

120

Traditional tile or beadboard was replaced with white-painted pressed tin to give a unique look to—and dress up—these bathroom walls.

121

An old wooden mantel installed next to a clawfoot tub serves as an elegant and convenient shelf for bath salts, candles, flowers, and other bath luxuries.

122

A skylight brings additional light and cheer to a small bathroom where a tiled shower provides refuge from the stresses of the day.

123

A chair can be used for all kinds of things in a bathroom. The slipcover should be a fabric that can be washed if lotion or bath oil is spilled on it.

124

If your space is big enough, consider the ultimate luxury of twin pedestal sinks in a master or guest bathroom.

125

Pouches of linen tied with delicate ribbons make pretty sachets for bath salts or potpourri ready for display in a guest bathroom.

126

An armoire can make up for the lack of a closet in any room. In a humid bathroom, one that is fronted with chicken wire allows air to circulate and attractive accessories to be displayed.

127

For the ultimate entertainment indulgence, this master bathroom mirror incorporates an LCD screen that's invisible unless the television is on.

128

For a bathroom imbued with country charm, consider floor-to-ceiling beadboard.

129

A circular shower rod gives just enough privacy in a freestanding tub, and you can experiment with different shower curtains to give the room the right feel.

130

Don't feel like you have to hide your bathroom supplies. Here towels are stored in open shelves under the sink.

131

A plain butcher-block sideboard
is transformed with decorative
trim and a collection of seashells
glued to the drawer. A starfish
becomes the drawer pull.

132

For small spaces, multifunctional pieces are key. This chrome-and-glass medical table in the bathroom has also seen use in other rooms as a bar for entertaining.

133

Tile extended up a wall and around a tub gives an almost sunken-tub feeling. Vary the tile pattern around the top and include a border for extra appeal.

134

Shells belong near water, so what better place for them than in the bathroom? This shell border was created by gluing the shells in place. The theme is extended to the chandelier over the tub.

135

Your vintage tub isn't complete without a shower curtain made from a chenille bedspread. First, hem to the correct length, then install grommets to hold the shower hooks.

136

Silver and cut crystal are timeless accessories and, in the bathroom, can be displayed in groupings, either empty or filled with toiletries such as swabs, cotton balls, and eau de toilette.

137

A vanity that is draped in silk resembles a skirt's bustle and is romantic to its core. Hang balloon shades from the window above for an even more decadent look.

138

Flea-market finds are the staple
of this high-energy bathroom.
A cerulean dresser desk has been
transformed into a vanity, and
a resin ceiling medallion has been
made into the mirror.

139

Make a new wall look old by
smearing spackling here and there,
spreading it, and then painting on
washes of browns in the same
palette, from soft creams to
deeper hues.

140

Linen is classic and versatile, and wears well for life's everyday items like hand towels, tablecloths, and upholstery used for seat cushions.

141

Translucent blue tile in an oversized shower is inviting and refreshing, and gives a watery effect that's perfect for the bathroom.

142

Cultivate a soothing atmosphere in the bathroom with simple lines, minimal accessories, and the peaceful yet cheery combination of white and pale yellow.

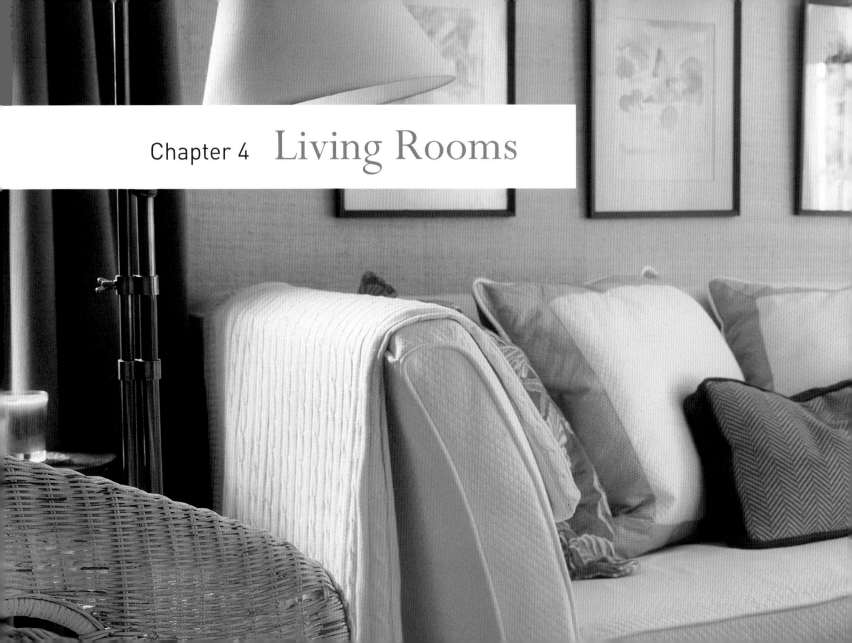

Chapter 4   Living Rooms

143

There's nothing like a fireplace to add warmth and hominess, and with gas and electric fireplaces providing almost carefree alternatives to burning wood, any home can be outfitted with one. The style options are plentiful as well.

144

Add visual interest to a plain painted wall with an application of a lighter or darker complementary shade applied through a stencil. You can even design your own stencils for a truly personal touch.

145

Tweed, plaid, velvet, and leather give this neutral scheme interest and vitality. Closely placed mismatched chairs add to the sense of coziness and comfort of this living room.

146

Details—such as piping that contrasts with the primary color scheme of window treatments while picking up other colors in the room—can complete the picture.

147

The flat-screen-television-as-art idea works here above a classically appointed mantel. The television is out of the way and is not the focal point of the room.

148

One distinctive fabric can set
the design tone of an entire
room. Here, the silhouette print
on the curtains is carried over
to the framed silhouettes on
the mantelpiece.

149

Oil painting portraits found at antique shows and estate sales instill a sense of history, especially when placed in a room filled with other antiques, such as the daybed shown here.

150

A filled bookcase can support a decoratively framed painting, which can be moved or changed to create different moods.

151

Frequent visits by two- and four-legged guests are accommodated with a durable carpet of sea grass. Fringes around the leather sofas can conceal shy cats and prevent scuff marks from the heels of children's shoes.

152

Slightly distressed leather club chairs are at once traditional and contemporary—and extremely comfortable.

153

The open shelves of an étagère display objects of differing sizes without taking up too much wall space.

154

There are many ways to divide a space. Here, a rescued piece of gingerbread railing has become an informal room divider.

155

The pale palette and gently worn furniture in this cozy but open living and dining area are accented with pieces whose dark edges lend drama.

156

Group items by color and shape for a classic look. Open shelves on either side of a double window in a living room provide ample space for displaying assorted collections—of trophies, vases, or candlesticks.

157

An old mantel is personalized with a handmade mosaic fashioned from broken teacups—making it truly a one-of-a-kind.

158

Mirrors break up a space and add light and visual appeal when placed against each other on top of a fireplace in a living room.

159

A simple earthenware jar is spruced up by an encircling dainty wreath of pine boughs and winter grasses, and is the perfect receptacle for a sprig of dried flowers.

160

A table and two chairs in front of a fireplace offer the perfect spot for enjoying a cup of tea or playing a game by the fire on chilly evenings.

161

Using period-appropriate stencils to create a simple yet elegant focal point above a fireplace mantle gives a living room style, authenticity, and a personal touch.

162

Bandboxes—popular as lightweight storage containers in the 18th and 19th centuries—make beautiful decorative storage units today, especially when paired with other antiques, such as books.

163

Establish a focal point with a single dramatic element in a living room, for example a tight grid of similarly themed prints flanked by matching urns.

164

Leaded-glass doors are used to extend the open look of the fireplace on either side of an expansive mantel.

165

Urns used as vases on a mantle or coffee table can complement a classic look and come in a variety of shapes, styles, and colors.

166

Silk window treatments pulled to one side allow for a touch of flounce in an otherwise demure room.

167

The impact of floor-to-ceiling windows is maximized with leggy furniture that allows light in from every direction. A touch of a mustard color in the room makes it even brighter.

168

When preparing for a party, dress up a modest ice bucket by perching it on a stool or plant stand and encircling it in the greenery of your choice.

169

The overall style of this cottage living room is designed to be an extension of what's outside—to play on color and light. The crisp cotton piqué slipcover showcases a host of blue- and green-themed pillows.

170

Grass cloth on the walls reflects the outdoor light and gives the room an organic, living, breathing quality.

171

A refurbished and truncated set of stairs makes a multi-leveled side table for easy access to an assortment of books and other accessories.

172

Let a collection of paintings set the tone of a living room, as the dramatic display of floral still lifes that hang in this room.

173

For a rich, homey feel, go with a brown palette and lots of texture. With brown it's easy to mix tweed with knit and wool; a wicker basket filled with rolled yarn contributes nuances of color and texture.

174

Yellow walls and ceiling capture sunlight from the wall of French doors, infusing the room with summer all year long.

175

Plenty of upholstered furniture in a large room keeps it cozy. Choose variety of pieces to give the room personality.

176

Dominant patterns can peacefully coexist when they're grounded, as they are here by the geometric grid in the rug and the floral motif throughout.

177

This homeowner went bold with a paint that matches an antique variety of fruit growing in her orchard, some samples of which are collected in a white bowl on the table.

178

A collection of stepstools—all different sizes and colors—forms the basis for an arrangement of books and other curios in built-in bookcases.

179

When a room is color-coordinated, all sorts of accessories will work in it, such as the eclectic shell mirror-and-candleholders on the far wall and shell-encrusted lamp on the near table.

180

Transform an armoire by painting it a soft shade of pink with white trim, and finishing the back with pink-accented wallpaper. It's the perfect showcase for all of your prettiest pink things.

181

Resist the urge to refinish or paint imperfect antique pieces—such as the coffee table, chairs, and chest shown here. Combining new and old furniture in a living room creates a homey, lived-in feel.

182

A neutral-patterned rug brings the entire room together, while a pink area shag rug unifies the seating space and adds some pizzazz.

183

A jumble of patterns could disturb the balance in this room, so pillows and throws have been carefully selected. The pink throws match the area rug, and the pillows pick up the color in the drapes.

184

Pink can be both a restful and exciting color. To keep it from overwhelming a space, balance it with plenty of white. The sofa and matching chairs, plus the white walls and trim, keep this room quiet so its pink accents can pop.

185

The formality of this room is established with dark walls and classic white trim. Red accents and a variety of fabrics used provide plenty of dramatic counterpoints throughout.

186

A sole distinctive chair covered
in a fabric that echoes the palette
of the rest of the room is a lovely
conversation piece and is perfectly
situated in a corner of the room.

187

A customized mirror replaces wood paneling in an alcove, helping enlarge the room. Short on wall space? Lean framed photographs or paintings against a wall or mirror, atop a shelf or mantle.

188

Cathedral ceilings are balanced with floor-to-ceiling bookcases, whose shelves can also be used to showcase artwork and other collectibles and knick-knacks.

189

Stone urns, more commonly
found in outdoor formal gardens,
bring a touch of formality and the
outdoors inside when "potted"
with artificial ivy.

190

The recessed spaces in this cabinet are painted a bright yellow to tie in with the other yellow touches in the room.

191

The sofa, chairs, and ottomans share a mustard and chocolate palette, though they are all upholstered differently.

192

To pull off an historical look in a Colonial house, work with simple antique pieces like iron candleholders and a basic rocker by an enormous fireplace.

Chapter 5 Dining Rooms

193

Toile wallpaper applied inside a
cupboard provides visual appeal to
a cabinet corner while helping to
showcase the sparsely displayed
collectibles inside it.

194

For a cool, dramatic, and chic look, accent a mostly white room with black-and-white-patterned upholstered dining room chairs, pillows, and other bold accessories.

195

Wood, wood everywhere: A collection of wooden bowls is supported on open shelving so that their colors can complement and contrast with those of the wall and floor.

196

Historically accurate paints set this space apart and add authenticity. If that's a direction you want to go, research the period and what your options are.

197

An easy, elegant, and accessible way of storing silverware is to put it—sorted by type—in vintage silver cups arranged on a silver platter.

198

Once you have a color scheme chosen, you can mix and match the patterns and shapes of your tableware for memorable settings. Match floral arrangements to the dishes.

199

A variety of textures defines this dining room, from the dramatic floor-length draperies to the Aubusson rug to the fanciful crystal chandelier that adds sparkle.

200

Slipcovers can transform dining room chairs—for a season or longer—while still allowing the beauty of the chairs to come through. Let them set the mood of the room.

201

One way to marry antique and contemporary styles in a dining room is to mount several vintage wine labels in handsome modern frames.

202

An oh-so-pale blue keeps a predominantly white dining room cool while adding a touch of contrast and color.

GIA O'KEEFFE A PORTRAIT BY ALFRED STIEGLITZ VIKING

PRIVATE PARIS

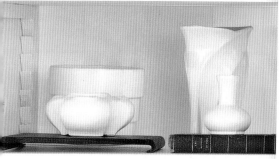

203

The monochromatic effect of displaying white pottery on white shelves is made more visually interesting by the addition of brown trays and books to support them.

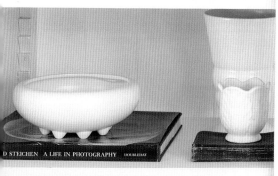

D STEICHEN A LIFE IN PHOTOGRAPHY DOUBLEDAY

MASTERS OF FRENCH PAINTING

HOME SIMPLE

204

Turn an antique silver trophy
into a handsome lamp and top
it with a modern, sleek black
shade to bring style and elegance
to a table.

205

A hooked rug can make an eye-catching wall hanging over an antique sideboard displaying a trio of vases.

206

What better way to relax and
entertain than around a 12-foot-
long farmhouse table with wicker
chairs? For special occasions,
pull the table and chairs out onto
a covered portico with a lovely
garden view.

207

Linen tea towels can make attractive and absorbant oversized napkins while adding character to a table setting for intimate gatherings.

208

Pairing gold-rimmed china with a plate featuring a vibrant green floral graphic gives an effect that's classic, fun, and completely up to date for your next gathering.

209

Unique napkin rings can be made from rhinestone-studded belt buckles—found in vintage shops, flea markets, or antique stores—threaded with ribbon.

210

Miniature watering cans filled with flowers make a spring table especially inviting when used as placecards that guests can take home with them.

211

The wonderful feeling of dining alfresco in the summer can be recreated "indoors" (under a canopy) with fresh flowers on the table, floral prints, and lantern light.

212

For a sophisticated look, place a few dark elements against a mostly white color scheme; use strong, simple shapes; and go for greater impact with a few large accessories rather than many small ones.

213

For a romantic look, think curves, textures, and patterns, as shown here with the variety of curvy ceramics, slipcovered chairs, a fringed tablecloth, and hints of pale green and rose in the fruits and floral dishware.

214

A wide natural-stone fireplace takes center stage in the large living and dining area of a cabin with a rustic yet comfortable and pampered feel.

215

Overstuffed armchairs flank the fireplace and give way to a dining area where chairs fashioned from branches and finished with plaid seat cushions complete the cozy feel.

216

Reclaimed bricks from an old factory were used for this floor to bring a sense of history to a new home.

217

A brick-red corner cupboard blends perfectly with the color scheme and serves as valuable storage space.

218

To further infuse the space with regional history and charm, wooden decoys and old baskets have been placed on the beams that support the roof.

219

A wide-planked wooden table says country; the rust-colored trim and blue-gray ceiling give an historical feel to this simple yet dramatic dining room.

220

Unique sterling serving pieces like this fish server (called a "slice") can make a dinner table elegant in an instant, and can be used at informal gatherings, as well.

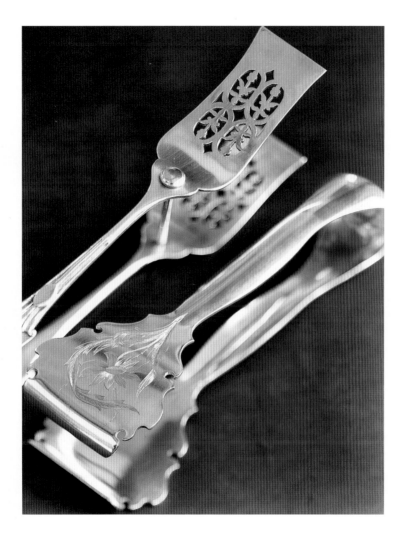

221

Decorative and fanciful sterling tongs come in a variety of sizes that allow for serving everything from asparagus to cherry tomatoes and can help grasp sugar cubes for tea or coffee.

222

Sleek and modern stemmed votives will brighten and beautify a dining table, creating just the right romantic or festive mood while preventing messy wax drips.

223

Using different sterling napkin rings is like having individual sculptures at every place setting and will surely be a topic of conversation during dinner.

224

Add an antique touch to your dining room table by using a collection of mismatched engraved silver napkin rings.

225

For a simple, summery floral arrangement, use the same color and style of candle in different sizes, then tuck freshly clipped flowers from your garden around their bases.

226

Make a dining room more dramatic and memorable by choosing a painting that incorporates the room's color scheme in a way that is big and bold and that creates a sense of balance.

227

Matching napkins with beautifully delicate roses stitched into the corners are the perfect addition to a lovely springtime table setting.

228

Setting a distinctive table is easy when you establish a strong central feature—such as color—to set the tone, letting everything else follow its lead.

229

Create a playful mood by making fanciful place settings—each charming and unique—from any ribbon, buttons, or old note cards you have stashed away.

230

Allow a color palette to capture your imagination and transform a room. Mismatched glass candlesticks with cream-colored candles work beautifully with white gold-rimmed teacups.

231

A winter dining table is graced with tiny paperwhites artfully and delicately arranged in white ceramic salt dishes for a beautiful, decorative touch.

232

Set an unusual table to entertain your guests using a collection of silver spoons engraved with different names, found in vintage and antique stores.

233

A collection of stick spatter bowls or dishes deserves to be shown off, as they are hard to find and wonderful to look at. Every piece is hand painted, the work of English and Scottish craftsmen from the 1830s to the early 20th century.

234

The colors in a painting of Provence inspired those in this warm dining room: a lemony yellow and the subtle variations of fine wood.

235

An easy-to-care-for sisal rug complements the carefree look and keeps the original, wide-planked floors from being scratched.

236

The large painting in this dining room is left unframed so it has a less formal feel. It offers a gorgeous view much like that of through a window.

237

This table "glows" with various yellows and creams, from the dinnerware to the candles and the flowers—even the label on the wine bottle.

238

Colorful toile curtains are formal
enough for the dining room, yet
sunny and cheery enough for the
kitchen, and serve to harmonize
the two rooms.

239

The intensity of the blue walls and cupboard interior in this room was achieved by applying two coats of royal blue and one of black. The color is picked up on the seat cushions and in the china on display.

240

White trim brings out the richness of the royal-blue walls; faux marble baseboards add a modern touch of distinction.

241

An old oil lamp serves as a
chandelier to cast a soft glow
over an outdoor table so that
intimate meals can linger from
the evening well into the night.

242

To add a romantic atmosphere to alfresco dining, a small collection of tapers in mismatched silver candlesticks is placed on a side buffet table.

243

Crystal, silver, votive candles, a crisp white tablecloth, and blue transferware combine for a traditional, formal table setting.

244

Fall's bounty makes a lovely arrangement on a dining room sideboard. The shapes and colors of gourds, apples, pears, and berries are accented with sprigs of greenery.

245

Warm colors like yellow, green, and red help set an active and stimulating mood, but can also cultivate feelings of welcome, intimacy, and coziness in a dining area.

246

You'll always find a spot for something special, so don't think your next captivating flea market find won't work in your house. This hot-air-balloon chandelier is a whimsical touch in an otherwise stately room.

247

Let each chair be unique, yet compatible, by mixing bold, colorful fabric patterns front to back on the same chair.

248

A 19th-century carved trencher filled with green apples makes a casual centerpiece for an antique—or any style—dining room table.

249

Don't be afraid to stray from the traditional. A vintage file cabinet can be used as a buffet with ample storage space.

250

Delight guests at a springtime luncheon with tiny, preseeded clay pots that serve as both place cards and party favors that can be taken home and enjoyed once the flowers bloom.

251

The candle chandelier is a local antiques find and is a bold focus for the room. The light cast by the candles creates a very intimate, romantic atmosphere.

252

The blue finish on top of the round white-weathered pedestal table is a unique touch that helps bring a sense of unity to the room.

253

Chairs are slipcovered in a waffle weave that's versatile enough to use indoors or take outside for alfresco dining in warm weather.

254

A collection of decorative silver platters in groups of three frame the French doors that lead to the sunporch.

255

Finishing touches help complete and define a room. Here, lighting in the cupboard brings attention to the collection of spoons and tea sets, while antique prints and paintings fill the walls.

256

Visit your local florist to find a few unusual items to mix with things you may have growing in your garden. The personalized centerpieces you create will add color, warmth, and charm.

257

Oyster shells make great salt and pepper dishes, especially for meals enjoyed outdoors in the summertime. Before using, boil the shells to ensure they're sanitary.

258

Silver-plated pieces once used in hotels are collector's items when they have the hotel's name engraved on them; even if they don't, silver pieces always look good displayed together.

259

Add kitsch to a modern dining room with a large unframed photograph, a mismatched set of chairs, and other eclectic artwork.

260

With the appliqué options
available in craft stores today,
monogramming all kinds
of things—including chandelier
shades—is now possible …
and easy.

261

Vintage frames discovered at flea markets can be painted and hung on their own or used to frame "floating art."

262

Transferware that's too fragile to use for serving food can be turned into art, as has been done in these matching compositions.

263

A keepsake—here, a menu from a favorite restaurant—can be framed and given a place of pride on a wall or shelf.

264

Mixing old and new items—
a basket, a candelabrum, vases,
a creamer—creates a standout
effect.

265

Repurpose a dark sideboard
by painting it a color of your
choosing that will work with
the rest of your room.

266

Accessorizing a table is the most fun part. Here, a tiny glass vase at each place setting welcomes guests with three delicate tulips and a card featuring the guest's first initial.

267

Bring joy to a spring table with this simple arrangement: Fill a medium-size bowl with damp moss and arrange the flowers around the outside of the bowl. Add a smaller bowl full of speckled candy eggs, sugared almonds, or pastel malt balls in the middle, and arrange the moss and flowers so the rim is hidden.

268

Gilded chairs are dressed up with tasseled, buttoned "ball-gown" slipcovers in a shade that nearly matches the table.

269

Silver candelabra full of white tapers are timeless, as are the small vases of daisies that will bring cheer to guests dining at each place.

270

Dress up and contemporize a dining alcove by putting bright slipcovers over the chairs and using leftover material to make placemats. Individual tumblers of flowers perfect the presentation.

271

A plain dining table and white slipcovered chairs are made more dramatic with a powerful arrangement like hydrangeas in large copper vases.

Chapter 6 Family and Great Rooms

272

Spruce up your sitting areas with pillows fashioned from hand-printed silks and linens in a variety of shapes and patterns, and with fringes and other adornments.

273

Touches of bold color can unify a room and a house, and create drama—as red does here in the throw, tablecloth, and fresh flowers in this mostly white room.

274

The muted sage-and-tan palette of this great room is accented by touches of red in the leather armchairs, pillows, wall decorations, and other accessories and knick-knacks.

275

Try replacing a traditional wood coffee table with a solid leather ottoman to add a touch of masculinity to a den or family room that is otherwise subtly feminine.

276

A single, large-scale piece like this armoire meets multiple storage needs while providing a clean, streamlined look and hiding a television, stereo, and other electronic equipment.

277

A perfectly fluted, small white vase is an elegant container for a collection of white marble eggs that would add beauty to a side table, mantle, or coffee table.

278

Breathe new life into a room and keep things simple by wallpapering just one small wall and adding complementary, patterned tablecloth—covered with a smaller, white tablecloth—to a buffet table.

279

Combining antique, vintage, and modern furnishings, unique accents, and playful surprises makes a room pop.

280

Use an antique cabinet with a space-saving foldaway desktop in a small den for versatility and to avoid clutter.

281

Earthy shades of green and brown set the tone for relaxation and meditation in this quiet nook that provides a desk for sketching, painting, or other work, and an overstuffed chair for relaxing with a book.

282

Old linen tea towels can be made into soft and ultracomfortable pillowcases. Wrap a modern-looking bow around one for a contrast that works.

283

Color and eclecticism will bring any potentially hidden corner into full view. Top an antique cupboard with a tightly arranged grouping of colorful vases, urns, and other collectibles.

284

Hand-carved Bible boxes hearken back to a time when few houses had doors that locked. One's most valuable possessions were secured in individual boxes with locks.

285

A wooden bowl full of rag balls for making rugs creates a colorful centerpiece when paired with a small vase of fresh flowers on a coffee table, side table, or buffet.

286

History is embodied in this arrangement of an old oil painting hanging above a 19th-century jelly cupboard displaying an antique wooden bowl and wedding-band hogscraper candlesticks.

287

A slipcover can be a way to add texture to a room. The pillows and other pieces in the room share the mix-and-match theme—even the wicker basket is covered in fabric.

288

A stone wall is left white while the flat wall is painted a robin's egg blue to play up the qualities of texture and color.

289

A vintage mantel and repurposed iron grate give character to an otherwise plain fireplace.

290

Wood (in the side table, chest, and dishrack), clay (in the sculpture and flowerpot), and fabric (the slipcovers of the chairs) all speak to a country rusticity and simplicity that unify this corner of a family room.

291

The fringed slipcovers on the
sofa, pillows, and ottoman give a
comfortable and relaxed feeling
to an otherwise streamlined
room. Handcrafted arrangements
of framed, dried flowers reflect
the tone of the room.

292

A chandelier's long cord is dressed in a fabric sleeve that is complementary to the rest of the room, and its lampshades are fringed, softening the piece to seamlessly fit into the room.

293

Making a room comfortable means providing inviting places to sit, like benches with thick pads and lots of pillows, and overstuffed chairs and ottomans.

294

A sunny vase of fiery dahlias is a sight for sore eyes and will brighten any room where it is placed.

295

A 19th-century linen press hides rainy-day diversions including a television, a movie library, CDs, and board games in this bright, open, yet comfortable family room.

296

Black-and-white prints in dark frames help ground a white and cream–paletted room that's further defined by the textures of the fabrics and the slats in the wall.

297

Creamy white walls and pure white trim give a small room breathing space and allow furniture to take center stage.

298

Antique game boards are used as decorations and echo the subtle checkerboard pattern in the rug.

299

A large stone hearth is accented with a slab of natural stone as a mantelpiece and is finished with dentil trim.

300

In a twist on tradition, the window rim and sills are rough-hewn while the walls receive the detail. Guitars are hung as art, and blankets are piled on the floor as cushions for game time.

301

Update your decor without completely redecorating by rotating your favorite artwork or photographs. Mix things up to see how different arrangements appeal to you.

302

Maximizing light and cheeriness is the objective of this room, where white walls shine and natural light bounces off the floral chintzes and antiques.

303

There can be many variations of white-on-white. In this room, a vintage basket filled with white chrysanthemums used as a planter is an instant brightener to a monochromatic room.

304

Keeping extra pillows handy without cluttering up a room can be tricky. This pale blue footstool solves the problem simply and elegantly.

Chapter 7 Bedrooms

305

A sepia and rose–colored palette imbues this room with softness and romance. The old photographs leaning on shelves hung above the bed cultivate a sense of history.

306

Fabrics like the slipcover on this chair can be aged by soaking and agitating them in a special "tan" dye in the washing machine.

307

Mixing antique and contemporary furnishings in a peaceful color scheme helps guestrooms appeal to those who may not like a particularly feminine or overly stylized touch.

308

Trunks have lots of storage potential when divided with lift-out trays that are packed efficiently. They can be left open for a decorative touch to display; or they can be stored in a closet or under a bed.

309

The white sails and soft blue skies in this pair of naval prints balance the white lamp and bowl of baby's breath for a striking composition in the bedroom of a seaside cottage.

310

Give an otherwise plain bedroom
a twist with a distinctive feature
like antique wall sconces that
instantly add distinction and
drama to the room.

311

Awaken refreshed and retire happy in a bedroom that sings of light and sunshine and a perpetually flowering garden.

312

Look for baskets that already mirror a theme (in this case, flowers), or paint them white and decorate them yourself. Then use them to store pillows and blankets.

313

A decorative window frame made into a mirror captures light, opening up a dark corner space.

314

Guest rooms are great places to indulge in a bit of decorative whimsy—as long as the overall effect is soothing. Wallpaper with lilies of the valley is a nice complement to shades of white, green, and blue throughout the rest of the room.

315

A wicker table is fanciful yet versatile, and can give a guest bedroom a gardenlike feel—especially when topped with a vase overflowing with fresh flowers.

316

Upholstered headboards are nice for guests to prop pillows against for reading in full comfort, and add softness and comfort to the room.

317

Ribbed cotton chenille bedspreads and shams are soft and soothing for summer, and provide a restful night's sleep.

318

An airy, restful master bedroom is accomplished by keeping things clean and simple with a white-on-white scheme complemented by deep earth tones and natural themes.

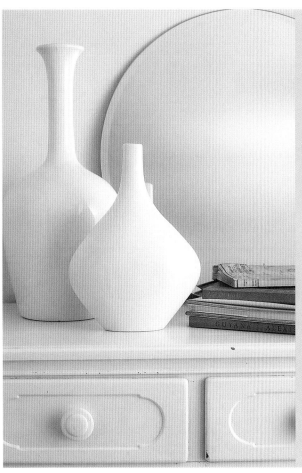

319

Arrange a round mirror with a pair of inexpensive white vases for a sleek, modern, and minimalist look in a bedroom.

320

Dried sea urchin shells—with their distinctive color, shape, and texture—form attractive and cool arrangements in simple white pottery bowls.

321

A built-in bed maximizes the space in a small guest bedroom, while colorful linens make the room inviting and a wall lamp allows guests to read before sleeping.

322

Mix stripes, florals, and solids in the same color family to get an eclectic but harmonious, vintage-inspired look without the vintage price tag.

323

Feelings of intimacy and repose
are brought out by warm colors,
such as those found in the drapes,
walls, and bedspread of this
master bedroom.

324

The blush-colored upholstery
is picked up in the room's
two side chairs.

325

A simple yet elegant floral arrangement is a quick way to energize a guest bedroom. A predominance of white and green creates a light and fresh feeling.

326

Fashion a unique and colorful bedskirt from a mismatched collection of floral handkerchiefs sewn onto a flat bedsheet and accented with "cotton ball" fringe.

327

A white lace bed skirt adds a soft, romantic touch to this bed that is otherwise bursting with color with its linens, piles of pillows, and duvet cover.

328

Add dimension and character to a dressing table. Giving a lampshade the power of a mini tableaux can make a dresser top really stand out.

329

To give a vintage look to new
fabric prints before making
them into pillows, tea-dye them
or leave them in the sun for a bit.
Then use old French linen dish
towels as backs.

330

A tonal palette of light pink and brown allows for a range of classic additions, like shells or lamps, that together create a sense of harmony and balance.

331

An antique, handpainted foldaway kitchen table makes an excellent, and charming, nightstand/desk combination perfect for a small guest room.

332

Two or three dominant colors in a room are all you need to create an eclectic mix without giving an overly busy appearance. The colors can be used in a variety of patterns, however—florals, stripes, and plaids, for instance, are all used here.

333

For an unconventional—yet charming—look, use a dining chair as a bedside table, topped with books and a reading lamp.

334

A floral area rug does wonders to anchor a room's layout and to provide visual interest to a room that features solid colors and very few patterns.

335

Keep plenty of soft blankets and quilts on hand for guests on chilly nights. Easily identify items in a linen closet by affixing handsome metal brackets and handwritten labels to each shelf.

336

This master bedroom's restful effect comes from soft green walls and a white-painted floor. A faux-lamb's-wool rug provides a plush, warm place for bare feet last thing at night and first thing in the morning.

337

A bed you want to sink into is calming and inviting, made so by the soothing neutral color scheme here that's broken up only by the ticking in the bedspread and a delicate floral-patterned blanket.

338

A small tray filled with shells is a lovely stage for a couple of white candles and will be the perfect welcome for guests after a long journey.

339

Add contrast to a two-story master bedroom by creating the illusion of a chair rail: divide a room with paint—a color on the bottom and white on top.

340

This small youth's chair—an antique found at a flea market—is the perfect perch for a big teddy bear and his precious little buddy—and the American flag for a dash of patriotism.

341

If closet space is tight, a ladder provides the hangers guests may need during their temporary stay in a guest room, and keeps everything easily within reach.

342

An armchair and a wall lamp provide a cozy spot for reading or relaxing by the fire, with plenty of books within reach on the shelves behind the chair.

343

A desk can be a welcome and practical addition to a master bedroom as a place to do serious work, write letters, sketch, or contemplate.

344

A great seasonal makeover for any small room is to change the color of one of the walls with a new shade of paint that can capture the feeling of that time of year.

345

Geometrics work with other geometrics as long as one pattern is dominant and all are within the overall color scheme, as with the plaid chair and checkered carpet here.

346

An upholstered paneled screen extends the concept of a headboard, creates a sense of coziness around the bed, and makes a long room more intimate.

347

A clear apothecary jar becomes a nice display vessel for a collection of antique eyeglasses on a dresser top or nightstand.

348

Paneling that's been painted a
dark blue enriches a room with
cherrywood beds and trim, and
helps the crisp matching quilts
really stand out.

349

A guest bedroom is the perfect
place to showcase a collection of
antique trunks found in vintage
shops or flea markets. They're
perfect for storing extra pillows
and blankets.

350

A floral-motif chandelier adorns a corner stenciled with water lilies and irises, and bathes the room in a romantic glow.

351

The drapes in this bedroom are a set of mix-and-match florals in colors that complement the rest of the room.

352

Pockets have been sewn into the sheer half-curtains to hold treasures from the garden.

353

Different floral linens were sewn together to create a unique bedspread.

354

An old barn door nailed to the wall makes a unique country-chic headboard that ties together the barn motif in the eclectic art and accessories.

355

To maintain a sense of serenity while adding a seasonal touch, consider wrapping presents in similarly themed and colored papers that match the room where they will be opened.

356

To create a simple yet rich look in a guest bedroom, decorate with a palette of only two colors. Here, dark blue and white make a dramatic combination.

Also by Leigh Montville

At the Altar of Speed

Manute: The Center of Two Worlds

TED WILLIAMS

The Biography of an American Hero

Leigh Montville

DOUBLEDAY
New York   London   Toronto   Sydney   Auckland

PUBLISHED BY DOUBLEDAY
A division of Random House, Inc.
1745 Broadway, New York, NY 10019

DOUBLEDAY and the portrayal of an anchor with a dolphin are
trademarks of Doubleday, a division of Random House, Inc.

Book design by Caroline Cunningham

Cataloguing-in-publication data is on file with the Library of Congress.

ISBN 0-385-50748-8

For . . .

The Garden Street Athletic Club

New Haven, Connecticut

I was in love with Ted Williams.
His long legs, that grace,
his narrow baseball bat
level-swung, his knowledge of art,
it has to be perfect, as near
as possible, don't swing
at a pitch seven centimeters
wide of the plate.

I root for the Boston Red Sox
Who are in ninth place
Who haven't won since 1946

It has to be perfect.

BASEBALL, A POEM IN THE MAGIC NUMBER 9

We wish we lived our lives—grace, level-swung, every day a seeking for perfection—as Williams lived his game; if only our lives could be the knowledge of the art of the game. That is worth rooting for, even if we remain in ninth place.

GEORGE BOWERING (1965)

Contents

Prologue

T ed Williams loved to tell the story about the alligator. He told it everywhere, told it for much of his life. There were different permutations
to fit different circumstances, but the basic story always stayed the same.

"Didja hear about the alligator?" he would ask.

His voice was loud. His presence was overwhelming.

"Bit that kid's leg off!"

He would be inside an elevator. He would be inside a restaurant. He
would be at some "sports fans" event, with people waiting in line to secure his autograph on a scrap of paper. He would be somewhere at a ballpark. He would . . . okay, this was one of the last recorded times he told
it . . . he would be standing in an aisle at Walgreens, holding on to a
walker.

Someone else would be with him, someone else to share the joke. Ted
Williams would nudge that person, wink, do something to let him know
what was taking place.

"Terrible thing!" Williams would say.

"What happened?" the co-conspirator would ask if he was sharp.

"Terrible thing," Williams would repeat if the co-conspirator was not
sharp. Get with the program, buddy.

Here the story would change to fit the circumstance. In Florida, easy,
the alligator simply had slipped out of the muck around a local swamp,
befuddled by the heat, walked down a city street or suburban subdivision,
and found the poor, unwitting kid and started snapping and chewing. In
New York, perhaps the keepers were taking the alligator to the Bronx
Zoo and he escaped. In Newcastle, New Brunswick, perhaps someone
had brought the alligator back from Disney World and slipped it into the

Miramichi River. In Boston, Minneapolis, Chicago, right at O'Hare Airport . . .

"Big alligator!

"Bit the kid's leg off at the knee!

"Kid's in terrible shape!

"Don't know what happened to the alligator!

"Still on the loose!"

Ted Williams would nudge the co-conspirator and advise him to watch and wait. The people who had overheard this dreadful tale—who had overheard it from Ted Williams no less, no farther away from me than I am from you; or at least had overheard it from some loud-talking, big son of a bitch at Walgreens—would pass the news. The next people would pass the news and pass and pass. The result would come back like a boomerang. Later in the day. Later in the night. Later in the week. Later.

"Did you hear about the alligator?" someone would ask the co-conspirator.

"Did you hear about the alligator?" someone would ask Ted Williams himself.

The following story is not about the alligator. This story is about the man who started all the talking.

1 Boston

Ted Williams of the Boston Red Sox looked as fit as an Indian buck. After a winter out of doors, including a month of lazy fishing at the edge of the Florida Everglades, he was tanned to a light mahogany. His brownish green eyes were clear and sharp, his face lean, the big hands that wrapped around the handle of his 34-oz. Louisville Slugger were calloused and hard. He had 198 pounds, mostly well-trained muscle, tucked away on his six-ft. 3¾ in. frame. He expected, he conceded, "to have a pretty good year."

But as usual Ted Williams had a number of worries at the back of his mind.

TIME, APRIL 10, 1950

The only other car in the parking lot was a cream-colored Cadillac Coupe DeVille with Minnesota license plates. Jimmy Carroll paid no attention.

The sun was coming up, beautiful, over the Atlantic Ocean. Six o'clock in the morning. Jimmy was supposed to meet some people to go out on some rich guy's yacht from Falmouth, Massachusetts, a town located at the fat beginning end of Cape Cod. One of the people, believe it or not, was supposed to be Ellis Kinder, the pitcher for the Boston Red Sox. Jimmy was a baseball fan. He had driven through the dark from Boston, excited, and arrived way too early.

The door to the cream-colored Cadillac Coupe DeVille opened. Theodore Samuel Williams stepped out.

"I didn't know what to do," Jimmy Carroll says, all these years later. "He started walking toward my car. I rolled down the window."

"Do you know Ellie Kinder?" Ted Williams asked. "Are you waiting for him?"

"Yeah," Jimmy blurted.

"Well, where the hell is he? Hi. I'm Ted Williams."

"No kidding!" Jimmy blurted again. "Jimmy Carroll."

"The sons of bitches are always late. Do you know a place around here where we can get some breakfast?"

"Well, yeah," Jimmy blurted yet one more time.

"Well, come on, let's get some breakfast."

There are other moments in his life Jimmy Carroll can describe with meaning and drama—marriage, divorce, births of children—but none are touched with the magic of that 1950s moment. The sun forever sits the same way. The car door always opens. The tall figure—Jesus, good Christ, it's him—unfolds.

Ted Williams becomes Jimmy Carroll's friend.

"We'd take rides," Jimmy says about the relationship that developed long ago. "He loved to take rides. He loved going along the Charles River. We'd make the whole loop, over to Cambridge, out to Newton and back. He'd be talking about all the places we passed, asking questions, making comments. We'd take walks. We'd go down Marlborough Street at night, really quiet and dark, a lot of college kids living there, come back up Beacon Street. Noisier. Cars would stop. People would shout.

"I took him all over the place. I took him out to Nantasket once, to the amusement park. Mobbed. We could only stay about five minutes. I took him to South Boston. Mobbed. He signed autographs for all these kids at the L Street Bath House. I took him . . . one day we're sitting around, doing nothing, and he says, 'Let's go somewhere. Where can we go?' I said, 'Why don't we go over and visit James Michael Curley, the former mayor of Boston? He's very sick.' Ted said, 'The guy who went to jail because he was taking money to help the little guy?' I said, 'That's the one. He threw out the first pitch on Opening Day a couple times. You know him.'

"We go. Ted Williams to see James Michael Curley! We get shown into a bedroom. There's two twin beds. Curley is in one of them. You can see he's close to dying. He's delighted to see Ted, though. He's a fan. Ted gets in the other twin bed! Curls up! They lie there, the two of them. Talked for an hour!"

Magic.

For the next eight, nine, ten years, there was magic.

"I'd drive him to the airport, pick him up," Jimmy says. "While he was on the road, he'd let me use the car. I was selling liquor at the time. I'd drive the big Cadillac Coupe DeVille to some place, park it right out front. I'd be having trouble with some clients, maybe the Greeks—they only wanted to buy from a Greek—and I'd point outside. 'You like that car? You know who it belongs to?' "

One night Williams let Jimmy use the car for a date. Jimmy took the woman to Hugo's Lighthouse, a restaurant in suburban Cohasset. As he parked the car, a large policeman appeared. The policeman asked if Jimmy was a baseball player. Jimmy laughed and said he wasn't, but why would someone ask? The policeman said, "Because you're driving Ted Williams's car." Jimmy asked how the policeman would know this. The policeman said he just knew, that a lot of people knew what Ted Williams's car looked like. Everybody did.

"Could I ask you a favor?" the policeman also asked, after all of this business was done.

"Sure," Jimmy said.

"While you're eating, while you're in the restaurant, would it be possible for me just to sit in the car? Ted's car?"

"Sure," Jimmy said.

He and his date ate their dinners. They came out of the restaurant. Six policemen—the original one and five of his friends—now were inside the car. Touching Ted's leather upholstery. Twirling Ted's chrome knobs. Trying to breathe Ted's air. Just once.

The fame of Ted Williams in Boston and in much of the country during his baseball life was different from the fame of today. There is no analogy to make, really, to the situation of some living, modern famous person. Williams was closer to a figure from mythology or fiction, to a comic strip character, to Spiderman, Superman, Popeye the Sailor Man. Or more.

"I met him once, when I was around nine years old," William Bulger, former president of the University of Massachusetts, says. "I was with some youth group at a ballgame. He came over to meet us. I looked up and I thought I was looking into the face of God. He spoke to me. He said, 'Are you a boo-er?' I didn't know what a 'boo-er' was. I said nothing. I just stood there."

The perpetual leftfielder of the Red Sox was famous in a time when heroes were constructed with the imagination and with words rather than force-fed and sold through a 21-inch or 56-inch color screen. The tape measure of the normal did not exist. He did things once, and you saw them once in person or heard them once on the radio or read about them forever. And they grew.

The few pictures at the start of his career in 1939 that came onto the movie screen during the Warner Pathe news before the feature film at the downtown theater were herky-jerky images, black-and-white, Ted Williams obviously posing for his swing before the ballgame began, sometimes not even in the batter's box, perfect lighting, crack, then everything turned grainy and too fast as the hard-to-see ball traveled over a grainy fence and he ran the bases in a speeded-up hurry. Even the pictures at the end on television, 1960, were not much better.

"I started doing the Red Sox games in 1951," broadcaster Curt Gowdy says. "We used three cameras to cover the entire game. One from first base, one from third, one behind the plate. I went to [owner] Tom Yawkey at the end of the season and said, 'I think we could use a fourth camera from centerfield to show the balls and strikes. I think it would be a great addition.'

"Yawkey surprised me. He didn't want it. He said the television coverage would become too good. People would stay home from the ballpark. We didn't get it."

For virtually all of Ted Williams's 19 big-league years, the assembled folk at the ballpark had to report to friends and neighbors what they had seen him do. There was no replay. There was no highlights package at 11. How far did that ball go? How mighty was that swing? How mad, exactly, did The Splendid Splinter become? The voices of Gowdy and other broadcasters had to explain. The sets of fingers on the typewriters in the press box—each set lined up in direct competition with all the other sets of fingers in the press box—had to find phrases and sentences, cocka-mamy analogies, to translate and reconstruct reality for the general public's edification. Word of mouth had to carry the brushfires further.

The figure that stepped from all of these words, from all of this thinking—the human being who actually came into a restaurant, sat down, and ordered a malted milkshake—had all the mystery of any unseen divinity. Each swallow, each bite of his sandwich, was an amazement.

Hyperbole trailed Ted Williams like a faithful hound.

"The Red Sox used to come to Harvard to practice in our cage on rainy days," Billy Cleary, 1960 U.S. Olympic hockey player and longtime Harvard athletic director, says. "We had the only indoor facility in the area at the time. I was an undergraduate then, and as soon as we saw it was raining, we'd all go down to watch the Red Sox, to watch Ted.

"One day there was a bunch of kids around the batting cage, Ted at bat . . . a pitch came in, and he didn't swing. One of the wise-guy college kids shouted, 'Strike!' Ted turned around and said, 'That was not a god-damned strike. What do you know about baseball?' Kids being kids, a bunch of them laughed. Ted was fuming.

"His turn was done, so he stepped out and somebody else stepped in. You could see Ted was still mad. Fuming. He was muttering about the kids and the pitch, getting madder by the moment. When his turn finally came around again, you could see him squeezing the bat, harder and harder, still muttering. He was grinding his teeth. The pitcher threw the ball, and Ted swung, and he hit it so hard . . . there was a net, you know, inside the building . . . the ball went right through the net, broke the cords, then went straight to the ceiling, where it hit a big light. Broke the light. Sparks. Stuff falling from the ceiling.

"Ted turned to us. He said, '*That* was a strike, goddamn it.' Walked away. It was the most amazing thing in sports I've ever seen."

Did it happen that way?

Really?

It did, because that was what the mind remembered and the words reported. There was no evidence to dispute them.

He lived at the Somerset Hotel on Commonwealth Avenue, Room 231, a suite, for the last half of his career. He would check in at the beginning of the season, check out at the end. Mae Carney, the head telephone operator, was instructed not to put any calls through to Room 231, never, under any circumstances. Messages were taken, and bellhops like Leo Pratt would hurry them to the room, sliding them under the door if no one answered a knock. Never enter the room! That was the rule.

Room 231 was his refuge. He had a vise and piles of feathers in his bedroom to tie flies for fishing, his major hobby. He had a tripod and a telescope in the living room. He could watch the stars. He also could watch the coeds in their dormitory at Garland Junior College.

Jimmy Carroll was a visitor.

"The suite was perfect for him," Jimmy says. "It was right next to the stairs. He could come in the back way or leave and no one would see him. He walked a lot of the time to the ballpark. He knew shortcuts and back alleys that no one else knew. He walked through the Victory Gardens [vegetable gardens planted by apartment dwellers during the Second World War in the park land of the Fenway] a lot."

Jimmy's office was at 120 Ashford Street, behind Braves Field, maybe a mile from the hotel. Ted would call. Jimmy would go to the hotel. There would be no great plan. They would just hang out sometimes. Talk.

They would talk about religion, about politics, about the stock market. Ted had still been paid by the Red Sox during his time in Korea, and his agent, Fred Corcoran, had put the money in the market. Something called IBM. He worried about the wisdom of the investment. Huh. The conversations could be about anything. Religion and politics combined.

"I was a Kennedy man," Jimmy says. "He was a Nixon man. He always was giving me the needle about the Catholic thing. I sold a whiskey, OFC. He said, 'OFC . . . that's Only For Catholics? Only For Cardinals? Only For Chiselers? What is it?' I told him the plans were already in place for Massachusetts when Kennedy took charge. The state was going to be split in two. High Mass and Low Mass."

Jimmy would bring over a case of Cutty Sark, another of his products, but never saw one of the bottles opened. Ted seldom drank, and when he did it was wine, sparkling burgundy. If he and Jimmy went out to eat, they often went to restaurants in the suburbs, quiet places. If they went out to eat in Boston, they went to the Union Oyster House on Union Street, a place Ted liked because management seated him in the back, a private room. Or to Steve McGrail's Linwood Grill on Kilmarnock Street, a place Ted liked because management would instantly fire up two steaks for him. Late at night, the few times he went out, Ted liked the bar at the Copley Plaza. Or the Darby Room. Or the Polynesian Room at the Somerset. Every place had to be dark. Every one of them, it seemed, was down a flight of stairs.

"I remember one night we're coming back from the Copley," Jimmy says. "Traffic was being rerouted, and we wound up going past the side of the Boston Public Library. Ted suddenly says, 'Stop the car.' I stopped. He pointed and said, 'What's that?' It was people, homeless, sleeping on the heating grates outside the library. Ted couldn't believe it. I remember him talking about that all night. How the hell could this country have people living like that? It really bothered him."

There were trips to prizefights, to see local guys like Tony DeMarco, Paul Pender, Red Priest, Tommy Collins. Ted liked boxing. There were double dates, Ted asking if Jimmy *really* was interested in that girl he was with. Why is that, Ted? Because if you're not, I'll take a shot at her. Ted liked women. There were trips to see sick kids and old people in hospitals. A lot of those trips. There was a trip to a driving range in Weymouth, a trip to Filene's Basement in Boston (mobbed), even visits to Fenway Park.

Jimmy wound up shagging flies during off-day workouts sometimes. Pete Cerrone, the Red Sox equipment man who also worked in Filene's Basement selling suits, would throw batting practice from behind a door he dragged out to the mound to avoid being killed by line drives back through the middle. Jimmy would be out in rightfield. Ted would hit the ball, and Jimmy would move in for the catch, and the ball would go over his head. He could hear it pass, a low *whoosh*, a jet engine in the air. The next sound would be a *clank* when it hit the seats.

"One day Ted told me I should hit," Jimmy says. "I told him I didn't want to do it. He said, 'Come on, every kid who grew up in Boston wants to hit the leftfield wall.' Okay, he was right. I went up there, and Pete was throwing underhanded, and I couldn't hit anything. Ted came over, showed me some things, adjusted my hands. He said to Pete, 'Throw it overhand and throw it in there.' I swung, I connected, the ball went out and hit the wall. I did it . . . I've told my son so many times about hitting the wall, he never wants to hear it again. But I did it. I hit the wall."

The relationship was one-sided perhaps, Ted always in control, but also perfect. Ted got to do whatever he wanted to do. Jimmy got to see what Ted wanted to do. That was enough. Jimmy sometimes laughed at his good fortune. How many people wouldn't want to be doing what he was doing? He wasn't trying to make a buck, a deal. He was inside the velvet ropes of celebrity, seeing what Ted saw. That was more than enough. Maybe he wasn't walking in Ted's size 10 or 11 baseball shoes, a different size for each foot, and maybe he wasn't taking a swing at a 3–2 fastball, but he was wearing one of Ted's sports coats for dinner. Size 46. Same size. His size. Ted was wearing Jimmy's camel's hair overcoat in the cold. Size 46. Same size.

What was it the two MDC cops called Ted when they stopped him for speeding? Ted was coming over to see Jimmy's mother, sick in Carney Hospital. The cops stopped him, looked at the license, and radioed back to the station, "We've got the Pope of Baseball here," then gave him an escort to the hospital. The Pope of Baseball! Jimmy could see what life was like to be the Pope of Baseball.

"We had a lot of fun, but there were times he would become really quiet," Jimmy says. "We'd be driving somewhere. His mind would be someplace else. You could tell. He'd have a look on his face. I'd wonder if he really was happy. I didn't think he was. I still don't."

Too much. Too much. Too much. That was Jimmy's thought. Too much. Sometimes the life of the Pope of Baseball could be way too much.

"The Colonel called me once, Dave Egan, the columnist from the *Boston Record* who Ted hated the most," Jimmy Carroll says. "He was a powerful figure, the Colonel. I was nervous. He said he'd heard that I was close to Ted. I said that I was. He said he'd heard Ted wasn't feeling well. Was this true?"

What to do? Jimmy figured he could tell the truth.

"He's okay," Jimmy said. "Except he's got diarrhea."

"Diarrhea?" the Colonel asked.

"Diarrhea," Jimmy confirmed.

The next morning the phone rang. Williams was furious. There was a story in the paper that "Ted Has Diarrhea." Why would Jimmy tell someone that?

"I didn't know," Jimmy still says. "I didn't think they'd put that word in the paper. 'Ted Has Diarrhea'?"

Stop the presses. This was the life of the Pope of Baseball.

He was the famous Ted Williams from the time he was 17, no more than 18 years old. The famous life was the only adult life he ever knew. From the time he joined the hometown San Diego Padres in the Pacific Coast League—he still hadn't graduated from Hoover High School—until the day he died in Hernando, Florida, 83 years old, he was the prize pumpkin at the county fair, prodded and pushed, examined, greeted with oohs and ahhs.

How do you handle this?

Because he could hit a baseball—an athletic feat in the national consciousness second only to knocking out a string of heavyweight contenders at the time—he could go where he wanted to go, do what he wanted to do. There might be a hassle involved, a crowd of bug-eyed gawkers and talkers in attendance, but he could be his own man.

The normal social restraints did not exist. He could pick his friends from the boardroom or the parking lot, whichever interested him, simply by offering his hand. He could pick his women from the Somerset lobby, any of them, sitting on the sofas, waiting for him to pass. He could travel or stay home, eat early or late. He could fart in church. If he wanted to go to church.

Is there such a thing as too much freedom? He was a test. A latchkey child from a broken home, unencumbered by an adolescence filled with parental dos and don'ts, he was raw and basic and naive when he arrived in the spotlight. No one had ever told him what to do in the past, and now, no matter how many people told him, he really didn't have to listen.

He was the famous Ted Williams. He could figure out what he wanted to figure out for himself.

"Vinnie Orlando, the visiting clubhouse guy, told me a story," Will McDonough, sportswriter for the *Boston Globe*, says. "Vinnie was about the same age as Ted and said that when Ted showed up for spring training the first time in 1938, he was like a Neanderthal. He was an animal.

"He didn't even know how to drive a car. He asked Vinnie, who had a car, if maybe they could double-date. If Vinnie could find some girls. Vinnie found the girls. He and Ted went to pick them up. 'How are you, how are you, etc. . . . .' Ted and his girl get in the backseat. Vinnie and his girl were in the front. Vinnie said he drove about three blocks. The girl in the backseat started screaming. Ted had just jumped her. He didn't know that maybe you were supposed to talk to each other, maybe eat dinner, whatever. He just jumped on her. He didn't know."

Where do you go from there?

The necessities of life bring conformity for most people. Get a job, get some money, get married, get a house, yessir, nosir, how high sir? What if all the necessities are covered by the single ability to swing a 32-ounce bat and hit a 5-ounce ball? Maybe you learn to drive and you learn the basics of dealing with the opposite gender, but how much else do you learn? There is no pot to confine growth to a prescribed area. You grow—or you don't grow—exactly in the ways you want.

The famous Ted Williams was able to pick and choose. If he wanted to fish for salmon or learn how to fly a plane or take pictures, he followed his inclinations to the maximum degree. If there was something he didn't want to learn, maybe something personal about relationships with a wife, a child, a friend, something that involved change and pain, well, he didn't have to learn. He could write a check, mumble, and move along.

Take me or leave me. I am what I am. If that was unacceptable, there always was a line of people who would not mind. He could bellow his opinions. He could charm a room, have everyone laughing and feeling good. He could shut down in a moment.

His refusal to wear a necktie, always a source of jokes, was actually a statement. The famous Ted Williams does what he wants. Take me or leave me. If you want somebody who wears a necktie, you want somebody else. Ted Williams was the one who would decide what was right and what was wrong for Ted Williams. Don't believe him? Then just listen.

His language was part of his freedom.

"The first time I ever saw him, first words out of his mouth were 'you motherfucken syphilitic piece of shit,' " Boston sportscaster Bob Lobel says. "He was playing golf. I don't know if he was talking to the golf ball, to himself, to what. I just know I've remembered every single word."

"I was in the U.S. Marines," former Red Sox batboy George Sullivan says. "They always talk about the language in the service. It didn't bother me one bit. The entire time I was a Marine, no one swore any better than Ted Williams. I'd had my basic training in that respect before I ever had basic training."

"I was a bodyguard for General George S. Patton during the Second World War," Al Palmeri, who was a director at the Ted Williams Baseball Camp for many years, says. "Yes, General Patton swore. No, he did not swear as well as Ted."

No one could swear as well as Ted. Not only were the words showstoppers—words like "cunt" and "cocksucker," dropped freely with f-bombs and modified with his favorite adjective, "syphilitic"—but there was a way he swore that made his outbursts special. He strung the words together to make elaborate, rococo, profane poetry. There was a cadence, a rhythm to his swearing. There was a blasphemous direction too, much of the anger addressed upward toward a syphilitic Supreme Being who had let humanity down just one more time.

"There was always a sequence," Dottie Lindia, wife of friend Joe Lindia, says. "Once the first word came out, you knew the other ones would follow. And if you ever could interrupt him in the middle, you knew he would have to start over again. The words had to come in the sequence."

For Williams, the language of the dugout was his language of the restaurant, the living room, the neighborhood store. That was simply the way he was. The social muffler that most people use—the one that keeps them from asking a second cousin to "pass the fucken potatoes" at Thanksgiving—never was developed. Never had to be. Never was.

He was the famous Ted Williams.

"I remember one time, though, we were at a restaurant, many years after he retired," Al Cassidy Jr., a longtime friend, says. "When we came in, I noticed a table with some mothers and fathers and some kids. I could see they got all excited. They were looking over at our table.

"Then Ted got going. The words were rolling out, one after another. I could see the mood change at the other table. Finally one of the fathers came over and read Ted out. Said there was no need for language like that. Ted took it. He didn't say anything, but he took it. He didn't swear again. Got very quiet. You could see he was embarrassed. He was like a little kid."

He *was* a little kid. Always. In a million ways.

That was what made him fascinating.

He preened. He pouted. He could be unbelievably kind, especially with money. He could be cold and remote. Women were a constant problem: a joy, a nuisance, a mystery, a lower life form put on earth mostly to entertain and complain. There were holes in his psychology that could be debated and studied nightly by academics and tavern regulars, third stool from the right. He was brilliant. He was dense. He was conservative, red white and blue. He still could have tons of liberal thoughts. He was an American hero, no doubt about that, a picture on a bedroom wall. He also could do things that were much less than heroic, everyday surrenders in everyday affairs. He was Ted Williams. He could hit a ball. More than anything, he could hit a baseball. He was famous.

Three wives. Two wars. Nineteen years in the major leagues. That was only a start.

He found his way to his own complicated Oz. He then had to stay there for all of his life.

A party was planned for Williams's 40th birthday on August 30, 1958. Nothing elaborate. He would throw it for himself in the suite. The guest list was comprised of the normal people, not teammates: the accountants and hotel operators and bellhops and lawyers and people who surrounded him in slack-jawed admiration and helped him live inside his bubble of fame. Jimmy Carroll was on the list.

He had an idea.

"You say to yourself, 'What do I get this guy for his birthday?' " Carroll says. "He has absolutely everything. What could I get him that might mean something to him?"

Carroll remembered a conversation in one of the many trips in the Coupe DeVille. He remembered exactly where it had taken place. They were going to the airport, down Commonwealth, and had just turned at Arlington Street, when he asked Ted if he had any idols. The night was rainy.

"No, never," Williams replied.

"You must have had an idol as a kid," Carroll said. "Ty Cobb? Babe Ruth? Someone like that. *You* were my idol."

"No. I grew up on the West Coast. I didn't even know much about those people then. Never followed the major leagues very close. I didn't have any idols. No."

Silence returned to the car. Carroll wondered if he'd asked the wrong thing. He drove around the Boston Common and was heading on to Charles Street, more silence, windshield wipers whacking, when Williams suddenly spoke.

"I take that back," he said. "I do have an idol. He's still my idol. Douglas MacArthur."

"Douglas MacArthur?"

"He's my kind of guy. He was my commander in the Second World War and the Korean War. I really respect him. Douglas MacArthur."

Douglas MacArthur, huh? Carroll decided that the perfect gift for Ted's birthday would be a signed picture from Ted's idol. Douglas MacArthur. One problem: how would a man get in touch with Douglas MacArthur? All Carroll knew was what he had read, that MacArthur now lived in the Waldorf Astoria in New York and worked for the Rand Corporation. How would a man get through the switchboard at the Waldorf Astoria?

Carroll approached the head bellman at the Somerset with his problem. He knew there was an alliance between bellmen at big hotels, one helping the other for odd requests. The bellman at the Somerset connected him with the head bellman at the Waldorf.

"You'll never get ahold of him," the bellman at the Waldorf said. "Not a chance."

"Ted Williams," Carroll repeated, invoking the magic name as often as possible. "This is for Ted Williams."

"Here's your only shot," the bellman finally said. "A driver picks the General up every morning at 8:15 to take him to work. The servants don't arrive until 9:00 A.M. If you call in those 45 minutes between 8:15 and 9:00, you might be able to talk to his wife. And you have to take it from there."

Carroll called the next day. The General's wife answered. She was cold. Carroll talked at his salesman's warp speed. Ted Williams! The ballplayer! General MacArthur is his idol! Ted Williams! Ted Williams! The General's wife warmed a little bit. She said that the irony was that the General also thought very highly of Ted Williams. He considered Williams to be the personification of the American ideal, the true man's man. Ted Williams? Okay, she gave Carroll the phone number and extension of the General's office. Good luck. Carroll dialed.

"I'm James Carroll of Boston," he said.

"How'd you get this number?" Douglas MacArthur replied.

The voice over the phone had dignity, force, strength. The only time Carroll ever had heard it was on the news, MacArthur telling Congress that "old *soldiers* never die, they just fade away." Never had Carroll been so nervous. Never had he talked so fast. Ted Williams! Ted Williams! Ted Williams!

Slowly, the General became interested. Yes, he truly admired Ted Williams, but he certainly couldn't go to Boston for a birthday party. Carroll said, "No! That wasn't what I wanted!" A signed photograph? Oh, that was different. How about something even better?

"I have a lot of oil paintings that people have sent me," MacArthur said. "They're paintings of me going back to the Philippines, most of them. I don't know why, people were inspired by my return to paint for some reason. Why don't I send you one of those? Would four feet by three feet be all right?"

The painting arrived in a crate at the house of Carroll's mother. He brought it to the Somerset on August 30. Irene Hennessy, famous in New England as the Narragansett Beer girl ("Hey, neighbor! Have a Gansett!") saw him in the lobby. She was a friend of Ted's.

"What do you have there, Jimmy?" she asked.

"You wouldn't believe it," he replied.

Unveiled in Room 231, the large face of MacArthur stared at the party group. The inscription read: "To Ted Williams—Not only America's greatest baseball player, but a great American who served his country. Your friend, Doug MacArthur. General U.S. Army." Williams was delighted. He placed the picture on the mantel above the fireplace.

Everyone stared in appropriate wonder. How far can a kid from nowhere in San Diego travel by hitting a baseball? This far.

This far indeed.

2 San Diego

The landscape of the past lies somewhere under the landscape of the present. That is a fact. An erector set of change might have been constructed to obscure the gridwork of memory—different buildings, different people, different trees, different signs, and different colors—but the past is still down there at the bottom.

If you can see it.

"This was all jackrabbits and snakes," Joe Villarino says, driving past the subdivision behind Herbert Hoover High School, house after house after house. "None of these houses were here. Just jackrabbits and snakes."

The clutter has to be removed.

That is the basic trick.

"Jackrabbits and snakes," Joe Villarino says again. "This was the edge of the city. Everything to the east was jackrabbits and snakes. Look at it now. My daughter has a house over in Spring Valley. Lives on what they call 'Dictionary Hill.' You know why they call it that? When they first cleared the land, they sold the lots for $60. And you got a free dictionary if you bought one. Now those lots . . . you couldn't touch one for under $200,000. And there's no dictionary."

Take away the Burger Kings and the Midas Muffler shops and the 24-hour pay-and-go convenience gas stations. Take away four of the six lanes on El Cajon Boulevard. Take away most of the cars too for that matter. Take away the fat concrete walls that make up the modern Hoover High, no windows anywhere, and replace them with a more gentle architecture from a more gentle time. Take away. Take away.

The old San Diego still sits there, population 100,000, maybe 150,000 tops, fresh air that you could breathe, people who would say hello (and you would say hello back), everyone knowing everyone else, everyone knowing everyone else's business. Take away the metropolis, population 1,223,400, the freeways with their important numbers, the 5 and the 8 and the 805 and all the rest. Take away the hustle, the bustle, the revved-up everything. The old San Diego still is underneath.

If you can see it.

"We didn't have a car," Joe Villarino says. "Not a lot of people did. My father, he paid a dollar a month for a trolley pass to get back and forth to work. I remember waiting for him to get home at night. He'd let me have the pass, and I'd just ride the trolley downtown and back, downtown and back again. Just to do it."

"This place right here was Powelson's Drug Store," Joe Villarino says, pointing at a Mexican restaurant named El Rodeo, the letters on the sign done in red and yellow. "The old man who ran it was very nice. He loved the baseball team, loved sports. We'd go in there every day."

"I had five brothers and two sisters," Joe Villarino says. "All of my brothers are gone. My sisters are still alive, but my brothers are gone."

Take away. Roll back. Everyone is still alive. The adventure of long ago is still there. The sun is up. The time is five minutes to eight, and the tall, skinny neighbor kid is coming down the sidewalk from his home at 4121 Utah Street toward Joe's house at 4335 Oregon. Every day. Clockwork. He already is a presence, the tall, skinny neighbor kid, loud in what he says, animated, almost goofy. He has opinions and dreams and confidence.

Joe is waiting for him on the steps of 4335 Oregon. Ted Williams would be here. Every day.

"I'd be right outside," Joe says, pointing at a squat apartment complex. "Except this isn't my house. The address is the same, but this building is new. . . ."

Off they go to Garfield Elementary School. The tall kid is excited. If they get there early, they will be first in line when the big playground box, looks like a coffin, is opened. They can take out the bats and the balls and get to work. The tall kid already has his glove. Ready to go.

"This is Garfield Elementary," Joe says, pointing at a one-story, modern school. "Except, of course, it's not the same one we went to. Same place, though. The principal used to park his car right here. It was an old Model T. . . ."

Take away. This is where it all began.

If you can see it.

Joe Villarino is now 85 years old. He can see.

"I'm looking for the water tower . . . there it is," Villarino says, pointing at a tower that rises maybe 150 feet off the ground. "Ted and I tried to climb that once. It was my idea. We talked about it and talked about it and one day we did it. We climbed the fence on the way home from school and got about halfway up before the guard came out and caught us. He was going to have us arrested. I was so scared. My mother would have killed me if I was arrested for climbing that tower. The guy just let us go.

"This . . . this was a reservoir," Villarino continues, pointing toward a large park. "There were dirt embankments on the sides. The whole thing was covered with boards. I don't know what happened to the reservoir. When we played baseball down there [the field at the end of the park] I made money by going onto the boards to get the foul balls. The boards were rotted and creaky. I was small. That's why I got the job. I'd hear those boards creaking and was sure that I was going to fall through. I got 35 cents for every baseball I brought back."

The park, North Park, was the starting point. The field . . . well, it is called Ted Williams Field now . . . was where the baseballs first started to fly over a short rightfield fence. This was the tall skinny kid's laboratory. From his porch on Utah Street a block and a half away you can see the baseball lights. Add some good, year-round California weather. Add a lot of free time. Add a lot of desperation, drive, whatever you want to call it, the yearning to step out of stifling circumstance. The result would knock the American League on its well-established keister.

"I suppose I knew him as well as anyone, maybe better," Villarino says. "We went all the way back to when we were six years old. My oldest brother even was going to marry his youngest aunt at one time. Wouldn't that have been something? We almost became shirttail relatives.

"I played marbles with Ted Williams before I ever played baseball with him. He had this big bag of marbles, bigger than anyone else. He always said that he'd won them, but I don't think so. I think he was buying marbles and putting them in his bag."

The old-timers, Villarino included, say the neighborhood has declined, now populated by new and threatening people, don't go there after dark, but it does not look threatening in the day. It looks much the way it did when Williams was a kid. A working man's neighborhood. The older houses mainly are wooden, tiny affairs, done in a style called "California bungalow." There are palm trees in front yards, orange and lemon trees in backyards. Kids' bicycles are left on their sides on crabgrass front lawns.

Williams's house ("There it is," Villarino says) is one of the California bungalows. There is a different tree in front and an aluminum awning over the porch and the street numbers—4121—curiously have been moved from the overhang of the porch to a side pillar, but not much else has changed. Two kids from next door are playing in front. Alas, they are kicking a soccer ball.

The owner of the house now is 62-year-old Tim Higgins. He is a retired postal worker and has lived here for 28 years. His mother lived with him until three years ago, when she passed away. He maintains her bedroom in the back, everything kept the way she had it, simply because he can't be moved to change the arrangement.

"I haven't changed a lot in the house," he says. "I've tried to keep it up as best I can. People come, once in a while, to take a look, but never anyone from San Diego. Always from somewhere else. I get letters too, people asking for a souvenir from the house . . . but what can I give 'em? I keep thinking that someone will come along, some wealthy man, somebody with deep pockets, make me a big offer because this was where Ted was raised, but I don't think it's going to happen. If this place ever sells, I'll have to sell it as natural real estate."

Higgins can rattle off what is old and what is new without even thinking. The kitchen is old, same stuff that was here when Ted was here. The venetian blinds, they're originals. The heating is new, central heating installed in 1970. The toilet fixtures definitely are old. A plumber once looked at them and said they might even be valuable they were so old. Said to never change them. To call the Smithsonian first.

The ceilings are very low, maybe eight feet. The rooms are cramped. Higgins can point out who slept where. He also can show the lines of an addition that Ted had carpenters add for his mother sometime after he began making money. The patio in the back, Ted had that added too.

"See how small the backyard is?" Higgins says. "That's where Ted used to go to swing his bat, I guess."

Higgins met Williams once. He remembers the date, July 8, 1992. Williams returned to San Diego for the All-Star Game with his son, John-Henry. John-Henry wanted to see the house. Higgins remembers how uncomfortable Williams was. An ESPN crew—some crew anyway—was taping the visit. Williams didn't even want to go inside the door. John-Henry insisted. Williams was reluctant at every turn.

"This house, Ted don't like it," Higgins says. "You could see it brought back a lot of bad memories. All he wanted to do was get out. He was nice to my mother, but I stayed back, didn't even ask for an autograph. People at the post office said, 'Hey, you should have got his autograph,' but I could see how Ted was feeling.

"This house, Ted don't like it at all."

Williams was the Huckleberry Finn character of this modest neighborhood, the undisciplined roamer, the kid who didn't have to be home at any particular time. Born on April 30, 1918, named "Teddy" after Teddy Roosevelt—a name Williams later formalized to Theodore Samuel Williams—he and his brother Danny were caught in the cold climate of a bad marriage. Their father, Sam, was a photographer who left for work early and stayed late and didn't smile much at home. A drinker. Didn't care. Their mother, May Venzor Williams, was a religious zealot. She was always working for the Lord. For the Salvation Army.

May Venzor Williams was the dominant figure in Ted Williams's young life. Or maybe the dominant nonfigure.

"She fell in love with the Salvation Army when she was very young," her nephew, Manny Herrera, says. "Her family was Mexican Baptists, religious enough, but not in the Salvation Army. The Army would hold revival meetings on the corner of Haley and State Streets in downtown Santa Barbara, where she grew up. When May was 11 years old, maybe 12, one of her sisters would come home and tell their father that May was down there singing. Mr. Pedro Venzor would get up, go down to Haley and State, and bring May home. She wouldn't fight. He'd say, 'Those people are crazy.' 'Yes, Daddy.' 'They're fanatics.' 'Yes, Daddy.' 'I don't want you going down there with them.' 'Yes, Daddy.'

"The next day she'd be back at Haley and State. Singing again."

That early love affair never ended. The only hiccup in her devotion came while she was training in Hawaii to become an officer in the Salvation Army. She met Sam. He was seven years older, finishing up his time in the U.S. Army, an enlisted man from Mount Vernon, New York, returning from the Philippines. He claimed he had served with Teddy Roosevelt in the famous charge up San Juan Hill during the Spanish-American War. There is some mystery to that—his birth certificate indicates he would have been 15 years old at the time—but whatever he told May seemed to work. She gave up her hopes for a Salvation Army commission (officers were not allowed to marry outside the Army) but kept her faith and went with Sam. The year was 1910.

They were an interesting couple for the time, May with a Mexican mother and a Mexican father with Basque roots, Sam a mixture of Welsh and English. They lived for a short while in Los Angeles, where Sam was a streetcar conductor, but by the time the boys were born, and after May apparently had suffered two earlier miscarriages, San Diego had become home. This was where May had been stationed, a foot soldier now in the service of the Lord. The family moved into the tiny white house on Utah Street when Ted was five years old. The price of the house was $4,000. The payments were $100 per month.

Sam wandered into his photography business, owning a shop on Fifth Avenue. May charged into her life's work. She went to nearby Tijuana to convince drunks of the error of their ways. She went to downtown Broadway in San Diego to ring a bell on Christmas. She went wherever money was being raised and the Word was being spread.

"I went with her to the bars a couple of times," Alice Psaute, an 80-year-old Salvation Army veteran, says. "You'd go in with pots. Men would throw money at the pots. You'd have to get on your hands and knees and pick quarters off the floors."

"You'd see May on the streetcars all the time," Frank Cushing, a friend of Ted's from San Diego, says. "There were only two streetcar lines at the time, the 7 and the 11, and she'd be on either one of them every day. So if you took the streetcar, you saw her. Praising the Lord."

She would wear her blue uniform with the familiar blue bonnet every day. She was tireless and fearless. She sang, she played musical instruments, she did magic tricks to attract the curious. She once—Alice Psaute says—held the world record for selling the most copies of *The War Cry*, the Salvation Army magazine, in a calendar year. The world record. Not San Diego. Not California or the United States. The world record. What kind of dedication does that take?

Too much, perhaps, if you have two young boys.

"May actually was ahead of her time," Manny Herrera says. "She was one of the first liberated women. She did what she wanted to do. She didn't want to cook . . . couldn't cook. That gal burnt everything she ever tried to cook. She didn't want to clean house. I was in her kitchen once, she had nine big stacks of newspapers in there. My aunt Sara, who raised me, May's younger sister, came down from Santa Barbara to cook and clean house when the boys were young. May didn't want to do it. She was a sweet woman, but she was no housekeeper. She was all Salvation Army."

The boys, who both cringed when they were brought by her to be part of the Army's street-corner revivals, eventually were left at home. They had that unsupervised heaven that all kids say they want but few can handle. Where to go? What to do? The dull lights of education, of course, offered no great attraction. The boys went for the two traditional dramatic enticements: Ted went for sports, for baseball, and Danny, two years younger, went for trouble.

"I was seven years behind Ted at Hoover High," Frank Cushing says, "so when I got there, Ted was already a big deal, famous in the big leagues. But my metals shop teacher always talked about Danny, the things Danny Williams did. Never talked about Ted."

The roles of the athlete and the delinquent almost seemed to have been handed down from a higher power. Ted was bigger, stronger, favored his father's light coloring. He looked Anglo. Danny was shorter, sickly, favored his mother. Darker. Danny Williams looked Mexican.

Would the roles have been reversed if the bodies had been reversed, the skin colors reversed? Hard to say. Ted did have the disposition, the mind, to pick up something and study it harder than anyone else around him. He fell into an all-consuming love with baseball the way the mathematics prodigy falls into an all-consuming love with the infinite variations of numbers. The fact that he looked like an athlete and an All-American boy certainly did not hurt when coaches looked to find their favorite students, the ones who had the chance to learn most, but the love was there at the beginning. Danny . . . Danny did have the disposition for trouble.

"He wasn't a bad kid," Joe Villarino says, "but he always had to challenge authority. He just did things. Like the playground was locked up every night and didn't open until nine. No one was supposed to be in there before nine. Danny just didn't care. He'd climb the fence and be in the playground by himself. The playground director would come at nine, find Danny, and ban him for a month. The month would pass and Danny would be allowed back, and a couple more months would pass and he'd climb the fence again and be banned again. It was like he had to do it."

He became the truant, the kid who went to a succession of schools, failing in most of them, the kid who maybe stole your bicycle when you were young and maybe stole your car when you were older. He gravitated toward the gray, if not toward the darkness. Ted would later tell the story of standing on the front porch with Danny, ten o'clock at night, waiting for their mother to come home to let them inside. There was a reason they were standing outside. Danny.

"When he had a key and got inside, he'd take things down to the what-do-you-call-it, the pawn shop," Manny Herrera says. "May would walk by the pawn shop and see her Salvation Army cornet in the window. What was this? She'd go inside and ask how it got there. The man would pull out a slip of paper and say, 'Do you know a Danny Williams from 4121 Utah Street?' May would have to pay to get her cornet back."

His edgy early life would evolve into his edgy later life. He would get into trouble and Ted would send him money, and he would get into more trouble and Ted would send more money. Ted would send a new set of furniture to his mother, and Danny would send the furniture to the pawn shop.

Danny's sons, Ted (named after Uncle Ted) and Sam, remember moving a lot as young kids, always ahead of bill collectors, going from El Paso to Chicago to wherever. They remember an embittered, often mean man at the wheel of the family car. They remember a pistol strapped to the shaft of the steering wheel.

"Dad had a hard time with authority," Ted Williams, the son of Danny, says. "The handgun was part of it. He figured that if the handgun was showing and he had a license, it was okay. Well, maybe it was in some states, but not all of them. We'd be driving and get stopped, and there'd be a big thing. Because of the handgun."

Danny wound up his travels exactly where they began, back at 4121 Utah Street, living with May. He came back to die. He had leukemia. His two sons moved into the bedroom he and his brother had shared. They listened to May talk about the Lord, saw her leave the house in her uniform and bonnet. They went to Salvation Army summer camp. They learned how to ride bicycles in North Park.

"May was very sweet," Danny's son says. "By this time she was still in the present, but she was winding down. Virtually every sentence she spoke did have some mention of the Lord. It was not a very happy time. My father was an unhappy, angry man. He always felt like he was owed something by somebody but never got it. His illness made him more unhappy and angry.

"I was eight years old when he died. He was just 39."

Ted, in his autobiography, *My Turn at Bat*, describes Danny as "the kind of guy who always wanted a motorcycle, but never got one." Danny was that indeed. He was the flip side of Ted. There is a mystery, always, when two brothers live in the same bedroom, are raised in the same circumstance, eat the same food, and use the same shower and then step out the front door and do truly different things.

How do you figure it? Danny found trouble and disappointment.

Ted found baseball.

"Ted was all baseball when we were kids," Joe Villarino says. "The rest of us would play other sports. Ted only cared about baseball. That's all he talked about. He never talked about girls, never had a date that I know of. Just baseball. I had a nice little girl, shared my locker at school. Not Ted. Just baseball."

"He'd walk down the street—I can see this—and put his hand along his nose, straight out, like he was looking on two sides of a door," Les Cassie Jr., teammate and friend from the neighborhood, says. "He'd close one eye, then the other, figuring out what he could see from each eye. He did this all the time. He was always figuring things out. I guess it had something to do with hitting. They'd talk later about how great his eyes were. Well, he worked at it."

"He was different from all the other kids, from the rest of us," Roy Engle, teammate and friend, says. "I don't know how else to describe him. He was just different."

He was serious about what he was doing. That was a major difference.

Maybe the other kids thought they were serious about baseball, wanted to go off to the great ballparks of the land, but they were hoping a lot more than working. Baseball to them was a lottery ticket. A maybe. The other kids, when baseball season ended, were playing the other sports, football and basketball, chasing the other lottery tickets. Ted was working. Baseball was a train ticket, not a lottery ticket, a train ticket to a glorious future. A definite. He had inherited May's devotional gene. He simply put his devotion into a more secular pursuit.

One of his earliest teachers was his uncle, Saul Venzor, one of May's four brothers. At family gatherings in Santa Barbara, Spanish spoken more than English, Saul would play catch with his eight-year-old nephew in the driveway. Saul had a semipro baseball history as a pitcher. There was a family legend that he once had struck out Babe Ruth, Joe Gordon, and Lou Gehrig during an exhibition. Whether the legend was true or not probably doesn't matter. The important part was that Saul was good enough to have it attached to him. He was a big guy and competitive.

"Saul was tough," Manny Herrera says. "If he played you in Chinese checkers, he had a ruler in his hand. He wanted you to think. If you made a wrong move, he'd whack your hand with the ruler. Why'd you make that stupid move? You wouldn't make it again.

"He taught Ted how to throw a baseball. Saul had a good fastball. Ted had a good fastball."

While Danny broke away from authority, Ted walked toward it. Authority controlled the bats and balls, the games. The knowledge. He played baseball at Garfield Elementary, starting out as a normal recess and after-school activity, but by the age of 12 he was into his obsessive mode, swinging the bat in the backyard, imagining a late-game situation at the faraway Polo Grounds in New York, runners on base, Williams at the plate. He was swinging the bat, swinging and swinging, drinking malted milkshakes, eating any food put in front of him, swinging the bat, looking for size and power and that perfect synchronization to send baseballs over the fence at North Park. The playground director wasn't a threat. He was a friend, a teacher.

His name was Rod Luscomb, and he was a big, good-looking guy, six or seven years older than Ted, a former minor league ballplayer who'd been thwarted in his climb upward by an injury. Luscomb saw the potential in a kid who was consumed by baseball. Luscomb also had been consumed. He became Ted's batting practice pitcher and confidant. "Instructor" would imply too much teaching. Ted pretty much taught himself, finding the uppercut swing that would be so different from the swings of most big-league batters in both style and performance.

"Lusk had pitched in the minors and was still pitching semipro ball on Sundays," Williams said in the book *Ted Williams: My Life in Pictures.* "He would throw me batting practice for an hour or more. Then I'd throw to him. I tagged after him, hung around that little playground for a good seven years. A wonderful, wonderful man. I can't give him *enough* credit for making me a ballplayer."

Luscomb was one of a number of neighborhood men who would respond to the want, the need, of an unregulated boy. If Sam didn't care and May was too busy with the Lord, there were other men who had time. Want to stay for dinner? Sure. Want to go fishing? Sure. Want to come along? Sure. Here was a kid who would savor things that their own kids perhaps took for granted.

Mr. Roetert, next door, was a game warden and took the kid fishing for bass. Mr. Lutz, across the street, was a great shot with a rifle and took the kid hunting for rabbit. Mr. Villarino . . . he had a trick where he could fold his eyelids back, make his eyeballs look like they were going to fall out. Could you do it again, Mr. Villarino? Mr. Cassie, well, Mr. Cassie did a lot of things with Ted Williams.

"They went fishing all the time, my father and Ted," Les Cassie Jr. says. "I went with 'em once. It was the most boring thing I'd ever done. I never went back. Still haven't gone back."

Mr. Cassie and Williams would go to Coronado Island at night, walk past the elegant Del Coronado Hotel, the chandeliers lit, rich people dressed and doing whatever rich people did, then fish for albacore until midnight. They would go to Mission Bay, pull down some bamboo sticks and make fishing poles on the spot to go fishing. They would talk, plan. They would be surrogate father and surrogate son.

"Ted was like part of our family," Cassie Jr. says. "He'd eat dinner a lot at our house. My mother loved him. She'd always make a place. We'd go to the pool hall and play snooker, Ted and me. There was only one table in the pool hall, and it was always open. The only people we ever saw playing were us. We both thought there was something suspicious going on, like a card game in the back, but we never knew. We'd play pool, then we'd go to my house for dinner."

The Williams story that Les Cassie Jr. has told the most—for over 65 years now—is Williams's introduction to Hoover High baseball coach Wos Caldwell. There is a Br'er Rabbit, word-of-mouth rhythm to it after all of these repetitions, Williams showing up at Hoover baseball practice after finishing his last day at Horace Mann Junior High School in February. The practice was one of those *Chorus Line* affairs, one of the first practices of the season. There were maybe one hundred kids, all trying out for the team, at a field—not the baseball field—next to the school. Williams shouts, 'Hey, coach, let me hit.' No answer. Williams sits on the steps of the print shop. 'Hey, coach, let me hit.' No answer. Finally, after a few more of these pleas, Caldwell relents. He is a big, quiet man who once played football with Red Grange at the University of Illinois. Okay, this will shut the kid up. Go ahead.

"The first one went on top of the lunch arbor," Les Cassie Jr. says, bringing in the proper majesty of the moment. "No one had ever hit one up there. Then he hit another. Then, when it's over, he tells Wos Caldwell, 'I'll be back tomorrow.' "

Okay, the kid could hit.

He also could pitch.

For the next three years, he was the hitting-pitching star of the Hoover High Cardinals. The league seasons were short, 12 games plus playoffs, because the road trips were long on the Southern California coast, schools spread apart, but Caldwell scheduled games everywhere against all manner of teams to keep his boys playing. Williams once estimated he played about 64 games a year with the high school. Then he estimated he played another 64 with other teams. With the Fighting Bob Post American Legion team. With the Texas Liquor House semipro team. With the kids' league in the mornings at North Park and again with the men's league in the afternoons. He went up to Santa Barbara, played on semipro teams with Saul Venzor, a 15-year-old kid with men.

He was a commodity. He could hit. He practiced even more than he played, single-minded and constant.

"If I gave you a quarter for each pitch you ever threw me in batting practice, how much do you think I'd owe you?" he asked Wilbert Wiley, another local kid, many years later.

"Start at $100,000," Wiley replied.

"Hundreds of kids have the natural ability to become great ballplayers," Williams would tell *Time* magazine, "but nothing except practice, practice, practice will bring out that ability. I used to go with another kid, Wilbert Wiley, who was just as enthusiastic as me. We'd take turns pitching to each other. . . . Come to think of it, one of my greatest thrills came when I was 14, the day I discovered I could hit whatever Wilbert threw me."

Williams hit brand-new baseballs. He hit old, scuffed-up baseballs. He hit baseballs held together with electrical tape. He hit imaginary baseballs, again and again. He walked down the street with a bat and hit flowers off their stems. He hit .583 in his junior year at Hoover High. He hit .403 in his senior year. He hit.

"We had a pretty good team," Joe Villarino, who was the third baseman, says. "But we were pretty good because we had Ted. He was something else. He talked about seeing the ball flatten out when it hit the bat. The rest of us would try to look, but none of us saw what he saw. I know I never saw the ball flatten out on the bat when I hit it.

"Always, the conversation was about hitting. I remember him wondering why some hitters let their little finger hang over the knob of the bat. He wondered if it did something, gave them more power. He tried it out. Said it didn't do anything at all."

"There was a game, a team put a shift on against Ted," Les Cassie Jr. says, a glimpse at future strategies. "Ted hit the ball to left. He was wily. He solved the mysteries of the game."

School was mostly a lark, a place you had to be to play baseball on the team. Rod Luscomb later remembered that the first time he met Williams at the playground was at two o'clock in the afternoon. Williams was supposed to be in school. He was ten years old and said that school wasn't important. He wanted to be a ballplayer. Luscomb told him that he couldn't be a ballplayer in North Park until 3:15 every day and had to go to school if he wanted the playground instructor to pitch to him. Williams went to school.

He was, for sure, a teacher's frustration, the smart kid who didn't care. He went for the laugh instead of the grades on the report card. He was the kid a teacher wanted to sit in the front of the room, the one to be kept under surveillance.

"Ted would speak his piece in class," Cassie Jr. says. "You knew he was there. He had that big, booming voice even then."

"We had a teacher for history, Mr. Maguine," Villarino says. "Ted would always mispronounce his name. He'd call him 'Mr. May-quin.' Mr. Maguine would say, 'It's pronounced Ma-gwynn.' Old Ted would say, 'Right, Mr. May-quin.' Then he'd just laugh. That would happen every day."

"He habitually stopped in the office to have a friendly chat with the principal, who, to him, was not a superior person, but a friend," Floyd Johnson, the principal at Hoover, remembered years later in a conversation with sportswriter Forrest Warren. "As these little conversations progressed, the conversations always turned to baseball and fishing, and I always have been extremely interested in both sports.

"If one had looked in on one of these visits, they would have seen Ted slumped down in his chair with his feet on the principal's desk. I was completely oblivious of Ted's posture. I thoroughly enjoyed the conversation. This was not impudence on Ted's part, because to him all folks on the campus were just the same—faculty, principal, or kids."

Fun outside of school was greasing the streetcar tracks on Halloween night, watching the cars slide. Fun was playing a game called "Big League" in the handball court at North Park, hitting a pipe that ran across the wall for a home run, playing "Over the Line," that old sandlot standby, Ted almost able to place the ball where he wanted. Fun was Ted going hunting with a kid named Wally Hebert. They had two bullets between them—bullets were expensive—but they came home with two rabbits. Fun was even pounding out the neighborhood bully. The kid was giving Joe Villarino trouble, and Villarino, small, was building up to a confrontation when the kid also crossed Ted. End of the bully. Ted could scrap. Fun was anywhere.

"You'd go to the movies with Ted, he always did this thing . . ." Cassie Jr. says. "He'd stop at the water fountain, get his hands all wet. Then you'd sit down in the theater, and Ted would do a loud 'Ker-chew' and flick the water on the people in front of us. We'd all start laughing."

"He didn't go to many movies, though, back then because he thought they might hurt his eyes," Villarino says. "But he'd go to anything that had Olivia de Havilland. For some reason, he just loved Olivia de Havilland."

The three years of high school went past in this kind of hurry—now a gauzy, Depression-era film clip—and the biggest award Ted received on graduation day was for typing. Bob Breitbard, who played football but not baseball at the same time at Hoover, remembers the principal, Floyd Johnson, standing on the front steps of the school and singling out both Williams and him. It was a moment.

"He said, 'I want to give Ted Williams and Bob Breitbard special recognition,' " Breitbard says. " 'They both were able to type 32 words a minute without an error. They finished first in their class.' "

Fun was typing?

"My sister still says she took the test for both of you," Joe Villarino says to Breitbard.

The interesting part of that graduation—besides the fact that Ted received exactly one gift, a fountain pen, from Mr. Cassie for graduating high school—was that it was held in February 1937, the class having gone all the way through school on an off-semester pace. By the time graduation was held, Ted already had played half of the 1936 minor league season.

He was a San Diego Padre veteran before he ever left high school.

The Padres were the new game in town in 1936. They were owned by Bill Lane, a crusty old-timer who had made a lot of money in gold in Utah and eventually brought a baseball team from Salt Lake City to Los Angeles. The team became the Hollywood Stars, part of the AAA Pacific Coast League.

After ten years of operating in L.A., playing at Wrigley Field, also home of the Los Angeles Angels, the rent suddenly had been doubled on Lane, from $5,000 to $10,000 for 1936. He thought he could do better than that, and he could. The city of San Diego was ready for minor league baseball.

How ready? Using the cheap and plentiful Depression-era labor of the WPA, a wooden stadium seating 11,500 was built in three months near the docks and the train tracks on the site of an old bus terminal. Or almost built. Certain amenities were skipped in getting the park ready for opening day—there was no backstop, for instance, so patrons had to be ready for foul tips at any moment—but Lane didn't mind. He had a clause in his contract with the city that if the park were not fully completed, he did not have to pay rent. The doors still could open, tickets were 75 cents apiece, and the nearby naval base had sailors with free time and the ballpark had beer.

The Padres were a hit. They would lead the PCL in attendance in 1936. Lane wouldn't pay rent for the entire year.

"It was a different kind of crowd," Autumn Durst Keltner remembers. "People dressed to go to the games. It was an event. My mother and I would dress for every game, then sit in the box for players' wives. It could get ugly sometimes—people yelling things at the wives if their husbands weren't playing well—but you dressed and you sat there and watched the game."

Autumn was 12 years old at the time. Her father, Cedric Durst, was a 36-year-old outfielder on the Padres. The PCL consisted of mainly players at one end or the other of their career, moving up or out. Durst, who'd played four years with the St. Louis Browns, then four more with the New York Yankees, including the famous 1927 "Murderers' Row" edition, was among the latter.

"He'd roomed for four years with Lou Gehrig," his daughter says. "That's why they had him room with Ted."

Durst was quoted about the experience in a 1960 series about Ted by Phil Collier in the *San Diego Union*. He remembered Williams as the most intelligent young hitter he'd ever met, the first kid he'd seen who had figured out what was taking place in the pitchers' heads, the strategies that were being used against him. Most kids swung and survived on reflexes. Williams already was using his head.

"He was a big, good-natured kid, and full of confidence," Durst said. "He woke me up one morning—he was jumping on his bed, beating his chest, and he said, 'Christ, Ced, it's great to be young and full of vinegar.'

"I said, 'Sure, Ted, but not at six o'clock in the morning.' "

Williams had wound up with the Padres in the middle of their season after a complicated bidding process that also involved the New York Yankees. Because he was a minor, either his father or mother would have to sign for him. Sam became involved with Bill Essick, a scout for the Yankees. Negotiations were proceeding, and it appeared Ted would be heading off into the Yankees' spread-out farm system. May, on the other hand, talked with Bill Lane.

It made sense for Lane to sign a local kid for a local team. It made sense for May that her son would play baseball close to home. Sense equaled sense. She extracted a promise from Lane that Ted would not be farmed out in the next two years and also extracted a small bonus. She signed the contract. The local kid was on the local team. He was paid $150 per month.

"I'd seen him before he ever signed," second baseman Bobby Doerr, another teenager who had played a year in L.A. with the Stars and moved with the team to San Diego, says. "Teams didn't have the big farm systems they later had. There were a lot of tryouts in those days, guys trying out before the games.

"I was standing by the right side of the batting cage for some reason that I don't know. I mean, I was a right-handed hitter, so that meant I usually stood on the left side of the cage, but somehow I was on the right this day. There's Ted, no more than eight, ten feet away from me. I remember him telling me he was six-foot-three, 147 pounds. I don't know why he told me that.

"The old guys—which was most of our team—were hitting and Frank Shellenback, our manager, was pitching. He said, 'Okay, now let the kid hit a few.' The old guys all were kind of grousing about that, but then Ted got in there and started swinging. After he hit six or seven balls, one of the guys said, 'Well, they'll sign this kid in the next week.'

"On Monday, there he was, waiting for us at the train station. He was on the team. Off we went to San Francisco."

Think of the excitement. This was possibly the first time Williams had ever ridden on a train, certainly the first time in a sleeping car. The wheels were clacking and the countryside was going past, and he was in this special car, filled only with ballplayers, *professional* ballplayers. He was going to the dining car, the seats in the special car then turned into beds while you ate, lowers and uppers, uppers for the rookies, lowers for the veterans, everyone sleeping for a night, still moving, then landing at some city you've never seen, going to some ballpark you've never seen, playing against players you've never seen (but maybe have heard about), playing baseball, baseball, baseball.

Maybe there was no air-conditioning anywhere, not in the hotels, not on the trains, where the windows were opened and the grit just covered everyone, and maybe the uniforms were that heavy, itchy wool, weighing 500 pounds by the seventh inning, caked with mud, not to be cleaned except once a week, and maybe and maybe, but this was heaven. The road trips were different in the PCL, due to the distances between cities. Teams would check into a hotel and play seven straight games in the same city. Monday was off for traveling. Games were played Tuesday to Sunday, a doubleheader on Sunday, the second game shortened to seven innings. Heaven. The Padres would have a curfew of six o'clock on Sunday if they were traveling, hurry to the train, travel all night, then travel all day and travel all night and half the next day, arriving just in time to take cabs to Civic Stadium in Seattle to play on a hard-rock dirt infield in the sun. Heaven.

"I caught the first ball Ted Williams ever hit as a professional," Bobby Mattick, who was playing for the Los Angeles Angels at Wrigley Field, says. "He came into the game as a pitcher. We were up on them pretty good, and Shellenback brought him in. When he got to hit, this lanky kid, all bones, he hit a liner to me at short. He got up again, but I don't remember what he did. I just remember that his first game was as a pitcher, and his first time at bat he hit the ball to me."

There are a couple of mistakes in Mattick's memory—Doerr's memory too for that matter. Williams's first at bat was a strikeout in San Diego on a Sunday, the day before the trip to San Francisco, a called third strike, looking, against Cotton Pippin, a righthander from Sacramento. But the important part was that this was the start. Firsts came one after another. Yes, on his next trip to the plate after Mattick's catch Williams collected his first hit. Yes, he collected another hit in his next at bat in the game. First two-hit day.

First catch in the outfield. First base on balls. First spit as a professional. Here were new eyes on an old parade. The kid chattered from morning until night, chewing his nails, booming out his words, asking questions that were followed by more questions. Why did a pitcher do this? Why did a batter do that? The kid swung any object that happened to be around, swung the bedroom pillows in simulation of the swing he would use at the plate. He swung nothing, just that imaginary bat, if no object could be found. Repetition brought subtle innovation. There would be baseball people, sportswriters, fans, who would wonder for years at his "natural" swing. Well, if it was natural, it was because he did it all the time.

Because of his size, so tall and so thin, and because of his age and because of his energy and because of his . . . well, because of his swing, he was noticed. He was a different sort of talent.

"I can see this now," Dominic DiMaggio, future teammate and friend says. "The first time I ever saw Ted, I was sitting on the bench for the San Francisco Seals, and our manager, Lefty O'Doul, went out and talked to him while they were taking batting practice. That was unheard of. He never did that, talk with someone from another team. All of us saw it and were wondering what he was doing. He came back to the dugout, and someone asked him. He said, 'I told him, "Never let anyone change your swing." '

"Lefty O'Doul was the most respected teacher of hitting in the entire league," Mattick says. "He was very big on hip action. When he saw that in Ted—remember you saw a guy for seven straight days in the Pacific Coast League—that was important."

Different. The kid stuck in your head.

"I remember the first game he played against us in San Francisco," Max West, another kid in the league, playing for the San Francisco Missions, says. "We played at Seals Stadium, which was located down by the water. Very windy. Very tricky. A big brewery was right across the street, and it got so windy that this foam from the beer would blow across and land on the field. New guys on the team were always told that if you ate some of the foam it would be like drinking beer. They'd give it a try and be washing out their mouths all night. It tasted bitter, awful.

"Anyway, Ted was up. He hit this long shot to right that looked like it was going foul, out of the park. He broke his bat on the hit. He didn't even run, went the other way, going back to the dugout for another bat. Well, if you knew the wind, you paid attention. Sure enough, that wind kept blowing the ball back and back, and when it landed it was a fair ball inside the rightfield line. Ted already was back to the dugout. Do you think he heard about that?"

Williams and Doerr became road-trip friends, pushed together by their age and situation and what they found was a common love for fishing and hunting. Doerr talked about fishing for steelheads and trout, Williams about fishing for bass and albacore. The day games would end early enough for walks at night, and the night games would free up time for walks during the day. The two young guys would walk and walk—stop for a milkshake every now and then to try to put on weight, more weight for more power—and wind up, say, down at the fish pier in Seattle. Look at the fish! All the way from Alaska! Arctic char! Halibut!

"We'd go to movies a lot, Westerns," Doerr says. "I remember coming out of a movie one time in Oakland. Bill Lane was out there. He was a mean old guy. He grabs Ted. He says, 'Hey, you're heading the list.' Ted says, 'What list?' Lane says, 'The overeaters list.' We got two dollars a day for meals. Ted said he couldn't live on that. He was charging for meals that were more than the two dollars a day.

"I don't know what he did for the rest of the year, but he did tell me that the next year, when he was playing every day and hitting, he ordered as much as he wanted and Lane didn't say a thing."

The baseball part of this new life started slow for Williams. The Padres had three veteran outfielders, and Williams was a reserve, playing only when Durst or Vince DiMaggio or Ivey Shiver was hurt or needed a rest. The plan was to allow this new kid a chance to watch and learn, maybe become a contributor next year. The plan fell apart, though, toward the end of August. Shiver suddenly announced he was quitting. He had a chance to become the football coach at the University of Georgia. Lane tried to convince him to stay, but Shiver saw coaching football as his future. The job was open, by default, for Williams.

He was solid, if not spectacular, during a stretch run, then quick elimination in the PCL playoffs. He finished with a .271 average on 107 at bats in 42 games. His only home run had come during an exhibition game and did not count in the statistics. The interesting part was that his future quietly had been settled.

"Red Sox general manager Eddie Collins came out to look at [shortstop] George Myatt and me," Bobby Doerr says. "While he was here, he saw Ted and became interested. He signed me, and he wanted to sign Ted. Lane told him Ted was too young and that he'd promised Ted's mother that Ted would be around for two years. Collins asked Lane to be called when the bidding opened. And Lane didn't forget."

"It wasn't hard to find Ted Williams," Collins later explained. "He stood out like a brown cow in a field of white cows."

In the 1937 season, after graduating from Hoover in the winter, and after a first two months with another stretch on the bench, Williams finally broke into the lineup on June 22 with an inside-the-park homer to Lane Field's deep, deep WPA centerfield to give the Padres a 3–2 win over Portland. Shellenback kept starting him after that, and Williams kept delivering base hits and homers. The Padres wound up winning the PCL title with eight straight wins in the two rounds of the playoffs. Williams wound up with a .291 batting average with 23 home runs.

His Hoover friends, like Villarino and Cassie and Roy Engle, were able to go to the park and watch it all unfold. Cassie remembers listening to the road games on the radio with his father. There was a pure excitement here, this skinny kid doing all this stuff in front of friends. Didn't he say he was going to do it? Here he was. He was doing it. Williams still was living on Utah Street. He still was taking batting practice at North Park, bringing scuffed-up balls from the pros back to the playground.

He had just passed his 19th birthday, and he was ascendant, taking this one last run around the familiar bases.

"Which pitch bothers you most?" veteran pitcher Howard Craghead asked him one day.

"Can't tell the difference," Williams replied. "They all look like they are hanging out in front of the plate on a string."

"The Boston Red Sox bought a champion when they acquired 19-

year-old Ted Williams . . . ," an unnamed West Coast correspondent breathlessly told the *Boston Globe* after Collins finally was able to corral the rights to Williams in December 1937. "If this lad doesn't make good, there will be many scribes and managers doing some explaining, but they are confident the youth will make a name for himself under the big tent. . . .

"Williams has good eyes and no 'fat' pitch ever gets by him. To give him one down the alley with nothing but the cover on the ball is like putting a match to a stick of dynamite. He'll murder the apple. Change of pace pitches and curve balls don't cross up the lad, either. . . . His supporters predict that he'll put Boston on the map and pack the people into the park to see this lanky 'stringbean' plaster the ball. And let us tell you, the kid really can smack that pea."

The correspondent, moving out of the produce department, then described a Williams home run that supposedly had traveled 126 miles. The ball, he said, landed in a boxcar in the rail yards behind Lane Field and was not found until the train reached Los Angeles. This statistic later would be repeated in a *Ripley's Believe It or Not* cartoon, but PCL historian Art Beverage says that similar home runs have been attributed to other PCL sluggers. Part of PCL myth, probably none of the hits were real. The correspondent also described another Williams homer that nearly knocked a kid out of a tree behind the Lane Field fence.

"There has been so much written about Williams' attitude that one would be led to believe the kid is a 'bad actor,' " the correspondent added. "But he isn't. There isn't a finer youth to be found anywhere. True, he's at that age where he doesn't like to take advice, believing that he knows everything and can't be told anything, but he'll come to earth before long."

The kid, however, felt he was traveling in the opposite direction. He wasn't heading toward restrictions; he was leaving them behind.

The deal that was made—the Red Sox trading the rights to four minor leaguers to Lane and shipping $1,000 to May and Sam—would not only send him off to the challenge he always wanted but free him from all the constrictions he felt on Utah Street. He would be out of the home life he always had hated.

"It was like this," Williams once explained. "My mother went one way, my father went another way, and I went yet another way. Three people. Three different ways."

May had not been part of that family section with Autumn Durst

Keltner at the Padres games. She had chosen her normal routine, circling outside the park, selling her magazine, ringing her bell, doing God's work. She was not averse to telling people, yes, sir, that was her son, Ted Williams, who was a star for the team. Yes, sir. This was the place Williams was leaving.

"I was talking with him not too many years ago," Manny Herrera says. "I told him, 'I loved your mother, man. She was a sweet lady.' She had come to live with us near the end of her life. Ted just said, 'Well, yeah, but she was. . . .' He then used some words that I wouldn't repeat. Hah. I had the feeling that he did not think she was a great mother."

Lane Field is long gone, replaced by a parking lot. Ted is gone. The teachers, the coaches, so many of the characters—May in her Salvation Army bonnet, Sam, Danny—are gone. There will be a time soon when the past will be buried even deeper, nobody around who can describe it, nobody who can pick it out from the picture of the present. Ten years? Fifteen? Twenty? There will be a time, but it is not now.

Joe Villarino still is playing ball.

"It's a good glove," he says, pulling a black first baseman's mitt from the trunk of his Japanese car. "My daughter bought it for me three years ago. For my 82nd birthday. I think it cost her $165."

He plays in the LaMesa Senior Slow-Pitch Softball League. Three times a week. There are over 200 players in the league, age 55 and over, average age 71. The games are played on Little League diamonds, the sound of an aluminum bat hitting a fat ball sending old bones into action. Joe Villarino is the second-oldest player in the league.

"We have guys who drop dead playing," he says. "I bet there have been six or seven guys who dropped dead since the league started. There was a guy just last year. He was on second base, and someone hit a ball into the outfield, and he tried to get from second to third. Never made it. Died right there between second and third."

Joe has played some form of ball for all of his life. From Hoover, he took a shot at the minor leagues, went to Kilgore, Texas, D League baseball. Found himself on the buses, playing on the dirt infields in the hot sun, no money in his pocket, and came home. Played in local hardball leagues. Then fast-pitch softball. Then slow-pitch. Took time out to go to Fiji and the Philippines with the U.S. Army during World War II, drafted.

Came back, got married, worked a career for the gas company. Raised a family. Kept playing ball.

"I can't throw anymore," he says. "I blew my arm out throwing curveballs to my son. I thought he could have been something—he was a good little ballplayer, but short, like me. It just didn't happen."

He stands in the parking lot next to the Little League field. The other old-timers are packing up. The question arises: would Ted have done well in this league?

"Ted would have hit a home run every time he came up," Joe Villarino says. He smiles.

He says he wishes he had seen more of Ted through the years. He wishes Ted would have retired in San Diego after baseball. It just didn't happen that way. Once Ted left, he never lived in San Diego again. Maybe it was the specter of his mother that kept him away, maybe it was Danny's troubles, maybe it simply was the attractions of other places, another, richer life. Who's to say? Maybe he was busy. He simply didn't come back much. Only on visits.

"The first time he came back was on December 25, 1938, after that first year in Minnesota," Joe Villarino says. "He showed up at my house on Christmas Day, driving a Buick convertible he got out there. Never had a car before that. Never drove. He had a woman with him too. Doris Soule, her name was."

Ted was out in the world.

3 Minnesota

Ted Williams hit one so high and fast yesterday that he rode over the city on it. He rode right into his new baseball home, into the hearts of opening day fans. That blow brought cheers for the lanky kid in right field, it helped bring a 14–4 victory over Louisville in the debut of the 37th [American] Association campaign at Nicollet Park. . . .

He came up a third time against Carl Boone with the singling Stan Spence on base and did it. A terrifically towering flyball sailed like a bird over Nicollet Avenue, over the front part of the roof across the street. For the fans, there was your ballgame.

HALSEY HALL, *MINNEAPOLIS STAR*, APRIL 30, 1938

The Kallas Café was the meeting point for the good folk of Princeton, Minnesota, one of those luncheonettes where everybody knows everybody and the smell of breakfast hangs around until it is replaced by the smell of lunch. John Kallas was the proprietor, and he had a couple of teenage sons who helped him out. They were helping out on the day Ted Williams suddenly materialized.

Jimmy Kallas, the 19-year-old, spotted Williams first. He had seen Williams's picture in the Minneapolis newspaper, another teenager, same age, knocking the cover off the ball for the Minneapolis Millers during the summer of 1938. Jimmy Kallas told Tony Kallas, the 18-year-old, the news.

"There's Ted Williams," Jimmy said behind the soda fountain.

"Nah."

"It's him."

Princeton was a small town, no more than 3,000 people, 50 miles north of Minneapolis. Not a lot of famous baseball players came through the café's door. Williams, it turned out, had arrived to do some fishing. The Millers were off, and Minneapolis outdoors writer Ed Shave was taking him along in search of some Great Northern. Shave, it turned out, had even told John Kallas, the father, that they would be stopping.

Introductions were made. Friendships were made.

The next time the Millers had a day off, Williams returned, stayed at the Kallas house, and went fishing with John. John caught four or five Great Northern. Ted caught none. How'd that happen? John Kallas was better than he was? Through the years he would come back again and again. He would use the Kallases' cabin up at Green Lake. He would stay at the Gagen Hotel, proprietor: A. M. Gagen, four dollars a week, meals included. He would walk the woods, fish the fresh waters.

Ted liked Princeton, Minnesota.

"I went duck hunting with him the first time he ever went," Frank Weisbrod, now 85 years old, says. "We went out to Little Rice Lake, three miles outside of town. The ducks are always around there because they like the wild rice. Ted just didn't know anything about duck hunting. He was shooting at ducks clear on the other side of the lake."

He soon got the hang of it.

"Dad would drive him out to Little Rice Lake at four in the morning to lay out the decoys," Jim Kallas told Luther Dorr of the *Princeton Union-Eagle*. "But Dad had to be at work at the café at noon. Ted said, 'That's okay,' and he'd walk the three miles back. If he did well, he'd walk inside the café with the ducks."

He wound up spending a lot of time at R. O. Benson's place, the Princeton Sports Shop, tying flies and talking hunting and fishing. Paul Westeman, who built silos when the weather was good, had nothing to do when the weather was bad. He'd sit around the shop too. R. O. Benson was his father-in-law.

"Ted's in there one day, tying flies and tossing them in a bucket," Westeman says. "In comes Doc Wetter, and he's chewing snuff, and he spits in the bucket. Oh, Ted was mad."

The rhythms of small-town, outdoors life simply seemed to fit. Ted's father, Sam, finally had called it quits in San Diego, divorcing May and going away with another woman to Sacramento. There never was a great rush to return home. Princeton seemed as good as any place to be. There were trips to South Dakota to hunt pheasant. There was good Greek cooking at the Kallas house, the pheasant and duck covered with gravy.

Only one thing was missing.

"Jim, make me a chocolate malt and put a lot of ice cream in it," Ted said one day at the café in the fall of 1938. "And hey, know any good-looking girls around here?"

Kallas said he did. He said he would call one and see if she would come down for a Coke at three o'clock.

Doris Soule arrived right on time.

W illiams shouldn't even have been in Minnesota. That was the thing. Never should have been there in the first place. He should have been playing in Boston. He should have gone to spring training in Sarasota, Florida, and been with the Red Sox for that 1938 season.

"I never figured it out," 85-year-old Max West, who traveled across country from California with Williams, still says. "I was going to camp with the Braves. He was going to the Red Sox. I made the team and he didn't. And he was better than me."

Hadn't the "stringbean" already proved himself in the Pacific Coast League? Wasn't he supposed to be "the best prospect to come out of the league since the Yankees' Joe DiMaggio at the end of 1935"? That was the advance notice. DiMaggio, golden and smooth, had glided into the American League to put together two remarkable seasons. In 1937 he'd led the league with 45 homers, hit .346, and finished second in both hits and runs batted in. He'd finished second by four votes for MVP to Detroit's Charlie Gehringer, done so well that he was holding out for a bigger contract, a subject that was the talk of all spring training.

Even if Williams couldn't reach DiMaggio's high mark on the wall on the first try, then shouldn't he at least be somewhere on the surface? Shouldn't he at least be in the league?

The baseball in the PCL was as good as could be found in the thirties without going to one of the 16 major league ballparks stacked on the east side of the Mississippi River. A number of players in the Pacific Coast League could have been playing in the majors but liked where they were. These were players who loved the sun or loved the West Coast (or whose wives loved the sun and the West Coast) or who found they could make more money in places like L.A. or San Francisco once they developed a local name and a following.

Minnesota—the Minneapolis Millers of the American Association—offered none of that. The Millers were a farm team mostly raising new talent for the big leagues. The veterans on the roster were there because they had no place else to go, being terminally deficient in some ability on a major league scout's list or coming back down the ladder and taking a graceful exit from the game. Minnesota, for the young player, mostly was a place to improve some area the big team thought was lacking.

The Red Sox and manager Joe Cronin wanted Williams to improve his head. They decided very fast that he was too young, too immature, too . . . wacky. Had anyone ever talked his way *out* of the big leagues? His first experience with his new employers was just a mess.

He arrived at the Sox 1938 training camp as a tall bundle of fidgets and bluster, fingernails bitten down to nothing, a motormouth covering his own insecurities. He later would say that he never even had thought he could play big-league baseball until he went to camp and saw that his abilities matched those of the other players on the roster, but that was not the way he acted. He talked and talked, his confidence touched with defiance.

"I remember him on the train," Max West says. "He'd keep saying things like, 'Well, if Cronin thinks this, then he's got another think coming.' Or, 'If Cronin thinks that, he'd better think twice.' I said to myself, He's never met Joe Cronin. What's this all about?"

The trip across the country—Williams on his way to that first meeting with the square-jawed player-manager—was an adventure before the big adventure even started. Bobby Doerr, who'd played the '37 season in Boston, was asked to take the train from his home in Los Angeles, meet the new kid in San Diego, and babysit for the rest of the long grind to Sarasota.

This plan was doomed when heavy rains and flooding hit the Los Angeles area. The Oscars were canceled for the first time, the flooding was so great. Tracks were washed out, and trains couldn't get in or out of Los Angeles. Williams was advised to take the train by himself from San Diego as far as El Paso. Doerr took a bus out to Indio, California, where he took another train to El Paso with Braves rookie West and veteran Babe Herman, who also was heading to Florida.

"Our train got to El Paso first," Doerr says. "Babe Herman had played there at some time in his career and knew a good restaurant in

Juarez, Mexico. So we went across the border, ate, and came back to the station three hours later and there was Ted."

Descriptions from the time always make him sound like some quirky character played by a young Jimmy Stewart in a comedic movie. Part science-project scatterbrain. Part fast-talking salesman. A large part kid from nowhere. Talking. Asking questions. Handing out opinions. Swinging anything that resembled a bat. Swinging the pillow in the Pullman car. Swinging his arms if nothing else was available, swinging his arms through the air.

West remembers waking up, the train stopped at a siding or maybe a station. He pulled open the shade and, sure, there was Ted, standing on a rail on the next track. He was balancing himself while swinging a rolled-up newspaper at an imaginary pitch. Talking to anyone. Talking to no one. Doerr mostly remembers the talking. Williams latched on to Herman, a hitter with some power during 12 previous big-league seasons, a man who had hit .393 in 1930. The talking never stopped. Almost never. Williams always had one more question, one more opinion, about hitting.

"In the dining car a woman turned to the porter and asked, 'Could you please make him keep quiet?' " Doerr says.

"I don't think he slept a minute the whole way," West says. "At least he didn't from what I saw."

When the train reached Tampa, two long and talkative days and nights after leaving Texas, West departed to Bradenton and the Braves camp. Herman already had left, headed to a minor league camp. Williams and Doerr continued to Sarasota, winter home of the Ringling Brothers Circus and spring home of the Red Sox and not much else.

The team had been at work for over a week when the two-man California contingent arrived. Doerr quietly folded again into the roster. Williams did nothing quietly.

The first character he met in the clubhouse was equipment manager Johnny Orlando. A few years older than Williams, Orlando was a direct opposite. He had a street-corner sophistication, the wise-guy knowledge not only of where all bodies were buried but how they got there. He had started working at Fenway Park when he was ten years old, a kid from nearby Chelsea, picking up papers so he could get into the games for free. He worked his way into the operation, moving up to run the clubhouse. He then brought his younger brother, Vinnie, off a construction site and onto the payroll. Vinnie was the visiting clubhouse man and the same age as Ted.

"Sarasota in 1938 was a hayshaker town," Johnny Orlando began, years later, in a 12-part series in the *Boston American* about his experiences with Williams. "You could shoot a cannon up Main Street from Five Corners and maybe only hit a rattlesnake. . . ."

He described how the other players, including stars like Jimmie Foxx and Lefty Grove, had been working hard for days and everyone was wondering where this "Williams kid" was. Then, finally, the door to the clubhouse opened and . . .

"This Li'l Abner walks in. He's got a red sweater on, his shirt open at the neck, a raggedy duffle bag. His hair's on end like he was attached to an electric switch. If anyone ever wanted a picture of a raw rookie, this was the time to take the shot."

"Where you been, kid?" Orlando asked. "Don't you know we been working out almost a whole week? Who are you supposed to be, Ronald Coleman or somebody, you can't get here on time?"

Welcome to the big leagues. Orlando gave the new arrival a uniform that did not fit. There was no uniform in the trunk for a six-foot-three, 172-pound stick, so Orlando simply gave him the biggest shirt and biggest pair of pants he could find. Two Ted Williamses could have fit inside. Orlando then said, "Come on, kid," and took the new arrival to the field for the first time.

Sitting in the stands, watching his players on the field, was Cronin. He spotted Williams immediately. He also noticed the big uniform.

"Hey, tuck your shirttail in," Cronin shouted. "You're in the big leagues now."

Williams reacted.

"Who's that wise guy up there?" he said.

"That's Joe Cronin, your manager, kid," Orlando replied.

Williams ran onto the field, trying to tuck the too-big shirt into his too-big pants, not exactly getting the job done. Welcome to the big leagues. They didn't fit any better than the uniform did.

Orlando's instant nickname for Williams, "Kid," not only stuck for his first spring training but would be with him for the rest of his life. The Red Sox veterans—especially incumbent outfielders Sam Chapman, Joe Vosmik, and Doc Cramer—also soon found other nicknames. Williams was "the San Diego Saparoo" and "the California Cracker" and a bunch of other names that never made the newspapers. Williams responded by calling everyone "Sport" or "Meathead." He called Joe Cronin "Sport." Cronin, in turn, called him "Meathead."

The unwritten rule at the time was for rookies to shut up, wait their turn, and be indifferent to all abuse heaped upon them by their elders. Williams did none of the above. He pushed his way into the batting cage, kept talking, and reacted to every remark. He made comments about the humidity in Florida, about the unfairness of Fenway Park (which he never had seen) for a lefthanded hitter, about the physical oddities of his new teammates.

An oft-repeated piece of dialogue between Doerr and Williams—DOERR: "Wait'll you see Foxx hit." WILLIAMS: "Wait'll Foxx sees me hit"—may or may not actually have happened, but it captured the moment perfectly.

"Here's a thing I've never seen written," Vinnie Orlando said years later. "Ted showed up with his own bat. He'd bought it at a drugstore or a five-and-dime somewhere in Florida on the way. A cheap bat. The veterans all were laughing at his bat. Then he started hitting, and they weren't laughing so much anymore. He used that bat for a couple of weeks."

The hitting, alas, seemed to sour when the games began. In his first exhibition on March 13, he went a quiet 0-for-4 against the Cincinnati Reds. Nerves, pressure, and youth, combined with the tougher pitching that he now faced, made his first week a struggle of adjustment at the plate. By the end of it, he was gone, shipped to the Millers, the Red Sox affiliate, one of the first cuts of the spring. His first big-league audition was done almost as soon as it started.

Of course, there was a story.

The Red Sox were scheduled to play the Braves in Bradenton on March 20. When the players assembled for the short bus trip in uniform, Williams still was in civilian clothes. He didn't think he was going. Cronin had posted a list of names for the trip. Williams hadn't read the list.

"Why aren't you on the bus?" Cronin asked. "You were on the list."

"When folks want me to do something, they come up to me and tell me, man to man," Williams replied. "They don't expect me to go around hunting for bulletins."

"Young man, you stay right here," Cronin said. "Don't bother about Bradenton."

"Okay, Sport."

The next day he was told to report to the Millers' training camp in Daytona Beach. He packed some forever unanswered questions along with his clothes. Wouldn't he have hit the way he always hit—the way he soon would hit in Minneapolis—if he'd been given more time, a longer look, in Sarasota? True, the Sox were set in the outfield, and true, it was an easy decision to say that a 19-year-old kid needed to go somewhere he could play every day, but wouldn't he have made these decisions harder if he had had a longer chance? He never gave himself that chance.

Johnny Orlando, his biggest ally and a first Red Sox friend, walked him to the bus stop. Williams was mad. He had confronted the veteran outfielders, Chapman, Vosmik, and Cramer, one last time in the clubhouse before he left.

"John, I'll be back," Williams said. "Don't have any worries about that. I told those guys that I'd make more money in one year than all three of them combined, and I will. How much would that be?"

Orlando said he figured the outfielders made $12,000 apiece. No more than $15,000 tops. He asked how much Williams had in his pockets at the moment.

"I got enough, John," Williams said. "I don't need much to get along. A bit for meal money. That's all I need."

"Kid, I got a finif [a five-dollar bill]," Orlando said. "I'll split it with you. That'll buy you a good steak. You just go out and have a good year. You've got a lot of time coming for you in the big leagues."

That was the way he left his first experience in the big leagues: with a bus ticket for Daytona Beach and $2.50 of Johnny Orlando's money in his pocket.

The best part about the Millers' camp was meeting Rogers Hornsby. A short-tempered veteran of 23 years in the big leagues, nine of them as a player-manager, Hornsby had retired at age 41 at the end of the 1937 season. His name was mentioned in any argument about who was the greatest hitter in the history of the game. He'd won the Triple Crown for best batting average, most homers, and most runs batted in twice in his career and just missed it another time. He'd batted over .400 three times, the highest at .424 in 1924. He now was a coach for the Millers for the spring, figuring out exactly what he would do next in his life.

Williams took care of any immediate plans. With the disappointment of being shipped to the minors quickly shelved, the confidence meter back to high, and his enthusiasm working noisily again, Williams latched on to Hornsby the way he had latched on to Babe Herman on the train.

"He was one of the most knowledgeable guys I ever talked hitting with," Williams said years later in a book he co-authored with Jim Prime called *Ted Williams's Hit List*. "Here I was, a 19-year-old kid, and he wanted to talk about hitting all the time. Boy, I sure took advantage of the opportunity to pick his brains."

(Williams put Hornsby fourth on his hit list after Babe Ruth, Lou Gehrig, and Jimmie Foxx.)

The questions fell out of Williams's mouth in a typical torrent. The veteran put into words a philosophy that the kid intuitively had been following.

Hornsby said, "Get a good ball to hit." The way to control the battle between the hitter and the pitcher was to force the pitcher to throw his best pitch in the worst situation. Use the rules of the game, four balls and three strikes, to carve the situation into what you want it to be. Don't chase pitches, don't give away strikes. Work the count to your advantage, 2–0 or 3–1, and force the pitcher to come to you.

Study the pitcher. Know what pitches—fastball, curveball, change of pace, whatever—he can throw. Know how well he throws each of the pitches. Know where he throws them best. Know when he throws them. Know what he likes to do when he is in trouble. Study, study, study. What did he try to do to you the last time? What do you think he will try to do this time? Study. Study. Get that good ball to hit.

This simple sentence would be the foundation of Williams's success, maddening at times for fans and teammates when he refused to swing at a fat pitch an inch outside the strike zone in important situations. Critics would call it a selfish approach, personal success over team success, but he never varied. Why would he ever want to give up any of his advantage to the pitcher, even a quarter of an inch? He would argue this point into his eighties, still yapping back when political columnist George Will suggested he should have swung more often at hittable pitches outside the strike zone. ("I like George Wills politically," Williams said. "But baseballically he was all wrong.") He had walked over 100 times in his second PCL season and would walk 150 times in Minneapolis and 2,019 times (second only to Babe Ruth) in his major league career.

To hear Hornsby say all the things he himself had been thinking was comforting to the kid. He spent hours in the batting cage with the middle-aged teacher, working on his swing before and after exhibition games, talking and talking, engaging in hitting contests with one of the greatest hitters who ever lived. They would bet on who could hit the most line drives. Hornsby was gone before the team broke camp, taking a job as a coach with the Baltimore Orioles, then moving along later in the season to become manager of the Chattanooga Lookouts, but while he was around the Millers, he was a captured resource for one special student.

This pattern would continue for the rest of Williams's life. He would seek out the greats of the game, ask questions, challenge the answers. He would talk with old Hugh Duffy, who hit .438 in 1894. He would talk with Bill Terry, who hit .401 in 1930. He would argue with Ty Cobb, who thought a man should hit down at the ball, while Williams thought a man should hit up. He would talk, as an old man, with Tony Gwynn and Nomar Garciaparra and Jason Giambi. Take away the segregated stars of the Negro Leagues and take away Shoeless Joe Jackson, banned from baseball for gambling, and Williams would talk hitting with virtually every great living hitter of the twentieth century.

The subject would never go stale for him. He would talk hitting with anyone who asked and with a lot of people who didn't. He would ask little kids and sportswriters and cocktail waitresses and senior citizens to show him their swings. He would adjust the batters' hands. He would preach hip action, concentration, the virtues of repetition. The act of hitting a baseball would fascinate him to the point of obsession, sending him to the physics laboratory at the Massachusetts Institute of Technology, to the lumberyard at the Hillerich and Bradsby bat factory in Louisville, Kentucky, to the batting cage at the end of the day, after everyone else had gone home.

A sportswriter remembers taking a blind man to meet Williams one day, years after Williams's career was finished. Williams nodded, shook hands, went through the celebrity motions, until the blind man mentioned he played softball. Williams perked up at that.

"How do you hit?" Williams asked.

The blind man explained that a special ball was used, a ball that beeped in sequence so the players could hear it approach. Wait for the beeps to draw close. Swing. Williams asked to see the man's batting stance. The blind man obliged, swinging a couple of times. Williams stood and made various adjustments to the stance. The blind man swung a few more times. Better.

"Now, here's what you gotta do," Williams said, holding the man in the new stance.

"Yes?" the blind man said.

"You gotta stand there," Williams said. "Don't swing early. Wait. You gotta wait until you hear that last fucken beep!"

Get a good ball to hit. The lesson of Rogers Hornsby.

M inneapolis turned out to be more playground than purgatory. Freed from the final, nagging constraints of San Diego—freed from living in the house on Utah Street, from playing in front of high school friends and teammates, the sound of the Salvation Army band in the background—Williams bought his first car, the Buick convertible, moved into a room in the rented house of married teammate Walter Tauscher, and let his last few inhibitions, if any, drop to the ground. He was a picture.

"Williams is tickled to death to be with the Millers, especially under the tutelage of Donie Bush, talks a blue streak, wants to know all about Minneapolis and Minnesota, when the duck hunting season opens, the fishing, would like to get his hands on the guy that started 'this second DiMaggio business,' " Dick Hackenberg of the *Minneapolis Star* said in a first description. "He smacks his lips over the 279-yard [*sic*] right field fence at Nicollet Park because he got 19 of his 25 home runs last year over the 340-yard [*sic*] right field barrier in San Diego."

The pieces seemed to fit. Bush, the 51-year-old manager, a stubby little man at five-foot-six, 160 pounds, was a former big-leaguer with a nononsense disposition and seemed to be a perfect character to try to channel his new star's eccentricities. The ballpark, Nicollet, was friendly to both a lefthanded hitter and an average and indifferent rightfielder. The situation was perfect. Rather than fight for a space in the veteran outfield in Boston, the new number 19 for the Millers was in the lineup every day, the team's certified star. And if there were any, uh, irregularities, they would take place a long way from Boston.

The Millers opened the season with a mammoth four-stop road trip heading north. Williams was hitless in his first 12 appearances in three games in Indianapolis, but when the team hit Louisville, he began to roll. He collected his first hit in the first game of the series on a day when he walked five times to tie an American Association record. (Get a good ball to hit!) He collected his first and second home runs, both inside-the-park shots to the wide-open 512-foot centerfield of Louisville's Parkway Field in the third game. The second shot traveled an estimated 500 feet on the fly.

When the Millers finally hit Nicollet on April 29, he went 3-for-4 in the home opener, including a long home run over the short fence in right, the ball landing on a roof across Nicollet Avenue. Two more home runs and a double would follow in his third game at home. The pattern of success was established.

"There was a furniture store and the President Café across the street on Nicollet Avenue," long-time *Minneapolis Star-Tribune* columnist Sid Hartman says. "The insurance company canceled its policies for plate-glass windows because of Ted. They had to put up some kind of bogus windows. Because of Ted.

"I was a kid when he played. I had dropped out of school then and was selling popcorn and peanuts at the park. He took a liking to me. I don't know why. He took me for a ride in his Buick one day. We were doing 100 miles an hour down Wayzata Boulevard. I was scared to death."

The season unfolded at this same 100-mph pace. The Millers were a .500 club, destined to finish sixth in the eight-team league, but Williams was a one-man offensive show. He hit long, impressive homers to places where homers never had been hit. He reeled off a 21-game hitting streak from Memorial Day until the middle of June. He won games at the plate, lost games in the field, and drove his stubby manager to distraction.

What do you say to an outfielder who slaps his glove on his thigh and yells, "Hi-yo, Silver," when he chases fly balls? What do you say when the outfielder turns his back to the action at the plate and works on his swing, taking imaginary cuts at imaginary pitches, oblivious to whatever else is taking place? What do you say to an outfielder who loses a fly ball in the sun because he won't wear his sunglasses? To an outfielder who keeps up a running dialogue with the scorekeeper inside the scoreboard in right? Who keeps up a running dialogue with the nearby fans, who have learned that if you yell at this particular animal in the cage he will yell back? Who says, "I got here by myself, I can find the way home," when you give him base-running instructions when he has landed on second with a double?

"Either he goes or I go," Donie Bush supposedly said to Millers owner Mike Kelley.

"You're a good guy and a fine manager," Mike Kelley supposedly said in return. "This, however, is the Red Sox star of the future, and if you're really threatening to leave, well, it was nice to know you. . . ."

Hyperactivity was the norm for Williams. If he had seemed a bit eccentric in San Diego, the "bit" part of the phrase was removed in Minneapolis. He always seemed to be doing something that was a little different.

He was riding around the outfield before a game on a bicycle borrowed from a Western Union delivery boy! He was climbing up the screen to the press box before another game, commandeering the public address system and announcing the names of his teammates as they went into the batting cage! He always was moving, talking, reacting, emotions as easy to read as the big M on the front of his shirt! He was doing jumping jacks in the middle of the game in rightfield! He was throwing rocks at guys sitting on boxcars watching the game over the fence in Louisville! He was driving *everyone* to distraction!

"I joined the team late, in the middle of June," Lefty Lefebvre says. "I was really surprised. Nobody wanted to be around him. He was just a cuckoo guy. A loner. I felt kind of sorry for him."

Lefebvre, a lefthanded pitcher, had been shuttled to the Millers straight from college. He had graduated from Holy Cross in Worcester, Massachusetts, on one day, then signed a contract in Boston the next morning to become a professional ballplayer for $600 a month. A strange and wonderful thing immediately had happened to him.

"The Red Sox had me dress for the game that day, just to see the park, meet a few of the players," he says. "The rules were different then. I sat on the bench for the game. They were playing the White Sox, and by the fourth or fifth inning the White Sox were just killing them. Joe Cronin looked down the bench and told me to start warming up."

The call from the bullpen came an inning or two later. Lefebvre was flabbergasted when he saw Cronin signaling from the mound that he wanted the lefthander. ("I almost shit," Lefebvre says, 65 years later.) The one-day college graduate hit the first batter he faced in the neck with his first pitch, but finished out the inning, and then another one. He figured, leading off the bottom half of the inning, he would be replaced with a pinch hitter.

"Go up and take a swing, kid," Cronin said instead, fed up with the mess the Red Sox were making in front of him.

On the first pitch, his first at bat in the majors, Lefebvre swung and made contact. The ball went up, up, and over the leftfield wall. Lefebvre, running hard into second base, didn't know what had happened. He noticed the fielders standing still. The second-base umpire, Bill McGowan, said, "Come on, kid, keep going, will ya?" Lefebvre had become the first player in major league history to hit a home run on the first swing of his first at bat. It was the only big-league home run he ever would hit.

"The pitcher was Monty Stratton, the guy who got shot," Lefebvre says. "I always told him, 'You were so embarrassed, giving up a home run to me, you shot yourself.' "

Moving along to Minneapolis, Lefebvre became part of the Millers' pitching rotation. Williams asked him one day to go to lunch. They were close in age. They were both rookies. Lefebvre felt sorry for the loner and also wanted to know him better. He said he'd be glad to go.

They drove from the park in the Buick, as fast as the Buick would travel. Top down. They screeched to a tidy halt in front of some sandwich shop. Williams led the way.

"He was loud," Lefebvre says. "We sat down at the counter. He said he wanted a chicken sandwich and a frappe. The sandwich came and he started smelling it. He said, loud voice, 'Is this chicken fresh?' The owner came over and told him it was. Jesus Christ, it was embarrassing. Ted smelled the chicken some more. He'd say things a nine-year-old kid wouldn't say. No control at all. Anyway, he eats the sandwich, drinks the frappe in about a minute, and says we're out of there. I've got three-quarters of a sandwich still to go.

"We go from there to another sandwich shop. It happens all over again! He orders the same thing, a chicken sandwich and a frappe. He says the same thing. Is this chicken fresh? He starts smelling the chicken. Eats the sandwich, drinks the frappe in a minute, and says we have to go. I'd been to two restaurants, seen him eat two meals, and I still hadn't eaten a whole sandwich.

"He was just cuckoo."

Williams's friends off the field were not ballplayers. He picked up people who interested him, people who shared his same love for hunting and fishing. The people could come from anywhere, do anything for a living. If they were interesting, he latched on to them. Hard. He once again found other, older men for guidance, adopted them and their families, and they adopted him.

"We lived in a nice neighborhood in South Minneapolis," Jack Bean says. "One of our neighbors was a widowed woman with a couple of kids. She would go to the beach for the summer and to make ends meet she rented out the house. Ballplayers were a good match, so she rented to players from the Millers.

"In 1939 she rented to Walter Tauscher and his wife, who had a baby.

Maybe two kids. And we heard that there also would be this other young ballplayer, 20 years old, who would live with them. That was Ted. My father was kind of a rambler, a first-class talker, a salesman for an ice cream company. He got talking to Ted and found that Ted liked to hunt, and my dad liked to hunt, and they just became friends. He liked Ted, this raucous young guy."

Bean was a couple of years younger, a gap large enough at that age to make him more onlooker than participant in the relationship between Williams and his dad. He spent more time with Tauscher, a sweet man, who would play catch with him in the driveway. He mostly watched Williams and was amazed. Williams was just so outrageous.

"Our family went to dinner one night at the Hoffmans' house, and we took Ted," Bean says. "It was a legendary night. Mr. Hoffman was an important guy, some kind of vice president for Woolworth's. He was sort of short and round. I remember Ted meeting him on the porch. He slapped Mr. Hoffman's stomach and said, 'Good evening, Whale Belly.' I couldn't believe he did that. Mr. Hoffman just looked at him and started laughing."

The night proceeded from there. Williams didn't talk through dinner. He shouted. When the potatoes came, he said, shouting, "No thanks." He then took two great servings. Same with the meat. "No thanks." Two great servings. Same with everything. "No thanks." He was a steam engine as he chewed.

"What do you do around here for fun?" he shouted when dinner was finished.

Tom Hoffman, the youngest Hoffman, ventured that sometimes everyone played ping-pong. Had Ted ever played ping-pong?

"No, but I know I can beat anyone in the house," Williams shouted.

"We played table tennis until about 12:30 that night," Jack Bean says. "Ted couldn't beat anyone in the house, especially Tom Hoffman, but that didn't stop him from trying. His face was all red. He got so mad. He'd still be playing if the kids didn't have to go to bed."

Good night, Ted. Good night, Whale Belly.

"We played an exhibition against a softball team during the season," Lefebvre says, remembering a similar kind of offbeat challenge. "The softball team had a great pitcher. Fast pitch. I said to Ted, 'I'll bet you five bucks you can't get a hit off this guy.' Ted ran for his money. First time up, the guy strikes Ted out. Ted owes me five bucks, and he's steaming. 'Ten bucks,' Ted says. Okay. He gets up there and hits a home run, maybe

400 feet, off this guy. Out of the park. He ran around the bases, just laughing and smiling. Like a little kid."

Every day was a different drama. Williams threatened to quit once, told Donie Bush he was going home to California. Bush calmly told him the club would pay his fare and he could come back when he felt better. (He never left.) A wild fastballer named Bill Zuber beaned him on August 3, knocking him out, sending him to the hospital with a concussion. Three days later he was back, hitting a homer and a double. And then there was the water cooler. Frustrated at fouling out with the bases loaded, he delivered a punch at the glass water cooler, sending glass all over the dugout. Bush went crazy again.

"One day . . . Doc Brown, the trainer, had a little cubbyhole in the clubhouse and was in charge of all the equipment," Lefebvre says. "Williams goes to him before the game and says he needs a ball to give to a kid. Brown wouldn't give it to him. Williams pouted. He goes out to rightfield, it's only 280 to rightfield, and he leans against the fence. He's still there when the game starts. A ball comes out to right center, and he doesn't move. Stan Spence had to run over all the way from centerfield to make the play Williams was supposed to make. He didn't move. He didn't give a shit. He was a big baby."

The free pass for all of this, of course, was that he could hit. Try any of it as a scuffling utility infielder, batting somewhere around .250, and you would be back in the family kitchen, eating Mom's home cooking. Hit .366, whack 46 home runs, collect 142 RBI—win the American Association Triple Crown—and even if you finish second in the MVP balloting, the sportswriters already looking at you a little strangely, your future is pretty much bulletproof.

"I remember Ted and my father having a discussion about money in the living room," Jack Bean says. "The Red Sox general manager, Mr. Collins, had sent Ted a contract for the next year. My father and Ted were talking about it. I remember Ted saying, 'You mean you think I should ask for more?' "

Andy Cohen, the veteran second baseman for the Millers, arranged a postseason barnstorming tour for the team. This was a way to make a few extra bucks, 15 exhibitions against local opposition in the small towns of northern Minnesota, even into the Dakotas. Williams signed on for the tour.

The team went around the state in personal cars. Tauscher drove one of them. Lefebvre and Spence rode in the backseat. Williams sat in the passenger seat. The term "riding shotgun" applied. Williams carried his shotgun.

"There was a thing during the season called Radio Appreciation Day," Lefebvre says. "Each player got to pick what gift he wanted. Most of us picked clothes, things like that. Williams wanted a case of shotgun shells. He brought the whole case with him on the tour."

Lefebvre and Spence would fall asleep. . . .

Blam.

"I thought I saw a jackrabbit," Williams said.

Lefebvre and Spence would fall asleep again. . . .

Blam.

"Another jackrabbit."

"He used up that whole case of shotgun shells," Lefebvre says. "I think he shot a few cats, a few dogs, anything that moved. Maybe a cow."

The love affair with Minnesota had begun for Williams. He never would play again in the state, but he would come back again and again in the off-season in the next decade. There would be other places he loved in the future, places where the hunting and fishing were good and easy, places where he could disappear and walk with ordinary people, far from the publicity storms he started somewhere else, but this was a first.

"He'd check into the King Cole Hotel downtown and come out and see my dad," Jack Bean says. "The hunting was so easy. You could go around the corner and find a pheasant. My dad and Ted and some other men would go to Green Isle, Minnesota, where my dad grew up, this little town with maybe 460 people, 458 of them Irish, and stay at our relatives' houses and hunt for three or four days at a time and love it.

"It was like Ted was part of the family . . . and here's the thing, neither my father nor I ever went to see him play baseball once. He was just a friend, outside of baseball. I think that's what he liked the most. My father would never show him off. Or anything like that. He was family."

Bean remembers Williams would let him use his car sometimes on these later trips. Bean decided to pay him back. He introduced him to a new great razor.

"It's called a Gillette," he said, presenting his gift in the car. "It's adjustable. You turn the dial and you get the kind of shave you want."

Williams adjusted the razor. He went to the highest setting. He took one swipe, no foam, no soap, and half his face was scraped off. The blood appeared immediately.

"I didn't know what to say," Bean says. "I didn't know what he was going to do. He would have been justified in doing just about anything. He looked at me and said, 'Jack, you're right. This razor is great.' Then he threw it out the car window as far as he could throw it."

Part of Williams's love affair with the state, along with his love for the hunting and fishing and the anonymity, eventually was an actual love affair. There was a definite reason to go back to Princeton. Doris Soule, the girl who had come down to the Kallas Café, seemed pretty interesting. The daughter of a fishing guide, she had been visiting her grandparents in Princeton in the fall of 1938 when he showed up after the end of the barnstorming tour. He was intrigued. She hunted, she fished, she argued with him. What could be better? Her grandfather was the town's last remaining blacksmith.

"The first time I saw Ted, he was an awful sight," Doris later said. "He hadn't shaved, he had a hole in the seat of his pants (though he did have another pair of pants under those), and he was wearing those earflap things. Taken all in all, I guess I wasn't very impressed."

"I just couldn't stand him," she said at another time. "We had arguments all that first evening, and I told him I never wanted to see him again. But I soon learned that when Ted fixes on an idea, he stays with it. He came back the next day."

Williams had told writers in spring training that he didn't smoke, didn't drink, and "was still a virgin." Lefebvre says he met Doris and thought she was "a nice-looking girl, very pleasant, and I don't know how the hell she could stand him."

Paul Westeman, 85, remembers her in Princeton.

"I remember that she was nice enough looking," he says. "I also remember that she was sexually active."

Really? How would you remember something like that 65 years later?

"She'd been sexually active with my best friend, Buddy," the 85-year-old man says.

Ted Williams had a girlfriend.

4 Boston

Young Ted's attitude changed suddenly this summer from the half-artless, calf-like good nature of a year ago. Something had happened to his ego and his clubhouse attitude toward his mates, the press and the public had become acid. Yet, as this writer wrote, earlier in the year, the Kid was hitting and hustling, so that his inner nature was between himself, his manager and his parson just as long as he splashed the outfield and fences with his wooshing drives.

AUSTEN LAKE, *BOSTON AMERICAN,* AUGUST 13, 1940

This time everything was supposed to happen right. The missteps of 1938, when the kid from San Diego arrived in Sarasota too full of himself, too arrogant, certainly had been adjusted. Hadn't they? He'd been sent to Minnesota, handed some humility. Maybe he'd been a little eccentric there too, a little flighty, but Lord he had hit, and he'd had another year to mature and he'd increased his value and there was a spot open for him now in the starting Red Sox outfield and the Red Sox maybe valued him half as much as he valued himself and it all certainly would work. Right?

He showed up three days late for spring training in 1939.

The Sox had sent him the same tickets for rail travel they had sent the previous year, but he was out in the world now, owned a car. He was *driving* from California, where he'd finally returned for Christmas. There were stories that brother Danny, unable to get the keys to Ted's Buick, had put it on blocks and sold the tires during the off-season, a good reason to take the car from San Diego, but whatever the case, Ted had asked Les Cassie Sr. to accompany him to Florida. Cassie Sr. agreed. They set out on a grand cross-country juggernaut.

They got as far as New Orleans.

"They would have been to Sarasota in time," Les Cassie Jr. says today, "but Ted got sick. They checked into a hotel in New Orleans."

He had the flu, a temperature of 102. Respiratory problems would bother Williams throughout his career, especially in the spring. He claimed to friends later that he'd been checked for tuberculosis once and was found to have been touched by the disease somewhere in his past. Coughing and hacking, knocked down by a high temperature, he would add the air itself to his list of villains during a season.

He arrived in Sarasota, looking "like shit," according to Cronin, but nothing could stop him this time. His new situation on the team was obvious from the beginning.

"Not since Joe DiMaggio broke in with the Yankees by getting 'five for five' down in St. Petersburg in 1936 has any baseball rookie received the nationwide publicity that has been accorded this spring to Theodore Francis [sic] Williams of the Red Sox," the Boston Globe's Gerry Moore reported as part of the general chorus of trumpets heralding Williams's new star status. "And unless we miss our guess Titanic Ted will continue to be given plenty of newspaper lineage and figure prominently in fan gossip through the regular season."

The headline on the article was "Ted Williams: The Answer to a Sports Writer's Prayer." Moore proceeded to list the new man's colorful qualifications.

"Everything about Williams shuns the orthodox," he wrote. "His 6 ft., 3 in., 175-pound stringbean physique, his inimitable nonchalance in fielding his rightfield position, his constant boyish chatter, seldom possessing any meaning, both on and off the field, and last, but by no means least, his frequent flair for committing eccentric or what is known in the baseball world as 'screwball acts.' "

The Sox had made room for him in rightfield by dispatching Ben Chapman to the Cleveland Indians, not a small move since Chapman had hit .340 in 1938. Williams inherited Chapman's number 9 as well as Chapman's job. (Williams had been number 5 in his first spring training.) Cronin mused publicly about whether to bat him third or fifth in the lineup.

In Sarasota he was still a bundle of fidgets and tics, still a motormouth, but his new status made his presentation a lot more bearable. He wasn't taking away someone's job; he had a job already.

The Boston newspapers noted that he still would say anything to anyone. He still called Joe Cronin "Sport." He shouted, after reserve Fabian Gaffke was beaned, "Look at that. This game is too risky. I'm taking the civil service exams." He even had political opinions. He walked into a group conversation about possible war led by Ivy-educated catcher Moe Berg and said, "Germany and Russia will go in together if there's any fighting," words that were dismissed immediately but came true in the next six months.

He still was a baseball-talking machine.

"I liked him," Elden Auker, a submarine-ball pitcher traded to the team from the Tigers, says. "He was just a young kid, full of energy. He had nothing on his mind except baseball. Some of the guys would get a little bored with him talking about it all the time. Some didn't want to ride in a cab with him . . . but I'd already been in baseball for six years and I wanted to help him."

Williams still wanted to know everything and know it now. He still wanted to do everything and do it now. He would tell Auker, "That guy's started off the last five hitters with fastballs," and ask what that meant. Auker would talk about pitching patterns, the way they worked. No other young hitter ever had paid as much attention. None that Auker had seen.

Spring training passed without incident, serious or goofy, until the Sox played an exhibition game in Atlanta. Johnny Orlando, Williams's buddy from the clubhouse, set him up for trouble.

"It was during batting practice in the Atlanta ballpark that I pointed to the rightfield and told the Kid that Babe Ruth had hit a ball that cleared all three fences," Orlando said in his series in the *Boston American*. "It was one of those big parks that had a high fence on the outside. One year, the Atlanta club had built a new fence inside this first one, just to make it easier for their lefthanded hitters to connect with home runs. But the second fence was still too far out, so they built another, still lower and closer to the plate.

"They looked like three steps going from the ground to the Sears Roebuck store on the far side of the street outside the ballpark."

Orlando had baited Williams. He said the first time up you could almost see the words "The Babe cleared all three" written across Williams's forehead. Strikeout. The second time up? Strikeout. Third time? Strikeout. Williams was steaming when he went back to rightfield. *The Babe cleared all three fences.*

Almost immediately, a short foul ball came down the rightfield line. Williams misjudged it first, letting it fall, then had trouble picking it up off the grass. Steaming. He finally picked up the ball, turned, and heaved it over the grandstand onto Ponce deLeon Avenue. Everyone in the ballpark just stared.

Cronin immediately called him in from the field. Williams waited to hand his sunglasses to replacement Gaffke, then loped back to the clubhouse. Only Orlando—and Williams—knew exactly what had happened.

"This was a rush of anger against himself that was prompted because he didn't live up to the Babe's example," Orlando said. "That was the only reason. But everybody was too busy lambasting him to understand."

Cronin said he had never seen this particular display in all of his years in baseball. He also said he would have "a nice fatherly talk" with his young outfielder that night. He also said the young outfielder would be back in the lineup the next day when the Sox faced the Atlanta Crackers again.

Next day? Williams pounded a pitch that cleared one of the Atlanta fences, if not all three. It was still a home run.

"With Ted it was never a case of envy," Orlando said, "just that he wanted to be as great a hitter as the Babe. Jealousy never entered into it. The kid wanted to be like the Babe. Often he hit a home run a mile and came laughing at me on the bench, asking, 'Did the Babe ever hit one that far?'"

The answer—and it came soon—sometimes was no. Williams had hit the big time, and he immediately would deliver rockets.

He came out swinging. That is all that can be said about his first two months in the major leagues. He hit a grand slam on the first pitch of his first at bat in New England in an exhibition game against Holy Cross in Worcester. He collected a double in his first major league game in New York and a single in his first Fenway game.

On April 22, his fourth game, he showed what all the fuss was about in a series-ending 12–8 loss to the Philadelphia Athletics. In the first inning he cranked a monster shot into the centerfield bleachers at Fenway into a section that had been reached only by Ruth, Gehrig, and the

Indians' Hal Trosky. In the third he just missed a homer by inches against "the tie sign" on the left centerfield wall, the ball dropping back for a double. In the fifth he singled into right. In the sixth he singled through the middle, a wicked line drive. In the ninth, the game really over but the fans waiting just to see what he did, he drove A's leftfielder Bob Johnson to the leftfield wall to spear a liner that was held back by the wind.

Welcome to the major leagues. Indeed. The headline in the *Globe* the next day read "Williams Revives Feats of Babe Ruth." Take that, Johnny Orlando.

"More than an hour after the game was over, there was Titanic Ted, surrounded by a hundred urchins in the parking lot near the players' entrance at Fenway Park," Victor O. Jones wrote. "He was shivering in the cold, but still showing kids how he broke his wrists to buggy-whip the ball. Guys that are that screwy about hitting always can hit and guys who take time out to be nice to kids usually last a long time in baseball."

The rockets had just begun.

The day that is remembered most from his debut swing around the league was May 3. He was introduced to Detroit's Briggs Stadium, which would become his favorite place to hit. He knocked balls to previously unexplored places.

The park was fully enclosed, and rightfield, which was short down the line at 325 feet, featured three decks of stands. The third deck was a press box added three years earlier. The height of all this was 120 feet. No one ever had hit a ball over the roof in rightfield, even before the press box was added. Williams hit three in one day.

The first was a foul ball, just foul, on the first pitch he saw against starter Roxie Lawson. He flied out to center to end the at bat. The second ball was fair, also hit off Lawson, in the fourth. High fastball. It hit on the roof above right center and bounced back onto the field only because the roof slanted that way. The third shot cleared everything.

Williams worked rookie reliever Bob Harris to a 3–0 count. Detroit catcher Rudy York said, "You wouldn't be swinging, would you?" "You bet I am," Williams replied. And he did.

"It was a climbing liner—as much of a liner as a drive could be which cleared a 120-foot barrier, straight as a string, over the whole works about a dozen feet fair," Gerry Moore reported in the *Globe*. "According to eyewitnesses outside the park it landed across adjoining Trumbull Ave. and bounded against a taxi company on the other side on the first hop."

Williams bounced around the bases, clapping and enjoying himself.

Tigers third baseman Billy Rogell asked him, "What do you eat?" York, at home, said, "You weren't kidding, were you?"

"That's about as good a drive as I can hit," Williams said.

"I don't know where the kid gets that power," Elden Auker said, discussing the physics of it all with veteran pitcher Monte Weaver, a former mathematics professor at the University of Virginia. "That last sock went 500 feet before it landed or I'm an Eskimo."

On Decoration Day, May 30, after he had blasted a 460-foot shot in St. Louis that also dropped jaws, a mammoth crowd appeared at Fenway to see what this new kid looked like. Newspapers estimated 50,000 people were turned away at the gate, a full house of 35,000 admitted. The opponent was the front-running Yankees, and Williams was not a disappointment.

In the first game he unleashed a bomb against Yankee ace Red Ruffing that landed deep in the bleachers, as far back in the seats as any of the writers could remember a ball landing. In the second game he hit another shot into the bleachers. He now had eight home runs on the season, four in the last four games.

This was all the way it was supposed to be. The Boston fans loved him. He loved back.

"At the start, he used to delight in tipping his cap," Barbara Tyler, Eddie Collins's secretary, said. "But he didn't really tip it. He was playing rightfield in those days, so when he'd hit a home run, he'd reach for the button on top of his cap with the tips of his fingers as he rounded first base. Then he'd lift it off his head about three inches and let it plop back on top of his head."

The only bump in the season was a down stretch in the middle of June. This was the time when most rookies have problems, when they have to make adjustments to the adjustments the pitchers are making the second, third, and fourth times they see a new hitter hit. His batting average dropped to .280, and he sat on a traveling trunk in the clubhouse and told Johnny Orlando he wished he were back in Minnesota. Orlando gave him a quick pep talk.

"I told him, right to his kisser: Kid, you're going to be all right," Orlando reported in his *Boston American* series. "You'll hit .335 for the year. You keep swinging and you'll have 35 home runs. And if the guys ahead of you keep getting on base, you'll drive in 150 runs."

Williams said he would buy Orlando a Cadillac if all this came true. It almost did. Williams wound up hitting .327. He hit 31 home runs. He led the league in RBI with 145. He finished fourth in the MVP voting and would have been the rookie of the year, no question, except the award had not been invented.

The season was an unqualified success. There were no bad incidents—okay, a couple of pouts when he failed to run out balls, one hit that popped off the wall and should have been a double instead of a single—and he was generally treated as the best thing to land in the region since the *Mayflower*.

After trial and error, he had landed at the Hotel Shelton on Bay State Road, next to the Charles River and within walking distance of Fenway. (One of the other residents would be Eugene O'Neill, the famous playwright. There are no recorded meetings between Williams and O'Neill for either breakfast or words. "There wouldn't be," former Shelton manager Paul Sonnebend says. "Eugene O'Neill was crazy. I mean just crazy.") Williams had found places to fish, even secured a permit to fish on local reservoirs. He had found some local friends like John Blake, a state trooper from Foxboro and Johnny Buckley, a theater manager in Cambridge. He seemed content, settled.

"I was married and lived in an apartment, so I had him out to the house for dinner maybe four times during the season," Elden Auker says. "He loved Mildred's fried chicken. Jimmie Foxx, my roommate on the road, was going through a divorce and living in a hotel, so I'd invite him and Ted. They'd talk about hitting."

The Red Sox, enthused at what they had seen, decided they would try to make good even better. Cronin talked about adding some rows of seats in right to bring the fences closer, making it easier for his new lefthanded slugger to reach. Even though he was an adequate fielder, there was talk about moving Williams to left, to make his life easier.

Auker remembers only one disquieting moment that turned out to be a preview of what was to come. It happened back in Sarasota, back in spring training.

"We were standing in the lobby of the hotel," Auker says. "A bunch of us had gone out to dinner. Ted, Jimmie Foxx, Mildred, myself, Bobby Doerr, and his wife, Monica. We were talking about going out to play putt-golf, picking teams. Ted was sitting down in a chair.

"Bill Cunningham came up to him. Cunningham was a columnist from the *Herald*. He'd been drinking. You could see it. He said, 'Well, come on, Ted. Let's go up to the room and get it over with. All the fans in Boston are waiting with bated breath to hear the story about the kid from Minneapolis.' Ted never moved. He just stared at Cunningham. He said, 'Mr. Cunningham, I'd rather do it later because I never give interviews to sportswriters when they've been drinking.'

"I remember thinking at the time, how many players would do that? I mean, Ted was right, but how many players would have just gone along? I think that's where it all started. With Bill Cunningham. He never had a nice word to say about Ted after that."

(Cunningham, years later, would type out a different memory. He said that Williams arrived at Sarasota as "a gangly, not surly, but very mouthie rookie." He attributed the following quote to Williams on a first meeting with the Boston press: "What are all you reporters doing down there around an old man like Lefty Grove?" he taunted. "From what I saw out there today he couldn't pitch for San Diego in the Coast League. And that Foxx! What's so special about him? You're all down there taking down his words and shooting pictures of him and I hit three balls out there today better than he did. I don't see any of you hanging around me for interviews. But I suppose you're no better than the sportswriters on the Coast, and they're about as lousy as you can get.")

Williams, after the season, went back to Minnesota—and the hunting and fishing and Doris. He stayed there for the entire winter. And everything was different when he came back.

The addition to Fenway turned out to be bullpens, not extra seats. The bullpens had been in foul territory on either side of the field, but now were placed inside an elongated, 20-foot-wide box that jutted from the bleachers in right. The 400-foot distance to the power-alley fence now was 380. The move was so obviously designed for Williams that the addition was called "Williamsburg." Great things were supposed to happen in Williamsburg.

The switch to left also had been made. There were assorted reasons— an easier field to play, less sun in the fielder's eyes, a chance for newcomer Dominic DiMaggio, fleet and sure, to play the wider spaces in right—all of them designed to make Williams's life easier. He had become the obvious designated star in the Red Sox operation.

Another change, also supposed to help, was a flip-flop in the batting order. Williams now was batting third. He had batted fourth a year earlier behind Jimmie Foxx, put there as a threat to make pitchers pitch to Foxx. Now the roles were being reversed, Foxx a threat to make pitchers pitch to Williams. A torch had been passed.

Hadn't it?

No.

Williams was not ready for any of this. The fans were not ready for any of this. Who was he to receive this kind of treatment this fast? He was 21 years old. He'd played one season. A lot of ballplayers had come through the Red Sox roster, and none of them had been handled this way. Not even the Babe. The image of Williams had shifted from phenom to slightly spoiled child. This was not a good thing.

The first boos from the leftfield stands at the new leftfielder came during the exhibition city series against the Braves. As if it were a new hat, a new pair of shoes, there was an entirely different fit to all of the new stuff. The new fit was worse than the old fit. There seemed to be a pebble in this shoe.

Williamsburg was a distraction rather than an aid. The typical Williams homer covered the extra 20 feet to the old fence, no problem, and all the new fence did was add to a public demand for more homers, all homers, all the time. The new spot in the batting order, Williams decided early, was a detriment. All that happened now was that he had less of a chance to knock in runs. Pitchers, especially righthanders, were not afraid to walk him to reach the 33-year-old Foxx. Behind Foxx, batting fifth, was Cronin, 34 years old. Pitchers chose to tackle the old, known poison rather than the new.

And left field? There seemed to be different fans in those seats, with different demands. There always was a negative voice somewhere in that crowd. What had happened to the kinder souls in right?

Williams moped and moaned about all of this through the early part of the season. His batting average was a respectable .317, but the homers weren't coming, the RBI weren't coming. He was miserable. He complained about his salary, about the sportswriters, about the fans, about anything that crossed his path. He was miserable to be around.

Cronin decided that this petulance—not to mention the power slump—should be treated. He decided he might bench Williams and discussed the reasons with Harold Kaese of the *Boston Transcript*. Though the benching never came, Kaese still wrote a column about all the reasons that Cronin had considered. Kaese painted the picture of a moody, immature star, finishing with a kicker that infuriated Williams.

"Can you imagine a kid, a nice kid with a nimble brain, not visiting his mother and father all last Winter?" Kaese wrote.

It was such a personal shot, low and cheap and ill informed, not even considering what problems Williams might have at home, that Kaese even tried to take it back. He called his desk asking to have the line dropped, but a series of mistakes let it run. Williams always remembered it.

"I mean [home] was never a happy place for me, and in 1939 my mother and father separated and there was more grief, so I just stayed away," Williams wrote in *My Turn at Bat*. "And do you know what Harold Kaese wrote the first time I did something to displease him? 'Well what do you expect from a guy who won't even go see his mother in the off season.'

"Before this, I was willing to believe a writer was my friend until he proved otherwise. Now my guard's up all the time, always watching for critical stuff. If I saw something, I'd read it twenty times and I'd burn without knowing how to fight it. How could I fight it?"

The uneasiness continued, aggravated now, even worse. The *Record* reported an incident that happened on June 30 at Fenway. Williams had become involved in one more stretch of theatrics with the fans in left. The headline was "Williams' Cussin' Probed by Cronin."

"There was a complaint that Ted Williams had yelled insulting words at the left corner of the grandstand, among which there were many women who have reported as having objected to Williams' language," the story said.

"I know they have been riding him from the bench all over the circuit and in some cases from the stands," Cronin said. "Even if he didn't do things to have warranted these verbal attacks, it is all part of baseball and players must learn to live with it."

Eddie Collins was asked how the situation would have been handled in "the old days."

"Some of his teammates would have punched him in the nose long before this," the general manager said. "But I think he'll pull out of it."

In Cleveland on July 21, Williams gave syndicated sportswriter Harry Grayson of the Newspaper Enterprise Association a bizarre story. He said he wanted to quit baseball and become a fireman. Grayson put it all in print. Across the country.

"My uncle was a fireman in Mount Vernon, New York," Williams explained years later. "I went out to see him on an off-day in New York and we were sitting there in the sun and he was telling me about the pension he was going to get when he was 50. I was getting booed because I wasn't hitting enough home runs and he was telling me I could get $600 a month if I took the pension at 50 and if I waited until I was 60, I'd get around $1000. I don't know. It sounded good at the time."

People read the newspapers. In Chicago, manager Jimmy Dykes outfitted his players with fireman hats and whistles and sirens to greet Williams from the dugout when he came to town. Who was this kid? He'd rather be a fireman than a baseball star? In New York, Lefty Gomez would pull the same fireman act.

The big explosion came in a quiet moment a few weeks later. Sent home from New York with an aching back, Williams went to Fenway for a treatment. He was hitting .336, but his power numbers were still down. He had only 13 homers and 71 RBI, and he was not happy. Austen Lake, the columnist for the *Boston American*, was in the locker room, and when Williams was dressed, Lake approached him for an interview. The locker room was filled with young amateur ballplayers who'd just worked out at the park.

"I haven't any time," Williams said, hurrying to leave. "I've got a date."

Lake persisted, following him through the tunnel to the field and then into the grandstand. Williams finally sat down in a box seat and mumbled out some answers about his back and the team. Lake could feel something was wrong.

"What's the matter with you, Ted?" Lake asked.

The floodgates opened. Lake said he listened to perhaps 20 minutes of "internal poison" being spewed. Williams called his $12,500 salary "peanuts." He said he wanted to be traded. He said he hated Boston, hated the fans, hated the newspapers, hated the trees, hated the weather, hated, just hated. The word "fuck" or some derivative was woven into most sentences. He wanted out.

"Plainly, Ted had been nursing this torrent of the spleen," Lake wrote the next day, August 13. "The week that he had spent alone in Boston with his sprained sacrum should have purged any superficial sourness in his system. But obviously this was no mere ballplayer's grouch, a passing black mood, no temporary curdle in his inner chemistry. He felt what he said with a vast conviction. He didn't like Boston's streets, the way the houses were built, the parks, the people, the riverway. Phooie!

"But most of all he didn't like the human crows who perch on the rim of the ballpark and write typographical sneers.

" 'I don't like 'em and I never will,' Ted said."

Lake said he gave Williams a chance to take all the words back. He said Williams declared, "You can print the whole so-and-so mess. I feel that way about it and I'll continue to feel that way about it." The story hit the city like a fine bombshell.

Ted Williams doesn't like Boston? Okay, Boston doesn't like Ted Williams.

"The logical place to send Williams is to Cleveland, a thriving and pleasant city on the shores of Lake Erie," columnist Dave Egan, the Colonel, wrote in the *Boston Record*. "In that city is a team known far and wide as the Cleveland Crybabies and it is my profound belief that there young Ted Williams would find the happiness and camaraderie which he seeks."

"Five or eight years from now, when mature judgement settles in and his adolescent muscle jerks and junior spasms disappear, [Williams] may take moral stock of his past and maybe tsk-tsk himself," Lake wrote. "For the lad is a high-strung nerve victim who thinks whole headfuls of thoughts at a time in a kind of cerebral chop suey instead of single ideas in a sequence like little pig sausages.

"Then, like Foxx and Cronin, he may learn to accept the sour with the sweet—maybe in Boston, maybe in Detroit or New York. Big money, quick fame, mass adulation, a celebrity at 22, have fogged his perspective."

The battle that would cover the rest of Williams's years in Boston had been joined. He would perform all of his future deeds—and misdeeds—in front of a yappy, gossipy, smart-ass chorus. Boston never has been a metropolis like New York or Los Angeles where an athlete could slide away from his notoriety and hide among the general population. In the forties and fifties the city was even smaller. To play baseball in Boston was to be analyzed and scrutinized, laid out on a municipal laboratory table and picked apart. To be a star, a star of the magnitude Williams became, was to have the process increased by a factor of ten. To watch Williams, irritated by it, fighting against it, giving it the big middle finger . . . his reactions were fine public entertainment.

There were no movie actors, no great singers, no personalities—save a few politicians and a mobster or two and Arthur Fiedler, conductor of the Boston Pops—to take away any of the heat of celebrity. Williams was a national figure now, stranded in local woods. Eight Boston newspapers, four in the morning and four in the afternoon, tried to bump, slam, elbow, and run around each other to get into the local living rooms and coffee shops and sweatshops. Every mill town and suburb also had a newspaper that wanted to get into the chase. Worcester. Providence. Lynn. New Bedford. Lowell. Fall River. Everybody wanted a piece.

No headline would jump sales any faster than a headline involving Ted and controversy. A story on Ted was the ultimate good business.

"Everybody had a different opinion of him," Clif Keane, former sportswriter from the *Boston Globe*, now 90 years old, says. "Talk to ten different people and you would get ten different opinions about Ted Williams."

There were writers who liked Williams, writers who despised him, writers who bounced back and forth. The ground troops were the baseball writers, appearing at the ballpark every day, chronicling what they saw in front of them. They were the irritants, buzzing around his head. The writers who moved *inside* his head were the columnists.

They were a varied lot, the columnists, some pompous, some meek, some absolutely brazen. They had a standing, an importance, that is hard to measure in modern terms. The written word meant much more without the talk shows of today, the television analysis, the rat-a-tat highlight chatter. The columnists were the sole important voices that people heard. There was no such thing as "the media." The columnists were the media.

"Bill Cunningham was from the *Boston Post*," Tim Horgan, former Boston sportswriter, says, going down a partial batting order. "A big guy, one of those guys who becomes an All-American 20 years after he played at Dartmouth. Full of shit. Nice to me, but full of shit. He was a presence, though, when he came into a room. He had a cane. Could play the piano. Could sit down and play dirty songs. . . .

"Austen Lake was from the *Boston American*. Tough guy. Aloof. He'd played college football at five different colleges, which you could do back then. He did birdcalls all the time. I remember sitting at a table with another writer and he invited Lake over and whispered to me, 'Don't be surprised if he starts doing birdcalls.' Sure enough, when there was a lull in the conversation, *tweet-tweet, tweet.* . . .

"Kaese, dignified, a great athlete, squash player. . . . Huck Finnegan used a bludgeon when he wrote about Williams. . . . Arthur Sampson, used to be a football coach at Tufts, a gentleman. . . . George Carens from the *Boston Transcript,* loved Ted, thought he did no wrong. . . . Eddie

Rummill from the *Christian Science Monitor*, looked like a preacher, looked exactly like he came from the *Christian Science Monitor*, except he loved broads. Had more broads than Ted Williams."

The cast of characters would change during the years—and the rankings of the names on Williams's personal shit list would change by the latest edition of the latest paper—but one constant would be the columnist at the *Boston Record*, Egan, known forever to his readers as The Colonel. Dave Egan would stay at the top of the list until the day he died. Even after he died.

Referring to Williams as T. Williams Esq., Egan would use wit, slander, good statistics and bad, feigned outrage, bias, and every opportunity possible to deliver his broadsides. There would be odd days, especially when the rest of the columnists would be coming down on Williams, when Egan would come to Williams's defense, but the next day he would be back with the ball-peen hammer. He sometimes was unfair. He sometimes was unscrupulous. He always was utterly compelling reading.

"The trains would go north to New Hampshire at night, and half the people waiting at the station in those little towns would be there to get the *Record*," Clif Keane says. "To see what Egan wrote."

A native of Newport, Rhode Island, Egan graduated from Harvard in three years and then graduated from Harvard Law School. He was, by all accounts, brilliant. He was also, by the same accounts, a terrible drunk. Quickly lurching from the law to sportswriting when his law office asked him to take a one-week *unpaid* vacation, he bounced around the various employers on Newspaper Row, Boston's answer to Fleet Street, before landing at the *Record* at 4 Winthrop Square in 1939. He had found a home. The *Record* and its sister tabloid, the *American*, were the local outposts of the Hearst Corporation, heavy on sensationalism, the subway readers' papers of choice. The marriage was perfect. An outrageous newspaper for an outrageous man.

"Every time I try to describe him, the only picture that comes in my head has him sitting at his desk next to the water cooler, typing, and he's bleeding from a half-dozen places," Jeff Cohen, son of *Record* sports editor Sam Cohen, says. "I was just a kid, and here was this star of the paper. He'd gotten into some altercation in one of the bars downstairs, and someone had beaten him up. And there he is, typing. Bleeding everywhere."

He was fast and lethal in his work. Lake, the columnist at the *American*, was a literary bleeder, agonizing over each paragraph. He would be in the midst of the process when Egan would come in, half-drunk, do a dance in an hour, and be gone. Lake would still be squeezing words through the typewriter four hours later. Egan's words would be the better-received words.

"He was just a great writer," Keane says. "And you didn't need a thesaurus to read him."

Pleasant and soft-spoken when sober, he was a mean, cantankerous drunk, ready to scream and punch. He would go on benders, disappear for days. Cohen and the other editors would try to find him. He would dry out at Dropkick Murphy's in Athol and other rehabilitation sites, phoning in his column, sometimes drunk again from bottles friends had smuggled in to him. There were stories that he would drive to Athol a few days before he knew he was scheduled to start a rehab stint, hide his own bottles in trees and bushes around Dropkick's grounds. Ready for rehab? Ready. He was an eminently resourceful drunk.

Cohen wrote some of Egan's columns when all efforts to find him failed. Alex MacLean, another writer, would do columns. Half the staff would do columns under the logo of The Colonel, a strange caricature of a Robert E. Lee look-alike. None of the replacements would have the bite and zest of Egan.

"I was a young guy, starting out," Keane says. "His advice was, 'Always take a little nip before you write. You'll write better.' It didn't work for me, but it worked for him."

Cohen even hired Bernie Drohan, a former vaudevillian known as "The Funniest Man in South Boston," composer of the song "Southie Is My Hometown," to watch Egan, to try to keep him sober. Drohan was overmatched. Everyone was overmatched.

"I covered a fight with Egan," Horgan says. "Tony DeMarco against Carmen Basilio. All week they locked Egan up in his room to keep him sober. Like an animal, they locked him up. In a cage. The night before the fight he somehow got out. There was this great search for Dave Egan. Where is he? Where is he? Finally they find him, shit-faced, about five hours before the fight. They pour coffee down him, get him to ringside, still shit-faced. He writes a helluva column."

There was a second unpleasant aspect to Egan: he was on the take. This was not unique at the time. Graft often was encouraged by the Hearst franchise and other papers to augment the generally low salaries of sportswriters. Egan took it to a journalistic art form. The racetracks, the boxing and wrestling promoters, anyone who wanted to put on a Boston event, found a way to slip him money.

"I went to work at the *American* after my paper folded, and I took a 33 percent pay cut," Horgan says. "I was told I could make it up by setting up a few 'accounts.' That's what they were called. Everybody had a few 'accounts.' I'd always wondered why the first editions of the paper were filled with stories about the new menu at Suffolk Downs or some fighter no one cared about. That was it. You had to get the clips to show your 'accounts.' Then, the next edition, the stories were taken out, replaced with the real stories."

Egan would call Wonderland, the dog track in nearby Revere, if the week's payment was a day late. He would mention that he was going to write a column the next day about how he and his wife had become sick after eating in the track dining room. The payment would be delivered post haste.

"Dave Egan was on the take from all of them," Keane says. "He'd steal the gold from your teeth."

For Williams, Egan mostly was an unseen enemy. None of the columnists ventured to the clubhouse very often, Egan virtually never. (The one recorded time he went to a game, injured third baseman Jim Tabor tried to hang him out of the press box by his heels before being stopped by Eddie Collins.) This was a war fought mostly from a distance. The ground troops, the baseball writers, would be involved in the direct confrontations.

"If you were a foot taller and 50 pounds heavier, I'd punch you in the mouth," Williams would shout later at tiny Hy Hurwitz, a former Marine working for the *Globe*.

"If I were a foot taller and 50 pounds heavier, you wouldn't dare," Hurwitz would reply.

The columnists would drop their bombshells from afar. How can you hit what you can't see?

Tension became an everyday constant. Williams would yell about the scene—"What do you get when you add water to a sportswriter?" Williams would ask. "Instant horseshit"—but he also would use it. He would show the bastards, the cocksuckers, the syphilitic sons of bitches. Egan. He would show him. The syphilitic son of a motherless whore. He would shut him up. Kaese, the constant chronicler of Williams's facts and foibles, and the other writers would note that in the times of the biggest controversies, Williams would hit best. He almost needed the emotion, the challenge. He fed on it.

This did not make the meals any more appetizing.

"Did I ever tell you how I met Williams?" former Boston sportswriter Leo Monahan says.

Monahan was an office boy, a Red Sox fan from South Boston. He would take the Colonel's columns off the phone, listening to the drunken man's ramblings and brilliance. He would write smaller stories, filler, do work in the office. He wanted a chance. Finally one day Cohen sent him to cover the Red Sox.

"How do I get into the game?" Monahan asked. "I don't have a press pass."

"Talk your way in," Cohen replied. "You're a newspaperman. You should be able to do that if you're a newspaperman."

Monahan went to Fenway, talked his way in. (He was, it turned out, a newspaperman.) He went to the battleground that was the Red Sox clubhouse. He saw the famous man alone in a corner. He decided to present himself. This was the dialogue:

"Mr. Williams, sir, I'm Leo Monahan from the *Record*," Monahan said. "Huck Finnegan is off, and I've been sent to cover the Red Sox. I'd like to introduce myself."

"You work at the *Record*?" Williams asked.

"Yes, sir."

"You know Huck Finnegan?"

"Yes, sir."

"You know Austen Lake?"

"Yes, sir."

"You know Dave Egan?"

"Yes, sir."

"Could you give them all a message for me?"

"Yes, sir."

"TELL THEM TO ALL GO FUCK THEMSELVES."

Yes, sir.

Far from all of this noise, the controversy around the public Ted Williams, the F-words and tantrums, another side was also being developed, another constant that would remain for all of Williams's Boston career. Who was Ted Williams? What made him tick? There always would be two sides to the argument. He had visited his first sick kid.

A 12-year-old named Donald Nicoll from West Roxbury had landed in Faulkner Hospital with a ruptured appendix in June 1939. This was serious business. The miracle antibiotic, penicillin, had not been developed, and the treatment at the time was to open the patient, drain the poisonous fluids, and hope for the best.

Nicoll's father, a night cashier at a cafeteria in Dock Square, looking for anything to cheer his stricken son, wrote a letter to Williams, asking him to visit. Sure enough, Williams arrived at the hospital room. And into the kid's life.

"The first time he came, I was out of it," Nicoll says. "I didn't know who anyone was. Then he came again. And again. He just came in and we talked. He always called me 'Melon Head.' "

After Nicoll went home on August 16, the visits continued. He had a lengthy recovery time, more than ten months, and the Boston schools sent a tutor to give him classes. Williams would arrive—"several times"—after the tutor left and help Nicoll with his homework. Or just talk.

"It was never anything elaborate," Nicoll says. "It was like he became part of our family. I can't even remember if he ever had dinner with us or not. He became friendly with my father, who was a big baseball fan, and they would talk about the season, about the games. We all would talk about anything.

"I think he liked it, being away from all the attention, and being part of someone's family. He was so different from all the things you were reading. I think he was just a very sympathetic person."

Some component of the relationship obviously struck Williams. It would develop almost into a need. He would always be the softest of touches, the most eager hand to help. Dozens of Donald Nicolls, hundreds, would receive the same treatment. The man who uniformly thumbed his nose at the masses would pick out the weakest of the particular and offer comfort, promise to hit a home run the next day, "Just listen to the radio, kid, I'm trying for you."

Was he following the lead of the grown men, neighbors and strangers, who had befriended him when he was a kid, men who had given him the simple but important gift of time? Was he following his mother, who gave *all* of her time to the Salvation Army, to the downtrodden and needy, even at the expense of her time with her own sons? Was he simply drawn to this one positive part of fame, the fact that a few words and a few minutes could make some suffering person's life much better on any given day?

Did he simply want to be, underneath everything else, a "good guy"?

There are athletes who march stiff-legged through this opportunity to help, scrawling out a few autographs for a photo shoot at the odd hospital ward, then jumping into their luxury automobiles, gone as soon as possible. There are other athletes, more than you might think, who jump into the situation, drawn to it by the comforting power they can have with one word, one touch, finding as much satisfaction in it as any satisfaction they might hand out. No one ever jumped deeper than Williams, who would wind up carrying an entire charity for sick children, the Jimmy Fund, on his back. He not only visited but befriended. Stayed involved.

Donald Nicoll was the start.

"When I got better, I'd go to games with him," Nicoll says. "I'd go to his hotel by myself the morning of the game, call up to his room, then wait in the lobby. He'd come down, and we'd go to Fenway Park together. The routine was that I'd walk in with him, talk a little bit, then hang around the grandstand until the game started, then find an empty seat. He snuck me in. That's what he did. I went to games with him until I went away to college."

One morning Williams said he had to stop and eat breakfast in the hotel coffee shop. Nicoll went with him. They sat at a table.

"Give him what he wants," Williams told the waitress.

"No, that's okay," Nicoll said.

"Give him what he wants," Williams said again.

"No, that's okay," Nicoll said again.

Williams insisted. The waitress joined the argument.

"Do you want the two eggs or the three?" she said.

"No, that's okay."

"Two or three?" Williams said. "That's your only choice."

"Two," Nicoll finally said.

He looked up at the waitress. And at Williams.

"Two is all I can handle," he said. "I already had breakfast once before I got here."

In August, Williams returned from the back injury and controversy to play his best baseball of the season during the last month and a half. Or at least he hit better. He pounded a home run in his first game back, part of a doubleheader loss to the Yankees, and added three more in the next week. The Red Sox were hopelessly out of the race, and he padded his numbers. He finished with a .344 average, 113 RBI, and 23 homers, only

9 of them at Fenway. Williamsburg was a bust. He'd hit 5 more homers in Boston as a rookie before the fences were moved.

The cloudy air from his explosion never really cleared. The papers kept stirring it up. The fans kept grumbling—not all of them, but enough for Williams to hear. Teammates, even quiet Jimmie Foxx, were quoted in their displeasure with the way their new star acted.

"Sir: What have Joe Cronin and Eddie Collins been doing all this time? We've been hearing rumours of Williams' incorrigible goofiness since the Spring. . . . blame the Red Sox bosses for not cooling The Kid off and saving all this fuss," P.I.T. from Boston wrote in a letter to The Colonel that made a very good point.

"Ans: The problem goes deeper than that," Dave Egan replied. "Cronin looked on Williams as a prominent spoke in his wheel. The Kid has been hitting and, except for occasion, hustled. The lad now as always has been an asset in Joe's pennant dreams. Once in the earlier season Cronin in exasperation warned Ted, 'How would you like to spend the rest of the season in Louisville?' To which Ted answered with a shrill ha-ha. 'Louisville, that #%&&*@**%,' he snorted. He knew that Cronin knew that without him, the Sox pennant bubble would be so much soapy mist."

Williams was on his own. That was the message from Sox management. The team's idea of public relations was a good pregame dinner and an open bar in the press room. There would be no great guidance here, no discipline. Williams was too good, too talented, to be pushed around the Parcheesi board like the normal baseball pieces, but at the same time there was no mechanism to give him help. For his entire career, he pretty much would be on his own.

Max West, who had taken that first train trip from California to that first spring training with Williams, had become a somewhat less controversial Boston addition to the Braves. He was a solid outfielder, had hit for a little power, indeed had croaked a three-run homer to give the National League a 4–0 win in the 1940 All-Star Game. He had two experiences with Williams during the season.

"You didn't see the guys on the Red Sox very often because when they were on the road we were home, and when we were on the road they were home," West says. "One place we did run into each other was the Hotel Commodore in New York on top of Grand Central Station. Both teams stayed there, and sometimes we'd both be in the same hotel at the same time."

The Braves were checking out this time at the end of a trip. The Red Sox were checking in. West hadn't been reading the Boston papers, so he didn't know what was happening. He spotted Williams in the midst of a group of players and went to say hello. He hadn't talked to Williams at all during the 1939 season.

"Hey, Ted," he said, California guy to California guy. "How're you liking Boston?"

"All the other players with him just started walking away, disappeared, just like that," West says. "Ted started talking about the city and the fans and the trees. All the stuff. I just didn't know."

West did know later in the season. He'd been bending over to get a drink of water in the Braves dugout when he was hit in the face by a foul tip from Paul Waner. The baseball had split West's mouth open, swollen his features. He clearly couldn't play, so the Braves went on the road without him.

Crazy with inactivity, he suggested to his wife one afternoon that they go to Fenway, "to see Ted." They had seats behind the visitors' dugout along the leftfield line.

"There was this one big dude, huge, with a big belly, who was sitting near us," West says. "He was riding Ted. A foghorn voice. Every time Ted came on or off the field, the guy would yell and Ted would run closer and closer to the line and stare at him."

"Watch this," West told his wife. "Something's going to happen here."

Going out to left to start the next inning, Williams stopped in front of the stands. He pointed at the beer-belly foghorn guy.

"You," he said.

"You know who you are," he said.

"You're a son of a bitch," he said.

West was amazed. He says he played later in his career in Pittsburgh, and thank God Ted never played in Pittsburgh. Ted thought Boston was tough?

"They'd have run him out of town in Pittsburgh," Max West says.

The season finally, mercifully, was done.

5 .406

Joe DiMaggio's perpetual-motion hitting streak, 54 consecutive games as of Monday, July 14, has put another up-and-coming young man in the shade. This is a pity because the party in question requires a good deal of shade, 6 feet 3 inches to be exact, and shade is scarce these days. It also is a pity because Theodore Francis [*sic*] Williams of the Boston Red Sox, clouting the ball at a clip close to .400, is making a serious bid for the magic mark that only four American Leaguers, Nap Lajoie, Ty Cobb, George Sisler and Harry Heilmann, ever have hit.

NEWSWEEK, JULY 21, 1941

The voices speak from the baseball season that grows larger and larger with time. A reconstructed innocence is built by people who later, at the end of 1941, would remember forever exactly where they were and what they were doing on December 7 when they heard the news that the Japanese had bombed Pearl Harbor.

This was the summer before the bad things happened. It is seen now as the last snapshot in the sunshine before the rain clouds broke, a time when two men hitting baseballs would have a sweet, inflated importance in the American consciousness. Maybe there is an exaggerated sweetness here, a self-editing process that is colored by all that came later. Then again, maybe not.

This was the summer Ted Williams became much more than another good ballplayer playing a game very well, the summer when he separated himself from the pack of other men who played this game before him and after him, the summer when he hit .406. He turned 23 years old in the middle of it.

The voices from that time are attached to eyes that watched every day of that summer unfold.

> JOHNNY ORLANDO: "The first day he showed up at camp, just me and Vinnie were there. We went out on the field at Sarasota because he wanted to play a little pepper. But pretty soon he started belting the ball all over the place."
>
> VINNIE ORLANDO: "The day he showed up everybody was looking for him. I was sleeping on the rubbing table. It was late afternoon. I didn't hear him come in, and he tipped the damn table over with a loud yell. It scared the hell out of me. Ted was really a jumpy kid in those days. He couldn't sit still. He was always doing something."

There are people who are dead in this report—people like Johnny, the home-clubhouse man; Vinnie, the visiting-clubhouse man; Joe Cronin, the player-manager—and there are people who still are alive, like Dominic DiMaggio and pitcher Charlie Wagner, now 90 years old, still nicknamed "Broadway" for his sense of fashion. They all speak with the same sense of wonder. They remember detail, nuance, feelings.

In 1967 columnist Edwin Pope of the *Miami Herald* was commissioned to write a book on one season in the career of Ted Williams as part of a string of books on different athletes for Prentice-Hall publishers called the Golden Year Series. Pope picked 1941, the obvious choice. He subcontracted a lot of the research to Will McDonough of the *Boston Globe*.

McDonough worked through the files of the *Globe* and interviewed a succession of people for the book. He turned his fat folder over to Pope, who was prepared to write when his editor at Prentice-Hall called. The editor said 1941 was not an acceptable choice because *Joe DiMaggio: The Golden Year, 1941* already was in the works.

Pope switched to a later Ted Williams season, sending McDonough back to the files and the dugout, but kept the notes. The quotes, as fresh as if they had been spoken yesterday, are used here for the first time thanks to Pope and McDonough. The voices are heard.

> JOE CRONIN: "Our clubhouse in Sarasota was a wooden building that was rat-infested. I think we had four showers in those days, and it was

very small. Our training field itself was huge. You had to hit a ball at least 400 feet to get it out of the park, and in rightfield it was about 440. In '41 we had put trees in around the outfield fence because we always had a prevailing wind blowing in from the ocean. We thought the trees would reduce the breeze.

"The players stayed in the Sarasota Terrace Hotel, right across the street. Ted roomed with Charlie Wagner. We had to be on the field at 10:00 A.M. in camp, and we usually worked out until one or two in the afternoon."

Williams was a week late in arriving at this paradise. That was how he started 1941. He drove from Minnesota, where he said he had been hunting wolves and lost track of the time.

There is life in the long ago.

The grumpy Ted Williams had disappeared somewhere in the off-season. The one virtue of phosphorescent anger, quick to ignite, is that it usually disappears in a hurry. The winter in Minnesota, clear and cold, had muffled the harsh words of the 1940 summer. Throughout his career, throughout his life, Williams would be able to take assorted steps back from his publicized confrontations. New morning. New day. He would become a master at turning pages, moving forward.

This was one of the many turns.

CLIF KEANE, FORMER *GLOBE* SPORTSWRITER. "Ted Williams, in the morning, never had a bad day. Every day started great. Things might happen during the day that would change all that—and they happened a lot—but in the morning he was great again."

He'd taken some extra-heavy 38-ounce bats back to Minnesota to swing and add strength. He'd moved his weight up to 185. He was filling into a man's body. A new contract—the newspapers guessed that it was for $20,000, up from 1940's "peanuts" at $12,500—had made him happy. Doris Soule was moving to Boston to live on Newbury Street with her brother, Donald, and to work as a cashier at the Parker House Hotel. The feuds and the requests to be traded were history. That was the idea. He was ready to go.

"How can they stop me from hitting?" he asked sportswriters. "They couldn't stop me my first year, and they couldn't stop me my second. They won't stop me my third."

One possible answer to his question soon arrived: he could be injured. Two weeks into his belated training camp, he broke his right ankle.

He'd twisted the ankle three days earlier when he slammed into the fence while making a catch. Now, playing an exhibition against the minor league Newark Bears in Sarasota, his right cleat caught in the dirt as he started to slide, stretching a single into a double. He limped off the field.

The immediate diagnosis was a sprain, so he stayed with the team. He couldn't run, feeling pain as he tried to move out of the batter's box, but found he still could hit. This was positive. Maybe even a bonus. The injury suddenly did not seem so injurious. He always had hated—and would hate—the spring training games, thought they pretty much were a waste of time. Now he didn't have to play in them. When the team took a boat to Cuba for an exhibition series in Havana, he stayed in Florida, went to Bradenton, and hit every day against the minor league Louisville Colonels. Perfect.

On the way north, the ankle still bothering him, he took daily batting practice and pinch-hit in games. Perfect. In Birmingham, Alabama, he finally had the injury X-rayed by a doctor, the brother-in-law of Tom Yawkey's wife. The X-rays revealed a slight fracture and bone chip. He went back to Boston for treatment. Perfect?

> JOE CRONIN: "I remember Ted hurting his leg and getting a lot of pain out of it. We thought it was just a sprain at first, but the X-rays showed it was fractured. Ted would have to play with that ankle taped every day that year."

Bobby Doerr would claim forever that the ankle injury was the foundation for Ted's season, that it forced him to take weight off his right foot in the batter's box, a move that made him lay back longer, wait, on a pitch. Williams forever would deny that thought. He said he was laying back because he was older, stronger, more in control. Whatever the case, he was laying back, waiting, and would hit better than ever.

After some pinch-hitting appearances and one false start, the ankle driving him back to the bench, he went into the everyday lineup on April 29 in Detroit and clocked a 440-foot homer and a long double to left. (Another bonus from the injury: he always hated the first few cold weeks of the season. The injury pretty much kept him out of that.) In Chicago, four days later, part of the same road trip, he belted a 500-footer into the rightfield seats at Comiskey Park against White Sox fastballer John Rigney in the third inning. The game, later tied, went into extra innings.

CHARLIE WAGNER, PITCHER: "Extra innings and it was getting dark. I was pitching, and Ted said to me, 'Roomie, you hold them the last half of this inning because I'm going to hit a home run and get us all the hell out of here.' I told him I'd do my best. He said, 'The hell with that, hold 'em,' because he was going to hit a home run. And that's just what he did, to win the game for us. At the time they said it was the longest homer ever hit at Comiskey Park."

The shot, also off Rigney, was described as 50 feet higher than the earlier homer. It landed on the grandstand roof. Guesstimates went as high as 600 feet. The fun had begun.

CHARLIE WAGNER: "I roomed with Ted in 1941. I roomed with him for five years, and he was always a clean-living guy, never smoked or drank or stayed out late. He loved to yak and talked baseball all the time. He was a good roommate. . . . In '41 I'd say his average day on the road went like this:

"He'd get up a little before seven o'clock, and first thing he'd do was turn on the radio. There wasn't any TV in those days, and Ted loved the radio. He always had the papers sent up to the room first thing in the morning. When he got them, he read every box score of every game in the league, paying particular attention to what the pitchers did. How long they lasted in a game. Whether they were wild or not. Things like that.

"After he finished the box scores, he went to the theater page. He used to cut out the timetable for all the movies downtown and in the neighborhood shows. Then he'd figure out how many he could see before he got to the ballpark and whether he'd want to see one after the game.

"Myself, Ted, and Lefty Grove were always the first ones to the park. Ted was a very intense guy, and he used to psych himself up for the games. The better he'd hit, the moodier he'd get because he was psyching himself. In the room the morning before a game he'd walk around talking out loud about the pitcher and what he was going to do to the guy. He loved to stand in front of a mirror like he was swinging a bat.

"I often tell the story—and it's true—about the time, and I'm pretty sure it was in '41, that I came back to our room one day and found a pile of shavings on my bed. By mistake, someone had shipped some new bats to Ted at the hotel. It was an off-day, so he took them to the room and started shaving the handles. He always carried a scraper around with him. So when I reached the room, there was this big pile of shavings.

"I said to him, 'Hey, Roomie, what the hell are you doing?' He said to me, 'Don't worry, Charlie, with these babies we're going to win a lot of games now.' As he said this, he took a vicious swing. With the follow-through, he hit the bedpost of my bed, and the whole damn thing fell on the floor. We had to send down and get another one."

The start of the two great baseball stories of the summer came on May 15, 1941. Williams and Joe DiMaggio both embarked on hitting streaks. Quietly. Williams had a single against the Indians. DiMaggio had a single against the White Sox. The two quiet hits, neither of them out of the infield, would start a strange rivalry from afar that would grow and grow, capturing headlines and lasting for generations.

Williams or DiMaggio? DiMaggio or Williams?

DiMaggio's single was the start of his 56-game hitting streak, an inconceivable event before it happened, untouched after it happened. Williams's single was the start of his own more modest streak of 23 straight games that would be the springboard to his .406 batting average, not inconceivable before it happened, but certainly untouched in future years.

The other supposedly untouchable records—Babe Ruth's 60 home runs, Ty Cobb's 96 stolen bases—would fall to bigger bodies or faster bodies in the future. The 56-game streak and the .406 average would only grow older and more impossible to match.

Williams or DiMaggio? DiMaggio or Williams?

They would edge back and forth in the national consciousness as the season unwound. One would capture the interest of the ordinary fan, then the other one would take it back. They were a tag team for attention. Williams tagged first.

Six days after the start of his streak, he went 4-for-5 against the

Yankees, then 3-for-7 in the next two days. He then went on a stretch of games in which he collected at least two hits per game. His average, which had been inching up in the first half of May, shot past the magic .400 mark on May 25 and went straight to .430. From May 17 to June 1, he hit .536. His average for the entire month of May was .436. Edge: Williams.

On June 8 he was held hitless in both games of a doubleheader against the White Sox. His streak was done. DiMaggio kept going. The Yankees, who had been in fourth place six and a half games behind the Cleveland Indians on May 15, now were rolling. DiMaggio became a day-to-day constant headline. The modern streak of 41 consecutive games with a hit had been established by George Sisler of the St. Louis Browns in 1922. There was a sold-out frenzy in Washington's Griffith Stadium when Di-Maggio tied the mark with a single in the first game of a doubleheader. Then, in the seventh inning of the second game, using a bat borrowed from Tommy Henrich after his own bat had been stolen between games, he singled to left off Red Anderson. Definite edge: DiMaggio.

Williams or DiMaggio? DiMaggio or Williams? They were walking separate tightropes across the sky. Everyone was looking up, waiting for either or both to fall.

As Robert Creamer points out in his book *Baseball in '41*, there is a tendency to look backwards now at the two men, through all of the moments that happened later, through all of the things each did during and after his career, through all of the history that happened, all of the images that were accumulated. DiMaggio was the Beatles! Williams was the Rolling Stones! DiMaggio was Bill Russell! Williams was Wilt Chamberlain! DiMaggio was Cary Grant! Williams was John Wayne! The comparisons could run forever. DiMaggio was elegance, grace, a seven-course meal! Williams was determination, noise, a fat steak, and a good baked potato! DiMaggio was *The New Yorker*! Williams was *Field and Stream*!

None of this thinking existed at the time. Most of the members of the Beatles and the Rolling Stones hadn't even been born. (A scary thought when you look at Keith Richards.) There were still wars to fight, pennants to be won or lost, actresses and models to be married, coffee machines and rowboats to be endorsed.

DiMaggio had played five seasons in the major leagues, Williams two. As Creamer states, the all-time outfield in 1941, no arguments anywhere, was Babe Ruth, Ty Cobb, and Tris Speaker. DiMaggio, as good as he had been, still played under the shadows left by Ruth and Gehrig. Williams was a possible star, an ingenue, no more than that. How many players had arrived in the big leagues, clicked off a couple of solid seasons, then fallen prey to curveballs or other demons? This was an odd-sized guy who could hit and he sure could talk. No more than that.

The spotlight hadn't really arrived to define either of the two men before 1941. The image of DiMaggio, the pulseless, urbane stylist, would begin to be typed into creation by the men watching the exploits of a 27-year-old Italian high school dropout in New York. The bombastic, big-talking, skinny kid in Boston would begin to become the bombastic, big-talking man. Enough major pieces would be added to the puzzle to make everyone pay attention.

Williams or DiMaggio? DiMaggio or Williams? Now the spotlight was on these two very different men. They were becoming what they would be.

DOM DiMAGGIO: "I think Ted was a little in awe of Joe when he first came up. I know he respected and admired him. He and Joe were just different people. Joe always was in Toots Shor's in New York. He always had a guy with him. There'd always be some guy. Ted went off by himself a lot more. He'd play the game and go off on his own.

"I know I liked him from day one. I came up in '40, and he'd had a year in already. I'd heard so much about him, and I said to myself, 'Now I've got to play with this guy?' But I liked him. I always sympathized with him when he had those problems with the media. I was quiet, and Ted would get talking about hitting in our little corner of the clubhouse—he never talked about fielding—and he would draw a crowd and after a while he'd turn to me and say, 'Dommie, you think I'm full of shit, don't you?' "

Williams was hitting .405 when the All-Star break arrived. He had 16 home runs and 62 RBI. Joe DiMaggio had hit in 48 straight games. The New York press had found a new goal for him, Wee Willie Keeler's 44-year-old "all-time" streak of 44 straight games, and he had tied, then broken it in a weekend series with the Red Sox. The All-Star Game was a celebrated pause in this daily soap opera.

Unlike today, the game was the second-biggest event in the season after the World Series. It was much more than a public relations showcase; the outcome was meaningful to all parties concerned. The leagues were very different. The American and National Leagues seemed as separated in culture and population as England and France. Which league was better? Which players were better? The All-Star Game was the test.

Williams had played in the 1940 game, 0-for-2, and was excited about his second appearance. He had brought along an eight-millimeter camera that he handed to Bobby Doerr, asking the second baseman to record the activities. He walked the premises at Detroit's Briggs Stadium with the confidence that befitted a .400 hitter.

In the American League lineup, he batted fourth, after DiMaggio. He had a double in the fourth to drive in a run, but by the eighth inning the National League had a 5-2 lead. The American Leaguers mounted a rally, loading the bases and scoring a run, but in the middle of it Williams struck out, looking at a fastball from pitcher Claude Passeau.

Then the ninth came along, another rally, another chance. Williams came to the plate with two outs, two men on base, one run in, the score now 5-4, and the crowd very excited. With two balls and a strike, he delivered the biggest home run of his young career, a shot that hit the facade in right. He bounded around the bases with the exuberance of a kid who has received a bicycle and an air gun on Christmas morn, jumping and waving his arms, running on air. American League 7. National League 5.

BABE PINELLI, HOME PLATE UMPIRE: "I remember well calling Ted out in the eighth inning due to a comment he and I had in the ninth. He came to the plate with two men on and two out. The National Leaguers had missed what appeared to be a cinch double play when Joe DiMaggio hit to the second sacker and [Arky] Vaughan threw low to [Frank] McCormick at first, which he couldn't handle.

"In the meantime, during the excitement, Ted talked to me. He asked, 'Babe, how was that pitch on me in the eighth inning?' I explained it was a real good pitch, high enough and tight. Ted's answer was a classic. 'Babe,' he said, 'it was a good pitch, and all umpires should call it a strike.' He walked to the plate, and when he hit the homer, I believe it was the same spot Passeau put it to strike him out in the eighth inning.

"Incidentally, Ted was one of the few batters who stood so close to the plate. As close as possible. His feet were right on the chalk line. Babe Ruth was another. Like all great hitters, both had tremendous quick wrists plus power."

DOMINIC DiMAGGIO: "I was the on-deck hitter when Ted hit that home run. It's funny, because I didn't think they were going to pitch to him. I thought they were going to walk him and pitch to me. Passeau was a righthander. When Ted came to the plate, their manager came out to talk to Passeau. That's when I thought they were going to walk Ted. To this day, I'd like to know what that conversation was about.

"Anyway, they pitched to Ted, and I remember he had a tremendous swing at a pitch that he fouled back. I recall saying to myself, If he ever hit that, he would have hit it over the roof. Then he almost did hit the next pitch over the roof. This was a line blast. It went off the facade on a line . . . this wasn't any fly ball."

Joe Cronin: "I was sitting in the dugout when he hit the home run, and I jumped up and ran as fast as I could to home plate to meet him. As soon as Ted hit the ball, he stood in the batter's box watching the flight of the ball. While he was watching it, his arms shot straight over his head like a football referee signaling a touchdown, and as soon as the ball hit the top of the facade, he started clapping his hands and jumping up and down. He did this all around the bases."

Tom Yawkey: "When Ted hit that home run, I jumped out of my seat and started jumping up and down and clapping my hands. Because I was watching Ted, who was doing the exact same thing as he ran around the bases."

This was the imaginary home run that Williams always wanted to hit during all those swings in all of those different places, from the backyard on Utah Street to the train tracks on the way to Florida, to the hotel room and Charlie Wagner's bed. Bottom of the ninth, he always would tell himself. Two outs, need a home run to win. He had walked into his own vision. He kept saying, over and over again in the clubhouse, "It's my biggest thrill."

Definite edge: Williams.

The attention returned to DiMaggio after the break and continued to grow as he continued to hit. When the streak finally ended in Cleveland on July 17, a couple of fielding gems by Indians third baseman Ken Keltner robbing him of the chance to grab a $10,000 endorsement offer from Heinz 57, the Yankees had moved into a six-game lead that would only grow and grow. His 91 hits during those 56 games were the obvious fuel for the charge.

Williams now had the spotlight to himself, unencumbered by even a pennant race for distraction. Except he was struggling. He too had fallen off his tightrope.

He had stayed in Detroit, joined by the rest of the Red Sox, for a series to open the second half of the season. The first game was rained out, and Williams went 0-for-4 against Buck Newsom the next day, and his average dropped from .405 to .398, easy as that. In the first game of a series-closing doubleheader he walked three times and popped out to drop his average another point. Taking a lead after one of those walks, trying to get back to first on a pickoff attempt, he twisted his bad right ankle. He sat out the second game, and for the next nine days his services were confined to pinch-hitting four times. One for three with a walk. His average was .396 when he returned to Boston and the starting lineup.

In the first game back, hitting against old friend John Rigney of the White Sox and switched from third to fourth in the lineup, behind Cronin instead of in front, he powdered a shot to the bleachers in right center to get rolling again. Twelve days later, after a 19-for-35 stretch, his average was back to .412. Ta-da. He was walking the wire again.

CHARLIE WAGNER: "During the whole season, but particularly in the second half, he'd get on the same kick every day—'I'm going to hit .400. I know I can do it. I'm determined to do it.' He was obsessed with the challenge. A funny thing about Ted, he hungered to hit against the pitchers who got him out more than he looked forward to the guys he could hit fairly easily. Most hitters want that guy they can clobber. Ted didn't. He wanted the challenge of getting a guy who had been getting the best of him.

"Another thing he had going was his thirst for knowledge about hitting. He was always bugging the great hitters of the past. When we were on a train, he'd bend Jimmie Foxx's ears so bad about questions on hitting he'd almost drive Jimmie crazy. When we went into other cities, he'd talk to great hitters like Harry Heilmann. I remember he always asked Heilmann to try to figure out why Heilmann only hit well every other year.

"I know he asked all these hitters about what they did to get out of slumps. Ted firmly believed that if a hitter never went into a bad slump, or could avoid long slumps, he'd be a great hitter."

The quest to hit .400 was a day-to-day constant. In August the *Globe* began running a daily comparison between Williams's efforts and the pace set by Bill Terry of the New York Giants, the last man to hit over .400 with .401 in 1930. The last American Leaguer to do it was Heilmann with .403 in 1923. The number of years that had passed was evidence of how hard the feat had become. Add into the equation the seldom-noticed change in sacrifice fly rules—there basically was no sacrifice fly in 1941; it was called an out—and a much easier ball to field than the mushballs used in the early days of the century when hitting .400 was not such a spectacular accomplishment, and Williams was moving into unknown hitting territory.

He was working angles that never had been worked.

VINNIE ORLANDO: "I don't know if this has ever been written, but Ted used umpires to help him that year. On the field, when he was on base, he'd strike up a conversation and ask the umpires how the pitchers were throwing in that last series in New York. See, the umpires usually came from another series someplace else. Ted would find out from them what the pitchers were throwing to certain hitters. How they were throwing. What they were throwing. If they were relying on the fastball or curve. Things like that. It was like having a personal scouting system. The umpires didn't mind because Ted never gave them any trouble.

"The league got wind of all this later, though, and made the umpires stop it. Although Ted and the umpires always got along great."

He was doing things hitters never had done very much.

CHARLIE WAGNER: "Ted loved to exercise in the room. He was always doing those fingertip push-ups. He used to challenge me and tell me he could do 25 more push-ups than I could, no matter what. If I did 25, he'd do 50. If I did 50, he'd do 75.

"About that time we got a pitcher named Ken Chase from Washington [actually it was the next year, 1942], and Kenny was a great exercise man. He and Ted used to compete against each other. Ted was always squeezing those hand grips to make his hands and wrists strong. I don't care who the athlete was, there was never anyone more dedicated to becoming a great hitter than Ted was. That's all he wanted."

He was caught in his own unforgiving battle against the hard and fast rules of mathematics. Man versus Long Division. Divide the hits by the number of at bats and that's the answer. There is no way to bend the numbers. The beauty of baseball is that it is the most honest, most measurable day-to-day job that can be found. Family connections and snappy patter and a good haircut matter not a bit. Subjectivity does not exist. Execution is all that counts. The numbers are the only judge.

Williams was alone against the numbers.

CHARLIE WAGNER: "In Boston, Ted would get up early in the morning, and he and I would go out to this lake, sit in a boat, and just fish a little. It was the most relaxing thing in the world before a game. This was when I think Ted just sat and thought about the pitcher he was facing that day and the things that could happen. We'd come back to the park after this and get dressed. During a game, Ted stayed pretty much by himself in the dugout. He wasn't trying to be difficult. I think he just wanted to concentrate on the pitcher and the game."

VINNIE ORLANDO: "In those days Ted would get up about five or six in the morning and go fishing up at a place called Sunset Lake in Framingham [about 20 miles west of Boston]. He'd fish for a few hours before coming back to Boston and eating breakfast. He'd eat in places where other people didn't go because he didn't want to be recognized. And he'd never eat where the other players did. In those days the games started at 3:00 P.M., and the players had to be at the park by noon. Ted would come in and grab a broom handle we had in the clubhouse and start swinging it. He did this all the time.

"After the games, he'd either take extra practice—and he did this a lot that year—or we'd go out to eat right away. This guy used to inhale ice cream by the quart. He was the fastest eater I ever saw. I remember once Dom telling him, 'For Christ's sake, Ted, why don't you stop long enough to chew?'

"After we'd eat, we'd either go on a double date or Ted would go to the movies. Ted and I used to double-date a lot in those days. He had a big Buick and was a wild driver. He'd scare the hell out of me the way he drove through town. . . . Ted loved movies. Once he told me, 'Vinnie, I sit so close to the screen watching those Westerns that the dirt flies up and hits me in the face when the horses go by.' He was really nuts about Westerns in those days."

August melted away into September, and he kept at his hitting pace. Two hits out of every five trips to the plate. Two out of five. Two out of five. That was the minimum syncopation to his struggle. Two out of five.

On September 1, he belted three home runs in a doubleheader against the Senators to take the American League home run lead. He suddenly had a good shot at the Triple Crown, since he was also in the mix with Charlie Keller and DiMaggio of the Yanks for the RBI lead, but that almost didn't matter. Two out of five. The math was what mattered.

Teams had tried various strategies, pitching around him (he would finish with 145 walks), shifting defenses (Jimmy Dykes, manager of the White Sox, even unveiled a full shift that was a precursor of things to come), but none had worked. When he left Fenway Park for the last two series of the year, three games each in Washington and Philadelphia, he was hitting .405. Two out of five. Two out of five.

Wouldn't he surely keep going?

Not necessarily. When he left Washington, he was hitting .401. Two out of ten. A trio of Senators pitchers—Sid Hudson, Dutch Leonard, and a rookie lefthander named Dick Mulligan—had pretty much kept him under control. His true average now was .4009, rounded off to .401.

Three games in Philadelphia would decide his fate. The drama was obvious.

The series consisted of one game on Saturday, followed by a season-ending doubleheader on Sunday. The original schedule called for three single games, starting on Friday, but A's owner Connie Mack shifted the Friday game to Sunday in hopes of pulling in one final good gate to Shibe Park.

Williams used the extra day off for extra hitting.

JOE CRONIN: "I've always thought that first game was rained out. I'm sure we had a storm or something Thursday which soaked the field. I know I got one of our coaches, Tom Daly, and told him to take Ted out to the park for some hitting practice on Friday to keep him loose. Maybe [Frank] Shellenback and [Frankie] Pytlak went along, I'm not so sure. . . .

"A thing I remember about the weekend was the concern Ted had about facing those Philly pitchers. They were all kids he never had seen before, and he hated this. Ted would rather face the best than someone he had never seen before. Part of Ted's great success as a hitter was the way he studied pitchers. Even then he got to know more about the pitcher than the pitcher knew about himself. With new kids he never had faced or seen before, he lost this edge. So he was worried about this."

Mr. Mack, the famed owner-manager who still directed his team from the bench in a business suit, had scheduled a trio of rookies to start the games. The first, on Saturday, was a righthanded knuckleballer named Roger Wolff. Williams also was not a great favorite of the knuckleball. He walked the first time he faced Wolff and doubled the next time to jump to .402, but then flied to right, fouled to first, and whiffed on a low knuckleball in the ninth to strike out for only the 27th time during the season.

One out of four. The hard math was not good. His average now was .39955. Official statistics were rounded off to three numbers, so he officially was hitting .400. A debate developed almost instantaneously about what he should do next. The debaters on the side of common sense said he should sit out the final day, walk away with his .39955, his official .400, and take a nice seat in the record books. Failing that, he should play only long enough in the first game to move his average above the .400 mark, unofficially and officially, no doubt, then take a seat.

There was precedence to do this.

In 1935, six years earlier, Joe Vosmik, then with the White Sox, went into the last day of the season with a two-point lead over Buddy Myer of the Senators for the batting title. Vosmik, playing at home, decided to sit out the final doubleheader. Word came from back east, alas, that Myer had gone 4-for-5 and edged into the lead. Vosmik quickly pinch-hit in the first game and played the second. He went 1-for-4 and finished second to Myer for the title, .349 to .348.

In 1938, three years earlier, Jimmie Foxx had a one-point lead over Jeff Heath of the Indians on the last day, .348 to .347. Foxx had a clause in his contract that said he would be paid a $500 bonus for the batting title. Even though he had 50 home runs and 175 RBI, he sat. Heath went 0-for-4 and 0-for-3 in a doubleheader. Foxx won the batting title and collected the $500.

So why shouldn't Williams do the same? Or a variation of the same? The opportunity was there, a rounded-off .400 looking the same as any other .400 to anyone in the future, but it did have a fine-print, legalistic stink to it. Williams never hesitated. He said that he would play.

His decision would be characterized later as bold or courageous, but

Williams always would downplay it. He would say that he didn't know .400 would be so important. Why should he? The feat had been accomplished 11 years earlier. He had talked with most of the men who had hit .400. Surely if he didn't hit .400 this year, he would hit that high the next year or the year after that. Or somebody else surely would.

"I'll tell you this," Williams always would say. "If I'd known how much it was going to mean, I would have thought about it [sitting out] a lot more."

His decision made September 27, 1941, a special day. The man on the tightrope was so far out there that some eyes couldn't even watch.

TOM YAWKEY: "I went to Philadelphia to watch the games, but left after the game on Saturday. Ted went 1-for-4, so I thought I was a jinx. I went to New York after the game and left instructions for [traveling secretary] Phil Troy to keep in touch with me the next day about how Ted was doing."

The eyes that could watch, watched closely. They studied the man next to them as he went toward his fate.

JOHNNY ORLANDO: "The night before the final game of the season I walked the streets of Philly with Ted. We walked for over three hours, and my feet were burning. Ted didn't drink, so from time to time I'd run into a bar room to get a drink, and he'd wait outside until I got finished, drinking a soft drink.

"During the whole conversation all he kept repeating, over and over, was how determined he was to hit .400."

JOE CRONIN: "The Saturday night before the Sunday doubleheader, Tom Daly and myself were sitting on a big sofa in the lobby of the Ben Franklin Hotel in Philadelphia. About ten o'clock or so Ted came into the lobby. He had been out walking with Johnny Orlando. When he came in, he sat with me and Tom talking about everything until about midnight. It was during this discussion that I asked him, 'How do you want to handle it?' He said, 'I want to play it out. I want to play it all the way.' As far as I was concerned, that was it."

CHARLIE WAGNER: "In the room that night he wasn't really nervous, but he was sky-high emotionally. He kept talking about the pitchers he was going to face and how they would pitch to him.

"The next day we got up early, ate breakfast in the hotel, and went out to the park in a cab together. The ride out was quiet. I remember thinking about how fast the cabbie was driving and that we'd probably get killed before we got there the way he was flying through the intersections. At the park, Ted took early batting practice. Ted wanted to play in the worst way."

The first-game pitcher was another rookie, Dick Fowler. Williams didn't come to the plate until he led off the second inning. Small snippets of nervous dialogue were extended. A's catcher Frankie Hayes told him that he was going to have to earn his .400, but that the A's pitchers were going to pitch to him, not walk him. Umpire Bill McGowan told him, "To hit .400, a batter has to be loose." Williams went into his classic upright stance, squeezing the bat, squeezing, squeezing.

After looking at two balls, he lined a single to right off first baseman Bob Johnson. He was on the way.

In the fifth, he blasted another Fowler pitch over the wall in right and onto 20th Street. . . .

In the sixth, facing reliever Porter Vaughan. . . .

JOE CRONIN: "I got worried when Mack brought that lefty Vaughan into the game. Ted was 2-for-2 and over .400, but I said to myself, Well, he's not only never faced this guy before, but the guy is lefthanded. . . . But it didn't make any difference to Ted. He had the challenge that day and he loved it."

Single through the middle. . . .

JOHNNY ORLANDO: "I remember Jack Malaney from the *Boston Post* running down to the clubhouse now and telling Cronin to take Ted out because he was over .400. Cronin told Ted he was coming out, but Ted said he was going to keep on playing."

Seventh inning, Vaughan still in the game. Single down the rightfield line. . . .

Eighth inning? Reached first on an error.

He thus was 4-for-5 in the first game, a 12–11 slugfest win. His average was .404. Was he going to hit .400? There pretty much was no doubt.

The numbers, the mathematics, had lost in the end. He was bulletproof for the second game. Play or not play? No debate. He played and had even more fun. . . .

FRED CALIGIURI, A'S ROOKIE STARTER: "I had just arrived in Philadelphia, and this was my fifth start. There was quite a lot of enthusiasm in that last game of the season with Williams shooting for .400, and also it was Lefty Grove Day, who was presented with gifts, etc. Grove started that day, his last appearance, and you can imagine what a thrill it was for me to pitch against Grove and Williams.

"I asked Hal Wagner how we were to pitch to Williams, as I never had faced him before, and Wagner said, 'You've got to be kidding,' or some such remark. Anyway, first time up, Williams pulled an inside curveball past [Crash] Davis, our first baseman. Davis told me between innings that I had better pitch Williams outside because he [Davis] did not see the last shot. He was kidding, of course.

"Next time up he hit a fastball against a loudspeaker situated on top of a fence in right centerfield, dropping back in for a double. Third time up he popped up to the infield. He was 2-for-3 in the last game."

The final number was .406. The final hit, the double in the fourth, was far more emphatic than Caligiuri's matter-of-fact description. Williams said after the game it was the hardest ball he had hit in his career. Accounts said it put a hole in the speaker before dropping to the ground. It was a grand, whiz-bang hit to finish a grand, whiz-bang, 6-for-8 day and an entire grand, whiz-bang year.

Portions of the crowd of 10,268 ran onto the field to surround Williams at the end. He had to grab his hat so it wouldn't be stolen, had to fight his way into the clubhouse, helped by a few teammates. He was relieved, pleased, overjoyed.

"In the clubhouse afterward, he was a different Williams," an "unnamed Red Sox veteran" later told Garry Schumacher of the *New York Journal-American*. "For the first time since I've known him, he liked to have other ballplayers around him, to take pleasure in their praise and backslapping. A year before, a similar feat would have revealed him a strutting, smirking braggart. Here, instead, he strove honestly and so very earnestly to make himself one of the gang."

Done.

JOHNNY ORLANDO: "I remember after the game, he grabbed me by the arm and took me to the men's room. All the photographers and writers were waiting for him, but he took me inside and told me, 'I'm a good hitter.' He said it just like he had proved something to himself. And after he said it, he kissed the bat he had in his hand."

W illiams's .406 was not seen as a profound achievement when it was posted on the wall. The Boston newspapers, only two days later, moved along to give all attention to the World Series between the Yankees and the Brooklyn Dodgers and the heavyweight title fight between Joe Louis and Lou Nova. The baseball writers in their Most Valuable Player balloting soon gave the award to DiMaggio for his streak and its assist in bringing the Yankees the pennant. Williams was second and there was no great uproar.

Time is what has given this baseball summer of 1941 its substance and charm. The summers that followed, 62 of them now and counting, have shown how hard it is to do what he did. Time cuts out the picture from 1941 and puts it in the wallet.

Who was Ted Williams?

This is who he was.

Various statistical analyses have shown the depth and meaning of the .406. Cronin always estimated that Williams had "at least" 12 sacrifice flies during the season, which would have built the final number to .419, which would have been the official stat both before and after Williams played. Ed Linn, in the book *Hitter*, points out that adding his 145 walks to his 185 hits gives Williams an on-base average of .574. The man was better than an even bet to reach first base every time he went to the plate! Stephen Jay Gould, the late Harvard anthropologist, laid out various tables in an essay entitled "Achieving the Impossible Dream" in *Ted Williams: A Portrait in Words and Pictures* to show that the .400 hitter already had become extinct before Williams reached .406, that the .406 was "the greatest achievement in twentieth-century hitting." He said, "Williams's .406 is a beacon in the history of excellence, a lesson to all who value the best in human possibility."

Time.

Charlie Wagner says that conversation about the war in Europe and the uncertain future took place in the Red Sox clubhouse every day in

1941. Of course it did. The Lend-Lease Act was signed before spring training even started, and Yugoslavia and Greece both fell to the Germans before Williams was ready to take his taped ankle into the starting line-up. The *Bismarck* was sunk 12 days after DiMaggio's hitting streak began, and Hitler invaded the Soviet Union five days after it ended. On September 1, when Williams made the turn for home in his bid for .400, all Jews in Germany became legally required to wear a yellow Star of David.

Citizen Kane was in the movie houses, and *For Whom the Bell Tolls* was on the bookshelves, and Tommy Dorsey was on the radio. In separate parts of the country, Neil Diamond, Bob Dylan, Jesse Jackson, Faye Dunaway, Dick Cheney, and both Simon and Garfunkel were being born.

The picture in the wallet contains none of that.

Men in hats cheer. Base hits land everywhere at the two-out-of-five clip. This 23-year-old young man, this self-confident perfectionist, does push-ups on his fingertips in his room, eats his ice cream in big gulps, watches Westerns and drives his Buick, and meets his challenges and wins. This is the foundation of his greatness, the reason for anyone to pay attention, 1941 and .406, forever present tense in a mostly past-tense world.

He kisses his bat. He smiles. He is who he wanted to be.

By the end of the next year he would be in an entirely different uniform.

6 World War II

He was a student of celestial navigation. He was a student of meteorology. Doors that had remained closed at Hoover High School, boring and uninviting, dull, now were wide open, and the reluctant and indifferent student in San Diego now was plowing through math and physics and a bunch of other subjects at one of the top colleges in the country, taking his obsessive mind in directions away from the study of the well-struck baseball. He was learning how to fly.

Ted Williams was going to war. His way.

"Why do you want to be a pilot?" reporters asked. "You probably could have found something less dangerous in the service."

"Because I like to hit!" Naval Aviation Cadet Williams (service number 705-53-11) replied.

He arrived at the postcard campus of Amherst College in the postcard town of the same name at the foot of the Berkshire Mountains in western Massachusetts on November 15 as the final leaves fell away from the fall foliage of 1942. He was a day late, of course, for the start of the Civilian Pilot Training Course and pulled up in the backseat of a Boston taxicab. The driver took his two bags into the lobby of Genung House, dropped them in the lobby, and accepted 25 bucks.

"Gee, kid, the best of luck to ya," newspaper accounts reported the cabbie said, shaking the new recruit's hand.

In June 1942 Williams had been spotted at the Harvard University graduation exercises watching Hugh Voorhees, a Hoover classmate, receive a bachelor's degree. Asked his opinion of the school, his comment was, "It's old, isn't it?" Now he was traveling from classroom to classroom in another old and prestigious New England school, wearing an ill-fitting green uniform from the Civilian Conservation Corps, tie and all, trying to fill in enough holes in his high school education to become a pilot.

"The colleges have changed because of the war," Dr. Warren Green, professor of astronomy and now coordinator of the CPT program, said. "They're all pitching in. Now we're teaching trades and forgetting theory. It's going to be hard to go back to the old method of teaching."

This was a crash course—hopefully not literally—to provide airmen for the sudden war. Campuses across the nation were being used as first-step facilities for fliers. The government was paying Amherst $12 per week for room and board for each cadet, plus $70 for each cadet who graduated, $55 for each cadet who didn't. The cadets themselves were receiving $75 per month.

"We lived in the frat houses," Johnny Pesky, also in the program, remembers, "and at Genung House. That's where Ted and I were at the beginning. Dr. Green was a big guy, a good guy. He'd won the Croix de Guerre in the French Foreign Legion in the First World War. There wasn't any fooling around. We even were doing some flying, little Piper Cubs and WACOs. It was beautiful country."

Reveille was at 05:45, sounded by a large bell taken from the Amherst Fire Department and installed on the front of the Chi Phi house. The college students, still in session, complained about the early morning noise. The cadets complained in return about the college students making noise all night.

Work began at 06:45. The cadets, half Army, half Navy, were split into two groups. One took a bus to the tiny Turner's Falls airport to fly those Piper Cubs in the shadows of Mount Tom and the Berkshire Mountains. The other group stayed on campus for ground training, learning the elements of navigation, aerology, recognition, and radio code. In the afternoon, the two groups switched.

The naval cadets were called "the baseball squad." In addition to Pesky and Williams, Buddy Gremp and Johnny Sain of the Boston Braves and Joe Coleman, property of the Philadelphia Athletics, were in the program. (Alex MacLean, one of the writers who filled in for the drunken Dave Egan, also was in the squad.) This was an eight-week course that would prepare the cadets for the more difficult training that lay ahead. A full calendar year would be covered before they could possibly receive their wings and head into combat situations.

"I'm just tickled to death to be in this thing," Williams said. "It's just what I want."

He did close-order drills with a ten-pound dummy rifle. He ran the commando obstacle course. He did morning calisthenics and tried to learn how to swim and looked at math problems until his head hurt, and he jumped into the tiny planes with his instructors and flew. The landscape was a carpet beneath him, the farms and rounded-off mountains, the Connecticut River and, oops, the power lines.

The military life, surprise of surprises, suited the loner, the incendiary public figure, the squeakiest of all celebrated wheels. He liked it. He was pretty good at it. Save for one public relations afternoon when a half-dozen Boston writers were allowed on campus, he was almost able to be another 24-year-old name and serial number in a vast sea of names and numbers getting ready to face the Japanese or the Germans, whatever was needed. No spotlight, no headlines, he was as close to being anonymous as he ever would be.

Not that there hadn't been headlines on the way to this little slice of artificial anonymity. No, probably no one else in the country had entered the war effort with more controversy and clamor, more noise surrounding him, than Ted Williams did.

Eleven months earlier, the bombing of Pearl Harbor had changed all lives in an obvious instant. The lives in baseball were no different. Bob Feller, the number-one pitcher in the game, had joined the Navy on December 8, the quickest, fastest change of all, the words of President

Roosevelt's "Day of Infamy" speech still resonating. A few other players had followed his lead, but the bulk of the major leaguers considered options. Enlist? Or wait? The military draft, which eventually would take more than 10 million young American men off to war, hung over all of them. Married players, players with children, were lower on the list, classified 3-A, but most single players were part of the great lump at the top of the 1-A draft pool. Indeed, slugger Hank Greenberg of the Detroit Tigers had been drafted during the 1941 season, an indication that athletic success was not grounds for deferment.

Williams, during his .406 heroics, had been classified 3-A as the sole support of his mother. He then was reclassified in January 1942 to 1-A, no different from the six other unmarried Red Sox ballplayers, Johnny Pesky, Dominic DiMaggio, Charlie Wagner, Eddie Pellagrini, Earl Johnson, and Bill Butland. Lefthanded pitcher Mickey Harris already had been called by the Army. The rest could be drafted at any moment.

Back in Minnesota, living at the King Cole Hotel in Minneapolis and the Gagen in Princeton, hunting and fishing and visiting Doris, Williams was called for his physical on January 8 in Minnesota. He passed.

"I guess they need more men," he told reporters as he left the physical.

"I can tell you baseball ought to be proud to have men like Ted Williams in the service," Eddie Collins said from Boston, certain of what would come next. "That's the way we feel about it. And he'll make a fine soldier."

The business appeared to be done, except . . . well, except two days earlier Williams had seen a lawyer. Something didn't seem right to Williams. Had the draft laws changed? Why was he being reclassified? Was it because the law had been changed or because he was the .406 hitter of 1941, a famous name? He was told the laws had not been changed. Then why, he wondered, had his status been changed? This did not seem right to him.

"Do you want to appeal?" the lawyer asked.

"Yes, I do," Williams replied and proceeded to fill out the paperwork, getting affidavits from May in San Diego, whom he now had not seen in almost two years.

The lawyer warned about the negative publicity. Williams said he had dealt with negative publicity just fine. What was right was right. Why should he be treated differently from anyone else? He said his mother was 50 years old, in poor health, and shouldn't be forced to work. He said he sent her $5,000 in the past year and wanted to keep up payments on three other annuities that would insure her future.

Two days later, Hennepin County Draft Board No. 6 in Minneapolis voted down his request, 5–0. He was tentatively scheduled to be inducted on January 24. He surely was gone again.

"Ted won't be hurt by the layoff," Joe Cronin said, already in Florida, certain of this outcome. "Other players have been out of baseball for a year or more and come right back. A lot of them did it during the other war. Uncle Sam comes first."

Not exactly. Williams's lawyer, Warren Rogers, went to see Colonel J. E. Nelson, head of the draft in Minnesota. Rogers asked if anyone else with the same file as Williams would be judged 3-A. Nelson said he probably would. Nelson also said "this case is an exception." Request was still denied.

The last chance was the President's Board of Appeal. Only Nelson or state appeal agent Harold Estram could appeal. Williams met with Estram in Minneapolis. Estram studied the case and decided that Williams had no more money than the average 23-year-old earning $35 a week. He agreed to carry the appeal the final step, essentially to President Roosevelt's desk.

On February 27, 26 days later, an order from Roosevelt was issued, changing Williams's status back to 3-A. He was free to go to spring training for the 1942 season.

The newspapers exploded. Not just in Boston, everywhere.

Who did he think he was? Hardship deferment? Hadn't he been making good money the past three years? Comparisons were made with boxer Jack Dempsey, who was deferred during World War I and labeled a "draft dodger." Wasn't that what Williams was doing? Dodging the draft while the guy down the street, who had real hardships, was packing his bags? The UPI pointed out that since the appeals law went into effect in October 1940, the state of Massachusetts had "no more than a dozen" appeals to the presidential board. No more than 1,500 people had appealed during the same time in the entire country.

"I am a bartender and a Ted Williams fan, but from now on you can count me off his list of supporters," William Lago, a South Boston bartender, said in a common opinion poll of "Mr. Average Man" in the *Globe*. "I am in the draft and I have a mother and child to support, but I know if I'm called my dependents won't starve."

Red Sox management reacted to Williams's possible return with cautious, muted pleasure. The public relations situation was obviously combustible.

"Naturally, I welcome him back with open arms," Cronin said in Sarasota, where Jim Tabor already was practicing in rightfield to be Williams's replacement. "I'm certain that his is a most worthy case and that Ted wouldn't hesitate an instant about jumping into the Army when and if he is called. If Uncle Sam says fight, he'll fight. Since he has said play ball, Ted has the right to play."

The story grew juicier when Williams at first said he had nothing to do with the appeal, didn't even know what his lawyers were doing. The draft board responded by saying that he personally had okayed the appeal. Williams admitted that he had, but said he did it on the advice of the attorneys, none of whom he had paid, people who simply acted on his behalf out of their own belief in his case.

He would claim years later in his autobiography that he suffered from a lack of advice. He had no help from his father or his mother, had no friends in baseball to give him counsel. He simply let the lawyers take charge. What did he know about the Germans, the Japanese, the war? He was not any great student of current affairs. The Sox already had sent him a contract for $30,000 for the next season, the most money he ever had made, and the figure burned in his head.

"There are a million ballplayers in 3-A—Joe Gordon played baseball that year, Joe DiMaggio played, Stan Musial played—but Ted Williams is the guy having trouble with the draft board," Williams said in his book. "I remember I had a contract to endorse Quaker Oats, a $4,000 contract. I used to eat them all the time. But they canceled out on me because of all this unfair stuff and I haven't eaten a Quaker Oat since."

Now he had plenty of advice. Cronin advised him to join the service, any service. Red Sox owner Tom Yawkey advised the same route. James A. Silin, his business adviser, sent a telegram.

"This is the biggest decision you ever have to make, Ted," Silin wrote. "Be sure you do the right thing. Your baseball career as well as your patriotism and your future happiness for many years to come are at stake. If you enlist you will gladden the hearts and stir the Americanism of thousands of kids to whom you have been and should always remain an idol. Don't let those kids down. You will never cease to regret it if you do."

Williams's head was spinning. What to do? Were all these people right? Maybe they were. He flew to Chicago to take a tour of the Great Lakes Naval Training Station with Mickey Cochrane, the former Hall of

Fame catcher for the Detroit Tigers. Cochrane was now in charge of the Great Lakes athletic program. Williams said, again in his autobiography, he liked what he saw. Cochrane, dressed in a blue uniform with bright brass buttons, drove him around the base in a Lincoln Continental with push-button windows. The place was buzzing with activity. He was ready to sign the papers.

Then Cochrane made a mistake.

"Gee, it's going to be awful tough to play ball," the old catcher said. "You try to play ball, they'll boo you out of every park in the league."

They will, huh?

This was no different from another voice yelling from the stands, a challenge, an affront. Who are you to yell at me? To tell me what I should or shouldn't do? Where are you in the crowd? Step up. I'll show *you*. No one had convinced him that he was wrong. There were "a hundred" guys in baseball with 3-A deferments. Why should he be any different from any of them? Forget Cronin and Yawkey and Quaker Oats.

The next day, back in Minnesota, he announced that he was heading south. He went to Princeton, picked up his things, kissed Doris good-bye, and headed for Sarasota. He was playing the 1942 season, would make the big money, and enlist at the end. The hell with everybody else.

He arrived at spring training, driving, at 6:30 at night on March 10, complaining that he had lost three hours on the ride in Nashville when he tried to cash a check and no one believed he was Ted Williams. The scene had an easy familiarity, only the Orlando brothers in the clubhouse as he dressed in a hurry and went out with them to the field. He stood at the plate and swung at imaginary pitches using Dom DiMaggio's bat. The Orlando brothers, done for the day, refused to give him balls.

A dozen sportswriters appeared when he was finished and was taking a shower. He proceeded to sit at his locker and explain his case for the next 50 minutes, answering all questions.

"I made this decision myself and I know what I'm in for," he said. "But I'm going to try my darndest. That's why I came down here.

"Baseball is awfully important to me. This war, of course, is more important, but I just feel that I am as much entitled to this season of baseball as anyone in this country with a legitimate 3-A classification for dependency."

He went into detail about his financial situation. He said he had lost money in his first year of baseball, broke even during his second, and made a little money in the third. That was why this season was important for him and for his mother.

"I know that I'll have to take abuse," he said, "but I'm going to try to take it."

The next day began a series of public auditions, the writers waiting with their built-in applause meters as Williams returned in front of the fans. How would people treat him? Cronin put him in the exhibition game that day as a pinch-hitter. Verdict? There was a warm welcome from the 800 assembled as he struck out in a 6–5 loss to the Cincinnati Reds. First exhibition before a crowd of servicemen? That came three days later in Tampa. The servicemen cheered and asked for his autograph. Boston? That was the question.

Williams said his mail generally was running 60 percent for him, 40 percent against. A lot of the "against" mail seemed to be from Ohio, where he had been taking a battering in the Cleveland papers. He said he hoped Boston would be kind. He speculated that the crowd would be 80 percent for him, 20 percent against. He said if it wasn't, he understood. He was worried mostly about one group.

"That's the kids," he told *Globe* sportswriter Gerry Moore. "I've always done everything I could for kids because I remember how I was once. I've never refused a kid an autograph in my life. I try to slip them old bats and balls every chance I get. If a middle-aged man boos me, I feel sorry for him because I think he ought to know better. But if the kids, even though I know they may be ignorant of the facts, start to get on me, I'm afraid that might prove a little too tough to take."

The verdict? The first game in Boston was an exhibition on April 12 at Fenway against the Braves. The welcome was warm. Williams was enthused. He said he heard only three negative voices in a crowd of 8,186, a loud guy in right and two kids in left. The cheering was even louder the next day at the Sox home opener. On his first time at bat, DiMaggio on second, Pesky on first, he labeled a 2–2 fastball from the Philadelphia Athletics' Phil Marchildon two rows into the bleachers behind the Sox bullpen. Collecting two more singles and hearing only positive noise in an 8–3 win from the crowd of 9,901 that included 1,200 servicemen, Williams declared the day his second best in thrills to the ninth-inning homer in '41 at the All-Star Game.

The verdict? He was going to be able to play baseball this season. The great draft controversy pretty much was done.

"By the beginning of 1944 every able-bodied man will either be in the service or replacing, in industry, the men who must fight," Major Ernest Culligan, public relations officer of the Selective Service System, said a few weeks later, ending most deferment squabbles. "We've got to start thinking in terms of a 10-million to 12-million-man Army and when we think of that we realize the shortage of manpower."

Williams officially finished all debate on May 22. He enlisted in the Naval Aviation Service.

"I've tried to do the right thing from the start," he explained in a low voice after being sworn in by Lieutenant Commander Thomas A. Collins at the Flight Selection Board at 150 Causeway Street, next to Boston Garden. "I didn't want to be pushed by anybody. I knew I was right all along. Then this thing came along. It was just what I wanted."

The thought process for this decision was the same process he would use for anything and everything for all of his life. The worst approach to him—be it asking him to go to war, to hit to leftfield, to tip his cap, to act nice around the house—was to try to force him. Don't tell him what he *should* do. Offer options, offer quiet opinions perhaps, but don't push. Never push. A push was a challenge. Never challenge. Left alone, he would figure out what he needed to figure out.

Everything about joining the new navy V-5 program, which offered flying to men with no college education, was done in secret. He went to Squantum Naval Air Station in Quincy on the morning of May 6 with Ed Doherty, the Red Sox public relations man, and Lieutenant Robert "Whitey" Fuller, the former PR man for Dartmouth College, now recruiting fliers for the V-5. They toured the facility in a beach wagon, met the commander. Williams was put in the cockpit of a Navy training plane, allowed to get the feel of it, play with the gadgets, let his imagination run.

He signed the forms in the beach wagon on the way back to Boston and an afternoon game. Done. Easy as that. His terms. His way.

"Ted is in the pink of physical condition," Lieutenant Frank R. Philbrook, the physician who examined Williams, proclaimed on the day of induction. "His nerves are very steady. His blood pressure is perfectly normal and his pulse is right at 60. He is perfect material for any type of naval aviation."

Philbrook then opened a subject that always would bother Williams: his exceptional eyesight. Stories and more stories would be written about his phenomenal eyes, about how he could read the label on a record as it spun on a turntable, about how he could see things that normal men could not. The stories would imply that Williams was a freak of nature, that he had a gift that most men did not. They implied he simply walked to the plate and was able to hit simply because of his eyes.

Williams always would argue with that idea. To him, concentration was the secret, not any phenomenal set of eyes. Practice was the secret. Who had ever swung a bat more times than he had? Who had ever swung a broomstick, a pillow, had ever swung anything more in a bat-hits-ball motion? Who had studied the components of the batter-pitcher confrontation more? The implication that his eyes gave him an edge degraded all the work he had done. Didn't it?

Philbrook, in his few words, unknowingly started the argument.

"The fact is, Ted has excellent eyes," the doctor said after Williams was tested at 20-15 eyesight. "He has an unusually high degree of depth perception, which is probably one reason for his success as a batter. He can easily judge where to hit the ball. This is of equal value in determining where the ground is in relation to a plane. He has normal reflexes."

The doctor said only four or five potential pilots out of a hundred had eyes as strong as Williams's. He said Williams could read a letter at 30 to 35 feet that an average man could only read at 20. Admit it or not, Williams had very good eyes.

As for hearing . . .

"Dr. Philbrook gave me a test," Williams said, laughing. "In a very low voice he asked, 'Can you hear me?' If he only knew how I could hear those hecklers up in the 40th row at the ballpark he'd know my ears were okay."

The enlistment basically ensured that Williams would be able to complete the 1942 season. Pesky followed him into the V-5 program a few weeks later, and the two of them were assigned to classes at Mechanics Arts High School, three nights a week, four hours each night, on navigation, aerology, physics, and advanced math. The classes started on July 13, and the instructor, unplanned, called Williams to the front of the 250 students to say a few words.

"I only hope I prove myself worthy to go through with you," he said, serious and humble, so different from his talk at the ballpark. "I give you my word I'll do my best."

The second sentence, about doing his best, had an added significance for the Red Sox fans in the group. Back at Fenway his effort was being questioned. The baseball season was chugging along, the Sox in a familiar chase after the front-running Yankees, and the man of the moment had landed on the front pages for a more familiar problem. His good hearing had gotten him in trouble again.

In the second game of a Red Sox sweep of the Washington Senators in a doubleheader on July 1, Williams responded to some members of the chorus in left. He gestured to them on the way back to the bench in the middle of the third inning, cupping his hand to one ear, and then proceeded to go through an obviously indifferent at bat against Jack Wilson, swinging at the first two pitches, no matter where they were, then lofting a fly ball to center. He threw his bat high in the air as he trotted toward first. He was booed for the action.

In the fifth he was even more indifferent at the plate. He took the first two pitches for strikes down the middle, then seemed to have a change of mind. He proceeded to concentrate on hitting foul balls down the left-field line, aiming directly at his most prominent hecklers. He later admitted he wanted to "knock some teeth out."

"It's a scene I remember to this day," Dominic DiMaggio says. "He had those guys in his sights. Who else would ever do something like that? Could do it?"

The fact that he made a mistake in his foul ball attempts—hitting a liner off the wall in left for a double—made no difference. He jogged slowly into second base on the hit. The people knew what he was doing and the boos increased. Cronin also knew what he was doing. He exploded when Williams leisurely scored a run and came back to the dugout.

"What's the matter, don't you want to play?" the manager asked animatedly in the dugout. "Get out of here then."

He sent Williams to the showers. Pete Fox, Williams's replacement, was cheered loudly as he trotted to left. ("Look at the son of a bitch," Fox remarked to Charlie Wagner before being called off the bench. "I bust my hump to try to get a hit and I can't. He gets one without even trying.") Cronin then fined Williams $250 the next day, an off-day before a big series began with the Yanks. Williams apologized in his own Williams way.

"I deserved to be put out of the game," he said. "I'm just thick-headed enough, screwy enough, dumb enough, and childish enough to let those wolves in the leftfield stand get under my skin. Someday I'm going to bring 25 pounds of raw hamburger out and invite those wolves down to eat it."

Contrition was mixed with the usual residue of anger.

"What do they want?" he asked. "I'm leading both leagues in runs batted in, home runs, runs scored, and bases on balls."

The Red Sox were three games behind the Yankees on the day Williams went into his pout. Twenty days later, they were 11 games out and the race was done. Though the rest of the season went more quietly and Williams wound up winning his first major league Triple Crown with a .356 batting average, 36 homers, and 137 RBI, the outburst and the Red Sox swoon were remembered more at the end of the year than all of his accomplishments.

When the Most Valuable Player votes were counted, second baseman Joe Gordon of the Yankees was the winner. Williams was second. The 24 members of the Baseball Writers' Association gave Gordon 12 first-place votes, Williams 9. Statistically, the result was laughable. Gordon led the league in only one category, strikeouts, with 95. He was 34 points lower than Williams in batting average, had 18 home runs (half as much), and was 34 RBI lower. Williams led the league in seven categories, including walks with 145.

He now had hit two rare offensive benchmarks in two consecutive years—the first man in 11 years to hit over .400 and the first man in eight to win the Triple Crown—and still had not won an MVP Award. (He also, remember, had captured the Triple Crown in the American Association and finished second in MVP voting.) The voters talked about Gordon's solid fielding and about the Yanks' overall success, but there was no doubt that this vote had more to do with personality than performance.

"I thought Gordon would get it," Williams said. "I'm sorry I couldn't win it, but that's all in the past. I'm playing a bigger game now."

He was quoted from Amherst and the Civilian Pilot Training Course. Diplomacy must have been in the curriculum.

Eight weeks in Amherst was supposed to send Williams and Pesky and the baseball squad to Chapel Hill, North Carolina, for an eight-week stretch in preflight training. Pesky and the baseball squad proceeded along. Williams stopped at the Chelsea Naval Hospital outside Boston, where he had an operation for a hernia, picked up in the cold at Amherst.

He was two weeks late in arriving at Chapel Hill, where he rejoined his class.

"Chapel Hill was the physical part, like basic training," Pesky says. "It wasn't a problem for any of us because we were in good shape from baseball . . . but they did run us through the wringer."

"Up by the light of the moon, double-time all day, to bed with the owls" was the way he described the routine to Austen Lake in 1943 in the *American*. "Drill till your tongue bulged. Sports, hikes, inspections. We played all games to test us for versatility—boxing, football, wrestling, swimming, soccer, and baseball. The object was to find if we had a nerve-cracking point. Some did.

"A lot of guys, knowing Ted's reputation as a pop-off, waited for him to explode. But he never blew any fuses or got a single bad behavior demerit. If anything, he took a little stiffer discipline than the others, sort of stuff like, 'Oh, so you're the great Ted Williams, huh?' "

All of this activity was on the University of North Carolina campus. The cadets stayed in the dormitories, took classes in the classrooms, used all of the athletic facilities. They played soccer in the football stadium.

Pesky remembers the wrestling training best. The final test for the wrestling course was a match against another cadet, the winner getting the better grade.

"I wrestled some little guy from Cape Cod," Pesky says. "Vinny Larkin was his name. He beat the shit out of me. Oh, he was quick. I couldn't find him. He killed me. Maybe three years after the war, I'm at the ballpark, and this little guy yells out to me from the stands, 'Hey, Johnny, I'm the guy who beat you in wrestling.' I took him down to the dugout. He had a beard now, had put on some weight. I told the guys, 'This is the guy who kicked the shit out of me.' They all said, 'Well, you didn't do a good enough job. Pesky's still standing.' "

Williams's training camp moment came in the boxing ring. The instructor was a former professional fighter—Pesky thinks his name was Allie Clark—and the fighter noticed Williams's fast reflexes. At the end of one session, some time left in the class, he brought Williams into the ring and said, "Let's see if you can hit me." They squared off, wearing big gloves.

"Ted was just swinging at first, and Clark got out of the way easy," Pesky says. "He was a boxer! Then Ted started to get the hang of it. He fakes! And then he unloads. Pow! He hits the guy. Then he fakes again. Pow. He hits the guy again. When the thing was over, the instructor says,

'Hey, how would you like to have me help you make a fast million bucks?' Ted says, 'How would you do that?' 'I'll train you as a boxer.' Ted says, 'Oh, no, not me.' Clark didn't even know who Ted was."

An interlude for Williams at Chapel Hill—a chance to go where people did indeed know who he was—came on Monday, July 12, 1943. He was shipped back to Boston. To Fenway Park.

Boston Mayor Maurice J. Tobin had arranged an exhibition game as part of the Mayor's Annual Field Day. ("Proceeds of the day are to be used to purchase artificial legs, glass eyes, eyeglasses, braces, and to furnish milk and food to underprivileged and undernourished school children," the press release said.) Twisting appropriate arms and calling in appropriate favors, Tobin had Williams freed from preflight school and Dominic DiMaggio freed from the Norfolk Naval Base to return to Boston to play on an all-star team against the Braves. The manager of the all-star team was Babe Ruth.

Now 48 years old, Ruth had been retired for eight seasons. He would be dead five years later. Part of the day's attraction was a home run hitting contest before the game between the Babe and Williams. This was a moment. Williams never had met Ruth.

"Hiya, kid," newspapers reported the Babe said when the meeting finally occurred in the clubhouse. "You remind me a lot of myself. I love to hit. You're one of the most natural ballplayers I've ever seen. And if ever my record is broken, I hope you're the one to do it."

"I was flabbergasted," Williams said, years later, recalling the moment. "After all, he was Babe Ruth."

The game was scheduled to begin at 4:30 to allow defense workers, whose shifts ended at 3:30, to attend. Prices ranged from $1.00 general admission to $2.75 for box seats. The crowd was disappointing, estimated between 12,000 and 20,000 people. The bleachers were empty. The home run hitting contest was scheduled to begin at four o'clock.

"Boston's my starting town," the Babe said over a microphone before the contest began. "I was mighty sorry to leave here for New York . . . of course, [*smile*] I got lots more dough when I went there . . . but here's the town I love."

The contest was no contest. Williams might not have played for the Red Sox for nine months, but he had been playing on the preflight team at Chapel Hill a little bit, and when he stepped into the batter's box, he pounded three shots into the seats. The Babe was not as fortunate.

On the second pitch from Red Barrett of the Braves, he took a big cut and fouled the ball off his ankle. He limped around for a little bit, tried again, but never hit a ball hard. Ted 3, the Babe 0.

In the game, Williams hit another homer, a 425-foot rocket into the bleachers in the bottom of the seventh to give the all-stars a 9–8 win. The Babe, who coached first base for most of the day, inserted himself as a pinch-hitter in the eighth, but popped to second base.

"See that uniform down there on the floor?" he said disconsolately to Mel Webb of the *Globe* in the locker room after the game. "It's the last I shall ever put on. I started right here in Boston . . . and I finished right here today."

The uniform on the floor was the home Yankees pinstripes, a special uniform the Babe brought with him for personal appearances, the uniform that he wore in a picture that was made before the game with Williams. Williams wore a 1942 Red Sox traveling uniform, gray, for the same picture. The two men stared at the camera, half-smiles on their wartime faces, captured in a shot that would hang in many Boston homes and taverns for the rest of the century and beyond.

Two weeks later, yes, of course, Babe Ruth took his retirement back. He wore that pinstriped uniform again in another exhibition game, this time at Yankee Stadium to benefit the War Fund. Williams also was there, part of the Chapel Hill Clodbusters, who played against an all-star team comprised of members of the Yankees and the Cleveland Indians.

Will Harridge, president of the American League, was at the game and told reporters about a conversation he had with Williams's commanding officer from Chapel Hill.

" 'You are going to be surprised at the boy we turn back to you when the activities are over,' [the officer] told me," Harridge said. " 'He is one of the finest young men we have in the entire school. . . . He has taken hold with all of the enthusiasm that could be expected of anybody and is the most agreeable person in the school. I understand he had ideas of his own in baseball which he insisted on carrying out. There hasn't been any of that since we've had him. He's just tops!' "

In September, Williams and Pesky and the baseball squad went from Chapel Hill to primary flight school at NAS Bunker Hill, Indiana. This was an 1,800-acre stretch of farmland seven miles south of Peru, Indiana, that had been converted into a training base a year earlier and was called by everyone the USS Cornfield. On four 5,000-foot runways and one

2,500-square-foot mat, this was where the cadets were taught how to take off and land airplanes.

The base population consisted of 1,000 students, 342 officers, 2,400 enlisted men, and 189 civilians, everyone working to churn out pilots like so many cans of beans. Now the instruction became hairy. Williams and Pesky each had only 35 hours of flying at Amherst, 15 solo. The serious flying now began. There would be 99 hours of flying in Indiana, 60 solo. Students were expected to learn precision landings, aerobatics, night flying, slow rolls, snap rolls, inverted spins. Everything in the book.

Pesky had problems. With the book.

"I could fly the plane all right," he says. "I just had no idea where I was going."

He was frustrated by the navigational charts, the math, the constant tests that asked him for answers he could not figure out. Williams was part of his frustration. Williams seemed to work less and do better. Pesky would complain.

"Why can't you get it?" Williams would ask. "You're a high school graduate, same as me."

"Yeah, I'm a high school graduate," Pesky would reply. "But I'm not Ted Williams."

The study skills that Williams had developed, virtually by himself, in his passion to dissect the art of hitting a baseball now were turned toward aviation. He had an active, inquisitive mind. He did not blow through the classes in Amherst—finishing with a grade of 2.98 out of 4.00—nor would he blow through Bunker Hill (2.97), but he certainly survived. His ability to concentrate and understand enabled him to jump past the college courses he had missed. There always would be a feeling with him about anything that "if he put his mind to it . . ."

The subjects that would interest him—fishing and photography at the top of the list after hitting—would be explored down to the core. He would develop a noisy interest in politics and history. He would become a reader of more than the sports page, fluent in the small talk of current events.

"You'd see him one day and talk about some subject he didn't know anything about," Lewis Watkins, a friend and business associate later in life, says. "The next day he'd bring up the same subject, and he'd know more about it than you did. He'd have gone home, researched it, and now he was telling you about it."

A newspaper account of Williams in the clubhouse during the 1942 season, when he already was taking preflight classes at Mechanics and Arts High School, showed this part of his mind and personality. He picked up a bat, held it like a machine gun, and sprayed phantom bullets around the room.

"*Dit-dit-dit-dit-dit-dit . . . bang,*" he said. "All right, you guys! What did Farragut say?"

"Who's Farragut?" someone ventured.

"What a bunch!" Williams shouted, bringing out his newest piece of knowledge, probably one day old. "Farragut was a great Navy hero in the Civil War. I bet every damn kid in the bleachers knows he said, 'Damn the torpedoes!' "

Full speed ahead. That was how Williams attacked the things he wanted to attack.

"You can tell from the way he acts around the training planes that he is a flying enthusiast," Captain D. D. Gurney said at Bunker Hill as that phase of training finished in December. "His flight instruction was completed more than two weeks ahead of schedule, and he was right up with his class in ground school subjects. He has an inquiring mind, and that is a splendid piece of flying equipment."

The splendid piece of flying equipment was off to Pensacola, Florida, and the final, advanced stage of pilot training. Johnny Pesky, alas, was not. His flying days were done.

He was not Ted Williams.

Pensacola Naval Air Station was a noisy, boisterous beehive. The skies were filled, night and day, with airplanes of every size. Bombers. Fighters. Transports. The background sound was a constant buzz as planes took off and—whoops, wait a minute, careful now, whew— landed, one after another. The Navy would issue 61,658 sets of wings between 1942 and 1945. Every one of those pilots had to train at either Pensacola or Corpus Christi, Texas.

The Navy called Pensacola "the Annapolis of the Air." Six auxiliary air stations were located within a 40-mile radius. A military man could arrive—and military men arrived from England, New Zealand, Canada, and Australia as well as the United States—and learn to fly a plane of just about any size, armed to perform just about any military function.

"The pilots, once they got to Pensacola, knew how to fly pretty well," Bob Kennedy, an instructor in 1943, says. "This was where you put the finishing touches on them."

Kennedy was the same Bob Kennedy who had been playing third base and in the outfield for the past four seasons for the Chicago White Sox. He had preceded Williams through the school, so when Williams arrived, who was there to teach him? Well, Williams didn't know who at first.

"I worked it so I was his instructor," Kennedy says. "We were flying what we called SNJs and what the Army called AT6s. They were little twin-seater fighter planes. When I saw a picture of the Japanese Zero, it looked exactly like the planes we were flying. The way training worked, I'd have a group of ten pilots. I'd go up with one, go through what we had to do, then come back, and I'd go up with the next one until the line was gone.

"I kept on my goggles and my headgear when I came up to Ted. I acted really military. Made him do some things you make new pilots do, like salute a lot and carry your chute to the plane. I was rough on him. I knew he was thinking to himself, What's the deal with this guy? We went up and flew, and when we came back, I couldn't hold myself any longer. I took off my goggles, and he looked and looked twice, and then he just started swearing."

Kennedy and Williams were stationed at Bronson Field, one of the six auxiliary stations. This was another hastily built facility for the war and hadn't been opened until the end of 1942. It consisted of four runways and a circular concrete mat. There were 892 students at Bronson.

The life was alternately invigorating and boring, with a lot of waiting time for available aircraft to train. A cadet could go to the theater at Bronson and see *Mr. Lucky* on Friday night, *Power of the Press* on Saturday, *Keep 'em Sluggin'* on Sunday, and *Wake Island*, *Captive Wild Women*, *Ladies Day*, and *Bombardier* for the rest of the week. (No report on whether Williams saw either *Power of the Press* or *Keep 'em Sluggin'*.) The base newspaper ran a daily contest, two airplane silhouettes, one an Axis plane, the other an Ally, under the heading "Which One Would You Fire At?" Times for church services were listed, denomination by denomination, with a final designation for "Colored Personnel Service" at building C13.

Williams fit in just fine.

"I'm in the air every morning," he told reporter Stephen White. "You know as soon as you make out in one plane, they put you in a bigger one.

First, way back at Amherst, we had Piper Cubs and nothing to worry about except keeping the motor going. Then, at every stage, they give you more and more complicated planes, two or three new things to think about.

"Right now, down here, we worry about course rules. Every field has different rules about coming in—this one you come in one way and let your flaps down, and in that one you swing around and don't let your flaps down until you're in a different position. You have to know everything and know it right. There's a lot of traffic around these fields and a lot of planes in the air. Make a mistake and somebody gets hurt."

His fitness report from Class 12b-C with Squadron VN5D8 from February 17, 1944, to April 29, 1944, ranked his performance in various areas. All marks were on a scale of 4.0. Outstanding was 3.9 to 3.8. Above Average was 3.7 to 3.5. Average was 3.4 to 3.2. Below Average was 3.1 to 2.5. Unsatisfactory was 2.4 to 2.0. Inferior was 1.9 to 1.0.

"Officer-Like Qualities—Intelligence 3.7, Judgement 3.4, Initiative 3.6, Force 3.5, Moral Courage 3.6, Cooperation 3.6, Loyalty 3.5, Perseverance 3.4, Reactions in Emergencies 3.4, Endurance 3.5, Industry 3.6, Military Bearing and Neatness of Person and Dress 3.6. Average: 3.53."

In pilot characteristics, he was ranked above average in skill, composure, enthusiasm, aggressiveness, combativeness, and endurance. The only category he was ranked average was judgment.

In personal characteristics, checks were placed next to straightforward, enthusiastic, cheerful, and cooperative. Interestingly, blanks for moody, irritable, stubborn, and erratic were unchecked.

"Cadet Williams has shown a good attitude while in this squadron," Lieutenant (jg) A. B. Koontz wrote under "Remarks." "He has been enthusiastic, industrious and cooperative. While in this squadron his progress has been satisfactory and he has performed all duties in an efficient manner. He possesses good moral and military character and is above average officer material. I would like to have him in my squadron."

Cadets were asked during their training whether they wanted to graduate into the Navy Air Corps or the Marines. They didn't get to choose but were allowed to indicate a preference. They also could indicate what type of plane they wanted to fly. Williams checked "Marines."

"I checked 'Marine Fighter' first and let the other choices just string down," he said. "Some of my buddies are in the Marines and anyway I like the idea of being alone up there with nobody to worry about but myself."

On May 2, 1944, he received his wings as a second lieutenant in the Marines. It was quite a day. He also married Doris Soule. It was a quiet wedding, the news divulged by her mother, Ruby, back in Minnesota. Ruby had learned about it from a telegram sent by the happy bride.

There had been rumors about a wedding for almost three years, since Doris first was pictured in the *Globe* with what looked like an engagement ring. Williams had denied and denied the possibility, both in Boston and in Minnesota. In the summer of 1942, reporters had speculated that the couple would have to wait until Williams graduated from flight school. Speculation was right. This became another wartime wedding.

"I always thought he *was* married," Major Bill Churchman (ret.), a longtime friend, says. "Pensacola, in those days, was like a Mardi Gras every night outside the base. He wasn't part of that. I always thought he was married to Doris. I know she was around."

Churchman could be confused about the timing, because after graduation Williams (and Doris) was still around. His assignment was to stay at Pensacola and train the succeeding waves of cadets. He was with Kennedy at Bronson. The usual next stop those days after getting your wings was a brief course in whatever your specialty might be, and then you were off to combat in either Europe or the Pacific. Kennedy had been ordered out of that progression, and now the same thing happened with Williams.

"I didn't ask for that," Kennedy says. "And Ted didn't either. I will say this, though, flying every day as an instructor did make you a much better pilot than you would have been just coming out of the school."

There were classes in the morning, in the afternoon, and at night. The night classes were the trickiest, maybe 50 planes in the air at the same time, everyone at different altitudes trying not to crash into each other. Kennedy didn't like the night flying very much.

"Ted and I and the other instructors, we'd teach the whole syllabus," Kennedy says. "Landings. Checking air speed. Formation flying. Some stunts to control the plane. Shooting at a fixed target. Shooting at a moving sleeve. Night flying. We taught everything."

For the next year, this was Williams's life. Not a bad life. He would fall in love with the weather and the fishing of Florida, later telling tales of how he would look for the good fishing spots while in the air. He would pick out an inlet where some old-timer was having some success, buzz down to see how many fish were in the boat, then fly back to the base, land the plane, and drive out to the inlet. The old-timer would be startled that anyone could find him. Williams would explain.

The Bronson Bombers—it was noted in the *Bronson Breeze*—finished first in the Pensacola baseball league during this time, no small thanks to Lieutenant Ted Williams, but he was not serious about the game in the service. His serious baseball thoughts were kept to the idea of returning to Boston.

"Dough's all that counts," he told the *Record*'s Huck Finnegan during his stay at Pensacola. "Who's going to care about me when I can't swing a bat? It doesn't take them long to forget you. I'm in a business that's a career against time! A big leaguer's got about ten years to pile it up. If he doesn't, nobody's going to kick in to him when he's through.

"I'm not reaching for the moon, but I've come down from $250 a day to $2.50 a day and that's a sharp drop. How do I know I'll be any good when I get back? I don't want much, just enough so I can open a sporting goods store and have plenty of guns around me. I love guns. And I want enough time to myself that I'll be able to do all the hunting and fishing that I please."

On August 18, 1945—12 days after the atomic bomb was dropped on Hiroshima, nine days after Nagasaki—Williams finally had overseas orders and headed toward Pearl Harbor and assignment for combat. He and Kennedy both had been sent in June for specialized fighter training in Jacksonville and were on their way. Unfortunately, or fortunately, depending on the perspective, the war was done.

What Williams truly was heading for in Pearl Harbor turned out to be . . . baseball. That was how he ended the war, playing baseball.

"It was the 14th Naval District League," Mel Brookey says. "There were ten teams in the league with a total of 116 major league ballplayers. We were in ninth place, the team from the Marine Air Corps. Then Ted Williams joined us in the middle of the season. We became a little better, if you know what I mean."

Brookey was a 19-year-old kid, drafted out of Henrietta, Oklahoma. He remembered hurrying to the newspapers, the *Tulsa World* and the *Daily Oklahoman*, every day during the '41 season to see how many hits Ted had collected on the way to .406 and whether or not DiMaggio had kept that 56-game hit streak alive. Now he was playing with Ted and against DiMaggio.

"They needed catchers," he says. "So there I was, getting good exposure to the best there was. DiMaggio and Joe Gordon and Stan Musial and a bunch of big-leaguers were playing the Army League, which also was on Pearl Harbor. We'd play two games a week in our league, then two more in exhibition against those teams.

"I'll never forget DiMaggio hit a liner down third base against us. Our third baseman leaped, and the ball went right between his bare hand and his glove. The ball was hit so hard it went all the way to the fence in left on the fly. The fence was painted Army green. The ball had to be thrown out of play because it took some paint off. . . . Musial, we played against him, he hit four doubles against us. They all were off the right-centerfield fence, and they all hit within two feet of each other. . . . Ted? Ted hit some massive home runs. The parks were all small, and he hit shots that looked like golf balls flying over the fences."

The remnants of the Japanese attack almost four years earlier still could be seen in the harbor, the twisted and burnt hulls of assorted ships. The remnants of the war in the South Pacific could be seen even more dramatically. Some games were played against hospital units, and GI patients in various stages of recovery would limp or be wheeled out to watch the action.

Bill Dickey, the New York Yankees catcher, was the commissioner of the league. Dan Topping, the owner of the Yankees, was in charge of the two Marine teams.

"We had good uniforms," Brookey says. "We had the best of everything. Topping made sure of that."

Pesky played in the league. Alvin Dark played. Ted Lyons of the Chicago White Sox, the toughest pitcher for Williams to hit in his big-league career, was the Marine Air Corps manager. Bob Kennedy played on the team. The competition level was high.

"Oh, yeah, especially for the guys who weren't major leaguers," Brookey says. "It was really life or death. Especially before the war ended. If you went 0-for-5, you could have found yourself in Okinawa or Guam."

The average crowds were 10,000, 12,000, all military. Williams and Musial and the biggest stars would put on hitting exhibitions. The service World Series, Army versus Navy, was held at the biggest stadium in the islands, Furlong Field, and attracted crowds of 40,000 for every game. The players said it was much better baseball than the baseball being played in the World Series back home between the Detroit Tigers and the Chicago Cubs.

As the war wound down, the league wound down. Release dates were based on the number of points each man had earned in service. Williams was released from the Marines on January 12, 1946, at Camp Miramar, California. He and Doris stayed in San Diego in the house on Utah Street with May until it was time to go to spring training. May, during the war, had served milk, coffee, and soft drinks to thousands of servicemen coming through town. Still in the Salvation Army, still working for the Lord.

Mel Brookey did not have the required number of points to be sent home. He was shipped to Peking, China. It didn't matter anymore that he could catch. Service baseball with a major league touch was finished.

The real baseball could begin again.

7 Boston

Myself, I am dancing lightly on the balls of my feet and keeping both hands high, for I already am on record stating, with some heat, that the Red Sox never will win the pennant so long as TWmsEsq. is around to throw sand and monkey wrenches into gears and machinery. . . . When he threw in the towel in other years, the air suddenly was full of flying towels. He discouraged easily and so did the remarkably complacent fellows who basked in the shadow of the great man, but it could be that where, in other years, the star was unable to carry the team along, this year the team may carry the star along.

DAVE EGAN, *BOSTON RECORD*, MARCH 19, 1951

There is no way to determine what would have happened for Ted Williams if World War II had not come along and taken away three full years of his career. There is no way, really, to determine what would have happened in the careers of any of the 540 major leaguers (out of a total of 580 players in the American and National Leagues) who left for the war.

Would Williams have hit .400 again? And again? And again? He was 24 years old when he left and 27 when he returned, prime years for any athlete, part of that brief time when body and mind work together as equal partners, still-youthful physical abilities seasoned by recently earned experience. How many home runs would he have hit? Fifty per year? Is that too far-fetched? How many runs would he have batted in? Would his personality have been tempered, changed? How? There are statistical ways to extrapolate the numbers, by looking at what he had done before he left and what he did after he returned, but statistics don't take into account the unforeseen, unknown odd bumps that can occur on the way to those averaged-out numbers.

Maybe he would have been injured in those three years. Maybe a Bob Feller fastball would have ended his career in a sad instant. Maybe he would have become disinterested in the game, frustrated by the fans and sportswriters, and run off to that firehouse or to some other more quiet, everyday place if he never had tasted everyday life the way he did in the Marines. Maybe, maybe . . . maybe baseball would not have taken the grand jump in popularity it took after the war.

There is a question in all lives—"What if I had taken that job in Bozeman, Montana?" All that anyone ever knows for sure is what actually happens. Three years might have flown off into the air above Pensacola, Florida, with Williams in those SNJs, but when he landed, all we know is that he was still able to do what he did before he left, and the American public was dying to see him do it.

"I was in Australia in the Navy during the war," Dominic DiMaggio says, talking about the baseball scene that awaited. "I'd been doing a lot of thinking. I decided I was a free agent. I even might have written a letter to the Red Sox saying I didn't belong to them anymore. I didn't think I did. I didn't think I belonged to anyone. Well, Joe Cronin came out to see me in San Francisco. He was really mad. The veins were popping out of his head. He said the Red Sox owned me, and he was there to sign me up for $11,000. This was not the figure I had in mind."

Part of DiMaggio's thinking was that baseball interest was going to explode. He worked Cronin up to $16,000 in salary negotiations and added an attendance clause.

"I know attendance was down to 450,000 people last year and you can't pay me what I want," he said. "So I'll take the $16,000, but if we draw 500,000 people, you give me another $500. And for every 50,000 people after that, you give me $500 more. Okay?"

The Red Sox tried to wheedle, capping the attendance figure at 750,000 in the final contract, but DiMaggio held firm. He said if the team drew more than 750,000, "You should give me even more." The Red Sox finally agreed.

"We drew 1,400,000 people," DiMaggio says. "I had it figured. People wanted to see baseball. And I knew we were going to be good."

The 1946 Red Sox that DiMaggio and Williams joined were very good. (Williams signed for $37,500, no arguments.) They had won 93 games in 1942, a respectable number, and the core of that young team was back, seasoned by life, if not baseball experience. Williams, Doerr, DiMaggio, and Pesky all were into their best baseball years. Tex Hughson, Mickey Harris, and Joe Dobson were returning frontline pitchers. Added to the cast were veteran slugger Rudy York, obtained from the Tigers, and pitcher Dave "Boo" Ferriss.

Ferriss, 24 years old, had returned a year earlier from the war, released after two years due to a severe asthma condition. Pitching for a woeful, seventh-place Red Sox replacement team in 1945, he had won 21 games. He was ready now for the real action. Everybody was. He would unfurl a 24-6 season.

"I think everybody was just really happy to be back," Ferriss says. "And I think the fans were happy to have us back too. I know I was excited just to be there, where I always wanted to be. In 1941 my college coach in Mississippi had gotten me a chance to play in the Northern League for the summer. I played in Brattleboro, Vermont. On July 25, an off-day, the manager up there took three or four of us down to Fenway Park to see our first major league game. We met Ted and Dom and Bobby, and then, when the season ended, the Red Sox had me come down again and I threw batting practice for ten days. They even took me to Yankee Stadium. There I was, throwing batting practice to Ted at Yankee Stadium, while he was going for .400. It was all a thrill.

"Then, to be up there and the way we started in '46 . . . I think we were 41-9."

If the wheels had lined up perfectly in 1941 to lead Williams to his best personal season, well, they had lined up now to put him on the best team of his career. He was aboard a true pennant express. There was, for once, for the only time, no legitimate carping in the local press about "What's Wrong with the Red Sox?" There was nothing wrong for an entire season with the Red Sox.

"Joe Cronin had caught the rest of the league with its pants down," Dom DiMaggio says. "We just ran away from everyone."

Williams was a major part of that. He weighed 195 pounds and had home cooking and a place of his own for the first time as a player. He was living in a rented apartment on Foster Street in Brighton with Doris and their German shepherd, Slugger. Tex Hughson and his wife lived in the same building. Williams seemed to be, for lack of a better word, "settled."

He went through a relatively incident-free spring, clocked a pair of homers in an 11–5 win in the annual exhibition series with the Braves, then cranked a gigantic, 460-foot shot into the centerfield bleachers of Griffith Stadium on the first pitch he saw in the season opener against the Washington Senators. The Red Sox swept the series, and Williams hit .500 with the homer, a triple, and two doubles, along with four intentional bases on balls. Senators owner Clark Griffith said he thought Williams "is going to be the best hitter of all time."

The good times proceeded from there. On June 9, in the first inning of the second game of a doubleheader sweep of the Tigers, as the Sox lengthened their lead to eight games, he uncorked the longest home run of his Fenway Park career. The bomb off Freddie Hutchinson—still memorialized at Fenway by a single red seat in a sea of blue seats—landed in the 33rd row of the centerfield bleachers. Actually, to be precise, it landed on the head of construction engineer Joseph Boucher of Albany, New York, then went even farther on the bounce. Boucher was wearing a straw hat at the time and removed it to discover the ball had put a nice hole in the top.

"I'd caught the first game in that doubleheader, and Williams had got four hits and nailed Pat Mullin to the right-field wall," Tigers catcher Paul Richards later remembered in the *Atlanta Journal* about that day and that home run. "Birdie Tebbetts was catching the second game and Hutchinson was pitching. Between games we're in the clubhouse and Hutch is saying he doesn't care if Williams is the superstar. He's not going to let him hit like that. He's going to brush him back.

"Well, the game starts now and Williams comes up. He stomps his foot and digs in and Hutch comes inside and Williams leans back. Next pitch, Hutch really comes inside and Williams hits the dirt. He gets up and digs in again. Williams hits the next pitch out of sight. I read later where he called it the longest homer he ever hit.

"By the third inning, Hutch was out. He's back in the clubhouse and he's really fuming, but I can't resist. I sneak back there and leave the door open so I can get back out. I said to Hutch, 'You really showed that Williams.' Here comes a chair, flying at me, but I beat it to the door."

By the All-Star break, Williams was in the chase for a second straight Triple Crown. The only goal that wasn't reasonable was another .400.

"I won't hit .400 and I didn't have to reach July to find that out," he told Carl Felker of *The Sporting News*. "No dice. I said in the Spring I wouldn't hit .400. Not this year."

He said missing three years of baseball hurt any chance for .400 for anyone. He said getting used to a bunch of new pitchers in the league hurt. New pitchers meant new problems to decipher. He said subtle changes in the ballparks also hurt. Changes? Only he could notice the changes. He said the mounds were different.

"In Fenway, the mound is low," he said. "In New York and Cleveland and Detroit it's high. In St. Louis it's different from any of them. As a result, the same pitch thrown by the same pitcher comes at you from a different angle if it's thrown in Boston or one of the other parks. That's quite a difference if you make a study of those things."

In the All-Star Game, held at Fenway, he made perhaps his most famous quick study of all time. With the American League whaling the National 8–0, Williams stepped to the plate against Rip "Showboat" Sewell of the Pittsburgh Pirates. Sewell had become famous for throwing what he called his "eephus pitch." It really was a soft, parabolic lob to the plate. The ball was as much as 30 feet off the ground before it came down, and the batter had to supply a different sense of timing and all of the power to hit the ball. No one ever had hit it for a home run.

"I was standing at the batting cage before the game," Boo Ferriss says. "I was there when Sewell came past Williams. Ted said, 'Hey, Rip, are you going to throw that thing to me?' Rip said, 'If I get in the game, I will.' Ted said, 'Oh, boy,' just like that. You could tell he was excited by the idea."

Williams already had collected a homer and two singles in the game when he stepped to the plate against Sewell. The entire ballpark knew what was coming next. Eephus number one was fouled into the third-base seats. A fastball then was a called strike. Eephus number two was outside for a ball. Eephus number three . . . eephus number three came into the plate looking to Williams like every harvest moon ever invoked in any love song. He moved up in the batter's box, swung as hard as he had in his life, and sent the ball into the rightfield bullpen.

"I was standing on the mound in the bullpen, warming up," Boo Ferriss says. "The ball was coming right at me. I was ready to catch it. Then Mickey Harris reached in front of me."

The homer was one of those sweet blends of sport and show business that mean nothing and everything at the same time, a precursor in style to slam dunks and end-zone celebrations. Oh, my. The impact was on the eye, the gut, the imagination, not the game. How did he do that? Oh-my-oh-my, oh, my.

Alfred W. Lemaire, a World War I veteran confined to his home for the past 12 years in Hudson, New Hampshire, sent an immediate wire of thanks. He had written Williams a letter a week earlier asking for a homer in the All-Star Game and now heard on his radio that it had been delivered. (Twice.) Williams, in postgame celebration, said, "My wife thinks I'm a pretty good hitter, what do you think?" In the morning six kids sat on the porch of his Brighton apartment looking for an audience with the star or his wife. They had to settle for Hughson, the neighbor. He said only Williams could have hit the pitch for a homer because of his "perfect eye, perfect coordination, and tremendous power." The star already had gone fishing.

Five days later he hit three home runs and added a single, collecting eight RBI in the first game of a doubleheader with the Indians. He counseled "a little boy with a stout heart and a brave smile" from Quincy, victim of an incurable disease. He then went 1-for-2, a double, in the nightcap. The Sox won both games for an 11-game lead. Oh, my. The Red Sox machine could not be stopped.

On September 13, they captured the pennant, their first since 1918 and the departure of Babe Ruth. Williams finished the season with 38 home runs, second to Detroit's Greenberg at 44. His batting average (.342) was second by 11 points to Washington's Mickey Vernon (.353). His 123 RBI were second to Greenberg's 127. For the first time in his life, associated with a winner, he was a runaway selection as the American League MVP.

The World Series awaited.

The fun, alas, was done.

The image of Ted Williams, the loner, the one-man band, the self-centered star, had been sketched into existence before the war by the Boston press, pencils moving across the paper to chart the odd things he did to counterbalance the spectacular. Nine days in October 1946 supplied the indelible India ink.

When he came to his biggest moment—what turned out to be his one and only chance at that moment—he was a bust. His one World Series experience was a nightmare.

In seven games against the St. Louis Cardinals, the Series ending with a memorable 4–3 loss in St. Louis, he batted .200. He had five hits, all singles, in 25 at bats. The man who fought against slumps had the biggest slump of his life.

"What would you change if you could change anything in your life?" he would be asked over 50 years later.

"I'd have done better in the '46 World Series," he replied instantly, a quiver coming immediately into his voice. "God, I would."

Was he distracted? Was he fooled by the Cardinals pitchers, notably Harry "The Cat" Brecheen? Was he too emotional, too stoked, too ready for the moment? Was he sick? Was he hurt? There would be arguments for all of these positions in the future, none of them put forward by Williams, one of those enduring riddles of subpar athletic performance. What happened?

The best physical explanation is that he was hurt. The race for the National League pennant had ended in a tie between the Cardinals and the Brooklyn Dodgers, necessitating a best-two-of-three playoff series. This left the Red Sox idle, a situation that worried manager Joe Cronin. How could he keep his team sharp? He scheduled a three-game series of exhibitions against an all-star team to keep his boys busy.

The first game drew only 1,996 fans to Fenway on a cold Tuesday afternoon, despite the fact that the all-stars had Joe DiMaggio in centerfield. The Sox had a 2–0 lead in the fifth when Williams held back on a curveball from Senators lefthander Mickey Haefner. The curve never curved, striking Williams directly on his right elbow.

"I saw the pitch spinning halfway to the plate," he said. "I laid back, waiting for the curve. But as it came at me I saw it was just spinning and wasn't going to curve. I tried pulling away from it, but it hit me on the elbow."

He left the game immediately, elbow quickly swelling, and was rushed to a doctor's office on Bay State Road for X-rays. The X-rays were negative, but the elbow now was "swelled up like a hard-boiled egg," according to Williams. The remaining two exhibition games were canceled. Team doctor Ralph McCarthy told Williams to rest.

"Gee, I would have liked to have gone fishing," Williams said, "but I guess I won't be able to cast lefthanded. I better take care of this."

He wouldn't swing a bat until the day before the Series, four days later, when he would report the elbow felt "sore," even though he hit a couple of batting practice homers. How sore did it really feel in the following seven games? How much did it affect him, physically and mentally? Who will ever know? There were rumors that he also had the flu, troubled by his usual respiratory ills.

A more public distraction already had developed. A New York newspaper had reported he was going to be traded to the Yankees for DiMaggio. Or maybe to Detroit for pitcher Hal Newhouser. Or maybe to Cleveland for Bob Feller. The Boston newspapers, led by the Colonel, had taken that news and run happily with it.

"Take a good long look at Williams if you are one of the fortunate ones to have a Series ticket, for it is the last look you will ever take of Ted Williams in a Boston uniform," the Colonel typed in an excited hurry. "Unfortunately, I do not regret his going, and if the members of the championship Red Sox team itself were as honest, they would say exactly the same thing. He does not associate with them. He would not even attend the victory party in Cleveland. He is utterly lacking in anything that bears even a remote resemblance to team spirit or team pride.

"First and last and all times in between he is for Ted Williams and Ted Williams alone. So he will go his frustrated way, to hate the population of New York next year as he hates the people of Boston, and all I can wish him, as he goes, is good luck. He may need it."

A Williams-for-DiMaggio trade had been the subject of perpetual Boston debate, tavern logic declaring that the layouts of Fenway and Yankee Stadium—a short leftfield at Fenway, a short rightfield in the Bronx—would enable each star to hit more home runs. The printed possibility, accompanied by "no comments" rather than denials by both Cronin and owner Tom Yawkey, brought out a civic buzz. (Yawkey, while saying, "No comment," also was asked if he might sell the team. He said he might, and then use the proceeds to "buy a couple of newspapers so I can fire some sportswriters.") Williams was not immune to the noise.

"I'd hate to be traded to the Yankees," he said. "I don't like New York. I just don't want to play there. I wish I had a clause in my contract saying that I couldn't be traded to a club without my consent."

The trade stories brought back the story of Williams missing the team's victory party in Cleveland when they clinched the pennant. He had won the game that day against the Indians, 1–0, with the only inside-the-park home run of his career, and the Sox had clinched the pennant more than an hour later when the second-place Tigers lost to the Yanks. The players had dispersed, off around the city, and had to be called back to the Hotel Statler for the champagne celebration. Williams never had been found to join the group.

Where was he? One Sox official said Williams had been off with fishing friends. Another said he had been at the bedside of a dying veteran. A whisper said that he was no farther away than his room, choosing not to join his teammates. Which was right? Wouldn't DiMaggio, a "team man," be celebrating with his teammates? Wouldn't anyone?

(A classic Boston press sidelight to the pennant-clinching party was a meeting on the elevator between manager Joe Cronin and *Record* base-ball writer Huck Finnegan, who had predicted the Sox would fold in the stretch. Cronin gloated and said, "Well, we did it." Finnegan said, "Well, you'll never do it again." Cronin came back with, "You can go fuck your-self." Finnegan came back to the comeback with, "Well, you can go fuck *your*self." *Bing!* This stretch of dialogue was delivered as the elevator doors opened in the lobby to a circle of conventioneers waiting to board.

Williams's me-first approach was illustrated by the ongoing debate about the "Boudreau Shift." Why wouldn't he hit the ball to leftfield? What was the story with *that*?

Frustrated by Williams's three-homer onslaught in the opener of that post-All-Star doubleheader, Cleveland manager Lou Boudreau had re-acted in the second game by moving the left side of his defense (the third baseman and shortstop) to the right side of second base every time Williams came to the plate. He also had moved the outfielders to the right, the leftfielder now playing center. The invitation was clear: hit the ball to left. Half the field was wide open. Just bunt and you can have the hit. The single.

Williams's basic reaction was to keep doing what he was doing, to pull the ball into the fat, toothy smile of the defense in right. If there were more infielders and outfielders, well, he would simply hit through them or over them. He stuck with his strength, his power. Why give in and do something you don't normally do? Why, for example, bunt for the easy hit? Go for the long ball.

His view, perhaps, had merit, but watching this little confrontation three, four, five times per game was maddening. Hitting to left would be so *easy*. Why wouldn't Williams do it? Pride? Even though his numbers didn't suffer, every out Williams made seemed to be an indictment of his own hard head. The door was open. Why wouldn't he take it? Wouldn't the team, the Red Sox, be better off if he took it?

Other teams had taken note of Boudreau's success.

"This audacious win-or-lose-everything strategy has been adopted by Eddie Dyer, freshman manager of the Cardinals," the Colonel would type in the coming week of the Series. "It is based on the assumption that [Williams] either can't or won't bunt the ball or pop it into leftfield; that he is a certain rightfield hitter who, pitched to with careful correctness, will hit into the milling mob of men who hurry to that sector when he steps to the plate.

"Some of the unthinking ones construe this as a compliment to the hitting greatness of Williams. It is no such thing. It is a sneer at his inability to hit successfully, except to one particular part of the lawn. It is a challenge, not to hit the ball where they are, but where they ain't, and he has been pitifully unable to cope with that challenge."

The World Series—oh, right, the World Series—seemed to be almost an afterthought. The only writer who seemed to be concentrating on the Series itself was Williams himself.

Midway through the season he had started to do a daily column in the *Globe*. It was a ghostwritten affair ("Can he hit a fast adjective on the inside corner?" the *Globe* asked. "Will he step up on metaphors the way he stepped up on Rip Sewell's blooper?") and mild. The ghostwriter was Hy Hurwitz, and the process was a daily exercise in mutual dislike. ("Now I have to talk to that son of a bitch," both men said separately after each game.) Williams mostly told anecdotes and praised teammates and the opposition. He did not change much here.

"Why they've made the Red Sox such heavy favorites is beyond me," Williams wrote in his pre-Series analysis. "Those Cardinals have two arms and two legs like we have. They've got guts and speed and pitching. Personally, I think the Series is an even-stephen proposition."

He predicted the Sox would win in six games. He kept talking (and Hurwitz kept typing) as the Series unfolded. His daily angst and frustration could be spotted only slightly as he fought another version of the shift and the Cardinals' confusing lefty, Brecheen.

Game one (Red Sox 3, Cardinals 2):
You could have knocked the bat out of my hand with a straw when I saw the Cardinals break out their tricky shift the first time I came up. I never expected it. The Cards had said they weren't going to try any funny defense on me. Boy, did they pull a fast one. . . . I did get a kick out of one thing. I got a single to rightfield over the third baseman's head. Brother, that's one for the books.

Game two (Cardinals 3, Red Sox 0):
I've had a feeling Brecheen would be the toughest pitcher for us to beat. He proved it today. Brecheen isn't the kind of a pitcher who'll blow you out of the batter's box. But, brother, he's careful . . . he was threading

needles all day. The guy looks nice to hit at, but when you try to hit, the ball just isn't where you think it's going to be.

Game three (Red Sox 4, Cardinals 0):
I don't know what the reaction was among the Cardinals when I laid down that bunt today. With the wind blowing in and nobody covering third base, I thought it was the only thing I could do. If the Cardinals wish to play me that way the rest of the Series, it's OK by me.

Game four (Cardinals 12, Red Sox 3):
Maybe this shellacking we received will spur us on. The Cardinal pitchers aren't going to keep stopping most of us the way they have so far.

Game five (Red Sox 6, Cardinals 3):
I think we've got a tremendous edge on the Redbirds. They have to win two games. All we need is one. . . . They tell me that [Enos] Slaughter's elbow is bad. I understand he got hit just like I did when we played the All-Stars in Boston about 10 days ago. If it's the same type of injury that mine was, I don't think he'll be able to play any more. Those things get sore and stiff.

Game six (Cardinals 4, Red Sox 1):
Brecheen is one of the smartest spot pitchers I've ever faced. What makes him so effective is you don't know what spot he's going to pitch to. He's high when you think he'd be coming low. And he's inside when you're looking for him to be outside. He isn't supposed to be fast, but today he threw a couple of fast ones that would shatter non-breakable glass.

The Series came down to a final, seventh game. Cardinals management scheduled a day off to sell tickets. Williams's frustrations remained as bottled inside his body as they did inside the calm words of his column. If he needed consolation, he only had to look as far as St. Louis star Stan Musial, who had led all of baseball in hitting but also was struggling around the .200 mark in the Series. Consolation, though, wasn't a factor. He needed hits.

On the off-night, a sportswriter walked past Williams's room at the Hotel Chase. The door was partially open, and the sportswriter knocked. There was no answer. He looked into the darkened room and saw

Williams, sitting in silhouette by the window. He knocked again. There was no answer. He left.

"It kind of scared me," the sportswriter said in this anecdote delivered in a 1952 *Sport* magazine article by Frank Graham.

The writer told his story to Grantland Rice, the dean of American sportswriters, the one sportswriter Williams liked best from the entire subspecies. Rice decided Williams would not spend another night like this on the eve of the big game and hustled him out to dinner. He and the first writer tried to keep him entertained, directing the talk toward Minnesota and hunting and fishing. Williams kept bringing the conversation back to the game.

"I'd give anything in the world if we could win that game tomorrow," he said.

"And if you could get a couple of home runs?" Rice said.

"I wouldn't care if I didn't get a single, unless it could mean winning the game," Williams said. "Naturally I'd like to get four singles. Or four home runs. But if I struck out four times I'd be happy—if we could just win. Tom Yawkey . . . Joe Cronin . . . all the fellows on the ballclub . . . have waited so long for this. I hate like hell to think they might miss it."

The words hang over the final World Series game Williams ever would play. How would his life have changed with a different result in this one game? How would the history of the Red Sox have changed? There was no Curse of any Bambino acknowledged to be at work here. There was no bittersweet legacy of losing, big moments squandered. This was the first big moment, the building block for a sad future.

What if it had been different?

The Cardinals beat the Red Sox, 4–3, with a final run in the eighth inning that came when Slaughter scored from first on a single. The piece of the drama that always is remembered is poor Pesky, taking the throw at short from backup centerfielder Leon Culberson, hesitating an instant, then turning and throwing late to the plate to catch Slaughter. Sic transit gloria.

Williams was 0-for-4 in the game. He hit a fly ball to each Cardinal outfielder in his first three appearances, but the out that is remembered came in the top of the eighth. DiMaggio had doubled home two runs to tie the game at 3–3, pulling a muscle in the process. His replacement, Culberson, was on second. Brecheen, the lefthanded nemesis, was on the mound in relief. He induced Williams into one final pop-up to second baseman Red Schoendienst.

"I had hoped my bat would do the talking for me in the Series, but it was tongue-tied by some great Cardinal pitching," columnist Williams said through his ghost. "I feel tongue-tied myself right now."

"Gangling Ted Williams, the batting hero of the Red Sox American League pennant campaign, was a pathetic figure," Hurwitz reported in his own story in the same paper. "Held hitless today, Williams took the defeat tragically. The boyish-looking Williams, almost on the verge of tears, sat for at least 30 minutes at his locker, looking at the floor. . . .

"Even as the Red Sox departed, Williams still sat there in deep meditation. Finally, he managed to kick off his shoes. Then he resumed his sitting. Every once in a while he would rub his forehead as if to sweep the depressing thoughts from his mind."

Happy Chandler, the commissioner of baseball, offered him consolation.

"God love you, Ted," Chandler said, putting a hand on Williams's shoulder.

"I never missed so many balls in my life," the slugger sadly replied.

The angry critics who followed him now had their best ammunition. *First and last and for all times in between he is for Ted Williams and Ted Williams alone.* The critics always had had opinion, invective, challenge, but he always had been able to turn it all back at them. What do you people know? The words had been his fuel. Performance had been his answer.

This time there was no performance.

As his long career unfolded, the 1946 Series always would be used as a trump card in the argument. What did you do when you had your chance? Forgotten, pretty much, would be the 6-for-8 finish in Philadelphia in 1941, to hit .406. Forgotten would be the other dramatic moments, the homer off Sewell's eephus, for instance, in '46. These were personal achievements. What about the team? What about the Red Sox? Each succeeding failure would be laid at the locker of Ted Williams.

He was a great player, but . . .

He was a great *hitter.* . . .

He was a dog in the clutch.

Every incident that came along would reinforce the image of the hitting diva, the mezzo-soprano who could give a shit what the orchestra was doing. There would be an unfairness to it all, for sure, 24 other players on the ballclub, everybody culpable, but he would not help. He would storm in and storm out of controversies, shut up and speak out. The graph line of his moods would go up and down and back again, his personal success forever diminished by his team's lack of success.

What did you do when you had your chance?

There would be no answer to that because there would be no more chances. The Red Sox teams for the next five years, built around the core of the '46 pennant winners, mostly would be glorious, infuriating underachievers.

Every spring they would be picked to win the American League. Every fall they would find a different way to fall short. They would look like the best team ever invented at home at Fenway. They would fall apart on the road, their heavy-hitting attack muted and their defensive inadequacies and lack of speed highlighted by different dimensions in the different stadiums.

The Sox would be good enough, time and again, to reach the big moment. They never could capitalize on that moment.

"I thought we had the best eight players on the field for a number of years," Williams once said. "But you have to have the backup guys who can go in there and cover up for the starters when they're out for five or six days. We never had the backup guys."

There never was a deep-enough bench. There never was enough pitching. There never was enough something. Enough heart? Enough organization? Enough luck? The seasons unwound in an infuriating row:

1947—The Red Sox hung close until July, when the Yankees put together a 19-game winning streak. Boston limped home in third place, 14 games behind their nemesis from New York. Three pitchers—Ferriss, Hughson and Harris—came down with sore arms.

1948—The Red Sox won the final three games of the season to tie the Indians for the pennant. The American League had a one-game playoff at Fenway on October 4 and new manager Joe McCarthy oddly picked Denny Galehouse as his starting pitcher. Galehouse was rocked, the Indians won, 8–3, and went on to whip the Braves, four games to two, in what would have been the only all-Boston World Series.

1949—The season came down to a final two games in New York. The Red Sox went 43–13 for the months of August and September to hold a one-game lead. One-of-two in New York meant the pennant. The Sox lost both games.

1950—Williams broke his elbow in the All-Star Game on July 11 and missed the next two months of the season. The Red Sox were supposed to die, but instead they rolled, coming to within a game and a half of the front-running Yankees. After Williams returned on September 15, alas, the team collapsed, finishing third, four games behind the Yanks.

1951—The end of the line arrived for the '46 pennant winners. They were in front in July but collapsed in September to finish 11 games out. The dynasty that could have been won only one pennant.

In each of these five seasons, the Red Sox were in the mix for at least a while. In two of them they lost the pennant on the last day. A slight change in any of dozens of variables could have brought a different result. Certainly in '49 and '50. Those were seasons when every player, alone at night, could look into a mirror and say, "Well, if I only. . . ." One play. One more hit instead of an out. One more high fastball, in instead of dead over the plate. One more something could have brought glory.

The one mirror everyone saw, though, was the mirror in Ted Williams's house. What could *he* have done differently? Wasn't he the star, the leader? His salary jumped from $50,000 in 1946 to $75,000 in 1947 to $90,000 in '48 to $100,000 for '49, '50, and '51. He was the highest-paid player in the game, made more money than Ruth ever had made. What more could he have done? Shouldn't there have been something? How many World Championships had Ruth won? (Seven.) How many had DiMaggio won? (Ten.) How many had Williams won? (Zero.)

As maddening as the results were for Red Sox fans, they were doubly maddening for Williams. He was very good for all of those five years:

1947—He won his second Triple Crown, leading the league at .343 with 32 home runs and 114 RBI. The writers bagged him again for MVP, giving the award to DiMaggio by a single point, 202 to 201, when a single writer (not a writer from Boston, as it is often stated) left him off his ten-place ballot completely. He should have been the MVP. He *was* truly the MVP.

1948—He led the league in batting average at .369, hit 25 homers, knocked in 127 runs. Forgotten in the aftermath of the playoff loss was the fact that Williams had been on base eight of ten times in the final two-day sweep over the Yankees that enabled the team to reach the playoff.

1949—Won the MVP easily. Had 43 homers, most he ever would hit in a season. Tied for the RBI lead with 159. Hit .343. Just missed the batting title with his .3427 average second to the .3429 of the Tigers' George Kell.

1950—Even though he missed 67 games with the broken elbow, he still had 97 RBI and 28 homers.

1951—Hit .318. Thirty homers, 126 RBI. Led the league in walks for the seventh out of eight straight years, missing only in the injury-shortened '50 season. Walked 832 times in the five years. Struck out only 246 times.

Wasn't all of that wonderful stuff? Was there anyone—no, there wasn't—who was doing better in all of baseball?

The knockers still knocked. The Colonel's favorite gambit was to print a list of the ten biggest games of Ted Williams's career and show how Williams had faltered. Forgotten were all of the other games that had put the Sox in these prime positions and forgotten too was the fact that the Colonel himself had made up the list, picking just the games he wanted, and forgotten was the fact that teams always walked Williams, pitched him very carefully in the big games and . . . a 1949 debate between a mythical pair of pro- and anti-Williams supporters distributed by the North American News Alliance spelled out the problem. The anti-Williams debater always had the final word.

"You must admit that he never has done anything in the big games, the clutch games down the stretch," Mr. Anti said. "The 1946 World Series . . . The post-season playoff in 1948 . . . Or the final two games of the 1949 pennant race . . .

"You may say it is coincidence, but I say he is up there waiting for the base on balls. . . . Waiting for the perfect pitch. Not looking to knock ANYTHING out of the park . . . Waiting for the sucker pitch that never comes . . . And, in the process, making an uninspiring ballplayer of himself."

Not everyone subscribed to the theory of "Get a good ball to hit." Not all the time.

W illiams's public image took a curious hit in the winter between the '48 and '49 seasons. It came with the birth of his daughter, Barbara Joyce Williams. Bobby-Jo. The blessed event happened on January 28, 1948, the off-season, at the Richardson House of Boston Lying-In Hospital. The baby, who would have been named Theodore Donald if it had been a boy, weighed five pounds, six ounces. The mother and daughter, the hospital announced, were "doing fine." The father was not in attendance.

He was fishing in Florida.

On January 6, he had left Minnesota for Miami to go fishing in the Keys and the Everglades, sending Doris to Boston to stay with Johnny Buckley and his family in Brighton. This was his vacation. The baby wasn't due until the middle of February. Williams already had bagged an appearance at the Boston Baseball Writers' Dinner on January 29, where he was scheduled to receive a shotgun as the most valuable Red Sox player for 1947, but planned to be in Boston in time for the birth. When the baby was two weeks early, he missed the moment.

The chorus that chronicled his life was not pleased.

Missing the writers' dinner was an intramural sin. This was always an awkward moment for Williams, the event where he was forced into a tuxedo the first time he went, into a tie in other years. Missing the dinner was definitely not a public relations plus, but how could the writers complain? Other players had missed other dinners. Missing the birth of a first child, however, opened all kinds of possibilities. The prodders prodded.

"Once again Williams finds himself standing in the corner wearing a dunce's cap . . . ," Harold Kaese wrote in the *Globe*. "The baseball writers, of course, are not surprised at Williams' absence when his first baby was born. Heck, he wouldn't come up here to get the $200 gun they're giving him tonight, would he?"

Kaese had another story in the same paper. A reporter on the *Globe* desk had reached Williams in Everglades City. The prodded new father had reacted. Kaese printed the unflattering exchange that was recorded on a Dictaphone:

REPORTER: "Hello, Ted, did you hear about the birth of Barbara Joyce? Congratulations."

THE KID: "Yeah, the Miami papers told me a little while ago and I got a wire from Johnny Buckley just now, but I don't want to talk to anyone about it."

REPORTER: "Are you coming to Boston, Ted? Everyone here wants to know whether you're flying up."

THE KID: "I don't know. What do I have to come up there for?"

REPORTER: "A good question, Ted, but after all your wife is in the hospital with your first born."

THE KID: "She's all right, isn't she? Are they OK?"

REPORTER: "Yeah, they're both doing well, the hospital tells us."

THE KID: "Well, what good can I do up there? By the way, what hospital is she in?"

REPORTER: "She's at the Boston Lying-in Hospital—the Richardson House there."

THE KID: "The Boston what?"

REPORTER: "The Boston Lying-in—the Richardson House."

THE KID: "Oh, yeah. OK."

REPORTER: "Well, can we say whether you're coming to Boston or not, Ted?"

THE KID: "I don't know what I'll do."

REPORTER: "Where were you today? Out fishing?"

THE KID: "Yeah, out fishing. That's right."

REPORTER: "Do you want to talk to one of the sportswriters, Ted?"

THE KID: "No, I want to talk to somebody I know up there."

REPORTER: "You mean Johnny Buckley?"

THE KID: "Yeah, where is he now?"

REPORTER: "He's at the Bruins hockey game. I think he's expecting you to call sometime tonight in reply to his wire. Why don't you call him at home a little after ten. He ought to be home by then."

THE KID: "Yeah, I'll do that."

This was not an exact transcription of the conversation. This was the newspaper version. The exact transcription was filled with "fucks" and other salty modifiers buzzing through the other words like so many angry bees. This transcription floated around the *Globe* for the next 30 years. It never failed to get a reaction.

What kind of guy was this Williams? What kind of marriage must he have? What kind of life? This wasn't any complicated situation. All he had to do was say how proud he was to be a father and say that he wished he were there, that he didn't know the baby would come early. What was this? Fatherhood seemed as if it were an imposition on his personal plans to go fishing. Was this how he really felt?

Yes, it probably was.

This was Ted.

He didn't hit Boston until five days later. The papers had been killing him. The Colonel, Egan, surprisingly had been one of his defenders in this case, but most opinions were that a man should be somewhere near at hand when his baby was born. At least not on vacation. Williams landed at 1:45 in the morning of February 2 on a flight from Miami that had been delayed by mechanical problems. The reporters were there to meet him.

"The heck with public opinion," he said as flashbulbs popped.

"It's my baby," he said. "It's my life."

"You are not a nice fellow, Brother Williams," the writer Paul Gallico wrote after the baby business. "I do believe that baseball and the sports pages would be better off without you.

"Where you are wrong in saying that the public cannot run your life is that we can. For I am a part of that public and I would no longer invest 10 cents to see you ply your trade because I have an aversion to finding myself in the same enclosure with a self-confessed mucker.

"When, oh when will you thick-headed athletes catch on that the public is your darling, that you may not disillusion us, that you cannot live as other men but live in glass houses and that this is the price you pay for wealth and success."

Gallico was wrong on all counts. First of all, the public loved to be in the same enclosure with a self-confessed mucker. Loved it then. Loves it now. Always will love it. A ticket was well worth the money. This mucker was a great show, great theater, as much as a great hitter. There always was the wonder about what he would do next because he would do anything.

"A kid once came up to me at my camp and told me his father always booed me," Williams said, years later. "He said his father told him he always really liked me, but he also loved to boo me. He wanted to see what I would do. I said to the kid, 'Really? I'd like to talk to your father about all this someday.' The kid said his father was dead."

The second count on which Gallico was wrong was about the glass houses. Williams realized very well where he lived. No one in all of organized sport was surrounded by more glass. That was one of the reasons he kept all the blinds tightly drawn.

He ventured hard to keep his private life private. He rented a big Tudor house in Waban, an upscale village in the upscale suburb of Newton. He made a rule that there would be no pictures taken of his new daughter, refusing even the big-money offers of the national magazines.

Except for an accident in 1946 in suburban Holliston when he was driving his own car to an exhibition game in East Douglas against the Cleveland Indians—Doris was slightly injured—he did not make headlines outside the sports page. The sports page headlines might be shifted to the front page, but he was not seen on the streets, wasn't out late, wasn't the instigator in any controversies outside the playing field.

He would say at the end of his career that he was late for curfew on the road only twice in 19 seasons. Both times by 15 minutes. Both with permission. He never was involved in any cabal against any manager. He never criticized teammates. He never criticized umpires.

The only people he criticized, really, were himself and the people who criticized him. He criticized himself more than anyone.

"Ted lived his life in a tunnel," Maurice "Mickey" McDermott says. "He didn't look one way or the other way. All he wanted to do was be the greatest hitter that ever lived. He went his own way."

McDermott, a lefthanded fireballer who came up to the Red Sox as a 19-year-old in 1948, was an avid explorer of the side of the Boston baseball life that Williams never joined. Williams never smoked, hated cigarette and cigar smoke. Williams seldom drank and never to excess. Everybody else seemed to smoke. Everybody else seemed to drink. McDermott followed the crowd. The "other" crowd.

"Ted liked me," McDermott says. "I think he did. He didn't let people in. That was his thing. He was private. He'd pick you out if he liked you. If he didn't like you, you'd get the look. That look. It was 'get out the door.' I think he let Bobby Doerr in as much as anyone. He loved Bobby Doerr. He loved Dominic DiMaggio. He and Bobby and Dominic and Johnny Pesky too, they were the four guys from the West Coast . . . and I think he let them all in a little bit, but I don't think he ever let anyone really in.

"He let me in a little bit because I think he saw a bit of himself in me. I was in the big leagues as a teenager, same as he was. I was from a poor background. He tried to tell me things, especially at the beginning. He said the key was 'discipline.' I just wasn't listening. Me? Discipline? I couldn't spell it. I didn't know what it meant."

The owner, Tom Yawkey, once was rumored to drink a bottle of whiskey a day. His second wife, Jean, called "a former showgirl" in Boston papers, drank. Eddie Collins drank. Cronin drank. The succession of managers hired by Yawkey drank. Joe McCarthy drank a lot. Yawkey had his own private bar in Fenway, hidden from strangers. He brought in his people and they drank. The writers drank in the press room. The lower-level personnel in the front office drank. The afternoon games ended at dinner hour and everybody drank. Most of the players drank. There was time.

Discipline?

"Every generation has its vices," McDermott says. "Ours was drinking."

McDermott, who wound up with a 12-year career and a 69-69 record, saw the things that Williams missed. While Williams was raging or thinking, dissecting the pitchers and his own swing, McDermott was looking around. He was well outside the tunnel. He is 75 years old now and has kept his alcohol-preserved notes in his head. He remembers postwar baseball in the fine, blue words of the time. (McDermott died in the summer of 2003, a year after this interview.)

Spring training . . .

"We'd be in Sarasota, they had sulfur in the water. Everything stunk terrible. So much sulfur, you'd light a match in the bathroom, pow, you'd be in fucken Cuba. . . .

"Walter Dropo had a beautiful girlfriend in Sarasota. Her name was Mona Knox. Gorgeous. John Ringling North, the owner of the circus, also owned the hotel. He was around all the time. A fucken nut. He always wore a black hat and a cape. Looked like he was from *The Shadow Knows*. One day he sends over two big guys to see Walter. John Ringling North also liked Mona Knox. The two guys tell Walter, 'Hey, you'd better lay off or we'll take care of you.' That was the end of Walter and Mona Knox. . . .

"The circus was always there when we were there. You'd walk down the street and you'd see some seven-foot-two cocksucker. Hello, how are you? Then you'd run into some four-foot-two cocksucker. How are you? A car went past, the Doll Family, all midgets. Looked like twelve-year-old kids, except they were smoking cigars. . . .

"There was a girl from the circus, high-wire act. She had enormous breasts. Ginger. Everybody loved Ginger. Ginger loved everybody back. She came to a game at Payne Park. Mel Parnell, I think, is pitching, and Danny Murtaugh is batting, and Birdie Tebbetts is catching. Ginger sits down behind our dugout. She's wearing a halter top. Everything stops. They're all looking. Murtaugh screams out, 'Will you look at the jugs on Ginger. . . .' "

Economics and life . . .

"I go up to talk to Cronin about my contract. I was with Windy McCall, a pitcher, a fucken nut. Had a plate in his head. He'd been hit by machine-gun bullets during the war. He goes in and comes out. Said he'd signed for $5,000. I go in and come out. I tell him I'd signed for $4,000. He goes crazy. Says I should get $5,000 too. He goes back into Cronin's office. I hear all this shouting. I got $5,000. I think Cronin was terrified of him. . . .

"You made no money and you had to pay for everything. I was with the Senators, and Bob Porterfield, a pitcher, wore out his hat. He had to pay $7.50 for a new fucken hat! Everything. You had to pay for your sanitary socks. And if you didn't give Johnny Orlando a big enough tip, he'd take an ice pick and punch holes in the socks. . . . Shoes! You had to pay for shoes. Walter and I would go over to Spot Bilt in Cambridge, buy seconds for $2.50. Shoes. . . .

"You had one uniform. You wore it every day. One hundred percent fucken wool. You'd sweat so much, you'd lose 20 pounds by the fourth inning. I pitched 17 innings one night in Chicago and wound up in the hospital for three days. You'd take off that wool uniform and your body would be covered all over with little pimples. . . .

"Ted one morning went fishing in the sun without a shirt. Got all sunburned. That afternoon we had a game. He covered himself with Noxzema so the sunburn wouldn't hurt. Then he put on that fucken wool uniform and went out there. The heat got working, he fucken died. . . ."

Sex . . .

"McCarthy calls me into his office. He says, 'What do you think about Lefty Gomez?' I said, 'Lefty Gomez is a great pitcher, one of the best in baseball.' McCarthy says, 'He lost his fastball in the sheets. Do you understand that, Maurice? He lost his fastball in the sheets.' Lefty was a wonderful guy. A sportswriter once asked him what was the toughest thing he'd ever done. Lefty said, 'Tried to fuck standing up in a hammock. . . .' "

Drinking . . .

"The first game I ever pitched, I got in because Ellis Kinder was drunk. He was an amazing man, Kinder, the strongest man I ever knew. He was always drunk. He showed up drunk for this game, everybody knew it, except McCarthy. Because *he* was drunk. Kinder starts. He goes out, throws one pitch into the backstop, high. He has no idea where he is. McCarthy came out. Kinder's falling off the mound. They call me in. Kinder's wandering around in back of the mound, he gives me the ball. Hiccup. Go get 'em. . . .

"I went drinking once with Frankie Fontaine. Remember him? Crazy Guggenheim? He was on *The Jackie Gleason Show*. He was from Boston. A great guy. He said, 'Come on, let's get a drink.' I said, 'Okay, but I have to pick up some lobsters for dinner first.' Three days later . . . we've hit every bar in Boston. Twice. The lobsters have been just sitting there. The car smells like 30 dead carp. Smells so bad I have to sell it. . . ."

Discipline.

Williams resisted this raucous, smoky scene that was covered by a fine alcoholic mist. He never charged the night life; he walked the streets instead. He walked with Bobby Doerr. He walked with Johnny Orlando. He walked by himself. He went to bed early, got up early, went fishing. His business agent, Freddie Corcoran, whom he hired with a handshake in 1946, was a total character of the time, a handshaker, a backslapper, a cocktail lounge schmoozer of the first order. Corcoran had to come to Williams to finalize the deals, the endorsements, find him in a hotel room or a fishing cabin. Williams wasn't where the deals were made.

He never received any credit for any of this, for the life he didn't lead, from the Boston press. Kinder, drunk, once slammed his car into a tree on the Fresh Pond Parkway in Cambridge at two in the morning. He appeared the next day at Fenway, all banged up, and told reporters he had swerved so he wouldn't hit a dog running across the road. He then smiled and asked, "What self-respecting dog would be out at two in the morning?" The reporters all smiled and laughed with him.

What would have happened if Williams were telling the same story? He never was involved in any of this.

"He was a great man, really, a man's man," McDermott says. "I think he was a very humble person, had a great deal of integrity. And he was brilliant. He could take a book, bing-bing-bing, and remember it. He had one of those photographic memories. He was thinking about things that none of us were thinking about."

McDermott, while he was pitching in Boston, fashioned a small night-club career on the side as a singer. He sang at Steuben's, a club near the Common. He did cocktail lounge songs, Sinatra stuff. (The Colonel, who called him "the Juvenile Delinquent," reviewed McDermott's act and said, "He can't pitch. He can't sing. And he has a nightclub pallor." He then came into the club once and met McDermott. "Yeah, you're a nice kid," he told the pitcher, "but who's going to buy a newspaper if I say that?" McDermott, the showman, understood the logic.) Rocky Palladino, the owner of a rival, bigger club, the Latin Quarter, came to McDermott with a proposition. He said he would book McDermott for $5,000 for three days if McDermott could convince Williams to play the piano for him. Williams wouldn't actually have to play, someone behind a curtain would do that, but Williams would receive $12,500 for the three days. Plus a new Cadillac.

"I go to Williams in the outfield, before a game," McDermott says. "I'm on my hands and knees, begging, 'Theodore, I could use the money.' For three days I would earn more than I earned for a year of baseball. He says, 'Bush, Jesus Christ, that's all I need, to be fucking around with a piano with those Boston cocksuckers in the audience. Somebody would say something the first night and I'd be off the stage in a minute, jumping on him.'"

To see Ted Williams do something stupid, you pretty much had to buy a ticket to the ballpark. That was where he was the public show.

Another view of Williams during this time came from George Sullivan, who later would become a sportswriter and then the public relations man for the Red Sox. In 1949 he was 15 years old and the visiting team batboy. He felt as if the Hand of God had picked him up and placed him where he was.

"Ted would give me rides home to Cambridge," he says. "He had two cars, a Cadillac and a Ford. He'd drop me off at my corner, Kerry Corner, right in front of the Varsity Spa, where everybody could see me. I was the kid who got a ride home from Ted Williams. I always wanted to say, real loud, everyone listening, 'And tomorrow be on time, will ya?' I never did."

Sullivan studied Williams on a daily basis. What was the great man doing? How did he handle things? Who was he? What was he? Sullivan noticed what the players themselves never noticed, the way the dressing room changed when Williams entered. The other players were in awe, the same way Sullivan was. Conversations stopped. Or changed immediately to what Williams would begin to spout about. He was in control. His voice boomed over everybody else's voice.

"The only one who ever gave him any grief at all was Jack Fadden, the trainer," Sullivan says. "Fadden would give it to him good. He'd be rubbing down Williams and he'd say, 'Can you throw like DiMaggio?' 'Can you hit like DiMaggio?' Williams would say, 'No, but I'm a better hitter.' And Fadden would say, 'Can you run like DiMaggio?'

"That's how that famous conversation developed. Williams said he was 'the greatest fisherman who ever was.' Fadden said he knew one who was better. And he went into the story of the loaves and the fishes. God. And Williams said, 'Well, you had to go way back to find one.' "

Sullivan received two dollars per game as visiting batboy and had to work, unpaid, running errands and cleaning on days when the Red Sox were off or on the road. On one Red Sox off-day, hurrying to the park at 2:30 in the afternoon, he heard a sound—*blam*—coming from the ballpark. A backfire? *Blam.* Maybe one of the beer trucks. *Blam-blam-blam.* The sound was coming from the field.

Sullivan came up through the stands and saw dead pigeons all over the field. He saw Williams in the visiting bullpen with a rifle. *Blam.* He saw another pigeon drop. This was the same scene—minus owner Tom Yawkey and infielder Billy Goodman in the picture—that sportswriters Hy Hurwitz and Tim Horgan would discover eight years later. They would write the story, and Horgan's boss, Arthur Siegel, would call the Humane Society. Just another round in the press-Williams wars.

There was no Humane Society involved here. Sullivan hurried to his tasks in the Red Sox locker room. Clomp, clomp, clomp. A familiar stride soon came up the stairs. A familiar arm came around Sullivan's shoulders. A familiar voice spoke.

"Hey, buddy, do me a favor. Get some garbage cans and pick up those birds, will ya?"

Three cans were needed to do the job. Maybe four.

"It was one of the most disgusting things I've ever done," Sullivan says. "The birds, all the guts hanging out. Disgusting."

The moods of his idol fascinated the 15-year-old boy. Williams could be exuberant, pleasant, kind. He also could be angry, mean. The language fascinated the 15-year-old boy. The foul words came out in wonderful sequences. The big word, the f-word, would be interspersed between syllables. Unfuckenbelievable! Unbefuckenlievable! The 15-year-old boy learned things he hadn't been taught by the nuns in parochial grammar school. He learned how to swear like his idol.

"There was a moment . . . this wasn't in '49, but later in his career, the late fifties, maybe even 1960 . . . that showed the switch that he had inside him," Sullivan says. "I'm not sure what year it was, but Willie Tasby, the outfielder, had just come to the team from Baltimore. He was one of the first few black guys the Red Sox finally had. It was before a game, and Tasby was just sitting in the dugout, had his hat pulled over his eyes. Resting. Ted came up the tunnel. You could hear him."

"Is he fucken here?" Williams shouted.

"Has he fucken come yet?"

"Is he here?"

He was walking with a photographer. He was supposed to meet some Little League hero. The Little Leaguer had saved some other kid from drowning or from some other sad fate and now was being honored by meeting the famous Red Sox star. The kid was here, in a first-base box. He was waiting. He was wearing his Little League uniform.

Williams came onto the field, spotted the kid, and the nice switch clicked. Hey, how are you? You play baseball? You hit? What's your average? You hit .538? You should be giving me tips! I should be asking for your autograph! The kid was thrilled, overjoyed. The photographer took the picture. Williams shook the kid's hand.

He turned, took no more than five steps back into the dugout. Somebody said something he didn't like.

"Virgin Mary, All-Clapped-Up Mother of God!" Williams shouted.

Willie Tasby, sitting at the end of the dugout, jumped off his seat as if touched by electricity. He never had been around Ted Williams.

"I ain't never going to ride in an airplane with you!" Willie Tasby exclaimed.

"That was Ted," Sullivan says. "The switch went both ways. He gave me my master's degree in cursing."

Sullivan, among all of his stories, remembers a strange moment. Since he was the visiting batboy in '49, he very seldom was in the Red Sox dugout during a game. One night, though, a hot summer night, very hot, he was working with the Detroit Tigers, and they ran out of towels. He had to scoot across the field, through the Red Sox dugout, and get some towels from the adjacent visiting clubhouse.

He went across the diamond after a third Tigers out, picked up the towels in the visiting clubhouse, and came back through the Red Sox dugout. The Red Sox were still batting. Williams was batting. Sullivan had to wait for the inning to finish before he could go back across the field. The score was 0–0, maybe the fifth inning, and Freddie Hutchinson of the Tigers threw and Williams swung and the ball flew through the sky, landing deep in the bleachers. Sullivan couldn't remember a longer homer from Williams.

The slugger ran the bases, didn't shake hands with next batter Vern Stephens at the plate, and came into the dugout in a huff. He yelled at himself even as his teammates came to congratulate him.

"Goddamn it," he said. "I never should have swung at that son of a bitch."

"It wasn't a strike," he said.

"Never should have swung."

The homer broke up a scoreless game, eventually won it for the Red Sox. The Red Sox were in the middle of a pennant race. Williams was mad at himself because he had swung at a bad ball and hit it 14 rows back into the bleachers? He was more worried about his own little code than the pennant race?

"What do his teammates really think of this?" Sullivan says he wondered. "What kind of team guy is this?"

It was the wonder of the time.

The final particulars for the debate between personal success and team success were assembled during the 1950 season. This was the final, ill-fated chase of the Yankees by the dynasty that never was. Williams was in the thick of it.

Even when he didn't play for eight weeks.

The debate itself was restarted in a taxicab traveling from Logan Airport to the Hotel Statler on the last day in January. Williams was in the cab, arriving to appear at the Baseball Writers' Association dinner and then for a stretch of appearances at the Sportsmen's Show at the Mechanics Building. The *Globe*'s Clif Keane, a yappy, combative addition to the Boston press corps, was also in the cab.

"What do you think of Ted Williams?" Keane asked the driver, who did not know who was in the car.

"I think he's a pretty good ballplayer," the cabbie said. "But he doesn't come through in the pinches sometimes. He's always trying to hit a home run. He'd be a better ballplayer if he tried to get singles to knock in runs once in a while."

"There it goes again," Williams said in the backseat with familiar frustration. "The same old talk. I'm supposed to be perfect all the time. If I hit home runs, they yell for me to get singles. When I try to hit to leftfield, they want home runs. What do these people want anyway?"

The debate was put into sign language on the afternoon of May 11. The Red Sox lost an important early doubleheader to the Tigers, and Williams and the Fenway crowd became direct adversaries.

In the first game, sixth inning, Williams dropped a soft fly behind short—yelling, "Mine," before he dropped it. The fans in left booed. Hy Hurwitz in the *Globe* reported that Williams "raised his two forefingers skyward to let the fans know how he felt about them." In the second game Williams misplayed Vic Wertz's single to left with the bases loaded, and all three runners scored, Wertz ending on third. The boos increased and followed Williams toward the dugout at the end of the inning.

"The first game boohs were mere ripples compared to the vocal going-over given Ted [now]," Hurwitz wrote. "So Williams increased the vulgarity of his gestures to match the boohing, repeating them three times to three different sections of the stands.

" 'I don't mind the errors,' Williams told reporters after the game, 'but those —— —— fans; they can —— —— —— and you can quote me in all the papers. They're —— ——.' "

"Williams removed himself from the ranks of decent sportsmen," the *American* quickly editorialized. "Yesterday he was a little man, and in his ungovernable rage, a dirty little man."

The obligatory forced apology from Williams, forced by Yawkey this time, was rendered the next day. The obligatory you're-our-guy ovation was rendered at the first at bat of the next game by the bulk of the fans. The uneasy dance continued.

At the All-Star Game—after the obligatory "Ted Wants to Be Traded" story came out of New York and was greeted by the obligatory Williams denial—he was injured. He broke his left elbow.

Tracking down a fly ball from the bat of the Pittsburgh Pirates slugger

Ralph Kiner in the first inning, Williams made a fine catch and crashed into the leftfield wall at Chicago's Comiskey Park. There was no cinder warning track, only a short, sharp rise in the field to give any indication the wall was close. Williams hit hard, but thought he had only bruised the arm and played until the eighth inning.

X-rays, back at Sancta Maria Hospital in Cambridge, told a different story the next day. A half-inch break in the radius was detected, then repaired a day later. The arm was put in a cast—the first cast of his life—and he was expected to be out of action for "about six weeks."

"Maybe you could watch some games out in left field," reporters suggested when Williams checked out of the hospital on July 20.

"I wouldn't sit out there with those meatheads," he replied.

A young *Globe* reporter, Ernie Roberts, had been assigned to cover the press conference at the hospital, but missed it. The scheduled starting time had been five o'clock, but the Red Sox played a day game that afternoon and finished early, so Williams held his press conference early. When Roberts appeared at the hospital, everyone else had come and gone.

"I was in a panic," Roberts says. "I covered college sports, never the Red Sox. I knew Williams had gone home, but I had no idea where he lived."

The only person Roberts knew who knew Williams was his uncle, George Nicoll, the father of Donald Nicoll, the first kid Williams ever had visited in the hospital. Roberts called his uncle, who gave him a street address in Waban. Roberts drove out Beacon Street, found the house, and rang the front doorbell.

"A maid answered," Roberts says. "I told her who I was and what I wanted. She kind of raised her eyes and said, 'Wait a minute.' Now Doris, Ted's wife, appears. Same thing. She kind of raised her eyes too, and said, 'Wait a minute.' She came back, pointed to a room at the side of the hall, and said, 'He's in there.' Then she went the other way."

Roberts went into the living room. Williams was pacing and muttering and quickly unloaded. The bad words came. The questions came. Can't you guys leave me alone? What do you think you're doing? Roberts, nervous, stammered out his situation. He couldn't even think of questions to ask.

Williams suddenly started talking. He explained his problems with his elbow, the things he would have to do before he could come back, talked about various subjects. Roberts wrote everything down in a hurry. Bobby-Jo came into the room. Doris came into the room. Everybody was talking. Roberts kept writing. Williams walked Roberts to the door.

"I think you know my uncle," Roberts finally said. "George Nicoll?"

"George is your uncle, Roberts?" Williams said, putting his arm around the writer's shoulder. "You should have said so."

Roberts left, dumbfounded. The word "mercurial" stuck in his head about the character he had just met. Williams, after this slight pause, returned to the old battles with the press.

His recuperation was filled with obligatory "exclusives" that he had reinjured the elbow and now would be "out for the season." These were followed by the obligatory denials. The obligatory story about Williams fishing in Calais, Maine, during this time was followed, of course, by the obligatory wonder of how a man could cast with a fishing rod if he could not swing a bat. Which was followed by the obligatory explanation that a normal man has two arms on a normal body. And Williams, in fact, was righthanded.

On September 15, he returned to the lineup. When he had left, the Sox were eight games out of first place. An 11-out-of-13 losing streak had sent Joe McCarthy back into retirement and brought in the religious Steve O'Neill to replace him. (O'Neill would finger his rosary beads in the dugout while Williams nearby would issue his medical reports on the private parts of the Virgin Mary.) Williams's injury seemed to be the final killer, except . . . except the Red Sox played better without him than they did with him.

They hit like crazy—even Mickey McDermott was hitting over .300 as a pitcher—and they ran off strings of wins, the most impressive a 16-for-17 stretch in August. When Williams came back in style with a homer and three singles to help the Sox beat the Browns, 12–9, in St. Louis, they moved to within a game and a half of the first-place Tigers, a game behind the second-place Yankees.

Alas, 9 of the remaining 15 games were on the road. Alas, the grand one-day return was not sustainable. The elbow still was tender, still hurt. Alas, alas. The Red Sox finished four games back at the end.

"Ted Williams was an objet d'art—and just about as useful," Jim Murray of the *Los Angeles Times* would write, years later, when Williams became eligible for the Hall of Fame. "He should be in the Louvre, not Cooperstown. He was probably the greatest pure striker of a baseball who ever lived. But this translated into exactly one pennant for his team. . . .

"Ted Williams was of the Red Sox, but not on them, a subtle but nonetheless real distinction. He gave recitals. The business of winning or losing appeared to belong at a different level. He played the Yankees four times a game. The rest of the team played them nine innings."

The knockers were free to knock forever. Williams never would play on another end-of-the-season pennant contender, never play another meaningful game in a team sense. The 1951 chase would be done by the middle of the summer, and then he would be off to war and then. . . .

"To get a real line on Williams you have to see his face in the clubhouse after a game which the Red Sox have won and in which he's gone hitless," Jack Orr wrote in the *New York Compass* during the middle of the 1950 season. "That tells the story."

The Colonel in the *Record* called him "a malingerer" and "the most overpaid buffoon in the history of baseball."

He would be seen as a solo act for the rest of his career, whether he wanted to be or not.

8 Korea

Ted Williams, one of the great hitters of all baseball time, hasn't had a bat in his hands for 14 months now. But his hands haven't been idle. He's been fingering the stick of a 500-mile-an-hour Panther jet fighter plane over Korea. The war-scarred countryside of that unhappy peninsula has become as familiar to him as the big-league baseball parks where he performed for cheering fans.

Where once he exploded base hits for the Boston Red Sox, he switched to blasting the North Korean and Chinese Communist armies with bombs, rockets and napalm (flaming jellied gasoline) for the United Nations. And he belly-landed a badly shot-up jet last February as skillfully as an old pro hooking a slide into third base.

MARVIN KRONER, *COLLIER'S*, JUNE 1953

The idea that Ted Williams could be called back to the Marines had been bubbling deep in the news pages for the past year. No one simply had noticed.

The advent of the Korean War in 1950 had caught the Marines flat-footed. They really needed pilots. The last days and months of World War II had shown that there would be many changes in modern warfare. Nuclear weapons, jet airplanes, and helicopters had all been unveiled. These advances brought questions about the very existence of the Marines.

Would an amphibious landing force—the basic role of the Marines—even be necessary anymore? One nuclear weapon could knock out an entire expeditionary force as it approached from the sea. And if the Marines were necessary, wouldn't helicopters be the best, most mobile way for them to travel?

A tight postwar budget had scaled down the expectations for Marine aviation. The newest, fastest planes were sent to the Air Force. The hottest pilots followed. Marine aviation was in disarray. There still were debates about whether the program should be disbanded, when the forces of Kim Il Sung stormed across the 38th Parallel on the afternoon of June 25, 1950, and changed the situation in a moment. Maybe new wars wouldn't be all that different from old wars.

The Marines now needed planes. . . .

The Marines now needed pilots. . . .

The planes were hurried into production, a budget quickly appropriated by Congress. The pilots were not rushed into production. They were found in the hall closet, where they had been hanging for the past seven or eight years. Williams was one of them.

"Why were you still in the reserves?" a friend later asked.

"Aw, I don't know," Williams replied. "They gave me some papers one day, something about a discharge, and I put 'em in my back pocket and forgot about 'em."

"You had a choice when World War II ended," Lloyd Merriman, an outfielder for the Cincinnati Reds in the same situation as Williams, says. "You could go into the inactive reserves and go home immediately. Or you could go to China and finish out your tour. I myself didn't want to go to China."

Who did? There were no meetings in the inactive reserves. There were no summer camps. Pilots' names simply were put on a list in a file cabinet somewhere and stayed there. Now, seven and eight years later, the file cabinet suddenly was open, the dust swept away, and the names were being called.

Williams's name was called on January 9, 1952.

He was scheduled for a physical on April 2 at Squantum Naval Air Station, the base where he had signed his name on the enlistment papers the first time. Williams was on a fishing expedition in the Keys, unavailable, when the news broke, but agent Fred Corcoran issued a statement that he said came from Williams: "I'm no different from the next fellow. If Uncle Sam wants me, I'm ready."

There are strong doubts that Williams actually spoke those words, and if he did, Corcoran had his arm twisted well behind his back. Williams was livid. All of the recalled pilots were livid. Their war was behind them. They had survived and bought houses, mowed lawns, lived lives, led the American League in hitting. Now they had to go back? They all felt an unfairness.

It would take five years and the combination of an airplane delay in New Orleans and the typing of a well-lubricated New Orleans sportswriter named Crozet Duplantier to get Williams's true feelings into public print. Thinking he was talking off the record to another former Marine in 1957, introduced to Duplantier by former Marine Hy Hurwitz, Williams blasted the Corps and the "gutless politicians."

"I wouldn't have resented it if they recalled everyone in the same category as myself, but they didn't," Williams said in the New Orleans airport. "They picked on me because I was a ballplayer and widely known. I was at the height of my earning power. I had already served three years. My career was short enough without having it interrupted twice."

Stung by the reaction to his words the next day, especially to the report that he had spit on the ground after mentioning the names of Senator Robert Taft and President Harry Truman, Williams explained that he thought he was off the record and retracted the spit. He did not retract the basic thought.

"I'll tell you about the Marines," he said. "They got the government to appropriate a lot of money. They said they had all the pilots they needed, but needed planes for them. Actually, they had no pilots, so when they got the money, they had to recruit 1,100 guys, including guys like me."

That was how he felt. That was how virtually all of the retread pilots felt.

The news of his recall was greeted with appropriate doom in Boston. A few stories suggested the possibility that he might flunk the physical, due to his elbow operation in '50, but most stories laid out the possibility that his career was finished. He was 33 years old and probably would be 35 if and when he returned. True, Ty Cobb and Honus Wagner and a bunch of other players had played past 35, but Rogers Hornsby was done and Jimmie Foxx was done and Joe Cronin was done. Joe DiMaggio was done.

There was no excess of sentimentality from the typists. Harold Kaese thought he should have been traded.

"The Red Sox might just have won the [coming] 1952 pennant without Williams if they had traded him for players who could have helped them on the field without demoralizing them in the dugout and the clubhouse," Kaese wrote in the *Globe*. "It seems impossible for the Sox to win through the simple expedient of being rid of him. If, by some miracle, they should, there will be no stopping the anti-Williamses, who will make this a city of earaches by shouting from the house-tops, 'I told you so.' "

This was written on the day Williams received his notice.

"As for the baseball writers, their sentiments must be mixed this morning," Kaese finalized. "The Red Sox dressing room will be easier and more pleasant to enter—but will it be worth getting in to?"

Williams decided to move into the season as if nothing were going to happen. If he flunked the physical, fine, he would keep playing. If he passed, he would start flying. He went to spring training on March 1, signed a one-year contract, and worked out and waited. On April 2 he took the physical in Jacksonville, Florida, not Squantum, and passed easily. (An observer noted that the doctors didn't even take time to look at the X-rays of the elbow before they pronounced Williams fit.) He decided to keep playing until he was scheduled to report for active duty.

On April 30 he played what could have been his final game with the Red Sox. Mayor John B. Hynes declared the Wednesday afternoon "Ted Williams Day." A string of gifts were presented, including a set of No. 9 cuff links from the department store Filene's, a Paul Revere bowl from the city, a projector from his teammates, and a memory book from the *Boston Traveler* signed by 400,000 fans. The big gift was a light blue Cadillac from the Red Sox.

(A resolution passed in the Massachusetts State Senate for Ted Williams Day called him "an inspiration not only to the youth of our country, but to the youth of Massachusetts." Dave Egan, ever the sentimentalist, disagreed. "Williams has stubbornly and stupidly refused to recognize this responsibility to childhood," Egan wrote in the *Record*. "The Kid has set a sorry example for a generation of kids. He has been a Pied Piper, leading them along a lonely, bitter road. He has done much harm and now it is one minute before midnight. If this should be his final hour, then he should capitalize on it by apologizing to all boyhood everywhere, and by telling them that the social niceties are of the utmost importance, if only because they raise man above the level of the beast."

The players from the visiting Detroit Tigers and the Red Sox were strung across the field in the formation of a bird's wing. Everyone held hands and sang "Auld Lang Syne." Williams, in the center at home plate, held on to Dominic DiMaggio with his left hand and with his right held the hand of Private Fred Wolfe, an injured Korean War veteran in a wheelchair.

"This is a day I'll always remember," Williams said at the close of his brief, choked remarks to the crowd of 24,764, "and I want to thank you fans, in particular, from the bottom of my heart."

He waved his cap, already in his hand, at the fans in three different directions. In a final, dramatic good-bye, he clocked a two-run home run in his last at bat in the bottom of the seventh off Dizzy Trout to give the Sox a 5–3 win. He did not, no, tip his cap as he went into the dugout.

"It was a good pitch," he explained in the clubhouse, talking about the home run, the perfectionist more than the dramatist. "A curveball, and I hit it pretty well. But the foul ball I hit against Virgil Trucks [in the third] was better."

He went to a party in his honor that night at Jimmy Keefe's, a Boston sports nightspot, and spent the next day preparing to leave for active duty. He had no idea what, exactly, was going to come next.

A story in the *Globe* by Washington reporter Ruth Montgomery estimated that the recall of Williams was going to cost the federal government more than $75,000 per year. In addition to the $50,000 the government was going to lose in taxes from Williams's salary and the $25,000 it was going to lose on taxes from his endorsements, he was going to be paid $608.25 a month.

Montgomery also had a tale about Williams's World War II career. Remember how he had been shipped out for action as the war ended? This apparently was not an incidental matter.

Late in the war, Speaker of the House John W. McCormack, a congressman from South Boston, apparently had asked Marine headquarters in Washington for an appearance by Williams at an Irish event in Boston. A Marine general apparently had spotted the request, called for Williams's file, and discovered that Williams still was in Pensacola.

"We're not running a war to provide any pink teas for congressmen," was the quote from the unnamed general. "Why wasn't this fighter pilot sent into combat long ago?"

That was how Williams wound up in Honolulu the last time. There was no mention whether or not the general was still in charge this time.

W illiams left Boston for Willow Grove Naval Air Station, located outside Philadelphia, on the morning of May 2. Doris kept the Cadillac—the new light blue Cadillac—and headed with Bobby-Jo for Florida and the house in Miami. Williams drove his wife's Ford. He eluded the reporters and photographers at the Hotel Shelton and made a rendezvous with two other recalled Marine pilots.

"He had us meet him at the junction of Routes 9 and 128," Raymond Sisk says. "He'd called me the night before and told me not to come to the hotel because the reporters would be all over the place. I was coming from Medford, and the third guy, Bob Skowcroft, was coming from Needham, so we picked a spot in between.

"It was crazy with the press. I stayed the night before I left at my folks' house. My father spotted a reporter staking out the front door. He was just sitting in a car, and he still was there in the morning. We had to sneak out the back door, sneak to my father's car, and sneak out of there. Then we met Ted, threw my luggage in his car, and we were off."

Sisk had been with Williams in flight training during World War II. They'd met in Chapel Hill and gone along to Bunker Hill and then to Pensacola. In the alphabetical socialization process of the military everywhere, Sisk (S) and Williams (W) were close enough to share a bunch of the same experiences.

"When we first showed up at Pensacola, we were in the same six-man flight group," Sisk says. "We had a second lieutenant in charge of us who was a real son of a bitch. He didn't like Ted. The second lieutenant just had something against Ted because Ted was famous. We'd go up every day and come back, and this guy would be all over us. He'd ream us up one side and down the other. But especially Ted. You could see he was after Ted.

"Finally, after a few days of this, Ted let him have it. He went right after him, nose to nose, this second lieutenant. Ted said, 'You're not going to take it out on these guys just because of me.' He stormed off, went to headquarters.

"So who did they give us to replace this second lieutenant? They give us [baseball player and Ted's friend] Bob Kennedy. It was a lot better after that."

Now, ten years later, Sisk had read about Williams's recall in the newspapers on a Wednesday and told his wife, "Jeez, if they got Ted, they're gonna get me." On that Saturday, his orders had arrived in the mail. He was 30 years old and had the same feelings about the recall that Ted did. He had married and graduated from Boston College Law School in the seven years since he left the service. He also didn't need another war.

"I guess we bitched all the way to Willow Grove," Sisk says. "That would be about right."

The trio stopped for lunch at a diner in North Jersey—Ted signed about 40 autographs—and arrived at the base late in the day. Sisk had taken over the driving because he had been stationed at Willow Grove during the last war and Williams asked him to "just drive by" when they first arrived. He wanted to see if reporters had gathered, because "those Philadelphia writers, they're the worst."

"We drove by and there wasn't a soul at the gate, just the guards," Sisk says. "So we went down a block, made a U-turn, came back, and pulled up at the gate. The writers, the photographers, came from everywhere. I have no idea where they'd been when we went by the first time."

A press conference had been scheduled at headquarters. Williams said, "I already miss my little girl," and "being back in uniform is okay, but I'd rather be playing baseball," and "I'm going to do the best I can." He posed for photographers, changing a Marine Corps recruiting poster that read "Ask the Man Who Was One" over his picture to "Ask the Man Who Is One." When the press conference ended, reporters were told to leave, but one of them followed Williams into the street.

"One more question. . . ."

"Goddamn it, I told you, 'I'm going to do the best I can,' " Williams shouted. "Now get the hell out of here."

The training at Willow Grove was easy, a refresher course on flying. Williams had flown exactly once since he had left the service. The retreads flew the same little SNJs and Corsairs they'd used for training during World War II. They needed 30 hours in the air before moving along to Cherry Point, North Carolina, to fly the new jets.

Old skills seemed to come back easily. Raymond Sisk found his instructor was Joe Durkin, a guy from Boston who had been in his unit during World War II. Durkin told Sisk to sit in the front seat and fly around a little and they could go for coffee. Easy as that.

Williams wound up practicing dogfights with Bill Churchman, a friend from Pensacola in the last war. They flew around and around, each trying to get the upper hand. Churchman lost Williams.

"Where the shit are you?" he asked into the radio.

"Look in your rearview mirror," Williams replied.

The group finished training on May 27 and went to Cherry Point and the jets. Doris came up with Bobby-Jo, and they found an off-base apartment. Bob Kennedy also had been called back, but had left his wife and kids home. Williams invited him to the apartment for a home-cooked dinner.

"Ted's driving in the Ford," Kennedy says. "I'm in the passenger seat.

Bobby-Jo is in between us. I'll remember this forever. She must have been four years old, five. She turns to Ted and says, 'You're right, Daddy. He is a big blue-eyed son of a bitch.' I laughed . . . I couldn't wait to get back to the barracks that night to call my wife and tell her."

Williams stayed at Cherry Point through the rest of the baseball season and into November. The training was all makeup work, learning how to fly the new jets in a hurry. There was none of the physical training from World War II. Williams looked around and felt lucky.

"It's those fat and bald guys who were sitting with soft jobs behind desks I feel sorry for," he said. "They're the ones who are having it tough. I have an idea going through this is plenty rugged for them."

"You were in a different time in your life," Raymond Sisk says. "World War II you'd go up and you'd touch wings with other guys. You'd try to do it. Now it was 'Stay the hell away from me, I'm married and have two kids.' You had more to lose."

Sisk was lucky. The Marines found out he had gone through law school and put him in the Judge Advocate's Corps. Kennedy was lucky. His appeal—married, two kids—was granted. He was sent home. Williams was not lucky.

On November 14 he was given orders to report to the Marine Air Station, El Toro, California, by January 2, 1953, to await his transfer overseas as a replacement. It was reported that he told a friend he thought he was going to die. He was going to Korea.

The mimeographed "Standard Operating Procedures for Tactical Flight Operations for VMF-311" spelled out the dangers in businesslike language. The cartoon squadron logo of a cat, sitting on top of a falling bomb, was on the cover. The cat looked suspiciously like Sylvester, going after Tweetie one more time, but the nonsense stopped on page 1 of the restricted document.

The third item on the page was "103 Survival Equipment."

1. Each pilot will wear on all flights a life vest equipped as follows:
    a. Two (2) dye markers
    b. One (1) shark repellant
    c. Two (2) flares
    d. One (1) whistle
    e. One (1) Vest Type Flashlight

2. In addition to the above, all pilots will if available carry the following minimum of survival gear:
   a. First Aid Kit (Including tourniquet)
   b. Signaling Mirror
   c. Knife (Readily Accessible)
   d. Pistol (w/ammunition)
   e. Compass
   f. Flashlights
3. Bail out bottles are carried in all parachutes.
4. Parachutes, life rafts, and radios are carried in all aircraft.

The fourth item was "104 Escape and Evasion Equipment."

1. Each pilot will have the following items of Escape and Evasion Equipment in his possession on all flights above the bombline.
   a. Cloth Map of Korea
   b. Blood Chit
   c. Pointie Talkie Sheet
   d. Cerise Panel
   e. Barter Kit.

Ted Williams finally had reached a combat situation. He arrived in the first week of February 1953 and was assigned to VMF-311. The V in the designation meant that his squadron flew airplanes. The M meant the pilots were Marines. The F meant they flew fighter planes. VMF-311 had been the first Marine fighter squadron to arrive in Korea and had a fine history. Charles Lindbergh, one of Williams's favorite characters of history, had flown with the squadron as a civilian adviser during World War II.

The base was K-3, one of 55 U.S. air bases now spread across the terrain of South Korea. K-3 was located in P'ohang, a city located in the southeast corner of the peninsula on the Sea of Japan, maybe 50 miles from the big city of Pusan. The Japanese had used the base in World War II, sending Zeros into the air to tangle with U.S. planes. Now the United States was using the same short runway, 6,000 feet, carved onto the top of a hill, to send F-9 Panther jets off toward the north. The area was cold and grim.

"Korea in 1953 was the Old Orient of peasants, low buildings huddled among harsh hills, and a populace that walked or pedaled from here to there and supplemented their meagre wardrobes with surplus military clothing," Senator John Glenn, another pilot in VMF-311, wrote in *John Glenn: A Memoir* to describe the environment. "It was a land of small rice paddies and kimchi, a Korean staple food consisting of cabbage, onion, radishes, and a lot of garlic, left to ferment and solidify. Kimchi literally had an air about it; if you were downwind when someone had the jug open to slice kimchi for the next meal, it wasn't something you'd forget.

"The Koreans wasted nothing. In P'ohang each morning, shuffling men in dark clothes hauled barrels of human excrement to use as fertilizer. About once a week they came to the base to clean out our six-hole outhouse. Officially it was 'night soil' they hauled away, but we called the barrels 'honey buckets,' as if the stench demanded euphemism."

Korea was the first real test of jet warfare. The Air Force had the glamour role, flying the newer, faster F-86 Sabre jets in search of the newer, faster Russian-built Communist MiG-15s, a more than worthy opponent. The Marine fliers, with the slower, less maneuverable F-9 Panthers, were assigned to ground support. The Panthers carried a 3,000-pound bomb load, plus rockets and napalm, and attacked both prescribed targets and whatever unfriendly trucks and equipment and troops they could find.

Pilots would fly as many as three missions a day, crossing what they called "the bombline," the stretch of real estate where the ground war was being fought. The ground war tactics had evolved into a close approximation of World War I, a stationary front with marginal wins and losses every day. Virtual trench warfare. The skies were where the modern battles were being fought.

The F-9 Panther had a reduced fuel capacity and the bombline had moved north, so the VMF-311 fighters had to fly maybe 175 miles, drop their payloads, and fly back, all within an hour and 45 minutes. There wasn't a lot of time. They often had to stop at other bases to refuel.

The big worry was antiaircraft fire. The North was heavily fortified with guns from the Russians, many of which had been captured from the Germans in World War II. So the planes that took off from the former Japanese base were being attacked by former Nazi guns in a battle between present Communism and present Democracy, although present Democracy was on the side of present Korean dictator Syngman Rhee. It all was a fine and deadly geopolitical stew.

Williams was in the middle of it. He lived in a room in a Quonset hut with two other pilots, Jim Mitchell and Lee Scott, his footlocker shoved under his cot in a corner. The highlight of the room was a bathing beauty on a calendar from an auto parts store in Columbus, Ohio.

"Who's from Columbus?" reporter Jim Lucas of the *New York World Telegram* asked on a visit.

"Oh, her," Williams answered. "She was here when I arrived. But I think she's nice. So I keep her. Wouldn't you?"

The standard operating procedure for new pilots was to take two flights over the bombline to familiarize themselves with their planes and with the topography before they went into actual combat on their third flight. The new men were at the most risk the way this war was being played out, bombing runs conducted by seniority first. By the time the new men dived toward the target, the antiaircraft guns had had time to adjust. The new men had to be ready.

Williams took his two flights for familiarization, then went into combat on the third. And was almost killed.

The raid was a big one. The Allies sent 200 planes to attack a Communist troop and supply center in Kyiomipo, 15 miles south of Pyongyang, the North Korean capital, on Monday, February 16, 1953. The distance was so great for VMF-311 that the fliers were scheduled to land for fuel on the way back at K-13, the Air Force base at Suwon, outside Seoul, closer to the bombline.

Williams, filled with the mixture of excitement and nervousness of a new man, followed the plan of attack. He dropped from the sky at the prescribed time, dove lower than the 2,000 feet necessary to drop his bombs, let them go, and pulled back on his controls and felt great as the plane followed his command. He had passed his first test, gone through the enemy fire, and come out the other side.

Then the trouble began.

The light indicator said his wheels were down.

What is this? he wondered.

He hit the appropriate controls. The wheels came back up.

Then the stick started to shake in his hand.

What is this?

He tried to call one of the other pilots, but the radio was dead.

What?

He had been hit. He hadn't felt a thing, no explosion, no sound, no bump or jostle, but something had hit his plane someplace somewhere.

The particulars of his situation came through his head in a flash: he was flying a wounded plane over hostile territory, 15 miles no less from the capital of North Korea. He decided at first to abort all original flight plans and head for the Yellow Sea, where he could ditch the plane and be rescued. This was what the "Standard Operating Procedure" suggested.

1100. Search and Rescue Operations

1. Each pilot should carry pertinent S&R information with him on every hop. This information is covered at every Group Briefing.
2. Although it isn't possible to cover all that a pilot should do when forced down because of variations of the situation, these are some general rules that should normally be followed:
   a. If possible, get out over the water (except in cold weather) or away from the target area.
   b. Try to call and give the nature of your trouble, the extent of injuries if any, and your intentions before ejecting or landing.
   c. After landing, try to signal your condition to the ResCap and then hide until the helicopter arrives.
   d. Try to be near a clear area at least 100 feet in diameter so that the helicopter can land.

Williams almost immediately changed that. He found a couple of problems with the SOP. First, this *was* the winter, and the Yellow Sea had big chunks of ice floating in it, and a human being dropped into that water would not last very long. Second, he did not want to eject from his plane. The ejection seat was part of the new equipment for this new jet war. The first-generation ejection seats so far had not worked very well.

Williams, at six-foot-three, was only one inch shy of the maximum requirement for a fighter pilot. He filled the cockpit, stuffed it. Previous pilots who had ejected had suffered broken legs, broken backs, other serious injuries. Williams felt, big as he was, that his legs would be gone if he ejected. He surely didn't want that.

Hurtling through the air, first actual combat mission, he was left with life-and-death choices. What to do? The loner was as alone as he ever had been.

Or was he?

Flying behind him was a 22-year-old pilot from VMF-311 named Larry Hawkins. Hawkins, from Pine Grove, Pennsylvania, was a veteran in this war and in the F-9 Panther. The call-up of the retreads had created a curious situation in Korea. The most experienced pilots were the young pilots. The old-timers, called back, had learned how to fly in the old propeller-driven antiques of World War II, then had been hurried into the jets seven years later. The young pilots had grown up with the jets from the beginning.

Hawkins was as young as a fighter pilot could be. He'd joined the Marines two days after graduation from high school as an enlisted man, then applied for OCS and the flight school. He was coming through the pipeline just when the Korean War started. His mother, who didn't like the idea, had to be convinced to sign a release form so he could receive his wings under the age of 21.

He already had flown between 40 and 60 of the 111 missions he would fly during the war. He was used to the cold of the cockpit of the Panther, the cabin pressure maddeningly low. He was used to landing on fumes, the tanks almost empty from the long trip back from the bombline. He was used to the peculiarities of his job.

All of his personal deals with danger had been made. Danger was danger. It simply was there. He had seen planes drop from the sky on fire. In one of them he had seen the pilot, good guy, couldn't remember his name but everybody called the guy Cornpone, struggling with the ejection equipment. The fur collar on Cornpone's bomber jacket had become caught in the Plexiglas canopy. The seat never ejected. The plane and pilot went straight into the sea.

Things happened. Four Marine pilots, only a couple of weeks earlier, had flown into a mountain, everyone keyed into the group leader's radio, everyone dead. Hawkins by now was bold enough to throw himself into the flak, machine guns firing, the smell of cordite in his nose, but experienced enough to watch for irregularities that could happen at any moment.

He saw an obvious irregularity with Williams's plane. It was going the wrong way.

"I didn't know who it was, because I didn't know Ted then," Hawkins says. "I just saw this plane heading north. Our evacuation route was toward the Yellow Sea, but he was heading toward Pyongyang. This wasn't good. Get up around Pyongyang, and that's where all the big antiaircraft stuff was. Dug in. That was the capital."

Hawkins peeled away and followed Williams. He tried unsuccessfully to establish radio contact, then flew close for a visual check. He flew below, around, and on top of Williams's plane looking for damage. He saw a liquid being discharged that he thought was hydraulic fluid. He flew close to Williams and signaled by hand for Williams to follow him. Williams signaled back. Hawkins turned them west toward the coast and an eventual route south, back toward Suwon.

. "I've got a wounded duck," he radioed to his commander.

Williams flew on the left side. Hawkins watched him closely. Small puffs of smoke continued to come from the back of Williams's plane. They worried Hawkins. If this were hydraulic fluid, it should be gone by now. Why wasn't it gone? Maybe it was something else. Wait, was it fuel? Had to be. Either the main fuel cell or one of the fuel lines had been hit.

This increased the problem. A fuel leak meant the possibility of fire. The biggest worry was that if the fuel pooled at the bottom of the engine, the plane would blow up. The way to stop the pooling was to fly higher and faster. Hawkins took Williams up to 25,000 feet, and they zipped through the sky.

Everything was improvised. Hawkins was thinking as he flew. How did a 22-year-old pilot know all this stuff?

"I'd paid attention," he says. "I'd studied the books."

Finally, the pair reached the sky over K-13 in Suwon. The other planes already had landed. Hawkins led Williams into a circling pattern, the standard beginning to a flameout landing. They were down to 7,500 feet when Hawkins gave the signal for Williams to drop his wheels. The wheel-doors opened, and the plane caught on fire.

Hawkins was right. This was fuel. The reduction in speed had caused the fuel to pool in the wheel wells. The fuel was catching on fire.

"You're on fire!" Hawkins yelled into the radio. "Eject!"

Williams's radio, of course, did not work.

"Eject," Hawkins nevertheless yelled.

Williams already had rejected that idea. He had heard the sound of the fire igniting in the back of the plane. At least he had heard something. He kept his wheels down and continued to spiral toward the field. He had decided to crash-land.

"He's on fire and he's coming in," Hawkins yelled over the radio to the tower.

The landing strip at K-13 was 11,000 feet long. If all this had been happening at Williams's home base, K-3, with its 6,000-foot strip, there would have been no chance for survival. He would have been dead.

He cleared a fence and hit the far end of the runway at over 200 miles an hour and began to slide. He clamped his foot down hard on the brakes. Flames and sparks and pieces of the plane flew off around him. He could see people running out of his way. He could see people in the Korean village at the end of the runway getting out of the way.

He slid for maybe 9,000 feet, off toward the left. And stopped.

"I was right after him," Hawkins says. "I had my wheels down, my flaps down, and as I went past I could see this tall figure getting out of the cockpit as fast as he could. I think he was getting out before the plane ever stopped. Because he was afraid the plane was going to blow."

The plane did not blow. There was not enough fuel left.

The leftfielder for the Boston Red Sox was alive and well.

The news of Williams's escape was big not only in Boston but around the country. "Williams Crashes Jet, Walks Away Uninjured," the *Globe* said on the front page. An accompanying story from the Associated Press was headlined " 'Golly, I'm Glad He's Safe,' Says Ted's Wife, in Miami."

"It's enough to scare you to death," Doris said. "I think it's awful. It's an awful close call—too close. And he just got there!"

Bobby-Jo had heard the news first on television. She'd called Doris into the living room, "Mommy, there's something about Daddy on TV!" That was how Doris heard the news.

"I ran into the living room," Doris said. "But I only heard the end of it."

Williams, back at K-3, described the crash for the AP the next day. He already had flown another mission safely in the morning.

"When I stopped at the air base again today the operations officer told me the plane I crash landed yesterday was really clobbered and full of holes," he said. "They [the Communists] hit me in a good spot. They put my plane out of commission and they almost put me out of commission, too."

Woody Woodbury, another pilot, later to gain a measure of fame as a comedian and the game-show host replacing Johnny Carson on *Who Do You Trust?*, probably had a better view of the crash than anyone. Even Williams. Flying one of the F-9 Panthers that landed before Williams did, Woodbury had figured out from the radio messages what was going to happen. Ted Williams was going to crash-land! Woodbury pulled up a front-row seat.

"When you landed, there was a truck that had a sign that said 'Follow Me' in big letters," he says. "The truck was going to lead you to a spot a long way from the active runway. I gave the guy a signal that there was something wrong with my plane—and there wasn't—and I pulled over to the side on the taxiway. I wanted to see what was going to happen."

Sure enough, the Panther with number 19 on the tail, Williams's plane, came over the fence at the end of the field and hit the runway and started skidding. Woodbury watched it all come toward him, the debris and the smoke and the flames. It stopped no more than 60 yards away. He watched Williams climb out.

"I can see it all in my mind right now," Woodbury says. "Ted pops out and he's moving away from the plane in a hurry. A staff car had pulled up. An old, old green Plymouth. A guy got out, a colonel, and he was holding a piece of paper. Ted goes up and salutes. The colonel salutes back and hands Ted the piece of paper."

Woodbury asked Williams a few days later what had happened. They were flying together on a transport plane.

"Why'd the colonel hand you the paper?" Woodbury asked.

"I just got my ass blown off," Williams replied. "I'm fucken lucky to be here. And this guy asked me for my fucken autograph!"

He was Ted Williams, even when he almost had been killed. That was inescapable fact. He was the .400 hitter. He was the MVP, the shoulda-been MVP, the All-Star, the guy who tagged the eephus pitch. He was the news.

Lloyd Merriman, the outfielder for the Cincinnati Reds, also was in VMF-311. He also had a spectacular crash a few weeks later. Hit by antiaircraft fire during a raid, now coming into the short landing strip at K-3, he had no hydraulics system, which meant no brakes. The ground crew had rigged a wire across the field so he could hook on, as if he were landing on an aircraft carrier. Merriman, another World War II retread with a wife and two kids, had never practiced this kind of landing very much. He came in too fast, missed the wire and kept going.

"Okay," he said, "I'll just go back up, come around, and try it again."

His speed, alas, had dropped to 120 knots. He needed 150 knots to become airborne again. He didn't have them. The plane hit the ground at the end of the runway and went into the rice fields beyond. One rice field. Two rice fields. Three rice fields. He stopped in the fourth rice field after breaking through three levees. The plane broke in half. Merriman climbed out unhurt, but smelly.

"The canopy had blown off," Merriman says. "And all those rice fields had been heavily fertilized. The cockpit was filled with fertilizer when I climbed out."

The fire truck came. Other trucks. The ambulance.

"You're okay," the medics said.

"Thanks," Merriman said.

"Could you do us one favor, though?"

"Sure."

"You're supposed to ride back in the ambulance, but could you, uh, ride in the back of a pickup truck instead?"

There were crashes everywhere. Jerry Coleman of the New York Yankees, the third of the three recalled baseball pilots in Korea, sustained a fierce crash in a Corsair. Carrying a full bomb load, his plane's engine failed. He crash-landed. The bombs somehow did not explode, but the Corsair flipped and Coleman almost strangled on the straps of his helmet. John Glenn, the future astronaut and senator, was hit three times in his first ten missions and was given the nickname Magnet Ass. Every day, every other day, every third day, something happened to somebody.

The crash that was remembered, though, was Williams's crash. He was the news. There never before had been anything like this in American popular history. There had been military heroes and there had been athletic heroes and there had been athletes who had become military heroes, but there never had been such a high-profile mix. The biggest names almost always had drawn the softest military assignments. None had been involved in such a moment of danger and, okay, adventure.

The crash put Williams into a separate category of folk hero. A category of one. If the 1946 World Series forever tagged him with the image of the me-first personal achiever, the crash at K-13 in the F-9 Panther jet more than compensated. He had his own trump card.

Who had done what Ted Williams did?

Not Babe Ruth. Not Cobb. Not DiMaggio. Not Joe Louis. Not Red Grange. Not anyone.

The emotions and achievements of sport are artificial. They are meaningful, as meaningful as can be, because man gives them value, says they are important. They are still fantasy, artificial. The worst defeat, bad as it may feel, is not in the same universe as the news that can be delivered in one sentence in a cancer ward. The greatest athletic accomplishment, no matter what it might be, can do no more than bring a momentary smile to a lot of faces. It changes nothing.

The athletic hero, while worthy of all the kind words and polished trophies, is an artificial hero. The real hero operates in a real world, usually a common man showing uncommon bravery or reactions in a moment of peril.

What happened to Ted Williams on that landing strip at K-13 on that February afternoon brought him to a different level of public veneration. The artificial and the real were married. There was no asterisk after his name on any list of American heroes.

Williams slipped into the daily life of VMF-311 and K-3. The big social scene was at the O Club. The Japanese had left behind some corrugated-tin huts. Various clubs had sprung up at various huts. The O Club was for the pilots. They drank beer, played cards, shot dice, bullshit with great regularity, and sang songs. Sandbags on top of the tin roof kept it from blowing away into the Korean night.

"We had a piano," Woody Woodbury says. "John Glenn got together the money, and he and I went to Japan on R&R and bought the piano. John Glenn shepherded that baby all the way back."

Woodbury was the piano player. He improvised songs like "I Always Wanted Wings Until I Got the God Damn Things" and "Cruisin' Down the Yalu Doin' 680." He became so famous in the tin hut that he was asked to fly to Seoul to put on a show for troops.

"I flew up with him, two planes," Lloyd Merriman says. "I guess the theory was that if something happened to one of us on the way, the other one could come back and describe what it was."

Williams joined the crowd now and then, but spent more time away from the noise. He read books. He wrote letters. He fell in love with photography. He hunted ducks. He hunted ducks a lot.

"I'd finished my missions, but the Marine Corps kept me at K-3 as a chief warrant officer," Edro Buchser says. "That meant I was the sheriff of the place. I had my own canvas tent, away from everyone. I had my own jeep. I had my own men, who I sent out on patrol. I told them to look for North Korean spies and for ducks."

Buchser was a longtime hunter from Kentucky. He had bought a shotgun on *his* R&R trip to Japan. He'd added a couple more by various means. He'd collected a bunch of guns, in fact, not the least of which was a Thompson submachine gun he had in the back of the jeep. Buchser was the man in the know and the man in charge of hunting ducks.

Williams soon opened the flap to Buchser's tent. A nice friendship was formed.

"We shot a lot of ducks," Buchser says. "We did this mainly because my men had been out and we knew where the ducks were. They were mallards, just like the ducks back home. We'd sometimes, Ted and me, kill 100 ducks a day between us. He was the better duck hunter, so I'd say he killed three for every two that I'd kill.

"We'd give the ducks sometimes to the peasants, because they needed food to eat. Sometimes we'd bring them back and have them cleaned at the mess, and we'd put on a big duck dinner for all the officers. We must have done that about three times."

Fishing was a possibility, but the water was a distance away and the territory was a little sketchy with "spies" and you needed a boat, and so the expedition would take an entire day. Hunting was easy. You could just go and hunt for an hour. Partridge were in the fields. Deer too, except they were small. Looked like little dogs. Ducks were the best.

Mostly, Williams and Buchser went alone. They enjoyed each other's company. They spoke the same four-letter language. They liked the same things. Woody Woodbury, who was one of Buchser's roommates, came along one day and didn't appreciate the solitude of the task. He seemed too noisy. Buchser grabbed Woodbury's fatigue cap and threw it into the air. Williams shot it, both barrels. The pieces of the hat floated down to the ground.

"I went duck hunting with Ted once," Lloyd Merriman says. "I wasn't much of a duck hunter, don't even know if I shot one all day. What I remember is that Ted could see those ducks. He'd point and say, 'There they are.' I couldn't see anything. He'd start counting them off. I still couldn't see anything."

News came down one day that a certain General McGee wanted to go duck hunting with Buchser and Williams. What do you do when a general calls? You ask what time he wants to go.

The general, who arrived with his own shotgun, turned out to be a good guy, an older hunter from Virginia. His aide, a major, also arrived. Turned out to be some Ivy Leaguer from Harvard or someplace. Not a good guy. An asshole.

The hunters spread out in separate blinds. Buchser was at one end of the line. The general and major were in the middle. Williams was at the other end. The ducks appeared in the sky. The major jumped up and shouted, "There they are, General. Shoot 'em." The ducks flew away.

"We told the major you couldn't do that," Buchser says. "I don't think he listened. Ted was really pissed off."

The ducks appeared again. The major jumped up again. "General, there they are. Shoot 'em." The ducks disappeared again.

Silence.

Williams stood up. He was holding his shotgun.

"Major," he said, "if you do that again, I'll blow your fucken head off."

"The general got all upset at that," Buchser says. "He made Ted go sit in the jeep. That was the end of Ted's hunting for the day. Ted was all upset."

Buchser worried about his friend's temper. Buchser had been in the Marines long enough to know the points where a man had to shut up and swallow. Williams didn't seem to know.

In the O Club one night he became involved with a bird colonel in a big argument about Korea and the U.S. presence and the war. Williams said all the things that all the pilots wanted to say, about how the war was unfair, that they were fighting with one arm tied behind their backs, that they should be able to chase the North Koreans into China or Manchuria or wherever the North Koreans went. The rules were stupid.

"Old Ted was just booming it all out," Buchser says. "I was kicking him under the table, hard, trying to get him to stop. I thought he was going to get a court-martial."

Reporters would arrive every now and then, trying to interview the famous baseball player. He talked to most of them, but threatened bodily harm to the one who woke him up at three in the morning in search of a few snappy comments. There were a few other star-turn differences— Williams was invited to a reception for Adlai Stevenson, for instance, during one R&R trip to Japan (didn't go)—but mostly he was left alone. He was part of the group.

"We gave one baseball clinic," Lloyd Merriman says. "The field was terrible, full of rocks. We showed some enlisted men a few things about hitting."

Williams interested Buchser in photography, convincing him to "get rid of that piece-of-shit camera" and buy a knockoff Japanese version of a Leica. They went around in Buchser's jeep, taking pictures of the local population. They carried pistols in case the local population had different political sentiments about U.S. troops. Buchser always had a walkie-talkie to call for help if needed.

Buchser took Williams into the neighborhood at the edge of the base filled with houses of prostitution. The houses were all posted with OFF LIMITS signs and were patrolled regularly by Buchser's men. One of the establishments had a swinging door on the front, like a saloon from the Old West. Buchser took a picture of Ted, squatting down, trying to look under the swinging door.

"Ted liked women," Buchser says. "Not in those places, but Ted liked women. He didn't drink or play cards or hang around a lot, but women were something that stirred his interest."

There was a M*A*S*H quality of absurdity to it all. Fly a bombing run in the morning. Shoot ducks in the afternoon. Go to visit nurses on a day off. Vacation in Japan every five weeks. Buchser knew a nurse from his hometown at an Air Force base, K-2, maybe 45 miles away. He arranged to make a trip to K-2 on business, called the nurse, and told her he was bringing a friend, Ted Williams, the baseball player. Maybe she could find a nurse for Ted?

"This captain heard we were coming," Buchser says. "So he arranged a big party, honoring Ted. Oh, Ted was really mad at that. Steaming."

Williams had one more combat adventure when he was hit by a large rock during a bombing run. The explosions from the bombs of the previous plane had sent the rock as high as 2,500 feet in the air, knocking a perfect hole in the fuselage of Williams's plane. He landed without incident. There was another scare when his rockets were late in firing and shot across the front of some surprised fellow pilots, but otherwise the missions went smoothly.

Williams had developed medical problems, though, which often kept him grounded. His shaky respiratory system did not like the constant cold. He was hospitalized for 22 days for pneumonia early in his tour on the USS *Haven*, a naval hospital ship. He came back, flew some more, but had problems with his ears and nose. The lack of good pressurization in the F-9 Panther inflamed his eustachian tubes at high altitudes. He had earaches, sinus problems.

"A lot of the older guys had those problems," Larry Hawkins says. "If you were over 30, the lack of pressurization killed you."

After five and a half months, 39 missions, the problems getting worse rather than better, Williams was given an early release from combat. There were pilots on the K-3 base who thought he was being given a release simply for being Ted Williams, public relations. Maybe they were right, maybe wrong, but he did have problems with his ears at altitude.

That was fact. He told reporters that perhaps his impaired hearing would help against the wolves in leftfield.

On July 1, 1953, he was sent home.

He was preceded by a path of newspaper clippings pondering his future. When would he be released? Some said he would be in the Marines until August, some said until October, out for the rest of the '53 season. Some said he might be released on a medical discharge when he reached the States. What would he do? What could he do? Would he want to play immediately? Could he play immediately? He was approaching his 35th birthday in August. How much could be left? This would be his third comeback, if you counted the return from his broken elbow in 1950. How many comebacks were too many?

He stopped in Japan. He stopped in Honolulu. He arrived at Moffett Field in northern California on July 9. Arthur Sampson of the *Boston Traveler* reached him as he went to a press conference. Sampson was one of the Boston writers Williams liked. Williams dictated his own long paragraph about his feelings to Sampson:

> The Kid is back home. He had 39 combat missions overseas. He's going to try to get to that hospital in Oakland sometime before the afternoon is over. He's happy to see the Sox doing so well. He'd like to see the All-Star Game. He'd like to play baseball again if he can. If he can't he'd like to go fishing or something. And that's all there is to it so far as I know it as of this moment.

He was shipped to Bethesda Naval Hospital in Maryland for treatment, but was indeed allowed to attend the All-Star Game in Cincinnati on July 14, where he was greeted as a returning hero. He threw out the first ball to Roy Campanella, the catcher for the Brooklyn Dodgers, bantered with ballplayers, received a standing ovation. In a pregame interview he drew a laugh when he mistakenly called the American League dugout "the cockpit." Yogi Berra of the Yankees asked him if he had seen Jerry Coleman in Korea.

"Nope," Williams replied. "I never saw him, but I heard he was doing a great job. The last I heard he was down in the boondocks somewhere. I'd enjoy this more if he and all the other fellows over there were here with me."

The activity in Korea was winding down. Coleman would fly 63 missions before he left. Lloyd Merriman would fly 87. Edro Buchser, the duck hunter, would stay at K-3 almost until the end of the war. The peace treaty called for a cessation of hostilities on July 27 at 19:10 hours, military time. On that afternoon, VMF-311 flew a maximum mission into the north, bombing the Communists one last time. Captain Bill Armagost of VMF-311 flew the last jet mission of the war 35 minutes before the cease-fire began.

Why would the Allies do that?

"I was gone by then," Buchser says, "but I talked later to some of the boys who went on that raid. I guess the thinking was that they [the Communists] had killed some of us, so we'd go kill some more of them while we still had a chance."

On July 28, one day after the cease-fire, Williams was discharged from the barracks of the U.S. Naval Gun Factory in Washington, D.C. He headed straight for Boston.

George Sullivan, the 15-year-old batboy from 1949, now was George Sullivan, the 19-year-old aspiring sportswriter. He was a sophomore at Boston University, but also had a job at the *Cambridge Chronicle*. He was writing a column called "I Was a Big League Batboy," wisely using the contacts he had made at Fenway to get his new career moving.

On July 28, he had scheduled a coup. He had arranged an interview with Tom Yawkey, who seldom talked to anybody in the press for the record. Yawkey remembered Sullivan as a batboy and said he'd be pleased to talk with him.

"That morning, though, I pick up the paper and there's a headline, 'Williams Expected Back,' " Sullivan says. "I knew he'd been at the All-Star Game a few days earlier, and I knew this would be a big day if he came back to Fenway. I called Yawkey's office and asked if he wanted to postpone the interview. Yawkey's secretary asked him and he said, 'No, no, come on in.' "

Sullivan was sitting in Yawkey's office when Williams came back from Korea. He watched the warm reunion, team owner and team star, shaking hands and hugging. He listened to their conversation putting the missing year and a half into place. He was amazed at what happened next.

"Why don't you go down and hit a few?" Yawkey suggested.

"Nah, I'm tired," Williams said. "I just flew up from Washington."

"Come on."

"Nah. I haven't hit in a long time."

"Come on."

"Nah. I don't think so."

"They were like two little kids," Sullivan says. "Yawkey was really excited. He really wanted to see Ted hit. Ted . . . you knew he wanted to do it, but he had to be talked into it. They went back and forth, and finally Ted said, 'Oh, all right,' and went down to the clubhouse to put on a uniform."

Sullivan "made a beeline" to the batting cage to get a good position. He knew what almost nobody else knew in the park. He waited to see what would happen.

"The gates hadn't been opened yet," he says. "The Red Sox were in the cage, and some of the players from the other team were throwing on the sidelines. The only people in the park were the concession kids and the ushers, maybe 200, 300 people total. When Williams came out, though, there was a roar. You would have thought you were in Yankee Stadium. Everything just stopped. Everybody was watching."

The batting practice pitcher was Paul Schreiber, who had roomed with Williams for the '47 season on the road, Williams's last roommate. Williams stepped up to the plate, limbered up, asked Schreiber to start throwing. Sullivan's face was against the net of the cage, his hands on the metal bar. He was no more than three feet away from Williams.

"He hit a few balls," Sullivan says. "Maybe as many as six, maybe as few as two, I don't remember, but it wasn't a lot. Then he started hitting the home runs."

One.

Two.

Three.

"Throw the fucken ball," Williams shouted as even Schreiber turned to watch the balls go into the stands.

Four.

Five.

"Don't wait. Throw it."

Six.

"Throw the son of a bitch!"

Seven.

Eight.

Nine.

Sullivan had been counting in his head. The 200, 300 people were going crazy. Nine home runs in a row! He looked at Williams's hands, gripping the bat. Blood was running through his fingers and onto the knob. His soft hands already had ripped open. He walked out of the cage, straight to the dugout. Nine home runs in a row.

"It was the greatest thing I'd ever seen," Sullivan says. "I don't care if it's Little League, nine balls over the fence in a row! I was so excited that I skipped school the next day to be back at the park to see what he would do next."

The results weren't nearly as impressive. A bigger crowd had gathered, including all the sportswriters. Williams's tender hands were hurting. He wore a pair of golf gloves, which had been given to him by Claude Harmon, the golfer. He didn't put on the same show.

He did, however, have an observation. He saw general manager Joe Cronin for the first time in the midst of his swings.

"Hey, Joe," he said. "What'd you do to the fucken plate while I was gone?"

"What do you mean?" Cronin asked.

"It's crooked."

Cronin brought in a surveyor in the next few days. Home plate was off an inch. The problem was corrected.

Ted Williams was home from the war.

9 Boston

It is often said that Williams could have been another Ruth except for his vicious personality, but there is not the slightest truth to this canard, for Williams could have been only a substitute for the Babe and a poor one at that. He lacks the ability that the Babe had and lacks it in every department, including that of batting. . . . I've gone thirty years without using the word, but now that the word has come into polite usage by the gutter tactics of our great man, I shall say that Babe Ruth could spit farther than [Ted Williams] can hit a ball and that there is no basis for comparison between the two even in the one department in which Williams has won shameful fame.

DAVE EGAN, *BOSTON RECORD*, AUGUST 10, 1956

Things had changed with the Red Sox while Ted Williams was away at the war. The little corner of the Fenway Park clubhouse he once inhabited with Doerr, DiMaggio, and Pesky now had new residents. Williams's neighbors now were Ted Lepcio, Dick Gernert, and Billy Consolo. Kids.

The Red Sox had gone for a youth movement.

"I graduated from Seton Hall in 1951," Lepcio, a shortstop, says. "So I was late reporting. It was June and I was going to the minor leagues. The problem was that this was a very good year in the Red Sox farm system. Every team in the farm system was in either first or second place, except for Louisville, the Triple A team, which was having problems.

"The Red Sox didn't want to break up the combinations on any of those winning teams, so they thought it over and said, 'Why not send him to Triple A?' So I went to Louisville, straight out of college. I did okay, and in February of '52 the team brought 25 prospects, including me, down to Sarasota to get a look at 'the Red Sox of the Future.' These were guys who were going to play in three or four years.

"The first day, though, the news came down that Bobby Doerr had retired. It was like a shock wave. Everything changed. There were meetings everywhere. It was like now they were looking for players to play right away. One year out of college, I made the Boston Red Sox."

Doerr had retired at age 34 with a chronically bad back. The game had become too uncomfortable to play. The Red Sox, with new manager Lou Boudreau, decided this was the beginning of the end for the present roster, the time to take a look at the future. They decided to get the replacements ready in a hurry.

In June 1952, a month after Williams left for Korea, they put the 32-year-old Pesky in a package with Walter Dropo, Bill Wight, Fred Hatfield, and Don Lenhardt for Dizzy Trout, George Kell, Johnny Lipon, and Hoot Evers. ("Broke my heart," Pesky says. "It was never the same.") In the spring of 1953, Dominic DiMaggio quit. Always proud, always with a sense of business, quiet and tough, would have been better than his brother if he had his brother's size, DiMaggio walked away when he felt the team no longer had confidence in him. He was 35.

"I'd told Joe Cronin five years earlier that if I had the ability to be in centerfield and I wasn't there, I'd be out of here so fast your head will spin," DiMaggio says. "I'd hit .294 a year earlier, and they were talking about this kid, Gene Stephens. He was a nice kid, a likable kid, but he couldn't hit. I said, 'I'll bet you $1,000 he won't hit 210.' And he didn't. He hit .206.

"The Red Sox just let me walk off. They didn't try to trade me, anything. To this day, I still can't figure it out. I had value and they let me just leave."

All of this left Williams with the kids.

The 1953 Opening Day lineup had only one player from the 1952 Opening Day lineup, Jimmy Piersall, 23 years old, and he had been switched from shortstop to rightfield. Kids. They came in a production line of promise and press clippings through Williams's last seven seasons, Piersall and Tommy Umphlett and Stephens and Marty Keough and Don Buddin and Milt Bolling and Norm Zauchin and Harry Agganis and Ken Aspromonte and Carroll Hardy and even Pumpsie Green, the first African

American player on the last team to have an African American player. They were 22, 23, 24 years old, coming through, trying and mostly failing.

Williams would look around him and see all kinds of kids. Lepcio was 23 years old in 1953; Gernert was 24. Consolo was the youngest kid of all. He was 18.

He came to the Red Sox straight out of Dorsey High School in Los Angeles. The major leagues had a new rule, designed to keep signing bonuses down. If a player signed for a bonus of over $4,000, he had to immediately be put on the big-league roster and had to stay there for two seasons. Consolo had signed for $60,000. He was on the roster. He never played much, finished with a .220 career batting average, but for the next six seasons he watched every move this guy Williams made in the clubhouse.

He had a very good seat.

"Ted comes back from Korea, walks in the room," Consolo says. "I didn't know who he was when he came through the door, but I knew he was someone. They had all the big cameras then. Not television cameras, those big newspaper cameras. The photographers are all following him, snapping flashbulbs. He poses here. He poses there. They take out his uniform. He poses with the uniform.

"His uniform! You made the major leagues those days, you got two sets of whites and two sets of grays. Maybe Johnny Orlando asks you for your waist size. That's it. Ted! They pull out seven or eight white uniforms. Mr. McAuliffe, the guy who provided the uniforms, was even there. Seven or eight pairs of pants. Seven or eight shirts. Here comes this little Italian tailor into the room. Nobody ever had seen him before. He starts measuring the uniforms on Ted! It's like Ted's getting a tuxedo! His uniforms were custom-tailored. He didn't like anything around the neck—the no necktie thing—so every shirt was cut lower. Just for Ted."

Bats . . .

"Ted tells Johnny Orlando, 'Johnny, let's get going. Get me 24 bats from Louisville for tomorrow,' " Consolo says. "I'm thinking, this is crazy. There's no way those bats can get here from Louisville that quick. Next day, two big boxes are in front of his locker. Two dozen bats. I can't believe it. Ted takes out this little weighing machine, this scale. He opens the boxes and starts studying the bats. He weighs them, looks at the wood, grips them like Arnold Palmer on the tee.

"He'd say, 'This bat is no good,' and he'd throw it on the floor. Wood

Ted *(left)* his mother, May, and brother, Danny. [Sporting News]

Ted, in a portrait taken by his photographer father, Sam.
[Sporting News]

May *(guitar, glasses)* with the Salvation Army band. Ted forever hated that part of his mother's life. [Sporting News]

Danny, the brother who took the other road. [May Williams Collection]

EVENING TRIBUNE
SAN DIEGO, CALIFORNIA
Tuesday, Mar. 29, 1960 a-23

D. A. Williams, 39, Kin of Ted, Dies

Daniel Arthur Williams, 39, brother of Ted Williams, the big league baseball player, died last night in Mercy Hospital after a long illness.

Mr. Williams lived at 4121 Utah St., North Park. He was a painter and decorator but had been disabled the last 2½ years.

The hospital said death was from a malignancy of the bone marrow. He had been in and out of the hospital, entering there the last time Wednesday.

Besides his brother, Theodore Samuel Williams, 41, the Boston Red Sox outfielder, Mr. Williams leaves his widow, Betty Jean, and two sons. They are Samuel, 9, and John Theodore, 8.

He also is survived by his mother, Mrs. May Williams, a widow who is a member of the Salvation Army.

Mr. Williams was born and reared in San Diego.

Funeral arrangements are pending at Benbough Mortuary.

DANIEL WILLIAMS
Native San Diegan

J. Monjo of Coronado, and 11 grandchildren.

Private services are pending at Coronado Mortuary. Cremation is planned.

Jesse N. Douglas

The tallest kid in the back is the one who would become famous from the
1936 Hoover High baseball team. [San Diego Hall of Champions]

Breaking in as a pitcher with
the Padres: an idea that didn't
last long. [San Diego Hall of
Champions]

Life in exile in Minneapolis. The message was to "grow up," but don't change that swing. [Jerry Romolt]

The grip would stay the same.
[BOSTON PUBLIC LIBRARY]

Confident rookie, 1939.
[BOSTON PUBLIC LIBRARY]

New man finally can read his stats
in *The Sporting News*. [RED SOX]

"Meathead" and "Sport," Ted and player-manager Joe Cronin. [Boston Public Library]

Photography, gadgets, always would be interesting. [Boston Public Library]

The first game of 1942. Joe DiMaggio *(left)* is back from his 56-game hitting streak in 1941. Ted *(center)* is back from hitting .406. Dominic DiMaggio is brother of one, friend and teammate of the other. [BETTMANN/CORBIS]

Going . . . going . . .
yes, gone. [RED SOX]

Safe. Jim Hegan is the catcher. [RED SOX]

The Colonel, Dave Egan, Ted's nemesis.
[BOSTON HERALD]

Fishing during '41. Escaping the
rigors of the chase for .400.
[Red Sox]

Jimmy Foxx and Ted, caught in
the stern obligations of celebrity.
[Boston Public Library]

Induction physical for World
War II. [Boston Public Library]

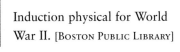

Taking the oath.
[BOSTON PUBLIC
LIBRARY]

Saying good-byes. [RED SOX]

The "Baseball Squad" from Amherst. Ted
and Johnny Sain are in the back. Johnny
Pesky, an unidentified officer, Buddy Gremp,
and Joe Coleman are in the front. [RED SOX]

The hand-eye coordination had not left. [BOSTON PUBLIC LIBRARY]

Ted and the Babe, exhibition at Fenway during World War II. [RED SOX]

Graduation and marriage to Doris Soule, all on the same Pensacola day. [Associated Press]

Back! A pennant in 1946. [Boston Public Library]

Ted with necktie, a rare picture. Look on Red Sox GM Eddie Collins's face shows how rare. [Red Sox]

Hitting that other white ball in exhibition with Babe Didrikson Zaharias. [Red Sox]

Ted and kids: always a combination. [RED SOX]

Mickey McDermott, explorer of late-night culture. [RED SOX]

This big! Fish story with Eddie Collins and Joe Cronin. [BOSTON PUBLIC LIBRARY]

Fishing exhibition at Jamaica Pond. [BOSTON PUBLIC LIBRARY]

Tying flies, showing the results to
Doris. [Associated Press]

Looking—belatedly—at daughter,
Bobby-Jo. [Boston Public Library]

Batting practice, the best fun of
all . . . [Boston Public Library]

Sometimes. (Note bat thrown into
the air.) [Boston Public Library]

Good-bye, heading to Korea. Would he ever play again? [Red Sox]

The Panther jet, a new challenge in a different war. [Jerry Romolt]

Cargo to be delivered to North Korea. [Frank Cushing]

Life vest that would not be used.
[Frank Cushing]

Ted's Panther jet that he crash landed.
[Frank Cushing]

Ted on R & R in Kyoto,
Japan. [Frank Cushing]

floor. The bat goes rolling across the room. Johnny runs over and picks it up. Next bat, 'This bat is no good,' same thing. Johnny goes running. Out of 24 bats, Ted picks two. He says, 'Send those other damn bats back.' Johnny says, 'Yeah, they're not worth a damn.' "

More bats . . .

"A few days later, Ted says, again, 'Johnny, get me another couple dozen bats from Louisville,' " Consolo says. "I say to myself, This can't happen. They haven't even had time in Louisville to make the new bats since the last shipment. Next day, there's the boxes on the floor. Ted has the scale out again. Same thing.

"What I notice this time is that Johnny Orlando puts the lousy bats back in the boxes. The next time Ted wants new bats from Louisville, Johnny just tapes up the boxes and gives them to Ted all over again. Same bats."

Always, bats . . .

"At the end of a game, the first things that went back in the clubhouse were Ted's bats," Consolo says. "Johnny's assistant, Donnie Fitzpatrick, would grab Ted's six or seven bats and go through the tunnel. Then the team. Nobody would move until Ted's bats went back to the clubhouse. Then the team. Then Fitzie would come back for the rest of the bats."

Everything Williams did seemed interesting. He now seemed to be a giant walking among young and mortal men. A few of the young and mortal men—like pitcher Frank Sullivan and catcher Sammy White— might snicker behind the giant's back, but the rest mostly stared. These were people who had been in high school, junior high, grammar school, when he hit the .406. They had grown up with his name, his image, in front of them. They felt like they were in the same room with Babe Ruth. The people who had known him, seen him when he was hitting the .406, were gone.

"I just could not keep my eye off the man," Consolo says. "He was phenomenal."

The staring didn't just happen in Boston. It happened everywhere. The returned Ted Williams was the biggest attraction in the game. The Red Sox would go into the batting cage and the other team would linger in foul territory, not go back to the dugout. The players wanted to watch Williams hit. How does he do it? What is his secret? The stars would watch him hit. Everyone would watch him. When Williams was done, everyone else would go back to what he was doing.

"We played an exhibition one year in the Polo Grounds for the Jimmy

Fund," Consolo says. "I get goose bumps thinking about it. There's a home run hitting contest between Ted and Willie Mays. Ted hits nine straight home runs into the Polo Grounds seats. There's 65,000 people and they're screaming. Then he hits the next three *out* of the Polo Grounds."

He seemed like the master of some obscure Oriental art. Weighing the bats . . . who weighed bats? Who else had a scale? Williams weighed his bats every day, scraping them clean of olive oil and resin, weighing them again. He would talk hitting, two and a half hours straight in the clubhouse for a rained-out exhibition in Minneapolis, and the kids would listen to every word.

All he needed, it seemed, was the name of a pitcher to formulate a plan for a given game. Dick Gernert remembers Williams asking the clubhouse boy to find out who was pitching for the Indians on a particular day in Cleveland. The answer was "Mike Garcia." Williams said, "Sliders. I'm going to hit a slider out of here today."

Gernert watched and waited. Williams struck out in his first at bat, grounded out in his second. In his third trip to the plate, he smoked a home run into the second deck.

"The fucken guy finally threw me a slider," Williams said. "I told you I'd nail it."

Who had that kind of patience? To wait all day for a particular pitch? Who had that kind of talent? To absolutely nail the pitch when it came? Williams knew more than anyone else knew. He was a marvel.

"You'd finish batting practice, and everybody else would go into the clubhouse, play cards, have something to eat," Gernert says. "Ted would come in, change his shirt, and run back out. He wanted to watch the opposing pitcher warm up."

The pitchers warmed up next to the dugouts then, rather than in the bullpens. Williams would walk over, stand behind the catcher. Was that intimidating? Gernert went with him sometimes. Williams would dissect the pitcher's curveball, point out what location the pitcher liked, how much the ball curved, what indications there were that the curve was coming. Gernert would listen so hard his head would hurt. He felt he was seeing the same things Williams was seeing, but he wasn't seeing them at all.

"I'd get nervous at the plate when I got down in the count," Gernert says. "Ted would say, strike one, okay, you've seen his fastball. Okay, strike two, maybe you've seen it again. Now you've got him . . . I never felt that way. I could never relax like that."

A White Sox pitcher, Dick Donovan, once explained the pitcher's point of view. He was a Boston guy from Quincy, and Williams called him over before a game. He said, "I'm going to tell you what you're going to throw me today." He proceeded to spell out, word for word, exactly what Donovan's pitching plan for the afternoon was going to be. He spelled it out better than Donovan could spell it.

"It was eerie," Donovan reported. "Like he was clairvoyant."

There might have been a different strike zone for Williams, a little smaller than it would be for an average utility infielder, guys nodding in the dugout at called balls they knew would have been called strikes for them, but that had been earned. The returned Williams had an added stature, a place. He was a link to past glories, legitimate, a survivor of random inequities.

Even the Boston writers, for the moment, were inclined to give him a little breathing room. At least at the start. For just a moment. Just one.

"Williams stands as a symbol for the voiceless, selfless U.S. kids who were victims of war's adversity," Austen Lake wrote in the *American*. "Ted went—twice—without a grumbling murmur, leaving in the midst of life's most fruitful period. He did it with superlative grace and performed a distasteful task with dignity. So there is something of EVERY American combat man in Ted.

"As far as I'm concerned, he can wear a wreath of spinach on his head, sleep in the Public Garden pansy beds, eat oysters for breakfast and commit any shenanigan he wishes. I'm sold on the guy, just as I'll buy ALL our ex-combat dogfaces, leathernecks and gobs! They are the solid, sterling core that gives America hope."

"It may be that on some future day and in some future season he will deserve the succulent raspberry tart, but I would suggest that first he must do something to deserve it," Dave Egan wrote in the *Record*. "Personally, I do not hoot people from memory, nor dislike them from here to eternity. Williams is certainly an older and quite possibly a different man, playing in another year and on a completely new team that has a far more fiery spirit, and I insist that he must be judged with as much impartiality as possible not on something that happened in 1948, but on what happens now.

"It makes no difference to me what he did or did not do against the

Cardinals in the World Series of 1946, nor what he did or did not do in the gas-pipe series in the Yankee Stadium. At the risk of being misunderstood, I should also like to add that it will make no difference to me what he did or did not do in the skies over Korea."

From Williams's second at bat on his return—a 420-foot, pinch-hit rocket off a Garcia fastball on August 9, 1953, against Cleveland—until the end of his career, he was the Red Sox show. The rest of the game was busywork, window dressing packaged around his trips to the plate. How good was he? Straight from Korea he batted .407 for the rest of the season. He had 13 home runs in 91 at bats, a slugging percentage of .901. Who else could do that? No one.

"I once interviewed a blind guy who went to the ballpark every day," former sportswriter Tim Horgan says. "I asked him why he would go, since he couldn't see anything. He said he just loved the sound of the ballgame, being there. The part he liked best was when Williams came to the plate. He said that when Williams just stood up in the dugout he could tell. The sound of the ballpark would change."

Consolo brought his entire family to the park one day in Cleveland. Everyone in the family except his parents lived in Cleveland. There might have been 35 Consolos in the park. He gave the best seats to his two uncles, who worked construction, drove bulldozers, didn't know a thing about baseball. Between them, they might have seen four baseball games in their entire lives.

"Who's that number 9?" one of the uncles asked after the game.

"That's Ted Williams," Consolo said.

"Well, I don't know who he is, but he's a good hitter."

"He's the best hitter in the game!"

"I don't know about that, but he can hit. He's the only one who looks like he can hit up there. Everybody else, they look scared. He looks like he knows what he's doing. . . ."

"Ted Williams."

"Number 9. Whoever he is. He's the only one who can hit."

A change also had taken place in Williams's personal life. He confided to a nurse, years later, that he had returned from Korea with a social disease. If true—and why would he invent something like that?—syphilis was a final blow to a marriage that was much shakier than it ever had been portrayed in public.

Doris filed a petition for separate maintenance in a Miami court on January 19. She said Williams had "indulged in a course of conduct" for the past six years in which he had "mistreated and abused" her. She said he had used "language that was profane, abusive and obscene" and that he swore at her "in both public and private." She said he had beat her and struck her. She asked for "reasonable sums," plus the Miami house, the light blue Cadillac, and custody of Bobby-Jo, who now was six.

"I don't think he ever wanted to be married," Doris later would tell reporters.

She probably was right. He certainly didn't want to be married to *her*. He seldom was home during their marriage. On the road for half of the baseball season, he immediately was off to the fishing holes of America in the off-season. One friend says Williams also used to rent hotel rooms under an assumed name—often the friend's name—to "get away" during the season at home. The flap about his absence for the birth of Bobby-Jo was inevitable. He always was gone.

Every big off-season controversy or news break seemed to contain the words "contacted at So-and-So, where he was on a fishing trip," or "Williams was unavailable for comment, off on a fishing trip." There never was the sentence "Williams, contacted while watching *I Love Lucy*, put down his newspaper and answered questions at his front door."

Doris often had been quoted as saying she "doesn't like baseball much" and seldom was seen at Fenway Park with the other baseball wives. She also was not fond of the Florida fishing life. This did not seem to be a good mixture for a man whose life, whose every day, centered on baseball and the outdoors.

Gerry Hern of the *Boston Post* contributed this unattributed anecdote:

"An admirer commenting on the domestic situation said the other day, 'I knew a long time back that the marriage would have a tough time. On his honeymoon, Ted took his wife to the Everglades to fish. He went to a deserted area where a man could fish in peace and calm. His wife stayed in the cabin while he fished. She didn't like snakes.

" 'Finally, Ted talked her into coming out one day. He assured her there was nothing like it for the soul and there weren't any snakes. They left the cabin and headed down a path toward his favorite spot with Ted leading the way. Suddenly, his wife screamed. A huge snake crossed the path between them. Well, how could he deny that? He took her back to the cabin and went fishing alone. How did he know that some silly snake would take just that time to cross the path?' "

There were rumors that Williams was involved with other women. There were rumors that Doris had developed a drinking problem during his many absences. The press at the time, while charting every movement he made in a baseball uniform, mostly wrapped the rest of his life in a veil of discretion. None of this was put into print. He himself also worked hard to keep that veil of discretion tight.

"I've been fishing a lot," he reported in an "exclusive" interview about his off-season activities with Arthur Siegel of the *Traveler* on January 18, a day before the petition for separation was filed. "Got a kick out of winning that Palm Beach tournament. Then went to Cuba for a week and caught 40 bonefish on a fly. That's considered really good.

"I haven't done any special walking or anything for my legs. I haven't touched a bat. They tell me that fishing helps my hands. I might be about ten pounds overweight. But I'm not sure.

"I've been so busy down here that I haven't done more than think about the baseball season."

One day later the papers were duly filed. Not exactly a great "exclusive." The boundaries were kept. Baseball was baseball. Williams's marital situation would become public only when it became public record . . . seven days after the papers were filed.

The discord in the marriage, though, was public knowledge for a long time for anyone who knew the couple.

"My wife, Emily, and I were in Miami one winter," Dominic DiMaggio says. "I said, 'Let's go over to see Ted.' I had the address in Coral Gables, but we got lost. I stopped at a police station and told him who I was looking for. They were nice enough to have a couple of officers lead me to the house in a patrol car.

"Doris answered the door. She saw the patrol car and said, 'What's he done now?' She really meant it. We calmed her down. We waited for an hour or two, but Ted never showed up."

"I wound up stationed in Miami while Ted was in Korea," Raymond Sisk, the pilot-lawyer who returned to active duty with Williams, says. "My wife and I would take Doris out to lunch every few weeks. I remember saying to my wife that we shouldn't get too friendly with Doris, though, because I didn't think they were going to be a couple for very long. There was nothing particular that made me feel that way, just a bunch of things Ted said. I told my wife it would be awkward if we became too friendly with Doris because we were Ted's friends."

"Did Ted like women?" Max West, the old Boston Braves outfielder, asks. "Does a cat have an ass? Those Red Sox teams were filled with guys who liked women. I remember one year . . . we had the city series at the start of the season, the Braves and the Red Sox. For some reason, they put both teams in the same hotel. I'm in the lobby, and a bunch of the Braves' wives were going to go up to a room to play bridge, maybe five or six of them. The elevator opens and Ted walks out. The wives go on. Ted looks at 'em and he goes back on the elevator too."

The suit for separate maintenance was dropped on February 12, but the march toward divorce had begun. Williams had moved out, living now on the Florida Keys in Islamorada, one of his prime fishing spots. Doris stayed in the house in Miami with Bobby-Jo. Williams agreed to pay her $125 per week.

A stewardess for National Airlines, Evelyn Turner, told the Associated Press on February 9 that she was "surprised" at a radio report that she would become the next wife of Ted Williams. She said she knew Williams, that "Ted's a real wonderful fellow and we've been friends for a long time—but strictly friends."

"After all, he's still married," Evelyn Turner said.

The marriage was done.

O n March 1, two weeks after the suit was dropped, Williams reported to Sarasota. The first day of spring training for 1954 had a traditional, show-biz look for the Red Sox. They dressed in their home whites in the old rat-infested clubhouse and came out the door together for the only time of the year for the still photographers. Then they ran around the field together for the first time, the only time of the year. Another shot for the still photographers.

The niceties completed, batting practice began. Hitters began to hit, and the rest of the players ambled to different spots on the field to shag fly balls. Williams was a shagger.

He stood in left and renewed acquaintances. He had been the last Red Sox player to arrive, leaving Islamorada at 6:45 in the morning and driving for almost five hours, accompanied by team physician Dr. Russell Sullivan. Sullivan had been Williams's guest for a few last days of fishing before the start of camp.

Talking now with Piersall in left, Williams spotted a soft line drive hit by reserve outfielder Hoot Evers coming their way. He was late starting for the ball and had to reach low for it and . . . he fell down.

Pop.

No great dramatic moment here. No All-Star Game heroics. No jet plane landing. He had an awkward middle-aged tumble. A loss of balance, maybe from a few too many pounds. A 215-pound man, no longer a skinny kid, simply teetered and fell. He was back talking with Dr. Sullivan again, but lying on his back on the ground. He had broken his collarbone in the first few minutes of his first baseball workout of the year.

"His technique [trying to catch the liner] was reminiscent of the form of an original Bloomer Girl," Frank Fox, referred to as "a former Notre Dame featherweight boxer," said in the *Globe* in a description of the fall. "It is said that the report of the breaking bone was deafening, but I did not hear it due to the fact that Joe Cronin, next to me, coincidentally cracked a peanut."

The injury took a couple of days to be diagnosed, but eventually Williams was shipped back to Boston for an operation at Sancta Maria Hospital in Cambridge. (The *Globe* ran an "exclusive" of the X-ray.) The writers, gathered at the Eastern Airlines terminal for his 11:30 P.M. arrival on March 7, were informed that he would be the last person off the plane. After 25 people exited, there was a lull in the line and then a big thud at the top of the stairs. The writers squinted to see what had happened to Williams now, but it was a young girl who had fallen, and they continued their vigil. No one inquired about the condition of the girl.

A bone fragment an inch and a half long was found floating in Williams's shoulder. It was fit back into place, and the pieces of the shoulder were held together with cat gut and steel wire. The wire, one-sixteenth of an inch thick, six inches long, was referred to as a "pin." Dr. Sullivan, the fisherman, performed the operation. He estimated Williams would be out of action for the next eight weeks, which included the first 21 games of the season.

Williams stayed overnight in the hospital, then stayed in a Boston hotel for 13 days before going back to Florida to recover. He would not play again until May 15, when he pinch-hit in the seventh inning of a 2–1 loss in Baltimore and batted again in the ninth, going 0-for-2. He said he felt terrible with the pin still in his shoulder. Doctors had told him he was the first baseball player to try to return with a pin in his shoulder. Athletes in other sports had done it, but he was a baseball first.

"The pin hurt me," he said. "I felt it each time I swung. I swing one way, the pin seems to be going the other. I don't know, I might have to have them take the pin out if it keeps hurting and retarding my swing."

The next day—second day back—he went 8-for-9 in a doubleheader in Detroit.

He had two home runs, a double, and five singles. It was one of the greatest statistical days of his career. He still felt terrible.

"It hurt me all day," he said. "The worst jolt came when I swung and missed in the eighth inning of the second game. I'll try it for a couple more days, and if it still troubles me, I'll talk with the doctor and arrange for him to take the pin out."

The shoulder would continue to be a story for the rest of the season—Yankees manager Casey Stengel would suggest that he was going to insert a pin in the shoulder of all of his hitters if this was what it did for Williams—but a more interesting story had formed during Williams's recuperation. He had announced that he was going to retire at the end of the '54 season.

Paid $30,000 by the *Saturday Evening Post* for a series of as-told-to articles with New York writers Joe Reichler and Joe Trimble, personal favorites, Williams said, under the headline "This Is My Last Year in Baseball" in the April 10 issue, that this, well, was his last year in baseball. He said that he had made up his mind well before his injury.

"I'll be 36 in October [actually August] and, as ballplayers' ages go, an 'old man,' " he and Reichler-Trimble wrote. "How many men of that age, other than pitchers, are playing regularly in the majors? . . . I can't think of a ballplayer I saw who looked as if he belonged in a major-league uniform after the age of 36—again excepting pitchers, who work only once a week when they're old."

No other reasons for retirement were given. He was just "too old." He filled out the first installment by admitting that he had "rabbit ears" and then whacking the people who yelled into them. The Boston sports press led the list.

"There aren't many of them I like," Williams-Reichler-Trimble wrote. "There are some nice Joes in Boston, but some of them are wrong guys. They knew where they stood with me right from the beginning. I certainly am not going to play politics and soft-soap them so they'll write nice things about me now. . . . Some sportswriters today don't care about facts and figures. All they're interested in is your personal life. Give the fans figures, records, scores. That's what they want, not what Joe Doakes had for breakfast in the morning."

The Boston sports press was not amused. Williams's opinions were bad enough, but to have spoken them through two *New York* writers (to whom he had given $10,000 of the $30,000) was even more heresy. The local boys started typing. The postwar honeymoon was done.

"Perhaps it would be an excellent idea if baseball's terrible-tempered Mr. Bang would retire now, instead of at the end of the season," Dave Egan, the Colonel, wrote in the *Record*.

"I know that by remaining he will make a contribution to Ted Williams, the only person he loves, but it is highly questionable he will do anything of a sensible and constructive nature in the building of a team for tomorrow.

"The man, of course, should be lying on a cot, talking things over with a psychiatrist and possibly unraveling his twisted mental processes. He should be pitied, of course, rather than censured, for he's not the only one who lacks a few buttons and marbles, yet on the other hand mere boys like Billy Consolo and Tom Brewer and Ellis Kinder (how in the hell did he stick his nose in here?) are entitled to protection against the venom that this misanthropic mauler likes to spread."

"He came into baseball a sour, mixed-up kid, wearing chips for epaulettes, and with his holsters strapped high," Bill Cunningham wrote in the *Herald*. "Despite fame, fortune, and the impact of two wars, that's what he still is here 16 years later. Other men, especially those who've been blessed with success, mature, mellow, expand, develop graciousness, tolerance, the ability to laugh even at themselves—but not our Teddy."

Strangely, the retirement announcement was not treated as the big news. The feud with the writers was bigger. The retirement was pushed to the side on the sports pages. The *Saturday Evening Post*'s quarter-page ads for the story were bigger than any of the stories about it.

Something seemed fishy about the announcement from the beginning. Retirement made no sense. Williams obviously still could hit. He was making big money. He liked baseball, and was even a bigger star than when he left. Why quit? The unspoken, unwritten guess was that this all was related to his divorce proceedings. If his income were less, wouldn't the settlement be less to Doris? No Red Sox officials expressed great amazement or fear for the future. The retirement seemed a pro forma exercise designed to sell a few magazines and help in the courtroom.

The Colonel, for one, was unconvinced.

"For the sum of thirty grand, Ted Williams revealed to the readers of the *Saturday Evening Post* that he will retire at the end of the season,"

Dave Egan wrote. "For nothing but the literary exercise and a mere pittance, I shall reveal to the readers of the *Sunday Advertiser* that he definitely will not retire at the end of the season.

"The chief reason he will not retire is he will do unto Tom Yawkey what Tom Yawkey always had done to him. . . . As a friend, Williams will play for Yawkey next year and the year after, and quite possibly the year after that as well. . . . Not a person in the entire organization has speculated, publicly or privately, on the most vital decision that would confront them if Williams were serious in saying that he will retire at season's end. Nobody has asked the enormous question, who will be our leftfielder when Williams retires and nobody need ask it, for he is not going to retire."

For the rest of the season, Williams would continue to say he was going to retire. Virtually no one believed him. The Red Sox were terrible, but he was solid. As the young team flopped and floundered to finish 42 games behind the pennant-winning Cleveland Indians, Williams collected 29 home runs, 89 RBI, and hit .345 in a season that was further shortened by two weeks in the hospital with pneumonia in June. Only his lack of 14 more at bats kept him from winning his fifth batting title.

Was this a man who was going to retire? There were no festivities, no good-bye gifts, before his supposed final game on September 26, 1954, against the Washington Senators, no nostalgic tributes written about his home run off Constantine Keriazakos on his next-to-last at bat. There was a nice ovation when he was removed, two outs in the ninth, by manager Lou Boudreau and replaced by Karl Olson. That was it.

That was it?

"You think I'm kidding, but I'm not," he told writers.

He took a special train to Portage, Maine, as a guest of the Bangor and Aroostook Railroad the next day to start a fishing expedition. At each stop—a crowd of 500 waiting in Presque Isle—he signed autographs and repeated his promise as if he were a politician campaigning on a strict policy of negativity. The Associated Press in the following days reported that he caught his limit of brook trout at Round Pond, his limit of salmon at Fish River Lake, and flew by pontoon plane to Ferguson Pond for more fishing. His promise stayed the same.

"I'm not going to be a sandlot player," he said.

The oddness continued through the winter and into the spring. Williams said he would be fishing for marlin in Chile in May, for salmon in Nova Scotia in June. The newspapers reported that Hillerich and Bradsby had received an order for Ted Williams bats. Williams was described as "relaxed and happy" in Islamorada. The newspapers reported that he had taken two 54-ounce bats with him from Boston and already was seen swinging them in Miami. Williams was incommunicado. The Red Sox reported to spring training and his equipment was laid out. Just in case.

Only after spring training began—Williams still not in camp—did the importance of the divorce proceedings in Miami start to be mentioned. Speculation grew that once he was divorced he would return to baseball. Arthur Siegel of the *Traveler* was the one writer to draw Williams to a phone. Siegel called from his Montreal hotel room one morning after watching the Boston Bruins lose, 2–0, to the Montreal Canadiens a night earlier. He told the operator, who said Williams wasn't home, that this was "an emergency." He waited.

"Who's this?"

"Arthur Siegel."

"What the [string of bad words]. Why would you say it was an emergency? The cops got me to come to the phone. [More bad words. Siegel estimated about a minute of bad words.] How'd the Bruins do?"

"They lose, 2–0."

"Well, give 'em my regards."

Siegel asked the important questions. Williams didn't answer.

"I've got so much on my mind, I can't talk about anything else right now. And then you complicate it by putting in an emergency call from Canada. I start thinking about who I know in Canada and what can be wrong."

Siegel apologized.

"Are you going to play ball this year, Ted?"

"No comment, Arthur."

Gerry Hern of the *Post* reported on February 28 that "for the first time in history the fate of the Red Sox may be in the hands of a woman." He said lawyers for Williams and Doris were involved in "conferences." If the conferences resulted in a situation where Williams could keep part of his salary in a divorce settlement, he would continue to play. If the "ante, plus taxes, is to be his entire salary, he probably will sit on the sidelines."

The indications clearly were that Williams would play if possible. The Colonel held out one last hope. . . .

"The hit and run . . . the stolen base . . . the squeeze . . . the big hitter getting the big hit off any pitch he can reach . . . that's baseball and it's what we never have known in all the years Williams has been here," Dave Egan wrote on March 14 in the *Record*.

> That is why I earnestly wish him well with his fishing and piously hope that the sardine and the tuna (in cans, if he wants them that way) will hurl themselves onto his hook and die, content with the knowledge that they have done so for the greater glory of the Boston Red Sox.
>
> My mail indicates this feeling is shared quite generally by baseball fans up and down the stern and rock-bound coast. In letter after letter the hope is expressed that he will keep on fishing and leave the Red Sox to whatever their fate may be and I shall guarantee you that it will not be worse without him than it was with him.

. . . but the Colonel soon was left with his own diabolical dreams.

On May 9, after all the guessing and the back-and-forth wondering, the season already a month old, Doris Williams was awarded a divorce in circuit court in Miami. She received $50,000, payable within two years in a lump sum, $12,000 court costs, $100 per month in child support, the $42,000 house in Miami, and the light-blue Cadillac worth $4,000. Williams received his freedom. Despite an "I don't know" answer about his baseball future on the courthouse steps, he was back in Boston four days later and taking batting practice. Twelve fresh uniforms, already tailored, were in his locker.

"I knew all along he'd be back," Johnny Orlando said. "Ted told me last fall he'd be back and play 100 games."

Huh.

Williams played in 98 games. He hit .356, which again would have led the American League if he'd had enough at bats. He had 28 homers and 83 RBI on a young team that hung around in the pennant race until September. His back hurt him during the year, his shin hurt so much from foul balls he began wearing a shinguard, he was hit with pneumonia again, and he was exhausted, whipped at the end, but said he would be back for more. He was named "Comeback Player of the Year."

Williams gave an interview to Grace Davidson of the *Boston Post* in the off-season. He told her he hated holidays because of the loneliness. He said he probably never would get married again. He said he had a secret longing to adopt a son, an orphan, but that it would be impossible.

"I'm not married, they'd never give me one," he said ("wistfully" in Davidson's description). "I've my little girl, Bobby-Jo. You should see her. An iddy-biddy little thing, pretty and sweet, just as sweet as she can be. She can hit a ball straight as an arrow. Is she smart! She can do anything, that iddy-biddy little thing."

Williams always talked differently with women writers. Through the years, the few looks into his personal life, into his deeper thoughts, his more complicated feelings, were primarily drawn out by women sent from a different section from sports in the newspaper to do a feature. There always would be a courtliness to his disposition in their stories, an affability, a different set of words. The stories by men would be about the now, the game today, the game tomorrow, the chatter-chatter of baseball. The perpetual fight. Women would draw out the measured, reflective responses. Ted Williams is a nice guy, after all! Virtually all the women writers would say that.

The interview would be held in a restaurant or in his hotel room. He would be helpful, ready to explain. He would order dinner. There always would be a description of how tanned and handsome he was. In an interview with Joan Flynn Dreyspool for *Sports Illustrated* in July 1955, he even spread pictures of Bobby-Jo across a coffee table.

"Just look at her," he said. "She's minus a few teeth there, but look at those eyes, that mouth. They're just like mine, aren't they?

"She can run like a little reindeer. I wish I could run like her. Ever since she was three years old she'd throw a baseball right at me, never off-line . . . the most important thing in my life is my little girl."

Charming.

"When I was a kid I used to do different exercises to develop my arms and chest because I was so skinny and didn't have much strength," he also told Dreyspool. "I have to laugh now. Fifteen years ago, every night before I went to bed I'd eat a quart of ice cream or have a big malted milk with eggs in it because they said that would put fat on me. I'd still like to do it, but I can't. As it is, I think I've gained a couple of pounds these last few days. You sit on your tail on that bench and you eat and eat and nothing happens. Then, 'Blimpo.' "

Humble.

In an interview with another woman, Leslie Lieber of *This Week* magazine, four years later, he told an interesting story about why he came out of retirement. It had nothing to do with his divorce, with a sudden need for money, with any of the reasons that had been speculated across the headlines. It had to do with history and ego. Ego definitely was part of the equation. Maybe the biggest part.

One morning, late in the '54 season, Williams was waiting at Union Station in Baltimore for a train to Washington, the next stop on the Red Sox road trip. He had a newspaper close in front of his face at the customary six inches, a reading trick he had developed to help focus his eyes better. A man still recognized him.

"Excuse me, Ted," the man said, "but I've been bothered by all that talk about your quitting baseball. You were kidding, weren't you?"

"Why should I kid about a thing like that?" Williams said.

"Look here, Ted," the man said. "You're crazy if you think you're going to quit baseball now. You can't. You can't."

The man's name was Eddie Mifflin. He was a businessman from Swarthmore, Pennsylvania, and a sometime Pennsylvania state legislator. He also was a statistical freak in love with baseball. He knew Williams's career numbers better than Williams did. His argument was that by missing almost five years due to military commitments, Williams was nowhere near the place he truly should be in baseball history. This was a travesty.

If Williams could keep playing, Mifflin argued, he would leapfrog up the ladder in some statistic virtually every time he did *anything*. Singles, doubles, triples, home runs, runs batted in, runs scored, slugging percentage, batting average, walks! He could advance in all categories dramatically. Wasn't that reason enough to keep playing? History?

"Do you even know how many hits you've racked up?" Mifflin asked.

"No," Williams admitted.

"You've got 1,930 in all, including yesterday. It won't take much to reach 2,000. And in home runs you're not even among the first ten in lifetime totals. But if you stick around. . . ."

"Who are you?" Williams asked, interested.

"Just a helluva fan," Mifflin said before jumping on a train for Philadelphia.

"Get in touch with me," Williams said.

Later in the season, Mifflin met with Williams in a New York hotel room. Mifflin laid out a gridwork of "approaching milestones" and promised to find more. He would become a constant in the close-out years of Williams's career, calling every few weeks, sending Western Union telegrams of congratulation with each step of the ladder that was climbed.

Goals. Ted Williams always was very good at chasing goals.

H is relationship with the Boston sportswriters—all male—remained at its cranky norm. It was roughly the same relationship South Korea had established with North Korea since the war. The two sides didn't talk much, and when they did it was in angry outbursts. Williams and the writers stared a lot across their own 38th Parallel, each waiting for the other to make some foolish, provocative move to begin hostilities again.

Williams long ago had lobbied Red Sox management for a postgame cooling-off period for the players, a designated time limit when sportswriters would not be allowed to come into the clubhouse. The limit was up to 15 minutes now. Williams sometimes would pull his chair right to the door, jam the back of the chair under the handle and sit there to make sure nobody entered. Many times the writers, when they finally came into the room, deadlines pounding in their heads, found it mostly was empty. This was a constant irritant and made the job of describing the triumphs and many pitfalls of the local nine much harder.

Edgy skirmishes between Williams and the writers broke out here and there, an unkind column from the Colonel or Bill Cunningham or Austen Lake or Harold Kaese on one side, a fast torrent of hard words about "gutless cocksuckers" and "syphilitic fucken so-and-sos" on the other, but the big boom did not arrive until the 1956 season. Saliva lubricated the wheels of discord, made them move much faster.

"I'm on vacation in Milford, Connecticut," Tim Horgan says. "I'm standing in the water at Silver Sands Beach. A guy comes walking across the sand, all dressed up. He comes up to me and says, 'Are you Mr. Horgan?' I say, 'Yes, I am.' He says, 'I have a telegram for you.' "

Horgan's mind ran through the quick Rol-a-dex of potential personal disasters. Deaths of loved ones. Fire back at the house. Stolen car. Bank failure. What?

"It was from my boss, Arthur Siegel," Horgan says. "Ted had just spit at the fans. I was supposed to hurry back to do a story the next day about what fans in the leftfield seats thought."

Actually, this was the third spit, the big one. Williams had stumbled upon this act of protest on July 18, the occasion of his 400th home run. The homer was a dramatic shot, giving the Red Sox a 1–0 win over

Kansas City, and as he crossed home plate he looked up at the press box behind the plate and spit toward the assembled writers. Three days later, he spit again, same circumstance, in a game against the Tigers that was billed as Joe Cronin Night, an occasion to honor the Red Sox general manager's selection to the Hall of Fame.

"I went up to Williams after the game against Kansas City," George Sullivan says. "I was a sportswriter now, working for the *Herald*. I'd never had any problems with him, so I said, 'Hey, what were you doing when you crossed home plate? Did you say, 'Fuck you,' to the press box? It was hard to tell.' He had a little smile on his face. He said, 'I spit at you cocksuckers. And I'd do it again.' I said, 'Does that include me?' And he said, 'Yes, it does.'

"I'd learned as a batboy that the only way to handle Williams was to give it back to him. I said something, using the same language, and he said something back and then we were into it. 'Fucken this' and 'fucken that.' Shouting. Everybody was watching us. The other writers were all writing it down."

The first spit—or maybe the second, he isn't sure—lives brightly in the memory of Earl Duffy, an assistant manager at the Somerset. He remembers the agitation around one of those two spits. He remembers Williams hit a home run and let loose and then everything at the hotel let loose.

"My secretary was in a state of excitement," Duffy says. "She said, 'There's a man on the phone. He's calling from Fenway Park . . . something about an emergency regarding Ted Williams.' I picked up the phone and heard a highly excitable voice, 'I'm calling from the front office at Fenway Park. Is there any way we can get Ted Williams into the hotel without going through the lobby or other places where people gather?' 'Yes,' I said. 'We have a locked door on the swimming pool side of the hotel [Charlesgate West]. Ted knows where it is. I'll have the door unlocked and I will be standing on the street.' "

Duffy headed to his appointed spot.

"In no time at all, I spotted a car making a quick turn off Commonwealth Avenue," he says. "The car screeched to a halt and Ted Williams leaped out. He had a grim look on his face as he barreled past me. I ran behind him. 'Take the first door on your right!' He almost tore the door off its hinges and he raced up the stairwell to his suite."

The lobby was soon filled with reporters and photographers. They wanted to know which room belonged to Williams. Hotel management would not divulge the information.

"One of the reporters found a way to get it, though," Duffy says. "He went up to the suite and knocked on Ted's door. The slugger called down and said if the man were not removed there just might be a homicide committed outside his suite."

The sportswriters, interestingly, did not chide Williams much for either of the first two spits. The actions were seen simply as another example of Ted being Ted and of the general hostilities around the ball club. The team was not doing well and the fans were booing. Williams was not the only target. Jackie Jensen was being booed in right. Don Buddin, the young error-prone shortstop, was being booed unrelentingly. (Fifteen years later, Buddin long gone from Fenway, there still was a piece of graffiti in the men's room at the Dugout, a Commonwealth Avenue bar, that read "Don Buddin lives! There is a little bit of him in all of us.") The atmosphere was not good.

"Why should I talk to you?" Piersall asked Horgan one day. "I make three times as much as you."

On August 7, 1956, the situation blew apart. A crowd of 36,530 fans, the largest Fenway crowd since World War II, gathered to see the Red Sox meet the Yankees on a Wednesday afternoon. Jensen had a small problem before the game even began, heading toward the stands to confront a man who kept calling him "Mr. Doubleplay." This was a gathering of the tormentors and the tormented.

The game was a pitchers' duel, Willard Nixon of the Sox against Don Larsen of the Yanks, and went scoreless straight into extra innings. In the top of the 11th, the trouble started. Mickey Mantle hit a high fly ball to left, and Williams lost it. The day had been touched with intermittent showers, and he was staring up into the rain and the ball wound up bouncing off his glove for a two-base error. The boos came from everywhere.

Williams atoned for his mistake on the very next batter, making a solid running catch of Yogi Berra's liner to end the inning, but the sound of the boos remained in his head. The same people who were cheering now had been booing two minutes ago! Who could he trust? The two-sidedness, the injustice of it all, worked in his head. There were still a few people who were booing!

He was steaming.

"Oh, boy, now the Big One," Billy Consolo says. "I watched the whole thing, best seat in the house. Ted comes in from leftfield and spits a couple times, and everybody's booing and there's a fan, right on top of our dugout, standing on the dugout itself, just giving it to him. Ted stops and looks at the guy. Just then, someone threw a golf ball. Fenway doesn't have a second deck, but there's a roof and there's people up there. One of them threw a golf ball and it landed right on the plank that's the top step of the dugout. The ball bounced way high in the air, right in front of Ted. He watched it.

"That set him off. He reached back and got a big gobber and just let it go at that guy on the dugout."

The press officially recorded three spits. Included was a spit at the Yankees' dugout, where the players had been riding him about his last two spitting incidents. Then Williams went into the Red Sox dugout and became really mad.

"There's a runway, a tunnel that goes back to the clubhouse," Consolo says. "Players would go in there to smoke during the games. There's a water fountain in there too. One of those big metal water coolers, bolted to the concrete wall. Ted just knocked it over, ripped it off the wall. Water started spurting everywhere."

The Red Sox still had to bat in the bottom of the 11th inning of the scoreless game. Improbably, they loaded the bases and Williams came to the plate. Yankees pitcher Tommy Byrne, working carefully to this obviously enraged man with a bat in his hands, walked him, sending home the winning run. Williams tossed his bat 30 feet high in the air at this indignity, seemed for an instant as if he were going to go back to the dugout instead of taking the walk, then loped to first base to end the game.

"So now we're going to go back into the clubhouse," Consolo says. "Except we can't. There's five feet of water in the tunnel. It's flooded. We have to take our stuff, go up through the stands, just like you'd do in the minor leagues."

The players went into the clubhouse. Quiet. They'd won the game, but there was none of the usual celebration and happy talk. Everyone sat in front of his locker and waited for what would come next. Everyone looked, out of the corner of his eye, to see what Williams was doing. Williams was sitting down, saying nothing.

"Here's that wooden floor again," Consolo says. "You hear the *clomp, clomp, clomp* of spikes. It's Pinky Higgins, the manager. He goes over to Ted's locker and says, 'Kid, that's the lousiest thing I've ever seen in baseball.' Ted, he just looks up at him and says, 'Hey, I might not be here tomorrow.' Ted couldn't care less. He said to Gene Stephens, 'Kid, you better get your rest. You're probably going to play tomorrow.' "

The reaction this time was immediate. This spit had flown over some invisible but well-recognized barrier. Tom Yawkey, the owner, had been listening to the radio broadcast in his suite at the Hotel Pierre in New York. He quickly called Cronin and fined Williams $5,000. It was a huge sum at the time. Only Babe Ruth ever had been fined as much by any owner.

The writers were in a tizzy. Some of them followed Williams again to the Somerset. This time they got results. After threatening homicide again, Williams answered questions through the locked door. Bob Holbrook of the *Globe* reported a sanitized version of the exchange:

"I'd spit again at the same people who booed me today."

"Will you be at the ballpark tomorrow?"

"Probably. Because I can't afford a $5,000 fine."

"Why do the boos bother you?"

"I just can't help it."

"Don't you think you are a little bit to blame for this situation?"

"Not a damned bit. You writers are responsible for this . . . the whole thing. I'm no rockhead, you know. If it didn't bother me I wouldn't be as fired up as I am now. . . ."

Williams wanted to make sure he was quoted correctly.

"Now you got that quote . . . two things. . . . First, I'd spit at the same people who booed me today. Second, I wouldn't be at the ballpark tomorrow if I could afford a $500 . . . $5,000 fine every day. . . . Got it? Read it back to me. . . ."

"Is Ted Williams considering quitting? Is this his last year?"

"Probably. . . ."

Yawkey from New York, said, "Why the man does these things is something I can't figure out." Yawkey sounded anguished. "I can't. I can't can't. O, so many times I've tried to figure it out. I can't. I can't. I can't." Cronin said the fine definitely would be taken from Williams's pay. The sportswriters said . . . well, Harold Kaese said that Williams should quit.

"He is getting too old for the game—old physically and old mentally," Kaese wrote. "His body is wearing out and so, apparently, is his nervous system. He never could take it very well. Now he is near the point where he can't take it at all.

"What Williams goes through now during a season can't be worth whatever he is being paid. . . ."

The next game was a night game, Family Night, against the Baltimore Orioles. The prospects for confrontation were so great that a bunch of the New York sportswriters stayed in town for the show. They found, instead, a love affair. The fans cheered for Williams from the moment he set foot on the field. When he homered in the sixth to break up a 2–2 tie, they cheered even louder. He responded by elaborately placing his hand over his mouth as he ran toward the dugout.

A change happened in Williams's head that night. He said he realized, finally, after 17 years associated with the city, 17 years of grinding against whatever discordant noises he heard, the bulk of the people were not against him. The cheers on this one night did what the gifts and standing ovations and constant attention never had been able to accomplish—they made him feel loved. The forest stood out from the louder, yapping trees.

"From '56 on, I realized that people were for me," he explained years later. "The writers had written that the fans should show me they didn't want me. And I got the greatest ovation I ever got."

A half-dozen funds were started to pay his fine. A legislator from South Boston introduced a bill to have uncouth spectators at Fenway fined. Public reaction everywhere was on Williams's side and against the side of the sportswriters, his persecutors. The *Globe* ran a page of letters, "What Globe Readers Say About Ted." The letters were 100 percent against either the writers or the "loudmouths" in the stands at Fenway, who did not speak for everyone. A reader, Phil Resnick of West Roxbury, had a common thought:

"A nonunderstanding, cruel press has gone the limit in crucifying a brave man and I want to reply to their viciousness," Resnick wrote. "Ted had two hitches on combat missions. Ted had marital trouble. Ted had several severe injuries. Ted received a continuous barrage of abuse in the papers. Ted was booed while hitting .372.

"If the above facts aren't enough to ruin anybody's 'nerves,' I'll eat a regulation bat, ball and catcher's equipment. In my opinion, Ted deserves a rest, a good doctor, and a little help, not censure."

The sportswriters were the problem! They made good fans do bad things, misled the fans! That was Williams's flash-of-light revelation. The fans seemingly agreed.

The press was left to explain itself. The writers blustered and dragged out past transgressions. The typists definitely were on the defensive. Unable to use the words they often heard, they tried to find a way to describe what it was like to be called "gutless syphilitic fucken cocksuckers" on a regular basis. They were reeling.

Dave Egan wrote from underneath his Confederate hat in the *Record*: "If he does such things [as spit] on Joe Cronin Night, which was to have been one of the most heart-warming nights in many years, and if he does them in front of the largest crowd in the post-war history of the Red Sox, I ask you to stretch your imagination to its most elastic limit and surmise, if possible, what he does in the privacy of the clubhouse where his conduct and his language have been known to shock young players who came to the Red Sox prepared to idolize him. He has been a disturbing influence on this club since his second year in the big leagues and I have dinned it into your ears for many years that the Red Sox could not possibly be a team and play as a unit so long as he was the prime ballerina.

"This will be a better team without him than it ever can hope to be while he is going his lonesome, sorry way, for it never will be a team while he has any connection with it. I have written this sentence so often that it now rolls automatically off the typewriter, but it was true when I first wrote it 15 years ago and it is equally true today."

Austen Lake cried from the pages of the *American*: "Truth is that Williams, systematically, has gone far out of his way to smear the writers with every obscenity he can dredge from his cranial frogpond. And believe me, that man has a genius for indecencies. From the time he joined the Red Sox in 1939 as a green kid, he was a one-man Indian uprising with an obsession for the writers' scalps.

"It's half-past time the writers told the stark, naked truth about this johnny jump-up who paints himself a martyr to sports-page oppression. For time upon time I've heard him squawl indelicacies at the writers whose job it is to travel with the Boston Red Sox. And for the times I've witnessed his frenzied tirades, there've been hundreds I didn't. No reason needed! He invents the occasions!"

Harold Kaese concluded in the *Globe*: "Someone has to come to the defense of Boston sportswriters, even if it has to be a sportswriter. On the word of one man—Ted Williams—public opinion generally has classified them with Gen. Nasser, the Chinese Reds and the measles. To be a sportswriter now is to be cousin to the devil. Why? Because Ted Williams says Boston sportswriters are no good.

"This is unfortunate, because no city except New York has as high a standard of sportswriting as Boston."

Williams's response was three home runs in the four games after the spit. Stick that, boys, in a place where the snappy adjectives don't shine. He had found a peace of mind. He finished the season with a .345 average, second to Mickey Mantle. There were no further spits.

In the noisy court of public opinion, this was a showdown Williams pretty much figured he had won. And he pretty much had. The Red Sox and Yawkey never collected the $5,000 fine.

10 Boston

Like a feather caught in a vortex, Williams ran around the square of the bases at the center of our beseeching screaming. He ran as he always ran out home runs—hurriedly, unsmiling, head down, as if our praise were a storm of rain to get out of. He didn't tip his cap. Though we thumped, wept, and chanted "We want Ted" for minutes after he hid in the dugout, he did not come back. Our noise for some seconds passed beyond excitement into an immense kind of open anguish, a wailing, a cry to be saved. But immortality is non-transferable.

JOHN UPDIKE, *THE NEW YORKER*, OCTOBER 22, 1960

The 1957 season was his late-career masterpiece. If 1941 and the .406 batting average was his work of inspiration—a 23-year-old rising star startling everyone with his fresh approach, his energy, his fire—1957 was the triumph of experience. The young man has to overcome the things he doesn't know to succeed. The old man has to overcome the things he no longer can do.

That was what Williams did here. He was 38 years old at the beginning of the season, 39 at the end, and unsure each day of what surprises his body might have for him. He was a senior citizen, an elder statesman, a relic in his environment. He hit .388 and led the American League in batting.

"When did you come up to the big leagues?" he asked Red Sox broadcaster Curt Gowdy one day.

"I was up in 1949," Gowdy replied. "I was with the Yankees for two years before I came here in '51."

"Then you saw me when I was really great," Williams said. "I'm glad you saw me when I was really great. Before Korea."

The pin from 1954 was still in his shoulder and bothered him at night. Not in the games, just at night. Sleeping. His elbow, the one he broke in the All-Star Game in '50, still bothered him in the cold. He never felt that his swing had come all the way back from that injury. His respiratory system, never good in the spring and fall, now was a time bomb. Since Korea, when he caught a cold, pneumonia seemed a step away.

He was susceptible to all the aches and pains and twists and turns of a man approaching 40 who asks too much of his body. He had missed a bunch of games and been bothered for a long time by a bad ankle when he slipped off a shower clog in the 1956 season. Slipped off a shower clog! He was at an age when the healing process now took time.

All of this caused him to go to Sarasota with questions in his head. How many games would he play? How well would he stay together? He had a feeling that this was it, 1957, the end. There was no public pronouncement, no magazine article, not this time, but that was how he felt. Why not give it his best shot? Not that he ever didn't give it his best shot.

"I never did anything special in the off-season, just fish and hunt," Williams said. "Off-season work is just important that you don't get a hell of a lot out of shape. Way overweight. Hell, I hadn't played in a year and a half when I was in the service and I was playing in ten days. Fellows hurt themselves drinking and getting fat."

He arrived in Sarasota in this good shape, took a dollar from traveling secretary Tom Dowd after Dowd bet him he couldn't hit a ball over the distant rightfield fence in a certain exhibition game (he hit two), and stayed in shape. He started well, hit well, and took a couple of different approaches: he hit the ball to left and he kept quiet.

This was the spring he made headlines with his comments to sportswriter Crozet Duplantier in the New Orleans airport lounge about the Marines, about being recalled to Korea, about Harry Truman and Senator Robert Taft and other "gutless politicians." He never thought he would be quoted, and when he was, he was embarrassed. After issuing all the appropriate apologies and explanations, he basically decided to keep his mouth shut.

"I was so mad about the New Orleans incident I wouldn't say anything to anybody," he explained ten years later to Miami sportswriter Edwin Pope. "You might say your boss or some political candidate is lousy in a rhubarb session, but you don't write that . . . things that are unfair or untrue or prejudiced always made me fired up and go hit better."

Pope, whose first choice of 1941 for a Williams book was rejected by the editors of the Golden Year Series because it was in conflict with a book about Joe DiMaggio's 56-game streak, substituted 1957 as Williams's golden year. He interviewed Williams extensively about the season, collecting all the words the famous man held back while he flat-out stunned the American League one more time.

The key to 1957, it turned out, was the bat as much as the batter.

"I picked up a 34½-ounce bat on the way north from spring training, a little heavier than what I had been using," Williams explained. "I tried it out and, boy, I was ringing the ball with it. Boom, right through the middle. I said, 'Hell, I'm going to start the season with this bat.' It was about two ounces heavier than the bat I normally used. It had iron in it. I started the season with it, and I never hit the ball consistently harder than that year."

The heavier bat stopped him from pulling the ball as often. As early as the second game of the season, against the Yankees, *bang*, he had a hit to left against the shift, straight through the shortstop hole. *Bang*, another one. Next game, three for five. *Bang*. He used the bat through the spring, and soon the mouth-to-ear-to-mouth telegraph of pitchers and managers started to spread a new message: maybe Williams can't get around on the fastball anymore. The shift started to be shifted back toward normal dimensions.

Williams's crucial time for accumulating average, proven fact, always was the spring, when the weather was cold. If he started well in the spring, the summer months would carry themselves. After the first two weeks of the season, he was hitting .474 with nine home runs. He was rolling. This was the best start of his career.

"So when it gets warmer, I go back to a little lighter bat," Williams said. "Where I hadn't been getting hits between first base and second base, now I'm getting them. They couldn't shift me so much and I'm going to pulling again. Balls are going through for me that hadn't been going through for five or six years. This was the beginning of the breakthrough for me. This was the real secret of this year."

Quietly, unannounced, virtually unnoticed by the chorus in the press box, he finally had solved the Boudreau Shift. He also had solved the slider, the pesky third option that pitchers had been adding in recent years. Forget the fastball with some pitchers, forget the curve. Want to get cute with the slider? He simply watched the curveballs and fastballs go past. He waited for the slider! He drilled it. He drilled everything.

He had three home runs against Chicago's Bob Keegan on May 8. This was his first three-homer game in a decade. He had three more homers in a game against Early Wynn and Bob Lemon on June 13. This was the first time in American League history a man had two three-home-run games in a single season.

On May 16, Jim Bunning of the Detroit Tigers gave him momentary pause. Bunning struck him out three times, and Tigers catcher Frank House told him, "You're swinging too hard. You're grunting and groaning." Williams's reply was "I only grunt when I miss." He was, to put it mildly, mad. Pissed.

"He came back to the dugout after that third strikeout," Billy Consolo says. "I don't know how to describe the bat rack. The bats go in sideways into little cubicles, you know? The knobs are at the end with your number written across, so you know which bat to take.

"Ted comes down the stairs in the dugout. He throws his bat in the cubicle. Then he takes his fist, swings as hard as he can, punches into the cubicle into the middle of the bats. He swung so hard he knocked little pieces off the knobs of four or five of the bats! His arm is all the way in there, and when he pulls it out, his hand is just covered with blood. He was madder than a hornet."

Williams had a routine. "Bottom of the ninth, two on, two out, Briggs Stadium in Detroit, Williams at the plate . . . ," was the situation he had loudly described for himself in the batting cage for concentration ever since his All-Star home run in 1941. In the following days, his teammates heard a little addition. "Bottom of the ninth, two on, two out, Briggs Stadium in Detroit, *Jim Bunning* on the mound. . . ."

The rematch came on July 12. Consolo sat on the bench and said, Holy Jeez, what's going to happen? Everyone remembered the bloody hand. Williams bet Red Sox PR director Joe McKenney 25 cents he would hit a home run off Bunning. First time up, slider, home run off the top of the third deck at Briggs. Second time up, fastball, deep into the second deck. No need for the imagined home run in the bottom of the ninth.

"The ball came up and in on a slider from Bunning, instead of down," Williams said. "That gave me trouble. I'd be looking for it and swing from my ass and be, ugh, just underneath it. I was missing the fucken sliders and he had that little extra speed. I made up my mind I was going to get on top of the fucken ball. Pssssshhh! That's what I did."

His competition for this batting race was Yankees wunderkind Mickey Mantle. Now in his seventh season after seamlessly replacing Joe Di-Maggio in centerfield for the Yanks, the switch-hitting, 26-year-old Mantle not only had outlasted Williams for the title in 1956, the saliva season, with a .353 average to Williams's .345, but also had won the Triple Crown, leading the league in homers and RBI.

The press tried to make the competition into a prizefight, indicating that Williams was mad, furious, about Mantle's success a year earlier. Williams wasn't talking, so the stories continued. At the end of August, the two men virtually were tied. Williams had come through the summer heat with a .377 average and 33 home runs. Mantle was at .376 and had one more home run. The pennant race was done for the Red Sox, of course, so this was the closing show of the season.

"I wasn't mad at Mantle at all," Williams said. "Every year, whoever I thought I had to beat, they were my targets and I'd watch and see what they were doing. It was just a goal in yourself. Not anything to publicize. Never anything personal."

In the first week of September, working the prizefight analogy, both boxers went back to their corners and stayed there for a while, exhausted. On September 1, Williams checked out of the lineup with a cold and checked into Sancta Maria Hospital one day later with what turned out to be pneumonia. Almost at the same time, Mantle checked out of the lineup with shin splints and on September 6 checked into Lenox Hill Hospital in New York with what turned out to be torn ligaments around his left ankle.

Mantle never recovered. He hit only one more home run the rest of the way, and his average fell to .365, still the highest of his career. Williams went in the other direction. After missing two weeks—a Hy Hurwitz article in the middle of this period predicted he would miss the entire season and probably was finished forever—Williams informed Mike Higgins on September 17 that he felt well enough to pinch-hit against Kansas City if needed.

In the eighth inning, the call came. The Red Sox were trailing, 8–6, and he blasted a two-run shot off Tom Morgan to tie the game. The fun had begun. The Red Sox had two days off and then opened a series in New York. In the first game, Williams pinch-hit to lead off the ninth and whacked a 2-2 pitch for a homer off Whitey Ford. In the second game, he hit a grand slam off Bob Turley in the second inning, the 15th grand slam of his career, then walked three times. In the third game, he homered off Tom Sturdivant, singled and walked twice.

He had hit four home runs in his first four official times at bat after being in the hospital with pneumonia. The fact was even tougher to comprehend than the numbers.

"It's a lot tougher to hit four home runs in a row this way than in a single game," Williams said. "You're playing at night, during the day, different places, four different pitchers. It's a lot tougher than doing it in four at bats against the same pitcher on the same day."

The accomplishment was doubly satisfying because most of it came at Yankee Stadium. He would finish his career with a .309 batting average at the Stadium, 30 home runs, 94 RBI, but always was frustrated by the number of times the Yankees walked him. Given a chance, Yankees manager Casey Stengel always walked Ted Williams.

"I'm gonna guess I walked more times there than anybody else who ever stepped into that stadium," Williams said. "Without question. I know I walked more there than I did in any other park."

The four home runs in four official at bats became part of another streak to mark Williams's return. He reached base 16 consecutive times. No one ever had kept records for something like this, but it certainly seemed like a record.

On September 23, the streak was stopped in Washington when he grounded out against the Senators' Hal Griggs, but in the next at bat he homered. The end of the season simply belonged to him, the old man in the race, the 39-year-old tortoise against the 26-year-old hare. On September 28, he went one for three against Sturdivant at Fenway, to finish with a .388 average.

Jimmy Carroll drove him to the airport after the game.

"He was going to Labrador to go fishing," Carroll says. "He had to fly to some place in Canada, then take a small plane to Labrador. I thought about that. I said, 'Ted, I wouldn't be getting on some small plane to fly to . . . Labrador.'"

"Well, I would," Williams replied.

He always would list the .388 as his greatest baseball achievement, better than the .406, because of what it involved. This was the product of hard labor as opposed to the 1941 product of joy. If he could have run at all, he would have hit over .400. All he needed were eight more hits, bleeders, bang-bang, beat the throw. Wouldn't he have collected the eight more hits if he could run?

The writers again snubbed him in the MVP voting, announced in November. Mantle received 233 votes. Williams received 209. One writer had Williams listed ninth on his ballot, another tenth. Red Sox owner Yawkey called the two writers "incompetent and unqualified to vote." This was the fourth time Williams had finished as MVP runner-up, second in the .406 season to the Yankees centerfielder, second in the .388 season to the next Yankees centerfielder. He had won the award twice.

"No comment," Williams said when asked his reaction.

He was in San Juan, Puerto Rico. He was making a fishing film.

His life outside the ballpark during this time was only a rumor to the younger men who played with him. He was dominant in the clubhouse, talkative on the trains and planes, even sat down now and then to play gin rummy, then he disappeared. On the road, he stayed in a different hotel now under a pseudonym (Al Forrister was one of them) to keep away from the autograph seekers and the noise. At home, he simply wasn't around once the game ended.

He often was gone before the final out.

"I was his official pinch runner," Consolo says. "Gene Stephens was his 'caddy,' who would come in to play the final inning or two, but I was the pinch runner. In 1956 I scored more runs than I had at bats. I had 11 at bats. I scored 13 runs. Is that a record? We'd come into the clubhouse after the game and he'd be gone."

When Williams wasn't gone, Consolo often would watch him leave the parking lot. Consolo walked to the games from the Hotel Kenmore, where he lived. Williams drove from the Somerset. Consolo would linger sometimes, unnoticed, to watch his exit. Fans would be gathered outside the gates of the cramped lot waiting just for Williams. He would drive through them in the Cadillac. It was pandemonium.

"I always was waiting for someone to get killed," Consolo says. "He'd floor it, hit the brakes, floor it, hit the brakes. It was all stop and go until somehow he got through."

Where did he go? What did he do? He was from another generation now. He never was part of any married social scene with the Red Sox, even when he was married. He had never been part of the single social scene, and now, older than everyone else, he wouldn't know where to start. He had his own scene.

"Ballplayers wouldn't ask me to go out and drink because they knew I wouldn't," Williams said. "Besides, I didn't want to talk only baseball. Most ballplayers are so damn dumb you can't get anything from them. I wanted to talk about pitching, world events, something different from what the others did. I never believed in replaying the game. What happens when you replay the game? You second-guess somebody always. The guy you're talking to will go back and tell the other guy, 'You know what Williams said?' Instead of saying we were discussing it with Joe Kluttz, because who gives a shit what Joe Kluttz said?"

He had his guys. Johnny Buckley, first in Brighton, then in Lexington, was the theater manager in Cambridge who first met Williams when he told him to put his feet down from the seat in front while watching a movie. John Blake was the state trooper from Foxboro who stopped him back in 1939, rookie season, and became his friend forever. There were always guys to call. Abby Gordon. Fred Corcoran, the agent. Jimmy Carroll. Joe Lindia in Cranston, Rhode Island.

"Joe was always a big Ted Williams fan. Ted was his guy," Dottie Lindia says about her husband. "We had a restaurant in Cranston. One day, Joe's brother, Eddie, calls from Florida. He was down there on vacation with his wife, Muriel. Eddie was out fishing, and his wife was waiting for him, back at the marina. She was drinking a Narragansett beer. Ted Williams came in and spotted the Narragansett beer, from New England, and started talking to Muriel. She was pretty cute. Ted asked, 'What are you doing?' She said she was waiting for her husband, who was out fishing.

"They got talking, and when Eddie came in, he was flabbergasted. Ted asked Eddie to go fishing with him the next day. That's when Eddie got on the phone to Joe and said, 'You'll never guess who I'm going fishing with tomorrow.' Joe heard the name and said, 'Guess what? I'm going fishing with you too!'

"He closed the restaurant. He got a plane to Miami that night. He took a bus to the Keys. When he got off the bus, early in the morning, Eddie and Ted were waiting for him. Ted said, 'Hey, I understand you want to do a little fishing.' They went from there."

"I always thought Ted had a genuine feeling for people," Jimmy

Carroll says. "I remember driving with him the day after Herb Score, the Cleveland pitcher, had been hit in the eye with a line drive against the Yankees. Ted was really shook up. Really, really shook up."

Carroll's experience with his mother and Williams confirmed his thought. His mother dropped to the sidewalk from a stroke at South Station one afternoon, waiting for the City Point bus on her way home from work. Carroll didn't learn the news until he came home, 1:30 in the morning, after hanging around with Williams at the Somerset. He went to Carney Hospital, stayed with his mother until 4:30 A.M., when the doctors told him she was stable and he should go home and get some rest. He fell dead asleep.

"The phone rings at eight o'clock," Carroll says. "It's Ted. He was supposed to go do something on the North Shore, and I had made plans to drive him. He's shouting, 'Where the hell are you, bush?' He's just going on. I couldn't get a word in, because that's Ted. Finally, I'm able to tell him about my mom going to the Carney with a stroke. He just melted. The line went dead. He said something low in his voice and then he hung up. I went back to bed."

Carroll showed up at the hospital in the afternoon. His mother was now the star, getting the best treatment in the place. What had happened? Ted Williams had showed up! The place had been crazy. Williams had gotten directions to the hospital, drove, become lost, was stopped for speeding, and was escorted to the hospital—the Pope of Baseball—with the sirens screaming. He wound up visiting patients up and down the hall, then said, "I have to go to work now," and played an afternoon game at Fenway.

"Then he calls me up that night to have dinner with him," Carroll says. "The Union Oyster House. Upstairs. We got talking about death, I remember. He was very interested in cremation. He wanted to know what the Catholic Church thought about it. I said I didn't know. He said cremation was for him. He couldn't see lying in a box, all those people coming past. Waterman's, the biggest funeral home in Boston, was right up the street from the Somerset. He said he hated seeing the crowds there. Not for him. It was one of two times he talked about cremation. The other was when we went to visit Harry Agganis at Sancta Maria Hospital."

Agganis was the tragic story of Boston sport. Named Aristotle George Agganis—"Ari" Americanized to "Harry" early through mispronunciation—he grew up in Lynn, one of the many mill towns north of the city. He was handsome as any Greek sculpture, a triple-threat quarterback who took Lynn Classical High School to a mythical national championship at the Orange Bowl in his junior year, then played to crowds totaling over 160,000 people in his senior year.

Scorning scholarship offers from around the country to stay near his widowed mother, he was an all-American at Boston University. Scorning pro football offers after college, he signed a fat bonus contract to play baseball for the Red Sox. He was Consolo's roommate at Sarasota when they both were rookies in 1953. Consolo remembers the phone ringing every day, a phone call from Paul Brown of the Cleveland Browns encouraging Agganis to quit baseball and quarterback the Browns.

In 1954, after a year in minor league Louisville, Agganis hit .251 with the Red Sox with 11 home runs and 57 RBI in his first season in Boston. In 1955 he was hitting .313 when he became sick. On May 16 he complained of chest pains. He went into the hospital, came out, went back in again. On June 27, while doctors tried to help him sit up, he died from a pulmonary embolism, a tragic end.

Williams was the only Red Sox player allowed to visit him in the hospital. Carroll drove him to Cambridge and back.

"What do the Greeks think about cremation?" Williams asked on the ride home.

"Nah, you wouldn't know," Williams answered before Carroll could speak. "You don't even know what the Catholics think."

"He went into it again, about how he wouldn't want to be laid out in a funeral parlor," Carroll says. "That's all we talked about coming back."

Williams was now conscious of age and mortality. He *felt* old. The routines of, say, the .406 season, had changed. He did not fish anymore on the day of games. He did not show up before everyone else at the ballpark and did not stay later than everyone else. He still had a bat in his hands at all times at the ballpark, feeling the wood, swinging, measuring, but he also was measuring his body. He saved his energy.

"When you get older, it takes all of your stamina to get loose," he said. "It's a fight to get loose before you get tired. In a lot of cities I'd walk to the park to get loose. Not New York, but a lot of cities. In Detroit, you'd walk through a slum area. You'd be stopped by 40 drunks, four whores and a lot of sick people. They wouldn't know who you were, but they thought that anybody who would walk through in decent clothes was a millionaire."

The suite at the Somerset was home base. He could admit who he wanted into his life, keep out the rest. He would watch Jack Paar on the television, would eat ice cream straight from the quart container, would look down from his window at the traffic and the people on Commonwealth Avenue. He would call who he wanted on the phone, all calls in return stopped by the switchboard for clearance. He would order room service more often than not. This was the environment he could control.

Most of the time.

"The air conditioner wasn't working one day," Jimmy Carroll says. "He called down to send someone up. No one came. He called down again. No one came. Ted was pissed off. He fooled with the air conditioner and it didn't work. He kicked it. Hard. It fell off the wall into the room.

"The guy finally came up. The air conditioner's just sitting there. It's all beat up. He said, 'What happened here?' Ted said, 'I don't know. The air conditioner fell off the wall.' 'How the hell did it fall off the wall?' 'I don't know.' 'Did you kick it?' 'No.' The thing had a big dent. Ted had such a grin on his face."

There were women in his life. Yes, there were women. The name of a different woman would surface every few years in the paper, the woman claiming that she was going to be the next Mrs. Ted Williams. She usually would be a model or an actress from New York, and the headline would not hurt her career.

"We talked about bubble gum," one of the women breathlessly told UPI when quizzed about her phone calls with Williams. "Some company was going to put his picture in bubble-gum packages."

Maureen Cronin, the daughter of Joe Cronin, was a kid, just about the same age as Bobby-Jo. She had a crush on Williams and tried to see him wherever he was. She stood in line one day at an autograph event. Some women were in front of her. They had their baseball signed, and when they looked at the ball as they walked away they all started screaming, laughing. Cronin followed them.

"What's so funny?" she asked.

The women showed her the ball. It read "Room 231, Hotel Somerset."

"Women chased him everywhere," George Sullivan says. "I was sitting with him once in the dugout in Washington, just the two of us. This woman must have lay down on top of the dugout because all of a sudden her head is right in front of us. Hanging over the edge. Upside down. She had long, long hair. It hung way down. Two feet, maybe three. She's talking to Ted, asking to meet him, basically asking, 'Can I screw you?' Ted played along with her a little bit, but then got tired of her and told her to get the fuck off the dugout. I guess he didn't like the way she looked upside down."

"I was pitching for Washington, maybe the Yankees, after I left the Red Sox," Mickey McDermott says. "I had something going with a woman in Boston. I asked Ted if I could use his room, because I didn't want the manager to know. Ted gave me the key. I went in and there was a bottle of wine, chilled, waiting for me. A little plate of cheese and crackers. The stereo was set up with a record by that colored guy, the piano player—Erroll Garner? It was all laid out for me. He did have some style, Theodore."

Williams's laundry was brought to the suite a couple of times per week by Arthur D'Angelo. Arthur worked at the Somerset as a primary job and ran a souvenir business with his twin brother Henry in his extra time. They were young, immigrant entrepreneurs from Italy, selling pennants and autographed baseballs and whatever other trinkets people would buy from two little carts on Jersey Street. Some of the balls and pictures and other merchandise had Ted Williams's signature on them.

"We had a stamp with his autograph," Arthur, who now owns half of Jersey Street and whose Twins Enterprises supplies souvenirs for the entire country, says. "We just stamped his name on things. He'd tell me sometimes, 'I know you fucken guys are making a lot of fucken money off me,' but he never asked for any of it.

"It was different back then. The games mostly were during the days, and the crowds weren't anything like they are today. You didn't sell a lot of stuff, and Ted really didn't care that much about the money. Not like the guys today."

At the Somerset, Arthur had the only extra key to the suite. He would run assorted errands for Williams, deliver the clean clothes, mostly when Williams was on the road. Every now and then, though, when Williams was at home, Arthur would stumble into social situations. He would see some women. Nothing scandalous, understand, just a woman in the room here, a woman there. Arthur was surprised at the women. He did not think they always were particularly attractive.

"Ted," he finally said, "Joe DiMaggio is married to Marilyn Monroe. What's the deal? You could have any woman you want. These women I see, I hate to say it, mostly are dogs."

Williams made a crude anatomical remark about all women being basically the same. He wasn't looking for Marilyn Monroe.

The next three years, the closeout to his Red Sox career, were marked by the same kinds of battles he had with his body in 1957. He constantly was trying to keep the parts working. The Associated Press voted him Athlete of the Year for 1957—ahead of World Series hero Lew Burdette, middleweight champ Carmen Basilio, Texas A&M running back John David Crow, and Stan Musial (Mantle was 13th)—but the Athlete of the Year was not exactly ready for four-minute miles and handstands. He mostly was trying to keep his athletic self together.

The magic of the .388 year didn't linger. He was hurt a week after the season ended. Trying to reach a landlocked trout in Labrador, he caught his left foot between two rocks and twisted his ankle. The injury lingered through the winter and into spring training for 1958.

When the ankle started to get better, he hurt his side. He was just demonstrating his batting stroke. The side seemed to feel better, then he hurt it again, demonstrating again. On Opening Day, he was sick with food poisoning from eating tainted oysters a night earlier. He missed the game.

The best start of his career in '57 was replaced by the worst start of his career in '58. The league had mandated the use of protective headgear at the plate for the first time—"miner's caps," the players called the helmets—and Williams took the least-protective, least-obtrusive route, inserting a plastic liner inside his regulation cap, but even that didn't feel right.

He was hitting .225 on May 20. Mel Ott, the Hall of Fame outfielder for the New York Giants who retired in 1947, sympathized in the *Globe* with the idea of an old man playing a young man's game.

"Here is a man, almost 40 years old . . . ," Ott said. "When I reached 40, I'd hung 'em up long ago. I had to. I ran out of gas.

"It was plain murder trying to play when I was only 37. Bill Klem, the old umpire, gave me a helpful hint one time. He suggested that every night I got five pounds of raw epsom salts and drop them into a steaming tub and jump in. I'd spend half an hour in the tub, then crawl into bed, exhausted. I barely made it. Every bone and muscle in my body ached."

Only three players in the big leagues—Murry Dickson, Enos Slaughter, and Mickey Vernon—were older than Williams. On May 21, there was another indication of how old Williams was: the Colonel, Dave Egan of the *Record*, his biggest and most persistent critic, died.

Egan was found in the living room of his Wakefield home by his wife, Mary. He had been having assorted health problems, but his death by natural causes was still a surprise. He was 57 years old and already had worn out his body.

His wake at the Horace A. McMahon Funeral Home and his funeral at St. Joseph's Church were large affairs. Archbishop Richard J. Cushing, soon to become Boston's most famous cardinal, officiated the Mass. He eulogized Egan as a man "blessed with a great natural talent."

"He had a powerful pen and a facility for turning the English language into a most effective form of writing," the archbishop said. "He accomplished a great deal of good. For many people, the sports pages of the newspaper are the most important section. While all the people who read his columns didn't agree with him, they all appreciated him. They enjoyed him. And to bring joy to people is a great thing."

Egan left a complicated legacy. He was the only writer in Boston who had complained loudly about the Red Sox' racist outlook under Yawkey, the only one who saw the shame in a forced, half-baked, no-chance tryout in 1945 for Negro League stars Jackie Robinson, Sam Jethroe, and Marvin Williams. He was often credited or derided as one of the major forces in the Boston Braves' decision in 1953 to leave town. He was a different voice at all times, making fun of the powerful and successful, siding with the unpowerful and unsuccessful . . . and, of course, there were his "accounts" at the racetracks and boxing rings.

His columns about Williams were remembered more than any others. He had been a defender of Williams in personal situations—the controversy surrounding the birth of Bobby-Jo, for instance—but a constant critic on all other matters. No one had attacked Williams more often.

"I used to sell the *Record* at the ballpark when I was a kid," Ray Flynn, later the mayor of Boston, says. "It cost three cents, and I'd always fish around in my pocket, looking for change, hoping the guy would say 'keep the two cents.'

"Ted Williams was my idol. Whenever the Colonel would write something bad about him, I'd go through all my papers and rip out the page that had the Colonel's column on it. It was my own little tribute to my hero. I swear on my mother I did this."

Honorary pallbearers at Egan's funeral included owner Walter Brown and star Bob Cousy of the Boston Celtics, Milt Schmidt of the Boston

Bruins, boxers Tommy Collins and Tony DeMarco, race track owner B. A. Dario, and Joe Cronin of the Red Sox. Egan's space in the newspaper the next day was taken by Larry Claflin, a young *Record* columnist.

"Hardly a day passed when someone wouldn't ask you if you knew the Colonel and what kind of man he was," Claflin wrote. "It was a difficult question to answer and it still is. He was a man of frequently short temper. He would have all the patience in the world with those who interrupted him if he liked them, but none if he didn't like the visitor. He had a savage typewriter when the occasion demanded, yet a beautifully gentle one at times. His typewriter seemed to always have the right word at the right time, but only when he sat at it. . . .

"And you thought to yourself that the Colonel was a man with whom you just had to disagree at times, because he always took a strong stand, but he was a man you just had to read," Claflin concluded. "And you thought about the time Ted Williams called you 'the poor man's Dave Egan' and you admitted that you always felt that was a compliment."

Williams was on the road for all of this. On May 23, the day Egan was buried, the wheels and levers to calibrate his swing all seemed to slip back into place. After reading an Egan-esque column in a Kansas City paper suggesting that he was finished, done, he went 4-for-4 against the A's, including a grand slam homer. The long climb to statistical respectability began.

He was close to .300 in June and was at .308 by the All-Star Game, where Casey Stengel had to add him to the roster, the first time he was not chosen for the starting lineup. He continued at this pace, slowly climbing through the second half of the season. There was a spitting incident in Kansas City when he didn't run out a ground ball and was booed and fined $250. ("I'm sorry," he half-apologized. "Principally, I'm sorry about the $250.") He had a game in Detroit where he hit two monster home runs, one of them off Jim Bunning. He missed time with both a sore wrist and his usual respiratory woes.

When late September came, he found himself in a late race for the batting title. His unlikely opponent was slap-hitting second baseman Pete Runnels, his teammate. Runnels, traded from the Senators to the Sox in the off-season for Albie Pearson and Norm Zauchin, had benefited from the fact he batted second in the lineup and Williams batted third. Pitchers had to throw strikes to Runnels because they knew they still had to be careful when Williams came to the plate.

On September 22, Runnels was leading the chase by six points. Williams was struggling, hitless in his last seven at bats. He was not a happy man. The opponent at Fenway was the Senators. In the first inning, Runnels singled and Williams grounded into a double play. The unhappiness grew. In the third, Runnels singled again. Williams was called out on a third strike down the middle of the plate from Bill Fischer. The unhappiness became fury.

Angry at himself, not the umpire, he turned away from the plate and took the swing he should have taken at the fat strike. He went to release the bat toward the dugout in disgust on his follow-through, but his hand stuck for an instant on the mixture of olive oil and resin that he used for grip. The bat flew out of his hand and out of control and into the stands. The knob end struck the head of 60-year-old Gladys Heffernan, the housekeeper for Joe Cronin, sitting in her boss's box seats.

Williams was mortified. It was an accident, of course, but one of those accidents—"Don't run with that pencil in your hand, you'll poke your eye out!"—that kids have when they're doing something they shouldn't do. He rushed to the box and apologized to the bleeding woman. He went to the first aid room to see her. He cried. The fans booed.

"I don't see why they had to boo him," the plucky Heffernan said, not seriously injured. "I felt awfully sorry for him. He came into the first aid room to see me, and you could tell by the look on his face how badly he felt. It was an accident."

Williams said, "I wanted to die."

Once again, his emotions had become a public spectacle. How did this happen? Why did it always happen to him? Dr. Sidney Farber, the head of Children's Hospital and the Jimmy Fund, an associate and friend of Williams's, already had given the best explanation in a quote in a story called "How Ted Williams Became Popular" in the June 1958 issue of *Sport* magazine.

"My two teenage boys watch Ted at Fenway Park and we have some serious talks around the dinner table about baseball and Ted," Dr. Farber said. "Here's what I tell my boys. There is a man running 100 yards in 10 seconds and he steps on a little pebble and falls down and breaks his neck. The same man, walking 100 yards at his leisure, would never even have noticed that pebble. There is that tremendous strain to strive to do so well in Ted. That intenseness, that fight toward perfection. Here is a man with greatness as an athlete. I can't understand why people sometimes boo him. If he bats .400, which is considered as near to perfection as a player can get, it means also that he has failed 600 times. I think we should remember the 400 times he has hit safely and not dwell on the rest."

The typists in the press box again decided to dwell on the rest. Williams, who doubled in his last at bat in the game, surrounded by boos from the Fenway crowd, was fined $50 for the incident by league president Will Harridge. The typists thought Williams was handled quite lightly.

"Consider what would have happened if a less important and popular player—say Julio Becquer of the Senators—had thrown the bat after taking a third strike," Harold Kaese suggested in the *Globe*. "He probably would have been (1) kicked out of the game, (2) fined much more than $50 and suspended, (3) arrested, and (4) told to go back to Cuba and stay there."

"It is the excuse of Williams' partisans that disgust with himself provoked him into throwing the bat that struck the old lady," Jimmy Cannon wrote for the North American News Alliance. "I agree with Williams' opinion of himself."

The words were nothing but a late-season tonic to the perpetrator of the dastardly deed. Always focused by personal crisis, he began a wondrous stretch of hitting, his double setting him off on a .500 pace for his final 28 at bats. On the next-to-last day of the season, he was tied to the ninth percentage point with Runnels at .322. The difference in the math was that his .322 was on 130 hits in 403 at bats, while Runnels was 180 for 558. Every hit meant more to Williams.

"I'm watching this whole thing on the next-to-last day, and it's just terrific, all this pressure," Billy Consolo says. "Pete and Ted, one after the other. Pete gets up the first time and hits a triple, and I say, 'Pete's got it.' Ted walks. Second time up, Pete gets a single, and I say, 'Well, that's it.' Then Ted gets a single right behind him. 'Maybe not.' Then Pete gets up and hits a home run. 'Pete's got it.' Then Ted hits a home run, *right after him!* 'Wow.' Then Pete hits a long fly ball that Roy Sievers catches, great catch, and Ted gets a single. Pete's got three hits and he loses the lead. It was just amazing."

Runnels wound up 3-for-6 on the day. Williams was 3-for-4. For the first time all season, final day of the season, he was at the top of the list. On that final day, with a double and a homer while Runnels went hitless, he clinched the batting title. His sixth. He resembled one of those aging Gary Cooper gunfighters, brought back to the dusty street, still able to do what he did on the right day and in the big moment. He was the American League batting champion at age 40.

"Consolo and I were watching him during a game, I don't remember the year," Ted Lepcio says. "He hit a ball that almost killed the first baseman. We started wondering about how it was possible to hit a ball that hard. Mickey Vernon was with us, sitting on the bench. He said, 'Listen, when he first came around, he hit three shots a day down the line like that. I remember when I played against him I asked the manager not to have me hold the runners on first because that son of a bitch hit the ball so fast down there you didn't have a chance."

In 1959 all that stopped. This was the year the body took control and won the battle over the mind.

A few weeks before spring training began, Williams was swinging a bat underneath a coconut tree behind his house in Islamorada, Florida. He was telling a friend what a good year he was going to have. Something twanged at the base of his neck on the right side during one of the swings. A little something. A "hey!" An "ow!" He thought nothing of it. Except that was his season, right there.

The Red Sox had switched training sites from Sarasota to Scottsdale, Arizona. They opened their exhibition schedule with three games against the Cleveland Indians in San Diego. In the second of the three exhibitions, midway through the game, Williams again felt that small pull at the base of his neck on the right side. A crick. That's what it was, a crick in the neck. The crick in the neck—a pinched nerve—would never leave.

He wound up going to Boston from Scottsdale and straight into traction at New England Baptist Hospital for three weeks. He wound up wearing a cervical collar. He wound up missing the first month and a half of the season. He wound up going 1-for-22, an .045 average, to start his comeback. He wound up benched on June 14 by manager Pinky Higgins. His average now was .175. He was 18-for-103. The Red Sox were in last place in the American League.

"We'll give Teddy a few days' rest," Higgins told reporters.

"Did Williams suggest this himself?" they asked.

"I just figured it would do him some good," the manager said.

"But did Williams make the suggestion?"

"No. He's got in a little rut. A few days off will help anybody."

The move was shocking. For all of his career after the first two seasons, Williams basically had been his own manager. He decided when he would or wouldn't, could or couldn't play. Very few players before him, maybe none besides Babe Ruth, had been given that kind of latitude. Now Williams was being treated like another struggling name on the roster.

"The inevitable has happened: For the first time Ted Williams has been benched for reasons other than his own choosing or through injury, war service or marital mixup," Austen Lake wrote in the *American*. "Did we ever imagine we'd see the day when old No. 9 with his droopy pant-legs would be tweezed from the Red Sox lineup because of (1) light hitting— and him the Albert Einstein of the bat, (2) gimpy gallops in pursuit of balls to his outfield sector and (3) inability to get around the bases?

"I report this with a sense of melancholy. For there seemed to be a sense of 'permanency' about TSW, an 'imperishable' quality, which went with his super physique and rugged resistance to the ordinaries of life. Who, him? It is a bit of a shock to find he is fashioned of plain meat and bones."

The time on the bench didn't help. Nothing really helped. Williams would feel uncomfortable at the plate for the entire season. He couldn't turn his head far enough to get a good look at the pitcher. He was back in the pack of the normal, the average, the everybody-else, guessing and swinging and going back to the dugout befuddled. He hit as low as sixth in the order. He was human, normal.

The one leftover constant from his star-power life was his greatest irritant: the attention. He still was Ted Williams, and everything he did was news. Bad news now. He outlined a three-step program to get rid of the problem for Tommy Holmes of the *New York Herald Tribune*.

"Sportswriters," he said. "First I'd like to find uranium. Then I'd buy a major league club. Then I'd bar all writers from the park."

He hit .254 for the sad season, 10 homers, the numbers of a utility infielder, only edging the figures that high when the neck loosened a little toward the end and he started to swing a little better.

"I had a miserable year," Williams said in *My Turn at Bat*. "The worst of my career by far. I could barely turn my neck to look at the pitcher. I wasn't getting nearly enough of a look, and I thrashed around all year near .250. A lot of times, I wouldn't even go to the dugout between innings if I didn't think I would get to bat. I'd just wait in the bullpen. I seemed to go from slump to slump. . . . As was pointed out to me by some of my friends in left field, I could spit farther than I was hitting."

The easy idea would be to quit, to pack it in, to go home. The oft-told story—told by Williams himself—is how he went to see Yawkey on the day after the season ended at Yawkey's suite at the Ritz-Carlton, not knowing what he was going to do. How the owner told him to quit. *You've had a great career, you were hurting this year, and I don't want to see you hurt more. Listen, why don't you just wrap it up?* How the words struck his ears wrong, one more catcall from the chorus, one more challenge. The faithful follower of Williams's career can almost hear the reply in Williams's head, steam starting to turn the engines. *Quit? Go fuck yourself! I'll say when I fucken quit!* Not that he said those words out loud. Just that he thought them, chewed on them, used them to make his decision.

One more year. His terms.

He knew he still could hit. That was the one important fact that everyone else seemed not to notice. He was hitting better at the end of the season. If he could keep the parts on the old car lubricated, top off the radiator, and rotate the tires one more time, he could drive out in some semblance of style. Maybe the neck would quiet down with a winter of rest. Maybe nothing new would develop. Maybe he could do this one last thing. The telegrams from Eddie Mifflin listed a string of achievements that could be reached. Eight more homers and Williams would have hit 500. Why not? One more year.

He appeared in the office of Red Sox business manager Dick O'Connell with a strange request in January 1960. In Boston for his now-annual dual-purpose visit for the Sportsmen's Show and contract signing, Williams proposed that he take a pay cut. He'd been paid $125,000 in 1959, the highest salary in baseball, and hadn't played like the best player in baseball. The Red Sox could take back $35,000 for 1960. He would work for $90,000. Fair?

O'Connell tried to talk him out of the idea. Williams was insistent. That was the new contract, $90,000. More than a 25 percent pay cut.

"I don't think that will ever happen again," O'Connell said, years later, after hundreds of subsequent contract negotiations. "Nowadays, if you want to cut a salary, the players' association is ready to take you to court."

"I was surprised at first and later I wasn't," Yawkey said. "You have to know Ted. He's an unusual person. He does what he wants and doesn't give a damn what other people think."

Ted Williams at a discount. One more year. The Filene's Basement Hall of Famer. How would this work?

"The most we can expect from him is 100 games," Billy Jurges, now the Red Sox manager, said. "The least we can expect is pinch-hitting."

W illiams arrived in Scottsdale for spring training still wondering what would come next. The pain in his neck was still there. The best encouragement he had received was from a doctor from Johns Hopkins who had stayed in Islamorada for vacation. The doctor told Williams he had suffered from the same type of neck problem and that one day, poof, it simply had disappeared. No reason.

Maybe that would happen here. Maybe not.

Williams's mind also was on events in San Diego in the old house on Utah Street. It turned out he had been more involved with his family than anyone ever knew. His brother Danny, sick for three years with leukemia, would die on March 28. Far from the noses of the Boston press, certainly never mentioned by him, Williams had been involved in Danny's fight against the illness. He had chartered flights for Danny to go to Salt Lake City for treatments. He had provided money to keep Danny's family afloat. He had visited.

"There's been a mythology built up that Ted Williams hated his family," his nephew, Ted Williams, Danny's son, says. "I just finished David Halberstam's book, *The Teammates*, that repeats it. That disappoints me. Something gets started and is just perpetuated without research, just a retelling of the old story.

"It's simply not true. There's a quote in Halberstam's book from Bobby Doerr, who says Ted said he hated his family. I'm sure Ted said it. He said a lot of things. The way he talked . . . he said things that sounded a lot worse than they really were. The truth is that he did a lot of nice things for his family. I was just at a gathering, maybe 40 family members, all from the Hispanic side, and they all had stories of things Ted did for them. He took care of everybody at one time or another.

"I think he was as close and as friendly with his family as a loner could be. He really didn't have the time or interest to be around a lot, but he visited. There are pictures of him at some Mexican restaurants, everybody there from the family. He certainly was involved financially."

Williams would call his relatives on his mother's side "the Mexicans" when talking with his brother. Not, it seemed, in a deprecating way. A Ted Williams way. If he was ashamed of his Mexican heritage, he never said so. If he was proud, he never said so. He never said anything about any of this. He handled his family matters the way he handled his charity work: quietly. He did what he did and shared the facts with no one.

When he was in California, throughout his career and then for the rest of his life, he would pop in and out of Santa Barbara, the home of "the Mexicans." The visits primarily were to see his aunt, Sara Diaz, who had helped to raise him. Maybe he wouldn't even spell the family name right in his autobiography—"Venzer" instead of "Venzor"—but Danny Venzor lived next door to Sara and other Venzors lived in the immediate neighborhood, and when he visited, he would see most of them.

"I went to live in New York for a while," Dee Allen, daughter of Saul Venzor, the pitcher who first taught Williams to hit, says. "I went to a game at Yankee Stadium. We sat near the third-base thing, and I asked an attendant to call Ted. Gave him my name. He came right away. We had a nice talk."

Thirty, forty years later, Williams still was involved. He called Allen and said he had heard that Sara's house needed some help. What was wrong? Allen made a list. He asked Allen to oversee the rehabilitation of the house. She collected estimates to fix the roof, fix the windows, add screens, put a chain-link fence around the property. She called Williams and he okayed the different projects and sent the funds.

"That's the best money I ever spent," he told a friend.

Was that someone who hated his family? He wrote a letter to Danny in the spring of 1959 that fit his situation perfectly. It was the letter of the still-concerned loner: short, self-absorbed, repentant, but still trying to be involved.

Dear Dan and Jean,

As you probably know, I'm in Phoenix for Spring Training. Right now I'm sore all over. Trying as hard as I can to get in shape to get one more year and be of some good to the club.

Sorry I haven't called or written sooner, but have been so busy getting packed and out here. Its really a rat race.

Saw the people that own the apartment next door and they spoke awfully nice about you folks. He is sure a nice fellow and so is she. She said the Lutz's were all right.

Hope Danny is getting along. Apparently the new medicine is helping. With summer coming on the heat will help him.

Will call next week.

Best, as always,

Ted

Hello to Sam and Ted

Danny had found some stability toward the end of his life as a house painter and carpenter. His son also dislikes the oft-repeated descriptions of his father as a "criminal." He says his father was angry a lot, exploding at simple situations—which seemed to be a family trait—but was far from a criminal.

"He always wanted things the easy way," Ted Williams, the son, says. "He could work hard, but then he would make bad decisions. I remember him building the barbecue in the back at Utah Street. I remember him rebuilding the porch. He wasn't afraid of work. The problem was, he'd work hard, say make $80, and then go gambling with it. I guess his idea was that he could make it $300 instead of $80, but that wouldn't happen. He'd come home broke again.

"His anger was an internal situation. He had it, Ted had it, May had it. I'll bet Ted's father, Sam, had it too. My father was like Ted. He could go along, la-de-dah, la-de-dah, then something would boil up and he would cross the line. He'd stomp around the house. Hit people. I remember one time he sent my brother and me to bed and we were in the bedroom, flipping quarters. One of the quarters fell off the bed and made a sound. Rolled across the floor. My father came in, furious, just beat the shit out of both of us. It wasn't what we were doing—we were kids, just playing—it was something inside him. He couldn't stop himself."

Williams went to Danny's funeral, then arranged to have May move from Utah Street to Santa Barbara to live with Sara, then in a rest home. May was 68 years old, unhinged by the fate of her youngest son. She would be dead within a year. Williams also had a promise for Danny's widow. The boys? His nephews? When they were ready for college, he would pay the bills.

"My mother remarried not too long after my dad died," Ted Williams, the nephew, says. "We didn't see Ted for maybe the next ten years. Then, when I graduated high school, my mother said, 'Here's his number. Give him a call. He said he'd send you to college.' I called and that's just what he did for me and for my brother. I'd call him every semester—right around the time tuition payments were due—and give him a progress report. And he'd send a check."

None of this was ever in the newspapers or the magazines or even his own book. This was family, personal. He didn't talk about family, personal. Not that he didn't carry the personal with him. It seemed to be on his mind when he returned to Scottsdale. The neck still hurt. The body still hurt. The death of his brother still hurt.

He clearly was struggling.

"I keep thinking, 'Williams, you're dying hard,' " he told Milton Gross of the *New York Post*. "I keep saying to myself, 'Your neck hurts, your ankle hurts and your back hurts and you are dying so damn hard.' "

Gross had a unique interview style. He would whisper his questions. It would be maddening to a crowd of sportswriters trying to overhear the answers because the natural reply to a whisper is a whisper. The entire interview would be conducted sotto voce.

"Why did you come back to try it another year when it is so hard?" Gross whispered. "Is it the money? Is it your record, hitting below .300 for the first time in 20 years?"

"I'm not wealthy," Williams whispered in return. "I can certainly use the money. But that's not all of it. I'd kind of like to redeem myself for last year. Another of the important reasons I came back is that I want to reach 500 home runs."

The Red Sox offices at Fenway had been swamped with remedies for his strained neck. Fans sent information on miracle salves, miracle diets, miracle doctors, miracle chiropractors. A woman from San Francisco said the neck pain would go away if he massaged his big toe. An ex-Marine from Fort Worth advised rubbing face cream along the "back" of his spine.

"We have a formula which has for years kept our racehorses free of such a condition as you are now troubled with," a processing manager wrote from Michigan. "When a racehorse is in training for the season he often encounters a condition like yours. This formula heals him while he continues training. Be pleased to send you some if you will use it. There is no charge."

Nothing seemed to work. The spring was a grind. He never felt right. His comments always would include an "I don't know" and a "maybe I'm done," and his body still seemed to be screaming at him to go home.

And then the screaming stopped. Opening day in Washington.

"I've been traded to the Senators," Billy Consolo says. "I'm actually playing. The first inning, I hit a home run. I run the bases, sit in the dugout, and feel pretty good about myself. I can see the headlines about Consolo in the next day's papers. Then Ted gets up in the second inning. He hits a ball off Camilo Pascual that is one of the longest home runs ever hit in Griffith Stadium. I don't think my home run even was mentioned in the stories the next day."

The shot went almost 500 feet to dead centerfield, clearing a 31-foot wall. Williams hadn't hit a home run in the entire spring in Arizona. Three-two count. Waist-high fastball. He had hit one now in his first at bat in the regular season.

"I put something on it," Pascual said. "I throw it real good, but it looks like he no care."

"I think the umpire and I were still watching the ball when Williams came home," catcher Earl Battey said.

On the next day, the home opener in Fenway against the Yankees, he hit a second shot, curving a Jim Coates waist-high fastball around the foul pole in right. True, he'd be out of the lineup for almost a month from pulling a muscle just running bases in that home run trot, and true, he would then be hit with the annual virus to miss some more games, but the neck was good. He was back.

His final season became a sweet baseball encore, not a pull of the curtain. The home run off Pascual had tied him at 493 home runs with Lou Gehrig, fourth lifetime, and the home run off Coates put him ahead. As the schedule unfolded, he knocked off one after another of Eddie Mifflin's list of goals. He slammed number 495 off Ralph Terry on his return to action on June 5 at Yankee Stadium and went from there. He would hit seven home runs in the next two weeks, 12 in 80 at bats, the best power pace of his career.

In the midst of that streak, he hit number 500, a magic mark, on June 17 against the Cleveland Indians off rookie Wynn Hawkins. He then announced to *Cleveland Plain-Dealer* columnist Hal Lebovitz, not the Boston writers, that he was going to retire at the end of the season. For sure this time. He also said he was never going to be a manager. He didn't want the pressure.

"Big guys . . . well, I don't want to say I'm a big guy, but I've been under pressure because I'm a hitter," he explained. "I guess I've been under pressure all the time.

"I'll give you an example. One time I came into Cleveland here. I can't remember just the circumstances. It may be I was just back from Korea and hadn't been hitting. Anyway, I hadn't been hitting and I was sick.

"But we got here to Cleveland and there was a big headline, 'Score to Face Williams.' Well, Score had been pitching right along. And I hadn't been hitting. Besides, I was sick. But because of that headline, I had to play. That's the sort of thing I mean. If I became a manager, I'd go right on being under that same pressure. I've had it for 20 years."

Back in Cleveland in August, he hit homer number 511 off Jim Perry to tie Mel Ott for third place on the all-time list, then soared past Ott with two more shots the next day. On the plane to Baltimore that night, he bought champagne for everyone on the flight, including the sportswriters.

"So scientists think getting to the moon is an accomplishment?" Clif Keane asked the next day in the *Globe*. "Know what happened to the baseball writers yesterday on the flight here from Cleveland?"

The Red Sox were terrible again, heading toward a seventh-place finish, 32 games out of first, their worst finish in 27 years. The games meant nothing. The rest of the season was a nostalgic last lap around the league for their star. Williams spurned all offers of special presentations at other ballparks and was saluted instead at each stop after a final groundout or pop fly to right only by the standing ovations of a knowledgeable baseball public.

The quotes about him now frequently were in the past tense. The pieces of his career were laid out, a string of cards that went back to 1939. The numbers had become remarkable.

"Do you realize that I'm only six months older than Ted and this is the ninth year I've been gone from baseball?" Bobby Doerr said on a visit to Boston. "I couldn't imagine myself out there trying to do what Ted is doing."

"He never missed a bus," Joe Cronin, now president of the American League, said to sportswriter John P. Carmichael in Chicago. "He'd take an upper or a lower on a train. He was a 'loner' from the beginning. From the first day he appeared, he said: 'I'd like to leave my playing on the field.' He went along. He took his pitches and he never moaned. That wasn't his nature.

"Ted Williams was built to accept a challenge. He was always at his best. He had a goal for hitting and home runs and he never lost sight of it."

Cronin sympathized with Williams's path as a loner. The buzz around him often seemed so unnecessary.

"He had his own public relations within himself," Cronin said. "It could have been better with the press, but so often they wrote about him just to torment Ted and get him going. He was a kid. He had some careless moments when you'd have to yell at him . . . but he never was a disturbing element on the club.

"He'd just get mad at something and there he'd go. His fault was listening to the fans. Players could say the same things to him and he'd laugh, but he'd get mad at the customers. But in his heart he didn't mean it. I always felt that about him."

On September 25, after the Yankees finally had won the American League pennant, the Red Sox announced that Williams officially was retiring. His final appearance at Fenway Park would be three days later, a Wednesday afternoon game against the Baltimore Orioles.

"Dear Boss: This is it," wrote John Gilooly, sitting in the Colonel's old chair at the *Record*, for the morning of Williams's final game. "Deal me out. I am through.

"Get another boy and give him a new ribbon and let him take over the keyboard. This is my official resignation. Williams has retired. He won't be back. Neither will I. My old job as a lifeguard at an uptown car-wash is still open. I can return at the same salary.

"The loss of Williams to a Boston sports columnist is like a bad case of athlete's fingers to Van Cliburn. You just can't pound the keys any more. The song has ended."

The sentiment was perfect. What would the Red Sox do for a left-fielder, for a powerful, consistent bat, a perpetual All-Star? Who cared? Where would all the words go? That was the important question. Take away the haystacks or the water lilies and what would Monet paint? This was a sunset of the imagination, the object of inspiration disappearing forever. If there were no Tintern Abbey, how could there be discussion about what flew around its belfry?

"Our Hemingway," Gilooly called Williams. "Oh, the stories he has written for us."

The Great Ted Williams Essay Contest was ending. There never had been anything like it in Boston. The mountain of words around this one man was larger even than his accomplishments on the field. He had been the finest civic entertainment imaginable for 21 years, chin stuck out, taking on all varieties of comers. Yip had been countered with yap, bite with snarl, barbed-wire similes with 450-foot round-trippers. What a wonderful show! Generations had grown up in New England, jumping for the newspaper, gasping or laughing to start the day, taking a side and enjoying it all.

Now it was done?

Almost . . .

Two out-of-town contestants had arrived for the final day. One was the 28-year-old novelist John Updike, simply following his nose to the event. Already celebrated for *The Poorhouse Fair* and *Rabbit Run*, on a course to become the preeminent man of letters for an entire generation, he brought a fan's sensibilities to the moment, a hero-worshiper's love. The second writer was Ed Linn, a 36-year-old nonfiction craftsman of sports features and books, on assignment from *Sport* magazine. He brought the insider's look, the durable cynicism of a Boston native who had followed Williams's entire career with fascination and had spent considerable time inside the ropes with the famous man in mouth-to-mouth combat.

Two perspectives. Updike would describe the flavor and aroma of the gourmet sausage in *The New Yorker*. Linn would describe how it was made in *Sport*. The words would be saved and shown to college students in the future.

"On the afternoon of Wednesday, Sept. 28th, 1960, as I took a seat behind third base, a uniformed groundskeeper was treading this [leftfield] wall, picking batting-practice home runs out of the screen, like a mushroom gatherer seen in Wordsworthian perspective on the verge of a cliff," Updike wrote. "The day was overcast, chill and uninspirational. . . ."

"Ted came into the locker room at 10:50, very early for him," Linn wrote. "He was dressed in dark brown slacks, a yellow sports shirt and a light tan pullover sweater, tastily brocaded in the same color. Ted went immediately to his locker, pulled off the sweater, then strode into the locker room. . . ."

The poetic elegance of the situation, final game, all these years, all of this struggle, would be placed against the cantankerous reality of the competitive man. Updike would describe the ecclesiastical joke he heard behind him from Boston College sophomores. Linn would describe Williams telling some photographers to kiss his ass. Updike would describe the tilt of Williams's head, the nuances of his stance, the busywork of his hands. Linn would describe Williams sweet-talking some unidentified redhead. Back and forth. This was all of it. The whole picture.

The crowd was small, 10,454, everyone bundled against the cold. The Red Sox never had been big on public relations, on show. The largesse of Tom Yawkey, it was said, stopped at the last name on the player payroll. There was confusion too about the day. Was this Williams's last game at Fenway? Or was it his last game period? The Red Sox would head for three more games at Yankee Stadium to close out the schedule. The retirement announcement had been ambivalent about whether Williams would play in those games.

If he was going to New York, well, there probably was bigger Red Sox news to consider on this day. Bucky Harris, the general manager and drinking buddy of Yawkey, had been fired at the tag end of this sad campaign and Jackie Jensen, the hard-hitting rightfielder, had returned. Afraid of flying, Jensen had sat out the year but grown itchy in California. He was on hand to announce that he would be back.

Williams's final game at Fenway was sort of crammed into the middle of all of this. The small crowd indicated how little emphasis had been placed on the moment.

The ceremonies before the game were brief, a few politicians and broadcaster Curt Gowdy speaking. Gowdy's speech was on the fly, off the top of his head, extemporaneous. ("Ted asked me for a copy once," Gowdy says. "There was no copy.") Williams's speech was pure Williams, with a shot at the sportswriters and a quick good-bye.

"Despite the many disagreeable things said about me by the Knights of the Keyboard [pointing at the press box]—and I can't help thinking about them—despite these things my stay in Boston has been the most wonderful thing in my life," he said. "If I were asked where I would like to have played I would have to say Boston with the greatest owner in baseball and the greatest fans in America."

His final day on the job began.

Baseball is different from other American games. Football, basketball, and hockey are played at an edge-of-the-seat pace. They are car chases, action films, the spectator as pulled into the activity as the participants. Baseball is a drawing-room drama. The spectator sits back, analyzes, discusses. The best big moments arrive at the end, everyone sitting around a long table as Hercule Poirot begins to divulge exactly who done it. That is when the spectator moves to the front of his seat. That is what happened here.

Williams walked in the first inning. . . .

He flied to center in the third. . . .

He flied to right in the fifth, this time forcing outfielder Al Pilarcik to the wall. . . .

He did not come to the plate again until the eighth. . . .

In the on-deck circle was Jim Pagliaroni, one of the many kids in the Red Sox lineup, 22 years old, a catcher. He remembers feeling the moment, knowing that something was going to happen. The excitement.

He had grown up in Long Beach, California, and had turned down a larger offer from the Los Angeles Dodgers and signed with the Red Sox for $85,000 in 1955 simply because his hero was Ted Williams. Brought to the big club immediately under the bonus rule, he had met the man himself for the first time in the bathroom of the clubhouse. Pagliaroni was at one urinal. Williams stepped up to the next urinal and said hello. Pagliaroni had a confused bathroom reaction.

"I almost crapped in my pants," he says.

The Red Sox had told him to join the Army to get both his military commitment and the weird bonus restriction out of the way, so two years in the service and two more years in the minors had passed, and now he was back with the Red Sox. Ted Williams still was his idol.

"Two things I always tell people," he says. "First, a few years later I was in the National League. Stan Musial came up to me and asked how I'd liked playing with the Kid. I said, 'Great,' and he said, 'You know, people always would compare the two of us. Well, there was no comparison. Ted Williams was the best. He's the only hitter I've never seen check his swing. Not once. Every other hitter, and I've seen most of them, has checked his swing a bunch of times. Never Ted.'

"Number 2, I myself eventually caught behind a lot of great hitters. Musial. Mantle. Roberto Clemente. Hank Aaron. Name 'em. Ted Williams was the only hitter . . . I'd put my glove up, sure I was going to catch the ball, and he would swing and hit it. That was how late he was, how quick. Nobody else ever made me think I was going to catch a ball that was hit."

Pagliaroni stared now, along with everyone else. What was going to happen? What would Ted do? He came out to a respectful ovation, the 10,454 folk clapping hands, noisier perhaps than if the park had been full, the sound whirling around the empty seats.

On the mound was Oriole reliever Fat Jack Fisher, who had surrendered the last two fly balls to Williams. He was a fastball pitcher working to a fastball hitter.

Williams stood in that familiar straight-up stance, left foot molded to the back of the batter's box. The first pitch was a ball, low. The second was a slider, high. Williams swung and missed it. The next pitch was a fastball. A fastball pitch to a fastball hitter. Williams did not miss it.

"From the moment Ted swung, there was not the slightest doubt about it," Linn wrote. "The ball cut through the heavy air, heading straightaway to center field toward the corner of the special bullpen the Red Sox built for Williams back in 1941."

"The ball climbed on a diagonal line into the vast volume of air over center field," Updike wrote. "From my angle, behind third base, the ball seemed less an object in flight than the tip of a towering, motionless construct, like the Eiffel Tower or the Tappan Zee Bridge. It was in the books while it was still in the sky."

Convergence.

Euphoria.

Pagliaroni started walking from the on-deck circle to the plate. He was crying. It was the first time he ever had cried at a baseball game. Another kid, Bill Monbouquette, a pitcher from nearby Medford, was in the bullpen. He couldn't believe what he was seeing as the ball came closer, closer to where he was. He had tried to will the earlier two fly balls through the sky and failed. This one required no help. The ball came over his head and hit an aluminum canopy over the bench where he and the other pitchers were sitting.

"What a noise it made!" he says, more than 40 years later. "It was a joyful, eerie feeling. You were so happy for Ted—what a way to go—but you also realized that this was it for him. You knew you won't ever see this again."

Monbouquette and the other bullpen pitchers yelled, "Tip it, tip it," as Williams circled the bases, hoping that he would tip his hat at last to the fans. He never did. Pagliaroni waited at home plate to unload the big hug. He received the fast handshake as Williams hurried past. Business as usual.

Williams put on his blue jacket in the dugout and sat at the end of the bench near Pinky Higgins. The game was held up for four minutes as people cheered "We Want Ted" and asked him to come out for a curtain call. His teammates urged him to do it. He never moved.

"Gods do not answer letters," Updike wrote, his most famous line.

"I had the impression—maybe I shouldn't say this because it's just an impression—that he got just as much a kick out of refusing to go out and tip his hat to the crowd as he did out of the homer," Linn wrote, a quote from an unnamed teammate. "What I mean is he wanted to go out with the home run, all right, but he also wanted the home run so he could sit there while they yelled for him and tell them all where to go."

Higgins sent him back into left for the start of the ninth, then sent kid reserve Carroll Hardy out to replace him. One more ovation. "Tip your hat," Don Gile, the kid first baseman yelled as Williams passed. Never happened.

The show was closed, done.

The Red Sox quickly passed out word in the press box that Williams would *not* be going to New York. In the middle of the game, they had announced that his number 9 would be the first number to be retired in club history. If he had been going to go to New York—Linn pointed out that his equipment bag had been packed—it really didn't matter. This was the closeout that everyone had wanted.

The home run was Williams's 521st, leaving him behind only Babe Ruth and Jimmie Foxx. The hit itself was his 2,654th, just enough to move him past Tris Speaker and into 10th place in career batting average at .344. He had missed five years in the prime of his career due to military service, a sixth due to his assorted injuries and bronchial problems. More than anything, he had persevered, kept going. He had not given up, not given way, not knuckled under to anyone.

He had become—and this was a question to win a dollar bet in any taproom—the first player in history to steal a base in four decades (even though he only had 24, lifetime). He had touched 4,884 bases in his career, knocked in 1,839 runs, and scored 1,798. He had walked 2,019 times, struck out only 709.

A picture of Hitler saluting an all-day troop review in honor of his 50th birthday at Charlottenburgen Chasseau, seven miles outside of Berlin, had been on the front page of the *Record* the day Williams made his Boston debut in 1939. Men's topcoats were on sale at Filene's for $9.00, $12.00 for herringbone. An electric iron was on sale for a buck at Jordan Marsh. The mother of Amelia Earhart, the local girl who flew away and never returned, was on a vigil. Carole Lombard and James Stewart were starring in *Made for Each Other* at the Loew's State and Orpheum. Fred Astaire and Ginger Rogers were in *The Story of Vernon and Irene Castle* at the Keith Memorial. Lindbergh was meeting with FDR at the White House.

On this final day, Castro was moving out of the Hotel Theresa in Harlem with "300 pieces of luggage, an unfinished case of whiskey, and two containers of white rice." Khrushchev was at the UN, dismissing the disarmament speech of British Prime Minister Harold McMillan. JFK was in Albany and Richard Nixon was in Vermont, two days after their first televised debate. *Hiroshima Mon Amour* was at the Fenway Theater, Steve Reeves was appearing in *The Last Days of Pompeii* at a number of Loew's theaters. Two-trouser suits were for sale at $54.95 at Jordan Marsh. A 21-inch black-and-white table model was available for $89.95 at Tip-Top TV.

"A day for some of your especial assets and for assisting others, establishing achievement and a well-run place or activity," Williams's horoscope had read in the *Record*. "*You* can make unusual gains when you try."

Updike reported the letdown of the fans, inevitable after such a high moment. Linn reported the movements of Williams in the clubhouse, the dazed look on his face, the beer in his hand, the last tirade at a last reporter (Linn). Forty-five minutes after the game, Williams was gone, out the back gate underneath the bleachers in his Cadillac. Jimmy Carroll says he was at the wheel. Back to the Somerset.

"Ted had thrown his shoes in the trash can," Carroll says. "I grabbed 'em. Johnny Orlando said, 'Hey,' but Ted said, 'No, that's okay.'"

Harold Kaese, the last remaining columnist of the original typewriter combatants, quoted Shakespeare in the morning *Globe*—"Forever and forever, farewell, Cassius! If we meet again, why, we shall smile; if not, why, then, this parting was well made." Huck Finnegan in the *Record* took a more traditional approach.

"Outside of the theatrics, what did it all mean?" Finnegan asked. "He hadn't won the game. Wertz' pinch double in the ninth (he tipped his cap) and Klaus' error on a DP toss had done that. In fact, if Tasby had fanned, it would have been Williams' turn to bat again with three men on and the Sox needing one run to tie. And there he was OUT OF THE GAME.

"In retrospect, hasn't that been the story of the Red Sox since Williams joined them? Winning always has been secondary to individual accomplishments. Even the year he hit .406 the Sox finished 17 games behind the Yankees. So it was this year. His great hitting LIFTED the Sox from the FIFTH spot they occupied at the close of 1959 to SEVENTH, the worst record they have compiled since Yawkey bought the club in 1933."

Updike's story, "Hub Fans Bid Kid Adieu," became a sports classic, generally recognized as the best American sports story ever written. Linn's story, "The Kid's Last Game," became expanded into a fine book, *Hitter: The Life and Turmoils of Ted Williams*. The other stories wrapped the requisite number of daily sea bass.

The subject of all this?

The chroniclers had missed one important moment. Somewhere in his time in the clubhouse Williams quickly had found a telephone and laughed and shouted, "Well, I did it, I hit a home run on my last at bat." He had called a woman in Chicago.

He was in love.

11 Cooperstown

THEODORE SAMUEL WILLIAMS. "Ted." BOSTON RED SOX. A.L. 1939–1960. Batted .406 in 1941. Led A.L. in batting six times; slugging percentage 9 times; total bases 6 times; runs scored 6 times; bases on balls 8 times. Total hits 2,654 included 521 home runs. Lifetime batting average .344. Lifetime slugging average .634. Most Valuable A.L. Player 1946 & 1949. Played in 18 All-Star games, named Player of the Decade, 1951–1960.

Plaque, Baseball Hall of Fame,
Cooperstown, New York, July 25, 1966

The marriage took place quietly on September 26, 1961, at the East Cambridge district courthouse on Thorndike Street in Cambridge. The *Boston Record* reported the bride wore "a cream-colored dress." The groom, it was noted, wore "a cream-colored sport shirt, open at the neck, no tie, a blue check sports jacket, blue slacks and white buckskin shoes."

Even out of baseball, Ted Williams was the star of whatever Boston show in which he took part.

"Ted was a nervous bridegroom," old friend Johnny Buckley, the best man, said in the *American*. "The ceremony lasted about 15 minutes and then we all drove back to my place in Lexington where pictures were taken in the front room and then outside on the lawn. The four of us then went to a private wedding reception at the Carriage House in Lexington. We had filets and lobster and champagne. Then we went back to my house and about 9 P.M. Ted loaded his luggage into his car and they drove off."

If there were any doubts about whether Williams would be able to keep busy without baseball—and there shouldn't have been, not with his many interests—they were gone now. In less than a year out of the game, he had added a new job with the Sears, Roebuck and Company department store chain as the company's public face, had become involved with his own baseball camp, had hunted and fished in parts of the world as far away as New Zealand, and now was married again.

He had vowed, loudly and profanely, that he was never going to go back to the altar after the failure of his first marriage, but that had changed in the final couple of years of his career. He even had proposed to a woman from Alabama and been turned down.

"It wouldn't have worked," the woman says, preferring that her name not be used. "I was divorced and had two boys, and Ted really didn't want to be a father. I went my own way and married someone else. And Ted went his own way and married someone else."

In the winter before his last season, he had met 36-year-old Lee Howard of Chicago. She was also divorced, had two teenage kids, and was vacationing with her parents in Florida. She first met John Blake, the state trooper friend of Williams, liked him, and he said, "Oh, I've got someone for you to meet. Wait till he gets a load of you."

"I met Ted the next day," she says. "I was gone, right from there. He was handsome, plus. There were so many things to like about him. There was definitely a mutual attraction. From that day on, there wasn't a single day that we didn't either see each other or talk on the phone."

Howard was beautiful—tall and slender and blond. She had been raised outside Chicago in Riverdale, Illinois, as Lee Houda, but had changed her name to Howard when she went to Hollywood to work in movies. A model from the time she was in high school, appearing in Marshall Field's ads and walking the runway in both the spring and fall fashion shows in Chicago, she had been picked to be in movies in a scene right out of the movies.

"I was in a nightclub with some friends in Chicago, and a man came over and introduced himself and said he wanted to make me into a movie star," she says. "I didn't believe him, of course, thought it was some kind of joke, but he gave me his card and said, 'Call me.' I called the next day and it was all true.

"I went to some interviews. This famous man . . . I forget his name. The one who made Deanna Durbin famous . . . came in from California.

He offered me a seven-year contract for MGM. I said, 'Why not?' I never really wanted to be an actress, but it didn't sound bad."

She went to Hollywood, appeared in a bunch of movies, "but just as part of the crowd, somewhere in the background," and went to the studio-recommended school for acting lessons. She also went to the beach and mostly had fun. She met a man named William Charly, just out of the service, and they married and she became pregnant. That was the end of Hollywood.

"I just walked out of the contract," she says. "We came back to Chicago, and I went back to modeling. When the marriage ended, I went back to live with my parents with my children."

Her relationship with Williams had developed through the year and a half they had known each other. He was closing out his career, and she was able to adjust her modeling schedule to the Red Sox schedule. Whenever they played in the Midwest, she would come over to Detroit or down to Cleveland or Kansas City. She also went to Boston to the Somerset. Never a big baseball fan, she had her own observations about her future husband on the diamond.

"I saw him running after a ball at Fenway, and I told him afterward, 'I was afraid you were going to have a heart attack,'" she says. "He just loved that. Everyone we saw, he'd say, 'She saw me run after a ball and was afraid I was going to have a heart attack.'"

The proposal for marriage came in the form of an order. Williams was in Chicago on business, out of baseball in 1961, and he and Lee went out for the night, and then she had to leave to go back to her parents' house. He said, "This is ridiculous. We're getting married." That was it. That was the proposal. The prospective bride didn't mind that there wasn't a question mark on the end of the sentence. She took the order. Gladly.

"He was a handsome man," she says. "And I loved him. When I met him, he was truly handsome. I've seen pictures of him when he was younger, and he was so skinny. When I met him, he was filled out. Just handsome."

The wedding was held in Cambridge because that was where it could be arranged by Buckley quietly. There never was the question of a church service. Williams flew up from Florida, leaving a fishing tournament early. Howard flew in from Chicago. The ceremony was performed by assistant city clerk Paul Healy. Buckley and his wife were the witnesses.

"On Friday afternoon from my office in my theater in Central Square, I telephoned Healy at City Hall," John Buckley said to reporters. "I told him that a person I was interested in wanted to arrange a marriage, and I asked Paul to come to the theater with the necessary forms. When he arrived, I introduced him to Williams."

The word "Reserved" was written on marriage intention blank 874. The names were filled in on Monday and the ceremony performed. The *PM Globe* the next day, in a sidebar to the story of the wedding, had a headline "Was Ceremony Legal? Clerk's Status Clouds Ted Williams' Wedding." The paper had learned that Healy was the acting city clerk, and now a city councillor was going to conduct an investigation to see if Healy legally could perform marriages and so on and so on. Nothing had changed. Anything Williams did still sold newspapers.

"Your dancing and party days are over," he told his new wife about her new life.

"I don't care," she replied.

The honeymoon was scheduled for Antigua, but a hurricane had hit the Caribbean island. The couple drove instead to the fishing camp Williams owned on the banks of the Miramichi River in New Brunswick, Canada. The new life began.

"We went to Florida, to Islamorada, after Canada," Lee Williams says. "Ted would wake me up at 5:30 in the morning, making the sound of a bugle through his fist. He was so happy every day to get up, get going. I was not so happy. It was 5:30 in the morning."

The job with Sears was an economic salvation. The contract was for $100,000 per year, same as his contract for most of his later baseball years. The money allowed him to put baseball aside for sure, rejecting a late offer to be a pinch-hitter for the New York Yankees that would have been a sad distortion at the end of his career, as sad as the sight of Babe Ruth in another uniform at the end, swinging at fastballs he could not catch. Sears ensured Williams's dignity.

The five-year deal was announced on December 27, 1960, in Chicago, three months after his closeout home run and nine months before he married Lee. George H. Struthers, vice president for merchandising for Sears, had first proposed the idea in a meeting at the Somerset a day after the last-game home run. Struthers said full details of Williams's role still had to be worked out, but when they were, the details were perfect.

Williams basically was paid to live much the same life he always had led, except he no longer had to play baseball. And he had to talk to people.

He became head of the "Ted Williams Sears Sports Advisory Staff," a group of athletes who field-tested, endorsed, and helped market sporting goods for the largest department store chain in the country. Williams was in charge of hunting and fishing and baseball. His name went on rods and reels and shotguns and bats and balls and gloves.

"He tested them too," basketball Hall of Famer Jack Twyman says. "He'd make the buyers cry. They'd have some new product and he'd say, 'This is just a piece of crap.' "

Twyman was the basketball representative. Buddy Young was football. Doug Ford and Shirley Englehom were golf. Butch Bucholz was tennis. Bob Mathias was track and field. There were advisers for arcane sports like archery, horseshoes, ping-pong. Ed Lubanski was the bowler. George O'Day was the sailor. Sir Edmund Hillary, conqueror of Mount Everest, was in charge of mountain climbing.

This was the preeminent sports marketing operation in the country, long before a time when sports marketing was a course in college and athletes had multimillion-dollar contracts simply to wear a pair of shoes. Be like Ted. That was the message before all the other messages began. His face was the big face on top of all the other faces.

"We'd have meetings of the board perhaps twice a year," Twyman says. "There were a lot of strong personalities in one room. Think about it. To get to the top level in any sport, you'd better have a strong personality. What kind of fortitude and patience does it take to climb Mount Everest? These were strong-willed people. Ted was very strong-willed."

Williams called Twyman "the Glandular Case" because of his size. Twyman called Williams "the Swollen Splinter" because of *his* size. They would get on elevators and Ted would do his "Didja hear about the alligator that attacked that woman in Lake Michigan?" or, better yet, in the middle of Chicago, "Didja hear about that light plane that flew into the John Hancock building?" Twyman would marvel at Williams's enthusiasm for the job, for the day, for life.

There was a certain magic in the fact that all these athletes, disparate champions, were gathered together. Anything could happen.

"We were making a film with Bob Mathias, the decathlon champion, one day," Carl Lind, who ran the advisory staff program for a number of years, says. "We were at a track someplace. Bob is dressed in a suit. There was a high-jump pit. He spotted it. He said, 'You know, I've been wondering about this Fosbury Flop that they're doing now in the high jump. That wasn't around when I was jumping. I wonder how I'd do.' "

Mathias took off his suit jacket, loosened his tie, went to the high-jump pit, and jumped over the bar backward. The bar, Lind figured, was set at least at six feet. Mathias just did it. Just like that. Pulled up his tie and put on his jacket. Back to work.

Lind spent a lot of time with Williams. He remembers taking Williams to meet some Sears vice president who fancied himself a fly fisherman. The vice president bragged to Williams that he had bought a "new pole."

"We only deal with rods in this business," Williams quickly said. "Poles are for cat fishing."

One of the big promotions was for an unsinkable fishing boat the company produced and sold. Williams was the centerpiece. In a commercial, he used an auger to drill a hole in the bottom and the boat did not sink. He then took a chainsaw, sawed the boat in half, and the boat still did not sink. It was all very dramatic.

The company invited writers from the big outdoors magazines—*Field and Stream, Outdoor Life,* and *Sports Afield*—to see this boat and other new products at the Sears test base in Fort Myers, Florida. Williams was there for interviews. One of the writers had the audacity to ask whether the chairman of the Ted Williams Sears Sports Advisory Staff actually had sawed the boat in half and still ridden in it without sinking.

"Hell, yes," Williams replied.

He had the manager of the test base bring out the power half of the boat that had been sawn in half. Williams sat in the half of the boat, fired up the engine, and drove into the middle of an inlet. He was careful to keep his weight back so the boat would plane. See?

Then he got cute. He inched forward to see what would happen. The half-boat did not plane anymore. The half-boat took water and sunk. The chairman of the Ted Williams Sears Sports Advisory Staff sunk with it.

"Ted can't swim," a man said to Carl Lind on the shore.

George O'Day, the expert sailor, quickly sailed to the rescue in a Sears Seawind sailboat. Alas, Ted Williams, hunter and fisherman, did not want to be seen even halfway dead in a sailboat. A sailboat! He hung on to the half-boat with one hand, the sailboat with another, and waited until someone else came out in a Sears aluminum fishing boat. Then he consented to be rescued.

"A big promotion was with our fishing rods, which were made by Shakespeare," Lind says. "Ted would test their rods. His appraisal was: butt for strength, middle for action [flex], and tip for feel. Our Sears Ted Williams rods were made with a special weaving process that enabled you to grab the rod at the tip, lift it up with reel attached to the butt without breaking it. Other rods, made by another process, were brittle and would break while applying our 'tip test.' We featured Ted in a number of ads with 'the tip test.' "

The first five-year contract evolved into a second five-year contract and kept on going. The relationship obviously worked. Williams appeared at Sears stores around the country, casting for invisible fish in the parking lots to big crowds. Sears sold a bunch of sporting goods. Williams had a pleasant job.

"The Sears people always were very nice," Lee Williams says. "They'd send a private plane down, and we'd go off to some different place."

One of the places every year was New Haven, Connecticut, where Winchester made the Ted Williams shotgun. Williams would tour the plant, then have dinner at night with Winchester executives. At the end of one of those dinners, heading toward the car, he stopped to relieve himself against a wall. A Winchester vice president named John McDonald heard the following dialogue at the booth of the parking lot.

WOMAN: "There's some guy urinating over there against the wall. Can you do something about it?"
ATTENDANT: "I'll check." [Attendant leaves, returns.]
ATTENDANT: "That's not some guy, ma'am. That's Ted Williams."

Domestic life was uneven. Lee Williams soon discovered that her husband was a complicated man. He had cursed when they had been dating, used the four-star, four-letter words every now and then, but after the marriage the words emerged more and more often. He became angry more and more often.

"All I want is peace and quiet," he would say.

Then he would do something to disrupt the peace and quiet.

There was no rhythm to his anger, no way to predict when it would erupt. He would become angry at friends, strangers, situations. He would become angry at his wife. Things would set him off. Small things. Big things. Nothing. Something. Just about every day.

"Like we were in the kitchen one day," Lee says. "He went to touch something . . . I forget what it was. Something that was broken. Something that he shouldn't be touching . . . I said, 'Uh-uh-uh. . . .' "

Gone.

The words came in a torrent, a thunderstorm of abuse that seemed to arise from nowhere over the Gulf of Mexico, drench the lawn furniture on a previously sunny Florida day, then slide out of sight again. It was like nothing had ever happened for Williams when the clouds left, over and done, the sun back again, but the people around him still would feel awfully wet. Lee Williams would feel soaked.

"You were just waiting for the bomb to go off," she says. "You just didn't know where or when."

Her husband could be nice, sweet sometimes. He would bring coffee to her in bed in the morning. He would buy her gifts in a moment. Bring him into a store and he would say, "Do you like this?" Maybe it was jewelry. Maybe ceramics. Anything. If she nodded, yes, he would shout, "Give me half a dozen of these." He bought in bulk. Laughing.

He bought her a sewing machine, even though she said she didn't know what to do with it any more than he did. What the heck. She read the instructions. She made him a pair of khaki Bermuda shorts, longer in the leg, because that was how he liked them. He wore the Bermuda shorts until they fell apart, that was how much he liked them. She had to admit that she too liked the Bermuda shorts. She liked the way they looked on her husband.

"We did have some nice times," she says.

She never had been very big on the outdoors. Her idea of outdoor sport was golf. He would play golf with her, a panic, really, as his frustrations built. The clubs would fly. He would yell at the ball, the woods, the sand traps, and the water, yell at himself. The big outdoor sport, of course, was fishing. He could yell at the fish. Or whomever else was fishing.

One of his first gifts to her was a pair of waders. He bought her the entire fishing rig. He taught her how to tie flies, which was much more complicated than she could imagine. She would do everything she was supposed to do, cast once, and the fly would fall apart in the water. He taught her how to cast. She liked that, casting.

She caught a 9½-pound salmon on the Miramichi. She still isn't sure how she did it. She spent hours on the water in Florida, looking for bonefish and tarpon. She still doesn't know how she did it.

"You have to stand up in the boat," she says. "That's what Ted said. You never could sit down. You'd just stand there for hours."

She was standing in the boat one day, her back to her husband. He was standing the other way. She heard a splash from behind her. She thought he had caught a fish. She turned to see. He had fallen from the boat and was cursing in the shallow turquoise edge of the Atlantic Ocean.

She couldn't stop herself from laughing. Neither could he, once he stopped the cursing.

The normal fishing experience, however, was not good. He would get mad at someone or something, and there would be awkward moments after he kicked the tackle box in frustration. She found herself begging off the trips, saying that she had to stay home to buy something. She always felt her husband seemed happiest at the end of fishing days, talking with men about fishing or about baseball. Men talk. She was not involved.

He was a mystery to her.

"It was strange," she says. "We'd go out to eat. He always would say we had to go somewhere where he wouldn't be recognized. We'd go off to some corner. Then he'd start talking in that loud voice and people would turn and see him and recognize him. He didn't want the attention, but also he did."

In the year before the marriage, his brother Danny had died of cancer in the house on Utah Street. On August 27, 1961, less than a month before the marriage, Williams's mother May died in Santa Barbara. Williams went to California for both funerals but never asked Lee to go with him, never seemed to consider it.

He talked very little about his time in San Diego, about his youth. He never talked about his father. He never talked about the fact he was half-Mexican, though Lee already had been told that by someone else. The few conversations Williams had about his mother were about the Salvation Army and how embarrassed he had been when she made his brother and him go with her to the street corners to solicit money, about how he had to grit his teeth every time he went because he hated it so much. He never talked about his mother's personality, about her hopes for him, about any of that.

"You'd have thought when she died it would have been a natural time to talk about her," Lee says. "It just didn't happen."

Lee's teenage children, a boy and a girl, stayed with her parents after she married Williams. They already were in high school and already were familiar with their surroundings. They would come to visit, and Williams always would be pleasant, would joke around, but he never was asked to take the role of surrogate parent and never took it. Bobby-Jo also came to visit. She was 12, 13 years old, and these visits were less pleasant.

"Ted set such a high standard for her," Lee says. "He'd get mad at her for the smallest things. She'd forget her house keys. Or something like that. Things kids do. With Ted, it would be the end of the world.

I'd take her shopping to get her out of the house. She'd say, 'Lee, I don't want to go fishing again.' I'd say, 'Come on, let's get you some school clothes.'

"I met her mother, Doris. Ted set it up. He thought we should know each other because of Bobby-Jo. I liked Doris. She was very pleasant and was remarried to this man who I also liked. Ted had a problem with him. I forget what it was. I liked Doris, though. I understood she'd had a problem, but I liked her."

The problem Doris had was her drinking. She drank virtually every day at a local bar or at home. Bobby-Jo was caught between a lenient mother who drank and an absent father who demanded perfection. There was a push-pull sadness to her situation.

"Ted was all discipline," Daria Stehle, wife of one of Williams's Korean War buddies, says. "We'd go to visit and it was always 'Sit up straight. Put your hand in your lap at the dinner table.' He was very loud. Our kids were terrified of him. Bobby-Jo was caught in a situation where her mother just let her do anything, no discipline, and Ted, who was very strict. It was tough for her."

"I wondered if it would have been better if she were a boy," Lee Williams says. "I think it would. I always thought Ted had trouble understanding women. He was always the man's man.

"I remember spending a lot of time with Bobby-Jo at the camp. That was where we were for a lot of the summer and that was when she would come to visit."

Williams went to spring training with the Red Sox in Scottsdale, Arizona, in 1961 in his make-do role as "executive assistant." He fell into a shouting match with Larry Claflin, part of the new generation from the *Record*, a quick ten-rounder just for old times' sake, but made few other headlines. He found that the Sox management had little interest in his opinions or advice. They had their own little agendas now that did not include him.

This did not matter. His baseball life had shifted from the big-league diamonds to a smaller, unpressurized, gentler environment. In the summer of 1961 and in the immediate summers to follow, Williams's major baseball interest was in his camp—the Ted Williams Baseball Camp in Lakeville, Massachusetts. This was a kids' camp, a boys' camp, ages eight to nineteen, baseball everywhere. Laughter. Fun. He gave hitting clinics. He practiced his casting on the parade grounds. He talked baseball and fishing and played a little golf in the morning.

This was a long way from Fenway Park. He was in charge.

"He'd come through to inspect the cabins," Al Cassidy Jr. says. "We were all afraid of him. He had that big voice. *He* was big. Everything had to be military styled. He'd look at you and say, 'You're going to have to get a haircut.' And you got it."

Cassidy's father, Al Sr., a small-town entrepreneur, one-third owner of a drive-in restaurant in Lakeville, a town on the edge of Cape Cod, had put the deal together for the camp. The idea came from Cassidy. The money came from Ted. The charm of the deal was the way it all happened. The two men didn't know each other.

They started out as strangers.

"My father had no money," Al Cassidy Jr. says. "He was running the drive-in with his brother and his brother-in-law. It was kind of like the place on *Happy Days*, and they were just about taking home enough to live. He always had ideas, though, my father."

Cassidy heard the local Boy Scout camp was up for sale in the late fifties, went to the bank, and asked for a loan. The directors of the bank, alas, noticed that he had no other money and also had no experience running a camp. They told him the only way a venture like this could succeed was if he had someone famous involved, a name that would attract customers.

Cassidy—who always told his five kids that the most important part of the word "American" was the last four letters, "I Can"—thought about possible famous names in the neighborhood. He picked the closest one he could find, driving up Route 24 to nearby Brockton. He talked to Rocky Marciano.

The heavyweight champion of the world, the Brockton Bomber, Marciano was a notoriously frugal and suspicious figure. Cassidy worked on him for months. He hung around the gym. He went to fights. Finally, the champion agreed to put his name on the operation. Cassidy, a happy man, hurried back to the bank to report he had signed up Marciano.

"Rocky Marciano is a boxer," the bankers replied, speaking the obvious.

"No mother and father in their right minds are going to send their kids to a boxing camp," the bankers also replied, again speaking the obvious. "Who wants to see his kid come home with a broken nose and a fat lip?"

No loan. No camp. Cassidy was momentarily frustrated. He asked what, exactly, he should do.

"You need a really famous name," the bankers explained. "Someone parents know. Someone like Ted Williams."

Ted Williams?

"My father put together a scrapbook," Al Cassidy Jr. says. "He went to the camp, took a bunch of pictures of the buildings and the lake, had them developed, and put them in this leather scrapbook. Then he went to Fenway Park early one day when the Red Sox were playing. He bribed an usher ten bucks to get into the park early, while the Red Sox were taking batting practice."

This was 1957, the middle of the .388 season. Cassidy, carrying his scrapbook, went down to the front row of the stands. He waited for Williams to come past. He never had met Williams, knew nothing about him except the things he had read in the papers. Huh. They were not exactly encouraging.

"Hey, Ted," Cassidy shouted when Williams appeared, heading toward the batting cage.

"My name is Cassidy," Cassidy said when Williams looked up. "Can you come over here for a minute? I have a proposition for you."

"Wait until I'm done hitting, okay?" Williams said.

After batting practice was finished, Williams came to the stands. The two men talked. Williams talked loud. Cassidy talked fast. He pulled out the scrapbook. Look at this camp! Look at how beautiful it is! This would be a baseball camp! Teach kids baseball! The idea actually was unique for the time. There were few specialty camps in the fifties, none of the music camps and soccer camps and computer camps and adventure camps that would follow, places where kids could go to concentrate on one particular interest. A baseball camp! The Ted Williams Baseball Camp! Williams said he was intrigued . . . but he didn't have any time for camps right now. He didn't get involved in business during the season.

"Give me your number," he said. "I'll call you when the season is done."

Cassidy went home defeated. He was sure he'd gotten the brush-off. A nice brush-off perhaps, but certainly a brush-off. The season ended. The phone rang. The loud voice was on the other end. Cassidy was back in business.

Williams came down to Lakeville, toured the camp, and liked it. He said he had been to a charity camp when he was a kid in San Diego, a place that treated the campers as if they were in a maximum-security prison. He later learned that Art Linkletter, the television host, was one of the counselors. A camp . . . okay, Ted Williams wanted to be involved in this camp. This was going to be a great camp. No prison here. Kids were going to love it. He said his agent wasn't going to like the idea, not at all, but Ted Williams liked it. He went right to the phone, right there, and told Fred Corcoran that he was getting involved with a camp, and he didn't care what Corcoran thought, he was going to damn well do it.

Cassidy returned to the bank with his new name. Williams wouldn't go with him, but said he would talk to the bankers on the phone if necessary. Cassidy told the loan officer who was now part of the picture. The loan officer called his boss. His boss called *his* boss.

Pretty soon Cassidy was sitting in the office of the president of the bank with a half-dozen men, the entire food chain of bank officials. He dialed a number. The loud voice came on the phone. The bankers were amazed. The bank had been trying to sign Williams for years as a promotional figure, but never had even received an interview. Now he was part of Al Cassidy's plan?

"This is very impressive," the bankers said at the end of the phone call.

"But we still won't give you the loan," the bankers also said. "This still sounds too risky to us."

Cassidy, defeated again, went home and phoned the sad news to Williams. So much for the camp. Nice idea. Williams said he might have another option. He was friendly with the head of the Middleboro Savings Bank. He would make a call.

The Middleboro Savings Bank approved the loan.

"You look at the deal," Cassidy Jr. says. "The camp cost $60,000. Ted put up the down payment. Ted put up his name. Ted, in the end, arranged the financing. My father and my two uncles put up nothing. Ted then insisted that they all were equal partners, 25 percent apiece. Who makes a deal like that? With people he didn't even know? This deal changed my family's life forever. Right there. Ted changed my family's life."

Williams had only one condition for the partnership. He held his two hands, palms up, six inches above a table in the bank office, and said, "This is how it has to be." He then put his hands under the table and said, "Never like this." He and Cassidy then shook hands.

The camp covered 130 acres. The Boy Scouts left three baseball diamonds, and soon there were five. Four batting cages were added. A long stretch of waterfront along Loon Pond was used for swimming and boating. The heart of the operation was baseball—the kids received daily instruction and every camper played in at least three games every two days—but there also were the arts and crafts and ghost stories and all the pieces of a typical boys' camp.

The doors opened in the summer of 1958, but the star of the production still was playing in Boston. He made it clear that he could not become very involved until he retired, whenever that might happen.

For the first couple of years, as his Red Sox career grew longer and longer, the camp wobbled on the edge of financial failure. Cassidy ran around, paying bills at the last moment, plugging financial holes. Sporting goods suppliers extended credit, then more credit, then more.

The highlight of those early camp sessions was a trip to Fenway Park. The campers would sit in Section 5, and in between a designated inning, Williams would wave across the diamond to them and they would cheer back at him, sitting in their little Ted Williams Camp uniforms that still were being carried on the books at Steve Stanley's sporting goods store in Middleboro.

"It was always a mess at the end of the games," Al Palmeri, one of the early employees at the camp, says. "You'd go outside and there would be a hundred yellow buses from camps all over New England. Every year, one of our kids would get on the wrong bus and go back to the wrong camp. And some kid from some other camp would get on our bus. The next day, someone always would have to take a trip back to Fenway to bring a kid back to a director from some other camp. It was like a prisoner exchange."

By the time Williams appeared in 1961, the camp was a marginal, if not truly solvent, enterprise. The arrival of Williams made it go. For the next eight summers, and stretches of summers after that, the camp was his home.

"He'd come into the office every day, and there'd be a big pile of those pink 'While You Were Out' messages for him," Al Cassidy Jr. says. "Every day he'd pick up the pile, read the first two or three messages, then throw the whole pile into the wastebasket."

One day a message came from the President of the United States, John F. Kennedy. The President of the United States wanted Ted Williams to come to some gathering at Hyannisport. Cassidy's father, Al Sr., one of the owners of the camp, put this pink message on the top of the pink-message pile.

"Ted came in, same routine, read the top messages, threw everything in the wastebasket," Cassidy Jr. says. "The Kennedy people called back. My father put the message on the top. Ted threw it away. The Kennedy people called back. This happened for three or four straight days."

"Ted," Cassidy Sr. finally said, "did you see that message from the President of the United States?"

"I did," Williams said. "I threw it away."

"You've gotta tell 'em something."

"No, I don't."

"I've seen that message every day for three or four days. They really want you. Shouldn't you tell 'em something?"

"Tell 'em I'm a Nixon fan," Williams said.

Williams hired Wos Caldwell, his old high school coach, to work at the camp. He hired Roy Engle, his old Hoover High catcher, to come. Engle, now a high school coach, would pack his family in an Airstream trailer every summer for the better part of a decade and travel back and forth across the country from San Diego. His youngest son, Dave, would wind up as an All-Star catcher for the Minnesota Twins.

The rest of the staff mostly were local guys, high school coaches and teachers and administrators. One of them from nearby Fairhaven was Joe Camacho, principal at the Otteweil School. Camacho was a former minor leaguer, a prospect once in the St. Louis Browns system, a guy who had hurt his knee and dropped off the trail to the big leagues in Fargo, South Dakota.

"We had a guy on the team, Roger Marras," Camacho says. "He had to change his name because all the fans would call him Mar-ASS. Roger Maris."

Camacho and Williams became good friends. They would go to the batting cages, and Williams would say, 'You should have been a better hitter. You must have been really fucken dumb.' They would play golf, Ted hitting a five-iron a ton, but in different directions, Doug Ford golf balls from Sears landing in strange places, Ted breaking four or five clubs every round from the unlimited supply he received from Sears. He shattered a plastic tee marker one day at a local course, sheepishly dropping fifty bucks on the pro shop counter. Keep the change. Then there was blooper ball.

"It was a game played with an oversized softball on a Little League diamond," Camacho says. "I beat out Ted Williams for the home run championship in blooper ball, a fact I always reminded him about. The difference was, my home runs were liners. He hit balls that went into outer space."

The all-star team from the camp made up of the most talented kids would play in the local city league, the New Bedford Twilight League, against men. Williams would sometimes show up to watch. Yogi Berra and Whitey Ford sent their sons to the camp. A basketball operation was added. Calvin Murphy was around. Jerry Lucas. There were no other camps like this. This was sports and fun.

"Our team played every year at Norfolk Prison," Camacho says. "There's Ted, standing in the corner with the warden, asking, 'What do these guys eat?' He just wanted to know everything."

The phone would ring in the camp office. Carl Yastrzemski from Fenway Park. Williams would pick up the receiver. Everyone would listen.

"You're standing too far back in the batter's box!" Williams would say. "You dumb, goddamned Polack!"

Williams rented, then bought a house on a local lake. The old Roche estate. Bobby-Jo went to a companion girls' camp one year. Williams bought her a horse. She had a crush on a kid named Bobby Fredricks.

Williams would show up for breakfast at six in the morning at the rec hall and ask for a plate of eggs and a big vanilla frappe. At night he would take any number of staff to local restaurants like the Town and Country for dinner. Nobody else was allowed to pay.

"He did everything," Al Cassidy Jr. says. "He even saved my father's life. My father was feeling lousy but wouldn't go to a doctor. Just wouldn't go. Ted says to him one day, 'Al, take a ride to Boston with me.' My father goes and says, 'Where are we going?' on the way. Ted says, 'I'm going to see my doctor. And when he's through with me, he's going to look at you.' My dad had colitis. Ted came to the house with a blank check and said, 'Anything he needs.' "

Cassidy says if he could pick one age of his life to be locked into forever, he would pick eight or nine or ten years old. He would be walking across a field in Lakeville, and Ted Williams would be telling him to get a haircut.

Lee Williams filed for divorce on April 3, 1964, in Dade County Circuit Court in Miami after two and a half years of marriage. Her petition cited behavior by Williams that was "erratic, irresponsible and wholly unpredictable." That was the court language, true enough, perhaps, but to her it sounded much more harsh than it should, words the courts needed at that time to justify a divorce.

There hadn't been any final scene, any cataclysmic battle. Lee Williams simply had given up the fight.

"I still loved him and he still loved me," she says. "I'd given it my best for two and a half years, and I had nothing left to give. We just couldn't live together."

They were from two different places, the fisherman and the model. That was the final decision. She couldn't handle the way he lived. He couldn't live any other way. She couldn't handle the rages. He couldn't do anything but rage when the feelings came.

He agreed once that he would put a dollar in a jar every time he swore. Ten dollars were in the jar before an hour passed. God was invoked in half the curses, and while Lee wasn't overly religious, a once-in-a-while Presbyterian, she shuddered at the words she heard. Williams didn't believe in any of that God stuff. Loudly didn't believe.

"I'd tell him that he should be thankful for this gift that he received, this gift that not many people ever see," Lee says. "I also told him that maybe he should look toward God for the answers to why he was mad so much. Ted would listen, but that was it."

She wasn't a fighter. Ted's friends always said that it was good to stand up to him, that he admired people who stood up to him. That wasn't her personality. She left the room rather than fight. That was her answer.

She was bothered when he yelled at other people as much as when he yelled at her. Johnny Buckley was a best friend, quiet and sweet. Ted yelled at him. Frank Tiernan was another best friend, also sweet. Ted yelled at him. Ted yelled at everyone he liked.

She wonders now if one of the modern behavior medications were around at the time, Prozac or Ritalin or some other concoction, he could have found an answer for his rages. She thinks he surely would have been a candidate for at least one of those drugs.

The part of him that bothered her most was that she never heard him say he was sorry. That was something he could not do. She never heard him say he was sorry to any of his friends. She never heard him say he was sorry to her.

He wanted everything his way. Every day belonged to Ted Williams. He would share some of the day gladly, make people happy, do inordinately nice things, but he never would change the day. Life was lived on his terms. Change was what made him unhappy.

"I remember we were in that big sports place in New York, whatever it is," she says with a smile. "Abercrombie and Fitch? We were buying stuff for Canada. I was looking around, trying to find things that match. Ted screamed out, 'Jesus Christ, it's as if we're furnishing a penthouse on Fifth Avenue.' "

They were different people. She filed for "at least $2,000 per month" for separate maintenance. Her affidavit said Williams was worth $200,000 in real estate, $100,000 in cash and bonds, and had an income of $8,000 per month.

She went back to Chicago. He stayed in Florida.

His public disposition—as opposed to his private disposition—was a different story. It had begun to soften the moment he stopped playing baseball. His public problems always had been with criticism, with the yapping chorus in the press box, with the discordant voices in the crowd, with the people who somehow did not, could not understand his interior battles. *Now there was nothing left to criticize.* The job was done. The heat was gone.

His softened disposition was a surprise to strangers. Wary because of all they had read, intimidated by his (growing) size and his booming voice, they still approached with great caution. When they found even a half-pleasant character inside the old image—Where ya from? Whadda ya do? Now, isn't that interesting!—they quickly shelved their preconceptions. What a nice guy! It was the sportswriters, after all, who had created the problem.

Consciously or unconsciously, Williams developed a character for social situations, The Public Ted, large and outrageous, an amplified version of himself. Friends said he changed in public. He became . . . more Ted. His voice moved closer and closer to actor John Wayne's voice. His opinions became like judgments, not open to debate. He did not leave strangers disappointed. If they were looking for someone larger than normal life, they certainly received it. When they met Ted Williams, they met someone with force, with a load of rough charm, an easy laugher, a positive thinker, a straight shooter. (You should hear the language, though, Martha.) The clothes of his character fit him quite well.

He was on the road a lot for Sears, for fishing trips, for the camp, for assorted ventures. He could show up anywhere. Woody Woodbury, the pilot from Korea who watched Williams's crash landing, now owned a hotel and nightclub in Fort Lauderdale, the Baha Hotel. Williams came bustling in one night, a woman on his arm. Jackie Gleason also was in the crowd. The proceedings froze right there. Woodbury, doing his act, said no eyes were on the stage, only on Gleason and Williams. The smell of testosterone filled the room.

"People went bananas," Woodbury says.

Williams went to the Little League World Series in Williamsport, Pennsylvania. He went to the American Legion World Series in Keene, New Hampshire. He went to New Zealand on assignment to catch a big game fish and a trout and to shoot a deer, all within 24 hours. (His time was 10 hours, 35 minutes. He finished off by shooting two deer in Ruatahuna within a minute.) Stand around long enough in the same spot and Williams probably would appear.

In Los Angeles, he showed up at Billy Consolo's barber shop.

"I was out of baseball, running my father's 16-chair barber shop at the Hilton Hotel," Consolo says. "An order came down from one of the rooms for a $1.00 bottle of Stephan Hair Tonic with Oil. The bellhop says, 'Check out the signature on the bottom.' It was Ted. I sent up the hair oil, and on the slip I wrote in real big letters. 'NO CHARGE,' plus my name. Five minutes go by and Ted calls and says, 'I'll be right down.' "

Williams suggested they go to dinner after the shop closed. (Consolo never had eaten in a restaurant with him during their big-league time.) Consolo said sure. He didn't know where to go. He finally took Williams to a restaurant owned by George Metkovich, an outfielder on that 1946 Red Sox team, a ten-year veteran of the big leagues. The choice was a hit.

"George was so happy to see Ted, he started to cry," Consolo says. "He took us to a back room, just Ted and me and George, and we talked for a while, and then George excused himself for a moment. What he did, he got on the phone. He must have called every guy he knew from the old Pacific Coast League, guys who had played with and against Ted back in '36, '37. They started coming in, one after another. Ted was just so happy to see them all. There must have been 25 guys by the end, all telling the old stories."

Williams was so happy he told Consolo the next day they should play golf. Consolo said sure again. He was in a quiet panic. He knew how to play golf, owned clubs, but didn't play much. He was a barber! He didn't belong to a country club, had no connections. What to do? He took Williams to the best public course in Los Angeles.

"It was one of those places where guys sleep overnight in their cars for tee times, just booked solid," Consolo says. "I went up to the pro in the clubhouse. I said, 'I don't know you and you don't know me, but I'm going to ask you for a favor. I've got Ted Williams here and he wants to play golf and I don't know what to do. Can you help me out?' The pro squinted through the window. Ted was on the putting green. 'That's him?' the pro said. 'That's Ted Williams?' I said, 'That's him.'

"There were four guys on the first tee. The pro shouts, 'Hold it right there. Mr. Williams, Mr. Consolo. You're on the tee.' He sent two assistant pros out with us. And we played golf."

Sears wanted to keep Williams's name in front of the public and hired Mike Todd Enterprises and famed agent Bill Doll to find ways to do that. Williams wound up with a syndicated newspaper column, a cartoon strip, and a radio show. There also was a movie, all set, script written, ready to go, that was never completed because the man in charge at Sears had a heart attack while on a safari in Kenya and his successor didn't like the idea of a movie.

"It was a TV documentary about Ted's life," Jordan Ramin, a vice president in charge of music publishing at Todd Enterprises, says. "Believe it or not, we had contacted, among others, John Wayne to narrate. However, another actor who said he'd love to narrate it was someone we thought would be terrific to play Ted in a real movie. Do you remember Robert Ryan? To this day, I can still see Ryan striding to home plate, scowling better than John Wayne."

When Ramin heard the firm needed a ghostwriter for Williams, he asked to submit a proposed column. Ramin wasn't a writer by trade, but Williams was his boyhood idol. Simply meeting the famous man would be a treat. Surprisingly, Williams picked Ramin's entry as the winner, saying, "This guy writes the way I think." The two men became once-per-week collaborators for four years. The *Boston Globe* ran the column on the front page of the entire paper. Ninety papers across the country ran it.

"Ted had to approve every column, and I'd make every single change he wanted," Ramin says. "Not only did I speak with Ted when he disagreed on a particular column, he sometimes corrected my grammar."

Williams and Ramin wrote about subjects ranging from the plight of the American Indian (bad) to the need to show more basketball on television (big) to the rap on boxing (bad). There was a lot of baseball too, comments on the issues at the moment, memories from the past. The radio spots were for NBC's national show *Monitor.* Williams would come to New York and knock off four or five at a time. Again, he was involved in the production.

Ramin still owns a tape of Williams disagreeing with a commentary about baseball cards. He is supposed to talk about bubble-gum companies wrapping up young ballplayers to long-term contracts (bad). He says he has problems saying the words.

"Because I started it all," he says. "I had a deal with Topps, $500 for the season, but there wasn't an exclusivity clause. Fleer comes to me in 1959. . . ."

He gives the play-by-play of the negotiations with the companies, pitting them in a bidding war. He wound up with a five-year exclusive deal with Fleer for $12,500, which is still in effect. How can he knock the exclusivity clause when he is the reason it was put into the game?

"Let's just do the other four commentaries," a voice says from the control room. "We won't worry about this one."

Ramin, with his musical background, even wrote a Ted Williams song as part of the plan to keep Williams in front of the public. The song was recorded and would have been part of the documentary.

> *Ted Williams is his name, Ted Williams is his name,*
> *The kid from San Diego,*
> *Whose bat would bring him fame*
> (refrain)

> *The year was 1960.*
> *On September 28th,*
> *All time stood still a moment*
> *As he walked up to the plate.*
> *His playing days were ended*
> *As he faced the setting sun*
> *And in that moment of glory*
> *He belted his last home run. . . .*
> (sample verse)

"There were two versions, the children's version and the bossa nova," Ramin says. "Ted liked the bossa nova version."

One stop Williams made almost every year during his perpetual travels was at the Sportsmen's Show in Boston. He had been going to the show since 1946 as it moved from Mechanics Hall to the Commonwealth

Armory and eventually to Hynes Auditorium. This was where The Public Ted had first emerged. The show was held in late January, early February, a time when the wounds of the previous summer were well healed, the new wounds not yet open.

Williams would arrive, complain about the weather, go indoors, and have fun. His foil was Jack Sharkey, the former heavyweight boxing champion, who would wear a little hat and always called Williams "Marblehead." Williams would call Sharkey "Bush." They would appear at the casting pool, Bush and Marblehead, exchanging shots, funny, bring out their fly rods, and try to hit targets in the water.

The press coverage mainly was from the outdoors writers, whom Williams liked. The conversations were sometimes boisterous, but pleasant. A little baseball, a little fishing, a little life.

"It was far better for me to go to the minors and play every day than it would have been to be kept by the Red Sox," he said one year in the *Globe*, describing the start of his career. "I might have played about 80 games that year. I might have hit about .260 or .270. I think I would have hit well enough for the majors, but I would have made so many mistakes in so many other ways that I couldn't have helped the Sox because I was so damn young at the time."

"I started fly casting at Lake Cochituate in Natick," Williams said another year in the *Globe*. "That was back in '39 or '40. I had a date with me, and to avoid being hit she was lying flat in the boat as I was casting. A fellow came over in his boat to see what was wrong."

"I have never been happier in my life," he said in 1963. "Sure, I miss baseball. I think I could still hit, but I'd probably have a heart attack running in from left field."

Curt Gowdy had tried hard to have NBC hire Williams as his color man for *Game of the Week* back in 1961 ("I thought he would have been great," Gowdy says. "He's the most intelligent man I ever met"), but the network executives had balked in the end. Something about a sponsor conflict between automobile companies. No matter. Williams's life was far from dull.

He was making more money than he had ever made. He was a salesman for Sears, for baseball, for fishing, for the U.S. Marines, for talking loud. For himself. The Public Ted was a character the country wanted to see. He played him well.

Woody Woodbury remembers he watched The Public Ted on television one night during the lull between games in some godforsaken doubleheader. Some broadcaster was asking incredibly basic, stupid questions, the equivalent of a reporter asking Einstein the sum of two plus two. Williams was returning answers that were five times, ten times more thoughtful than the questions. Woodbury at first found the process almost embarrassing to watch.

"How does Ted do it?" he wondered. "How does he even put up with it?"

Woodbury then remembered a moment at the Flamingo Hotel in Las Vegas. He and his wife were having dinner with Cary Grant. A stranger came up, sat down, and began asking Grant questions. Woodbury thought Grant knew the stranger because Grant answered a few of the questions. As the dialogue continued, though, it became obvious that the man was an interloper. Grant finally said, "That's enough, you'll have to go." The stranger became indignant.

"Just who the hell do you think you are?" he asked.

Grant was polite and devastating in a polite and devastating Cary Grant way.

"I know who I am," the actor said. "But do you know who *you* are?"

The quote seemed to fit here with Ted. He knew exactly who he was. He was an intelligent man, a voracious reader, Ted Williams. He wasn't the one with the problem. The reporter didn't have a clue who *he* was.

Woodbury decided his friend did remarkably well in this celebrity life, walking through fields of idiots. The Public Ted worked fine. He knew who he was.

The five-year wait before he became eligible for election to the Hall of Fame thus went quickly for Williams. He had disc surgery in 1964 at New England Baptist Hospital, but otherwise he was on the move. The Public Ted. He was virtually never seen at Fenway Park but was seen everywhere and anywhere else.

On January 20, 1966, he was back at Fenway. The selections for the Hall were scheduled to be announced at ten o'clock in the morning in the rooftop press room behind home plate.

"I feel like a lamb in the den with the lions," Williams joked as he stood before the notebooks and cameras.

His entry was not assured. The election was held among the baseball writers of America, and they had been known to be a tough group. Joe DiMaggio, no less, had been forced to wait three extra years before being selected. There was a possibility that also could happen to Williams, especially with his history with the baseball writers of America.

"DiMaggio had to wait, wait, and wait some more before the room clerk found him a space at the Inn of the Immortals," John Gillooly warned from the Colonel's chair in the *Record*. "So don't be startled if The Kid is asked to sit in the lobby for a while. There's no telling how the voting will be in other cities. The Kid, remember, was no politician. He kissed few babies (under 20, that is) along the trail. He shook few hands, patted few backs."

Williams had arrived in town a night earlier to attend a testimonial dinner for Jack Fadden, the longtime Red Sox trainer. Fadden, talkative and bright and wise, had been a career-long counterpoint to Williams, a conservative Abbott to the famous man's excitable Costello.

Dialogue (from the *Globe*):

WILLIAMS ON TRAINING TABLE: "What's that stuff you're rubbing me with, anyhow?"

FADDEN: "I call it 'Temperamental Salve.' "

WILLIAMS: "Yeah? I never heard of it. Feels good."

FADDEN: "I never use it on anyone except you."

WILLIAMS: "Is that right?"

Fadden was an interesting character. He loved to travel, but not by conventional means. When he finished his career with the Red Sox, his wife deceased, he would book passage on freight ships, going wherever their cargo took him. He would send out a mimeographed letter to friends every year about his visits to Cairo or Karachi or Mozambique. Or all of the above.

Even after his time with the Red Sox, he continued to be the head trainer at Harvard, sending the future congressmen and future corporate poobahs into Ivy League football battle. He would rub them down and tell them tales about Williams, about how Williams hated needles and how he was afraid of radiation because it might hurt "his equipment."

"He was very proud of his equipment," Fadden would say.

His admiration for Williams was considerable. He thought Williams was not only one of the most exceptional athletes he'd ever met but one of the most exceptional people. A broadcaster once asked if Williams would have been a good football player if he had gone to college. Fadden's reply was quick.

"He'd have been an all-American," the trainer said. "More than that, he'd have been Phi Beta Kappa."

The Public Ted charmed the gathering at the Hotel Statler ballroom. He spoke easily and graciously about his old friend. He choked up when he spoke about what might happen in the morning.

"It's possible I might get the highest honor a pro ballplayer ever can get," he said. "I certainly hope so."

At 10:01 A.M. the next day, Hy Hurwitz, a daily combatant during Williams's career, opened a large manila envelope in the Fenway press room. He pulled out a sheet of paper and announced, "Elected to the Hall was Ted Williams with 282 votes. That's a record, 93.3 percent of the votes. No one else was elected."

Again, Williams was humble and charming.

"This," he said, "completes everything a ballplayer ever dreams about or hopes happens to him."

Only 20 of the 302 ballots cast did not include his name. Casey Stengel, who would be selected as a manager for the Hall in 1966 in a later procedure, philosophized about the 20 voters who skipped Williams: "If they'd had to pitch to him, they'd have voted for him."

The induction ceremonies were held six months later on Monday, July 25, in Cooper Park in back of the library at the Baseball Hall of Fame in Cooperstown, New York. Past ceremonies had been held on the other side of the building on the front steps, but with Williams from Boston and Stengel from New York, the crowd was at least double the size of past years. The park was filled, people climbing into the elm trees and oaks to see. Loudspeakers were set up in the old location in front so late arrivals, unable to get into the park, at least could hear the speeches.

Williams had worked on his during the day on Sunday. He had been scheduled to travel to Oneonta to watch a minor league game with Red Sox farm director Neil Mahoney, but stayed behind to work on the speech. He then had gone to dinner with 22 friends, played some ping-pong at the Onestoga Inn with bellhops and kitchen help, then returned to his room to finish the speech.

New baseball commissioner Bill Eckert was forced to stop five times during his short introduction at the ceremony because of fans cheering for Williams. When the man of the moment finally came forward to a standing ovation, he stood in the sunshine and talked for six minutes:

I'm happy and I want to emphasize what a great honor it is to have the new commissioner of baseball here, General Eckert. The general and I have at least one thing in common, we have done some flying. He was in the Air Force and I was a Marine, and I want to tell you, no matter what you might have heard, there were many times when the Air Force went out first and the Marines had to go out to hit the targets they missed.

I guess every player thinks of joining the Hall of Fame. Now that the moment has come for me, I find it difficult to say what is really in my heart. But I know it's the greatest thrill in my life.

I received 280-odd votes from the writers. I know I didn't have 280-odd close friends among the writers. I know they voted for me because they felt in their minds, and some in their hearts, that I rated it, and I want to say to them, "Thank you, thank you from the bottom of my heart."

Today I'm thinking of a lot of things—I'm thinking of my playground director in San Diego, Rodney Luscomb; my high school coach Wos Caldwell; my managers who had such patience with me and helped me so much, fellows like Frank Shellenback, Donie Bush, Joe Cronin, and Joe McCarthy. I'm thinking of Eddie Collins, who had such faith in me, and to be in the Hall of Fame with him, particularly, as well as the other baseball players is a great honor. I'm sorry Eddie isn't here today.

I'm thinking of Tom Yawkey. I have always said it and I would like to repeat it today, Tom Yawkey is the greatest owner in baseball. I was lucky to have played on the club he owned, and I'm grateful to him for being here today.

But I'd not be leveling if I left it at that, because baseball players are not born great. They're not born hitters or pitchers or managers, and luck isn't the key factor. No one has come up with a substitute for hard work.

I've never met a baseball player who did not have to work harder at learning to play baseball than anything else he ever did. To me it was the greatest fun I ever had, which probably explains why today I feel both humility and pride because God let me play this game and learn to be good at it, proud because I spent most of my life in the company of so many wonderful people.

The other day, Willie Mays hit his 522nd home run. He has gone past me, and he's pushing ahead and I say to him, "Go get 'em, Willie."

Inside the building are plaques to baseball men of all generations. I'm proud to join them. Baseball gives every American boy a chance to excel. Not just to be as good as someone else, but to be better than someone else. This is the nature of man and the nature of the game. And I've been a very lucky guy to have worn a baseball uniform, and I hope some day the names of Satchel Paige and Josh Gibson in some way can be added as a symbol of the great Negro players who are not here only because they weren't given a chance.

As time goes on, I'll be thinking baseball, teaching baseball, and arguing for baseball to keep it right on top of American sports, just like it is in Japan, Mexico, Venezuela, and other Latin and South American countries.

I know Casey Stengel feels the same way, and I'm glad to be with him on his big day. I also know I'll lose a dear friend if I don't stop talking. I'm eating into his time and this is unforgivable, so in closing I'm grateful and know how lucky I was to have been an American and had a chance to play the game I love—the greatest game of all—baseball.

The startling part of the speech was the paragraph about including players from the Negro League in the Hall. No one ever had said this from this podium. The major leagues were seen as "real" baseball, anything else inferior. Negro League players never had been on the ballot. This was a first crack in a door that ultimately would open and include Paige and Gibson and other Negro League stars in the shrine.

For Williams, the request was all about simple fairness and justice. His politics always would be aligned with conservative, Republican men, all the way back to Herbert Hoover, his favorite president, the man whose name was on his high school uniform, but he always had a liberal social conscience, a feeling of doing "what's right." Perhaps this came from lessons from his Salvation Army mother, May, lessons he never noticed hearing that nevertheless stuck. Perhaps it simply was his own idea. He always comforted the sick. He always was free with time or money to help friends. He was—and even his worst critics would have admitted it—a constant ally of the downtrodden and neglected.

Larry Doby, the first black ballplayer in the American League in 1947 with the Cleveland Indians, always acknowledged that Williams was one of the first stars to be friendly. (And conversely, Joe DiMaggio was not.) Pumpsie Green, the first black ballplayer on the Red Sox, always said that Williams was one of the first players to warm up with him. Race was never a factor with Williams. He had become a jazz buff, friendly with pianists Erroll Garner and Oscar Peterson. People mattered, not race.

"What did you think when you were in the major leagues and they were all white at the beginning of your career?" he once was asked.

"I never thought about it," Williams said. "Isn't that funny? It never crossed my mind. We'd go into Washington or some place and I'd talk with one of the ushers or the ground crew and he'd say that Josh Gibson had hit one 'way back there' somewhere in the stadium two days ago. I'd look and I'd say, 'Wow. I could never hit one that far. I wish I'd seen that.' But I never thought about the situation. I just didn't. That was just the way it was."

The one controversy from the induction day came courtesy of that long-ago antagonist, The Colonel. Just before the speech, when Williams received his plaque from General Eckert, a fan from Boston in the crowd shouted, "What would Dave Egan say now?" Tim Horgan, working for the *Boston Traveler*, thought he saw Williams turn toward the fan and say, "Fuck Dave Egan."

Horgan was sitting next to Neil Mahoney in a group of Red Sox officials. This was a very good seat.

"What'd he say?" Horgan asked.

Everyone in his neighborhood seemed to think they heard the same thing.

Horgan wrote a story about the grand day, about Williams's speech, the honor. He never mentioned the "Fuck Dave Egan" part. He did, however, mention it on the phone with his managing editor. The managing editor put it in the paper. Under a headline that read "Ted Mars Ceremony." The story was under Horgan's byline.

At Fenway, four days later, Horgan was asked to go to Tom Yawkey's private office. He had never been to Yawkey's office. Not many people had. Virtually no sportswriters. Sitting behind a desk were Yawkey, general manager Dick O'Connell, and former catcher Haywood Sullivan, now in the front office. They had a tape recorder. They played a tape that they said conclusively showed that Williams said "the heck with Dave Egan." Or something like that. Horgan heard the words "Dave Egan" from the tape but could not pick out the words before the name. Too much static. Yawkey played the tape again. Horgan was unconvinced.

Yawkey now yelled at Horgan. Horgan threatened to punch Yawkey in the nose. Yawkey calmed down and demanded a retraction. Horgan calmed down and brought the demand back to his office.

The *Traveler* printed the retraction under the headline "Ted Williams, We Apologize." Horgan was not happy.

"The Red Sox games were broadcast on WHDH, which was owned by the *Herald*," Horgan says. "It was in their interests to make a retraction. But . . ."

Yes?

"I still think he said it."

Ted Williams was in the Hall of Fame. The heck with Dave Egan. Or something like that.

Unnoticed in any of the reports from Cooperstown was the presence of a Mr. and Mrs. Steven Tomasco as the guests of the famous inductee. They had stayed in a room at the Onestoga Inn, next door to the other inductee, Casey Stengel. They had been driven from Philadelphia to the event by Major Bill Churchman, Williams's old friend from the Marines.

Mrs. Steven Tomasco was Bobby-Jo, Williams's daughter. She was married now. She was 18 years old. She was pregnant.

"She and Steve had gone to Elkton, Maryland, to get married," Churchman says. "Eloped. I think she waited five or six weeks after they did it to tell Ted. Ted was not happy about it. He said to me, half-kidding, 'Jesus, Churchman, I put you in charge of my daughter and she runs off with some goddamned dago.' "

Williams's oft-stated dream for his daughter was a college degree. He always hoped she would fill in that one important line on her résumé that he always felt was lacking on his. Education. That was the ticket. She would wear a cap and gown, and he would be the happiest father at the graduation ceremonies.

That was not going to happen now.

Bobby-Jo had traveled through assorted teenage troubles. When she met Tomasco in 1965, she was a patient at the University of Pennsylvania Hospital Institute, a psychiatric treatment center. That alone showed how troubled she had been.

"She'd had a tough time," Tomasco says. "Living with an alcoholic mother in Florida . . . a distant relationship with a famous father . . . it was not the best. She always said Ted made her act like this little Barbie doll. It was all strange, right down to the name, the boy's name, Bobby-Jo.

"When she was 16, maybe just turned 17, she became pregnant by some guy. Everybody, I guess, knew except Ted. The idea was that she was going to have an abortion. The only one who could pay for it, though, was Ted. Her mother said, 'You're going to have to tell your father.' Barbara was terrified of telling him. She tried to commit suicide. She slashed her wrists."

Williams thus was told by his ex-wife, Doris, that his daughter was pregnant and also had tried to kill herself. This must have been a memorable conversation. How would news like this hit a combustible character who could rage about the way his wife parked the car in the family driveway, about how slow the service was in a restaurant?

In Florida, attempted suicide at that time was viewed as a criminal offense. Bobby-Jo could not stay in Florida. Williams called friends who looked around for a noncriminal treatment facility. Churchman found one at the University of Pennsylvania Hospital, the Institute, a place where such famous patients as Marilyn Monroe and Judy Garland had been treated.

Now a Philadelphia businessman, Churchman facilitated the move. He picked up Bobby-Jo at the train station, noticing the long scars from her wrists to her elbows, and found her a place to live and counseled her about her problems for a year and a half. The abortion was performed in Pennsylvania, the procedure legal now owing to her psychiatric history. Bobby-Jo was near the end of her treatment when she met Tomasco, the son of the local distributor for the Armstrong Racing Form, at a party. She had gone to the party with a date. Tomasco had gone with a buddy.

"She was a little bit heavy from all the medications, just getting ready to leave the hospital," Tomasco says. "I guess she had been extremely promiscuous, one guy after another. We just kind of hit it off. We met at the party, left together—she left her date and I left my buddy—and we basically stayed together after that."

Tomasco's introduction to Ted was in a suite at the Warwick Hotel in Philadelphia. This was when the couple was dating. Williams was pleasant, ordered a room service dinner. He always was pleasant, but distant, even after the marriage.

"He asked me to call him 'Mr. Williams,' and I did," Tomasco says. "He always called himself 'Old Teddy Ballgame.' "

Tomasco also met Doris. He found a sadness in his new mother-in-law. Doris, indeed, drank a lot. When he and Bobby-Jo would visit Florida and sit down for a family dinner, Doris would prepare and serve the dinner for however many people were at the table. She would not serve herself.

"I'll eat when I finish my drink," she would say.

She would never finish the drink. She quietly would refresh it again and again, still be drinking the same drink when she retired to the bedroom for the night.

"She tended to live in a combination of the past and the present," Tomasco says. "I think she really missed the life she'd had with Ted. There was a certain place she went to . . . the restaurant at one of the big hotels of the time on Miami Beach. She'd go there every Thursday, dress up for this upscale restaurant, and have lunch. Then she'd come back, cook, have dinner ready for everybody to eat except her.

"She talked all the time about how much she hated Ted, but I always had the feeling that she still cared for him."

Williams's support for the new couple was minimal. The newlyweds pretty much were on their own. They moved in with Tomasco's parents at first, then to their own apartment outside Philadelphia. Williams sent $600 to put Tomasco through three months of computer school, responded to some of Bobby-Jo's financial requests, but became even further removed from his only daughter.

Gone were the pictures spread across a coffee table for the female feature writers. Gone were the tales of the little girl who could throw a ball like a boy. Gone was most mention of Bobby-Jo. She became, like the family in California, a private relationship. He would have contact through the years, bits and pieces, visits, but his only public comments would be remarks like "Kids, you know, they break your heart." Best friends would hear his anger about Bobby-Jo but never understand where it originated.

On October 13, 1966, more than two and a half years after it was filed, the divorce from Lee became final. Williams told her that he hadn't answered his phone for the two and a half years because he didn't want to hear her lawyer tell him the marriage was finished. He said he still loved her and still wanted to get back together. She said that she still loved him but they couldn't get back together.

Circuit judge Harvie Duval awarded her $50,000 plus $10,000 in attorneys' fees. She received $15,000 in cash plus monthly alimony of $850.

"Do you think there is any chance at reconciliation?" the judge asked in the courtroom.

"Are you kidding?" Lee Williams replied.

12 Washington

The sweep of Williams' success was the greater because he was not only a rookie manager, untutored in the leadership of men, but as a baseball figure he was covered with the rust of nine years away from the game.

Everything appeared to be against Williams as a successful manager, including his own initial reluctance to take the job. Against him was his reputation as a loner and a brooder who had stood apart from his own Red Sox teammates during those many years. . . . But now, in retrospect, it is remembered that there never was any ceiling on the potential of Ted Williams on any pursuit he chose for himself.

SHIRLEY POVICH, *WASHINGTON POST*, OCTOBER 21, 1969

Russ White was a sportswriter for the *Washington Daily News*, the undisputed third newspaper in Washington, D.C., in 1969. He was 32 years old, scuffling against the bigger names from the *Washington Star* and the almighty *Washington Post*. He wasn't the product of some famous journalism school; he was a high school graduate who simply had started writing professionally after getting out of the service. There was nothing he liked better than getting a scoop, making the big-timers choke on their master's degrees when they read the headline over his story in the *Daily News*. He covered baseball.

Millionaire businessman Bob Short, former chairman of the Democratic Party, was the new owner of the perpetually grim Washington Senators, and White had been quizzing him about the vacant manager's job. White thought he had found a story. The NFL Washington Redskins had just hired Vince Lombardi as their coach, creating a bunch of local interest, and Short said he wanted to create the same kind of interest. He too was thinking of a big name.

White, the journalist, tried to figure out what names might be considered big—Vince Lombardi big—in baseball, and whittled down the list to two. White decided either Joe DiMaggio or Ted Williams, the two biggest baseball names possible, probably would become the next manager of the Senators.

He made calls and made more calls, and the more he talked to people, the more convinced he became that Short would choose Williams. The final convincing call was to a fishing guide in Islamorada who grunted, "Yeah, Ted's going to take it." White still wanted confirmation.

He never had talked with Williams in his life, but had tracked down Williams's home number in Islamorada. White called and received the answering machine. With a sudden flash of inspiration, he left a message, "Ted, hi, this is Bob Short. Can you call me at once at this number?" White then gave his own number.

He was sitting in his boxer shorts in the den of his starter home in McLean, Virginia, when the phone rang. Ted Williams, at the other end, said, "Hi, Bob."

What to do now?

"Don't hang up," White said. "This isn't Bob."

All the stories of all the problems with the press that Williams had in Boston came fluttering through White's mind as he tried to keep talking. How mad is this guy going to be? How soon is he going to rip my head off? Was this the end of a young career in journalism? White bluffed and said that he knew that Ted was the new manager and . . .

"You cover the team?" Williams asked.

"Yes."

"What kind of hitter is Mike Epstein? What kind of pitcher is Darold Knowles? Does he have a curveball? What . . . ?"

The interview became an interview in reverse. The worry was unnecessary. Williams asked all the questions. White gave all the answers. The conversation lasted a solid 15 minutes. Was Williams going to take the job? Of course. The story became a headline on page 1.

The *Post* and *Star* denied it. The *Post* even had its own exclusive that Nellie Fox, the old second baseman with the big chew of tobacco perpetually in his cheek, was going to be the manager. White followed up his first story with a story that Williams was going be a team vice president as well as the manager. The *Post* also denied that. On the third day, the press conference set, the *Post* finally agreed with White.

Ted Williams was coming back to baseball to manage the Washington Senators.

"Y ou couldn't pay me enough to manage," he had said, much more than once.

Now he was a manager? With the Senators?

Why not the Red Sox?

The Red Sox never had called. No, that wasn't right. They had called at least twice, once during the middle of Williams's playing career. They even had offered the general manager's job at least once. They never had romanced. That was their failure. They never had been serious. They had never offered inducements or twisted wrists.

Did they ever really want him? They never really had shown that they did.

His postretirement relationship with the club had been quiet. He was announced as a vice president on the day he was named to the Hall of Fame, but that was only another in a string of half-ceremonial posts he filled as he continued to receive deferred salary from the team.

Various reasons had been advanced for why he wasn't more active. Were other Red Sox executives afraid to bring such a strong figure onto the scene? Perhaps. Were there doubts, after his public relations miseries with the press, that he could survive in Boston? Perhaps. To hire Williams was to put yourself in a position someday to fire Williams. That was a Boston problem right there.

He also didn't fit into owner Tom Yawkey's old idea of a nightly companion, a drinking buddy. Again, for all the kind words spoken between them, they were very different people with different interests. After Yawkey finally was scared into abstinence in 1966 and dried out by his doctors, he had cleaned house. The manager he chose, disciplinarian Dick Williams, had brought a pennant in 1967.

"And Dick Williams, for one, wanted no part of Ted Williams," *Globe* sportswriter Will McDonough says.

Ted also never had pushed the issue. He never seemed interested. Since retirement, he had spent most of his time in each spring training working with minor leaguers rather than the stars. He never even showed up for the '67 World Series, preferring to keep fishing on the Miramichi River.

When he made a visit to Fenway during that season, he sat with Yawkey for the game. Yawkey was focused, living his daily death with the Red Sox. Williams was not.

"What's that new building going up downtown?" he asked, pointing toward the skyline during the winning rally.

He was sold on the Senators by Short, the owner. A dynamic character, Short once had bought and moved the Minneapolis Lakers to Los Angeles and made a $5 million profit when he sold them to Jack Kent Cooke. He was promising great things with the perpetually moribund Senators he recently had purchased for $9.5 million.

"I cannot immediately deliver a new team, but it is possible to get a storybook manager," Short declared.

"This man is one of the most exciting individuals I've ever met," Williams said about Short. "It really pleased me that he thought I actually could do something for Washington, the nation's capital. I was impressed."

The money was reported to be a million dollars for five years, plus a bunch of stock options. Williams called Carl Lind at Sears, and Lind told him he could keep the Sears job, that the company liked the idea of his name out front again. The timing simply was right. He was 50 years old, and if he was ever going to try this managing business, this would be a good time to do it.

One other thing: he was married again.

"Ted had been calling me, asking me to come back," second wife Lee Williams says. "We had nice conversations, but I didn't want to do it. Then one time he called and he said he probably wouldn't be calling anymore. He had a problem. He'd gotten a woman pregnant, and while he wondered if the baby really was his, he pretty much thought it was. He was getting married."

The bride was Dolores Wettach, a 32-year-old fashion model. The wedding was held quietly in Vermont. The honeymoon—Jimmy O'Loughlin thinks—was held in Waterbury, Connecticut.

O'Loughlin, a Waterbury detective, ran yearly benefits for the Jimmy Fund. He had been a minor leaguer in Ocala, Florida, in 1947 in spring training, trying out for a spot in the Red Sox system, and approached Williams for an autograph in centerfield. This was considered a no-no, a reason for immediate dismissal, a minor leaguer approaching a star during practice. Williams told him he would get in trouble. O'Loughlin said,

"I don't give a fuck. Give me your autograph." Ted said Jimmy reminded him of his brother, crazy. They had been friends ever since. Williams often went to Waterbury for Jimmy Fund events.

"Ted pulls up in the car with Dolores," Jimmy says. "I'm pretty sure it was their honeymoon. Ted jumps out, angry, gives me the keys and says, 'Jimmy, show her around town for the weekend. You're in charge of her.' I said, 'Ted, what do I show her in Waterbury?' He said, 'Just show her.' He was steaming. He stormed off. I drove Dolores around.

"He was so mad he wouldn't go to dinner that night. He made me take Dolores. We'd had this special dinner, boiled chicken baked with potatoes, prepared just for him. His favorite. He loved that. He said to me, just as I took her out the door, 'Bring me back a plate of that stuff.' "

Dolores, like Lee, was beautiful. She had been in the pages of *Vogue*. She had auditioned in London for the role of Pussy Galore in the James Bond film *Goldfinger*, rejected only because her voice was too soft. She was not the traditional picture of motherhood.

"Puttering in the kitchen of this Florida Keys fishing retreat . . . Mrs. Williams looked about as much like a housewife as Zsa Zsa Gabor looks like a nursemaid," Myra MacPherson would write in a *Washington Post* profile when Williams took the Senators job. "She is 5 feet 9 inches tall, model slim, with a large-eyed face. She was wearing a shirt tied at the midriff and low-slung hiphugger blue jeans. She was opening a bottle of French champagne for lunch.

"It's not too early for wine," she said. "Some people have it for breakfast."

Champagne for lunch? This did not seem like a good fit with the outdoorsman. Williams did not like the idea of a baby at this stage of his life. He also did not particularly like the idea of marriage to this woman. He railed against both ideas. Loudly.

In her pregnancy, Dolores found an ally at Williams's fishing camp on the Miramichi River in New Brunswick, Canada. Ding Dussault, a summer neighbor, the track coach at Tufts University outside Boston, was another Williams friend. He understood the problems of late-in-life fatherhood because he'd had a son, Eddie, at age 50. He also understood the many moods of Ted. He, like most of Ted's friends, had learned how to handle the thunder and rain.

Dussault counseled Dolores about Williams's sudden rages, about the four-letter words, about the way her new husband was. He wrote letters to her when she left the Miramichi, and she responded, worrying about "all the prickhound women" and the corporate big-timers who always wanted "to rub off" on Ted. Dussault told Dolores again and again to hang in there, maybe it all would work out when the baby was born.

"Maybe it'll be a boy," Dussault said. "That would help."

On August 26, 1968, the baby was born in Brattleboro, Vermont. Williams missed the moment again. He was fishing.

The baby was a boy. Williams wanted to name him John-Henry Williams after John Henry, the steel-driving man, Lord, Lord, a symbol of all things masculine. Dolores agreed, but added a middle name, Dussault, in honor of her new friend and adviser. John-Henry Dussault Williams. She called the baby "Dusey."

"Ted Williams is a composite," Bob Short said, six months later, announcing his new manager on February 21, 1969. "He is the .400 hitter, two wars, 20 years in baseball, fishing, hunting, problems with the press, obscurity to fantastic fame.

"All that he is and was makes the guy and the man I hired. Take some of that out of the mix and he's probably not my man. I want him to be Ted Williams as part of the Tell-It-Like-It-Is set, possibly 25 years ahead of his time. This is the reason that we made him the first million-dollar manager in baseball history."

On February 25 in Pompano Beach, Florida, the great experiment began as spring training opened for the Senators. Williams wore a shirt with number 9 on the back, formerly the property of large-sized slugger Frank Howard, who now wore number 33. Williams's large-sized pair of pants once had belonged to some unnamed large-sized relief pitcher. He talked to his troops. He met the press. The Hall of Fame outfielder and father of a five-month-old boy was on the job.

The *Boston Globe* sent Bob Sales to Pompano Beach to write a six-part series on Williams's return to the game. Sales was not a character from the belligerent Boston past. He was part of the new breed of sportswriters, "chipmunks" New York old-timer Jimmy Cannon called them for the way they chattered and ran around and collected facts. Sales had sixties long hair and a beard. He often wore love beads and a dashiki. He never had met Williams.

"Jesus Christ, what do we have here?" Williams said in his little

Pompano Beach office. "I know, I know, you hate the war, you hate the government, you hate this, you hate that."

Sales, who had a gravel voice, snarled something back. Williams laughed. No problem.

The Public Ted was in charge here every day. The sportswriters who had covered his career couldn't believe the change. The new breed wondered what the big fuss had been about when he played. (Those old-time sportswriters must have been idiots!) He had gone from churl to kindly grandfather, gathering everyone round to tell stories and lay out philosophies. He was a foul-mouthed teddy bear.

"Hitting is such an individual talent," Sales suggested. "Are there things you tell your players to help them hit better?"

"Certainly you can help hitters," Williams replied. "No question! Can a golf pro help a golfer? Can a swimming coach help swimmers?"

The baseball maxim was that great players usually do not become great managers. Able to manage their own success on the field, they traditionally had been frustrated by the lack of similar talent or ambition or both in the players they now had to direct. To find a great player who had become a great manager, writers had to go all the way back to John McGraw in the first two decades of the century.

Could Williams be the next McGraw? He was inheriting an awful team, the worst in baseball, and he had never managed any team anywhere at any level of the game. He had been the consummate loner as a player, the exact opposite of the cheerleading, backslapping utility infielder who traditionally was considered the best fit as a manager. Could he overcome all of that? He had a lot of work to do.

One interesting move he made at the beginning was to create a new coaching position. Williams knew his inadequacies with baseball rules and baseball strategies, when to play the infield in, where to shift the outfield, how to make many of the long-tested moves. He wanted a bench coach to assist him on all of that.

He offered the job first to Johnny Pesky, but Pesky declined. He had moved into a short-lived broadcasting career as a color announcer, even was going to speech classes. He said he couldn't bail out on his commitments this close to the season. Williams then offered the job to Joe Camacho, the blooper-ball home run hitter and grammar school principal from the camp at Lakeville.

"My first reaction was, 'No, I'm not going,' " Camacho says. "I had two kids. I had tenure. Then I got thinking about it. The pension was very good. Where else can you work four years and take out a $30,000 a year pension? I went."

The other coaches were incumbents Nellie Fox, Wayne Terwilliger, and Sid Hudson, plus old-time former Red Sox coach George Susce. Williams also offered O'Loughlin, the Waterbury detective, the equipment job. O'Loughlin decided against the move. He had *four* kids and couldn't handle the travel. Williams understood.

"Then, in the middle of that season, my wife died," O'Loughlin says. "Now I have four kids and I'm raising them by myself. What do I do? There's Ted. He's on the phone right away. He saved me. He hired a full-time housekeeper so I could keep going to work."

The players in Pompano Beach were almost overwhelmed by the first sight of Williams. It was as if a face from Mount Rushmore had come down to give advice. His voice boomed. His messages were direct. He was Ted Williams! People paid attention.

"I'd grown up in Pittsfield, Massachusetts," Tom Grieve, a 21-year-old rookie outfielder in that first camp, says. "In our neighborhood we had 10, 15 kids, and all we did all day was play baseball. Morning until night. Play baseball. Talk baseball. I'd get the *Springfield Union*, six o'clock in the morning, and rip it open to the sports pages to see what had happened. Read everything.

"Everyone else was a Red Sox fan. I was a Yankees fan. So Ted was my antihero, but he was just so large. My dad would take us to a doubleheader in Fenway one year, a doubleheader in Yankee Stadium the next year. Ted would always go 3-for-3, and Mickey Mantle always would go 0-for-3, and my sisters would always kill me on the way home.

"To stand next to this guy, to have him talk to you . . . I was in constant awe. I could see his lips moving, but I couldn't hear what he was saying."

Williams's general philosophy was summed up early in spring training. Camacho and Fox were in the infield discussing various options for third-base cutoff plays. Each coach had an opinion. They went back and forth. Williams listened in on this for a couple of minutes, then said, "Fuck it, let's hit." Hitting practice began.

The subtleties of the game of baseball, "inside baseball," never would be part of his approach. There weren't even any signs for him to give to Terwilliger at third base. Terwilliger ran that show. There weren't any signs to give to the catcher except a shout or an exaggerated motion now and then to throw a curveball or slider. The catcher ran that show. The subtleties of hitting, ah, were a different matter.

"Ted would say things like, 'In the first seven innings I always tried to hit the top half of the ball because I wanted to hit line drives,' " catcher Rich Billings says. " 'Then, after the seventh, I always tried to hit the bottom half of the ball for a better chance at a home run.'

"Guys would look at each other. I'm going up there against Nolan Ryan, and he's throwing 95 miles an hour, and I'm trying to hit a particular half of the ball? They'd never heard anything like this."

Hitting was the game. Pitching was a necessary evil. Williams didn't tinker with stances or strokes as much as he tinkered with heads. *Get a good pitch to hit.* The game was to work the pitcher to a 2-0, 3-1 count, forcing him to throw a fastball or his favorite pitch. Wait for that favorite pitch in a particular zone. Swing. Hit it! Don't be late.

"Here it is," Williams would shout from the dugout when the count reached the proper numbers. "Be ready . . . aw, Jesus Christ. How can you be so late? What are you doing? Jesus Christ."

The material took time to absorb. He did not have any budding .406 hitters on the roster. The Senators lost nine of their first ten exhibition games, then lost the season opener, 8–4, to the Yankees before a sellout at Robert F. Kennedy Stadium. President Richard Nixon threw out the first ball, three of them actually. Williams said that he not only had voted for the president but had contributed money to his campaign.

"I don't think too many people are any happier than I am that he is the president," the manager said.

Nixon would return the compliment. He would attend five games during the season . . . and for good reason. The Senators were fun to watch.

They won their next game, 9–6, over the Yanks, won two after that, lost six in a row, then settled into the win-one, lose-one pace of a middle-level team. The doormats were doormats no more. They fit nicely into that well-appreciated category of spunky overachievers. The same guys who had stunk a year ago stunk no more. They were respectable.

By July 2, they had edged over the .500 mark (41-39). By July 14 (now 49-45), they had edged past the previous year's entire attendance mark of 542,042 when 23,831 patrons arrived to watch a 3–0 win over the Tigers. The next McGraw had arrived.

"We're the same guys," catcher Paul Casanova said. "But we're a different team."

"The first time he ever talked to me," Tom Grieve says, "he told me to go into my swing, then stop at the point where I made contact with the ball. I had no idea. I never had thought about that. Not once.

"I went into my swing, and I remembered coaches always saying to be 'out in front.' I stopped somewhere maybe a foot, 18 inches past where it turned out I actually hit the ball. He looked at me, told me to think about it, then come back to him in a few days and do it again. I passed the word about his question, and everyone went around figuring out where he hit the ball."

Think. Be smart. That was the big change in the Senators. Concentration. Interest.

Even the pitchers seemed to profit. Though Williams was constant in his shots at the profession—"The only thing dumber than a fucken pitcher is two fucken pitchers"—there were lessons he could teach.

"I just listened to everything he said to the hitters and turned it around," pitcher Casey Cox says. "If this was the situation they wanted to create, the 2-0, 3-1 count, then it was the situation I wanted to avoid. The important thing was to throw strikes."

Williams wanted all of his pitchers to throw the slider, the toughest pitch for him to handle as a player, the slider in on the hands. Cox threw the slider, more sliders than he'd ever thrown. He changed his positioning on the mound, took different sides of the rubber now for righthanded and lefthanded hitters, making it easier to get that slider inside on the hands.

Dick Bosman, the ace of the staff, was on the way to a 14-5 season. Joe Coleman Jr., a graduate of the Ted Williams Baseball Camp, would be 12-13. Casey Cox was on the way to the best year of his career, 12-7, with a 2.78 ERA.

The whole thing worked. Williams was encouraging, forceful, involved. The players fed on the buzz from his notoriety. People finally were paying attention to them! If any other inspiration were needed, they simply had to stand near the clubhouse wall on some days.

"The Redskins had their locker room right next to us," Tim Cullen says. "You could hear Lombardi talking to them. Every word. That was pretty good."

After the Skins finished practice across the street at the D.C. Armory, Lombardi would stand behind the batting cage with Williams and they would talk. Lombardi always wore baseball pants and a baseball hat for practice. He looked like he belonged.

"I was there when Ted Williams met Vince Lombardi for the first time," Russ White says. "It was at a dinner. Ted says to him in that big voice, 'I understand that you can walk on water.' Lombardi said, 'I understand that you can too.' "

The only controversy of the year was small. The All-Star Game was held in Washington, and there was a celebration for the centennial anniversary of major league baseball. A large dinner was held at the Shoreham Hotel. Williams didn't go, even though he lived at the Shoreham Hotel.

He had learned that Joe DiMaggio was going to be given an award for "The Greatest Living Player," and that, along with the fact that the dinner was black-tie formal, kept him in his suite. Dolores, angry at him, wearing a blue dress, took the elevator to the ballroom and accepted Williams's award as "The Greatest Living Hitter."

"Maybe some people will say, 'Hey, that's Old Ted,' " Ray Fitzgerald wrote in the *Boston Globe*. " 'One of a kind. Nobody can tell him what to do.' That's what some people will say. It's not what this person says. What this person says is that Theodore Samuel Williams has colossal gall, inconceivable conceit, to insult the profession that has made him a household name to anyone that ever held a bat in his hands."

The controversy came and went quickly. Nothing could derail the good works of the season.

The sprint home was fun. The once bedraggled, lowly Senators won eight of their final nine games, including a season-ending 3–2 win over the Red Sox. Each of the players and coaches had found a new Ted Williams fishing rod and reel in his locker stall a day earlier. A thank-you. Williams received a standing ovation from the 17,482 spectators before the final game when he took out his lineup card. Another thank-you.

"Ted, that's for you," one of the umpires said about the noise as Williams continued to talk.

He lifted and twirled his cap in appreciation. There wasn't even time to think. He tipped his cap—sort of tipped it—for the first time since he was a rookie in 1939.

The numbers, in this game most judged by numbers, were startling. The team batting average had jumped from .224 to .251. Every starter hit better in 1969 than he did in 1968. Shortstop Ed Brinkman, the poster child for the surge, had jumped from .187 to .267. The team had scored 170 more runs, collected 156 more hits, and 174 more walks. There were jumps in the number of doubles, triples, and homers, and a decrease in strikeouts.

"You can't prove you can manage in one year," Williams said modestly on the last day. "But this year gave me more confidence."

The voters decided he could manage, picking him American League Manager of the Year. It was a considerable feat. He had been out of baseball, virtually uninvolved, and led this team of cast-offs and rejects to the Senators' first winning record in 17 seasons. The team that was supposed to finish at the bottom of the standings was a respectable 86-76, fourth place in the American League East. Williams had charmed the press, sold tickets, and produced a solid team.

What couldn't this man do when he put his mind to it?

A local high school basketball coach named Don Newbery had developed a different sort of hobby for the time. Equipped with a portable tape recorder, he patrolled the locker rooms of the D.C.-area professional sports teams, interviewing the coaches and players. This was long before ESPN and sports radio, long before tape recorders had become handy-dandy, compact machines.

"Sometimes I'd sell 15-second, 20-second sound bites to radio stations for two or three dollars, but this certainly wasn't a moneymaking business," he says. "I was just interested in sports. The PR guys were very nice and would give me credentials. Sometimes I'd play the interviews at clinics."

At the end of the 1969 Senators season, Newbery convinced Dolores Williams to do an interview. He met with her on the roof of the Shoreham Hotel, her suggestion, because it was a sunny, pleasant day. She brought along John-Henry, who was slightly over a year old now.

Newbery was looking only for a breezy, happy spot, one of those smiling interviews with the smiling wife of the famous man of sport. That is not what he received. With the sounds of the baby in the background, squeal here, squeal there, every now and then the rattle of a plastic toy, Dolores opened windows into the personal life of Ted Williams that never previously had been opened in public.

The following is the text of that long interview, printed in its entirety for the first time. Newbery has a broadcaster's echo-chamber voice, unremittingly cheery as he tries to return to safer ground. Dolores Williams has a soft voice. She is hesitant and shy at the beginning, but speaks more and more freely as the interview progresses. Her candor eventually becomes uncontainable:

DON: This is Don Newbery. My guest today is Mrs. Ted Williams. I've had Mr. Ted Williams on my program quite a number of times, and I feel very honored to have this lovely wife of Ted as my guest, and I'm very appreciative of the fact she is giving not just me but all of my listeners a chance to hear from her and hear some of her thoughts.

DOLORES: Oh, aren't you nice.

DON: Mrs. Williams, first of all, I think most of my listeners would like to know something of your background. Where you grew up. What kind of schools you went to.

DOLORES: My word, I could fill up your whole hour on that. I grew up on a farm in Vermont, and I went to a one-room schoolhouse where all the eight grades were in this one room, and we walked to school a half a mile, and we used to have races back and forth to see who could make it all in one trip. . . .

DON: You're talking about your grammar school. Would you go on now with your high school and so forth.

DOLORES: Well, then, from grade school we went to high school, but at that time if you were a girl in the country, they felt education was wasted. So here I started to have a little bit of an argument with my father about going to high school. And it was a problem because we had no transportation for the students in Westminster to go to this high school. So it meant I would have to room out. Anyway, I went to high school in Bellows Falls and from there got a scholarship to go on to the University of Vermont.

DON: Oh, wonderful. Beautiful country. Beautiful school.

DOLORES: Oh, I loved it. Listen, I used to say, whenever my battery ran down, I'd go home and hug the trees to get it recharged.

DON: Wonderful. From the University of Vermont . . . okay, what did you major in, and then what happened after college?

DOLORES: I majored in nursing, and I minored in agriculture and basic principles of single combustion engines and electricity.

DON: Oh, my. What did you do with all of this?

DOLORES: I'll tell you what. Because my father was so against education . . . and we had a farm . . . I wanted to prove to him that if I was educated it wouldn't go to waste. And you see, I was the oldest girl, and we didn't have any boys in the family till the bottom of the patch, so Daddy, with all his animals, I figured I'd be the clever gal and come home with some of these new collegiate ideas on how to raise animals more effectively.

DON: Very good. Now when you graduated from Vermont . . .

DOLORES: Wait. I have good things to tell you . . . while in college I won the livestock showmanship in my class of the year because I was probably about the only girl handling animals up there. And . . . wait a minute . . . because we had a mink ranch on the farm . . . and because I was my father's partner, I had to skin all the animals and cut up the meat to grind for the animals. . . . The man from Grand Union came up there to our department, and he was demonstrating, and just to be funny he brought me up to, you know, hand me the knife to explain different cuts of meat. When he found out how well I could cut, he offered me a job for $60 a week at his meat counter.

DON: Oh, my goodness. Well, what happened with it?

DOLORES: Oh, no, I turned that down.

DON: Marvelous.

DOLORES: Then, to top it all off . . . uh, no, I guess I won't tell you that. No, I won't tell you that. Because it sounds conceited. . . .

DON: You mean you won something. We'd like to know about that. We'd like to know your diversifications and, you know, all the abilities you do have. . . .

DOLORES: No, you see, I was very self-conscious. Being I came from the farm, and also the oldest, I was also a very skinny girl, and I had a lot of chores to do on the farm, so I thought I was known as a deadbeat in school. As a joke, when I graduated from high school and you know they give you class gifts, the president called me up and he said he understood I not only was sweet 16 and never been kissed but also sweet 17 and never been kissed, and they didn't want me to graduate without a kiss, so they said they were going to give me one right then and there . . . and I tell you I started to cry, and I ran and hid in the curtains, and they all laughed and said, "Don't cry, it's only a candy one, so turn around," so they laughed some more . . . so the joke of the matter was after being known as a deadbeat and not getting any kisses or dates, in college I was mysteriously appointed—the newspaper called me up and said one of the professors in school said I was the type of girl who should represent Vermont in the Miss Universe contest. And I won it!

Don: Wonderful.

Dolores: Yeah, I think it was because of the animals.

Don: Are you kidding? He knew what he was talking about. No question about that.

Dolores: But that was my biggest thrill, because I remember feeling so sad in school because no one liked me and I was so ugly and so skinny and then to come off and be Miss Vermont. Because I used to wish when I was little that I was pretty. I'd wish, "If I could only be Miss Vermont someday."

Don: And your wish came true.

Dolores: And I wished to make a lot of money too, when I was little. So we wouldn't have it so tough. And that wish came true [as a model].

Don: Yes, it did. Very much so.

Dolores: Of course, what I call a lot maybe no one else calls a lot.

Don: I don't know about that.

Dolores: Well, it was a lot for me. I was able to get what I wanted for my parents.

Don: All right, now let's go now from the University of Vermont. Where did this Miss Vermont contest project you? What did it do for you?

Dolores: I think it drove deep into my values, of what I had back home. I had always thought that things on the other side of the fence were greener and bigger and better and because you deserved it and you were someone special, and what I found out, my goodness, what I had back home in my own backyard was far more precious and special than any of these wealthy people or famous people or even these beautiful people that I met. . . . I was very disappointed by the contest and the girls and the people in it. . . . When you pick a girl, it's a matter of taste. Every girl is beautiful. Every girl it's just a matter of who's the sponsor, a matter of who's teaching her to do what and where. And you can't make a choice. It was a shame to see so many people heartbroken and try to cut each other's throat because it meant so much to them. And I once had a doctor say to me—you know, because I studied nursing—"Just remember, none of us can pick the hole we came out of." . . . and it's terrible when you're judged by something as physical as that. You're kind of like a piece of meat. So that was disappointing.

Don: Right.

Dolores: Though I think I deepened my values and I know too that people back home said that I was going to become jaded, that I wouldn't be the same again because I'd go off and be Miss Vermont and "she'd really think she was something." That's why I prefaced before I didn't want to say anything because I didn't want to sound conceited. I sort of had that fear that somehow that would happen. . . . Anyway, I went to New York. I wanted to go on with my studying and be a licensed midwife, and it was while I was nursing that two photographers spotted me. And they asked if I would come over to their studio and have *Vogue* magazine meet me. They thought I'd make a good model. It happened that I photographed with a very strong resemblance to Jacqueline Kennedy, and this, of course, was what *Vogue* at the time wanted to keep in fashion. So this step put me into the modeling world, and then I was nursing and modeling, and I never did get to go to Johns Hopkins and get my license in midwifery because then I was making so well in the photographic field, I was getting sent around the world on different trips. And that's how I met Ted.

DON: All right, let's stay with this modeling bit just a little while. Suppose there are some girls listening right now and all they see is the glamour and lots of money that certain girls do make in modeling. . . . What do you think the opportunities are? Is the chance a good chance or is it . . .

DOLORES: Your best chance is if you don't go knocking on their doors and ask them to look at you. Your best chance is if for some way they spotted you. Because it's really a matter of luck. You can knock your brains out, and if they don't want you, no matter how pretty you are, they don't want you. They go through a fad. Like, say it was the Jacqueline Kennedy look. If I didn't look like Jacqueline Kennedy, it wouldn't have mattered who I was, how I photographed, whose friend I was, or no matter what kind of favors were done anywhere along the line, it's a matter of luck. And the type of a feel . . . the type of fad or fashion they're playing up at the time. But if you're persistent and you're versatile enough, you might be able to lend your body to this particular fad. Like, it seems right now they're on a . . . like, when they were on the Twiggy look . . . a very skinny, bony, nebbish type of girl, a female who doesn't denote too much sex, doesn't denote so much sophistication. It's sort of an inbetween . . .

DON: Uh-huh.

DOLORES: They once took a . . . believe it or not, they put models in IBM machines. And the machine told them, believe it or not, I could never go on the cover of *Vogue* because I would emote too many emotions. I wouldn't sell the magazine. You have to be sort of a neuter so you don't offend the women and that the men don't like you . . .

DON: Well, how do they do that? What kind of information do they put on this machine? Do they ask you questions?

DOLORES: No, no, they put down their observations. Like, they'll put down your measurements, put down your coloring, I guess everything. Somehow the machine comes out with whether you're sexy or whether you're neuter or you don't offend anyone or whether you will offend someone.

DON: Very interesting.

DOLORES: Unfortunately, it said, "Dolores, the way you are, only men will like you." I had to change. I had to take off a lot of weight and do a few other things.

DON: Oh, my goodness. That is interesting . . .

DOLORES: But if a girl really has it and she wants to be a model because she enjoys selling clothes and she's not a hard person and she can also mend maybe her insides to her inner feeling, perhaps to the clothes, this helps. Because they're looking for something besides just a pretty girl. That doesn't make a picture. But they don't want a girl that's so conceited and so concerned about herself that all you see is that pretty face, because you're not helping out the client at all. He's not selling his clothes, he's selling the girl. And he doesn't want to sell the girl. It's all to make money.

DON: Right . . . okay, you said this was the way you met Ted. Uh, can you tell us now where and when did you meet Ted Williams.

DOLORES: Let's see. In March, it's going to be six years ago I met him, and we were both coming back from Australia and New Zealand. He was down there on a trip, and I was down there for *Vogue* magazine. And as you know, that's a pretty long plane trip. And we were of course sitting in first-class, and cocktails and champagne are being served, and it wasn't too long before spitballs were landing in my lap! And I turned around, and here's this guy popping these spitballs at me. And there are notes in them. He wants to know who I am. Well, I'll tell you, we, the *Vogue* group, had been so close to each other . . . well, it had gotten to the point that the other model and I weren't talking, and it was like the world was just too closed in. And this was a breath of fresh air. This fresh guy throwing spitballs. . . . I thought, Oh, boy, this was great. So I did a pantomime back at him as to who I was. I pantomimed some poses out as a model. So I wrote back on the note, and I threw it back at him. I said, "Who are you?" Of course, he didn't pantomime back as a fisherman. He threw back a note saying he was "Sam Williams, a fisherman." And he said, "What's your name?" So I wrote down my name and threw it back. And then he wanted me to have dinner with him when we landed in San Francisco. [missing part on tape] and there he was sitting there in the lounge, waiting for me to get out [of the bathroom], and he said something very bold and personal that, well, really knocked me off my feet. So I said, "Well, don't let this pickup line scare you." So I said something appropriate. . . .

DON: Ha.

DOLORES: And I couldn't get rid of him. But I said to myself, I'd like to see you try it [what he suggested] on the airplane! . . . Well, when that plane landed, I was running ahead of the crowd, trying to lose him at the gate and so forth. And I had a date, this doctor was meeting me in San Francisco. But he wasn't there, and I sat there on the bench, and Mr. Williams, the Fisherman, kept asking me to have dinner with him. He was getting off there, but the plane was going on to New York. I said no, and I sat and my date never showed up, and the phone would ring right there on the counter. . . . Now, I don't know how Mr. Williams got the phone, right there at the counter, next to where I was sitting . . . but it would be him, checking in every ten minutes, wanting to know whether I was still there or not, and lo and behold, the doctor finally sends me a telegram that he can't make it because he has to go to court the next day or something. So I book out on another flight. Now, if you remember about six years ago, there was that big nationwide smog-fog-in?

DON: Yes, yes.

DOLORES: Where everything was grounded for two days? Well, that was it. My flight got grounded. And where do you suppose the airline put me up? Where do you suppose? Or else he just happened to be at the same airport motel. I understand he does stay pretty close to the airport. Well, of course, I did wind up having dinner with Mr. Williams . . . but it wasn't until after three dinners with him that I discovered he wasn't Sam Williams the Fisherman.

Don: It was after three dinners . . .

Dolores: Yes! And the only reason I found out was because he took me to this mai-tai or luau kind of place in California, and one of the little Oriental girls at the coat-check counter said, "Oh, I know who you are." He said, "Yeah, really?" She said, "You're Ted Williams, the baseball player." He said, "No, I just look like him." But then I began to wonder . . . sure enough, that's who he was.

Don: Well, had you ever heard of Ted Williams the baseball player?

Dolores: I'd heard of him, but that was it. If anyone asked me who I knew in baseball, it was Ted Williams, Babe Ruth, and Joe DiMaggio. That's all I knew. Just the names. Nothing else. Whether they were alive, dead, or what.

Don: And when you found out about this, what was your first reaction to it, that this is Ted Williams, the great baseball player. What was your first thought?

Dolores: If I'd known who he was, I'd have never gone out with him. I said, "These famous people are so spoiled, they can have anybody they want." I said, "Darn it, why didn't I know that beforehand!"

Don: All right now, you found out this was Ted Williams the baseball player. It's after the third dinner. You both now enjoy each other's company . . .

Dolores: Oh, no. No. That's about the time we started fighting. Listen, if you go through three days with him, you're in luck. You're lucky. That's it. The honeymoon's over in three days. Then the fights start. And then he acts like a little boy and you love him all over again, and then it's smooth rolling and then, whooops, there you go again . . .

Don: Well, tell me this . . .

Dolores: Listen, we split up on the streets of San Francisco. I walked one way and he the other, and I got in a cab and I said, "I don't need your kind of treatment at all. I don't care who you are or how famous you are." . . .

Don: How about when he asked you to marry him? What happened then?

Dolores: Well, I'll tell you . . .

Don: And were you expecting him to ask you to marry him . . .

Dolores: Oh, I was expecting him to ask me to marry him for three years.

Don: Oh, okay.

DOLORES: And it was the most back-around way of asking me. It was, "Are you sure it isn't a mistake?" That's the way . . . "Are you sure it wasn't a mistake?" and—what was it?—"Have I gotten you so you can't get along without me?" That's what he wanted to know, yeah.

DON: And what was your reaction?

DOLORES: I said, "Yesss." He said I was the most voluptuous female that he knew and that I meant more to him than any dame he knew.

DON: Wonderful . . . all right now, you get married to this famous man. What happens after you get married? Where do you go to live? And why? Why do you go to this certain place?

DOLORES: Well, there's no problems there. We went everywhere. I went back to New York and worked some more as a model. He had trips and commitments with Sears Roebuck which took him around the country to different factories. And he had—he still does have—a baseball camp in Massachusetts. So in the summer we lived there. We bought a home and fixed that up. When fall comes, we went to New Brunswick, Canada, and salmon-fished till the frost set in. Then we moved down to my farm in Vermont for Christmas and the snow to set in, then back to Florida. And that was how we did it.

DON: Where did you finally locate?

DOLORES: We're not finally located anywhere.

DON: When you finally decided to settle down. In other words, you're going from one place to another, wasn't it finally in the Florida Keys? That's where everybody seems to think that Ted Williams really migrated to and stayed, all year round. Is this true?

DOLORES: No. No, he's split up in three different places. Now four. There's the Keys, Lakeville, Massachusetts, Vermont, and New Brunswick, Canada. Blackville.

DON: Okay. But when Bob Short finally got ahold of him, he was in the Florida Keys, right?

DOLORES: Yes.

DON: Okay, now, when Ted first mentioned to you he was even considering this business of managing a major league baseball team, what was your reaction then?

DOLORES: Oh, I thought it was great. I thought it was a real good idea.

DON: I'm sure you did. Why?

DOLORES: Well, because I thought he needed a bigger challenge in life than what he was receiving at the time. And I figured, if there was something big that he could get his teeth into, perhaps he would be a happier individual. Because I think there's nothing more frustrating than not feeling proud of yourself. Or feeling you're no longer necessary or needed. . . . And this was his biggest talent, where he had worked all his life in achieving. Baseball . . . Goodness, after they talked to him, he'd hang up the phone and start cursing a blue streak. "I'll be such-and-such if I do that!" "I'm sick and tired of it, I'm glad it's over. Crap. Blah-blah." . . . He rolled on. On and on. Then he'd get a second thought. "But you know, sweetie, I'm sure as hell I could do it. Christ, I know I could do it. If I could get the right managers here," and he'd start snapping his fingers . . . he'd get up and, you know, he has a kind of sway to his hips, you know, sometimes he goes up to the plate, you know how those hips kind of rock forward . . . he goes up there, and you could see the excitement charging up, and then aw, black would come back up and aw, he'd slam it down again . . . that was the finish. He'd had it. Then someone would call up and he'd start right in again with the enthusiasm. It just went up and down again like a seesaw. Until he finally met Mr. Short. And Mr. Short was a very intelligent man in that he let Ted have his way completely in everything. He gave him all the loopholes he wanted, so he didn't feel caged, that he could get out if he had to. If he was a failure, he could withdraw without being embarrassed. Or move upstairs. He also was assured he could have anybody he wanted. It wasn't going to be that kind of problem that you have to work with who I give you. And Mr. Short gave him the big-league style of going first-class. Go to the top. He had all the professional people if you want to get a job well done. . . . And Ted liked this. He's a perfectionist himself. He doesn't want to fool around with any namby-pambies or, uh, it's too bad we can't swear on this program because Ted's got some beautiful descriptive words that would come in so well here.

DON: All right, he accepted the job. And all of a sudden, the publicity hounds started coming down there . . .

DOLORES: Oh . . .

DON: What was happening then?

DOLORES: Oh, oh, oh . . . this is the first time I really got a glimpse of why Ted has such a hate for some of them. I tell you, they're rude.

They're animals! I don't understand how they can be human beings. Absolutely bold, vulgar, it's like just because you're somebody they have the right to claw and get a piece of you.

DON: I know just what you mean.

DOLORES: Oh, it's terrible. I mean, I've got the baby. We have a house hidden way in the back. There's no sign, no mailbox. Only by way of mouth can you find out where we are. A big spike fence around the place with signs, BEWARE OF THE DOG. I've got a German shepherd attack-trained dog there. And wouldn't you believe they're climbing the fence and sneaking and poking behind the palm trees with their cameras in their hands. And I'll tell you, if I hadn't caught the dog, they would have been eaten . . . well, not eaten really, but they would have got a good hunk taken out of them. (My father said I should have let the dogs do it.) I got so angry, I went up to them and said, "Just what do you want?" They said, "Oh, nothing. We're just tourists." They really don't think that privacy means anything at all. . . . And there he just boldly sort of goes back out to his car, he left his car there . . . I went out. I had the baby in my arms. And wouldn't you know he had enough nerve, in the car, he turned around and took another picture. This time to get the baby and me in the picture.

DON: Well . . .

DOLORES: At first he was just satisfied taking a picture of the grounds and the house, hoping to see someone . . . but the dog was, I was really worried the dog was going to get him because then Ted would be angry because we'd have a suit on our hands about the dog attacking someone. So then I made sure that the dog was fully insured. In case someone did get bitten.

DON: Okay, then spring training begins . . . and how did this whole season go for you? Let's reflect back. Just give us your feelings now of being the wife of this man Ted Williams, who has been greatly publicized and has taken the fancy of everyone over again, not only because of his personality but because of his success. Can you reflect over the whole year, how has it been for you?

DOLORES: Heartbreaking. It's the toughest relationship going when you live with someone as famous as he is. And who is as volatile as he is. And as expressive. And can work under his pressures. Also, he's very insecure, and he wants so badly when he's doing something new to do it to the best possible. And absolutely nothing can come in his way. I mean, if I even ask a question, then it's termed an argument. And they say you hurt those you love the most, but boy, he could come home and just take everything out on me, and it was tough. And of course, I don't know baseball, and to have me even show some interest was annoying. Because, you know, you can't be bothered with a greenhorn. And this now became the most important thing in his life, and everything else was secondary. So it was tough.

DON: So did you get over a particular hump, a place where you felt everything started to smooth out a little bit? Any part of the season? The latter part of the season? Any part of it?

DOLORES: Oh . . . did I get over a hump? I think in the beginning I was kept out of everything and I was not knowing why. I was told I couldn't come. I couldn't go to the training. I couldn't be there at practice. I couldn't go to the games. I wasn't allowed to go on the trips, and I had all these imaginations: Why? Why didn't he want me? What's happened? Where have I failed? This was what was bothering me, bugging me, and of course with all this tension coming home I began, "Oh, dear, all these other women." . . . the female plague. Pure jealousy. And of course they were mobbing him. And of course Ted is charming . . . I mean, he could charm the leaves off a tree . . . and this was eating at me. And then, of course, his hostility that he's capable of . . . you know, when you're not married to someone, you don't know how unpleasant it is to be married sometimes. I always had the most wonderful relationships . . . until you get married. Then, all of a sudden, the romance went out the window. No longer, it seems like I'm not an equal anymore. . . .

DON: Don't you hear that often?

DOLORES: Yes, I think so. But I never listened before. I always thought these other wives, they just were failures and it wouldn't have mattered . . . it's just that old, I don't know what you think, until it happens to you and then you realize there's something to the story. But it was tough, and it was getting to me . . . I was getting upset, losing weight, I just had to finally make up my mind that it wasn't going to bother me . . . and Ted did take me on one trip, which helped a lot. Because I saw more of what was going on. And just the idea of knowing . . . it was not knowing what was going on, not knowing what happens at the games, and I just had never been to a baseball game before. I had never seen a baseball player. Ted Williams was, I mean, I met him on the airplane, he was an ex-ballplayer. He wasn't playing ball. I just didn't know what this was and all this staring, all this mob excitement, and all these big shots talking and the way they handle people, and I wasn't aware at all of all the things that had to take place behind the scenes. The problems. The money contracts. The . . . I don't know, even the personnel problems. That was it. It was very tough. No one in my family or . . . I had no friends who could help me out with the problem. It seemed like there were lots of problems because Ted can be a Dr. Jekyll and a Mr. Hyde, and everything he says is a half-truth and a half-lie. He means what he says at the time he says it, but then five minutes later he doesn't mean it anymore. And knowing this pressure was on him, this part of him was coming out which I wasn't as aware of before, and I was just . . . I was just going up and down the flagpole. It was awful.

DON: All right. How do you feel now that the season is over?

DOLORES: Mixed . . . mixed. I'm glad it's over because it's ended and you know it can't unravel. If it kept on going, maybe we'd slip back farther and farther. It's a great place where we ended. Ted's happy. The team's happy. And everyone can be proud. It's like it was worthwhile, all the struggle, and I'm glad it did come to an end. On the other hand, it's sort of sad because it's final. It did end. I guess it's like life itself. It is sad when it does end, but I am glad it did end. And they'll all get together and start again. New hopes.

DON: First of all, I want to tell you, you're not in a boat by yourself. You're really not in a boat by yourself. I know many so-called big-time coaches and managers, both on the college and professional level, where the pressure really is there and I mean big-time. And I would say at least 95 percent of the wives express themselves similarly as you do . . . that same feeling. Same words, Dr. Jekyll and Mr. Hyde . . . uh, this business of perfectionism, being left out of it, not knowing why they can't say this and can't do that . . .

DOLORES: You know what it's really like? It's almost like when you go back to your early schooldays. When the boys didn't like the girls. I don't want to be bothered with "a dumb girl" or "a sissy girl," "she's only a girl." All of a sudden, you feel like you're a dirty slop rag and you're picked on, and "Get out, don't give me any arguments, and don't try to get in the act, Christ, I don't think it's any place for you and John-Henry," and it's this sort of talking down to you all of a sudden. It's like, I suppose, any professional person. If they're on the stage, they bring the work home with them. They're acting that part. I suppose with baseball it's another world, another cut, a cross-section of people, and I suppose to be a successful manager you have to talk boy-talk or somehow men must talk tough to men because women are never allowed in there and it's where all the sort of unheard-of things happen. And I don't even know what the locker-room talk is unless it's what Ted comes home with, and that's what I find is pretty rough, and not so much the words but the inflections and the intonation. That's what hurts. But it's a matter of, I guess, just my understanding and going with it. Not letting it bother me. Because it takes more out of me than it does from someone who's dishing it out. That's pointless.

DON: All right. Are you . . . I guess you're looking forward to this break. What are you going to do? Are you two going to go off somewhere? Do you have any plans?

DOLORES: You know what Ted's up to. He's going to Africa.

DON: What about you, though?

DOLORES: No, I can't go. No place for a girl! No place for a girl! He has to go first for himself and find out how it's all arranged, and then when he knows his way around, he says, "Then I'll take you. I'll be your guide." See how charming he can be? He'll be my personal guide. He said, "Sweetie, it won't matter. We'll go there a couple weeks, and you'll have your belly full of it, and we'll go around and, Christ, it'll be a wonderful time. I'll take you! I promise. I'll take you." But I'm beginning to think he never will.

DON: But what happens to you now? Do you go back up to Vermont or New York?

DOLORES: No, I go to Vermont. Take the baby home to the farm. Well, first we go to New York. Ted and I are going to spend a couple days in New York getting ready for the safari. Then go to the farm.

DON: All right. Okay. I'm really happy I've had a chance to talk with you. You know I've wanted to talk with you for a long, long time.

DOLORES: I don't know if I'll be happy I talked to you.

DON: Well, I'm sure you will. You came across just the way I thought you would. There . . . as I said before, there's a truthfulness to you. You react to people. I mean, you react! And when anybody reacts, they're not holding back, and you know then that there isn't a phony among your midst and that's you. You're a true human being, and I think everybody who comes in contact with you appreciates that and loves you for it. I think that's what makes one person fall in love with another. When they're talking with someone or meet someone and they get a true reaction from them when you're talking with them . . .

DOLORES: Honesty is awfully important. I love that most of all. Honesty and freedom. It really is. It goes way back again to when I talked to you about the beauty contest and how disappointed I was with the dishonesty and lies. That's not nice. Like I say, hug the trees when things get tough. . . . I worry because sometimes, you see, I think that I'm not born at the right time. Or I worry that I'm the wrong kind of person. Sometimes I think I don't fit here. Because I *do* worry about what I say. Then sometimes I think maybe I too am a Jekyll and a Mr. Hyde. Sometimes I get stronger and I say, "The heck with him. Why do I care? Why should I live my life to please those people? When I'm dead they won't care. When I'm dead they won't care at all. So what a foolish mistake it would be if I try to act and say what I think would make other people happy when I can't be myself. There, I've lost my freedom, again." . . . And it's terrible if you feel that somebody won't like what you're doing and they're going to be embarrassed, and it's just marvelous if you happen to be with someone who, even if you do wrong, they love you for it. That's what I hope for. Because I'd love to be able to make mistakes. Or do something wrong. Or say something wrong. And have Ted say, "I love you anyway. Even for all your faults."

DON: All right, well, I want to thank you, Mrs. Ted Williams, for giving me the time. Really. It's really been my pleasure. I'm glad you gave me the opportunity because, as I said before, I'm sure all my listeners are very glad to hear from you because anything you do or say comes from in your heart and . . .

DOLORES: But it may not be put together right . . .

DON: Well, it'll be put together right . . . I don't think there's any question about that. I want to thank you again.

DOLORES: You're welcome. Thank you too very much for helping me so much. And for making it come out so well.

DON: Thank you.

Don Newbery played the interview for his wife that night.

"You can't put that on the air," she immediately said.

"You're right," he agreed.

"I had two major reasons for holding the tape back," Newbery says.

"Number one, Ted would be embarrassed. Number two, Ted would be angry. I also had promised Dolores I would hold the tape until I thought it was appropriate."

He put the cassette tape in a box in his Montgomery County basement, and there it sat for more than 30 years.

The glow of managing began to disappear in the second year. The Senators reverted to their old selves. Williams had less and less interest in the busywork of managing. The job. He still was interested in hitting. He would talk hitting forever. He would talk photography, grilling the photographers who came around the team so much they stayed away from him. He would talk fishing.

Baseball? The game? He'd sometimes rather talk about something else.

"We're playing an exhibition in West Palm Beach," Tom Grieve says. "The game is going on. Ted spots a big spider on the floor of the dugout. He starts screaming about the spider. . . ."

"Holy shit," Williams screams. "Look at the size of that fucken spider."

Some of the players look.

"Look at it! That's the biggest fucken spider I've ever seen."

The rest of the players look. It *is* a big spider. Just then a lizard, smaller than the spider, appears. The lizard sticks out his tongue, grabs the spider, and starts to have lunch.

"Holy shit!" Williams shouts. "The fucken lizard is eating the fucken spider!

"Holy shit!

"Look at this!"

The entire team is watching. In the game, Mike Epstein has just struck out. He comes back to the dugout, mad, throws his bat. The lizard gets scared, runs through a crack in the floorboards. The spider, saved, runs through another crack. Williams is incensed.

"Jesus Christ," he shouts at Epstein. "Can't you see what we're fucken doing?"

Epstein has no idea.

The enthusiasm simply was gone. For Williams. For the players. His honeymoon as an idol, an icon, a dispenser of great truths from a diamond-shaped pedestal, was well finished. He was another boss now, remote and hard to figure. His stories all had been told. Told again—and again—they sounded flat. The days when the job seemed to be a challenge, a crusade, came less and less often.

"One thing that would still get Ted's attention was superstars," Grieve says. "Whenever we were playing a superstar, Ted always got excited. It was like a personal thing. Spring training, we're playing the Braves. Joe Coleman is pitching. Ted tells him he doesn't want him to throw any fastballs to Hank Aaron. No fastballs, Coleman gets Aaron out the first time. Second time, no fastballs, he gets him out again. Third time, Coleman, who has a good fastball, figures he has to at least show it once, just to let Aaron know he has it. He doesn't even try to throw it for a strike, throws it way outside . . . Aaron still hits it out of the ballpark. Ted just goes berserk. Absolutely berserk. It was spring training, but it was like we just lost the World Series."

The players, one by one, seemed to realize they were not going to be the next Ted Williams. No matter how much he talked, they never were going to have his talent. The bar was too high. They never could get there. The ball-strike count would reach the proper numbers, 2-0, 3-1, and they would look toward the dugout and see Williams gesture and hear him say, "Fastball, right down the middle." The pitch would come—indeed, a fastball right down the middle—and they would swing and foul it back. They would look in the dugout. Williams would be pounding the wall, muttering the bad words.

His patience was gone. There was a subtle turn in his comments, the positives soured to negatives.

"What do you do in the off-season?" he asked one day as Tim Cullen settled into the batting cage.

"I'm in investments," Cullen said. "Stocks and bonds."

"I hope you're good at it. Because you're not good at this."

The youngest players were frustrated most. They were from a generation that wanted answers, explanations. Why? Williams was from a generation that didn't explain. If you were sat down, you were sat down. No one told you why.

"I'm in the lineup, batting fifth," lefthanded hitter Bernie Allen says. "The first four guys get hits. The other team makes a pitching change to a lefthander. Ted pinch-hits for me. Am I upset? I tried to go after him, but Nellie Fox held me back. That happened four or five times. I tried to go after him."

The crowds became smaller and smaller at RFK. Short, it turned out, had bought the team with short money. Financial problems had returned. Worry about the future of baseball in Washington had returned. Williams's voice would rattle around the empty seats when he yelled at the opposing starter.

"That's right," he would yell. "There's nothing dumber than a fucken pitcher."

Remembering his own pitchers, he would turn to them on the bench and add, in a lower voice, "but I don't mean you guys."

His first instincts had been right. Managing stunk. He would walk all the time on the road, carving up the long wait for night games with explorations in search of a shrimp boat. Caught by the image of writer Zane Grey, maybe the first celebrity fisherman on the Florida Keys, Williams had a grand dream. Like Grey, he would own a shrimper and pilot it around, port to port, in search of all the great fish possible to catch. In each town the Senators visited Williams would find marinas, boatyards, maritime experts. He would bring Joe Camacho with him. They would walk everywhere. In Anaheim they were walking on the freeway. A highway patrolman stopped and asked what they were doing. Looking for a shrimp boat?

The close games all seemed to go in the other direction now. The .500 mark of respectability slipped and slipped away. The big close of 1969 was replaced by a big flop at the end of 1970.

On the final day of the season, Cullen and reserve first baseman Dick Nen were in a cab to Memorial Stadium in Baltimore to play the Orioles. The Senators were in a 13-game losing streak. The Orioles were on their way to the World Series. This was the flat, downbeat end to the year.

Cullen spotted Williams walking toward the park. He had the cab driver pull over and asked if Williams wanted a ride. Williams grunted and, okay, got in the cab.

"You know, Dick, you're a smart hitter," Williams said to Nen during the ride. "You've got a good swing. If you keep applying yourself, you can do damn well in this league."

Silence.

More silence.

"What about me?" Cullen, hitting .211 with one home run, asked. "What kind of a hitter am I?"

"Timmy, you're one of the dumbest fucken hitters I've ever seen in my life," Williams answered.

"Yeah," Cullen agreed. "But at least I know what my problem is. My bat's too short."

"Your bat's too short! That's a new one!"

"Well, it is."

"How do you know?"

"My bat's too short," Cullen said, "because I can't reach that slider on the outside of the plate from the bench."

Silence.

Williams started to laugh. The players laughed. The cab reached the ballpark. The Senators were bounced, 3–2, to finish with a 14-game losing streak. They had the lowest team batting average in the major leagues.

Managing stunk. The glow officially had faded, and eight days later it officially was gone. Bob Short traded the left side of the infield—Eddie Brinkman and Aurelio Rodriguez—along with pitcher Joe Coleman to the Detroit Tigers for troubled, sore-armed Denny McLain. General manager Joe Burke hated the trade. Williams hated the trade. Short loved the trade. It was one of the worst trades in baseball history.

McLain was the kid everyone's mother had said to stay away from at school. Too old for his years. That was Denny McLain. Too fast. Too shifty. He was only 27, but his odometer read much higher. He had made baseball history as a 24-year-old, winning 31 games in 1968—a feat on a par with Williams's .406 season, done only once now in 69 years. He had won the MVP and the Cy Young Award, and the Tigers had won their first World Series championship in 23 years. He had followed that by setting out on a course of self-destruction.

After a 24-9 finish in 1969 to win a second straight Cy Young Award, he had been suspended for the start of the '70 season by Commissioner Bowie Kuhn for investing in a bookmaking operation. Back on the team, he was suspended by the Tigers for dousing a couple of sportswriters with a bucket of water. Back on the team again, he was suspended for the end of the season by Kuhn for carrying a revolver on a team flight.

Now he belonged to Ted. He was charismatic, goofy, and sly. He flew airplanes. He played the organ and sang in Vegas lounges. He was married to Lou Boudreau's daughter. He hated Ted from the beginning. Ted hated back.

"Denny McLain was a conniver," Joe Camacho says. "He always was subterfuging everything we'd try to do."

"I don't think there was any one thing that happened," Rich Billings, who was McLain's roommate, says. "I know he didn't like the way Ted talked about pitchers. His ego was as big as Ted's. It was like, 'I'm still Denny McLain. And I'm going to do it my way.' "

He showed up at camp with his own airplane and invited players to go to the Bahamas for lunch. He wasn't a drinker or a smoker, but he had a constant can of Coca-Cola with him, and his body had started to fall apart, and his arm was definitely shot. He would slide away for secret cortisone injections simply to keep pitching. His arm already had started to calcify from all the injections.

He said he wanted to pitch every fourth day because that was how he won 31 games. Williams said he would pitch every fifth day, same as everyone else. Back and forth. He wanted to play golf all the time, another sport he could play quite well. He seemed to know half the golf pros in America. Williams put in a $1,000 fine for anyone caught playing golf during the season.

"I was the player rep," Bernie Allen says. "I had to go in to try to get Ted to take back the ban on golf. I also played golf all the time."

"You play golf, it throws your baseball swing out of whack," Williams said.

"No, it doesn't," Allen replied. "Not me."

"How can you say that?"

"Because I bat lefthanded, but I play golf righthanded."

"Really. Why do you do that?"

"Because I don't want to ruin my golf swing."

"No golf."

The roles were established. Williams became the crotchety old teacher. McLain became the leader of the unruly classroom making fun of him. It was all sophomoric stuff. Kid stuff. McLain called the players opposed to Williams "the Underminers." He had nicknames for everyone. He was the leader in all impromptu bitch sessions. The subject always was Williams and his coaches.

A lack of talent was not the only reason to wind up with the worst team in baseball. The roster was filled with malcontents, squeaky wheels that had been abandoned elsewhere. The audience was willing to listen. McLain was more than willing to talk. He seemed to stay up at night figuring out ways to drive Williams crazy.

Cab story number 1: McLain and Allen went out to play golf in Kansas City, the threat of the $1,000 fine in the background. They left the hotel at 8:00 A.M., a suspicious time for any major league ballplayer even to be awake. They jumped into a cab. Turning around, they saw two of Williams's coaches jumping into another cab.

"Denny says to the cab driver, 'Take us to a place that has exits on two different streets, then come around and pick us up at the other exit,'" Allen says. "The guy stops, we get out. We can see the coaches pull up behind us. We go through the building, out the other door, the guy picks us up, and we play golf. It was like spy stuff. Stupid."

Cab story number 2: "We get into Milwaukee late one night because we'd played an extra-inning game in Chicago," Rich Billings says. "Denny and I hurry out to get something to eat because there's a 12 o'clock curfew. We have a day game the next day. We go to this bar where all the players go, and most of the team is there. We eat and leave with maybe a half-hour until curfew.

"On the way back in the cab, we spot Ted and George Susce walking down the street. I duck down, natural instinct. Not Denny. He's rolling down the window, shouting, making sure they see us. Then he tells the cab driver to turn around and go back to the bar.

"He walks in—most of the team still was there—and says he just saw Ted, and Ted said that curfew had been pushed back an hour because of the extra-inning game. Hallelujah. He says the next round is on him. Then we leave.

"Sure enough, maybe 20 minutes after 12, Joe Camacho comes around, checking for curfew. I open the door and Denny's in the bed, pretending to sleep, making these big snoring sounds. You could see that Camacho didn't know what to think. Twenty-one players out of a 25-man roster missed curfew. Williams knew it was Denny who had set it up. He never fined anyone."

There was at least one good confrontation, McLain and Williams f-bombing each other to death behind the closed door in the manager's office, but never any resolution. The team was awful. The situation was awful. The players, as much as they were entranced by McLain, knew that the trade had killed whatever chances they had to win. Brinkman and Rodriguez might have been the two most valuable players on the field.

In the middle of May, Short unloaded the home run–hitting Epstein and solid pitcher Darold Knowles to the Oakland A's for two unknowns and enough cash to make his payroll. He was tapped out, done. The team was up for sale and almost definitely was going to move.

Even the legendary McGraw couldn't have done anything with this mess. The one hope of every Washington Senator was to no longer be a Washington Senator.

"I was traded at the end of the season to the Yankees," Bernie Allen says. "Ralph Houk, the manager, said they had been trying to get me for eight years, but the Twins and then the Senators would never let me go. He said, 'You must have really done something to piss off Williams.' I said, 'I tried the best I could.' "

In the middle of September, Short announced that the team was moving to Arlington, Texas. Who cared about anything now? The final game of the season—the final game forever in Washington—was played on September 30 at RFK. A paid crowd of 14,000, plus an estimated 4,000 people who had snuck in for the moment, watched the Senators take a 7–5 lead into the ninth against the Yankees. One out. Two outs. With the home team one out away from the win, the fans rushed the field in bizarre celebration. The umpires awarded the game to the Yankees, 9–0, a forfeit, when it became obvious that clearing the field was not possible.

The final edition of the Senators finished with a 63-96 record, 37½ games out of first place. McLain finished with a 10-22 record, a 4.27 ERA. The entire sad lot of cares and woes was now shipped to Texas. Williams inexplicably went with it.

The marriage to Dolores was done. The two of them had fought and clawed it to death. ("She heard people saying 'fuck' around the ballpark and said it was no place to bring up children," Williams explained once to a friend. "Aw, there was no chance.") Players and people around the team had seen edges of the discord. In a California coffee shop there was an argument, Williams pushing the table one way, Dolores back, Williams back, Dolores back, Williams flipping the table and walking out. In Minneapolis there had been a memorable moment during Williams's first year on the job.

"Bob Short had a big house in Minneapolis, and he threw a party for the team and the traveling party after a game," Russ White, the sportswriter, says. "Dolores was on the trip. The game ended, and everybody got on the bus to go to Short's house. Dolores still was talking to some people outside the clubhouse. Ted is steaming. He says, real loud, 'We'll get going as soon as this Fucken Cunt gets on the bus.' Dolores heard.

Everybody heard. She got on the bus. The entire trip was done in complete silence."

White wound up playing chess with Dolores in a corner during the party. He felt compelled to say something.

"I really felt sorry for you back there," he said. "There was no need for that."

Dolores looked at White.

"He'll get his," she said in an even tone.

A daughter, Claudia, was born after the separation. Williams missed the birth. His attendance at his children's births was now a consistent 0-for-3.

He appeared in Pompano Beach, then Texas, alone and grumpy, not wanting to be where he was. McLain was gone, traded to the Oakland A's, but the problems remained. Now renamed the Rangers, the team still stunk. Managing stunk.

"Ted was just angry all the time," Rich Billings says. "He didn't want to be in Texas. He let everybody know. I honestly think he had a blood-sugar problem. He'd slam his door after games. He sometimes didn't even take a shower. Just drop his pants, put on his street clothes, and leave. He'd be gone sometimes before all the players were off the field."

"The clubhouse was in centerfield," Tom Grieve says. "So you had to walk all the way out there. It became a game, going through the door. You'd see maybe his jacket on the floor, then his uniform shirt, then his T-shirt, then his pants, then his spikes, all leading toward his office. And he'd be gone."

Why had he come back in the first place? Some of the players suggested loyalty to Bob Short was the reason, making the franchise look more appealing to a potential buyer. Some suggested loyalty to his coaches—especially Joe Camacho—was the reason, a chance to get another pension year for everybody. Some suggested Williams himself needed the money.

Whatever the reason, it was not a labor of love. He checked into a hotel for the season, spent a lot of time at Gaylen's bar-be-cue with its big fish tank, and sat in the middle of the bench at Arlington in his self-generated cloud of bad words. The image of the batboy, the son of Arlington mayor Tom Vandergriff, frozen at one end of the dugout, afraid to go through the barrier of Williams's language to the other end of the dugout, became fixed in players' minds.

The manager was not a happy man.

"Outside of the clubhouse, he'd be an entirely different guy," Billings says. "At the park, though, he didn't want to be there."

There was one moment in Boston when all the nonsense stopped. A divine Fenway Park interlude. A home run hitting contest between radio personalities and retired ballplayers was held before the Rangers' game with the Red Sox. An announcement in the press box had said Williams would *not* be part of it, but the fans started chanting, "We want Ted, we want Ted, we want . . ."

The Rangers players watched their manager. He was wearing the blue zipper jacket to cover his big stomach. He was muttering.

"You want me to hit, you cocksuckers?" he said. "You fucken syphilitic blank-blank-blank. You want me? I'll show these fucken . . ."

"Why don't you wave to them?" someone suggested.

"I'm gonna fucken hit," Williams said, grabbing a bat from the bat rack.

The bat didn't feel right. He grabbed another. Didn't feel right.

"Anybody here got a W-183?" he shouted.

Tom Grieve used a W-183 Louisville Slugger. He suddenly realized— why hadn't he thought of this before?—that the "W" meant Williams. He used a Ted Williams bat. He handed it to his manager.

"Yeah, this will do the job," Williams said.

He marched toward the plate with Grieve's W-183 as the crowd went wild. His players, caught in the last-place woes of their situation, never had heard this kind of ovation. They also never had seen the look on the face of their manager that he had now. What was it? Determination? That was an understatement. He ripped off the blue jacket on the way, never stopped, threw it on the ground, cursing with each step. He stood at the plate. All the old demons had returned. Same place. All over again. The Colonel could have been typing in the press box.

Red Sox coach Lee "Stinger" Stange was the pitcher. He threw a couple of lollipops toward the plate. Williams let them go past, stepped back, and made a motion to Stange that translated to "Bring it, come on, will ya?" Stange threw the next pitch with speed.

Williams sent it back at him with faster speed. A liner. Next pitch? Another liner. Next pitch? Next? Next?

"It was the most electrifying thing I've ever seen in my life," Rich Billings says. "He hit line drive after line drive. He hit them everywhere.

the paper every day. I was batting fourth in the order behind Frank Howard. It was a great start.

"I come in for batting practice one day, and Ted's talking with five or six writers. He's talking about the book. He says, real loud, pointing at me, 'Look at this big dummy. He should hit 20 homers every year. He just sits there, though, and waits for the slider.' Everybody laughed. I laughed. I thought he was making a joke."

"Did you read my book?" Williams then asked. "I'll bet you didn't even read my book."

Everybody laughed. Billings laughed.

"Just because you read a medical book, that doesn't make you a surgeon," Billings replied, joke to joke.

Everybody did not laugh. The reporters laughed, but Williams did not laugh.

"Get your ass out to the bullpen where you belong," he said. "Get!"

Billings skipped batting practice, went to the bullpen. When he returned for the start of the game, his name had been scratched from the starting lineup. He sat for the next three days.

The book was serious. All three of the books were serious.

I slamorada, after a while, began to call itself "the Sportfishing Capital of the World." Williams was the face on the Sportfishing Capital of the World. The off-season stories about him always mentioned Islamorada. There was an exotic quality to the place. Hemingway was linked forever to Key West at the end of Route 1, even though he didn't live there very long. Williams was linked to this spot in the middle of the Keys. He lived there for more than 35 years.

"People would come in and ask to sit in the same chair where Ted Williams sat," Manny Ortiz, owner of Manny and Isa's, Williams's favorite restaurant, says. "They'd ask what Ted Williams ate and then they'd order it.

"Ted Williams saved my business. No one was coming here. Then he started coming three or four times a week. And the people followed."

People had come looking for Williams from the moment he arrived on Islamorada. When he was drafted back into the Marines for Korea in 1952, reporters had tracked him down to Jimmie Albright's house. Williams hid in the closet, suffering from the heat, while Albright smiled and brought the reporters into the living room and kept the conversation

He hit them off the wall. He hit a home run that was just foul. Everything was a shot. Guys in the dugout were just looking at each other. Staring. How old was he?"

The date was August 25, 1972. He was five days short of his 54th birthday.

"The players were just stunned," Grieve says. "Most of them, in their hearts, were hoping that he'd look foolish, maybe whiff on a bunch of balls. The old thing . . . yeah, well maybe it isn't as easy to do it as you say it is. Too see him do *that*."

"You would have thought he was 22," Billings says. "I never have seen a batting practice exhibition like that from anyone of any age. Had he been taking batting practice in secret getting ready for this? Or did he just step up there and do it? No one knew."

Ten swings, maybe 15, and Williams was done. He came back through the cheers, threw the W-183 bat down, and stormed back into the runway toward the clubhouse and his office. He never said anything to his players about the moment, and they never said anything to him.

You want me to hit? Okay, I'll hit.

The forced march ended in Kansas City on October 4, 1972. The Rangers lost to the Royals, 4–0, on the final day of the season, their 100th loss. The managing career of Ted Williams was done. He was back to what he loved to do. He was a fisherman again. He never would manage another major league game.

13 Fishing at Islamorada (The Saltwater Life)

People who know me are aware that I have a dream of one day owning a seaworthy vessel big enough to carry a couple of skiffs on deck. The plan is to live on the big boat and fish out of the small ones as I cruise from port to port. I've been looking for the perfect boat for about 40 years now, and perhaps it's just a dream that will remain forever out of reach.

But it really doesn't matter because I've done as much fishing as I could do in this great country of ours and I've enjoyed every minute of it. Fishing has given me a lot in life and the reason I've made such strong statements regarding the future is that I'd like to give something back. We've got the best country in the world for fishing right here in America. Let's do everything we can to keep it that way.

TED WILLIAMS, *POPULAR MECHANICS*, MAY 1989

The voices carried across the water on any given morning for over 40 Florida winters. The heat and the humidity would keep everything down; the waves, the air, the day itself. The eye would have to search across the flats, along the horizon, maybe find the shapes. A boat? Two men? Fishing? The silhouette would be as much as five, maybe six miles in the distance. The voices would carry, seemingly from nowhere. The words would not be confused with any spiritual messages.

"You dumb cocksucker. You don't know what the fuck you're doing. . . ."

"I don't know what the fuck I'm doing? You sad son of a bitch. . . ."

The first foul voice, of course, belonged to the famous baseball player. The second, of course, belonged to the famous fishing guide. There were two of those famous fishing guides in Islamorada, Florida, Jimmie Albright and Jack Brothers, equally conversant in the language of expletives, and it was pretty certain that either one of them would be out on the water on any given day with Ted Williams.

They owned the water. Jimmie, Jack, and Ted.

"They were the three big figures in Islamorada fishing," Rick Ruoff, guide and writer and broadcaster, says. "For a long time, they just scared the crap out of me. Jimmie would be out there fishing with no shirt on, barefoot, a pair of khakis rolled up. Caustic. Tough. Jack was like a longshoreman. A good guy, just a tough case. Jack drank a lot, which Jimmie didn't, but they'd both rib you, ride you. Ted . . . Ted was Ted Williams."

The famous man lived his life in compartments. Most people do this to varying degrees, lines drawn between work and home and, perhaps, other ventures—different environments, different friends. Williams built fences between his compartments. Very few friends or associates were allowed to move from one environment to another. The baseball people were the baseball people. The Boston friends were the Boston friends. The California family was in California. The camp people, the Sears people . . . Williams split up his calendar year into neatly defined segments. Like a child at the dinner table, he did not like the different servings on the plate to touch each other. Each was a separate pleasure.

Fishing was his dessert, his favorite compartment of all. He had a separate life in Islamorada. He was with Jimmie and Jack on the water, away from all of the stuff. The tarpon and the bonefish never asked for an autograph or wrote a bad word. This was his fun.

The term the guides used to describe taking a client onto the water was "to fish" the person. Jimmie fished Williams for tarpon for over four decades. Jack fished him for bonefish for more than three. There were variations to the routine—Jimmie certainly fished Williams more than anyone, all kinds of fish, plus sometimes Williams used other guides—but that was a general rule. The two guides fished him for almost four decades.

"Jimmie and Jack were very much the same," John Sutter, another Islamorada guide, says. "This is a very competitive business, kind of a testosterone contest. There were a lot of strong personalities trying to establish who was top dog when I got here. Jimmie and Jack were the top dogs."

The two guides had the same type of reputation Williams had on the baseball field. They seemingly had been in the business forever. They definitely knew everything there was to know. They were the old pros, grand masters in their art.

Sutter, who is six-foot-nine, became a guide in 1978. He came into the business from the National Basketball Association. A former all-American at Tulane, he had played for the Indiana Pacers and the Portland Trailblazers. He could recognize written and unwritten testosterone rules that already had been well established.

"I told myself right away that I had to defer to these guys," Sutter said. "It was obvious. I'd been around basketball all my life, and believe me, Jimmie and Jack got as much deference as anyone I'd ever seen in basketball. More."

When Williams was still playing with the Red Sox, he would block out his dates for the winter before he ever left for spring training. He would follow the schedule, same as baseball, except in this sport he had to pay to play instead of being paid for it. The price for a guide for a day was $40 a day, beginning its climb to the present $400 a day. Williams would be there for most of the climb, paying his money, fishing.

"Ted liked to go early," Cecil Keith, another guide who fished Williams, says. "He'd go as early as 6:30 in the morning if you were fishing for tarpon. Bonefish, you'd have to go a little later because you couldn't see 'em. You could see the tarpon because they're so much bigger."

Sight fishing was the game. See the fish. Go after them. The bonefish—the biggest one Williams ever caught was 12¼ pounds—would give themselves away when they fed. Their silver-green tails would stick out of the water. There! The trick was to be able to cast into the middle of them, drop a fly close enough for them to turn in their feeding and take a bite, soft enough not to startle them. The task required precision, touch, definite technique. Skill.

The tarpon, some weighing 100 pounds or more, were easier to spot, dark shapes in the shallow water. Everything took place in shallow water. The intrigue was important, hide and seek. There were other ways to fish both bonefish and tarpon, easier ways, trolling with live bait or waiting at a bridge for the fish to come past, but this was the sportsman's way. Fly fishing. Light tackle. The lighter the better. This was the challenge. See the fish. Make him bite. Let the fight begin.

"I went fishing with Ted once in Islamorada," Billy Reedy, a friend, says. "I caught a fish. I was proud. I caught a fish with Ted Williams! He still hadn't caught one. He said, 'But did you see the fish? Did you see him?' I had no idea what he meant. I thought I'd done a good thing, catching a fish."

"But did you see him?" Williams asked again.

"No," Reedy finally admitted.

"Jee-sus."

The jump was the amazing moment in catching a tarpon. The big fish would realize his predicament, jump out of the water to try to free himself—there! the picture!—and the fight would begin. With the bonefish, the first run would be the moment, line flying out of the reel, a rocket suddenly attached to the end. No fish would fight harder to get away. None. Jack Brothers said he had seen two bonefish in his life die of heart attacks because they were trying so hard to escape, fighting until their own death.

Williams would spend an adult lifetime looking for these moments. Plotting, planning, spending big cash. These weren't commercial fish, good eating on the family table. They were sport fish, alive only for the fight. Williams would come to that fight with all the care and ritual of Manolete meeting the bull on the sand at the Plaza de Toros in Madrid, sunscreen on his face, options in his tackle box, passion in his heart. When he was younger, he would stand on the dock at the end, the victor, posed for a picture next to his vanquished foe. When he was older, smarter, he would release the fish, send it back into the arena, a competitor for another fight on another hot day.

The Keys still had the feel of tropical wilderness when Williams first arrived during World War II. This was virgin fishing territory, opened up by technology. The outboard motor was an invention that came out of the war. New places along the coastline could be explored. A guide could anchor a big boat offshore and take his clients out in little skiffs that could be maneuvered around the flats with the new 7½ horsepower motors.

The fish were everywhere, pretty much undisturbed forever. The water was clear, like looking through a plate-glass window on a still day, sediments undisturbed, pollutants from back in Homestead and Miami still not seen.

"We'd order four motors at a time," Cecil Keith, a guide at the beginning, says. "There weren't any mechanics around back then, anyone to fix 'em. We'd put two motors on the boats, then use the other two for parts to fix the first two."

The only place for a tourist to stay on Islamorada was Beard's Cabins. Three cabins, take your pick. The only tourists mostly were fishermen. The place was being invented. The sport was being invented. It was a brand-new time.

"The hurricane of 1935 had cleared everything out," Keith says. "Everything had to be rebuilt."

The Hurricane of 1935 was one of the most devastating storms in U.S. history. It struck directly at Matecumbe Key, the center of a string of islands that make up the town of Islamorada. An 18-foot tidal surge and winds as high as 200 miles per hour hit the island. Sixty of the sixty-one existing structures in Islamorada were destroyed. The official death toll from the storm was 463, but the true figure probably was much higher. People were swept out to sea, never seen again.

Many of the victims were disgruntled World War I veterans, "Bonus Marchers" sent to the Keys to work on the construction of a highway proposed from Miami to Key West. Many others were local residents, herded onto a rescue train, people who had just boarded at Islamorada when the storm struck. A series of mistakes brought the Flagler Railroad cars up from Miami into town too late. With no highways between the islands, with boat travel impossible, the one-track Flagler train, the lifeblood of the Keys since 1912, was the only possible means of escape. And it didn't work.

"I was four years old," Cecil Keith says. "Our family got on the train, and we hadn't traveled much when it got knocked over. Our car landed on its side and on top of a pile of lumber in a lumberyard. That's what saved us. All the men stood on the bars, the poles, in the car and held all the children over their heads to keep us from drowning. We made it. The other cars . . . a lot did not."

A first highway across the Keys was built on the remains of the railway trestles, tiny two-lane bridges, and opened in 1938, but the advent of World War II slowed most development. The area still was being put back together when Ted Williams first appeared in 1943. Jimmie Albright was one of the people arranging the pieces.

"Ted had fallen in love with fishing in the Everglades during the war," Rick Ruoff says. "He bought a house in Miami. He'd go out along the Tamiami Trail, fishing for snook. One of the guides, Red Greb, told him,

'Hey, if you like this so much, you should go out on the Keys for bone-fish.' That's how he went out to Islamorada and met Jimmie."

Jimmie, one rival guide said, was "the Meriwether Lewis" of the Keys. He charted out the entire area. He made the wilderness—the fishing wilderness—manageable. He came down to Florida from Detroit in 1942 to go fishing. He basically never left. He always said that he showed up for the first time in Islamorada on a hot afternoon and stopped in a little store to buy a five-cent Coke. The proprietor thanked him for being the first and only customer of the day. There was no water, no electricity, and there were no fishing guides on the island. Albright remedied the last of these problems.

He married a blond girl from Alabama named Frankee—one of three sisters who all married fishing guides—bought a big 37-foot boat that he named *Rebel*, and went into business. There was a slight stall when he was commissioned into the Coast Guard for the war, but he came back and went to work. Using the new outboards, he began exploring the local waters on both the ocean and gulf sides. He took note of where the fish could be found. The fish were everywhere perhaps, but some spots were better than others. Jimmie discovered one small stretch of water off Buchanan Bank that was positively magical.

"The tarpon start migrating in the spring, around March," guide Buddy Grace says. "That's when they start to appear around here. They keep moving through until the end of July, middle of August. The theory is that they're going out to spawn. The University of Miami says they spawn 80 miles out in the Sargasso Sea grass. We just know they come through here.

"When they get near Buchanan Bank, they head into this little indentation. Then they have to turn around. Nobody knows why. They all do it."

"It's an area no more than 30 feet long and 30 feet wide," former guide Hank Brown says. "That's what Jimmie found. Tarpon probably had been turning around there for thousands of years, but nobody ever had noticed."

The area became known as "the Pocket." Want to catch a tarpon? Go to the Pocket. Florida Bay covered maybe 500 square miles, and this little 30-foot by 30-foot cul-de-sac was the best spot of all. This was where the tarpon were.

"The first one out to the Pocket in the morning put his stake down and had control," Joe Johansen, a guide, says. "That became the rule. Jimmie and Jack would each try to be the first out there. They had a rivalry at the Pocket."

Jack Brothers appeared in Islamorada in 1953. He came down from Brooklyn with a buddy and decided to stay. An employment agency sent him to the Theater of the Sea, a small-time operation on the island, one of the first marine parks in the country. The job was to be a tour guide in the theater, talking about the attractions, answering questions.

"The place had two guides," Brothers's son, Frankie, says. "My dad took the tour with one of them to see what you had to do. The guide was a woman. She reached down into the tank to pick up a nurse shark and picked up a sand shark by mistake. The sand shark took all the skin off her arm."

After the woman was sent off to the hospital and normalcy returned, Brothers took the next tour of the day with a male guide. This guide reached into the tank and was stung by a moray eel. He also went to the hospital. What kind of place was this? Two tours. Two people in the hospital.

"My dad took the job," Frankie Brothers says. "He stayed there for two years."

Brothers married a local girl, a conch, and set up shop. Around this time, fly fishing in saltwater started to become popular. The sport had been all spinning rods and reels until then, but developments in equipment and a change in perception brought fly fishing on to the scene in the fifties. Jack and Jimmie and Ted were in the middle of it.

Again, everything was new. What kind of flies worked? What kind of hooks? What kind of line? This was a puzzle that had to be figured out, a sport that had to be constructed by trial and error. Jimmie figured out a knot—the Albright Special—to tie two different diameter pieces of line together. The knot is still used today by every guide on the dock. The Albright Special.

"Jimmie was one of those frontier guys," Hank Brown says. "Not only in the techniques of fly fishing but in the location of the fish. Everything. Jack was right behind him."

Jimmie story: John Sutter worked on the same dock as Albright. For two years after Sutter arrived, Albright never said a word to him, acted as if a six-foot-nine former NBA basketball player did not exist. Finally, he spoke.

"Are you from Marion, Indiana?" he asked.

"Yes, I am," Sutter replied, startled.

"I used to live in Marion. On Boot Street."

"I used to walk down Boot Street every day to school," Sutter said. "It was five minutes from my house."

Jimmie walked away. Sutter was dumbfounded. Welcome to Islamorada.

Jack story: He had taken a client into the flats, and they had found some tarpon. The client was not getting any bites.

"Change the fly, Jack," the client said. "Something else would work better."

"I really don't think it's the fly," Brothers said. "I think it's the presentation. Try it again."

No luck.

"Change the fly, Jack."

"I really don't think. . . ."

The dialogue was repeated a number of times. The client started to become hot. Brothers became hotter. He finally took the client's rod, reeled in the line, bent over, and bit the feathers off the fly. A smoking man, he snubbed out his cigarette, then peeled the paper off the filter. He put the filter on the hook, cast once, and almost immediately pulled in a tarpon.

"It wasn't the fly," he told the client as he brought the fish into the boat. "It was the presentation."

"Jack's in a tackle store one day, just to shoot the breeze," Hank Brown says. "Two very heavy guys from Texas are in there, talking with the owner about going fishing. The owner asks Jack if he wants to take the guys out. Jack looks at them and says, 'If you think I'm going to drag your two fat asses around in a boat all day, you've got another think coming.' That was Jack. Public relations didn't exactly matter. Jimmie was just like him."

Jimmie and Jack. And Ted. He fit in with these two characters as if he were their brother. They all had the same hard edge, same hard language, same curiosity, same idea of fun. They all had the same short fuse.

"I'd fish Ted on Saturday mornings for my father in the seventies," Frankie Brothers says. "I was just a kid, 13 years old. He called me 'Porky.' I called him 'Mr. Ted.' He'd give me five bucks for the morning. Sometimes I'd fish too. (Something the real guides never would do.) One morning we were out and I was fishing for snook and he was fishing for redfish. I caught a snook, a big one, maybe 18 to 20 pounds. Mr. Ted got all upset. I'd caught a fish and he hadn't. He said, 'Take me in.'

"For six months after that, he never used me. I was a kid. I caught a fish. He never said anything and I never said anything, and then, six months later, it was suddenly, 'Hey, Porky, Saturday morning?' And it was like nothing ever had happened."

The Islamorada that Williams discovered in 1943 on that early tip from Red Greb gave him all the things he wanted. Friends. Fishing. Privacy. He could have lived anywhere in the off-season—Minnesota, California; indeed, he often had talked about buying a place on Cape Cod—but he chose here.

The house he bought in 1953 after his first divorce was a small, spartan bunker on the ocean side of the island next to the grounds of the Villager, the first motel-resort complex. This was definitely a bachelor's quarters. A military bachelor's quarters. Curt Gowdy and his wife visited once and both were struck by the cleanliness and order of the house. Everything had a proper place. Everything was in that proper place.

"My wife, I remember, wanted to do something for Ted in appreciation of his hospitality," Gowdy says. "There was nothing really to buy, because he had everything, and he had taken care of all the meals. He was a very good cook. My wife said, 'What can I do for him?' What she did, while Ted and I were out fishing, she put shelf paper on all of his kitchen shelves. Ted just thought that was the greatest thing. Every time he saw my wife, he'd thank her for the shelf paper."

Retiring from baseball in 1960, getting serious with Lee Howard, thinking about the future, Williams decided to sell the bunker at the end of the season and find something larger. He offered the house to Gowdy, who said he liked it.

The two men talked about the deal during the 1960 World Series between the Pittsburgh Pirates and the Yankees, when Williams was a "correspondent" for *Life* magazine and Gowdy a broadcaster for NBC. Williams returned to Florida from the Series first. Gowdy was scheduled to fly down a day later.

"I got to the airport, it was a night flight," Gowdy says. "I was going to buy the house. My wife didn't want me to buy it, but I was going to do it. At the airport, though, I realized I'd forgotten my wallet. I called my wife, and she was still mad and refused to bring it. I missed the last flight of the night and went back home. I still was going to buy the house.

"The next morning Ted called. He told me not to bother. He'd gotten home and the house had been wiped out. Hurricane Donna."

The storm had hit Islamorada on September 9, not as powerful as the Hurricane of 1935, but very close. The wind had gusted to as much as 150 miles per hour. The storm surge was 13 feet. Not a leaf was left on a single tree on the entire island. Homes were destroyed. Everybody ran for cover on the gulf side.

"I went to Jimmie's house," Cecil Keith says. "We had the big boat and four skiffs over there, and they rode out the storm all right. My house didn't do as well. The roof and the walls were gone. The only parts of the house that were in the same position were the sink and the toilet."

Williams found that his house, while the walls and ceiling remained, had been cleaned out. All of the mementos from his baseball years had been strewn around the island. Neighborhood kids for the next few years would make a game of going through the brush and weeds near the house, looking for trophies or cards or bats or whatever pieces of his famous baseball life they could find.

The new house, larger and nicer, was on the gulf side, a waterway in the back, big palm trees in the front. The address was 140 Madeira Road, not far from the Islamorada Yacht Basin and the Islamorada Fishing Club. Though he still traveled a lot, this was his home in retirement, his given address.

Williams could walk down every day to talk with the other fishermen, with the guides. What kind of luck did you have? Where were the fish? What were you using? He could practice casting from his backyard, aiming at a float. Without a guide many days, he could take his own boat out for a day on the water, alone or with friends. He had a spot he liked off Long Key, a spot the guides called "Ted's Spot."

"You'd see him out there all alone," Buddy Grace says. "Just fishing. Ted's Spot."

Williams's home life in the new house would go through various permutations—different wives and lovers, visiting children, and assorted resident dogs—but the constant was the fishing. Jimmie and Jack and the water. The lure of fishing, the game, was bigger than the lure of anything else. He would sacrifice anything for the fishing. He did.

"It's hard for a woman in Islamorada," Williams once told Billy Reedy. "The men go out fishing during the day, and what does the woman do? There isn't anything. If she doesn't have some job, some interest, she's going to be bored an awful lot."

For men, men of a certain outdoors disposition, the place was easy.

For women . . . it took a different kind of woman to survive in Islamorada. Especially if she was with Ted Williams.

Louise Kaufman arrived in Islamorada in 1952 with her husband, Bob, and their five kids. They bought one of the biggest houses on the Key, a three-story affair on the Gulf of Mexico.

She was the daughter of Walter Magruder, a businessman who had been involved in lumber and had owned two brick and tile plants and also had been a lobbyist in Washington. In 1942, nine years after his daughter was married, Magruder bought and reopened a metal cookware company in Carrollton, Ohio. The company made stainless steel mess trays, pots, pans, and serving utensils for the government during the Second World War. The company did very well.

Bob Kaufman, Louise's husband, joined his father-in-law in the business and became the president when Walter Magruder died in 1947. The company had switched to the peacetime economy, making stainless steel cookware, utensils, and sinks.

The Kaufmans first lived in Canton, Ohio, but as their family grew, they kept moving to larger houses. They eventually owned a 650-acre horse farm four miles outside Carrollton and lived in a ranch house designed by Louise. They were very comfortable. The Islamorada home was a vacation home. It replaced a home they had owned in Coral Gables, Florida.

"In those years, Carrollton Mfg. prospered and the Islamorada home [soon] was expanded," Louise's son, Rob, writes in background notes on his mother. "It was supported by a vacation plan for outstanding sales by the cookware direct sales people. Lou had weekly guests from the north who had sold enough to win the Florida Keys Vacation Prize. This plan paid for a full-time captain/fishing guide to maintain and operate the sportfishing yacht and the bonefishing skiffs.

"Louise was an avid fisherman and caught all of the important Keys gamefish. Both offshore and backcountry. She caught a women's world record tarpon on bait casting (#14 line) that weighed 152 pounds. This was about 30 pounds more than she weighed. She also caught bluefin tuna in Bimini as well as dozens of sailfish, white marlin and wahoo off Islamorada. Fishing was her passion for years. She belonged to the International Women's Gamefishing Association."

Louise loved the Keys. She was a gardener and planted an elaborate orchid walk to the big house. Bob had helped keep the marriage together in 1949 when he had given up golf, which he played at a scratch handicap, to spend more time with her and the kids, but now Louise had her own interest. The house in Islamorada was a new stress. She spent a lot of time in Florida. He spent a lot of time in Ohio.

The inevitable happened, a divorce in the summer of 1957. Louise's mother had died in January, and she and Bob had inherited 75 percent of the company. In the divorce, she received the house in Islamorada and gave up the house in Carrollton and her stock in the company. The kids stayed in Ohio, and Bob eventually married his secretary.

As for Louise, she had fallen in love with Ted Williams. She had fallen hard.

"All those things she gave up in the divorce," her son says. "That was the price she paid to be with Ted Williams."

Williams had been brought to her house the first time by Jimmie Albright. Williams, after his own first divorce from Doris, lived in the small bunker on the ocean side of Route 1. He didn't have a phone, didn't even have a television set. Albright brought him to Louise's big house to watch a heavyweight fight because Louise had everything. She certainly had a black-and-white television set.

Born in 1912, she was six years older than Williams, so that put her in her early forties and him in his late thirties when they met. She liked a bunch of things he liked, primarily fishing, and she could churn out a four-letter word on her own, here and there, and she had an edge to her. She would battle him a little bit. They got along fine. More than fine. They became buddies and lovers.

The buddy-lover quotient almost certainly was different for each of them—extremely different—but they worked out their own sort of relationship. Ted was Ted. Louise was there. They each found satisfaction at their own level of interest.

"The first time I saw Ted, I said, 'That's the most attractive man I've ever seen," Evalyn Sterry says. "He had the most infectious smile, just a great smile when he wanted it to be there."

Evalyn was Louise's best friend from Ohio. She had known Louise since they were 16 years old, going to tea dances. When Louise eloped with Bob Kaufman, 20 years old, Evalyn eloped with her own first husband. It was the Depression. They all went together to Wheeling, West Virginia, and were married on the same day, January 3, 1933. The friendship had continued. Evalyn lived now in Delray Beach with her third husband, Saunders Jones, close enough to Louise to visit.

"Come on," Louise said on one of those visits. "We're going over to Ted Williams's house for a drink."

This was Evalyn's first meeting with Ted. There was a second man in the house, but Evalyn was too spellbound by the baseball star to catch the other man's name. She figured he was a local fishing guide. Wasn't everyone in Islamorada a fishing guide? The evening wore on, and suddenly Ted and Louise were laughing at her.

"You don't have any idea who this is, do you?" he said.

"No," Evalyn said. "I don't."

"Evalyn, say hello to Benny Goodman."

She remembers riding in the backseat of Ted's car with the famous clarinet player. Ted was doing about 90 miles per hour on Route 1, maybe the most dangerous stretch of highway in America. Everyone except Ted was terrified. The famous clarinet player was digging his fingers into Evalyn's arm.

"Ted, this is making me really nervous," she finally said, since no one else would speak. "Could you please slow down?"

She remembers that Ted was a gentleman and slowed down. She also remembers . . . and this was odd . . . that Benny Goodman had brought down his latest recording. She wanted to hear it back at the house. Louise wanted to hear it. Benny wanted to hear it. Ted wouldn't play it. What was that? He simply refused. A macho thing? I am the lord of my house? What?

"We went out fishing the next day, the four of us," Evalyn says. "Ted kept his eye on Benny all the time, watched him cast. It was like he was judging Benny, did Benny know how to fish? We rode around, didn't get any fish, but I remember Ted judging Benny."

Louise, at any rate, had fallen hard for Ted. They had the same kind of mind. "Industrious" is the word Evalyn uses. Louise had learned how to paint and did fine impressionistic still lifes. She was a reader of nonfiction, never novels, a collector of facts. She was passionate about the subjects that interested her, studying them, mastering the talents necessary to be involved in them. She was passionate about Ted.

He would go off to Boston and play baseball and live in Room 231 and come back, and they would be together in the Keys. He would go off and come back, and they would be together. He would go off . . . and retire . . . and come back . . . and tell Louise he had something im portant to talk about. He was going to marry a woman named Lee Howard.

"Ted was really broken up about telling her," Lee says. "He said that this was the hardest thing he'd ever had to do. I know it really bothered him."

It bothered Louise even more.

"She was devastated," Evalyn Sterry says. "She wound up going to live in Paris for four or five months. She rented an apartment over there. I was really hoping she was going to meet some man and get over Ted."

This did not happen. Before she left, she appeared outside Ted's house, looking through the windows, the night he returned with Lee from their Canadian honeymoon. Lee was startled by the noises and spotted her. ("It had to be her," Lee says. "This was Islamorada. There wouldn't have been any other older women peeking around Ted's house.") Now back from Paris, also after spending some time with her sister, Alice, who was married to Grant Stockdale, the ambassador to Ireland, Louise was on the telephone to Ted.

"She'd call and tell him I was going to get pregnant and take all his money," Lee says. "That was what she always said."

When the marriage ended with Lee not pregnant and not with all Ted's money, Louise was back. She moved her clothes back into his house and was back into his life.

"She just loved him," Evalyn Sterry says.

Two years later, when Ted was married a third time, the quick wedding to Dolores Wettach, Louise was devastated again. This time she sold the three-story house on Islamorada and moved to an apartment in Delray Beach to be close to Evalyn. She eventually bought a house in Delray Beach.

This time the love of her life surely was gone. Wasn't he?

"Ted shouldn't be marrying this girl," Louise told John Underwood, a writer. "He should be marrying me."

Underwood, a senior writer at *Sports Illustrated*, had become friends with Williams. ("Williams Befriends Sportswriter!" "Man Bites Cocker Spaniel!") They had met casually at a horse show in Miami, Underwood tentative, Williams charming, asking the writer to sit in his box for an hour. They had been pushed together again in a boat by Edwin Pope, the *Miami Herald* columnist.

"I thought it would be a great thing to go fishing with Ted Williams in the Keys," Pope says. "I knew him a little bit, but not well enough to ask him to do that. I figured, though, if I could get my friend Underwood to have *Sports Illustrated* do the story, maybe Ted would go for it."

Underwood pitched the story to the magazine. The magazine liked it. Underwood pitched the idea to Williams. Williams said, "Come on down." Underwood and Pope went. The result was a terrific *SI* article in August 1968 called "Going Fishing with the Kid," one of those bonus stories in the back that ran forever and left the reader feeling at the end as if he were sunburnt and wearing a Hawaiian shirt and sitting in Ted's living room.

"An open boat with The Kid does not happen to be the place for one with the heart of a fawn or the ear of a rabbit," Underwood wrote. "There are four things to remember: 1) he is a perfectionist; 2) he is better at it than you are; 3) he is a consummate needler; and 4) he is in charge. He brings to fishing the same unbounded capacity for scientific inquiry he brought to hitting a baseball."

Lovely stuff. Everyone shook hands at the end of the day and thought the story was done. Except for Pope.

"Underwood doesn't just write about people," Pope says. "He marries them. Every one of those long pieces he ever wrote for *SI*—Bear Bryant, for instance, John McKay—he wound up best friends with the subject. They do *books* together."

A first best friend Underwood had made in this case was Jack Brothers, the guide on that fishing day. Brothers invited him to return to the Keys to fish for tarpon. Underwood, a fisherman like his dad, took Brothers up on the idea. They went out together and almost had a giant tarpon into the boat when Brothers made a mistake and the fish swam free. The fishermen had been so close to capturing the tarpon that it had left a pile of scales on the side of the boat.

Underwood scraped up the scales for a souvenir and, on impulse a few days later, put them into an envelope and sent them to Williams with a note about the misadventure, the old story of the one that got away. Williams sent a note back saying that he hoped Underwood had given Brothers hell, but scrawled over the text "Not really!" He also complimented Underwood on the *SI* story. He said the story "had captured me."

The *SI* editors in New York also liked the story. They wondered if there might be more.

"Do you think Williams would want to sit down to do his life story?" managing editor Andre Laguerre asked.

"I'll find out," Underwood said.

Williams sputtered, changed his mind, changed his mind again, then finally agreed to do it. Underwood went to see him in Ocala, Florida, where he was working with Red Sox minor leaguers. The start of the project was rocky. Underwood found a grumpy Williams. He saw the dark side.

"Ted came down for breakfast and he was just angry," Underwood says. "He was angry about everything. Tight. Everything was tight. His eyes got real small and his mandibles jumped when he said something. I tried to pay for the check and he grabbed it out of my hand and said, 'Don't be a big shot,' slammed some money down, and walked away. I just sat there, saying to myself, 'I'm not going to put up with this.' The editors at *SI* would back me if I decided not to do it. I decided that I didn't want to do it."

Underwood confronted Williams at the ballpark. He said he couldn't work with someone who acted that way. The story was done. Williams didn't argue, said nothing. Underwood was back at the motel, packing, when there was a knock at the door.

"It's time for dinner," Williams said. "Do you want to go eat?"

"It was his way of apologizing," Underwood says. "He never said anything more about it. He never got that look again with me, as long as we knew each other. He got mad, but never got that look again."

The partnership was back in business. The result was the longest four-part series *SI* had ever run, "Hitting Was My Life." Make that a five-part series. Williams added a fifth part.

"That was all his idea," Underwood says. "He wanted to do a part just on hitting. He even had the title, 'The Science of Hitting.' That came from him."

The words again rolled across the page. This was Williams talking, cleaned up perhaps, but loud and opinionated and funny. He told his side of his story that had been written by so many other people. His worst critics harrumphed that a bunch of the facts were wrong, the situations not exactly as he described them, but facts usually are wrong in arguments, aren't they? This was his argument.

He was absolutely candid. The thoughts came out of him with a rhythm, the way he talked, with a bluster and cadence and sense of passion. He had been wanting to say these things for a long time, whether he knew it or not.

"The best thing is that Underwood recorded everything on one of those big old reel-to-reel tape recorders," Edwin Pope says. "He took them to be transcribed by some lovely Spanish woman he knew in Miami. She called him the next day and said, 'Mr. Underwood, I am very sorry. I cannot do this. I have never heard language like this.' "

An editor at Simon & Schuster wound up asking Underwood and Williams to convert the words into a book. The one book became three books. The results were *My Turn at Bat*, an instant best-seller on the nonfiction charts, *The Science of Hitting*, still the best instructional book ever written about swinging a round bat at a round ball, and *Fishing the Big Three*, a memoir and guide about fishing for tarpon, bonefish, and the Atlantic salmon.

Underwood and Williams became so close that Underwood nearly cringed at some of the things Williams revealed about himself. Bobby Doerr was a friend, all right? A friend for a lifetime? Williams would say things, personal things, here that Underwood knew would never be said to Doerr. The conversations went far beyond subjects for the book. None of these words ever would be in any book. Williams seemed as if he wanted to talk, to divulge, to be intimate. He somehow chose Underwood as the person to listen. The writer always wondered why. He thinks it had to do with education.

"I wish I was smart like you," Williams would say.

"Ted, you're smarter than I am," Underwood would reply with conviction. "You're probably the most intelligent man I've ever met."

The writer found sides to Williams he didn't know existed. On a trip to Africa after the 1969 Senators season, he noticed his new friend had become quiet. He couldn't figure out why. They were in Zambia, hunting various animals for an *American Sportsman* show on ABC. Underwood was there only for the first half of the trip because he had to return for work. Why wouldn't Ted talk?

"Then I realized what it was," Underwood says. "He was upset that I was leaving. He didn't want me to go. He was pouting. Like a little kid."

Williams liked all three books. He toured for them, did signings. Finally someone had gotten it all right. (He had. He and Underwood.) This was what he really thought. This was what really had happened.

The first two books were published while he was managing. He wondered if his players had read them. Especially *The Science of Hitting*. He let it be known it would be a good idea if they did.

"I had a great start in the 1972 season, a great first month in Texas," catcher Rich Billings says. "I was in the top ten in hitting. Right there in rolling, just to keep Williams suffering. Jimmy Carroll, the friend from Boston during the fifties, remembers just showing up one day at the small, first house.

"I was in Miami, and I met some retired Boston firemen, all guys in their seventies," Carroll says. "They wanted to meet Ted. I said I would take them. I put two in the backseat, two in the front, and we showed up. Louise Kaufman was outside. She said, 'Oh, boy, he's going to love this. I'm getting out of here.' People didn't just drop in on Ted.

"We go in and he's upset at first, but one of the firemen, Clarence Brodie, had a great face. He just did, he had a great, friendly face. Ted got hooked on Clarence Brodie, just talking to him. Liked the way he laughed. Ted wound up cutting up some grapefruit for all of us, serving it with sherbet. We spent a couple of hours there.

"On the way out, he said, 'Jimmy, can you do a favor for me?' I said, 'Anything.' He said there was a woman in the bedroom. I should take her back to Miami. She was a good-looking woman. Ted told her she was going back with us. She didn't want to go. She thought Ted was going to take her to meet Cary Grant. They were filming *Operation Petticoat* down there. Ted, I guess, had said that they would see Cary Grant. Now he said, 'Back to Miami.' She came back with the four firemen and me. A real good-looking girl."

Through the years, the area pretty much grew up around Williams. The tiny bridges constructed on the railroad trestles were replaced by modern, wider expanses. The Keys became a tourist destination. The 126-mile road from Miami to Key West became a boulevard of attractions and lodges, blinks and winks to entice the curious traveler. Every year civilization intruded one step closer.

The famous man was not happy with the idea.

"The Cheeca Lodge was built," Hank Brown says. "Ted went there to eat one night. He was told that no one could eat in the dining room without a tie. He went home and came back wearing a tie. Over his V-necked T-shirt. It was a famous moment. The Cheeca Lodge decided to throw out its dress code."

"I got him interested in buying a condo at the Ocean Reef," John Underwood says. "He was going to do it. Maybe he even did it. I can't remember. He didn't like it, though. He didn't like the rules at the pool. Or in the dining room."

This was another stuffy dining room. Neckties required on Saturday nights. Williams ordered a bowl of soup with conch fritters. He tucked his napkin into his V-necked T-shirt this time. The soup arrived. He picked up the bowl and started drinking. The excess soup rolled down the napkin, across the front of the T-shirt. He finished the bowl, walked out, and never returned.

"He looked like a slob when he did that," Underwood says. "But he was anything but a slob. He was just making his statement."

No condo. Thank you very much.

The second house, the one on Madeira, was his anchor. There was little night life in Islamorada—though the one local tavern boasted that it had no front door because it was open 24 hours a day, every day—and Williams wouldn't have been involved in it anyway. He entertained at home, kept his early-to-bed schedule. He would rather argue with Jimmie or Jack in the kitchen about proper fishing tackle than go out on any town.

A cypress-paneled den on the second floor was Williams's sanctuary. Rick Ruoff, a neighbor, remembers being brought up there and seeing trophies and baseball pictures on the wall and feeling privileged. The living room gave no indication of who lived in the house, except when Williams was married to Dolores. Then it gave an indication that Dolores lived there.

"There was a painting of Dolores in the room," Millard Wells, an Islamorada painter and gallery owner, says. "She said Ted had commissioned it from a famous New York artist. It was quite striking."

It was a seminude, Dolores staring out of the frame with her jeans unbuttoned and a sleeveless shirt unbuttoned. Half of the shirt covered one breast. Dolores's hand covered the other. Her hair blew in the breeze. The word "Vermont" was painted in the background. She looked sensuous, beautiful.

The plan was to have a second painting of Ted in the room. Dolores commissioned Millard Wells to paint it. She said she wanted a fishing painting that showed off Ted's muscular body.

"I didn't know what exactly that was," Wells says. "The usual pictures I paint show the fisherman catching a fish, involved in the fight, the tarpon in midair. Muscular? I painted a picture of Ted bringing a tarpon into the boat. No gaff, just Ted doing it by himself. The muscles were glistening.

"Dolores didn't like it. To this day, this is the only commissioned painting a customer ever has refused. What she wanted, it turned out, was

Back! Still can throw . . . [Boston Public Library]

Still can talk with the Knights of the Keyboard.
[Boston Public Library]

Billy Consolo, the bonus baby. [Red Sox]

Ted and Cardinal Cushing. [Red Sox]

Ted and Jimmy Piersall.
[Red Sox]

Exhibition at Cooperstown in 1955.
[Red Sox]

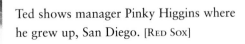

Ted shows manager Pinky Higgins where he grew up, San Diego. [Red Sox]

Ted signs his 1956 contract with Red Sox owner Tom Yawkey. His $110,000 salary makes Ted the highest-paid player in the game. [Bettmann/Corbis]

What kind of question was that? [Red Sox]

Another crisis. Another press conference in the Fenway press room. Ted's the only one who looks comfortable. [Boston Public Library]

Endorsement opportunities.
[Boston Public Library]

Ted and Ty Cobb. They differed in
batting philosophies. [Red Sox]

The Lion in Winter. No longer the skinny kid. [Jerry Romolt]

Fighting the aches of age.
[BOSTON PUBLIC LIBRARY]

Final day at Fenway,
followed by the hordes.
[RED SOX]

Homer on last at bat. Shakes Jim Pagliaroni's hand. [ASSOCIATED PRESS]

Marriage to Lee Howard.
[Associated Press]

Steve Tomasco, Ted, and daughter
Bobby-Jo Tomasco. [Red Sox]

General manager Dick O'Connell
(left) and baseball writer Hy Hurwitz
announce Williams's election to the
Hall of Fame at Fenway. [Red Sox]

Ted and Casey Stengel at
Hall of Fame induction in
Cooperstown. [Red Sox]

Dolores Williams, wife No. 3, with son John-Henry as a baby. [Bettmann/Corbis]

Manager of the Texas Rangers. [Red Sox]

A magic night at the plate as Rangers manager. [Red Sox]

Don Zimmer and Ted.
[RED SOX]

Back in a Red Sox uniform in the
spring. Vinnie Orlando checks the fit.
[RED SOX]

Still opinionated. [RED SOX]

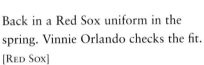

Pesky and Williams
(early.) [Red Sox]

Pesky and Williams
(late.) Same uniform.
[Red Sox]

Old-timers' reunion. Jackie
Jensen, Jimmy Piersall, and Ted.
[Red Sox]

Eye on the ball. [Red Sox]

Old-timer's swing.
The erstwhile Splendid
Splinter. [Red Sox]

Ted and Louise Kaufman, the love of his life. [Frank Cushing]

Bud Leavitt and John-Henry Williams. [Frank Cushing]

Ted on the job. Older Ted signs pictures of the younger Ted. [Jerry Romolt]

Ted and Joe DiMaggio, 1991 All-Star Game in Toronto. [ASSOCIATED PRESS]

Ted and George Carter. [GEORGE CARTER]

Opening of the Ted Williams Tunnel in Boston. Governor William Weld *(left)*, Ted, and John-Henry. [STAN GROSSFELD]

The Kid's Kid, member of the Fort Myers Red Sox. [ASSOCIATED PRESS]

Secular sainthood. Ted, more than half blind, throws a celebrated strike to open the 1999 All-Star Game at Fenway. Tony Gwynn of the San Diego Padres tells him where to throw the ball. [REUTERS NEWMEDIA INC./CORBIS]

Hitter.net hat. Hitter.net shirt. Hitter.net smile. [Stan Grossfeld]

A last visit to the Dana-Farber cancer ward, a last trip for the Jimmy Fund. [Stan Grossfeld]

One thing you have to remember to do . . . [Stan Grossfeld]

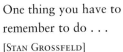

Get a good pitch to hit. [STAN GROSSFELD]

A kiss from Elden Auker at the Hitters Hall of Fame, the last public appearance of Ted Williams. John-Henry is behind the wheelchair. Claudia Williams is behind John-Henry. [STAN GROSSFELD]

The Kid. Teddy Ballgame. Theodore Samuel Williams (1918–2001).

[STAN GROSSFELD]

the same painting I did for everyone else. I sold this one to somebody else. There never was a painting of Ted."

Williams's years with Dolores in Florida were the same as they were in Washington. Storm clouds followed wherever the couple went. John Underwood, doing the books, saw the highs and lows. He found Dolores alternately tough and delightful. He liked her. She battled with Ted with all guns working, foul word for foul word, sarcasm for sarcasm. Ted battled back.

"One day I came in the house and Dolores had her head in the gas oven," Underwood says. "I ran across the room. I thought she was trying to kill herself. I really did."

" 'No,' Dolores explained, 'the pilot light went out.'

"I thought, though, that this was the marriage that was going to work for Ted," Underwood says. "I think he loved Dolores at the start. He definitely was trying. If you saw a picture of her in a checked shirt, some denim shorts, she was the perfect woman for him. She loved the outdoors. Smart. She could keep up with him.

"Who knows why marriages fail? Only the two people who are in the marriage can know that."

Underwood remembers taking Dolores to a dinner in New York. Williams asked him to do it. He showed up, and Dolores was wearing some orange taffeta dress by some famous designer. He suddenly was hit by the fact that, yes, she was a *Vogue* model. She looked like a *Vogue* model.

"She was real good-looking," Joe Johansen, a guide, says. "I was a young guy, and I'd be looking at Ted's house when I went by in the boat. But not really to see Ted."

The end to the marriage was evident when Williams appeared at Millard Wells's gallery one day in 1972 with the painting by the famous artist in New York. Dolores was gone, and Williams wanted the "damn thing" out of his house. He asked Wells to pack it and send it back to her. This did not happen. Dolores had decided to stay in Islamorada. She had rented a cottage on the ocean side and purchased a skiff to give nature tours to schoolchildren. No shipping was necessary. She came to pick up the painting.

Wells and his wife were in the studio. Wells remembers the conversation.

"I don't know why Ted doesn't want to keep this," Dolores said, pointing at the work. "It's a beautiful painting by a great artist. The things he did. The atmosphere he created. The use of sunlight. You can see the sun sparkling on my box. . . ."

The three people stared at the painting, the jeans unzipped. What did she say? Did she say what I thought she said? Millard looked at his wife.

"She's talking about her jewelry box," he said.

Millard's wife looked back.

"You can see it glistening on my hair. . . ."

"Maybe socks."

Dolores took the painting.

What to do now? Williams had tried just about all the ways a man can get married. He had married his first love, his first girlfriend, Doris. That didn't work. He had married the gorgeous second wife, Lee, the actress and model, for love. That didn't work. He had married out of necessity and duty, Dolores. Another gorgeous woman. That certainly didn't work. What was left?

He had lived the single life during different stretches, women available any night he wanted. That didn't work. He was 55 years old.

He did the logical, sensible thing—he married for companionship. Louise was back by the end of 1974.

True, there would never be another ceremony in front of another justice of the peace. True, he told one and all, especially Louise, he never would marry anyone again. True, he was now as married as he ever had been.

Louise had won the race. She was the only one who could take him. The screaming, the words, the flashes of cantankerousness, she understood. The infidelities, she understood. Or at least could handle. She had learned how to hunker down and survive. He had called his second wife, Lee, in 1974 and begged her to return, to try again.

"If you come back, I'll even go to church," he promised.

"What does that mean?" she wondered. She never had asked him to go to church.

Lee eventually had relocated in California after the divorce. She had obtained her real estate license and worked at a large development in Marina Del Rey. She loved her life, what she had put together, yet she still thought about his offer. She had kept in contact and still loved him and he still loved her. She thought hard.

"No," she finally said. "I just can't do it."

Louise had no second thoughts. She moved back in with her framed original Audubon print and her sterling silver and her crystal and her furniture and filled the oceanside home. She had proved to be, after grand trial and grand error, the one woman who could fit inside the blast area. He was, if there ever had been, a man who needed unconditional love. She had it to give.

"She was a strong character like him," Louise's friend Evalyn Sterry says. "She truly loved him, and I think, really down deep, he loved her. I don't know what it was with those two marriages after she met him . . . maybe he was looking for someone younger, better-looking? I don't know."

Louise had reached her sixties now. Williams was still leading-man handsome, if overweight. The wrinkles in his face were friendly battle ribbons from a life lived outdoors. The wrinkles were not as friendly to Louise. She looked old, much older than him. People who did not know Williams and met him with Louise would not understand their relationship.

At least one writer, doing a story on Williams the Fisherman, thought she was the maid. Johnny Pesky, who did not really know her, reached for a description and said, "Oh, you mean Grandma." The same guides who had drooled over Dolores referred to Louise as "that old woman."

She fit, though, into Williams's life. She gave it order, structure. She cleaned his clothes, cooked his meals, poured him a big cocktail. He liked his cocktails now—"a Ted Williams Special," a big drink, one bottle of rum only enough to pour two. The alcohol sometimes was not a pleasant addition. He would become noisier, more abrupt, quicker to hit the blowup button. The language would come tumbling out, quicker and louder and more forceful. He was not a drunk, but he was not a good drinker.

"My wife and I were at the house one night for dinner," Gary Ellis, a guide, says. "We finished dinner, and Ted asked if I wanted another drink. I said I'd have one if he had one. He said, 'Sure.' Then he changed his mind. Just like that. 'I don't want another drink. Going to bed now. Bye.' That was the end of the evening."

Little else really had changed. His life still was his life. The Public Ted still startled and charmed vacationers around the island, telling the alligator story, booming opinions, curt or pleasant, depending on the moment. He still fished with Jimmie and Jack, battling all the time. He still fished by himself. Battling all the time.

"I was watching him one day," Rick Ruoff says. "I was fishing a client. Ted was out there alone. He made a mistake bringing a tarpon in. Lost him. I see him bring the rod up, break it across his knee, and throw it on the bottom of the boat. Then I see him reach down, pick up another rod, and break that one over his knee and throw it on the bottom of the boat. Then he hits the push-pull, *rrrrrr,* and he's gone."

Ruoff lived almost next door to Williams. He was constantly amazed at the famous man's energy and bluster. Louise had brought a dog into the relationship, a Dalmatian named Slugger. Ruoff owned a brown English setter with white spots. One morning, 7:00 A.M., Williams was driving past Ruoff's house in his blue Suburban. Ruoff's dog was on the front lawn. Williams hit the brakes on the Suburban, came back in reverse, stopped, and got out.

"Hey, Bush," he shouted. "What kind of dog is that?"

"Now there's shrubs in front of my house," Ruoff says. "I know he couldn't see me on the porch. I know it! It's seven o'clock in the morning, and he's just shouting. He's Ted Williams! He figures someone's going to answer!"

"It's an English setter," Ruoff replied.

"That's close enough," Williams shouted. "Slugger, my dog, needs a girlfriend."

He got back into the Suburban. He drove away.

"He was this bombastic, iconoclastic guy," Ruoff says. "He was hard of hearing, you know? So you'd go to dinner, and you know how people speak louder when they're hard of hearing? He'd say, 'PASS THE GOD-DAMNED BUTTER,' and you'd pass it real fast."

The daily push and pull between Williams and Louise in this returned relationship was best examined by Richard Ben Cramer in a 1986 piece for *Esquire* magazine. Ben Cramer used a wonderful device to describe Williams's out-of-proportion approach to everything by capitalizing almost every word Williams spoke. Williams was definitely a capital-letters man for all of his life. Every person who ever met him, from the earliest days in San Diego, always remarked about how he always was SHOUT-ING. Evalyn Sterry says, "He talked in italics."

Ben Cramer showed Williams's affection for Louise in the story and showed her affection for him, but one stretch of description and dialogue near the end details the perils of living with Ted Williams. He has become angry at just the memory of Bobby-Jo not going to college:

"... *THAT BURNED ME.* ..."

The switch is on. Lou calls it the devil in him.

"... A PAIN IN MY HAIRY RECTUM!"

"Nice," says Lou. She is fighting for him. She has not flinched.

"Well, DID," he says through unclenched teeth. "AND MAKES YOU HATE BROADS! ..."

"Ted. Stop." But her Ted is gone.

"... HATE GOD!"

"TED!"

"... *HATE LIFE!*"

TED! ... JUST ... STOP!"

"DON'T YOU TELL ME TO STOP. DON'T YOU *EVER* TELL ME TO STOP."

Lou's mouth twists up slightly, as she snorts: "HAH."

And that does it. They have beaten it, or Lou has, or it's just gone away. Somehow it's past, and Ted sinks back in his chair. His jaw is unclenched. He grins slyly. "You know I love this girl like I never ..."

Lou sits back, too, and laughs.

This was the written example of the unchoreographed doom that three marriages couldn't survive. This was the part that Louise could handle, would handle, did handle, the moldy spot that had to be consumed on an otherwise fine slice of everyday life. She was strong enough—her love was strong enough—to get past it.

Williams was upset by the *Esquire* piece when it was published, grumping and fuming. Louise told him to keep quiet. The writer had captured him.

"Ted," she said, "that's you."

She wrote a letter to Richard Ben Cramer, thanking him and congratulating him on his achievement.

14 Citrus Hills, 1987-1993

In the end, the greatest desire of 95 percent of the people who come to the Red Sox spring camp—fans, players, other managers and (especially) reporters of all kinds—is to have some kind of demonstrable contact with Ted Williams, and to take away a memento of same. Which is perfectly logical, for to behave otherwise would be like visiting the Grand Canyon and ignoring the part by the river. In his 65th year of life, Williams has transcended the beloved-uncle role baseball usually gives its retired stars and has earned the status of full-blown national monument, a monument that walks around enjoying the hell out of itself.

MICHAEL GEE, *BOSTON PHOENIX*, APRIL 12, 1983

The finished product would be a Technicolor fantasy. The short film, an advertisement, would make the new Citrus Hills development in Hernando, Florida, look as inviting as a combination of midtown Manhattan and an island in the Bahamas. Tampa was right next door! Symphonies! Culture! Orlando was right next to the other door! Disney! The Gulf of Mexico awaited! Rivers! Lakes! Golf courses! Average temperature: 72 degrees! (But no humidity!)

The two hours of hard, back-roads driving to either Tampa or Orlando would not be mentioned. Nor would the fact be mentioned that most of the golf courses were still either under construction or dots on a contractor's map. Nor would the general, sleepy-eyed, fast-food, gun-rack-in-my-pickup environment around the 500 acres of resort living on vast stretches of former cattle and watermelon farms be mentioned.

No, this was a paradise. How good was it? Hey, Ted Williams lived there already.

That was the most undeniable fact in the presentation.

"Hi, I'm Ted Williams," he said into the camera, the first take en route to the finished product. "If you've ever dreamed of owning a place in Florida . . . (*big noise in the background*) . . . awww, now a fucken airplane."

Two developers from New Hampshire, Sam Tamposi and Gerry Nash, had begun buying up property in and around Hernando in the sixties. They had done big things in New Hampshire, accounting at one time for over 50 percent of the industrial growth in the state, and had more big ideas for Florida. Tamposi's brother, Nick, a pilot for Pan Am, had scouted out the state from the air on his many flights to South America and picked out this area of high ground and undeveloped promise. Nash and Tamposi had bought and sat on the land for 15, 20 years and waited.

By 1987 they were ready to move.

"Hi, I'm Ted Williams. If you always dreamed of a place in the sun, come to the outdoor wonderland of Citrus County. Citrus Hills. On Florida's Gold Coast . . . now it's a goddamned tractor. Fuck it, let's do it again."

Tamposi, a minority owner in the Red Sox after Tom Yawkey died in 1976, had become friends with Williams. They met at Fenway in a roof box, liked each other, and stayed in touch. Nash and Tamposi decided Williams would be the perfect spokesman for their newest enterprise. He was perfect for their demographic: older New Englanders looking to escape the cold. Longtime Red Sox fans! They'd love to be with their idol! Live with Ted! Nash and Tamposi flew down to Islamorada to talk with their man.

A couple of factors were working in their favor. Number one, Sears finally had dropped Williams as its prime spokesman. The Ted Williams Sports Advisory Staff was no more. Number two, Williams was ready to get out of Islamorada. The fish had left and the people had arrived. No longer could you find those great schools of bonefish or tarpon. Every day just trying to cross Route 1 in Islamorada you could be flattened by a family of four hurrying toward Key West in a camper from Michigan. Or, even worse for a Marine Corps veteran, a carload of hippies. This was not Williams's idea of retirement living.

"Do you know why he left?" Rick Ruoff, the Islamorada friend and neighbor, says. "He told me once that he was leaving because he couldn't take a left turn on to Route 1 anymore. There was too much traffic. It was as simple as that.

"I think he just gave up. He couldn't stand to see what had happened to this paradise where he once lived. He never came back much after he left. Maybe three or four times. And he had changed. He was cranky and old. He'd lost his comfort and identity. He wasn't the Ted Williams who once had owned Islamorada."

Nash and Tamposi offered money, land, a challenge. Williams took them all. He already knew the area from fishing trips around Homosassa Springs. Louise was ready to move too. At least she said she was.

"Hi, I'm Ted Williams. If you've always dreamed of a place in the sun . . . now it's going to rain! Look at those clouds. Going to get our ass good and wet."

He would be the lead character in the presentations that would be shown to the sad, snowbound old-timers of the North. He would catch their ears; the golf courses and the modern homes would catch their eyes, and the prices would capture their pocketbooks and minds. Nash and Tamposi leased a bunch of airplanes to fly prospective clients on junkets to see their futures. Flights left every weekend.

Williams put his home in Islamorada up for sale, and he and Louise first moved into a condo in Citrus Hills in Hernando, then moved to a model home, then had a bigger house built on top of the biggest hill on the Florida peninsula. The Keys were history. Business was business. Hernando was home.

He stared into the camera and talked.

"Hi, I'm Ted Williams. If you always dreamed of a place in the sun, come to the outdoor wonderland of Citrus County. Citrus Hills. On Fla's Gold Coast . . . fuck it, let's do it again. . . ."

He threw a golf club, a putter, about 30 feet in the air. Mrs. Cronin's housekeeper was not in the area, as she had been almost 30 years earlier at Fenway Park.

"Hi, I'm Ted Williams. If you always dreamed of a place in the sun, come to the outdoor wonderland of Citrus County. Citrus Hills. On Florida's Gold Coast. It's truly a sportsman's paradize . . . para . . . para . . ."

He strangled on the word.

He stopped.

He stared into the camera and steamed.

"Cocksucking fucken syphilitic Jesus."

He stared into the camera some more.

He started talking again.

He did not smile.

"Hi, I'm Ted Williams. If you always dreamed of a place in the sun, come to the outdoor wonderland of Citrus County. Citrus Hills. On Florida's Gold Coast. It's truly a sportsman's paradise. Fishing, golf, tennis, and more. Citrus Hills has something for everyone. Including a spacious country club with the best dining around. I love it. I know you would too."

Perfect.

The contractor for both the first house and the second house was Ted Johnson. He was a young guy from Crystal River, 33 years old when the first house was built. He didn't know much about baseball, didn't care, and had no interest when Williams called him the first time, or the second time to come to the first house for a drink. He finally . . . oh, it was Christmas . . . went the third time.

"We sat and chitchatted, and it was nice," Johnson says. "Then, before I was going to go, Ted gave me an envelope. He said, 'I know you didn't make a lot on this job, so maybe this can help make it up.' I tried to refuse, but Ted put the envelope in my coat. Ted was Ted. Forced me to take it."

Johnson stopped his car as soon as he was out of range of the house. His curiosity was killing him. He opened the envelope and took out $2,500.

"Pretty good, huh?" Johnson says. "Well, that was probably the smartest $2,500 Ted ever spent in his life. I can't tell you how many times in the following years I went up there, did work for him, never charged him a cent. He got that $2,500 back."

Johnson and Williams became friends. Maybe more than friends. Johnson felt they both found a niche in their relationship. Johnson's father had died, and spending time with Williams seemed easy, natural. There were lessons to be taught about fishing and life. There was a student and there was a teacher. It all worked.

"He was eager to teach me and I was eager to learn," Johnson says. "We'd go fishing all the time. He'd beat my ass if he could. He was a great competitor. We'd go out on the bonefish flats, and even at his age, he'd spot the bonefish a long ways away."

Johnson started out at the beginning in the sport, buying a fly-casting rod, and wound up bumping around the Bahamas and Mexico and Belize with Williams. Going to Canada. They never talked baseball. They seldom talked World War II or Korean War. They always talked fishing.

"We'd go down to Andros Island, to a lodge owned by a giant black man named Rupert Bleeker," Johnson says. "Ted loved Rupert Bleeker. Called him 'King Farouk.' "

Typical trip down at King Farouk's: All the other fishermen in the lodge were doctors. There were 16 of them. They got so drunk one night one of the doctors fell on all of their fishing poles, breaking half of them. Fun guys, except for one sourpuss. The sourpuss doctor wanted no part of the fun.

"He comes down to dinner one night, and there's Ted . . ." Johnson says. "There's 18 of us at the dinner table."

TED: How're you doing today?

SOURPUSS: Grump, grump.

TED: Well, glad you're concerned about Old Ted Williams. Because Old Ted Williams is pretty good today. It's nice that you would show that concern.

SOURPUSS: What?

"Ted was just grinding him," Johnson says. "The guy was looking at Ted like 'Who the hell are you?' Ted just kept grinding, though, and you know what? The guy broke down and had fun and turned out to be a really nice guy."

When Johnson built Williams's second house, he followed plans laid out by Louise. This house was built on the top of the big hill, the tallest hill on the Florida peninsula, land that had been part of Ted's deal. Louise was in charge of everything. Williams's one request was that it be built next to the oak trees on the hill. Johnson built in a special fly-tying bench for Williams in the garage. The house was finished in the fall of 1991.

"It was a house, back then, that had a lot of life," Johnson says. "Louise was a good decorator. The den had a lot of paneling."

This was now home. The Gulf of Mexico had been traded for privacy. Williams, now 72, convinced Joe Lindia to move to Citrus Hills. He couldn't convince Jimmy O'Loughlin. ("Jesus, Ted. There's nothing there," Jimmy said.) The guest list shrunk dramatically, simple geography keeping people away. To see Williams now you had to be going to see

Williams. You didn't just stumble on him. There were no drive-bys, no drop-ins. Citrus Hills was a gated community. The gawker factor was cut way down.

Williams and Louise settled into the slowed-down life of the development. They had reached that level of separate-bed togetherness that couples married for 30 years find. They bitched, they fought, they knew they were in the long grind together.

"Ted was funny," Ted Johnson says. "We'd come back from some of those trips, and he'd be saying in the car, 'I can't wait to get home to my Louise.' Then he'd be home five minutes, storming around."

"The first time I met the two of them, I said to myself, These two old people are going to kill each other," another friend says. "The old man is going to try to strangle the old lady, and she's going to stick a fork into him, and one of them is going to die. The more I knew them, though, that was just the way it worked."

Williams had few obligations to fulfill for Citrus Hills. He mostly had to live there. Every day he called Tamposi and they talked for hours, just yapping. He was retired, perhaps, sharing the same feelings and worries of his neighbors, men who finally had walked away from the shop, the office, the nine-to-five burden, but at the same time he was not retired. He was Ted Williams. That was still a full-time position.

W illiams had spent more than half his life in hotel rooms and cabins. There was no reason to stop now in his later years. Two examples of trips during the retirement life of Ted Williams:

Trip number one (with Louise)—Frank Cushing danced with older women. That was his job. He worked for a cruise line. The population on any given cruise usually was overstocked with single, aging women. Cushing was hired to talk with these spinsters and widows at dinner, to dance with them at the dances, to laugh and help them be merry. There was no sexual side to the job—a sexual relationship would have been cause for dismissal, in fact—only travel and companionship.

Cushing had known Williams at various stages, growing up in San Diego, serving in Korea, and had become a friend while Williams was the manager of the Senators. He brought Williams and Louise on a cruise early in 1991.

"I've always wanted to go on a cruise," Williams said.

"Tell me where and when," Cushing said. "I'll set it up."

The trip was 15 days through the Panama Canal on the *Golden Odyssey*. Cushing wrangled to be on the same trip. The captain told him his only assignment was "to make sure Mr. Williams and Miss Kaufman have a nice time." Cushing said he could do that.

Ted didn't dance, never danced, so there was no dancing, but he went to the buffets and the shows, walked around the boat figuring out how everything worked. He inspected the Canal, made sure it was still a good idea. He had fun. Ted Williams on a cruise! Interesting.

"On one of the last days I got Ted to do a little presentation," Cushing says. "He didn't want to do it, of course. He said, 'Who wants to listen to an old, over-the-hill ballplayer?' and, 'I'm not very good at public speaking,' but in the end he did it. Everybody on the boat came. It was the highlight of the trip.

"He talked for about 45 minutes and after that answered questions and after that signed autographs. Some other activity was planned for the ballroom, but he was still going. People wouldn't leave. The captain later asked him if maybe he wouldn't want to get into the business, that they could run a 'Ted Williams Cruise,' but Ted didn't want any part of that."

One cruise was enough.

Trip number two (without Louise)—In the summer of 1991, Williams went fishing in Russia with Indiana basketball coach Bobby Knight and Jerry McKinnis, host of ESPN's *The Fishing Hole*. Knight often had been cited as the American sports figure closest to Williams in philosophy, temperament, intelligence, and use of the four-letter word. Knight had pursued the friendship, and Williams had gladly accepted. The trip to Murmansk in the Arctic Circle during the last official days of the Soviet Union—the final leg to the fishing camp in a Red Army helicopter, fat red star on the side—was a final bond.

McKinnis, who had the trip filmed for his show, watched the interaction between his two traveling partners. He was fascinated.

"On the flight over, which took forever, they got into an argument," McKinnis says. "Ted would argue with you. Bobby would argue with you too. This one was about how you do a proper back cast. They both wound up standing in the aisle of first-class demonstrating how they did their back casts. They were two big men, arms moving everywhere, telling each other they were wrong. I don't know what the other people thought."

Knight was McKinnis's friend, which was how the whole trip started. Knight asked Williams to go. Williams, who didn't know McKinnis, called him at Knight's urging and asked to go. McKinnis almost fell down.

"I was a Stan Musial fan as a kid in Arkansas," he says. "I knew Ted was better—he was—but I loved Stan the Man. Every morning I would pull out the sports page and check the box scores. Stan against Ted. How they did would determine my entire day.

"Now Ted Williams is calling me on the phone, asking me to come on this trip. I'm in my office and we talk and I'm really excited when I put down the phone. The problem was, it was a Friday afternoon and everyone had gone. I went downstairs, out into an alley, where a carpenter was working. He had two sawhorses set up. I went over and told him that I had just talked to Ted Williams. Because I had to tell someone."

The Soviet Union had just begun to fall apart in 1991. There was still a Cold War edge to every place the visitors stopped. The poverty was eye-opening. Williams asked questions everywhere about how things worked, about how people lived, about what they had for dinner. On the Umba River, the formerly Communist fish seemed to have no resistance to biting on a capitalist fly. Atlantic salmon were Atlantic salmon.

Williams was a little shaky in the river because of the rocky footing, so McKinnis and party improvised. They put him in an inflated inner tube for balance. He did just fine. McKinnis found that Williams the fisherman was not overrated. Knight also was very good.

"Coach Knight caught an awful lot of fish," Williams said. "He used my rod sometimes. I was rigged up just right."

The trip lasted a week. All problems in baseball, college basketball, and geopolitics were solved. No one in any of the small towns knew who either of the two men were. They had a grand time.

The interpreter was a man from Moscow named Oleg. He described the local cultures, explained the political change, advised when and when not to pay a proper amount of rubles for bribes. His Russian was much better than his English, but he was the most interesting part of the trip. Oleg was a survivor, a provider.

"Oleg," Williams asked one night in a Russian bar, "do they have rubbers in Russia?"

"Rubbers?" Oleg replied. "I don't understand."

"Rubbers."

"Rubbers?"

Williams searched for the appropriate word, "condoms," and showed visually what he wanted. Condoms! Yes! Russia had condoms.

"Are they made in Russia?"

"Yes, they are."

"Are they any good?"

"Better than what you have now."

Williams asked Oleg to buy him some condoms. He had met a woman. She didn't speak English and he didn't speak Russian, but they seemed to like each other. Maybe there would be a use for condoms.

"I may have to have you stay out of the room for a little while tonight," Williams told Knight, his roommate. "I may have to use it for a little while. You know?"

"Je-sus," Knight said.

The assignation never did happen, but it could have. Williams told a friend back in Hernando that all the pieces were in place, but he was afraid of those Russian condoms. Who knew what they would be like?

He was now 73 years old.

The alliance with Tamposi opened another door for Williams. His strong political opinions always had been known to anyone around him—*hate* the Kennedys, *hate* most politicians in general, vote Republican—but they never had been put before the public. He never had campaigned for anyone, never had been part of the political process.

Tamposi convinced him to change that in the winter of 1988. The result, it could be argued, may have bent the course of history.

"You look at all the things Ted did in his life," Al Cassidy Jr., longtime friend, says, "and the biggest thing he ever did, bigger than hitting .406, bigger than anything he did in baseball, was to campaign for George Bush in the New Hampshire primary in 1988. The government of the United States would not be the same as it is if it weren't for Ted Williams."

An overstatement? Perhaps. Out of the question? Not really.

This was the situation: Ronald Reagan was finished in the White House after eight years. Bush, his vice president, was part of a crowded field of candidates trying to replace him. The New Hampshire primary, the traditional springboard toward nomination, was one week away. Bush was floundering.

The results of the Iowa caucus, the first chance for voters to pick and choose, had been a shock. Senator Bob Dole finished a strong first, and the Reverend Pat Robertson, the televangelist favored by the newly powerful Christian Coalition, had been a stunning second. Bush was a tired third.

The numbers had fallen in New Hampshire. The *Manchester Union-*

Leader, a voice of conservatism, mindful of late publisher William Loeb's one-word description of Bush as a "wimp," had backed Pierre "Pete" Dupont, governor of Delaware. Throw in Senator Jack Kemp, the former quarterback of the Buffalo Bills, another candidate. Bush had problems. He now was five points behind Dole in the polls.

"This was a tough week," John Sununu, the former governor of New Hampshire who was running Bush's campaign, says. "There was no doubt about it.

"Bush had done the work. He'd done a ton of work in the past year, coming to the state often. That was what originally had given him the lead in the polls. Now the lead was gone. What we had to do was reconnect him with the people. That was our word, 'reconnect.' He somehow had to show people again that he was the same guy they had met earlier. Nothing had changed."

Williams was a prime part of the reconnection. He didn't know Bush, but he certainly knew Tamposi, who was part of the political stew in New Hampshire. Tamposi was a big Republican contributor in the state, an unseen and unelected presence, a "man behind the man" type of character. He had helped Sununu become governor and now was committed to helping Bush win the White House.

Tamposi and Sununu talked to Williams. Sununu had met him before but really didn't know him. Would he do something like this?

"It turned out he was a closet political junkie," Sununu says. "He was a strong, conservative Republican. As I got to know him, we had a lot of talks about politics. I think he was liberal on social policy, but he loved the Republican financial policy, loved the Republican foreign policy commitments. In all our conversations, he always talked in one way or another to the character of people."

Williams agreed to travel from Florida to New Hampshire to help. The question now was how to use him.

"We scheduled a trip for Bush to North Country to a bunch of small places," Sununu says. "All the experts told us it was a crazy move. The weather was terrible that winter. Snow all the time. Who would come out to see the vice president in these little places? We sent Ted with him.

"I forget the exact stops, but I know they went to a lake in Laconia where people were ice fishing, and I know they went to a big thing in Wolfeboro. They were together all that time."

The crowds were terrific. The attraction—nobody ever claimed otherwise—was Williams, still the New England heartthrob. The people went straight toward him. He signed autographs, talked, introduced his new best friend, "the next president of the United States." The next president of the United States definitely had second billing.

"We were somewhere . . . I forget exactly," Steve Kennedy, a Sununu aide, says. "A man said he had a fishing rod he wanted to give to Ted. Ted said, 'Okay,' and we take the governor's car and we follow the man to his house. The man came out with this old antique bamboo fly rod with all these silver fittings. Ted knew exactly what it was. The make and model. He loved it."

"Why would someone give me something like this?" Williams asked in the car on the way back to the campaign trail. "This is really valuable."

"Ted," Kennedy said, "people love you."

"They'll never know how much I love them back," Williams said.

The next morning Kennedy was supposed to pick up Williams at seven at the Hawthorne Inn in Hanover. Williams was not there. The woman at the front desk said, "Some Shriner came and picked him up at six." Williams had met someone who mentioned a sick, elderly woman who "loved Ted" and would love to see him, and he had bought a couple of cups of coffee and . . . he had left directions for Kennedy to the house.

Was this grassroots politics? Or what?

"Primaries are different in New Hampshire," Sununu says. "The state is small. People really take the face-on measure of the man they're voting for."

The measure here was good for Bush. The reconnection was established. Bush was the walkaway winner with 59,290 votes. Dole was second with 44,797. Kemp was third with 20,114. The juggernaut was back on course. The flow of campaign contributions returned and multiplied. The New Hampshire primary sent Bush off toward the White House. No doubt about that.

"Thank you, New Hampshire," he said when he left the state.

"Thank you, New Hampshire," he repeated, nine months later, when he was elected.

What part did Williams play? Who can say? Sununu says that when the votes were analyzed, Bush had won approximately 39 percent in the cities of southern New Hampshire, 55 to 60 percent in the North Country. Any of dozens of factors—including a late round of attack ads against Dole—could have accounted for the win, but Williams would have been one of them. A big one. Could he really have been enough to put Bush over the top? Sununu doesn't say that, but also doesn't argue against the idea.

"This was a tough week," he repeats.

Williams and Bush became friendly and stayed friendly. They had a lot in common. Bush had been a Navy pilot in World War II, had played baseball at Yale, loved to fish. They talked a common language.

"I have a picture in my office of George Bush and Babe Ruth," Sununu says. "It must have been taken around 1941. Bush was the Yale baseball captain, and a lot of the Babe's artifacts somehow were donated to the Yale library. There was a connection. Ruth went up for the presentation; and he posed for the picture with the baseball captain. The president is in his baseball uniform.

"Ted saw it one day and liked it. I think he liked the idea that the president was a player, not just some guy who liked baseball."

Sununu became Bush's chief of staff. A lifelong baseball fan, he conjured up two special moments for Williams at the White House.

The first was a luncheon in the Rose Garden with Bush and Joe DiMaggio on the afternoon of the 1991 All-Star Game. This was the 50th anniversary of both the .406 season and DiMaggio's 56-game hitting streak. After the luncheon, everyone flew aboard Air Force One to Toronto for the game.

"I put that together with Fay Vincent, the commissioner of baseball," Sununu says. "The idea behind the whole thing was that we could ride on ·the plane for an hour and a half and have these two guys to ourselves and listen to them talk. It was wonderful."

The second event was the presentation of the Presidential Medal of Freedom. Sununu called Williams and informed him that the president wanted to give him this medal, the highest civilian honor possible.

"No thanks," Williams said.

"No thanks?"

"I don't want to do it."

Sununu asked Vincent to persuade Williams or at least find out what the problem was. Vincent called Williams and then called Sununu. Williams didn't want to do it because he didn't want to wear a tuxedo. Sununu said he didn't have to wear a tuxedo, but did have to wear a tie. Was that all right?

Williams received the Presidential Medal of Freedom. Sununu has the tie Williams wore, autographed and framed, in his office.

"Pretty good, huh?" Sununu says, talking about the rewards of a political career. "I also have a baseball signed by Ted Williams, Joe DiMaggio, and Hosny Mubarak, the president of Egypt. Not many people have that."

The only time Williams was in a baseball uniform now was for a month in the spring. He had returned to the Red Sox in 1978 as a batting instructor. The Yankees first had made him an offer, and then the Los Angeles Dodgers did, after he said on a radio interview that he "wouldn't mind working with young hitters in spring training." The Red Sox finally jumped into the bidding and made an offer, and he accepted.

He became slightly emotional on the first day of camp at Winter Haven, Florida, when someone asked him about putting on the Red Sox uniform again.

"It feels good . . . pretty damn good," he said. "I'd like to tell you how I really feel about putting this uniform on again. But I won't. No, I'd better not. Just say this . . . this will be the only uniform I'll ever want to wear."

The job was only for the spring. The Red Sox made it sound like a year-round position, and for the next 15 years they would travel to every regular-season series on the road with a packed bag containing a number 9 gray shirt, gray pants, hat, shoes, the works, but Williams never would appear once to use them. His job, he decided, was to work with the kids in the spring, the younger the better. Winter Haven was his last baseball compartment. More than enough.

He would appear in the morning at Winter Haven, give a nod to the gathered sportswriters ("The Knights of the Keyboard! Good morning, Knights!"), a special nod to any woman in their midst ("And good morning to you, Gail!"), jump on a golf cart, and head down to the minor league complex. Four diamonds were clustered around one central spot, a tower in the middle. Williams would sit on the cart at the base of the tower, able to watch the action at four different home plates simply by turning his head. The hopefuls would parade past, swinging at baseballs, and Williams would deliver his critiques. Some of the players, faithful readers of worn-out copies of *The Science of Hitting*, knew exactly who he was. Many had no idea. To them, he was simply another big, important man with a big mouth.

"You've got a great swing there," he would boom. "Whaddya hit last year?"

"Uh, .227."

"Well, okay. How many homers?"

"Four."

"Four!"

(Pause.)

"Jesus Christ. You've got to shit or get off the pot!"

His philosophy of hitting was at variance with the philosophy now in use in the Red Sox system. He would cringe when he saw a hitter like Dwight Evans swing *down* at the ball. A man should swing *up!* The Red Sox batting coach in the late seventies and much of the eighties was Walter Hriniak, a disciple of the Charlie Lau, down-at-the-ball approach. That had become the dominant hitting theory.

"One day Hriniak comes to me," Don Zimmer, who was the manager from 1976 to 1980, says. "He says he's teaching kids to hit the ball down. Ted is teaching kids to hit the ball up. What should he do? I said, 'Jesus, can't you teach 'em to hit the ball in the middle, a line drive right past the fucken pitcher?' "

Zimmer didn't know Williams at the beginning. They became friendly soon enough, and Zimmer asked Williams to come out to dinner, Zimmer and his wife and Ted. Williams declined. He said he knew the conversation would be all baseball. He didn't want that. It would bore Zimmer's wife. Zimmer protested, asked and asked again, and Williams always declined for the same reason.

"Finally, I grab my wife and we go over to where Ted's staying, and we just get him one night," Zimmer says. "He agrees to go, but only on the condition we don't talk baseball. I agree. Promise. Not one word. We go, and for four hours we don't talk about a fucken thing *except* baseball. And we had a hell of a time."

The camp life was low-key, easy. For 15 years, starting in 1978, Williams would deliver a few pronouncements on the state of the young hitters today—"By God, I like 'em"—for whichever media members (new word: media) might come past. He would watch the minor leaguers, shower, and go back to his condo apartment. Joe Lindia or Johnny Buckley or both would be down, helping him out, cooking dinner, hanging around.

The condo for spring training always was provided by Al Cassidy. The former promoter and co-owner of the Ted Williams Baseball Camp in Lakeville had moved to Winter Haven and become a developer. His family, four sons and a daughter, had followed. Williams had been involved with him in a few business deals and remained a good friend. He would call Cassidy almost every day during the year, stop by every day during spring training.

"He was always around," Al Cassidy Jr. says. "My father finally would have to kick him out of the office, saying he had to get some work done. Ted would just come in the house, sometimes go right to the couch, curl up, take a nap. Then he'd wake up, say bye, and be gone."

Cassidy Jr. always thought the Williams at the house was a different Williams from The Public Ted. He would seem almost shy. Cassidy Jr. saw a wistfulness to him at family barbecues, family events. He had nicknames for everybody, questions about everybody's lives. He wanted to belong, wanted to be part of all this. He always had inserted himself into other people's families—back to the Cassies in San Diego, the Beans in Minneapolis, the families of most of his friends. He always remembered the little ticks of family business, always found an overweight someone to call "Porky." He almost seemed to have a need. When he moved to Citrus Hills, only an hour and a half from Winter Haven, he would visit the Cassidys even more frequently.

"I always thought, Ted looking at our family, this was something he'd always wanted," Cassidy Jr. says, "and yet he never had. Even with all the things he did."

Cassidy Jr. would notice a change when he went with Williams around the town. One person, two people, there would be no change. Once the third person came, once the crowd followed, the voice would become louder and the opinions stronger. The wistful, sweet feeling would disappear. The Public Ted would take charge.

"He'd have to be who everyone expected him to be," Cassidy Jr. says. "Ted Williams."

The Public Ted still played very well at the ballpark. He was a prime roadside attraction. Elderly snowbirds from New England would stand, transfixed, mute in his presence, nervous as all get-out. Interest him in something you said, which was not hard, and he would talk for ten minutes, ask questions. Say something wrong or boring—or even worse, say nothing at all—and he would grunt.

He had added tennis to his sports dossier somewhere along the way. The first year in camp, 1978, he challenged everyone. Loudly. He played

Carl Yastrzemski in a celebrated postworkout match, George "Boomer" Scott serving as ballboy, Williams losing in straight sets. Next? Someone told him that former Red Sox manager Eddie Kasko, now a scout for the team, was the best tennis player in camp. Williams didn't know Kasko, but looked for him.

"Hey," he shouted when he found Kasko. "You play tennis? I understand you're the number-one seed."

"Well, I don't know about that," Kasko said.

"Well, I don't know either," Williams said. "You can't be number one until you beat number nine!"

They set up a match at four o'clock on the courts of the nearby Ramada Inn after the workouts. Williams walked through the orange groves between the ballpark and the hotel and appeared, racket in hand. They played. Kasko looked up midway through the match. There had to be 200 people gathered around the court. Many of them had brought lawn chairs.

"Tomorrow, 7:30," Williams shouted at the end, Kasko still number one. "Rematch."

They would play for more than a decade. Williams never would win a match, not one, but he would shout, boast, throw his racket against the fence in anger. His intensity would keep the competition going. Tomorrow! Rematch! He played righthanded. His special shot was the lob. His extra-special shot was his slam in return when Kasko would try the lob against him.

One year Kasko told him two friends were coming down from Virginia. They played doubles. Maybe Kasko and Williams should be doubles partners against them. Williams didn't like the idea.

"I don't know how to play doubles," he said.

"It's easy," Kasko said. "It's just like you have a rope tied to my hip. I go forward, you go forward. I drop back, you drop back."

"Nah, I don't want to do it."

"It's easy."

"Nah."

"The thing is, these two guys think they can play. They think they're really hot shit."

"Really?"

The doubles matches became part of the annual routine. Neither of Kasko's two friends ever really believed he was playing with Ted Williams. The first friend said after the first match, "I couldn't move. My legs felt like lead." The second friend said, "Couldn't move? I couldn't breathe."

In the spring of 1982, George Sullivan, the former batboy-sportswriter, had become the Red Sox publicity director. One of his first ideas was to schedule an old-timers game during the season. The Yankees had an old-timers game yearly, with great success. Sullivan thought the Red Sox should try one too.

His biggest worry was convincing the most famous Red Sox old-timer to play. He brought up the subject in Winter Haven, and the conversation went exactly as planned. Williams first said he wouldn't do it, no, never, that was the dumbest idea he ever heard. Then he said, Okay, when is it, where is it, what is it. He would do it.

"I'm in my office late a few days later," Sullivan says. "The day is done. Everybody's gone. I hear *crack* . . . *crack* . . . *crack* coming from the major league field. What's that? I had my suspicions. I had to go look. Sure enough, there's Ted. He's got a guy throwing to him. He's taking batting practice. Nobody around."

(Williams ultimately enjoyed the game. He called Sullivan into manager Ralph Houk's office and said, "Thanks. That was one of the best days of my life." Even though he was hitless, he made a running catch of a soft Mike Andrews liner.)

Baseball, though, was mostly now a spring sport. The famous man was mostly a retired consultant in Florida.

Al Cassidy Jr. always tried to get Williams to go to Boston. Cassidy Jr., working for his father, would travel north often for business commitments. Williams always declined. Nah, too much hassle. He declined most invitations. The White House would call and he would decline. Nah, too much hassle. A good trip was a fishing trip. The rest were nonsense, hassle.

That was why Cassidy Jr. was surprised in November 1988 when Williams accepted an invitation to go to Boston. Williams even said he would set up the hotel room.

"We fly to Boston," Cassidy Jr. says. "From the minute we get off the plane, people are yelling to Ted. 'Hey, Ted. How're you doing?' In the cab, people are yelling from the streets, from other cars. I'm amazed. I ask Ted if it always has been like this in Boston. He says it has, pretty much, but it's increased as the years have gone by.

"We get to the hotel. Ted has a suite. A huge suite. The presidential suite. Ted says, 'Oh, by the way, there's a place I have to go tomorrow night. A thing I have to do. Can you go with me?' I say, 'Sure.' "

The next night arrived. Cassidy, cleaned up, golf shirt and khakis, presented himself, ready to go with Ted. Wherever it was.

"Jesus, Bush," Williams said. "Don't you have anything better to wear than that? Did you bring a tie?"

Cassidy was dumbfounded. Ted? A tie? Williams was *not* a creature of fashion. He never had talked about clothes once. A tie? Cassidy Jr. changed, was approved, and went with Williams in a cab to the Wang Center, the biggest theater in Boston. They got out—what the heck is this?—and went into a reception room in the theater, and Cassidy Jr. found himself in a celebrity wonderland.

"There's Joe DiMaggio," he says. "There's David Hartman. There's Tip O'Neill. There's John Glenn!"

The event—"A Night with Ted Williams"—was a tribute for all of Williams's work with the Jimmy Fund, the Boston charity that benefits the Dana-Farber Cancer Institute. The stage was set up like an old fishing cabin, and the celebrities came out, one after another, to talk about their experiences with the man of honor. Glenn brought down the house with his tales from the Korean War. The event raised over $225,000 for the charity.

"It was all set up, planned," Cassidy Jr. says, surprised even now. "And he didn't tell me any of it."

The quickest way to get Williams to stop talking—well, one of the quickest—was to ask him about his charity work. This was personal, private, no cameras or attention allowed. He would go public, help raise enough money to keep the Jimmy Fund alive, vibrant, all by himself, but the visits to kids were almost always done in secrecy. There are very few pictures of him in the wards, sitting down, asking kids the names of their pet animals. Virtually none from when he played.

"You hear some of the stories and they're amazing," Mike Andrews, onetime Red Sox second baseman, now the director of the Jimmy Fund, says. "Like the kid who was dying and wouldn't let go of Ted's finger. Ted just pulled a cot next to him and slept there all night, the kid holding Ted's finger.

"The way Ted got to know kids was remarkable, came back to see them, again and again, always remembered their names. He'd show up anytime."

Bill Koster was the director of the charity when Williams played. Koster would set up the visits, set up the events. He was one of the few people with constant, easy access to Williams. Williams would grump and moan, "Koster's got me doing this thing, I'm only staying 15 minutes," then go to wherever the itinerary directed and stay for three or four hours.

"I'd go with him sometimes to hospitals," Jimmy O'Loughlin says. "I'd be the guy to bring the baseballs. He'd say, 'Jimmy, bring a couple of baseballs.' I'd bring two and they'd be gone in a minute. He'd say, 'Jimmy, go back down to the car and get a couple more baseballs.' I'd be running up and down, in and out from some hospital. Finally, I figured I'd better just stuff baseballs in all my pockets when we went to one of these places."

"He'd call me up," Jimmy Carroll says. "He'd say, 'Bush, there's a place we have to go.' We'd visit some person who was in a lot of pain. We'd do this all the time."

Williams did things other athletes couldn't or wouldn't do. Named chairman of the Jimmy Fund for a number of years, he personally endorsed all checks over $1.00. Want Ted Williams's autograph? Send a check to the Jimmy Fund. He appeared at drive-ins, going from car to car with a canister. He appeared at bowling alleys and pool halls and Masonic lodges.

People in outposts in New Hampshire and Connecticut, Rhode Island and Maine, people who never had seen him play in person, had a chance to see him at the local Kiwanis Club smoker. There was a famous big dinner at the Hotel Statler when he returned from Korea in 1953—"A hundred dollars a head, everybody pays, even the head table," was his one demand—but the small events were better. They were personal, usually done with friends.

"He'd do things in these small towns . . . he could have made five times the money if he did them in Boston, but he was loyal to his friends," Mike Andrews says. "He liked doing things with them. Just ordinary guys."

Williams would go to Joe Lindia's restaurant in Cranston, to Frank Bertallini's restaurant in East Hartford, to a benefit softball game in Somerset. He went five times to Waterbury, Connecticut (once on his honeymoon), to events run by O'Loughlin, his friend, the Waterbury detective.

Two of them were memorable softball appearances against Raybestos Brakettes pitcher Joan Joyce. Each visit drew as many as 20,000 people, more than twice the capacity of Municipal Stadium, people standing everywhere. They still are the two biggest sports events in the city's history. Both times, in 1961 and 1966, Joan Joyce struck him out.

"She'd come to the camp when the idea was first proposed," Joe Camacho says. "Ted hit against her there and hit her pretty well. Then, the night we went to Waterbury, we'd stopped for dinner on the way. Ted had a couple of glasses of wine. Ted was not a drinker. He wasn't at his best. She blew that ball right by him."

O'Loughlin remembers a sixth event he had planned for Williams in Waterbury in the late sixties. Williams didn't want to go. He said he had been to the city five times, "and people are sick of me." He suggested O'Loughlin find someone else to head the show. O'Loughlin took the challenge.

"Who're you going to get?" Williams asked.

"I'm going to get Joe DiMaggio," O'Loughlin said.

"Good luck."

O'Loughlin went to New York with some other Waterbury cops. The other cops went to drink beer. O'Loughlin had an appointment with the retired Yankee Clipper.

"I went to see Joe DiMaggio at 11:30 in the morning," O'Loughlin says. "I left the other guys at a bar called Sonny's that was behind a police station. It was a cop bar, and it was a Cosa Nostra bar. All at the same time. Sonny was very connected, but he liked cops.

"I go to the Hotel Pierre, I think it was. I go to a suite. I say to this guy, 'I want to see Mr. DiMaggio. I have an appointment.' Joe comes down. He gives me this big-shot routine. I tell him why I'm there, and right away he says, 'No, I can't do that.' Then he says, 'How much are you guys paying?' I tell him, 'Nothing.'

" 'Nothing?' DiMaggio said. 'If you don't pay, you're not going to get anyone to go.'

" 'We've never paid,' I said. 'And we've gotten plenty of people.'

" 'Who'd you get?'

" 'We got Ted Williams. We got your brother Dominic to come. For nothing.' "

DiMaggio said Waterbury was not going to get him. A large-sized man appeared and said the interview was finished. O'Loughlin went back to the bar. He was, in his words, "really pissed." He told the story to Sonny, the proprietor. Sonny was sympathetic.

"Let me make a couple calls," he said.

When Sonny returned, he told O'Loughlin to go back to the Pierre.

DiMaggio would see him again. This time there was a different atmosphere. DiMaggio seemed amenable. There was a question about what would be the proper date in August, but that was resolved. O'Loughlin promised billboards with DiMaggio's picture to hype the event. The two men shook hands. O'Loughlin returned to the bar in triumph.

"He's not going to do it," Sonny said. "He has a conflict. He called."

"But he said . . . ," O'Loughlin said.

"He's not going to do it," Sonny said. "How important is this to you? If you want me to try some more, make a few more phone calls. . . ."

"Never mind," the detective said.

Edge: Williams.

The famous man never had been hurt by his lifelong tendency to find his friends at random, friends like O'Loughlin, picking up whatever interesting folk might come across the shadow of Ted Williams. Someone once said, "You go into a room full of people with Ted and watch, he'll find one guy who will interest him. He'll pick that guy out and they'll become friends." The strategy never had brought him riches—picking out hunting guides and firemen and storekeepers instead of dancing with the confirmed business nobility—but it never had cost him money either.

Until he met 47-year-old Vince Antonucci. Aka Vince Addison. Aka Nick Addison. Aka William Addison. Aka Vincent Villa. Aka Vincent Hurst. Aka John Shuffle.

In 1988, home at Citrus Hills, time on his hands, the 70-year-old Williams wandered into a memorabilia store called Talkin' Baseball in nearby Crystal River, Florida. Antonucci later would claim Williams was enticed by a phone call saying, "We have a package here for you," but former partner Barry Finger thinks "that was Vince's romantic version. Ted just was driving by one day and stopped."

Antonucci put on the charm. Arrested 30 different times and convicted at least seven times on charges ranging from writing bad checks to second-degree grand theft, he was a certified con man. He worked this con very well. He had a wife, Kim, and a daughter, Nicky, maybe three years old, who soon was calling Williams "Uncle Ted." Uncle Ted soon was a partner in Talkin' Baseball.

"You look at it, Vince had stumbled on to a gold mine," Barry Finger says. "He's in the memorabilia business, and he has exclusive rights to Ted Williams! Ted's not only in the business but has paid money to be in it! He's a partner! You couldn't do any better than that, but Vince . . . Vince was one of those guys who would rather work an angle to make 50 cents than work legitimately to make 75. He was always working the angle."

Finger, a memorabilia collector, says he unknowingly had bought the same package from Antonucci, stopping at the store to look at cards and winding up a partner. He says he saw very soon after Williams joined the group that bad things were going to happen. He wanted out.

"I called Ted's attorney, Robert McWalter, and asked, 'What does it take to get me out of this?' " he says. "I could see the wheels were going to fall off the cart in a hurry. I told Ted that too, but Vince was accusing my wife and me of the same things he was doing. Ted chose to believe Vince."

The autograph market had exploded in recent years as baby boomers, hitting their big-earning years, looked to buy little pieces of a romanticized boyhood past. No sport was more attractive to that demographic than baseball. Stars from the forties, fifties, and sixties—hell, nobodies from the forties, fifties, and sixties—now had new careers signing their names. They did card shows. They did personal appearances. They did stuff for mail-order companies.

The shows were instant money. Need a few bucks? Do a show. Williams had become a prestigious part of the marketable crowd.

"I think I might have had Ted for his first show in 1986," Jim Hawkins, a former promoter in Detroit, says. "We had him come out to Dearborn. I think we paid him $12,000 a day for two days. We charged $9.00 an autograph. You know, number 9."

Hawkins says Williams was unique in the autograph business. DiMaggio was ridiculous, a list of demands. Mantle was fine until he had a few drinks. Willie Mays was tough. Williams was a joy. He had fun with the trip, dropping f-bombs across the countryside. He enjoyed the people. He didn't even care about the money.

"Don't give it to me," he said when Hawkins tried to hand him the check. "I'm going fishing. I'll lose it. Send it to Stacia, my secretary. Uh-uh."

He terrorized an early-bird special crowd of old ladies at a Dearborn steakhouse (Ted liked to eat early) with conversation about "cock-high fastballs" and "fucken sliders." He charmed a surprised barber with the shout, "That's the best damn haircut I've ever had!" He signed, smiled, and went fishing again.

Hawkins had Williams back for a second appearance in Toledo in 1988. There was a little concern about that show. Three days before it was going to be held, Hawkins still hadn't heard from Williams. The phone rang at seven in the morning. Hawkins had been sleeping.

"Hello?"

"This is Captain Williams."

Hawkins did not make the connection.

"Who?"

"Captain Williams. I've got to know where I'm supposed to be."

"I'm sorry. Captain Williams? I'm afraid I don't know who you are." Hawkins still was confused.

"You never did know what the fuck was going on!"

"Oh! That Captain Williams."

There was a Midas touch quality to the business, though, for the old-timers. Yes, they would make money for their signatures. Yes, also, they became the object of attention from wise guys and chiselers. Who was to say a particular person signed a particular object? Forgeries jumped up everywhere. Certificates of authenticity were simple pieces of paper. This was a business touched with greed much more than nostalgia.

"If I've learned one thing from looking into Vince Antonucci," Herb Hoskins, investigator from the Florida State Attorney's Office, says, "it's that I wouldn't believe I had a real autograph from someone unless I saw them sign it in front of me."

The situation was made for Antonucci-like characters. Williams liked the idea of the money from the new business, of course, but seemed to like the work even more. He would show up early, maybe eight o'clock, sign what he had to sign for two hours before the shop opened at ten, and return home. The shop was next to a Winn-Dixie supermarket, and sometimes Finger would arrive, see Ted's SUV parked already in the lot, and wonder where Ted was. He'd look into the Winn-Dixie, and there was Ted, pushing the shopping cart, going through the aisles.

"Really, you want to know why he became a partner?" Finger says. "I think he was just looking for something to do. He was bored. He just liked coming around."

When Finger left, Williams bought his share of the business. Williams was now a two-thirds partner, Vince still with one-third. The partnerships, of course, really didn't matter. Antonucci wanted to take everything. Friends were worried.

"It didn't sound like a good deal, so Sam Tamposi even had Antonucci checked out," Al Cassidy Jr. says. "He told Ted what he found, that Antonucci had been arrested all those times and everything. You know Ted. His response was, 'Everybody deserves a second chance.' If Ted made up his mind on something, he wasn't changing it."

"I never met Antonucci, but I knew his reputation," Jim Hawkins says. "I told Ted. He said, 'Awww, you're just jealous I went with someone else, not you.' I told him that wasn't the case at all."

Finally, the economics of the situation convinced Williams late in 1989 that something was wrong. He was signing all these articles—"You take a ten-cent root beer tin and Ted signs it and now it's worth $100," Hoskins says—and he was putting his own money into the operation, and nothing was coming back. Where was it all going? He asked questions. Antonucci ran out of answers.

"What Vince did, he ran a succession of things on Ted," Lewis Watkins, a graphic artist who also was bilked in the scheme, says. "Vince always thought he was going to be caught. He'd steal something . . . and when he didn't get caught, he'd steal something else . . . and when he didn't get caught, he'd do it again . . . until he finally got caught."

Williams brought a civil case against Antonucci. Antonucci filed a civil case in return against Williams. A criminal case involving the theft of a $37,800 check was filed against Antonucci in February 1991. Looking for representation, Williams sought the advice of Major League Baseball. He was referred to John Dowd, the big-time Washington lawyer who had handled the investigation in the Pete Rose betting case for Major League Baseball. Dowd was from the big-time Washington firm of Akin, Gump, Strauss, Hauer and Feld LLP. Williams hired them.

Again, friends told him he was making a mistake. Did he need big-time lawyers to attack a small-time con artist? Williams didn't budge. If he needed a cannon to get rid of that mosquito in the bedroom, he would get the cannon. It was a costly move.

"There's only two people in the world I ever heard Ted say that he hated," Frank Cushing says. "The first was that sportswriter in Boston, The Colonel, Dave Egan. The second was Vince Antonucci."

"These lawyers would come down from Washington in their private jet," Watkins says. "They'd bring down baseballs for Ted to sign. He'd sign 'em and think he was getting a good deal. He wasn't. The clock was running all the time those guys were here."

Antonucci brought in a big-time lawyer of his own, George Evans, a flamboyant character from Miami. Evans was the master of the delay, the continuance, the challenge. ("I didn't like him," Lewis Watkins says, "but I'll tell you what, if I'm ever arrested for murder, I'm calling George Evans first to be my lawyer.") Four different judges would hear the case before it was done.

When Williams finally went on the stand, Evans grilled him for almost four hours. Louise watched in the courtroom. Williams, reading glasses hanging from his neck with fishing line, seemed frail in that setting, suddenly old, under the weather, but refused an offer from the judge to break early and come back the next day.

"The defense attorney was bringing up all kinds of picky stuff, trying to trip him up," investigator Hoskins says. "Mr. Williams was not an astute businessman. One time, though, the attorney was questioning him about being in Crystal River on a particular day. Mr. Williams said that was impossible. The attorney asked how he could be so sure. Mr. Williams pulled out an appointment book and put on his glasses. He said, 'Because on that day I was fishing in the Ural Mountains with President Gorbachev and President Bush.' Everybody started laughing."

The verdict was guilty. The final judge in the case was Jack Springstead. After he sentenced Antonucci to five and a half years in jail and ten and a half years' probation and ordered him to repay the money taken from Williams, Springstead returned to his chambers. His clerk came in and said Williams wanted to see him. Springstead said that was fine.

Williams thanked the judge, and then they started talking. Springstead was a Marine and a fisherman. Williams was interested in all of that. The conversation ended with the judge saying, "I'm sorry you had to see the bad part of Florida like that. If you want to see the good part, give me a call and we'll take you fishing."

And Williams did just that.

"He came up to my dad's camp up at Lemon Grove, and we went out on airboats, fishing for red fish," Springstead says. "Ted didn't even fish. He brought a camera and just took pictures of everyone. It was a great day. My son was there, and my dad and his friend Al Copeland were there, and when we got back, we fried up the fish with some beans— 'Boston beans' I called 'em in honor of Mr. Ted—and sat around and talked. Al Copeland said he'd work a whole day back in the thirties to make a quarter so he could take the bus from Brookville to St. Petersburg to watch Ted hit."

The good side of the instant-friendship business was back at work. Springstead and his family wound up traveling to Williams's house to watch pay-per-view prizefights. (The Mike Tyson–Peter McNeely night was a short night.) Williams had added another family to his collection.

"I'll give you the tale of the tape on Ted Williams," Springstead says. "On March 13, 1993, a terrible storm hit Hernando County. The 'No-Name Storm' it was called. It did a lot of damage farther up the East Coast, but it also hit us real bad. An 11-foot storm surge came through. My father's fishing camp was filled with four feet of water.

"That was on a Saturday. On Sunday, about noon, we're cleaning up the house and who comes up the driveway? There's Ted, 73 years old. He'd been to the house exactly once in his life. He's asking, 'What can I do? How can I help?'

"That was Mr. Ted."

There was an addendum to the Antonucci story. He was paroled in August 1993 after only a year and a half of jail time. Williams successfully had blocked an even earlier attempt at parole, but was unsuccessful here. Antonucci soon skipped town. Reports began to arrive from around the country of a man peddling bogus Ted Williams memorabilia. The man knew a lot about Williams and said he once had been Williams's business partner.

"He bragged about how he had scammed his way into Ted Williams's life," Robin Leonard, a poker dealer at the Mesquakie Indian reservation in Tama, Iowa, told sports columnist Tom Grace of the *Citrus County Chronicle*. "He read every book he could get his hands on about Ted. This guy has a hell of a memory. He talked about all the stuff he has stored away: bats, balls, Sears ads, lithographs, and some videotapes of Ted talking about baseball. He also claimed to have some signed documents that will give him the rights to many of the autographs and memorabilia after Ted dies. He said he was going to make a fortune and cheat Ted's kids out of their inheritance."

Antonucci had surrendered only about one and a half pages of items from a 65-page list of inventory at the end of the trial. Jim Hawkins from Detroit said even the items returned were lacking.

"He gave back all the junk," Hawkins, who appraised the items for Williams, says. "He'd kept all the good stuff for himself."

Williams was angry at this latest turn, Antonucci running free. He agreed to have the case presented on *America's Most Wanted*, the television show designed to capture at-large criminals. Lewis Watkins appeared on the show. One day after it aired, March 25, 1995, Antonucci was arrested in Anacortes, Washington, 70 miles south of Seattle. Over 100 calls had been received, all with sightings of the con man, three from Anacortes. Antonucci went back to jail. Williams appeared on *America's Most Wanted,* thanking people for their help.

Williams and Watkins both went to see Antonucci sentenced again and led away in leg irons. Estimates of the cost to Williams from this con man's scheme and capture and conviction ran from $1.5 million to $3 million. That was only the money. Seven years had passed since the start of the sordid business, and a lot had changed in Williams's life.

"You look back and Vince Antonucci was the start of Ted's decline," Lewis Watkins says. "This took a lot out of him. It was personal. This was the feeling of rape, someone coming into your home and violating you. That's what Vince did."

The second step in the decline took place at Williams's favorite place in the world: the Miramichi River in New Brunswick, Canada.

15 Fishing on the Miramichi (The Freshwater Life)

We strained our eyes to see Ted as he worked his pool. From inside we could hear Edna straightening up the pots, waiting for Roy to take her home. Outside it was quiet, and Bud had turned up the collar on his jacket. Down below we could see the twitch of motion, Ted's line hitting the water. As the dusk deepened, even that was lost, and all we could do was sit and wait for Ted to come back.

MEL ALLEN, YANKEE, APRIL 1982

The light in the basement workroom always would be lit when Roy Curtis or Edna Curtis or, later, their son Clarence arrived at the cabin. This would be early in the morning, six or seven, still halfway dark, and their feet would crunch in the gravel of the driveway as they came to work and saw Ted through the window, already at his bench, head down, engrossed, not even hearing them pass, fully dressed for the day and tying flies.

The light was his own invention, of course, an aluminum funnel strung upside down over a bulb that hung by a cord from the ceiling. This way the illumination was focused on his hands, his long fingers doing their delicate work, cutting the dyed deer hair and arranging and shaping, maybe adding feathers, twisting and tying the thread around the barbless hook, inventing a daydream, an image, a flash of color and excitement that would attract a hard-to-attract fish.

The river awaited.

"I'd go sit on the porch when I got here," Clarence Curtis says, sitting on the same porch now. "I'd watch the river. See which way the wind was blowing. See if I could spot any jumps or rolls. See where the fish were. My mother would go inside and cook breakfast."

The river was the Miramichi, running across the Canadian province of New Brunswick from Fredricton to Miramichi Bay at Newcastle, maybe the cleanest long river in the entire world. The opponent for two months of every summer for over 30 years was the Atlantic salmon, maybe the heartiest, smartest game fish in the world. The competition was everything.

The salmon were making their annual trip up the river to spawn. Where were they now? Was the water low in the river? High? Which way was the wind blowing? Where were they? Where would they stop? What kind of day was it going to be? Warm? Cool? Rain? How would that affect the fish? What color, what pattern, what little dance would intrigue them? Stand out there, cast and cast, and some days you wouldn't see a fish. Stand out there other days and drama would unfold, the fish taking the fly and fighting and running and fighting until fisherman and fish, both sides, were exhausted. Take the hook out of the son of a bitch's lip, marvel at his beauty, send him back into the water. Start again.

For Ted Williams, this was baseball without all the noise. This was another puzzle that never could be solved but still could be attacked, analyzed, cut down to a size that few men had ever seen. This was the game he could love for itself, away from the hoo-ha and the assholes. Purity. This was where the purity was, the battle as pure as the freshwater that flowed around his waders.

If there was one place he could be, one thing he could do . . . *Edna, that's the best breakfast I ever had! Thank you, Ted . . .* this was it. He would go fishing. Here. Not Islamorada. Not anyplace else in the world. Here.

"He first came up, I think, about 1956," Jack Fenety of the Miramichi Salmon Association says. "Maybe a year or two earlier. The Tourism Board invited him up. Got him interested. This was when he still was an active player."

Maybe there was that schmooze at the beginning—Ted would be good for business! Let's get him up here!—but better than any salmon who ever looked at a bouncing flash of color, he bit and bit hard.

"The fresh air, colorful scenery and clear, unpolluted waters are out of this world," he said in public-relations-speak in the *Boston Traveler* on his first visit (in October 1955). "I'll be back again next year for more of the same."

He had caught nothing on his first day, two 12-pound salmon on the second day in the rain, and three more on the third day. He wound up coming here in the middle of every summer for the next three decades and more. He became a perpetual spokesman for New Brunswick and the salmon. He honeymooned with his second wife here. He came here with his third wife. He came here with the kids, John-Henry and Claudia. He came here with Louise. This place was the longest-running constant in his entire life.

"He was going to buy another camp, further up the road, but he bought the land for this one in 1961," Clarence Curtis says on the porch of Ted's cabin. "It was ready in 1962. My father helped build it."

The house is in Blackville, not far from Renous and Quarryville, down a gravel path, hidden from the road, perched high on the banks of the river, maybe 100 feet above water level. No problems with floods here. A tiny guesthouse is behind the main house. This is the place you might rent unseen for your family of four in Maine, basic and homey, but away from everything, *National Geographics* stacked in a corner for the rainy days. Half, two-thirds of the family might scream for action, lights, some entertainment to make a vacation a vacation. One or two might see the excitement.

The fish are right outside the front door.

"Roy worked for Ted for 28 years," Edna Curtis says. "Every summer. Met him when Ted was fishing up at the Browns' camp. Ted needed a guide. He hired Roy, eventually hired him for the entire summer. Not many people did that, hired a guide for the summer. I went to work for him in '65 as his housekeeper and cook. Roy stayed with Ted until he died in 1988 from lung cancer. Hadn't smoked in 28 years. Quit, in fact, when he started working with Ted because Ted hated cigarette smoke. Then Clarence, our son, became the guide after Roy died."

The word for the customer in Miramichi salmon culture is "sport." Ted was the sport. There is an edge to the word, the image of some crass fat-boy businessman from New York City showing up with all the most expensive fishing gear he can find, crashing and thrashing around the river, not knowing what he is doing, the locals winking and smiling behind his back. Ted was not like that. He knew what he was doing. He might not have been "the greatest fisherman that ever lived," as he would be described, probably wasn't as good as he thought he was, but he certainly was very good and very dedicated. He was a very good sport.

"We were with him for a long time," Edna says. "He was our livelihood. We were raising ten kids in our house at one time with no plumbing, no electricity, a big woodstove for heat. Most everyone along the river, the men, are guides. That is how they make their living. Guide in the summer. Collect unemployment in the winter. That's what we'd do. I'd leave the kids in the morning—if you have ten kids, the older ones take care of the younger ones pretty much—and take care of Ted."

The river is 200 miles of good fishing, 400 miles if you add in the tributaries. Drive along Route 8, the Miramichi River Highway, the picture of a salmon on the logo on the road signs, and fishing is everywhere. The only industry is the paper mill at the mouth of the river in Newcastle, and it is highly regulated, the annual log run long ago replaced with trucks. The rest is fishing. There are no rapids, no dams or impediments to stop the salmon's grand march to the spawning grounds. Only men with fly rods.

Roy and Ted would work up and down the river. Roy was perfect for Ted, never a baseball fan, unimpressed and ignorant about all the baseball things Ted had done. If Rocket Richard or Dickie Moore or some other Montreal Canadiens great had been on the river, ah, that would have been a different matter. Hockey, the greatest sport there was. Jack Dempsey or Gene Tunney? Ah, boxing. Baseball was just that American game.

The rules of the relationship between guide and sport were established early. In the first few days in 1959, in fact, when Ted was still playing with the Red Sox. Heading off road, into the woods, in Ted's Ford station wagon, Roy said he should drive. He knew the woods. Ted said, no, he knew how to drive in the woods, damn it. Roy said, Ted said, Ted drove into the woods. Ted got the station wagon stuck in the mud. Ted started cursing, yelling at Roy. Roy did not like this.

"I worked before you got here and I'll work after you leave," Roy said. "I don't have to listen to this."

He got out of the station wagon. He started walking.

Silence.

More silence.

"Hey, come back here," Ted said.

Roy stopped.

"I wasn't mad at you," Ted said, as close to an apology as he could get. "I was just mad at myself, mad at the mud . . . awwww, just mad."

That was Ted. Roy came back, drove the station wagon out of the woods. That was Roy.

The partnership lasted long enough, well enough, to have both guide and sport elected into the Atlantic Salmon Hall of Fame in Doaktown, Roy first, Ted the next year. Ted—it was said, again and again—always worked best with people who stood up to him, who gave back the same medicine he gave out. Roy always gave back. He mostly was a quiet man with sad eyes, so quiet that he didn't even own a phone. He tried one once, but found that people kept using it. Took it out after a year. To talk to Roy, you had to call one of his sons, George. George would take the message to Roy's house.

"Roy and Ted got along," Edna says. "Roy liked Ted."

The best way to fish the Miramichi was to own a "pool," a private piece of the river. The public pools, where anybody could fish, could become crowded. A line of fishermen would work toward the front, each taking three or four casts at a spot, then moving forward in rotation, the first in line going to the back. The private pool afforded time and maneuverability.

Ted owned the pool in front of his house, the length of his property line, halfway across the river, and at different times owned or leased other pools along the river. The pools were different depths, each of them better for different conditions. Ted and Roy would study the conditions and make their choices. They would fish after breakfast, fish after lunch, sometimes fish after dinner.

Before and after he managed the Senators, as a player and as a sporting goods salesman and as a golden age retiree, Ted would drive up in July, then leave in the first week of October at the end of the salmon season. Edna would go up to Newcastle at the start and buy a side of beef, a quarter of a hog, and more chickens than she could count. She would add a box of bacon and another box of sausages to the order. The meals for the summer would be covered.

With minimal complications and interruptions, the master of the house could do his work. A sign on the kitchen wall spelled it out: GIVE US THIS DAY OUR DAILY SALMON.

"Salmon fishing isn't for everyone," Vin Swazey, another guide and Ted's friend, says. "It's an expensive sport. If you're a nonresident, you have to fish with a guide. A guide costs . . . I don't know, at least $100 a day. I have to think that Ted paid Roy that. There's a lot of equipment. The flies. The time. It's like driving a Cadillac. Some people get to do it, others don't. Some people get to fish for salmon. If you can't afford it, there's a lot of bass and trout out there."

The challenge of the sport is to divert a single-minded fish from a grand purpose. The salmon is on its way home, back from the Atlantic to the freshwater spot where it was born. That is where it will spawn. The females will deposit their eggs in the salmon beds. The males will fertilize the eggs. Old fish and new then will return toward the sea and begin the trip back again the following spring. To catch a salmon is to pull off a trick that involves athleticism, guile, ingenuity, free time, feathers and thread and cement, and varying amounts of good luck. The fish does not take the fly as food, as nonfishermen might think, but is attracted to the movement, the colors. No one knows exactly why the fish takes the fly. The guess is that the same curiosity that might kill the family cat is what lands the salmon on a hook at the end of a fishing line.

For Williams, the deception was the best part, the basic challenge. The intrigue. The figuring out, the planning. He tied flies, experimented, throughout his adult life. Maybe he didn't tie the quarter-million flies that Wallace W. Doak, up at W. W. Doak outfitters in Doaktown, supposedly tied in a lifetime, but he tied a lot. He was deep into the fly-tying culture.

"In 1957 I was a student at NYU Law School," fisherman Ted Rogowski says. "I was friendly with Charlie DeFeo, an artist, who lived at 33 West 67th Street. Charlie called me one day and said to be at his house at nine o'clock the next morning. He said he had a surprise.

"I showed up. He wouldn't tell me what the surprise was. There was a knock at the door. There was Ted. He came in, and we all tied flies for two hours in an apartment in the middle of New York City. I remember he was upset about the press corps, said they were all lying and cheating and making things up. Around eleven o'clock, he stood up and said, 'Well, I have to go to work now.' The Red Sox were playing the Yankees."

Tying flies was something Williams always did. It was his release. It focused his mind. It kept him out of trouble. Dottie Lindia remembers going with her husband and Ted to the suite at the Somerset after the game in 1958 when Ted threw the bat and it hit Joe Cronin's housekeeper. They all were supposed to go out to dinner, but Ted was very upset. He went into his room and tied flies for an hour. He was calm when he came out.

"Ted tied very good flies," Rogowski, who later became Williams's lawyer and friend, says. "He was very inventive. He invented a fly called 'the Spotlight,' red, yellow, and green. He said, 'Why do I have to figure out which color is going to attract the fish? Put 'em all out there. Let them decide.' He invented one called 'the Bear Hair.' Black. He invented a range of tarpon flies . . . made them interchangeable. No one ever had done that. He was innovative. A perfectionist."

While on the river fishing, he would share knowledge and theory easily. He would talk to anyone. What flies are you using? Catching anything? He would take out his own fly collection for the day and trade, barter. He became friendly with the fly tiers of the river, stopping at George Rutledge's shop in Renous, buying materials, talking about fish, two or three times per week. He would stop to see Emerson Underhill, creator of a famous fly called "the Green Machine," in Bernardsville. Underhill had broken his back as a young man, flipped his car no more than a quarter-mile from his house and was thrown out. He would have landed all right except he had a hunting knife in his back pocket. The knife made the landing worse, crushing the vertebrae at the base of his spine. He had been confined to a wheelchair ever since. Tying flies.

Each year Underhill would hunt for a deer during season, sitting in a car with his rifle near a parking lot. The deer would come out of the woods, try to cross the parking lot, Emerson would stick the rifle out the car window, and the deer would become part of Emerson's projects. The hair would go on the flies. The skin would become part of wallets he made. The meat would become a succession of dinners.

"Ted showed up one day, just to see the flies," Underhill says. "He kept coming. We'd sit and talk. Every year for a while he'd bring me a big fish for dinner. You just knew he knew how to cast a line. He was so tall, which helps. I'd sell him some flies. The 'Green Machine.' The 'Orange Blossom Special.' The 'Undertaker.' "

Another stop was at W. W. Doak. This was the preeminent outfitting store on the river. A crowd of fishermen always could be found. The proprietor, W. W. himself, was a religious man, a Christian. Ted was a walking broken commandment. At least when he talked. He would come into the shop and drop a few selected vulgarities, and W. W. would steam for a moment, then react. Ted would be banned to the parking lot for a designated amount of time.

"I have another friend who also was banned for bad language," Tom Balash, a fisherman and friend of Ted's, says. "You'd have to stand outside, say, for ten minutes, and then you could go back in. And you had to talk right."

Ted would come back for more. Or he would call. He would call a lot. He would be back in the cabin after fishing in the morning and would call Doak's and ask W.W. how the fishing was going on other parts of the river. W.W. would explain that, like Ted, other fishermen also were taking their midday break and many of them had decided to buy some equipment, unlike Ted. The store was packed. Ted would keep on talking. W.W., very busy, would hand the phone to his son, Jerry, with the words, "Here, you talk to him." Jerry was 12 years old.

"I got to meet some famous people that way," Jerry Doak says. "My father had me wait on some quiet guy one day in the store, everything busy. I could see the guy was a little upset, being outfitted by a 12-year-old kid, but he went along with it and bought some stuff. He gave us a check and signed his name. I was waiting on Benny Goodman.

"I got to know Ted. He was an enigmatic fellow, to say the least. I called him 'Captain Williams.' He called me 'Junior.' Ted, as a guy . . . he'd be nice when you were alone. He took me out back and taught me about casting. Taught me a lot. People would come in the store, though, and it would be the big voice, 'You're putting on weight, Junior. I've never seen a fat Doak.' He would be different.

"In October of 1978, I was preparing to get married. I remember he said, 'Anything you want to know about marriage, you just come to me.' "

To fish with Williams was to stand in a defined second place. He was the acknowledged leader of all expeditions. Roy, the guide, took a natural second place. Ted would be first in line in the river, casting into the new water first. Roy, if he fished instead of just watching, would stand second. Ted would explore a stretch of water, move along. Roy would move into the already explored water.

That also was the usual rotation for visitors. Ted first. He would critique all parts of the visitor's skills, starting with clothes and equipment and moving right into technique. If the visitor was unsure of himself—or, God forbid, did not know much about fishing—the critique would last for the entire day. Friends often would fish once with Ted, then never fish with him again.

"He was a great guy, in my opinion, if you didn't mind what he said to you," Swazey, the guide and friend, says. "Because he'd say anything. Myself, I never let what people say bother me."

Swazey and Ted closed out one Miramichi season fishing together. Ted first. Swazey second. At the end of a long day, no fish around, Swazey had a hit and reeled in a fat ten-pound salmon. Ted was furious. How could Swazey have caught a fish and Ted hadn't? Ted had been fishing that same stretch of water. What had Swazey done differently?

"He was so mad," Swazey says. "I knew when he came back the next year, he'd do something. Sure enough, soon as he got here, he called me up. Wanted to go fishing."

Ted said the rules had changed. Swazey should go first. Ted would go second. They went into the river, and after a while, sure enough, Ted had a hit. He fought the fish, brought it home, exulted, released it. What do you think about that? What do you think of Ted Williams now? Swazey showed him his rod. He had only a bare hook at the end of his line.

"Are you happy?" he said. "Maybe now I'll use a fly."

Ted went crazy.

"I went out with him one time," Rogowski says. "He's first, I'm following. There's a bar that goes through the river, sort of an elevation of rocks and pebbles. The water is high, and Ted is going farther and farther out. The water is up to his chest, and he's a big man. I'm five-foot-seven. I say, 'Ted, for chrissake' . . . and then I fall off the bar. 'What do I do?' I shout. 'Swim to shore,' he says. I had to dogpaddle. Ted shouts up to the house, 'Start the bonfire. You've got a puppy dog coming to shore!' "

The fishing would vary from year to year, much like baseball. A good year would have a lot of rain and not a hot summer. The salmon would move higher and higher up the river, encouraged. A bad year, no rain, very hot, the trip would be much shorter. The great years, like 1986 and 1992, would be balanced by a bad year like 1968, no action anywhere. The economic effects of a bad year—"Think about it," Swazey says, "if you went somewhere to fish for a week or two weeks and never caught any fish, would you be back the next year?"—would put an economic headlock on the region for two, three years to follow.

Not for Ted, though. He would be back.

"He was a very good fisherman, an outstanding fisherman," Swazey says. "For an American [smile] a good fisherman. He spent as much time on this river during a summer as I did."

Swazey says this as he sits on the bank of the river near his own camp in Boiestown. During a conversation that takes no more than 45 minutes on a sunny August morning, five deer can be seen crossing the water no more than 200 yards away, a bald eagle can be seen flying overhead, and two salmon jump from the water, pop, just like that.

"Not bad for 45 minutes," he says. "Do you see why Ted liked this place?"

The camp was where Ted spent the most time with his two youngest children as they were growing. Edna Curtis remembers rocking John-Henry when he was six weeks old. A good-looking baby. She remembers Claudia almost as young. The kids, as they grew, trailed around after her as if she were a surrogate grandmother.

"Those kids loved me when they were little," Edna says.

She worked through the variations in Ted's personal life with adaptability. Who was there was who was there. That was her strategy. She didn't judge.

The second wife, Lee Howard, did not seem particularly charmed with the place. She didn't fish much. The third wife, Dolores, "could cast a mean line," but always seemed to be fighting with Ted. The divorce came along, and sometimes the kids would be at the camp without Dolores for their three-week visit and sometimes she still would come too. Edna handled it all. And then there was Louise.

"I was coming around the side of the house one day," Edna says, "and Ted was there with this white-haired woman and said, 'Edna, isn't this the prettiest 62-year-old woman you've ever met?'"

Edna and Louise got along. Louise brought a steadiness to the house. She knew how to let Ted run until his batteries were worn down. Dolores would charge back at him, but Louise would let his rages just fall apart on their own. Ted was Ted.

Edna and Roy and Louise and Ted would go out to eat once in a while. Edna and Louise would go shopping in Newcastle. Every year, somewhere around the end of August, everybody would go out for a joint birthday celebration. Edna's birthday was on the 18th, John-Henry's on the 26th, Ted's on the 30th. Edna would bake a four-layer chocolate cake, just huge, as part of the celebration.

The kids and Ted and fishing were not a good combination. He had no patience. He would treat the kids, no matter what their ages, the way he would treat another visitor who had trouble with the subtle dos and don'ts of this complicated sport. Why are you doing that? What do you think you're doing? Jesus syphilitic fucken Christ.

"John-Henry didn't like fishing," Clarence Curtis noticed. "At least he didn't like fishing when Ted was around."

Edna noticed a difference in the way Ted treated his two children. John-Henry, she noticed, drew most of the attention. Claudia, more often than not, was just there. She was a girl. John-Henry was the boy. Clarence noticed the same thing. Neither of the kids enjoyed fishing with their father. He was too demanding.

Edna also noticed another thing. Louise did not particularly like John-Henry.

"She thought he was spoiled," Edna says. "She said, 'That John-Henry has a bad case of the gimmes.' "

Williams's best times on the river came with men. He made friends with men in the small towns and camps, could drive along and spot someone fishing and recognize him—"There's So-and-So"—simply by the way the man cast a line. He also would import friends. Bobby Doerr came to the camp and resumed the perpetual argument about hitting theories. Curt Gowdy came. Ted Rogowski came. Fisherman guys. Not many people from Islamorada ever came (and no one from the Miramichi, not Roy, not Clarence, not W. W. Doak, ever went to Islamorada). The different spheres of his life pretty much stayed separate.

"We did go up once, Jack Brothers and myself," Millard Wells, the artist from Islamorada, says. "Ted had us up in the morning and out there. The thing I remember most . . . Ted took us back to the airport. There was some time to wait, so we all went into the restaurant for breakfast. We wanted some more coffee and the waitress wasn't coming. We were sitting behind this big partition. Ted got fed up and climbed the partition. Then he climbed back with the pot of coffee. 'Here you go, boys.' Ted would do things like that."

An annual visitor was Bud Leavitt, the sports columnist and outdoors writer for the *Bangor Daily News*. Leavitt was another big man, robust, about the same age, a guy who had graduated high school, went to work in the mill in Bangor for one day, came home covered with dirt, and showed up at the newspaper the next day looking for a job. He covered all sports, including baseball.

In 1939, Williams's first year in Boston, Leavitt was at Fenway Park. He was self-conscious, the small-town guy from the small-town paper, working the same turf as the big-timers for a weekend. He was sitting at the end of the dugout before a game when Williams spotted him.

"Hey, Bush," Williams said. "Come over here. I hear you're from Maine. I bet there's some pretty good fishing up there."

Leavitt did not know that Williams called everyone "Bush." He thought Williams was making fun of him for coming from a small town. He got mad.

"I'll come over and talk to you," he said. "But only if you ask me right and if you use my name."

Perfect.

The friendship spanned all of Williams's career and beyond. Leavitt probably knew—and took to his grave—more about Williams's inner workings than anyone. Leavitt's house in Bangor was a stop on the way up and on the way back from the Miramichi. Every summer the two men would go off somewhere to fish. Leavitt would go down to spring training, before and after Williams retired, and they would do more fishing.

"The two of them, they were like two old ladies about it all," Leavitt's daughter, Liz Polkinghorn, says. "They'd go back and forth, yipping at each other, one insult after another. They'd wear each other's clothes! You'd see Dad in a sweater one day and the next day Ted would be wearing that sweater. Or vice versa."

Mel Allen, a writer at *Yankee* magazine, went to the Miramichi with the two men in 1981 and wrote a profile. He caught the back-and-forth banter so well that Williams and Leavitt were recruited to do some fat old men commercials for Nissen Bread in New England. The commercials were back-and-forth classics, all on the lines of "What do you know about bread, Bush?"

There were strains in the relationship, one of them refusing to call the other for a stretch of time. Williams once said or did something at Leavitt's house that upset Leavitt's wife—Liz Polkinghorn doesn't remember what it was—and then sat down and wrote out an apology, saying he would never say or do whatever he said or did again. The scratches always healed, and the relationship continued until Leavitt died of cancer in 1994.

Leavitt once brought Red Smith of the *New York Times*, the dean of American sportswriters, to the Miramichi with him. Williams outlined his love of the Atlantic salmon for the two of them.

"After the salmon are spawned, they might go back down river more than 200 miles to grow up," Williams said. "Then they fight their way back to the original spot where they were bred, by instinct alone, to spawn. This gorgeous fish battles river obstructions, lawbreakers, natural predators and fishermen. It's a miracle this precious creature has lived to return around another time to spawn. The Atlantic Salmon is very, very special in my mind.

"The greatest single experience a fisherman can have is to hook an Atlantic Salmon," Williams continued. "There is nothing else in angling like it. One word tells it all—anticipation! One word—anticipation! You make five hundred, six hundred and even one thousand casts . . . you make the perfect one. Bam! Now it's the salmon and you . . . wow!"

In the summer of 1993, Louise became sick at the camp. She had not been feeling well in Florida, troubled by a bowel obstruction, but thought she could handle Canada. She knew that Ted would be going, no matter what, the annual highlight of his year, and once on the river would be there for the summer. She postponed medical treatment in Florida to be with Ted. She figured she could go to her doctors when she returned in the fall.

"She called me before she left," Evalyn Sterry, Louise's best friend, says. "It was the last time I ever talked to her. She had planted all her flowers at Citrus Hills, and they were just coming up, beautiful, and she said she almost didn't want to go to Canada. But she did, to be with Ted.

"This was not the first time she'd had an obstructed bowel. When she was living at Delray Beach, she also had a problem. She had an operation and needed a place to recuperate. I was up in Harbor Springs, Michigan, for the summer. I said, 'Louise, we've got two extra bedrooms and a bathroom. Get up here.' She stayed for two months."

When she became sick, Ted and Clarence took her to the hospital in Newcastle, where doctors looked at her problem. They suggested she be transported to Moncton, New Brunswick, for an operation. Her daughter, Barbara Kovacs, came to the camp, and Louise had the operation. She did not handle it well, slipping into a coma. Then suddenly she slipped back out. She seemed fine, her memory sharp. Everybody was relieved.

Ted and Clarence saw Louise on a Monday, and the plan was that she would come home on Tuesday. The plan never worked out. She said she felt awfully cold on that Monday, and by Tuesday her condition had changed again. She was back in a coma and was transferred instead to the intensive-care unit.

Ted and Clarence kept visiting every other day, but the news never was good. The final news came on August 10, 1993.

"Ted was out there in the middle of the river, fishing," Clarence says. "I was on the shore. My mother came out on the porch and yelled down that the hospital wanted Ted to come fast. He knew what it meant. I remember he looked so all alone. He looked so sad. He was just crying."

Williams later told friends that he was the one who had to sign the papers to have the life support systems shut down. He said Louise's daughter told him that it was his responsibility.

The funeral was held in Columbia, South Carolina. Claudia, 21, met Bobby-Jo, her 45-year-old half-sister, for the first time at the wake. Williams came into the room at the funeral parlor and boomed out some words, and Claudia saw a middle-aged woman flinch. "That's the same way I react," Claudia said in an interview in *Boston* magazine. "That must be her." And it was. Herb Hoskins, the investigator for the Antonucci business, drove up from Inverness, Florida, just to pay his respects.

Barbara Kovacs said the relationship between her mother and Ted was "like Katharine Hepburn and Spencer Tracy, a 50-year love affair." There were some similarities for sure, the couple that never wed, never finalized the deal. Lou was the one woman Williams loved. Or thought he loved. That is what he sometimes said. "The one woman who could take his shit," more than one mourner said. She put up with the infidelities and the disappearances. She rode out the storms and enjoyed the calm in between. Two marriages to other people and still she stayed. She loved *him*, there was no doubt about that.

She was mother and lover. He was Ted. There always had been the feeling between them, both spoken and unspoken, that she was going to outlive him. She would take care of him until the end. Louise dying first was not the way it was supposed to go.

"I'd say their relationship was half-mother, half-goddamn-that-son-of-a-bitch-Ted," Bill Churchman says. "I think she was the one love of his life."

Williams returned to the Miramichi with Claudia after the funeral and finished out the season. He was not in good shape emotionally or physically. He was 75 years old and suddenly seemed his age.

"One of the last times I was out with him, he lost his balance and fell in the river," Vin Swazey says. "It was sad. I helped him out and told him he was crazy to be out there in waders. The rocks are slippery. Anything can happen. He said he knew. To fish now, he'd have to go out in a boat. But you just knew that wasn't what he wanted to do."

John-Henry, 24, was with him for the drive back to Citrus Hills at the end of the 1993 season. Clarence was there to say good-bye.

"Ted would get emotional about leaving every year," Clarence says. "This time, though, was different. More emotional. There were tears in his eyes when he was leaving. He was just taking a long look at the river. I think he knew the chances were that he never would be back."

A reporter from the *Saint John Telegraph Journal* caught him before he left. There were problems with the salmon stock in the river. Commercial fishing in the salmon feeding grounds in the Atlantic, net fishing by Indians at the mouth of the river, and sportfishermen who brought fish home as food and trophies had helped deplete the numbers. Williams, grieving the loss of the one woman he loved, unsettled by his own health, spoke with emotion about the problem. He said that killing a salmon was the equivalent of murder.

"I'm going to cut my throat right here if it doesn't stop," he said. "I would almost feel as if I put a knife in my vein and bled a little bit if I ever took a salmon out of this river."

The headline in the *Sunday Bangor Daily News* was "Williams Vows to End Life to Save Miramichi Salmon." Jack Fenety of the Miramichi Salmon Association put the words into perspective.

"Ted is a John Wayne type who is the master of his own ship and steers his own course," Fenety said. "Talking about how he would kill himself for the salmon is how he wouldn't tip his hat for the fans at Boston. He's a lone eagle.

"His devotion to the Miramichi River and the Atlantic salmon is unquestionable. Ted Williams' affinity with the river and its fish borders on the spiritual."

After 1993, he never saw the river again.

16 A Changed Life

Heads turn as John Henry Williams, 21, lopes down the steps of Fenway Park's Box 54. And not just because he is six feet, five, movie-star handsome, and coming in as if he owns the place. No, the regulars are staring because the kid looks so much like The Kid, circa 1940, it's scary.

HAROLD J. BAULD, *BOSTON*, NOVEMBER 1990

The loneliness of the big house on the biggest hill on the Florida peninsula was obvious. Ted Williams came home at the end of the 1993 Atlantic salmon season, pulled down the blinds, and wrapped himself inside. The emotional hurt with the loss of Louise was compounded by a physical hurt. He had fallen down at the Miramichi, broken a couple of ribs. He didn't want to see a lot of people, do a lot of things.

One person he did see was Lewis Watkins. Watkins had something positive to show him.

"The first day he came back, I took him to the construction site," Watkins says. "We sat outside in his Chevy Suburban. He was amazed. He started crying. He said, 'Jesus Christ, I never expected anything like this.' "

The building under construction was the Ted Williams Museum, the first museum ever built in the United States for a living athlete. Sam Tamposi donated a prime hunk of Citrus Hills land right on North Citrus Hills Boulevard. The excavating company donated excavating at cost. The construction company donated construction at cost. The groundbreaking had been in July, and work had begun in September, and the opening was scheduled for February. The building was rising in a hurry.

"The museum was Ted's idea," Watkins says. "Back in 1990, maybe 1991, we were talking about presidents one day. Nixon . . . he loved Nixon. Bush. Somehow we got talking about presidential museums. Ted said he'd like to have his own museum. I said, 'Really?' He said, 'Yes.'

"It was so out of character for him, something you'd never expect him to say, that it really hit me. I said, 'This has to be something that he'd really like.' "

The conversation ultimately led to the construction. Watkins, a man with an active entrepreneurial mind, was in charge of everything. The rise of the museum was therapy for Williams. He talked every day now with Watkins, fighting the sadness of Canada, keeping busy. Watkins knew some of the sadness Williams felt.

"I talked to Louise on the phone in those three days when she was out of the coma," Watkins says. "Everything seemed fine. She wanted my wife, Mindy, and me to come up. She even had a list of things she wanted me to bring, stuff that was expensive in Canada, baby powder and certain canned goods. That was Louise. She made me smile. I was supposed to lug all this shit up through customs so she could save $20. She and Ted, they both still thought prices were back in the fifties. Ted forever was thinking that something that cost $140 would cost $39.95.

"It was all so strange. She sounded perfectly healthy. Then she was back in the coma, and then she died."

The museum was a needed positive against the negatives of the summer. Williams would tell people, "This was Lewis's idea. I told him, 'If you want to do it, do it. Just leave me out of it,' " but the truth was he wanted to know everything that was taking place. Watkins kept him informed.

The graphic artist had been introduced to the famous man by Vince Antonucci. Eventually, Williams and Watkins both were touched by Antonucci's scam. Watkins hadn't even known Williams was a baseball player when he met him. He only knew that Antonucci wanted him to paint a picture of someone.

"The first print I did in color, Ted didn't like the way the uniform hung on him," Watkins says. "He said it was 'too baggy.' I said, 'Well, that's the way it looked in the photograph,' but I did another one in black and white, pen and wash. He didn't like this one either. He said the hands were wrong on the bat, the lips had to be tighter, a bunch of things."

Watkins refused to do a third print. The hell with that. He waited a couple of weeks and brought the second print back to Williams.

"Jesus Christ, that's perfect," Williams said. "You got it."

"I knew he'd say that," Watkins says. "Because he thought he had some input, he loved it now."

The opening of the museum on February 9, 1994, was a gala Citrus County event. Watkins induced 37 Hall of Famers to come to the out-of-the-way weekend. He brought in Nashville singers (Lee Greenwood performed), movie actors (Roy Scheider was the biggest name), famous athletes from other sports (Bobby Orr of the hockey Bruins came from Boston), the Marine Corps Band, politicians and high-rollers, and thousands of common folk. The stars of the show, besides Ted, were Joe DiMaggio and Muhammad Ali. Three living legends.

"Muhammad Ali was wonderful," Watkins says. "I wasn't a big fan before he came, but he was one of the greatest people I've ever met. He came in four days early and did all kinds of advance publicity. News helicopters were following him around. I took him on a tour of the museum. He sat down and cried when he read Ted's induction speech. Ali loved Ted Williams. Ted loved Ali.

"They had dinner together one of those nights at Andre's. Just Ali, Ted, myself, and Howard Bingham, Ali's friend and photographer. Ted had the greatest time. They must have talked for two and a half, three hours. Talked about everything. I remember Ted questioning Ali about Louis Farakhan. Ali said Farakhan was 'too radical.' Ted had studied up. He had all kinds of questions about boxing. Howard Bingham said, at the end of the night, that this was the most Ali had talked to anyone in the past three years."

"You know what Muhammad Ali said to me?" Williams said. "He said, 'Ted, all I want to do for the rest of my life is make people feel good.' That's the nicest thing I ever heard."

DiMaggio was his prickly self. He refused to share his limousine with any other Hall of Famers for the breakfast on the day of the opening, then sat in the limo with his lawyers and confidants for 40 minutes at the front door of the restaurant deciding whether or not to go in while everyone was forced to walk around the car. When the other Hall of Famers left for the ceremony, he was late, so late that Williams left before him.

"It was all his lawyers," Watkins says. "They wanted him to have the grand entrance. His limo pulled up as we were getting out. There were

6,000 people in the tent, plus another 15,000 gathered outside. I could hear Joe telling the lawyers, 'No, this is Ted's day, I've got to go in before him.' He came hurrying up. Ted put his arm around him and said, 'Joe, let's walk over here.' They went in front of the crowd outside the tent. Ted punched Joe with his elbow and said, 'Wave at the people. They came here to see us.' They both waved, Joe DiMaggio and Ted Williams."

The event went fine. Williams talked, light and easy. ("Dominic DiMaggio is here. We had perfect communication when I played left and he played center. He said, 'I've got it,' and I said, 'You take it.' Worked all the time.") Joe DiMaggio talked. Ali talked. The monies raised and the services donated ensured that the museum already was paid off on the day it was opened.

Ali stayed so long signing autographs that a side of the tent had to be taken down, his car backed right to his seat to take him away. Williams and DiMaggio exited together, guarded by 17 sheriff's deputies, and went back to the house on the hill. They were joined by Stan Musial, and the three of them talked into the night. The Splinter, the Clipper, and the Man. It might have been the longest single stretch of conversation between Williams and DiMaggio in their entire lives. It definitely was the first time one had visited the other's house.

"The ceremony the next year was just as big, maybe bigger," Watkins says. "George Bush came. We had a flyover, two Harrier jets. We had the secretary of the Navy, the commandant of the Marine Corps. Ted was promoted to colonel . . . should have been made a fucken general, that's what I wanted, but it didn't work out. Willie Mays was there. Ty Cobb's son. Babe Ruth's daughter . . . Bob Costas, Michael Bolton."

There was one difference.

The star of the show could not see much of what happened at the second ceremony.

Ten days after the opening of the Ted Williams Museum, he suffered a stroke that could have killed him. His life had been changed forever.

A woman named Lynette Simon, a contemporary of Louise, had moved into the big house in the months before the museum opened. Williams was almost apologetic about the move. Was this too soon after the death of Louise? Was this inappropriate? He asked Watkins. The artist said that whatever a 75-year-old man did in this situation was just fine.

Williams asked if Watkins and his wife would go on double dates with the new couple, the same as they did when Louise was alive. Watkins said sure.

"Ted was almost courtly with Lynette Simon," Watkins says. "He'd open her car door, pull out her chair. She was the same with him, kind of prissy. It was fun to watch. They were like two high school kids."

Simon had been around the Islamorada scene, a friend of both Louise and Williams. The courtliness obviously worked. She left her home in Lakeland, Florida, and settled into the big house. She probably saved Williams's life.

"Ted was taking a hot shower," Watkins says. "He loved hot showers. He had a stroke as he came out. He fell to the floor. If Lynette hadn't been there, he probably would have stayed on that floor for a day, day and a half, until someone—probably me—came to the house. There's no telling what kind of damage could have happened. Lynette found him right away and called me and called 911."

She also called Rich Eschen, a local friend who had been helping Williams sort out the aftermath from the Vince Antonucci memorabilia business. Eschen and his son hurried to the big house. They found Ted on the floor, conscious, but unable to move.

"I think I can move," Williams said, "but I just don't want to."

"Stay right there," Eschen said. "We'll get an ambulance."

This was not the first stroke Williams had suffered. In December 1991, while he was having dinner at a Bennigan's in Clearwater, Florida, with his secretary, Stacia Gerow, and Jimmy O'Loughlin and O'Loughlin's wife Beverly, plus their daughter April, he complained of a headache and said that his eyes weren't working right.

"I can see you," he said to April.

"But I can't see you," he said to Beverly, who was sitting right next to her daughter.

He passed off the situation as momentary discomfort, part of the ir-regularities of growing older. Beverly wasn't so sure of the diagnosis. When she went back to the hotel room with her husband, she said, "Something's wrong with Ted." Jimmy agreed. She called Stacia's house at eight in the morning, looking for Williams.

"He's gone," Stacia said. "He left at five."

The trip back to Citrus Hills took about two hours. Williams drove his Suburban through an altered landscape. His peripheral vision was gone. He worried himself when he clipped a traffic cone that he hadn't even seen. The exceptional eyesight that other people said was such a secret to his success—and he always downplayed—was now a subject to be discussed in the past tense.

"He got back and saw his doctor," Beverly says. "That's when he learned he'd had a stroke. Twenty-five percent of his vision was gone."

Doctors now determined that he also had suffered a second stroke early in 1992. These first two strokes had given him pause but hardly altered his life. He still was able to travel. Even though he was unsteady and fell on the rocks at the Miramichi, he still fished, read, took walks, was active. A few weeks before the museum opened, at a fund-raiser for a similar museum for Bob Feller, he'd picked a baseball off the ground, thrown it into the air, and hit it with a bat.

This third stroke was a very different business from the previous two. Now he was missing 75 percent of his vision. His peripheral vision was totally gone. He described looking through a tunnel. He could only see people directly in front of him. The blood clot that had traveled from his heart to the right side of his brain had numbed the left side of his body. His balance was affected. Walking was a problem. The baseball that he hit at the Bob Feller fund-raiser was the last baseball he ever would hit.

"I had my tee shirt and my shorts on the bed, and I started to reach for my shorts," he said in a 1996 issue of *Sports Illustrated*, describing the moment the stroke hit after he left the hot shower. "Jeez, I got down on my knees, then I'm lying on the bed and I couldn't move. Finally I got my shorts, crawled and got my shirt. But I couldn't do anything else."

He was taken to Shands Teaching Hospital in Gainesville, Florida. Hospital spokesman Daniel Moore characterized the stroke as "minor," but the effects were far from minor. The 75-year-old Williams stayed in the hospital for nine days, then was taken to a rehabilitation hospital to learn how to walk again. He would need nursing care for the rest of his life.

Five months after Lynette Simon found him on the floor, he sat down with the *Boston Globe*'s Dan Shaughnessy. A third- or fourth-generation successor to the columnist seat of Harold Kaese, Shaughnessy had an entirely different relationship with Williams than Kaese ever did. Shaughnessy, 40 years old, never had seen Williams play, certainly never had seen the angry side. Williams was the loud and lovable legend, an aging wonder, a line of jaw-dropping statistics in the record book. A great guy.

In 1993 Shaughnessy's eight-year-old daughter, Kate, had contracted leukemia. The day the diagnosis was made Shaughnessy was supposed to go to a business meeting with Williams's son, John-Henry. Shaughnessy called from the hospital room at the Dana-Farber Cancer Institute to cancel, explaining why. Ten minutes later the phone in the room rang, and a large voice asked for Kate.

"You're going to beat this thing," Ted Williams boomed. "You're going to be okay."

Now the cancer was in remission, doing exactly what Williams had predicted. Williams had his own thing to beat.

"If there was ever a candidate for [a stroke], it was me," he told Shaughnessy. "That museum was a big project . . . and I had some business things that were preying on me and I was just trying to do too much. They want me to go to so many places.

"I had too much going on and too many stresses and worries and stuff. It was harder as I got older, because no matter what, there were more demands on me."

His vision probably wasn't going to return. The doctors had told him that. He was adjusting to seeing through the tunnel. He was going to speech therapy, which really was reading therapy. The therapist magnified the daily sports pages, and Williams was learning how to move his head to read the words, not move his eyes. It was pretty certain he never again would drive a car.

Other parts of his body were returning slowly. Therapy was working here. He had gone from a wheelchair to a walker to a cane. The hardest part of walking was that he couldn't see where he was going very well. The left side of his body had improved—his left arm was stronger than ever due to the workouts—but sometimes it would feel "sleepy." The tips of his fingers often felt strange.

He wasn't complaining.

"Jesus," he said, shaking his head, "I see people every day . . . Holy Jesus . . . that have it real tough."

The Red Sox had sent down a 46-inch television, plus a dish for the satellite, so he still could watch games. He knew about the different players, knew swings and pitching strategies, also knew the Red Sox were not doing very well. He hungered for behind-the-scenes stuff. What was going to happen next?

"I hope they don't fire [manager] Butch Hobson," he said. "But they're really giving him a rough time up there, aren't they?"

"I'm afraid I'm one of the ones giving him the rough time," Shaughnessy admitted.

Williams laughed.

The sports-page battles could have happened a billion years ago. Shaughnessy was a tough critic of the Boston sports scene and its central figures. He had written a book about the history of Red Sox failure, *The Curse of the Bambino*, in 1990. The title, suggested by his editor at E. P. Dutton, had jumped into popular culture, a whisper that now accompanied every bouncing ground ball to every Red Sox middle infielder. Long ago, no doubt at all, Shaughnessy and Williams would have tangled. Now they danced lightly.

Williams said, "They say I'm still all there in my brain . . . but I don't know about that." He laughed again. His spirits were good on this day. He described a recent dream he had—a baseball dream—that was almost mystical.

"I was laying there and I was having a lousy night," he said. "I was kind of resting and then I started to dream. Randy Johnson was pitching. I said, 'Jeez, I can't hit him. I just had a stroke and I'm not even seeing very good.' But they kept teasing me and I thought, 'Aw, Christ.'

"So I started to get up there and he was throwing a couple and I'm saying, 'Jeez, he's got pretty good stuff.' So I said to myself, 'I'm not going to try to pull him.' That's the first thing I said in my dream. 'I'm not going to try to pull him. I'm going to try and hit one hard through the middle.'

"He threw one pitch and it was a ball. I seen his speed. He threw another one for a strike. He threw another one and it was right there and I just punched it through the middle."

Late in the interview, Shaughnessy asked an obvious question that never had been answered in all the stories, all the words that had been written about Williams: why did the famous man hit lefthanded? He was righthanded in everything else that he did. He fished righthanded, wrote his name righthanded, opened doors righthanded. Why did he change for this one act that, as he would say, "made a little history"?

"I just did," he said. "Why, I don't know."

"Nobody ever told you to?" another voice asked.

"No. I just did it by myself."

The second voice belonged to John-Henry Williams. The interview was held in the office of Grand-Slam Marketing, which now was located in a strip mall on the edge of Citrus Hills. John-Henry was in charge. He was the president of Grand-Slam Marketing, and his girlfriend, Anita Lovely, was the vice president, and all operations now were run out of Hernando,'Florida.

This was the biggest poststroke change of all in Ted Williams's life. John-Henry had arrived and was in charge of everything.

An anecdote by Armand LaMontagne, an artist from Scituate, Rhode Island, described the relationship between strong and active men and their children.

In 1984 LaMontagne was commissioned by Tom Yawkey's widow, Jean, to carve a life-sized wooden statue of Williams for the Baseball Hall of Fame. He had done a similar statue of Babe Ruth a year earlier for the Hall and Mrs. Yawkey thought Williams should be standing right there with the Babe.

The finished product was unveiled at Cooperstown in 1985. Williams was in attendance, his first trip back since he was enshrined. He was delighted. His likeness had been carved from a single 1,400-pound piece of laminated basswood, everything true to scale, even the tiniest details down to the buttons and folds in Williams's shirt.

LaMontagne followed with similar sculptures of Boston icons Larry Bird, Bobby Orr, and Harry Agganis. He did a second sculpture of Williams the fisherman, waders and vest, fish and all. LaMontagne became known as an artist who captured the strength and spirit of strong men.

One of his commissions was a large oil painting of General George S. Patton for the Patton Museum in Fort Knox, Kentucky. Before the public unveiling, Patton's 80-year-old daughter had a private showing. She never had looked at the work in progress. LaMontagne was worried. What would she think of the final result?

The old woman appeared at the museum at the appointed time. She stood in front of the painting and the large cloth was removed. Her father stood in front of her.

She said nothing.

She didn't move.

She said nothing.

She didn't move.

Finally, after the longest time, she sat down on a nearby bench. Her eyes had never left the painting. She began to talk.

"Now," she said, eyes never leaving the painting, "you finally have to listen to me. . . ."

LaMontagne saw similarities with the situation that had developed with his earlier client. The stroke kept Ted Williams in one place. He had to listen to his children now.

W illiams's relationships with his children—first Bobby-Jo, then John-Henry and Claudia—had been as complicated as his relationships with his wives. He had no patience for the job of fatherhood. An autograph and a few questions about "what position you play" might work for other people's kids but did not work here.

A friend once said, "You don't argue with Ted Williams, he just reads you out." That was doubled if you were his kid. He played the role of the divorced father well enough, sent the checks and made some big moments and spent more time with his kids than most people thought he did (weeks in the summer, assorted trips), but Williams was not good at the day-to-day combat of normal living. He was strict and foreboding, intractable. If other people—pretty much everyone around him—jumped when he shouted, why wouldn't his own kids jump? He pretty much became disinterested, lost heart for the task, when they didn't.

Bobby-Jo was a first example.

"I always thought Barbara and her father, once we were married, had a relationship of keeping in touch, rather than as a father and daughter," Steve Tomasco, Bobby-Jo's first husband, says. "Not a family relationship. 'How's your weight?' 'How are the kids doing?' Everything was kept at a certain level. Ted and Barbara would never get deep down to the real issues."

Bobby-Jo's problems had continued. The teenage marriage to Tomasco lasted for five turbulent years. He describes a horror of infidelities, drug abuse, second chances, and mental institutions. Bobby-Jo had come out of the Institute at Pennsylvania Hospital with a liking for prescription medications, Tomasco claims. When upset, she would take the pills. She was upset a lot.

Two daughters, Dawn and Sherri, arriving in quick succession, complicated the situation. Williams had paid for a three-month computer course for Tomasco, and the young husband was in the workforce, trying to start out with his young family. This was not easy. He always had to be worried what his young wife was doing at home.

On more than one occasion, he says, there was another man involved. She ran away to New York with a neighbor, a drug-culture character, came back, ran away again with the neighbor to Florida, then came back when the neighbor became abusive. She fell for the man at the 7-Eleven, for another neighbor, for a succession of someone elses, he says. Tomasco kept trying to restart the family situation. It kept falling apart.

"No matter what she had, it never was enough," Tomasco says. "Barbara had no patience. She always wanted things right now. She wanted a house, wanted a new car . . . we were just starting out. It takes time to get those things. She'd never understand."

Her impatience often involved her father, whom she called "Daddy." She would call Daddy to get things. That was a basic part of their relationship. She would ask; he would give.

"He'd complain about it every time, probably deliver a 20-minute lecture," Tomasco says. "But in the end, he'd give her what she wanted. That was the way it always went."

Williams gave her money to have plastic surgery to repair the long scars, wrist to elbow, on the insides of both arms. He gave her money to help buy a car. He set up accounts at Sears, where she could buy at a discount. He was happy about none of it.

The Williams temper was not hidden from his son-in-law. Tomasco saw Williams, upset with a phone ringing in the background while he tried to talk, throw the phone against a wall. He saw Williams destroy an air conditioner in anger. He heard the bad words, "like a movie, some Chevy Chase movie, where they just string together 20 swear words in a row." Tomasco also saw the anger in his wife. Bobby-Jo also used the words. Bobby-Jo also threw things . . . at her husband.

"Knives, plates, anything," Tomasco says.

In the late stages of the marriage, the couple lived in an apartment in Devon, outside Philadelphia. Tomasco was starting to succeed in the computer business, working for a firm in nearby King of Prussia. Bobby-Jo, on a particular day, wanted him to come home for lunch. He said he had too much work, couldn't leave. She said if he didn't come she was going to take a fistful of pills and kill herself.

"So I rush to the house," Tomasco says. "I go in the living room and my daughters are crying and she's knocked out on the floor. I called the hospital and she was committed. She was in the hospital for three or four months, electric shock, the whole treatment."

Tomasco hadn't brought the couple's troubles to Williams in the past. He didn't know how much Williams knew, didn't know what Bobby-Jo had told him. Had Bobby-Jo told Williams that her husband was at fault? Tomasco didn't know. Just thinking about telling his father-in-law some of the things that had happened, he envisioned "Ted's head just getting redder and redder, blowing up like a balloon." The son-in-law worried what would happen with the explosion.

This time he called. He explained the situation.

"Ted sent his wife, Dolores, up as an emissary," Tomasco says. "Her message basically was, 'Ted can't be responsible for all of the medical bills and all that's going on.' I wound up placing my two daughters in a foster home for the four months. There wasn't anything I could do. I had to work to pay the bills, so I couldn't stay home with the kids."

When the marriage broke up, according to Tomasco, after one more infidelity, one more guy, Bobby-Jo took the girls to Florida. Tomasco, head spinning, tried to put his life back together. He would hear from Bobby-Jo from time to time, often late at night, wee hours in the morning, drink in her voice. She seemed to move from man to man, place to place. He never could keep track.

"After we were divorced, it's funny, but things got much better for her financially," Tomasco says. "I understand Ted started giving her $1,800 a month, eventually bumped it up to $2,500–$3,000 before the kids were grown."

Tomasco's oldest daughter, Dawn, now with two kids of her own, says that Williams was involved with her mother's life and her life and her sister's life as a child in those moving-around years. She remembers calls, no matter where they lived, every Sunday morning at seven o'clock, the two girls and Bobby-Jo waiting around the phone. She remembers vacations in Islamorada, the two girls living with Ted and Louise and a couple of Louise's kids or grandchildren for a month. She remembers Ted Williams's Famous Eggs, cooked for about three seconds, served almost raw, very hard to eat. The kids still would ask for seconds. Her grandfather was a presence.

"He'd walk into a room and he'd command respect," Dawn says. "It was 'Yes, sir,' and 'No, sir.' He'd always be checking our fingernails. When we got older, it was 'How's your weight?' 'How long is your hair?' 'Where'd you get that nose?' I always answered, 'I got that nose from you, Grandpa.' He'd say, 'Goddamn it, you sure did.' "

John-Henry and McCarthy and Brian O'Connor, now serving as the Polaroid host. O'Connor looked at his friend, still surrounded, and didn't like what he saw.

"His health wasn't good," O'Connor says. "I hadn't seen him for a couple of years and was surprised at how much he had slipped. His talk was only baseball. He got very tired."

"It was just a great weekend for him, though," Dan Shaughnessy says. "I was there when he met Matt Damon, the actor. Matt Damon's just in awe. He's from Brookline. His dad's a baseball coach. He tells Ted he grew up reading his book on hitting. Ted says, 'You did, huh? What's the biggest lesson in the book?' Damon says, 'Get a good pitch to hit.' Ted's face just lit up.

"He got tired, but when you talked to him about baseball . . . he was almost dozing when I asked him about something the coaches had told my son. They'd said he should be a little pigeon-toed at the plate. I asked Ted. Why pigeon-toed? Here he was, almost asleep, and bang, he was standing up, going into the stance, talking a mile a minute."

The only lingering question was the cap.

What about the cap? Hitter.net. What really happened?

"We had the two hats, the Red Sox hat and the Hitter.net hat," Dave McCarthy says. "We're in the tunnel. There was some debate about which hat to wear. John-Henry asked me what I thought. I'm thinking, he wears the Boston hat, but I say, it's John-Henry's decision.

"John-Henry talks to a couple more people about it. I don't know how he decided. Maybe being at NASCAR the day before, where everyone is wearing a hat advertising something, had something to do with it. I don't know what happened. Except Ted wears the Hitter.net hat.

"I honestly don't think John-Henry had an idea what the ramifications would be. I didn't have any idea either."

A public decision. A public mistake.

"When John-Henry was on a trip, Ted always wore the Hitter.net garbage," John Gard, who was the nurse on the All-Star trip, says. "When Ted came just with me, I got him to wear other stuff. He had a bunch of other hats and shirts, Red Sox logos. When we went to the World Series in Atlanta, John-Henry wasn't along. Probably figured there wasn't any money in it. Ted wore the Red Sox cap."

The crowd in Atlanta cheered as loudly as the crowd at Fenway had. The ovation for hometown hero Hank Aaron was paltry compared to the

Bobby-Jo eventually remarried in 1976, after meeting ASCAP copyright enforcer Mark Ferrell in a Fort Lauderdale bowling league. They eventually moved to Nashville when her kids were nearly grown. Tomasco eventually remarried. He has had little contact with his daughters since they headed to Florida with Bobby-Jo, but "four or five years ago" met with his youngest daughter, Sherri Mosley, in Nashville.

He asked what her mother had told her about him. Sherri said Bobby-Jo told the girls Tomasco had abandoned them, that he was in and out of mental institutions, and that he was crazy. Tomasco took a deep breath. He told his daughter that was not exactly the way it happened. He told his story.

"Thinking back, I liked Ted Williams," Tomasco says. "He never said anything bad to me. He didn't like the fact that Barbara and I both smoked. He didn't like the beard I had at the time. But he was all right. Every time one of the girls' birthdays arrived, when the girls were young, a big box from Sears would arrive filled with little dresses. He gave me a nice eight-track player for Christmas one year.

"I had some enjoyable times with Ted Williams. More than I had with his daughter."

Williams's youngest daughter, Claudia, 25 years younger than Bobby-Jo, younger even than Bobby-Jo's children, Ted's grandchildren, was determined to avoid the pitfalls of her older half-sister. She had heard the stories about Bobby-Jo's troubled teenage years, and by the time she was 16 she was living in France. She didn't want any part of being the famous man's daughter. She wanted a father, not the famous Ted Williams.

"I never heard him say a good thing about Bobby-Jo," Claudia said in a September 2002 article in *Boston* magazine by James Burnett and Doug Most. "And that scared me, because I didn't want him to talk about me like that."

The story Claudia tells often is about applying to Middlebury College. The prestigious Vermont school, which she wanted to attend, rejected her one, two, three times. Williams finally heard about all this. He made a call. The school now was more than ready to accept her. She wouldn't go.

"If I wasn't good enough to be admitted before I was Ted Williams's daughter," she says, "then why am I suddenly good enough now that I am Ted Williams's daughter? I wouldn't want to go to that kind of place."

She went to Springfield (Massachusetts) College instead, returning after graduation to Europe, where she eventually taught English in Germany. She was an athlete on her own, a triathlete, tall and muscular, touched by the genes of both her father and her mother. She was anonymous in Europe. Herself.

Claudia's relationship with Williams, at best, was a version of the same superficial dance that Bobby-Jo had experienced. Plus, Claudia had the impediment of her brother, three years older.

The fact was clear to anyone who saw the dynamic in action—Ted with the two children from his third wife, Dolores—that John-Henry was the favored figure. He was the boy. Williams had the old-world, old-time approach to his children. The son was the successor to the family name, front and center, daughters in the background. Everyone knew the rules. Claudia knew the rules. Her full first name could have been "And Claudia." John-Henry . . . And Claudia.

"I never really knew my father," Claudia says. "The way I know him best is through John-Henry. My brother's my link. He's the one who knows all the things I want to know. He's the one who can tell me."

Claudia would come back to the United States in 1996, encouraged by her brother, leaving Germany and settling in St. Petersburg, 60 miles to the south, close enough to see her father, far enough away to be free. Bobby-Jo and Mark would come down in 1999, driving a mobile home, eventually building a house less than a mile from the big house.

As for John-Henry . . . John-Henry was different. He was the boy.

The stories about him often said that he looked like his father, an eerie reminder of long-ago glories, but the truth was that John-Henry Williams looked more like his mother. Dolores Williams's modeling career was driven by her resemblance to Jacqueline Kennedy, and her son could have been Jacqueline Kennedy's son. He looked very much like John Kennedy Jr., the ill-fated publisher of *George* magazine, classically handsome, almost pretty. Both Bobby-Jo and Claudia looked much more like Ted.

"I always would hear about John-Henry's resemblance to Ted, but I told people they should have seen Dolores's brother, John," Mary Jane Ryan, a Red Sox employee who grew up near the Wettach family in Westminster, Vermont, says. "That man was a hunk. John-Henry looks just like Dolores's brother."

John-Henry had edged into public perceptions of Ted's life when he was 13 years old. First at the 1982 Old-Timers' Game at Fenway, when he appeared as the batboy and Ted made a shoestring catch off Mike

Andrews, then at Red Sox spring training in Winter Haven, Florida, he was an instant curiosity. Ted Williams, 63 years old, had a teenage son? People had forgotten the one-year-old who sometimes had been around the dugout when Ted managed the Washington Senators.

Since the divorce in 1972, when John-Henry was four, Dolores pretty much had kept Claudia and him away from professional baseball and the celebrity life that she found distasteful and false. When he was 13, she finally allowed him to edge into his father's public glow.

The glow was certainly a different existence. People would look at the son almost the same way they looked at the father. What would it be like to be Ted Williams? What would it be like to be his son? Different.

"We asked him one day to come with my family to Epcot Center," Michelle Orlando MacIntyre says. "He said he wanted to go, but he couldn't. His father wouldn't let him. We asked why. John-Henry said, 'Because he's afraid I'd be kidnapped.' "

MacIntyre was the granddaughter of clubhouse man Vinnie Orlando and was approximately the same age as John-Henry. She and her cousin, Denise, befriended him early in spring training. They all hung around together, watching the baseball, hitting when the batting cages were open, swimming at the pool . . . going to Epcot Center.

"My grandmother convinced Ted to let John-Henry go," Michelle says. "I was decided to be all right for John-Henry by Ted. Because I was Vinnie's granddaughter, I was 'Ted Williams Approved.' "

Michelle and John-Henry wound up with innocent, first-love crushes on each other, a tale she describes in a yet-unpublished children's book. She wondered at his life. He lived on a farm in Vermont, and his mother made clothes for him, and his father, who sometimes bought clothes for him, always bought them too large. He had been places, seen things, had lived with a family in France on an exchange program. He had been to the Amazon River on one of those Outward Bound kind of trips. His mother had thought it was safe because Bill Cosby's son was going too.

"What nationality are you?" Michelle asked.

"I'm a Heinz 57," John-Henry replied. "I'm a mix."

He seemed naive sometimes, not knowing a lot of things that most kids knew. He seemed experienced at other times, knowing things that most kids didn't know. He was a practical joker, funny. He was different, coming from a far different life than most kids have.

"I thought he was great," Michelle Orlando MacIntyre says. "I will love him forever."

"I remember him being around," former batboy George Sullivan, the Red Sox PR man at the time, says. "One memory in particular. Ted was in my office for something, and John-Henry came running in with two baseballs. He said a guy outside wanted Ted to sign the balls.

"Ted didn't want to do it. John-Henry pleaded. Ted said, 'No.' I got involved. I said, 'How about this? Tell the guy if he writes out a check for $25 for the Jimmy Fund for each ball, your father will sign. Is that all right?' Ted agreed. John-Henry came back with the checks. Ted signed.

"I remember John-Henry was real proud of himself for the deal. He'd made the Jimmy Fund some money. I think now . . . what did I do? Did I get him started in the autograph business?"

Ted Williams's son.

What would it be like to be Ted Williams's son?

By the time John-Henry was four, Claudia newly born, his parents had split. Dolores took the kids to the rented house on the other side of Islamorada. Louise eventually moved in with Ted in the house on the bay. The buffer of a stepmother was established.

"Louise was not nice to those kids," Jack Brothers's son, Frankie, says. "She would be mean to them. She didn't do it when Ted was around, but she did it other times. I felt sad for them. I liked John-Henry when he was young. He was a good kid."

Both John-Henry and Claudia started their education at Island Christian School in Islamorada, a private school started by Reverend Tony Hammond. John-Henry went through fourth grade in the school. Reverend Hammond, a conch, a native, one of those kids who grew up searching for Ted Williams's trophies in the aftermath of Hurricane Donna, remembers Ted at events. Never at church on Sunday, but at events at the school. And games.

"John-Henry was a good athlete," Reverend Hammond says. "He was the biggest kid in the class, and he carried himself well. I remember thinking that he was going to be something, that this was what an athlete looked like as a kid."

After John-Henry finished fourth grade, Dolores moved back to Vermont, taking the kids. They lived on the 60-acre farm in Putney. The farm was at the base of a mountain with a view of another mountain. Dolores's parents lived in the neighboring house, their door open, two grandparents active every day in raising their grandchildren.

Chickens and farm animals roamed the property. Dolores kept her high heels on top of a grand piano in case any of the chickens sneaked into the living room and starting looking for a leather lunch. The house was large and rustic. The portrait of Dolores from Islamorada hung on one end of the wall, a baseball portrait of Ted at the other end.

Ted was still a part of the conversation, even if he was not part of the marriage.

"There was a big brick wall around the house," Mary Jane Corea says. "Dolores said she had built it herself. I said, 'You built this wall yourself? How did you ever do it?' Dolores said, 'It's easy. Anybody could do it if they've ever been married to Ted Williams. It's a Frustration Wall.' "

Corea, her daughter Joanne, and her sister Ruth, Johnny Pesky's wife, visited the farm a couple of times in later years. They had become friends first with John-Henry at spring training, then with Dolores. Corea got a kick out of Dolores. Dolores would stop the car in the middle of the road on the way to a restaurant, open the windows, and say, "I love that smell." The smell was from a skunk. Dolores would say anything.

"She took Joanne's wallet and opened it," Mary Jane says. "Joanne said, 'What are you doing?' Dolores said, 'I want to see your pictures. Is that all right?' Joanne said, 'Fine.' "

The first picture showed a young man.

"Who's that?" Dolores asked.

"That's my boyfriend," Joanne said.

"Lose him," Dolores said with authority.

Next picture. Another young man.

"Who's that?"

"That's my brother."

"He's cute."

Next picture. An older man.

"Who is that! Now we've got something! He's really good-looking!"

"That's my father."

Dolores looked at Mary Jane, the wife of the good-looking man. Dolores looked hard.

"Are you still married?" Dolores asked.

"Yes, we are," Mary Jane said.

Dolores shook her head.

"And to think I kept my body so good-looking for Ted Williams," Dolores said. "And he still left me."

"She didn't go so far as to call me a fat little bastard, but she just about did," Mary Jane says. "I laughed. She's right. I am a fat little bastard. My husband laughed when I told him."

Dolores was protective with her kids. There was no television in the house. She monitored the news from the outside world on the radio, telling John-Henry and Claudia what she thought they should know. They had chores. They had meals served from two antique stoves. They had basic farm life. Dolores wanted them to enjoy the security of an insulated, rural cocoon, the same cocoon she had known as a child.

"You think about it, John-Henry grew up in about as different a life as possible from his father's life," Mary Jane says. "When John-Henry came out to see his father, he was in this celebrity world. Then he would go back to the mountain. That had to be hard. I think it would be sad to go back to the mountain."

For high school, he attended Vermont Academy, a blueblood prep school about eight miles from the house. For the first two years, he was one of the 70 day students, commuting from the farm. For the second two years he was one of the 180 boarding students.

"He was a kid who wanted to please," former headmaster Bob Long says. "He seemed more at ease with the adults in the community than he did with the kids. He wasn't a kid who was in the corner being picked on, but he also wasn't a leader of the pack. He was somewhere in the second half. I remember he did want to be an athlete, but he just didn't have the skills."

Both his mother and his father were noticed during his four years at the school. Ted mostly would just appear. There was no advance notice. He would show up to visit a couple times a year, usually toward the end of the schoolday, almost an apparition from the great outside of hustle and bustle. He would say little to the people at the school, just appear to visit his son.

"The coach of the JV baseball team was an older man, Francis Parkman, a descendant of the famous Francis Parkman who wrote about the West," Long says. "Parkie was not really a coach. He mostly knew how to line up nine people without anyone hurting themselves.

"One day, a JV game, Vermont in April, snowing and blowing, nobody watching, Ted shows up. Parkie was just beside himself. Here he's running the baseball team and the Thumper himself is watching. Ted Williams definitely left a lasting impression on Mr. Francis Parkman."

Dolores made a noisier impression.

"She would fly off the handle periodically about something that bothered her at the school," Long says. "She said that Claudia never would go to the school (and Claudia didn't), but she did keep John-Henry there for the whole four years. She always seemed troubled to me. There was a look to her face, her eyes. She must have been in her fifties then. I heard she was a beautiful woman once in a time. And you could see it was there. But she was always so tortured. Something always was wrong."

One visit came when something definitely was wrong. Dolores arrived at Long's office with John-Henry and a large bag of coins. A few days earlier the money box in a first-generation video game had been robbed, an estimated $150 now missing. Theft was a major offense, cause for immediate expulsion. An investigation had found nothing.

Dolores discovered the bag of coins in John-Henry's possession. She quizzed him and brought him and the coins to the office. John-Henry apologized.

"This presented quite a dilemma," Long says. "The rule was automatic expulsion. Here was John-Henry, though, with the coins and the apology. He's there because his mother made him come, not because he wanted to be there. What do I do? I remember there was considerable debate among the staff. We decided on some form of punishment—I forget what it was—but we let him stay."

In his senior year, John-Henry was burned badly in an odd accident. A cat had died on the farm, and John-Henry tried to burn the corpse, as he had seen his grandfather do with other dead animals. He put the cat in a 55-gallon metal drum his grandfather used for animal cremations, poured a flammable liquid on top, and lit a match. The fumes ignited instantly, burning him on the arms and chest. He wound up in Boston at the Shriners Burns Institute.

For a number of weeks, recuperating, he lived with Johnny and Ruth Pesky in suburban Lynn. Sherm Feller, the Red Sox public address announcer, would shuttle him back and forth to the hospital for treatments. Michelle Orlando MacIntyre was one of his visitors at the hospital a few days after the accident first happened.

"He was crying," she says. "He has a voice that sometimes can sound so sad. Like the world's coming to an end, like the whole world is against him, like everybody's abandoning him. He showed me the scars on his chest. Just awful."

Recovered from the burns, self-conscious about the scars, he returned to Vermont Academy, made up his work, and graduated. Ted and Louise were at the ceremony. John-Henry was off to Bates College in Lewiston, Maine.

"Ted and John-Henry had looked at Bowdoin the day before they came here to visit," Chick Leahy, the former Bates baseball coach, says. "At Bowdoin, there was a big fuss, reporters from the local newspaper, pictures. People here were wondering what to do. I said, 'Do nothing. Just let them come and look at the college.' "

Ted became involved in the process of selecting a school. His greatest regret was not having a college education. The one place he ever seemed intimidated, almost in awe, was in the presence of a sharp, educated mind. How many times did he lament the fact that Bobby-Jo didn't go to college? Education, that was the ticket for the big ride.

The search for a school for John-Henry had narrowed down to a handful of small, semi-elite New England private colleges. Babson in Wellesley, Massachusetts, had been rejected after Ted spotted some lascivious writings on a bulletin board. Bowdoin . . . Bates . . . they had the extra attraction of being in Maine, where Bud Leavitt and other friends lived, close enough to give help to a college freshman. Close to Vermont and the farm. Bowdoin . . . Bates . . . the low-key approach worked.

The admissions director at Vermont Academy was surprised John-Henry was admitted to Bates, but figured Ted Williams's son was Ted Williams's son. That must have counted for something in the selection process. John-Henry enrolled in September and appeared for baseball tryouts.

"I told Ted and John-Henry during the visit that we have open two-week tryouts in the field house," Chick Leahy says. "I also told them there would be a cut."

Leahy had called Vermont Academy after John-Henry was admitted and already knew that he was not getting the Second Coming of Ted Williams. The tryouts reinforced that idea. Bates was a Division III school, low on the NCAA food chain, but neophytes did not play. The kids were still high school standouts, had played three or four years of American Legion baseball, had played on town teams throughout New England. John-Henry had done none of that, and it showed.

A vacation interrupted the two-week tryouts, and Ted came to pick up his son. John-Henry asked if he and his father could use the field house for practice. Leahy fed the pitching machine and watched.

"Ted was very good with his son," Leahy says. "He didn't shout. He just gave tips. Keep your head up. He wasn't pushy at all."

"How long have you been the coach here?" Ted asked while John-Henry showered.

"Thirty-four years," Leahy said.

"Wow."

The two men talked for a while about hitting theories and about the history of the field house—"We used to hit at a place like this at Harvard when I was with the Red Sox," Ted said—and then the father collected his son and went home. A few days after vacation, never having left the field house, John-Henry was cut. He wasn't close to making the roster.

"I told him what I tell all the freshmen I cut, that he should go play more baseball and come back and take another crack at it if that was what he really wanted to do," Leahy says. "I said the seniors would be moving on and spots would open and he should just say, 'Next year I'll show you some stuff.'

"It never happened. John did not have a good year academically and was gone from Bates."

The next stop was the University of Maine at Orono. This was the closest facsimile to a college baseball powerhouse in New England, a Division I school that had sent six teams to the College World Series. Again, John-Henry tried out. This time the coach was Ted Williams's friend.

John Winkin had worked for 15 years at the Ted Williams Camp in Lakeville. He had been in charge of the two-week clinic at the end of every year for the best players. He loved Williams. They had talked in the night at the camp about everything, even Williams's failed marriages and his ineffectual attempts at parenthood. They had watched Red Sox games together. He wanted, very much, for Williams's kid to succeed.

This did not happen.

"We had tryouts in September," Winkin says. "We had two fields. The varsity field and the freshman field. John-Henry showed up with his own bats and a bag of balls and started toward the varsity field. I said, 'Where are you going?' I told him that the varsity field was for the varsity. The new guys had to go to the other field. He turned around and left."

Williams called Winkin that night. He asked what happened. Winkin explained about the two fields. Williams said that was fine.

"The next day, the same thing," Winkin says. "John-Henry showed up with his bats and balls and headed for the varsity field. I said, 'Didn't you talk to your father?' He turned around and left. And that was it."

He would hit sometimes in the field house during the rest of his time in college, but never again try out for the team. The players would watch him with curiosity, but never became his friends. "His swing looked like his father's, except it was from the right side and certainly didn't have the same results," Ted Lovio, one of the players, says. Winkin watched out for him, saw him around, talked with him, but always felt ill at ease.

"You had to watch him like a hawk," the coach says. "That was the feeling I had. I thought he was a sneaky guy. I sensed that in him. I'm not sure he had a normal growing up."

He left school in 1989—later said he played semipro baseball in Fresno, California, took a look at acting as a career, tried out for the Toronto Blue Jays, all against his father's guidance—and then came back to school. He drove an expensive car around the Orono campus and seemed to move with confidence. The baseball players mostly thought he was stuck up, a prima donna.

In the summer before his senior year, John-Henry and his father were in Maine to visit President George Bush at his summer retreat in Kennebunkport. Air Force One was scheduled to land at Pease Air Force Base in New Hampshire, and John-Henry and his father were part of the welcoming committee. Rodney Nichols, a young Maine state trooper, was part of the motorcade.

"The plane was about three hours late, so everyone was just hanging around," Nichols says. "Dave McCarthy, with the New Hampshire state police, asked me if I wanted to meet Ted Williams. He took me over and we talked and Ted introduced me to his son. John-Henry and I got talking. He was very interested, for some reason, in law enforcement. We talked for a long time, and when I was leaving—they were staying in York, Maine—I told him a bunch of us were going out that night and I invited him along. I gave him my phone number. I never thought he'd call, but he did. And he came out with us."

A friendship began. John-Henry lived off campus and didn't seem to have a lot of college friends. Nichols filled a void. John-Henry was trying to market home sites at Citrus Hills at the same time he finished school and almost every weekend was taking a client down to Florida on the Nash-Tamposi airlift from Nashua, New Hampshire. Nichols went along most of the time, staying at the big house, playing golf in the middle of winter, talking with Ted.

"Ted gave me a lot of time," Nichols says. "He liked me because I was his son's friend. He probably had more in common with me than with John-Henry. We'd play golf a lot. Ted treated me better than he treated John-Henry. If the two of them didn't holler at each other once during a day it was a rare day."

The golf with John-Henry would be money sport, $100 a hole. The golf with Ted would be for bragging rights, a lot of conversation and yapping. Competitive. Nichols remembers the final hole of one round, all even, his ball and Ted's ball each about 40 yards away from the 18th green, a pair of sand wedges out of the golf bags. Nichols shot first.

"Ted's really getting on me," Nichols says. "He's saying, 'Don't think about that water in front of the green, don't think about the sand traps to the right, don't think about the woods.' Well, I stick it real close to the pin. I start giving it to him. Same thing. And he duffs the shot! Knocks it right in the fucken water. I just started laughing. He was so mad. John-Henry's giving me signs, shaking his head, telling me not to laugh, has the fear of God in him, but I can't stop myself. It was funny."

Nichols wound up going to the Miramichi, salmon fishing for six hours one day, standing in the river with Ted, just talking, learning everything about the sport. For a few years, he felt he was as friendly with John-Henry as anyone was. He attended John-Henry's graduation at UMaine with Ted, Claudia, Bud Leavitt, and Brian Interland, a family friend from Boston. He saw Ted's pride in having a first member of the immediate family finish college. Ted Williams cried at the ceremony.

"Here's the thing, though," Nichols says. "You know how proud Ted was? How he always preached education to his kids? John-Henry comes back off the stage, opens the binder or whatever it is that they give you, and there's nothing inside. He tells Ted there must have been a mix-up and he'll straighten it out.

"It turns out that John-Henry didn't really graduate. The school let him go through the ceremony, but he still needed another course. He didn't tell Ted that. He signed up for a summer course at some school in New Hampshire. He never went to class, but before the final exam he went down to New York to the Spy Store and bought some miniature walkie-talkie thing. A kid I know from York sat out in the car and read the answers from the book to John-Henry in the classroom during the test. That's how he got the diploma."

"He made a big production out of presenting his diploma to Ted at the house," Rich Eschen says. "He didn't just hand it to him. He put it in a big, elaborate box with pictures and all kinds of stuff. It was definitely a production."

"I don't think Ted ever knew what happened," Nichols says.

In his senior year, 1991, John-Henry also made a first move into the sports marketing business. This was the 50th anniversary of the .401 season, and he and Interland, a Boston-area businessman, put out a commemorative T-shirt. The T-shirt was a modest business success.

Finished with college, John-Henry stored his belongings in the basement of the house of Rodney Nichols's father in Eliot, Maine, and started to put his business degree to use. He eventually moved in with Interland outside Boston and began a memorabilia operation called Grand-Slam Marketing. Interland's friend in music promotion, Jerry Brenner, put up the seed money.

Interland had known Ted Williams since 1960. Williams was his idol. Working as an intern at a Boston television station while going to Northeastern University, Interland had finagled a trip to see the famous man in Lakeville at the Ted Williams Camp on an off-day on the Red Sox schedule. The reporter from the station told Williams about "this kid" who knew more stats about Williams than Williams himself knew. Kid and hero met. Hero was impressed. Hero invited kid to see him on a Sunday morning at the Somerset and took him to the game. They had been friends ever since.

"I even bought a condo in Islamorada," Interland says. "Just because Ted was there. There was a moment . . . I took my kids to meet Ted. He asked them if they'd had lunch. They hadn't. He started making something for them—he's a very good cook—and I was watching, thinking, Ted Williams is buttering my kids' bread. He is my idol and he's buttering my kids' bread."

Now Interland was involved with Williams's kid.

The Antonucci fiasco was still in the courts, fresh in everyone's minds. Ted was staggering financially from the costs of the lawyers. That was Interland's impression. John-Henry's idea was that he was going to resurrect and improve the family business, bring some money to his father. He also was going to protect his father from future versions of Antonucci. That was also Interland's impression.

"More than anything, I think John-Henry wanted to develop his relationship with his father," Interland says. "How would it be, if you're a kid, and everybody else knows your father better than you do? I remember getting a call from John-Henry when he was maybe 16 years old. He was crying. He said, 'I just don't know why my dad doesn't love me.' I said, 'John-Henry, he talks about you all the time.' I know how much he wanted to be loved by his father. I think in the business he wanted to show his father what he could do."

Three companies eventually were formed: Grand-Slam Marketing, Major-League Memorabilia, and the Ted Williams Card Company. The goal was to bring some order to the marketplace, to add some more luster to the Williams name. John-Henry charged into the action as if he were rousting money-changers from the temple.

"I think John-Henry was influenced by Ted's reaction to Antonucci," Interland says. "Ted talked about Antonucci all the time. The veins would be popping out of Ted's neck he was so angry. That's what John-Henry saw. Ted had been very accepting of people and he'd been burned. John-Henry wasn't going to let that happen again."

The Ted Williams signature was clean and precise, easy to copy. ("The old guys like Ted and DiMaggio they all had much better handwriting than these guys today," one dealer says.) Besides some forgeries Antonucci had dumped onto the market, besides the many autographs Johnny Orlando had signed for Ted, there were countless other fakes on the scene.

John-Henry was determined to expose these fakes and sell people the real autographs that he, of course, could provide. He said he could determine at a glance whether a ball or bat or picture had been signed by Ted. He was Ted's son! He would know!

"He showed up at an auction I ran at the Kowloon restaurant," Phil Castinetti, a memorabilia dealer from Everett, Massachusetts, says. "That's the first time I ever saw him. He started saying that all the Ted Williams stuff I had was fake. I asked who he was. He said he was Ted Williams's son. I said, 'Well, your father did a show up here last month, and I was there when he signed every one of these things.' The kid finally shut up."

The scene would be repeated at varied shows and card shops. A famous story, later told, was that John-Henry accused one dealer in Atlanta of selling fake autographs and the dealer, like Castinetti, asked John-Henry who he was. John-Henry said his name, and the guy said, "Well, if they're fake, I want my money back. Because you sold them to me three months ago." John-Henry was not gentle in his approach to people.

"You didn't have to be perspicacious to figure out John-Henry," Jerry Romolt, a longtime memorabilia dealer from Phoenix, says. "All you had to do was be around him for an hour. He was an open book. There were times he could charm your socks off, but he always had an agenda. You always knew it."

Castinetti wound up helping both John-Henry and Interland. He hooked them up with the computer whiz who had designed the website for his store, Sportsworld. He talked with John-Henry two or three times per week. He invited Interland to his wedding, arranged for Interland to stay at his father's condo in Florida.

"I felt a little sorry for John-Henry," Castinetti says. "I went with him to a card show in St. Petersburg, maybe in 1991 or 1992. I'd never really met his father, who seemed like a grouchy old guy to me.

"We're down there and Ted was signing and John-Henry broke through the line. He had a bunch of balls in his hands. He said, 'Sign these, Dad.' Ted looked at him like he wanted to kill him. He said, 'John-Henry, you know how much I have invested in you?' Then he spread out his thumb and forefinger on his right hand. 'That's how much.'"

The approximate length of a penis.

The relationship between father and son still had obvious gaps. Ted could still be tough, and Louise was still alive and she was in control. She did not want Ted working a lot. John-Henry still made her nervous. There was a scene about a missing picture from the mantel in the big house. Louise was not happy.

John-Henry's visits to Florida would last for two or three days of conflict, then he would be gone to the marketplace.

"He'd bring down a stack of pictures for Ted to sign," Rodney Nichols says. "Ted would sign every single one of them, but he would bitch as he signed every single one of them."

The businesses, as they evolved, were not skyrockets. The small profits that were made were sent to Ted. There were no profits left for the other parties. Interland had quit his job and was working for $500 a week. He was struggling.

The business the partners had thought would do best, the Ted Williams Card Company ("The cards were beautiful," Interland says. "If there had been a Pulitzer Prize for baseball cards that year, we would have won it"), was hit by the baseball strike of 1994–95. All of the three businesses were hit. Baseball had dropped off the top shelf of public interest.

Brenner and Interland dropped out of the business.

"What we did, virtually, was give the companies to John-Henry," Brenner says. "He'd been a good partner. Honest. Worked hard. He had amazing contacts. The White House would call the office. All these top FBI agents would call. We just weren't making money."

"All kinds of little things hurt," Interland says. "Like we had great hopes for this print of Ted, Larry Bird, and Bobby Orr. Who in Boston wouldn't want something like that? We took out a full-page ad in the Sunday *Boston Globe*. Very expensive. Well, the 800 number in the ad was wrong. We got nothing from it. That was the kind of thing that happened."

John-Henry, now with control of three companies not making a lot of money, also had added a fourth. He opened the Ted Williams Store, retail, in January 1994 at the Atrium Mall in Newton, Massachusetts.

"The store was as dead as dead can be," Steve Sherman, partner in the enterprise, says. "The Atrium Mall was new. Everything about it was wrong. Number one, it was too high-priced. There were a lot of nice stores, but they were very expensive. Number two, it was on the wrong side of the highway, Route 9, going into Boston instead of out of Boston. People didn't want to make the U-turn to shop."

The store was on the third floor of the dead mall, behind a large pillar that obscured most of its front window. Sherman still figures that if John-Henry had rented or leased more expensive space downtown at Faneuil Hall, the tourist and shopping mecca in Boston, sales would have skyrocketed. John-Henry took no advice on the matter. He went for the better deal that turned out to be the worst deal.

"He didn't listen to anybody," Sherman says. "He was ostentatious, obnoxious. Kind of a sleazy individual."

The biggest moment for the Ted Williams Store came on July 28, 1994. Ted Williams came to the store. This was a look into the future. Louise now was gone. Ted was still recovering from his stroke in February. The visit was only three weeks after he talked with Dan Shaughnessy in his first poststroke comments in Florida. John-Henry had put the day together.

The *Globe*'s John Vellante reported that "The Splendid Splinter looked fatigued and walked with a cane, but his voice was loud and clear. His vision is probably permanently impaired, but his signature was bold and authoritative." The event was the sale of a lithograph signed by Williams and Dominic DiMaggio, Johnny Pesky, Bobby Doerr, and Eddie Pellagrini, the Boston College baseball coach, who also had played with

Williams. They all were in attendance, along with 600 ticket-holders and customers. The 521 lithographs—for Ted's 521 home runs—were sold for $175 apiece. The *Globe* did not report that an aide had to place Williams's hand on the proper part of each print to sign his name.

"Dad being here was really his idea," John-Henry said in the paper. "When I told him what I was doing, he said, 'What would you think if I joined in? It might be fun to get away from here [Florida] and see some of the guys.' It's the first time he's been out of Florida since suffering the stroke."

Was that the way it happened?

The first well-tangled questions about love and commerce had arrived. Was this what the famous man really wanted to do less than six months after his stroke? Wouldn't he be better off at a beach somewhere? Was this fun or work? Was John-Henry the loving caregiver? Or was he the mercenary manipulator? Was he a combination of both? He already had hired nurses and a cook for the big house at Citrus Hills. He was flying back and forth to Boston, making plans and decisions. He would be living in Florida by December. The distance between his father and himself would be closed to nothing.

"Now, you finally have to listen to me. . . ."

Steve Sherman remembers that there was no warning to the rest of the staff about the Ted Williams Store closing. One night the store was open. The next morning it was cleaned out of inventory. John-Henry was gone.

He was off to take care of his father.

17 Citrus Hills, 1994–1999

Williams is 78 now. Since falling in his driveway and breaking his left shoulder two years ago, he has been unable to drive. This year, for the first time in five decades, he didn't go fishing. His buddies Jack Brothers, Joe Lindia, Sam Tamposi—and, worst of all, his long-time, live-in girlfriend, Louise Kaufman—have died in the past five years, and the lines in Williams' face have sunk deeper with each loss. His voice carries a jagged weariness, a residue of seeing bits of his rich life fall away one by one.

S. L. PRICE, SPORTS ILLUSTRATED, NOVEMBER 25, 1996

George Carter was a former Marine, a former sergeant major in the U.S. Army, a former Pawtucket, Rhode Island, policeman, a former truck driver for Cumberland Farms, and more than a little uncertain in the summer of 1994 about how his new profession was going to work. He didn't know if he was going to like being a male nurse.

"People all think male nurses are gay," he said. "Well, I'm not gay."

Fifty-eight years old, a large and expressive man, he had relocated in Florida with his wife and searched for a new occupation. He enrolled in a program called Green Thumb at Withlacoochee Vocational Tech in Inverness, a program to retrain people over 55 for late-in-life careers. Nursing was a growth field in old-age Florida. It made sense.

He graduated in 1994, the only male in his class, and signed up with Interim Health Care. The company made its male nurses wear red polo shirts and white pants. He felt like an awkward clown. Especially on his first interview.

"We have a live-in position . . . ," his new bosses at Interim told him.

"I specified that I didn't want to do live-in," Carter said.

"The client requested a male nurse," the bosses said. "It's a celebrity client, and you're the only available male nurse on our list."

"Who's the celebrity?"

"We can't tell you until we get to the interview."

The meeting with Ted Williams was held at the big house on top of the biggest hill on the Florida peninsula. Carter wasn't a Ted Williams fan, wasn't a baseball fan, but certainly knew who the potential client was. He was impressed. He sat on the couch in the living room with the 12-foot ceilings. Williams sat on the chair. Slugger, his pet Dalmatian, was next to him.

"Look out for the dog," Williams said in his big voice. "He'll bite your arm off."

A joke? Carter wasn't sure at first. He looked at the big, infirm man with this big, healthy voice. Williams was fresh out of the hospital from his stroke, still spinning, dealing with his new, altered life. John-Henry was closing up shop in Boston. The famous man clearly needed around-the-clock help. Carter decided that maybe he wanted this job.

Now he had to survive the interview. He gave Williams a rundown of his previous life, perhaps emphasizing the manly parts because of the, you know, misconception people sometimes have of male nurses. Williams perked up at the mention of Rhode Island.

"Do you know Bill Powers, the judge?" Williams asked.

Carter almost fell off his chair.

"My father grew up with Bill Powers," Carter said.

"No kidding," Williams said.

Carter said that Powers had grown up in Valley Falls, Rhode Island, which is right near Cumberland, Rhode Island, and was the attorney general when he, Carter, was a policeman. Powers later became Supreme Court justice of Rhode Island and was "blind as a bat." Carter even knew how Powers had become blind. The judge was fixing a radio as a boy and a wire hit him in one eye and he must have gotten an infection and the blindness spread to the other eye, and that was how he had to spend the rest of his life.

"Bill Powers was my friend," Williams said.

"Thank God," Carter said to himself.

He had the job. He was plunged into a situation that neither Withlacoochee Tech nor Interim Health Care ever had envisioned in their Green Thumb brochures. For stretches of the next eight years, he bathed, dressed, cajoled, fought, drove, walked, befriended, and ultimately loved the famous man. He woke him in the morning with reveille, tooting into an imaginary trumpet formed by his right hand. ("Will all military personnel please fall out on the flight deck," Carter would shout. "Williams, get your ass out of bed.") He sent Williams to the bedroom at night, same imaginary trumpet, with taps or, more often, "The Marine Corps Hymn." He pulled the covers high over the famous man's sleeping body at two in the morning to make sure the famous man was not cold.

The days were never boring. There were intermittent trips to famous places, dinners, events, everyone standing and applauding Ted Williams's glorious past and his pluck at handling the adversities of the present. There were more frequent trips to Walgreen's, where Williams would start to boom out the alligator story, holding on to his walker, and Carter would stand next to him, dressed in a nurse's whites, the two of them looking for all the world like a patient and his keeper out on a pass from the loony bin. There were stops at Kentucky Fried Chicken, where Williams would order the eight-piece bucket and eat it all, everything except the cardboard.

Famous people would stop at the house. John Glenn would visit to retell war stories. Senator John McCain would ask for an endorsement. (And be refused.) George Bush would be on the phone. (Mostly the father.) If the question from the baseball-card curious always had been, "What is Ted Williams really like?" George Carter had more answers than anyone who ever had lived. He was with the famous man for 24 hours a day at long stretches, sharing not only the most intimate moments but all moments, every one of them. He was the famous man's surrogate eyes and ears and surrogate legs. He did everything.

How far did the limits extend? Slugger, the dog, came down with cancer of the penis. George Carter administered salve to the affected region. Every day.

"This dog loves me," he would tell the famous man. "He don't love you."

"I know why he loves you," Williams would reply.

The relationship that developed between the caretaker and the cared-for became a nice mixture of the gruff and the sweet. Carter wouldn't take any shit and Williams wouldn't take any shit, and they growled affectionately at each other through the days, weeks, months, and years. Carter became very protective of his client. He felt that protection was not only his job but his wish. His heart. He grew to love Ted Williams, that cranky old goat.

He did not grow to love Ted Williams's son.

"I thought sometimes I lived in a madhouse," Carter says. "I couldn't believe what was taking place."

The arrival of John-Henry in December 1994 brought a different dynamic to the big house. Lynette Simon, the girlfriend who replaced Louise, soon was gone. Lynette didn't fit. Stacia Gerow, Ted's longtime secretary in Islamorada, who had moved up to Clearwater simply to keep working for him, was gone. Stacia didn't fit. The friends and family of Louise found that their calls to Ted were unanswered. Gone.

John-Henry had his own approach to how things would be.

"It became increasingly harder to get through to Ted," old friend Frank Cushing says. "John-Henry would let famous people like Tommy Lasorda get through, people he thought could do something for him, but Ted's old friends had problems."

Starting with George Carter, a string of nurses and aides and cooks would come through the premises, most of them hired and ultimately fired by John-Henry; sometimes, like Carter, hired and fired again, sometimes offering frustrated resignations instead. The view of the famous man's son sometimes seemed to be universally negative.

From the beginning, he ruled with an air of privilege that the famous man never had. He was not afraid to spend the money earned on Ted Williams's name. The son bought his own condominium at Black Diamond, the trendiest of the competing developments that had sprung up around Citrus Hills. He drove a BMW 740IL and a 1978 Porsche 930. He had his Miss Massachusetts girlfriend, the former secretary from Boston. He was 26 years old when he arrived and could be brusque and demanding, overbearing. The workers soon thought he was arrogant, greedy, and, worst of all, incompetent. He, on the other hand, pretty much thought that they were a bunch of thieves.

Paranoia churned through the house as if it were part of the air-conditioning. The only one who didn't feel it was the prime resident.

"The one regret I have from all the time I worked with Ted Williams is that I never told him how bad his son was," George Carter says. "Everyone kept it from Ted because Ted loved the kid, no matter how many times the kid disappointed him. Somebody should have told him. I should have told him."

When John-Henry moved to Florida, an arm of the Ted Williams memorabilia business already had been established in Hernando, located in a storefront office in the Hampton Place strip mall. The office informally was called Grand-Slam South. Rich Eschen was running things on a low-key basis.

"It was a lot of fun," Eschen says about the first days of the operation. "This was before Ted got sick. He would come in, sign some things in the morning, talk with the visitors—and there were a lot of them—and then we'd go to lunch and then we'd play golf. I couldn't think of anything better."

Eschen had been working in real estate when he met Williams at Citrus Hills six years earlier in 1988. He was paired with Williams to play doubles by the development's tennis pro. Tennis evolved into golf, which evolved into a business relationship and friendship. When the judgments in the Antonucci case were delivered, Williams asked Eschen to go around and collect whatever Talkin' Baseball inventory was still available. Eschen did this, visiting stores, bringing packages back to Williams's house, where it quickly filled the dining room, packages everywhere.

Eschen suggested that maybe Williams should rent an office for all the stuff, plus any memorabilia work that had to be done. Louise, alive and in control of the business situation at the time, quickly endorsed the idea. Get the stuff out of the house. John-Henry agreed from Boston. The 1,200-square-foot office thus was already there, ready for John-Henry's schemes and dreams when he arrived. The dreams also were his father's dreams.

"Ted really wanted John-Henry to be a success," Eschen says. "He looked at his friends, like Al Cassidy, like Sam Tamposi. Their kids were established, running the family businesses now. That's what he wanted for his own son."

The difference in this business was that the major ingredient was not office buildings or developments; it was Ted Williams's right hand. The Williams signature, placed upon a bat or baseball or eight-by-ten glossy or uniform shirt or anything else was necessary to inflate the value and sell the item. This father, unlike Cassidy or Tamposi, still had to work to make the business go. He was at the core of production.

John-Henry stepped up this production. When Louise was alive, she and Eschen filtered through the many deals and demands that came to Williams's mailbox, picking out only the best ones. Williams himself bagged a lot of the offers. When John-Henry arrived, the selection process became much more liberal. Solicitation now mixed with selection. Even though he was sick, Ted would sign more than he ever did. Ted would visit more shows, more events.

"Ted wound up going to all kinds of things when he was sick," old friend Jimmy O'Loughlin says. "He wouldn't do any of that shit when he was healthy."

"I worked with Joe DiMaggio and Ted Williams for years," Jerry Romolt says. "Joe was preoccupied with money. I did a thing with Joe in 1993 . . . I made him three and a half million dollars for eight hours' work. He signed 1,941 bats, and we put 'em on a shopping network and they sold out. Joe, for the longest time, didn't sign bats. We built a demand for these bats. Joe made the three and a half million; I put a new room on my house.

"Ted didn't care to do all this. He didn't care about money the same way."

The autograph market had gone upward. This was the high point, the peak of the memorabilia craze. Prices varied, but on average a picture signed by Williams could be sold at retail for $300. A bat went for $700, $800. A jersey went for $1,000. Signing became a part of Williams's daily schedule. John-Henry always would say signing was therapy for his father, an activity that gave him direction, purpose. The nurses would say this was an activity that gave John-Henry money, that everything was based on making money. The debate would intensify as the years passed, as Williams grew sicker.

"John-Henry always had him signing," Jack Gard, one of the string of nurses, says. "For me, the worst was when we went to San Diego for vacation one year. We went for a week. John-Henry sent stuff out there for Ted to sign by UPS, all these boxes. That's when I had it out with John-Henry. I told him, when we got back, 'That's just not right. The man deserves a vacation.' That's what got me fired."

The worst sin in the big house was to let an autograph go out the door for free. John-Henry would become furious when his father signed autographs for an old ballplayer, a friend. Mickey McDermott remembers sneaking into Williams's room on a freight elevator in Las Vegas during an autograph show to have five balls signed. He felt as if he were in a spy movie. The kid can't know! The kid will be mad! Williams signed. He told Mickey to keep quiet about it. Mickey kept quiet.

The employees were told never to ask for an autograph. Video cameras were installed around the house, tape rolling 24 hours a day, to make sure no extra signatures were being signed. Extensions were installed so John-Henry could monitor calls. Call with the wrong name or the wrong message and the phone suddenly would go dead. The number was changed often. The keyboard combination to open the front gate—forever 1-9-4-1—was changed.

"John-Henry brought a guy down from Boston to install the cameras," John L. Sullivan, one of the nurses, says. "There were two in the kitchen, one in the living room, one in Ted's bedroom. We found out when some roofers came. There were leaks forever in the dining room, and when the roofers came, they said, 'What the hell are all these wires doing up here?' The wires were from the cameras."

Williams apparently did not know about any of this. Apparently, no one ever told him. There were a bunch of things he was not told.

"John-Henry forever was promising his father that he and Anita, his girlfriend from Massachusetts, were coming for dinner," George Carter says. "He'd actually show up maybe one in 20 times. The other times, the food would be sitting there, getting cold, and Ted would say, 'Where the hell is John-Henry?' He'd get antsy. I'd know John-Henry wasn't coming, so I'd say, 'He told me earlier that he was going to take Anita out to dinner.' Ted would say, 'Well, good. He should take Anita out. She deserves it.' "

John-Henry and Anita were the ruling couple. They would make a date to marry once—September 9, 1999 (9/9/99)—but that never happened, never seemed serious in the first place. They seemed more like business partners or friends than lovers. Anita handled the busywork of the business operation. John-Henry seemed to handle the big dreams. They shared their free time. They played a lot of video games.

"They played the same game, I forget the name of it," Frankie Brothers, hired as one of the nurses, says. "They'd stay up until four in the morning. Then they'd show up late at the office. Ted would say, 'John-Henry, you're running a fucken business. You can't stay up until four in the morning playing some fucken game.' "

Nothing, though, stopped the business of autographs.

Brothers invented a stand to hold bats to make signing them easier. John-Henry had it built. Williams signed. There were different experiments on how to validate the Williams signature—holograms, certificates, eventually Polaroid pictures—and John-Henry tried them all. Williams signed under all conditions.

There were days when the signing went easy, everything light. There were days when the signing went bad. Williams would hit a point . . . John-Henry would ask for more . . . Williams would throw his pen against the wall. Jesus!

"I hope you can eat, John-Henry," Williams shouted one day. That session was finished.

The famous man's days still began notoriously early. He had a paper route of names he liked to call on the phone at 7:00 A.M. ("Come on, let's wake up So-and-So.") He still liked big, mega-cholesterol breakfasts, more bacon, please, forget the doctors. ("When this man dies, I'm going to be the guy who has killed him," Bill Hogerheide, one of the cooks who came and went, would say to himself as he worked at the stove, grease spattering everywhere.) He still had curiosity. ("What new thing are we going to learn today?")

There were trips to Ocala to the rehab clinic three or four times a week, rehab sessions at home with a physical therapist on other days. There still were visitors, the trips, the ever-present autographs, and lots and lots of opinions. The restricted, different life was still a full and busy life.

"We'd stop at the office around ten on the way back from rehab, talk with John-Henry, sign the autographs," Frankie Brothers says. "We'd do an hour, two hours. John-Henry would piss him off and he'd say, 'Come on, Frankie, let's get out of here.' At 11:30, 12, he'd go to bed, watch the History Channel or the Discovery Channel and take a nap. Around 2:30, he'd be back up. 'Frankie, who called?' He'd go back on the phone. Loved to talk to his friends. Four o'clock, we'd have dinner."

Brothers, son of Jack Brothers, Williams's fishing guide in Islamorada, was recovering from his own problems. He had been addicted to cocaine, in and out of rehab, and this was a good chance for him. He was straight and helping his father's friend. He found joy in his job. Mr. Ted, Colonel Ted still was a hoot.

"When Ted would eat . . . he had the tunnel vision, you know, but the left eye was the worse eye," Brothers says. "He would only eat the food on the right side of his plate. I'd get up, spin the plate around. Ted would say, 'What's this? I didn't ask for fucken seconds.' I'd tell him what I'd done. He'd say, 'Shit,' and start eating some more."

If the Red Sox were playing on television, Williams's night was made. He would call his old bench coach with the Senators, his friend from the Ted Williams Camp, Joe Camacho in Fairhaven, Massachusetts, and they would stay on the line for the entire game. The hell with the bill. Camacho's wife had died in 1988, and he was living with his grown son, Jimmy. A scratch golfer, Jimmy would get on the phone extension to talk about how golf was a much harder sport to play than baseball, part of a continuing argument, but mostly his father and Williams would talk about the game.

"I think that last pitch was a slider," Ted would boom into the phone.

"Yeah, a slider," Camacho would reply.

"Nomar's hands seem a little higher now. Do they seem a little higher to you?"

"I don't know. . . ."

The unseen, often unmentioned, value of baseball—the blue light in the nursing home, a shut-in pleasure, a reason for enduring the complicated day—was shared by the widower and the convalescent. Every night. Night after night. Funny, after knowing virtually every famous name in the game, the convalescent's best friend was the minor leaguer who blew out a knee and became a school administrator.

"In May of 1986, Ted came to my father's retirement party at Thad's Steak House in New Bedford," Jimmy Camacho says. "There were all these school administrators and teachers and Ted. He was in town for the Old-Timers' Game. Brought John-Henry with him. John-Henry was about 16, 17, this quiet, naive kid. Ted was eloquent when he spoke. He'd skipped the dinner for the old-timers just to be with my dad."

After Williams's stroke in 1994, the Camachos would come down to Citrus Hills once a year to visit, usually around St. Patrick's Day. Other visitors would appear. Jimmy O'Loughlin would show up, find that the punch code didn't work at the gate, and simply drive the car around the end of the fence and across the lawn to the front door. Dominic DiMaggio would appear. Billy Reedy would arrive from Detroit, bringing hams from a company he owned. He also would bring baseball old-timer Clete Boyer. They would sit in the living room and replay the games of the past.

Reedy had been best friends with former manager Billy Martin. He was in the car with Martin when they crashed on Christmas night of 1989 in Johnson City, New York, and Martin died. The first words Reedy heard, coming out from the sedatives after his operation, were "Do you know Ted Williams? He's on the phone for you."

"Why are you so friendly with Billy Martin?" Williams once asked. "I never really liked him very much."

"Well, you should like him," Reedy said. "Billy's from California. You're from California. Billy loves baseball. You love baseball. Billy loves hunting and fishing. You love hunting and fishing. And not to get too personal here, but Billy's had some problems with women and marriage, same as you. Ted, you and Billy Martin are the same guy!"

Dolores, wife number three and John-Henry's mother, also would come down now from Vermont to visit. The doors to the house were open to her again after the big stroke and Louise's death, no other woman on the scene, John-Henry in charge. Claudia soon was back from Germany, the triathlete, the jock, living and working in St. Petersburg, sometimes riding her bike 60 miles to visit her father. There was a hole in the Frustration Wall that Dolores long ago had constructed in her head as well as on the farm in Vermont. Couldn't she visit her son and daughter? Williams would shudder at her arrival. The nurses would shudder as she unpacked. Chaos would be part of her traveling ensemble.

"One of the first times she came was for the museum ceremonies when George Bush appeared," Carter says. "She had brought down a revealing, low-cut dress for the dinner. She said to me, 'The only way I can wear this is if you tape my breasts back.' So there I was with a roll of tape, taping her breasts back."

"She would sunbathe naked by the pool," John Sullivan says. "The landscapers would be out there, mowing the grass. There'd be one part of the grass that would be mowed to nothing . . . right by the pool."

"She came down once and said she was going to marry Ted again," Carter says. "She brought down a homemade wedding dress. Ted wanted no part of the whole idea."

She once, at the dinner table, informed Carter that "a fat man like you is a bad fuck." Carter didn't know what to say. Williams was so upset at the remark that he threw his napkin on the table, stood up, stalked to his bedroom. He didn't even use the walker.

Carter wound up quitting once in his on-again, off-again stint at the house because of Dolores. He says Dolores was supposed to go back to Vermont, but John-Henry was late arriving to give her a ride to the airport. Ted was agitated. He wanted Dolores gone. He transferred his anger to George. George's strategy—each of the nurses had different strategies for handling Ted—was to return anger for anger.

"Goddamn it, I don't want to hear another word, Ted," he said.

"Well, where's John-Henry . . . ," Ted said.

"I don't know where the little prick is," Carter said.

Dolores heard this exchange. She grabbed Carter's wrist, dragged him into a bedroom, and locked the door.

"Who the fuck are you to talk to Ted Williams like that?" she asked.

"I'm not doing this, lady," Carter said, unfreeing his hand, unlocking the door.

"I go out the door and into the hallway," Carter says. "She gives me a good, swift kick in the ass. Really hurt. I turn around and say, 'Go fuck yourself,' and I'm out of there."

Seldom were the days dull. The nurses had to be on constant guard for a mishap. In 1994, Thanksgiving Day, pushing himself to come back from the big stroke too fast, Williams took an exercise walk with Kay Munday, nurse at the time. The walk went longer than expected and when they got back, while Munday answered the phone, Williams fell in the driveway and broke the same shoulder he had broken at the All-Star Game. Now there was no operation, no headlines. The broken shoulder was another situation that he had to accept. He couldn't lift his left arm.

In 1997 he fell again. His physical therapist wasn't paying attention this time. The dog, Slugger, knocked Williams to the living room floor, breaking his hip. He underwent hip replacement surgery. Falling was a constant worry. His health was a worry.

The Florida thunderstorm of anger also still could arise in a hurry. There were still moments when Williams would lose control, steam and pout and react. His anger still could be undiluted, fierce. The nurses had to work with that.

"When Ted had his hip done at Citrus County Hospital, John-Henry called me at 2:00 A.M. and told me to get over there because they said Ted was whipping out," Frankie Brothers says. "I get over there, and he'd yanked out the catheter that goes into the main artery beside your heart to monitor your blood pressure. That could have killed him right there. He was screaming and yelling. The nurses in the hospital couldn't do anything with him."

"Colonel, it's Frank," Brothers said, grabbing Williams's arm. "I'm right here."

"Oh, Jesus, Frankie," Williams said. "Goddamn it, they're trying to hurt me."

"They won't hurt you."

"I hope so. Goddamn it, Frankie, don't leave."

"I won't leave."

"Anger was his fuel," Brothers says. "Ted got pissed, he became the most focused person in the world. Most of us get flustered when we get angry. Ted was the opposite. When he hit home runs, that's how he did it. He got angry. Most people screw up. He hit home runs."

The words sometimes were still tough to hear. . . .

"Claudia, you're becoming a cunt, just like your mother!"

How do you say that to your daughter?

"John-Henry, you're the abortion I wanted!"

How do you say that to your son?

"When he'd get upset at both of his kids, he'd start yelling, 'Wettach, Wettach, Wettach,' their mother's maiden name," nurse John Sullivan says. "Like all the bad things in them came from the other side of the family."

The moment would pass. Life would resume.

The times the nurses liked best—better even than the occasional trips to events, the occasional minglings with the famous—were the times when no one else was in the house. The battles with John-Henry would be done. The autographs, the schedule would be done. Maybe Williams couldn't sleep, just wanted to talk. The disorientations and agitations gone, he would be fascinating.

"I wish I could remember all the names of the people in his stories," George Carter says. "He told about the time an attendant came down in Washington and invited him up to meet President Eisenhower. He never went and really regretted that. Eisenhower was one of his heroes. Richard Nixon . . . when Nixon died, Ted cried. He loved Nixon. It was like his father had died."

"He knew everything about baseball," Frankie Brothers says. "He'd studied it. He'd talk about the Bernoulli Principle, which is the law in physics for why a curveball curves. Other guys didn't know anything about it. We were at Cooperstown one year, though, and he said to Sandy Koufax, 'Sandy, have you ever heard of the Bernoulli Principle?' Sandy said, 'Ted, you know better than to ask me that.' Ted said, 'Goddamn it, that's why I'm glad you were in the other league!' "

Brothers asked Williams one night what was the longest game he'd ever played. Williams replied, "Seventeen innings, but I wasn't there at the end. I came out in the tenth." He said he left the ballpark and went back to the team hotel. On the way back to his room, he passed the room of a teammate. (Unnamed.) The door was open. The teammate's girlfriend was in town and was watching the game and her boyfriend on television. She invited Williams to join her. They drank champagne and watched baseball.

"And I gave her a little bump," Williams said.

Brothers was confused by the word. In his drug past, a "bump" was a line of cocaine. Ted Williams gave his teammate's girlfriend a line of cocaine?

"No, you dumb shit," Williams said. "I popped her. We had sex. That's a bump."

He still was an obvious flirt when pretty women came around. Anita Lovely, John-Henry's girlfriend/fiancée, could charm him in a moment. John-Henry would send Anita to talk to him when he was being obstinate, when there were problems with the autographs. Anita would bring calm. Ted still liked women and women liked him. He called them all "queens."

"How's the queen today?" he would ask.

"Whoa, take a look at these queens around here," he would say.

He kept gifts in the house for pretty women. For a while, he had watches. Then he had Estee Lauder perfume. Brothers had read a story that Williams was a virgin until he was 20 or 21 years old, that baseball was his passion until then, that he had no time for girls. Brothers asked if this was true. Williams said it was and proceeded to deliver a play-by-play of his first sexual encounter. He had a twinkle in his eye as he described the finish.

"I said, 'Hell, this is pretty good!' " Williams said. " 'This is almost as much fun as baseball!' "

Alas, the long sexual run for a very sexual man had ended now. Williams was at the rehab clinic one day with Carter, sitting in the waiting room, wearing his normal outfit of faded shorts and old shirt and Velcro-tie sneakers. A receptionist noticed that his fly was unzipped. She said, "Psssst, Mr. Williams, your fly is open."

He gave her a nice octogenarian smile.

"If it can't get up, it can't get out," the famous man said. He made no move for his zipper.

The marked increase in autograph production from his father, coupled with the memorabilia craze, began to pay off for John-Henry's companies after a while. The cash began to flow. A Boston businessman, Brian O'Connor, a Polaroid executive and former Marine, was asked by Ted to give John-Henry advice.

"I went on a seven-day fishing trip with Ted and John-Henry in Mexico in 1996, maybe 1997," O'Connor, who had met Williams as a Jimmy Fund director, says. "I think it was the last time Ted ever went fishing. We had to work a way to strap him into the boat. It wasn't too long after he'd tripped over the dog.

"We were fishing for permit, a game fish down there. The way you do it, you spot the permit and then cast to the fin. I was Ted's eyes. I'd spot the permit and then Ted would cast to where I told him. I'd have to kind of hold him so he wouldn't fall over when he cast . . . it worked all right."

The message Williams wanted O'Connor to bring to John-Henry was to stay on the straight and narrow in business, not to "go off like a gunshot." O'Connor repeated the message every night on the trip, and on the phone, and in ensuing trips to Florida. He pointed out that a company selling $500,000 worth of memorabilia at a whack had to be run differently from a company selling $50,000 at a whack. There had to be more prudence.

"I think John-Henry was listening at the beginning," O'Connor says, "but over a period of two years, as his revenues grew, his listening power diminished."

O'Connor's view of John-Henry was: "hard worker, not the brightest soul in the world, zero social graces." The number of companies worried the adviser—especially with the addition of Hitter.net, an Internet service provider, a company unrelated to baseball. The accounting practices in all these cross-hatched companies worried the adviser as well.

"Try to do one thing well," O'Connor advised.

John-Henry heard. Or maybe didn't.

Everything was spinning.

"The kid was spending a lot of money," Frankie Brothers says. "I'd never seen anyone spend money like him who wasn't a drug dealer. Spending it on shit. I was running the house on an American Express card. Anita was doing the finances. One month she sent me a photocopy of the wrong statement. His statement. The kid had charged $38,000 that month in shit. All shit. Fifteen thousand dollars for a fish-eye lens. It was ludicrous."

Several business situations had hit the newspapers. The first was a lawsuit from Upper Deck Authenticated, the trading card company. Ted had signed an exclusive, three-year, $2 million contract with Upper Deck in 1992. Part of the deal was that if he were incapacitated, he still would be paid, even if he no longer could sign autographs.

Indeed, since the bad stroke, he had not signed for Upper Deck and had not been paid. John-Henry's lawyers mentioned this fact. Upper Deck's lawyers then mentioned the fact that Ted *had* signed—had done a public signing at the Ted Williams Store, in fact, with the lithographs six months after the stroke—and still was signing for John-Henry's operations. Where were the autographs due Upper Deck? The card company sued. An out-of-court settlement was reached.

"So Ted had to sign to pay off the lawsuit from Upper Deck," nurse John Sullivan says. "The guy from Upper Deck came, Monday through Friday, three straight weeks, and Ted signed every autograph."

In the middle of the process one day, Williams turned to Sullivan. He was not happy.

"I'm eighty-whatever," he said. "And I'm still fucken working."

A second set of headlines around John-Henry came from a bizarre situation back in Boston. Rodney Nichols, the former Maine state trooper and friend of John-Henry's, now worked at a Toyota dealership. He and a friend had become jammed up with debts to a bookie. Rodney had given the bookie Ted Williams's World Series rings from 1946 and 1986, hoping they would be enough to pay the debt.

The bookie, wondering if the rings were authentic, gave them to a New Hampshire man who brought them to Phil Castinetti, the Everett, Massachusetts, memorabilia dealer. Castinetti said they were authentic, but wondered if they were stolen. Nichols assured everyone that they were not.

"John-Henry had left all that stuff in my father's basement," Nichols says. "It had been there for years. My father got sick of seeing it. There was some food in the boxes and mice had gotten in there. My father called John-Henry and told him to come and get it, that if he didn't, it all would be sold at a yard sale. John-Henry said he didn't want anything, except his skis and maybe he'd like to sell a king-sized bed he'd bought new so his father could visit him in Maine. My father bought the bed, paid $600 for it.

"Going through the stuff for the yard sale, my father found the rings and some other memorabilia. He put the rings in a drawer. He kept the other memorabilia. I called John-Henry about the rings. He just said, 'So that's where they are.' He didn't say anything about coming up for them.

"When I needed the money, I remembered the rings."

Castinetti was prepared to sell the rings at public auction. He invited a crew from the New England Sports Network to his store to film the rings, to start the publicity. The reporter tried the rings on her hand. He advertised the fact that he had the rings.

He also called John-Henry. John-Henry called the FBI.

"I wanted to offer the rings to John-Henry because I knew him," Castinetti says. "His reaction was, 'I gotta get those rings back. My father will be pissed.' I said I'd sell them to him."

John-Henry told the FBI the rings were stolen. A sting operation was established to arrest Castinetti. A hidden camera in a Boston hotel room captured an undercover FBI agent and John-Henry handing over $90,000 in a metal suitcase to Castinetti and his assistant Danny Dunn. Dunn gave the FBI agent the rings. The door opened and agents flooded the room. Castinetti thought at first he was being robbed.

("It's all here on my videotape," Castinetti says now in his family room, slipping a cassette into his tape machine. "I call it my '$30,000 videotape' because that's how much I had to pay my lawyer."

("Oh, don't play that," his wife says from across the room filled with toys. "The kids get scared when they see the men burst in with the guns.")

At the trial in March 1998, John-Henry contended that the rings were stolen by Nichols. He said that he had picked up whatever memorabilia he had left with Nichols's father. The rings had to be stolen. Nichols's father came to the stand. He brought along a box from his basement that contained hundreds of Ted Williams photographs, plaques, and his address book. How did John-Henry explain this?

Castinetti, Dunn, and another man were found innocent. Rodney Nichols was not so lucky. In a separate trial in Maine, Nichols was convicted and sentenced to six months of house arrest. John-Henry received the rings.

"I never have stolen a thing in my life," Nichols still says. "I wanted my lawyer to call Ted as a witness, but he never did. I'd heard Ted was telling John-Henry to just let it go, that he shouldn't be doing this to a friend. I don't know. I tried to call Ted and John-Henry cut it off and called the FBI. They told me I would be charged with tampering with a potential witness if I called again."

Police had to stop Castinetti from attacking John-Henry outside the courthouse in Maine after Nichols's trial ended. Castinetti was mad at John-Henry, Brian Interland, the FBI, everyone associated with John-Henry. He instituted an annual 50 percent off, one-day sale on all Ted Williams memorabilia in his store. He was quoted early in all future stories about Ted Williams's son.

The son, however, seemed bulletproof.

Hitter.net was another ascendant star in the NASDAQ, dot-com revolution. The company was providing Internet service, mostly in Florida, to places not reached by the bigger service providers. The subscriber list was up to 18,000. The possibilities were varied. Should John-Henry go public? This was the time of the instant-success IPOs. Should he sell to a bigger company? A number of them were romancing him, one prepared to pay $7.5 million for Hitter.net. Should he simply become bigger and bigger himself, challenge the big boys?

The mishmash of John-Henry's companies opened the possibility of taking memorabilia money and pumping it into the dot-com company. The Ted Williams name, golden, made investors and loan officers listen. In 1996 John-Henry had been granted power of attorney for his father. He now pretty much *was* Ted Williams, although Ted's signature was needed on certain documents. This was not a problem.

"I was with Ted at the house one day, and a bank officer had some things for Ted to sign," John Sullivan says. "Ted asked me to read them because he couldn't read very well. The bank officer said, 'No, they're all right, John.' I said, 'Let me read them.' The contracts were blank. I told that to Ted. He said, 'I'm not signing any blank contracts.' John-Henry showed up and then the donnybrook began.

"He was having his father sign all kinds of things. He was having him sign blank contracts. Ted had no idea what he was doing."

A Florida businessman, Steve Southard, recommended by Al Cassidy Jr., had done good work closing the Boston companies and basing everything in the memorabilia business in Florida. He was seen as a reasoned voice of caution in the background. He eventually quit. He found John-Henry didn't need a voice of reason and caution. John-Henry didn't listen to any voices except his own.

"This kid is the Son of Satan," Southard said to George Carter. "He's built a whole house of cards, and it's all going to fall down."

"The president of Sprint came down to see John-Henry," George Carter says. "I'm sure he was here mostly because he wanted to meet Ted—that happened a lot—but he talked with John-Henry for a long time. I was around.

"The president of Sprint said, 'John-Henry, you're not a very good businessman.' He turned to me and said, 'Isn't that true, George? Why isn't he a good businessman?' I said, 'Because he won't listen to anybody.' The president of Sprint said, 'John-Henry, listen to him . . . because he's telling you the truth.'"

The kid would self-destruct. That was the prevailing business thought. The night of July 13, 1999, was used as another illustration. That was the night of the 1999 All-Star Game in Boston, one of the greatest moments in Ted Williams's life.

The All-Star Game hadn't even been scheduled for Fenway Park in 1999, the last season of the 20th century. The Milwaukee Brewers, opening their new stadium, Miller Park, were supposed to have the honor. The Red Sox were supposed to host the game in 2002.

A construction accident in Milwaukee, part of the stands falling down, killing three workers, had rearranged things. Miller Park would not be ready for the 1999 season, and baseball commissioner Bud Selig, also the owner of the Milwaukee Brewers, executed a switch with the Red Sox.

A convergence of factors had begun that would create an extraordinary moment.

The game would be held at the place where Ted Williams's career had been played out. The people in the stands would be the people who watched him or descendants of the people who watched him. They would know his story the way schoolkids know the story of George Washington. . . .

The situation for the game was unique. Major League Baseball, to celebrate the end of the century, was going to unveil an All-Century team at the World Series. The living nominees for that team—33 men from a list of 100 names—would be flown into Boston, brought onto the field, one by one, and introduced by actor Kevin Costner in a virtual real-life replay of the movie *Field of Dreams*.

Willie Mays, Hank Aaron, Sandy Koufax, Cal Ripken, Juan Marichal,

Al Kaline, Bob Feller, Yogi Berra . . . they would be joined by the present All-Stars . . . Mark McGwire, Sammy Sosa, Mike Piazza, Derek Jeter, Nomar Garciaparra . . . and they would all stand under the lights and the stars and the fireworks and the flyover. Never had such a gathering of baseball talent been held.

And Ted Williams would throw out the first ball. . . .

Mickey Mantle had died in 1995. Joe DiMaggio had died only five months earlier in 1999. Babe Ruth was dead and Lou Gehrig was dead and Ty Cobb was dead and Ted Williams was still standing. Shaky, perhaps, three-quarters blind, 80 years old, almost 81, but he still was there. He had won whatever race had been set out. Survived. The oldest of the living All-Century candidates. Alone at the top of his class.

He could be caught one last time in this late curtain call for a generation. World War II veterans supposedly were dying at a rate of 1,056 per day now, a layer of history being peeled off the top, but there was still time for one more wave, a good-bye, a wet-eyed standing ovation. He was wrapped in the flag, wrapped in all the sweet childhood memories of baseball, in the promise of youth, the sadness of old age, wrapped in noise and emotion. He was elevated to some level of secular American sainthood.

Theodore Samuel Williams, from 4121 Utah Street in San Diego, Teddy Ballgame, the Splendid Splinter, the Kid . . .

"With the Citgo sign pulsating behind him, a giant No. 9 stenciled into the outfield grass, and the ancient theatre shaking on its landfill foundation, Williams stood in front of the mound, flanked by Mark McGwire and Tony Gwynn," Dan Shaughnessy would type for the *Boston Globe*. "Behind homeplate, dressed for dinner, but wearing a catcher's mitt, was Carlton Fisk.

"Strike.

"Bedlam."

And the game that followed would mean nothing. And the players around him would be only so many supporting actors from the drama of Ted Williams's days. And he would remove his cap—yes, he did—and wave it at everyone in triumph.

His Hitter.net cap.

The cap on Williams's head became an instant story. Every other player on the field except a hatless Carl Yastrzemski wore a cap from his present or former team. Only the guest of honor, the star of the show, was different. Williams wore not only the hat but also a blue Hitter.net golf shirt.

The fashion decision immediately was seen as the most heinous of John-Henry's public crimes. Detractors said he had turned his poor, sickly father into a billboard. He had taken a pure, historic moment and turned it into a commercial opportunity. There was an observed impropriety here, a sadness. The greatest living baseball player resembled one of those old-timers visited at the nursing home, a once-dignified businessman now with a large soup stain on the front of his T-shirt.

The hat, the cap, was the soup stain. Hitter.net.

"The kid got a lot of grief for that," Peter Sutton, John-Henry's attorney, says in defense, "but what people don't realize is that without Hitter.net, Ted wouldn't even have been at the All-Star Game. Baseball wouldn't have had one of its greatest moments."

Sutton says Williams originally didn't want to go to the game. He didn't want the hassle, the inconvenience. He would be in a wheelchair most of the time, jostled and touched, surrounded by strangers, gawkers, bugged.

Sutton says he tried to convince Williams of the importance of the moment. John-Henry tried. The Red Sox tried. Major League Baseball tried. Williams couldn't find a reason for going.

"The thing that changed his mind was when a couple of firms inquired whether or not he was going because they wanted to make deals," Sutton says. "Ted turned them down, but then he said to John-Henry, 'Tell me this: if I went for your company, would that help you?' John-Henry said it sure would. Then Ted said, 'Then I'm going. For you.' "

"That's true that Ted didn't want to go," Brian O'Connor agrees. "Ted had no great love for the Red Sox front office. All those years, he'd want to go to a game sometime in the summer, take some friends? The Red Sox would give him the tickets, then send him a bill. Ted Williams had to pay to go to the Red Sox games!"

From not going, no, can't do it, the trip became an expanded expedition. O'Connor, still a director of the Jimmy Fund, lobbied hard for Ted to make a visit to the Dana-Farber Cancer Institute. The charity recently had located its original poster child, "Jimmy," a 63-year-old Maine man named Einar Gustafson. For years, Jimmy had been presumed dead, a victim of his cancer. Now he had stepped forward.

"Ted has to meet him," O'Connor said.

John-Henry balked. He could see no commercial possibilities here.

"John-Henry," O'Connor said, "Ted *has* to do this."

John-Henry finally agreed.

"How are you, Jimmy baby?" Williams shouted on Friday afternoon, July 9, at the hospital when he finally met Gustafson, cameras clicking everywhere. "This is the biggest thrill of my trip, right here! Jeez, you look great! You're an inspiration to everybody."

One more time Williams went around the wards, talking with sick kids. They had no idea who he was, but they certainly knew he was someone as he bellowed and laughed and more pictures were taken. *What a good-looking kid you are! I'll bet you're not going to be here very long!* This was a sweet reprise.

Two days later, he was at something entirely new for him. He was the grand marshal of the Jiffy Lube New England 300 NASCAR race at the New Hampshire International Speedway. The visit was arranged by Dave McCarthy, the New Hampshire state trooper who headed a three-man voluntary security force for Williams on road trips. McCarthy, previously a bodyguard for New Hampshire governor John Sununu, had noticed people crawling around and over Williams at an autograph show and had offered his services. He had become bodyguard and friend.

"So I set this up, and Ted's in the car, ready to go on the track, and I go to check something," McCarthy says. "I'm walking back and I hear all this cheering. What's that? The car is gone. They took him out already, went without me, and he's going around the track, waving at people. The people are just going nuts."

Hitter.net was a presence on Williams's hat and shirt and at the track. Special Ted Williams Hitter.net baseball cards were distributed. Hitter.net even sponsored a 16-year-old kid, Kenny White, in a number 9 car in an earlier Busch Northern race. ("He's not going to die, is he?" Ted asked.) Williams had little experience with NASCAR but was a big hit with the drivers. They all wanted their pictures taken with him.

"You just tell me where he's going to be," Dale Earnhardt told McCarthy. "I'll be there."

The plan was for Williams to leave before the race, but on the way out McCarthy wheeled him to the fence for the start. He wanted Williams to feel the power come past. When that happened, the 42 cars revved up, snorting and blowing, thundering into the afternoon, here and gone in a noisy instant, Williams shouted, "Holy shit! You don't get that on television."

He stayed at the Four Seasons in Boston for the weekend, the Somerset long ago converted to condominiums. He did interview after interview, the last real walk around the block for the Public Ted, dissecting the game of baseball for newcomers, boosting the cause of the modern-day player against the long-ago star, rare for any retired athlete. He dozed off, woke up, came back for more.

On Tuesday night, the All-Star Game, he was driven from centerfield to the pitcher's mound by Al Forrister, a grounds crew employee who once had shagged balls for him. Forrister had started at Fenway in 1957. He once had warmed up Ryne Duren. Yankees manager Ralph Houk had used every other player in the bullpen except Duren during a game and now wanted Duren. The only people sitting in the bullpen were Duren and Forrister. Forrister grabbed a glove to catch the pitcher. He had been around so long that Williams had used his name as an alias for years when checking into hotels.

"I drove him out from the same place in centerfield in 1991 for the Equitable Old-Timers' Game," Forrister says. "He and Joe DiMaggio came out together that night. Another guy and I, we had to time it just right. He went one way, I went the other, and we landed at home plate at the same time. Joe and Ted.

"This time, I went to the mound. I knew the way."

When they reached the mound, All-Stars new and old surrounded the golf cart. Forrister called out their names for Williams, who could not see. Mark McGwire. Sammy Sosa. Here's Cal Ripken Jr.! Williams had words for each of them, everybody mingling in the noise as the ovation continued even past a public address announcement to leave the field. Who cared? This was history. Or at least it felt like history.

When the time came to throw the first pitch, Gwynn steadied Williams, pointed him in the right direction. The pitch went through the air, no bounce, and landed in Fisk's glove. The crowd cheered even more. This was the moment of the weekend.

"Tears were coming out of Ted's eyes," All-Star Larry Walker of the Colorado Rockies said. "I had to turn away because tears were coming out of my eyes too."

When the ceremonies were done, Forrister took Williams up the many ramps to luxury box 22, the Polaroid box. Williams was reunited with

ovation for number 9, the Splendid Splinter, Teddy Ballgame. One last stadium shook one last time, and then the shaking stopped and the players and the 1999 World Series began.

The long, wet good-bye was done.

The advance of Williams's physical problems was unrelenting. Back at Citrus Hills, he would become disoriented more often, have to be led from room to room. There always was the worry that he would fall. He was tired much of the time, out of breath. He needed longer and longer naps, his life becoming more and more constricted. He was taking assorted medications for his assorted problems.

One-half of a Zoloft pill, an antidepressant, had been prescribed every day to help him through the first years of his situation. He was up to two full Zolofts a day now, and still the anger would seep out.

"If these are the golden years," he said to Curt Gowdy, the broadcaster, "my question is: how long do they have to last?"

He would wake up in the mornings some days and the perversity, the hopelessness, of his situation would almost overwhelm him. He would stand at the side of his bed and talk to God as if God were some negligent waitress, some bellhop who had arrived too late to solve the day's latest problem. The anger would unroll.

"You're a black-bearded Jewish son of a bitch and your mother is a whore," Williams would say, eyes toward the ceiling of his bedroom. "And I don't believe in either one of you."

There was a general belief—Johnny Pesky said, flat out, "Ted was an atheist"—that Williams didn't believe in God. Never a churchgoer, never a confidant of priests and preachers, almost vicious in his descriptions of his mother's work with the Salvation Army, able to string out blasphemies at any moment (see above), he did little to change that opinion. He seemed, if anything, a direct opponent of God.

Which was the point.

How do you spend so much time cursing and damning a Someone who doesn't exist? John Underwood, the writer of *My Turn at Bat*, remembers that most of Williams's curses seemed to have God or Jesus Christ or some religious figure involved. Williams seldom knocked off an idle "goddammit," just a little verbal seasoning to his language. His goddamns were direct and personal, requests to bring fire and necessary brimstone against a car that wouldn't start, a window that wouldn't open, a situation that had become unhinged.

God was an everyday character in Williams's life. An inhibitor. A black-bearded Jewish son of a bitch who did bad things. Why couldn't God be good? Better at least? If God knew everything, then how could He allow all of that suffering in all of those hospital wards? Couldn't He see all of those little kids at Dana-Farber with their shaved, bald heads and their dull eyes? If a baseball player could see and feel, why couldn't God?

"I had one conversation with Ted about God later in life," Russ White, the sportswriter from the *Washington Daily News*, says. "I told him I had become a religion writer. That I felt it was my calling.

"I remember this perfectly: he wished me good luck and said, 'You know, I never have gone much to church and all that, but I've always tried to live by the Golden Rule. Do unto others . . . I've always tried to do that.' He was absolutely sincere."

This was true. He had led his life by adhering to codes. Maybe they were his own codes, drawn from different influences, but they resembled codes that came from religious teachings. He had comforted the sick, helped the needy. Money never had been his false god. The hurts he delivered to people mostly were unintentional, not calculated. Humility had been part of his package, buried perhaps underneath braggadocio, but certainly there. He never had gone "big time." He had shared his good fortune easily with others.

Russ White considers Williams "one of the most spiritual people I've ever met." He says Williams thought about God daily, battled Him, yet still tried to conform to His stated rules. In Williams's own way, he was more involved with God than a whole congregation of churchgoers might be. God was with him for every at bat. God was with him at every fishing hole. God was with him everywhere. God just pissed him off an awful lot. God was often the enemy.

"It sounds silly, but I have dreams about Ted," White says. "He is in heaven, talking the way he talked. We're sitting at his feet. It is all very spiritual."

The case of Tricia Miranti was exhibit A in Williams's discomfort with God. When Williams first began rehabilitation for his stroke, he met a small 17-year-old girl in a wheelchair at the Ocala clinic. Her therapy sessions ran at the same time his did, so the famous man and the small girl saw a lot of each other. He thought she was a cute girl and maybe not that bright. She obviously had a list of problems. He challenged her to a game of checkers just to be nice. She beat him.

"I'm figuring I'll be nice and maybe I'll let the little girl win," he told her mother, Vicki. "Then I notice she's doing some moves here, some moves I didn't expect. Then she beats me. She actually beats me!"

Tricia Miranti, who was very bright, became his latest and last cause, the sick kid at the end of all the sick kids, a one-girl, personal Jimmy Fund crusade. When she was five, she had suffered a cerebral hemorrhage that almost killed her. She had been a normal kid and now was in a wheelchair. Her mind was not affected, but her body was changed forever. She had to relearn everything from how to speak to how to sit to how simply to hold her head up. There were things she never would relearn. Talk about the whims of God.

"She was perfectly normal when she was five years old," Vicki Miranti says, describing how Tricia's problems started in 1981. "A few days after Thanksgiving, there was a sale and I bought her this Pink Panther bicycle she really wanted for Christmas. Then on December 10 she was hit by all of this. I had hidden the bike at her grandparents', and I kept it there for over a year, hoping . . . and then I just gave it away to a little girl who lived next door."

Williams gave his failing heart to the teenage Miranti. The sweetest sound became her giggle. He tried to bring out that giggle as hard as he could. The sick old ballplayer and the sick kid became fast friends. Vicki would drive Tricia to the big house, where she would leave her with Ted and Frankie Brothers and Slugger for long afternoons at the pool. Williams never had used the pool, never would, never learned to swim, but Tricia would splash and do her therapy, and Williams would smile and talk with her.

He and Lewis Watkins set up a foundation for her. The goal was to send her to college (she went and graduated from the University of Central Florida) and provide for the many expenses in her life not covered by insurance. They ran one fund-raiser, a big-money luncheon at George Steinbrenner's hotel in Tampa for Williams's 80th birthday. The fund-raiser and other donations did the job.

"I never saw Ted Williams as a great baseball player," Vicki Miranti says. "I saw him as a great man. He was my angel."

His question was: if he was the angel, where were the supposed real angels? How could God do this to Tricia? What had she done to Him?

The injustice of her situation would cause Williams to unravel strings of his curses, all the bad words, delivered in anger. Anger overtook him when he talked about what had happened to Tricia Miranti.

"You shouldn't talk to God like that," George Carter said. "He'll punish you."

"How will he do that?" Williams asked.

"He'll make you stay here even longer."

That would be the cruelest trick of all. Stay here? For what? The many pleasures in Williams's life had disappeared, one by one. Eddie Barry, a former Boston Bruins hockey player and a friend, used to take him for rides on a golf cart around the local courses when he first became sick. Even that was too dangerous now. He was pretty much homebound. His last pleasure was food. Eating.

"He lived for food," Jacques Prudhomme says. " 'That's all I have left,' he would say. He lived for TV, companionship, and food."

Prudhomme became his personal chef in 1999. A French-Canadian world traveler, married and divorced five times, he answered an ad on the Internet for the job. He had owned restaurants, been a personal chef for millionaires, lived a wandering life that started when he was 13 years old in the back reaches of Quebec and his mother sold him to a circus. He was a perfect, new, accented voice in the household.

"People say to me, 'Jacques, it is so bad that your marriages did not work out, that you did not find love,' " Prudhomme says. "I say to them this is not so. I have found love five different times with five different, wonderful women. I have lived five different lives. I consider myself more lucky than people who only have found love once."

Prudhomme's idea was to clean up Williams's diet. The previous chefs had been intimidated by the famous man's bluster and cooked whatever he wanted. Prudhomme tried a strategy that involved psychology and white lies. He conned Williams out of the cholesterol.

Williams would demand bacon. . . .

"Mr. Williams, I am trying to develop a low-fat sausage," Prudhomme would say. "Would you help me? I want to get it right. We will put a lot of garlic in it. Help me try that."

Williams would ask for a Reuben sandwich. . . .

"Oh, Mr. Williams, I am sorry. I already have made a rack of lamb. I am such an asshole. Would you help me out and eat this rack of lamb? If it's no good, I will make you a Reuben sandwich."

Every meal was another exercise in finesse. Prudhomme would cut up

Williams's food and wait for the results. He knew he was doing well when he heard Williams on the phone with former President Bush, saying, "You've got to get your butt down here! We've got some of the best god-damned sausage you ever ate!"

Prudhomme quickly became friends with George Carter, who was back on the job after Williams begged him to return. They worried about the famous man, about his health, about his welfare, about the daily machinations of John-Henry. How had the famous man landed in this situation?

The component both Prudhomme and Carter thought had been missing from Williams's life most was love. They would talk about this often. How can a man who has been loved by so many people be missing love? He didn't seem to know how to give love, and he did not know how to receive it. Love always had seemed to arrive with a price tag for Williams, the request for a favor.

"Ted was like a little boy," Carter says. "Somewhere along the line he'd missed love in his life. If you got to know him at his vulnerable points, he was a little boy. He would put on that facade when he was around people, he'd get on the phone and you couldn't even hear yourself think, but, ahh, deep down inside he was a little boy who didn't have much love in his life."

"People had loved him all the way up as an idol, but never as a person," Prudhomme says. "You know when you are 82, 83 years old, you think about these things, and at the end I think his eyes opened up and he could see who was really giving him love."

Before he left every day, Prudhomme would take Williams's hand and say, "I love you, Mr. Williams." Williams would ask him what he wanted, what he needed. Prudhomme would say, "All I want is your love." Williams would say, "Well, you have that."

"Jacques," Prudhomme says Williams asked one day, "how come my son never tells me that he loves me?"

"I don't know," Prudhomme replied.

The next time John-Henry was around, Prudhomme says he made a point to say, "I love you, Mr. Williams," and then said, "John-Henry, you love your dad too, don't you?" "Yeah, I love you, Dad," John-Henry said. Prudhomme thought the words were cold, mechanical. He thought that John-Henry also didn't know how to give or receive love.

"It was with his friends that he had the greatest love," Prudhomme says. "With Joe Camacho. With Billy Reedy. With Bob Breitbard. There he could feel the unconditional love. He was a complicated man, but when he opened up, there was a flow of love."

Even the love of life itself was now a problem. Williams's first 74 years had been an exercise in that love. Had anyone ever grabbed life harder by the ears, shook it, pummeled it, enjoyed it more? The last years had been an erosion of that love, piece by piece by piece. What was left?

"We talked about suicide one night," John L. Sullivan, one of the nurses, says. "I'd been reading the book *Final Exit*, and Ted was very interested. The basis of the book was that you could control the end of your life. It told you what symptoms to fake to have control over your fate. You faked the symptoms and certain drugs were prescribed. You didn't take the drugs, you squirreled them away. When you had enough, you could check out when you wanted. The problem—I'd read this too—was that it didn't work. People were taking the drugs thinking they were going to die and they still were alive. And the drugs had terrible side effects."

"You know what I think?" Williams said. "I think when you're 65 years old the government should give you a little green box. Inside the green box there should be a black pill. Whenever you needed to take it, it would be right there."

"Jesus, Ted, I'm getting close to 65," Sullivan said. "Couldn't you make it a little later?"

"Sixty-five," Williams said.

The big decline in Williams's health came quickly. Both Carter and Brothers say that worry over money was one of the major reasons for the turn. Money and John-Henry. Money because of John-Henry.

"Ted would fuck his brain when he went to bed," Carter says. "He was one of those guys, if something was bothering him, he couldn't let it go. John-Henry got him all worked up."

The situation had begun years earlier, even before Williams became sick. One of the people who had come back into his life was high school classmate Bob Breitbard.

A precise and energetic little man, Breitbard had become a millionaire in the dry cleaning business since those Hoover High days. He was active in San Diego, the creator of the San Diego Hall of Champions, a well-known local figure. He once had owned the San Diego Rockets in the National Basketball Association.

Williams stayed in Breitbard's house for a week when the Hoover class of '36 held its 50th reunion. The Hall of Champions, with Williams as a prime member and Breitbard as the director, was another tie between the two men. When Williams went to San Diego with John-Henry in 1992 after the first stroke for the 1992 All-Star Game and for festivities naming a nine-mile stretch of Route 59 Ted Williams Parkway, Breitbard was the host.

Breitbard now would visit Williams once a year for at least a week in Florida and talk with him almost daily on the phone. Williams would visit Breitbard in San Diego. The longtime bonds of friendship had increased.

"How are you fixed for money for retirement?" Breitbard supposedly asked Williams after the Antonucci business.

"I'm okay," Williams said.

"Well, if you need it, I can give you a million dollars."

Williams refused, but John-Henry in 1991 asked Breitbard for a loan of $500,000 to get started in business. Breitbard made the four-month loan, interest-free, without Williams's knowledge. John-Henry missed the four-month deadline and nine years later on August 1, 2000, still owed $265,000. Williams found out about it.

"He asked Bob, and Bob said John-Henry still owed him the money," Frankie Brothers says. "Bob told him, 'I don't want to be an asshole, Ted, but I'm 81 years old and you're 81 years old, and neither of us knows how long we're going to be around. That's money for my kids. You should know that after we're gone, my kids are going to have to go after your kid.' Ted was really upset. He thought the kid had taken care of it.

"The next day John-Henry declared bankruptcy. Ted went off the wall."

The bankruptcy was a coincidence of poor timing. Hitter.net, John-Henry's grandest scheme, had joined the first wave of dot-com failures, filing for Chapter 11. The company that once had attracted an offer of $7.5 million now was worth nothing. Less than nothing. The *St. Petersburg Times* later would say the company had "racked up debts of $12.8 million." "When the new business took off, he expanded," Peter Sutton, the lawyer for John-Henry, says. "He wanted to go nationwide. Then the economy hit him. He had put on too many people, bought switches, equipment. He had, like, 50 people on staff. Then the dot-coms died. He didn't take a salary, didn't want to restructure, firing a bunch of people. Plus, he was worried all the time about his dad dying. He gave up the whole business."

"John-Henry always had eyes the size of pie plates when he started a business, but he'd never see the thing through," Rich Eschen says. "He never had enough sense not to go for the big hit, to just establish your business and go from there. You look at the contacts he had. Ted would introduce him to anyone he wanted to meet. CEOs. Famous people. Presidents. Anyone. He had the world at his feet, and he kind of blew it."

The worst part of the bankruptcy for Ted Williams was not the death of the company but the debt to Breitbard that now couldn't be paid. Williams was apoplectic.

"The next three or four days were hell," George Carter says. "Ted was on the phone everywhere. He wanted to sell the place in Canada for the money. He was trying all kinds of things. He was out of his mind. Then on the third or fourth day, when I was washing him, I saw all these red things that had broken out on his back. He had the shingles."

"He had a red rash on his left shoulder," Frankie Brothers says. "Very painful. That was the beginning. That was August. In October, he had the pacemaker put in in Gainesville. In January of the next year, he had the open-heart surgery in New York. It was all downhill. The kid started it . . . and he's too stupid to know what he did."

The nurses claim that John-Henry had squandered most of Williams's money in attempts to go big-time with the Internet company. They said houses that had been paid off in Citrus Hills now had second and third mortgages. Investment properties had been sold or claimed by the banks. Ted Williams pretty much was broke.

On October 30, 2000, Williams was rushed to Shands Hospital in Gainesville when he had difficulty breathing. This began the long process of surgeries and increased medical troubles. Three nights earlier the following auction item had appeared on eBay, the merchandise computer website:

Description: This is a 10 foot by 15 foot USA Flag. It has been flying at Ted Williams' house for the past 6 months. Florida weather during the summer has worn the color a bit and it was replaced by a new Flag. We took this Old Flag and decided to give it a place in History forever. Ted Williams signed it in blue Sharpie on a white stripe in big bold letters. This is the only flag of its kind in existence. The other flags were not as lucky as this one.

John-Henry Williams.

The item sold for $3,050. There were 28 bids.

"Somehow," columnist Will McDonough wrote in the *Boston Globe,* "I don't think Ted Williams, a former Marine pilot, would have signed his name on a flag if he had known that U.S. Code Title 36, Section 176, paragraph (g) reads: 'The flag should never have placed upon it, nor on any part of it, any mark, insignia, word, figure, picture or drawing of any nature.' Paragraph (i) reads: 'The flag should never be used for advertising purposes in any manner whatsoever.' "

The Internet business was gone. The autograph business clearly was in trouble. The famous man was sick. What next?

"You look back now and the All-Star Game was the high point for both Ted and John-Henry," Brian O'Connor, the former business adviser, says. "After that, they both started dying. Dying in different ways, but dying."

18 Hospitals

Ted Williams, Beantown's ever cranky, but much beloved "Splendid Splinter" and baseball's last .400 hitter, died Friday. The Boston Red Sox treasure, who made good on his goal to be known as the greatest hitter ever, was 83. The Hall of Famer was pronounced dead of cardiac arrest at 8:49 A.M. at Citrus Memorial Hospital in Inverness, spokeswoman Rebecca Martin said. He had suffered a series of strokes and congestive heart failure in recent years.

ASSOCIATED PRESS, JULY 6, 2002

George Carter and Frankie Brothers split the days into two 12-hour shifts while the famous man was in Shands Hospital in Gainesville in the first week of November 2000 to have his pacemaker installed. They told the resident physicians and nurses they weren't there for medical reasons, only for the comfort of Ted Williams. He did not like to be alone.

The first schedule had George working overnight, Frankie during the days. This did not last long. An officious, know-everything nurse worked the night shift. She and George tangled, and George asked Frankie to change shifts because "I'm going to punch her lights out if I stay on nights." The change was made.

Frankie found the nurse as unbearable as George had described. He, instead, waited to see what would happen.

"Know this about Ted: he doesn't like anyone touching his feet," Brothers says. "He's peculiar, quirky about certain things. His feet were one of them. I wouldn't even dry his feet after he'd take a shower. I knew. The only one who could touch his feet was Claudia. She'd give him a rub, do a pedicure. She was all right for some reason."

Brothers explained this and other conditions to the night nurse. She heard, but didn't listen, nodded as if a truck driver were talking about physics. She was the nurse.

On one of the nights before his surgery, Williams awoke and asked Frankie what was on television. Frankie said, "CNN." The two of them settled back to watch CNN. The nurse came into the room on her rounds.

"She flips up the covers and grabs Ted's feet to take his pulse," Brothers says. "Ted goes wild. He had his urinal right there, the bedpan. He just throws the urinal at the nurse. Everything goes flying! I looked at her and started laughing. It was the funniest thing I ever saw. The nurse . . . she got off the night shift. They eventually got rid of her."

This was one of the few moments of actual humor in the next 20 months. Williams was off on a grim climb through the American medical system. He certainly was no stranger to hospitals, his body having been tweaked and repaired in the past to keep him on the ballfield and walking without pain on the city streets, but this was different. He was sleeping most of the time now. He was often disoriented when he was awake. His heart wasn't pumping enough blood to his head. This was a trip for survival.

The decision to insert the pacemaker came after days of discussion. The various heart medications no longer were working. Williams's arteries were clear enough—he'd had both carotid arteries cleaned—but his heart was firing too fast, overworking itself. Perhaps the pacemaker could control that.

"He did great," Dr. Anne Curtis, the surgeon who performed the operation, said on November 6 in the *Boston Globe*. "The surgery went very smoothly and quickly. The problem lately is that Mr. Williams has a rapid heartbeat [atrial fibrillation]. That can lead to deterioration in the heart and we had to slow it down. We implanted a single chamber pacemaker."

Williams's trip to the hospital had brought the first public worries about his possible demise, especially in Boston. He talked with Dan Shaughnessy on the phone the night before the operation and said, "I really don't need it [the pacemaker] but I'll do whatever they want me to do. . . . I'm pretty good. I don't know where everybody's getting the news that I'm near death's door and all that crap."

"He's very aware of what's going on," John-Henry said. "I'm just glad it got done and I'm looking forward to Dad getting better and getting on with his life. This had been very stressful."

Two weeks later, Williams was released from the hospital. He said that he "really felt better" and was looking forward to going back to Citrus Hills to eat a home-cooked breakfast. The truth was much darker than his words.

The pacemaker, alas, was not the answer. The breathing problems continued. The heart problems continued. He was now a candidate for more substantial, life-threatening surgery. Options were discussed for the next two months, John-Henry consulting various heart specialists. The final decision was made to send him to New York Weill Cornell Medical Center in Manhattan to repair the valves in his heart.

It was a risky surgery for anyone, extra risky for someone 82 years old and in ill health. Dr. Jeffery Borer, a famous New York cardiologist who had repaired the hearts of TV talk-show stars David Letterman and Jack Paar, would do the job. Williams's heart would be removed from his body. A leak on the mitral valve on the left side of the heart would be repaired with tissue from a pig. The tricuspid valve on the right side would be tightened with sutures. Everything would be put back together, and he hopefully would be better than he had been at the start.

The prospects were laid out for Williams at Shands. He had a 50–50 chance of survival.

"I was in the room when Dr. [Rick] Kerensky told him," Frankie Brothers says. "Dr. Kerensky said, 'Till now we've been treating you with medication and we've put in the pacemaker, but it's just not working. Your only option now is open-heart surgery.' Ted said, 'Well, what chance do I have?' Dr. Kerensky said, 'To tell the truth, it's about 50–50.' Ted said. 'You know what? I've had a hell of a life. I have no regrets. If I have to die on an operating table, so be it.' That's a direct quote."

Williams was flown to New York by private jet on January 14, 2001, and the surgery was performed the next day. A team of 14 doctors, nurses, and technicians worked on him for nine and a half hours. He came out of the operating room attached to six IV lines. A tracheotomy tube had been inserted to control his respiration. Dr. Borer told John-Henry that his father would have been dead within five days without surgery.

For the next five weeks Williams stayed in the New York hospital. Rumors that he was near death began to circulate again, but were squelched.

He was an old man, a sick man. That was the reply. This would take time. Not included in the reply was the fact that he had another problem now—his kidneys were failing.

"The operation was a success," Frankie Brothers says. "George and I couldn't see Ted until five or six days later, but when we did he looked and sounded good. The next day, though, he started running a fever. He never looked or sounded good again.

"A staph infection had set in. To stop the staph infection they had to give him vancomycin, the strongest antibiotic there is. The problem with vancomycin . . . it gets rid of the infection, but it kills your kidneys in the process. They wound up giving Ted vancomycin twice. Ted wound up on dialysis."

"He opens his eyes in response to his name being called, mouths words from time to time and shakes his head appropriately in response to certain questions—all of which represent high-level responses and things he wasn't able to do two weeks ago," Dr. Borer said optimistically on February 6 in the *Globe*. "We've now shifted into a phase of chronic recovery, of rehabilitation. That's an interval during which progress can be expected to be slower. It's not that good things aren't happening. It's just that they happen at a far slower rate than during the first couple of weeks."

On February 19, Williams was transferred to Sharp Hospital in San Diego for continued rehabilitation. There were other options, notably Shands in Gainesville and the Spaulding Hospital in Boston, but the transfer to San Diego, to a hospital no more than five miles from Utah Street and the North Park playground, was facilitated by Bob Breitbard. He arranged for two condos, one for John-Henry, another for Frankie and George, and set up the hospital. He wanted to see his friend come back to the old hometown.

The visit would last for four months. Williams would spend most of his time listed in either intensive or critical care. Another staph infection brought a final round of vancomycin. The dialysis would wear him down. It was news when he simply could talk.

"How is he?" were his reported first words since the surgery in New York.

John-Henry was telling him on March 15 that John Glenn had called. Williams interrupted with his question. John-Henry was heartened by the cognitive process that had to take place: listening to the conversation, knowing who John Glenn was, forming the question, asking the question.

A second question—a request for red wine—also was noteworthy. On April 29, he talked with Dr. Borer on the phone, the first time Borer had heard him speak. Williams remembered that the doctor had promised him a glass of red wine if all went well. Where was the red wine? This also seemed encouraging, "the sign of a functioning intellect," Borer said.

The time in San Diego was strange. The nurses, Carter and Brothers, say that John-Henry mostly was absent from the scene. The first thing he did was install five computers in the condo. He played his games for days and traveled the Net and did business. He seldom visited the hospital, often disappearing altogether on weekends. Where did he go? Frankie and George found the public comments about John-Henry and his concern for his father laughable. Where was he?

John-Henry, on the other side, complained to friends that the nurses on the West Coast took liberties, weren't around as much as they should have been. They thought they were on some kind of paid vacation instead of taking care of his father.

Who was right?

The nurses complained about the people who had access to Ted. John-Henry turned away most visitors. He kept telling Bobby-Jo's daughter Dawn, who lived in Anaheim, that Ted was "too tired" or too something for a visit every time she called. Old friends like Joe Villarino from San Diego were refused. Tommy Lasorda was allowed. Bobby Knight was allowed.

"Dolores showed up," George Carter says. "She was allowed to visit. She tried to feed Ted some homemade remedy from a jar. All the monitors went crazy. She could have killed him. They threw her out of the hospital."

The split between the famous man's son and the famous man's caregivers grew larger and larger, ever more obvious, and finally became a total rupture. On "May 18 or May 19," Brothers says, "John-Henry came in, threw a couple of plane tickets at George and me, and said, 'You guys are going home.'" The nurses felt terrible, as if they were leaving a best friend in peril.

"We went to the hospital that night. Ted cried like a baby when we told him," Brothers says. "Ted was crying, George was crying, George's wife, Barbara, was crying, I was crying. I felt so bad for Ted. At the time, I wished I was a man of means, so I could say to John-Henry, 'Screw you, you don't have to pay me. I'm staying here with your father.' George felt the same way."

The nurses returned to Florida. A month later, Williams followed. John-Henry brought him back to Shands in Gainesville. He would stay there for two months, then return to the big house in Citrus Hills on August 30, 2001, his 83rd birthday. Frankie and George were not rehired. New nurses were brought into the house.

"I'm feeling pretty good," Williams would report in a whisper to Dan Shaughnessy in the *Globe*. "But my whole life has been knocked out of joint. Oh, boy, I've never been through years like I've been through in the last four years. There's nothing I can compare it to in my life. I really have been through hell."

"It's still taking some time for Dad to kind of wake up," John-Henry said. "But I can only imagine what it's like to be under the weather for eight months. He's definitely not as strong as before the surgery, but he's getting stronger every day. This is so different from what happened to poor Joe DiMaggio. Joe went home to die. Dad hasn't come home to die. He's come home to live and get better."

Despite the sweet, hopeful words of a dutiful son, the picture of John-Henry had not changed for many people around him. While Dr. Kerensky praised John-Henry, remarked on his caring, other staffers at Shands were not so sure. They didn't like the way he dealt with them or with his father. They noticed a strange instruction on his father's chart: nothing was to be done to possibly impair range of motion of his right arm. No IVs were to be inserted into the right extremity. The right extremity was off-limits.

"Why is that?" they wondered.

"So he'll be able to sign autographs again," they were told.

On September 11, the day of the terrorist attacks in Washington and New York, Jacques Prudhomme went to the big house to visit Williams. John-Henry had asked the cook to remain available for Williams's return, but when the time came, he offered a salary half as large as Prudhomme had been making. Prudhomme refused.

He visited now as a friend, bringing along half of a Reuben sandwich for Williams for lunch. He sat in amazement in the kitchen he had redesigned, watching the news on the television, the destruction of the World Trade Center in New York. He also stared in amazement at what was in front of him.

Williams was undergoing physical therapy. All of the exercises, all of the work, were being done to restore strength and mobility to his right arm, his right hand.

"Just for the autographs," Prudhomme says. "It disgusted me. I went into my car and cried. I said I would never come back to this place again. It was all too sad."

The mystery of where John-Henry was during those missing weekends in San Diego was solved. He had been doing research, looking into a future medical procedure for his father. He called Bobby-Jo with the results while Ted was at Shands. He was excited.

"Have you ever heard of cryonics?" he asked.

The question struck her as odd. She had indeed heard of the speculative science of freezing bodies for a possible space age cure and afterlife. News about medicine was one of her hobbies. She had seen a television report about cryonics somewhere. She thought the concept was bizarre.

"Yes," she replied. "I've heard about cryonics."

He asked her what she knew. She answered and he was impressed.

"What do you think about it?" he asked.

"I think it sucks," she replied.

"Well, let me ask you something. What do you think if we did that with Dad?"

"You're not serious about this, are you? You have to be kidding."

"No, I'm not."

"That's insane. It's totally off-base. It's not going to happen."

"Why not?"

Bobby-Jo repeated the dialogue—her version—in a story two years later by Peter Kerasotis in *Florida Today*. She said she started taking notes about the time John-Henry said he wanted to have their father frozen. She continued through the part where he said, "We don't have to take Dad's whole body. We can just take the head." She said he talked about the possibilities of making money from Williams's DNA, with "all these little Ted Williams's running around." The idea made her sick. She thought John-Henry was sick.

He asked her to go to Scottsdale, Arizona, to a company called Alcor, which processed, froze, and stored the bodies. He had been fascinated by what he saw. She refused.

Could this really happen? Could her father's body be frozen when he died?

"I didn't know what to say," Bobby-Jo says now. "We were flabbergasted. We wanted to say something, but we didn't know how. We're asked, 'Why didn't you call reporters in June when John-Henry first contacted you about all this shit?' If we did, people would have said, 'Oh, my God, she's gone off the deep end.' "

The relationship between Bobby-Jo and her two half-siblings never had been close. Since she had arrived at Citrus Hills in 1999 with Mark, the two generations of children had looked at each other with great suspicion. Each side thought the other had mercenary motives.

"I told John-Henry once, 'You know why everything you touch turns to shit?' Mark Ferrell says. " 'It's because you're full of shit.' "

Ferrell and Bobby-Jo were aware of John-Henry's stranglehold on her father's financial situation before they even moved. They had visited him in Citrus Hills and knew the nurses who had worked for him, had heard all the stories about the autographs. They knew about Hitter.net and the worries about where all the money was going. That was one of the reasons they moved.

"My mom never had the courage to confront John-Henry," Bobby-Jo's daughter, Dawn Hebding, says. "I think she was afraid of him. Everyone told her, 'This is your father. Why are you allowing all this to take place? Pack your shit up and get down there. Have people see what's going on.'

"My grandfather eventually asked her to move down. That's why she and Mark did. I also think it was a last-ditch effort on their part to possibly get a piece of the pie."

When they first arrived, living in their RV next to the Crystal River while their house was constructed on one of the three Citrus Hills lots Williams had distributed to his children, they had some access to the big house. Mark, a man with his own bluster, would do the verbal dances with Williams, telling him that the great athletes were the NASCAR drivers, not the baseball players. Williams would dance back. Everyone said Williams had a respect for Mark for straightening out Bobby-Jo's life. Williams, Ferrell says, was interested in the construction of the house, interested in what it was like to live in a trailer, interested in his daughter.

There was never a doubt, though, that John-Henry was in charge. There also never was a doubt that John-Henry was not happy that she and Mark had arrived.

"He didn't want Bobby-Jo to see her father," George Carter says. "Ted loved Bobby-Jo. He said so many times. John-Henry just didn't want her around. We finally got her and Mark up to the house for dinner one night. It was very nice. Ted was happy. I went to the window once, though, and looked out. I could see John-Henry on the porch of this neighbor's house, a doctor. John-Henry was watching everything with binoculars."

"We went up there one Thanksgiving, my wife and I and Bobby-Jo and Mark, for Thanksgiving," Jack Gard says. "My wife made a dish, turkey stuffed with oysters, that Ted really liked. We invited everyone. Claudia stayed down in St. Petersburg. John-Henry said he was going back to Massachusetts with Anita to her parents for the holiday.

"Halfway through the meal, John-Henry showed up. Out of nowhere. Hadn't gone to Massachusetts. Killed everything. He just had to know what was going on."

Dawn Hebding visited the house once with her son and daughter, Ted's great-grandchildren. She says she was surprised, seeing pictures everywhere in the house, that there were no pictures of the great-grandchildren. She had been sending them for years. Her thought was that John-Henry had grabbed the pictures, never shown them to his father.

Other things also bothered her. Anita arrived at almost the same time she did, and stayed and seemed to monitor the conversation. And then there were the cameras. Hebding had been warned about the cameras by John Sullivan, the nurse. She found them intrusive.

"The cameras were on in Grandpa's bedroom," she says. "They were trained right on the bed, and the picture was shown on the television in the living room. There's Grandpa in his underwear. All this construction was going on in the house, remodeling the kitchen, all these people working, and Grandpa didn't have any privacy at all. I really didn't think that was right. Everybody deserves some privacy."

Eric Abel, the lawyer for both Williams and John-Henry, also the lawyer for Citrus Hills, disagrees with the notion that John-Henry kept Bobby-Jo and her father apart. Abel says Ted Williams was the one who wanted the distance. He wanted nothing to do with Bobby-Jo.

"I bet I talked to Ted ten times about Bobby-Jo," Abel says. "Every time, he'd call her 'that fucken syphilitic cunt.' I wondered what she had done to make him feel that way. The final straw, I know, was when he had the problem with his granddaughter."

Bobby-Jo's youngest daughter, Sherri, was a pharmacist's assistant. Dawn Hebding says Sherri told Williams that she wanted to go to pharmacy school to become a registered pharmacist. He agreed to send her. At the start of every semester, she requested money. He provided it.

Hebding says John-Henry was suspicious. He checked with the pharmacy school where Sherri was supposed to be a student. There was no record of her enrollment. She simply was spending the money. He told Ted.

"My grandfather was enraged, he disowned my sister," Dawn Hebding says. "My mother and my sister and Mark, they all blamed John-Henry. I said, 'Well, wait a minute here. He wasn't the one who wasn't enrolled in pharmacy college.' All I saw, to tell the truth, was my grandfather surrounded by money-scrounging weasels. My family included.

"That's why I moved to California, just to get out of there. California was as far away as I could get."

Williams dropped Bobby-Jo from his will. Eric Abel says Williams wanted her to be completely shut out, all past provisions and trusts changed. Abel says he salvaged one trust for Bobby-Jo in the end. Williams was not happy, but agreed with the move.

Abel now told Williams that he, the father, would have to meet with his daughter to tell her the news. Williams did not want to do this. Abel persisted, and finally Bobby-Jo and Mark came up to the big house for a breakfast meeting.

Abel says he did most of the talking at the meeting. He tried to put everything in a positive light. "Ted felt he had contributed more to Bobby-Jo throughout her life than he had for his other two younger children, blah-blah." "There still was one 1986 irrevocable trust in her name, blah-blah, so you're still going to get something." He asked Bobby-Jo at the end of his presentation if all of this was all right.

"She said, 'That's fine with me, but Daddy, I want to hear it from you,' " Abel says. "Ted looked at her and said, 'It's what I fucken want.' He said it just that way. I felt bad for her. That was a bad day."

Bobby-Jo says her refusal to accept John-Henry's cryonics proposition was what ended her contact with her father. She had seen Williams at Shands four days before his birthday return to Citrus Hills, but when she called and asked John-Henry when she could come to the house with a cake and balloons, John-Henry said her visiting days were done. If she appeared at the house, he would have her arrested.

"Why would you do this?" she says she asked.

"Because you're not a team player," she says John-Henry replied.

In the following months, she would hire three different lawyers in attempts to see her father. Nothing would work. She felt her father was too ill to know what was happening to him and around him. John-Henry now not only had power of attorney but had moved into the big house after Williams's pacemaker surgery. He said he had moved to be closer in case something happened. His critics said he had moved to establish legal residence so that he'd be able to claim the contents of the house, including the many pieces of memorabilia, when his father died.

Bobby-Jo felt that John-Henry not only had control but was planning a terrible thing. The idea of cryonics, her father's body frozen, ate at her. She told some friends, but no one else. Who would believe her? Would John-Henry really do this?

Eric Abel, John-Henry's lawyer, again tells a different story. Again, he says Ted did not want to see her. Again, he says he told Ted it would be good to see her. Again, Ted declined with bad words. This time Abel says Williams called his daughter "that dried-up cunt."

"It's sad," Abel, who at the time lived next door to Bobby-Jo, says. "She fancies herself his great champion, and he could give a shit about her."

In the late fall of 2001, there was a sweet interlude. The happy past intruded, just for three days, on the grinding present. Dominic DiMaggio and Johnny Pesky appeared at Citrus Hills. David Halberstam would tell the story of their visit in his short book called *The Teammates*.

"For many years, the glue that held them together as friends was Williams; someone that great, one of the very best ever at what they all did, had rare peer power," Halberstam wrote. " 'It was,' Pesky once said of him, 'like there was a star on top of his head, pulling everyone toward him like a beacon, and letting everyone around him know that he was different and that he was special in some marvelous way and that we were much more special because we had played with him.' "

The winner in the business game after baseball had been Dominic. After leaving the Red Sox prematurely in 1953, he started a fabricating company that made padding for dashboards and car doors. For a long time, it was virtually the only company that made padding for dashboards and car doors. He also added a company that made rugs for cars.

He had an entire second career in business and did very well. He is a wealthy man, retired now, but still spends most of his days in his den watching the scrolling CNBC fluctuations of the stock market across the bottom of his big-screen television.

He never tried very hard to bring Williams into his business, figuring

Ted had advisers and opportunities and was living in Florida, but he did offer Pesky a chance. Pesky declined.

"Dominic," Pesky said, "I'm a jock. I was born a jock and will die a jock. They'll cut the uniform off me."

(Pesky, coaching with the Red Sox, once appeared on talk radio with Dr. Joy Browne, a psychologist whose show was on the station that broadcast the Sox games. Pesky was asked how the interview went. "Great," he said. "She doesn't know a fucken thing about baseball and I don't know a fucken thing about anything else. We had a wonderful conversation.")

DiMaggio and Pesky both wound up staying in the Boston area. Pesky lived in Lynn and married Ruth, a local girl—Mickey McDermott lived with them for a year as a rookie and said "it was like living with your father"—and then bought a ranch house in Swampscott. He has been with the Red Sox for pieces of seven decades as player, manager, broadcaster, and coach. He still puts on the suit, 84 years old, and hits fungoes to young outfielders. He is a local treasure, a friendly and perpetually kind man.

DiMaggio, troubled with assorted ailments, including the rare Paget's disease, which left him walking in a hunched-over position, raised his kids in his wife Emily's hometown of Wellesley Hills, and then they moved to Marion, on the water, next to Cape Cod. They also bought a home in Ocean Ridge, Florida, near Palm Beach.

In late September, early October, the weather growing cold, DiMaggio was making plans to go from Marion to Ocean Ridge for the winter. Emily was flying down early, Dominic to follow on a flight a few days later, but now he had second thoughts. The 9/11 disaster a few weeks earlier had made air travel a hassle. He said he didn't need the hassle.

"I'm going to drive down," he said one night over cocktails. "I'll stop off and see Ted."

"Dominic, you can't drive down," Emily reminded him with great logic. "You're 84 years old."

A third participant in the conversation was 64-year-old Dick Flavin. A former local Boston television commentator, Flavin now is a toastmaster and after-dinner speaker and producer of a play on the life of Boston politician Tip O'Neill. DiMaggio was Flavin's boyhood idol—the nice tale of a fourth-grade kid with glasses finding inspiration in a major leaguer with glasses—and the two men have been friends for over 30 years. Flavin was into his third glass of chardonnay when Dominic proposed driving and Emily proposed not driving.

"I can drive!" Flavin said, surprising even himself. "I'll go with you!"

The plan quickly was finalized and expanded over more chardonnay. It became a nice little adventure, maybe not a trip down the Amazon, but a challenge. Drive down to see Ted! Pesky was called and was an instant addition. DiMaggio was scheduled to appear at a reunion for members of the Philadelphia Athletics Historical Society. There would be a stop in Philadelphia for that, another stop in Virginia for rest, then a flat-out push to Florida. This would be an old men's road trip. They would travel in Dominic's steel-gray Jaguar.

"We go to Philadelphia and it's wonderful," Flavin says. "The reunion is held in some function room of a Best Western, and there's all these old ballplayers and fans. Packed. Maybe 500 people. Johnny and Dom both talk and the people love it. They sign a million autographs. A guy gets up and says, 'If we'd had crowds like this for the Philadelphia Athletics when they played here, they'd still be the Philadelphia Athletics.' "

"Eddie Joost was there and he looked terrific," Pesky says. "I thought I was doing okay, but he was terrific. He was a good-looking guy, of course, when he played. And he was still good-looking now."

"Bobby Shantz was there," DiMaggio says. "I could never hit that little bastard."

Back on the road the next day, Flavin and DiMaggio shared the driving. Pesky sat in the backseat. His contribution was that he wouldn't smoke any of his cigars for the entire trip. The miles passed with good conversation and laughter. DiMaggio and Flavin did most of the talking. Pesky did a lot of the laughing, looking from the window in some place, Lancaster, Pennsylvania, perhaps, and saying, "I think I used to manage in this fucken town!" More laughter. The language deconstructed as the miles passed, the bad words of the clubhouse and baseball brought back and savored.

"Dominic and I thought we were the funniest guys on the planet the way we made Johnny laugh," Flavin says. "We were really proud of ourselves. Then in Florida, Johnny and I share a room and he walks in, sits down, and clicks on *The Golden Girls*. He laughs just as hard as he did at Dominic and me."

The travelers never had turned on the radio during the entire trip, just talking, but in the last stages DiMaggio slipped in a Pavarotti CD. He sang along with the famous singer. Opera. His brother, Vince, it was noted during the conversation, used to sing opera in the outfield between pitches.

The three men pulled into Hernando early on a Monday evening, then went to Ted's house in the morning. Dominic had seen Ted during Ted's recent decline, visiting him in San Diego, waiting two days just to get a reaction. Flavin recently had buried his mother and was steeled a bit to the effects of disease and age. Pesky was unprepared for what would come next, Williams's weight now down around 130 pounds.

"We go in the house and the first thing we can see is Ted," Flavin says. "He was at the end of the long living room, next to the window, in profile, that famous face, but he was sort of huddled over in his wheelchair. He heard us coming, but couldn't see. Dominic shouted, 'Teddie, it's Dommie.' He started running on his bad legs. He went over close so Ted could see him. 'Hello, Dommie,' Ted said. His eyes welled up. They hugged. Pesky, who wasn't ready for this, just started bawling. It was a scene. Dominic is running as fast as he can on those old legs. Pesky is holding back."

For the better part of the next three days, the three old ballplayers, old friends, told stories, told lies, rolled through the events that had happened as young men. Flavin watched it all, part of it and not part of it, entranced.

"They'd talk about who was the toughest pitcher for each of them," Flavin says. "Pesky said it was Spud Chandler. Dominic said it was Early Wynn. Williams said it was Ted Lyons, said he never could figure Ted Lyons out."

Dominic would ask Williams how he ever could stand as close to the plate as he did. Williams would ask Dominic how he never could figure out what pitch struck him out. Remember that?

Dialogue after DiMaggio struck out:

WILLIAMS: What did he get you on?
DiMAGGIO: I don't know.
WILLIAMS: What do you mean you don't know?
DiMAGGIO: I don't know.
WILLIAMS: You stupid son of a bitch.

Williams told the story—again—of his first trip to spring training, about the flood in Los Angeles and meeting Bobby Doerr in El Paso and arriving in Sarasota. There was talk about obscure names, about pitchers like Frank Baumann, "who could have been great if he hadn't been hurt."

Ted posed the question, who was the most underrated clutch hitter they ever had played against. Mickey Vernon? Larry Doby? No, Eddie Robinson. That's the guy!

There was conversation about everything, all the funny moments of a shared time, a shared experience long ago that shaped all three men's lives forever. The Red Sox. Teddy. Dommie. Johnny. Kids' names on old men. There was singing.

"I sang Ted an Italian song," DiMaggio says. "Then I told him the story behind the song. It was about two best friends who loved the same girl. Then we sang, 'That Old Pal of Mine'—'The pal that I love, stole the gal that I love'—and the Ted Lewis song, 'Me and My Shadow.' We even sang 'When You're Smiling.' Then Flavin sang some Irish songs and did his poem."

For years, starting when he was in college at Georgetown, performing in bars for free drinks, Flavin had done a dramatic rendition of "Casey at the Bat." Before the trip, with appropriate apologies to Ernest Lawrence Thayer, he had reworked the poem into "Teddy at the Bat." He performed it now for the subject, moving close to be inside Ted's restricted tunnel vision, doing all the elaborate windups and swings and grimaces:

> The outlook wasn't brilliant for the Red Sox nine that day,
> The score stood four to two with but one inning left to play.
> So when Stephens died at first and Tebbetts did the same,
> A pallor wreathed the features of the patrons of the game.
>
> A straggling few got up to go, leaving there the rest
> With the hope that springs eternal within the human breast.
> They thought if only Teddy could get a whack at that—
> They'd put even money now with Teddy at the bat.
>
> But Dom preceded Teddy and Pesky was on deck.
> The first of them was in a slump. The other was a wreck.
> So on that stricken multitude a deathlike silence sat,
> For there seemed but little chance of Teddy's getting to the bat.
>
> But Dom let drive a single, to the wonderment of all,
> And Pesky, of all people, tore the cover off the ball.
> When the dust had lifted, and they saw what had occurred,
> There was Johnny safe on second and Dominic on third.

Then from that gladdened multitude went up a joyous yell,
It rumbled in the mountains and rattled in the dell.
It struck upon the hillside and rebounded on the flat,
For Teddy, Teddy Ballgame, was advancing to the bat.

There was ease in Teddy's manner as he stepped into his place,
There was pride in Teddy's bearing and a smile on Teddy's face.
And when, responding to the cheers he lightly doffed his hat,
   (I'm making that part up)
No stranger in the crowd could doubt 'twas Teddy at the bat.

Ten thousand eyes were on him as he wiped his hands with dirt,
Five thousand tongues applauded as he wiped them on his
      shirt.
Then when the writhing pitcher ground the ball into his hip,
Defiance gleamed in Teddy's eyes, a sneer curled Teddy's lip.

And now the leather-covered sphere came hurtling through the
      air,
And Teddy stood a-watching it in haughty grandeur there.
Close by the sturdy batsman the ball unheeded sped.
"That ain't my style," said Teddy. "Strike one!" the umpire
      said.

From the benches black with people went up a muffled roar,
Like the beating of the storm waves on the stern and distant
      shore.
"Kill him! Kill the umpire!" someone shouted on the stand,
And it's likely they'd have killed him had not Teddy raised his
      hand.

With a smile of Christian charity great Teddy's visage shone.
He stilled the rising tumult and bade the game go on.
He signaled the pitcher, and once more the spheroid flew.
But Teddy still ignored it, and the umpire said, "Strike two!"

"Fraud!" cried the maddened thousands, and the echo
      answered "Fraud."
But one scornful look from Teddy and the audience was awed.

They saw his face grow stern and cold, they saw his muscles strain,
And they knew that Teddy wouldn't let that ball go by again.

The sneer is gone from Teddy's lip; his teeth are clenched in hate.
He pounds with cruel vengeance his bat upon the plate.
And now the pitcher holds the ball, and now he lets it go,
And now the air is shattered by the force of Teddy's blow.

Oh, somewhere in this land of ours the sun is shining bright,
The band is playing somewhere, and somewhere hearts are light,
And somewhere men are laughing, and somewhere children shout.
And they're going wild at Fenway Park 'cause Teddy hit one out!

Everybody cheered at the end. Williams loved the poem. During the three days, Flavin performed it five times. Every time, there was the same reaction. The days developed a pattern. The three visitors would arrive for breakfast, stay through the morning, then leave so Williams could rest. They would be back at 4:30, the customary early dinner hour, then stay till Williams was tired again. Pesky left a day early, flying back to Boston, and Flavin and DiMaggio came back for one more dinner and one more breakfast.

DiMaggio had become closer and closer to Williams through the years, closer at the end than he was to his brother Joe. The death of his brother on March 8, 1999, was actually a final bond between Dominic and Ted. Williams had called virtually every day while Joe hung in a coma. How's Joe? Is he any better? Joe's death hit Williams on a personal level, a family kind of death, the loss of an odd and remote brother, the one man who knew the complications of Williams's life better than any other man on the planet. Never close, friendly enough, but never friends, the two superstars had been forced to deal with the same adulation, the same attention, the same artificial sainthood. They were the two lead characters in the same myth. Could anyone else understand what that had been like? Joe and Ted, they understood best the demands of each other's lives.

Dominic, as much as anyone else, understood what those demands had done. He was familiar with the insecurities underneath both halos.

"I remember we were at a barbecue once at Al Cassidy's," Dominic says. "Teddy said to me, 'Dommie, I admire what you've done. You're successful in business. You married well. You're a clean-cut guy. You've lived a wonderful life.'

"I said to him, 'Well, what about you? You've done great.' Ted said, 'Aw, if it hadn't been for Sears Roebucks, I'd be flat on my fanny.' He was really down. I said, 'Teddy, you've done better than 99 percent of the chief executives of the corporations in this country. If anyone should argue that with you, you should just spit in their eye. You've done as much as any man can do in this life.' "

Williams, he remembered, nodded. But didn't seem convinced.

The three days done, DiMaggio and Flavin drove off toward Ocean Ridge. Ted stayed where he was, captive to the machines and to the parts of his body that were clogged up, shutting down, and turning off.

The last time Williams appeared in public was on February 17, 2002. The occasion was the Ninth Annual Hitters Hall of Fame induction ceremonies at the Ted Williams Museum. John-Henry was the promotional hand behind the production.

A year earlier, Williams had missed the event for the first time because he was in the hospital in San Diego. The few people who had seen him since his return, his bedroom now resembling a hospital room, dialysis every day, were almost certain he would not appear this year. John-Henry was noncommittal.

"We'll see what kind of a day he's having," the son said. "We'll see how he's feeling."

For high-rollers, who paid $1,000 a head, there was a weekend of activity featuring a golf tournament and a fishing tournament on Saturday, followed by a country club banquet at night. The rollers mainly were longtime associates of Williams's, friends, or longtime fans or collectors who specialized in Williams memorabilia. The induction ceremony on Sunday was held in a white rent-a-tent outside the museum and was open to the public.

A number of former recipients of awards, plus former teammates and baseball friends, including DiMaggio and Pesky, McDermott, Enos Slaughter, and 91-year-old Elden Auker, were in attendance. Honorees for this year included Cal Ripken Jr., recently retired from the Baltimore Orioles, and Jason Giambi, Don Mattingly, and the late Roger Maris from the Yankees. The master of ceremonies was former Los Angeles Dodgers manager Tommy Lasorda.

Lasorda was halfway through the program, rolling out his usual jokes about Italian men and long-suffering wives, when there was sudden activity at the side of the white tent. A flap was pulled back and a blue van could be seen, engine running, side door open, something happening. The something was the arrival of Ted.

He was in a wheelchair and was lowered from the van by one of those hydraulic lifts. He was wearing a blue sports coat and a blue cardigan sweater and a red hunting shirt and had a blue blanket with a Red Sox logo on the front tucked up to his chest. John-Henry directed the unloading, then took charge of the wheelchair. He pushed his father up a ramp onto the back of the stage. Claudia joined them.

"We have a special guest," Lasorda said, interrupting his patter. "Let's wait a few seconds until he gets here."

"Ladies and gentlemen, the greatest hitter that God ever put on earth, Ted Williams," Lasorda finally announced.

The crowd rose, applauded, but not with the type of reaction that might have been expected. A large number of Baltimore fans were there to see Ripken, another large group of Yankee fans to see Giambi and Mattingly. Ripken, Giambi, and Mattingly all would receive larger ovations during the afternoon.

This was far from the scene of 1999 at Fenway at the All-Star Game. The face of the man in the wheelchair hardly resembled the face on the lids from the Dixie Cups, the covers of the *Life* magazines, the special edition lithographs all the collectors owned. The drawn skin was almost transparent. The gray hair was a lifeless winter grass. The eyes were unfocused. A tracheotomy tube was stuck in Ted Williams's throat.

The high-rollers were shocked. Some of the former ballplayers and friends cried. Enos Slaughter, who would be dead within the year, blubbered. The rest of the crowd—the Orioles fans and the Yankees fans and the drive-by curious off the Florida highways—simply stared at the sadness as if it were a traffic accident.

Lasorda helped Williams, now at the front of the stage, make a brief two-fingered wave. John-Henry dropped to one knee at one side of his father. Claudia went to the other side.

"We knew this day was coming for a few weeks," John-Henry said to the crowd. "We never clearly realized what it would mean to be on the same stage here with my dad and my sister, breathing the same air everyone else is breathing, and knowing how valuable life is and what love is, from a daughter to a father and from a son to a father.

"I don't think there are two children luckier in the whole wide world than my sister and I. All I want him to know is that I know the hell that he and I have gone through in the last year and a half, and I and my sister could not have done it without him. Dad, we love you."

The words, normal enough on the printed page, had a surreal quality in the situation. What was the point? Why had John-Henry brought Williams here? To tell him something he could have told him in private 100 times per day? Was this a show of love, togetherness, what? Was this a photo op, a marketing idea? What? It clearly wasn't a show of returned health or vigor. Was it supposed to be a sentimental good-bye? Wouldn't the words have been different? What? What was the point? Again, this was the mystery with John-Henry.

Bobby-Jo wasn't in the crowd, even though she lived close enough to walk to the ceremony. Mark Ferrell said he and his wife were watching the Daytona 500 on television instead. He said they wanted nothing to do with John-Henry's "exploitation" of her father.

"Ted can hardly talk," Elden Auker, who had visited Williams in the morning with Lasorda and another friend, told the *Boston Globe*. "He's got this thing on his throat, he's on dialysis every night, and now he's lost his appetite and is losing weight. His face is very pale. They're just keeping him alive. It just isn't right. He's in a wheelchair, he can't take care of himself, he's got someone around him 24 hours a day. It's just sad to see.

"It's like he's on display. Of course people were thrilled to see him, but to see him in that condition, to see him like that? I've known him since 1939. We've been friends all these years. To see what he's going through, just keeping him alive . . . it just doesn't seem right. But I guess that's life. I guess there's nothing you can do about it."

Williams said nothing during the entire ceremony. Lasorda tried to prod him, saying, "What about all those pictures, perfect swing, ball always going out of the park . . . didn't you ever hit a ground ball? Didn't you ever hit into a double play?" Nothing. Never had a joke fallen so flat. Lasorda peeled away, realizing the impropriety. Nothing.

The one thing Williams did was chew gum. He chewed while John-Henry brought him out. He chewed while John-Henry talked. He chewed while John-Henry wheeled him back, down the ramp, back into the van, and back to the big house on the biggest hill on the Florida peninsula. He chewed with a ferocity, as if chewing was the one outlet for expression left after all the other outlets had been dimmed to subsistence levels. He chewed and chewed and chewed.

George Carter, the nurse, said that Williams had a habit of grinding his teeth when agitated. He had ground them down so low that they had been bonded so he wouldn't grind them to nothing.

The van pulled out. The ceremony continued. Less than five months later, Ted Williams was dead.

John Butcher came to work at two o'clock in the morning on July 5, 2002. That was how the night shift ran now at Ted Williams's house. The dialysis nurses would work until two, running Williams's blood through the machine in his bedroom, and then the night nurse would arrive and work until ten in the morning. A nurse's aide and a sleeping nurse-practitioner also were in the house.

The easy, ad hoc camaraderie of Frankie and George, George half-sleeping on a big chair in the living room, Williams creeping out at 3:00 A.M. to try to scare him, George jumping up to say "Boo," was gone. These were more professional nurses hired to take care of a very sick man. No less compassionate than Frankie or George or John Sullivan or Jack Gard, they simply did not know their patient as well. He had been a very sick man from the moment they were hired.

"We didn't talk much," John Butcher says. "He was tired and sick most of the time. If you would ask questions, sometimes he would answer, depending on how he felt. I don't know much about baseball, so we couldn't talk about that. The only thing I could talk about with him was fishing."

The life of Ted Williams had become more and more quiet. The goals had become smaller and smaller. A good day had been when he could walk a few steps, and then it was when he could stand up, and then it was when he could sit up, and now, what next? He went in and out of the present. There was little doubt that he was wearing down.

Dominic DiMaggio called every morning.

"I'd gone up to see him again in April, on the way back north," DiMaggio says. "Ted wasn't in the best condition. It was apparent to me that he was surrounded by a lot of people who didn't know anything about baseball. I thought he needed baseball. That's why I started calling every day. I'd fill him in on what was happening. Sometimes we'd talk for a while, he'd seem alert. Sometimes not."

If talk of baseball was lacking, the sound of the game was still around. The background noise to Williams's days in the past months, oddly enough, had been the whack of a bat hitting a baseball. John-Henry, at age 33, was giving the sport one more try.

A batting cage now sat next to the big house. John-Henry had purchased a high-technology, $100,000 pitching machine, the most advanced pitching machine on the market. Some major league teams didn't have such a high-tech machine. Videos of the best pitchers in the game—Roger Clemens, Randy Johnson, whoever—could be projected on a screen in the background. The machine could be programmed to throw the pitches that the individual pitchers threw: sliders, sinkers, big sweeping curves, 100 mph fastballs.

John-Henry had bulked up, filled with the food supplements of modern athletes. He had hired a personal batting coach. Every day, he swung against the virtual Cy Young Award winners, sending baseballs into the virtual seats in the nets.

"I went out to see Ted in the spring," Rich Eschen, the former employee at Grand-Slam Marketing, says. "Before I got to the house, I ran into John-Henry outside the batting cage. We talked, and he asked if I wanted to hit a few. I said I didn't know. I'd played college baseball, but I was 50 years old. He said, 'Give it a try.'

"I went into the cage and I'm wearing, you know, a pair of Docksiders, and he cranked up the machine, and pretty soon I was swinging at 100-mile-an-hour fastballs. I'd never *seen* 100-mile-an-hour fastballs in my life. I hit for a while, then went in to see Ted. He was in his bed, connected to the machines. He was not good. I don't think he really recognized me."

Rumors abounded about John-Henry's reasons for swinging in the cage. What was he trying to do? Maybe he was getting ready to play Ted in a movie. Maybe he was getting ready to actually try baseball. ("He thinks he can do anything," Arthur "Buzz" Hamon, a former director of the Ted Williams Museum, a critic, said. "He can drive a fucken race car. He can climb Mount Everest. He can play baseball. He's fucken delusional.")

On June 20, he signed a contract with the Gulf Coast League Red Sox in Fort Myers, Florida, for $850 per month. On June 26, he made his professional baseball debut by going 0-for-3. He definitely was trying to play.

The sportswriters and sportscasters at the game, mostly from Boston, out-numbered the fans.

"He has to get it out of his system," his sister Claudia said. "Good for him. Wasn't there that movie, *The Rookie?* If that guy could do it, why couldn't my brother? I know he wants to do this."

Other opinions were uniformly negative. This was crazy! The only reason this kid—no, this man—was being given a chance at his age and with his nonbaseball background was that he was Ted Williams's son. This was a free pass. No one walks into baseball at 33 and plays.

"It's a total embarrassment," a "high-ranking Red Sox official" said in the *Boston Globe.* "He couldn't make a good high school team. We let him hit against two of our lower-level Gulf Coast League pitchers, and in 16 at bats he only managed five foul balls."

"I have one thing that's a total unknown," John-Henry replied in the same article. "And that's the blood rushing through my veins and it's from a guy that did do it."

The argument was soon moot. On June 27, John-Henry broke a rib crashing into the stands while chasing a foul pop-up. Two games into his career, still hitless, he was on the injured list, out for five or six weeks. He decided to stay with the team in Fort Myers, getting treatment for his injury.

That left his father home alone, pretty much on his own, with the new nurses. He lived in his own private nursing home.

"He would tell us sometimes how he appreciated us," Virginia Hiley-Self, one of the nurses, says. "Then sometimes, when he'd get mad at us, he'd tell us otherwise."

Hiley-Self had worked at the big house pretty much since Williams returned from Shands. She had grown to love him through the months, hearing his stories about a trophy fish caught off the coast of Peru, about a crash landing in Korea, about baseball in Boston. She had pushed him outside in his wheelchair on good days, laughed when Dominic and Johnny and Flavin brought life to the house, smiled when Tricia Miranti, Williams's teenage friend from rehab, brought a smile to his face.

"He was just so articulate," she says. "He was so comfortable in what he said."

A Christian, she directed some conversations toward religion. The last time he had been rushed to Shands with flu-like symptoms in January he had shouted in the emergency room, "*You know who did this to me? Jesus Christ did this to me!*," but she says he was receptive to what she said. Her message was that God forgives and can provide eternal life. She says Williams eventually accepted that.

"He prayed," Hiley-Self says. "He knew that Christ was his savior."

In June, on Father's Day, just before John-Henry left for baseball, Williams talked to Bobby-Jo for the first time in ten months. Claudia called her and said, "Dad wants to talk to you." Bobby-Jo, who still hasn't figured out how or why the call was made, told her father in a rush how much she loved him, how much he meant to her, how much she missed him.

"Where are we going to meet?" a strained voice asked.

"Daddy, where do you want to meet?"

"At the park."

"Where at the park?"

"At the damn gate at the park, where we always meet."

The park he meant was Fenway Park. He was the famous baseball player. She was the little Barbie doll girl. Time was frozen, long ago. This was the last time she ever talked to him. The door was closed again.

"He was out of it," Bobby-Jo says. "He'd been out of it since the operation. John-Henry would say these things in the press about him that would make you laugh. Daddy didn't even know where he was most of the time."

In the first week of July, his condition quietly worsened. Virginia Hiley-Self worked on Tuesday, July 2, and thought, "It won't be long." Williams was very weak. The dialysis knocked him out. He was breathing all the time through the tracheotomy tube and respirator. All of the nurses knew his situation.

On July 4, DiMaggio made his daily call. *Hello, Dommie. Hello, Teddy.* The rest was silence. Williams had fallen asleep. A nurse came on to the line and said, "Ted is having a tough day."

In the middle of that night, the early hours of July 5, John Butcher sat and watched while Williams had a restless sleep. When the famous man was conscious, there was no conversation because of the tube in his throat. As the night passed, he simply seemed to get weaker and weaker. There was no precipitating event that caused a change in his condition. Around 7:00 A.M. his oxygen reading decreased to a worrisome level. Butcher, 30 years a paramedic, called 911, then awakened the nurse supervisor and the nurse's aide. He rode with Williams in the ambulance.

No one else close to the famous man came with him to the hospital. John-Henry was in Fort Myers with the Gulf Coast Red Sox. Claudia was in St. Petersburg, getting ready to fly to Boston. Bobby-Jo was home, less than a mile away. The hundreds, thousands, millions of people who had put the picture of number 9, leftfielder, Boston Red Sox, on their walls and in their imaginations, worshiping and wondering, entranced by his abilities, now awakened or slept in various time zones and went about their daily business.

At 8:49 A.M., July 5, 2002, after an eventful 83 years and 300 days, Ted Williams died in the emergency room at Citrus Memorial Hospital in Inverness, Florida. John Butcher, who did not like baseball, was with him.

"I would say he passed a natural death," Butcher says.

Ted Williams, easy with words, massaged, surrounded, assaulted, built up, and taken down by words, had no final deathbed words. He died quietly.

Then the words began again.

19 Refrigeration

Ted on ice. Freeze-dried Ted. The Frozen Splinter.

Could this be any worse?

Stripped of any chance for a dignified burial or cremation, the body of the greatest hitter who ever lived rests in a cryonic warehouse in Scottsdale, Az. There will be no funeral, no memorial service. And his children soon will be fighting one another in court.

DAN SHAUGHNESSY, *BOSTON GLOBE*, JULY 8, 2002

Al Cassidy Jr. was knee-deep in the Atlantic Ocean when he heard that Ted Williams had died. He was at a family gathering in Ponte Vedra, which is near Jacksonville, Florida. The plan was to break the news to him gently in the living room, a cousin coming down to the beach and telling him that Uncle Bernie had fallen and needed help back at the house, but Cassidy said, "Hey, the whole family's up there, someone else can help." The cousin was starting to persist, bending the truth even further, when another cousin arrived.

"Hey, Al," the new cousin said, unaware of the plan, "did you hear that Ted died?"

Cassidy's first thoughts went in 87 different directions. Of course he thought about Ted and good times and then about Ted's suffering at the end. He thought about his father too, who had died around this time exactly five years earlier. He thought most about John-Henry and Claudia.

How were they taking this? How were they doing?

Back at the house, he called John-Henry's cell phone. John-Henry answered. He said he had been at the ballpark, City of Palms Park, when he heard his father died. He now was at the airport in Ocala, Florida, watching his father's prepared body being placed aboard a private jet to be taken to the Alcor Life Extension Foundation in Scottsdale, Arizona.

Cassidy was not surprised at this news.

"I'd known about the plan for cryonics for a while," he says. "Mark Ferrell, in fact, had called me about it almost a year earlier. But I knew about it before he called."

The science-fiction scenario John-Henry had sketched for Bobby-Jo—and for Cassidy—actually was taking place. His father's body was going to be drained of fluids, refilled with antifreeze solution, frozen, placed in a refrigerated cylinder in Scottsdale, and left there in the long-shot hope that generations from now science would be able to fix and replace the organ and body parts that had failed. Life after death. John-Henry actually was taking a shot at it with his father. With Ted Williams.

What kind of stir was this going to cause?

"I'm going to come down to the house," Cassidy said. "I'll meet you there."

"I'll be late," John-Henry said. "I have to go to Tampa. Claudia went to Boston this morning, and she has to turn around and fly back. I'm going to pick her up at the airport."

Cassidy and his wife, Gloria, and their youngest son, Brian, went to the big house in Citrus Hills. There was a weirdness being there, walking around Ted's rooms, everything still in place, messages on the kitchen corkboard that had been received by the nurses before they left. Former President Bush had called. John Glenn had called three times. Dominic DiMaggio had called. Cassidy thought he and his wife and son would stay for a while after John-Henry and Claudia arrived, then probably drive the rest of the way to their home in Winter Haven.

He wound up staying "four, maybe five" days. By the time John-Henry and Claudia arrived, the outside world had started to stir at the news of what was happening. The outside world was not happy.

"The surprise was Bobby-Jo," Cassidy says. "No one thought she would do what she did. She was calling newspapers, causing a fuss."

Bobby-Jo's message was that not only had her father's body been frozen, but the procedure had been done against his will. He never would have agreed to something like this. He wanted to be cremated, his ashes strewn across the waters off the Florida Keys. Everyone knew that. An outrage had been perpetrated on her daddy.

People who never once in their lives had considered the option of being frozen after death listened sympathetically. The phone at the big house began to ring with calls from news outlets.

"John-Henry was secure in what he had done," Cassidy says. "You could see it when he and Claudia came home with Eric Abel. Claudia was devastated, just the way you would be if your father had died. John-Henry didn't feel that his father had died at all. Everyone was going to meet up again. That's what John-Henry thought. He wasn't devastated one bit."

The news outlets, particularly the Associated Press, said they needed a response on Williams's death by midnight if any statement was going to appear in the morning papers. Cassidy, his wife, and Abel composed it in the kitchen, two hours of work for one paragraph.

> Ted Williams was a private person in life and in death he wished to remain private. He did not wish to have any funeral or any funeral services.

No mention of cryonics. Nothing controversial. The late work meant that Cassidy and family would stay overnight.

"We were going to stay at a motel, but John-Henry said we should stay at the house," Cassidy says. "I asked him where we should sleep, and he gave us his room. He said, 'I'll sleep in Dad's bed.' Claudia slept on the couch."

The next day, the story broke, full force. The phone calls came from national outlets now, CNN and NBC, all the rest, camera crews at the door. John-Henry decided to talk to none of them.

Already the tone had been set by Bobby-Jo and the first commentators: the duplicitous son had done another bad thing to his famous father, probably, almost certainly, for money. The failed businesses and the Hitter.net cap at the All-Star Game and the FBI sting gone wrong all were mentioned. The former employees at the big house and other people John-Henry had offended all had begun to talk and would keep talking. The *Boston Herald*, in coming days, would learn that John-Henry had slept in his father's bed since his father died. There, another sign of weirdness.

"John-Henry would go to the computer and print out all the stories from the different papers in the morning," Cassidy says. "They weren't nice. He decided just to hunker down."

The big house became the outpost from the media storm. Step outside and someone would take your picture. The pluses and minuses of cryonics were being debated on the outside, the minuses winning in a landslide. The public referendum on John-Henry was raging, 99 percent negative. The sad state of the greatest hitter who ever lived was being turned into late-night television humor on Letterman and Leno.

On the inside, John-Henry and Claudia were making peace.

They had been feuding before their father died. More than feuding. They had been suing each other. Ted long ago had given each of them 1,000 autographed bats as an inheritance. Two months earlier, Claudia had tried to sell her bats to Jerry Romolt in Arizona for $1.2 million. According to the terms of the irrevocable trust, John-Henry had an option of matching any bid. He exercised the option, but failed to come up with the money. Claudia wanted to sell the bats to Romolt. John-Henry had an injunction slapped on her. Claudia sued back. John-Henry, enraged, had taken a baseball bat to Claudia's car, breaking all the windows.

This was a high-octane form of sibling rivalry, not the first time something like this had happened. John Sullivan, the nurse, often described an incident when Claudia, mad at John-Henry, drove her Geo Metro at full speed at John-Henry's car, braking only at the last possible moment. Claudia had complained in the past too that she, like Bobby-Jo, was being denied access to her father. There had been times when Claudia and John-Henry weren't talking. These were Ted Williams's kids. The anger was part of them.

"I didn't know about the bats," Al Cassidy says. "When it came up and when they started shouting at each other, my wife and I did what we do with our own kids. Claudia went into the kitchen with Gloria. I stayed in the living room with John-Henry."

Claudia's angry voice could be heard from the kitchen, talking about her brother and the bats. Her brother smiled.

"Isn't she great?" he said. "The way she sticks up for herself? That's just great. My sister's a fighter."

As the four, maybe five days passed, Cassidy was bothered most by an absence of phone calls. The phone did ring, but it always was another reporter on the other end of the line, another television station looking for the exclusive interview. Where were the calls of condolence? Where were Ted's longtime friends?

"Here were Ted's kids and their father had died," Cassidy says. "Where were the people who all said they loved Ted? If you loved Ted, wouldn't you want to see how his kids were doing? Nobody called. It was sad."

The answer was that the people who loved Ted did not love his son. If they had loved him before, or even had been ambivalent, they did not love him now.

The son was pretty much alone with his decision.

Had there been an announcement to the world that Ted Williams himself had opted to be preserved and frozen upon his death, there would have been a public reaction. What was he thinking? Cryonics? That hokey science-fiction enterprise? Had he lost his mind? People would have been incredulous, not angry.

As the claim surfaced that *Ted didn't want this,* there was an outcry. When Bobby-Jo and the nurses and other friends stepped forward, the situation moved from the bizarre to the criminal. This was wrong! People were screaming.

"Anyone recall the old Patty McCormack movie *The Bad Seed?*" Bob Ryan asked in the *Boston Globe.* "Oooooo, there was a wicked child.

"Now consider this: if that evil little girl had a twin brother, it would have been John-Henry Williams. Make no mistake: The Kid's kid is Very Bad News, and he has saved his best/worst move for last, managing to besmirch a weekend that should have been 100 percent devoted to a celebration of his father's truly remarkable life. But how can we focus completely on Ted's accomplishments when his ever-manipulative son has had the gall to violate the wishes of his two siblings and, more importantly his father himself, with this just-about-incomprehensible move to involve his late father's body with the controversial world of cryonics?"

"During the past couple of years, as Teddy Ballgame battled health crisis after health crisis after health crisis, there had been cruel, whispered jokes that The Kid's kid, John-Henry Williams, would somehow attach some entrepreneurial spirit to his father's death," Steve Buckley wrote in the *Boston Herald.* "A pay-per-view funeral, perhaps. Or the old man's clothing landing on eBay. But this? The horrible spectre of Ted Williams' head being frozen and mailed to an Arizona-based cryogenics firm? DNA for sale? Would Ted Williams have wanted this?"

This was the tone of most comment from the media.

Bobby-Jo, liberated from her silence, went on the offensive. She described the back-door way she heard about her father's death, a phone call from a friend at Citrus Memorial. She told how she confirmed that her father's body was on the way to Arizona with a call to the *Boston Herald*. She cut John-Henry into a few thousand pieces. She said that money was behind everything, John-Henry proposing to sell their father's DNA so there would be "hundreds of little Ted Williamses running around."

"In my 53 years, my dad has told me, and anyone that was around him knew, that his wishes were to be cremated," Bobby-Jo told the *Globe*. "My dad would flip out if he could see what was going on. And he would flip out if he thought his son was going to do that to him."

Bobby-Jo initiated legal proceedings to free her father's body. Boston television stations camped outside the county courthouse in Inverness as if they were covering the first stages of the Scopes Monkey Trial, interviewing anyone who walked through the doors. The Ted Williams Last Wish Fund was established to help pay for legal expenses.

The friends and former employees of Williams uniformly backed Bobby-Jo. Friends, like Bill Cushman, talked about being shut out of Williams's life. They said that every time they called they were told that "Ted was resting" or some variant on that theme. Eventually they called no more. Workers, the nurses, described the many incidents at the big house, the stranglehold John-Henry held on his father's life. They reported that in 1998 the Florida Department of Children and Families had paid a visit to investigate abuse of a senior citizen: Ted.

"The doorbell rang and there were two guys in suits," George Carter said. "Jacques and I were there. We thought the guys were real estate agents. Instead, they were investigating Ted's condition. Someone had turned in a complaint."

Citrus County sheriff's detective David Wyllie was one of the two men. He said he found nothing wrong.

"Williams told us he liked signing bats," Wyllie told the *St. Petersburg Times*. "He said it gave him a reason to get up in the morning and there was nothing going on that he didn't approve of."

The Stockholm Syndrome was mentioned by friends like Joe Camacho's son Jimmy, comparisons made to the last days of entertainers Groucho Marx and Martha Raye, both of whom had been dominated by their caretakers. Was this the case here? The idea of Ted being a willing participant in cryonics was disputed, time and again.

"I was there when John-Henry brought up cryogenics," Frankie

Brothers said in the Keys. "Ted said, 'You're out of your fucken mind.' John-Henry said that they didn't have to freeze the whole body, just your head. Ted said, 'Fuck you,' and walked back into his room by himself. That's what he did when he was pissed. He would walk without his cane or his walker.

"The whole thing has been something straight out of Hollywood. You know what the kid had? He had dollar signs in his eyes for his father. That's all he had. All his father was to him was a meal ticket, right down to the dying."

"I have to hand it to Louise," Lee Williams, Ted's second wife, said. "She was right, after all. She always told Ted that I was going to get pregnant and take all his money. She wasn't right about me—I didn't get pregnant and I didn't take all his money—but look at what happened in his next marriage."

The baseball All-Star Game was held in Milwaukee four nights after Williams's death. (Ironically, this was the game that was flip-flopped with Boston in 1999.) Major League Baseball not only honored Williams but announced that its MVP Award for the game forevermore would be named after him. John-Henry and Claudia went to Milwaukee, but left before the game, John-Henry citing death threats. The game itself was a mess, ending in an embarrassing 7–7 tie after 11 innings. Then a decision was made not to award the new Ted Williams trophy.

"I'm watching the game, and they said that the trophy wasn't going to be awarded, and I started laughing," Brian O'Connor, the Polaroid executive brought down to help John-Henry in business, says. "I told my wife, 'John-Henry had to ask them for some money at the last minute. I can never prove it and no one ever has said anything, but I would bet that John-Henry was looking for money from Major League Baseball.'"

The Red Sox held a tribute for Williams on July 22, almost a funeral in absentia. There was no game that night, only the ceremony, which attracted a crowd of over 20,050. A 77-foot-long number 9 was fashioned in left field from roses, carnations, and other flowers. A giant American flag covered the leftfield wall. A number 9 was spelled out in the many windows of the Prudential Building, a skyscraper beyond right field.

Friends and acquaintances—from John Glenn to Nomar Garciaparra to Johnny Pesky to Curt Gowdy and Jimmy Fund director Mike Andrews—rotated through a trio of easy chairs at home plate to tell their Ted Williams stories to the crowd. Dick Flavin performed the "Teddy at the Bat" poem. Jack Fisher, the Baltimore pitcher who threw the ball, stood in a spotlight on the mound as a video of Williams's last home run was played on the megaboard. Players from the present and past, wearing their Red Sox uniforms, were introduced, and they ran or jogged or walked haltingly to leftfield, where each player added a red rose to the floral arrangement. A solitary Marine bugler played taps.

Missing from all of this emotion were John-Henry, Claudia, and Bobby-Jo. Locked down in their dispute, they hadn't been invited. The sole mention of the cryonics situation came from Dominic DiMaggio.

"I am saddened by the turmoil of the current controversy," he said. "I hope and pray this controversy will end as abruptly as it began and the family will do the right thing by honoring [Ted's] final resting place and may he rest in peace."

DiMaggio's words drew the largest standing ovation of the night. He said Red Sox officials hadn't wanted any mention of the situation, but he couldn't help himself.

"This," DiMaggio said, meaning cryonics, "was not what Ted wanted."

Williams's choice of cremation, his ashes distributed off the Florida Keys, and no funeral was spelled out in his final will that was presented to the Florida court system. Written in 1996, the will that cut Bobby-Jo from the proceeds ("It's what I fucken want") also backed her contention about what her father wanted to happen after his death.

John-Henry and Claudia countered on July 25 with a handwritten note they said spelled out Williams's desire to be frozen. Dated November 2, 2000, which was four days before he underwent surgery to implant his pacemaker, the handwritten note read, "JHW, Claudia and Dad all agree to be put into bio-stasis after we die. This is what we want, to be able to be together in the future, even if it is only a chance." The signatures of John-Henry, Claudia, and Ted were at the bottom.

At first glance, it was almost a laughable document. It looked like a poorly written note shoved into a teller's window by a bank robber or a demand from a kidnapper. John-Henry said he had folded it, thrown it in the trunk of his BMW, and it had been stained with oil. Bobby-Jo and the nurses pointed out that Williams always had been signing blank sheets of paper at the house, often just "to get the flow" before tackling another autograph session. Bobby-Jo also pointed out that her father always signed his legal documents as in his will, "Theodore S. Williams," not the "Ted Williams" that was on the note, which was the same way he signed his autograph. The argument was that this was a Ted Williams practice autograph on a blank piece of paper and John-Henry and Claudia could have written anything, added their signatures, and sworn that this was an agreement with their dad. There were no witnesses.

John-Henry and Claudia released a statement defending their position. They said this was the "clear-cut, definitive" evidence of their father's wishes. He wanted to rejoin them in the future.

"Our father knew, as we did, that our decision to have our bodies preserved would seem odd, even crazy, to many, particularly those of his generation," the statement read in part. "What happens to people's bodies upon their death is largely a matter of religious tradition. Our father was not a religious man. The faith that many people place in God, we place in science and other human endeavors. Every day, we see countless examples of scientific achievement—space travel, the Internet and various medical advances—that would have seemed impossible to prior generations."

The key person in the dispute turned out to be Al Cassidy Jr. Ted long ago had named him executor of his estate. Cassidy said, again and again, that his total allegiance was to Ted. Starting with that first moment when Ted sat down with Cassidy's father and listened to the plan at Fenway Park after batting practice and looked at the scrapbook of pictures for the proposed Ted Williams Baseball Camp in Lakeville, the famous man had been the most important figure in the Cassidy family's success and happiness. Cassidy Jr. absolutely wanted to do what Ted would have wanted.

Cassidy decided that Ted would have wanted to be in the freezer, if that's what his kids wanted.

"Ted loved those two kids," Cassidy says. "Of all the people who have come forward, there hasn't been one who could say Ted didn't love those two kids. Everybody knows that Ted loved those kids! All his life, Ted was looking for family, and in the last stages he finally had it, and it was beautiful to see."

Cassidy backed the note, said it was real. His judgment made the note real in front of the Florida courts, unless proven otherwise. That proof would involve long and costly legal proceedings, and even then might not matter because John-Henry's lawyers had filed a motion for dismissal, saying the Florida courts had no jurisdiction because Ted's body now was in Arizona.

Bobby-Jo was stumped. She didn't have the money to keep pursuing the matter in court. She said she already had spent $82,500, mostly from her retirement funds, "and never seen a judge." The public outrage at what had happened was not backed with dollars. Logic dictated: would a charitable donation be better spent toward a cure for cancer or a scholarship at some school than toward freeing an old man's dead body from a refrigerator, no matter who the old man might be? The Ted Williams Last Wish Fund did not flourish. It had raised only $8,200, $5,000 of that from Bob Breitbard.

This would not do the job. Bobby-Jo estimated that she would need at least $60,000 to keep fighting.

"The whole ploy was to break me down," she told the *Boston Globe*. "Without fan support, that probably will happen. John-Henry has unlimited resources. He could tie me up in court for many years. He has the golden pot."

On December 20, 2002, Bobby-Jo settled. She received $215,000, which had been freed from the one 1986 trust that still had her name on it. Cassidy could have held up payment for ten years. In exchange, she promised not to pursue her court battle and not to speak publicly about the situation.

"I am sorry that I could not achieve the goal of having my father released from the laboratory in Arizona and have his life-long wishes fulfilled," she said in a statement. "Through these many months of negatives I have been blessed, too, at the same time. So many people reached out to me, prayed for us, and encouraged us throughout the entire proceedings. 'When a door is closed, a window will be opened.' I believe in this. And because of this, I have peace in my heart: knowing that I did the right/correct/and moral thing."

Peter Sutton, John-Henry's attorney, had a different view.

"It was about the money," Sutton said. "It always was about the money. This was never about cryonics. It was about the money from the beginning. Now Bobby-Jo and Mark have it."

The potential witnesses for the-court-case-that-never-was-heard were disappointed. George Carter and Frankie Brothers were prepared to testify that the cryonics note never had been signed on November 2, 2000, because between them they were in Williams's room for all 24 hours and they never saw the signing take place. They also said that Claudia wasn't even at the hospital on that day, didn't even know her father was at Shands.

Nurses at Shands were prepared to say that the note wasn't signed because John-Henry, suffering from chicken pox, was quarantined from his father that day. One nurse had another bit of information.

She said that five days after Williams died, she received a call from John-Henry. She started to offer her condolences, but John-Henry brushed them away. She said he had one urgent question: what were the dates my father was in the hospital for his pacemaker?

None of this testimony ever would be heard. Ted would stay in Arizona.

"The rumors always have been that Walt Disney was frozen," Dr. Jerry Lemler said at the Alcor Life Extension Foundation in Scottsdale. "They are not true. Walt Disney, to the best of our knowledge, was cremated, his ashes thrown somewhere over the Pacific Ocean. He had talked about the idea of being frozen, but it did not happen.

"I've always thought, though, that if we had a celebrity here, it would help us immensely. We're a small organization. We've been in business for 30 years and we have only 600 members. Only 53 people are in our facility at the moment. This will grow, of course, as our members age and die, but we have not been able to get the word out. I always thought a celebrity would help.

"Thinking about who that celebrity would be, I had no idea. Entertainers . . . I don't know. It would be a controversial thing. I don't know who would want to risk it. Politicians? Probably not. If I could have anyone, I decided, I would love to have Dr. Billy Graham. Who doesn't like Dr. Graham? He would be perfect."

Ted was a solid second choice.

He had brought a definite notoriety to the tiny company located in a warehouse-like structure in an industrial park next to the Scottsdale airport. The word was definitely out. The procedures and the hopes of cryonics were being explained to an interested, if not accepting, public.

Who didn't know Ted? Joe Falls, a sportswriter for the *Detroit Free Press*, conducted an unscientific survey a number of years earlier, maybe 15 years after Williams had last swung a bat or hit a ball. Falls, just for the hell of it, walked Deerfield Beach, north of Miami, and asked 100 people, "Who is Ted Williams?" He found that no one didn't know who Ted Williams was. Not one of the 100 people.

Maybe Ted was better than Dr. Billy Graham.

"The response has been incredible," Dr. Lemler said. "In the time before the news came out about Ted, we only averaged about 5,000 hits a day on our website. After the news came out, we jumped to 600,000 hits a day. Ted put us on the map. He made people who never heard of cryonization want to know what it was all about."

Williams's body had been flown to the facility on July 5 after his death, presumably tended by a "crash team" from Alcor. The exact time schedule and the details were left murky by Lemler because, wink-wink, he couldn't even confirm that Williams was a resident due to the possibilities of a court case.

If everything had happened as everyone presumed, though, Williams's body would have been treated for four and a half hours in a quasi-operating room at Alcor, 14 people in attendance, then submerged in a tub-like contraption filled with dry ice. The temperature of the body would have been lowered to minus 76 degrees Celsius, then the body would have been placed, hung, inside a sleeping bag, upside down inside a steel vat called a "dewar," where it would stay, frozen in a liquid nitrogen environment, until some future day when science would thaw out the various residents and repair the flaws that stopped their breathing and the beating of their hearts.

The listed price for the procedure and perpetual maintenance was $120,000. The cheaper procedure, freezing only the decapitated head, cost $50,000. Each dewar, looking like something from a microbrewery, could contain four full bodies and five heads. According to Dr. Lemler, four of eight dewars in the warehouse-like room at Alcor were filled with bodies, a fifth with the liquid nitrogen supply. *If* Ted were at the facility, he would have been one of the newer residents in a sixth, partially filled dewar.

There was no indication at all in the room or on the dewars of what was stored inside. There was no indication anywhere in the facility that the greatest hitter who ever lived was a resident.

"There's a lot more we can say when the court situations are all cleared up," Dr. Lemler said. "But until that time, we are bound by confidentiality agreements."

A round little man with a gray beard and glasses, a psychiatrist who looks like a psychiatrist, Dr. Lemler said he stumbled upon cryogenics in a Barnes and Noble bookstore. He picked up a copy of *The Engines of Creation* by Dr. Eric Drexler, a pro-cryonics book, and idly began reading. He was fascinated. He said the experience can best be described as looking at a hologram and finding the picture immediately.

"You know how most of the time you have to twist the hologram around until you get just the right angle and can find the picture?" he said. "This was instantaneous. I looked and it all seemed obvious to me."

He was practicing in tiny Speedwell, Tennessee, at the time. He decided to follow his impulses. His wife and two children might have had more problems finding the picture in the hologram, but he eventually sold them on the idea. They all became members of Alcor. He became the director in 2001. He was a steady-volume proselytizer for his company.

"A lot of things have to happen for all of this to come true, for life to be restored, but it is possible," he said. "That's all we're saying, that it's possible. First, we have to learn how to bring people back from the frozen state. That has never been done. Second, we have to discover cures for the diseases that killed these people. I myself think we eventually will have a disease-free world. We will learn how to eliminate disease. Stem cells, nanotechnology, things we never heard of two, five years ago, will allow this. Finally, maybe hardest of all, we will need an enlightened, peaceful society that will want to bring us back. We have to hope for that.

"What you're doing with cryonics is playing the lottery. The chances of winning are very small, but if you win . . . you win the greatest gift of all. Look at the money people spend to stay alive for a year, for six months, for two weeks. They will do anything. They will try anything. This is an attempt for a whole lot more than that."

His vision of what would happen was understandably unclear. The cryogenically frozen dead people whom he called "patients" will be captives to the advancements of science. The Alcor hope is that science will find ways to repair and replace all the major organs and parts of the body. "Patients" will return as they wish to return and be placed at whatever age or physical condition they want. They can spell out that condition in a videotape, in a letter, whatever means they want. Each patient is allowed to fill at least one one-foot-square box with whatever mementos or wishes he or she might want to see in the future. The box is buried one mile below the earth in a salt mine in Hutchinson, Kansas.

"You can buy more boxes if you want," Dr. Lemler said. "We have one man—he was a writer for *The Carol Burnett Show*—who buried 19 boxes. He had a lot to say."

Ted?

What would happen to Ted if all this worked? What would be the instructions in Ted's box at the bottom of that salt mine?

Dr. Lemler knew a little bit about baseball.

"Ted Williams would come back as the young Ted Williams if he wanted," he said: "If he wanted, he'd be able to run and throw and hit, just the way he did. I don't know if they'll still have baseball then, but if they do, he'll break all of those records that Barry Bonds will set."

The controversy mostly had dimmed by July 5, 2003, the first anniversary of Williams's death. Bobby-Jo and Mark Ferrell, who had been trying to keep interest alive in unfreezing Williams's body with an e-mail campaign to different media outlets, mostly under Ferrell's name owing to Bobby-Jo's agreement in the court settlement not to speak publicly, were hoping for a boost in attention with the anniversary, but it really didn't arrive.

The television network HBO did a segment on *Real Sports* on the situation, but told nothing new. Ferrell said nasty things about John-Henry. George Carter, Frankie Brothers, and Jacques Prudhomme retold their stories. Carter wept at the end. Buzz Hamon, the former director of the Ted Williams Museum, described a last phone call from Williams a month before his death.

"I had it on the speaker phone, so there are witnesses," Hamon says, repeating the tale. "Ted said first that he wanted me to get together with John Underwood to write a book about the last 20 years of his life. Then he said he was 'a prisoner.' He said, 'I made a mistake. I need a lawyer. . . .' Then there was a click and the phone went dead. I tried to call him back, but I never talked to him again."

The few newspaper stories, again, were a retelling of the old story, "Ted's Kids Still at War over Still-Frozen Body." There was little interest on the outside about any of this. The circus had moved along to other sideshows. The Red Sox were hot on the Yankees' trail! War in Iraq! Ben and J-Lo! Even friends who had been outraged now had accommodated to the news.

"I was really bothered when the news came out," Billy Reedy said from Detroit, a common thought. "Then, the more I thought about it, this was family business. What's the difference? Ted's dead."

John-Henry and Claudia never had explained themselves. The big television shows all wanted them—Barbara Walters, Larry King, *The Today Show*, all the rest—but the two children rejected the invitations. Dolores kept quiet in Vermont. Anita Lovely, no longer the fiancée/girlfriend of John-Henry but still friend and business associate, kept quiet.

Ferrell kept talking. He called Al Cassidy "that lying little piece of shit from Winter Haven" and called Claudia "Fraudia" and said Ted had called Eric Abel "that whoralific Jew lawyer." Bobby-Jo mostly was silent. Ferrell kept her that way. He refused to let her talk to a lot of people. Friends now worried about Bobby-Jo. They couldn't get through to *her*. Ferrell was in charge. Was she all right?

"Her story is her inheritance," Ferrell said. "That's all she's got. If we give away the candy, there's nothing left in the candy store. Do you know what I mean?"

Claudia had come out to appear at the Ted Williams Museum induction ceremonies in February and to run the Boston Marathon in April in honor of her father, donations requested for the Jimmy Fund, but she deflected questions about the dispute and cryonics. John-Henry returned to baseball, playing in the lowest-level independent minor leagues. He still couldn't hit. Ferrell and Bobby-Jo sent out happy e-mails after each story appeared about his struggles.

"Daddy told me," Bobby-Jo said. "He said, 'John-Henry doesn't have it.' " The scene had settled into a peculiar stand-off. Ted was frozen and the kids hated each other and most other people had moved along to other subjects. Period. And then the August 18, 2003, issue of *Sports Illustrated* hit the stands and mailboxes across the country. The headline across the top of the cover read "What Really Happened to Ted Williams." The sideshow began again.

A disgruntled, disgusted Alcor employee, chief operating officer Larry Johnson, had contacted Bobby-Jo and her Cleveland attorney, John Heer. Johnson had a story to tell, with pictures, tapes, and memos to back it up. Heer called Jerry Romolt, the memorabilia dealer in Arizona, looking for advice. Romolt sent Johnson to *SI* with a ready-made exclusive.

Where to begin? Ted Williams's body was *not* hanging upside down in one of those dewars. Not the entire body. The head had been mistakenly separated during preparations and now was in a neuro-can, which resembled a high-tech paint can, filled with nitrogen. Not only that, but cracks had appeared in the head because the freezing had faltered in another container called a Cryostar. Nine cracks in all. The cracked head was in the paint can, the body was in the dewar.

The *SI* story said the enterprise apparently had been botched from the beginning. Williams never had signed the consent form. That was signed by John-Henry *after* Williams was dead. Williams never had met with

Alcor representatives in Florida. They had met with John-Henry at the big house, while Williams shouted incoherently in his bedroom. John-Henry had not made his first visit to Alcor or met with Lemler until six months *after* Williams and his two children had supposedly signed their oil-stained pact for bio-stasis at Shands.

There was more. John-Henry and Claudia, despite the promise in the pact, still had not signed agreements to be frozen at Alcor. In fact, John-Henry still owed the company $111,000 from the $136,000 bill (including air transport) for his father's interment. Alcor was aggressively pursuing payment, and one of Johnson's tapes recorded a board member and an adviser joking about throwing Williams's body away, posting it on eBay, or sending it in "a frosted cardboard box" to John-Henry's doorstep.

Johnson, the former employee, had pictures of Williams's head and body. He said a number of people had been taking pictures of the body during the preparation for freezing. Johnson even ran some pictures on his personal website, charging $20 per viewing, but soon junked the scheme under public pressure. *SI* didn't run the pictures, but senior writer Tom Verducci looked at them.

"That was the worst part," Verducci says. "Looking at the operation. I was naive enough to think decapitation would be a clean and precise medical procedure. Not at all.

"I saw a picture of the head . . . at least they said it was Ted Williams's head. It was sitting benignly in a clear plastic box. The only thing that stopped me from getting sick right there was that it looked so bizarre. Too bizarre, like it was from some grade B science-fiction movie."

In a sidebar to the five-page story, *SI* said 8 of 182 recorded samples of DNA from Williams's body were missing. Where did they go? It also reported the fact that Lemler, on March 12, 2001, was "placed on two years' probation and fined $1,000 by the Tennessee Department of Health for unprofessional conduct related to his operation of a weight-loss program between 1997 and 2000."

Lemler, citing confidentiality agreements, refused to comment. He also soon resigned. Alcor denied that it had done anything wrong, but didn't go into specifics.

The laugh machines started everywhere.

When Williams's body first had been frozen, the jokes about "Ted-sicles" and frozen foods at least had to compete with a backdrop of dignity, a sympathetic respect for the recently dead. There were no inhibitions now. Time muted sympathy. The tales from Alcor opened all doors.

"I turned on Martha Stewart this morning," David Letterman said. "She was showing how to thaw Ted Williams's head."

A Boston radio station, WBCN, started running "The Tasteless Ted Williams Joke of the Day." (Example: Q. What is Ted Williams's favorite musical group? A. The Talking Heads.) More than one commentator suggested that Ted's Head be a candidate along with all of the other oddities for governor of California. Bloggers typed out long, involved conversations with Ted's Head.

"Ted Williams rests not in peace, but in pieces," Tim Sullivan wrote in the *San Diego Union-Tribune* in a description of the atmosphere. "His head has been severed, shaved, drilled and repeatedly cracked. The rest of his remains are preserved in a separate tank of liquid nitrogen in an Arizona industrial park.

"Thirteen months after Williams' death, his landmark life is recalled now mainly as prelude to his macabre afterlife. He has become the gruesome grist of callous comedians, the last of the .400 hitters and the first ballplayer to actually embody the frozen rope."

"We have no choice but to go in and physically take Ted's body away," columnist Steve Oulette suggested in the *Plattsburgh* (New York) *Press Republican*. "Four or five people armed with crow bars and righteous indignation should do it. . . .

"We don't need scientists, engineers and medical technicians because we don't care about preserving the frozen body. Break the cylinders open and take what never belonged there. We'll get the remains to a crematorium as soon as possible. Then the ashes will be sprinkled as Ted always expressed, to friends and in his will:

" 'Off the coast of Florida where the water is very deep.' "

Ric Ridgeway, chief assistant state attorney, announced that he was going to look into the situation, but quickly backed away, again proclaiming the oil-stained note a legal document. Bobby-Jo and Mark asked why Ridgeway never had looked at sworn statements from George Carter and Frankie Brothers, never had talked to the nurses at Shands. There was no answer. Frustrated, Bobby-Jo and Mark turned their attention on Arizona, asking the state's attorney general to launch an investigation into Alcor. Maybe that was a way to set her father's body free, close the company that had it.

John-Henry and Claudia remained silent. John-Henry now was playing in Louisiana for the Baton Rouge River Bats. He previously had played for the Selma (Alabama) Cloverleafs in the same league, but engineered his own trade to the River Bats.

"We had lunch," owner and sometimes manager L. G. Dupuy says. "He said he could help us with our marketing program if I could help him with his hitting. I agreed to do it, and it worked out for both of us."

John-Henry, hitting .091 before he joined the River Bats, hit .256 after he joined them. Dupuy said he had convinced John-Henry to try for base hits, just hit the ball, instead of swinging for the big home run. The strategy seemed to help. The River Bats rolled along and won the playoffs and the league championship. John-Henry, alas, did not roll with them. He had left the team before the playoffs to take care of "some personal business."

One more shocker was on the way: he was sick. John-Henry had acute myelogenous leukemia.

He eventually told the *Citrus County Chronicle* in October that he first felt sick at the end of 2002, but didn't see a doctor until February 2003. He played most of the baseball season but felt weaker and weaker, cutting down on practice time just to play the games near the end. He had gone to UCLA Medical Center in Los Angeles on October 9, 2003, where the disease had been diagnosed. He was undergoing chemotherapy treatments. Claudia was with him and being tested as a possible bone marrow match.

"It's been such a hard road since Dad died," Claudia said in the *Chronicle* article. "It seems like it hasn't stopped yet. John-Henry and I are very positive people. We're certainly not going to be negative. We're going to persevere."

Ironies abounded. Hadn't Ted spent his entire public life working with the Jimmy Fund to find a cure for kids with cancer? Here was his own kid with cancer. Hadn't Ted's brother, Danny, died of this same disease at the age of 39? Here it was again in the next generation. Was this, the cancer, part of that supposedly precious Williams DNA? Was this the ultimate test of John-Henry's convictions? Did he really believe in cryonics? Would he truly want for himself what he gave to his father?

"How about this?" Mark Linehan, a Red Sox fan from Roslindale, Massachusetts, asked. "Suppose Claudia's bone marrow doesn't match. Suppose the only match out there is Bobby-Jo?"

Nothing now seemed out of the question. Nothing could be considered too weird. Mark Ferrell had been quoted in the *Boston Herald* in September when the first rumors about John-Henry's disease appeared.

"I certainly hope that John-Henry Williams does not have leukemia," Ferrell said, "because I want him to live a very long life and think every day about the hell he did to his father and everyone who loved him."

The legacy of Ted Williams was the loser in all of this postmortem news. The flash card of name recognition now brought up "Ted's Head" or "Frozen" instead of pictures of a perfect baseball swing, a perfect fly cast, a Panther jet streaking across the sky, flames coming out the back, the pilot wondering what the hell to do next. The man who once inhabited the frozen, detached body when it was whippy and new or middle-aged and thick, back when it was loud and opinionated and drop-dead handsome, almost was forgotten.

This was the shame.

"I didn't go to see him in those last couple of years," Joe Camacho, the friend who called him every day after his stroke to watch the Red Sox games, says. "I didn't want to see him like that. I wanted to remember him as he really was. I saw the pictures, when he went to his Hall of Fame for the last time in the wheelchair; he looked like Sid Caesar. I didn't want that."

Ted Williams wasn't that character at the end. He wasn't the upside down, headless body in the dewar. He wasn't the body in the hospital bed or the wheelchair. Ted Williams was . . . Ted Williams. He walked, he growled and swore, intimidated. He hit baseballs with great regularity. He charmed strange women. He wove feathers and glue and fishhooks together and put them on the end of a fishing line and dropped them right in front of the nose of an Atlantic salmon. He lived.

His curiosity was boundless, his mind active. He loved what he liked, hated what he didn't like, never suffered fools gladly or any other way. He did absolutely, positively what he wanted to do in any situation under all conditions. Consequences seldom were a consideration.

One of the new nurses near the end knew little about him. She went home, punched his name into her computer's search engine, and read stories into the night. She was amazed.

"Mr. Williams," she said the next day, "I read up on you last night. You didn't tell me. You're a great American hero."

"Well, you got that right," Williams replied from his hospital bed.

He is in at least nine halls of fame, including his own, and undoubtedly will be named to more. ("I accepted for him at the Atlantic Salmon

Hall of Fame," Jim Prime, his co-author from *Ted Williams's Hit List*, says. "I didn't wear a tie. It felt good.") He has a tunnel named after him in Boston ("Congestion entering the Ted"), a stretch of highway named after him in California, the road alongside his museum named after him in Florida.

Children, many of them growing old now, are named after him. Dogs, many of them with a cantankerous nature, carry his name as they search for trouble. He once, when Sears was king and he was king, seemed to have his name on half the outdoors. At least the sporting goods half.

"I named my son Ted Williams Ziegler *before* I ever met Ted," Bill Ziegler, the trainer for Williams's Washington Senators teams, says. "Ted was my idol. The way I got the job . . . I was a young guy, an assistant trainer at Florida State. I saw Ted was made the manager of the Senators, and I sent in an application, just hoping for a rejection letter. If I got the letter and he signed it, I had his autograph."

The letter did far more than Ziegler ever expected. He had a tongue-tied interview. He was given the job. He found himself with his idol in Pompano Beach, Florida, for spring training. Wait! His idol now was asking him to go to lunch. Lunch with his idol.

"We go to some Polynesian restaurant that Ted liked," Ziegler says. "I'm nervous. Just as we get to the door, Ted stops. He says, 'When we go inside, turn to your right and check out the tits on the cashier.' My idol! I do just what he says."

He was earthy, petulant, real. He was big. Very big.

The baseball moments, the numbers, all are in the record books. The subtleties are lore. Computers do now what he did in his head, breaking down tendencies of individual pitchers, factoring in the weather, the length of the grass on the infield, the direction of the wind, the unsure hands of the centerfielder, the common cold shared by three spectators in a first-base loge box. Williams did it better, instantaneously, every pitch of every at bat. Every day.

Coaches now try to teach his swing. Videotapes. Pitching machines. Gadgets. Who gets it right? No one. Not the way Ted Williams got it. The exact opposite theory of hitting a baseball, down instead of up, is the predominant theory. Why? It is easier. His swing was his invention, analyzed by him, adjusted by him, calibrated. He talked to every teacher he could find, but he was his own guru.

His Hispanic heritage, virtually unknown and never discussed during his career, now is a historical landmark. The game virtually runs on Latin blood. The biggest stars, from Sammy Sosa to Pedro Martinez to Alex Rodriguez, are predominantly Hispanic. He was the first, the first Latin superstar. Ted Williams, undercover Mexican, May Venzor's son.

Even his attitude, flipping off the fans, feuding with the sportswriters, sometimes reluctant to run out ordinary ground balls . . . does that sound familiar? If he was not the first to do this, and he wasn't, he certainly was the most noticeable. He was ahead of his time, the superstar diva. The best at this too, if not the first.

"The later sportswriters all have him wrong," Boston sports commentator Clark Booth of WCVB says. "They never saw him play. They saw him as some kindly old father figure telling stories and saying bad words. Lovable. Ted Williams wasn't *lovable*. He was *interesting*, *fascinating*, the same way Napoleon or Charlemagne or Winston Churchill was interesting, fascinating. He did great things despite great flaws. That's the beauty of Ted Williams."

Tromping through the woods, flying his fighter plane into the night, refusing to tip his hat, he was a caricature of the manly man who inhabited the pulp magazines of his time. His obligations never kept him from adventure. If there was no time for the give-and-take dynamics of family, no patience for his children, well, there was more time for fishing.

His weakness was his anger, and his anger was his strength. He made the hard and damnable trade of conformity for greatness that most very successful men seem to make. He went where his anger took him, trying not to leave too many pieces of shrapnel in his wake.

"He had big trouble with women," someone suggested to one of his friends. "Three wives, Louise, the affairs, troubles with his daughters."

"He had no trouble with the women who went home in the morning," the friend replied. "They seemed to like him."

He could be charming and he could be mean. He could be superficial and deep. Take something he wanted to do, something that interested him, and he could break it down to its smallest components, study it until he absolutely understood it. Take something he didn't want to do, but maybe should do, and he could throw it away in a moment.

He was smart, if not always wise.

"I'm a real smart son of a bitch," he said during a 1998 interview with Scott Rabb in *Esquire* magazine. "I'm an old, dumb ballplayer and a real smart son of a bitch."

His end was nothing short of a Gothic horror. The body that carried him to such glory, such achievement, turned against him. His sins of omission and commission gathered up and tied him down—the son he didn't want to be born taking control, the wife he didn't want to marry returning to the house, the daughters he never understood fighting in the background, the press he always distrusted and despised, now free to pick through the laundry of the personal life that he always carefully folded and kept hidden.

His end was not his story.

"The part people sometimes forget," Al Cassidy Jr. says, "is that while Ted had a tough last eight years, he had a wonderful 75 years before that. He was healthy, strong, active. He was Ted Williams."

His head was on his shoulders for all that time. His heart was on his sleeve. He once took Claude Passeau very, very deep. He once tackled long division and won. He survived his two wars, his three marriages, and he spit anywhere he wanted. He once watched a lizard try to eat a spider.

He went past in a whoosh and a rush and assorted sonic booms. He was different from everyone else, if not necessarily better. He would walk into a room—Bill Ziegler remembers this—and his presence alone would make people talk even if they didn't know who he was. Ziegler once saw a lady approach, wanting to know who exactly Williams was. Did he, perchance, once play sports?

"You got me," the famous man said. "I was with the Green Bay Packers."

There was an outsized quality about him that was undeniable. Drumbeats and horns were his music, never orchestral strings. The things he did were broad, oil-based strokes on a large canvas, never pastels or watercolors. He was an electric light in the midst of everyday, nine-to-five gray. He captured the imaginations of strangers.

"A Fall River baseball fan made a brief appearance on television yesterday," a story in a clipping from a long-ago edition of the *Fall River Herald*, date and author unknown, begins. "Joe (Gee-Gee) Valton created a stir at Fenway Park during the Red Sox–White Sox game when he leaped out of the stands for a chat with Ted Williams as the Bosox slugger awaited his turn to bat in the eighth.

"A great admirer of the Splendid Splinter, Valton left his seat to present $10 to Ted as chairman of the Jimmy Fund. Ted accepted the donation and told Valton to 'beat it or you're liable to get arrested.'

"Before he took Williams' advice, Valton embraced his idol, then shook hands with Umpire Red Flaherty and leaped back into the grandstand. Police collared the Fall Riverite and took him to the law enforcement room at the park. There he was told it would cost him $50, but Valton answered, 'It's worth $50 to shake hands with Ted Williams.' "

The body of the famous man might be frozen in some goddamned, clapped-up, syphilitic fucken steel can, but his life is frozen in memory and daydream, recollection and tall tale. He did not hesitate often on his walk across this American landscape.

He was Ted Williams.

Epilogue

Didja hear about the alligator?
No!
Bit that kid's leg off. . . .

A former Sears salesman named Steve White told a story in the *Sylva* (North Carolina) *Herald and Ruralite*. He was taking Ted Williams on a tour of six stores in central Florida, and there was some downtime in the middle of the day. Williams asked if White knew any place to go fishing. White took him to Lake Harris near Leesburg and stopped at a bait store to rent a boat from a man he knew as "Bubba."

"I need to rent a boat," White said. "I've got Ted Williams in the car, and he wants to go fishing."

"Yeah," Bubba replied, crinkling his eyes at the information. "And I've got Santa Claus back there drinking a Budweiser."

What's an alligator doing around here?
Don't know. Just got loose somehow . . .

"I shined shoes outside the Hotel Somerset," Ray Flynn, the former mayor of Boston, says. "The doorman was from South Boston, and he let one kid from Southie work the front every year. I was that kid for a few years.

"Ted Williams lived at the Somerset, and the Yankees also stayed there when they came to town. One afternoon, the Yankees all were coming down from their rooms, heading to Fenway. They were waiting out front for cabs. I got a piece of paper and an old pen, and I went up to a couple of the players and asked for their autographs. The pen didn't work!

"Jerry Coleman reaches into his suit jacket and takes out a gold pen. He signs and hands the pen to someone else and someone else, and now Joe DiMaggio is there. For some reason, he thinks I'm Jerry Coleman's nephew or something, and he smiles and takes the gold pen and signs.

"While he's signing, Ted Williams comes down. He comes over to Joe and me. He takes the gold pen and signs. They're talking, Ted Williams and Joe DiMaggio, how are ya, back and forth, and for some reason Williams thinks that I'm DiMaggio's nephew or something. He says, 'Hey, it's getting late. Let's get to the ballpark.' We get into the cab, Ted Williams, Joe DiMaggio, and me. I leave my shoeshine box right on the street because that would be a giveaway, you know?

"I ride in the middle of the backseat. I have Joe DiMaggio on one side of me. I have Ted Williams on the other side. I have both of their autographs. And I also have Jerry Coleman's gold pen in my pocket. Who ever has made out better than this? Williams and DiMaggio figure it out by the time we get to Fenway that I'm nobody's nephew, but for that short time. . . ."

You see it?
Walked right by me . . .

"He was down at his camp one summer," former Red Sox manager and scout Eddie Kasko says. "He calls me at my office at Fenway Park. He wants me to go with him to Lynn [Massachusetts] to see a minor league game. The New Britain Red Sox were playing, and he wanted to check up on some kids. I didn't want to go, but he's Ted and he's insisting. I say I'll go."

Williams said he would be waiting outside Fenway, the door at 4 Yawkey Way, at precisely 4:30. Kasko came out of the door at 4:30. Williams's station wagon was pulled up onto the sidewalk. He was standing outside. He was giving hitting lessons to a kid who appeared to be about 14 years old. The kid's father was watching.

"No, that's not right," Williams shouted. "You gotta get your hips in front of your hands.

"Hips in front of your hands . . .

"Hips in front of your hands . . ."

The kid was swinging and swinging. Sweating.

"No! Hips in front of your hands . . ."

Kasko announced his presence. Williams said to the kid, "Bye, keep-working-on-it, gotta-go," and jumped into the station wagon with Kasko. They roared off at Ted Williams speed.

Kasko turned and looked back at the father and son. They were staring at the departing station wagon.

"I'm thinking, here's a guy, probably takes his son to buy some Red Sox tickets," Kasko says. "They're outside Fenway Park and Ted Williams pulls up, jumps out, and starts teaching the kid how to hit. Is that a dream or what? They were standing there, not knowing if they could believe what just happened.

"They probably still don't believe it."

Hips in front of your hands.

They catch the son of a bitch yet?
    Uh-uh. Still on the loose.

"I brought like five baseballs with me on the fishing trip to Russia," Jerry McKinnis, the television fisherman, says. "I didn't want to push, or be an idiot or anything, but if the moment was right I thought I'd ask Ted to sign them.

"Well, it turned out I could have brought two dozen baseballs. He was just a great, great guy."

While Williams wrote his autograph, he explained the etiquette of signing baseballs. On each baseball there is one place where the seams come close together, a virgin stretch of white leather, that is called "the Sweet Spot." Only the true stars of the game can sign their names in that place. The other players, the competent but ordinary players, can sign anywhere else, but that spot is reserved for only the best. The good player always defers to the better player in signing on "the Sweet Spot."

"Okay," McKinnis said, fascinated by the concept. "Suppose I'm here with you and Mickey Mantle? What happens?"

Williams considered the question.

"In that case, you better have two goddamn baseballs," he said.

That's just amazing. An alligator. Here. Who'd have ever thought?
    Biggest damn alligator you ever saw . . .

Vinnie Orlando wound up working for the Red Sox for 58 years as a clubhouse attendant. Johnny Orlando died in 1986 and had left the team years earlier, but Vinnie didn't retire until 1990 at the age of 74. He was a cranky old man much of the time at the end, had that old man's attitude that he had seen it all, done it all, no need for anything else. The major leagues were done. Everything now was the minors. There were times, though, a rain delay, some quiet moment, when he would become expansive.

He would sit on a trunk in the old clubhouse in the old ballpark and talk about old players and old times. New ears would be amazed.

"Lou Gehrig was a prick," Vinnie Orlando would say.

"A prick?" the new mouth under the new ears would reply. "Lou Gehrig? The Pride of the Yankees?"

"A cheap prick. Hated kids. Wouldn't sign autographs."

"Lou Gehrig?"

"Babe Ruth was another prick."

"Babe Ruth?"

"He'd push kids out of the way. 'Get out of here.' "

"Babe Ruth."

"Mel Ott was pretty good. Good guy."

The list of Hall of Famers would be run through quite rapidly—most of the famous names described as pricks—and then Orlando would settle into his favorite subject, his favorite ballpark character of all time. Theodore Samuel Williams. Not a prick. No. Good guy. The best of them all. The stories would roll out, one after another. Ted and the Press, Ted and Women, Ted on a Cloudy Day in Cleveland. A doubleheader.

The best story of all was Ted Back from Korea. Vinnie Orlando would talk about the special workouts held at night, after the ballgame had been played, everyone gone from Fenway. Ted was getting his swing back, you know? Gone almost two years. Needed the work. Wanted the work. The lights would stay lit, the ground crew kids would drag out the batting cage, Vinnie would go to rightfield with a glove, and Pete Cerrone—the guy from Filene's Basement—would pitch from behind the old door on the mound.

Pete would take the baseballs from a basket next to him. One pitch would follow another, each sent back on a line. Pete would pitch and pitch and Ted would swing and swing. The middle of the night. Vinnie would run down the line-drive results in the outfield. No one around. Ted would hit the ball and hit the ball and scream at the top of his well-developed lungs.

Whack.

"Ted Williams! The greatest fucken hitter that ever lived!"

Whack.

"Ted Williams! The greatest fucken hitter that ever lived!"

Whack.

"Ted Williams . . ."

Whack.

Vinnie would throw the balls back to the mound. Pete would collect them, put them into the basket, and deliver them once again to the plate.

Author's Addendum

In the late summer of 1999, I was asked by *Sports Illustrated* to write an obituary for Ted Williams. I was a senior writer, available for assignment. The call from the editor was a bit of a surprise because I never had written an obituary for the magazine and because, as far as I knew, Ted was still alive.

"Has something happened?" I asked the editor. "I haven't been watching the news."

"No, nothing," the editor replied.

"What's the deal?"

"I saw him on television last month at the All-Star Game in Boston," the editor explained. "He didn't look good to me."

Huh. I did know that as cold as the appraisal seemed, the assignment of an obituary for a living person was not unusual. Newspapers and magazines and television networks often prepare "packages" when the elderly and famous start to cough or go into the hospital for "routine" surgery. There had been a rush of typing at *SI* at the deaths of baseball icons Mickey Mantle and Joe DiMaggio, nothing written in advance. The magazine wanted to be ready this time.

I was the choice for the job, I suppose, because I was a Boston resident, a New England native, onetime sports columnist at the *Boston Globe*, a lifelong follower of both Ted and the Boston Red Sox. The magazine didn't even know half of it. *Ted Williams was my boyhood idol.* Okay, there, I said it.

The editor sent me a pile of clippings from the *SI* library, and I put them next to a couple of books I already owned and tried to figure out what to do next. I remembered a guy from my newspaper past who wrote these kinds of premature obits, a heavy-handed character who called friends and family of the not-yet-deceased and said, "I'm writing an obituary about So-and-So," and then heard great wails and laments from the other end of the phone before he could explain the person was still alive. No, I did not want to do that.

Then, what? My first obligation, I decided, was to imagine what would happen when Ted died. What would the newspapers do? What would be on the television, both local and national? I envisioned a string of tributes to the ballplayer, "the greatest hitter who ever lived"; to the veteran, the Marine Corps airman from two wars; to the hunter-fisherman, the ultimate man's man; film clips in black and white, home runs dropping over long-ago fences, interviews of this brash and loud and often profane character. I could read the stories before they even were written.

How could I be different? My story would appear as much as a week later, maybe even later than that, after all these other stories had landed. I sat in my little office on a late summer night, considered possibilities, and then, in a rush, started typing. I never looked at the pile of material next to me, just wrote, memory taking charge, yanking me along. A lifetime of Ted Williams. I left the initials TK ("TO KOME" in copyreaders' shorthand) to indicate the blanks for the numbers and dates that would be filled in with Ted's eventual demise.

This was the finished product:

IN MEMORIAM: If you grew up watching Ted Williams hit a baseball, well, you simply kept watching what he did, everything he did, even when he stopped hitting baseballs. That was the way it was. From the day he arrived at Fenway Park in Boston in 1939 as a slender 20-year-old outfielder with a swing for the ages, until TK, when he died at the age of TK in TK, he was part of your life.

He might have changed and you might have changed and times might have changed as years passed, but he always was a fascinating character. He was a superstar before the word was invented. He was a man's man, icon of all icons. Watch? You had to watch.

At least I did. . . .

TED 1—The postcard from Ted Williams came to 80 Howe St., New Haven, Ct., on a late summer day in 1953. That is the best I can figure.

I tried, just now, to pull the card carefully from the lined, loose-leaf notebook page where I glued it, apparently 46 years ago, but the postmark was lost in the process.

I say the late summer of 1953 because that was when I was an autograph demon. Most of the other cards in my old notebook—George Kell, Maurice (Mickey) McDermott, Jimmy Piersall, a bunch of forgotten Boston Red Sox names—have postmarks from the summer of 1953. I was on the case in 1953. I was 10 years old.

I lived in a six-story apartment house, an only child, and I somehow discovered, alone in my bedroom, that if you write to your athletic idols, *they sometimes will write back.* I was a writing fool. My basic message on a penny postcard was "Dear So-and-So, I am your biggest fan! You are great! Please send me your autograph!" I finished with my name and address, sent out my cards and waited with the anticipation and faith of a trout fisherman on the banks of a fast-running brook on a Sunday morn.

The arrival of the mail every day became true adventure. Our brass mailbox was in the middle of a bank of brass mailboxes. I would look through the little holes in the brass door to see if anything had arrived. I would hurry the key into the lock, rifle through the bills and the circulars, the grown-up and the mundane, looking and looking until . . . one magical day, Ted Williams.

He was the biggest fish of them all. I might not remember the exact date his postcard arrived, but I remember the feeling. Even now I cannot think of another piece of mail that has made me feel happier, not college acceptances nor good reports from doctors, nothing. The Ted Williams postcard was unadulterated bliss, wholly equivalent to a letter straight from heaven. Better. Straight from Fenway Park.

I had never seen a major-league player in person, had never been to a major-league stadium, never had seen a major-league game. Television had not arrived at my house. Ted Williams was a mythical figure, a creation of radio words and black-and-white newspaper pictures. He had the purity of Sir Lancelot, the strength of Paul Bunyan, the tenacity of, say, Mighty Mouse. Distance, to be sure, made heroes much more heroic than they ever can be today.

Williams had returned from the Korean War in July of 1953. He was 35 years old. He had been flying F-9 Panther jets for 14 months in Korea, fighting the Communists in their sneaky MiGs, real-life versions of the same model planes I had made from Revell plastic kits, maybe without the blotches of excess glue on the side. He was back and he was hitting as well as he ever had, a .407 average in the final 37 games of the season, 13 homers, a .901 slugging percentage. He could do anything, everything. He was No. 9. He was The Kid, Teddy Ballgame, The Splendid Splinter. He hated to wear a tie! (I hated to wear a tie!) He was invincible.

I remember staring at the postcard for hours. Had he actually signed it? No doubt. The blue ink was a different color from the rest of the card. He was in the finish of a swing in the black-and-white pose. His eyes seemed to be following a baseball he had just hit, probably into the bullpen in right. He seemed focused, serious, divine. I imagined him reading my own card by his locker, thinking about me. Should he reply? He could tell by my writing that I was an honest kid, a hard worker in school, obeyed my parents. Of course he should reply. I could see him pulling out this postcard from a special place, taking out his pen.

"Capital T," he wrote, with a big flourish, "e-d. Capital W (another flourish) i-l-l-i-a-m-s." He dotted the i's high, maybe a half inch above the rest of the writing.

"You know," an older sportswriter told me a number of years later, "he never signed any of that stuff. The clubhouse guy, Johnny Orlando, his buddy, signed everything. Johnny Orlando could sign Ted Williams's name better than Ted Williams could."

I look at the postcard now. I somehow have kept it through college, through marriage, divorce, changes of jobs, a half-dozen changes of residence. Forty-six years.

I don't know. Johnny Orlando?

I think Ted might have made an exception. Just once.

TED 2—The sound of his voice preceded him. Or at least that is what I remember.

The year must have been 1978. Or maybe 1979. The Red Sox clubhouse at Chain O'Lakes Park in Winter Haven, Fla., was divided into two rooms. The smaller room was reserved for selected veterans and the coaching staff. They shared the space with a pair of enormous washing machines. The machines were at work, taking out the stains from another spring training day. I was a sportswriter now, working for a Boston newspaper. I guess I was talking with someone about something to do with the coming season.

"Tell me this," the new voice said, loud, very loud. "What detergent do you use to clean these uniforms?"

Everybody turned toward the noise because there was no alternative. There he was, Ted, himself, huge, instantly dominating his surroundings. He was wearing a Hawaiian shirt. He would have been 60 years old. Maybe 61. He was tanned and robust, looking as if he had just returned from the high seas or the deep woods. A pair of sunglasses hung from his neck on a piece of fishing line.

"Tide," an equipment man said. "We use Tide."

"Now why do you use Tide?" the voice boomed. "Is it better than all the other detergents? Is it cheaper? Is there some secret ingredient? Why do you use Tide?"

The fun began. Somehow, in my sportswriting life, I had never been in the same room with Ted Williams, never had talked to him, never had been around him. This was going to be interesting. What would he be like? Would he fill out the picture I'd had in my head for so long? Or would he—like so many famous figures, encountered without their press agents and handlers—be a mean-spirited disappointment? What? At first glance, I had to say he looked like John Wayne. He talked like John Wayne. He was John Wayne.

He was on the scene as a hitting instructor. For a number of years he had skipped the rituals of the baseball spring, off to search for salmon or bonefish or do whatever he did, but for some reason he had decided to return for this season. He was here mostly to work with minor leaguers.

He would show up every morning in his old Ford station wagon, identifiable with the "If Guns Are Outlawed, Only Outlaws Will Have Guns" bumper sticker on the rusty bumper. He would change into his uniform, then head to the minor league complex, someone driving him on a golf cart. He would sit on the cart at a point where he could see the activity on four different diamonds. The entire Red Sox farm system was laid out in front of him.

"What's your name?" he would ask some kid in a batting cage. "Get over here. Where are you from? Mississippi? Let's see what you're doing here."

He would jump from the cart, adjust the kid's stance. He would take the bat, squeeze it hard, swing with emphasis. See? Pow! He would talk baseball, baseball, more baseball, laying out hypothetical confrontations between pitcher and batter, each ball and strike forcing the pitcher to alter his strategy, finally forced at 3-and-2 to come in with a fastball and, oh, brother, here it comes! Pow! The kid from Mississippi would return to work looking slightly dazed.

I stood with other members of the new generation of Knights of the Keyboard, Williams's term for his long-time adversaries in the press box. I listened to his declarations. (If you were in the state of Florida, you pretty much couldn't avoid them.) I did the obligatory Ted-is-here column.

He was charming and frank. He actually listened to the questions, actually thought out the answers. He laughed easily in large sonic booms. The writers who had tormented him during his career, Col. Dave Egan and Austen Lake and the rest, were dead. The torment also was dead. The uncomfortable star, reacting to all criticism, spitting in the direction of the clacking typewriters, was long gone. Williams wore his middle age as if it were a bathrobe and slippers. He could care less what anyone wrote.

He would pose for pictures with a daily stream of worshipers, penitents, strangers. ("You gonna take that lens cap off before ya take the shot?" he would bellow. "Here, let me do it.") He would argue with anyone about politics, sport, detergent, anything. He would question. He would tell stories. He would interact, 24 hours a day. There was a liveliness about him that was different from the ordinary. He was larger than larger than life, if that makes any sense. He was Ted Williams and he knew who he was. He played his own role. Himself.

The highlight of the spring came when he set up a public tennis match against Carl Yastrzemski, then the Red Sox star. He didn't just challenge Yastrzemski to the match; he promoted it for an entire week. He told the world. Time, date, place, probable outcome. (A huge Williams win.) He was like a professional wrestling star, booming out the particulars. He made side bets. The tennis match became more important than any of the baseball taking place every day. Williams vs. Yastrzemski! When the great day came—Yastrzemski won easily, making the big man move too much and lurch for shots—there must have been 1,000 people surrounding one of those apartment-complex courts. All because of this event Williams simply invented.

"Is he always like this?" I asked his friend Joe Lindia, a guy from Cranston, Rhode Island, who was his driver, friend, roommate for the three weeks. "Is he always . . . Ted?"

"Always," Lindia said. "You go with Ted, anything can happen."

Lindia told a story. In one of Williams's last seasons as a player, the Red Sox trained in Scottsdale, Az. Lindia went out to visit. One day, an off day, Williams said they should take a ride. They drove to the far edge of the town and went to a seedy motel. Williams directed Lindia to a certain room at the back. Lindia had no idea what was happening. Williams knocked on the door. An old man, looking as seedy as the motel, itself, answered.

"Joe," Williams said. "Say hello to Ty Cobb."

They went into the room with Cobb. A bottle of whiskey was opened. Cobb and Williams talked baseball for a number of hours. Cobb, it seemed, had one theory about hitting. It was directly opposed to Williams's theory. The argument became intense. The two men were shouting at each other. They looked as if they might even begin to fight.

"Look, I know how we can settle this," Williams finally said. "Ty, you say one thing. I say another. Joe, what do you say?"

"Funny, huh?" Lindia said. "The two greatest hitters in the history of baseball. I'm supposed to break the tie. I couldn't hit a baseball for a million dollars."

On one of the last days of training camp, I went to dinner with my young family at one of those steak houses with an all-you-can-eat salad bar. My son was five years old. Maybe six. I guided him to the salad bar to fill up his plate. On the way back to the table, I noticed Williams was in a booth with four or five people. Lindia was one of them. I was going to keep going, but Lindia waved and said hello. I waved back. Williams looked and saw my son.

"Hey," he said in that loud voice. "That's a great-looking kid."

My son had no idea who the man was. He smiled.

"I mean he's exceptional," Williams said, even louder now. "A great-looking kid."

I could feel the eyes of everyone in the restaurant turning in my direction. It was like one of those "my broker says . . ." commercials. People were looking at Williams, then staring at my son. People were nodding their heads in agreement. Yes, a great-looking kid. My son.

"Looks like he'd be a pretty good hitter," someone at the table suggested.

"I don't give a s—— about that," Williams said, loudest voice yet. "I'm just saying he's a great-looking kid. Look at him."

It was a moment. My son is 27 years old now and I still talk to him, maybe once a year, about what happened. He rolls his eyes.

TED 3 — The idea was that Ted was going to be dead pretty soon. That was what the producer said. Ted was going to hit his 80th birthday in a couple of weeks and he'd had the three strokes and he was half blind and he didn't get around much, didn't submit to many interviews. Anything could happen, you know. This might be the last television interview he ever would do.

This was the summer of 1998. I was the interviewer. I showed up with two cameramen and the producer around noon on the appointed day at Williams's house in Hernando, Fla. The house was relatively new, part of the Citrus Hills development, which featured a bunch of streets named after former Red Sox players and officials. It was not the kind of house you would imagine for Williams. There was a commercial aspect here, a lack of dignity.

Buzz Hamon, the curator at the Hitters Hall of Fame, also located on the Citrus Hills property, briefed us on what to expect. There would be 30 minutes, no more than 45, with Williams. His attention would wander after that. He would be ready for his afternoon nap. He had a cook and an aide who helped him daily. Hamon said it had been a tough stretch for Williams. Not only had the strokes affected him; virtually all his friends had died. Joe Lindia had died. Williams's long-time companion, Lou Kaufman, had died. His dog had died. He pretty much had outlasted his generation.

I feared the worst. When Williams came into the den, where we had set up our lights, he was using a walker and was helped by the aide. He was shrunken, frail. The robust character of 20 years earlier was gone. The baseball god of 40, 50 years ago, was long gone. He was helped into the easy chair and landed with a grateful thud. And he was wonderful.

I have a copy of the tape. From the core of that besieged and worn-out body, Ted Williams emerges. The voice is still loud, challenging, authoritative. It is him. His right hand might wander, almost out of control, and he might dab now and then at a little saliva, coming from the side of his mouth, but he is funny and definitive and certainly in charge.

I have my little list of questions, but they are mere starting points. He drives the conversation wherever he wants it to go. I am only along for the ride. *Oh, brother . . . Now here's something interesting! Glad you brought that up!... Oh, that's in all the books. Go read about it.... Where are you from? This is inside stuff you're getting, buddy.* He talks about fishing with Bobby Knight in Russia. He talks about how he thinks George Will knows a lot politically, but not too much "baseballically." He talks about Joe Jackson, who should be in the Hall of Fame, damn it. He talks about Mark McGwire, LOVES Mark McGwire, talks about Nomar Garciaparra, LOVES Nomar, talks about Joe DiMaggio and Willie Mays and Ken Griffey Jr. LOVES Ken Griffey Jr.

He takes a myth and deflates it. Remember the old story about the final doubleheader in 1941, when he could have finished with a .400 average simply by sitting out? The story is that manager Joe Cronin gave him the option and Williams scoffed. Sit it out? He played the two games, went 6-for-8, finished at .406. He upheld the sanctity of the game, something no one would do in modern, stat-conscious times. Wasn't that how it went? Not exactly.

"I never thought about sitting out," he says. "Not once. But I gotta say this. I didn't realize how much .400 would mean to my life. I mean it had happened only 10 years before I did it and I thought someone else would do it pretty soon. I felt there certainly would be other .400 hitters. I said that. Always said that. Now here it is, 50, 60 years later."

He talks about hitting the slider, invented during the middle of his career. That new pitch. He talks about hitting against the Williams shift, stepping back an inch or two from the plate to be able to punch the inside pitch to left. He talks about flying in Korea in the squadron of eventual astronaut John Glenn. He talks . . . and then he stops.

"You've got enough," he says. "Bye."

Just like that.

Fifty-one minutes. Twenty-two seconds. Exactly.

The tape does not show the conversation after the interview was finished. He talked informally for another 10 or 15 minutes. He was lively, friendly. He was funny. He took out the needle.

"This isn't a paid interview, is it?" he said. "There's no money for this. Right?"

I said there wasn't. No.

"Well, I enjoyed it, and I'd do it again," Williams said. "But the next time there should be a little remuneration. Do you know what I mean? Remuneration. Some compensation."

"Maybe we could send you a hat," I suggested.

"You know where you could put that hat," Williams said.

He asked me who my boss was. I said I had a lot of them. He asked who was the biggest boss, the boss of all the bosses. I thought about it. I said I guessed Ted Turner was the biggest boss. This was a CNN deal.

"Well, you tell Ted Turner that Ted Ballgame would like some remuneration, OK?" Williams said. "Tell Ted that Ted would like something he could fold and put in his pocket. You know?"

I said that since this was an interview to celebrate his 80th birthday, maybe we could work something out, come back for his 100th. He laughed. He said, ha, if we were back for that, he would do that interview for free. Ha. For sure.

The good news was that he didn't die soon after this day. The interview was far from his last. Within a year, he seemed to be everywhere. He was the lead character in all celebrations for the end-of-the-century all-star team. He was at the All-Star Game at Fenway, the World Series in Atlanta. He was at Cooperstown. He was at the Yogi Berra Museum in Montclair, N.J. He was with Ted Koppel late at night, with the *Today Show* in the morning. He talked cooking with Molly O'Neill in the pages of the *New York Times Sunday Magazine*. He had a last triumphant tour.

I remember him going to his bedroom with the walker for his afternoon nap at the end of the CNN interview. Final picture. The big event at night was going to be a Red Sox game on television off the satellite. He wanted to rest. The cameramen were breaking down the equipment. Suddenly chimes rang out from the bedroom. They played the tune "Hail, Hail, the Gang's All Here." They were a signal that Williams required assistance. The aide hurried to the room. A minute later he returned. He was laughing.

"Ted just wanted me to tell you one thing," he said. "Don't forget the part about the remuneration."

Not a disappointment. No. Never.

The obituary eventually appeared in the issue of July 15–22, 2002. Ted had died, of course, on July 5 at the age of 83. Almost three years had passed and a bunch of stuff had changed since I had written what I had written. I was part of that stuff. I no longer worked at *SI*, opting to take a small buyout and become a book writer. Oddly enough, the first book I was writing in my new life as a full-time author was this biography of Ted.

I had been on the case for six months, edging into my subject, luxuriating in this new, slower pace of journalism, collecting phone numbers, and interviewing friends and associates of this famous man. The next year and a half became a rush, a crush of activity as the publisher juggled the date of publication in response to the notoriety and controversy that came out of Ted's death and the cryonics business and the squabbles between his children. Other books were on the horizon. Indeed, sometimes it seemed as if half the people I called were in the process of writing their own books.

I look now at my finished product, the book. . . .

I also look again at my obituary. . . .

The book is certainly a much darker cat. Lewis Watkins, the first director of the Ted Williams Museum, said one day, "When you do a book like yours, you're reaching down to the bottom of the ice chest, where you touch all the dirt and the strange things." This is true. My fingers are still a little numb.

And yet . . .

My wife framed that little penny-postcard, maybe-autographed picture of Ted Williams at the beginning of all this. It has sat on my desk for all of the phone calls, for all of the typing, Ted looking at me as I punched out the bad words that he sometimes spoke and the troubles that he sometimes had. His face never has changed. He is in the finish of a swing, his eyes looking upward at the certain home run that he has just hit. (To rightfield.) He is still young and perfect and indomitable, able to do any damn thing he wants to do.

And I am still ten years old.

Leigh Montville
January 30, 2004

Acknowledgments

I talked with over four hundred people for this project. I thank all of them for their kindness and interest. I have learned about fishing, flying, fame, human nature, medical science, dozens of different subjects, including the fine art of hitting a baseball. (Wait for a good ball to hit.) I asked a lot of uneducated questions and received a lot of thoughtful, informed answers. Time, handed to an inquisitive stranger, is a wonderful gift.

I thank everyone who gave me that gift.

The map of Williams's baseball career has been laid out well in several books that I read, notably *Hitter: The Life and Turmoils of Ted Williams* by Ed Linn; *Ted Williams: A Baseball Life* by Michael Seidel; and *Ted Williams: A Portrait in Words and Pictures* by Dick Johnson and Glenn Stout. *My Turn at Bat*, Williams's autobiography, written with John Underwood, still captures his voice as if he were sitting in the same room. *Ted Williams: The Pursuit of Perfection* by Jim Prime and Bill Nowlin and *I Remember Ted Williams* by David Cataneo are sweet collections of interviews of people who knew, saw, or were touched in any way by the famous man. Edwin Pope, whose book *Ted Williams: The Golden Year* is an overlooked gem, gave me a fat loose-leaf binder filled with the research for both that book and for his unwritten book about the 1941 season. Thanks are not enough.

From the newspaper and magazine side, thanks to all contestants, living and dead, in The Great Ted Williams Theme Contest. Their words gave the famous man's life as much substance and character as anything he did on the field. Special thanks to sports editor Don Skwar and the librarians at the *Boston Globe*.

Ted's nephew, Ted Williams, provided some photographs of Ted's mother and brother that had never been published. Frank Cushing, Ted's friend, provided some other new, remarkable shots from the Korean War. Thanks also to Jerry Romolt, George Carter, and Lewis Watkins for pictures from their personal collections. Thanks to Stan Grossfeld at the *Globe* and Debbie Matson at the Boston Red Sox.

Finally, thanks to Jason Kaufman, my editor; to Esther Newberg, my agent; to Bill Nowlin and Clark Booth, my sounding boards; to my children, Leigh Montville and Robin Moleux and her husband, Doug; to my stepchildren, Alex, Ashley, and Matt; and to Samantha, my wife, friend, copy reader, and heart.

Bibliography

Auker, Elden, with Keegan, Tom. *Sleeper Cars and Flannel Uniforms: A Lifetime of Memories from Striking Out the Babe to Teeing It Up with the President*. Chicago: Triumph Books, 2001.

Baldassaro, Lawrence, ed. *The Ted Williams Reader*. New York: Fireside Books/Simon & Schuster, 1991.

Cataneo, David. *I Remember Ted Williams: Anecdotes and Memories of Baseball's Splendid Splinter by the Players and People Who Knew Him*. Nashville: Cumberland House Publishing, 2002.

Corcoran, Fred, and Bud Harvey. *Unplayable Lies*. New York: Duell, Sloan and Pearce, 1965.

———. *Ted Williams: The Seasons of the Kid*. New York: Prentice-Hall, 1991.

———. *Joe DiMaggio: The Hero's Life*. New York: Touchstone/Simon & Schuster, 2000.

———. *What Do You Think of Ted Williams Now? A Remembrance*. New York: Simon & Schuster, 2003.

Creamer, Robert. *Baseball in '41*. New York: Viking Penguin, 1991.

Curtis, Wayne. *River Guides of the Miramichi*. Fredericton, N.B., Canada: Goose Lane Editions, 1997.

DiMaggio, Dominic, with Bill Gilbert. *Real Grass, Real Heroes: Baseball's Historic 1941 Season*. New York: Zebra Books/Kensington Publishing, 1991.

Glenn, John, with Nick Taylor. *John Glenn: A Memoir*. New York: Bantam Books, 1999.

Gowdy, Curt, with John Powers. *Seasons to Remember: The Way It Was in American Sports 1945–1960*. New York: HarperCollins, 1993.

Halberstam, David. *Summer of '49*. New York: HarperCollins, 1989.

———. *The Teammates*. New York: Hyperion, 2003.

Hirshberg, Al. *What's the Matter with the Red Sox?* New York: Dodd Mead, 1973.

Johnson, Dick, and Glenn Stout. *Ted Williams: A Portrait in Words and Pictures*. New York: Walker Publishing Co., 1991.

Kaplan, Jim. *Lefty Grove: American Original.* Cleveland: Society for American Baseball Research, 2000.

Linn, Edward. *Hitter: The Life and Turmoils of Ted Williams.* Orlando, Fla.: Harcourt Brace & Co., 1993.

McDermott, Mickey, with Howard Eisenberg. *A Funny Thing Happened on the Way to Cooperstown.* Chicago: Triumph Books, 2003.

Mersky, Peter B. *U.S. Marine Corps Aviation: 1912 to the Present.* Baltimore: Nautical and Aviation Publishing Co. of America, 1997.

Pope, Edwin. *Ted Williams: The Golden Year.* New York: Prentice-Hall, 1970.

Prime, Jim, and Bill Nowlin. *Ted Williams: The Pursuit of Perfection.* Sports Publishing, L.L.C., 2002.

Seidel, Michael. *Ted Williams: A Baseball Life.* Lincoln: University of Nebraska Press, 1991.

Stout, Glenn. *Impossible Dreams: A Red Sox Collection.* Boston: Houghton Mifflin, 2003.

Tebbetts, Birdie, with James Morrison. *Birdie: Confessions of a Baseball Nomad.* Chicago: Triumph Books, 2002.

Underwood, John, and Ted Williams. *Fishing "the Big Three."* New York: Simon & Schuster, 1982.

Williams, Ted, with David Pietrusza. *Ted Williams: My Life in Pictures.* Kingston, N.Y.: Total Sports Publishing, 2001.

Williams, Ted, and Jim Prime. *Ted Williams's Hit List.* Indianapolis: Masters Press, 1996.

Williams, Ted, with John Underwood. *My Turn at Bat: The Story of My Life.* New York: Simon & Schuster, 1969.

Williams, Ted, and John Underwood. *The Science of Hitting.* New York: Simon & Schuster, 1970.

The Baseball Encyclopedia: The Complete and Official Record of Major League Baseball, 7th ed., edited by Joe Reichler (New York: Macmillan, 1988), was a major resource material for statistics. *The 2003 Boston Red Sox Media Guide* was a resource for Red Sox statistics and facts. The Internet sites baseball-almanac.com., baseballlibrary.com, and baseball-reference.com also were very helpful.

Index

357

Help a dark room feel warm and inviting by going with a cool, neutral wall color rather than trying to brighten the space. Think subtle and soft and comforting.

358

A weathered cupboard is the perfect repository for a collection of tweed, leather, fine fabrics, and even a small wooden barn model.

359

An armoire doesn't have to be closed. Leave it open and let it speak to your personal style, reflected in your arrangement of the contents.

360

Standing lamps provide light for readers without requiring space for a table. Different heights accommodate the preferences of the bed's occupants.

361

An antique stool is a handy bookstand that can support one or several titles and keep nighttime reading material easy to reach.

362

When a bed is as unique as this
Louis XV piece—which still has
the handles that were used to
move it toward a fire or an open
window more than 250 years
ago—the best way to dress it
is with something simple like a
scalloped-edge blanket.

363

White satin and white cotton meet in the white chiffon spread covering this decadently soft and welcoming guest bed.

364

For an all-out romantic look, pile on silk pillows and complete the look with pink sheer emblazoned with gold stars and a plush shag rug underfoot.

365

Boldly patterned wall coverings can dramatize a room's already striking and unique features, like an arched door, high window, or cathedral ceiling.

366

When you're short on closet space, finding attractive places to hang things becomes a challenge. Look for decorative shelves and wall hooks that give you enough room to allow items to fall well away from the wall.

367

Mixing and matching prints isn't a no-no when they're organized around a theme or color scheme, like these striped, plaid, solid, and patterned pillows and linens— all in red, white, blue, and gold.

368

To make a small room with lots of different floral prints appear more expansive, a giant antique mirror is used as a headboard, reflecting light from the windows and creating the illusion of more space.

369

Transform an inexpensive lamp with silk flowers applied with a glue gun. Finish the look by affixing a fanciful ribbon along the bottom edge of the shade.

370

A rail of hooks above a bed makes a unique way to hang artwork. The rose theme of the paintings is carried over to the bouquet on the side table.

371

Transitioning from a bright color like the yellow of this hallway into a soft color like the pale blue of this bedroom sets a relaxing mood for retiring.

372

This bedroom's sense of vitality comes from the many ways flowers and plants are woven into its design: the curtains, the pillow shams, the prints on the side table, and, of course, the pot of daisies.

373

Dried lamb's ear in a white pot complements a simple cupboard painted the palest shade of green but with a white top.

374

Sheer bedcover fabric can be
fashioned over plain pillows and
decorated with fanciful hooks,
buttons, fabric flowers, and
even photos.

375

Create a private space for yourself by transforming a nook in a bedroom. This space gets some of its definition from the striped shade and matching chair fabric.

376

To customize and give formality and elegance to an otherwise plain wood finish, look for pieces like these column toppers that can be glued into place.

377

Note that the wall at the bottom and back of the space under the desk is painted a different color than the upper part of the wall. This provides visual separation.

378

Allow yourself the luxury of
something really striking, even if
you just move it around in your
room for variety. A fine silk throw
in pale colors is the luxurious
item here.

379

Mix and match accessories at will,
but be careful to stay within a
complementary palette to avoid a
cluttered look that clashes.

380

A guest room's dramatically dark carved oak beds are enlivened with colorful pillows made of vintage floral fabrics. An ornate lamp with a floral, fringed shade complements the intricacy of the beds.

381

A round mirror over a simple bedside table can give a feeling of harmony and coziness, and offers guests a means of checking their appearance in the privacy of their room.

382

Heavy curtains on a canopied bed
bring drama and authenticity to
a bedroom decorated in a style
similar to the late 1700s. Curtains
originally served to keep out
drafts and preserve warmth.

383

A collection of antiques in a palette of subdued reds, grays, and blues gives period quality to this corner of a bedroom. Fresh flowers introduce the present to the past.

384

Wallpapers can be used to cover storage containers, trash bins, even peg rails, and can be an inexpensive way to give a bedroom instant character and charm.

385

Ottomans need not always be accompanied by chairs. Here is one that can be used for a stool or a handy place to toss clothes or throws.

386

Romance doesn't have to be soft and demure. Heat it up with red floors and hot-colored pillowcases and bedspreads.

387

Transform a new wooden dresser by giving it an aged patina look and crystal knobs, lending it an old-fashioned, classy look.

Chapter 8 Kids' Rooms

388

Even a young girl will love the assortment of prints and patterns put together here—it's simple, soothing, and something that can be grown into.

389

Fashion an easy art center where kids can enjoy "drawing on the walls" by painting a bottom panel of a door with several coats of blackboard paint.

390

The tone of this room is cool, with basic blue walls and crisp white trim. It can change as the child whose room this is grows.

391

A bedspread can establish or support a theme, and can also be easily changed. In this room, the theme is surfing.

392

Kids can be rough on rooms, so you can bring in no-worry furniture that looks good by finding "distressed" pieces like this bookcase, or wear-proof pieces like the rolltop desk and bench.

393

A large globe is an endless source of fascination and learning for kids of all ages. Place it on a desk or nightstand where it will get lots of use.

394

For organizing those first pairs of shoes, try using decorative ceramic, plastic, or leather trays that can be displayed for easy access or stowed away under a bed or in a closet.

395

Victorian pressed-glass curtain tiebacks are as cheerful today as they were more than 100 years ago, and will certainly make little girls happy.

396

Consider your child's current tastes and allow for room to grow by using favorite colors and accenting with collections of personal items that can be replaced or added to over the years.

397

Rooms can be made to feel larger than they really are by using patterns consistently. The checked pattern here is repeated in the draperies, walls, and area rug; florals are repeated on the quilt, pillow, and artwork.

398

Daybeds can double as sofas when friends visit. Baskets can be stored under the bed to hide clutter.

399

Matching upholstered sleigh beds are made for crib-sized mattresses; when the beds are outgrown, they can still be used as daybeds or benches at the end of full-sized beds.

400

When setting up your child's workspace, think basic and light, and use stackable boxes and a bulletin board to help keep clutter under control.

401

For a cozy feel, striped fabric panels were added to the head- and footboards of this antique bed tucked in the corner of a small child's room.

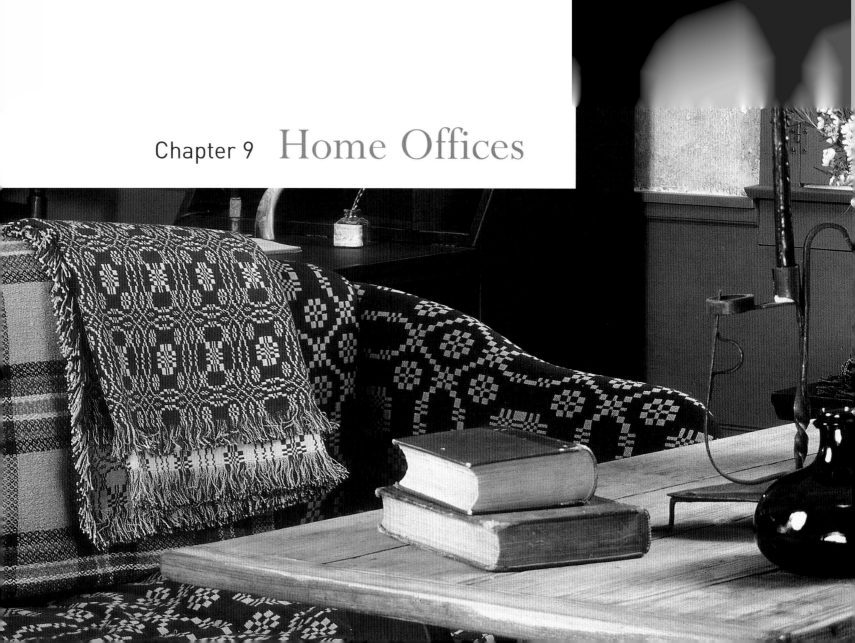

402

Create a keepsake of summer seashore collectibles by mounting shells and sea glass inside a frame and hanging it over your desk to remind yourself of the sand and sea air.

403

A collection of glass jars provides a looking glass into a world of white buttons of different shapes and sizes, and creates a unique, interesting accent in a sewing room.

404

Sterling silver is very versatile. It can be used in many ways and always looks great. Here, a toast rack does duty as a mail sorter.

405

The desk is usually the focal point of a home office and needs to be treated as such. If yours is wood, select office accessories that warm up the earth tones.

406

A great clutter-buster is a bulletin board, which can also become an inspiration board for you when filled with favorite photos, postcards, or decorating swatches.

407

Stackable and portable are qualities to be desired in desk accessories. Old wooden drawers and leather in-boxes work for this office.

408

Convert an alcove space into a home office by dividing the space with a drapery panel and painting the office space a contrasting color.

409

A converted closet just large enough for a desk and chair makes a handy home office that can be concealed with decorative curtains.

410

Decorative hardware for doors and cabinets is "jewelry for the home." Incorporating it into a door for a home office can make that utilitarian space more attractive.

411

You may want to try something unique in your private office space. A stencil in an expressive pattern can be just the thing to wake up the wall in front of you. A word to the wise: Practice on paper first!

412

Create a faux bookcase on the door to your office by applying narrow "shelves" to the surface of the door, then sawing off the spines of out-of-date reference books and gluing them above the shelves. Plan the shelves ahead of time so you can accommodate books of a variety of heights.

413

Warm up an off-white foldaway
drawer desk with pink accents
and fresh flowers for inspiration.
A floral seat cushion adds comfort
and style to the desk chair.

414

Any room can be made into a home office. Here, a wicker desk has been added to a sunroom to create a bright, cheerful workspace.

415

Recycle a pretty gift box or vintage boxes and fill it with letters, postcards, photos, and special mementos to remind you of many wonderful things at once.

416

Keeping ribbons in sight means they have a better chance of being used. Find interesting clear jars in which to display them and keep them where you'll feel inspired.

417

Centuries-old character comes from paneled wainscoting, half shutters that help conceal the contemporary size and style of the windows, and paint sponged on the walls.

418

Add visual interest to a study with a tall bookshelf made to look like a ladder. It's also the perfect place to display other collectibles.

Chapter 10　Small Rooms

419

If you're inspired by the delicate colors of spring's first blooms, bring the greens and pinks inside. A green wall can serve as a backdrop for floral prints and other collectibles in various shades of pink.

420

Color adds excitement and personality to small rooms—these citrusy stripes of paint and bouquet of fresh tulips punch up the energy of this space.

421

To make the most of a small space, think balance and simplicity of form—as in the matching love seats—and of color—with a neutral palette.

422

Create a nifty nook practically anywhere by defining the space with one eye-catching object. In this space, it's an iron chair softened with a floral pillow and dressed up with antique lace and a silver tea set. And don't forget fresh flowers.

423

Transform a plain lamp into something quirky with buttons. Using plain or patterned buttons and a strong adhesive, begin affixing them around the top of the lampshade and work your way down to the bottom.

424

This area is stylish yet remains comfortable by combining simplicity with comfort, eclectic with classic. The unfinished wooden chest pairs nicely with the unfinished wicker chair; the mix of fabrics complements and contrasts; the silver candelabrum, crystal bowl, and wrought-iron plant stand add classic elements; the angel and the hanging oar bring in personality and whimsy.

425

The soft shades of pink, blue, and green in the ceramics on display are picked up in the different floral pillow fabrics that both contrast and complement each other.

426

Covering a small wall with squares of wallpaper can bring the art of collage to a whole new creative level. Plan the design first by pinning up the squares, then draw chalk outlines on the wall and begin affixing the squares from the center outward.

427

An unframed abstract painting provides a dash of color against the brick wall, further supported here by colorful chairs beside a warm wooden drop-leaf table.

428

Keep a breakfast nook informal with wooden folding chairs that can be painted to complement or contrast with the surroundings. Their simple design allows other elements to take center stage, such as bright colors on doors and a large painting.

429

Create a private Eden by positioning plants of different sizes and types around a bank of sunny windows. Interspersing statuary adds further refinement.

430

The bright color of the yellow wing chair is the focal point of a garden sanctuary and makes the room much more alive.

431

A flower room with a large sink and plenty of storage space can also serve as a handy out-of-the-way wet bar during gatherings.

432

Use an assortment of handled wicker baskets to store shears, planters, and other gardening supplies in a flower room.

433

A stainless steel–topped island separates a working kitchen from a casual playroom/den where the furnishings are practical and comfortable.

434

Sliding glass doors between two rooms provide additional quiet and create a more distinct space while still allowing light to flow from one room to another.

435

To offset bold fabrics like velvet and chenille, use natural elements that provide texture. In this room, these include a shelled mirror and a raffia floor pillow.

436

If you want "cozy elegance" in a room, include linen in your mix of fabrics. A faded finish and traditional pattern lend a sense of heritage.

437

A large drum-shaped lampshade covered with textured silk has a rich appearance both on and off. When lit, it casts a flattering glow on the room.

438

For a shot of nostalgia and old-fashioned fun, introduce a chiffon throw that's reminiscent of the lacy gowns and lingerie of the 1920s.

439

A white-on-white palette unifies a mix of old and new as a Victorian crib repurposed as a settee pairs with a painted coffee table and an assortment of knick-knacks.

440

An intimate dining nook is created by positioning a small table under a crystal chandelier and opening up the space with a tall, narrow mirror hung on the wall.

441

Make old windows new again by
fashioning them into wall decor,
as with this tall, gothic-style frame
hung over an antique daybed.

442

It takes discipline to keep from filling up a space, but the result of keeping it simple can mean tremendous tranquillity, as in this attic furnished with a hammock for solitary relaxation.

443

A simple stenciled border along the walls, just below the ceiling, picks up the palette and tone of the country mural on the wall by the staircase.

444

The rich earth tones of an eclectic pottery collection help bring the display together and create a sense of unity in the small nook.

445

For comfort and to soften the appearance of this primitive bench, a seat cushion with a hand-sewn cover is added, maintaining the rustic look of the piece.

446

Nooks like this closet converted
to a butler's pantry make great
spaces for displaying colorful
collections, for storing cookies
and other treats, and for hiding
some kitchen appliances.

447

A linen slipcover, pillow, and half-curtains enhance the country ambience of a room otherwise dominated by wooden furniture.

448

If you crave a place in your home where you can feel calm, resolve to make one. Here, a small space is furnished simply with a welcoming pair of matching wing chairs.

449

Their individuality, fragility, and lovely patterning make these quail eggs worthy of a special spot. They are displayed in a nest of hay in a white enamel vase.

Chapter 11 Laundry Rooms

450

Accessibility maximizes efficiency, which is why laundry and work rooms in particular benefit from long, open shelves, where often-used items can be stored neatly and within reach.

451

Conceal an open under-the-sink or under-counter area—a natural spot for storing unsightly cleaners—with simple curtains hung on a securely fitted rod.

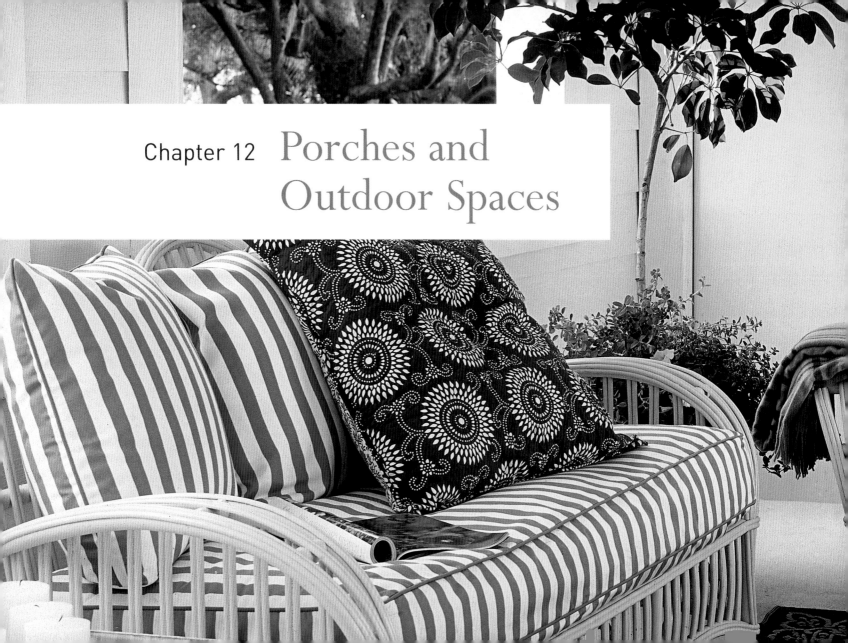

Chapter 12 Porches and Outdoor Spaces

452

Hammocks don't have to go between trees. They can be secured to porch railings, where the addition of a blanket and pillow will make it the most sought-after spot in summer.

453

Brighten up a patio with colorful rugs, pillows, flowers, dining chairs, and even curtains fashioned from fabrics designed to withstand the effects of the sun and rain.

454

Assess the unique nature of a plant
to find the pot that's right for it.
A low-growing plant is handsome
in a stately urn; modulated leaves
look nice in a plain container.

455

Floral porcelain teacups perched on old balustrades are used as charming bumblebee drinking stations in a lush garden.

456

Window boxes cleaned of summer's flowers make great receptacles for fall's festive bounty, like colorful pumpkins and gourds.

457

Why not bring the inside out? If you know it's going to be a nice day, put away the plastic patio chairs and treat yourself with some fine furniture.

458

Make a grand porch cozy by creating small seating areas— with loveseat and chairs and also an eating table. Add plenty of pillows to make it inviting and comfortable.

459

Overstuffed pillows on wicker
chairs invite rejuvenating breaks
on the porch—perhaps even an
afternoon nap—with a peaceful
view of a garden or the woods.

460

Bold stripes add color and
distinction on the floor of a
sunporch. When considering
paints and styles, choose a paint
that's designed to stand up to
heavy foot traffic and the effects
of the elements.

461

In that wonderful transitional time between spring and summer, make an occasion out of a meal by moving your dining room table outside and using less casual chairs gathered from other rooms.

462

Cobalt and white–striped fabric on porch furniture brings the cool blueness of the sky right to the house and creates a peacefulness that promotes relaxation.

Chapter 13 Seasonal Decorating

463

No Memorial Day or Fourth of July celebration is complete without flags. A grouping of flags of different sizes placed in an umbrella stand is at the ready for anyone who gets the urge to wave one.

464

A couple of classic benches and a solid wooden table all painted crisp white become a "picnic table" that stands up to informal and formal meals.

465

Transform a shed into a festive eating area to celebrate fall. A gourd-festooned centerpiece and seating places adorned with chinaberries are eye-catching against a plain table and chairs.

466

Vintage greeting cards and dried flower bouquets secured to chairs with twine combine color, texture, history, nature, and a simple greeting all in one decorative accent.

467

Atop a mantle, pair vintage ornaments with other antique display pieces, like this hand-painted ball ornament resting on a McCoy cornucopia vase.

468

Miniature Christmas trees (live or fake) make a beautiful mantel display. For a special family project, assign each member of the family one to decorate, then group them together.

469

Combining treasures is a
wonderful way to bring magic
and meaning to your holiday
decorations. Here, a vintage
transferware compote dish
becomes a home for a lovingly
worn teddy bear holding a
prized bauble.

470

For the myriad occasions when a simple gift is called for, cookies and treats stashed into decorative tins are the perfect thing. Packed properly, the food will stay fresh for several days. The containers make festive decorations—and easily accessible gifts—for the kitchen or dining room.

471

Infusing a Christmas tree with ornaments of every color calls for other decorations to be more refined, like garlands of pine boughs and gifts wrapped in earth tones of gold, green, and rich brown.

472

Get creative with organizers,
especially for holiday items.
Here, a vintage egg carton now
makes an excellent storage unit
for ornaments that need to be
handled with care.

473

Cardboard coasters and plain paper goods become novel gift tags by simply lacing a beautiful ribbon through a hole and attaching them to packages.

474

Green and gold are elegant color choices for the holidays, and they get a new twist when the greens are muted and aqua-hued, and the gold is more yellow. If you don't have a fireplace, you can still hang stockings from a banister or, as here, from a piano.

475

The holidays are the perfect occasion to decorate with themed collectibles, like the vintage Santas displayed on this mantel and table.

476

Turn plain manila tags into personalized Christmas tree ornaments by gluing them on vintage holiday cards and decorating with glitter.

477

Add a festive touch to your front door—or any door in your house—by hanging a collection of small bells that will add merriment to the season every time the door is opened or closed.

478

Early-American Christmas trees were decorated with paper chains, strings of cranberries, dried quinces, painted walnuts, feathers, and cookies for children.

479

Wreaths fashioned from fresh
evergreen boughs are both
fragrant and elegant. They can be
accessorized in many ways. This
one has nature in its theme,
incorporating dried flowers,
milkweed pods, pinecones,
and a feather.

480

Amaryllises wreathed in pinecones and boxwood make a stunning seasonal centerpiece for a dinner table, entry table, or coffee table.

481

A white corner cupboard is an excellent display case for seasonal items in the traditional Christmas colors of red and green in all their variations.

482

Now's the time to bring out any fun or funky boxes you found at flea markets throughout the year so that they can be used as gift boxes. Ribbons and ornaments make them extra special.

483

To turn your cards into a nifty decoration. Center a piece of narrow ribbon over a wider one and sew at the top to secure. Using holding clips from an office-supply store, sew them onto the ribbon, leaving enough space in between for cards. Next, glue buttons over the stitching.

484

Brightly patterned seasonal tablecloths can be sewn into beautiful stockings, which are especially meaningful when they're personalized with someone's initials.

485

Festive poinsettia glasses on a two-tiered vintage pie stand add the perfect touch to your seasonal decorating.

486

Special take-home holiday goody bags are simple to create and beautiful outside and in. Stack cookies in a baking cup, trim the cup with ribbon, put the cup in a cellophane bag, trim the bag with zigzagged pinking shears, and secure with a ribbon. You can also include the recipe and a personalized gift tag.

487

Working with nontraditional holiday colors, such as lilac, plum, and silver—this homeowner's favorite colors—creates a romantic holiday atmosphere.

488

A long mantel is home to cream-colored pillar candles of all shapes and sizes, which complement the lights on the tree and add an extra-warm glow to the room.

489

Simple festive touches are sometimes all that's needed to bring the holidays home. Here, miniature spruce trees are grouped and surrounded by red pears. Red pillar candles accent the centerpiece.

490

Create a welcoming holiday arrangement composed of candles wrapped in seasonal papers, with bows, sprigs of holly, and Christmas tree ornaments.

491

A cozy cottage's white theme makes for an almost anything-goes setting for the holidays. An all-natural tree evokes Christmases past and fills the room with the scent of fresh pine.

492

To give a bedroom a festive touch, a string of red glass beads is laced through a bed frame and accented with wreaths of paperwhites.

493

Stray from the expected by introducing a nontraditional color into the holiday scheme. Here, teal-blue balls and tree skirt add a modern touch to gold stars and ribbon.

494

Antique needlework and blooming agapanthus show off holiday postcards from the early 20th century, supported in old frogs (ornamental flower holders).

495

Vintage letters bring Old World
character to this traditional red,
green, gold, and silver tree,
and a small ladder next to the
tree provides a lovely perch for
small gifts.

496

The new take on an old Christmas tradition is easy to make: this Advent calendar is fashioned from flash cards, paper clips, and ribbon, with tiny ornaments as treats.

497

An enclosed wraparound porch is a favorite spot for seasonal decorating. Here, synthetic green trees with simple white lights complement the already established black-and-white theme.

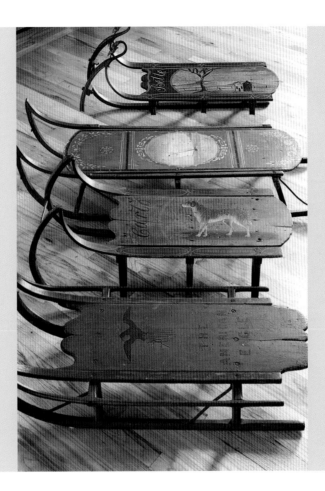

498

Antique sleds make wonderful wintertime display pieces, to be admired on their own or piled high with gifts.

499

A small tinsel tree with a glittering gold star is the perfect topping for a small coffee table and is a modern foil to the big, traditional tree in the back of the room.

500

Go for an 18th-century country look by making a pineapple—the classic symbol of hospitality—the centerpiece of a decorative mantel.

Photo Credits

Page 2: *Keith Scott Morton*

Page 5: *Gridley & Graves*

Page 6: *Michael Luppino*

Page 9: *John Gruen*

Page 10: *Michael Luppino*

Page 12: *Andrew McCaul*

Page 13: *Chuck Baker*

Page 14: *Gridley & Graves*

Page 15: *Keith Scott Morton*

Page 16: *Beatriz Da Costa*

Page 17: *Anastassios Mentis*

Page 18: *Keith Scott Morton*

Page 19: *Michael Luppino*

Page 20: *Michael Luppino*

Page 21: *Andrew McCaul*

Page 22: *Jessie Walker*

Page 23: *Stacey Brandford*

Page 24: *Natasha Milne*

Page 25: *James Merrell*

Page 26: *Robin Stubbert*

Page 27: *Ann Stratton*

Page 28: *Andreas von Einsiedel*

Page 30: *Andrew McCaul*

Page 31: *Michael Luppino*

Page 32: *Keith Scott Morton*

Page 33: *James Merrell*

Page 34: *Andreas von Einsiedel*

Page 35: *Steven Randazzo*

Page 36: *Gridley & Graves*

Page 38: *Keith Scott Morton*

Page 39: *Keith Scott Morton*

Page 40: *Gridley & Graves*

Page 41: *Gridley & Graves*

Page 42: *Michael Luppino*

Page 43: *Jonn Coolidge*

Page 44: *Susie Cushner*

Page 46: *David Prince*

Page 47: *Steven Randazzo*

Page 48: *Susie Cushner*

Page 49: *Keith Scott Morton*

Page 50: *Keith Scott Morton*

Page 52: *Michael Luppino*

Page 53: *William P. Steele*

Page 54: *Michael Luppino*

Page 55: *David Prince*

Page 56: *Jonn Coolidge*

Page 57: *Michael Luppino*

Page 58: *Keith Scott Morton*

Page 59: *Natasha Milne*

Page 60: *Ray Kachatorian*

Page 61: *Adrian Briscoe*

Page 62, 472: *Keith Scott Morton*

Page 63: *Keith Scott Morton*

Page 64: *William P. Steele*

Page 65: *Gridley & Graves*

Page 66: *Jeff McNamara*

Page 67: *Robin Stubbert*

Page 68: *Keith Scott Morton*

Page 69: *Simon Bevan*

Page 70: *Simon Bevan*

Page 71: *Tim Street-Porter*

Page 72: *William P. Steele*

Page 73: *Keith Scott Morton*

Page 74: *William P. Steele*

Page 75: *Jim Bastardo*

Page 76: *Michael Luppino*

Page 77: *Michael Luppino*

Page 78: *Keith Scott Morton*

Page 80: *Ann Stratton*

Page 81: *Keith Scott Morton*

Page 82: *Keith Scott Morton*

Page 84: *© Kindra Clineff/ Terry John Woods*

Page 85: *William P. Steele*

Page 86: *William P. Steele*

Page 87: *William P. Steele*

Page 88: *Keith Scott Morton*

Page 90: *William P. Steele*

Page 91: *Keith Scott Morton*

Page 92: *Keith Scott Morton*

Page 93: *Keith Scott Morton*

Page 94: *Keith Scott Morton*

Page 96: *Jeff McNamara*

Page 97: *Robin Stubbert*

Page 98: *Jeff McNamara*

Page 99: *Andrew McCaul*

Page 100: *Jonn Coolidge*

Page 101: *Jonn Coolidge*

Page 102: *Keith Scott Morton*

Page 103: *Keith Scott Morton*

Page 104: *Minh + Wass*

Page 106: *David Montgomery*

Page 107: *Keith Scott Morton*

Page 108: *Keith Scott Morton*

Page 109: *Grey Crawford*

Page 110: *Keith Scott Morton*

Page 111: *Michael Luppino*

Page 112: *Stacey Brandford*

Page 113: *Keith Scott Morton*

Page 114: *Michael Luppino*

Page 115: *Debi Treloar*

Page 116: *Keith Scott Morton*

Page 117: *Keith Scott Morton*

Page 118: *Keith Scott Morton*

Page 119: *Jonn Coolidge*

Page 120: *Jonn Coolidge*

Page 121: *Jonn Coolidge*

Page 126: *Keith Scott Morton*

Page 127: *Minh + Wass*

Page 128: *Michael Luppino*

Page 130: *Steven Randazzo*

Page 131: *Gridley & Graves*

Page 132: *Keith Scott Morton*

Page 133: *Gridley & Graves*

Page 134: *Steven Randazzo*

Page 135: *David Prince*

Page 136: *Rob Melnychuk*

Page 137: *Miki Duisterhof*

Page 138: *William P. Steele*

Page 139: *Steven Randazzo*

Page 140: *Michael Luppino*

Page 141: *Steven Randazzo*

Page 142: *Michael Luppino*

Page 143: *Jim Bastardo*

Page 144: *Gridley & Graves*

Page 145: *Gridley & Graves*

Page 146: *Jim Bastardo*

Page 147: *Keith Scott Morton*

Page 149: *Keith Scott Morton*

Page 150: *Jonn Coolidge*

Page 151: *Steven Randazzo*

Page 152: *Michael Luppino*

Page 154: *Michael Luppino*

Page 155: *Jim Bastardo*

Page 156: *Ann Stratton*

Page 157: *Keith Scott Morton*

Page 158: *Keith Scott Morton*

Page 159: *Jonn Coolidge*

Page 160: *Keith Scott Morton*

Page 161: *Michael Weschler*

Page 162: *Keith Scott Morton*

Page 164: *Keith Scott Morton*

Page 165: *Keith Scott Morton*

Page 166: *Donna Griffith*

Page 167: *Keith Scott Morton*

Page 168: *Keith Scott Morton*

Page 344: *Gridley & Graves*

Page 345: *Gridley & Graves*

Page 346: *Michael Weschler*

Page 347: *Keith Scott Morton*

Page 348: *Natasha Milne*

Page 349: *Gridley & Graves*

Page 350: *William P. Steele*

Page 352: *Robin Stubbert*

Page 353: *John Gruen*

Page 355: *Andrew McCaul*

Page 356: *Steven Randazzo*

Page 357: *Charles Schiller*

Page 359: *William P. Steele*

Page 360: *Simon Bevan*

Page 361: *Keith Scott Morton*

Page 362: *William P. Steele*

Page 363: *Michael Luppino*

Page 364: *Gridley & Graves*

Page 366: *David Montgomery*

Page 367: *Steven Randazzo*

Page 368: *Beatriz Da Costa*

Page 369: *Steven Randazzo*

Page 370: *Keith Scott Morton*

Page 371: *Philip Clayton-Thompson*

Page 372: *Adrian Briscoe*

Page 373: *Steven Randazzo*

Page 374: *Keith Scott Morton*

Page 375: *Keith Scott Morton*

Page 376: *Colin McGuire*

Page 377: *John Gruen*

Page 378: *Gridley & Graves*

Page 379: *Keith Scott Morton*

Page 380: *Keller & Keller*

Page 382: *Caroline Arber*

Page 383: *Ann Stratton*

Page 384: *Keith Scott Morton*

Page 386: *Jonn Coolidge*

Page 387: *Catherine Gratwicke*

Page 389: *Jonn Coolidge*

Page 390: *Keith Scott Morton*

Page 391: *Adrian Briscoe*

Page 392: *Michael Luppino*

Page 393: *Andreas von Einsiedel*

Page 395: *Gridley & Graves*

Page 397: *Jeff McNamara*

Page 398: *Keith Scott Morton*

Page 399: *Keith Scott Morton*

Page 400: *Keith Scott Morton*

Page 402: *Steven Randazzo*

Page 403: *Miki Duisterhof*

Page 404: *Keith Scott Morton*

Page 405: *Keith Scott Morton*

Page 406: *Keller & Keller*

Page 408: *Keith Scott Morton*

Page 409: *Grey Crawford*

Page 410: *© Kindra Clineff/ Terry John Woods*

Page 411: *Robin Stubbert*

Page 412: *Keith Scott Morton*

Page 413: *Keith Scott Morton*

Page 414, 427: *Keith*

Scott Morton

Page 416: *Michael Luppino*

Page 417: *Gridley & Graves*

Page 418: *Colin McGuire*

Page 419: *Donna Griffith*

Page 420: *Steven Randazzo*

Page 421: *Jeff McNamara*

Page 422: *Miki Duisterhof*

Page 423: *Gridley & Graves*

Page 424: *Roy Gumpel*

Page 426: *Keith Scott Morton*

Page 428: *Robin Stubbert*

Page 430: *Michael Luppino*

Page 431: *Keith Scott Morton*

Page 432: *Steven Randazzo*

Page 433: *Robin Stubbert*

Page 434: *Steven Randazzo*

Page 435: *Simon Bevan*

Page 436: *© Kindra Clineff/ Terry John Woods*

Page 437: *© Kindra Clineff/ Terry John Woods*

Page 438: *Keith Scott Morton*

Page 440: *Steven Randazzo*

Page 441: *Steven Randazzo*

Page 442: *Steven Randazzo*

Page 444: *Keith Scott Morton*

Page 445: *Andrew McCaul*

Page 446: *Keith Scott Morton*

Page 447: *Gridley & Graves*

Page 448: *Gridley & Graves*

Page 449: *Gridley & Graves*

Page 450: *Steven Randazzo*

Page 451: *Steven Randazzo*

Page 452: *Keith Scott Morton*

Page 453: *Steven Randazzo*

Page 454: *John Gruen*

Page 455: *James Worrell*

Page 456: *Donna Griffith*

Page 458: *Gridley & Graves*

Page 459: *David Prince*

Page 460: *Robin Stubbert*

Page 462: *Robin Stubbert*

Page 463: *Andrew McCaul*

Page 464: *Robin Stubbert*

Page 466: *Keith Scott Morton*

Page 467: *Susan Gentry McWhinney*

Page 468: *Donna Griffith*

Page 469: *Michael Weschler*

Page 470: *Gridley & Graves*

Page 471: *Gridley & Graves*

Index

COLLINS GUIDE TO THE WILD FLOWERS
OF BRITAIN AND NORTHERN EUROPE

The Wildlife Trusts are working for a UK richer in wildlife. Their extensive network covers all parts of the countryside and reaches into cities as far apart as Belfast and Ipswich. They care for more than 2,300 nature reserves: from rugged coastline to urban oases, remote islands to flower-rich meadows.

With more than a third of a million members, The Wildlife Trusts provide an unrivalled source of expertise on wildlife and conservation issues, offering advice that helps local landowners and communities care for their local wildlife. This work also includes the implementation of rescue plans for nationally rare species, including the Red Squirrel, the Dormouse and its ancient woodland home, the Marsh Fritillary butterfly and the Otter.

The Wildlife Trusts also campaign for better protection for wildlife at the local, national and international level, and recognize that people are a vital part of the solution to the challenges they face.

Joint projects like this one between The Wildlife Trusts and Collins Natural History are important, not just because they help raise vital funds for wildlife in the UK (for each copy of the book sold 30p will be donated to The Wildlife Trusts), but also because they show people the wonders of the natural world though the medium of first-class photographs, which encourage their interest and commitment to protect it.

COLLINS WILDLIFE TRUST GUIDE
WILD FLOWERS

*A photographic guide to the flowers
of Britain and Northern Europe*

Peter Heukels

Photographs assembled by Natural Image

HarperCollins*Publishers*

HarperCollins*Publishers*
77–85 Fulham Palace Road
London
W6 8JB

The HarperCollins website address is:
www.fireandwater.com

First published 2000

2 4 6 8 10 9 7 5 3 1

01 03 05 04 02 00

Titles in the series include:

Birds of Britain and Europe, John Gooders

Butterflies of Britain and Europe, Michael Chinery

Mushrooms of Britain and Europe, Régis Courtecuisse

Trees of Britain and Europe, Keith Rushforth

Night Sky, Mark Chartrand

ISBN 0 00 220139 9

Edit and page make-up by D & N Publishing, UK

Colour origination by Colourscan, Singapore
Printed and bound by Rotolito Lombarda SpA, Milan, Italy

CONTENTS

Preface

The landscapes of northern Europe have been continuously occupied by Man since the last ice age came to an end approximately 10,000 years Before Present (B.P.). It took thousands of years for the forests to reconquer their lost territory on the tundra and steppes that had survived in the area between the sheets of land ice advancing from the north and the high, extensively glaciated mountains in the south. Migrating tribes with a hunting-and-gathering mode of life soon began to exert a moderate influence on the natural vegetation. However, Man's impact on his environment became significant only after the introduction of agriculture, which began to spread from Asia Minor as early as 8,000 B.P. and eventually reached Western Europe about 6,000 B.P. Forests dwindled as Man began to use slash-and-burn techniques to clear areas of land for cultivation. By the beginning of Roman times, a semi-open, cultural landscape had replaced the forest in much of Europe except in the boggy and mountainous areas, and in the cold regions of the far north.

For centuries, this agricultural revolution led to an increase, rather than a decrease, in biodiversity, for the agricultural landscape offered sustenance for many species that otherwise could not have lived here. After the industrial revolution in the 19th century, however, agricultural management intensified. Fertilizers and pesticides came into use on a large scale, enabling farmers to reclaim the 'badlands', which had hitherto been inaccessible to them and had therefore served as a refuge for the native flora and fauna. Today, less than 3 per cent of Europe is true 'wilderness', and such terrain is restricted to the Arctic tundra, the sea-coasts and the highest mountains. Since the Second World War, the urbanized area has multiplied three- or fourfold. The agricultural landscape has come to resemble the barren steppes that the first nomadic tribes hesitatingly entered 10,000 years ago, but in many ways it is now even less hospitable to life than it was then, and the 'Red Lists' of extinct and endangered species grow longer every year.

Yet, outside the bulging cities, at least some glimpses of the native flora and fauna can still be had. In Europe, there is a tradition of spending one's leisure time in the countryside, looking for flowers and other living things. This book has been written primarily for the amateur naturalist who wants a basic understanding of the landscape he is visiting. It is not intended for the trained professional, who will find any information he needs in detailed regional floras. However, between these scientific works and the many existing amateur guides there yawns a large gap, especially when major areas like northern Europe are considered. In being more detailed and less incomplete than most amateur guides, this book intends to bridge that gap to some extent. Included are all herbs and dwarf shrubs that have a wide range or are regionally common in the northern and central European lowlands, the far north, and the foothills of the great mountain chains running across the old continent – the Pyrenees, the Alps, and the Carpathians to the south, and the Urals to the east. Most of the plant species are illustrated and fully described; where appropriate, the main characteristics, habitat and range of any lookalike species are briefly outlined in the text. Wherever there is a chance of confusing a species with others, the reader is alerted.

Peter Heukels, Leiden

MAP OF EUROPE

The area covered by this book (white).

INTRODUCTION

To bring a plant to name, one generally needs a field guide, a hand-lens (10 times magnification), and some basic knowledge of the plant structures that can be observed through the lens. The aim of this section is to help the reader become familiar with the botanical jargon used in the species descriptions in this book.

Major Plant Types
The general morphology of flowering plants is understood by anyone: they possess roots, stems, leaves and flowers. The difference between trees, shrubs and herbs will be equally obvious: **trees** possess a woody bole or trunk, **shrubs** have several woody stems rising from the ground, and **herbs** have no wood at all, i.e., no secondary or thickening wood (although herbs do possess thin strands of primary wood-vessels in the stem, transporting water from the roots to the leaves). **Half-shrubs** have woody, permanent stems near the ground, and herbaceous stems higher up, the latter dying each winter. **Deciduous** trees and shrubs shed their leaves in autumn; **evergreen** plants carry them through the winter, as most conifers and many Mediterranean shrubs do. Herbs are divided into three groups: **annuals** and **biennials**, which blossom only once before they die (in their 1st or 2nd year, respectively); and **perennials**, which blossom each year (or, at least, have the potential to do so).

Most plants possess the green pigment **chlorophyll**, which enables them to synthesize their own food (sugars) from aerial carbon dioxide and water from the soil. The leaves are the main green organs of a plant, absorbing the sunlight that provides the energy for making sugars. Many **saprophytes** (living from dead organic matter, often through symbiosis with a fungus) and **parasites** (stealing what they need from a living host) have lost their chlorophyll and may present themselves in all shades of white, yellow, red, violet or brown. **Hemi-parasites** depend on their host for water and dissolved minerals, but make their own sugars in their green leaves. **Epiphytes** grow on other plants (often trees), but without taking anything away from them; they content themselves with a few crumbs of dust or debris collecting in fissures of the bark, and some rainwater or dew. Often they have features of **xerophytes**, i.e., plants adapted to a life in deserts and other dry environments. Such adaptations can take the form of special tissues or organs for the storage of water, or measures to reduce evaporation, such as having tiny leaves, and dense, reflecting hairs or a waxy layer on the surface. **Hydrophytes** or aquatic plants are adapted to a life under water; they often possess air-channels in their stems. Their leaves may be submerged or floating, but often their flowers are emergent. Plants from marshy environments (**helophytes**) often show mixed characters of terrestrial and aquatic plants; for instance, both submerged leaves, and emergent, aerial ones.

Stems and Branches Stems may be upright (**erect**) in posture, or prostrate (**trailing**, if not rooting along their length; otherwise **creeping**). When a stem is prostrate before rising from the ground, we call it **ascending**. Plants, undirectionally searching for support on neighbouring plants or other objects, are **scrambling**; when their stems turn spirally to catch a hold, they are **winding** (clockwise, or anticlockwise). Plants that use their normal stems, branches and leaves to anchor themselves to trees, walls, and rockfaces, or have special adhesive organs for this purpose, are called **climbing**. Many perennial herbs possess specialized, creeping, underground stems (**rhizomes**), enabling them to survive the winter or a dry period when the overground parts die; from the rhizomes, new aerial stems are sent up every year. **Corms** are thickened underground stem-bases that grow vertically and serve the same purpose. Stems are often **terete** (rounded), but can also be **angular** (often triangular, or square) in cross-section. Their surface can be lengthwise grooved, ribbed, fluted, or even broadly winged. Stems can be simple, or variously ramified, sending off **branches**. In woody plants, the youngest, still flexible and leaf-bearing branches are called shoots or twigs, while older, heavier, leafless branches are called boughs. Branches can be drooping (as in Weeping Willow), horizontally spreading, or ascending (to almost erect, as in Lombardy Poplar). Many herbs and shrubs propagate by means of **stolons** (specialized, creeping or even underground branches), forming young plants at regular intervals; aerial stolons are also known as **runners**. Trees and shrubs can do a similar thing, through **suckers** rising up from their root system. In herbs, the stem may be strongly reduced to seemingly absent, so that all leaves are crowded together in a **basal rosette**. This is often the case in biennial herbs after their first growing season; in the next spring, the flowering stem or **scape** will rise up from the centre of the rosette. Occasionally plants possess **cladodes** (small branches imitating green leaves), while the true leaves are absent or reduced to scales. Wild Asparagus is an example, displaying clusters of needle-like cladodes; in Butcher's Broom the cladodes are flattened, and they resemble normal leaves. The parasitic Dodder species have only thin winding stems without chlorophyll, and no apparent leaves at all.

Floral Parts A flower consists of several whorls of leaves, some of them still recognizable as such, others modified into sexual organs. These **floral parts** usually occur in definite numbers. In **trimerous** (or 3-merous) flowers, multiples of three are found in each whorl; other common basic numbers are four (in **tetramerous** or 4-merous flowers) and five (in **pentamerous** or 5-merous flowers). The outer whorl, called the **calyx**, is often green, and is made up of individual **sepals**. The next inner whorl is the **corolla**, usually the showiest part of the flower. The corolla leaves are individually called **petals**. Often, the corolla bears dark markings (stripes, or dots), which serve to guide visiting insects to the centre of the flower.

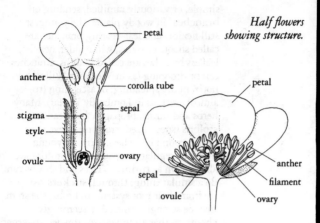

Half flowers showing structure.

Collectively, sepals and petals form the **perianth**. Sometimes there is not much difference between the sepals and the petals, as often in the Lily family where they are both attractively coloured; in these cases the perianth lobes are usually named **tepals**. The calyx can even be the most colourful part of the perianth, in which case the petals can be transformed into smaller, fragrant **honey-leaves**. Inside the perianth is a whorl of strongly modified leaves, the **stamens**, producing the **pollen** in the **anthers** on top of a thin stalk (**filament**). Stamens can be modified into honey-leaves as well, or back into petal-like (petaloid) structures. At the centre of the flower are one or more **pistils**, each consisting of a swollen, basal **ovary** (containing the **ovules**, later to develop into seeds), and one to several sleek **styles**, each with a **stigma** at the top. Styles can be reduced, bringing the stigma right on top of the ovary (as in poppies). Ovaries have a definite number of compartments (**locules**), clearly visible in cross-section; therefore, we speak of 1-, 2-, 3-locular ovaries, and so on. In principle, the number of locules corresponds to the number of **carpels** (fruit-leaves) from which the pistil is composed. Consequently, 1-locular fruits consist of 1 folded carpel; a 5-locular fruit is made from 5 fused (**connate**) carpels. When the fruit is ripe, it often splits along the seams of the original carpels, which are then called **valves**. When the outer floral parts (calyx, corolla, stamens) are inserted at the base of the ovary, the ovary is called **superior**; when they are inserted at the top, the ovary is called **inferior**. An intermediate arrangement is called hemi-inferior. As the carpels can be connate, so can the petals. The corolla then takes on the shape of a dish, a cup, or even a tube. The same holds for the sepals, which are often fused into a tube with a fixed number of marginal teeth. Even the stamens can be connate (as in the pea family).

Flower Types When all floral parts are equal, and regularly placed in a radially symmetrical fashion (like the spokes in a wheel), the flower is called **regular** or **actinomorphic**. This is a common arrangement, beautifully displayed in buttercups (with free petals) and bell-flowers (with connate petals). Yet, in many species the flowers are **irregular** or **zygo-morphic**, with a vertical axis of symmetry along which the two halves of the flower mirror each other (bilateral symmetry). Well-known examples are the flowers of peas, vetches, brooms and other **papilionaceous** plants (with free or only slightly connate petals), and also the deadnettles and allies (with connate petals). Many irregular flowers are to some extent connate, in which case their calyx and corolla often show distinctly different **upper** and **lower lips**. Most orchids show an enlarged lower tepal (also called lip), while the remaining 5 tepals are unchanged and free. In **apetalous** plants, the corolla or the whole perianth is absent – as in many species that rely on wind or water to disperse their pollen, and do not need a showy perianth to attract insects.

Many flowers contain both stamens and pistils (**bisexual** or **hermaphrodite** flowers). But sometimes, especially in trees and shrubs, the flowers are **unisexual**, in which case part of the flowers have only stamens (in male flowers) or pistils (in female flowers). Where male and female flowers are present on the same plant, as in oaks and pines, we call the species **monoecious** (meaning 'with one house'). Where males and females are on different plants, as in willows and poplars, we call the species **dioecious** ('with two houses'). In herbs, bisexual flowers are quite common, but monoecism also occurs, especially in the Daisy Family. Herbs can also be dioecious (e.g. the Stinging Nettle), but this is not a frequent phenomenon.

Fruit Types   After flowering (anthesis), the petals are usually shed and the pistil develops into the **fruit**. The style and the stigma often perish in the process, but sometimes they remain on the fruit as a prolonged **beak**. The fruit may be fleshy or even juicy, as in **berries**, with many seeds dispersed in the pulp; or in **drupes**, with normally a single seed (stone) enclosed in a rock-hard wall (cherries); or in **pomes**, with several seeds in a tough, membranous or leathery core (apples). There are also several types of dry fruit. In **nuts** the fruit contains but one loose seed and does not open mechanically; very small nuts are called **nutlets** or **achenes**. In **capsules** there are many seeds, and the fruit-wall opens through cracks, splits or pores to set them free. Occasionally this happens suddenly and with such force that the seeds are hurled away over a considerable distance (**ballistic fruits**). Capsules originating from a single, free carpel have been given special names: **pods** (the Pea family), which usually split up along two seams into equal halves; or **follicles** (Marsh Marigold), which open along one seam. In the Cress family (e.g., Mustard), the fruit is called a **siliqua**, which is composed of two carpels (valves) falling off separately, and often leaving a thin **septum**, as – very conspicuously – in Honesty. Very short siliquas are called **silicules** (well-known from Shepherd's-purse). The shape of fruits is usually described in general stereometric terms, like spherical, cylindrical, conical, etc. Other terms are ellipsoid (oblong with rounded ends), spindle-shaped (oblo tapering ends), and ovoid (egg-shap

Compound fruits can develop i containing more than one pistil (o This often happens with ache deadnettles and other Labiates (always 4 achenes clustered together), and in the mallows (many achenes assembled in a ring). In Strawberries, numerous achenes are attached to the outer surface of the swollen, egg-shaped flower-base (**hypanthium**), which does not belong to the fruit proper. In the hips of roses several achenes are enveloped by a concave, jar-shaped hypanthium. Compound drupes (with numerous drupelets) are found in brambles and raspberries, amongst others. Honeysuckles are apparently developing compound berries.

Leaves The first leaves of a plant are the **seed-lobes**, often already discernible in the seed, and variously specialized. In **monocots** there is only one seed-lobe (e.g. grasses, sedges, lilies, orchids and the like). In **dicots**, which form the bulk of flowering plants, there are two seed-lobes (and in conifers there are even more). For our purposes, the leaves of adult plants are better guides. Leaves are always inserted on an **axis** (a stem, or a branch). The place of insertion is called a **node**; the stretch of the axis between two nodes is an **internode**. Many plants have **simple leaves**, consisting of an undivided **blade** and a **leaf-stalk**, or petiole. The base of the stalk may be widened into a **leaf-sheath**, enveloping the stem near the node. Instead of a sheath, a flappy pair of small, supporting leaflets (**stipules**) may be present here. In **sessile** leaves the stalk is altogether lacking, so the blade connects directly to the stem. In **subsessile** leaves the stalk is very short but still visible. Sessile leaves whose blades are much reduced are called **scale-leaves** or simply scales. We often find them in the vicinity of the flowers, and at the stem-base. Of course, they are hardly functional in catching sunlight, so they have frequently lost the green pigment. However, in plants growing in dry or very sunny places (e.g. Common Heather), the functional leaves are often reduced to green scale-leaves.

In normal leaves the blade may be variously shaped. In judging leaf-shape, the length to width ratio (l:w) is important.

Extremely narrow leaves (l:w = 10 or more) are called **linear**. Leaves with a l:w ratio of between 10 and 3 are **lanceolate** (narrowly or broadly so, depending on their closeness to one of either extremes). Still wider leaves (l:w between 3 and 1.5) are called (narrowly to broadly) **ovate**; they graduate via **suborbicular** leaves into **orbicular** leaves (l:w = 1). In ovate and lanceolate leaves, the greatest width is usually in the lower part of the blade. Blades that are widest near the top are called **obovate** or **oblanceolate**, respectively. If the greatest width is exactly in the middle, the blade is often called **elliptical**. Narrowly oblanceolate or linear leaves with a slightly widened top are called **spatulate**. Special names have been coined for other blade-shapes deviating from the regular, ovate-lanceolate-linear strain with gently curved margins. Often these names are self-evident: triangular, sword-shaped, strap-shaped, spoon-shaped, etc. The top of a blade may be **truncate** (cut off straight), or **rounded**, or **acute**. In **acuminate** or **pointed** leaves the (acute) top looks drawn out from the (generally rounded) blade, so the margins are curved in an S-shape. In **emarginate** or **notched** blades the top has a shallow incision. If the leaf-top wears a needle-like protrusion, the leaf is **awned**. The base of a blade can also be truncate, rounded, or acute. If its margins are straight, an acute leaf-base is called **wedge-shaped**. In **cordate** (heart-shaped) leaves the blade is ovate with a more or less pronounced incision (**sinus**) at the base, between rounded **basal lobes**. An orbicular leaf with a sinus and rounded basal lobes is called **reniform** (kidney-shaped). An ovate to lanceolate blade with a sinus and sideways divergent basal lobes is **hastate** (spear-shaped); when the lobes point backwards it is **sagittate** (arrow-shaped). In sessile leaves, the basal lobes are often adjacent to the stem, and then we call them **auricles**. When the auricles enclose the stem, we call the leaf **clasping**; when they are connate around the stem, the leaf is **perfoliate**.

Leaf-blades consist of a thin, webbed, green tissue, suspended between the **veins** – like the flying skin between the digits of a bat. Especially in monocots the veins may be **parallel** (straight or arched), without obvious bifurcations (though small fibres run between them). In dicots the veins are often variously **ramified**. Frequently one observes **pinnately veined** leaves, with one main, or middle vein sending off several smaller side-veins. Less often the leaves are **palmately veined**, with an odd number (5 or more) of equally important main veins all fanning out from the blade-base at the insertion of the leaf-stalk. The **leaf-margins** may be **entire**, or variously sculptured or incised. For a start, they may be only shallowly toothed. In this case, when the teeth are blunt, with sharp notches in between, the leaf is **crenate** (or **crenulate**, if one can hardly see the teeth). When the teeth are acute, but the indentations are rounded, the blade is **dentate**. When both the teeth and the indentations are acute, the blade is **serrate**. Finally, when both are blunt, the blade is **sinuous**. When the blade is more deeply incised – at least one tenth of the distance to the middle nerve (in pinnately veined leaves), or to the blade-base (in palmately veined leaves), but to no more than one third of the way – the leaf is **lobed** (pinnately, or palmately lobed, respectively). In this case, there is usually one major (side-) vein for each lobe. Leaves with very deep incisions (nearing the middle vein or the blade-base without actually reaching it) are called **divided** (pinnately divided or **pinnatifid** in pinnately veined leaves, and palmately divided or **palmatifid** in palmately veined leaves, respectively). In this case, the lobes of the blade are often called **segments**. Leaves with 3 segments are called **tripartite** (3-partite). When the incisions actually reach the middle vein or the blade-base, so that no green webbed tissue is left there and the segments are distinctly stalked, we speak of **compound leaves**.

Compound Leaves Here, again, the branching pattern of the veins is decisive. A compound, pinnately veined leaf is called a **pinnate** leaf; it is usually composed of pinnately veined **leaflets (folioles)** separately attached to the middle vein (which is then often called the **rhachis**). Usually, there is a **top-leaflet** at the end of the rhachis, and a varying number of **side-leaflets** laterally. In some groups, the top-leaflet may be wanting altogether, or it may be modified into a sleek winding organ (**tendril**); even adjacent side-leaflets can be transformed into tendrils (as in many vetches). The leaflets may be variously incised again (lobed, divided or pinnate themselves). In the last case, the leaf is **bipinnate** (2-pinnate). Through a repetition of the dividing process, the leaf may be three- or four-times pinnate (3-pinnate, 4-pinnate), or even manifold pinnate, but then we often stop counting and call it, more loosely, **finely dissected**. Sometimes we observe **ternate** (or trifoliolate) leaves, which in their simplest form are well-known to us in the shape of the clover leaf: a pinnate leaf with one top-leaflet and only two opposite side-leaflets. When the leaflets of a ternate leaf are ternate themselves, the leaf is called **biternate** (doubly ternate or 2-ternate; e.g., columbines). Again, further subdivision can occur, as illustrated by the Lesser Meadow-rue (up to 4-ternate). Examples are known of pinnate leaves with only a top-leaflet and no side-leaflets at all, thus imitating a simple leaf; yet, making this distinction here would be too academic a practice, and such plants will be treated as simple-leaved ones.

A compound, palmately veined leaf is called a **palmate** leaf for short. As a rule, palmate leaves have 5 or more pinnately veined leaflets (e.g., Horse Chestnut, and Hemp). When considering the general outline of a compound leaf (mentally drawn along the tips of the outermost leaflets), the same categories can be distinguished as in simple leaves; thus we speak of: bipinnate leaves, ovate in outline, and so on.

Phyllotaxis   When leaves (whether simple or compound) are inserted on the plant in a regular fashion, the phenomenon is called phyllotaxis. In many species they are **alternate**, that is spirally placed at regular intervals along the axis. The leaves can be pointing in several directions, especially on vertical axes, as are found in many herbs. But they can also be spread out in a horizontal plane, as often on shoots of woody plants (e.g., Beech), or stacked in two opposite rows, like a fan (e.g., Bog Asphodel). In all these cases there is only one leaf per node. Frequently, however, the leaves are **opposite**: placed in pairs at the same node. Then, successive pairs are frequently at right angles to each other (**cross-wise opposite** leaves). When there are 3 or more leaves inserted on each node, we speak of **whorled leaves**. This arrangement is more or less typical for certain groups like water-milfoils and the Bedstraw family.

Indument All minor appendages on the surface of a plant are collectively called the indument. Frequently one sees **hairs**, which can be straight, curly, or branched. Straight hairs are **appressed** to the surface (making a plant **silky**), or more or less **erect** (making it **hairy**). Sometimes, the hairs are bent down sharply (**deflexed**). If only the leaf-margins are hairy, the leaf is **ciliate**. Special terms exist for different types of hairiness: **pubescent** (hairs erect and soft), **villose** (hairs erect, soft, and very long), **lanate** (hairs curly, soft and long, like wool), **tomentose** (hairs tangled, forming a thick mat, like felt), **cottony** (hairs very thin, like cobweb-threads), **mealy** (hairs very small and brittle, easily coming off).

Hairs can be simple, or variously branched: **furcate** (forked), **plumose** (feathered), **stellate** (star-shaped), etc. Flat hairs are called **scales** (not to be confused with scale-leaves). **Tubercles** are short and blunt, like warts. Stout, prickly hairs are called **bristles**, making the plant **rough-hairy**. **Prickles** are much stronger, and usually placed on stems, stalks or major veins, as in roses and brambles; they can be straight, curved, or hooked; thin, straight prickles are called **needles**. **Spines** and **thorns** are modified leaves or branches; as such, they typically contain a trace of wood-vessels, so they cannot be easily detached from the plant (think of Gorse, or Hawthorn). **Glands** are hairs, bristles or tubercles producing watery or oily liquids; these are often of a sticky nature, like resin, or volatile (when they usually give the plant a notable scent). A glandular plant is more or less covered with glands and, if it is also hairy, we call it glandular-hairy. A special kind of glands are the stinging hairs of nettles. Some plants have **pruinose** stems or leaves, characterized by a bluish or whitish, waxy bloom.

Roots The roots of a plant take up water and mineral salts from the soil. They are attached to the stem-base, or to the nodes of rhizomes or stolons. In many herbs, the roots are **fibrous**, i.e. thin and much-branched. Roots can be used for the storage of food (often starch or sugars), and then they are often appreciably thickened to a **tuber**, be it spindle-shaped as in the Carrot, or more or less ovoid or spherical as in the Beet. Rhizomes or corms, being stems not roots, can be similarly thickened, and we often loosely speak of a tuber in this case, too. In some monocots (e.g., onions) the underground stem-base wears tightly packed and thickened storage leaves, collectively forming a **bulb**.

Inflorescences Flowers are often combined into an inflorescence, borne on a common stalk (**peduncle**). Each flower in an inflorescence can possess its own flowerstalk (**pedicel**), but sometimes they are unstalked (**sessile**). An inflorescence with stalked flowers inserted on an unbranched, central peduncle is called a **raceme**; if the flowers are sessile, we speak of a **spike**. In an **umbel**, stalked flowers are inserted at the top of the peduncle, whereas the pedicels (usually called **rays** here) radiate in all directions. Umbels can repeat this way of division more than once (**compound umbels**). The rays are often of unequal length, in such a way that all flowers are held approximately in the same (flat or domed) plane. Often the peduncle is branched. In **cymes**, all main branches of the peduncle end in a (stalked or sessile) flower, but growth continues from one adjoining side-branch (as in the **monochasial cymes** of the forget-me-nots), or from two opposite side-branches directly below (as in the **dichasial cymes** of the Pink family). In a **panicle**, the peduncle branches all along its length in several directions; the side-branches may themselves be ramified again, and the lower branches are often longer, giving the inflorescence a pyramidal outline. If, in a raceme or panicle, the flower-stalks or side-branches are of unequal length, so that all flowers are held in one plane, we call it a **corymb**, as in (racemous) roses, and (paniculate) Mountain Ash. For simplicity's sake, we often speak of umbel-shaped racemes or panicles rather than corymbs.

In many species, the flower-stalks and the branches of the inflorescence have undergone extreme reduction, bringing together the flowers in a dense cluster at the top of the peduncle; then we speak of a **flowerhead (capitulum)**. Numerous examples can be found in the Pea pamily (think of clover), the Teasel family, and typically in the Daisy family. In the Mint family, the strongly shortened inflorescences appear like clusters in the axils of the (opposite) leaves. Thus, they tend to form pseudo-whorls **(verticillasters)** around the stem, and these can be so closely set that the inflorescence resembles a spike. From this may already be inferred that normal leaves can be present in the inflorescence, and then we speak of a leafy spike, raceme, etc. Any such leaf carrying one to several flowers in its axil is called a **flower bract**; then the flowers are **axillary** to that bract (as opposed to **terminal**, when placed at the end of an axis). Often flower-bracts are much reduced in size, as in many members of the Carrot family (having a whorl of tiny bracts directly under the umbel), and also in the Daisy family (with an **involucre** of small bracts tightly surrounding the flowerhead. In some groups the whole (young) inflorescence is enveloped in a bract, named **spatha**; the spatha may be attractively coloured (as often in the Arum family).

THE PLANT DESCRIPTIONS

All descriptions in this book follow the same pattern. Under the name, all the information is supplied that is needed for a correct determination; then, under different captions, details are given about the distribution, mode of life and other facts of potential interest to the reader.

Classification and Names Plants are grouped according to what we know about their evolutionary relationships. Of course, we are all familiar with the concept of a **species** (plural, species). Although it is not easy to define that concept, we have a natural grasping of what it means, since we ourselves belong to one (the human species). Species are mutually related to a varying degree (like us, the chimps and the earthworms). The closeness of the affinity of species is judged by their anatomical and morphological similarities. Very similar species are grouped together in a **genus** (plural, genera). Several related genera will form a **family**; in their turn, families will form an **order**. Still higher categories are defined in likewise manner: classes, phyla, and regna – at which fundamental level we are distinguishing between plants, moulds and animals. A genus or a family that contains but one species is called **monotypic**. For us it will normally suffice to know the names of species, genera and families. In this book, the families are treated alphabetically (departing from the **scientific names**), and so are the genera within each family, and the species within each genus. To denote a species, we always mention its genus name, followed by its species name, e.g. *Calluna vulgaris* (Common Heather), or *Galium boreale* (Northern Bedstraw). Behind the species name ideally appears an indication of the botanist who first described that species – often in a shortened form if he won great fame by doing so. The inventor of this system of double names or **binary nomenclature** is the best known of all, and briefly denoted 'L.', which stands for Carolus Linnaeus (alias Carl von Linné), a Swedish naturalist who lived from 1707 to 1778. In his days, L. described a few thousand species of flowering plants; now we know approximately a quarter of a million of them, world-wide. Within many species, so-called **subspecies** are distinguished on the basis of characters thought less important. Subspecies have distinct geographical distribution patterns; if no such designation can be made, we speak of **varieties**. A **cultivar** is an artificial variety, gained in horticulture.

Of course, I have also tried to indicate a current **English name** for every species treated here. However, in many cases an English name does not exist, especially for plants restricted to the European mainland, and then only the scientific name is given.

Description: For every species in this book, the characters are given, starting with the general aspect (**habit**) of the plant in its adult life-form, its typical dimensions, and the way it completes its life-cycle (perennial, biennial, and so on). Next the stems and leaves are described, followed by the flowers and the fruits, again with relevant dimensions. Prominent diagnostical features of the species are highlighted italic. Each description should be read under simultaneous consultation of the photograph, to which the number before the species name gives a cross-reference: description and illustration are often complementary.

Flowering: This section gives an indication of the normal flowering time of the species. Of course plants may flower relatively late at northerly latitudes, and at higher elevations. In a mild autumn, many perennial species may flower for a second time; grazing or hay-making can produce the same effect. In freak climates warm spells may occur during winter, often inducing shrubs and trees to blossom out of season. Some annual herbs can produce several generations yearly, and may be found blossoming in all seasons if the weather is not too cruel.

Habitat: This section gives a concise description of the typical habitat of the species: the environment in which it is likely to be found. The habitat is firstly characterized by climatic factors (also dependent on the altitude), further by local hydrological and soil properties (edaphic factors), and also by the surrounding vegetation or – sometimes quite directly, as in pastures – by the animals present at the site (biotic factors). If the habitat is a special type of wood or scrub, the dominant woody species are often mentioned. Naturally, man plays an important role in determining the habitat of plants, nowadays. A general survey of the commonest habitats and their associated vegetation types will be given under here.

Range: In this section, the area of distribution is roughly outlined.

Similar species: If closely related species occur in northern Europe, they will be listed here, with details necessary for their recognition, and a brief indication of their habitat and range. Cross-references are given to other species that could cause confusion.

At the end of the main entry, additional information that may be of interest to the reader will be given (e.g. special uses made of the plant, its poisonous properties, causes of decline, and so on). The variability within the species is also discussed here, as are any infraspecific categories (subspecies, varieties), with their characteristics.

ENDANGERED SPECIES

In all European countries rare and endangered plants are protected by the law. Orchids are categorically protected almost everywhere. The list of protected species varies from one country to another. Penalties can be quite severe, even for possessing small fragments of protected plants. Generally, it is wise to leave all plants untouched. Digging up plants to cultivate them in your garden rarely makes any sense because your garden is very unlikely to be the right habitat for wild plants, and they will soon perish. If you want to start a reference herbarium, do it in a professional way. Always ask the owner of the grounds permission to collect plants, and report your interesting finds to a local botanical institute.

THE MAIN HABITAT TYPES OF NORTHERN EUROPE

The Tundra In the High Arctic, a very low dwarf-shrub vegetation occurs; dominant species are dwarf birches, some humble willows, crowberries, and members of the Heath family; also the curious Dryas can be found here. To the north, this tundra peters out against the barren polar, or Arctic desert, where – apart from lichens and mosses – only a few annual herbs manage to reproduce during the short summer, living through the winter as seeds. Herbs are found in the tundra as well, often profusely, giving the landscape a very colourful aspect in the flowering period (June–July). Common elements are saxifrages, buttercups, poppies, and cinquefoils; grasses and sedges are locally abundant. Mosses and lichens are very important constituents of the plant cover; reindeer use Reindeer Moss (a lichen, technically) as a staple food during the cold season. Evaporation is slow in this cold climate; therefore the precipitation, though rather scarce, keeps the land moist in summer, and thickly clad in snow during winter. The soil is permanently frozen from a few inches down (permafrost soils), causing melting water and rain to collect in stagnant pools and marshes, where moss-peat forms. Owing to the high latitude, the summer days are very long, which compensates to some degree for the short duration of the growing season. Towards the south, the scrub becomes taller, and richer in species. Here, also, the first stunted trees appear – mostly Downy Birch and Scots Pine, and (in northern Russia) Siberian Spruce. In the shelter of stream valleys we also find taller shrubs, like willows and alders.

The Taiga To the south of the tundra, a broad belt of coniferous or needle-leaf forest extends from Scandinavia through northern Russia all the way to northeastern Siberia: the northern or boreal taiga. These taiga forests are poor in tree species: mainly Norway Spruce and (on poorer soils) Scots Pine; in northeastern Russia there are some Siberian conifer species. The undergrowth can be quite rich, with mosses, club-mosses, ferns, diverse species of wintergreen, bilberries and crowberries, several orchids, and the Twin-flower *Linnaea borealis* as a characteristic species. Winter temperatures are very low; the summer is bearable, though short. On better soils, as often in stream valleys, isolated deciduous trees occur; Downy Birch and Aspen are the commonest species. Birches also play an important role in regenerating the forest after calamities like woodfires or felling. With their minute, winged seeds they can easily reach new growing places, and they are fast-growing, which gives them an initial advantage over the needle-leaf trees. However, the conifers will be slowly marching in under the translucent foliage of the birches and, being evergreen (and therefore capable of making longer use of the sunlight), will oust them in the end. In the taiga zone we also see the first *Sphagnum* bogs, with sedges, cotton-grasses, cloudberries, Cassandra, and Labrador Tea.

The Mixed-forest Zone Further to the south, the climate gradually improves; the growing season increases in length, temperatures are generally higher, and the sunlight falls in steeper. This favours broadleaf deciduous trees. In eastern Europe a typical mixed-forest zone can be discerned, transitional between the boreal taiga and the deciduous, broadleaf forests in the south. Here, we find Pedunculate Oak, Small-leaved Lime, Ash, diverse elm species, Norway Maple, Hornbeam, Silver Birch and Common Alder. Aspen and Downy Birch are still common, recolonizing the ground after felling or fire, as in the taiga; they often maintain themselves well in the stable end-phase (climax) of the forest. Again, the main coniferous trees in these forests are Norway Spruce and Scots Pine, the latter especially on sandy soils. Calcareous soils are richer in broadleaf species than acid soils. The shrub layer is well-developed, with Mountain Ash, Bird Cherry, Hazel, Spindle-tree and Fly Honeysuckle. The herb layer is rich, containing not only species from the northern taiga, but also many central European forms. East of the Volga River, Siberian Fir appears in increasing numbers, while, with the exception of the Lime, deciduous trees gradually fade out. Likewise, several central European elements in the undergrowth are gradually replaced by Siberian species.

Comparable mixed forest communities occur in southern Scandinavia, and throughout central Europe, with isolated outposts as far as the Belgian Ardennes and central France, but with a growing admixture of 'Atlantic' tree species (such as Silver Fir, Yew, Sycamore, Wild Cherry, White Oak, and Beech) missing in the east. In central Europe, conifers such as Norway Spruce, Silver Fir and Scots Pine have been extensively planted, and monocultures of these species have widely replaced the original mixed forest; also, much of it has been turned into cropland or pasture, in central and eastern Europe alike. In wet places, as along rivers, willows, alders and poplars are the dominant tree species. Birches and alders colonize the margins of *Sphagnum* bogs, which are quite common in this zone, especially in the humid west.

The Broadleaf-forest Zone In eastern Europe only a narrow band of broadleaf forest exists between the Mixed-forest Zone and the steppes in the south, from the famous forest of Białowieża in the west, to the foothills of the Ural Mountains in the east. Here, Pedunculate Oak is the dominant tree species, with Ash, Lime, Norway Maple, and elms; a lower tree layer is composed of Hornbeam, Crab Apple, Wild Pear, Field Maple, Tataric Maple and Mountain Ash, while the shrub and herb layers are well-developed (though species fade out again towards the east). Mosses are rare, owing to the thick litter. Going south, the forest becomes thinner and patchy, loses its lower tree layer of Hornbeam, and finally retreats to the river valleys, forming lush, green ribbons in the wide expanse of treeless steppe – which is largely replaced by cornfields nowadays. It is supposed that, in glacial times, part of the recent flora of these broadleaf forests survived in the southern Urals, and possibly in the Balkan peninsula.

An obvious zone of broadleaf forest has never developed in central Europe; here, the conifers always had an important share in the forest composition. In western Europe, however, the broadleaf forest zone is present again, and even wider than it is in the east. It once occupied all lowland to submontane areas from the southern tip of Sweden to the foothills of the Pyrenees and Alps in the south, including the British Isles. But the original forest has been wiped out almost completely, and for the most part early in history. The whole area has been taken into cultivation, and most extant woods are planted – often with exotic conifers like Douglas Fir, Western Hemlock and Sitka Spruce (from North America), or European relatives like Scots Pine, Norway Spruce and European Larch; but even the latter do not really belong here. Planted woods of Beech and (White or Pedunculate) Oak are also frequent, and the older examples can come rather close to the natural forest types that once existed here. They shelter many native shrubs and herbs; the undergrowth shows central European affinities, but to the west the 'Atlantic' element becomes stronger, with several species of a more or less endemic character. This western European forest flora is supposed to have sprung from refugial centres in the Iberian peninsula and southern France, after the ice age ended.

The Montane Zone Large parts of Europe are framed in high mountains with a flora of the alpine type, in several ways reminiscent of the Arctic tundra and the polar desert: the Urals and the Caucasus in the east, the Carpathians, Alps and Pyrenees in the south, and the Scottish Highlands and the Norwegian mountains in the west. Originally, when ascending the slopes of these high mountains, one traversed a mixed-forest belt, merging into a conifer forest, before reaching the alpine vegetation above the tree limit. These montane forest belts had much in common with the mixed-forest and taiga zones in the far north: the same dominant tree species were found here, as well as many of the typical shrubs and herbs. Since the Middle Ages, however, much of the montane mixed forest has been supplanted by Norway Spruce.

Lower mountain ranges pervade the old continent in all directions: the Central Massif, the Jura and the Vosges in France linking up to the Ardennes in Belgium and the mountains of southern and middle Germany (Eifel, Black Forest, etc.). Further eastwards lie the Bohemian Forest, the Ore Mountains, and the Sudetes. Originally, several types of submontane broadleaf forest occurred here; only the highest peaks had mixed forest communities. Formerly, cattle and swine were periodically driven into these woods to feed on foliage and nuts respectively, and to this aim certain tree species were spared or even nurtured by the farmers. For this reason, oaks have remained an important element in the landscape, even in the humid west, where in all likelihood the Beech, being more competitive, would have eliminated most other species if left to itself. Often the forest trees (oaks, mostly) were coppiced, in order to harvest the timber without actually killing the tree and losing the fodder. Some of these coppiced woods are still in existence; they are usually rich in undergrowth species, thanks to the improved light conditions.

The Hydrosere Europe receives much rain, especially in the oceanic regions of the west, and on the weather side of mountain slopes. Numerous streams and rivers carry the water back to the sea; in drainless terrain-depressions it tends to accumulate into stagnant pools or lakes. In general terms, these aquatic environments are much the same throughout the continent, and so are their characteristic plant communities. Flowing waters have their own set of characteristic species; most of them grow permanently submerged, as pondweeds, water-crowfoots, and starworts. However, most European streams and rivers are embanked, regulated and also heavily polluted, and little room is left for the original vegetation of riverbeds. Stagnant waters tend to become filled up with peat – the dead-litter of plants growing at their margins. Normally, a marked succession of vegetation types (hydrosere) can be observed here, starting with true aquatics, such as pondweeds and water-lilies, via swamp and marsh communities to a wet forest with alders, birches, and willows, with diverse transitions to the surrounding, drier types of forest typical of the region.

Mires, Fens, and Bogs In the wetter parts of Europe, peat forming can continue even after the water surface has been reached, in which case we speak of a mire. Peat tends to absorb and retain rainwater. Thus the thickening peat layers will lift the water up, over the surface. In this way, large lens-shaped peat-domes (up to several metres high) may form. If ground or surface water with a high mineral content still significantly contributes to the general supply of moisture, we speak of a fen. The peat will be formed here by plants adapted to high or moderate nutrient levels (eutrophic to mesotrophic environments); examples are Common Reed, Great Fen-sedge, and taller, true sedges. Comparable vegetation can be found in coastal dune-slacks. When the peat has risen so much that it loses contact with the ground water and has to depend completely on rain, the mineral levels fall steeply. Then a bog develops with plant communities adapted to low levels of nutrients, or even a deficiency in them (oligotrophic to dystrophic); characteristic plants are *Sphagnum* mosses and sundews. In cold, Arctic regions, with their low evaporation rate, and in the extreme west of Europe, where precipitation levels are high, mires (fens or bogs) can even develop on bare ground if the water does not run off easily. In this way, large areas were covered in blanket-bogs, following the undulating contours of the landscape; the finest examples are in Ireland. The coastal plains along the North Sea are mainly built up from alternating layers of clay and peat, ending with a long sequence of the latter; this stratification reflects the successive phases of marine transgression from the past, alternating with peat build-up in bogs. For many centuries these lands have been artificially drained and used as pastures, and few of the original bogs have been preserved. Moreover, large stretches of peat have been dug out for fuel production. In central and eastern Europe, fens and bogs are less frequent, smaller in extent, and confined to wet places, such as stream valleys, drainless depressions and lake margins; generally, they are not found here in any quantity south of the mixed-forest zone. Fens, being more fertile, show a natural tendency for developing into wet woods. On the other hand, bogs are so poor in nutrients that they can effectively prevent trees from growing; birches and Scots Pine will often try to settle themselves in drier climatic periods, only to be choked and engulfed in the *Sphagnum* mosses when wetter conditions return.

Heaths On poor, sandy soils, and on oligotrophic peat, the grazing of sheep has led to the forming of heathlands; dominant species are Common Heather on drier grounds, and Bell Heather in wet places. This process must have taken place since prehistoric times, and by the 19th century large tracts of land were used in this way. The animals were driven back to the farm daily so that the manure needed for the arable fields round the village could be collected. Nowadays, sheep flocks are rare, and much heathland has been turned into forest or fields. In nature reserves, rotational burning is often used to keep the heath from being recolonized by birches and Scots Pine. Heath is especially common in the regions where formerly mixed or deciduous forests existed; the richest examples are found in the wet, Atlantic, western parts of Europe.

Humid Grasslands On eutrophic peat, but also on damp mineral soils (especially clay and loam) humid grasslands are a frequent phenomenon. Most of these are created by Man, obviously to accommodate his stock of cattle; again, the history of these grasslands may reach back into prehistoric times. Roughly, humid grasslands can be divided into two types: pasture and hay-meadow. Pasture is used for grazing cattle, and the soil is often artificially drained; the turf is firm and, as a rule, manure or artificial fertilizer is being applied to raise production. Hay-meadows are generally wetter and less well-drained, often with a weak topsoil allowing the grazing of only young cattle, or sheep; their main function is the harvest of hay, and they are often sparingly manured. Pastures, being frequently to almost constantly grazed, have plant communities quite different from those of hay-meadows, the latter being usually richer in species, and more colourful on account of the many flowering herbs. Modern techniques have enabled farmers to convert many of their hay-meadows into drained pasture. Furthermore, mechanical traction makes it possible to grow wheat and other commercial crops on clay soils, formerly too heavy to be tilled with horses or oxen; this has led to a general reduction of the grassland area in Europe. However, coastal lowlands and the steeper slopes of hills and mountains still abound in pasture land, and some hay-meadows have been preserved along streams and rivers, especially on periodically inundated forelands.

A special kind of humid grassland is found along the sea-coasts. The lower mud-flats, still subject to daily flooding by the tides, are dominated by Eel Grass and glassworts; they catch the silt and bring about accretion of the land. As the land rises, it will be flooded less frequently or only during winter; then, a saltmarsh is formed, colonized by salt-resistant plants (halophytes) such as Sea Lavender, Sea Purslane, Annual Sea-blite, and Sea Aster, and later on salt-tolerant grasses and other herbs; in summer, these are often grazed by sheep or cattle. At a slow pace, these coastal forelands are embanked in polders, used for permanent grazing or crop-raising. Since the 10th or 11th century, much of the land along the North Sea has been reclaimed in this way. Different halophyte communities can be found on sandy or gravelly beaches, and on maritime cliffs. Some halophytes can also occur inland, in places where salty ground-water wells up, or – recently – along major highways, which are frequently salted when there is snow or black ice in winter.

Dry Grasslands On coarse and sandy, or even loamy soils – wherever the soil develops a seasonal deficiency in water – another type of grassland can be found. This is characterized by short turf and many drought-resistant herb species. These often have special provisions for the storage of water, like bulbs or tubers; examples are pasque-flowers, pheasant's-eyes, wild onions and many orchids. In Europe, dry grasslands tend be more natural than humid ones. In western Europe they are mainly found on maritime sand-dunes; characteristic species are Marram Grass, and fescues. A more impressive example is found in the steppe vegetations of southern Russia, of which the puszta in the Pannonic Plain is a slightly smaller version. Here, feather-grasses define the summer aspect with their waving, long-awned spikes. Smaller fragments of these steppe vegetations can be found further to the west, along the Vistula and Oder rivers in Poland, and even (in a much impoverished form) on river-dunes in the catchment area of the Rhine. These dry grasslands are vaguely reminiscent of the cold steppes that covered much of Europe during the ice age. These, however, were often dominated by different plant species, especially mugworts. As Europe has not only become warmer, but certainly a lot wetter since, comparable types of steppe vegetation can nowadays be observed only in central Asia. But some species may have maintained themselves after the retreat of the land-ice, at least on barren and exposed places like dunes, where trees could not settle. Also, several eastern steppe species have immigrated to western Europe after cereals were introduced. Cornfields have a lot in common with the steppe environment. The cereals themselves were originally steppe plants in western Asia.

Modern Cultural Landscapes

Generally speaking, the given classification of more or less discrete and recognizable vegetation zones and landscape types can only be applied to Europe as it was in the past. It has already been pointed out that, in the case of the Mixed-Forest and Broadleaf-Forest Zones, much has changed through reclamation and afforestation. In fact, this holds for Europe's plant cover as a whole. Truly natural vegetations can no longer be found here. What we see are only fragments of natural communities, often strangely mixed with cultural elements into what could be called a semi-natural vegetation at best. About 20 per cent of the wild plant species of Europe have been brought in from other continents by human intervention (often accidentally); these are only natural-ized. Two groups can be distinguished: *archeophytes* and *neophytes*, depending on whether they were introduced before the end of the Middle Ages (1492), or later, respectively. They tend to occur in dynamic, unstable environments, like the ruderal places accompanying all human settlements. They cannot compete with the indigenous species in a more natural environment; few exotic species have successfully naturalized in stable forest or mire vegetations. Urbanization continues ceaselessly, however, and the native flora is clearly receding before the noisy immigrants. What we are left with is always 'more of the same'.

Europe is relatively rich in nature reserves, where at least semi-natural vegetation types can still be observed; but their management is often impeded by a general drop in the ground-water table, emissions of fertilizer and pollutants, or disturbance by recreation and tourism. For many wild plants the future is uncertain, as is illustrated by the increasing length of the 'Red Lists' of endangered species. The introduction of ecological or biological methods of agriculture and forestry would help in preserving the wild flora. Unfortunately, 'market forces' and sheer unfamiliarity with such agricultural methods have severely obstructed this development up to the present day.

How to Use this Guide

Arrangement by Colour Flower colour is an easily observable character by which plants can be distinguished. It has some drawbacks, however: plants do not blossom throughout the year, and in many species the colour of the flowers may vary between individual plants, or even during the flowering time. Still, for practical reasons, the illustrations in this book have been arranged in colour groups. The colour series starts with brownish and greenish: the hues of many inconspicuous flowers that are pollinated by the wind, or water. The series continues with the more attractive colours of the many plants that are usually pollinated by insects; these are arranged in the following sequence: white, yellow, orange, red, pink, purple, violet, and blue. One should keep in mind, however, that a plant with a deviating colour may show up on a page other than expected. Especially when dealing with pink or purplish flowers, it is useful to search within wider limits: under 'red' or 'violet'. Normally pink, or (less often) yellow flowers may occasionally be white, so if you have a whitish flower that you cannot find at first, consult 'pink' and 'yellow' as well.

Flower Subgroups Within each colour group, the species have been grouped on the basis of some other, easily observable characters. There are six subdivisions: (1) irregular, bilaterally symmetrical flowers; (2) simple, regular, radially symmetrical flowers, occurring singly; (3) the same, but placed in elongated clusters; (4) the same, but placed in rounded clusters; (5) the same, condensed into compact flower-heads; and (6) vines, shrubs and dwarf-shrubs with distinctly woody stems, irrespective of the morphology of the inflorescence. For further details, *see* the explanation of the thumb tabs on p.39.

Here are two examples of the procedure to be followed when determining a species:

Example 1: *Yellow Flower in an Open Field*
In an open field you have found a yellow

flower that stands out by itself, is radially symmetrical, and has 5 showy, yellow, petal-like structures.

1. Turn to the colour-plate section marked *Yellow Simple Flowers*. Among the photographs in this group are several buttercups resembling your flower. The captions under the photographs give the page numbers of the relevant text descriptions.

2. On reading the species descriptions of the various buttercups, you find that your plant matches the one with backward-curving sepals, and that the terminal lobe of its 3-partite leaf is distinctly stalked. The root, you may find, is bulbous, as indicated by its common name, for it is the Bulbous Buttercup, which grows in open fields, especially in grasslands. In the case of large genera with many species, a crude key is given at the beginning of the genus, so always look first at the genus description for some more help.

Example 2: *Yellow Flower in a Wetland*

In a wet area you have found a plant with yellow, star-like flowers grouped together in an elongated cluster, and with lanceolate, opposite leaves.

1. Turn to the colour plates labelled *Yellow Elongated Clusters*. Among these, your flower resembles one of the loosestrifes.

2. Turn to the descriptions of the various species of loosestrife. There you find that the description of Yellow Loosestrife matches your example.

ABBREVIATIONS

Dimensions of plants, floral parts, and so on, are given in the metric system: metres (m), centimetres (cm) and millimetres (mm). Altitude above sea-level is given in metres.

Generic names in the text are often abbreviated to their first capital letter (e.g., *E. parviflorum* for *Epilobium parviflorum*) when it is clear from the context which genus is meant.

PART I

COLOUR PLATES

Key to the Colour Plates

The colour plates are divided into eight colour groups:

- ▨ brownish, pp.40–6;
- ▨ greenish, pp.43–83;
- ▨ whitish, pp.84–175;
- ▨ yellowish, pp.176–242;
- ▨ orange or red, pp.243–5;
- ▨ pink or pale purplish, pp.246–308;
- ▨ purple or lilac, pp.309–22;
- ▨ violet or blue, pp.323–47.

Within these colour groups the flowers are further divided by their individual shape and the general form of the inflorescence into six subgroups:

 irregular, bilaterally symmetric flowers, as in snapdragons, orchids or peas – irrespective of the general morphology of the inflorescence;

 simple, regular, radially symmetric flowers, occurring singly or in a diffuse pattern on the plant, as in anemones or Field Bindweed;

 the same as the previous subgroup, but placed in elongated clusters (racemes, spikes, sleek panicles, etc.), as in evening primroses or forget-me-nots;

 the same as the previous subgroup, but placed in rounded clusters: umbels, like those of Cow Parsley, or head-like clusters lacking a common wrapping (involucre), as in onions;

 the same as the previous subgroup, condensed into compact flowerheads composed of several small, tube- or strap-shaped flowers with a common wrapping (involucre) of green scale-leaves, as in daisies and dandelions;

 vines, shrubs and dwarf shrubs, with distinctly woody stems, like heather and roses, irrespective of the morphology of the inflorescence.

Each subgroup is indicated by a symbol (as shown above) on a thumb tab at the left edge of each double page of plates.

Water Figwort *Scrophularia auriculata* p.1061
Common Figwort *Scrophularia nodosa* p.1062 *(right)*

Lady's-slipper Orchid *Cypripedium calceolus* p.818
Bird's-nest Orchid *Neottia nidus-avis* p.837 *(right)*

Lizard Orchid *Himantoglossum hircinum* p.834
1. habit; 2. inflorescence

Violet Helleborine *Epipactis purpurata* p.829 *(left)*

Asarabacca *Asarum europaeum* p.365 *(above)*

Deadly Nightshade *Atropa belladonna* p.1081

Buck's-horn Plantain *Plantago coronopus* p.873

Greater Plantain
Plantago major p.874

Sea Plantain
Plantago maritima p.875

Carline Thistle *Carlina vulgaris* p.480

Least Bur-reed *Sparganium natans* p.1087 1. habit;
2. inflorescence; 3. fruit

Bog Myrtle
Myrica gale
p.795 1. habit;
2. inflorescence

Man Orchid *Aceras*
anthropophorum p.813
1. habit; 2. inflorescence

Bog Orchid
Hammarbya paludosa
p.832

Common Twayblade
Listera ovata p.836
1. habit; 2. flowers

False Musk Orchid
Chamorchis alpina p.816

Fen Orchid *Liparis loeselii*
p.835 1. habit; 2. inflorescence

Musk Orchid *Herminium monorchis*
p.833 1. habit; 2. inflorescence
Frog Orchid *Coeloglossum viride*
p.817 (*right*)

Prickly Saltwort *Salsola kali* p.457 *(left)*
Procumbent Pearlwort *Sagina procumbens* p.422

Annual Pearlwort
Sagina apetala p.420

Smooth Rupturewort
Herniaria glabra p.411

Annual Knawel *Scleranthus annuus* p.424

Parsley-piert *Aphanes arvensis* p.972

Hampshire Purslane *Ludwigia palustris* p.809

Herb Paris *Paris quadrifolia* p.777
1. flowering habit; 2. fruit

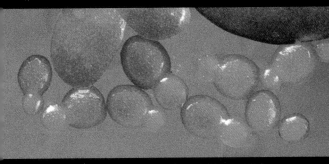

Rootless Duckweed *Wolffia arrhiza* p.754

Common Duckweed *Lemna minor* p.753

Ivy-leaved Duckweed
Lemna trisulca p.753

Fat Duckweed
Lemna gibba p.752

Greater Duckweed *Spirodela polyrhiza* p.754

Blunt-fruited Water-starwort *Callitriche obtusangula* p.384

Intermediate Water-starwort *Callitriche hamulata* p.383

Various-leaved Water-starwort *Callitriche platycarpa* p.385

Mare's-tail *Hippuris vulgaris* p.663
1. habit; 2. flowers

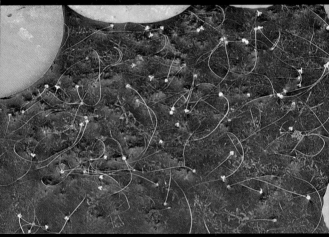

Nuttall's Water-thyme *Elodea nuttallii* p.664

Opposite-leaved Pondweed *Groenlandia densa*
p.904

Rigid Hornwort *Ceratophyllum demersum* p.443

Spiked Water-milfoil *Myriophyllum spicatum*
p.662 1. general aspect; 2. inflorescence

Tape Grass *Vallisneria spiralis* p.667

Beaked Tasselweed *Ruppia maritima* p.1020

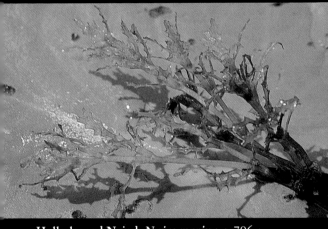

Holly-leaved Naiad *Najas marina* p.796

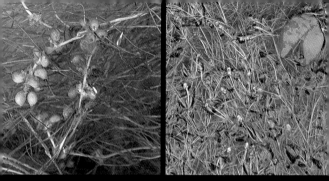

Fennel Pondweed *Potamogeton pectinatus* p.911
Lesser Pondweed *Potamogeton pusillus* p.912 *(right)*

Hairlike Pondweed *Potamogeton trichoides* p.914

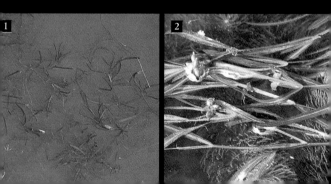

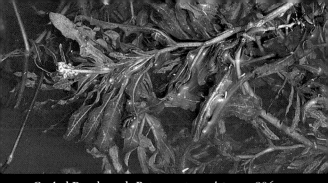

Curled Pondweed **Potamogeton crispus** p.906

Perfoliate Pondweed **Potamogeton perfoliatus** p.911
Reddish Pondweed **Potamogeton alpinus** p.905 *(right)*

Shining Pondweed *Potamogeton lucens* p.907

Broad-leaved Pondweed *Potamogeton natans* p.909

Perennial Glasswort *Arthrocnemum perenne* p.443
1. habit; 2. flowering spikes

Glasswort
*Salicornia
europaea*
p.455
(*above*)

**Long-spiked
Glasswort**
*Salicornia
procumbens*
p.456
1. habit;
2. flowering

Sea Beet *Beta vulgaris* p.449 1. flowering habit; 2. fruiting

Fat Hen *Chenopodium album* p.449 *(left)*
Oak-leaved Goosefoot *Chenopodium glaucum* p.452

Many-seeded Goosefoot *Chenopodium polyspermum*
p.453 1. habit; 2. fruit

Halberd-leaved Orache *Atriplex prostrata* p.448

Frosted Orache *Atriplex laciniata* p.444

Annual Mercury *Mercurialis annua* p.635

Sea Arrowgrass *Triglochin maritima* p.672 (*above left*)

Navelwort *Umbilicus rupestris* p.559 (*above*)

Rannoch-rush *Scheuchzeria palustris* p.1039

Black Bryony *Tamus communis* p.606

Pellitory-of-the-wall *Parietaria judaica* p.1136 (*left*)
Annual Nettle *Urtica urens* p.1138 (*middle*)
Stinging Nettle *Urtica dioica* p.1137

French Sorrel
Rumex scutatus p.900

Fiddle Dock
Rumex pulcher p.900

Common Sorrel *Rumex acetosa* p.892

Sheep's Sorrel *Rumex acetosella* p.893

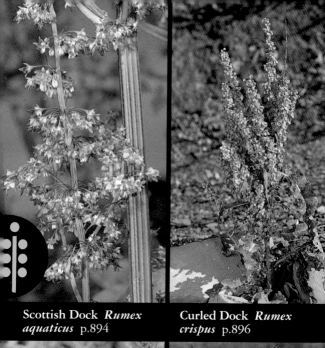

Scottish Dock *Rumex aquaticus* p.894

Curled Dock *Rumex crispus* p.896

Lords-and-Ladies
Arum maculatum p.361
1. habit; 2. fruit

Mountain Sorrel *Oxyria digyna* p.884
Sweet Flag *Acorus calamus* p.360 *(right)*

Alchemilla vulgaris p.971 *(left)*
Alchemilla glaucescens p.970

Alchemilla glomerulans p.971

Smooth Lady's-mantle
Alchemilla glabra p.970
1. habit;
2. ssp. *wichurae*

Hairy Lady's-mantle
Alchemilla filicaulis p.969
(*below*)

Alternate-leaved Golden-saxifrage
Chrysosplenium alternifolium p.1025

1

2

Moschatel *Adoxa moschatellina* p.351 *(left)*
Dwarf Spurge *Euphorbia exigua* p.630 1. habit; 2. flowers

Petty Spurge
Euphorbia peplus p.635

Sun Spurge *Euphorbia helioscopia* p.631

Cypress Spurge *Euphorbia cyparissias* p.629
1. habit; 2. inflorescence in late stage

Sea Spurge *Euphorbia paralias* p.633 *(left)*
Marsh Spurge *Euphorbia palustris* p.632

Pineapple Mayweed *Matricaria discoidea* p.525 *(le...)*
Ragweed *Ambrosia artemisiifolia* p.466

W...d *Artemisia [v]u[lg]aris* ...

Field Wormwood *Artemisia campestris* p.472
Mugwort *Artemisia vulgaris* p.473 *(right)*

Jersey Cudweed *Gnaphalium luteo-album* p.500
Heath Cudweed *Omalotheca sylvatica* p.527 *(right)*

Field Cudweed *Filago arvensis* p.497

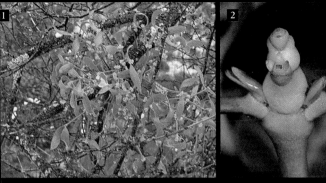

Mistletoe *Viscum album* p.1154
1. habit; 2. flower

Redcurrant *Ribes rubrum* p.1028
1. flowers; 2. fruit

Gooseberry *Ribes uva-crispa* p.1029
1. habit; 2. fruit; 3. flowers

Mountain Currant *Ribes alpinum*
p.1026 1. flowers; 2. fruit

Hop *Humulus lupulus* p.397
1. fruiting habit; 2. inflorescence

Dwarf Willow *Salix herbacea* p.1021
1. flowering habit; 2. fruit

Climbing Corydalis *Ceratocapnos claviculata* p.864 *(left)*
White Ramping-fumitory *Fumaria capreolata* p.864

Subterranean Clover *Trifolium subterraneum*
p.743 1. white form; 2. pink-veined form

Hairy Tare
Vicia hirsuta p.746

White Melilot
Melilotus albus p.729

Wood Sage *Teucrium scorodonia* p.704
1. habit; 2. inflorescence

White Horehound
Marrubium vulgare p.689

Catmint *Nepeta cataria*
p.693

Gipsywort *Lycopus europaeus* p.688

White Deadnettle *Lamium album* p.684

Field Pansy *Viola arvensis* p.1143
1. habit; 2. colour sport

**Common
Cow-wheat
*Melampyrum
pratense*
p.1053
(*above*)**

**Alpine
Butterwort
*Pinguicula
alpina*
p.755
(*above right*)**

**Ivy Broomrape
*Orobanche
hederae* p.853**

89

Oxtongue Broomrape
Orobanche loricata p.854 *(left)*
1. habit; 2. inflorescence

Thistle Broomrape
Orobanche reticulata p.858 *(above)*

Marsh Helleborine *Epipactis palustris*
p.828 1. inflorescence; 2. flower

Lesser Butterfly-orchid *Platanthera bifolia* p.846
1. habit; 2. flowers

Small White Orchid *Pseudorchis albida*
p.847 1. habit; 2. inflorescence

Summer Lady's-tresses *Spiranthes aestivalis*
p.848 *(left)* 1. habit; 2. inflorescence
Dense-flowered Orchid *Neotinea maculata* p.837

Creeping Lady's-tresses *Goodyera repens* p.830

Ghost Orchid *Epipogium aphyllum* p.829

Coralroot Orchid *Corallorhiza trifida* p.817 *(left)*
White Helleborine *Cephalanthera damasonium* p.815

Marsh Speedwell *Veronica scutellata* p.1078
Mudwort *Limosella aquatica* p.1049 *(right)*

Whorled Solomon's-seal *Polygonatum verticillatum*
p.778 1. habit; 2. fruit

Common Solomon's-seal *Polygonatum multiflorum*
p.777 1. habit; 2. fruit

Butcher's Broom *Ruscus aculeatus* p.779
1. habit; 2. flowers and fruit

Wild Asparagus *Asparagus officinalis* p.766
1. ssp. *officinalis*; 2. ssp. *prostratus*

Snowdon Lily *Lloydia serotina* p.773 *(left)*
Sand Crocus *Romulea columnae* p.671

Water Purslane *Lythrum portula* p.788

Sea Sandwort *Honkenya peploides* p.412

Shoreweed *Littorella uniflora* p.872

Knotgrass *Polygonum aviculare* p.885

Sea Knotgrass *Polygonum maritimum* p.890

White Water-lily *Nymphaea alba* p798

Mousetail *Myosurus minimus* p.943

River Water-crowfoot *Ranunculus fluitans* p.954

Common Water-crowfoot *Ranunculus aquatilis* p.948

Three-lobed Water-crowfoot *Ranunculus tripartitus* p.956

Ranunculus ololeucos p.959

Ivy-leaved Water-crowfoot *Ranunculus hederaceus* p.956
Fan-leaved Water-crowfoot *Ranunculus circinatus* p.952 *(right)*

Glacier Crowfoot *Ranunculus glacialis* p.955

Wood Anemone
Anemone nemorosa p.936

Green Hellebore
Helleborus viridis p.941

Frogbit *Hydrocharis morsus-ranae* p.665

Water Soldier
Stratiotes aloides
p.666 1. habit; 2. flowers

Grass of Parnassus
Parnassia palustris
p.1025

English Stonecrop
Sedum anglicum
p.555

White Stonecrop
Sedum album
p.555

Cloudberry *Rubus chamaemorus* p.1001
1. habit; 2. fruit

Mountain Avens
Dryas octopetala
p.974

Chickweed Wintergreen
Trientalis europaea
p.926 1. habit; 2. fruit

Wood Sorrel *Oxalis acetosella* p.860

Diapensia *Diapensia lapponica* p.606

Sea Stork's-bill *Erodium maritimum* p.649

Thornapple *Datura stramonium* p.1081
1. habit; 2. fruit

Water Chestnut *Trapa natans* p.1089

Floating Water-plantain *Luronium natans* p.355

Dwarf Cornel *Cornus suecica* p.552
1. flowers; 2. fruit

Marsh Pennywort *Hydrocotyle vulgaris* p.1113

Field Mouse-ear
Cerastium arvense p.402

Thyme-leaved Sandwort
Arenaria serpyllifolia p.401

Fringed Sandwort *Arenaria ciliata* p.401

Bog Stitchwort *Stellaria uliginosa* p.441

Common Chickweed *Stellaria media* p.439

Lesser Stitchwort *Stellaria graminea* p.437

Greater Stitchwort *Stellaria holostea* p.439

Wood Stitchwort *Stellaria nemorum* p.440 *(top)*
Water Chickweed *Stellaria aquatica* p.437

Knotted Pearlwort *Sagina nodosa* p.421
1. habit; 2. inflorescence

Fine-leaved Sandwort *Minuartia hybrida* p.415

Teesdale Sandwort *Minuartia stricta* p.416

Spring Sandwort
Minuartia verna p.416

Three-veined Sandwort
Moehringia trinervia p.417

Upright Chickweed
Moenchia erecta p.418

Coral Necklace *Illecebrum
verticillatum* p.413

Corn Spurrey *Spergula arvensis* p.433

Bastard Toadflax
Thesium humifusum
p.1022 (*above*)

Thesium pyrenaicum
p.1023 (*right*)

Reddish
Stonecrop
Sedum rubens
p.557 *(above)*

Drooping
Saxifrage
*Saxifraga
cernua* p.1032

Rock Cinquefoil *Potentilla rupestris* p.988

Barren Strawberry *Potentilla sterilis* p.989

Wild Strawberry *Fragaria vesca* p.976
1. flowers; 2. fruiting habit

Spring Pasqueflower *Pulsatilla vernalis* p.944
1. flowers; 2. fruit

Blinks *Montia fontana* p.902

Chaffweed *Anagallis minima* p.916

Springbeauty *Claytonia perfoliata* p.901

One-flowered Wintergreen
Moneses uniflora p.928
(*above*)

Summer Snowflake
Leucojum aestivum p.357

Snowdrop *Galanthus nivalis* p.357

1

2

Common Gromwell ***Lithospermum officinale*** p.374 *(left)*
White Bryony ***Bryonia cretica*** p.604 1. habit; 2. fruit

Starfruit *Damasonium alisma* p.353

Lesser Water-plantain *Baldellia ranunculoides* p.?

Bogbean *Menyanthes trifoliata* p.793 *(left)*

Water-pepper *Polygonum hydropiper* p.888 *(above)*

Buckwheat *Fagopyrum esculentum* p.883 *(top)*
Four-leaved Allseed *Polycarpon tetraphyllum* p.420

Berry Catchfly *Cucubalus baccifer* p.406

White Campion *Silene latifolia* ssp. *alba* p.428

Night-flowering Catchfly *Silene noctiflora* p.429

Small-flowered Catchfly *Silene gallica* p.427
1. habit; 2. flowers

Nottingham Catchfly
Silene nutans p.429

Spanish Catchfly
Silene otites p.430

Yellow Wintergreen *Pyrola chlorantha* p.930 *(left)*
Nodding Wintergreen *Orthilia secunda* p.929

Common Meadow-rue *Thalictrum flavum* p.964 *(left)*
Greater Meadow-rue *Thalictrum aquilegifolium*
p.963 1. habit; 2. pink-flowered specimen; 3. pink flowers

Swallow-wort *Vincetoxicum hirundinaria* p.366
1. yellowish form; 2. fruit; 3. white form

White False Helleborine
Veratrum album p.783
1. habit; 2. flowers

Scottish Asphodel *Tofieldia pusilla* p.782
May Lily *Maianthemum bifolium* p.773 *(right)*

Lily-of-the-valley *Convallaria majalis* p.767 1. habit; 2. fruit
Star of Bethlehem *Ornithogalum umbellatum* p.776 *(right)*

Kerry Lily *Simethis planifolia* p.781 *(left)*
St Bernard's Lily *Anthericum liliago* p.765

Irish Saxifrage *Saxifraga rosacea*
p.1037

Rue-leaved Saxifrage
Saxifraga tridactylites
p.1038

Mossy Saxifrage
Saxifraga hypnoides
p.1035

Sea Kale *Crambe maritima* p.581

White Ball Mustard *Calepina irregularis* p.570

Large Bittercress *Cardamine amara* p.572
1. habit; 2. flowers

Cardamine bellidifolia p.573

Hairy Bittercress *Cardamine hirsuta* p.574 *(left)*
Narrow-leaved Bittercress *Cardamine impatiens* p.575

Shepherd's Purse *Capsella bursa-pastoris*
p.572 1. habit; 2. flower

Shepherd's Cress *Teesdalia nudicaulis* p.602 *(left)*
Garlic Mustard *Alliaria petiolata* p.560 1. habit; 2. flowers

Hoary Alison *Berteroa incana* p.566

Hoary Cress *Cardaria draba* p.578

Rock Whitlowgrass **Draba norvegica** p.585 *(left)*
Hoary Whitlowgrass **Draba incana** p.584

Watercress *Rorippa nasturtium-aquaticum* p.597

Common Whitlowgrass *Erophila verna* p.586
1. habit; 2. flowers

Wild Candytuft

Hutchinsia *Hornungia petraea* p.589

Narrow-leaved Pepperwort *Lepidium ruderale* p.592

Perfoliate Pennycress
Thlaspi perfoliatum p.603

Field Pennycress *Thlaspi arvense* p.602

Awlwort *Subularia aquatica* p.601

Hairy Rocket *Erucastrum gallicum* p.587 *(left)*
Ranunculus platanifolius p.960

Dyer's Woodruff *Asperula tinctoria* p.1007 *(left)*
Round-leaved Sundew *Drosera rotundifolia* p.612

Heliotrope *Heliotropium europaeum* p.373 *(left)*
Corn Gromwell *Buglossoides arvensis* p.370

Round-leaved Wintergreen *Pyrola rotundifolia* p.931
Common Wintergreen *Pyrola minor* p.930 *(right)*

Brookweed *Samolus valerandi* p.925

Fairy Flax *Linum catharticum* p.784

Allseed *Radiola linoides* p.786

Enchanter's Nightshade *Circaea lutetiana* p.801
1. habit; 2. flowers

Alpine Enchanter's Nightshade *Circaea alpina* p.801

Yellow Bird's-nest *Monotropa hypopitys* p.928

Pyramidal Saxifrage *Saxifraga cotyledon*
p.1032

Meadow Saxifrage *Saxifraga granulata* p.1033 *(left)*
Alpine Saxifrage *Saxifraga nivalis* p.1035 *(middle)*
Kidney Saxifrage *Saxifraga hirsuta* p.1034

Biennial Saxifrage
Saxifraga adscendens
p.1030

Goat's-beard Spiraea
Aruncus dioicus
p.972 1. & 2. plant

Meadowsweet
Filipendula ulmaria p.975

Dropwort *Filipendula vulgaris* p.975

Dewberry *Rubus caesius* p.1000
1. flower; 2. fruit

Raspberry *Rubus idaeus* p.1002
1. flowers; 2. fruit

Bramble *Rubus fruticosus* p.1002
1. fruit; 2. flowers

Spiked Rampion *Phyteuma spicatum* p.395 *(left)*
Umbellate Chickweed *Holosteum umbellatum* p.412

Sticky Mouse-ear *Cerastium glomeratum* p.404

Strapwort *Corrigiola litoralis* p.406

Wild Madder *Rubia peregrina* p.1018

Cleavers **Galium aparine** p.1009 *(left)*
Wall Bedstraw **Galium parisiense** p.1014

Glaucous Bedstraw
Galium glaucum p.1010

Northern Bedstraw
Galium boreale p.1010

Hedge Bedstraw
Galium mollugo p.1011 o

Common Marsh-bedstraw
Galium palustre p.1013

Sweet Woodruff *Galium odoratum* p.1012 *(left)*
Fen Bedstraw *Galium uliginosum* p.1017

Limestone Bedstraw *Galium sterneri* p.1015

Dwarf Elder *Sambucus ebulus* p.399
1. habit; 2. fruit

Black Nightshade
Solanum nigrum p.1083
1. habit; 2. flower

Northern
Androsace
*Androsace
septentrionalis*
p.917 *(above)*

Ramsons
*Allium
ursinum*
p.763

Great Masterwort
Astrantia major p.1099

Sanicle *Sanicula europaea*
p.1128

Scots Lovage *Ligusticum scoticum* p.1115

**Garden
Angelica**
*Angelica
archangelica*
p.1094 *(above left)*

Wild Celery
*Apium
graveolens*
p.1097 *(above)*

Milk-parsley
*Peucedanum
palustre*
p.1126

Masterwort *Peucedanum ostruthium* p.1125

Knotted Hedge-parsley *Torilis nodosa* p.1135

Upright Hedge-parsley
Torilis japonica p.1134

Hartwort *Tordylium
maximum* p.1134

Wild Angelica *Angelica sylvestris* p.1095
Cowbane *Cicuta virosa* p.1107 *(right)*

Rough Chervil *Chaerophyllum temulum* p.1106 *(left)*
Wild Carrot *Daucus carota* p.1109 1. habit; 2. inflorescence

Moon Carrot
Seseli libanotis p.1131

Pepper-saxifrage
Silaum silaus p.1132

Bur Chervil *Anthriscus caucalis* p.1096

Cow Parsley *Anthriscus sylvestris* p.1096

Hogweed *Heracleum sphondylium* p.1113

Greater Water-parsnip *Sium latifolium* p.1132

Lesser Water-parsnip *Berula erecta* p.1100

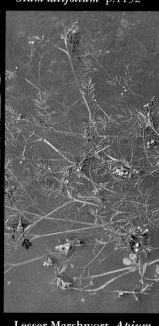

Lesser Marshwort *Apium inundatum* p.1098

Fool's Water-cress *Apium nodiflorum*
p.1099

Rock Samphire *Crithmum maritimum* p.1109

Corn Parsley *Petroselinum segetum* p.1123

Shepherd's-needle *Scandix pecten-veneris*
p.1129

Sweet Cicely *Myrrhis odorata* p.1117 *(left)*
Parsley Water-dropwort *Oenanthe lachenalii* p.1120

Hemlock Water-dropwort
Oenanthe crocata p.1119

Fine-leaved Water-dropwort
Oenanthe aquatica p.1118

Tubular Water-dropwort *Oenanthe fistulosa* p.1119

Burnet-saxifrage *Pimpinella saxifraga* p.1127
Spignel *Meum athamanticum* p.1116 *(right)*

Yarrow *Achillea millefolium* p.464

Daisy *Bellis perennis* p.476

Scented Mayweed *Matricaria recutita* p.526
Oxeye Daisy *Leucanthemum vulgare* p.524 *(right)*

Canadian Fleabane
Erigeron canadensis p.496

Mountain Everlasting
Antennaria dioica p.466
1. & 2. plants

Small Teasel *Dipsacus pilosus* p.608

Bilberry *Vaccinium myrtillus* p.625 1. flowers; 2. fruit

Matted Cassiope *Cassiope hypnoides* p.618 *(left)*
Privet *Ligustrum vulgare* p.799 1. flowers; 2. fruit

Field Rose *Rosa arvensis* p.991 1. flowers; 2. fruit

Burnet Rose *Rosa pimpinellifolia* p.995
1. habit; 2. hips

Umbellate Halimium *Halimium umbellatum* p.461

Cassandra *Chamaedaphne calyculata* p.619

Tree Heather *Erica arborea* p.616

Hop Trefoil *Trifolium campestre* p.735

Lesser Hop Trefoil *Trifolium dubium* p.736

Black Medick *Medicago lupulina* p.726 *(left)*
Spotted Medick *Medicago arabica* p.725

Common Bird's-foot Trefoil *Lotus corniculatus* p.723
Greater Bird's-foot Trefoil *Lotus uliginosus* p.724 *(right)*

Kidney Vetch *Anthyllis
vulneraria* p.707

Tall Melilot *Melilotus
altissimus* p.729

Wild Liquorice *Astragalus glycyphyllos* p.709

Yellow Milk-vetch *Oxytropis campestris*
p.733
(above left)

Yellow Vetch
Vicia lutea
p.747 *(above)*

Yellow Vetchling
Lathyrus aphaca
p.716

Meadow Vetchling
Lathyrus pratensis p.720

Horseshoe Vetch
Hippocrepis comosa p.715

Common Gorse *Ulex europaeus* p.744
1. habit; 2. flowers

Broom *Cytisus scoparius* p.712 1. flowers; 2. fruit

Hairy Greenweed *Genista pilosa* p.713

Petty Whin *Genista anglica* p.712 *(left)*
Winged Broom *Chamaespartium sagittale* p.710

Yellow
Archangel
*Lamiastrum
galeobdolon*
p.683 *(above left)*

Downy
Hemp-nettle
*Galeopsis
segetum* p.680
(above)

Large-flowered
Hemp-nettle
*Galeopsis
speciosa* p.681

Annual Woundwort *Stachys annua* p.698

Lesser Bladderwort
Utricularia minor p.757

Greater Bladderwort
Utricularia vulgaris p.758

Sand Toadflax *Linaria arenaria* p.1049 *(left)*
Common Toadflax *Linaria vulgaris* 1051

Sharp-leaved Fluellen *Kickxia elatine* p.1047
1. habit; 2. flower

Yellow-rattle *Rhinanthus minor* p.1060 *(left)*
Moor-king *Pedicularis sceptrum-carolinum* p.1058

Yellow Bartsia *Parentucellia viscosa* p.1056

Large Yellow Foxglove *Digitalis grandiflora* p.1041
Touch-me-not *Impatiens noli-tangere* p.367 *(right)*

Mountain Pansy *Viola lutea* p.1147
1. yellow form; 2. white form

Yellow Wood-
violet *Viola
biflora* p.1144
(above left)

*Orobanche
lutea* p.855
(above)

Knapweed
Broomrape
*Orobanche
elatior* p.852

Elder-flowered Orchid *Dactylorhiza sambucina*
p.823 1. habit (yellow and red forms); 2. whitish form

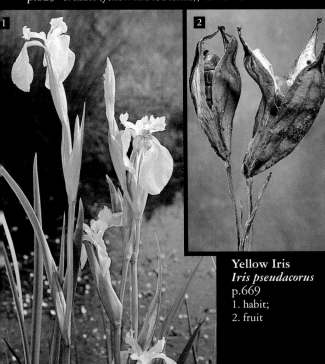

Yellow Iris
Iris pseudacorus
p.669
1. habit;
2. fruit

Welsh Poppy
*Meconopsis
cambrica* p.868
(*above left*)

Arctic Poppy
*Papaver
radicatum*
p.871 (*above*)

**Yellow Horned-
poppy** *Glaucium
flavum* p.868
1. habit; 2. flower

Greater Celandine *Chelidonium majus* p.862

Yellow Water-lily *Nuphar lutea*
p.797 1. habit; 2. flower

Yellow Pheasant's-eye *Adonis vernalis* p.936
1. flower; 2. habit

Yellow Anemone *Anemone ranunculoides* p.937

Marsh Marigold *Caltha palustris* p.938

Great Spearwort *Ranunculus lingua* p.957 (*left*)
Celery-leaved Crowfoot *Ranunculus sceleratus* p.963

Corn Crowfoot *Ranunculus arvensis* p.950 *(left)*
Snow Buttercup *Ranunculus nivalis* p.958

Small-flowered Buttercup *Ranunculus parviflorus* p.959
Annual Stonecrop *Sedum annuum* p.556 *(right)*

Tormentil *Potentilla erecta* p.985 *(left)*
Creeping Cinquefoil *Potentilla reptans* p.988

Trailing Tormentil *Potentilla anglica* p.980

Silverweed *Potentilla anserina* p.981
Potentilla supina p.990 *(right)*

Alpine Cinquefoil
Potentilla crantzii p.984

Grey Cinquefoil
Potentilla cinerea p.983

Creeping Jenny
Lysimachia
nummularia
p.919 *(above left)*

Trailing St
John's-wort
Hypericum
humifusum
p.658 *(above)*
1. habit;
2. flowering shoot

Yellow Centaury
Cicendia
filiformis p.640

Yellow-wort *Blackstonia perfoliata* p.636
Fumana *Fumana procumbens* p.460 *(right)*

Fringed Water-lily *Nymphoides peltata* p.794
Spotted Rockrose *Tuberaria guttata* p.463 *(right)*

Purslane *Portulaca oleracea* p.902

Upright Yellow Sorrel
Oxalis fontana p.861

Wild Daffodil *Narcissus*
pseudonarcissus p.358

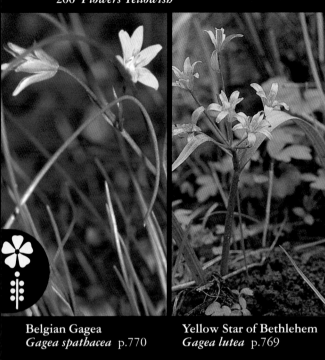

Belgian Gagea
Gagea spathacea p.770

Yellow Star of Bethlehem
Gagea lutea p.769

Weld
Reseda luteola p.966

Buckler Mustard
Biscutella laevigata p.566

Charlock *Sinapis arvensis* p.599 *(left)*
Bastard Cabbage *Rapistrum rugosum* p.595
1. flowers; 2. fruit

Hoary Mustard *Hirschfeldia incana* p.588
Small Alison *Alyssum alyssoides* p.560 *(right)*

Creeping Yellowcress
Rorippa sylvestris p.598

Marsh Yellowcress
Rorippa palustris p.597

Gold-of-pleasure
Camelina sativa p.571

Black Mustard
Brassica nigra p.567

Wild Turnip
Brassica rapa p.568

Wild Cabbage
Brassica oleracea p.568

Medium-flowered Wintercress *Barbarea intermedia* p.564
Common Wintercress *Barbarea vulgaris* p.565 *(right)*

Wallflower Cabbage *Coincya cheiranthos* p.580
Flixweed *Descurainia sophia* p.582 *(right)*

Perennial Wall-rocket *Diplotaxis tenuifolia* p.583
Treacle Mustard *Erysimum cheiranthoides* p.587 *(right)*

Lesser
Meadow-rue
*Thalictrum
minus*
p.965 (*above*)

Wolf's-bane

Lesser Spearwort *Ranunculus flammula* p.954
Hairy Buttercup *Ranunculus sardous* p.962 *(right)*

Multiflowered Buttercup *Ranunculus polyanthemos* p.961
Meadow Buttercup *Ranunculus acris* p.947 *(right)*

Yellow Saxifrage *Saxifraga aizoides* p.1031
Wood Avens *Geum urbanum* p.978 *(right)*

Cut-leaved Potentilla
Potentilla multifida p.986

Snowy Cinquefoil
Potentilla nivea p.986

Hoary Cinquefoil *Potentilla argentea* p.981

Large-flowered Evening-primrose
Oenothera erythrosepala p.811 *(left)*
Common Evening-primrose *Oenothera biennis* p.810

Small-flowered Evening-primrose
Oenothera parviflora p.811

Slender St John's-wort *Hypericum pulchrum* p.661
Hairy St John's-wort *Hypericum hirsutum* p.657 *(right)*

Imperforate St John's-wort *Hypericum maculatum* p.658
Mountain St John's-wort *Hypericum montanum*
p.659 *(right)*

Perforate St John's-wort *Hypericum perforatum* p.660
Marsh St John's-wort *Hypericum elodes* p.657 *(right)*

Yellow Loosestrife

Centaurium maritimum p.638 *(left)*
Crosswort *Cruciata laevipes* p.1007

Great Mullein *Verbascum thapsus* p.1067 *(left)*
Moth Mullein *Verbascum blattaria* p.1064

Dark Mullein *Verbascum nigrum* p.1066
1. habit; 2. flowers

Bog Asphodel *Narthecium ossifragum*
p.775 1. habit; 2. flowers

Primrose *Primula vulgaris* p.924

Oxlip *Primula elatior* p.922 *(left)*
Tufted Loosestrife *Lysimachia thyrsiflora* p.920

Roseroot
Rhodiola rosea
p.553 (*above*)

**Reflexed
Stonecrop**
Sedum reflexum
p.556 (*left*)

Sibbaldia
*Sibbaldia
procumbens*
p.1005
(*below*)

Alexanders *Smyrnium olusatrum* p.1133
Wild Parsnip *Pastinaca sativa* p.1122 *(right)*

Hog's Fennel *Peucedanum officinale* p.1124

Birthwort *Aristolochia clematitis* p.364

Alpine Hawkweed *Hieracium alpinum* group p.503
Hieracium lactucella p.505 *(right)*

*Hieracium
praealtum*
p.507
(*above left*)

*Hieracium
cymosum*
p.504 (*above*)

*Hieracium
amplexicaule*
group p.504

Common Hawkweed
Hieracium vulgatum group
p.511

Hieracium laevigatum group p.505

Hieracium murorum group p.512 *(left)*

Leafy Hawkweed **_Hieracium umbellatum_ group** p.510 *(below left)*

Savoy Hawkweed **_Hieracium sabaudum_ group** p.509 *(below)*

Leopard's Bane
*Doronicum
pardalianches*
p.494

**Marsh Hawk's-
beard** *Crepis
paludosa*
p.493

Rough Hawk's-beard *Crepis biennis* p.491 *(left)*
Smooth Hawk's-beard *Crepis capillaris* p.491

Cottonweed *Otanthus maritimus* p.529
Wall Lettuce *Mycelis muralis* p.527 *(right)*

Autumn Hawkbit *Leontodon autumnalis* p.523
Rough Hawkbit *Leontodon hispidus* p.523 *(right)*

Dandelion *Taraxacum officinale* s.l. p.546

Spotted Cat's-ear *Hypochoeris maculata* p.516

Smooth Cat's-ear *Hypochoeris glabra* p.515
(*below left*)

Lamb's Succory *Arnoseris minima* p.470
(*below*)

Nipplewort
*Lapsana
communis*
p.522

**Prickly
Lettuce**
*Lactuca
serriola*
p.521
(below left)

Least Lettuce
*Lactuca
saligna*
p.520 *(below)*

Nodding Bur-marigold *Bidens cernua* p.476
1. habit; 2. inflorescence

Trifid Bur-marigold *Bidens tripartita* p.477
1. habit 2. flowerhead
Arnica *Arnica montana* p.470 *(right)*

Corn Marigold *Chrysanthemum segetum* p.484
Yellow Chamomile *Anthemis tinctoria* p.468 *(right)*

Golden Samphire *Inula crithmoides* p.519

Goldilocks Aster
Aster linosyris
p.475

Cone-flower
Rudbeckia laciniata
p.533 *(below)*

Prickly Sow-thistle *Sonchus asper* p.543

Perennial Sow-thistle
Sonchus arvensis p.542

Marsh Sow-thistle
Sonchus palustris p.544

Early Goldenrod
Solidago gigantea
p.541 *(above left)*

Goldenrod
Solidago virgaurea
p.542 *(above)*

Tansy
Tanacetum vulgare p.545

Viper's-grass *Scorzonera humilis* p.533 *(left)*
Goat's-beard *Tragopogon pratensis* p.547

Colt's-foot *Tussilago farfara* p.548

Marsh Fleawort
Senecio congestus p.534

Field Fleawort *Senecio integrifolius* p.535
Common Ragwort *Senecio jacobaea* p.536 *(right)*

Shrubby Cinquefoil *Potentilla fruticosa* p.979

Tutsan *Hypericum androsaemum* p.656

Halimium *Halimium alyssoides* p.461 *(left)*
Common Rock-rose *Helianthemum nummularium* p.462

Lilium bulbiferum
p.771
1. habit; 2. flowers

Tuberous Pea
Lathyrus tuberosus
p.721 *(above)*

Grass Vetchling
Lathyrus nissoli

Long-headed Poppy *Papaver dubium* p.870 *(left)*
Summer Pheasant's Eye *Adonis aestivalis* p.935

Water Avens
Geum rivale p.977

Scarlet Pimpernel
Anagallis arvensis p.915

Salad Burnet *Sanguisorba minor* p.1004 *(left)*
Great Burnet *Sanguisorba officinalis* p.1004

Common Fumitory *Fumaria officinalis* p.866

Common Ramping-fumitory *Fumaria muralis* p.865
Bulbous Corydalis *Corydalis cava* p.863 *(below)*

Bird's-foot *Ornithopus perpusillus* p.732
Hare's-foot Clover *Trifolium arvense* p.735 *(right)*

Upright Clover *Trifolium strictum* p.742

2

Strawberry Clover *Trifolium fragiferum* p.737
Sea Clover *Trifolium squamosum* p.741 (*right*)

Red Clover *Trifolium pratense* p.740 *(left)*
Narrow-leaved Everlasting-pea *Lathyrus sylvestris* p.720

Bitter-vetch *Lathyrus linifolius* p.717

Marsh Pea *Lathyrus palustris* p.719

Crown Vetch *Coronilla varia* p.711

Sainfoin *Onobrychis
viciifolia* p.730

Common Restharrow
Ononis repens p.731

Wild Basil *Clinopodium vulgare* p.678
Marjoram *Origanum vulgare* p.694 *(right)*

Hairy Thyme
Thymus praecox
p.705
1. habit; 2. flowers

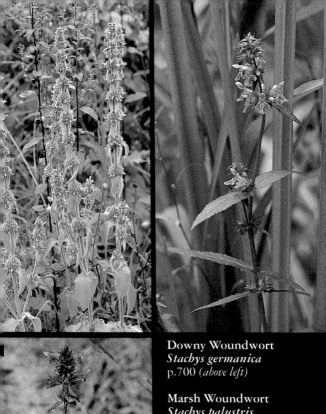

Downy Woundwort
Stachys germanica
p.700 *(above left)*

Marsh Woundwort
Stachys palustris
p.701 *(above)*

Water Mint *Mentha aquatica* p.690 *(left)*
Pennyroyal *Mentha pulegium* p.692

Water Germander *Teucrium scordium* p.703 *(left)*
Cut-leaved Germander *Teucrium botrys* p.702

Henbit Deadnettle *Lamium amplexicaule* p.685
Spotted Deadnettle *Lamium maculatum* p.686 *(right)*

Red Deadnettle *Lamium purpureum* p.686

Common Hemp-nettle
Galeopsis tetrahit p.682

Broad-leaved Hemp-nettle
Galeopsis ladanum p.679

Lesser Skullcap *Scutellaria minor* p.697
Gratiole *Gratiola officinalis* p.1046 *(right)*

Field
Cow-wheat
*Melampyrum
arvense* p.1052
(*above left*)

Crested
Cow-wheat
*Melampyrum
cristatum*
p.1052 (*above*)

Lousewort
*Pedicularis
sylvatica*
p.1059 (*left*)

Marsh

Foxglove
Digitalis purpurea
p.1042 *(above)*

Common Broomrape
Orobanche minor
p.855 *(far left)*

Bedstraw Broomrape
Orobanche caryophyllacea
p.851 *(left)*

Thyme Broomrape *Orobanche alba* p.850
1. habit; 2. young plant

Greater Broomrape *Orobanche rapum-genistae* p.858
Toothwort *Lathraea squamaria* p.1048 (right)

Pale Butterwort *Pinguicula lusitanica* p.756
Calypso *Calypso bulbosa* p.814 *(right)*

Heath Spotted-orchid *Dactylorhiza maculata* p.820
1. ssp. *elodes*;
2. ssp. *ericetorum*

Early Marsh-orchid *Dactylorhiza incarnata* p.819 *(left)*
Broad-leaved Marsh-orchid *Dactylorhiza majalis* p.822

Vanilla-orchid *Nigritella nigra* p.838 *(left)*
Fragrant Orchid *Gymnadenia conopsea* p.831

Monkey Orchid *Orchis simia* p.845 *(left)*
Green-winged Orchid *Orchis morio* p.843

Early Purple Orchid *Orchis mascula* p.842

Lax-flowered Orchid *Orchis laxiflora* p.841 *(below left)*

Narrow-leaved Marsh-orchid *Dactylorhiza traunsteineri* p.824 *(below)*

Broad-leaved Helleborine *Epipactis helleborine* p.826
Late Spider Orchid *Ophrys holosericea* p.839 *(right)*

Red Helleborine *Cephalanthera rubra* p.816
1. habit; 2. flowers

Sand-spurrey *Spergularia rubra* p.435 *(left)*
Greater Sea-spurrey *Spergularia maritima* p.434

Red Campion
Silene dioica p.426

Sand Catchfly *Silene conica*
p.426

Ragged Robin *Lychnis flos-cuculi* p.413 1. habit; 2. flowers
Sticky Catchfly *Lychnis viscaria* p.414 *(right)*

Large Pink *Dianthus superbus* p.409 *(left)*
Maiden Pink *Dianthus deltoides* p.407

Mossy Stonecrop *Crassula tillaea* p.553
1. habit; 2. flowers

Purple Saxifrage *Saxifraga oppositifolia* p.1037

Marsh Cinquefoil
Potentilla palustris p.987

Herb Robert *Geranium robertianum* p.653

Hedgerow Crane's-bill *Geranium pyrenaicum* p.653
Marsh Crane's-bill *Geranium palustre* p.652 *(right)*
1. habit; 2. flower

Cut-leaved Crane's-bill *Geranium dissectum* p.650
Dove's-foot Crane's-bill *Geranium molle* p.651 *(right)*

Common Mallow *Malva sylvestris* p.792
Cut-leaved Mallow *Malva alcea* p.790 *(right)*

Dwarf Mallow *Malva neglecta* p.791

Marsh Mallow *Althaea officinalis* p.790

Rough Mallow *Althaea hirsuta* p.789

Eight-stamened Waterwort *Elatine hydropiper* p.613

Field Bindweed *Convolvulus arvensis* p.550
Sea Bindweed *Calystegia soldanella* p.550 (*right*)

Chickweed Willowherb *Epilobium alsinifolium* p.803 (*left*)
Alpine Willowherb *Epilobium anagallidifolium* p.803

Pale Willowherb
Epilobium roseum p.807

Broad-leaved Willowherb
Epilobium montanum p.805

Square-stalked Willowherb *Epilobium tetragonum* p.808
Marsh Willowherb *Epilobium palustre* p.806 *(right)*

Hoary Willowherb *Epilobium parviflorum* p.807
Great Willowherb *Epilobium hirsutum* p.804 *(right)*

Sea Milkwort *Glaux maritima* p.918

Bog Pimpernel *Anagallis tenella* p.916

Grass-poly *Lythrum hyssopifolia* p.787
Twin Flower *Linnaea borealis* p.398 *(right)*

**Snake's-head
Lily** *Fritillaria
meleagris*
p.768
1. habit;
2. white form

Meadow Saffron *Colchicum autumnale* p.767
1. flowering habit; 2. fruit

Martagon Lily *Lilium martagon* p.772
1. habit; 2. flowers

Perennial Centaury *Centaurium scilloides* p.639
Lesser Centaury *Centaurium pulchellum* p.639 *(right)*

2

Common Centaury *Centaurium erythraea* p.637

Felwort *Gentianella
amarella* p.643

Squinancywort *Asperula
cynanchica* p.1006

1

2

Mezereon
Daphne mezereum
p.1088 1. flowers; 2. fruit

Cuckooflower *Cardamine pratensis* p.576 *(left)*
Coralroot Bitter-cress *Cardamine bulbifera* p.574

Tall Rockcress *Cardaminopsis arenosa* p577

Annual Gypsophila *Gypsophila muralis* p.410

Sea Rocket *Cakile maritima* p.570

Hoary Stock *Matthiola incana* p.594

Amphibious Bistort *Polygonum amphibium* p.885
Redshank *Polygonum persicaria* p.890 *(right)*

Bistort *Polygonum bistorta* p.887

Soapwort *Saponaria officinalis* p.423 *(left)*
Whorled Water-milfoil *Myriopyllum verticillatum* p.663

Water Violet *Hottonia palustris* p.919 1. habit; 2. flowers

Common Sea-lavender *Limonium vulgare* p.879

Matted Sea-lavender *Limonium bellidifolium* p.877
Rock Sea-lavender *Limonium binervosum* p.878 *(right)*

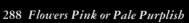

**Rosebay
Willowherb
*Chamerion
angustifolium***
p.800 *(above left)*

**Purple
Loosestrife
*Lythrum
salicaria***
p.788 *(above)*

**Vervain
*Verbena
officinalis***
p.1142

Common Comfrey *Symphytum officinale* p.381
1. habit; 2. yellowish form

Orpine
*Sedum
telephium*
p.558

Houseleek
*Sempervivum
tectorum*
p.558
(below left)

Common Stork's-bill
Erodium cicutarium p.648

Greater Dodder
Cuscuta europaea
p.551 *(above)*

Common Dodder
Cuscuta epithymum
p.550 *(left)* 1. habit;
2. inflorescence

Flowering Rush *Butomus umbellatus* p.382
(right)

Wild Leek *Allium ampeloprasum* p.759

German Garlic *Allium senescens* p.763

Crow Garlic *Allium vineale* p.764 1. habit; 2. sprouting bulbils

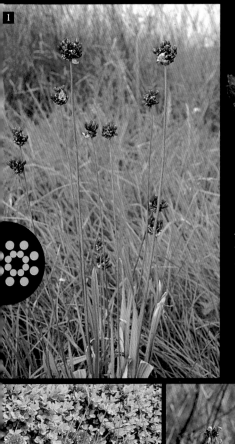

1

2

Sand Leek
Allium
scorodoprasum
p.762 1. habit;
2. flower

Chives *Allium*
schoenoprasum p.761

Field Garlic *Allium*
oleraceum p.760

Common Valerian *Valeriana officinalis* p.1139
1. habit; 2. white form

Narrow-fruited Cornsalad *Valerianella dentata* p.1140
Marsh Valerian *Valeriana dioica* p.1138 *(right)*

Hemp Agrimony
Eupatorium cannabinum
p.497 *(above left)*

Blue Fleabane
Erigeron acris
p.495 *(above)*

Butterbur
Petasites hybridus p.530

Scotch Thistle *Onopordum acanthium* p.528 *(left)*
Red Star-thistle *Centaurea calcitrapa* p.481

**Brown Knapweed *Centaurea jacea*
group** p.482 1. habit; 2. flowerhead

Welted Thistle *Carduus acanthoides* p.478 *(above)*

Nodding Thistle *Carduus nutans* p.479
1. habit; 2. flowerheads

Slender Thistle *Carduus tenuiflorus* p.479 1. habit; 2. flowerheads

Creeping Thistle
Cirsium arvense p.486

Meadow Thistle
Cirsium dissectum p.487

Dwarf Thistle
Cirsium acaule p.485

Melancholy Thistle
Cirsium helenioides p.488

Spear Thistle *Cirsium vulgare* p.489 *(left)*
Salsify *Tragopogon porrifolius* p.547 1. habit; 2. flowerhead

Wild Cotoneaster *Cotoneaster integerrimus* p.973
1. flowers; 2. fruit

Cinnamon Rose *Rosa majalis* p.994

Dog Rose *Rosa canina* p.992
1. flowers; 2. habit

White-stemmed Briar *Rosa vosagiaca* p.999
1. flowers; 2. fruit

Red-leaved Rose *Rosa glauca* p.993
1. habit; 2. fruit; 3. flowers

Sweet Briar *Rosa rubiginosa* p.996
1. flowers; 2. fruit

Bearberry *Arctostaphylos uva-ursi* p.617

Cranberry *Vaccinium oxycoccus* p.626
1. flowers; 2. fruit

Bog Rosemary
Andromeda polifolia p.616

Mountain Heath
Phyllodoce caerulea p.624

Mountain Azalea *Loiseleuria procumbens* p.623

Bell Heather
Erica cinerea p.621

Cross-leaved Heath
Erica tetralix p.621

Dorset Heath
Erica ciliaris p.620

Cornish Heath *Erica vagans*
p.622 1. habit; 2. flowers

Heather
Calluna vulgaris
p.618 *(left)*

Saint Dabeoc's Heath
Daboecia cantabrica
p.619 *(above)*

Crowberry *Empetrum nigrum* p.615
1. male; 2. female; 3. fruit

Lucerne
Medicago sativa p.728

Bush Vetch
Vicia sepium p.750

Wood Vetch *Vicia sylvatica* p.750

Sea Pea *Lathyrus japonicus* p.716

Lesser Calamint *Calamintha nepeta* p.677
Horse Mint *Mentha longifolia* p.691 *(right)*

Pale Toadflax *Linaria repens* p.1050 *(left)*
Common Eyebright *Euphrasia rostkoviana* p.1043

Wind Eyebright **Euphrasia nemorosa** p.1045 *(left)*
Ivy-leaved Speedwell **Veronica hederifolia** p.1073

Purple Toothwort
Lathraea clandestina
p.1047

Germander Broomrape
Orobanche teucrii
p.859 *(below left)*

Orobanche amethystea
p.850 *(below)*

Early Dog-violet
Viola reichenbachiana
p.1151 *(above)*

Marsh Violet *Viola palustris* p.1149 *(right)*

Wild Pansy *Viola tricolor* p.1152

Dark-red Helleborine *Epipactis atrorubens* p.825
1. habit; 2. flowers

Burnt-tip Orchid *Orchis ustulata* p.846 *(left)*
Common Pasqueflower *Pulsatilla vulgaris* p.945

Henbane
Hyoscyamus niger p.1082
1. habit; 2. flowers;
3. dark flowers
(*above*)

Monk's-hood
Aconitum napellus p.933

Common Lungwort
Pulmonaria officinalis
p.380 *(above)*

Hound's-tongue
Cynoglossum officinale
p.372 1. habit; 2. flowers *(left)*

Large Venus's-looking-glass
Legousia speculum-veneris
p.392 *(above)*

Water Lobelia *Lobelia dortmanna* p.393 *(left)*
Spreading Bellflower *Campanula patula* p.388

Small Scabious *Scabiosa columbaria* p.610
Wild Teasel *Dipsacus fullonum* p.607 *(right)*

European Michaelmas Daisy *Aster amellus* p.474

Alpine Fleabane *Erigeron borealis* p.496
Blue Lettuce *Lactuca perennis* p.519 *(right)*

Lapland Rhododendron *Rhododendron lapponicum* p.616

Common Vetch *Vicia sativa* p.748
Tufted Vetch *Vicia cracca* p.745 *(right)*

Northern Milk-vetch *Oxytropis lapponica* p.734
Purple Milk-vetch *Astragalus danicus* p.708 *(right)*

Ground Ivy *Glechoma hederacea* p.683
Bugle *Ajuga reptans* p.674 *(right)*

Skullcap *Scutellaria galericulata* p.696

Basil Thyme *Acinos arvensis* p.673

Selfheal *Prunella vulgaris* p.694 *(left)*
Meadow Clary *Salvia pratensis* p.695 1. habit; 2. flowers

Irish Eyebright *Euphrasia salisburgensis* p.1044

Long-leaved Speedwell *Veronica longifolia* p.1074

Brooklime
Veronica beccabunga
p.1072

Blue Water-speedwell
Veronica anagallis-aquatica p.1070

Wall Speedwell *Veronica arvensis* p.1070 1. habit; 2. flowers
Fingered Speedwell *Veronica triphyllos* p.1079 *(right)*

Green Field-speedwell *Veronica agrestis* p.1069

Common Field-speedwell *Veronica persica* p.1076 *(left)*
Germander Speedwell *Veronica chamaedrys* p.1072

Heath Speedwell
Veronica officinalis p.1076
1. habit; 2. flowers

Breckland Speedwell *Veronica praecox* p.1077

Spring Speedwell *Veronica verna* p.1080

Sweet Violet
Viola odorata p.1148

Heath Dog-violet
Viola canina p.1145

Hairy Violet *Viola hirta* p.1146

Hemp Broomrape *Orobanche ramosa* p.857 *(left)*
1. habit; 2. flowers
Yarrow Broomrape *Orobanche purpurea* p.856

Hepatica *Hepatica nobilis* p.942

Nigella *Nigella arvensis*
p.943 *(above)*

Lesser Periwinkle *Vinca minor* p.359 *(left)*
Madwort *Asperugo procumbens* p.369

Slender Gentian *Gentianella tenella* p.646 *(left)*
Fringed Gentian *Gentianella ciliata* p.644

Blue-eyed Grass *Sisyrinchium bermudianum* p.671
Spring Crocus *Crocus vernus* p.668 (*right*)

1

2

Forking Larkspur *Consolida regalis* p.940 1. habit; 2. flowers
Common Columbine *Aquilegia vulgaris* p.938 *(right)*

Common Milkwort *Polygala vulgaris*
p.882 *(above)* 1. blue form; 2. pink form

Thyme-leaved Milkwort *Polygala serpyllifolia* p.882 *(left)*
Dwarf Milkwort *Polygala amarella* p.881 *(above)*

Fen Violet *Viola persicifolia* p.1150

Giant Bellflower *Campanula latifolia* p.388
Harebell *Campanula rotundifolia* p.391 *(right)*

Peach-leaved Bellflower *Campanula persicifolia* p.389 1. habit; 2. flowers

Bearded Bellflower *Campanula barbata* p.386 *(left)*
Creeping Bellflower *Campanula rapunculoides* p.390

Jacob's-ladder
*Polemonium
caeruleum* p.880
1. habit;
2. inflorescence
(above)

Oyster Plant
*Mertensia
maritima*
p.374 *(left)*

Changing Forget-me-not
Myosotis discolor p.376

Field Forget-me-not
Myosotis arvensis p.375

Wood Forget-me-not
Myosotis sylvatica p.377

Water Forget-me-not
Myosotis palustris p.376

Blue-eyed Mary *Omphalodes verna* p.379
Alkanet *Anchusa officinalis* p.369 *(right)*

Bugloss *Anchusa arvensis* p.368
1. habit; 2. flowers

Viper's Bugloss *Echium vulgare* p.372 *(left)*
Purple Gromwell *Buglossoides purpurocaerulea* p.371

Pulmonaria angustifolia p.379
1. habit; 2. flowers

Bittersweet *Solanum dulcamara* p.1083 *(left)*
1. habit; 2. fruit

Blue Woodruff *Asperula arvensis* p.1006 *(above)*

Tassel Hyacinth *Muscari comosum* p.774 *(left)*
Common Grape Hyacinth *Muscari neglectum* p.774

Alpine Squill *Scilla bifolia* p.779

Spring Squill *Scilla verna* p.780 *(left)*
Bluebell *Scilla non-scripta* p.780

Cross Gentian *Gentiana cruciata* p.641 1. habit; 2. flowers
Clustered Bellflower *Campanula glomerata* p.387 *(right)*

Round-headed Rampion *Phyteuma orbiculare* p.394
Sheep's-bit *Jasione montana* p.391 *(right)*

Sea Holly *Eryngium maritimum* p.1111 *(left)*

Eryngium planum p.1112 *(above)*

Common Globularia *Globularia vulgaris* p.655

Sea Aster *Aster tripolium*
p.475 1. habit; 2. flowerheads

Chicory *Cichorium intybus* p.485
1. habit; 2. flowerheads

Cornflower *Centaurea cyanus* p.481
1. habit; 2. flowerheads

PART II

FAMILY AND SPECIES DESCRIPTIONS

The number preceding each species description in the following pages corresponds to the page number in the colour section on which that species can be found.

351

MOSCHATEL FAMILY, ADOXACEAE

A monotypic family of dicots, containing 1 species. Northern hemisphere. Flowers hermaphrodite, regular, 6–8 mm in diam., usually 5 together in a terminal, subglobose head up to 8 mm in diam.; side-flowers with 5 petals, 5 bifid stamens, and a trifid calyx, the top flower in each head with only 4 petals, 4 bifid stamens and a bifid calyx (hence the Greek name *Adoxa*, meaning against the rule). Pistil has 3–5 free styles and a hemi-inferior, 3–5-locular ovary. Fruit a greenish drupe with 3–5 stony seeds.

p.74 **Moschatel** *Adoxa moschatellina* L.

Description: *See also* the family characteristics. A perennial plant, to 15 cm high, with creeping rhizomes and long, slender stolons, forming loose carpets. Stems erect, simple. Basal leaves long-stalked, ternate with lobed segments, or doubly ternate. Stem-leaves 2, opposite, short-stalked, ternate. Leaves slightly fleshy, glabrous, and shiny pale green. Flowers greenish.

Flowering: (March) April–May.

Habitat: Deciduous woods (of oaks and beech) on moist, sandy or loamy, basic to slightly acid, fertile soils, often near streams or ditches; also in shaded road verges and (in the mountains) on rock-ledges.

Range: All Europe, but absent from Ireland, Iceland and much of N Scandinavia; from sea level to 2,400 m.

Moschatel can grow in deep shadow and is often the only herb living at the site. The leaves have a faint musky scent, especially when wilting.

WATER-PLANTAIN FAMILY, ALISMATACEAE

A nearly cosmopolitan family of mostly perennial, glabrous herbs of marshes and shallow waters; about 100 species in 11–13 genera. Monocots. Leaves often all basal, simple (ribbon-like to elliptical or sagittate), entire-margined, parallel-nerved, with sheathing bases; in some species the leaves are floating and alternately arranged along the stem. Flowers hermaphrodite or unisexual, regular, often in distinctive whorls, with 3 thin petals, 3 sepals, and 6–many stamens. Ovaries 6–many in each flower, free or fused at their bases, superior, 1-locular. Fruit a cluster of achenes.

---

p.119 **Common Water-plantain**
Alisma plantago-aquatica L.

Description: Plant 30–120 (–170) cm high, erect, glabrous. Leaves basal, mostly aerial (emergent), long-stalked; leaf-blade broadly lanceolate to ovate, pointed, with a rounded to slightly cordate base and *a length:width ratio of 1.5–3.5.* Flowers hermaphrodite, 6–10 mm wide, in a much-branched, whorled inflorescence; petals 3, white with a yellow base and often pink margins; sepals 3, at most half as long as petals. Stamens 6. Ovaries numerous, free; *style straight*, at least as long as the young achene, *the stigma shorter than the rest of the style.* Achenes smooth, flattened, with 1 shallow groove on the back; style withered on the ripe fruit.

Flowering: June–August.

Habitat: Freshwater ditches, pools, lake margins, banks of slow-moving streams, reed-swamps, marshes and fens, in more or less eutrophic environments.

Range: Most of Europe up to 70°N.

Similar species: **Narrow-leaved Water-plantain** (*A. lanceolatum* With.) has narrower, lanceolate leaf-blades (length:width ratio 3–6.5), slightly curved styles, with stigmas longer than rest of style, and usually pink to purplish petals; some fruit have 2 grooves on the back. In similar habitats, northwards to Scotland and S Scandinavia.

Ribbon-leaved Water-plantain (*A. gramineum* Lej.) has narrowly lanceolate to almost linear aerial leaves, and ribbon-like submerged leaves; flowers small (4–7 mm wide, petals barely longer than sepals), in branched inflorescences; style strongly curved outwards and much shorter than the young achenes; fruits all with 2 grooves on the back. In eutrophic to mesotrophic, fresh waters, northwards to Denmark, S Sweden and Estonia. In the Baltic region and Russia (from Lake Ladoga southwards to the Upper Volga basin) the last species is replaced by the very similar *A. wahlenbergii* (Holmb.) Juz., differentiated mainly by its lack of aerial leaves.

Parnassus-leaved Water-plantain (*Caldesia parnassifolia* (L.) Parl.) has broadly elliptical or ovate, deeply cordate, blunt-tipped, floating or aerial leaves (all basal and long-stalked), white flowers 8–12 mm diam., with 6–10 ovaries developing into small cluster of ribbed achenes with hard, woody core and persistent styles. In shallow, stagnant or slow-moving fresh waters of S and C Europe, northwards to N France and S Germany, and eastwards through the Ukraine to the Urals.

---

p.119 **Starfruit** *Damasonium alisma* Miller

Description: A smallish, annual or short-lived perennial, up to 30 cm. Stem emergent, sometimes very short in terrestrial forms. Leaves all basal, long-stalked, floating or submerged (rarely aerial); *leaf-blades elliptical with rounded tip* and rounded to truncate or slightly cordate base. Flowers hermaphrodite, 5–6 mm wide, in whorls of 3 forming a short raceme or panicle, or sometimes in a single umbel; petals white, yellow-based, longer than the sepals. Stamens 6. Ovaries 6 (rarely more, –10), superior, 1-locular, fused at their bases only, developing into *star-shaped whorl of green to brownish, tapering follicles*, up to 12 mm long.

Flowering: June–September.

Habitat: Margins of pools and ditches, often on grazed and well-trodden places, on mud or in shallow fresh water.

Range: A southern species, in W Europe nowhere frequent, northwards to S Germany, France and (very rare) in SE England, and eastwards to Russia.

Easily recognized by the star-shaped fruit clusters that remotely resemble those of Marsh Marigold, which has almost circular to reniform, bluntly toothed leaves and yellow flowers.

---

p.119 **Lesser Water-plantain**
Echinodorus ranunculoides (L.) Ascherson

Description: An erect (rarely prostrate) perennial, up to 50 cm. Stems smooth, rounded, to 3 mm thick. Leaves mostly aerial, all basal, narrowly lanceolate to almost linear, the *blade tapering into a long stalk*. Flowers 12–16 mm diam., long-stalked, in 1 umbel or in 2 (rarely more) whorls of 10–20 flowers each. Petals 3, white or pale pink, rounded; sepals 3, ovate, about half as long as petals. Stamens 6. Ovaries numerous (–45), developing into achenes; achenes not placed in a ring (as in *Damasonium alisma*) but *spirally arranged* in globose fruiting head up to 8 mm diam.; fruit-stalks erect or ascending.

Flowering: June–September.

Habitat: Shallow, oligotrophic to mesotrophic fresh waters on sandy soil, often in slightly acid heath-fens, but also in calcareous, slightly brackish dune-slacks.

Range: W Europe, northwards to S Scandinavia, and from Ireland eastwards to W Russia; mainly Atlantic; rare inland.

Similar species: **Creeping Water-plantain** (*E. repens* (Lamk.) Kern & Reichgelt) has short-stalked, tufted, narrowly lanceolate leaves, and slightly bigger flowers (up to 22 mm diam.), with broadly ovate sepals much smaller than petals; up to 5 flowers to a whorl, either seemingly basal (emerging from the tuft) or on a short (to 20 cm), thin (1 mm) flowering stem; fruit-heads smaller (to 5 mm diam.), with up to 20 achenes and a recurved stalk. Usually propagates vegetatively by means of long, creeping stolons, and can form dense, green mats under water. W Europe, northwards to the Netherlands; a Mediterranean–Atlantic species.

p.105 **Floating Water-plantain**
Luronium natans (L.) Rafin.

Description: A perennial aquatic with basal tufts of linear, submerged leaves on the nodes of a creeping rhizome rooting in the mud, and *thin, trailing stems* bearing long-stalked, elliptical, blunt-tipped, submerged to floating leaves. Flowers 12–16 mm diam., floating on the water, and *borne singly on long stalks* in stem-leaf axils. Petals white, with yellow base; sepals broadly ovate with rounded tip, deflexed after anthesis. Stamens 6. Fruits globose, with up to 15 greenish achenes in an irregular ring.

Flowering: May–August.

Habitat: Shallow, mesotrophic, slightly acid, permanent fresh waters (often on peaty soil), such as ponds, ditches, canal margins, and slow-moving streams.

Range: W and C Europe, from Wales eastwards to Poland and Moldavia, and locally northwards to S Norway; mainly Atlantic.

The species has dramatically declined owing to water pollution.

p.118 **Arrowhead** *Sagittaria sagittifolia* L.

Description: A stout perennial, with erect, triangular stems to 1 m. Leaves all basal; aerial leaves, on long, triangular stalks, are *sagittate* (arrow-shaped) with ovate to lanceolate front piece and backward-projecting, lanceolate to linear basal lobes; floating leaves also long-stalked but ovate or elliptical, without basal lobes; submerged leaves linear, strap-shaped. *Flowers unisexual* (lower ones female, upper ones male), 20–26 mm diam., with stout stalks, in superimposed whorls (often 3 to a whorl) at the end of stem; inflorescence sometimes branched. Petals rounded, white with purplish base; sepals broadly ovate, with rounded tip and pale margin. *Stamens numerous*, with purplish anthers. Ovaries numerous, developing into globose cluster of blackish achenes.

Flowering: June–September.

Habitat: Shallow, mesotrophic to eutrophic, stagnant or slow-moving, fresh waters.

Range: In Europe, except the far north; especially frequent in W Europe.

Similar species: *S. natans* Pallas, from Sweden, Finland and N Russia, has narrowly elliptical to lanceolate, floating leaves; aerial leaves (if present) have short, blunt, deflexed basal lobes; flowers slightly smaller, with plain-white petals and yellow anthers; inflorescence is also small (a few whorls, or only 1 3-flowered umbel).

Broad-leaved Arrowhead (*S. latifolia* Willd.), a large ornamental plant from N America, has locally naturalized in C Europe; some aerial leaves very wide, with ovate basal lobes, others narrower, ovate to lanceolate, and unlobed; petals plain white, anthers yellow.

Canadian Arrowhead (*S. rigida* Pursh) has locally naturalized in SW England; aerial leaves are broadly lanceolate, without basal lobes.

The ovate, floating leaves of Arrowhead are not always present on the plant. Young plants with only linear, thin, submerged leaves are frequently mistaken for Tape Grass, which however has creeping stolons. In rapidly flowing streams there is a permanently submerged, rarely flowering form, with supple, strap-shaped, diaphanous leaves up to 3 m long and 10–30 mm wide; often the blade is slightly widened where normally the basal lobes would be.

DAFFODIL FAMILY, AMARYLLIDACEAE

A cosmopolitan family of perennials with about 1,100 species in 75 genera. Monocots. Plants have bulbs and linear, basal leaves; stem-leaves usually absent. Flowers borne singly or in an umbel, wrapped in a membranous bract (spatha). Flowers hermaphrodite, 3-merous, with 6 subequal tepals; stamens 6. Ovary usually 3-locular, developing into a many-seeded capsule. In some genera the tepals carry appendages at their base, often connate into a dish- or pitcher-shaped *corona*. Most species are terrestrial and even typical of dry environments; a few are aquatic.

p.117 **Snowdrop** *Galanthus nivalis* L.

Description: A small perennial herb up to 30 cm, with egg-shaped bulbs up to 12 mm wide. Basal leaves few (often 2 or 3), linear, 3–7 (–10) mm wide, flat, *greyish-green*, blunt-tipped; flowering stem erect, with a linear, finely notched spatha high up under the flower. *Flowers solitary*, terminal, nodding on thin stalks, scented; tepals 6, the outer ones elliptical, 15–25 mm long and pure white, *the inner tepals much shorter* (8–11 mm), white, with a crescent-shaped, greenish blotch on the outside, near the shallowly *2-lobed tip*. Stamens 6, with greenish anthers; ovary inferior. Fruit a greenish, 3-valved capsule.

Flowering: February–April.

Habitat: Deciduous woods, on periodically wet, mesotrophic to eutrophic soils, especially along streams and rivers; often persevering in meadows created by tree-felling.

Range: Temperate parts of Europe, from C France eastwards to Asia Minor, and northwards to S Norway; mainly naturalized in the northern parts of its range.

A traditional harbinger of spring, and a well-known ornamental plant in parks and gardens. The flowers have a heady, sweet scent. Flowering starts when the leaves are only half-developed. Cultivars can have double flowers. The whole plant is rather poisonous.

p.116 **Summer Snowflake** *Leucojum aestivum* L.

Description: A rather stout, bulbous perennial up to 60 cm, forming dense tufts. Scape laterally compressed, with 2 broad wings and 1 high-placed, lanceolate, pale-green spatha up to 5 mm long. Basal leaves few, *bright green*, linear (strap-shaped, with a blunt tip), 7–20 mm wide, often equalling flowering stem. Flowers usually clustered (*2–7 together*), slightly nodding, on stalks of unequal length, in a 1-sided umbel; tepals 6, *all equal, rounded or shortly pointed*, 14–18 mm long, white with a triangular, green patch near the tip. Stamens 6, with orange anthers; ovary inferior. Fruit an egg-shaped, 3-valved capsule, brownish when ripe.

Flowering: April–June.

Habitat: Marshes, margins of ditches, pools and rivers; also in wet meadows on mesotrophic to eutrophic, muddy or peaty soils.

Range: Locally in W Europe, northwards to S Ireland and the Netherlands, and eastwards to S Germany; more frequent in S and SE Europe.

Similar species: **Spring Snowflake** (*L. vernum* L.) is smaller, with stems up to 30 cm, narrower leaves (5–15 mm wide), and solitary or paired, nodding flowers with 6 equal, yellowish-tipped tepals; it flowers early (February–April). In moist, deciduous forests on mesotrophic soils, in S and C Europe (from W Russia westwards to Belgium, with isolated outposts in S England and N Germany).

Both species are kept in gardens, and have locally naturalized.

---

p.199 **Wild Daffodil** *Narcissus pseudonarcissus* L.

Description: A bulbous, tuft-forming perennial, to 50 cm. Flowering stems laterally compressed with 2 sharp ridges; glabrous and with lanceolate, whitish to brownish spatha that soon withers. Leaves erect, equalling stems, linear, 6–12 mm wide, with blunt tip. Flowers solitary, more or less nodding, 40–60 mm diam., with 6 divergent, yellow tepals and *a deep-yellow, crenate, cup-like corona*.

Flowering: March–May.

Habitat: Wet and humid woods, copses and meadows, often on peaty soil in stream valleys, from sea level to 2,200 m.

Range: W Europe, northwards to N England and Germany; naturalized only in the further north.

Northern forms (ssp. *pseudonarcissus*) have an almost straight, cylindrical corona, and rather small, horizontal to nodding flowers with pale-yellow tepals. The southern forms, especially those from the Pyrenees (ssp. *major* (Curtis) Baker) have a widening, trumpet-shaped corona subequalling the (bright-yellow) tepals, and the flowers often point slightly upwards; this form (in several cultivars) is commonly kept in gardens. The plant is quite poisonous; regular handling of the bulbs can cause severe illness.

PERIWINKLE FAMILY, APOCYNACEAE

A family of perennial herbs and woody shrubs or vines, often containing latex, with 1,500 species in 180 genera, mainly in the tropics. Dicots. Leaves simple, often opposite (or whorled). Flowers regular, 5-merous, with a connate, bell- or trumpet-shaped corolla; corolla lobes 5, overlapping and turned (contort) in bud. Stamens 5, inserted on the inner wall of the corolla tube. Ovaries 2 (rarely 5), more or less superior, free, with a common style. Fruit a many-seeded capsule or follicle, usually double or forked.

p.333 **Lesser Periwinkle** *Vinca minor* L.

Description: A low half-shrub up to 30 cm, with creeping or trailing non-flowering stems forming loose mats, and ascending or erect flowering stems. Leaves opposite, shiny dark green, short-stalked, ovate to broadly lanceolate, with an acute base and *entire, glabrous margins*. Flowers solitary in the leaf-axils, violet-blue (rarely white), 20–30 mm diam.; calyx 5-lobed, with short, glabrous, lanceolate teeth up to 5 mm. Corolla has long, tapering tube (hairy inside), and 5 widely diverging, *obliquely truncate lobes*. Stamens 5; ovaries 2, hemi-inferior, free but closely set, with a single, joint style; stigma has 5 tufts of hairs. Fruit a double, spindle-shaped capsule, 15–25 mm long.

Flowering: (February) April–May.

Habitat: Deciduous or mixed woods, coppices and hedges, on moist, oligotrophic to mesotrophic, preferably basic, sandy or loamy soils, from sea level to 1,300 m; also on rocks in the mountains.

Range: A southern species whose native range extends eastwards through C and SE Europe to C Russia and Asia Minor. Reaches S England and the Netherlands, but rarely fruits in these areas; locally naturalized further north to Denmark and S Sweden.

Similar species: **Greater Periwinkle** (*V. major* L.) is larger in all parts, with rounded or slightly cordate leaf-bases, and hairy margins on both leaves and calyx teeth; flowers 30–50 mm diam.; fruit 40–50 mm long. A Mediterranean species, locally naturalized in W and C Europe.

V. herbacea Waldst. & Kit., found in EC and SE Europe, dies down completely in winter, and has narrower, cuneate leaves.

All species are poisonous.

ARUM FAMILY, ARACEAE

A cosmopolitan family of terrestrial, climbing, or aquatic herbs, with about 2,000 species in 110 genera. Monocots. Plants often have thick, creeping rhizomes (or, in climbers, aerial roots). Leaves often all basal, sometimes alternate, often pinnately veined (which is rare in monocots). Flowers usually unisexual, condensed in a fleshy, club-shaped or spike-like structure (spadix) enveloped in a large, often colourful bract (spatha); plants then often hermaphrodite, with female flowers below the male ones on the same spadix. Bisexual flowers occur in several genera, though. Perianth 4–8-partite (as in *Acorus* species), or absent (as in the other European genera). Stamens 1–many. Ovary superior, 1–3-locular. Fruit often a berry.

p.71 **Sweet Flag** *Acorus calamus* L.

Description: A glabrous, aromatic, tufted perennial up to 120 cm, with thick (2–5 cm), whitish, rather brittle, creeping rhizomes, marked with scars from dropped leaves. Flowering stems simple, *2-edged or flatly triangular*, with a terminal, cone-like spadix, which seems laterally attached as the spatha directly continues the stem. Leaves all basal, pale or yellowish-green, *linear* (sword-like), 1–2 cm wide, *often with a crinkled margin*, otherwise entire, tapering into a fine point; *midrib thickened, not quite central*. Spadix narrowly conical, slightly ascending, 5–10 cm in

length, many-flowered, greenish or
yellowish; spatha leaf-like. *Flowers hermaphrodite*, spirally arranged on the spadix; each
flower has 6 *small perianth parts*, a 2–3-locular
ovary, and 6 stamens. Fruit is berry-like.

Flowering: June–July.
Habitat: Shallow, eutrophic, fresh or brackish
waters, reed-lands and swamps.
Range: Naturalized in all of Europe except the
Arctic; native to C and SE Asia and W
North America.

In Europe the plant never fruits; it
propagates vegetatively, through fragmenta-
tion of the rhizomes. The species was
introduced from SE Asia in 1557, and soon
became naturalized in many European
countries. All parts of the plant are aromatic
when bruised; the sweet-tasting, odorous
rhizomes are used medicinally in stomach
bitters. Vegetative plants could be confused
with *Iris pseudacorus* (see p.669); however,
Sweet Flag is easily distinguished by its
asymmetrically veined, crinkled leaves and
its aromatic scent; *I. pseudacorus* leaves are flat,
broader, and often glaucous or greyish-green.

p.71 **Lords-and-ladies** *Arum maculatum* L.

Description: A perennial herb with flowering stems up
to 45 cm (often much shorter), with a
horizontally creeping, tuber-shaped rhizome.
Leaves all basal, long-stalked, broadly
hastate to saggitate, the basal lobes
obliquely backward-pointing or upturned;
blade shiny, bright to dark green, *with green
veins*, and often with dark-brownish
blotches. Spatha pale green to yellowish,
with *purple or brownish blotches*, purple-
rimmed, often purplish all over on the
inside. Spadix has protruding, club-shaped,
grey or purple, sterile upper part. Flowers
unisexual, naked (without a perianth),
aggregated at the base of the spadix, hidden
in the spatha, the male flowers (with 3–4
stamens) over the female ones; thread-like
sterile flowers also present. Ovary superior, 1-
locular, developing into rounded, orange-red

berry, up to 5 mm diam. *Fruiting spike short (40–50 mm).*

Flowering: April–May.

Habitat: Deciduous woods, scrub, also under hedges, on moist, basic, oligotrophic to mesotrophic soils.

Range: S, W and C Europe, northwards to N England, the Netherlands and S Sweden, and eastwards to W Russia.

Similar species: **Large Cuckoo Pint** (*A. italicum* Miller) has larger, spear-shaped leaves, a plain yellow-green spatha, a yellow spadix, and fruiting spikes up to 15 cm long; the leaves may be plain green, dark-spotted, or whitish-veined. Native to S and W Europe (northwards to France and S England), and locally naturalized in the Netherlands.
A. orientale Bieb. from E Europe has green, unblotched leaves and vertical, discoid, tuber-like rhizomes (corms); its leaves appear in spring.
A. elongatum Steven has leaves appearing in autumn. In woods and scrub of the Balkan region and the Ukraine.

Lords-and-ladies, also called Cuckoo Pint, is often planted in woods or shaded lawns on estate grounds; it naturalizes easily, mostly in the northern part of its range. When flowering starts, the club-shaped spadix distinctly warms up and emits a disgusting smell of decaying flesh. This attracts certain tiny moth-like insects, which after entering the kettle of the spatha are trapped by the hair-like, sterile flowers until these have withered.

---

p.117 **Bog Arum** *Calla palustris* L.

Description: A short, aquatic perennial to 30 cm, with long rhizomes, rooting in the mud or trailing in the water. Leaves held over the surface on long stalks, individually rising from the rhizome, with tongue-shaped scale-leaves at the base of the stalk; leaf-blade bright green, *ovate with a cordate base*, pointed, with arched side-veins. Flowering stems stout, axillary to the leaves, pale green, emergent. Spatha more or less flat (*without a closed kettle*), greenish outside, *white inside*. Spadix 10–30 mm long, narrowly egg-shaped. Flowers greenish, naked, hermaphrodite or partly unisexual. Stamens 6–many. Ovary 1-locular, developing into an onion-shaped, pointed, shallowly grooved, red berry up to 5 mm diam.

Flowering: (May) June–August.

Habitat: Swamps, ditches, dead arms of rivers, shallow pools and lakes, usually on mesotrophic, peaty soils in the lowlands.

Range: N, C and E Europe, westwards to France, Belgium and the Netherlands, northwards to Scandinavia, and eastwards to E Russia; only locally naturalized in the British Isles.

IVY FAMILY, ARALIACEAE

A polymorphous family of woody trees, shrubs, (especially) vines, and (rarely) perennial herbs, with 700 species in 55 genera in warmer regions of the world; in Europe only *Hedera* occurs. Dicots. Leaves alternate, opposite or whorled, simple or compound (simple in *Hedera*). Flowers mostly in umbels (or heads, racemes, spikes, panicles), regular, 5-merous, with calyx often reduced, and 5–10 (rarely 3) free petals alternating with as many stamens. Ovary inferior, usually 5-locular, and developing into a berry or a drupe.

Ivy *Hedera helix* L.

Description: An evergreen, woody vine, capable of climbing high up in trees, clinging to the bark with *specialized anchoring roots*; the plant can also climb walls and rockfaces, or scramble over the ground. Leaves alternate, leathery, deep green, often with paler veins, spear-shaped to almost palmately lobed (*with 3–5 rather acute lobes*); leaves of flowering stems often unlobed, ovate to cordate, shiny and (in full light) red-tinged. *Flowers in rounded umbels*, greenish or yellowish, 7–9 mm diam., with small, 5-toothed calyx and 5 ovate petals. Stamens 5. Ovary hemi-inferior, 5–10-locular. Fruit berry-like, globose, with a rim at the shoulder and a short, permanent style, brownish to black when ripe.

Flowering: September–December.

Habitat: Deciduous woods on moist, oligotrophic to mesotrophic, often acid, soils.

Range: S, C and W Europe, northwards to the Shetland Isles, S Norway and Latvia, eastwards to the Ukraine.

Similar species: **Irish Ivy** (*H. hibernica* hort. ex (Kirchner) Bean) has large, cordate to almost reniform leaves, with 5–7 blunt, shallow lobes, on the non-flowering shoots; this is possibly a cultivar of hybrid origin, once found in the wild in Ireland, and frequently cultivated elsewhere.

The tree-climbing habit is usually most developed in humid, Atlantic regions. The plant does little harm to the tree it settles upon, but smaller trees can be damaged by the sheer weight of the plant's foliage. Damage to brickwork is insignificant. The late flowering makes this plant a welcome nectar source for autumnal insects.

BIRTHWORT FAMILY, ARISTOLOCHIACEAE

A family of herbs and vines, with 7 genera and 625 species in tropical to warm-temperate regions. Dicots. Leaves alternate, simple. Flowers hermaphrodite, 3-merous, regular or irregular; perianth connate, tube-shaped. Stamens 6, 12 or many. Ovary inferior, 4–6–locular. Fruit a many-seeded capsule.

p.221 **Birthwort** *Aristolochia clematitis* L.

Description: A perennial herb with erect, unbranched stems to 90 cm. Leaves glabrous, stalked, dull green, deep-veined, and entire-margined; leaf-blade ovate to suborbicular with cordate base and blunt tip. Flowers clustered in the leaf-axils; perianth pale yellow, irregular, 20–30 mm long, *tube-shaped, with a distinct upper lip*. Stamens 6, *connate to the style*. Ovary ovoid or spindle-shaped, developing into a large, ovoid, brownish capsule up to 40 mm long; perianth not persistent on the fruit.

Flowering: May–June (September).

Habitat: Wood margins and hedges, also in shaded, ruderal places, on rather dry, eutrophic, calcareous soils, mainly in lowlands.

Range: C and S Europe, eastwards to E Russia; probably native only in the east and southeast, but an archeophyte further northwards to Britain, the Netherlands, Germany, and Poland.

An old medicinal herb, formerly used to induce childbirth or abortion. The plant has a nasty smell and is poisonous.

p.42 **Asarabacca** *Asarum europaeum* L.

Description: An evergreen perennial to 15 cm, with *creeping, hairy stems*. Flowering stems short, ascending, with 2 ovate scale-leaves near base. Leaves long-stalked, alternate to almost opposite, or seemingly in whorls of 3, shiny green, with reticulate veins and entire margins; leaf-blade reniform, with deeply cordate base. Flowers close to the ground, inconspicuous, single, terminal, nodding on a short stalk, *regular*, pitcher- or bell-shaped, 12–15 mm diam.; *perianth* greenish-brown and hairy outside, *purple-brown inside*, and with *3 incurved, pointed lobes*. Stamens 12, free. Ovary semi-globose; fruit a small, hairy, rounded, irregularly splitting capsule, crowned by the persistent perianth.

Flowering: March–August.

Habitat: Woods, copses, scrub and hedges, on rather dry, oligotrophic or mesotrophic, calcareous soils.

Range: C Europe northwards to Belgium and S Sweden, and eastwards to S Finland and E Russia.

Formerly used in medicine as an emetic and purgative. Poisonous!

SWALLOW-WORT FAMILY, ASCLEPIADACEAE

A large family of herbs and often winding shrubs, with 2,000 species in 250 genera, mainly in the tropics. Dicots. Leaves simple, opposite (sometimes whorled or alternate). Flowers regular, hermaphrodite, 5-merous; calyx 5-partite; corolla 5-lobed. Stamens 5, alternating with the corolla lobes, connate around the style. Ovaries 2, superior, free, but with connected stigmas. Fruit a many-seeded, double follicle.

p.126 **Swallow-wort**
Vincetoxicum hirundinaria Medicus

Description: A tufted perennial to 120 cm, with erect or arching stems. Leaves opposite, short-stalked (up to 10 mm), glabrous or slightly hairy, entire-margined; leaf-blade ovate to broadly lanceolate, with cordate to rounded base. Flowers in loose cymes, *inserted sideways between the axils* of the upper leaf-pairs; calyx has 5 lanceolate teeth; corolla whitish (grading to greenish or yellowish), 5–10 mm diam., deeply 5-lobed, with a short tube; *corolla lobes contort (turned) in bud*. Stamens 5, connate under the stigma. *Fruit a pair of spindle-shaped follicles*, 40–60 mm in length, glabrous, brownish when ripe; seeds small, with white, silky plumes.

Flowering: May–September.

Habitat: Margins of deciduous woods, scrub, shaded banks and verges, on dry to moist, calcareous, sandy or rocky soils, from sea level to 1,800 m.

Range: S and C Europe, northwards to Belgium, the Netherlands, S Sweden, and S Finland, avoiding the Atlantic coast; eastwards through C Russia to the Ob basin; also in N Africa.

A very poisonous plant. The Mediterranean *V. nigrum* (L.) Moench, with deep purple flowers, has extended its range northwards along the French Atlantic coast, and has recently naturalized in the sea-dunes of the Netherlands.

BALSAM FAMILY, BALSAMINACEAE

A subcosmopolitan family of herbs or half-shrubs, with 2–4 genera, of which *Impatiens* contains nearly all 600 species. Dicots. Leaves simple; stems more or less succulent. Flowers irregular, hermaphrodite, basically 5-merous, with 3–5 sepals (the lower one sac-like and with a spur). Petals 5, the upper one free, the lateral ones united in pairs. Stamens 5, alternating with the petals, with connate anthers. Ovary superior, 5-locular; style short or absent; stigma 5-lobed. Fruit a many-seeded, explosive (ballistic) capsule.

---

p.187 **Touch-me-not** *Impatiens noli-tangere* L.

Description: An erect, glabrous, annual herb up to 80 cm, with red-tinged, somewhat diaphanous, often branched stems. Leaves alternate, stalked, ovate, bluntly serrate to crenate, with short-awned teeth. Flowers pendulous, 20–35 mm in length, 3–6 together in lax, axillary racemes; sepals and petals yellow, sprayed with red dots; *lower, sac-like sepal strongly inflated, tapering into a stout, curved spur.* Capsule spindle-shaped to almost linear, opening with 5 coiling valves.

Flowering: June–September.

Habitat: In spring areas and along brooks in mostly deciduous woods on mesotrophic to eutrophic soils, from lowland to 1,500 m.

Range: Most of Europe, except the extreme north, and eastwards to E Russia.

Similar species: **Small Balsam** (*I. parviflora* DC.) has sharply serrate leaves and small yellow flowers up to 15 mm, with tiny spurs. Native to C Asia, and naturalized in W and C Europe, in moist woods and on riverbanks and disturbed ground.

The often man-sized **Himalayan Balsam** (*I. glandulifera* Royle) with purple or pink (rarely white) flowers up to 40 mm in length, is grown in gardens and has naturalized on riverbanks and disturbed ground in large parts of Europe.

BORAGE FAMILY, BORAGINACEAE

A cosmopolitan family of herbs (rarely shrubs), with about 2,000 species in 100 genera. Dicots. Leaves simple, alternate; plants often rough-hairy. Flowers mostly hermaphrodite, regular or irregular, basically 5-merous, in gradually unfurling monochasial cymes (cincinni or 'scorpioid' cymes), in racemes or panicles or (rarely) solitary. Sepals and petals partly connate; corolla tube often has scales on the inside. Stamens 5, sometimes partly sterile, inserted on the corolla. Ovary 2–4-locular (rarely 10-locular), with 1–2 ovules per locule; style usually descending between the locules and entering at their bases; stigma 1, sometimes 2-lobed. Fruit usually a cluster of 4 achenes, sometimes a capsule or a (compound) drupe. As a result of shifts in the acidity of the cell sap, the corolla of many species changes from pink to blue when the buds open, and again to reddish after pollination.

---

p.341 **Bugloss** *Anchusa arvensis* (L.) Bieb.

Description: A rough-hairy perennial (sometimes biennial) with ascending to erect, scarcely branched stems up to 60 cm. Leaves entire-margined to sinuous, or even with some blunt teeth; basal ones narrowly oblanceolate, tapering into long stalk, upper ones lanceolate, sessile and *half-clasping*. Flowers in a leafy cyme. Calyx deeply divided, with 5 teeth. Corolla 4–6 mm diam., with 5 rounded lobes, *slightly irregular* (the lower pair of lobes smaller), pale blue (rarely white or pink), with white midveins radiating from the throat, and a white, *twisted tube* up to 7 mm long; throat of tube closed with 5 short, triangular, hairy scales. Stamens hidden in corolla tube. Ovary 4-locular, forming a cluster of 4 irregularly egg-shaped, netted, 1-seeded achenes up to 4 mm.

Flowering: May–September.

Habitat: Dry grasslands, dunes, arable fields and road verges, on sandy or loamy, oligotrophic to mesotrophic soils, mainly in lowland.

Range: Most of Europe, eastwards to E Russia.

Similar species: **Green Alkanet** (*Pentaglottis sempervirens* (L.) Tausch ex L.H. Bailey) has sessile but hardly clasping upper leaves, regular flowers 8–10 mm diam., a straight corolla tube, and weakly 2-tipped scales at throat. Native to SW Europe; often kept in gardens, and locally naturalized in shaded places in S England and the Low Countries.

p.341 **Alkanet** *Anchusa officinalis* L.

Description: A rough-hairy perennial or biennial herb
to 1 m. Stems erect, unbranched, and with
erect bristles. Leaves lanceolate, up to
20 mm wide, the lower ones long-stalked,
the upper ones sessile. Flowers in *leafless,
coiled cymes* that later straighten and
become much elongated. Calyx deeply
incised, the teeth subacute, *with a green
margin.* Corolla deep blue to violet (rarely
white or pale yellow), 9–15 mm diam.;
corolla lobes rounded; tube closed with 5
triangular, white, hairy scales, concealing
the 5 stamens. Ovary 4-locular; fruit a
cluster of 4 obliquely truncated, unstalked
achenes.

Flowering: May–September.

Habitat: Dry grasslands, dunes, banks, verges and
waste places, on poor, sandy or stony,
preferably calcareous soils, from sea level to
1,800 m.

Range: Originating from the Pontic area, this
species has expanded over continental
Europe (except the extreme north)
westwards to Germany and France.

Similar species: **Yellow Alkanet** (*A. ochroleuca* Bieb.) has
appressed bristles on stem. Flowers always
pale yellow or whitish; achenes stalked;
calyx teeth have pale margins. In E Europe,
westwards to Hungary, and locally
naturalized further west.

An extract from the roots of *A. officinalis*
was formerly used as a colorant in make-up
rouge.

---

p.333 **Madwort** *Asperugo procumbens* L.

Description: An annual herb with prostrate to
ascending, often scrambling, brittle,
angular stems with hooked bristles. Lower
leaves alternate, oblanceolate, narrowing
into the stalk; *upper leaves opposite* and
sessile, lanceolate to narrowly ovate.
Flowers regular, few (1–3) in the axils of
the upper leaves. Calyx has 5 unequal teeth.
Corolla up to 3 mm long, 5-lobed, the

lobes violet (turning blue during anthesis) or rarely white; corolla tube white, with white scales at throat. Stamens 5, concealed. Ovary 4-locular. Fruit a cluster of 4 ovoid achenes, surrounded by the now *greatly enlarged, coarsely dentate, laterally compressed calyx.*

Flowering: May–July (November).

Habitat: Dry, ruderal places, cultivated fields, road verges and farmyards, on sandy or stony, calcareous, preferably manured soils, from sea level to 2,600 m.

Range: N, E and EC Europe, from Fennoscandia southwards to the Netherlands, Germany and Italy, and eastwards to E Russia.

---

p.141 **Corn Gromwell**
Buglossoides arvensis (L.) I.M. Johnston

Description: A hairy *annual* with mostly simple, (sub)erect stems and a vertical taproot. Leaves oblanceolate to almost linear, up to 50 mm in length, *blunt-tipped*, sessile, *with indistinct side-veins.* Flowers in terminal, leafy cymes. Calyx deeply incised, with 5 tapering teeth, at least equalling the corolla tube. Corolla 6–9 mm long, *with whitish (rarely pale-blue) lobes*; tube violet or bluish, scaleless at throat, but with *hairy longitudinal folds inside*; tube conceals 5 stamens. Ovaries and achenes 4, the latter *hard and wrinkled, grey-brown*, angular, with an acute top.

Flowering: April–June (September).

Habitat: Cereal (especially winter-cereal) fields, and open, ruderal places, on moist, preferably calcareous soils from sea level to 2,300 m.

Range: Widespread but declining in all of Europe, except Iceland and some Atlantic islands.

The description given above pertains to ssp. *arvensis*; **Blue Gromwell** (*B. a. permixta* (Jord. ex F.W. Schulz) R. Fernando), from France and S Germany, has blue flowers with a calyx shorter than the corolla tube.

p.342 **Purple Gromwell**
Buglossoides purpurocaerulea (L.) I.M. Johnston

Description: Rather like *B. a. arvensis* (*see above*), but *perennial* with prostrate to ascending stems, and lanceolate to almost linear, *long-tapering, acute leaves; flowers twice as long* (12–19 mm) as in *B. a. arvensis, turning from violet to bright blue* during anthesis; *achenes ovoid, smooth, shiny white.*

Flowering: April–June.

Habitat: Scrub and wood margins, on moist, calcareous soils from sea level to 1,200 m.

Range: S and SC Europe, northwards to S England, Lorraine, C Germany and Poland, and eastwards to E Russia.

p.215 **Lesser Honeywort** *Cerinthe minor* L.

Description: A biennial or short-lived perennial to 60 cm, with erect, sparingly branched, *glabrous stems*. Leaves ovate or obovate, sessile, *clasping the stem* with 2 rounded basal lobes, *bluish-green*, often with whitish blotches, hairless but *roughened by minute tubercles*. Flowers, in overhanging cymes, have elliptical bracts and 5 free, elliptical, ciliate sepals. Corolla regular, tube-shaped, with *5 erect, lanceolate teeth equalling tube*, yellow (often with 5 purple spots below the teeth), scaleless at throat. Stamens 5; *anthers much longer than their filament*. Ovary 2-lobed, each lobe with 2 locules. *Fruit a pair of 2-locular, 2-seeded achenes.*

Flowering: May–July (September).

Habitat: Pastures and road verges, also cultivated ground, on loamy or sandy, calcareous soils (often over limestone) in the montane zone between 1,200 and 2,300 m.

Range: C and E Europe, westwards to C France, northwards to S Germany and Poland, eastwards to C Russia and Turkey.

Similar species: **Smooth Honeywort** (*C. glabra* Miller) has smooth leaves, glabrous sepals, very short, recurved corolla teeth, and anthers equalling their filament. In C and S Europe, westwards to the Pyrenees, and northwards to the Jura Mountains, S Germany and the Carpathians.

---

p.318 **Hound's-tongue** *Cynoglossum officinale* L.

Description: A *softly grey-downy* biennial or short-lived perennial to 80 cm, with simple, erect stem. Leaves lanceolate, the lower ones narrowed into a stalk, the upper ones sessile. Flowers in axillary cymes that are curved only at the tip. Sepals 5, almost free, broadly lanceolate. Corolla regular, funnel-shaped, 5–7 mm diam., with *5 rounded, wine-red lobes*, turning muddy violet after anthesis; corolla tube with 5 hood-shaped scales at throat, conceals 5 stamens. Ovary 4-locular; common style persistent on the hypanthium. Fruit a cluster of 4 dark-brown, *flattened achenes covered with hooked bristles* and with a *thickened border*.

Flowering: May–August.

Habitat: Dry grasslands, scrub, dunes, and open wasteland, on oligotrophic, sandy or stony, calcareous soils, from sea level to 2,400 m; most frequent near the sea.

Range: Most of Europe (except the extreme north and south), westwards to Ireland, northwards to S Fennoscandia, and eastwards to E Russia.

Similar species: **Green Hound's-tongue** (*C. germanicum* Jacq.) has upper leaves slightly clasping, sparsely rough-hairy and bright green above (but densely pubescent below); achenes have no thickened border. In woods and hedgerows on calcareous soils in W and C Europe, northwards to C England, Belgium, Germany and Poland, and eastwards to C Russia and the Caucasus.

---

p.342 **Viper's Bugloss** *Echium vulgare* L.

Description: A roughly hispid biennial (rarely perennial), with erect, simple stems to 1 m. Leaves lanceolate to almost linear, the lower ones stalked, the upper ones sessile with an acute or rounded base; *side-veins indistinct*. Flowers in strongly recurved, scorpioid cymes. Calyx regular, deeply divided, with 5 lanceolate teeth. Corolla funnel-shaped, 10–20 mm long, purplish in bud, turning deep blue at opening (rarely white or pink), *irregular*, with an oblique throat and 5 ovate, slightly unequal lobes; *corolla tube slightly bent*, throat scaleless. *Stamens long-protruding*, though attached deep down in the corolla tube. Ovary 4-locular, with long-protruding style and bifid stigma. Fruit a cluster of 4 rough, angular achenes.

Flowering: May–September.

Habitat: Dry grasslands, dunes, and open wasteland, on sandy or rocky, oligotrophic, calcareous soils, from sea level to 1,800 m.

Range: All Europe, except the extreme north.

Similar species: **Purple Viper's Bugloss** (*E. plantagineum* L.) is a Mediterranean-Atlantic, softly hairy plant to 60 cm; stem-leaves have cordate bases and prominent side-veins; flowers larger (up to 30 mm), blue or violet. In dry, sandy places in S and W Europe, northwards to W France and SW England; also in S and C Russia.

---

p.141 **Heliotrope** *Heliotropium europaeum* L.

Description: An annual herb to 50 cm. Stems erect or spreading, branched, with dense, appressed hairs. Leaves ovate to elliptical, narrowed into the stalk, hairy, pale green or greyish, with prominent veins. Flowers in *strongly recurved, forked, scorpioid cymes*. Calyx deeply divided, with 5 spreading, narrowly lanceolate teeth. Corolla funnel-shaped, 3–4.5 mm diam., *white or lavender, with yellow throat*, and small teeth between rounded, spreading corolla lobes; tube conceals 5 stamens. Ovary 4-locular, often 2-lobed, with a *terminally inserted style* (unlike all other Boraginaceae treated here). Fruit a cluster of 4 achenes (often clinging together in pairs).

Flowering: May–August.

Habitat: Open, waste or cultivated places, and roadsides, on dry, sandy, loamy or rocky soils, from sea level to 1,500 m.

Range: A Mediterranean species, expanding northwards from S, C and W Europe to N France, S Germany, and Austria, and eastwards to E Russia.

In E Europe, several closely related species can be found.

p.118 **Common Gromwell**
Lithospermum officinale L.

Description: A perennial herb, often tufted, to 1 m, with a thick, non-creeping rhizome and numerous erect, branched stems with *appressed hairs*. Leaves lanceolate, *long-pointed*, up to 10 cm long and 2 cm wide, with prominent veins, (sub)sessile with a rounded base, and appressed hairs. Flowers regular, in leafy cymes. Sepals 5, linear. Corolla 4–6 mm long, funnel-shaped, greenish, whitish or cream, with 5 white, hairy scales at the throat. Corolla tube conceals 5 stamens. Ovary 4-locular, developing into 1–4 ovoid, smooth, shiny, *pearly-white, very hard achenes*.

Flowering: May–August.

Habitat: Wood margins, scrub, hedgerows, dune-thickets, grassy banks and slopes, on dry to moist, oligotrophic, calcareous soils, from sea level to 1,600 m.

Range: Most of Europe except the far north.

p.339 **Oyster Plant**
Mertensia maritima (L.) S.F. Gray

Description: A *hairless* perennial herb with trailing, slightly angular, reddish stems to 60 cm long. *Leaves blue-green*, fleshy, the lower ones spoon-shaped and stalked, the upper ones ovate and sessile. Flowers in ascending, leafy cymes, long-stalked in fruit. Sepals 5, broadly lanceolate to ovate, becoming enlarged in fruit. Corolla regular, to 6 mm diam., with 5 rounded, erect lobes, pink in bud, later turning blue inside; *corolla tube constricted near throat*, but without scales. Stamens 5. Ovary 4-locular; achenes fleshy.

Flowering: June–August.
Habitat: Sandy shores and shingle; a halophyte, often colonizing old floodmarks of wrack.
Range: Coasts of N Europe, from Iceland, Ireland and N Britain eastwards to Denmark, SW Sweden, and along the Norwegian coast to N Russia and Spitsbergen.

---

p.340 **Field Forget-me-not**
Myosotis arvensis (L.) Hill

Description: A hairy annual or short-lived perennial with branched, erect stems to 60 cm (but often much shorter); stem-hairs spreading. Basal leaves short-stalked, oblanceolate; stem-leaves sessile, elliptical to lanceolate. Flowers regular, in coiled, leafless, strongly elongating cymes in the upper leaf-axils; terminal cymes forked. Calyx deeply incised, with 5 lanceolate, appressed-hairy teeth; *calyx tube has hooked bristles*. Corolla up to 5 mm diam., pale blue, with 5 concave, rounded lobes and 5 yellow scales at the throat; corolla tube shorter than calyx. Stamens 5, concealed in corolla tube. Ovary 4-locular. Fruit a cluster of 4 dark-brown achenes; *fruit-stalks 3–6 times as long as calyx*, obliquely rising; calyx teeth erect in fruit.
Flowering: April–October.
Habitat: Arable land, dry grasslands, road verges, scrub, open woods, and waste areas, on dry to moist, mesotrophic, preferably sandy soils, from sea level to 2,000 m.
Range: Almost all of Europe.
Similar species: **Early Forget-me-not** (*M. ramosissima* Schultes) rarely exceeds 15 cm; upper stem has appressed hairs; flowers smaller (up to 3 mm) in cymes that eventually become longer than rest of plant; fruit-stalks barely equalling calyx, spreading or ascending; calyx teeth patent in fruit. On dry, sandy, often calcareous soils (often in dune areas) in most of Europe except the extreme north.
M. stricta Roemer & Schultes has hooked hairs on lower stem and on undersurface of leaves; fruit-stalks are short, and point

stiffly upwards. In continental Europe, in dry, sandy or loamy places.

---

p.340 **Changing Forget-me-not**
Myosotis discolor Pers.

Description: Much like *M. arvensis*, but *corolla pale yellow in bud*, changing to pale blue during anthesis; corolla tube often pinkish, *becoming longer than the calyx*. Leaves have straight hairs below. Fruit-stalks short and straight, rising obliquely upwards.

Flowering: May–July.

Habitat: Grassy places, but also cereal fields, open woods and trodden banks, on dry to moist, mesotrophic, sandy or loamy soils, from sea level to 2,000 m.

Range: Europe, eastwards to the Baltic States, the Ukraine and C Yugoslavia, and northwards to Iceland and S Fennoscandia.

---

p.340 **Water Forget-me-not**
Myosotis palustris (L.) L.

Description: A hairy, perennial herb with creeping rhizome, long stolons, and soft, ascending stems to 50 cm; stems rounded or weakly angular, hairless or with appressed hairs, sometimes also with erect or deflexed hairs below. Flowers regular, in curved, usually leafless, cymes. Leaves elliptical to bluntly lanceolate, with appressed hairs; only the lowest leaves stalked. Calyx has 5 *short, broadly triangular teeth* (at most half as long as calyx tube), and *only with appressed hairs*. Corolla 4–9 mm wide, sky blue (rarely pinkish or white); corolla tube has 5 yellow scales at throat. Stamens concealed. Ovary 4-locular; achenes black, shiny; *fruit-stalks at most twice as long as the calyx*.

Flowering: May–September.

Habitat: Marshes, and on banks of stagnant or flowing fresh waters, often floating on the water, or even partly submerged, forming a belt by the waterside, on sandy to clayey or rocky, eutrophic soils, from sea level to 2,000 m.

Range: C and N Europe, westwards to France and
Ireland, and eastwards to E Russia.

Similar species: **Tufted Forget-me-not** (*M. laxa* Lehm.)
lacks stolons, and only the stem has
appressed hairs. Calyx deeply incised (with
teeth equalling calyx tube), and usually
some leaves present in the cymes; flowers
2–5 mm wide. In comparable wet places in
most of Europe, but less frequent in the
south.

Creeping Forget-me-not (*M. secunda* A.
Murray) has stolons, erect stem-hairs,
leafless cymes, a deeply incised calyx with
erect hairs, flowers of 4–8 mm diam., and
reflexed fruit-stalks 3–5 times as long as
calyx. In wet places of W Europe, from
Portugal to Ireland and France; in the
south, found only on mountains.

Forms of *M. secunda* with small flowers
(less than 5 mm) and bluish-green leaves,
from the mountains of N Britain and
Iberia, are distinguished as *M. stolonifera*
(DC.) Gay.

Biennial forms of *M. palustris* without
stolons are often distinguished as ssp.
nemorosa (Besser) Berg & Kaastra.

---

p.340 **Wood Forget-me-not**
Myosotis sylvatica Hoffm.

Description: A mostly short-lived perennial (sometimes
biennial), with branched flowering stems
to 50 cm, as well as basal, *non-flowering
tufts of large, long-stalked, elliptical or
oblanceolate leaves*. Plant soft-hairy, with
erect hairs. Stem-leaves sessile, lanceolate
to ovate. Flowers regular, in coiled,
leafless cymes. Calyx deeply incised,
5-toothed, *with some hooked hairs* at base.
Corolla 5-lobed, 6–9 mm diam., turning
from pink to sky blue (rarely remaining
pink in some garden selections); *lobes flat,
rounded*; corolla tube equals calyx, and has
5 yellow scales at throat. Stamens
concealed. Ovary 4-locular; achenes 4,
brown; fruit-stalks spreading, less than
twice as long as calyx.

Flowering: April–July.

Habitat: Damp woods (especially Beech) and mountain grasslands, on moist, oligotrophic, calcareous soils, from sea level to 2,000 m.

Range: Much of Europe, but absent from the southwest; northwards to Belgium, Germany, S Sweden and Poland, and eastwards to C Russia.

Similar species: Wood Forget-me-not can be rather difficult to separate from *M. arvensis*; look for the presence of non-flowering leaf-tufts.

Alpine Forget-me-not (*M. alpestris* F. W. Schmidt), which is also treated as a subspecies, has fruit-stalks that hardly equal the calyces, which are silvery-hairy; achenes black. In mountains of Europe, from Scotland and Spain eastwards through Germany and Poland to W Russia; there are several closely related, endemic species in S and E Europe.

M. decumbens Host. has creeping rhizomes and a corolla tube distinctly longer than calyx. In N, SW and C Europe, mainly in the mountains.

The genus *Lappula* differs from the genus *Myosotis* in having achenes with *straight, barbed bristles*.

Bur Forget-me-not (*Lappula squarrosa* (Retz) Dumort.) can be recognized by its erect fruit-stalks and flowers up to 4 mm diam.; the achenes have 2–3 rows of barbed bristles on their angles. In cultivated fields, vineyards, road verges and dry, waste or disturbed places, in most of Europe, westwards to France, northwards to Germany and S Sweden, and eastwards to C Russia; probably only naturalized north of the Alps.

Deflexed Bur Forget-me-not (*Lappula deflexa* (Wahlenb.) Gürcke) has deflexed fruit-stalks and larger flowers (5–7 mm wide), while the achenes have barbed bristles in single rows. In rocky or grassy places in Russia and Fennoscandia, also in the mountains of C Europe, and westwards to the Pyrenees.

p.341 **Blue-eyed Mary** *Omphalodes verna* Moench

Description: A mat-forming, *glabrous or slightly hairy*,
perennial herb with a creeping rhizome and
long, creeping stolons; flowering stems erect or
ascending, up to 20 cm high. *Leaves ovate*
with a rounded to cordate base and entire
margins; *basal leaves long-stalked*, upper ones
short-stalked to sessile. Flowers few, in a lax
cyme; bracts few or absent. Calyx 5-parted.
Corolla 5-lobed, *blue with whitish seams*, 8–
15 mm diam. (sometimes all white); corolla
tube has 5 *whitish scales* at the throat. Stamens
5, concealed. Ovary 4-locular; *achenes hairy*.

Flowering: March–May.

Habitat: Woods (often Beech), on moist, humus-rich
soils, mainly in the mountains.

Range: C Europe, from the W Alps to Romania,
but truly indigenous only in the SE Alps
and S Carpathians; often cultivated, and
locally naturalized along streams and on
estate grounds elsewhere in Europe.

Similar species: *O. scorpioides* (Haenke) Schrank is biennial,
with branched stems, and elliptical to
lanceolate leaves; it lacks stolons. In C and
E Europe, westwards to Germany.
O. littoralis Lehm., which has blue-green,
narrowly elliptical leaves and white flowers
to 5 mm wide, is a rare endemic in the sea-
dunes of W France.

p.342 *Pulmonaria angustifolia* L.

Description: A rough-hairy, tufted perennial to 40 cm.
Leaves greyish-green, *unspotted*, the *basal
ones narrowly lanceolate*, tapering into the
stalk, and covered with *bristles of equal
length*; stem-leaves sessile. Flowers in dense
cymes, regular. Calyx cylindrical, with 5
lanceolate teeth. Corolla violet-blue (deep
pink in bud), 12–20 mm long, with 5
rounded lobes; corolla tube scaleless at
throat, but with 5 tufts of hair inside.

Flowering: April–July.

Habitat: Grasslands, heaths and open woods, on
moist, oligotrophic to mesotrophic,
calcareous or slightly acid soils, mainly in
elevated country, to 2,600 m.

Range: E and C Europe, westwards to E France and S Germany, and northwards to Poland and the Baltic States.

Similar species: **Narrow-leaved Lungwort** (*P. longifolia* (Bast.) Boreau) has smaller flowers (8–12 mm long), narrowly lanceolate, usually white-spotted, glandular-hairy leaves (bristles unequal, glands small and scattered); inflorescence remains dense throughout flowering period. In deciduous woods and scrub, on loamy or clayey soils, from Iberian Peninsula northwards to Britain and France; northern populations often seem to grade into *P. montana*.

---

p.318 **Common Lungwort** *Pulmonaria officinalis* L.

Description: A rough-hairy perennial herb to 40 cm. Basal leaves hibernating, *ovate, with a rounded or truncate to cordate base*, green with *whitish blotches*, abruptly narrowed into a long, winged stalk; stem-leaves ovate, sessile to half-clasping. Flowers regular, in dense, *densely glandular cymes*. Calyx teeth 5, triangular, less than 1 third the length of calyx tube. Corolla purplish to violet (pink in bud), 13–18 mm long; corolla tube has 5 tufts of hairs at throat (but no scales). Stamens 5, hidden in corolla tube or slightly protruding. Ovary 4-locular; style either long and protruding, or short and concealed (when stamens protrude). Achenes ovoid.

Flowering: March–May.

Habitat: Deciduous and mixed woods, on moist, humus-rich, oligotrophic to mesotrophic, calcareous soils, from near sea level to 1,900 m. Also kept as an ornamental, and often naturalized on estate grounds.

Range: W and C Europe, from France eastwards to C Russia, and northwards to the Netherlands, S Sweden and Poland.

Similar species: *P. obscura* Dumort. has plain-green or vaguely spotted, truncate or slightly cordate basal leaves on long, unwinged stalks, and scarcely glandular cymes; basal leaves are lost in winter. In C Europe, northwards to Belgium, C Sweden and N Russia, on heavy, calcareous soils.

Mountain Lungwort (*P. montana* Lej.) has unspotted, lanceolate, glandular-hairy basal leaves (glands few, hairs 2 mm long, rough), tapering into unwinged stalk; flowers blue, in elongating, hardly glandular cymes. In W and WC Europe, from Belgium to Germany, Switzerland and France, in damp woods and mountain grasslands.

P. mollis Wulfen ex Hornemann has unspotted, broadly lanceolate, tapering leaves with softer, short hairs (to 1 mm), and blue flowers (15–20 mm long) in densely glandular cymes. In C and SE Europe, west to Germany (close to Belgium), and north to Poland and C Russia, in open woods.

Common Lungwort is an old medicinal herb, formerly used to treat tuberculosis.

---

p.289   **Common Comfrey** *Symphytum officinale* L.

Description: A stout, *densely hairy* perennial with creeping rhizomes and erect, *rather brittle, broadly winged stems* to 120 cm. Leaves elliptical to lanceolate, the basal ones large (to 40 cm long and 15 cm wide) and stalked, the upper ones sessile and *running down onto the stem*. Flowers regular, in strongly curved, forked cymes. Calyx deeply incised, 5-parted. Corolla bell-shaped, 12–18 mm long, violet, purple, pink or cream, with 5 short, recurved, triangular lobes; corolla tube cylindrical, with 5 *sleek (almost lanceolate) scales* alternating with anthers. Ovary 4-locular; achenes wrinkled, shiny black.

Flowering: April–August.

Habitat: Damp, grassy, often somewhat ruderal places, along canals, ditches, pools, and rivers, on mesotrophic to eutrophic, peaty or clayey soils, from sea level to 1,600 m.

Range: Most of Europe, northwards to Fennoscandia (but naturalized only in the extreme north).

Similar species: **Tuberous Comfrey** (*S. tuberosum* L.) has tuberous rhizomes, leaves running down over a short distance only (so stems hardly winged), always creamy-yellow flowers

with short, reflexed lobes, and dull,
granular achenes. In W, C and S Europe,
northwards to England, France, S Germany,
Poland, and C Russia.
Rough Comfrey (*S. asperum* Lepechin)
from SW Asia has unwinged stems, pink
flowers turning blue during anthesis, erect
corolla lobes, and granular achenes.
Formerly cultivated for fodder, it has locally
naturalized in ruderal places in W and N
Europe.
Russian Comfrey (*S.* × *uplandicum*
Nyman), a hybrid with *S. officinale*, also has
pink-turning-blue flowers and has similarly
naturalized.

FLOWERING RUSH FAMILY, BUTOMACEAE

A monotypic family of glabrous aquatic herbs with creeping
rhizomes, and erect, rounded flowering stems to 1.5 m.
Monocots. Leaves all basal, almost equalling the flowering
stem, erect (emergent), linear, gradually tapering (often
twisted at the top), distinctly triangular below and
sheathing at the base. Flowers regular, hermaphrodite, 3-
merous, in a terminal umbel with unequal, ascending rays
and an involucre of brownish, lanceolate, pointed bracts.
Perianth 15–25 mm diam., with 3 ovate, pink sepals and 3
slightly larger, rounded, pink or white petals. Stamens 9,
with blackish anthers. Ovaries 6, superior, 1-locular, connate
only at their bases. Fruit a cluster of 6 brownish, flask-
shaped, many-seeded follicles.

---

p.292 **Flowering Rush** *Butomus umbellatus* L.

Description: *See* the family characteristics above.
Flowering: June–September.
Habitat: In shallow, stagnant or slow-moving, fresh
or slightly brackish, mostly eutrophic
waters, on clayey or loamy soils, especially
in lowland areas.
Range: In most of Europe, northwards to Lapland,
and from Ireland to the Urals.

This species suffers badly from water
pollution and habitat destruction, and is on
the decline; it should be protected, as
indeed it is in several countries.

STARWORT FAMILY, CALLITRICHACEAE

A subcosmopolitan family of monoecious aquatic herbs, with only 1 genus and 17–30 species. Dicots. Leaves opposite, simple. Flowers naked (without a perianth), usually solitary in the leaf-axils, often accompanied by 2 tiny, membranous bracts; female flowers have only 1 stamen, a 4-locular ovary, and 2 free, thread-like styles. Fruit a cluster of 4 1-seeded, flattened achenes. Most species are amphibious, developing terrestrial forms when the habitat dries up. The species are extremely variable, and often difficult to distinguish from each other; ripe fruits (present from June to August) are essential for reliable identification.

p.52 **Intermediate Water-starwort**
Callitriche hamulata Kütz. ex Koch

Description: A perennial aquatic to 80 cm long, with linear, 1-veined, submerged leaves to 25 mm long, and a *somewhat deepened rosette* of elliptical to spatulate, 3-veined, round-tipped floating leaves (not always present); submerged leaves emarginate, with a widened, symmetrical, 2-horned, *pincer-shaped tip*. Flowers solitary, axillary, subsessile, submerged. Fruit cluster 1.5–2.5 mm diam., suborbicular in side-view, with narrowly winged achenes, and *deflexed, appressed style remnants*. Land forms have smaller, elliptical (sometimes linear) leaves, and distinctly stalked female flowers.

Flowering: April–September.

Habitat: Shallow, slow-moving, cool, clear, oligotrophic fresh waters, on acid, sandy or loamy soils, from sea level to 2,000 m.

Range: In NW and C Europe, southwards to Italy, and eastwards to Bielorussia and Bulgaria; also in Greenland.

Similar species: **Pedunculate Water-starwort** (*C. brutia* Petagna) has submerged leaves with shallowly notched, often asymmetrical tips, and broadly winged achenes (1–1.4 mm long). In W and S Europe, northwards to S Scandinavia (but absent from the Netherlands and Germany).

Autumnal Water-starwort
(*C. hermaphroditica* L.), to 50 cm, is permanently submerged, always devoid of floating rosettes, and never develops land forms; stems greenish; all leaves linear, 1-veined, diaphanous, yellowish green, mostly longer than 10 mm, with a tapering, distinctly emarginate tip; fruit a suborbicular cluster of 4 broadly winged achenes, 1–3 mm diam., with soon-falling styles. In fresh or slightly brackish, often basic waters on sandy, peaty or clayey soils, in most of Europe (more frequent in northerly regions).

Short-leaved Water-starwort (*C. truncata* Gussone) is also permanently submerged. Stems reddish; leaves short (less than 10 mm), blue-green, truncate to shallowly emarginate; achenes little-fused. A rare species from SW Europe (northwards to Britain and Belgium), not often forming ripe fruits.

---

p.52 **Blunt-fruited Water-starwort**
Callitriche obtusangula Le Gall

Description: A perennial aquatic herb to 60 cm, with linear, deeply emarginate submerged leaves, and rosettes of *narrowly obovate to diamond-shaped, rounded to subacute floating leaves* (often with a pale-green base). Flowers mainly in the axils of floating leaves. Fruit broadly elliptical, 1.5 mm long, 1.3 mm wide, with 4 *slightly keeled (not winged) achenes*; styles erect or diverging. Land forms have rather fleshy, elliptical to narrowly diamond-shaped leaves.

Flowering: April–September.

Habitat: Slow-moving, fresh or brackish, often eutrophic, basic waters, on sandy or clayey soils, from sea level to 1,600 m, but mainly in the lowland.

Range: W and S Europe, northwards to the Netherlands and Germany.

Similar species: *C. cophocarpa* Sendtner has rosettes of broadly ovate to elliptical, round-tipped floating leaves and small, wingless fruits (0.8–1.2 mm long). Rare, but widely distributed in base-rich waters (often estuaries) of Europe, northwards to Iceland and Scandinavia.

p.52 **Various-leaved Water-starwort**
Callitriche platycarpa Kütz.

Description: A perennial aquatic herb to 80 cm, with linear, emarginate submerged leaves and slightly *convex rosettes* of obovate, *distinctly stalked floating leaves* (often deep green). Flowers mainly in the axils of floating leaves. Fruit clusters suborbicular in side-view, with 4 narrowly winged achenes, pale brown when ripe; styles erect, diverging or recurved, but not appressed to fruit.

Flowering: April–October.

Habitat: Slow-moving, eutrophic, fresh (rarely brackish), basic waters on sandy, rocky or clayey soils, from sea level to 2,000 m, but more frequent in the lowland.

Range: NW and C Europe, southwards to N Spain and Switzerland, and eastwards to Hungary and Poland.

Similar species: *C. palustris* L. has linear, round-tipped submerged leaves, stalked, broadly obovate to suborbicular floating leaves, and flowers often in pairs; fruits dark brown to blackish, and longer than wide (1.0–1.4 mm long, broadly obovate), while achenes are narrowly winged only near the top. In oligotrophic to mesotrophic, often acid, fresh waters and marshes, in Europe southwards to the Pyrenees and Italy, and eastwards to the Urals; in the south, found mainly in mountainous regions.

Common Water-starwort (*C. stagnalis* Scop.) has elliptical to obovate submerged leaves and rounded, pale-green floating leaves, suborbicular fruits to 1.8 mm diam., and pale-brown achenes with very wide wings all round. In fresh or brackish, often eutrophic, basic waters; also in springs and on wet paths in woods; a subcosmopolitan species, in Europe eastwards to Estonia, the Ukraine and Greece.

All these species may develop land forms.

BELLFLOWER FAMILY, CAMPANULACEAE

A family of herbs or half-shrubs, with about 600 species in 35 genera world-wide, predominantly in the northern hemisphere. Dicots. Leaves alternate (rarely opposite or whorled), simple. Flowers mostly hermaphrodite, often in racemes or spikes, sometimes in a rounded flowerhead with a common involucre of bracts. Calyx connate only at its base, with 5 (rarely 3 or 4) long teeth. Corolla usually 5-lobed, regular (irregular in *Lobelia*). Stamens often 5, alternating with the corolla lobes, free or basally connate to the corolla tube; anthers sometimes fused. Ovary (hemi-)inferior, 2–5-locular, with 1 style and a 2–5-lobed stigma. Fruit a many-seeded capsule.

Several species make fine ornamentals for gardens. The Campanulaceae or their immediate predecessors are believed to be ancestral to the Compositae.

---

p.339 **Bearded Bellflower** *Campanula barbata* L.

Description: A *rough-hairy* perennial herb with non-creeping rhizome and erect, usually simple, stems to 30 cm. Basal leaves oblanceolate, wavy-edged, blunt-tipped, narrowing into the stalk; *stem-leaves absent or few* (then narrowly lanceolate). *Non-flowering rosettes* also often present. Flowers few (usually less than 6), *pendulous*, in lax, 1-sided raceme. Calyx has 5 lanceolate teeth and *5 small, ovate lobes* in between. Corolla pale blue, bell-shaped, 20–30 mm long, with 5 recurved, triangular lobes, and with *long white hairs inside*. Stamens 5. Ovary 3-locular, hemi-inferior, with a 3-lobed stigma. Capsule opening through lateral pores.

Flowering: June–August.

Habitat: Moist grasslands, open woods and scrub, on acid, often stony soils, mainly in mountainous areas, to 3,000 m.

Range: C Europe, westwards to C France, northwards to S Germany (also in S Norway), and eastwards to Poland and Yugoslavia.

Similar species: *C. sibirica* L., with branched flowering stems, softer hairs, and lacking non-flowering rosettes, occurs in E Europe (westwards to NE Germany).
Canterbury Bell (*C. medium* L.) is biennial, with glabrous, violet-blue to deep-lilac, or white flowers, 30–50 mm long, in broad panicles, a 5-locular ovary, and a 5-lobed stigma. From SE France and Italy; kept in gardens and locally naturalized in Britain and Germany.

---

p.345 **Clustered Bellflower**
Campanula glomerata L.

Description: A *hairy, sometimes even greyish-downy* perennial with creeping rhizomes and erect, unbranched flowering stems to 50 (80) cm. Basal leaves long-stalked, ovate to lanceolate, crenate, with *rounded or cordate base*; stem-leaves alternate, short-stalked to sessile (then often half-clasping), broadly lanceolate. Flowers erect, *sessile*, clustered in upper stem-leaf axils, the majority forming a *rounded, terminal head*. Calyx deeply incised with 5 narrowly lanceolate, *acute teeth*. Corolla violet-blue (rarely pale blue or white), 15–30 mm long, with 5 long, ovate, diverging lobes. Stamens 5. Ovary 3-locular; stigma 3-lobed. Capsule opening through pores.

Flowering: June–August (October).

Habitat: Moderately dry to moist grasslands, open woods and scrub, grassy verges, and also waste places, on calcareous, mesotrophic, sandy, clayey or stony soils, from sea level to 1,700 m.

Range: Most of Europe except Ireland and the far north.

Similar species: *C. cervicaria* L. is rough-hairy, with strongly angular stems, and narrowly lanceolate basal leaves long-tapering into stalk. Flowers pale blue to almost white, to 16 mm, with exserted styles, in a few superimposed whorls at top of stem; calyx teeth blunt. In continental Europe, northwards to Belgium, S Fennoscandia, and eastwards to the Urals; more common on acid, sandy soils.

p.338 **Giant Bellflower** *Campanula latifolia* L.

Description: A tufted perennial herb with erect, unbranched, *bluntly angular*, more or less hairy stems to *1 m or more*. Leaves softly hairy, alternate, ovate to broadly lanceolate, bluntly serrate; lower ones to 20 cm long, pointed, gradually narrowing into a winged stalk, upper ones subsessile. Flowers stalked, placed singly (rarely 2–3 together) in the axils of the stem-leaves to compose a *leafy raceme*. Calyx deeply incised, with *large, slightly dentate, lanceolate teeth*. Corolla bell-shaped, blue or pale violet (rarely white), 40–55 mm long, with 5 ovate, diverging lobes; *corolla tube glabrous inside*. Stamens 5. Ovary 3-locular; stigma 3-lobed. Capsule opening through pores.

Flowering: June–August.

Habitat: Deciduous and mixed woods, scrub, streambanks, and shaded grassy places, on moist, mesotrophic, acid to calcareous soils; prefers higher altitudes, to 1,600 m.

Range: In C and E Europe, westwards to C France and Britain, northwards to S Scandinavia and the Baltic States, and eastwards to the Urals. Often cultivated in gardens, and locally naturalized in W Europe, e.g. the Low Countries.

Similar species: **Nettle-leaved Bellflower** (*C. trachelium* L.) is rough-hairy, and has sharply angular stems; basal leaves to 10 cm long, ovate, abruptly narrowed into stalk, coarsely serrate (indeed reminiscent of nettles); flowers blue, 30–40 mm long, with narrowly triangular calyx teeth and long hairs inside corolla tube. In most of Europe except the far north, in forest margins, scrub, and under hedgerows; also cultivated in gardens.

---

p.319 **Spreading Bellflower** *Campanula patula* L.

Description: A slender perennial or biennial herb with thin roots and simple, erect, usually rough-hairy, stems to 70 cm. Leaves glabrous or sparsely hairy, the lower ones obovate to oblanceolate, stalked, bluntly serrate, the upper ones scattered, lanceolate to linear, sessile, crenate. Flowers erect, in *very lax panicles* with long, diverging branches; flower-stalks have 2 small bracts near the middle. Calyx has 5 *linear, awl-shaped, remotely dentate teeth*. Corolla funnel-shaped, 20–25 mm long, with 5 *narrowly ovate lobes*, blue-violet or lilac, rarely white. Stamens 5. Ovary 3-locular; stigma 3-lobed. Capsule erect, 10 veined, opening through pores.

Flowering: July–September.

Habitat: Meadows, open woodland and scrub, on moist to wet, mesotrophic, sandy, loamy or rocky, preferably acid soils, from sea level to 1,600 m.

Range: E and C Europe, westwards to S England, northwards to S Scandinavia and Finland, and eastwards to the Urals.

Similar species: **Rampion Bellflower** (*C. rapunculus* L.) is biennial, and has thickened roots, wavy leaf-margins, and a slender panicle with short, erect branches; flowers slightly smaller (10–20 mm), pale violet-blue (rarely white); flower-stalks have 2 small bracts at their base; calyx teeth entire-margined. In forest margins, meadows and waste places of continental Europe northwards to the Netherlands, the Carpathians, and SC Russia; formerly cultivated as a vegetable, and naturalized in Britain, Denmark and S Sweden.

---

p.338 **Peach-leaved Bellflower**
Campanula persicifolia L.

Description: A glabrous, perennial herb with creeping rhizome and erect stems to 90 cm; no stolons. Leaves stiff, glabrous, bluntly serrate, the *lower ones narrowly ovate to lanceolate*, narrowed into the stalk, the upper ones lanceolate to linear, subsessile. Flowers erect or ascending, in *lax racemes*, with 2 small bracts at base of stalk. Calyx has 5 erect, *lanceolate teeth*. Corolla sky-blue or pale violet (rarely white), widely bell-shaped, 30–40 mm long, with 5 *short, rounded or slightly pointed, diverging lobes*. Stamens 5. Ovary 3-locular; stigma 3-lobed. *Capsule erect*, opening through pores.

Flowering: June–August.

Habitat: Wood margins, scrub, shady road verges and meadows, on moist to rather dry, oligotrophic, sandy, loamy or rocky, preferably basic soils, mainly in hilly or mountainous areas, to 2,000 m.

Range: Most of Europe except the British Isles and the extreme north, generally avoiding coastal areas. Also kept in gardens, and locally naturalized in Britain.

---

p.390 **Creeping Bellflower**
Campanula rapunculoides L.

Description: A hairy or subglabrous perennial herb with creeping rhizome and *creeping, underground stolons* forming dense mats. Flowering stems simple, erect, bluntly angular, short, sparse hairs. Leaves bluntly serrate to crenate, sparsely hairy or glabrous, the lower ones ovate to broadly lanceolate with a *cordate or rounded base*, long-stalked, the upper ones lanceolate, subsessile. Flowers in more or less *1-sided, leafy racemes*. Calyx has 5 lanceolate, *spreading or deflexed teeth*. Corolla bright bluish-violet, bell-shaped, *pendulous*, 20–30 mm long, with 5 narrowly ovate, diverging, *ciliate lobes*. Stamens 5. Ovary 3-locular; stigma 3-lobed. *Capsule pendulous*, opening through pores.

Flowering: June–September.

Habitat: Wood margins, hedges, shaded road verges, railway embankments and waste places, rarely in arable fields, on moist to rather dry, mesotrophic, sandy, clayey or loamy, often calcareous soils, from sea level to 2,000 m.

Range: Continental Europe, except the far north, and eastwards to C Russia; also cultivated in gardens, and locally naturalized in Britain and Ireland.

p.338 **Harebell** *Campanula rotundifolia* L.

Description: A glabrous or short-hairy perennial herb
with *creeping stolons* and erect or ascending,
slender, rounded flowering stems to
40 cm. *Basal leaves reniform to ovate*,
coarsely dentate, long-stalked, with blade
rarely longer than 15 mm; *stem-leaves
narrowly lanceolate to linear*, entire-
margined, the upper ones sessile. *Flowers
drooping* (but erect in bud), in lax, few-
flowered panicles. Calyx has 5 linear,
spreading to deflexed teeth. Corolla bell-
shaped, 12–20 mm long, pale blue to
blue-violet (rarely white), with 5 short,
triangular lobes. Stamens 5. Ovary 3-
locular; stigma 3-lobed. Capsule
pendulous, opening through pores.

Flowering: June–October.

Habitat: Dry grasslands, banks, road verges, open
woods and scrub, on dry, oligotrophic to
mesotrophic, sandy, loamy or stony, acid
soils, from sea level to 2,200 m.

Range: All Europe.

Similar species: *C. gieseckiana* Vest., has suborbicular basal
leaves, few lanceolate stem-leaves, flowering
stems hardly exceeding 10 cm, only 1–3
drooping flowers, and erect calyx teeth.
Arctic tundra.
Arctic Bellflower (*Campanula uniflora* L.)
has a creeping rhizome and erect to
ascending, simple stems to 15 cm,
oblanceolate to linear-lanceolate, subsessile,
entire or finely crenate leaves (upper ones
often with some blunt teeth), and solitary,
terminal, drooping, deep-blue flowers to
8 mm diam.; fruit erect, elliptical, to
15 mm long, dark blue or blackish. In
grassy places on stony or rocky, calcareous
soils in the tundra zone of N Europe,
southwards to C Norway.

p.345 **Sheep's-bit** *Jasione montana* L.

Description: A tufted or spreading, hairy annual or
biennial (sometimes short-lived perennial)
herb with vertical roots and ascending to
erect flowering stems to 50 cm; no stolons.

Leaves alternate, to 50 mm long, entire-margined (sometimes wavy-rimmed), the lower ones narrowly obovate to oblanceolate, blunt-tipped, the upper ones shorter, lanceolate to linear, acute. *Flowers in dense, globular heads* (15–20 mm diam.), with appressed involucre of several ovate, entire-margined bracts, borne terminally on *long, leafless peduncles*. Calyx tiny, with ovoid tube and 5 persistent, lanceolate teeth. Corolla regular, 5–8 mm long, blue (rarely pink or white), *deeply incised* (almost to the base), with 5 linear lobes. Stamens 5, not protruding; anthers connate before flowers open. *Ovary 2-locular*, with long-protruding style and *2-lobed stigma*. Capsule small (*c.* 3 mm), globose to club-shaped, 5-angular, and *opening distally with 2 short valves*.

Flowering: May–August.

Habitat: Dry grasslands, heaths and sea-dunes, on sandy, stony or rocky, oligotrophic, predominantly acid soils, from sea level to 1,700 m, but especially frequent near the coast.

Range: C and S Europe, westwards to Ireland, northwards to S Scandinavia and the Finnish Gulf, eastwards to the Urals.

Similar species: *J. laevis* Lam. is perennial, with creeping rhizomes and stolons, non-flowering tufts of almost linear leaves, and dentate bracts under the blue flowerhead. In SW Europe northwards to NE France and S Germany, usually at higher elevations.

---

p.318 **Large Venus's-looking-glass**
Legousia speculum-veneris (L.) Chaix

Description: An annual herb with slender, branched, downy to stiff-hairy, often reddish, erect or ascending stems to 40 cm. Leaves alternate, more or less hairy, ovate to elliptical, predominantly sessile. Flowers in *lax panicles*. Calyx deeply incised with 5 *spreading, linear teeth* (not quite equalling the corolla), persistent on the fruit. Corolla 15–20 mm diam., with a short, white tube and 5 spreading, broadly ovate, deep-purple or violet lobes. Ovary 3-locular, narrowly ellipsoid; style rather short, with 3-lobed stigma. Capsule linear, 10–15 mm long, angular, opening with 3 slits.

Flowering: May–August.

Habitat: Cereal fields, open road verges and waste places, on moderately dry to moist, mesotrophic, loamy or clayey, calcareous soils, from sea level to 1,200 m.

Range: Continental W Europe northwards to the Netherlands and Germany, eastwards to Hungary, and southwards all round the Mediterranean Sea; from sea level to 1,600 m.

Similar species: **Venus's Looking-glass** (*L. hybrida* (L.) Delarbre) has much smaller flowers (5–10 mm diam., the corolla shorter than the more erect calyx teeth) in terminal clusters. In S and SW Europe, northwards to the Netherlands and S England, in cultivated places on calcareous soils.

Both species have become rare.

p.319 **Water Lobelia** *Lobelia dortmanna* L.

Description: A glabrous, tufted, perennial aquatic with stolons and *hollow, erect, emergent flowering stems*, with milky latex, to 70 cm. The plant can form submerged, non-flowering mats in clear water to a depth of 3 m. Leaves submerged, predominantly basal, linear, elliptical in cross-section, with *2 wide, longitudinal air channels*. Flowers in a lax, drooping raceme; bracts shorter than flower-stalks. Calyx obconical, with 5 subequal, triangular teeth, persistent on the fruit. *Corolla irregular*, 15–20 mm long, white or pale lilac, with an upturned, deeply 2-lobed upper lip, and a forward-protruding, 3-lobed lower lip; corolla tube cylindrical, *cleft to the base posteriorly*. Stamens 5, with connate, hairy anthers. Ovary hemi-inferior, 2-locular, with a 2-lobed stigma. Capsule many-seeded, narrowly ovoid, opening terminally with 2 slits.

Flowering: July–September.

Habitat: Acid, oligotrophic lakes and pools, often in heathland regions, on sandy or rocky soils, mainly in lowland areas.

Range: N and NW Europe, from N Russia to Scandinavia, the Baltic coasts, N Germany, the British Isles and W France.

Similar species: **Heath Lobelia** (*L. urens* L.) has solid stems with alternate, oblanceolate to linear, bluntly dentate leaves, and deep-purple or violet flowers to 15 mm long. In grasslands, heaths and open woods on wet, acid soils in France and S England.

Water Lobelia is strongly declining; in the Netherlands it is nearly extinct. Both species are poisonous.

---

p.345 **Round-headed Rampion**
Phyteuma orbiculare L.

Description: A glabrous or slightly hairy perennial with erect, unbranched stems to 40 cm. Basal leaves long-stalked, narrowly ovate with a rounded or cordate base, crenate; stem-leaves lanceolate, short-stalked to sessile, crenate. Flowers in *dense, subglobular heads* (10–25 mm diam.), and not elongated after anthesis; bracts under the head ovate to broadly lanceolate, bluntly dentate or entire-margined, shorter than the flowers. Calyx has 5 narrowly triangular, often 3-veined teeth. *Corolla at first tube-shaped, curved*, later splitting into 5 spreading, linear lobes, *blue or violet-blue*. Stamens 5. Ovary mostly 3-locular, with a protruding style; stigma usually 3-lobed. Fruit a globose capsule, opening with 3 pores.

Flowering: June–August.

Habitat: Dry to moist grasslands and scrub, on mesotrophic, mostly calcareous, stony soils, mainly in the mountains, to 2,600 m.

Range: S and C Europe, westwards to N Spain, NE France (with an isolated outpost in S England), northwards to C Germany and S Poland, and eastwards to Latvia and C Russia.

Similar species: *P. tenerum* R. Schultz has usually 2-locular
ovaries (and 2-lobed stigmas); calyx teeth
broadly triangular, always 1-veined; stem-
leaves sharply dentate, and grading into
lanceolate bracts under flowerhead. In SW
Europe, and northwards to NE France.

Several closely related species occur in the
Alps.

p.148 **Spiked Rampion** *Phyteuma spicatum* L.

Description: A glabrous perennial herb with erect,
unbranched, hollow stems to 80 cm. Basal
leaves bluntly serrate to crenate (often
doubly so), long-stalked, ovate with a
cordate base, often with dark blotches; stem
leaves short-stalked, broadly lanceolate
with a rounded base, crenate to serrate, the
highest ones much reduced, almost linear,
and sessile. Flowers in dense, *ovoid (finally
cylindrical) spikes* to 60 mm long, 20 mm
wide; spike-bases have a few linear, deflexed
bracts that are usually shorter than the
flowers. Calyx small, with 5 lanceolate to
linear teeth. *Corolla at first tube-shaped,
curved*, later *splitting from base* into 5 linear,
ultimately spreading lobes, *creamy yellow*
(or, especially in top flowers, tinged with
green or blue). Stamens 5, free, shorter than
the corolla, with widened bases. *Ovary 2-
locular*, with long-exserted style and *2-lobed
stigma*. Fruit a globose capsule, opening
with 2 pores near the middle.
Flowering: May–July.
Habitat: Moist to wet deciduous woods and
grasslands, often along streams, on
oligotrophic or mesotrophic, loamy, usually
acid soils, from near sea level to 2,100 m.
Range: W and C Europe, northwards to SE
England, the Netherlands, Denmark and
S Norway, eastwards to Estonia and
C Russia, and southwards to N Spain, Italy
and Albania.
Similar species: **Black Rampion** (*P. nigrum* F.W. Schmidt),
sometimes treated as a subspecies, has
(more often singly) serrate or crenate,
usually unblotched basal leaves, and

dark-violet (rarely pale-blue or whitish) flowers with a 3-locular ovary and a 3-lobed stigma. In continental W Europe, northwards to the Netherlands and Germany, in moist woods and meadows, often (but not exclusively) on calcareous soils, to 1,200 m.

Both species have become rare and are protected in most countries.

---

p.334 **Ivy-leaved Bellflower**
Wahlenbergia hederacea (L.) Reichenb.

Description: A delicate, glabrous perennial herb with *thread-like, branched, trailing or creeping stems*, to 15 cm high. *Leaves reniform*, 10–20 mm diam., pale green, with *broad, shallow lobes*, only vaguely reminiscent of Ivy leaves. *Flowers solitary* in leaf-axils, on long, ascending stalks. Calyx 3–4 mm long, with cup-shaped tube and 5 lanceolate teeth, persistent on the fruit. Corolla pale blue or lilac (rarely white), funnel-shaped, 6–10 mm long, with 5 triangular-ovate lobes. Stamens 5. Ovary 3-locular, with a 3-lobed stigma. Capsule globular, opening with 3 valves.

Flowering: June–August.

Habitat: Wet meadows, moist streambanks, and marshy heathlands, on acid, oligotrophic, sandy, rocky or peaty soils, to 1,000 m.

Range: W Europe, northwards to Scotland and the Ardennes in Belgium (extinct in the Netherlands), and eastwards to S Germany.

The species has severely declined.

HEMP FAMILY, CANNABACEAE

A small family of dioecious, aromatic herbs, with 2 genera and only 3 species – *Humulus* (2 winding species) and *Cannabis sativa* (Hemp) – in temperate regions of the northern hemisphere. Dicots. Leaves opposite (sometimes alternate), palmately veined. Flowers unisexual, the male ones regular, with a 5-parted perianth and 5 free stamens, the female ones with an undivided, cup-shaped perianth (or naked), a superior, 1-locular ovary, and a bifid style or stigma. Fruit a nutlet (achene). *C. sativa* has erect, non-climbing stems, and compound, palmate leaves with 5–7 (9) narrowly lanceolate, serrate leaflets; the plant was widely cultivated for its fibres, which were used in cloth and rope industry from prehistoric times up to the 19th century; the Asiatic form is still grown for marihuana and hashish. The nutlets were used as a narcotic as early as 2,600 BP, by the Scythians in S Russia.

p.82 **Hop** *Humulus lupulus* L.

Description: A climbing perennial herb to 6 m, with square, rough-hairy, (clockwise) *winding stems*. Leaves opposite, simple, long-stalked, *palmately divided* with 3–5 coarsely serrate or dentate lobes, the upper ones often shallowly lobed or not incised, then ovate with a cordate base. Male flowers 4–5 mm diam., stalked, in lax, axillary panicles, with 5 oblong, greenish tepals and 5 short-stalked anthers; female flowers greenish, sessile, hidden in *axillary, pendulous, ovoid, cone-like spikes* (the hops) to 30 mm long, borne singly or in small racemes, and composed of numerous green (later brownish, and papery), overlapping bracts strewn with shiny glands secreting a yellow, powdery resin. Ovary 1-locular, with 2 long, hairy stigmas. Achene globular or ovoid, enclosed in the persistent perianth.

Flowering: July–September.

Habitat: Deciduous woods, scrub and hedges, on moist to wet, mesotrophic to eutrophic, sandy or loamy soils, from sea level to 1,500 m.

Range: Most of Europe except Ireland and the extreme north; often as a relic of former cultivation, dating back to the 9th century.

The cone-like hops are traditionally used for flavouring beer; to this purpose the plant is still cultivated in some areas, especially in S Germany. The hops have soporific properties; insomniacs may profit from sleeping on a pillow flocked with them.

HONEYSUCKLE FAMILY, CAPRIFOLIACEAE

A family of trees, shrubs, climbers, and some herbs, with about 450 species in 18 genera in the northern hemisphere and also in the Andes. Dicots. Leaves simple or pinnate, opposite. Flowers regular or irregular, hermaphrodite, 5-merous. Stamens 4–5, alternating with the corolla lobes and inserted on the corolla tube. Ovary inferior, 2–5-locular, with 1 style. Fruit a berry or drupe, rarely a capsule. Well-known European trees and shrubs from this family include Elder (*Sambucus nigra* L.), Guelder Rose (*Viburnum opulus* L.) and Honeysuckle (*Lonicera periclymenum* L.). Several exotic species are kept in gardens, e.g. Snowberry (*Symphoricarpos albus* (L.) Blake), native to N America. In many cases, the plants in this family are more or less poisonous, especially the berries.

---

p.279 **Twin Flower** *Linnaea borealis* L.

Description: A tiny, mat-forming dwarf shrub with *thread-like, creeping, slightly woody stems*. Leaves simple, opposite, short-stalked, suborbicular to obovate, to 25 mm long, slightly leathery, coarsely crenate to shallowly lobed. *Flowers pendent and borne in pairs* on a common, ascending to erect, glandular-hairy, axillary stalk (to 15 cm), with 2 opposite leaves near stalk-base and a few tiny, opposite, lanceolate, persistent bracteoles under the flowers. Calyx 5-parted, glandular-hairy. Corolla pink on outside, violet-streaked inside, bell-shaped, 6–10 mm long, almost regular, with 5 rounded lobes. Stamens 4, of 2 different lengths, inserted on the corolla tube. Ovary inferior, 3-locular, with thread-like style and rounded stigma; only 1 locule is fertile. Fruit a rounded, glandular-hairy drupe with 1 seed and a leathery wall.

Flowering: May–August.

Habitat: Needle-leaf forests, mossy tundras and heaths, on moist, sandy or peaty, acid soils, to 2,200 m; rare in the lowland, more frequent in mountainous areas (especially to the south).

Range: In N Europe (except Iceland), from the Arctic southwards to Scotland, the Netherlands, E France, S Germany and S

Poland, and eastwards to N Russia and the Urals.

Carl von Linné chose this plant as his personal emblem; it often figures in his portraits.

---

p.153 **Dwarf Elder** *Sambucus ebulus* L.

Description: A tall, hairless *herb* to 2 m, with erect, grooved stems and creeping rhizomes. Whole plant emits foetid odour. Leaves opposite, *pinnate*, with 7–13 lanceolate, serrate leaflets and *2 conspicuous, ovate stipules* at the base. Flowers in erect, flat or domed, umbel-shaped panicles to 16 cm diam. Calyx small, with 5 teeth. Corolla regular, to 8 mm diam., white (often pinkish on outside), with short tube and 5 acute, ovate lobes. Stamens 5, exserted, with *brick-red anthers*. Ovary inferior, mostly 3-locular, with short style and 3-lobed stigma. Fruit a globose, shiny-black berry to 7 mm diam.

Flowering: June–August.

Habitat: Shaded verges, hedges, dikes along rivers, and wood margins, on moist, mesotrophic, calcareous soils, from sea level to 1,600 m.

Range: S, W and C Europe, northwards to the Netherlands and S Poland; naturalized in Britain, Denmark and S Sweden.

Also known as Danewort. The berries are poisonous. Other European *Sambucus* species are shrubs or even trees.

PINK FAMILY, CARYOPHYLLACEAE

A very large family of herbs and dwarf shrubs, with about 2,000 species in 80 genera, mainly in temperate regions. Dicots. Leaves simple, mostly opposite. Flowers in dichasial cymes, regular, usually hermaphrodite, basically 5-merous. Sepals 4–5, free or connate. An epicalyx is found in some genera (e.g. *Dianthus*). Petals 4–5, or absent. Stamens 1–10, often in 2 whorls. Ovary superior or hemi-inferior, 1-locular or incompletely 2–5-locular (with septums only at the base). Styles 1–5. Fruit a capsule or (rarely) a berry.

For easy recognition of some major genera with small white flowers, the following observations may be useful. In all *Arenaria* species the petals are ovate, with a blunt top. In *Stellaria* (with ovoid, mostly 6-toothed capsules) and *Cerastium* (with cylindrical, 10-toothed capsules) the petals are deeply notched or even bifid. Rounded petals are also characteristic of *Minuartia, Sagina, Scleranthus*, and the Spurreys (*Spergula, Spergularia*), but these genera have linear or even awl-shaped leaves, as do some *Moehringia* species (the rest of *Moehringia* having 3–5-veined, ovate leaves). *Corrigiola, Illecebrum* and *Herniaria* have whitish stipules (like the Spurreys), but oblanceolate to obovate leaves.

---

p.268 **Corncockle** *Agrostemma githago* L.

Description: A striking, annual, grey-silky herb to 1 m, with erect, terete stems and opposite, narrowly lanceolate to linear leaves. Flowers regular, *30–50 mm diam.*, long-stalked, *borne singly*. Calyx tube rough-hairy, 10-veined, with *5 linear teeth exceeding corolla*. Petals 5, rounded or slightly notched, purple or deep pink, with a whitish base (rarely all white), and some dark veins. Stamens 10. Ovary 1-locular, with 5 styles. Fruit a brownish, ovoid, many-seeded capsule, splitting with 5 short teeth.

Flowering: May–August.

Habitat: A weed of cornfields, also in waste places, on moist to dry, preferably loamy, mesotrophic, calcareous soils, from sea level to 2,000 m.

Range: All of Europe except the Arctic, but rare now in westerly and northerly regions; an archeophyte, native to the Mediterranean area.

The black seeds are poisonous; they used to cause illness when baked in bread. Being of similar size and weight to rye grains, they were difficult to remove from the sowing seed; improved seed-cleaning methods and the use of herbicides have almost exterminated the species now.

p.107 **Fringed Sandwort** *Arenaria ciliata* L.

Description: A low, perennial herb, to 10 cm, with thin, *rough stems*. Leaves opposite, elliptical to oblanceolate or spoon-shaped, *1-veined*, to 8 mm long, *ciliate at least at the base*; no stipules. Flowers terminal, regular, solitary or in small cymes, 12–16 mm diam. Sepals 5, ovate, *shorter than corolla*. Petals 5, elliptical, white. Stamens 10, with *white anthers*. Ovary 1-locular, with 3 styles. Fruit an ovoid capsule, splitting with 6 teeth.

Flowering: July–August.

Habitat: Meadows and trodden places, on moist, calcareous, rocky soils in the mountains; 1,000–3,200 m in C Europe.

Range: C Europe, Scandinavia; an isolated station in Ireland (Ben Bulben).

Similar species: *A. gothica* Fries, from Gotland, S Sweden and the French Jura, is annual or biennial, with slightly smaller flowers.
A. humifusa Wahlenb., from Spitsbergen and N Scandinavia, is perennial, hairless, and forms stolons; flowers small (to 6 mm diam.), with purple anthers.
Arctic Sandwort (*A. norvegica* Gunnerus) is a tufted, subglabrous perennial, with dark-green, somewhat fleshy leaves, flowers to 12 mm diam., and yellowish anthers. Local in W Scandinavia, Iceland, and N Britain.
Alpine Sandwort (*A. montana* L.) is a greyish, hairy perennial, to 30 cm, with narrowly lanceolate, finely pointed leaves to 16 mm long, very large flowers (16–24 mm across) in lax cymes. In SW Europe, extending northwards to Brittany; locally naturalized in Britain.

p.107 **Thyme-leaved Sandwort**
Arenaria serpyllifolia L.

Description: A small, prostrate or ascending, much-branched, rough-hairy, greyish annual or biennial, to 25 cm, with (sub)sessile, ovate to elliptical, pointed, *3–5-veined leaves* to 8 mm long. Flowers 5–8 mm diam., in lax cymes. *Sepals 3–4.5 mm long, much longer than petals*, lanceolate. Petals minute, elliptical, white. Stamens 10, with yellowish anthers. Ovary 1-locular, with 3 styles. Fruit a pear-shaped capsule, inflated at base, *splitting with 6 teeth that exceed sepals*.

Flowering: April–September.

Habitat: Open vegetation such as heaths, dunes, and arable fields, on dry to moist, oligotrophic to mesotrophic, sandy or loamy, preferably calcareous soils, from sea level to 3,200 m.

Range: All Europe except Iceland, N Fennoscandia and Spitsbergen.

Similar species: **Lesser Thyme-leaved Sandwort** (*A. leptoclados* (Reichenb.) Guss.), also treated as a subspecies, is more delicate, with sepals to 3 mm long, equalling the small, conical or cylindrical capsule. In S, W and C Europe northwards to Scotland and S Sweden, and eastwards through Germany, Czechia, and Romania to the Crimea.

Thyme-leaved Sandwort is a common, polymorphic species. Lesser Thyme-leaved Sandwort is less frequent.

p.107 **Field Mouse-ear** *Cerastium arvense* L.

Description: A slightly hairy, *perennial* herb with creeping stolons and ascending flowering stems to 25 cm. Leaves opposite, sessile, lanceolate, blunt-tipped. Flowers in lax dichasial cymes, *relatively large* (12–20 mm diam.), the opposing bracts with narrow, whitish, scarious margins. Sepals lanceolate, with long, straight hairs and scarious margins. Petals deeply notched, white, elegantly curved outwards, *much exceeding calyx*. Stamens 10, with yellow anthers. Ovary 1-locular, with 5 styles. Fruit a straw-coloured, cylindrical, slightly curved, many-seeded capsule, splitting with 10 minute teeth.

Flowering: April–August.

Habitat: Common in grasslands and open places, on dry to moist, sandy or loamy, oligotrophic to mesotrophic, basic or slightly acid soils, from sea level to 3,100 m.

Range: Europe northwards to Scotland, Denmark and the Baltic States; naturalized in Fennoscandia.

Similar species: **Alpine Mouse-ear** (*C. alpinum* L.) is densely grey-hairy (or even white-woolly with some glandular hairs in ssp. *lanatum* (Lam.) A. & G.), and has larger flowers (18–25 mm diam.). In Iceland, N Britain, Fennoscandia and N Russia; also in the Alps, Pyrenees, Carpathians and Balkanic mountains.

Arctic Mouse-ear (*C. arcticum* Lange) has short white hairs and still larger flowers (18–30 mm diam.), with shallowly notched petals and herbaceous bracts lacking white margins. In Iceland, Scandinavia, Spitsbergen and N Britain. A subspecies (*C. a. edmondstonii* (H.C. Watson) A. & D. Löve), with more rounded, purplish leaves, is endemic to the Shetland Isles (Unst).

C. regelii Ostenf. is cushion-forming, almost hairless (except leaf-margins), with underground stolons producing deciduous buds. On tundra of Spitsbergen and N Russia.

Starwort Mouse-ear (*C. cerastoides* (L.) Britton), from (sub-)Arctic Europe (incl. Scotland), the Alps and Pyrenees, and the Balkan Peninsula, has only 3 styles and 6 capsule teeth.

C. dubium (Bast.) O. Schwarz, also has only 3 styles and 6 capsule teeth, but is annual, with glandular, sticky stems. From SE and C Europe westwards to W France and C Germany.

Dusty Miller (*C. tomentosum* L.) is densely hairy, with inrolled leaf-margins and spreading capsule teeth. From S Europe, but occasional garden escape in W Europe.

C. biebersteinii DC., from the Crimea, differs from *C. tomentosum* mainly in having flat leaf-margins and erect capsule-teeth.

In all these species the petals are at least 1.5 times longer than the sepals; in the following *Cerastium* species, petals are equal or only slightly longer.

p.106 **Common Mouse-ear**
Cerastium fontanum Baumg.

Description: A more or less hairy, perennial herb, with short, basal or axillary *vegetative shoots* and ascending, flowering stems to 30 (50) cm. Leaves opposite, lanceolate, sessile. Flowers in lax dichasial cymes, 6–10 mm diam.; the bracts usually have white, scarious margins. Sepals 5, lanceolate, 3–5 (9) mm long, with narrow scarious margins. *Petals equal to or slightly longer than sepals*, white, deeply notched. Stamens (usually) 10, with yellow anthers. Ovary 1-locular, with 5 styles. Capsule cylindrical, distinctly curved, straw-coloured, with 10 erect teeth.

Flowering: April–November.

Habitat: Grasslands, road verges and other grassy places, and also brackish environments, on moist, more or less eutrophic, usually basic soils, to 2,600 m, but predominantly in the lowland.

Range: All of Europe except Spitsbergen.

A very common, polymorphic species, with several, often weakly defined subspecies and varieties.

p.149 **Sticky Mouse-ear**
Cerastium glomeratum Thuill.

Description: A *yellowish-green*, prostrate to erect, *glandular-hairy annual* with stems to 40 cm. Leaves opposite, ovate to lanceolate or elliptical. Flowers 5–8 mm diam., *subsessile, in compact cymes* immediately subtended by a ruff of ovate, *herbaceous bracts* lacking white, scarious margins, and ciliate to the top. Sepals 5, lanceolate, with scarious margins. Petals 5, shallowly notched, equalling the sepals, white. Stamens (usually) 10. Ovary 1-locular, with 5 styles. *Capsule short-stalked* (stalk not exceeding calyx, *never deflexed*), almost straight, cylindrical, opening with 10 fine teeth.

Flowering: April–October, sometimes even in winter.

Habitat: Open grasslands, road verges, fallow fields, and gardens, on dry to moist, eutrophic, mineral or peaty soils, from sea level to 1,500 m.

Range: S and W Europe, northwards to Iceland and C Fennoscandia, and eastwards to C and S Russia.

Similar species: **Grey Mouse-ear** (*C. brachypetalum* Pers.) is grey-hairy, with less obviously clustered flowers; fruit-stalks 2–4 times longer than calyx. From S, W and C Europe northwards to S Sweden, and eastwards to Lithuania, the Carpathians and the Crimea.

Little Mouse-ear
Cerastium semidecandrum L.

Description: A glandular-hairy annual to 15 cm, with ascending to erect stems. Leaves opposite, subsessile, ovate, the lower ones oblanceolate. Flowers in rather lax dichasial cymes, often *deflexed after anthesis*, 5–8 mm diam. *All bracts have white, scarious margins*, even the lowest pair. Sepals 5, lanceolate, with scarious margins. Petals 5, white, *shorter than sepals*, shallowly notched or with some irregular teeth. *Stamens 5*. Ovary 1-locular, with 5 styles. Fruit a cylindrical, slightly curved, straw-coloured or whitish capsule, opening with 10 fine teeth.

Flowering: March–June.

Habitat: Open vegetation, on dry, sandy, oligotrophic to mesotrophic, slightly acid to basic soils, from sea level to 1,300 m.

Range: All Europe except Iceland, the Faeroes, N Fennoscandia, N Russia, and Spitsbergen.

Similar species: *C. s. macilentum* (Aspregen) Moschl. is a hairless subspecies in S Sweden.

Dwarf Mouse-ear (*C. pumilum* Curtis) has erect fruit-stalks; the lowest pair of bracts is wholly herbaceous, the higher bracts have very narrow white margins. In all Europe except the far north, but rather scarce in the west. Forms with 6–10 stamens and pale-green leaves are attributed to ssp. *pallens* (F.W. Schultz) Schinz & Thell.

Sea Mouse-ear (*C. diffusum* Pers.) also has erect fruit-stalks, but all bracts are herbaceous, and some flowers are 4-merous. In dry, grassy places (e.g. sea-dunes), mainly in coastal regions of W Europe, from Portugal to S Scandinavia, also more inland in the British Isles and NW Spain.

In all these species the petals are distinctly shorter than the sepals.

---

p.149 **Strapwort** *Corrigiola litoralis* L.

Description: A small, glabrous, annual herb with thin, often reddish, spreading to ascending stems to 30 cm. *Leaves alternate*, subsessile, *bluntly oblanceolate* to almost linear, grey-green, with whitish, pointed, *membranous stipules* at their base. Flowers very small (to 2 mm diam.), in dense, terminal cymes. Sepals 5, free, bluntly ovate or rounded, green or reddish with a white margin. Petals 5, rounded, much *smaller than sepals*, white or pink, soon falling. Stamens 5. Ovary 1-locular, with 1 very short style and 3 stigmas. Fruit a triangular, 1-seeded, achene-like capsule, surrounded by the persistent calyx.

Flowering: June–October.

Habitat: Open, often trodden, vegetation, on moist to dry (but seasonally wet), mesotrophic, sandy or gravelly soils, mainly in the lowlands.

Range: Continental W Europe, northwards to Denmark and eastwards to W Poland; very rare in Britain (Devon).

---

p.122 **Berry Catchfly** *Cucubalus baccifer* L.

Description: A short-hairy perennial herb with widely branched, weak and often straggling stems to 1 m. Leaves short-stalked, ovate, acute or pointed, green or blue-green. Flowers drooping, to 18 mm diam., in lax, leafy cymes. *Calyx connate, inflated*, bell-shaped, *10-veined*, yellowish-green, with 5 triangular teeth. Petals 5, oblanceolate to strap-shaped, *deeply notched* at the top, *greenish-white*, with scales at throat. Stamens 10, protruding. Ovary incompletely 3-locular (only at the base), with 3 styles. Fruit a rounded, *shiny-black berry* to 8 mm diam.

Flowering: July–September.
Habitat: Woods, scrub and hedges, on moist to wet, eutrophic soils, mainly in river valleys.
Range: In continental Europe, northwards to the Baltic Sea and eastwards to C Russia.

p.289 **Deptford Pink** *Dianthus armeria* L.

Description: A *densely hairy* annual or biennial herb with ascending or erect stems to 50 cm. Leaves opposite, *dark green*, linear, 1–3 mm wide, connate at their base (forming a sheath of at most 5 mm long). Flowers 8–15 mm diam., *in more or less flattened, terminal clusters surrounded by green, hairy bracts*. Calyx tube-shaped, with 5 short, triangular teeth, and epicalyx of crosswise opposite, lanceolate, green scales equalling calyx. Petals 5, with long, whitish claw and ovate, toothed, deep-pink to red-purple limb (to 6 mm) with *numerous white dots*. Stamens 10. Ovary 1-locular, with 2 styles. Fruit a cylindrical capsule, splitting with 4 teeth.
Flowering: June–August.
Habitat: Open, grassy vegetation, on dry, mesotrophic, sandy or rocky (calcareous) soils, from sea level to 1,250 m.
Range: S, W and C Europe, northwards to England, Denmark and S Sweden, and eastwards to WC Russia.
Similar species: **Carthusian Pink** (*D. carthusianorum* L.) is hairless, biennial or perennial, with leaf-sheaths up to 20 mm long, and brownish, abruptly narrowed epicalyx scales shorter than calyx. In C Europe, westwards to NE Spain, C France, and the Ardennes, and northwards to the Baltic Sea.
Sweet William (*D. barbatus* L.) is a well-known garden ornamental with broad, umbel-shaped inflorescences. Native to mountains of S Europe; naturalized in C Europe and W and C Russia.

p.270 **Maiden Pink** *Dianthus deltoides* L.

Description: A perennial herb with ascending, short-rough-hairy stems to 40 cm. Leaves opposite, linear, blunt-tipped. Flowers 14–20 mm diam., long-stalked, borne singly or in lax, few-flowered cymes. Calyx tube-shaped, with 5 short teeth, and epicalyx of 4 lanceolate, pointed, hairy scales much shorter than calyx. Petals 5, with long, whitish claw; limb rounded, toothed, purplish, with *numerous white spots and dark band* (rarely plain white), *bearded at throat*. Stamens 10. Ovary 1-locular, with 2 styles. Fruit a cylindrical capsule, splitting with 4 teeth.

Flowering: June–September.

Habitat: Grasslands, road verges, and grassy banks, on dry, sandy or rocky, oligotrophic, preferably acid soils, from sea level to 2,000 m.

Range: Most of Europe except Ireland, Iceland, Arctic Fennoscandia and N Russia; rare in the south.

---

p.270 **Jersey Pink** *Dianthus gallicus* Pers.

Description: A *downy* perennial, forming lax tufts, with ascending or erect flowering stems to 30 cm. Leaves opposite, short (to 20 mm), linear, *greyish or blue-green*, rather stiff, blunt-tipped. Flowers 20–30 mm diam., solitary or 2–3 together. Calyx tube-shaped, 5-toothed, with short epicalyx of *narrowly ovate, long-pointed scales*. *Petals plain pink or pale violet* (occasionally white), deeply toothed (incisions to a third of the limb length), *not bearded at throat*. Stamens 10. Ovary 1-locular, with 2 styles. Fruit a cylindrical capsule, splitting with 4 teeth.

Flowering: June–August.

Habitat: In dry, grassy places in coastal sand-dunes.

Range: Along the Atlantic coast of N Spain and W France; also on Jersey.

Similar species: **Common Pink** (*D. plumarius* L.) has very acute, rough-edged leaves to 40 mm long, and plain-pink or white flowers (also deeply incised) to 35 mm diam. From SE Europe; locally naturalized in grassy verges and banks, on dry, calcareous soils and old walls.

Clove Pink (*D. caryophyllus* L.), ancestor to the garden carnation, has plain, pink or white flowers to 35 mm diam., bearded petals with short teeth (incised to less than 1 sixth of the limb length), short, ovate (not long-pointed) epicalyx scales, and smooth-edged leaves. From S Europe, locally naturalized in W Europe.

Cheddar Pink (*D. gratianopolitanus* Vill.) has rough-edged leaves to 60 mm long, plain-pink flowers, to 30 mm diam., with bearded, short-toothed petals, and short, ovate epicalyx scales. On dry and sunny, rocky soils in mountainous areas of C Europe, westwards to E France, and northwards to Belgium, C Germany and C Poland; also in SW Britain (Cheddar Gorge).

All 3 of the similar species are hairless.

---

p.270 **Large Pink** *Dianthus superbus* L.

Description: A rather stout, hairless, branched perennial with erect or ascending stems to 60 cm. *Leaves green*, opposite, linear, 3-veined, 5–10 mm wide, acute (the lower ones often narrowly lanceolate and blunt-tipped). Flowers large (30–50 mm diam.), in lax cymes. Calyx tube-shaped, with 5 teeth; epicalyx scales narrowly ovate, long-pointed, reaching to a third of the calyx length. *Petals deeply fringed* (more than halfway incised), with linear, forked segments; *pink, with a patch of greenish spots* at the throat. Stamens 10. Ovary 1-locular, with 2 styles. Fruit a spindle-shaped capsule, splitting with 4 teeth.

Flowering: June–September.

Habitat: Shaded grasslands, scrub and open woods, on dry to moist, oligotrophic to mesotrophic, acid, sandy, loamy or rocky soils, from sea level to 2,400 m.

Range: E and C Europe, westwards to France (Massif Central, Pyrenees), Germany and Denmark, and northwards to S Sweden, N Finland and the Baltic States.

Similar species: Ssp. *speciosus* (Reichenb.) Pawl. has greyish-green leaves; flowers have brown dots at throat. C European mountains.

D. arenarius L. has white, often pink-margined, fringed flowers to 30 mm diam., and narrower leaves. In open, grassy places of NE Europe, from C Russia westwards to S Sweden and E Germany, and southwards to Hungary and N Romania.

In C and S Russia numerous other *Dianthus* species can be found (*see* regional floras).

---

p.284   **Annual Gypsophila** *Gypsophila muralis* L.

Description: A slightly hairy, more or less erect, *annual* herb to 30 cm high. Leaves opposite, linear, to 25 mm long, greyish-green. Flowers numerous, small (to 4 mm diam.), in *much-branched, lax inflorescences*. Calyx bell-shaped, 5-veined, 5-toothed, *with membranous seams* between the connate sepals. Petals clawed, the limb obovate, often notched, pink or white, with purple veins. Stamens 10. Ovary 1-locular, with 2 styles. Fruit a small, ovoid capsule, splitting with 4 teeth.

Flowering: June–October.

Habitat: Banks of pools, lakes and rivers, humid fields, and along paths in woods, on moist to wet, mesotrophic, sandy or clayey soils, from sea level to 1,500 m.

Range: C and E Europe, extending westwards to France, Belgium and the E Netherlands, and northwards to S Sweden and S Finland.

Similar species: **Fastigiate Gypsophila** (*G. fastigiata* L.) is a much larger plant (to 1 m), glandular-hairy above, with linear leaves to 80 mm long, white or pale-pink flowers (to 8 mm diam.) in dense, umbel-shaped cymes. In NE Europe, from Baltic States westwards to Germany and SE Sweden, and southwards to W Russia and Hungary.
G. paniculata L. is hairless, with narrowly lanceolate leaves, and lax cymes of white or pink flowers (2–4 mm diam.) with oblong, rounded petals. From C and S Russia westwards to E Poland, Czechia and Hungary, and southwards to Bulgaria; frequently cultivated in gardens, and locally naturalized in Germany and W Poland.

Alpine Gypsophila (*G. repens* L.) is prostrate, hairless, with lax cymes of pink or white flowers (8–10 mm diam.); petals slightly notched. Mountains of C Europe.

These 3 similar species are perennial. In Russia, some more *Gypsophila* species can be found (*see* regional floras).

---

p.49 **Smooth Rupturewort** *Herniaria glabra* L.

Description: A low, prostrate, *hairless or slightly hairy* annual or short-lived perennial herb, with creeping stems to 20 cm long. Leaves *turned flat to the ground*, opposite to *apparently alternate* (the members of each pair very unequal), narrowly obovate to elliptical, to 10 mm long, glabrous or weakly ciliate at the margin, often noticeably *yellowish-green*, with small, rounded, *membranous stipules*. Flowers minute (1–2 mm diam.), in *small, dense, axillary clusters*. Sepals 5, connate only at base, greenish, glabrous or sparingly ciliate. Petals 5, *threadlike*, whitish, hardly visible. Stamens 5. Ovary 1-locular, with short, bifid style. Fruit a tiny, ovoid, 1-seeded capsule.

Flowering: May–September.

Habitat: Open vegetation, also along rivers, railway yards in and along gravelled roads, on dry to moist, oligotrophic, sandy or gravelly soils, from sea level to 2,000 m.

Range: Europe northwards to E England, C Sweden, the Baltic States, and C Russia.

Similar species: **Ciliate Rupturewort** (*H. ciliolata* Melderis) is a low, dark-green, perennial herb with woody stem-base, large stipules, fleshy leaves, and sepals with markedly hairy margins; stem hairy along 1 side. In open, sandy or rocky places along coasts of Iberia, W France, the Channel Isles and SW Britain (Lizard Point).
Hairy Rupturewort (*H. hirsuta* L.) is annual; stems, leaves and sepals grey-hairy all over. On coasts, and inland, on sandy or rocky soils to 1,500 m, in W, C and SE Europe.

p.148   **Umbellate Chickweed**
Holosteum umbellatum L.

Description: An annual, with erect flowering stems to
25 cm, often glandular-hairy. Leaves
opposite, sessile, lanceolate or elliptical,
greyish or blue-green, glabrous, or
glandular-hairy at margins only; flowering
stems have 2–3 pairs of leaves. Flowers
7–10 mm diam., *5–10 together in an umbel*
with 2 small bracts; flower-stalks of unequal
length, deflexed for some time after anthesis.
Sepals 5, lanceolate, free. Petals twice as long
as sepals, finely toothed, white or pale pink.
Stamens 3–5 (rarely 10). Ovary 1-locular,
usually with 3 styles. Fruit a many-seeded,
spindle-shaped, yellowish capsule to 10 mm
long, opening with 6 recurved teeth.

Flowering: March–May.

Habitat: Open grasslands, cereal fields and disturbed
places, on dry, oligotrophic, slightly acid,
sandy soils, and also on walls and roofs,
from sea level to 2,000 m; mainly at low
altitudes in the north.

Range: Continental Europe, northwards to the
Netherlands, Denmark and S Sweden, and
eastwards through Poland to C Russia.

A strongly declining species.

p.96   **Sea Sandwort** *Honkenya peploides* (L.) Ehrh.

Description: A prostrate perennial herb with
quadrangular stems and ascending branches
to 30 cm, but usually much lower. *Leaves
crosswise opposite, stiff and fleshy*, subsessile, to
20 mm long, glabrous, narrowly ovate,
subacute, yellowish-green or glaucous.
Flowers 6–10 mm diam., *partly unisexual*,
stalked, in few-flowered, leafy cymes (or
apparently solitary in leaf-axils). Sepals 5,
ovate, free. Petals 5, white, spoon-shaped,
alternating with, and slightly shorter than,
sepals. Stamens 5, alternating with petals.
Ovary 1-locular, with 3 styles. Fruit an
ovoid to spherical, greenish to brownish
capsule to 12 mm, splitting with 3 valves.

Flowering: May–August.

Habitat:	Coastal beaches and young dunes, often on floodmarks, on sandy or gravelly, brackish to saline soils; very tolerant of salt-spray.
Range:	Atlantic coasts of Europe, northwards to N Russia, and around the Baltic Sea.

p.111 **Coral Necklace** *Illecebrum verticillatum* L.

Description:	A hairless annual with prostrate, threadlike, reddish stems to 20 cm long. Leaves opposite, to 10 mm long, obovate with rounded top, sessile, green; *stipules small, membranous*. Flowers to 2 mm diam., *crowded in the leaf-axils*, forming *verticillasters*, and surrounded by small, *silvery, membranous bracts*. Sepals 5, free, *white*, ovate, *hooded, awned, swollen and spongy after anthesis*. Petals 5, threadlike, alternating with sepals, hardly visible. Stamens 5, much shorter than sepals. Ovary 1-locular, with 1 reduced style and a simple or bifid stigma. Fruit an ovoid, pointed, 1-seeded, achene-like capsule, surrounded by the persistent sepals.
Flowering:	June–October.
Habitat:	Seasonally wet places in fields, along paths and at pool margins, on moist, oligotrophic, acid, sandy soils, from sea level to 1,200 m.
Range:	Mainly in W and SW Europe, northwards to S Britain and Denmark, and eastwards to Poland.

Submerged forms can attain a length of 60 cm.

p.269 **Ragged Robin** *Lychnis flos-cuculi* L.

Description:	A rough-hairy perennial to 90 cm, with erect, branched, often reddish stems. Leaves opposite; basal ones spoon-shaped to oblanceolate, narrowed into a stalk, upper ones lanceolate to almost linear, sessile. Flowers 30–40 mm diam., in rather lax cymes. Calyx cylindrical to ovoid, glabrous or ciliate, *purple-tinged, with 10 dark veins* and 5 short, triangular teeth. Petals 5, clawed, *the limb dissected into 4 linear*

segments, pink (rarely white), and bearing 2 bifid scales at throat. Stamens 10. Ovary 1-locular, with 5 styles. Fruit an ovoid, brownish, many-seeded capsule to 15 mm long, splitting with 5 recurving teeth.

Flowering: May–August.

Habitat: Meadows, marshes, damp woods, and ditches, on wet to moist, mesotrophic, peaty or mineral soils, from sea level to 2,500 m.

Range: All of Europe except Spitsbergen; rare in the Mediterranean.

---

p.269 **Sticky Catchfly** *Lychnis viscaria* L.

Description: A tufted, glabrous or slightly hairy perennial to 60 cm; flowering stems erect, simple, with distinctive, purplish, *sticky-glandular rings under the nodes*. Basal leaves lanceolate to almost linear, narrowed into a stalk; stem-leaves few, opposite, linear and sessile, *with purplish bases*. Flowers 18–22 mm diam., in dense cymes contracted into *2–4 superimposed verticillasters*. Calyx trumpet-shaped, 10-veined, with 5 short, triangular teeth. Petals 5, clawed; *limb obovate, often shallowly notched*, deep pink (rarely white), bearing 2 notched scales at throat. Stamens 10. Ovary imperfectly 5-locular, with partitions only at base. Fruit an ovoid, brownish, many-seeded capsule, *stalked inside calyx* and bulging over calyx rim, splitting with 5 recurving teeth.

Flowering: May–August.

Habitat: Grassy places, on dry, oligotrophic, preferably acid, sandy or rocky soils, in mountainous areas, 300–1,800 m.

Range: C and E Europe, northwards to C Scandinavia and S Finland, westwards to Belgium and SE France (and isolated in Wales and Scotland). Often cultivated in gardens.

Similar species: **Alpine Catchfly** (*L. alpina* L.) lacks sticky rings under nodes, and has deeply notched to bifid petals; a typical boreo-alpine species. In Iceland, Fennoscandia, N Russia, a few places in N Britain, and (at high elevations, over 2,000 m) in the Alps and Pyrenees.

Sandworts, *Minuartia* L.

A complicated genus with numerous, closely related species, all characterized by having 3 styles (not 4–5, as in *Sagina*), rounded (never notched or bifid) petals, and linear to awl-shaped, 1–3-veined leaves.

---

p.110 **Fine-leaved Sandwort**
Minuartia hybrida (Vill.) Schischkin

Description: A delicate, *loosely branched annual* with thin, ascending, glabrous or slightly glandular-hairy flowering stems to 25 cm; *lacks sterile shoots*. Leaves linear to awl-shaped, to 15 mm long, 3-veined near base. Flowers to 6 mm diam., on thin stalks much longer than calyx, in lax cymes. Sepals 5, free, lanceolate, short-awned, green, with *narrow, white, scarious margins*. Petals 5, narrowly ovate, rounded, distinctly *shorter than sepals*, white. Stamens 10. Ovary 1-locular, with 3 styles. Fruit an ovoid, yellowish-brown capsule to 5 mm long, splitting with 3 valves.

Flowering: May–September.

Habitat: Open grasslands and cereal fields, on dry, calcareous, sandy, loamy or stony soils, and also on walls, from sea level to 2,000 m.

Range: S and W Europe northwards to N England (very rare in Ireland), the Netherlands (just), and Germany; absent from C Europe, but occurs in S Russia.

Similar species: **Sticky Sandwort** (*M. viscosa* (Schreber) Schinz & Thell.) is also annual, always stickily glandular, with stems branched up from middle; flowers smaller (3–4 mm diam.); capsule does not exceed sepals. In dry, sandy places, in C Europe from Denmark and S Sweden southwards through Germany to E France, and eastwards to Poland and S Russia.
M. rubra (Scop.) McNeill is biennial, glabrous or slightly hairy; flowers, up to 8 mm diam., on stalks about equalling the 1-veined sepals.
M. mediterranea (Link) K. Maly is annual, and has comparably short flower-stalks, and 3-veined sepals. Mainly Mediterranean; also found in W France (Normandy).

M. setacea (Thuill.) Hayek, a perennial, forms dense tufts (containing sterile shoots); flowers to 5 mm diam., with petals slightly longer than sepals; leaves rough, erect, bristle-like. In SE and C Europe, westwards to C France.

p.110 **Teesdale Sandwort**
Minuartia stricta (Swartz) Hiern

Description: A low, *hairless perennial* with tufts of sterile shoots bearing awl-shaped, *1-veined leaves*, and ascending flowering stems to 10 cm. Flowers 7–8 mm diam., *very long-stalked*, terminal, *mostly in 3-flowered cymes* (or solitary). Sepals free, lanceolate, all green *without white margins*, short-awned. Petals slightly shorter than sepals, narrowly obovate, rounded, white. Stamens 10, with *yellow anthers*. Ovary 1-locular, with 3 styles. Fruit an ovoid capsule exceeding calyx, splitting with 3 valves.

Flowering: June–August.

Habitat: Tundra, mountain grassland, flushes, and on screes, on wet, peaty or rocky soils, from sea level to 1,800 m.

Range: A boreo-Alpine species, occurring in Iceland, the mountains of Scandinavia, in N Britain (Teesdale), and in the Jura mountains (very rare over 800 m) and S Germany.

Similar species: *M. rossii* (R. Br.) Graebner, from Spitsbergen, Greenland and Arctic N America, has vegetative shoots in upper leaf-axils of the (prostrate) flowering stems.
M. biflora (L.) Schinz & Thell. has strap-like, blunt leaves; flowers larger (7–12 mm diam.), white or pale lilac, often borne singly or in pairs. In Iceland, Scandinavia, Spitsbergen, N Russia. and the Alps.

These 2 similar species are perennial as well.

p.111 **Spring Sandwort**
Minuartia verna (L.) Hiern

Description: A tufted, often slightly glandular-hairy perennial, with sterile shoots and erect flowering stalks to 15 cm. Leaves linear,

3-veined, stiff, flat above and rounded or keeled beneath, pointed. Flowers 6–8 mm diam., in few-flowered cymes (often 3 together). Sepals to 3 mm long, 3-veined, narrowly ovate. Petals slightly longer than sepals, rounded, white. Stamens 10, with *purplish anthers*. Ovary 1-locular, with 3 styles. Fruit an ovoid capsule hardly exceeding calyx, and opening with 3 valves.

Flowering: May–September.

Habitat: Grassy places on dry, calcareous, rocky soils, and also on zinc-bearing mine-spoil heaps near lead workings, from sea level (in the north) to 3,200 m (in the Alps).

Range: C and S Europe, westwards to Belgium, C France and the Pyrenees; also in the mountains of Britain and Ireland, N Russia, and the Caucasus.

Similar species: **Mountain Sandwort** (*M. rubella* (Wahlenb.) Hiern) has petals shorter than sepals, and 1–2-flowered cymes. In Iceland, the Faeroes, Scotland (Perthshire), and the mountains of Scandinavia and N Russia.

Compare also with *Sagina nodosa* (*see* p.421), which has petals at least twice as long as sepals, and yellow anthers.

p.111 **Three-veined Sandwort**
Moehringia trinervia (L.) Clairv.

Description: A prostrate or straggling annual, with weak, trailing or ascending stems to 40 cm; *stems hairy all round*. Leaves opposite, subsessile (the lower ones stalked), ovate, acute, *conspicuously 3–5-veined, ciliate*. Flowers 4–7 mm diam., long-stalked, solitary in leaf-axils or in few-flowered, terminal cymes. Sepals 5, free, broadly lanceolate, 3-veined, with whitish margins, *ciliate*. Petals 5, obovate, rounded, *much shorter than sepals*, white. Stamens usually 10. Ovary 1-locular, with 3 styles. Fruit a rounded capsule, much shorter than calyx, and opening with 6 recurved teeth.

Flowering: April–July (September).

Habitat: In shaded scrub and deciduous woods, on dry, oligotrophic or mesotrophic, slightly acid to basic soils, usually on thick humus, from sea level to 1,800 m.

Range: All Europe except the Arctic, but only on mountains in the south.

Similars species: *M. lateriflora* (L.) Fenzl is perennial, with narrowly ovate, 1–3-veined leaves, and petals exceeding the hairless sepals. Near water, in damp woods and other shaded places, in N Finland and N and C Russia.

---

p.111 **Upright Chickweed**
Moenchia erecta (L.) Gaertner, Meyer & Scherb.

Description: A bluish-green, hairless annual, with erect flowering stems to 10 cm. Leaves stiff, narrowly lanceolate to linear, pointed. Flowers 7–8 mm diam., long-stalked, solitary or 2–3 (4) together in terminal cyme. *Sepals 4*, free, broadly lanceolate, *white-margined. Petals 4*, elliptical, with rounded or weakly truncate tops (*never notched*), shorter than sepals, white. *Stamens 4*. Ovary 1-locular, with 4 (rarely 5) styles. Fruit a yellowish, many-seeded, cylindrical capsule to 7 mm long, opening with 8 (rarely 10) teeth.

Flowering: April–June.

Habitat: Open, grassy vegetation, on dry, oligotrophic, sandy, gravelly or loamy soils, from sea level to 1,000 m.

Range: SW and W Europe, northwards to S Britain, Belgium and C Germany, eastwards to W Poland; also in Bulgaria and Greece.

---

p.289 **Proliferous Pink**
Petrorhagia prolifera (L.) P.W. Ball & Heywood

Description: A hairless annual with stiff, simple (rarely branched), erect or ascending stems to 50 cm. Leaves opposite, very narrowly lanceolate to linear, sessile with a short sheath (about as long as wide), to 40 mm long, 3-veined, rough-edged, greyish-green. Flowers 6–8 mm diam., 2–6 together in *compact, spindle-shaped to ovoid flowerheads*, completely surrounded by *brownish, bluntly ovate, papery bracts*. Calyx tube-shaped,

10–13 mm long, with 5 short teeth, and with 5 veins separated by membranous bands. Petals 5, clawed, the limb obovate, shallowly notched, *pale pink without darker veins*; scaleless at throat. Stamens 10, enclosed. Ovary incompletely 4-locular, with 2 short styles. Fruit a club-shaped, dark-brown capsule, splitting with 4 valves.

Flowering: May–August (October).

Habitat: Open, grassy places, on dry, preferably calcareous, sandy or rocky soils, and also on old walls, from sea level to 1,200 m.

Range: Continental Europe, from NE Spain north to the Netherlands, Denmark and S Sweden, and eastwards through Poland to C and S Russia; only on mountains in the south.

Similar species: **Childing Pink** (*P. nanteulii* (Burnat) P.W. Ball & Heywood) has leaf-sheaths twice as long as wide, and stems hairy in the middle. On sandy or gravelly soils, often near the coast, in SW Europe; isolated in W France (Normandy) and S England.

---

p.269 **Tunic Flower** *Petrorhagia saxifraga* (L.) Link

Description: A delicate, hairless, mat-forming perennial, with prostrate stems and ascending flowering branches to 30 cm. Leaves linear (almost threadlike), rough-edged, pointed. Flowers solitary, long-stalked, 5–6 mm diam., with epicalyx of *2–4 short, whitish, papery bracts*. Calyx trumpet-shaped, with 5 short teeth, and membranous bands between the 5 veins. Petals 5, with short claw and shallowly notched, obovate limb, *pale pink with purplish veins*; scaleless at throat. Stamens 10. Ovary incompletely 4-locular, with 2 styles. Fruit a broadly club-shaped capsule, splitting with 4 valves.

Flowering: June–August.

Habitat: Open, grassy places and fields, on dry, siliceous or calcareous, sandy, gravelly or rocky soils, and also on walls, from sea level to 1,300 m.

Range: Mainly in S and C Europe, extending northwards to E France and S Germany; naturalized in Britain, Poland and S Sweden.

p.121 Four-leaved Allseed
Polycarpon tetraphyllum (L.) L.

Description: A glabrous annual herb with spreading to erect, often reddish stems to 15 cm. Leaves subsessile, obovate to elliptical, to 10 mm long, the lower ones opposite and short-stalked, the higher ones subsessile and *apparently in whorls of 4; stipules present*, membranous, silvery. Flowers 3–4 mm diam., long-stalked, in rather lax, *repeatedly branched panicle*; bracts in the inflorescence minute, membranous. Sepals 5, free, broadly lanceolate, keeled, white-margined. Petals 5, obovate, much smaller than sepals, white. Stamens 3–5. Ovary 1-locular, with 1 style and 3 stigmas. Fruit an ovoid capsule with a papery wall, splitting with 3 valves.

Flowering: May–August.

Habitat: Bare ground or open vegetation, sand-dunes, and fields, on dry, sandy or rocky soils, and also on walls and between paving bricks, from sea level to 400 m, predominantly inland.

Range: Mainly Mediterranean, extending northwards through W France to the Channel Islands and SW Britain; also locally in SC Europe.

Similar species: *P. alsinifolium* DC., also primarily Mediterranean, has broader, mostly opposite, fleshy leaves, and slightly larger flowers with 5 stamens. In sandy, saline habitats along coast of W France (to Normandy).

---

p.49 Annual Pearlwort *Sagina apetala* Ard.

Description: A delicate, sparsely branched *annual*, with erect to ascending, threadlike stems to 10 cm; *no sterile shoots*. Leaves all cauline, opposite (not in bundles), linear, tapering into a fine awl, glabrous, or ciliate near base only. Flowers solitary, terminal, in upper leaf-axils, 2–4 mm diam.; flower-stalks long, glabrous or glandular. *Sepals 4*, free, ovate, to 2 mm long, *pale green*, glandular or glabrous, *spreading on the fruit*. Petals 4, *much shorter than sepals*, obovate, notched, soon falling. Stamens 4. Ovary 1-locular, with 4 styles.

Fruit an ovoid, yellowish capsule to 3 mm, splitting with 4 valves.

Flowering: April–August.

Habitat: Open, grassy vegetation, bare ground, sea-dunes, fields, and along paths, on dry, mesotrophic, acid to calcareous, sandy, loamy or rocky soils, and also on railway yards and walls, from sea level to 2,200 m.

Range: Europe northwards to the British Isles, Denmark and Poland, and eastwards to Romania and Asia Minor.

Similar species: **Sea Pearlwort** (*S. maritima* G. Don) has fleshy, blunt, at best very short-awned leaves, larger flowers (to 6 mm diam.) with purple-edged sepals appressed to and equalling the fruit, and minute or even absent petals. Mainly in coastal habitats (dune-slacks, cliffs) of W and S Europe, northwards to the Lofotens; locally on mountains inland to 1,500 m.

p.110 **Knotted Pearlwort** *Sagina nodosa* (L.) Fenzl

Description: A polymorphic, usually tufted *perennial* to 25 cm, with threadlike, ascending to erect flowering stems as well as *sterile shoots* rising from a *tiny leaf-rosette*. Leaves linear, short-awned, opposite, the upper ones markedly shorter and with bundles of young leaves in their axils, thus *seemingly whorled* (hence 'knotted' – knotty to the touch). Flowers 5–10 mm diam., terminal, solitary or 2–3 per flowering stem, on erect stalks to 10 mm long. *Sepals 5*, ovate, to 3 mm long. *Petals 5*, obovate, *up to 3 times longer than sepals*. Stamens 10, *with yellow anthers*. Ovary 1-locular, with 5 *styles* (not 3, as in *Minuartia verna*). Fruit an ovoid or shortly cylindrical capsule, splitting with 5 valves.

Flowering: July–September.

Habitat: Open places in damp heaths, short turf, marshes, also coastal habitats (dune-slacks and green foreshores), on wet, oligotrophic, basic, fresh or brackish, mostly sandy soils, and also on damp walls, from sea level to 2,000 m.

Range: All Europe except the Mediterranean and Spitsbergen.

Similar species: **Snow Pearlwort** (*S. nivalis* (Lindblad) Fries) rarely exceeds 30 mm. Leaves short-awned, to 6 mm, all opposite (without bundles of young leaves); flowers solitary, 4–5-parted, to 6 mm diam., with petals slightly shorter than sepals (these with a purplish mark near the top), and 8–10 stamens. From Arctic Europe, the Faeroes and the Scottish Highlands.

S. caespitosa (J. Vahl) Lange forms dense cushions (interspersed with dead leaves); flowers to 6 mm diam., solitary or paired, hardly protruding from the leaf-mass, 4–5-parted, with purple-marked sepals (slightly shorter than petals), and 8–10 stamens. In rocky or gravelly habitats to 1,670 m in Iceland, W and N Scandinavia and Spitsbergen.

Heath Pearlwort (*S. subulata* (Swartz) C. Presl) forms low cushions or dense mats of 'knotted' stems; flowers solitary, terminal, 5-parted, to 5 mm diam. (sepals equalling petals), on often glandular stalks rising 20–40 mm above the leaf-mass, and nodding for some time after anthesis. Widely distributed in Europe, northwards to Iceland, C Norway, and eastwards to S Sweden, Poland and the W Balkan region; also cultivated in gardens.

All these similar species are perennial, usually forming sterile shoots. In mountainous regions, several closely related species can be found, but their taxonomical status is often rather obscure (*see* regional floras p.416).

---

p.49 **Procumbent Pearlwort**
Sagina procumbens L.

Description: A low, glabrous, mat-forming *perennial* to 7 cm, with *creeping stems* centred on a small leaf-rosette. Stem-leaves opposite, linear but *slightly broadening in the middle*, shiny green, acute, awned, normally with *bundles of young leaves* in their axils. Flowers 2–4 mm diam., solitary in leaf-axils, on long, erect stalks, nodding for some time after anthesis. *Sepals 4,* bluntly ovate, green. *Petals 4*, white, minute (less than 1 mm) or even absent. Stamens 4. Ovary 1-locular, with 4 styles. Fruit an ovoid, yellowish capsule, splitting with 4 valves.

Flowering: May–September.

Habitat: Bare ground, open grasslands, lawns, and along paths, often in trodden places (very common between paving bricks), on moist to dry, mesotrophic to eutrophic, sandy, loamy or rocky soils, and also on walls, from sea level to 2,600 m.

Range: All Europe except Spitsbergen; subcosmopolitan.

Similar species: **Alpine Pearlwort** (*S. saginoides* (L.) Karsten), from Arctic Europe, Scotland and the C European mountains (to the Balkans), has 5-parted flowers with 10 stamens, petals subequalling sepals, and permanently nodding, 5-valved fruits.

Both these species form sterile, natural hybrids (*S. × normaniana* Lagerh.) with intermediate characters (e.g. less than 10 stamens).

p.286 **Soapwort** *Saponaria officinalis* L.

Description: A hairless or slightly pubescent perennial, with stout, whitish, creeping rhizomes and erect, slightly rough flowering stems to 80 cm. Leaves opposite, up to 15 cm long, elliptical to broadly lanceolate, acute, the lower ones stalked, the upper ones sessile, with *3 (5) prominent, arched veins. Flowers large* (25–40 mm diam.), in rather dense, leafy cymes. Calyx tubular, cylindrical or spindle-shaped, with 5 erect, appressed teeth, green or striped with red, but without membranous bands between the 15–25 rather inconspicuous veins. Petals 5, with *long claw* (exceeding calyx teeth), the limb broadly oblanceolate with a rounded tip, *pale pink* to whitish, spreading to slightly deflexed, with sleek, whitish, scaly appendages at throat. Stamens 10, exserted. Ovary superior, 1-locular, with 2 styles. Fruit a narrowly ovoid, many-seeded capsule equalling calyx, and splitting with 4–5 irregular teeth.

Flowering: June–September.

Habitat: More or less disturbed or ruderal places, road verges, river dikes, hedgebanks, and wood margins, on dry to moist, oligotrophic to mesotrophic, preferably calcareous, sandy soils, from sea level to 1,600 m.

Range: Probably native to S and C Europe (in damp woods, to about 55°N), but frequently kept in gardens and widely naturalized in W and N Europe, to Denmark and S Fennoscandia.

Formerly used as a substitute for soap; the rhizomes have a high saponine content.

---

p.49 **Annual Knawel** *Scleranthus annuus* L.

Description: A more or less prostrate, *stiff or even prickly annual* to 20 cm, with slightly rough-hairy stems. Leaves opposite, sessile (*connate around stem*), linear, tapering to a fine point, ciliate, stiff. Flowers numerous, 4–5 mm diam., short-stalked, 1–3 together in leaf-axils *all along the stems*. Calyx 3.2–4.5 mm long, with cup-shaped tube and 5 slightly longer, diverging, lanceolate, *acute teeth* with very narrow (0.1–0.2 mm), white margins. Petals absent. Stamens 5, *implanted on rim of calyx tube*, and alternating with calyx teeth. Ovary superior, 1-locular, with 2 styles. Fruit an ovoid, *1-seeded*, achene-like capsule (3–5.5 mm long), *not opening*, detaching itself together with the persistent, hardened calyx.

Flowering: May–October.

Habitat: Arable fields and open, grassy or ruderal places, and along unmetalled roads and heathland paths, on dry, mesotrophic, acid, usually sandy soils, from sea level to 2,000 m.

Range: All Europe except Iceland, the Faeroes, N Fennoscandia and Spitsbergen; also in temperate and subtropical Asia and Africa.

Similar species: Forms from S and W Europe, with small flowers (to 3 mm), short, acute, narrowly edged, erect calyx teeth, and often yellowish-green foliage, are often given specific rank (*S. polycarpos* L.).

Perennial Knawel (*S. perennis* L.), obviously perennial, has non-flowering shoots and a lignified stem-base, and is often greyish-green. Flowers restricted to upper leaf-axils, calyx rarely exceeding 3 mm; calyx teeth short, blunt, spreading, with relatively wide white margin (to 0.3 mm). In comparable habitats, in most of Europe northwards to C Scandinavia, the Baltic States and C Russia.

Catchflies and Campions, *Silene*

A genus of annual or perennial herbs with 5-merous flowers; calyx tubular, 10–30-veined; petals clawed, often bearded at the throat. Most species have 3 styles, an incompletely 3-locular ovary (with septums only at the base), and a capsule opening with 6 teeth. Some species (formerly attributed to the genus *Melandrium*) possess a truly 1-locular ovary, often 5 styles, and a 10-toothed capsule.

---

p.267 **Moss Campion** *Silene acaulis* (L.) Jacq.

Description: A hairless, *cushion-forming perennial* with creeping rhizomes, *sterile shoots*, and short flowering stems to 10 cm. Leaves opposite, thronged, bright green, small (to 10 mm long), linear-lanceolate. *Flowers terminal, solitary*, usually hermaphrodite, (6) 9–12 mm diam., often very short-stalked (then hardly raised over leaf-cushion). Calyx cup-shaped, 10-veined, with 5 triangular teeth. Petals 5, the limb obovate, *shallowly notched*, in diverse shades of pink. Stamens 10, protruding. Ovary incompletely 3-locular, with 3 styles. Fruit an ovoid to subglobose capsule, splitting with 6 teeth.

Flowering: June–August.

Habitat: Rocks, screes, in short turf on mountains, also Arctic tundra, on moist, preferably calcareous, stony or rocky soils, 1,900–3,700 m in C Europe, down to sea level in the far north.

Range: Iceland, N and W Scandinavia, the Faeroes, Scotland and adjacent islands, Wales, N

Ireland, N Russia and Spitsbergen; also in
the high mountains of C Europe.

---

p.268 **Sand Catchfly** *Silene conica* L.

Description: A glandular-hairy, scarcely branched
annual, with erect stems to 45 cm. Lower
leaves oblanceolate and stalked, the upper
ones linear and sessile. *Flowers 4–5 mm
diam.*, in small, leafy cymes (occasionally
solitary in meagre specimens). Calyx at first
cylindrical, later *inflated, ovoid to conical*
(abruptly narrowed to truncate at base),
short-hairy, *green*, with *30 prominent,
brownish veins*; calyx teeth 5, narrowly
triangular. Petals *pink or purplish* (rarely
white), long-clawed, with short, spreading,
shallowly notched limb. Stamens 10, hardly
protruding. Ovary incompletely 3-locular,
with 3 styles. Fruit an ovoid, many-seeded
capsule, opening with 6 teeth.

Flowering: May–June (August).

Habitat: Open, grassy places and dunes, on dry,
oligotrophic, calcareous, preferably
disturbed, sandy soils, from sea level to
500 m, but more frequent near the coast.

Range: S and W Europe, northwards to Britain, the
Netherlands, C Germany, Czechia and
Hungary, and eastwards through SE Europe
to the Crimea; naturalized further north, to
Denmark and Poland.

---

p.268 **Red Campion** *Silene dioica* (L.) Clairv.

Description: A hairy, mostly perennial herb (sometimes
biennial), with a creeping rhizome and
erect, sparsely branched flowering stems
to 90 cm. Leaves opposite, broadly
lanceolate to slightly obovate, pointed,
hairy, the lower ones short-stalked, the
upper ones sessile. Flowers 18–25 mm
diam., stalked, in lax panicles, *unisexual,
dioecious* (male and female flowers on
different plants), opening in daytime, not
scented. Calyx elliptical or cylindrical,
purplish, 10-veined in male flowers, larger
(to 15 mm long) and 20-veined in female

flowers, with 5 narrowly triangular teeth. Petals 5, clawed, the limb broadly obovate and *deeply incised, deep pink*, with short, whitish appendages at throat. Stamens 10 (in male flowers), not protruding. Ovary (in female flowers) 1-locular, with *5 styles*. Fruit a broadly ovoid, many-seeded capsule to 12 mm long, opening with *10 recurved teeth*.

Flowering: (March) May–October (November).

Habitat: Deciduous woods and scrub, along wood margins or under hedges, often in river valleys, on moist, mesotrophic, preferably basic, sandy, loamy or rocky soils, from sea level to 2,400 m.

Range: Mainly in W and N Europe (except Iceland and Spitsbergen); less frequent in the Mediterranean and E Europe.

Similar species: **Sweet William Catchfly** (*S. armeria* L.) is much smaller, scarcely branched, hairless, usually annual, with slightly sticky upper stems and narrower, glaucous leaves. Flowers hermaphrodite, to 16 mm diam., sleeker, reddish, with 10-veined calyces and 3 styles; petals shallowly notched, pink. From S and SC Europe westwards to C France, the Ardennes and S Germany, and eastwards to W Russia, the Balkans and Asia Minor; also kept in gardens, and has naturalized in some places in W Europe, including S England.

Fertile hybrids of *S. dioica* and *S. latifolia alba* are far from rare; they usually have pale-pink flowers.

p.123 **Small-flowered Catchfly** *Silene gallica* L.

Description: A glandular-hairy annual or biennial with erect, branched stems to 50 cm. Leaves opposite, lanceolate, sessile (the lower ones often elliptical and short-stalked, or even spatulate). Flowers (6) 8–12 mm diam., solitary in leaf-axils, subsessile (forming a *1-sided, spike-like raceme*), erect. Calyx spindle-shaped to narrowly ovoid, green, with 10 brownish, glandular-hairy veins, and 5 sleek, long-tapering teeth. Petals 5, long-clawed, the limb obovate, rounded or shallowly notched, white or pale pink, and with short, white appendages at throat. Stamens 10, not protruding. Ovary incompletely 3-locular, with 3 styles. Fruit an ovoid, many-seeded capsule, opening with 6 short teeth.

Flowering: (May) June–October.
Habitat: Arable fields, road verges, and waste places, on dry to moist, mesotrophic, preferably calcareous, sandy, loamy or gravelly soils, from sea level to 800 m.
Range: S and W Europe, northwards to E Britain and Belgium, and eastwards to Germany; naturalized in NC Europe, to Poland.

Southern forms often have petals with a large, dark-red blotch (var. *quinquevulnera* (L.) Koch).

---

p.122 **White Campion** *Silene latifolia* Poiret

Description: A glandular-hairy, branched biennial or short-lived perennial (rarely annual) with erect flowering stems to 1 m. Leaves opposite, lanceolate, the upper ones sessile. Flowers 25–30 mm diam., in lax, leafy cymes, *dioecious*, opening at nightfall, then faintly sweet-smelling. Calyx cylindrical to broadly ovoid (markedly inflated in fruit), greenish-white with darker-green veins; in male flowers 10-veined, in female flowers larger (to 20 mm long) and 20-veined. Petals long-clawed, the limb obovate and *deeply incised, white*, with short appendages at throat. Stamens 10 (in male flowers), not protruding. Ovary (in female flowers) 1-locular, with 5 *styles*. Fruit a broadly ovoid, many-seeded capsule, opening with *10 erect to spreading teeth*.

Flowering: May–October.
Habitat: Shaded field margins, road verges, hedges and copses, often in ruderal places, on dry to moist, mesotrophic, preferably calcareous, sandy or loamy soils, from sea level to 1,400 m.
Range: All Europe except Iceland and Spitsbergen.

The plants from W and N Europe belong to ssp. *alba* (Miller) Greuter & Burdet; the typical subspecies occurs in S Europe.

p.122 **Night-flowering Catchfly** *Silene noctiflora* L.

Description: A hairy annual to 45 cm, glandular above.
Leaves opposite, sessile, lanceolate (the
lower ones often stalked, spatulate). Flowers
16–20 mm diam., few together in lax, leafy
panicles, opening at nightfall and then
strongly sweet-scented. Calyx narrowly
ovoid, glandular-hairy, with 5 linear teeth
and 10 greenish to purplish veins. Petals 5,
long-clawed, *the limb deeply incised*, often
inrolled in daytime, *pale pink inside but off-
white or yellowish outside*, with short
appendages at throat. Stamens 10. Ovary 1-
locular, with *3 styles*. Fruit an ovoid, many-
seeded capsule, opening with 6 *recurved teeth*.

Flowering: June–September.

Habitat: Cereal fields, road verges and ruderal
places, on moist, mesotrophic, calcareous,
loamy or clayey soils, from sea level to
800 m.

Range: NW and C Europe, from Britain and
Belgium to E Russia; rare and often only
casual in the west.

p.124 **Nottingham Catchfly** *Silene nutans* L.

Description: A hairy perennial with a basal leaf-rosette,
leafy sterile shoots, and simple flowering
stems to 60 cm, glandular above. Basal
leaves spatulate; stem-leaves opposite,
oblanceolate to almost linear. Flowers to
18 mm diam., stalked, *drooping*, 1–3
together in axillary cymes composing a
sleek, *raceme-like, 1-sided panicle*, opening at
nightfall, very fragrant. Calyx glandular
(not hairy as well), narrowly ovoid to
spindle-shaped, with 10 purplish veins and
5 short, triangular teeth. Petals long-
clawed, white, sometimes cream or pinkish
outside, the *limb deeply incised, inrolled at
day*, with small appendages at throat.
Stamens 10, *protruding*. Ovary incompletely
3-locular, with *3 styles*. Fruit an ovoid,
many-seeded capsule, opening with 6 teeth.

Flowering: May–August.

Habitat: Grassy places and scrub, at field boundaries
and wood margins, and also on coastal cliffs

and inland chalk-outcrops, on dry, oligotrophic, preferably calcareous, sandy, gravelly or rocky soils, from sea level to 2,200 m.

Range: Most of Europe, northwards to C Scandinavia and S Finland, and eastwards through C Russia to the Urals.

Similar species: **Italian Catchfly** (*S. italica* (L.) Pers.) differs in having branched flowering stems, wavy-edged leaves, and short-stalked, erect (not drooping and 1-sided) flowers with a glandular-hairy calyx. In S and SC Europe (to S Germany and Czechia, and eastwards to the Crimea); locally naturalized in Britain.

White Sticky Catchfly (*S. viscosa* (L.) Pers.), a robust, densely glandular-hairy biennial or short-lived perennial to 90 cm; also has wavy leaf-edges. Flowers larger (18–22 mm), erect, on short stalks (seemingly whorled) in cymes contracted into an almost spike-like panicle; calyx cylindrical, green, 14–24 mm long, with 5 acute, lanceolate teeth; petals white, without appendages at throat. In grasslands, fields and road verges, also along railways, on dry, sandy or gravelly soils, mainly in the steppe zone of E Europe, northwards to C Russia; also in Denmark, S Sweden and S Finland.

S. tatarica (L.) Pers. is almost hairless, and (being perennial) possesses sterile shoots; flowers smaller (14–18 mm), often creamy or greenish-white, with shorter calyx (to 13 mm long). In dry grasslands and rocky soils in E Europe, from S Russia westwards to E Germany.

Many more *Silene* species can be found in the SE European steppe region (*see* regional floras).

p.124 **Spanish Catchfly** *Silene otites* (L.) Wibel

Description: A glandular-hairy perennial with sterile shoots and simple flowering stems to 60 cm. Leaves spatulate to oblanceolate, mostly basal, short-hairy; stem-leaves opposite, few. *Flowers small (3–4 mm diam.), mostly dioecious*, numerous, in lax cymes composing a lengthy panicle. *Calyx cup-shaped, glabrous*, with 10 greenish veins, and 5 triangular, glabrous or short-hairy teeth. Petals 5, clawed, with *small, almost linear, round-tipped limb, yellowish or greenish-white, without appendages at throat*. Stamens 10, protruding. Ovary incompletely 3-locular, with 3 styles. Fruit an ovoid, many-seeded capsule, exceeding calyx, and opening with 6 teeth.

Flowering: (May) June–September.

Habitat: Heaths and grasslands, dune-pastures, road verges, often in slightly ruderal or disturbed situations, on dry, oligotrophic, basic to slightly acid, preferably calcareous, sandy or stony soils, from sea level to 2,000 m.

Range: Europe westwards to W France, E England (Breckland), the North Sea dunes (not in Belgium), northwards to Denmark, and eastwards to Latvia and N Greece.

---

p.123 **Rock Campion** *Silene rupestris* L.

Description: A *hairless, greyish-green or glaucous* perennial, with sterile shoots and erect or ascending stems to 30 cm. Leaves opposite, subsessile, lanceolate, blunt-tipped, the lower ones spatulate. Flowers 7–9 mm diam., long-stalked, in lax cymes composing a small panicle. *Calyx glabrous*, cup-shaped, 10-veined, with 5 short, *bluntly triangular teeth*. Petals 5, clawed, notched, white or pale pink. Stamens 10, protruding. Ovary incompletely 3-locular, with 3 styles. Fruit an ovoid, many-seeded capsule, opening with 6 teeth.

Flowering: June–September.

Habitat: Pastures, screes and rocks, on dry, oligotrophic, acid, siliceous, rocky soils, from sea level to 2,900 m (rarely below 800 m in the south).

Range: Fennoscandia and in the mountains of C and S Europe, westwards to C France and the Pyrenees, northwards to S Germany.

Might be confused with *Gypsophila repens* (*see* p.432), which has narrower leaves, a 5-veined calyx, and 2 styles.

p.124 **Bladder Campion**
Silene vulgaris (Moench) Garcke

Description: A mostly hairless, greyish-green, branched perennial to 90 cm; stem-base often somewhat lignified. Leaves opposite, sessile (the lower ones may be short-stalked), ovate (rarely narrowly lanceolate), pointed, occasionally ciliate. Flowers 16–18 mm diam., in lax, leafy cymes, fragrant. Calyx ovoid, *inflated*, bladderlike, translucently whitish with *20 green or purplish, interconnected veins* and 5 broadly triangular teeth. Petals 5, clawed, constricted at throat (and with small appendages there), white, with a rounded, deeply incised limb. Stamens 10, protruding, with purple anthers. Ovary incompletely 3-locular, with 3 styles. Fruit a globular, many-seeded capsule, opening with 6 erect teeth.

Flowering: (May) July–September.

Habitat: In grassy, often ruderal, places, in road verges and along field margins, on dry to moist, oligotrophic to mesotrophic, basic, preferably calcareous, sandy, clayey or rocky soils, from sea level to 2,200 m.

Range: All Europe except Iceland and Spitsbergen; also in Asia and Africa, and naturalized in the Americas.

Sea Campion (*S. v. maritima* (With.) A. & D. Löve) (*see* photograph p.124) has a straggling, mat-forming habit, glaucous, waxy-looking leaves, few-flowered cymes, and capsules with 6 recurved teeth. On cliffs and shingle-beaches of W Europe, from Portugal northwards to Iceland and the Kola peninsula, and round the Baltic Sea.
S. v. bosniaca (G. Beck) Janchen is comparable but has narrower leaves, and scarious (rather than herbaceous) upper bracts in the inflorescence. On calcareous mountains of W and C Europe.

p.267 **Northern Catchfly**
Silene wahlbergella Chowdhuri

Description: A characteristic, slightly hairy, tufted
perennial, with *erect, simple flowering stems to
25 cm*. Leaves mostly basal, oblanceolate;
stem-leaves opposite, bluntly lanceolate,
the upper pair often scale-like. Flowers
terminal, *solitary, nodding in bud*. Calyx
ovoid, *inflated*, 14–18 mm long,
translucently whitish, with 10 purplish veins
and 5 short, bluntly triangular, convergent
teeth. *Petals concealed in calyx*, showing only
at the mouth, pink or purplish. Stamens
10, not protruding. Ovary 1-locular, with 5
styles. Fruit an ovoid capsule, opening with
5, often bifid, teeth.

Flowering: June–August.

Habitat: Bare or grassy places, marshes and tundra,
on moist or wet, oligotrophic, calcareous,
peaty or rocky soils, from sea level to
1,900 m.

Range: W Scandinavia, Finland, and N Russia.

Similar species: *S. furcata* Rafin., from N Scandinavia, N
Russia and Spitsbergen, has branched
stems, smaller, always erect flowers, a less-
inflated calyx to 12 mm, and white petals.

---

p.112 **Corn Spurrey** *Spergula arvensis* L.

Description: A slender, prostrate to erect, often
straggling annual to 40 (60) cm, glandular-
hairy above. Leaves opposite, with bundles
of leaves in axils (thus *seemingly whorled*),
linear, fleshy, longitudinally furrowed
underneath; *stipules present*, membranous,
not connate around stem. Flowers 4–8 mm
diam., long-stalked, deflexed after anthesis,
in *lax, dichasial cymes*. Sepals 5, free, ovate,
green with narrow white margins. Petals 5,
obovate, rounded, white, almost as long as
sepals. Stamens 5–10. Ovary 1-locular,
with *5 styles*. Fruit a rounded to ovoid
capsule slightly exceeding sepals, and
splitting with *5 valves*. Seeds subglobose,
with *very narrow, hardly visible wing or keel*.

Flowering: (April) May–September.

Habitat: Arable fields and disturbed roadsides, on dry, mesotrophic, acid, sandy soils, from sea level to 1,500 m.

Range: All Europe except Spitsbergen; rare in the south.

Similar species: **Pearlwort Spurry** (*S. morisonii* Boreau) is more erect, and has non-furrowed leaves, rounded, overlapping petals, mostly 10 stamens, and lens-shaped seeds with broad, circular wing. In heaths, along paths, and in sand-drifts, on dry, oligotrophic, acid, sandy soils, in continental W Europe, from Iberia northwards to S Scandinavia, and eastwards through Germany and Poland to W Russia. *S. pentandra* L. has narrower, subacute, non-overlapping petals, usually 5 stamens, and broadly winged seeds. In arable fields and dunes, on dry, acid, sandy soils, in continental W Europe from Iberia northwards to S Germany and Poland; also locally in S and SE Europe.

Compare also Spergularia segetalis (see p.436), which is similar but has very small flowers (2–3 mm wide) and 3 styles.

---

p.267 **Greater Sea-spurrey**
Spergularia maritima (All.) Chiov.

Description: An almost hairless *perennial* with a *stout, lignified base* and spreading to ascending stems to 30 (50) cm. Leaves opposite, linear, *fleshy*, slightly concave, *acute, short-awned*, with a *unilateral tuft of leaves* in 1 axil of each leaf-pair; *stipules present, connate around the stem*. Flowers (7) 9–13 mm diam., long-stalked, in lax, *leafy, monochasial cymes*. Sepals 5, free, bluntly ovate, green with narrow white margins. Petals 5, obovate, slightly longer than the sepals, *white with a pink top or all white*. Stamens 9–10, partly sterile (especially in smaller flowers). Ovary 1-locular, with *3 styles*. Fruit an ovoid, many-seeded capsule, opening with *3 valves*. Seeds often broadly winged.

Flowering: May–September.

Habitat: Saltmarshes, on periodically (less often daily) flooded, wet to moist, saline to brackish, sandy or clayey soils; mainly coastal, but also inland at places with brackish seepage, near salt-springs, and along salted roads.

Range: Coasts of W and S Europe, northwards to C Norway, and eastwards to S Russia; occasionally inland (e.g. in the Pannonian Plain).

Similar species: **Lesser Sea-spurrey** (*S. salina* J. & C. Presl) is smaller, often slightly glandular-hairy, annual or biennial (rarely a short-lived perennial), with flat or convex, fleshy leaves. Flowers 4–8 mm diam., petals a deeper pink (but white at base) and shorter than sepals; stamens (0) 2–5 (rarely more, and usually all fertile). It has a comparable ecology, and an even wider distribution (coasts of W and S Europe, northwards to N Russia, eastwards to S Russia, also locally inland in S Germany and Hungary).
Rock Sea-spurrey (*S. rupicola* Lebel) is perennial, always densely glandular-hairy, with fleshy, slightly concave leaves, pink petals equalling sepals, and 10 stamens. A Mediterranean-Atlantic species, inhabiting coastal cliffs of W Iberia, W France, S and W Britain, and Ireland.

These 2 similar species usually have unwinged seeds.

p.267 **Sand-spurrey**
Spergularia rubra (L.) J. & C. Presl

Description: An annual or perennial with mostly prostrate or ascending stems to 20 cm. Leaves linear, *hardly fleshy, blunt, awned*, with a *unilateral tuft of leaves* in 1 axil of each leaf-pair; *stipules present, connate around stem*. Flowers 3–6 mm diam., in leafy *monochasial cymes*. Sepals 5, free, narrowly ovate to lanceolate, with narrow white margins. Petals 5, shorter than sepals, purplish-pink (often pale pink at base). Stamens mostly 10, occasionally less. Ovary 1-locular, with *3 styles*. Fruit an ovoid, many-seeded capsule, splitting with *3 valves*. Seeds always unwinged.

Flowering: May–September.

Habitat: Heaths, poor grassland, road verges, sand-dunes, and cliffs, on dry, oligotrophic to mesotrophic, slightly acid, sandy or stony soils, from sea level to 2,200 m.

Range: All Europe except Iceland, N Fennoscandia, and Spitsbergen.

Similar species: *S. echinosperma* Celak. is always annual, with small, pale-pink flowers (4–6 mm) in few-flowered cymes; stamens 2–5; seeds distinctly bristly (rather than smooth or granular). Locally in C Europe, radiating to N Germany; also in N France; on sand or rocks, often near water.

Greek Sand-spurrey (*S. bocconii* (Scheele) Aschrs. & Graebn.) is a densely glandular-hairy annual or biennial, with very small, solitary, short-stalked, axillary flowers 2–4 (5) mm diam. (forming a kind of 1-sided, leafy raceme), and white-based, pink or white petals. Very locally in Cornwall, Scilly Isles, Channel Isles, and W France; mainly coastal, in sandy or gravelly, often disturbed places; further in the Mediterranean.

S. segetalis (L.) G. Don always has white flowers; a delicate, hairless annual with prostrate or ascending stems to 12 cm; leaves opposite, linear, not fleshy, acute, awned, with unilateral tuft of leaves in 1 axil of each leaf-pair; stipules present, silvery, fringed; flowers very small (2–3 mm diam.), long-stalked, deflexed after anthesis, in very lax, not leafy, monochasial cymes with tiny opposite bracts; sepals membranous and white but for green midvein; petals obovate, much shorter than sepals; stamens 5, rarely 3 or 4. In furrows of cornfields, cart-tracks, and other disturbed places, on moist, often compacted, mesotrophic, slightly acid or calcareous, sandy or loamy (loess) soils, mainly in the lowland, in S and W Europe, northwards to France (extinct in Belgium), S Germany and W Poland. This rare and threatened species is reminiscent of a *Minuartia*, but can be easily distinguished by its small flowers and silvery stipules.

p.109 **Water Chickweed**
Stellaria aquatica (L.) Scop.

Description: A sizeable, though rather weak, perennial, with prostrate hibernating stems and erect or straggling, *quadrangular, glandular-hairy flowering branches* to 120 cm. Leaves opposite, sessile (lower ones sometimes short-stalked), *ovate with cordate to rounded base*, pointed, more or less glandular-hairy, often with wavy rim. Flowers 12–15 mm diam., in *lax, leafy cymes*; flower-stalks often deflexed after anthesis. Sepals 5, free, ovate, glandular-hairy, with narrow white margin. Petals 5, *much longer than sepals*, deeply incised (*bifid*), white. Stamens 10. Ovary 1-locular, with *5 styles*. Fruit an ovoid capsule slightly exceeding calyx, and opening with 5 *bifid teeth*.

Flowering: June–August (October).

Habitat: Marshes and fens, pond, river and ditch margins, and also damp woods, on wet, eutrophic, nitrogen-rich, peaty or mineral soils, from sea level to 2,300 m.

Range: In most of Europe, northwards to C Britain and Lapland, eastwards to the Urals, but rare in the south.

This species deviates from other *Stellaria* in having 5 (rather than 3) styles and as many capsule valves; it is therefore sometimes attributed to a genus of its own (*Myosoton*).

p.108 **Lesser Stitchwort** *Stellaria graminea* L.

Description: An almost hairless perennial with weak, prostrate to ascending, often straggling, usually branched, *smooth, quadrangular stems* to 90 cm. Leaves opposite, *narrowly lanceolate* to almost linear, *grass-green, ciliate near base*. Flowers (5) 7–12 (18) mm diam., long-stalked, in lax cymes; *bracts have narrow scarious margin, ciliate near base*. Sepals 5, free, 3-veined, narrowly ovate, acute, sparsely hairy, and with narrow, scarious margin. Petals 5, deeply incised, equalling or exceeding sepals, white. Stamens 10. Ovary 1-locular, with 3 styles.

Fruit a narrowly ovate capsule much exceeding calyx, and splitting with 6 teeth.

Flowering: May–August.

Habitat: Grassland, grassy heaths, road verges, and wood margins, on moist to rather dry, oligotrophic to mesotrophic, acid to somewhat calcareous, sandy, loamy or clayey soils; from sea level to 2,000 m.

Range: All Europe except Spitsbergen and the Faeroes (but only naturalized in Iceland); only local in the south.

Similar species: In Arctic and sub-Arctic Europe a number of comparable species occur:

S. ciliatisepala Trautv. from Spitsbergen has ciliate (not hairy) sepals.

S. longipes Goldie, from Spitsbergen, N Scandinavia, and N Russia, has almost linear leaves, often with lax vegetative shoots in their axils; flowers few, with hairless sepals.

S. crassipes Hultén, from the same area, has rigid, thickened, broadly lanceolate leaves, with short, compact vegetative shoots in their axils; flowers solitary, with hairless sepals.

S. longifolia Muhl. ex Willd. has rough, quadrangular stems, almost linear, rough-edged leaves, small flowers (4–8 mm) in lax cymes, and hairless sepals just equalled by petals. From Fennoscandia, N and C Russia and C Europe (from Germany and the W Alps to Romania).

S. crassifolia Ehrh. has creeping and ascending stems, ovate to lanceolate, glabrous, fleshy leaves, and sparse flowers, 5–8 mm diam., petals longer than sepals. From Iceland, Fennoscandia, N and W Russia, Poland, N Germany and Denmark.

S. humifusa Rottb. also creeps, forming dense mats; it is densely foliated, and has fleshy, glabrous leaves, axillary vegetative shoots, and flowers 8–16 mm diam., petals longer than sepals. From Iceland, N Fennoscandia, N Russia and Spitsbergen.

S. calycantha (Ledeb.) Bong. has pale-green, ovate to lanceolate, ciliate leaves, sparse flowers 8–12 mm diam., petals shorter than sepals, or altogether absent. From Iceland, Fennoscandia and N Russia.

See also *S. uliginosa* (p.441), and regional floras for more details of the various similar species.

---

p.108 **Greater Stitchwort** *Stellaria holostea* L.

Description: A prostrate, ascending or erect perennial to 50 cm tall, with rather weak, *quadrangular, rough-edged stems*. Leaves opposite, 30–70 mm long, narrowly lanceolate to almost linear, tapering to fine point, shiny *dark green, rough-ciliate* on the edges and the midvein underneath. *Flowers large* (18–25 (30) mm diam.), in lax cymes; *bracts ciliate, without whitish margins*. Sepals 5, broadly lanceolate. Petals 5, deeply incised (to halfway), *almost twice as long as sepals*, white. Stamens 10. Ovary 1-locular, with 3 styles. Fruit a subglobose capsule, opening with 6 teeth.

Flowering: April–June.

Habitat: Deciduous woods (mostly Oak and Hornbeam), wood margins, hedges, and shaded verges, on moist to rather dry, oligotrophic to mesotrophic, slightly acid to basic, sandy or loamy soils; from sea level to 2,000 m.

Range: Most of Europe, northwards to S Scandinavia, S Finland and N Russia.

Similar species: **Marsh Stitchwort** (*S. palustris* L.) has smooth, quadrangular stems, and blue-green, completely glabrous leaves and bracts; bracts have membranous margins. Flowers much smaller (12–18 mm), with petals cleft to base. In damp meadows, marshes, at watersides, in Europe northwards to C Fennoscandia and N Russia; very rare in the south.
S. fennica (Murb.) Perf. is much like *S. palustris*, but with rough-edged stems and even smaller flowers; it occurs in Fennoscandia.

---

p.108 **Common Chickweed** *Stellaria media* L.

Description: A prostrate or straggling annual. *Stems terete, with 1 line of hairs (alternating between the nodes), or glabrous*. Leaves opposite, ovate, acute or slightly pointed, often ciliate; lower ones stalked, upper ones sessile. Flowers 8–10 mm diam., stalked, in lax, leafy cymes; *flower-stalks glandular-hairy*, curved and deflexed after anthesis. Sepals 5, free, 3–6 mm long, broadly lanceolate, glandular-hairy. Petals 5, deeply incised (almost to base), subequalling sepals (occasionally rudimentary or even absent), white. Stamens (1) 3–5 (8). Ovary 1-locular, with 3 styles. Fruit an ovoid, many-seeded capsule, opening with 6 teeth.

Flowering: (January) March–November (December).

Habitat: Fields, gardens, open grassland and roadsides, all sorts of ruderal and disturbed places, and also shingle-beaches, on moist to dry, eutrophic, mostly mineral soils; from sea level to 2,500 m.

Range: All of Europe; one of the commonest weeds.

Similar species: **Great Chickweed** (*S. neglecta* Weihe) is larger in all parts, with stems to 80 cm long, leaves to 40 mm long, flowers 10–13 mm diam., with eglandular, stiffly deflexed stalks and usually 10 stamens. In damp, shaded places, woodland margins, watersides, from W and C Europe northwards to British Isles, S Sweden, and Latvia, and eastwards to W Russia and the Crimea.

Lesser Chickweed (*S. pallida* (Dumort.) Piré) is more delicate than *S. media*, with short-stalked leaves to 8 mm long, flowers 4–5 mm diam., sepals less than 3 mm, rudimentary or absent petals, and 1–3 (5) stamens. Range roughly as for *S. neglecta*; habitat more like *S. media*.

p.109 **Wood Stitchwort** *Stellaria nemorum* L.

Description: A rather stout perennial to 60 cm, with creeping stolons, and *terete, hairy* flowering stems. Leaves opposite, *ciliate, the lower ones long-stalked, ovate with cordate base*, the upper ones more or less sessile, narrowly ovate. *Flowers large* (20–24 mm diam.), in lax, leafy cymes. Sepals 5, free, *hairless*, broadly lanceolate. Petals 5, *twice as long as sepals*, deeply incised (almost to base), white. Stamens 10. Ovary 1-locular, with *3 styles*. Fruit an ovoid, many-seeded capsule, opening with *6 teeth*.

Flowering: May–July.

Habitat: Damp, deciduous woods (often with Ash and Alder) near flushes or along streams, on wet, mesotrophic to eutrophic, usually basic, sandy, loamy or slightly peaty soils; from sea level to 2,400 m.

Range: Most of Europe except Iceland, Ireland and much of W France; only on mountains in the south.

This species is much like *S. aquatica* (*see* p.437), but the latter has 5 styles instead of 3.

Plants with stalked lower and upper leaves, but scale-like bracts, are distinguished as ssp. *glochidisperma* Murb. In C and W Europe, westwards to Britain, northwards to S Sweden, and eastwards to the Balkan peninsula.

p.108 **Bog Stitchwort** *Stellaria uliginosa* Murray

Description: A *bluish-green* perennial with thin, creeping or ascending, branched, *smooth, glabrous, quadrangular stems* to 50 cm. Leaves opposite, up to 10 (20) mm long, elliptical to lanceolate, sessile, *ciliate near base*, otherwise glabrous. Flowers 5–7 mm diam., in lax, leafy cymes; *bracts largely membranous, and not ciliate*. Sepals 5, free, broadly lanceolate. Petals 5, deeply incised (almost to base, with *2 diverging lobes*), *much shorter than sepals*, white. Stamens usually 10. Ovary 1-locular, with 3 styles. Fruit an ovoid, many-seeded capsule, opening with 6 teeth.

Flowering: May–August.

Habitat: Swamps, damp meadows, near springs and flushes, ditches and streams, and in cart-tracks in woods, on wet, oligotrophic to eutrophic, acid or neutral, sandy or peaty soils; from sea level to 2,300 m.

Range: Most of Europe, northwards to C Scandinavia and N Russia.

p.269 Cow Basil
Vaccaria hispanica (Miller) Rauschert

Description: An erect, *regularly branched, hairless, glaucous* annual to 60 cm. Leaves opposite, to 50 mm long, narrowly ovate to lanceolate, acute. Flowers to 15 mm long, 10–15 mm diam., long-stalked, in lax cymes. *Calyx markedly inflated, with 5 prominent keels*, 15–25 indistinct veins, and 5 erect, triangular teeth; no epicalyx. Petals 5, clawed, the limb narrowly obovate, rounded or notched, pale pink (rarely white) with darker veins. Stamens 10, protruding. Ovary 1-locular (in fact incompletely 4-locular), with *2 styles*. Fruit a rounded or ovoid capsule, much shorter than the calyx, and *opening with 4 teeth*.

Flowering: May–July.

Habitat: Arable fields, on moist, mesotrophic, calcareous, loamy or clayey soils; from sea level to 1,600 m.

Range: Continental Europe, northwards to Belgium, N Germany, Denmark and S Poland, and eastwards to C and S Russia; also cultivated in gardens, and naturalized in the same general area.

A strongly declining archeophyte, now rarely seen in fields, but occasionally sown in borders (especially ssp. *grandiflora* (Fisch. ex DC.) Holub, which has ovate leaves to 90 mm long, and much larger, deep-pink flowers.

HORNWORT FAMILY, CERATOPHYLLACEAE

A family of submerged, barely rooting, aquatic herbs, with only 1 genus, *Ceratophyllum*, containing 2 or 3 variable species nearly world-wide; some authors distinguish up to 30 local species. Dicots. Stems freely branching; leaves whorled, 1–several times forked. Flowers solitary in the leaf-axils, sessile, regular, unisexual (monoecious). Perianth 8–12-parted, greenish in female flowers, whitish in male flowers; tepals linear. Stamens (10) 12–16 (20), with very short filaments. Ovary superior, 1-locular, 1-seeded, with long style remaining on the ripe achene.

p.54 **Rigid Hornwort** *Ceratophyllum demersum* L.

Description: *See also* the family description. Leaves (3)
5–8 per whorl, *dark green, 1–2 times forked*,
with 2–4 linear, *rigid, denticulate segments*.
Achene greenish, smooth, 4–5 mm long,
with *awl-shaped, permanent style at least
equalling rest of fruit*, and *2–3 long,
backward-pointing spines* at base.

Flowering: July–September.

Habitat: Ponds, lakes, and slow-moving rivers and
streams, usually in eutrophic, fresh or
brackish water, mainly in the lowland.

Range: All Europe except Iceland and Spitsbergen.

Similar species: **Soft Hornwort** (*C. submersum* L.) has soft,
bright-green leaves, mostly 3 times forked
(with 8 segments), and finely warty achenes
without basal spines; style shorter than
fruit. In eutrophic, fresh or brackish waters,
in Europe northwards to S Sweden.

Both species hibernate in the form of
detached buds clad in young leaves; fruits
may be scarce in northern regions.

GOOSEFOOT FAMILY, CHENOPODIACEAE

A subcosmopolitan family of herbs, and some shrubs, with *c.*
1,400 species in 102 genera. Dicots. Leaves usually alternate,
simple. No stipules (contrary to the Dock family,
Polygonaceae). Flowers hermaphrodite or unisexual, regular,
usually small and greenish (sometimes without perianth,
especially in female flowers), often in dense cymes or spikes
(rarely solitary). Perianth (if present) 1–5-lobed. Stamens 1–5.
Ovary superior (or, in *Beta*, hemi-inferior), 1-locular, with 1
style (sometimes very short, or deeply divided with 2–4
branches), and 2–5 stigmas. Fruit a small, 1-seeded achene
(nutlet), indehiscent or opening with an apical lid, and often
surrounded by the enlarged, fleshy perianth. Some genera are
succulent, living in dry steppes or saline habitats, and these
often have reduced, opposite leaves (e.g., *Salicornia*).

---

p.60 **Perennial Glasswort**
Arthrocnemum perenne (Miller) Moss

Description: A *perennial half-shrub* to 30 cm, with
lignified, *creeping, subterranean stem* and

numerous, ascending to erect, symmetrically branched, glabrous, *succulent, beaded stems*, often flushed with red; whole plant orange-brown in autumn. Sterile shoots present. *Leaves opposite, reduced to short, blunt, fleshy scales*, connate around stem. *Flowers hermaphrodite*, extremely reduced, greenish, subequal, 3 together in sessile clusters, axillary to scale-leaves and sunk into stem to form long spikes. Perianth parts usually 4, fused to small scale bearing *2 minute stamens and 1-locular ovary* with short style and 2 stigmas. Fruit a small, 1-seeded achene; seed covered with minute, *curved or hooked hairs*.

Flowering: August–October.

Habitat: Highest, only seasonally inundated, parts of saltmarshes, on wet, clayey or sandy, saline to brackish soils; occasionally on shingle-beaches.

Range: Locally along the coasts of W France, England, Wales and SE Ireland; also in Mediterranean region.

Similar species: *A. fruticosum* (L.) Moq. is a shrub to 1 m, with blue-green, prostrate (but not creeping) stems, and seeds with straight hairs. In comparable, saline habitats of W France (to Normandy). • *Compare Salicornia (see p.456)*, which contains annual species with unisexual flowers.

p.64 **Frosted Orache** *Atriplex laciniata* L.

Description: A mostly spreading, much-branched annual to 30 (60) cm. *Stems reddish, without longitudinal stripes*. Leaves to 20 mm long, ovate to diamond-shaped (often with short, forward-pointing basal lobes), bluntly dentate to sinuously lobed; *only the veins lined with green tissue*, but with whitish tissue in between; *leaves thickly clad in silvery scales* (at least when young). Flowers minute, unisexual, monoecious, in terminal, leafy panicles: male flowers have greenish, globose, 5-parted perianth and 5 stamens; females without perianth, but enveloped by 2 small, sessile, erect, *cordate or hastate, 3-lobed, halfway connate, silvery bracteoles*; ovary superior, 1-locular, with 2 short styles. Fruit a small achene, enveloped by the then enlarged, *lobed, hardened bracteoles*.

Flowering: July–September.

Habitat: Sandy and gravelly beaches, especially on floodmarks; often ephemeral.

Range: Atlantic coasts of Europe, from SW France to N Britain and S Scandinavia.

Similar species: *A. rosea* L. grows more erect, and has axillary, leafy panicles all along stem; leaves alternate, ovate to triangular, bluntly dentate, silvery; bracteoles ovate-triangular (not hastate), dentate, and bearing large dorsal appendages. Mainly coastal, but also in eutrophic, ruderal places inland, in S and C Europe.
A. tatarica L. has spike-like inflorescences (only terminal, or in highest leaf-axils), and much larger, alternate, coarsely (often acutely) dentate, silvery leaves to 10 cm long. In ruderal places, also on saline soils, in S and C Europe.

---

p.63 **Grass-leaved Orache** *Atriplex littoralis* L.

Description: A glabrous or slightly mealy annual to 90 cm, with *ascending to erect, grooved branches*. Leaves alternate, *narrowly lanceolate to linear*, to 15 mm wide, short-stalked to subsessile, tapering at both ends, entire-margined or bluntly dentate, green or grey-green. Flowers unisexual, monoecious, in long, interrupted, terminal and axillary spikes: male flowers 2 mm diam., with greenish, globose, 5-parted perianth, and 5 stamens; females without perianth, but with 2 broadly ovate to triangular bracteoles, and a superior, 1-locular ovary with 2 short styles. Achene compressed, broadly ovate, surrounded by the then enlarged, fleshy, triangular-ovate, *dentate bracteoles with prickly tubercles* on the back.

Flowering: July–October.

Habitat: Floodmarks and rarely inundated saltmarshes along the sea-coast, also in ruderal places more inland, on moist, brackish, sandy or clayey soils; mainly coastal.

Range: Coasts of S and W Europe, northwards to N Norway, also in the Baltic area; inland in the steppe belt of SE Europe.

---

p.63 **Common Orache** *Atriplex patula* L.

Description: A glabrous, often slightly mealy annual with *spreading to ascending, grooved branches*. Leaves alternate: lower ones stalked, with 2 forward-pointing side-lobes and a *narrowed, more or less cuneate base*, narrowly ovate to diamond-shaped, entire-margined or remotely dentate; upper leaves subsessile, lanceolate to linear, often entire and without side-lobes. Flowers unisexual, monoecious, in long, terminal and axillary spikes: male flowers have greenish, globose, 5-parted perianth and 5 stamens; females without perianth, but with 2 subsessile, diamond-shaped, pointed bracteoles (with 2 side-lobes). Ovary 1-locular, with 2 styles. Achene enclosed in enlarged, fleshy, 3-lobed but otherwise *entire bracteoles; bracteoles glabrous or with some tubercles* on the back. Var. *bracteata* Westerlund has narrower leaves; bracteoles long-stalked and wrapped around a number of smaller female flowers.

Flowering: July–October.

Habitat: Waste places, fields, along ditches and roads, on moist, eutrophic, mostly clayey soils, rarely in saline coastal habitats from sea level to 1,700 m.

Range: All Europe except Spitsbergen.

Similar species: *A. calotheca* (Rafin.) Fries has 3-lobed, irregularly toothed leaves and deeply dentate bracteoles. In coastal habitats of the Baltic region, westwards to S Norway and N Germany.
A. oblongifolia Waldst. & Kit. has narrower leaves with small or indistinct side-lobes, and rounded bracteoles. E Europe (from Germany to C Russia).

p.64 **Sea Purslane** *Atriplex portulacoides* L.

Description: A *greyish-green or glaucous*, strongly branched *perennial* with *ascending, often partly creeping stems* to 1 (1.5) m, with lignified stem-base and *axillary, non-flowering shoots*. *Leaves partly opposite* (only upper ones alternate), rather fleshy, elliptical to oblanceolate, entire-margined, with rounded tip. Flowers small, unisexual, monoecious, *yellowish*, in *terminal, hardly leafy panicles*: male flowers have globular, 5-parted perianth and 5 stamens; *females (sub)sessile*, without true perianth but enclosed in pair of *fused bracteoles* forming flattened, 3-lobed pseudocalyx. Ovary (in female flowers) superior, 1-locular, flattened, truncate above, with 2 protruding styles. Fruit *subsessile*; achene fused to persistent pseudocalyx.

Flowering: July–October.

Habitat: Marine saltmarshes; often forming dense vegetations along tidal gullies, on regularly inundated, wet, saline, sandy or clayey soils.

Range: Coasts of S and W Europe, northwards to Denmark.

Similar species: **Stalked Orache** (*Atriplex pedunculata* L.) is a more erect, less-branched, greyish-green annual (without non-flowering shoots) to 30 cm, with a leafy panicle; leaves mostly alternate. Flowers greyish: male flowers have globular, 4–5-parted perianth; females enclosed in the fused bracteoles, forming flattened pseudocalyx with 2 large, divergent side-lobes; flower-stalks become much extended after anthesis. In rather open vegetation of saltmarshes, on wet, saline, preferably sandy soils; coasts of W and N Europe, from Normandy to S Sweden and Estonia (extinct in Britain); also inland, near saline pools in C Germany and the steppe belt in SE Europe and Asia.

These 2 species are often placed in a separate genus (*Halimione*).

p.64 **Halberd-leaved Orache**
Atriplex prostrata DC.

Description: An annual herb with prostrate to erect,
              quadrangular, longitudinally striped stems
              to 90 cm. *Leaves opposite* (but often
              alternate higher up stem), stalked, to 60
              (90) mm long, *triangular to sagittate*,
              coarsely dentate to nearly entire-margined;
              lower ones have truncate base (cuneate
              base in var. *longipes* (Drejer) Meijden);
              basal lobes acute, spreading or pointing
              back; leaves often have dense, silvery scales
              below, at least when young. Flowers
              minute, unisexual, monoecious, in dense
              panicles: male flowers have globular, 5-
              parted perianth and 5 stamens; females
              without perianth, but enveloped by 2
              small, sessile (partly stalked, in var.
              longipes), erect, broadly ovate or diamond-
              shaped, *dentate bracteoles* (these *connate only
              at their base*). Ovary superior, 1-locular,
              with 1 style and 2 (3) stigmas. Fruit a
              small achene, enveloped by enlarged,
              spongy (not hardened) bracteoles.

Flowering: July–October.

Habitat: The highest, rarely inundated zone of
              coastal saltmarshes, floodmarks, and also
              inland in arable fields, roadsides, gardens
              and ruderal places, on moist, eutrophic,
              basic or brackish, preferably clayey soils;
              var. *longipes* is restricted to sandy coastal
              habitats.

Range: All Europe except Iceland and Spitsbergen.

Similar species: *A. praecox* Hülphers is a low, prostrate plant
              with only basally connate bracteoles
              3–6 mm long (instead of 5–20 mm); in
              coastal grassland and shingle-beaches in N
              and NW Europe.
              Babington's Orache (*Atriplex glabriuscula*
              Edmondston) is a prostrate, often reddish
              plant, with bracteoles halfway connate;
              leaves ovate-triangular, coarsely dentate,
              with short, spreading basal lobes. In sandy
              or gravelly coastal habitats of NW and N
              Europe, southwards to Brittany.

              The foliage of *A. prostrata* can be yellowish-
              green to dark green, and often turns red in

the sun; in coastal forms leaves are often
somewhat fleshy.

---

p.61 **Sea Beet** *Beta vulgaris* L.

Description: A biennial or short-lived, hairless
perennial to 80 cm, with stout (but not
much thickened) taproot and prostrate
to ascending or erect stems. *Leaves fleshy,
slightly leathery, shiny green*, ovate or
diamond-shaped, often subacute; basal
leaves in rosette, and *to 10 (15) cm long,
narrowed into stalk*; stem-leaves much
smaller, alternate, often wavy. Flowers
hermaphrodite, sessile, in clusters of
2–3 or solitary, with lanceolate
bracteoles, the clusters aggregated in
long, interrupted, terminal and axillary
spikes. Perianth 5-parted, green.
Stamens 5. *Ovary hemi-inferior*, 1-locular,
with 3 sessile stigmas. Fruit a rounded,
flattened achene, fused with the then
thickened, corky perianth.

Flowering: June–September.

Habitat: Floodmarks, shingle-beaches and sea-walls,
on moist, brackish soils.

Range: Coasts of S and W Europe, northwards to
Scotland, Denmark and S Sweden.

The description pertains to the wild form
(ssp. *maritima* (L.) Arc.), ancestor of the
cultivated beet (ssp. *vulgaris*), which has
broadly triangular-ovate, subcordate,
rounded, hardly fleshy basal leaves to 30 cm
long, flowers in clusters of 2–8, and a
strongly thickened root-tuber. Both
subspecies easily hybridize, and
intermediate forms are frequent.

---

p.62 **Fat Hen** *Chenopodium album* L.

Description: A dark-green, *usually mealy* annual, with
erect, green-striped, rarely reddish stems
to 1.2 m. Leaves alternate, stalked, often
mealy below, variously dentate or lobed;
lower ones ovate or diamond-shaped,
upper ones often narrowly lanceolate and

entire-margined. Flowers minute, hermaphrodite, clustered in leafy panicles; no bracteoles. Perianth globose, white-mealy, 5-parted. Stamens 5. Ovary superior, 1-locular, with 2 styles. Fruit a rounded achene with 1 black seed, enclosed in (not fused with) the persistent but non-fleshy perianth.

Flowering: June–October.

Habitat: Arable fields, ruderal places, open roadsides, building sites, and the like, on dry to moist, (highly) eutrophic, acid or slightly calcareous, sandy or clayey soils; from sea level to 1,700 m; a common weed.

Range: All Europe except Iceland and Spitsbergen.

Similar species: **Green Goosefoot** (*C. suecicum* J. Murray) is weakly defined by its narrowly ovate or 3-lobed, blue-green, hardly mealy leaves with large, subacute, forward-pointing teeth. In N and E Europe, southwards to Germany, Switzerland and C Russia.
Grey Goosefoot (*Chenopodium opulifolium* Schrader ex Koch & Ziz.) has broadly diamond-shaped to subquadrate, usually distinctly 3-lobed, bluntly dentate, bluish-green leaves. In ruderal habitats of S and C Europe, northwards to N Germany and Poland.

---

p.61 **Good-King-Henry**
Chenopodium bonus-henricus L.

Description: A mostly erect, green or red-tinged *perennial* to 70 cm, with stout rhizome; stems often red-striped. Leaves alternate, stalked, mealy when young, *triangular to diamond-shaped, entire-margined*, with *spreading or slightly backward-pointing, subacute basal lobes*. Flowers minute, hermaphrodite, clustered in terminal, hardly leafy, sleek (often spike-like) panicles; no bracteoles. Perianth globose, green, 5-parted. Stamens 5. Ovary superior, 1-locular, with 2 styles. Fruit rounded, exceeding the persistent (not fleshy) perianth.

Flowering: May–August.

Habitat: More or less shaded ruderal places, roadsides, manure heaps, often near farms, on moist, (very) eutrophic, nitrogen-rich, preferably calcareous, sandy or clayey soils; from sea level to 2,500 m.

Range: Europe northwards to C Norway and Estonia; formerly cultivated as a vegetable. An archeophyte in much of the area, but in decline.

Similar species: **Strawberry Blite** (*C. capitatum* (L.) Aschers.) has similar leaves, but flowers in globose clusters in upper leaf-axils; perianth on ripening fruit becomes fleshy and bright red. From N America; more or less naturalized in Europe, northwards to S Scandinavia and C Russia.

C. foliosum Aschers. has much smaller, globose, axillary flower-clusters; leaves triangular, with long, acute, spreading teeth. From SW, WC and SE Europe; locally naturalized in ruderal places further north, to the Netherlands, Germany, the Baltic States and C Russia.

---

p.62 **Fig-leaved Goosefoot**
Chenopodium ficifolium Smith

Description: A more or less erect, green, mealy annual to 90 cm. Leaves alternate, stalked, *3-lobed, usually red-edged*, with *cuneate base* and *2 forward-pointing side-lobes*; top segment larger, with *parallel margins* for much of its length, *weakly dentate* or subentire. Flowers minute, hermaphrodite, in leafy panicles with slender, spike-like branches. Perianth 5-parted, globular, mealy. Stamens 5. Ovary superior, 1-locular, with 2 short styles. Achene globose, loosely surrounded by (not fused with) persistent, non-fleshy perianth.

Flowering: July–September.

Habitat: Cultivated fields, disturbed road verges, building sites, manure heaps and ruderal places, on dry to moist, (very) eutrophic, sandy, loamy or clayey soils; mainly in the lowland.

Range: In Europe northwards to S Fennoscandia (but not in Ireland), and eastwards to Poland and the Ukraine.

p.62 **Oak-leaved Goosefoot**
Chenopodium glaucum L.

Description: A spreading to erect annual, to 50 cm.
Leaves alternate, *shiny green above, greyish-mealy below, elliptical, with cuneate base*, and *sinuate to lobed margins*. Flowers minute, hermaphrodite, greenish, in clusters forming axillary spikes; terminal flower in each cluster has globular, 5-parted perianth, *lateral flowers 2–3-merous*. Stamens 2–5. Ovary superior, 1-locular, with 2 styles. Fruit a rounded achene, enclosed by persistent, non-fleshy perianth.

Flowering: June–September.

Habitat: Ruderal, often periodically inundated, places, along ditches and rivers, manure heaps, disturbed road verges, on moist to wet, (very) eutrophic, nitrogen-rich, preferably clayey soils; mainly in the lowland.

Range: In Europe northwards to SE England, S Sweden, S Finland and N Russia.

Similar species: The Mediterranean *C. botrys* L. has comparable, bluntly lobed leaves, but can be easily distinguished by numerous short, yellow, scented glandular hairs; locally naturalized, northwards to the Netherlands and Latvia, mainly along railways.

---

p.62 **Nettle-leaved Goosefoot**
Chenopodium murale L.

Description: A rather stout, erect annual to 50 cm.
Leaves alternate, stalked, green (only slightly mealy in youth), *ovate to slightly triangular* or diamond-shaped, with *cuneate base* and *coarse, acute, incurved teeth*. Flowers small, hermaphrodite, in rather wide, leafy panicles. Perianth 5-parted, mostly mealy. Stamens 5. Ovary superior, 1-locular, with 2 styles. Fruit a rounded achene, completely enclosed by persistent, non-fleshy perianth; *seed has sharp rim*.

Flowering: July–October.

Habitat: Cultivated fields and gardens, ruderal places, also along walls, on dry, oligotrophic to mesotrophic, calcareous, preferably sandy soils; from sea level to 1,500 m.

Range: S and W Europe, northwards to Britain, S Sweden and Estonia.

Similar species: **Upright Goosefoot** (*C. urbicum* L.) has distinctly triangular leaves with short, blunt teeth, much narrower, hardly leafy panicles, fruits just exceeding perianth, and rounded seeds. In arable fields and ruderal places (to 1,500 m) in continental Europe northwards to Denmark, S Sweden and C Russia.

---

p.63 **Many-seeded Goosefoot**
Chenopodium polyspermum L.

Description: A hairless, mostly *not mealy*, spreading to erect annual to 60 (80) cm. Leaves alternate, stalked, ovate to elliptical, *entire-margined* but for *single tooth or small side-lobe* in 1 or both margins; often yellowish-green with *red edge*. Flowers *c.* 2 mm diam., in axillary spikes. Perianth greenish, glabrous, 5-parted (rarely 4-parted). Stamens 5. Ovary superior, 1-locular, with 2 styles. Fruit a rounded, somewhat compressed achene, visible between perianth parts.

Flowering: July–October.

Habitat: Arable fields, building grounds, on moist to wet, (very) eutrophic, nitrogen-rich, preferably sandy soils; from sea level to 1,200 m.

Range: Most of Europe, northwards to Britain, S Norway, S Finland and N Russia.

Similar species: **Stinking Goosefoot** (*C. vulvaria* L.) is greyish-green, very mealy all over, with comparable, often more rhombic, entire-margined leaves, and thick style with 2 stigmas. Notable for its nasty, fishy stench. In very eutrophic, ruderal places, often on manure heaps and along walls in farmyards, in S and W Europe, northwards to England and S Sweden, but severely declining in the northern part of its range.

p.61 **Red Goosefoot** *Chenopodium rubrum* L.

Description: A stout, hairless, spreading to erect annual to 1 m, often strongly flushed with red; stems usually red-striped. Leaves alternate, stalked, *shiny, more or less fleshy*, ovate to rhombic, with *cuneate base, coarsely dentate, often with one pair of prominent, acute side-lobes*. Flowers small, hermaphrodite, clustered in large, reddish, leafy panicles. Terminal flowers in each cluster (4) 5-merous; *lateral flowers usually 3-merous*. Perianth lobes connate at base only. Stamens 3–5. Ovary superior, 1-locular, with 2 styles. Fruit a rounded, slightly pointed achene, exceeding permanent, non-fleshy perianth.

Flowering: July–October.

Habitat: Ruderal places, arable fields, manure heaps, and along ditches, on moist or wet, often seasonally inundated, (very) eutrophic, preferably clayey soils, and also in brackish environments; from sea level to 600 m.

Range: In Europe northwards to Ireland, Britain, S Sweden, S Finland and N Russia.

Similar species: **Small Red Goosefoot** (*C. botryodes* Sm.) also has 3-merous lateral flowers in each cluster, but perianth is connate almost to top, concealing achenes; leaves fleshy, triangular or slightly 3-lobed, but hardly dentate otherwise. In saline or brackish, coastal habitats of S and W Europe northwards to Denmark; also inland in C Germany and the steppe belt in SE Europe. **Maple-leaved Goosefoot** (*C. hybridum* L.) has ovate to triangular leaves with short-cuneate to slightly cordate base and (2) 3–5 coarse teeth or angular lobes along each margin. In arable fields and ruderal places, in continental Europe northwards to S Sweden and Estonia. (Extinct in Britain and Finland.)

Polycnemum arvense L.

Description: A glabrous or slightly hairy annual with spreading or ascending, *spirally twisted branches* to 50 cm. Leaves alternate, linear, *stiff and needle-like, triangular in cross-section*, to 8 (12) mm long. Flowers small, axillary, *solitary* (rarely paired), supported by 1 linear-lanceolate bract and *2 small, opposite, lanceolate bracteoles*. Perianth 1–1.5 mm long, membranous, 5-parted, cup-shaped, about equalling the bracteoles; perianth lobes without appendages (even in fruit). *Stamens 3*. Ovary superior, 1-locular, with short style and 2 stigmas. Fruit an ovoid achene to 1 mm long.

Flowering: (June) July–September.

Habitat: Arable fields and other cultivated or disturbed ground, on dry, oligotrophic, preferably calcareous, sandy or loamy soils; from sea level to 1,300 m.

Range: Continental Europe, northwards to Germany, Poland, Lithuania, and C Russia.

Similar species: *P. majus* A. Braun has prickly, needle-like leaves to 15 (20) mm, and straight stems. In comparable habitats of S and C Europe, northwards to Germany, Pannonia and C Russia.

---

p.60 **Glasswort** *Salicornia europaea* L.

Description: An erect, annual herb to 40 cm, with spreading to ascending, crosswise opposite, glabrous, *succulent, beaded*, yellowish-green branches, often flushed with red when flowering. General habit often vaguely reminiscent of small Christmas tree. Main root thin, soon ramified, not deep-growing. Leaves opposite, reduced to short, blunt, fleshy scales, connate around stem. *Flowers unisexual*, extremely reduced, greenish, 3 together in sessile clusters, axillary to the scale-leaves and sunk into the stem, thus forming *rather short, slightly spindle-shaped spikes* 10–30 mm long (terminal spikes to 50 mm). Perianth parts fused to small, rounded scale; *central flower in each cluster male, with 1 minute, subsessile stamen*, and *anther less than 0.55 mm long*; both *lateral flowers female*, usually markedly smaller, *with 1 short style and 2 stigmas*. Fruit a small achene; seed densely hairy.

Flowering: July–October.

Habitat: Periodically- to daily-inundated saltmarshes, on wet, clayey or sandy, saline to brackish soils; also inland near saline pools. A typical halophyte.

Range: Coasts of S and W Europe, northwards to the White Sea, and also in the Baltic region; inland in NE France, C Germany, C Poland, and the steppe belt from Pannonia to S Russia.

Another common name is Marsh Samphire. In autumn the plant turns brick-red or purplish. Dark-green, somewhat glaucous forms are sometimes attributed to *S. obscura* P.W. Ball & Tutin. Dark-green forms with short spikes (5–10 mm long, terminal ones to 30 mm) are separated as *S. ramosissima* J. Woods. British forms with clearly protruding stamens and subequal flowers are *S. nitens* P.W. Ball & Tutin (a low plant with short branches, and terminal spikes to 40 mm long) and *S. fragilis* P.W. Ball & Tutin (stout, strongly branched plants with terminal spikes to 80 mm, and yellow hues in autumn). The taxonomical value of these species is disputed; experts often claim to be able to recognize them at great distance in autumn by their subtle but distinctive colour shifts. The smallish, short-branched *S. disarticulata* Moss can be separated more satisfactorily, having solitary flowers in the axils of the scale-leaves, and very short spikes to 6 mm; it occurs in the highest zone of saltmarshes, or at the foot of sea-walls, beyond the reach of normal (summer) tides, along the Atlantic coasts of W Europe, northwards to S Ireland, S and E England, and the Netherlands.

---

p.60 **Long-spiked Glasswort**
Salicornia procumbens Smith

Description: An annual herb to 40 (60) cm; stem ascending, *irregularly, often densely branched*, with long, erect, glabrous, *succulent, beaded*, dark-green branches (but often pale green in spring, and turning pale yellowish-brown in autumn). *Main root stout, deep-growing*. Leaves opposite, reduced to short, blunt, fleshy scales, connate around stem. *Flowers unisexual,* extremely reduced, greenish, 3 together in sessile clusters, axillary to scale-leaves and sunk into stem, thus forming *long, linear spikes* (50–120 mm). Perianth parts fused to small, bluntly triangular scale; *central flower in each cluster male, with 1 minute, subsessile stamen,* and an *anther 0.6–0.9 mm in length;* both *lateral flowers female,* often markedly smaller, *with 1 short style and 2 stigmas.* Fruit a small achene; seed often sparsely hairy.

Flowering: July–October.

Habitat: Frequently- to daily-inundated, lower parts of saltmarshes, often near tidal gullies, also on high mudflats, on wet, sandy or clayey, saline soils; rarely inland.

Range: Coasts of W Europe, from Portugal to S Norway, also in SE France.

The bushy habit is reminiscent of an old-fashioned heather-broom. This species generally occurs in more exposed places than *S. europaea.* Young glasswort plants (of all species) can be made into a refreshing salad (add some lemon juice), but their salt content is roughly proportional to that of the soil they grew in. *Compare* with *Arthrocnemum* (*see* p.443), a genus of perennials with hermaphrodite flowers.

p.49 **Prickly Saltwort** *Salsola kali* L.

Description: A greyish-green, rather prickly, much-branched annual to 50 cm, with rough-hairy, ascending to erect stems. Leaves alternate, sessile, linear, *rounded or weakly triangular in cross-section, fleshy, awned,* 20–30 mm long. Flowers 3–5 mm diam., hermaphrodite, sessile, solitary (occasionally 2–3 together) in leaf-axils, with short bract and *2 narrowly ovate bracteoles.* Perianth 5-parted (rarely 4-parted), whitish or pink, membranous, with pointed lobes. Stamens 5. Ovary superior, 1-locular, with 1 short style and 2 stigmas. Fruit an ovoid achene, surrounded by the then closed, cup-shaped, persistent perianth (6–10 mm diam.), each lobe of which develops a *transverse, lobed, membranous wing.*

Flowering: July–September.

Habitat: Coastal dune areas and high beaches, open places with drifting sand, also floodmarks, on dry or moist, brackish, sandy soils.

Range: Coasts of Europe, northwards to Ireland, Scotland, S Norway, S Finland, and the Baltic States; also in the Mediterranean area, and inland in the steppe belt of SE Europe, from Czechia and the Balkan region to S Russia.

Ssp. *ruthenica* (Iljin) Soó, found in ruderal, sandy, less saline places, both coastal and inland, has softer, more flexible leaves to 60 mm long, and fruits with curved, asymmetrical, occasionally unwinged perianth (3–6 mm diam.).

p.59 Annual Sea-blite
Suaeda maritima (L.) Dumort.

Description: A more or less branched, mostly prostrate or ascending, *hairless annual* to 50 cm; stems often purplish. Leaves alternate, sessile, 10–40 (50) mm long, linear (slightly widened at base), *fleshy (shallowly concave above, rounded beneath)*, soft, *subacute*, blue-green, *turning purple or bright red in autumn*. Flowers usually 2–3 together in leaf-axils, small (2–3 mm diam.); bracteoles minute. Perianth globular, 5-parted, *with fleshy lobes*. Stamens 5. Ovary superior, ovoid, 1-locular, with reduced style and *2 sessile stigmas*. Fruit an ovoid achene, surrounded by fleshy perianth that never develops wing-like appendages.

Flowering: July–October.

Habitat: Periodically (often daily) inundated parts of saltmarshes, optimally on decaying floodmarks, on wet, clayey or sandy, saline soils; mainly coastal, but also in strongly saline habitats inland.

Range: Coasts of W Europe, northwards to the Shetland Isles and C Norway, and the Baltic Sea; also near saline pools in C Germany and the steppe belt from Pannonia to S Russia. A typical halophyte.

Similar species: **Shrubby Sea-blite** (*Suaeda vera* Forskål ex J.F. Gmelin) is a much-branched half-shrub to 1.2 m, with shorter (5–18 mm), densely crowded, blunt, always blue-green, fleshy leaves (flat above, rounded beneath), and ovaries with 3 sessile stigmas. In comparable places, and also on shingle-beaches and sea-cliffs, in S and SW Europe, northwards to Normandy and England.

Hairy Seablite (*Bassia hirsuta* (L.) Aschers) is an often markedly grey-hairy annual to 40 (60) cm with spreading to ascending, flexuous branches. Leaves linear, blunt-tipped, fleshy, to 15 mm long. Flowers minute, hermaphrodite or female, mostly in pairs in leaf-axils; no bracteoles. Perianth green or reddish, membranous, hairy. Ovary with 1 style and 2–3 stigmas. Achene surrounded by perianth, each lobe of which develops a short, divergent spine. Maritime floodmarks, on saline, sandy soils or shell deposits along the coasts of N Germany and Denmark; more in S and SE Europe. This species has become very rare in NW Europe.

Corispermum leptopterum (Aschers.) Iljin is more or less hairy, with narrowly lanceolate, soft-awned leaves, and flowers in axillary spikes; perianth consists of single, membranous, pointed scale; stamens 2; ovary has 2 styles; achenes flattened, ovoid to suborbicular, narrowly winged. In S France and N Italy; locally naturalized in ruderal, sandy places and along railways, from Belgium to Latvia.

Kochia (*Kochia laniflora* (C.C. Gmelin) Borbás) is a more or less hairy (pubescent) annual to 1 m with erect branches. Leaves linear, 1-veined, soft, to 25 mm long. Flowers usually hermaphrodite, mostly solitary in leaf-axils; no bracteoles. Perianth green, membranous, hairy. Ovary with 1 short style and 2–3 stigmas. Achene surrounded by persistent perianth; each perianth lobe develops transverse wing. Ruderal places and arable fields, on dry, sandy soils, mainly in the lowland, in Germany (Rhine valley), W Alps, N Italy, Pannonia and SE Europe. *K. scoparia* (L.) Schrader is a bushy, subglabrous, yellowish-green annual (reddening in autumn), with narrowly lanceolate to linear, 3-veined, ciliate leaves to 50 mm, and green, lobed, transverse wing to each perianth lobe. From the steppes of SE Europe; cultivated for ornament and for breeding silkworms, and locally naturalized in SW Europe.

ROCKROSE FAMILY, CISTACEAE

A family of shrubs and herbs with *c.* 165 species in 8 genera, mainly in warm-temperate regions of Europe, W Asia, Africa and the Americas. Leaves opposite (less often alternate), simple. Flowers regular, hermaphrodite, with 3 or 5 (then often unequal) sepals and usually as many petals. Stamens numerous (10 or more). Ovary superior, composed of 3 or 5 carpels, 1-locular or incompletely 3–10-locular, with 1 style. Fruit a many-seeded capsule, opening with 3 or 5 valves.

p.198 **Fumana**
Fumana procumbens (Dunal) Gren. & Godron

Description: An evergreen dwarf-shrub to 20 (40) cm, often with prostrate, rather gnarled, woody stems, and ascending to erect, herbaceous, hairy, rather densely leafy shoots. *Leaves alternate, linear, needle-like,* 4–8 mm long, finely pointed, ciliate; no stipules. *Flowers solitary in some leaf-axils,* 1–4 per shoot, 8–12 mm diam.; flower-stalks hardly exceeding leaves, short-hairy, *recurved after anthesis.* Sepals 5: outer 2 small, narrowly ovate; inner 3 larger, ovate, scarious, with strong vein. Petals 5, rounded or slightly truncate, yellow (but often reddish in bud). Stamens numerous: inner, *fertile whorls surrounded by sterile ones.* Ovary 1-locular, with 1 threadlike, twisted style and 3-lobed stigma. Fruit an 8–12-seeded capsule, opening with 3 valves.

Flowering: May–July.

Habitat: Bare or grassy places, on dry, preferably calcareous, stony or rocky soils; from sea level to 1,200 m.

Range: S and C Europe, northwards to southernmost Belgium, Germany and

Czechia, isolated on Öland and Gotland, and eastwards through the Balkan region to W Russia and Turkey.

---

p.242 **Halimium**
Halimium alyssoides (Lam.) C. Koch

Description: An evergreen shrub to 50 (100) cm, with spreading to erect, woody branches. Leaves opposite, ovate to elliptical, dull green and stellate-hairy above, white-tomentose beneath. Flowers *30–40 mm diam.*, 2–5 together in small cymes in highest leaf-axils. *Sepals 3, equally large*, ovate, hairy. Petals 5, rounded, yellow. Stamens numerous, yellow. Ovary has *reduced (short and straight, or absent) style* and 3 subsessile stigmas. Capsule opening with 3 valves.

Flowering: May–June.
  Habitat: Scrub and heath, on dry, acid, sandy soils; mainly in the lowland.
   Range: From the Iberian peninsula northwards to W and C France.

---

p.174 **Umbellate Halimium**
Halimium umbellatum (L.) Spach

Description: A spreading to erect half-shrub to 50 cm, with tomentose (occasionally glandular-hairy), densely leafy shoots. Leaves opposite, *narrowly lanceolate*, dull green above, white-tomentose beneath; *leaf-margins rolled under*; no stipules. Flowers 20–25 mm diam., in small cymes in the highest leaf-axils, the terminal ones *more or less in an umbel. Sepals 3, equally large*, narrowly ovate. Petals 5, rounded, *white*. Stamens numerous, yellow. Ovary 1-locular, with *reduced style* and 3 subsessile stigmas. Capsule opening with 3 valves.

Flowering: (March) May–June.
  Habitat: Pine-woods and scrub, on dry, acid, sandy soils; mainly in the lowland.
   Range: Iberia, and SW and C France.

See also Helianthemum apenninum (p.463), the only white-flowering *Helianthemum* in the area.

p.216 **Hoary Rockrose**
Helianthemum canum (L.) Baumg.

Description: A prostrate to ascending, loosely branched
perennial herb, barely lignified. Leaves
opposite, narrowly elliptical to almost
linear, grey-green (with forked hairs) above,
white-tomentose (with stellate hairs)
beneath; no stipules. Flowers (8) 10–15 mm
diam., 3–5 together in *small, terminal
racemes*. Sepals 5, ovate, the outer 2 strongly
reduced in size. Petals 5, rounded, yellow.
Stamens numerous, yellow. Ovary 1-locular,
with long, twisted style and 3-lobed stigma.
Capsule opening with 3 valves.

Flowering: May–July.

Habitat: Open, short grassland, on dry, oligotrophic,
calcareous, stony or rocky soils; from sea
level to 1,600 m.

Range: S and W Europe, northwards to N France,
C Germany, Poland and W Russia.

Similar species: **Alpine Rockrose** (*H. oelandicum* (L.) DC.)
has narrow, hairy leaves, green on both
sides, and small yellow flowers to 12 mm
diam. Scattered through much of Europe,
northwards to S Sweden and N Russia; the
type (with glabrous, green leaves) is known
only from Öland.

Distinct, insular *H. canum* subspecies are
found: ssp. *canescens* (Hartman) Proctor,
from from S Sweden (Öland) has flowers
borne on lateral branches of annual shoots;
ssp. *levigatum* Proctor, from Britain
(Teesdale), has 1–3 terminal flowers, and
leaves dark green and subglabrous above;
ssp. *piloselloides* (Lapeyr.) Proctor, from W
Ireland, has persistent lower leaves.

p.242 **Common Rockrose**
Helianthemum nummularium (L.) Miller

Description: A prostrate to ascending half-shrub to 30
(40) cm, with woody stem-bases. Leaves
opposite, short-stalked, elliptical to narrowly
lanceolate, green (with *forked hairs*) above,
white-tomentose beneath, with *2 lanceolate
stipules* at base, exceeding leaf-stalk. Flowers

12–20 mm diam., up to 12 together in terminal racemes, *each flower with smallish bract*. Sepals 5, ovate, outer 2 strongly reduced, lanceolate. Petals 5, rounded, twice as long as sepals, yellow (rarely creamy white or orange). Stamens numerous, yellow. Ovary 1-locular, with 1 long, sinuous style and 3-lobed stigma. Capsule broadly ovoid, equalling sepals, and opening with 3 valves.

Flowering: (May) June–September.

Habitat: Short grassland and cliffs, on dry or moist, oligotrophic, calcareous, sandy or rocky soils; from sea level to 1,200 m.

Range: Most of Europe except Iceland, Norway and N Russia.

Similar species: **White Rockrose** (*H. apenninum* (L.) Miller) has white petals with yellow blotch at base, 2 linear outer sepals, and stellate hairs on upper surface of leaves. In S and W Europe, northwards to S England and W Germany.

In mountainous regions (at elevations 1,000–2,800 m), there are forms closely related to *H. nummularium*: they have broader leaves, and larger flowers with pink or red-blotched petals (*compare with Tuberaria guttata*).

p.198 **Spotted Rockrose**
Tuberaria guttata (L.) Fourr.

Description: A hairy *annual herb*, with rosette of oblanceolate leaves, and ascending to erect stems to 40 cm. Stem-leaves opposite (*upper ones often alternate, and with 2 lanceolate stipules*), subsessile, elliptical to lanceolate, blunt-tipped, variously hairy on both faces (often pilose above, stellate-hairy beneath), with *3 arched veins* (not pinnately veined, or 1-veined, as in *Helianthemum*). Flowers 10–20 mm diam., 2–6 together in terminal racemes, usually without bracts. Sepals 5, ovate, outer 2 strongly reduced, lanceolate. Petals 5, rounded, *yellow with scarlet or brownish blotch* at base, soon falling. Stamens numerous, yellow. Ovary 1-locular, completely *lacking style*, hence with sessile stigma. Capsule subglobose, equalling sepals, and opening with 3 valves.

Flowering: (April) May–August.
Habitat: Grassy places, heaths and open scrub, also in dune-slacks, on dry, oligotrophic, acid, sandy, stony or rocky soils; mainly in the lowland.
Range: S and W Europe, northwards to S Britain, the Netherlands and E Germany.

DAISY FAMILY, COMPOSITAE

A large, cosmopolitan family of herbs (or rarely, in warm regions, shrubs or small trees), with *c.* 25,000 species in 1,100 genera. Dicots. Leaves alternate or in basal rosette (rarely opposite or whorled), simple (though often pinnately dissected). Flowers (sub)sessile in compact flowerheads, basically 5-merous, implanted on common hypanthium (receptacle), and surrounded by common involucre of bracts; individual flowers (florets) usually small, often with membranous bracteole (scale) at base. Flowerheads variously arranged, often in panicles. Calyx of each floret reduced to pappus of hairs or membranous scales, or absent. Corolla of 2 types: either regular and tubular, with 5 equal teeth (in tubular flowers or disc-florets), or irregular, with straplike process (ligule) at top of tube (in ligulate flowers or ray-florets); flowerhead may contain only 1 of these flower types, or both (when both are present, the ray-florets are on the outside). Stamens 5, attached to inner wall of corolla tube, anthers very often connate into narrow tube all round style. Ovary inferior (in relation to pappus), 1-locular, with 1 style and (1) 2 stigmas. Fruit a nutlet (achene), often disseminated by wind, in which persistent or even enlarged pappus often plays an important role.

---

p.168 **Yarrow** *Achillea millefolium* L.

Description: A *strong-smelling*, usually hairy perennial, with *creeping stolons* and erect flowering stems to 60 cm. Leaves alternate, lanceolate in outline, *doubly pinnately divided, feathery*, with 30–50 almost linear segments, glabrous or slightly hairy. *Flowerheads to 6 mm* diam., numerous, in dense, flat-topped, *umbel-shaped panicles*. Involucre cup-shaped, to 5 mm wide. Receptacle has scales between florets. *Ray-florets often 5*, female, with spreading, truncate, 3-toothed ligule to 2 (3) mm long, pure white or occasionally pink. Disc-florets trumpet-shaped, yellow, hermaphrodite. Achene narrowly ellipsoid to obovoid, compressed, to 2 mm wide, grey or straw-coloured, often with thick, narrow lateral wings; pappus absent.

Flowering: July–October.

Habitat: Grassland, road verges, ruderal places, on dry to moist, mesotrophic, calcareous to slightly acid, mineral or peaty soils; very common, from sea level to 2,800 m.

Range: All Europe except Spitsbergen.

Similar species: *A. nobilis* L. lacks stolons, has broader leaves (ovate in outline) with less than 20 segments, smaller flowerheads (to 3 mm diam.), and very short (to 1 mm), creamy-white ray-florets. In drier places in S and C Europe.

A. millefolium is also commonly called Milfoil. In C Europe plants with velvety-hairy leaves and pink ray-florets are attributed to ssp. *sudetica* (Opiz) Weiss.

---

p.168 **Sneezewort** *Achillea ptarmica* L.

Description: A more or less hairy perennial with creeping stolons and erect flowering stems to 90 cm. Leaves narrowly lanceolate to *almost linear, 4–8 mm wide, sharply serrate,* often glabrous. *Flowerheads 12–18 mm* diam., rather scarce (up to 15) in *loose, umbel-shaped panicles.* Involucre cup-shaped, to 10 mm diam. Receptacle has scales. *Ray-florets c. 10*, female, with white, deflexed, 3-toothed ligule to 5 mm long. Disc-florets trumpet-shaped, pale yellow or greenish, hermaphrodite. Achene compressed, obovate, to 1 mm long; pappus absent.

Flowering: July–August.

Habitat: Grassland, marshes, along streams and ditches, on wet or moist, mesotrophic, acid to neutral, sandy, clayey or peaty soils; from sea level to 1,700 m.

Range: Most of Europe except the Arctic, southwards to N Spain, N Italy, SW Romania and SC Russia; only naturalized in Finland.

Similar species: *A. cartilaginea* Ledeb. ex Reichenb. has lanceolate, biserrate, densely hairy leaves to 17 mm wide, shorter ligules, and achenes

to 2 mm long. NE Europe, westwards to E
Germany and Romania.

Sand Ragweed
Ambrosia coronopifolia Torrey & Gray

Description: A hairy perennial with creeping rhizomes
and erect, branched flowering stems to
90 cm. *Leaves mostly opposite* (but alternate in
inflorescence), subsessile, pinnately divided.
Flowerheads either male or female,
monoecious: *male flowerheads drooping, in long
racemes* at end of branches, with numerous
bell-shaped, tubular florets (no ray-florets,
and no scales), surrounded by rough-hairy,
*connate involucre; female 'flowerheads' erect,
solitary* in upper leaf-axils, with *1 flower and
reduced involucre*, often visible as few (up to 4)
short, blunt teeth on achene; *corolla absent.*
Achene 3–5 mm long, with short beak to
0.5 mm; pappus absent.

Flowering: August–October.

Habitat: Open, ruderal places, on dry, oligotrophic to
mesotrophic, preferably basic, sandy soils;
mainly in the lowland.

Range: Native to N America, but locally naturalized
in continental W and NC Europe, northwards to Denmark, eastwards to W Russia.

Similar species: **(Common) Ragweed** (*A. artemisiifolia* L.)
(*see* photograph p.77) is also from N
America, but annual, with doubly
pinnatifid leaves, and achenes with 5–7
sharp involucral teeth and longer beak (to
2 mm). Naturalized in continental W and
C Europe, in comparable habitats.

---

p.170 **Mountain Everlasting**
Antennaria dioica (L.) Gaertner

Description: A mat-forming perennial, with creeping,
branching stolons giving off leaf-rosettes
from which ascending or erect flowering
stems rise to 20 cm. Leaves glabrous or
slightly hairy and *green above, white-tomentose
beneath*; rosette-leaves spreading, spatulate;
stem-leaves alternate, lanceolate, erect,
often appressed to stem. Flowerheads

6–12 mm diam., in small, terminal *clusters of 2–8*, male or female (*dioecious*); receptacle scaleless; involucral bracts in several rows, blunt-tipped, papery – outer ones woolly, inner ones with glabrous limb, imitating ray-florets. *Male plants have white involucral bracts* and white or pinkish disc-flowers; *females have pinkish bracts* and disc-flowers. Achene ellipsoid, to 1 mm long; pappus of *white hairs* in several rows.

Flowering: May–July.

Habitat: Poor grassland and grassy heaths, dune-pastures, on dry, oligotrophic, calcareous to moderately acid, sandy or rocky soils; from sea level to 3,000 m.

Range: Most of Europe except the far north.

Similar species: **Alpine Cat's-foot** (*A. alpina* (L.) Gaertner) has upper stem-leaves with scarious tip, and sessile flowerheads to 8 mm diam. in clusters of 3–5, with lanceolate, brownish bracts. A comparable form (*A. posildii* Elis.) has subglabrous rosettes, and lacks stolons. *A. nordhageniana* Rune & Ronning has yellowish, brown-spotted involucral bracts. *A. villifera* Boriss has purplish, white-margined bracts and yellow anthers, and lacks stolons. These 4 species are found in boggy places in the mountains of Fennoscandia and N Russia.
Carpathian Cat's-foot (*A. carpatica* (Wahl.) Bluff & Fingerh.) has dark-brown or blackish bracts (acute in male heads), and purple anthers; also lacks stolons. On grassy slopes in Scandinavia and the mountains of C Europe, to the Pyrenees.
Pearly Everlasting (*Anaphalis margaritacea* (L.) Bentham), a close relative from N Asia and N America, is tufted, to 60 cm, and has larger panicles, yellow disc-flowers, and numerous persistent, silvery involucral bracts. Often cultivated for dry bouquets; locally naturalized in N and C Europe.

p.169 **Corn Chamomile** *Anthemis arvensis* L.

Description: An *aromatic*, branched *annual*, with spreading or ascending stems to 45 cm. Leaves alternate, roughly ovate in outline,

2–3-pinnate with narrow segments, *often hairy beneath*. Flowerheads solitary at end of branches, long-stalked, 20–30 mm diam.; *receptacle conical*, with *broadly lanceolate, long-pointed scales* between florets; involucre cup-shaped, with several rows of bracts. Ray-florets female, narrowly elliptical, bluntly 3-toothed, *white*, deflexed after anthesis; disc-florets hermaphrodite, yellow. *Achene truncate with several smooth ribs on all sides*; pappus absent.

Flowering: June–July (Autumn).

Habitat: Arable fields and disturbed roadsides, on dry, mesotrophic, preferably calcareous, sandy or loamy soils; from sea level to 1,900 m.

Range: All Europe except Spitsbergen; an archeophyte, native to the Mediterranean and W Asia.

Similar species: **Stinking Chamomile** (*A. cotula* L.) has foetid odour and linear scales on receptacle; achenes have several knobby ribs all round. In comparable habitats of Europe outside the Arctic.

(True, or Roman) Chamomile (*Chamaemelum nobile* (L.) All.) is perennial, with creeping rhizomes, and flowerheads to 25 mm diam.; tube of disc-florets sags over the top of unilaterally 3-ribbed achene; scales on receptacle elliptical, with rounded top; leaves glabrous beneath. In grassland, along roads, on banks, also in arable fields, on dry, sandy soils; native to S and SW Europe, northwards to N France and S Britain; also cultivated for ornament and medical uses, and naturalized in C and E Europe.

Matricaria (the mayweeds) is similar but has no scales on the receptacle.

---

p.233 **Yellow Chamomile** *Anthemis tinctoria* L.

Description: A branched perennial to 60 cm, with ascending or erect stems. Leaves alternate, *pinnatifid*, with lanceolate, lobed to deeply serrate segments. Flowerheads 25–45 mm diam., terminal, solitary, long-stalked; *receptacle hemispherical, with linear scales*.

Ray-florets female, short, broadly straplike, *yellow*, subtruncate with 3 blunt teeth. Disc-florets hermaphrodite, yellow. Achene angular with 4 sharp edges; pappus very short, collarlike, membranous.

Flowering: June–September.

Habitat: Ruderal places, roadsides, old walls, railways, on dry, mesotrophic, sandy, stony or rocky soils; from sea level to 1,600 m.

Range: Continental Europe, northwards to S Sweden; naturalized in Britain and Finland.

Compare with Chrysanthemum segetum (see p.484).

---

p.297 **Greater Burdock** *Arctium lappa* L.

Description: A stout, branched, more or less hairy biennial or short-lived perennial to 1.5 (3) m. Leaves broadly ovate, entire-margined or with sparse, short teeth; lower ones cordate, to 50 cm long, with rather long, *solid stalks*; upper ones with rounded base, short-stalked. *Flowerheads 35–40 mm diam., long-stalked,* forming *umbel-shaped panicles*; involucre globose, with numerous linear, green, *subglabrous, long-pointed bracts, terminating in hooked bristle*; receptacle with bristle-like scales between florets. All florets tubular, narrowly trumpet-shaped, purplish (exceptionally white). Achene ellipsoid, rugose near top, with *short pappus of scabrid, yellow hairs*.

Flowering: July–September.

Habitat: Ruderal places, road verges, wood margins, on moist, eutrophic, preferably calcareous, sandy, loamy or clayey soils; from sea level to 1,800 m.

Range: Most of Europe except the high Arctic.

Similar species: *A. nemorosum* Lej. from N, C and E Europe has narrow panicles with flowerheads 30–35 mm diam., on short stalks to 30 mm.

Lesser Burdock (*Arctium minus* (Hill) Bernh.) has short-stalked, often cottony flowerheads 15–20 mm diam., in racemes forming narrow panicles, and hollow leaf-stalks. In most of Europe except the Arctic.

A. pubens Bab. is intermediate between *A. lappa* and *A. minus*, having rather short-stalked flowerheads 20–30 mm wide, and glabrous to thinly cottony involucres. In W, C and S Europe; very common.

A. tomentosum Miller has solid leaf-stalks, and densely cottony flowerheads 20–30 mm diam., in umbel-shaped panicles; inner involucral bracts truncate and awned. In continental Europe, but rare in the north and west.

---

p.232 **Arnica** *Arnica montana* L.

Description: A glandular-hairy perennial with erect, simple stem to 60 cm. Most leaves in basal rosette, elliptical or broadly oblanceolate, 20–40 mm wide, entire; *stem-leaves opposite*, few (1–3 pairs). Flowerheads *solitary, large* (60–80 mm diam.); involucre cup-shaped, with 1–2 rows of green, lanceolate bracts; receptacle convex, hairy between florets. Ray-florets up to 20, yellow, strap-shaped; disc-florets numerous, yellow. Achene ribbed; pappus of rigid, white hairs in 1 row.

Flowering: May–September.

Habitat: Meadows, poor pasture and grassy heaths, on moist, oligotrophic, slightly acid, sandy, loamy or stony soils; from sea level to 2,800 m, but rare in the lowland.

Range: Continental Europe, northwards to S Scandinavia and Latvia, and eastwards to C Russia.

Similar species: *A. angustifolia* Vahl from N Scandinavia and Arctic Russia has smaller flowerheads (35–45 mm diam.), and narrower rosette-leaves (5–20 mm wide).

Arnica is a highly valued medicinal herb.

---

p.230 **Lamb's Succory**
Arnoseris minima (L.) Schweigger & Koerte

Description: A nearly glabrous to slightly hairy annual, with leaf-rosette and ascending to erect flowering stems to 30 cm; stems little-branched, and *strongly inflated below flowerheads*. Leaves all basal, oblanceolate, coarsely dentate or acutely lobed. *Flowerheads small* (7–10 mm diam.), solitary, terminal; involucre cup-shaped, with 2 rows of bracts (outer ones short); receptacle flat, scaleless. All florets ligulate, yellow, with rather short, truncate ligule. Achene *c.* 2 mm long, narrowly obovoid or ellipsoid, with 5 paler ribs and truncate top; pappus absent.

Flowering: June–September.

Habitat: Cereal fields and disturbed road verges, on dry, mesotrophic, sandy soils poor in lime, from sea level to 1,000 m.

Range: Continental Europe, northwards to S Sweden.

---

p.77 **Wormwood** *Artemisia absinthium* L.

Description: A strongly *aromatic, greyish perennial*, with tufted, erect, silkily hairy stems to 1 m. Leaves *2–3-pinnatifid*, with blunt, narrow segments, *grey-silky on both faces*. Flowerheads small (*c.* 3 mm diam.), ovoid, nodding, in long, ascending to erect, axillary racemes (forming slender panicle); involucre with few rows of bracts; *receptacle has long hairs*, but no scales. All florets tubular, yellowish; outer ones female, inner ones hermaphrodite (all fertile). Achene ovoid; pappus absent.

Flowering: July–September.

Habitat: Ruderal and disturbed places, roadsides, industrial areas, on dry, oligotrophic, basic, sandy or rocky soils; both coastal and inland, from sea level to 2,000 m.

Range: Most of Europe except Iceland; an archeophyte, probably originating from E Mediterranean region.

Similar species: **Hoary Mugwort** (*A. stellerana* Besser), from NE Asia, has 1-pinnatifid, white-tomentose leaves and larger flowerheads (5–9 mm diam.); cultivated for ornament, and locally naturalized in Britain, Denmark and Sweden.

Wormwood was formerly used as a liqueur-flavouring until its toxic properties were realized.

p.78 **Field Wormwood** *Artemisia campestris* L.

Description: A moderately hairy, scentless perennial with tufted, erect, reddish stems to 1 m. Leaves *2–3-pinnatifid*, green or grey-green (soon losing hairs), with linear segments keeled below. Flowerheads small (2–3 mm diam.), ovoid, short-stalked, erect, in ascending to erect, axillary racemes; involucre with few rows of bracts; receptacle scaleless. All florets tubular, yellowish; *outer ones female, inner ones functionally male* (some infertile). Achene ovoid; pappus absent.

Flowering: August–September.

Habitat: Open, grassy places, road verges, banks, inland dunes, on dry, oligotrophic to mesotrophic, often basic, sandy soils; from sea level to 2,000 m.

Range: All Europe except Ireland and the far north.

Similar species: *A. rupestris* L. is a half-shrub, to 50 cm, with green, 1–2-pinnatifid leaves, nodding, yellowish flowerheads (5–7 mm diam.) with hermaphrodite inner florets, and pinnatifid, leaf-like bracts at base of stalk. In NE Europe, in scrub on rocky soils.

Several related species occur in the steppe belt of SE Europe (*see* regional floras). The ssp. *A c. maritima* Arc. has larger flowerheads (3–6 mm diam.), and fleshy leaf-segments rounded, not keeled below. In sea-dunes of W France; and naturalized in dunes of the Netherlands.

---

p.78 **Sea Wormwood** *Artemisia maritima* L.

Description: A *white-tomentose, strongly aromatic* perennial to 60 cm, often slightly woody below. Leaves *2–3-pinnatifid*, with linear segments. Flowerheads small (1–2 mm diam.), ovoid, short-stalked, nodding to erect, in ascending to arched, axillary racemes; involucre with few rows of *white-tomentose bracts*; receptacle scaleless. All florets tubular, yellow, *all hermaphrodite*. Achene ovoid; pappus absent.

Flowering: August–October.

Habitat: The higher zones of saltmarshes, on levees along tidal gullies, under sea-walls, on periodically to daily inundated, wet, saline, sandy or clayey soils; also saline places inland.

Range: Coasts of W and N Europe, from SW France northwards to S Norway and Estonia; inland in C Germany and the steppes of SE Europe.

Similar species: *A. oelandica* (Besser) Komarov is non-aromatic, and has 1–2-pinnatifid leaves; endemic on Öland.

p.78 Norwegian Mugwort
Artemisia norvegica Fries

Description: A characteristic, *dwarfish, grey-silky* perennial to 10 cm, with *basal rosette* of stalked, 2-pinnatifid leaves, and few, erect flowering stems. Stem-leaves few, the higher ones simply pinnatifid. *Flowerheads few (1–3), large* (to 12 mm diam.), long-stalked, nodding; involucre hemispherical; receptacle scaleless. Florets tubular, yellow, *with hairy corolla*; marginal flowers female, inner flowers male. Achene ellipsoid; pappus absent.

Flowering: July–September.

Habitat: Mountain tundra and lichen heaths, on moist, oligotrophic, acid, sandy, gravelly and peaty soils; 550–1,900 m.

Range: NW Scotland (W Ross), C Norway, and the N Urals.

p.78 Mugwort *Artemisia vulgaris* L.

Description: A tufted, somewhat aromatic perennial, to 1.2 m, with weakly hairy, *tough, purple-striped stems*. Leaves 1–2-pinnatifid, ovate in outline, with lanceolate segments (3–6 mm wide), subglabrous and *dark green above, white-tomentose beneath*. Flowerheads ovoid, to 4 mm long, very numerous, *sessile, in dense, axillary spikes*; involucre cylindrical, grey-hairy; receptacle glabrous, scaleless. All florets tubular, *yellow or brick-red*; outer ones female, inner ones male. Achene spindle-shaped, with truncate apex; pappus absent.

Flowering: July–September.

Habitat: Ruderal places, roadsides, industrial areas, building sites, railways, on dry to moist, (very) eutrophic soils; from sea level to 1,600 m.

Range: Most of Europe except the high Arctic.

Similar species: **Chinese Mugwort** (*A. verlotiorum* Lamotte), from SW China, is strongly aromatic, to 2 m, and has purplish florets, creeping rhizomes bearing leaf-rosettes and densely hairy stems with narrow (not wide) pith. Locally naturalized in ruderal places of W and WC Europe.

---

p.321 **European Michaelmas Daisy**
Aster amellus L.

Description: A hairy perennial to 60 cm, with ascending branches. Leaves alternate, broadly lanceolate, entire or bluntly dentate, short-stalked; upper ones sessile. Flowerheads large (30–50 mm diam.), terminal, *few (1–10) in loose, umbel-shaped panicles*; involucre cup-shaped, with 2–3 rows of broadly lanceolate bracts, these *1.5–3 mm wide, with blunt, recurved top*; receptacle scaleless. Ray-florets up to 30 in 1 row, female, violet or blue (rarely pink or white). Disc-florets numerous, hermaphrodite, yellow. Achenes narrowly ellipsoid; pappus of white or ruddy hairs.

Flowering: July–October.

Habitat: Scrub and rough grassland, wood margins, on dry, oligotrophic, calcareous, sandy, loamy or rocky soils; mainly in low mountainous areas, to 1,400 m.

Range: C and E Europe, westwards to N France, northwards to S Germany and Poland, and eastwards to E Russia.

Similar species: *A. sibiricus* L., with acute involucral bracts occurs in N and C Russia, and (isolated) in Norway.

Several N American species have naturalized in Europe: they often have narrow, acute involucral bracts (to 1 mm wide), and ray-florets in all hues from white and pink to violet and blue (*see* regional floras).

p.235 **Goldilocks Aster** *Aster linosyris* (L.) Bernh.

Description: A more or less tufted, *hairless* perennial to 60 cm, with erect or ascending stems. Leaves numerous, alternate, *linear, to 50 mm long*, sessile, *1-veined*, entire-margined but *rough-edged*. Flowerheads 10–18 mm diam., in umbel-shaped panicles; involucre cup-shaped, with narrowly lanceolate bracts in several rows (outer ones often recurved, inner ones pointed), with wide, scarious margins; receptacle scaleless. *Ray-florets absent*. Disc-florets yellow, hermaphrodite. Achene to 3 mm long, ellipsoid, truncate at apex, hairy; pappus of white or ruddy hairs.

Flowering: August–September.

Habitat: Open grassland, steppes, cliffs, on dry, oligotrophic to mesotrophic, preferably calcareous, sandy, loamy or rocky soils; from sea level to 1,000 m.

Range: In Europe northwards to N England (Lancashire), S Belgium, Germany, S Sweden, and eastwards through C and E Europe to C Russia, the Pontic steppes and the Caucasus.

---

p.347 **Sea Aster** *Aster tripolium* L.

Description: A tufted, *hairless* perennial or biennial, to 1 (2) m, with short, thick rhizomes, erect to ascending stems, and ascending branches. Leaves alternate, subsessile, up to 15 cm long, lanceolate, entire or with some blunt teeth, *fleshy, often glaucous*. Flowerheads 10–20 mm diam., numerous in large, umbel-shaped panicles; involucre cup-shaped, with 2–3 rows of broadly lanceolate bracts *1.5–3 mm wide, blunt-tipped, appressed*; receptacle scaleless. *Ray-florets up to 15* in 1 row, female, *lilac or pale blue-violet*, (rarely pink or white). Disc-florets numerous, hermaphrodite, yellow. Achenes 2–3 mm long, spindle-shaped, hairy; pappus of white or ruddy hairs.

Flowering: (April) July–October.

Habitat: Coastal saltmarshes and estuaries, also in saline habitats inland, on wet (periodically to daily flooded), saline or brackish, often clayey soils; more recently also along frequently salted motorways.

Range: Coasts of Europe, except those of the high Arctic; also inland, especially in C Germany and SE Europe.

Plants lacking ray-florets are far from rare (f. *discoideus* (Reichenb.) Vuijck). The leaves can be eaten as a vegetable.

---

p.168 **Daisy** *Bellis perennis* L.

Description: A hairy perennial with basal leaf-rosette and ascending to erect, *leafless flowering stems* to 15 cm. *Rosette-leaves spatulate*, crenate or with some blunt teeth, green. Flowerheads solitary, 15–30 mm diam.; involucral bracts blunt-tipped, in 2 rows; receptacle conical, hollow, scaleless. Ray-florets female, numerous, in 1 row, *white, the tip often reddish* on outside. Disc-florets numerous, yellow, hermaphrodite. Achene to 1.5 mm long, obovoid, compressed, with thickened margin, hairy; pappus absent.

Flowering: April–September (Winter).

Habitat: Pasture, lawns, road verges, on moist, mesotrophic to eutrophic, mineral or peaty soils; from sea level to 2,500 m.

Range: All Europe except N and E Russia.

A very common species. A cultivar with only white, ligulate florets (Hen-and-chicken Daisy) is often kept in gardens.

---

p.232 **Nodding Bur-marigold** *Bidens cernua* L.

Description: A hairless or slightly hairy annual with erect, branched stems to 90 cm. *Leaves opposite, simple*, sessile, *slightly interconnate* at base, lanceolate, serrate (rarely subentire). Flowerheads axillary (forming dichasial cymes), 15–25 mm diam., *nodding* on long stalks, with involucral bracts in 2 rows – the 5–8 *outer bracts much larger, leaf-like*, the inner ones narrowly ovate, and with membranous margins; receptacle flat, with scales between florets. Ray-florets often absent (otherwise short, broad, and yellow: var. *radiata* DC.). Disc-florets numerous, yellow. Achene 3–4-ribbed, *smooth* (but with *downward-pointing, spiny hairs on ribs*), and with *pappus of 3–4 rigid, barbed bristles*.

Flowering: July–October.

Habitat: Marshy places, along ditches, canals and other stagnant waters, sewage reservoirs, on wet, (very) eutrophic, nitrogen-rich, muddy or peaty soils; from sea level to 1,200 m.

Range: Most of Europe except the high Arctic and much of the Mediterranean.

Similar species: *B. connata* Willd. from N America has stalked leaves (occasionally with 2–4 small side-lobes along stalk), erect flowerheads, achenes usually covered with small tubercles, and pappus of 4–5 barbed bristles. Naturalized along ditches and polluted streams in NW Europe, from the Low Countries to Poland and Switzerland.

---

p.232 **Trifid Bur-marigold** *Bidens tripartita* L.

Description: A glabrous or hairy annual with erect, branched stems to 90 cm. *Leaves opposite, 3–5-partite, with lanceolate, serrate segments*, on winged stalks, upper ones subsessile and sometimes simple. Flowerheads 10–25 mm diam., axillary, erect on long stalks, with *5–8 large, leaf-like outer bracts*; inner bracts broadly lanceolate, with membranous margin; receptacle has scales. Ray-florets usually absent (otherwise short, yellow). Disc-florets numerous, yellow. Achene ribbed, *smooth* (but with *downward-pointing, spiny hairs on ribs*), and with *pappus of 2–4-barbed bristles*.

Flowering: July–September.

Habitat: Marshes, beside ditches, pools, sewage reservoirs, on wet (or seasonally flooded), eutrophic, basic to slightly acid, sandy or peaty soils; from sea level to 1,200 m, but mainly in the lowland.

Range: All Europe except Iceland and Spitsbergen, but rare in the extreme north and south.

Similar species: *B. radiata* Thuill. has 10–12 leaf-like outer involucral bracts, 3–5-partite leaves, and achenes with 2-barbed bristles. In similar habitats, mainly in NE and NC Europe, extending westwards to Germany and E France, and southwards to Austria and C Russia.

Beggarticks (*B. frondosa* L.) has 3–5-pinnate leaves (with lanceolate, serrate leaflets, and unwinged stalks), short, rarely leaf-like outer involucral bracts, and spinulous-hairy achenes with 2-barbed bristles. Native to N America; widely naturalized in wet places of S, W and C Europe.

---

p.299 **Welted Thistle** *Carduus acanthoides* L.

Description: A hairy biennial or short-lived perennial, to 2 m, with erect, spiny-winged stems. Leaves alternate, decurrent on stem, pinnately divided, lanceolate in outline, with ovate, prickly dentate segments; *prickles to 5 mm long*; leaves green above, thinly white-cottony beneath. Flowerheads 10–25 mm diam., solitary (or 2–3 together), *erect on short, unwinged stalks* at end of axillary branches (forming large panicle); involucre rounded, with numerous sharp, linear-lanceolate bracts with prominent middle veins; receptacle has dense, stiff hairs between flowers. All florets tubular, hermaphrodite, red-purplish, with hairy style. Achene ellipsoid; pappus of long, white, basally connate hairs in several rows.

Flowering: June–September.

Habitat: Rough grassland, road verges, river banks wood margins, scrub, ruderal places, on dry to moist, mesotrophic, sandy or loamy soils; from sea level to 3,000 m.

Range: C and E Europe, northwards to S Sweden and C Russia, westwards to Ireland, and eastwards to Greece.

Similar species: *C. crispus* has shorter prickles (to 3 mm); flowerheads subsessile, often in clusters (2–5 together); middle veins of involucral bracts become obscure in basal region. In comparable habitats in all of Continental Europe except the far north.

Great Marsh Thistle (*C. personatus* (L.) Jacq.) is soft-spiny, with unlobed upper leaves, and tightly clustered flowerheads. In the mountains of C Europe, westwards to the Vosges and C Germany, and eastwards to W Russia and Bulgaria.

p.299 **Nodding Thistle** *Carduus nutans* L.

Description: A short-lived perennial, to 2 m, with spiny-winged stems. Leaves alternate, decurrent, pinnately divided, lanceolate in outline, with narrowly ovate, spiny-toothed segments. Flowerheads large, (20) 35–70 mm diam., solitary or in small clusters, *nodding on long, hairy, unwinged stalks* at end of branches; involucre wider than long, with numerous sharp, recurved, linear bracts; receptacle hairy, scaleless. All florets tubular, numerous, hermaphrodite, red-purplish, with hairy style. Achene ellipsoid; pappus of long, white, basally connate hairs in several rows.

Flowering: May–September.

Habitat: Rough grassland, dunes, ruderal and disturbed places, on dry, oligotrophic, basic (often calcareous), usually sandy soils; from sea level to 2,500 m.

Range: Most of Europe, northwards to Scotland, Germany and W Russia.

Similar species: **Alpine Thistle** (*C. defloratus* L.), with leaves glaucous beneath, and solitary flowerheads (25– 40 mm diam.) on very long, unwinged stalks, occurs in the mountains of C Europe.

Another common name for Nodding Thistle is Musk Thistle.

p.299 **Slender Thistle** *Carduus tenuiflorus* Curtis

Description: A rather slim, erect *annual* (or biennial), to 1 m, with spiny-winged stems. Leaves oblanceolate in outline, pinnately lobed or divided, spiny-toothed, decurrent, yellowish-green above, white-cottony beneath. *Flowerheads small* (6–10 mm diam.), erect, in dense clusters on short, hairy, unwinged stalks, forming large panicles; *involucre ovoid, much longer than wide*, with glabrous, lanceolate, spine-tipped bracts; receptacle hairy, scaleless. All florets tubular, hermaphrodite, *pale pink*, with hairy style. Achenes ellipsoid; pappus of basally connate, white hairs in several rows.

Flowering: May–August.

Habitat: Open, sunny places, grassland, dunes, road verges, on dry, mesotrophic, basic, sandy or stony soils; from sea level to 900 m, but mainly coastal in the north.

Range: SW and W Europe, northwards to Britain and the Netherlands, and eastwards to Switzerland and N Italy.

---

p.44 **Carline Thistle** *Carlina vulgaris* L.

Description: A biennial or short-lived perennial, to 50 cm, with erect, simple or scarcely branched stem. Leaves alternate, lanceolate, spiny-dentate; lower ones short-stalked, upper ones sessile and clasping. Flowerheads 1–3 (5), at end of stem and branches, large (20–50 mm diam.); outer involucral bracts lanceolate, spiny-dentate, leaf-like; *inner bracts longer, linear, entire, shiny yellow, spreading*; receptacle hairy. All florets tubular, hermaphrodite, yellowish-brown. Achene ellipsoid; pappus of *feathery hairs* in 1 row.

Flowering: July–September.

Habitat: Open, grassy places, banks, dunes, heaths, on dry, oligotrophic to mesotrophic, preferably calcareous, sandy, loamy or stony soils; from sea level to 1,700 m.

Range: Most of Europe, northwards to Finland and N Russia.

Similar species: **Stemless Carline Thistle** (*C. acaulis* L.) has basal rosette of pinnately lobed, spiny-dentate leaves, short stem to 20 (40) cm, or no stem at all; flowerheads solitary, very large (5–13 cm), with silvery-white inner involucral bracts. In comparable habitats in the C European mountains, westwards to C France and C Spain, and northwards to the Vosges, C Germany, Poland and Belorussia.

p.297 **Red Star-thistle** *Centaurea calcitrapa* L.

Description: An almost glabrous, much-branched, short-lived perennial, to 60 cm. Leaves alternate, not decurrent: lower ones stalked, pinnately divided with broad segments, soon withered; upper ones sessile, lanceolate, pinnately divided with narrow segments or simple, serrate, awned. Flowerheads short-stalked, in axils of side-branches, or terminal, often with ruff of leaves; involucre ovoid, 8–12 mm wide, with lanceolate *bracts ending in long (to 15 mm), sharp, reflexed, yellowish spine*, and often with smaller lateral spines; receptacle bristly-hairy. All florets tubular, hermaphrodite, *subequal*, with 5 long teeth, *pink or purplish* (rarely white). Achenes ellipsoid, with (soon falling) pappus of short hairs.

Flowering: July–September.

Habitat: Open grassland, scrub, roadsides, banks, ruderal places, on dry, mesotrophic, often calcareous, sandy, loamy or clayey soils; mainly in the lowland.

Range: Mainly in S and SC Europe, extending northwards to C France, Bohemia and W Russia; more or less naturalized further north (to Britain, the Netherlands, Germany).

Similar species: **Yellow Star-thistle** (*C. solstitialis* L.) has yellow florets and long, deflexed spines to involucral bracts (much like *C. calcitrapa*). In S Europe, extending northwards to C France and W Russia; naturalized in C Europe.
Rough Star-thistle (*C. aspera* L.) has larger, purplish flowerheads (to 25 mm wide), and involucral bracts with much shorter, palmate, 3–5-parted, reflexed spine to 6 mm. In SW Europe, to W France, in sandy, often coastal habitats.

p.347 **Cornflower** *Centaurea cyanus* L.

Description: A greyish-green *annual*, to 60 cm, with erect, moderately branched stems. Leaves alternate, *not decurrent* on stem, cottony beneath: lower ones lanceolate, usually more or less pinnately lobed or dentate; upper ones linear, entire. Flowerheads terminal, 15–30 mm diam.; involucre cup-shaped, to 10 mm wide, with greenish, narrowly ovate, rounded bracts bearing *short, brown fringe around top*; receptacle bristly-hairy. Florets all tubular, with 5 long teeth: outer florets much enlarged, spreading, *deep blue*, and sterile; inner ones shorter, blue-violet, hermaphrodite. Achene ellipsoid, striped, with oblique base, and pappus of short hairs.

Flowering: June–August.

Habitat: Cereal fields, road verges, banks, generally in disturbed places, on dry, mesotrophic, sandy or loamy soils; from sea level to 1,800 m.

Range: All Europe except the high Arctic.

Similar species: **Perennial Cornflower** (*C. montana* L.) also has enlarged, blue marginal florets, but is perennial, with creeping rhizomes, decurrent, broadly lanceolate leaves (to 40 mm wide, instead of less than 10 mm), much larger flowerheads (60–80 mm diam.) with involucres to 15 mm wide. In calcareous grassland and open woods in the mountains of C Europe, westwards to the Pyrenees, C France, the Ardennes, northwards to C Germany and Poland.

Less than half a century ago *C. cyanus* was a very common weed of fields with winter cereals; it has strongly declined as a result of the use of herbicides.

---

p.298 **Brown Knapweed** *Centaurea jacea* L. group

Description: A hairy perennial with erect, rather scarcely branched stems to 1.2 m. Leaves rough-hairy: lower ones elliptical to lanceolate, often pinnately lobed; upper ones narrower, subentire, sessile, occasionally clasping stem with dentate auricles. Flowerheads solitary, terminal; involucral bracts elliptical, greenish, bearing membranous, *ovate, brown or blackish appendage* with long, brownish, *irregularly incised or deeply dissected fringe*; receptacle hairy. All florets tubular, subequal (or outer ones slightly larger), with 5 long teeth, *red-purplish*, hermaphrodite. Achene ellipsoid; pappus of short hairs, or absent.

Flowering: June–September.

Habitat: Meadows, rough pasture, road verges, scrub, and open woods, on dry to moist, oligotrophic to mesotrophic, basic or slightly acid, sandy, loamy, clayey or stony soils; from sea level to 2,000 m.

Range: Most of Europe except the extreme north.

Similar species: The *C. jacea* group contains numerous closely related species, all with long-fringed, abruptly widening appendages to the involucral bracts. **Common Knapweed** (*C. nigra* L.), also known as Hardheads, is the more easily recognizable – indeed common – species in the group; it has broadly lanceolate leaves, purple flowerheads (20–40 mm wide) with equal florets, and involucral bracts with triangular, blackish, long-fringed appendage. In comparable habitats, to 1,000 m, in most of Europe, northwards to C Scandinavia. For details on the many other microspecies in the *C. jacea* group, *see* regional floras.

Wig Knapweed (*C. phrygia* L.) is also comparable, though not belonging to the *jacea* group. Leaves elliptical to ovate, more or less toothed. Flowerheads solitary or slightly clustered, large (30–50 mm diam.), with pink or purplish florets; outer florets much enlarged and spreading (as in *C. scabiosa*); appendages to bracts very long, spear-shaped, recurved, with long, dark-brown or blackish, featherlike fringe. Mainly in N, C and E Europe, westwards to Germany, and southwards to N Italy and Bulgaria.

p.298 **Greater Knapweed** *Centaurea scabiosa* L.

Description: A stout, rough-hairy perennial with erect, little-branched stems to 1.2 m. *Leaves pinnately divided* (lower ones often doubly pinnatifid, and even the highest often with some lateral lobes), lanceolate in outline. Flowerheads terminal, solitary, large (30–50 mm diam.); involucre rounded, large (15–25 mm wide); involucral bracts green, with inconspicuous veins, and *narrow, blackish fringe around top* (almost like that of cornflowers); receptacle hairy. Florets all tubular, with 5 long teeth, *red-purplish* (rarely white): *outer ones much enlarged, spreading*, sterile; inner ones shorter, hermaphrodite. Achene ellipsoid; pappus of short hairs.

Flowering: June–September.

Habitat: Rough grassland, scrub, roadsides, on dry to moist, oligotrophic, calcareous, sandy, loamy or stony soils; from sea level to 500 m.

Range: Most of Europe except the high Arctic and the deep south.

Similar species: *C. rhenana* Boreau has smaller flowerheads (involucres up to 10 mm wide), markedly veined involucral bracts, with narrow, black fringe and short, apical awn. In C and SE Europe, westwards to NE France, and northwards to C Germany, Poland and C Russia, often in roadsides or along railways. *Compare also C. phrygia* (p.483), which has subentire leaves.

---

p.233 **Corn Marigold** *Chrysanthemum segetum* L.

Description: A hairless annual with erect, moderately branched stems to 60 cm. Leaves alternate, bluish-green, narrowly obovate to lanceolate; lower ones narrowed into winged stalk and deeply pinnately lobed, upper ones narrower, dentate, sessile and often half-clasping. *Flowerheads large* (35–55 mm diam.), solitary, terminal; involucre has 3 rows of narrowly ovate, green bracts; receptacle scaleless. Ray-florets broadly straplike, *yellow*, female, in 1 row; disc-flowers numerous, yellow, hermaphrodite. *Achenes of ray-florets have 2 wide wings*, those of disc-florets have 10 ribs but no wings; pappus absent.

Flowering: June–September.

Habitat: Arable fields, field margins, open roadsides, also in ruderal places, on dry to moist, mesotrophic, neutral or acid, sandy or loamy soils; mainly in the lowland.

Range: Native to Greece and Crete; an archeophyte in W and N Europe.

Similar species: **Field Marigold** (*Calendula arvensis* L.) has subentire, sessile leaves, small, deep-yellow flowerheads to 20 mm diam., and curved, transversely ridged achenes (5–25 mm long, instead of less than 3 mm). In arable fields and vineyards, in S and SC Europe, northwards to the Paris Basin, C Germany, Romania and W Russia.

p.347 **Chicory** *Cichorium intybus* L.

Description: A more or less rough-hairy, often slightly glandular, *latex-bearing perennial*, with erect, widely branched stems to 1.2 m. Leaves rough-hairy beneath, lanceolate; lower ones short-stalked, pinnately lobed or pinnatifid with backward-pointing segments, upper ones often subentire, clasping. Flowerheads 20–40 mm diam., in large, loose panicles; involucral bracts in 2 rows, glandular, outer ones ovate, recurved, inner ones lanceolate, long-pointed, erect; receptacle flat, scaleless. *All florets ligulate*, with spreading, *light-blue*, strap-shaped, *truncate, 5-toothed ligule*. Achene ribbed; *pappus of very short, erect scales in 2 rows*.

Flowering: July–August (October).

Habitat: Rough grassland, road verges, banks, field margins, on moist, mesotrophic to eutrophic, preferably calcareous, loamy or clayey soils; from sea level to 1,500 m.

Range: Most of Europe except Iceland and Spitsbergen; only naturalized in much of the north.

Formerly cultivated for medicinal purposes. Today, the roasted roots are used as a coffee-substitute. The popular vegetable chicory is the cultivar 'Foliosum'.

p.300 **Dwarf Thistle** *Cirsium acaule* L.

Description: A scarcely hairy perennial with long, creeping rhizomes, and basal leaf-rosette; *stem very short or seemingly absent, bearing 1 flowerhead (rarely 2–4 heads)*. Rosette-leaves lanceolate in outline, pinnately divided with ovate, usually 3-lobed, wavy, dentate segments with sharp, spiny teeth. *Flowerheads subsessile to short-stalked*, 20–40 mm diam.; involucre narrowly ovoid, with several rows of appressed, lanceolate, purple-edged, acute but hardly spiny bracts; receptacle hairy. All florets tubular, with 5 long teeth, red-purplish, hermaphrodite. Achene 3–4 mm long, obovoid; pappus of feathery hairs in several rows, connate at base.

Flowering: June–September.

Habitat: Pasture, fallow fields, roadsides, on dry to moist, oligotrophic, calcareous, loamy or stony soils; from sea level to 2,500 m.

Range: Most of Europe, northwards to Britain, S Sweden and the Baltic States, and eastwards to E Russia.

A strongly declining species.

---

p.300 **Creeping Thistle** *Cirsium arvense* (L.) Scop.

Description: A scarcely hairy perennial, with creeping stolons and erect, branched, unwinged stems to 1.2 m. No distinct rosette, so *leaves usually all cauline*, lanceolate in outline, *shiny dark green* and glabrous above, often slightly cottony beneath, deeply pinnately lobed with wavy, spiny-dentate segments; upper leaves sessile, clasping stem but never much decurrent (hence *stem without spiny wings*). *Flowerheads numerous, rather small* (15–25 mm diam.), long-stalked (rarely subsessile, in small clusters), forming *large, loose, more or less umbel-shaped panicles*; involucre ovoid or subglobose, with lanceolate, purple-tipped, *shortly awned bracts* in several rows; receptacle hairy. All florets tubular, deep pink or purplish (rarely white), *usually unisexual and dioecious* (then male plants with slightly larger flowerheads, and sterile pistils). Achene to 4 mm long, obovoid, slightly compressed, smooth, olive-green; pappus of long, basally connate, feathery, creamy to yellow hairs to 30 mm, in several rows.

Flowering: June–September.

Habitat: Arable fields, roadsides, in ruderal and disturbed places, on dry to moist, eutrophic, mineral or peaty soils, even in brackish habitats; from sea level to 2,000 m.

Range: All Europe except Spitsbergen; only naturalized in Iceland; a troublesome weed in fields and gardens.

Similar species: **Marsh Thistle** (*C. palustre* (L.) Scop.) also has numerous (but subsessile), small flowerheads (10–20 mm diam.) in clusters of 2–8 forming long, sleek panicles; flowers hermaphrodite; stem less branched (often simple), always spiny-winged (leaves decurrent); achenes to 3 mm; pappus to 10 mm. In marshes, meadows, along ditches, in damp woods and dune-valleys, on wet, oligotrophic to mesotrophic, slightly acid, often peaty soils; from the lowland to 1,800 m, in all Europe except the far north.

---

p.300 **Meadow Thistle** *Cirsium dissectum* (L.) Hill

Description: A usually *unbranched* perennial, with creeping stolons and erect, *white-tomentose, unwinged stems* to 30 (80) m. Leaves dark green and hairy above, *white-tomentose beneath, scarce* (2–5), *low on stem* (but hardly in distinct rosette), stalked, (ob)lanceolate, *subentire to regularly lobed or sinuously dentate, soft-spined*; often 1 or 2 small, sessile, linear, erect leaves higher up stem. *Flowerheads solitary* at end of stem, rather large (25–30 mm diam.); involucre broadly ovoid, with erect, narrowly lanceolate, very acute, purple-tipped bracts in several rows; receptacle hairy. All florets tubular, red-purplish, with 5 long teeth, hermaphrodite. Achene to 2.5 mm; pappus of basally connate, feathery hairs in several rows, to 15 mm long.

Flowering: June–August.

Habitat: Hay-meadows, marshy heaths, fens, on wet, oligotrophic, moderately acid, peaty soils; mainly in the lowland.

Range: W Europe, northwards to Ireland, Britain, the Netherlands and Germany; naturalized in Norway and Hungary.

Similar species: **Tuberous Thistle** (*C. tuberosum* (L.) All.) also has solitary flower, terminal on rather leafless stem, but leaves deeply pinnately lobed, pale green and only slightly cottony beneath; roots characteristically thickened, spindle-shaped (instead of thin and terete); involucral bracts narrowly ovate and subobtuse. In moist, calcareous grassland, in W Europe, northwards to S Britain, S Belgium and Germany.

Brook Thistle (*C. rivulare* (Jacq.) All.) also has deeply lobed leaves (pale green beneath), but subsessile flowerheads in stalked, terminal clusters of 2–8; roots thin. In marshes, moist grassland, along streams and ditches, on acid, peaty soils, in C and E Europe, westwards to the Pyrenees, and northwards to Germany, S Sweden, Poland and the Baltic States.

---

p.300   **Melancholy Thistle**
        Cirsium helenioides (L.) Hill

Description: Rather like *C. dissectum* in having solitary flowerhead (rarely 2), but *much larger*, to 1.2 m, with *numerous leaves along (wingless, cottony) stem*. Leaves *sessile, clasping stem with 2 rounded auricles*, ovate to lanceolate, *subentire* (lower ones occasionally pinnately lobed), with *soft-spiny margins*; dark green and glabrous above, *white-tomentose beneath*. Flowerheads large (35–50 mm diam.); involucre ovoid, with lanceolate bracts in several rows; receptacle hairy. All florets tubular, purplish (rarely white), with 5 long teeth, hermaphrodite. Achene 3–5 mm long, obovoid, compressed; pappus of long, white, feathery hairs in several rows, 20–30 mm long.

Flowering: July–September.

Habitat: Grassland, marshy heaths and damp woods, on moist, oligotrophic, usually acid, peaty or rocky soils; at low altitudes in the north, but mainly on mountains to 2,300 m in the south.

Range: N and C Europe, westwards to Britain and the Pyrenees, and southwards to N Italy and Romania, but absent from the Netherlands, and naturalized only in Belgium and Iceland.

p.170 **Cabbage Thistle**
Cirsium oleraceum (L.) Scop.

Description: A coarse perennial, with scarcely branched, *glabrous, unwinged stems* to 1.5 m. Leaves large (to 40 cm long), sessile, elliptical to ovate (lower ones often pinnately lobed or coarsely dentate), usually glabrous, *pale or yellowish-green, very soft-spiny* along margins; *upper ones clasping* stem with large, dentate basal lobes. *Flowerheads large* (25–50 mm diam.), *subsessile, 2–6 together in terminal clusters*, subtended by *ruff of ovate, leaf-like bracts*; involucre cup-shaped, with narrowly lanceolate, erect, brownish-green bracts; receptacle hairy. All florets tubular, *pale yellow or cream*, hermaphrodite. Achenes 4–5.5 mm long, obovoid; pappus of long, basally connate, feathery hairs in several rows, 15–20 mm long.

Flowering: June–September.

Habitat: Marshy places, often along streams, in fens, hay-meadows, damp deciduous woods (often with Alder or willows), on wet, mesotrophic, sandy, loamy or peaty soils; from sea level to 2,000 m.

Range: Continental Europe, westwards to C France and the Low Countries, and northwards to S Scandinavia, Poland, and N Russia; locally naturalized in Ireland, Britain and Finland.

The only yellow-flowering thistle in the area. The soft, hardly spiny leaves can be eaten as a vegetable.

p.301 **Spear Thistle** *Cirsium vulgare* (Savi) Tenore

Description: A robust, biennial or short-lived perennial, with *large basal leaf-rosette* and *spiny-winged, cottony stems* to 1.5 m, branched above only. Rosette-leaves persistent far into 2nd year, to 50 cm long, lanceolate in outline, pinnately divided or lobed, very spiny along margins; bristly-spinose on (dull green) upper face. Stem-leaves (from 2nd year) lanceolate, decurrent for some length along stem (hence stem spiny-winged, but not continuously so), coarsely sinuous-dentate, very spiny along margins, bristly on upper face, short-hairy or cottony beneath. Flowerheads usually large (20) 30–50 mm diam.), *numerous* in rather sleek (sometimes slightly umbel-shaped) panicles; involucre ovoid, more or less cottony, with many rows of narrowly lanceolate to linear, *straight bracts tapering into sharp, yellow spine*; receptacle bristly-hairy. All florets tubular, red-purplish (rarely white), with 5 long teeth. Achene 3.5–5 mm, obovoid; pappus of basally connate, feathery hairs in several rows, 20–30 mm long.

Flowering: July–August (October).

Habitat: Rough or overgrazed grassland, road verges, banks, forest clearings, ruderal or disturbed places, on dry to moist, eutrophic, often basic, sandy, loamy or clayey soils; from sea level to 1,600 m.

Range: All Europe except the high Arctic.

Similar species: **Woolly Thistle** (*C. eriophorum* (L.) Scop.) has unwinged stems, long-spined, wavy-lobed leaves, larger flowerheads (40–70 mm diam.), subspherical, very cottony involucres with bracts often slightly widened under terminal spine. In comparable habitats, also in rocky environments, to 2,100 m, in W and C Europe, northwards to N England, the SW Netherlands, Germany, eastwards to Poland, Romania and Greece. *Compare also Onopordum acanthium (see p.490)*

Hawk's-beards, *Crepis*

One of several genera with all-ligulate, yellow flowerheads in branched inflorescences. *Crepis* differs from *Hieracium* (hawkweeds) in having beaked or pointed (instead of truncate) achenes, usually pure-white (instead of straw-coloured) pappus hairs (but *see* p. 493 *C. paludosa*), and involucral bracts in 2 unequal rows (instead of several, subequal rows). Also, some *Crepis* species have deeply incised, pinnately lobed or divided leaves, whereas *Hieracium* leaves are coarsely dentate at most. The branched species of *Leontodon* (hawkbits) and *Hypochoeris* (cat's-ears) have several scale-leaves under flowerheads, feathery (instead of simple) pappus hairs, and involucral bracts in several rows. *Picris* (oxtongues) are bristly-hairy, with curved achenes and feathery pappus. In all these genera, except *Hypochoeris,* the receptacle is glabrous or hairy, but without flat scales, and the florets always have truncate ligules with 5 minute teeth. Stem-leaves, if present, are alternate.

---

p.227 **Rough Hawk's-beard** *Crepis biennis* L.

Description: A *rough-hairy biennial*, with erect, branched stems to 1.2 m. Basal leaves elliptical or oblanceolate, *pinnately divided or lobed* (often with backward-pointing lobes with large, forward-pointing teeth), and with short, winged stalk; stem-leaves sessile, lanceolate, deeply lobed, the higher ones linear and often entire-margined but for some teeth at base. *Flowerheads relatively large* (25–35 mm diam.), in large, loose, umbel-shaped panicles; involucre ovoid, glandular-hairy, with narrowly ovate, *recurved outer bracts*, and erect, lanceolate inner bracts *finely hairy on inside*. All florets ligulate, yellow. Achene straw-coloured, spindle- or narrowly flask-shaped, 4–8 (13) mm long, to 1 mm thick, with 13–20 ribs; pappus of white, soft, simple hairs.

Flowering: May–August.

Habitat: Grassland, road verges, field and wood margins, banks, on moist, mesotrophic, often calcareous, sandy, loamy or stony soils; from sea level to 2,000 m.

Range: Most of Europe, northwards to Britain, S Sweden and the Baltic States; naturalized in Ireland, Norway, Finland and N Russia, often introduced with grass-seed.

---

p.227 **Smooth Hawk's-beard**
Crepis capillaris (L.) Wallr.

Description: A *slender, subglabrous annual or biennial*, with erect, branched stems to 60 (90) cm. Leaves oblanceolate in outline, pinnately divided or lobed with broadly lanceolate segments and narrowly triangular or hastate, subacute end-lobe; basal leaves short-stalked, upper leaves sessile, linear, with some large teeth at base. *Flowerheads small* (10–15 mm diam.), in lax, umbel-shaped panicles; *all involucral bracts appressed, inner ones glabrous on inside*. All florets ligulate, yellow, often red on outside. Achene spindle-shaped, *not beaked, to 2.5 mm long, 10-ribbed*, straw-coloured or brownish; pappus of soft, white, simple hairs.

Flowering: June–November.

Habitat: Grassland, road verges, grassy heaths, ruderal places, on dry to moist, mesotrophic to eutrophic, sandy, loamy, clayey or rocky soils, also on walls; from sea level to 1,200 m.

Range: W, C and S Europe, northwards to Britain and the Netherlands, and eastwards to Poland, Romania and Greece.

Similar species: **Beaked Hawk's-beard** (*C. vesicaria* L.) is biennial, and much hairier in all parts. Leaves coarsely lobed (much like a dandelion); upper leaves clasping, with pointed auricles; flowerheads larger (15–25 mm diam.); florets deep yellow, often red beneath, styles green (not dirty yellow); at least inner achenes have long beak. In comparable habitats, preferably on calcareous soils, in continental Europe, northwards to the Netherlands, Germany, Austria, and also in the Balkan region; naturalized in Britain and Ireland.

Bristly Hawk's-beard (*C. setosa* Haller f.) is much like *C. vesicaria*, but has long, yellow bristles on involucral bracts, glabrous (not hairy) receptacle, yellow styles, and plain-yellow florets. In S and SC Europe; locally naturalized in lawns further northwards.

Stinking Hawk's-beard (*C. foetida* L.) is hairy, annual or biennial, with unpleasant smell of bitter almonds when crushed; flowerheads nodding in bud, 15–20 mm diam., on stalks with some small, scale-like bracts (as often in *Leontodon*); styles yellow; inner achenes long-beaked; outer ones with short, thick beaks. In dry, open, ruderal places, preferably on calcareous soils, in W, C and S Europe, northwards to Britain, the SE Netherlands, Poland and C Russia.

p.226 **Marsh Hawk's-beard**
Crepis paludosa (L.) Moench

Description: A *subglabrous perennial*, with *creeping rhizomes*
and *simple, erect stems* (branched only in the
inflorescence) to 1.2 m. Leaves ovate to
lanceolate; lower ones long-stalked and
more or less deeply lobed in lower half,
upper ones sessile, *cordate, sharply dentate,
clasping stem* with rounded, dentate basal
lobes. Flowerheads 15–25 mm diam., in
loose, umbel-shaped panicles; involucral
bracts usually black-glandular, lanceolate,
erect. All florets ligulate, *deep yellow*, with
dark-green styles. Achene spindle-shaped, not
beaked, 4–5 mm long, with *10 ribs; pappus
of yellowish or brownish, simple hairs.*

Flowering: (May) June–September.

Habitat: Marshes and fens, hay-meadows, along
streams and springs, also in damp woods,
on wet, oligotrophic or mesotrophic,
slightly acid, sandy, loamy or peaty soils;
from sea level to 2,300 m.

Range: N and C Europe, from Iceland and N
Russia southwards to N Spain, N Italy,
Bulgaria, and SC Russia.

Similar species: **Northern Hawk's-beard** (*C. mollis* (Jacq.)
Aschers.) has lanceolate, subentire or
weakly dentate leaves (upper ones only half-
clasping), and 20-ribbed achenes with
pappus of white hairs. In comparable
places, from Scotland to the Pyrenees,
eastwards to C Russia and Jugoslavia; more
frequent in the mountains (to 2,000 m).

p.227 *Crepis tectorum* L.

Description: A slightly hairy annual or biennial, with
erect, moderately branched stems to 1 m.
Basal leaves few, stalked, oblanceolate,
deeply dentate or pinnately lobed, in rather
indistinct rosette; stem-leaves sessile,
lanceolate to linear, dentate to subentire
(apart from pair of acute, half-clasping
lobes at base); leaf-margins often rolled
under. Flowerheads 15–25 mm diam., in
loose, umbel-shaped panicles; involucres
hairy (often glandular as well), with linear-

lanceolate *bracts silky on inside*; receptacle pitted, hairy to subglabrous. All florets ligulate, yellow, with *dark-green styles*. Achenes 3–4 mm long, spindle-shaped, *purplish-brown* (when ripe), attenuate but hardly beaked, with *10 slightly spiny ribs*; pappus of long, white, simple hairs.

Flowering: May–September.

Habitat: Arable fields, open grassland, roadsides, dunes, ruderal places, on dry, mesotrophic, sandy soils, also on old walls; from sea level to 1,800 m.

Range: Continental Europe, northwards to Fennoscandia and N Russia.

Similar species: *C. praemorsa* (L.) Tausch is smaller (to 60 cm), biennial or perennial, yellowish-green, subglabrous; leaves oblanceolate, subentire, all in basal rosette; flowerheads 25–30 mm diam., in loose (compound) raceme; involucral bracts glabrous inside; receptacle glabrous; florets pale yellow; achenes 3.5–5 mm long, pale brown, 20-ribbed. In C and E Europe, westwards to E France and SE Norway, and northwards to N Russia.

p.226 **Leopard's Bane** *Doronicum pardalianches* L.

Description: A hairy perennial, to 80 cm, with creeping, thickened rhizome, creeping stolons and tuberous roots; flowering stems erect, branched, rising from dense tuft of foliage. *Basal leaves long-stalked, cordate, with marked sinus* and rounded basal lobes, shallowly dentate. Stem-leaves alternate, ovate, sessile and clasping, with cordate base, weakly dentate. *Flowerheads 30–50 mm diam.*, rather short-stalked, often *2–6 together on long, axillary peduncles*, forming lax, more or less umbel-shaped panicles; involucral bracts lanceolate, pointed, ciliate; receptacle domed, hairy. Ray-florets female, yellow, with strap-shaped, almost round-tipped, 3-toothed ligule. Disc-florets short, 5-toothed, yellow, hermaphrodite. Achenes blackish, 10-ribbed; pappus of short, simple hairs (or absent in ray-florets).

Flowering: May–July.

Habitat:	Deciduous or mixed woods, scrub along streams, in ravines, on moist, oligotrophic to mesotrophic, often rocky (then acid or calcareous) soils; from near sea level to 2,200 m, but probably naturalized only in the lowland.
Range:	W Europe, northwards to Belgium and the Netherlands (doubtfully native), and eastwards to SE Germany and Italy; naturalized in Britain and NC Europe.
Similar species:	**Plantain Leopard's-bane** (*D. plantagineum* L.) has basal leaves abruptly narrowed into stalk, and larger flowerheads (50–80 mm diam.), solitary on axillary peduncles. SW Europe, northwards to N France, and eastwards to Italy; naturalized in Britain.

Both species are grown for ornament.

---

p.296 **Blue Fleabane** *Erigeron acris* L.

Description:	A slender, grey-hairy annual or biennial, with erect stems to 50 cm. Leaves alternate (and partly in basal rosette), elliptical to lanceolate, (sub)entire. Flowerheads (6) 10–15 mm diam., in loose, slender panicle; involucre ovoid, with 2 rows of lanceolate, hairy bracts; receptacle scaleless. *Ray-florets up to 45 in number, in 2 or more rows*, female or sterile, with *linear to threadlike, purplish, pink or lilac ligule*. Disc-florets numerous, yellow, 5-toothed, hermaphrodite. Achene ellipsoid; *pappus of whitish hairs in 2 rows*.
Flowering:	June–August.
Habitat:	Open grassland, road verges, fields, ruderal places, on dry to moist, oligotrophic, basic to slightly acid, sandy, loamy or stony soils; from sea level to 2,300 m.
Range:	All Europe except Iceland and Spitsbergen.
Similar species:	**Sweet Scabious** (*E. annuus* (L.) Pers.) has larger flowerheads (15–25 mm diam.), with 50–120 white or very pale-blue ray-florets in several rows; disc-florets have 1 ring of pappus hairs, and outer ring of pappus scales. Native to N America; naturalized in continental W and C Europe, eastwards to C Russia, on sandy roadsides, banks, and along rivers.

p.321 **Alpine Fleabane**
Erigeron borealis (Vierh.) Simmons

Description: A low, more or less hairy perennial, with erect stems to 30 cm. Leaves entire-margined: basal ones in rosette, stalked, elliptical to oblanceolate; stem-leaves alternate, sessile, narrowly lanceolate. *Flowerheads solitary* (rarely 2–3 together), terminal, 10–16 mm diam.; involucral bracts densely hairy. Ray-florets lilac; disc-flowers yellow. Achene with *pappus of whitish hairs in 1 row*.

Flowering: July–August.

Habitat: Arctic tundra and mountain pasture, on moist, oligotrophic, mostly calcareous, stony or rocky soils; mainly in the mountains, to 1,200 m.

Range: In Iceland, Scotland, Fennoscandia and N Russia.

Similar species: *E. humilis* R.C. Graham has solitary, subsessile flowerheads, with purplish-hairy involucral bracts, directly over leaf-rosette. In comparable habitats of Iceland and Fennoscandia.
One-flowered Fleabane (*E. uniflorus* L.), from the Arctic tundra and the mountains of N and C Europe, has short-stalked, solitary flowerheads, and involucres with long white hairs.

---

p.170 **Canadian Fleabane** *Erigeron canadensis* L.

Description: A slender annual, with erect, hairy stems to 80 (150) cm. Leaves alternate, subsessile, narrowly oblanceolate to linear, subentire, ciliate. *Flowerheads very numerous, only 3–5 (7) mm diam.*, in large, piramidal panicles; *involucral bracts almost equalling florets*, subglabrous. Ray-florets female, with *short, erect, whitish (or very pale-pink) ligule* to 1 mm (rarely absent altogether); disc-florets yellow, hermaphrodite. Achene to 1 mm long; pappus of whitish hairs in 1 row.

Flowering: July–October.

Habitat: Open, ruderal places, fallow fields, dunes, along railways, on dry, mesotrophic to eutrophic, sandy or stony soils; from sea level to 1,200 m.

Range: Native to N America; widely naturalized in Europe except Ireland and the high Arctic.

p.296 **Hemp Agrimony** *Eupatorium cannabinum* L.

Description: A hairy perennial, with erect, branched stems to 1.2 (1.7) m. *Leaves opposite, 3-partite* (occasionally 5-partite), with lanceolate, serrate segments to 15 cm long. Flowerheads small (2–5 mm diam.), numerous in large, umbel-shaped panicles; involucre cylindrical, with *c. 10 blunt bracts in 2 rows*; receptacle scaleless. All florets tubular, *3–6 in a head, pink* (rarely white), hermaphrodite. Achene spindle-shaped, 5-angular; pappus of white, simple hairs in 1 row.

Flowering: July–September.

Habitat: Marshes, reed-lands, damp woods, along ditches and streams, on wet to moist, mesotrophic, sandy, loamy or peaty soils; from sea level to 1,700 m.

Range: All Europe except the high Arctic.

Cudweeds, *Filago*

A group of white-tomentose annuals, with clustered flowerheads and only regular, tubular florets (no ray-florets). Marginal florets female, and placed in the axil of scale-like, inner involucral bracts. Receptacle is flat, and has no scales. Achene is spindle-shaped, slightly compressed, with soon-falling pappus of white, simple hairs in 1 row. Related genera are *Bombycilaena*, with marginal, female florets completely enveloped by scale-like bracts (*see under Filago minima*), and *Gnaphalium* (*see* p.500), which lacks scale-like inner bracts.

p.80 **Field Cudweed** *Filago arvensis* L.

Description: A white-tomentose annual, with erect stems to 40 (70) cm and *short, more or less erect side-branches* over the middle. Leaves alternate, sessile, erect, lanceolate, to 15 (20) mm long. Flowerheads small (3–6 mm diam., to 6 mm long), ovoid, in *small, mostly axillary clusters of 2–7*, often overtopped by adjacent leaves; involucral bracts broadly lanceolate, blunt-tipped, woolly, with yellow, scarious margins. Florets tubular, yellowish; marginal ones female, inner ones hermaphrodite.

Flowering: July–September.

Habitat: Arable fields, along rivers, on dry, oligotrophic, slightly acid, sandy or gravelly soils; from sea level to 1,300 m.

Range: Continental Europe, northwards to Fennoscandia and the Baltic States.

---

p.80 **Small Cudweed** *Filago minima* (Sm.) Pers.

Description: A white-tomentose, *tiny annual*, with erect to ascending, *forked stems to 15 cm.* Leaves alternate, sessile, erect, lanceolate, to 10 mm long. Flowerheads small (2–4 mm diam., to 4 mm long), *5-angled*, in *clusters of 2–7 in branch-axils, or terminal*; involucral bracts broadly lanceolate, blunt-tipped, *woolly only near base*, with yellow, scarious margins. Florets tubular, yellowish; marginal ones female, inner ones hermaphrodite.

Flowering: July–September.

Habitat: Fields, heaths, dunes, along rivers, on dry, oligotrophic, slightly acid, sandy or gravelly soils; from sea level to 1,000 m.

Range: Most of Europe, northwards to S Scandinavia and the Baltic States.

Similar species: **Narrow-leaved Cudweed** (*F. gallica* L.) has linear leaves (less than 1 mm wide, to 25 mm long), overtopping flowerheads. In fields and open grassland, on dry, sandy, loamy or gravelly soils, in S and SW Europe, northwards to N France and SE England. *F. neglecta* (Soyer-Willemet) DC. also has linear leaves, but ovoid, rounded (not angular) involucres with brownish (not yellow) involucral bracts. In arable fields on moist, sandy or loamy soil, in France and Belgium; possibly extinct. *Bombycilaena erecta* (L.) Smolj. has flowerheads in terminal clusters of 2–3, with yellow bracts, and marginal achenes completely surrounded by scale-like involucral bracts. A mainly Mediterranean species, reaching NC France, Czechia and Moldavia.

p.80 **Common Cudweed** *Filago vulgaris* Lam.

Description: A *white-tomentose* annual, with erect stems to 30 (40) cm, branched from the middle and always *forked above*. Leaves alternate, sessile, erect, lanceolate to almost linear, 10–20 mm long, entire. Flowerheads sessile, *10–30 in terminal or axillary clusters* 10–12 mm diam.; involucral bracts woolly, with red blotch and yellow, scarious margins, tapering into *straight, yellowish point*. Florets tubular, yellowish, female, mixed with sparse hermaphrodite florets in centre.

Flowering: July–September.

Habitat: Arable fields, heaths, dunes, waysides, along rivers, on dry to moist, oligotrophic, slightly acid to somewhat calcareous, sandy, loamy or gravelly soils; mainly in the lowland.

Range: Much of Europe, northwards to Britain, S Sweden and W Russia.

Similar species: **Broad-leaved Cudweed** (*F. pyramidata* L.) is branched from base, and has narrowly elliptical or spatulate leaves, involucral bracts with yellow, recurved point, and ruff of 2–4 (6) leaves below and exceeding flowerheads. In comparable habitats, in S and W Europe, northwards to S England, Belgium and Germany.
Red-tipped Cudweed (*F. lutescens* Jordan) also has broader, spatulate leaves, but whole plant yellowish-tomentose; involucral bracts have recurved, purplish to brown point; some normal leaves may subtend flowerheads. In comparable habitats, in S and W Europe, northwards to S England, Belgium, S Sweden, and Poland.

Gallant Soldier *Galinsoga parviflora* Cav.

Description: An *appressed-hairy* annual, with erect or ascending, branched stems to 60 cm. *Leaves opposite*, short-stalked to subsessile, ovate, pointed, 30–70 mm long, bluntly dentate. *Flowerheads small* (3–5 mm diam.), *in dichasial cymes*; involucre cup-shaped, with lanceolate, blunt-tipped, hairy bracts in 1 or 2 rows; receptacle conical, with *trifid* scales. *Ray-florets usually 5, short, 3-lobed, white,* female; disc-florets very short, 5-toothed, yellow, hermaphrodite. Achene obovoid, angular, with (at least in disc-florets) *pappus of ciliate scales.*

Flowering: May–October.

Habitat: Arable fields (especially with root-crops), gardens, on moist to dry, eutrophic, sandy or loamy soils; mainly in the lowland.

Range: Native to S America; widely naturalized in Europe except the far north.

Similar species: **Shaggy Soldier** (*G. quadriradiata* Ruiz & Pavon) (*see* photograph p.168) has densely pilose stems (with erect hairs), entire receptacle-scales, and awned pappus-scales. Native to C and S America; naturalized in much of Europe, northwards to Fennoscandia and C Russia, in comparable habitats.

---

p.79 **Jersey Cudweed** *Gnaphalium luteo-album* L.

Description: A *white-tomentose* annual or biennial, with *erect or ascending stems (only branched at base)* to 30 (50) cm. Leaves alternate, 30–60 mm long, lanceolate to linear, erect (*often appressed to stem*). Flowerheads to 5 mm diam., in *dense, terminal clusters, not surrounded by leaves*; involucre ovoid, with glabrous, *yellowish, membranous bracts* in several rows, spreading after anthesis; receptacle scaleless. All florets tubular, *yellow*, 5-toothed, female and fertile, or functionally male (with sterile ovary and undivided style). Achene ovoid, to 0.5 mm long; pappus (to 2.5 mm long) of white, simple hairs in 1 row.

Flowering: June–August (October).

Habitat: Dune-valleys, quarries, sandbars and flats, along fields and ditches, on wet to moist, oligotrophic to mesotrophic, basic, sandy soils; mainly in the lowland.

Range: Europe northwards to S Sweden.

Compare Helichrysum arenarium (*see* p.501), which has shiny golden, always erect involucral bracts, and nearly all florets hemaphrodite and fertile. *Compare also Omalotheca* (*see* p.527) p.79 **Marsh Cudweed** *Gnaphalium uliginosum* L.

Description: A *white-tomentose* annual with *spreading to ascending, branched stems* to 10 (20) cm. Leaves alternate, 10–30 mm long, linear-lanceolate, sessile with narrowed base, *spreading*. Flowerheads sessile, in small, *terminal clusters surrounded by much longer leaves*; involucre ovoid, with glabrous, *brownish, membranous bracts* in several rows; receptacle scaleless. All florets tubular, *yellowish*, 5-toothed, all fertile, or inner ones partly male (with sterile ovary and undivided style). Achene ovoid, 0.4–0.7 mm long; pappus of white, simple hairs in 1 row.

Flowering: June–October.

Habitat: Cultivated land, waysides, channels and ditches, even between paving stones, on wet to moist, mesotrophic, sandy, loamy or clayey soils; from sea level to 1,600 m.

Range: Most of Europe except the extreme north.

Compare Filago (see p.497) with ovoid (not cup-shaped) involucres, and yellowish involucral bracts (or else, yellowish-tomentose leaves).

p.221 **Immortelle**
Helichrysum arenarium (L.) Moench

Description: A *white-tomentose perennial*, with non-flowering shoots at base, and ascending to erect flowering stems to 40 cm. Leaves alternate, oblanceolate to linear, to 70 mm long. Flowerheads 3–4 mm diam., in *dense, terminal, umbel-shaped panicles* to 50 mm diam.; involucre cup-shaped, with erect, rounded, membranous, glabrous, *shiny golden or orange bracts* in several rows; receptacle scaleless. All florets tubular, *usually all hermaphrodite and fertile, yellow*. Achene cylindrical or slightly pentagonal, truncate; pappus of whitish, simple hairs in 1 row.

Flowering: May–August (October).

Habitat: Open grassland, waysides, quarries, on dry, oligotrophic, slightly acid to calcareous, sandy, gravelly or rocky soils; mainly in the lowland.

Range: Continental Europe, northwards to S Sweden.

Compare Gnaphalium luteo-album (see p.500), which has pale-yellow involucral bracts.

Hawkweeds, *Hieracium*

A very complex genus with some sexual species and many agamosperms (stable intermediates forming fertile seeds without pollination). New agamospermous forms may originate through mutation or occasional hybridization. The characters are often graded, recurring with various degrees of expression in different species. Of paramount importance are the characters of the indument (glandular hairs, stellate hairs, and simple, eglandular hairs), the number of flowerheads, the presence of stolons or basal leaf-rosettes, the number of stem-leaves, and the way these are attached to the plant (stalked, sessile or clasping).

All species are perennial, with only ligulate, yellow (rarely orange or brick-red) florets in the flowerheads; the involucre has lanceolate bracts in several rows; the receptacle is flat, pitted, glabrous or hairy, but scaleless; the achenes are oblong, more or less cylindrical, ribbed, never beaked (unlike *Crepis, see* p.490, and they usually bear a dirty-white to straw-coloured pappus. There are 2 subgenera: (1) *Hieracium (sensu stricto)* is usually agamospermous, lacks stolons, has achenes 2–5 mm long with ribs apically confluent into a smooth rim, and has a pappus of simple hairs in 2 rows; (2) *Pilosella* is often sexually reproducing, and possesses stolons, achenes up to 2.5 mm long, with ribs shortly projecting at the top, and a pappus of simple hairs in 1 row.

As a rule, these general characters will not be repeated in the following descriptions. To express the characters of the indument a formula is used, and this appears in the text between square brackets:

[E S G] = with dense eglandular, stellate, glandular hairs;

[e s g] = with sparse eglandular, stellate, glandular hairs;

[eE sS gG] = with sparse to numerous eglandular, stellate, glandular hairs;

[(S) (g)] = *occasionally* with numerous stellate, sparse glandular hairs, etc.;

[s↑ G↓] = with sparse stellate hairs *above*, densely glandular *beneath*, etc.;

[E! S! G!] = with *very* dense eglandular, stellate, glandular hairs.

The subgenus is indicated in the scientific names by (*H.*) and (*P.*) respectively. Following the practice of *Flora Europaea*, what has been described in the subgenus *Hieracium* are species groups centring around the name-giving species, which is typical of the group and often more common than the other members, which are not explicitly mentioned. The species groups that have most likely contributed genetically to a certain intermediate taxon are also given in a formula, e.g. *H. maculatum* group (= glaucinum|vulgatum). For details on the many microspecies within each group, *see Flora Europaea*, the better regional floras, and the copious specialized literature (although the latter is often scattered in periodicals); it is worth asking for advice from the staff of a professional herbarium.

---

p.222 **Alpine Hawkweed**
Hieracium (*H.*) *alpinum* group

Description: Stems low, to 15 (35) cm [E S (Gg)]; eglandular hairs 3–8 mm long. Leaves [E (S↓) Gg], glands especially frequent on leaf-margins; basal leaves, on winged stalks, to 10 cm long and 15 mm wide, elliptical or spatulate to lanceolate, entire to coarsely dentate; stem-leaves 0–3 (8), lanceolate to linear, upper ones often small and bractlike. Flowerheads 1 (2–3); involucre 12–20 mm long, 7–18 mm wide, with linear-lanceolate bracts [E (Gg)], eglandular hairs 2–5 mm long. Ligules usually with some hairs on outside, and ciliate at top. Stigmas yellow.

Flowering: July–August.

Habitat: Rocks, screes, grassland, on moist to dry, oligotrophic, preferably acid, stony or rocky soils; primarily in the mountains, 800–3,000 m.

Range: N and C Europe, from Iceland and Britain eastwards through Fennoscandia and Poland to N and C Russia, and back again westwards through Romania and Yugoslavia to S Germany and E France.

Similar species: The *H. nigrescens* group (= alpinum|murorum), occurring in the same general area, has wider basal leaves, and often more than 1 flowerhead with ciliate florets.

Forms with soon-withering basal leaves, more than 2 (often 3–9) flowerheads and 2–4 stem-leaves are frequent in Iceland,

Scandinavia and N Russia, especially the *H. plicatum* group (= alpinum|carpathicum|murorum).

In the same, northerly region (and in N Britain) occur plants apparently linking up with the montane *prenanthoides* group, with even more stem-leaves (up to 8 in the *H. dovrense* group, and up to 20 in the *H. truncatum* group).

p.223 *Hieracium (H.) amplexicaule* group

Description: Stem (10) 30–60 cm [(E) S G!]. Leaves [(E) G!], the basal ones numerous, to 20 cm long, 6 cm wide, on winged stalks, often yellowish-green or blue-green, obovate or spatulate to lanceolate, with rounded but finely pointed tip, subentire to broadly dentate; stem-leaves 3–6 (12), ovate, upper ones cordate, clasping stem with rounded basal lobes or auricles. Flowerheads 2–12 (25), on long, ascending stalks [S G!]; involucre 12–18 mm long, 9–16 mm wide, with linear-lanceolate, long-tapering, acute bracts [(e) sS G!]. Ligules densely ciliate at top. Stigmas yellow or discoloured.

Flowering: June–August.
Habitat: Dry, (mainly calcareous) cliffs and rocks in the mountains; 500–2,600 m.
Range: C and S Europe, from Portugal to Greece, northwards to France, S Germany, Hungary and Bulgaria.

Some species from this group have naturalized on old walls (Britain, Belgium, the Netherlands, Sweden). In its native realm the *amplexicaule* group is connected with several other groups by numerous intermediary forms. *Compare also Picris hieracioides* (*see* p.531) – a bristly-hairy plant with feathery (instead of simple) pappus hairs.

p.223 *Hieracium (P.) cymosum* L.

Description: Stolons very short or absent. Leaves of central rosette [eE] to 17 cm long, 25 mm wide, oblanceolate, acute or blunt-tipped,

usually entire-margined. Flowering stems
30–80 (100) cm [E sS (g)], with 1–4
(sometimes bract-like) stem-leaves.
Flowerheads numerous (up to 100), in
dense pseudo-umbel; involucral bracts
dark-glandular [E sS gG], to 8.5 mm long,
1 mm wide, linear-lanceolate, often acute.

Flowering: June–September.

Habitat: Grassland, open woods, rocks, railways, on
dry to moist, oligotrophic to mesotrophic,
sandy, gravelly or rocky soils; from sea level
to 2,700 m.

Range: Continental Europe, westwards to Norway,
Denmark, Germany, E France and the
Pyrenees; locally naturalized in the lowland
of W Europe, as in NW Germany.

---

p.222 *Hieracium (P.) lactucella* Wallr.

Description: Stolons long, leafy. Leaves of central
rosette to 70 mm long, 15 mm wide,
spatulate or oblanceolate, blunt-tipped,
glaucous, glabrous or [e] on margins and
midrib. Flowering stem 5–20 cm [(e) S
G] with 0–2 (3) half-clasping stem-
leaves. Flowerheads 1–5 in irregularly
cymose inflorescences; involucral bracts
linear-lanceolate, blunt-tipped [eE s
gG]. Florets yellow, sometimes red-
striped at top.

Flowering: May–July (September).

Habitat: Grassland, grassy banks, verges, along
streams, on wet or moist, oligotrophic,
slightly acid, sandy, loamy or clayey soils;
from sea level to 2,500 m.

Range: Continental Europe from Scandinavia to
Spain, Italy and Greece, and eastwards to N
and C Russia.

*Compare H. flagellare (see under H. praealtum,
p.508).*

---

p.224 *Hieracium (H.) laevigatum* group

Description: Stem 30–100 (120) cm [Ee S↑ (g↑)].
Leaves [Ee (S↓)], basal ones usually absent,
or few and at least withered during

anthesis; stem-leaves rather numerous (4–25 or more), stalked, to 15 (20) cm long, 40 mm wide, ovate to lanceolate, often deeply dentate, with acute top and attenuate or abruptly contracted base, upper ones sessile (but not clasping), becoming narrower and grading into bracts [(e) sS (g)]. Flowerheads numerous, in loose panicles; involucre 9–12 mm long, 6–12 mm wide, with subacute bracts [(sS) (eE) (gG) or glabrous].

Flowering: June–August (September).

Habitat: Deciduous woods, shaded road verges, rocks and walls, dry gullies, on dry to moist, oligotrophic, sandy, loamy or stony soils; from sea level to 1,600 m.

Range: Cool-temperate Europe, from Iceland and Fennoscandia southwards to the Pyrenees, N Italy and Bulgaria.

The *laevigatum* group is more or less intermediate between the *vulgatum* and *sabaudum* groups.

The *argillaceum* group has stems 30–100 cm [E↓ S↑ G↑ !], and leaves [eE], the basal ones few to numerous, stalked, to 11 cm long, 40 mm wide, elliptical or ovate to lanceolate, usually acute, more or less dentate, and with cuneate base; stem-leaves 4–20, lower ones stalked like the basal leaves, upper ones smaller and sessile, but not clasping; flowerheads often numerous (3–50 or more), on rather long stalks [(e) S G]; involucre 9–11 mm long, 8–10 mm wide, with acute bracts [S (e) G]; stigmas yellow or discoloured; ligules often ciliate at top. In open woods, scrub, quarries, grassy places, on dry to moist, oligotrophic, often calcareous and stony soils. from just above sea level to 2,300 m, in most of Europe except Iceland, Faeroes, Ireland, and the Mediterranean south.

The *H. diaphanum* group, widely distributed in N and C Europe, is similar to the *argillaceum* group, and contains several species mainly differing by sparse or absent stellate hairs on the involucre.

p.222 **Mouse-ear Hawkweed**
Hieracium (P.) pilosella L.

Description: Stolons long, slender, leafy. Leaves of central rosette to 12 cm long, 20 mm wide, oblanceolate to spatulate [eE S↓], green. Flowering stem 5–30 (50) cm [eE S gG], with only 1 flowerhead; involucral bracts 0.5–1.5 (2) mm wide, linear-lanceolate, acute, with eglandular hairs, stellate hairs and glands in different combinations. Florets yellow, usually red-striped at top.

Flowering: May–July (September).

Habitat: Short, poor grassland, heaths, waysides, rocks, on dry to moist, oligotrophic to mesotrophic, acid or calcareous, sandy, loamy or stony soils; from sea level to 3,000 m. A very common species.

Range: Most of Europe except Iceland and some Mediterranean islands.

Similar species: *H. peleterianum* Mérat has thick, but fewer, stolons, with large, crowded leaves; leaves of central rosette [eE S↓ G↓] green. Flowering stems [eE S gG], with 1 flowerhead; involucral bracts 1.5–3 mm wide, lanceolate, acute [E! (s) (g)]. Florets yellow, occasionally red-striped. In dry sandy or rocky places up to 2,600 m, in N, W and WC Europe from Scandinavia to Portugal and Italy, and from Britain to N Russia.

p.223 *Hieracium (P.) praealtum* Gochnat

Description: Stolons absent (in ssp. *praealtum*) to very long and leafy (in ssp. *bauhinii* (Besser) Petunnikov). Leaves of central rosette to 18 cm long, 12 (20) mm wide, oblanceolate or spatulate to linear-lanceolate, greyish-green, glabrous or [eE (sS↓)]. Flowering stems 20–60 (80) cm, glabrous or [(e) (sS) (g)], with 1–3 (9) stem-leaves (smaller than basal ones). Flowerheads few–numerous, clustered (occasionally on long side-branches); stalks [eE sS gG]; involucral bracts to 1 mm wide, linear-lanceolate, (sub)acute [eE sS gG]. Florets yellow, outer ones occasionally red-striped.

Flowering: May–August.

Habitat: Heaths, road verges, railways, mine-refuse heaps, cliffs and rocks, on dry, oligotrophic, slightly acid to calcareous, sandy, gravelly or stony soils; from near sea level to 2,600 m.

Range: Continental Europe from Fennoscandia to Spain and Yugoslavia, and from France to C Russia.

Similar species *H. caespitosum* Dumort. has stolons long and leafy; leaves of central rosette 5–20 cm long, 7–25 mm wide, oblanceolate to spatulate, (sub)entire, long-hairy [eE]. Flowering stems 30–50 (80) cm, long-hairy [E s g], with 1–3 (sometimes bract-like) stem-leaves; flowerheads (3) 15–30 (50), pale yellow, in dense, umbel-shaped raceme or panicle; involucral bracts [E s G], linear-lanceolate, to 1.25 mm wide, usually obtuse. In grassland, road verges, on grassy banks and along railways, on moist to dry, mesotrophic, sandy, loamy or clayey soils (to 1,200 m) in continental Europe, from Fennoscandia southwards to France, Austria, Hungary and Greece, and eastwards to C Russia.

H. flagellare Willd., intermediary between *H. caespitosum* and *H. pilosella*, has long, thick stolons, only (1) 2–6 (rather large) flowerheads on forked flowering stems [eE S G], acute, black-glandular involucral bracts [eE s G], and yellow, often red-striped florets. In N, W and C Europe (except Iceland and Norway), from Spain and Britain eastwards to N and C Russia, and from Sweden to Hungary and Romania. (*Compare H. lactucella* (*see* p.505), which also has few heads, but subglabrous leaves.)

H. verruculatum Link, a large plant from EC Russia and SW Asia, lacks stolons. Rosette-leaves [eE S g] to 20 cm long, and to 40 mm wide (but soon withering); stem-leaves 4–12, half-clasping. Flowering stems 45–110 cm [E↓ S gG]; flowerheads numerous (10–60), in more or less umbel-shaped panicles; involucral bracts 1–2 mm wide [(e) S G]; florets yellow.

Orange Hawkweed (*H. aurantiacum* L.)
has orange to brick-red florets, flowering
stems [E s g] with 2–12 (25) flowerheads,
and lanceolate involucral bracts 1.5–3 mm
wide [E sS g]. Native to the mountains of
N and C Europe, westwards to C France,
and eastwards to C Russia; often grown in
gardens; more or less naturalized in Iceland,
Britain, Denmark, and the Low Countries.

---

p.225   *Hieracium* (*H.*) *sabaudum* group

Description: Stem 50–100 (180) cm [E↓ e↑ sS]. Leaves
[eE (s↓)], all cauline, *numerous (20–50)*, to
18 cm long, and to 40 mm wide, ovate or
elliptical to lanceolate, usually acute, more
or less dentate; lower ones narrowed into
short stalk and often withered during
anthesis, upper ones sessile, half-clasping
with rounded or cordate base, grading into
the bracts [eE S] of the (large)
inflorescence. Involucres 10–12 mm long,
7–10 mm wide, with *round-tipped,
subglabrous or sometimes glandular-hairy
bracts* [(eE gG)]. Stigmas usually
discoloured (rarely yellow). Achenes dark
brown. At anthesis, these plants often have
leafless lower stems, with crowded leaves
immediately above; the same can be seen
in the *prenanthoides* group.

Flowering: August–October.

Habitat: Deciduous woods, scrub, shaded verges,
along streams and ditches, on dry to moist,
oligotrophic, slightly acid to calcareous soils;
from just above sea level to 1,000 m.

Range: Europe except for most of the north and some
islands.

Similar species: The *H. flagelliferum* group (= sabaudum|
vulgatum) has fewer (6–25) stem-leaves,
flowerheads on glandular stalks [gG], not
[eE gG], and narrower involucral bracts [S].
In C Europe, westwards to W France, and to
be expected further north.

The *H. prenanthoides* group has stems
30–120 cm [sS eE gG], leaves [eE], all
cauline, numerous (10–30 or more), to 14 cm
long, and to 35 mm wide, ovate to lanceolate

and often constricted towards the base, acute or pointed, subentire to dentate; lower leaves narrowed into short stalk (and often withered during anthesis), upper ones progressively smaller, often *cordate and clasping* with rounded auricles [eE (S↓)]. Inflorescence leafy, with shortish, ascending branches [(e) sS G]; flowerheads numerous; involucre 8–12 mm long, 6–8 mm wide, with bracts [(e) s G]; achenes pale, straw-coloured. In mountain grassland, on dry to moist, oligotrophic, preferably calcareous, stony or rocky soils; mainly in the mountains (1,000–2,400 m), throughout Europe except the south.

The *H. crocatum* group (= prenanthoides| umbellatum) has stems [s eE]; leaves mostly sessile, lanceolate to linear, acute, subentire to dentate, to 10 cm long [e(mainly on the margin) (s)], no larger leaves in inflorescence; involucral bracts [eE (s) G!]; achenes dark-brown. In N and C Europe (including the Pyrenees).

The *H. juranum* group (= murorum| prenanthoides) has a similar, montane distribution, but has fewer (5–15), partly stalked stem-leaves, smaller involucres (7–8.5 mm long), with bracts [G!] often lacking eglandular hairs, and dark-brown achenes.

Many connections with other groups are known, especially in N and C Europe; *compare* e.g. the *truncatum* group (*see under H. alpinum* group, p.504).

p.225 **Leafy Hawkweed**
Hieracium (*H.*) *umbellatum* group

Description: Stem to 100 (150) cm [Ee↑ s↑, or subglabrous]. Leaves [eE↓ sS↓, often subglabrous s↑] all cauline, very numerous, crowded, to 15 cm long, and to 10 (20) mm wide, linear-lanceolate, acute or pointed, sessile with narrowed or cuneate base, subentire to (remotely) long-dentate; upper ones grading into bracts. Flowerheads rather numerous, in (bracteate, rarely leafy) *umbel-*

shaped or storied panicles, with long, ascending to erect stalks [sS (e) (g)]; involucre 9–11 mm long, 9–10 mm wide, with *usually glabrous, recurved bracts* [(e) (g)].

Flowering: July–October.

Habitat: Open deciduous woods, scrub, woodland waysides, heaths and inner sea-dunes, on dry to moist, oligotrophic to mesotrophic, usually slightly acid, sandy soils; from sea level to 800 m.

Range: Most of Europe except Iceland.

The narrowest, truly linear leaves – in which margins are often entire, and rolled under – are found in plants from dry, sandy places (such as inner sea-dunes). Leafy Hawkweed is exceptional in subgenus *Hieracium* in having many sexually propagating forms, besides agamospermous ones; the frequent crossings make the delimitation of microspecies problematical. The group is connected by intermediate forms to several others, notably, in W Europe, to the *sabaudum* group.

p.224 **Common Hawkweed**
Hieracium (H.) vulgatum group

Description: Stem 20–80 cm [S E]. Leaves [eE↑ (s↓)], basal ones numerous, stalked, to 15 cm long, and to 45 mm wide, ovate to lanceolate, more or less dentate; stem-leaves 2–10 (15), lower ones like basal leaves, upper ones smaller, subsessile. Flowerheads (1) 3–20 or more, usually on long, ascending stalks [S eE g], occasionally without glands; involucre 8–11 mm long, 7–10 mm wide, with obtuse to acute bracts [sS E gG]. Ligules usually glabrous at top. Stigmas discoloured.

Flowering: June–September.

Habitat: Open woods, scrub, heaths, grassy roadsides, rocks, cliffs, and walls, on dry to moist, oligotrophic to mesotrophic, usually acid, sandy, loamy or rocky soils; from sea level to 2,500 m.

Range: Most of Europe except Iceland, but rare in the south.

Similar species: The *H. caesium* group has glaucous leaves (2–4 cauline, the rest basal), 1–10 flowerheads, with dark-based hairs [E] on involucre. In Britain and C Europe, northwards to S Scandinavia, Finland and N Russia, eastwards to C Russia and Romania, and southwards to N Italy.

The *H. ramosum* group (= caesium| laevigatum) has stems [s Ee]. Leaves [E(e↑) (s↓)]; basal leaves absent or few, then stalked, elliptical to lanceolate, often coarsely dentate, to 90 mm long, and to 30 mm wide; stem-leaves 4–15 (18), lower ones like basal leaves, upper ones smaller and sessile, lanceolate or ovate. Flowerheads, 3–15, on stalks [S (e)]; involucre 10–12 mm long, 8–10 mm wide, with blunt or subacute bracts [Ss Ee (g)], glabrous florets, and yellow or discoloured stigmas. In Fennoscandia, Denmark, and C Europe from Switzerland to Romania.

Spotted Hawkweed (*H. maculatum* group = glaucinum|vulgatum) has leaves often purple-spotted (not always!), basal leaves present, stem-leaves 2–4 (8); involucral bracts have hairs and glands [eE G]. Common in W and C Europe from Britain to Poland, Bulgaria and Yugoslavia, and southwards to Spain and Italy.

The *H. murorum* group (*see* photograph p.225) has stems 20–50 (80) cm [sS gG(at least ↑)]. Leaves [E(at least ↓) (S↓)]; basal ones numerous, stalked, to 15 cm long, and to 70 mm wide, (broadly) elliptical or ovate to lanceolate, obtuse or acute, entire-margined or variously dentate (to deeply and broadly lobed), with attenuate to truncate base; stem-leaves absent or 1 (rarely 2), stalked, like basal leaves (or bract-like). Flowerheads moderately numerous (4–15 or some more), often in umbel-shaped panicle, on ascending stalks [(e) S G]; involucre 8–14 mm long, 5–12 mm wide, with acute or blunt bracts [(e) Ss G]; stigmas yellow or discoloured; ligules often glabrous at top. In deciduous woods, on rocks and cliffs, also on walls, on dry to moist, oligotrophic, sandy, loamy or rocky soils, from sea level to 2,500 m, in most of Europe except some Mediterranean islands.

The *H. atratum* group (= alpinum|
murorum) has stems [E S↑ G↑], leaves
[eE] with minute glandular hairs on
margin, 1–2 (4) stem-leaves [eE sS↓],
2–10 flowerheads with erect stalks [E S G],
linear-lanceolate involucral bracts [(e) (s)
G!], ciliate florets, and discoloured stigmas.
In N and C Europe, from Iceland eastwards
to N and W Russia, and southwards to
Britain, France, Italy, and Yugoslavia, but
only in mountainous areas.

The *H. bifidum* group has stems [e sS],
glaucous leaves subglabrous above, few
flowerheads on long stalks [E], involucral
bracts [E S gG]. Widely distributed in cool-
temperate Europe, descending lower than
H. atratum.

The *H. glaucinum* group (= murorum|
schmidtii) has green or glaucous, often
purple-spotted, stiffly ciliate leaves,
involucral bracts [E G], and often ciliate
florets. From Ireland and Spain eastwards to
Sweden, Poland and Bulgaria, descending
almost to sea level.

The *H. umbrosum* group (= murorum|
prenanthoides) has stems taller (to 70 cm)
[eE s↑ g↑], leaves [E] often subglabrous
above, basal leaves few, with rounded or
narrowed base; flowerheads on stalks [(e) S
G], florets mostly glabrous at top. From
Arctic Russia southwards to Greece, C
Europe and the Pyrenees, but in the south
occurs only on mountains. In C Europe and
Scandinavia, the *umbrosum* group is further
connected with other groups (e.g., the
vulgatum group) by intermediate forms.

The *H. fuscocinereum* group has involucral
bracts with dense, pale, eglandular hairs
and some glandular hairs [E! G]. In N and
NC Europe (north of the Alps), from France
and Britain eastwards to N and C Russia.

The *H. schmidtii* group has stems 10–40
(50) cm [eE S↑ Gg↑]. Leaves thick, green
(rarely dark-spotted), with simple hairs and
glands (if any) almost restricted to leaf-
margins [E↓ (↑) sS↓ (↑) (g)]; basal leaves
numerous, to 11 cm long, 50 mm wide,
elliptical or ovate to lanceolate, subentire to
deeply dentate, outer ones with rounded or

truncate base, inner ones cuneate, long-stalked; stem-leaves absent or 1 (rarely 2), like inner basal leaves but short-stalked, or much smaller and bract-like. Flowerheads 2–12 (18), on long, straight stalks [(e) S G(!)]; involucre 9–12 mm long, 9–14 mm wide, with narrow, acute bracts [eE sS (gG)]; ligules usually ciliate at top. On (mainly siliceous, acid) rocks and cliffs in the mountains (400–2,600 m) in most of Europe except Russia and parts of the lowland (e.g., the Netherlands). This group has many connections to other ones, which accounts for its variability.

The *H. hypochoeroides* group (= bifidum| schmidtii) has ovate, strongly dentate leaves [E] with truncate base, and densely stellate-hairy involucral bracts [S!]. In C, W and S Europe, eastwards to Romania, mainly in the mountains.

The *H. sommerfeltii* group (= bifidum| schmidtii|vulgatum) has all leaves narrowly lanceolate, usually purple-spotted (subglabrous above, with rather rigid hairs on the margin), narrowed into stalk. Iceland, Norway, N Britain, and C Europe eastwards to Hungary.

The *H. onosmoides* group (= schmidtii| vulgatum) has stems [E S↑]. Basal leaves narrowly ovate to lanceolate, more or less dentate to serrate, often glaucous, rigid-hairy [E↑-margin (s↓) (g-margin)] narrowed into winged petiole; stem-leaves 2–12 (lower ones subsessile, upper ones sessile and bract-like). Flowerheads 2–25 (30) on stalks [eE S! gG], with involucres 9–12 (15) mm long, 9–12 mm wide; involucral bracts [E s G], narrow, (sub)acute. In C and W Europe, from Portugal to Ireland, Britain and S Scandinavia, eastwards to Hungary, but absent from the lowlands.

The *H. alatum* group has stems up to 80 cm [eE S↑ G↑]. Leaves [eE↓ (s↓)]; basal ones few, narrowed into winged stalk, to 12 cm long, and to 40 mm wide, (ob)ovate or elliptical to lanceolate, more or less dentate; stem-leaves 1–8, lower ones stalked, like basal leaves, upper ones ovate to lanceolate, sessile and clasping. Flowerheads (1) 2–25, on stalks [eE S! G!]; involucre 10–15 mm long and equally wide, with pointed or tapering, acute bracts [eE sS gG]; ligules often slightly ciliate at top; stigmas discoloured. On cliffs and rocks, in meadows, on moist to dry, oligotrophic, stony or rocky soils; mainly in mountains (to 2,500 m) in W Europe, from Iceland through Ireland and Britain to N Spain, and eastwards to Switzerland and N Italy. In Ireland, Britain and the Faeroes be aware of the occurrence of forms tending to both *H. schmidtii* – particularly *H. scoticum* F.J. Hanb. (= alatum|schmidtii|vulgatum), with short-stalked basal leaves with cuneate base, stalks under the flowerheads [e S (g)], and (sub)acute involucral bracts [E s g], and *H. caledonicum* F.J. Hanb. (= alatum|schmidtii), resembling *H. scoticum* but having only 1–3 stem-leaves, and blunt involucral bracts.

---

p.230 **Smooth Cat's-ear** *Hypochoeris glabra* L.

Description: A *subglabrous annual* with *basal leaf-rosette* and erect to ascending, scarcely branched flowering stems to 30 cm, thickened under flowerheads. Basal leaves obovate to oblanceolate, narrowed into short stalk, *sinuously dentate or pinnately lobed*, shiny green, glabrous or bristly-ciliate. Stem-leaves reduced to lanceolate *scale-leaves in inflorescence. Flowerheads solitary, terminal,* (10) 15–20 mm diam.; involucre cylindrical, almost equalling florets, with unequal, erect, dark-tipped bracts in several rows; *receptacle has lanceolate scales*. All florets ligulate, with short, yellow ligule (pale yellow beneath). Achenes 10-ribbed, spindle-shaped, *inner ones long-beaked*; umbrella-shaped *pappus of hairs in 2 rows, inner ones longer and feathery.*

Flowering: June–October.

Habitat: Poor grassland, dunes, fields, heaths, on dry, oligotrophic, slightly acid, sandy soils; from sea level to 500 m.

Range: Most of Europe, northwards to S Scandinavia and Latvia, eastwards to the Ukraine and Greece.

Similar species: **(Common) Cat's-ear** (*H. radicata* L.) is
perennial, and has bristly-hairy leaves and
stems. Basal leaves narrowly oblanceolate,
often deeply lobed, with broadly
triangular or rounded top. Flowerheads
larger (20–40 mm diam.) with involucres
shorter than florets; outer florets have
grey-streaked ligule; achenes often all
beaked. In comparable habitats, also in the
mountains (to 1,800 m) and generally
more common, in all of Europe except the
far north.

p.230 **Spotted Cat's-ear** *Hypochoeris maculata* L.

Description: A *bristly-hairy perennial* with *basal leaf-rosette*
and erect to ascending, scarcely branched
flowering stems to 60 (90) cm, thickened
under flowerheads. Basal leaves obovate,
short-stalked, narrowed into stalk or with
rounded base, *sinuously dentate to subentire*,
dark green with *purplish-brown blotches*,
bristly-ciliate. *Stem-leaves 0–1*; rarely also
some small, lanceolate scale-leaves.
Flowerheads solitary, terminal, 30–45 mm
diam.; involucre ovoid, much shorter than
florets, with unequal bracts in several rows;
receptacle has lanceolate scales. All florets
ligulate, with broadly strap-shaped, yellow
ligule. Achenes 10-ribbed, spindle-shaped,
always long-beaked; umbrella-shaped *pappus
of feathery hairs in 1 row*.

Flowering: May–July.

Habitat: Poor pasture, heaths, open woods, quarries
and rocky cliffs, on dry, oligotrophic, acid
or calcareous, sandy, stony or rocky soils;
from sea level to 1,800 m.

Range: Most of Europe except the Arctic and much
of the Mediterranean. (Extinct in the
Netherlands.)

Similar species: **Giant Cat's-ear** (*H. uniflora* Vill.) has
unbranched stems strongly inflated below
solitary, very large flowerhead (40–60 mm
diam.), blackish, fringed involucral bracts,
and often several (3–5) larger stem-leaves.
In meadows and woods in the mountains of
C Europe (1,500–2,600 m), westwards to C
France, and eastwards to the W Ukraine.

p.233 *Inula britannica* L.

Description: A slightly hairy perennial, with erect, leafy, *scarcely branched stems* to 75 cm. Leaves alternate, soft, narrowly lanceolate, *densely hairy beneath*; lower ones short-stalked, upper ones sessile and slightly clasping. *Flowerheads solitary or few* (up to 3) together in terminal clusters, *20–50 mm diam.*; involucre broadly cup-shaped, with numerous linear-lanceolate, recurved bracts in several rows, outer ones hairy; receptacle scaleless. Ray-florets numerous, with very long, narrow, strap-like, spreading, yellow ligule; disc-florets yellow. *Achene hairy*; pappus of simple hairs in 1 row.

Flowering: June–August.

Habitat: Marshes, meadows, grassy banks, rocks, wood margins, on wet to moist, oligotrophic, preferably calcareous, loamy or rocky soils; from sea level to 500m.

Range: Continental Europe, northwards to S Scandinavia.

Similar species: *I. hirta* L. has densely hairy, elliptical, dark-green, rigid leaves and involucres, sessile to half-clasping upper leaves, and solitary flowerheads (rarely 2–3 together). S, C and E Europe (northwards to C France, S Germany, Poland and C Russia).
I. helvetica Weber has stems to 1.5 m, densely grey-hairy, lanceolate, sessile (not half-clasping) upper leaves, and solitary or clustered flowerheads (30–45 mm across). SW Europe to S Germany and NW Italy.
Irish Fleabane (*I. salicina* L.) has leaves lanceolate to ovate, shiny green, subglabrous (often ciliate), upper ones clearly half-clasping with cordate base; flowerheads 25–40 mm diam., involucral bracts glabrous (only ciliate); achenes glabrous. Widely distributed in continental Europe (1 station in Ireland), but rare in the lowland.
Narrow-leaved Inula (*I. ensifolia* L.) has stalked to sessile, lanceolate to almost linear, entire-margined, glabrous (but ciliate) leaves with 3–7 parallel, arched veins; involucral bracts silky at base. In E and EC Europe, westwards to S Sweden (Gotland) and N Italy.

Elecampane (*I. helenium* L.), to 2.5 m, has leaves densely tomentose, ovate to elliptical, lower ones stalked and very large (to 80 cm long), upper ones clasping; flowerheads 60–80 mm diam., solitary or 2–3 together; outer involucral bracts ovate, leaf-like, wider than 4 mm, inner ones linear-lanceolate with widened top. An old medicinal and ornamental plant from SE Europe, naturalized (as archeophyte) in grassland, along ditches and hedges, in most of Europe except the far north.

p.233   **Ploughman's-spikenard**
Inula conyzae (Griesselich) Meikle

Description: A hairy perennial or biennial, with erect, leafy, branched, often purplish, stems to 90 cm. Leaves alternate, ovate to broadly lanceolate; lower ones stalked, upper ones sessile with cuneate base (not clasping). *Flowerheads small*, to 15 mm long, 8–11 mm diam., numerous in *large, more or less umbel-shaped panicles*; involucre cylindrical, with bracts in several rows, *outer ones recurved*, ovate to lanceolate, green, *inner ones erect*, linear-lanceolate, purplish; receptacle scaleless. *Ray-florets hardly longer than inner involucral bracts*, with very short (or absent), 3-toothed, yellow ligule; disc-florets yellow, 5-toothed. Achenes ellipsoid, angular; pappus of simple hairs in 1 row.

Flowering: July–October.

Habitat: Grassland, road verges, grassy banks, scrub, open woods, on dry to moist, oligotrophic, preferably calcareous, sandy, loamy or rocky soils; from sea level to 1,200 m.

Range: Most of Europe, northwards to Denmark, Poland and the Ukraine.

Similar species: **German Inula** (*I. germanica* L.) has clasping upper leaves, and ray-florets with slightly longer, erect yellow ligules, markedly exceeding involucre. In C and SE Europe, extending northwards to C Germany, Poland and C Russia.
Stink Aster (*Dittrichia graveolens* (L.) W. Greuter) is annual, smells of camphor, and has sessile, narrowly lanceolate, subentire

leaves and short-stalked flowerheads
(7–12 mm diam.), with very short ray-
florets, on spike-like, axillary branches all
along main stem; achenes cylindrical. In W
and C France, and the Mediterranean area.

p.234 **Golden Samphire** *Inula crithmoides* L.

Description: A hairless perennial, with lignified base
and branched, ascending to erect stems to
1 m. *Leaves fleshy*, alternate, to 50 mm
long, short-stalked to sessile, *narrowly
oblanceolate to linear*, with *blunt or 3-toothed
top*, and often with bundle of small, linear
leaves in axil. Flowerheads 20–30 mm
diam., in loose, umbel-shaped panicles;
involucre much shorter than ray-florets,
with linear, erect bracts; receptacle
scaleless. Ray-florets numerous, with
narrow, strap-like, spreading, yellow
ligule; disc-florets yellow. Achene
glabrous; pappus of simple hairs in 1 row.
Flowering: July–October.
Habitat: Coastal cliffs and rocks, shingle-beaches,
high, sandy saltmarshes, on wet to moist,
saline soils.
Range: S Europe, extending northwards along
Atlantic coast to W France, S Britain and
SE Ireland.

This species only superficially resembles
Crithmum maritimum (*see* p.1109), which has
fleshy, compound leaves.

p.321 **Blue Lettuce** *Lactuca perennis* L.

Description: A hairless, latex-bearing perennial, with
erect or ascending, much-branched, wiry
stems to 70 cm. Leaves alternate, *glaucous,
half-clasping with rounded auricles, pinnately
divided* with remote, linear-lanceolate
segments, rarely shallow-lobed.
Flowerheads 30–40 mm diam., in panicles;
involucre cylindrical, with unequal,
lanceolate bracts in several rows; receptacle
flat, scaleless. All florets ligulate, with
strap-shaped, truncate, 5-toothed, *pale-blue*

to *lilac* (rarely white) ligule. Achene
ellipsoid, laterally compressed, to 7 mm
long, black, ribbed, *with long beak* (to
7 mm); umbrella-shaped pappus of simple
hairs in 2 rows.

Flowering: May–August.

Habitat: Grassland, vineyards, sunny slopes and
rocks, on dry, mesotrophic, calcareous,
stony or rocky soils; from sea level to
2,100 m.

Range: C Europe, westwards to France and
Belgium, northwards to Germany, and
eastwards to Romania and Bulgaria.

Similar species: *L. tatarica* (L.) C.A. Meyer is a perennial
with creeping rhizomes, glaucous,
pinnatifid to subentire, half-clasping leaves
(lobes rounded), large panicles of pale-
violet flowerheads (18–26 mm diam.), and
buff to blackish achenes with white pappus.
Native to E Europe, and locally naturalized
in (or naturally extending its range to) N
and NW Europe, in ruderal places both
inland and coastal.
L. sibirica (L.) Maxim. has simple,
unbranched stem, clasping, lanceolate,
dentate to entire leaves, few flowerheads in
small, terminal, slightly umbel-shaped
panicle, and greenish achenes with greyish
pappus. In woods, scrub, and along rivers in
Fennoscandia and N and C Russia.
Purple Lettuce (*Prenanthes purpurea* L.) has
lyrate, glaucous leaves, and nodding
flowerheads with violet or purplish florets.
In mountainous areas of C Europe,
westwards to C and NE France and S
Germany.

---

p.231 **Least Lettuce** *Lactuca saligna* L.

Description: A hairless, latex-bearing annual or biennial,
with erect, ivory stems to 1 m. Leaves
alternate, *greyish-green, often erect*; lower ones
short-stalked, oblanceolate, sinuously
dentate to pinnately divided, upper ones
sessile and *clasping with pointed auricles,
lanceolate to linear*, entire-margined.
Flowerheads *c.* 10 mm diam., subsessile,
erect, in *spike-like, terminal raceme*; involucre

cylindrical, with unequal, green bracts in several rows; receptacle scaleless. All florets ligulate, with rather short, oblanceolate, truncate, *pale-yellow* ligule. Achene ellipsoid, compressed, *half as long as whitish beak*; umbrella-shaped pappus of white, simple hairs in 2 rows.

Flowering: June–August.

Habitat: Poor pasture, vineyards, road verges, ruderal places, along railways, also sea-walls and shingle-beaches, on dry, mesotrophic, calcareous, mineral and often stony soils; from sea level to 800 m.

Range: Europe northwards to S England, the Netherlands, C Germany, and C Russia.

p.231 **Prickly Lettuce** *Lactuca serriola* L.

Description: A large, green or glaucous, latex-bearing annual or biennial, with simple, erect, ivory stem to 1.8 m. Leaves alternate, sessile, broadly lanceolate, half-clasping with pointed basal lobes, spiny on margins, and with *spiny midrib beneath*, the *spines longer than 2 mm*; lower leaves often pinnately divided (not so in f. *integrifolia* Bogenhard), upper ones merely lobed or sinuously dentate, and often upcurved and turned in a vertical plane. Flowerheads 11–13 mm diam., in large, partly leafy, pyramidal panicle; involucre cylindrical, with unequal bracts in several rows; receptacle scaleless. All florets ligulate, yellow. Achenes ellipsoid, *to 3 mm long, 1 mm wide*, flattened, ribbed, whitish at first, *grey or pale brownish, often mottled when ripe*, and with whitish beak to 3 mm long; umbrella-like pappus of whitish, simple hairs in 2 rows.

Flowering: July–September.

Habitat: Ruderal places, dunes, scrub, vineyards, road verges, building sites, along railways, on sandy, stony or rocky soils; from sea level to 1,600 m.

Range: Most of Europe except Iceland, Ireland, much of Scandinavia and N Russia; strongly expanding, especially in urban areas.

Similar species: **Great Lettuce** (*L. virosa* L.) is biennial to short-lived perennial, and has all leaves lobed or dentate (not deeply incised), usually not placed in vertical plane; spines on midrib less spiny (with spines often less than 1 mm long); achenes 4–5 mm long, 1.5–2 mm wide, yellow or orange at first, and black or deep violet when ripe. In comparable habitats, in S, W and C Europe, northwards to Britain, Belgium and Germany, and eastwards to Romania.

L. quercina L. has green stems, thickened root, sinuously pinnatifid (lyrate) leaves lacking spines on midrib; achenes 2–3 times as long as (black) beak. In C and SE Europe, mainly in the mountains (between 400 and 1,800 m), northwards to C Germany, and isolated on Gotland.

---

p.231 **Nipplewort** *Lapsana communis* L.

Description: A slightly hairy annual, with erect, often (widely) branched stems to 80 (120) cm; no milky latex. Leaves alternate, with shallowly *dentate margin*; lower ones stalked, *pinnately divided with large, ovate end-lobe*, and small side-lobes diminishing towards base, *upper leaves sessile, ovate, undivided*. Flowerheads 10–20 mm diam., in lax, somewhat umbel-shaped panicles; involucre cylindrical, with lanceolate *inner bracts in 1 row, and few smaller, outer bracts at base*; receptacle scaleless. All florets ligulate, strap-shaped, truncate, 5-toothed, *yellow*. Achene 2.5–9 mm (outer ones much longer than inner), spindle-shaped with rounded top, slightly compressed, with 20–30 fine ribs; *pappus absent*.

Flowering: June–October.

Habitat: Wood margins, scrub, shaded roadsides, hedgerows, gardens, ruderal places, also walls, on moist, eutrophic, slightly acid to calcareous, sandy, loamy or stony soils; from sea level to 1,800 m.

Range: All Europe except Iceland and Spitsbergen.

Compare Mycelis muralis (see p.527), which has smaller flowerheads and an angularly lobed end-lobe to the leaf.

p.229 **Autumn Hawkbit** *Leontodon autumnalis* L.

Description: A glabrous or slightly hairy perennial, with basal leaf-rosette and erect, usually *branched stems* to 50 cm, and *several flowerheads*. Stem-leaves reduced to *small scales under flowerheads*; basal leaves stalked, oblanceolate, deeply pinnately lobed or divided, with remote, narrow, subacute segments. Flowerheads 20–30 mm diam., long-stalked, *erect in bud*; involucre narrowly cup-shaped, with linear-lanceolate, dark-green, glabrous or hairy bracts in several rows; receptacle scaleless. All florets ligulate, with strap-shaped, yellow ligule, *outer ones often red-striped beneath*. Achene 3.5–7 mm long, spindle-shaped, narrowed above (but not beaked), ribbed, reddish-brown; *pappus of feathery hairs* in 1 row.

Flowering: June–October.

Habitat: Grassland, road verges, grassy banks, also dune-valleys and highest, rarely inundated parts of saltmarshes, on moist to dry, mesotrophic to eutrophic, basic or brackish, sandy, loamy or clayey soils; from sea level to 2,600 m.

Range: All Europe except Spitsbergen.

Similar species: *L. keretinus* F. Nyl. has yellow-orange, unstriped florets, short-beaked achenes, and red hairs on involucral bracts. In grassy places, in Finland and N and C Russia.

---

p.229 **Rough Hawkbit** *Leontodon hispidus* L.

Description: A rosette-bearing, *rough-hairy* perennial with erect, *simple stems* to 40 cm; *hairs forked*. Basal leaves rough-hairy (occasionally subglabrous), oblanceolate, sinuously dentate to pinnately lobed, narrowed into winged stalk, and with broad, rounded end-lobe. Stem-leaves absent. *Flowerheads solitary*, 25–40 mm diam., nodding in bud; involucre cup-shaped, with linear-lanceolate, bristly-hairy bracts in several rows; receptacle scaleless. All florets ligulate, with strap-shaped, yellow ligule, *outer ones usually grey-striped*.

Achenes straight, spindle-shaped, *all with 2–4 mm long beak; pappus of hairs in 2 rows, inner ones feathery.*

Flowering: June–October.

Habitat: Grassland, road verges, grassy banks, rocks, on dry to moist, oligotrophic, preferably calcareous, sandy, loamy or rocky soils; from sea level to 2,700 m.

Range: Most of Europe except the high Arctic.

---

p.228 **Lesser Hawkbit** *Leontodon saxatilis* Lamk.

Description: A slightly hairy perennial, with basal leaf-rosette and simple, ascending to erect flowering stems to 40 cm; *some hairs forked, others simple.* Basal leaves oblanceolate, narrowed into winged stalk, sinuously dentate to pinnately lobed, hairy; stem-leaves absent, sometimes 1 or 2 scales. Flowerheads solitary, 12–20 mm diam., nodding in bud; involucre narrowly cup-shaped, with linear-lanceolate bracts; receptacle scaleless. All florets ligulate, with strap-shaped, yellow ligule, *outer ones usually grey-striped beneath. Achenes of 2 types:* those of inner florets straight, with short beak to 1 mm, and pappus of feathery hairs in 1 row, surrounded by row of short scales; achenes of marginal florets curved, not beaked but truncate, with pappus of short scales and no hairs.

Flowering: June–November.

Habitat: Open, grassy places, dunes, road verges, grassy banks, on dry to moist, oligotrophic, slightly acid to calcareous, sandy or loamy, rarely peaty soils; mainly in the lowland.

Range: S, W and C Europe, northwards to Britain, Germany and Poland; naturalized in Denmark and S Sweden.

---

p.169 **Oxeye Daisy** *Leucanthemum vulgare* Lamk.

Description: A subglabrous perennial, with short, creeping rhizomes and erect or ascending, branched flowering stems to 60 cm. Leaves alternate; lower ones obovate to oblanceolate, crenate-dentate to deeply dentate, narrowed

upper ones lanceolate and shallowly lobed or dentate. *Flowerheads large* (30–50 mm diam.), solitary or (more often) in *clusters of 2–3* at end of stem and branches; involucre globose, *wider than long*, cottony, with numerous linear, upcurved, spiny-tipped bracts; receptacle glabrous, but honeycombed, pitted, the *pits with dentate rims*. All florets tubular, red-purplish (rarely pale pink or white), with 5 long teeth, all hermaphrodite. Achene ellipsoid, flattened or slightly tetragonal; pappus of simple, basally connate hairs in several rows.

Flowering: (June) July–September.

Habitat: Ruderal places, roadsides, field margins, dunes, hedgebanks, on dry, eutrophic, calcareous to slightly acid, sandy, loamy or stony soils; from sea level to 1,500 m.

Range: S, W and C Europe, northwards to N France, S Germany and C Russia; naturalized in Britain, Denmark and Sweden.

Occasionally cultivated for ornament in gardens. *Compare Cirsium eriophorum (see p.490)*, which has mostly solitary flowerheads, unwinged stems, and involucral bracts widened under terminal spine.

---

p.228 **Cottonweed**
Otanthus maritimus (L.) Hoffm. & Link

Description: A curious, *white-tomentose*, tufted, *aromatic perennial*, with erect or ascending stems to 50 cm. Leaves alternate, *crowded, sessile, fleshy, elliptical* to broadly lanceolate, bluntly serrate to subentire, *blunt-tipped*, white-tomentose on both faces. *Flowerheads globose*, 7–10 mm diam., in terminal, somewhat umbel-shaped clusters; involucral bracts obovate, blunt, tomentose, in several rows; *receptacle has scales*. All florets tubular, *yellow*, 5-toothed; *corolla connected to ovary through 2 basal spurs*, persistent on fruit, becoming corky. Achene compressed, 4–5-ribbed; pappus absent.

Flowering: (June) August–October.

Habitat: Sea-dunes and stabilized shingle-beaches, on dry, basic or brackish, sandy or gravelly soils; coastal only.

Range: S and SW Europe, northwards to SW France, and isolated in SE Ireland.

p.296 **Butterbur** *Petasites hybridus* (L.) Gaertner, Meyer & Scherb.

Description: A large, *dioecious* perennial, with creeping rhizomes, erect flowering stems (appearing before leaves) to 50 (80) cm, and tendency to colonize large areas. Normal leaves all basal, stalked, ovate or suborbicular with cordate base, round-tipped, to 60 (90) cm diam., shallow-lobed and dentate, grey-tomentose beneath (at least when young); flowering stems have numerous lanceolate, scale-like leaves (often with degenerate blade at end). *Flowerheads numerous, in terminal racemes*, not fragrant, ovoid, (functional) female ones 3–6 mm diam., long-stalked, (functional) male ones 7–12 mm diam. and short-stalked; involucral bracts lanceolate, usually in 1 row; receptacle scaleless. Florets *purplish, pink, whitish or cream*; in male florets corolla tubular, 5-toothed; in females oblique tongue or filament often present (then better called ligulate). Achene linear; clock-like pappus of hairs in several rows.

Flowering: March–May.

Habitat: Meadows, stream- and riverbanks, damp woods, from sea level to 1,800 m.

Range: In Europe northwards to Scotland, N Germany and C Russia; naturalized in the Baltic region and Fennoscandia.

Similar species: **White Butterbur** (*Petasites albus* (L.) Gaertner) has cream or yellowish, fragrant florets, irregularly lobed leaves with markedly reticulate nerves beneath, and stays grey-tomentose throughout season. From S Norway and C France eastwards to Bulgaria.

P. spurius (Retz) Reichenb. has triangular leaves with (2 or 4) spreading side-lobes, and yellowish florets. On sandy lakeshores, and on riverbanks, in Russia and Romania, with scattered stations westwards to Denmark, NW Germany and S Sweden. *P. frigidus* (L.) Fries has only 5–12 flowerheads. In bogs and streambanks in Fennoscandia and N and C Russia.

Giant Butterbur (*P. japonicus* (Sieb. & Zucc.) Maxim.) from Japan and Sakhalin has leaves to 1 m diam., and sizeable bracts (20–40 mm wide) in base of inflorescence. Grown for ornament, and a garden escape (male plants only) in W Europe.

Compare also Tussilago farfara (see p.548).

---

p.234 **Bristly Oxtongue** *Picris echioides* L.

Description: A *bristly-hairy* annual or biennial, with erect, branched stems to 60 cm. Leaves partly basal, partly cauline: basal ones elliptical to oblanceolate, narrowed into winged stalk, entire but wavy-edged, and with *some bristles implanted on pale-green tubercle*; stem-leaves alternate, *sessile and clasping*, ovate to lanceolate. Flowerheads 20–25 mm diam., in terminal, more or less cymose panicles; involucre ovoid with *3–5 ovate, pointed, erect, leaf-like outer bracts* and 8 lanceolate, tapering inner bracts in 1 row, all bristly-ciliate; receptacle hairy but scaleless. All florets ligulate, deep yellow, outer ones often red-striped beneath. Achene ellipsoid, corrugated, with *long beak; pappus of white, feathery hairs in 2 rows*.

Flowering: (June) July–October (November).

Habitat: Rough grassland, road verges, riverbanks and dikes, streambanks, on moist, mesotrophic, calcareous, often heavy soils; mainly in the lowland.

Range: S and W Europe, northwards to Ireland, Britain, the Netherlands, Poland and Romania, but presumably only naturalized in the northern part of its range.

Similar species: **Hawkweed Oxtongue** (*P. hieracioides* L.) is biennial or short-lived perennial; lanceolate, spreading outer involucral bracts resemble (erect) inner ones; leaves dentate to remotely serrate, bristles never imposed on tubercles; achenes short-beaked, with creamy pappus.

In road verges and on sunny, grassy slopes, often on drier, poorer or even rocky soils, from sea level to 2,200 m, in all of Europe except Ireland, Iceland, Norway and Spitsbergen. This species does resemble some hawkweeds *Hieracium*, especially the amplexicaule group), but these have simple, never feathery, pappus hairs.

p.234 **Common Fleabane**
Pulicaria dysenterica (L.) Bernh.

Description: A *tomentose* perennial, with creeping rhizomes and erect, branched flowering stems to 60 (90) cm. Leaves alternate, ovate-cordate, *sessile, and clasping stem with 2 subacute auricles*, subentire, grey-tomentose (at least beneath). Flowerheads 15–30 mm diam., solitary at end of stem and branches; involucre broadly cup-shaped, with numerous, lanceolate bracts in few rows; receptacle scaleless. Ray-florets numerous, spreading, *exceeding involucre*, female, with strap-shaped, narrow, *yellow* ligule; disc-florets very numerous, 5-toothed, deep yellow, hermaphrodite. Achene to 1.5 mm long, ellipsoid, hairy on ribs; double pappus (*short membranous rim encircling ring of white, simple hairs*).

Flowering: July–September.

Habitat: Marshes, dune-valleys, meadows, damp road verges, along streams and ditches, on wet to moist, mesotrophic, basic or even brackish, sandy or clayey soils; from sea level to 1,000 m.

Range: Most of Europe except Iceland, Fennoscandia and N Russia.

Similar species: **Small Fleabane** (*P. vulgaris* Gaertner) has round-based, simply sessile upper leaves, and flowerheads to 10 mm diam., with short, erect to recurved, pale-yellow ray-florets hardly exceeding involucre. In seasonally flooded, sandy or clayey places along lakes and rivers, in Europe northwards to S England, S Sweden and C Russia; a rare and declining species.

Compare also the *Inula* species (*see* p.517), which have pappus of hairs only.

p.235 **Cone-flower** *Rudbeckia laciniata* L.

Description: A subglabrous perennial to 2 (3) m, with
erect, branched stems. Leaves alternate,
lower ones long-stalked, pinnately
divided, ovate, with 3–7 larger, dentate or
lobed segments, upper ones finally
undivided, (sub)sessile, ovate, serrate to
subentire. Flowerheads solitary, terminal,
large (6–12 cm diam.); involucre widely
cup-shaped; involucral bracts linear-
lanceolate, to 15 mm long, rough-hairy;
receptacle conical, elongating after
anthesis, with truncate, ciliate scales
partly enveloping achenes. Ray-florets
sterile, with large, narrowly oblanceolate,
yellow ligule; disc-florets yellow. Achene
to 5 mm long, ellipsoid, bluntly
tetragonal; pappus of 4 short,
membranous scales.

Flowering: July–October.

Habitat: Reed-lands, willow-coppices, along
streams, canals, rivers, on wet, eutrophic,
sandy or clayey soils; mainly in the
lowland.

Range: Native to N America; naturalized in W and
C Europe, northwards to Britain, Germany
and W Russia.

Comments: **Hairy Rudbeckia** (*R. hirta* L.), also from
America, has hairy, undivided leaves, and
reddish or brown disc-florets. Naturalized
in comparable habitats of NC and E
Europe, from France to E Russia.

---

p.238 **Viper's-grass** *Scorzonera humilis* L.

Description: A subglabrous perennial (often cottony or
hairy below), with stout, *vertical rhizomes*
and erect, simple flowering stems to 50
(80) cm. *Leaves entire-margined, lanceolate to
linear*; stem-leaves alternate and sessile,
progressively diminishing up stem, finally
scale-like. Flowerheads 25–30 mm diam.,
solitary (rarely 2–3); involucre cylindrical,
often slightly cottony, with unequal, *blunt-
tipped bracts* in several rows; receptacle
concave, scaleless. All florets ligulate, twice
as long as involucre, *yellow*. Achenes

7–11 mm long, linear, cylindrical, rough between smooth ribs; *pappus of dirty-white, feathery hairs* in several rows.

Flowering: May–July.

Habitat: Heaths, marshy meadows, forest clearings, pine-forests, on wet to moist (or even dry), oligotrophic, slightly acid, sandy or peaty soils; from sea level to 1,700 m.

Range: Most of Europe except Ireland and the high Arctic, eastwards to the Caucasus, but rare in most areas.

Similar species: **Cut-leaved, Viper's-grass** (*S. laciniata* L.) has very variable, pinnately divided leaves (lower ones often doubly so). Mainly Mediterranean, reaching N France, Belgium, S Germany, Poland, and W Russia.

Black Salsify (*S. hispanica* L.), from the Pyrenees, C and SE Europe, often has several flowerheads, and acute involucral bracts. Cultivated for its black, edible, tuberous roots; occasional escape.

Several other species occur in S and SC Europe, some with lilac flowers, e.g. **Purple Viper's-grass** (*S. purpurea* L.).

---

p.239 **Marsh Fleawort**
Senecio congestus (R. Br.) DC.

Description: A more or less hairy, *yellowish-green to fresh-green* biennial (or annual), with *large tufts of basal leaves* and erect flowering stems to 1 (1.5) m; *stems hollow*, 10–40 mm diam., ribbed, with sticky glandular hairs. Basal leaves stalked, sinuously dentate to almost pinnately divided, *slightly fleshy but soft* (rather like endive), often only slightly hairy; stem-leaves sessile to half-clasping, lanceolate, dentate to subentire. Flowerheads 20–35 mm diam., in leafy, umbel-shaped panicles, honey-scented; involucre cup-shaped, with lanceolate *involucral bracts in 1 row*; receptacle scaleless. Ray-florets 21, female, with *spreading, yellow ligule* to 10 mm; disc-florets numerous, hermaphrodite, yellow. Achene strongly ribbed, glabrous; pappus of white hairs.

Flowering: May–July (September).
Habitat: Marshes, along ditches, canals, lakes, sewage reservoirs, on wet, (very) eutrophic, basic or slightly brackish, sandy, clayey or peaty soils; mainly in the lowland.
Range: NW Europe, from the Netherlands southwards to NW France, eastwards through Germany and the Baltic region to E Russia; also in Siberia. (Extinct in Britain.)

This species is often abundant in recently enclosed, non-saline polders, such as those created in the 1960s in the Netherlands (Flevoland).

---

p.240 **Field Fleawort**
Senecio integrifolius (L.) Clairv.

Description: A grey-downy perennial with simple, leafy flowering stem to 50 (70) cm. Leaves alternate, *(sub)entire: basal ones flatly spreading*, to 10 cm long, obovate to oblanceolate, narrowed into *short, winged stalk; stem-leaves few*, alternate, erect, small, narrow, and bract-like. Flowerheads 15–25 mm diam., long-stalked, 1–12 together in umbel-shaped raceme (or even small pseudo-umbel, with crowded bracts at base); involucre has 21 lanceolate, green bracts 6–8 mm long and bearing tuft of hairs at top; receptacle scaleless. Ray-florets 12–15, female, with elliptical, yellow ligule; disc-florets yellow, hermaphrodite. Achene 2.5–4 mm long, cylindrical, glabrous or short-hairy; pappus of long, white hairs.
Flowering: May–July.
Habitat: Short grassland, grassy banks, cliffs, open woods, on dry to moist, oligotrophic, calcareous, sandy, loamy or stony soils; from near sea level to 2,200 m.
Range: Much of Europe, northwards to S Scandinavia, Poland and N Russia, but absent from large areas (e.g. the Low Countries), and extremely rare in Britain (Cambridge).
Similar species: *S. helenitis* (L.) Schinz & Thell. has spatulate basal leaves (often withered at

anthesis) narrowed into long, winged stalk (at least as long as blade); stem-leaves more numerous, well-developed, lanceolate; flowerheads 3–20 (with 15–20 ray-florets), and woolly involucral bracts with brown or purple tip. In moist grassland and open woods in W Europe, from N Spain northwards to Belgium and Germany, eastwards to Austria.

S. integrifolius ssp. *maritimus* (Syme) Chater has dentate basal leaves, more stem-leaves, and involucral bracts 8–12 mm long; endemic to W Britain (Anglesey).
Several other, comparable species occur in the mountains of C and S Europe.

---

p.240 **Common Ragwort** *Senecio jacobaea* L.

Description: A hairy to subglabrous biennial or short-lived perennial, with *vertical taproot* and erect, furrowed stems to 90 (150) cm; *no stolons*. Leaves alternate, pinnately divided (to doubly so) with curly segments, slightly hairy below: lower ones stalked (with 2 clasping auricles at base of stalk), upper ones sessile and clasping, with small, narrow end-lobe, basal ones usually withered at anthesis. Flowerheads 15–25 mm diam., numerous in umbel-shaped panicles; involucre cup-shaped, with erect, linear, *black-tipped bracts* in 1 row, and *1 or 2 small, green outer bracts at base*; receptacle scaleless. Ray-florets 12–15, female, with oblanceolate, yellow ligule (but ray-florets absent in ssp. *dunensis, see* below); disc-florets yellow, hermaphrodite. Achenes ellipsoid, *of 2 types*: hairy (in disc-florets) or (sub)glabrous (in ray-florets), both with pappus of white hairs. The subspecies *S. j. dunensis* (Dumort.) Kadereit & Sell lacks ray-florets, and as consequence has only hairy achenes; intermediate forms can also be found.

Flowering: June–October (November).

Habitat: Grassland, roadsides, banks, field margins, wasteland, ruderal places, on dry, oligotrophic to mesotrophic, preferably calcareous and often sandy soils; from sea level to 900 m.

Range: Most of Europe except the extreme north and south; ssp. *dunensis* occurs in coastal dunes of W Europe.

Similar species: **Marsh Ragwort** (*S. aquaticus* Hill) has upper stem-leaves less deeply divided, with large terminal lobe; basal leaves often present at anthesis, involucral bracts never black-tipped; even inner achenes often (sub)glabrous. In meadows, marshes, at watersides, on wet, mesotrophic, acid, sandy, loamy or peaty soils, in S, W and C Europe, northwards to S Scandinavia and W Russia.

Hoary Ragwort (*S. erucifolius* L.) has creeping rhizome, giving off stolons with non-flowering shoots (leaf-rosettes) at tip; leaves grey-cottony (at least below), with segments in 1 plane (not curly), and with down-rolled margins; flowerheads smaller (12–15 mm diam.), with 4–6 narrow outer involucral bracts up to half as long as (13) inner bracts. In rough grassland, roadsides, on banks and along ditches, on moist, calcareous soils, in Europe northwards to S Sweden and N Russia.

S. vernalis Waldst. & Kit., from E Europe and W and C Asia, is annual, to 50 cm; stems and leaves cottony (at least when young); leaves sinuously lobed, finely dentate; flowerheads (20–30 mm diam.) with 13 ray-florets and 21 linear, erect involucral bracts. Locally naturalized in roadsides and fields of C and W Europe.

Oxford Ragwort (*S. squalidus* L.), from S and C Europe, is also annual, to 40 cm tall; leaves flat, 1–2 times pinnately divided; flowerheads 15–25 mm diam., with 13 ray-florets and black-tipped involucral bracts. Locally naturalized in ruderal places and on walls, in W Europe northwards to Denmark.

Common Ragwort is poisonous, even deadly to cattle and horses. Marsh Ragwort is also poisonous.

p.240 **Wood Ragwort** *Senecio nemorensis* L.

Description: A more or less hairy perennial, with erect, leafy stems to 2 m; *stolons short* or absent. *Leaves to 20 cm long*, alternate, short-stalked to sessile, *broadly lanceolate* (upper ones narrower), bright-green, *serrate-dentate* (with symmetrical, spreading teeth), often hairy beneath. Flowerheads 20–30 mm diam., in lax, terminal panicles; involucre narrowly cup-shaped, with *(6) 8–10 linear, dark-tipped inner involucral bracts* in 1 row; receptacle scaleless. *Ray-florets (2) 4–6 (8)*, female, with long, yellow ligule; disc-florets yellow, hermaphrodite. Achene to 4 mm long, glabrous, longitudinally striped; pappus of white hairs to 12 mm.

Flowering: July–September.

Habitat: Damp woods, willow-coppices, along streams and rivers, on wet, eutrophic, acid, sandy soils; from sea level to 2,200 m.

Range: Continental Europe northwards to Belgium, Germany, Poland, and N Russia; naturalized in S Sweden.

Similar species: **Broad-leaved Ragwort** (*S. fluviatilis* Wallr.) has long stolons; sessile to half-clasping, elliptical to broadly lanceolate (rarely narrower), serrate leaves (teeth pointing forwards); 10–15 black-tipped inner involucral bracts; 6–8 ray-florets. In comparable habitats, mainly in the lowland, in E and C Europe, westwards to France and the Low Countries; naturalized in the British Isles.

The subspecies *S. n. fuchsii* (Gmel.) Čelak., more frequent in the lowland, has long-pointed, scarcely hairy, always short-stalked leaves.

p.239 **Fen Ragwort** *Senecio paludosus* L.

Description: An erect perennial, to 1.8 m, with tomentose, densely leafy stems. Leaves alternate, to 20 cm long, *narrowly lanceolate* to almost linear, *serrate, green above, white-tomentose beneath*; lower ones short-stalked, upper ones sessile and half-clasping.

Flowerheads 30–40 mm diam., in terminal, umbel-shaped racemes or panicles; involucre cup-shaped, with tomentose to glabrous bracts; receptacle scaleless. Ray-florets 12–20, female, with narrowly elliptical, yellow ligule; disc-florets yellow, hermaphrodite. Achene to 3 mm long, glabrous or sparsely hairy; pappus of white hairs to 10 mm.

Flowering: May–August.

Habitat: Marshes, reed-lands, willow coppices, watersides, along streams and rivers, on wet, eutrophic, sandy, clayey or peaty soils; mainly in the lowland.

Range: In Europe northwards to Britain, the Low Countries, S Sweden and N Russia.

Similar species: *S. inaequidens* DC., though quite unrelated, also has half-clasping, linear leaves, but these much smaller (to 80 mm long, 5 mm wide), and entire-margined to dentate; it is a bushy half-shrub with angular stems, flowerheads 10–15 mm wide, 10–14 yellow ray-florets, and 10–14 inner involucral bracts, surrounded by equally numerous outer bracts with fringed top. From S Africa; naturalized in ruderal places, along railways and roads in SW Europe, to N France and the Meuse region in Belgium and the S Netherlands; rapidly spreading.

p.239 **Groundsel** Senecio vulgaris L.

Description: A glabrous to slightly hairy (but never glandular), usually erect *annual* to 30 (50) cm. Leaves alternate, pinnately divided or lobed, irregularly toothed, slightly fleshy, often cottony beneath; upper ones sessile and half-clasping. *Flowerheads small* (4–5 mm diam.), in panicles; involucre cylindrical, with linear, black-tipped inner bracts (to 8 mm long) in 1 row, and *8–10 short outer bracts* at base; receptacle scaleless. *Ray-florets usually absent*; disc-florets hardly longer than involucre, yellow, hermaphrodite. Achene 1.5–2.5 mm long, cylindrical, short-hairy between ribs; pappus of white hairs.

Flowering: March–November (Winter).

Habitat: Cultivated land, gardens, ruderal places, on dry to moist, (very) eutrophic soils; from sea level to 2,300 m.

Range: All Europe except Spitsbergen.

Similar species: **Heath, or Wood Groundsel** (*S. sylvaticus* L.) is taller (to 80 cm), and has 13 green, slightly cottony, glandular involucral bracts in 1 row, with 2–5 very short outer bracts; ray-florets 8–15, short, recurved; achenes short-hairy. In scrub, open woods, clearings, ruderal places and field margins, on dry, oligotrophic to mesotrophic, acid, sandy soils to 1,200 m in most of Europe, northwards to Britain, C Fennoscandia and NC Russia.

Sticky Groundsel (*S. viscosus* L.) is entirely glandular, with sessile (hardly clasping) upper leaves, slightly larger flowerheads (6–8 mm diam.), 21 green inner involucral bracts, 2–5 outer bracts up to half as long as involucre, and *c.* 13 straight, spreading ray-florets; achenes glabrous. In wasteland, dry ruderal places, along railways, also in dunes and on shingle-beaches, in Europe northwards to Scotland, the Netherlands, Poland, and C Russia; naturalized in Fennoscandia.

Groundsel is a very common weed, producing several generations per year.

p.298 **Saw-wort** *Serratula tinctoria* L.

Description: A *subglabrous* perennial to 60 (100) cm, with erect, wiry, furrowed stems. *Leaves serrate*, alternate; lower ones long-stalked, ovate to lanceolate in outline, pinnate to pinnately divided, upper ones subsessile, lanceolate, often undivided. Flowerheads 15–20 mm diam., in lax panicles; involucre narrowly cup-shaped, with dark-purplish, lanceolate bracts in numerous rows; receptacle with long, hair-like scales. All florets tubular, with 5 long teeth, purplish (rarely white), (functionally) *male and female florets on different plants* (dioecious). Achenes ellipsoid; pappus of white hairs in several rows.

Flowering: July–September.

Habitat: Rough grassland, scrub, open woods, on moist, oligotrophic, slightly acid to calcareous, sandy, loamy or stony soils; from sea level to 2,400 m.

Range: Most of Europe, northwards to S Scandinavia, Poland, and the Baltic States.

Similar species: *Jurinea cyanoides* (L.) Reichenb., from E and C Russia westwards to Czechia and C Germany, has stalked, pinnately divided, otherwise entire-margined, leaves (cottony beneath, with margin rolled under), and broadly cup-shaped flowerheads with hermaphrodite disc-florets hardly exceeding involucre.

Both species vaguely resemble certain Knapweeds, but lack spine or fringed appendage to involucral bracts.

Canadian Goldenrod
Solidago canadensis Aiton

Description: A rather hairy perennial, to 1.5 m, with *long stolons*; stems hairy above. Leaves lanceolate, short-stalked to subsessile, *with 3 main veins, serrate, green, hairy beneath*. Flowerheads 5–7 mm diam., *sessile, erect, numerous, in long, arched, axillary spikes*; involucre 2–3 mm long, narrowly cup-shaped, with bracts in several rows; receptacle honeycombed, scaleless. Ray-florets 5–12, hardly exceeding involucre, yellow, female; disc-florets yellow, hermaphrodite. Achene 0.9–1.2 mm long, ribbed, short-hairy; pappus (to 2.5 mm) of white hairs.

Flowering: August–October.

Habitat: Ruderal places, road verges, along railways, riverbanks, on dry to moist, eutrophic, sandy to clayey soils; mainly in the lowland.

Range: Native to N America; widely naturalized in Europe, northwards to Britain, S Norway, Poland, and C Russia.

Similar species: Two other American species have naturalized in Europe, in comparable habitats: **Early Goldenrod** (*S. gigantea* Aiton) (*see* photograph p.237) has stems only hairy in inflorescence, and leaves 3–5-veined, glaucous and hairy only on midrib beneath (and ciliate); involucre 3–5 mm long.

S. graminea (L.) Salisb. has linear-lanceolate, entire-margined (but ciliate) leaves, and short-stalked flowerheads in dense, umbel-shaped panicles.

---

p.237 **Goldenrod** *Solidago virgaurea* L.

Description: An erect, more or less hairy perennial, to 1 m, with *lateral leaf-rosettes* at base; *stolons short or absent. Leaves pinnately veined* with several lateral veins, serrate; lower ones oblanceolate or narrowly obovate, long-stalked, upper ones sessile, linear-lanceolate. *Flowerheads relatively large* (14–18 mm diam.), in *narrow racemes or panicles* with short side-branches; involucre 5–8 mm long, with lanceolate bracts in several rows; receptacle honeycombed, scaleless. *Ray-florets 6–9, far exceeding involucre*, yellow, female; disc-florets yellow, hermaphrodite. Achene 3–4 mm long, spindle-shaped, often slightly angled, pubescent, truncate at apex; pappus (to 10 mm) of whitish or straw-coloured hairs in 1–2 rows.

Flowering: July–October.

Habitat: Open woods, wood margins, scrub, rough grassland, road verges, river- and streambanks, on moist to dry, oligotrophic, slightly acid, sandy, loamy or stony soils; from sea level to 2,800 m.

Range: Most of Europe except Iceland and the high Arctic.

The only indigenous *Solidago* species in Europe.

---

p.236 **Perennial Sow-thistle** *Sonchus arvensis* L.

Description: A green or grey-green *perennial*, to 1 (1.5) m, with *long, creeping stolons*. Leaves hairless, pinnately divided, spiny-dentate, the middle and upper ones less incised (only lobed), clasping stem with 2 rounded, appressed auricles. Flowerheads 20–50 mm diam., in lax panicles; involucre cup-shaped, with lanceolate bracts, in 3 rows, and yellowish glandular hairs; receptacle scaleless. All florets fertile ligulate, *deep yellow*. Achenes 2–10-ribbed, slightly compressed, brown; pappus of white hairs (solitary, soon falling ones, and soft, persistent ones in bundles).

Flowering: July–October.

Habitat: Cultivated and waste ground, ruderal places, open road verges, on moist to dry, (very) eutrophic, sandy, clayey or stony soils; from sea level to 1,700 m.

Range: Most of Europe except the high Arctic.

Var. *maritimus* G.F.W. Meyer (not to be confused with the species *S. maritimus*!) has deeply incised, very spiny, glaucous, greasy leaves, only upper ones lobed. In sea-dunes and on floodmarks along Atlantic coasts of Europe, northwards to N Germany.

---

p.236 **Prickly Sow-thistle** *Sonchus asper* (L.) Hill

Description: A grey-green *annual*, to 60 (100) cm, with *taproot*; no stolons. Leaves hairless, pinnately divided or lobed, spiny-dentate, the middle and upper ones less incised (only lobed), clasping stem with 2 rounded, appressed auricles. Flowerheads 20–25 mm diam., in lax panicles; involucre cup-shaped, strongly widened at base, glabrous or cottony or slightly hairy, but hardly glandular, with 35–45 bracts in 3 rows; receptacle scaleless. All florets ligulate, yellow, fertile, with *greenish styles*. Achenes *c.* 2.5 mm long, straw-coloured, longitudinally ribbed, *strongly compressed and narrowly winged*; pappus of white hairs, soon falling.

Flowering: June–October.

Habitat: Cultivated and waste ground, ruderal places, on moist, (very) eutrophic, slightly acid to calcareous soils; from sea level to 1,700 m.

Range: Most of Europe except the high Arctic.

Similar species: **Smooth Sow-thistle** (*S. oleraceus* L.) has more deeply incised, softly spiny-dentate leaves (clasping stem with 2 pointed auricles), involucres with less than 35 bracts, pale-yellow florets, and transversely corrugated, reddish-brown achenes *c.* 3.5 mm long. In comparable habitats, and as widely distributed.

p.236 **Marsh Sow-thistle** *Sonchus palustris* L.

Description: An erect *annual or biennial*, with angular, *hollow, chambered stems* to 2.5 (4) m high, 40 mm wide, and *thickened taproot* to 50 mm diam.; *no stolons*. Leaves lanceolate, finely serrate (hardly spiny), deeply pinnately dissected, upper ones often not dissected, clasping stem with 2 *pointed auricles*. Flowerheads 30–40 mm diam., in rather dense, terminal panicles; involucre covered with *dense, black glandular hairs*, and with lanceolate bracts in 3 rows; receptacle scaleless. All florets ligulate, yellow, with *yellow styles*. Achene angular, ribbed, *straw-coloured*; pappus of *dirty-white hairs*.

Flowering: July–September.

Habitat: Reedlands, watersides, often in estuaries, on wet, mesotrophic to eutrophic, basic or brackish, sandy, clayey or peaty soils; only in the lowland.

Range: In Europe northwards to England, S Scandinavia, Poland and the Baltic States.

Similar species: *S. maritimus* L., to only 60 cm, is perennial, with creeping rhizomes; upper leaves often undivided, clasping stem with rounded auricles; involucres white-hairy at base, with ovate (not lanceolate) outer bracts; achenes brown, corrugated. In moist or wet, more or less saline places and estuaries, along Atlantic coast from W France southwards.

---

p.169 **Feverfew**
Tanacetum parthenium (L.) Schultz-Bip.

Description: A *strongly aromatic* biennial or short-lived perennial, with much-branched, erect stems to 60 cm. Leaves alternate, 1–2 times pinnately divided (with 3–7 *bluntly dentate main segments*), ovate, *stalked to subsessile*, subglabrous. Flowerheads (10) 15–25 mm diam., in lax, rather leafy, umbel-shaped panicles; involucre cup-shaped, with narrow-ovate bracts in several rows; receptacle scaleless. Ray-florets female, with *short, broadly elliptical, white ligule* (occasionally very short or even absent); disc-florets yellow, hermaphrodite. Achenes to 1.5 mm long, obovoid, 5–8-ribbed; pappus (to 0.2 mm long) of *short, membranous scales*.

Flowering: June–September.

Habitat: Cultivated land, gardens, ruderal places, on moist, mesotrophic to eutrophic, sandy or loamy soils, also old walls; mainly in the lowland.

Range: Native to SE Europe; often cultivated in gardens and more or less naturalized (often close to habitation) in W and C Europe.

Similar species: *T. corymbosum* (L.) Schultz Bip. is perennial, with creeping stolons; leaves pinnately divided, scarcely aromatic, with 7–15 serrate segments (more like *T. vulgare*), but ray-florets white as in Feverfew. In Europe northwards to C France, Germany, Poland and N Russia.

---

p.237 **Tansy** *Tanacetum vulgare* L.

Description: A strongly aromatic perennial with erect, scarcely branched stems to 1 m and short, creeping rhizomes. Leaves alternate, lanceolate, to 10–30 cm long, pinnately divided, with 15–33 acutely *serrate segments, (sub)sessile*, subglabrous. Flowerheads 7–12 mm diam., in dense, umbel-shaped panicles; involucre cup-shaped, with broadly lanceolate bracts in several rows; receptacle scaleless. *Usually no ray-florets;* disc florets yellow, tubular, hermaphrodite, with 5 teeth; some female ray-florets may be present, with very short, white, 3-toothed ligule. Achenes to 1.5 mm long, obovoid, 5-ribbed; *pappus of short, membranous scales*.

Flowering: July–October.

Habitat: Road verges, grassy banks, field margins, ruderal places, on dry to moist, mesotrophic, preferably calcareous, sandy or loamy soils; from sea level to 1,500 m.

Range: Most of Europe except Spitsbergen, and only naturalized in Ireland.

Formerly used as an anthelmintic.

Dandelions, *Taraxacum*

A very complex genus with many hundreds of microspecies, often largely agamospermous (forming seeds without fertilization) but also regularly hybridizing, especially in W and C Europe. Important characters are found in the morphology of the involucral bracts and the achenes, and the way the leaves are incised and toothed. Since detailed treatment is not possible here, only general features of the whole complex are given below; the reader is referred to special literature, and to critical regional floras.

---

p.229 **Dandelion** *Taraxacum officinale* L. *s.l.*

Description: A rosette-bearing, usually subglabrous perennial, with variously pinnately dissected basal leaves, stout taproot, and several ascending to erect, leafless, hollow flowering stems (scapes) to 40 (60) cm; all parts contain milky latex. Flowerheads solitary, terminal, 20–60 mm diam.; involucre cup-shaped, with lanceolate, erect inner bracts in 1 row, and several more or less recurved outer bracts; receptacle glabrous (rarely hairy), scaleless. All florets ligulate, yellow, outer ones often with red, purple or greyish stripes, inner ones shorter. Achenes narrowly ellipsoid, 10-ribbed, with small spines or tubercles near top; long beak bears umbrella-shaped pappus of simple, white hairs apically connected to adjacent pappus hairs to form the well-known, spherical 'clock'.

Flowering: April–May (Autumn).

Habitat: Grassland, road verges, dunes, wasteland, ruderal places, on dry to wet, oligotrophic to eutrophic soils of all types; from sea level to 2,600 m.

Range: All Europe, even (recently introduced) on Spitsbergen.

To determine microspecies, use only plants collected in early summer, as autumnal forms usually are very difficult to identify, especially after hay-making has taken place.

p.301 **Salsify** *Tragopogon porrifolius* L.

Description: A hairless biennial or short-lived, latex-bearing perennial, with thickened, cylindrical taproot, and erect, leafy, simple or branched stems to 1.2 m; *stems strongly inflated under flowerheads*. Leaves alternate, *linear-lanceolate, parallel-veined, entire-margined*, more or less erect, cauline ones sessile with *sheathing base*. Flowerheads terminal, solitary, 25–50 mm diam.; involucre with (often 8) *linear, long-tapering, spreading bracts in 1 row*; receptacle scaleless. All florets ligulate, *at most equalling involucral bracts, lilac to red-purplish*. Achenes 30–40 mm long, almost linear, ribbed, *spiny to warty on ribs*, narrowed into *long beak* bearing pappus of interwoven feathery hairs in 1 row, apically connected to pappus of adjacent achenes to form large, spherical 'clock'.

Flowering: May–August.

Habitat: Road verges, ruderal places, ditch-sides, banks and by canals, on moist, mesotrophic to eutrophic, acid or calcareous, sandy to clayey soils; mainly in the lowland.

Range: Native to Mediterranean region; naturalized in W Europe, northwards to the British Isles, the Low Countries, Denmark, and S Sweden.

Formerly cultivated for its edible roots and leaves ('white salsify').

---

p.238 **Goat's-beard** *Tragopogon pratensis* L.

Description: Much like *T. porrifolius*, but stalks of flowerheads hardly thickened, *florets yellow*, with yellow, dark-tipped anthers, *involucral bracts exceeding florets*, and achenes 10–25 mm long (including beak), more or less squamose.

Flowering: May–July.

Habitat: Rough grassland, road verges, ruderal places, on dry to moist, mesotrophic to eutrophic, sandy, loamy or clayey soils; from sea level to 2,600 m.

Range: Most of Europe except the high Arctic.

Similar species: *T. dubius* Scop. has very long achenes (25–35 mm including beak), florets much shorter than involucre, and inflated stalks

under flowerhead. On calcareous soils in
E and C Europe, extending westwards to
N France.

Goat's-beard closes the flowerheads early each
afternoon, hence its other name 'Jack-go-to-
bed-at-noon'.
T. pratensis ssp. *orientalis* (L.) Čelak. has larger
flowerheads (to 65 mm diam.) with florets
much longer than involucral bracts, and
brown-striped anthers. In E and C Europe,
westwards to the Low Countries.
T. pratensis ssp. *minor* (Miller) Wahlenb. from
W and C Europe has comparable
distribution, but pale-yellow florets much
shorter than involucre, and plain-yellow
anthers.

---

p.238 **Colt's-foot** *Tussilago farfara* L.

Description: A low perennial, with creeping rhizomes and
erect flowering stems to 20 cm, appearing
before leaves. Normal leaves all basal, stalked,
suborbicular with cordate base, shallowly and
rather angularly lobed, to 20 (30) cm diam.,
cottony above (at least when young) and
white-tomentose beneath; flowering stems
have numerous lanceolate to ovate, greenish
to purplish, scale-like leaves. *Flowerheads
solitary, terminal*, 15–30 mm diam., erect in
bud, nodding after anthesis; involucre cup-
shaped, with lanceolate bracts in 1 row
(sometimes with some small outer bracts at
base); receptacle scaleless. Ray-florets
numerous, female, with *spreading, linear,
bright-yellow ligule*; disc-florets functionally
male, 5-toothed, yellow; plant therefore
monoecious. Achene to 3 mm long, linear;
clock-like pappus of hairs in several rows.
Flowering: February–April (May).
Habitat: Arable fields, road verges, wood margins,
ruderal or disturbed places, on moist to rather
dry, eutrophic, often clayey soils; from sea
level to 2,600 m.
Range: All Europe except Portugal.

Compare with Petasites species (*see* p.530),
which grow much larger.

BINDWEED FAMILY, CONVOLVULACEAE

A family of herbs and shrubs, primarily winding climbers, with *c.* 50 genera and 1,800 species, in tropical and temperate regions world-wide. Dicots. Leaves alternate, simple; in the parasitic genus *Cuscuta*, leaves are reduced to minute scales. Flowers usually regular, hermaphrodite. Sepals (4) 5, usually (nearly) free. Petals (4) 5, connate, corolla more or less bell- or funnel-shaped, (4-) 5-lobed. Stamens (4) 5, alternating with corolla lobes. Ovary superior, 1–2-locular (occasionally incompletely so, or rarely 3–5-locular), with 1–2 styles. Fruit a capsule with 1–4 (rarely more) seeds.

---

p.105 **Hedge Bindweed**
Calystegia sepium (L.) R. Br.

Description: A climbing perennial herb, with glabrous, wiry, twining stems to 3 (5) m. Leaves alternate, stalked, glabrous, ovate-cordate to triangular-hastate, with *rounded or truncate basal lobes and a blunt to subacute tip*, entire-margined. Flowers axillary on long stalks with 2 opposite, *ovate-cordate bracts enveloping calyx*. Sepals 5, ovate. Corolla 30–50 mm diam., broadly funnel-shaped, circular (hardly lobed), white (rarely pale pink). Stamens 5. Ovary 1-locular (or incompletely 2-locular), with 1 long style and 2 elliptical stigmas. Capsule globose or ovoid, 3–4-seeded, opening with 2 valves.

Flowering: June–September.

Habitat: Reedlands, scrub, hedges, ruderal places, on moist to wet, mesotrophic to eutrophic, mineral or peaty soils; from sea level to 1,500 m.

Range: Most of Europe except Iceland and the high Arctic.

Other common names are Bellvine and Larger Bindweed. Ssp. *roseata* Brummitt has pink flowers and hairy stems. In coastal habitats, in the highest parts of saltmarshes, and on beaches and in dunes, in W Europe northwards to Denmark.

p.276 **Sea Bindweed**
Calystegia soldanella (L.) R. Br.

Description: A glabrous perennial herb, with spreading (rarely climbing) stems to 2 m, often buried in the sand. *Leaves rather fleshy, reniform,* suborbicular, entire-margined, long-stalked. Flowers axillary, long-stalked, with 2 large, cordate, *overlapping bracts* hiding calyx. Sepals 5, ovate. Corolla 30–50 mm diam., circular (hardly lobed), pink with 5 white stripes. Stamens 5. Ovary 1-locular, with 1 style and 2-lobed stigma. Capsule ovoid to flask-shaped.

Flowering: May–September.

Habitat: Sea-dunes and beaches, on dry, brackish, usually drifting sands, also on shingle-beaches.

Range: S and W Europe, northwards to Scotland and Denmark.

---

p.276 **Field Bindweed** *Convolvulus arvensis* L.

Description: A subglabrous perennial herb, with slender, climbing or prostrate, winding stems. Leaves alternate, stalked, ovate-hastate with *pointed basal lobes and rounded tip.* Flowers axillary, long-stalked, stalks with *2 small, lanceolate, opposite bracts somewhere in middle.* Sepals 5, ovate, blunt-tipped. Corolla 15–25 mm diam., circular, very widely funnel-shaped, pink with 5 broad, white stripes, or all white or pink. Stamens 5. Ovary 2-locular, with 1 style and 2-lobed stigma (lobes threadlike). Capsule ovoid, glabrous, 5–8 mm long, with 4–5 seeds.

Flowering: June–September.

Habitat: Fields, short grassland, roadsides, along railways, on dry to moist, mesotrophic to eutrophic, sandy, loamy or stony soils; from sea level to 2,000 m.

Range: Most of Europe except the extreme north.

---

p.292 **Common Dodder** *Cuscuta epithymum* (L.) L.

Description: A winding parasite, lacking chlorophyll, tens of centimetres long, tangled; *stems much-*

branched, threadlike, often red or orange. Leaves absent. Flowers in dense, globose clusters to 10 mm diam. Sepals connate at base, forming cup-shaped calyx with 5 acute teeth, reddish; corolla cup-shaped, whitish or pink, with 5 acute or pointed, triangular teeth. Stamens 5, inserted on corolla tube, over 5 rounded, ciliate scales. Ovary 2-locular, with 2 divergent styles. Capsule globose, *c.* 2 mm diam., usually 4-seeded.

Flowering: June–October.

Habitat: Heaths, scrub, dune-valleys, cliffs, parasitic on diverse number of other plants: *Ulex, Genista, Trifolium, Lotus, Calluna, Erica, Galium verum*, and *Thymus pulegioides*. From sea level to 2,200 m.

Range: Most of Europe except the far north.

Similar species: *C. lupuliformis* Krocker has only 1 style, with 2 ovoid stigmas; capsules ovoid, to 7 mm long; corolla has 5 short, blunt lobes; sepals much shorter than corolla tube. On shrubs and trees – *Salix, Rubus, Quercus, Prunus padus* – in E and C Europe, and along Rhine valley to the Netherlands.

---

p.292 **Greater Dodder** *Cuscuta europaea* L.

Description: A winding parasite, lacking chlorophyll; stems much-branched, threadlike, reddish or yellowish. Leaves absent. Flowers in dense, globose clusters, these 10–15 mm diam. Sepals connate at base, calyx cup-shaped with 4–5 blunt teeth, pink or yellowish. Corolla cup-shaped, with 4–5 blunt, triangular teeth, pale pink or yellowish. Stamens 5, inserted on corolla tube, over 5 bifid scales. Ovary 2-locular, with 2 divergent styles. Capsule globose, 2.5–3 mm diam., usually 4-seeded.

Flowering: June–October.

Habitat: Scrub, watersides, usually on *Urtica dioica* or *Humulus lupulus*. From sea level to 2,000 m.

Range: Most of Europe except Ireland and the far north.

Similar species: **Flax Dodder** (*C. epilinum* Weihe) has yellowish-green, scarcely branched stems, and yellowish flowers in clusters to 10 mm, with rounded, ciliate scales inside corolla tube. On flax. Formerly a troublesome weed, Flax Dodder has strongly declined, and is extinct in many regions (e.g. Britain, the Low Countries).

DOGWOOD FAMILY, CORNACEAE

A family of shrubs and trees, rarely herbs, with *c.* 100 species in 13 genera world-wide. Dicots. Leaves simple, often opposite. Flowers regular, 4-merous, hermaphrodite or unisexual. Sepals 4, usually small but free. Petals 4, occasionally absent. Stamens 4, alternating with petals. Ovary inferior, 1–4-locular (often 2-locular), with 1 style and 1 stigma. Fruit a drupe or a berry, with 1–4 seeds. Well-known shrubby species from Europe are **Cornelian Cherry** (*Cornus mas* L.) and **Dogwood** (*Cornus sanguinea* L., see photograph p.175).

p.106 **Dwarf Cornel** *Cornus suecica* L.

Description: A hardly woody, perennial herb, with creeping rhizomes and erect, simple or short-branched (annual) stems to 30 cm. Leaves opposite, sessile, ovate, subacute, entire-margined, with 2–3 pairs of arched side-veins. Flowers 2–3 mm diam., in dense, terminal umbel with large, common involucre of 4 white, suborbicular to broadly ovate, often red-tipped, bracts. Sepals 4, minute. Petals 4, purplish-black. Stamens 4. Ovary inferior, with 1 style. Fruit a globose, red drupe, *c.* 5 mm diam.

Flowering: May–July (September).

Habitat: Arctic tundra, mountain heaths, moors, wood margins, on moist, oligotrophic, acid, sandy or stony soils; from sea level to 1,300 m.

Range: N Europe, from the Arctic southwards to Britain, the NE Netherlands, N Germany, Poland, and C Russia.

Occasionally grown for ornament.

STONECROP FAMILY, CRASSULACEAE

A family of succulent herbs and half-shrubs, with *c.* 1,500 species in 35 genera world-wide. Dicots. Leaves usually simple, often alternate or in basal rosette. Flowers regular, mostly hermaphrodite, often 3–5-merous (but occasionally up to 30-merous). Stamens 1–2 times as many as petals. Ovaries 3–30 (as many as petals), free or partly connate. Fruit a cluster of follicles, each with several small seeds. Many species are kept as garden ornamentals or houseplants.

---

p.271 **Mossy Stonecrop**
Crassula tillaea Lester-Garland

Description: A tiny, often reddish annual, with spreading to ascending stems to 5 cm. *Leaves crosswise opposite*, crowded, sessile and *basally connate around stem, to 2 mm long*, ovate, fleshy, semicircular in transection. Flowers 1–2 mm diam., sessile, axillary. Sepals 3 (4), ovate, reddish. Petals 3 (4), lanceolate, white or pink, *shorter than sepals*. Stamens and ovaries 3 (4); ovaries free, developing into pear-shaped, pointed, *2-seeded follicles*.

Flowering: April–September.

Habitat: Cart-tracks, woodland rides, ditch- and streamsides, on periodically wet, otherwise moist, oligotrophic, acid, sandy or muddy soils; mainly in the lowland.

Range: S and W Europe, northwards to England, the Netherlands and NE Germany.

Similar species: **Pigmyweed** or **Water Tillaea** (*C. aquatica* (L.) Schönl.) has less-crowded, linear-lanceolate, fleshy but flat leaves to 6 mm long, 4-merous flowers, petals longer than sepals, and many-seeded, ovoid, pointed follicles. In comparable habitats, occasionally permanently submerged, in N and C Europe (including Iceland), southwards to N Germany, Austria and C Russia.

---

p.219 **Roseroot** *Rhodiola rosea* L.

Description: A hairless, usually *dioecious* perennial with stout, creeping rhizomes sending up dense clusters of flowering stems to 30 cm. Leaves alternate, crowded, obovate to oblanceolate, to 40 mm long, fleshy, toothed, often purple-tinged. Flowers 5–8 mm diam., *4-merous*, in dense, terminal cymes; male flowers with abortive carpels. Sepals 4, minute. Petals 4, oblanceolate, dull yellow, often absent in female flowers. *Stamens 8, with purple anthers.* Ovaries 4, developing into flask-shaped, *orange follicles.*

Flowering: May–August.

Habitat: Rocks, screes, coastal and inland cliffs, on dry, oligotrophic, calcareous or acid, stony or rocky soils; from sea level to 3,000 m.

Range: Most of Europe, but outside the Arctic only on mountains, southwards to the Pyrenees, C Italy and Bulgaria.

The rhizomes are fragrant, like Sweet Violet. *Compare with S. telephium (see p.558),* which has 5-merous, hermaphrodite, pink (or occasionally yellowish) flowers.

---

p.194 **Biting Stonecrop** *Sedum acre* L.

Description: A glabrous perennial, with creeping rhizomes and ascending or erect flowering stems to 10 cm, *forming dense mats.* Leaves alternate, to 6 mm long, sessile, ovate, thick and fleshy, *convex above, slightly flattened beneath,* green or reddish. Flowers 10–14 mm diam., starry, hermaphrodite, in small, terminal cymes. Sepals 5, ovate, blunt-tipped. Petals 5, broadly lanceolate, pointed, *bright yellow.* Stamens 10. Ovaries 5, developing into swollen *follicles with a recurved point.*

Flowering: May–July.

Habitat: Sunny, open places, dunes, heaths, rocks, also pavements, walls and roofs, on dry, oligotrophic to mesotrophic, basic, sandy or rocky soils.

Range: All Europe except Spitsbergen.

Similar species: **Tasteless**, or **Insipid, Stonecrop** (*S. sexangulare* L.) has cylindrical leaves to 9 mm long, with short spur at base, yellow flowers to 8 mm diam., and erect follicles. In comparable habitats, in C Europe, westwards to C France and the Low Countries, and northwards to Finland.

Biting Stonecrop has a pungent taste, hence also its other common name Wallpepper.

p.102 **White Stonecrop** *Sedum album* L.

Description: A spreading to ascending perennial, to
15 cm, forming loose mats. Leaves
alternate, to 10 mm long, *glabrous*, fleshy,
subcylindrical, subacute, green or reddish.
Flowers 6–9 mm diam., hermaphrodite, in
rather loose, glabrous or slightly glandular,
terminal cymes. Sepals 5. Petals 5,
lanceolate, *white or pale pink*. Stamens 10.
Ovaries 5, developing into erect,
cylindrical, pointed, pink follicles to 5 mm
long.

Flowering: June–August.

Habitat: Rocks, screes, walls, road verges, on dry,
oligotrophic, usually acid, rocky, gravelly or
sandy soils; from sea level to 2,500 m.

Range: Most of Europe, northwards to S
Scandinavia and S Finland; naturalized only
in Ireland.

Similar species: *S. hirsutum* All. has glandular-hairy leaves
often crowded in a terminal rosette on
vegetative shoots. In SW Europe,
northwards to NC France and N Italy,
mainly on mountains.

---

p.102 **English Stonecrop** *Sedum anglicum* Hudson

Description: A spreading to ascending perennial, to 5
(10) cm, forming dense mats. Leaves
alternate, to 6 mm long, 4 mm wide,
glabrous, fleshy, oblong, *flattened above*,
subacute, greyish-green or reddish, densely
crowded on vegetative shoots. Flowers to
12 mm diam., hermaphrodite, subsessile in
small, terminal cymes. Sepals 5. Petals 5,
lanceolate, *acute, white inside and pinkish
outside*. Stamens 10, with dark anthers.
Ovaries 5, developing into suberect, red
follicles.

Flowering: June–September.

Habitat: Rocks, grassy banks, short turf, dunes,
shingle-beaches, on dry, oligotrophic, acid,
sandy, stony or rocky soils; from sea level to
1,800 m.

Range: W Europe, from Iberian peninsula
northwards to Ireland, W Britain, C
Norway, and SW Sweden.

Similar species: **Thick-leaved Stonecrop** (*S. dasyphyllum* L.) has equally short, broad leaves, but these mainly opposite, always grey-green and glandular-hairy. In acid, rocky habitats of S and C Europe, westwards to Normandy; locally naturalized (often on old walls) in the British Isles, the Low Countries and Denmark.

---

p.194 **Annual Stonecrop** *Sedum annuum* L.

Description: A hairless, green *annual* or biennial, with spreading to erect, branched stems to 15 cm; all stems flowering. Leaves alternate, to 6 mm long, *fleshy but often slightly flattened, blunt-tipped*, green or reddish. Flowers 3–5 mm diam., subsessile, few together in terminal clusters. Sepals 5. Petals 5, *yellow*. Stamens 10. Ovaries 5, developing into green or red, spreading follicles.

Flowering: June–August.

Habitat: Rocks, screes, moraines, open grassland, on dry, oligotrophic, acid, stony or rocky soils; from sea level to 2,800 m, but only on mountains in the south.

Range: In Greenland, Iceland, Fennoscandia, N and W Russia, and C Europe, westwards to the Pyrenees, and eastwards to the Caucasus and Asia Minor.

---

p.219 **Reflexed Stonecrop** *Sedum reflexum* L.

Description: A rather stout, mat-forming perennial, with creeping rhizomes and ascending or erect, reddish *flowering stems to 40 cm*. Leaves alternate, greyish-green, cylindrical, *linear, 8– 20 mm long, pointed, soon falling when dead*. Flowers 12–15 mm diam., in dense, terminal, umbel-shaped cymes that nod before anthesis. *Sepals acute*, to 3 mm. *Petals 6–7*, lanceolate, *bright yellow*. Stamens 12–14, *ciliate at base*, with yellow anthers. Ovaries 6–7, developing into erect, yellowish follicles (5–7 mm) with recurved, tapering style to 8 mm.

Flowering: June–August.

Habitat: Bare or open, grassy places, banks, roadsides, rocks, also walls, on dry, oligotrophic, slightly acid to calcareous, sandy, stony or rocky soils; from sea level to 2,000 m.

Range: Continental Europe, northwards to C Norway and S Finland, and eastwards to the Ukraine; naturalized in the British Isles.

Similar species: **Rock Stonecrop** (*S. forsterianum* Smith) has leaves crowded terminally on vegetative shoots (like a tassel), persistent dead leaves at base of flowering stems, and glabrous filaments to stamens. In comparable, though often damper, habitats, in continental W Europe, northwards to S Scandinavia and Germany; extinct in the Netherlands.

---

p.113 **Reddish Stonecrop** *Sedum rubens* L.

Description: A greyish-green, usually red-tinged *annual*, with ascending or erect stems to 10 cm. *Leaves cylindrical, linear, 10–20 mm long*, blunt-tipped. Flowers 9–11 mm diam., subsessile, in *small, spike-like racemes* (often with 3 branches). Sepals 5. Petals 5, *white or pale pink* with reddish vein. *Stamens 5* (rarely 10). Ovaries 5, developing into ascending, glandular follicles to 3.5 mm, with straight style to 1 mm.

Flowering: May–July.

Habitat: Cultivated and wasteland, vineyards, roadsides, gravel-pits, rocks and old walls, on dry, oligotrophic to mesotrophic, sandy, stony or rocky soils; from sea level to 700 m.

Range: S and W Europe, northwards to Belgium and Germany, and eastwards to Romania and the Crimea.

Similar species: *S. andegavense* (DC.) Desv. has 4–5-merous flowers, short, ovoid, partly opposite leaves, and erect, slightly roughened follicles. In comparable habitats in SW Europe, northwards to C France.

Hairy Stonecrop (*Sedum villosum* L.) is a glandular-hairy biennial or perennial, with short vegetative shoots, broadly linear leaves to 8 mm long (flattened above), distinctly stalked 5-merous flowers (stalks longer than flower), and 5–10 stamens. In grassy places along streams, on moist to wet, basic (often calcareous), stony or rocky soils, in W, C and N Europe.

p.290 **Orpine** *Sedum telephium* L.

Description: A glabrous, often greyish-green perennial, with erect flowering stems to 60 cm; no vegetative shoots. Leaves alternate to opposite or whorled, subsessile, *rounded to obovate*, 50–80 mm long, fleshy, *bluntly dentate* or lobed. Flowers 8–10 mm diam., in dense, umbel-shaped cymes, terminal or in highest leaf-axils. Sepals 5. Petals 5, lanceolate, pink or purplish, occasionally yellowish. Stamens 10. Ovaries 5, developing into erect, pointed follicles.

Flowering: July–September.

Habitat: Shaded road verges, wood margins, scrub, ditch-sides, banks and rocks, on moist, mesotrophic, calcareous to slightly acid, sandy, loamy or rocky soils; from sea level to 2,500 m.

Range: All Europe except Iceland and the high Arctic.

A polymorphic species, with several subspecies. *Compare Rhodiola rosea (see p.553), which has 4-merous, always yellow flowers.*

p.290 **Houseleek** *Sempervivum tectorum* L.

Description: A succulent perennial, with dense, vegetative, *basal leaf-rosettes* to 12 cm diam., and *erect, leafy flowering stems* to 50 cm. Leaves fleshy, *bristly-ciliate* (otherwise glabrous), bluish-green, red-margined and red-tipped (or flushed with red all over); basal ones obovate to oblanceolate, *spreading*, cauline ones lanceolate, alternate, crowded (in tight spirals). Flowers 20–30 mm diam., in dense, cymose, terminal clusters. *Sepals and petals 6–20* (often 12 or 13); petals pink, slightly connate at base. Stamens twice as numerous as petals. Ovaries 6–20, developing into ring of green, erect, glandular-hairy follicles with recurved, glabrous, purplish styles.

Flowering: June–September.

Habitat:	Grassy places, rocks, walls and roofs, on dry, stony soils.
Range:	Native to the mountains of S, W and C Europe, from the Pyrenees to the SE Alps (to 2,800 m); often cultivated elsewhere in gardens and on rooftops and walls.
Similar species:	**Hen-and-chickens Houseleek** (*Jovibarba sobolifera* (J. Sims) Opiz) has globose basal rosettes, to 30 mm diam., of incurved, green, often red-tipped and glandular leaves; petals usually 6, yellowish, fringed and ciliate. In dry grassland and sandy places, in NC and E Europe, from C Germany via the Carpathians to C Russia, from 2,000 m down to 400 m; also cultivated in gardens and on walls.

Houseleek was once thought to give protection from fire by thunderstorms; this is probably because it was seen to thrive well on buildings that were not prone to being struck by lightning in the first place.

---

p.66 **Navelwort** *Umbilicus rupestris* (Salisb.) Dandy

Description:	A hairless perennial with ascending to erect flowering stems to 40 (60) cm. Leaves mostly basal, fleshy, green, long-stalked, with stalk *attached to middle of orbicular, crenate to lobed blade*; upper surface of blade has depression at the point of leaf attachment on underside; stem-leaves absent or few, often with a laterally attached stalk. Flowers 8–10 mm diam., *bell-shaped, pendent, in long, terminal racemes*. Sepals 5, short, lanceolate. Corolla whitish or greenish, with long tube and 5 short, triangular teeth. Stamens 10, inserted on corolla tube. Ovaries 5, developing into flask-shaped follicles.
Flowering:	May–August.
Habitat:	Rocks, stone walls, on dry to moist, oligotrophic, preferably acid, stony or rocky soils; from sea level to 500 m.
Range:	S and W Europe, northwards to NW France, W Britain and Ireland, and eastwards to Greece.

CRESS FAMILY, CRUCIFERAE

A large family of herbs (rarely shrubs) with over 3,000 species in *c.* 380 genera world-wide, though primarily in temperate northerly regions. Dicots. Leaves alternate, simple or compound. Flowers in terminal or axillary racemes, hermaphrodite, usually regular, with 4 sepals and 4 petals (hence the name Cruciferae, or cross-bearers), the latter alternating with the first. Individual flowers always without bracts. Stamens usually 6 (2 outer, 4 inner), standing before petals. Ovary superior, 2-locular. Style 1, often persistent on fruit as a beak. Fruit a siliqua (at least 3 times longer than wide) or silicule (relatively shorter), opening with 2 valves that after falling leave behind a membranous septum framed in the persistent placentas (bearing the seeds).

---

p.132 **Garlic Mustard**
Alliaria petiolata (Bieb.) Cav. & Grande

Description: A hairy biennial with erect, usually simple, leafy stems to 90 cm. Leaves alternate, *stalked, reniform to ovate with cordate base* and deep sinus between rounded basal lobes, bluntly dentate, thinly hairy (with only simple hairs). Flowers 6–10 mm diam., in terminal racemes; sepals 3–4 mm, lanceolate; petals clawed, *white*, with rounded limb. Fruit an ascending, linear, *tetragonal siliqua, 35–60 mm long*, on stalk to 6 mm, with 3-veined valves.

Flowering: April–July.

Habitat: Open woods, scrub, gardens, shady verges, hedges, on moist to dry, mesotrophic to eutrophic, preferably calcareous, often sandy or loamy soils; from sea level to 1,800 m.

Range: Most of Europe, northwards to C Norway, S Sweden and S Finland, and eastwards to C Russia.

When crushed, the plant smells strongly of garlic.

---

p.202 **Small Alison** *Alyssum alyssoides* (L.) L.

Description: A densely hairy annual, with ascending or erect, branched stems to 15 (25) cm. Leaves alternate, short-stalked to subsessile, narrowly obovate to oblanceolate, blunt-tipped, with stellate hairs. Flowers 3–4 mm diam., in elongating terminal racemes. Sepals 2–2.5 mm, *persistent* on fruit; petals to 4 mm, oblanceolate, with *notched tip pale yellow*, almost white after anthesis. Stamens 6, the 2 outer ones shorter, and with *2 bristles at base of filament*. Fruit a compressed, stellate-hairy, *suborbicular to broadly obovate, 4-seeded silicule to 4.5 mm* long, slightly notched at apex and with very short style to 0.5 mm.

Flowering: April–June.

Habitat: Open grassland, roadsides, arable fields, waste places, rocks, along railways, on dry, oligotrophic, calcareous, sandy, stony or rocky soils; from sea level to 1,900 m, but mainly in the lowland.

Range: Most of Europe except Iceland and the high Arctic.

---

p.133 **Thale Cress**
Arabidopsis thaliana (L.) Heynh.

Description: A hairy annual or biennial with erect stems to 30 cm, and spreading basal leaf-rosette; branches of inflorescence long, steeply rising. Basal leaves oblanceolate, short-stalked, dentate to subentire, with *simple and forked hairs; stem-leaves few*, alternate, subsessile, much smaller. Flowers 3–4 mm diam., in elongating racemes. Sepals to 2 mm long, narrowly ovate; petals white, with rounded limb. Fruit a linear, bluntly tetragonal to subterete, *ascending siliqua, 10–16 (20) mm long*, on *spreading stalk* to 10 mm; *valves 3-veined* (middle vein strong); beak short (to 0.4 mm); seeds in 1 or 2 rows.

Flowering: March–May (autumn).

Habitat: Arable fields, gardens, roadsides, waste places, grassy banks, on dry, oligotrophic to mesotrophic, slightly acid to calcareous, often sandy soils; from sea level to 2,000 m.

Range: Most of Europe except Iceland and the high Arctic.

Similar species: *A. suecica* (Fries) Norrlin has pinnately lobed to divided basal leaves, and slightly larger flowers. Confined to stony places in Fennoscandia and N Russia.

Braya (*Braya linearis* Rouy) from the mountains of N Scandinavia is a slightly hairy, mat-forming perennial to 30 cm; leaves lanceolate, stalked to subsessile, dentate to entire, partly in a rosette, partly cauline. Flowers white or pink, 2–3 mm diam.; fruit a short, linear siliqua, 8–15 mm long, to 1.2 mm wide, with *c.* 10 seeds. *Braya purpurascens* (R. Br.) Bunge has all leaves in rosette (or 1 leaf along stem), and very short, ovoid or spindle-shaped siliquas 4–10 mm long, 1–3 mm wide. In comparable, stony habitats, in Arctic Norway, N Russia and Spitsbergen.

Compare also Cardaminopsis arenosa (see p.577) which has compressed siliquas and teeth on petal claw; and the *Arabis* species, with mostly clasping stem-leaves, and 1-veined, flattened valves.

---

p.134 **Tower Mustard** *Arabis glabra* (L.) Bernh.

Description: A subglabrous biennial, with erect, unbranched stems to 1 m; *stems hairy beneath only.* Basal leaves oblanceolate, stalked, *sinuously dentate, stellate-hairy,* often withered at anthesis; stem-leaves numerous, alternate, to 60 mm long, *glabrous, glaucous,* erect, lanceolate, usually *entire-margined,* sessile, *clasping stem with 2 blunt basal lobes.* Flowers 5–7 mm diam., in elongating terminal racemes. Sepals lanceolate, to 3 mm long; petals 4–6 mm long, *cream or pale yellow,* with rounded limb. Fruit a linear, slightly compressed, *tetragonal siliqua, 40–70 mm long,* to 1.5 mm wide, erect, *appressed to stem,* with *seeds in 2 rows* (in each locule).

Flowering: May–July.

Habitat: Grassy slopes, heaths, sunny roadsides, scrub, wood margins, on dry, mesotrophic to eutrophic, sandy, loamy or stony soils; from sea level to 1,500 m.

Range: Most of Europe except Ireland, Iceland and the high Arctic.

Similar species: **Tower Cress** (*A. turrita* L.) also has pale-yellow flowers (to 9 mm diam.), but plant hairy to the top, siliquas much longer

(10–14 cm), arched and spreading to one side, with seeds in 1 row. In calcareous, rocky, wooded places and on old walls, in S and C Europe, northwards to C France, S Germany, Czechia, and C Russia; locally naturalized further north.

A. pauciflora (Grimm) Garcke is quite hairless, even on the long-stalked, entire-margined basal leaves; stem-leaves narrowed in middle, white or pinkish; seeds in 1 row. In open woods and rocky places, on dry, calcareous soils, mainly in the mountains, in S and C Europe, northwards to Belgium, S Germany and Czechia.

p.134 **Hairy Rockcress** *Arabis hirsuta* (L.) Scop.

Description: A hairy biennial or short-lived perennial, to 1 m; *stems hairy to the top*, branched only in inflorescence. Leaves have forked hairs; basal leaves oblanceolate, stalked, bluntly serrate, in a rosette; *stem-leaves 7–20 (30)*, erect, alternate, lanceolate, serrate-dentate, sessile; *auricles absent or small and rounded*. Flowers 3–5 mm diam., in elongating terminal racemes. Sepals lanceolate, to 3 mm long; petals 4–6.5 mm long, *white*, with rounded limb. Fruit a slightly compressed, *erect, linear siliqua to 50 mm*, appressed to stem; valves 1-veined to top.

Flowering: May–August.

Habitat: Grassland, dunes, grassy banks, rocks and walls, on dry, oligotrophic, calcareous, sandy or stony soils; from sea level to 2,000 m.

Range: Most of Europe except Iceland and the high Arctic.

In ssp. *sagittata* (Bertol.) Gaudin, middle vein of fruit-valve is obscure in upper half; stem-leaves 25–35 (45), sessile, with acute, spreading auricles; hairs on stem-base mostly simple. In dry, calcareous grassland and on walls, in S and C Europe, northwards to the Netherlands, Germany, Hungary, Romania, and N Russia. In ssp. *planisiliqua* Pers., fruit-valves have no distinct middle vein at all; stem-leaves 20–55, sessile, sagittate, with appressed, blunt auricles; siliquas constricted between seeds; stem-base has many forked hairs. In calcareous fens, in S and C Europe, northwards to France, Germany, Poland and N Russia. Both subspecies are also treated as separate species.

A. borealis Andrz. ex Ledeb. is much like ssp. *planisiliqua*, but has fruit-stalks 5–20 mm long (not 3–7 mm), seeds winged all round (instead of only apically), and stems with many forked hairs all over (instead of only basally). On dry, calcareous slopes in N Russia and Finland.

---

p.133 **Horse-radish**
Armoracia rusticana Gaertn., Meyer & Scherb.

Description: A *hairless perennial*, with *stout taproot*, short stolons, and erect or ascending stems to 1.2 m. *Basal leaves tufted, very large* (to 50 cm long), stalked, oblanceolate to narrowly elliptical, crenate; stem-leaves much smaller, alternate, lanceolate, the lower ones often deeply lobed, the upper ones (sub)sessile. Flowers to 9 mm diam., in elongating racemes forming large panicle. Sepals narrowly ovate, 2–3 mm long; petals 5–7 mm long, white, with rounded limb. *Fruit an obovoid silicule to 6 mm long*; style to 1.5 mm.

Flowering: May–July.
Habitat: Ruderal and waste places, road verges, riversides, along railways, on moist, eutrophic soils; mainly in the lowland.
Range: Native to S and C Russia and W Asia; frequently naturalized in all of Europe except the far north.

A form of horse-radish is frequently cultivated for its thickened, whitish roots, which are grated and pickled to make a sauce or side-dish.

---

p.206 **Medium-flowered Wintercress**
Barbarea intermedia Boreau

Description: A slightly hairy or glabrous biennial, with ascending or erect, branched stems to 60 cm.

Leaves all pinnately divided, alternate, sessile, clasping stem with 2 ovate, *ciliate auricles*; lower leaves with 3–7 pairs of side-lobes, upper ones with 1–3 pairs of side-lobes and a *narrow-ovate to lanceolate end-lobe*. Flowers to 6 mm diam., in elongating terminal racemes. Sepals narrow-ovate; petals yellow, with rounded or slightly notched limb. Fruit a *linear, tetragonal siliqua to 30 mm long*, erect, on short stalk to 5 mm, and with thick, blunt style to 1.5 mm.

Flowering: April–August.

Habitat: Grassland, roadsides, cultivated land, waste and disturbed places, streamsides, on moist, mesotrophic, sandy, loamy or peaty soils; from sea level to 1,700 m.

Range: S and W Europe, northwards to the Netherlands and S Germany, eastwards to Austria and Yugoslavia; naturalized in the British Isles and Denmark.

Similar species: **American Wintercress** (*B. verna* (Miller) Aschrs.) has fruits 30–70 mm long, and basal leaves with 6–10 pairs of side-lobes. Native to SW Europe, in grassland and along rivers; also cultivated as a vegetable (eaten raw, in salads), and more or less naturalized in the British Isles, the Low Countries and Denmark (and also in N America).

---

p.206 **Common Wintercress**
Barbarea vulgaris R. Br.

Description: A hairless, rather bushy biennial or perennial, with erect, branched stems to 90 cm. Leaves alternate, the lower ones pinnately divided with 2–5 pairs of side-lobes and an obovate, cordate-based end-lobe; *upper leaves undivided* (or with only 1 pair of side-lobes), ovate, lobed or bluntly dentate, clasping stem with *2 glabrous auricles*. Flowers 7–9 mm diam., in elongated terminal racemes forming large panicle. Sepals to 3 mm long, broadly lanceolate, *glabrous*; petals to 7 mm long, yellow, with rounded or slightly notched limb. Fruit a linear, tetragonal siliqua to 30 mm long, obliquely rising, with *tapering style to 3 mm long*.

Flowering: April–August.

Habitat: Grassland, road verges, grassy banks, along ditches, streams and rivers, on moist, mesotrophic to eutrophic, sandy or loamy soils; from sea level to 1,300 m.

Range: Most of Europe except the high Arctic, and only naturalized in Iceland.

Similar species: **Small-flowered Wintercress** (*B. stricta* Andrzj.) has lower leaves with elliptical end-lobe, flowers 5–6 mm diam., more erect siliquas with a squat, thickened style to 1.5 mm long, and sepals hairy at the top. In comparable habitats in N and E Europe, southwards to Britain, the Low Countries, Hungary, and SE Russia.

---

p.133 **Hoary Alison** *Berteroa incana* (L.) DC.

Description: A *grey-hairy annual*, with ascending to erect, branched stems to 50 cm. Leaves alternate, elliptical to lanceolate, blunt-tipped, usually *entire*, subsessile, *covered with stellate hairs*. Flowers 5–8 mm diam., in dense, elongating terminal racemes. Sepals to 3 mm long; petals 5–6 mm long, white, *deeply notched to bifid*. Fruit a slightly compressed, *ellipsoid silicule to 8 (10) mm long*, densely stellate-hairy.

Flowering: June–October.

Habitat: Road verges, ruderal places, cultivated land, rocks and stony slopes, on dry, mesotrophic, sandy, stony or rocky soils; from sea level to 1,000 m.

Range: E and C Europe, westwards to Switzerland; naturalized (often near flour-mills) in Britain, the Low Countries and Fennoscandia.

---

p.200 **Buckler Mustard** *Biscutella laevigata* L.

Description: A hairy perennial, with creeping, slightly lignified rhizomes, and erect stems to 50 cm. Leaves hairy, (ob)lanceolate, serrate-dentate to pinnately divided; basal ones narrowed into a stalk, cauline ones subsessile. Flowers 6–10 mm diam., in strongly elongating racemes. Sepals to 4 mm long, broadly lanceolate; petals clawed, with rounded, *elliptical, slightly hastate limb, pale yellow.* Fruit a strongly compressed, *2-lobed, 2-seeded silicule*, the *lobes suborbicular*, to 6 mm diam.; fruit-stalk ascending to almost spreading; style threadlike, 3–4 mm long.

Flowering: May–August.

Habitat: Grassland, open scrub, rocks, on dry, oligotrophic, preferably calcareous, stony or rocky soils; mainly in the mountains (to 2,600 m), descending to 100 m in river valleys.

Range: S and C Europe, westwards to Portugal and France, and northwards to S Belgium, Germany, Poland, and W Russia.

The lobes of fruit represent the strongly keeled valves; the membranous septum between them is very narrow.

p.205 **Black Mustard** *Brassica nigra* (L.) Koch

Description: A glaucous or dark-green annual, to 1 m; stems bristly-hairy beneath. Leaves alternate, *stalked*: lower ones pinnately divided with 1–3 pairs of side-lobes and an ovate or rounded end-lobe, *bristly-hairy* (with only simple hairs); *upper leaves undivided*, ovate to lanceolate, *short-stalked*, dentate to subentire. Flowers 10–15 mm diam., in strongly elongating racemes forming large panicles. Sepals lanceolate, *glabrous*, spreading at last; petals clawed, yellow, with rounded limb. Outer stamens markedly shorter than inner ones. Fruit an erect, slightly compressed *linear siliqua to 25 mm long, appressed to stem*, on stout stalk to 5 mm, and with beak to 5 mm long; *fruit-valves have prominent midvein.*

Flowering: June–September.

Habitat: Arable and wasteland, ruderal places, road and railway verges, groyns, riverbanks, sea-cliffs, on moist, eutrophic, sandy, clayey or stony soils; mainly in the lowland.

Range: Most of Europe except Iceland and the high Arctic.

Occasionally cultivated for the mustard seed.

p.205 **Wild Cabbage** *Brassica oleracea* L.

Description: A *hairless* biennial or perennial, with erect stems to 1.5 m, becoming woody at base. Leaves often glaucous; lower ones large (to 30 cm long), deeply pinnately lobed or divided with rounded, crenate or curly-margined segments; upper ones unlobed, sessile, at most *half-clasping stem* with 2 rounded auricles. *Flowers large* (25–35 mm diam.), in terminal racemes; *buds overtop open flowers*. Sepals lanceolate, yellowish, *always erect*. Petals 15–25 mm long, clawed, yellow. Stamens subequal, all erect. Fruit a *linear, subterete siliqua to 70 mm long*, with *conical beak to 15 mm* (less than a quarter the length of the valves), on an ascending stalk.

Flowering: May–September.

Habitat: Coastal cliffs and rocks, on dry, oligotrophic, stony soils.

Range: N Spain, W France and S Britain, also on Helgoland, and in the W Mediterranean area.

The cabbage described here is the wild form (ssp. *oleracea*), from which stem the many cultivars grown as a vegetable (various cabbages, cauliflower, brussel sprouts, borecole, etc.).

Rape (*B. napus* L.) probably originated from a hybrid between Wild Cabbage and *B. rapa*; it has a thickened taproot, slightly hairy lower leaves, smaller flowers (15–25 mm diam.), obliquely divergent sepals, and fruits with a long beak (to 25 mm); the 2 outer stamens are shorter and ascending. It is often cultivated for fodder, for the oil from the seeds (especially ssp. *oleifera* (DC.) Metzger, with thin roots) or for the strongly thickened, edible root (Swede, var. *napobrassica* (L.) Reichenb.) or stem-base (kohlrabi).

p.205 **Wild Turnip** *Brassica rapa* L.

Description: An erect annual, to 80 cm, with thin, lignified taproot. Lower leaves pinnately divided with several side-lobes and a rounded to ovate end-lobe, short-stalked to sessile, green, *bristly-hairy* (with only simple hairs); upper leaves ovate to lanceolate, subentire, sessile, clasping *stem with 2 rounded auricles, glabrous*, often glaucous. Flowers 12–20 mm diam., in elongating terminal racemes forming large panicles; *open flowers overtop buds*. Sepals broadly lanceolate, spreading at last; petals 7–11 mm long, yellow, clawed, (rounded) limb longer than claw. Fruit a *linear siliqua to 65 mm long, with long beak* (to 20 mm, up to half as long as valves), *obliquely rising* from thin, *long stalk* equalling fruit.

Flowering: April–August.

Habitat: Arable and wasteland, roadsides, riversides, on moist, eutrophic, sandy, loamy or clayey soils; from sea level to 1,800 m.

Range: Most of Europe except the extreme north.

The description pertains to ssp. *campestris* (L.) Clapham, the wild type. Ssp. *sylvestris* (L.) Janchen is biennial, with a distinct basal leaf-rosette and thin roots. Ssp. *rapa* is also biennial, and has thickened, fleshy taproots (turnips). The biennial forms are cultivated as a vegetable, and for the seeds; they are often found naturalized.

---

p.204 **Warty Cabbage** *Bunias orientalis* L.

Description: A rough-hairy biennial or perennial with creeping rhizome and erect, branched flowering stems, with *glandular tubercles*, to 1 m. Leaves alternate, rough-hairy; lower ones stalked, lanceolate to lyrate, deeply pinnately divided, with *acute, spreading to backward-pointing side-lobes* and large, *triangular to hastate end-lobe*, the lobes sinuously dentate; upper leaves lanceolate or hastate, dentate. Flowers 8–10 mm diam., in elongating terminal racemes. Sepals more or less erect; petals to 6 mm long, yellow, with long claw and *notched, obovate limb*. Fruit an ovate, *1–2-locular silicule, 5–10 mm long*, covered with blunt warts, *not splitting*, with short, oblique beak.

Flowering: May–August.

Habitat: Road verges, ruderal and waste places, on moist, eutrophic, sandy, clayey or stony

soils; from sea level to 2,100 m.

Range: E Europe, extending westwards to Poland, Hungary and Yugoslavia; locally naturalized in C and W Europe.

Similar species: *B. erucago* L. has slightly larger flowers, and tetragonal silicules with irregularly lobed, spiny wings. From the Mediterranean region, northwards to C France; naturalized in ruderal places in Britain and C Europe, often on loamy soils, to 1,300 m.

---

p.284 **Sea Rocket** *Cakile maritima* L.

Description: A slightly succulent, *hairless* annual, with ascending, branched stems to 60 cm. Leaves alternate, ovate to lanceolate, pinnately divided to only sparsely lobed, *glaucous, fleshy*. Flowers 8–14 mm diam., in elongating terminal racemes. Sepals lanceolate, erect; petals 6–10 mm long, lilac, pink or white, clawed, with rounded limb. Fruit a short, hard, corky, non-splitting siliqua, 10–25 mm long, with 2 superimposed locules (each with 1 seed) separated by a constriction and set on short, thick, divergent stalk; lower locule has blunt lateral knobs or horns.

Flowering: June–October.

Habitat: Maritime sands, beaches, dunes, on dry to moist, brackish, sandy soils; mainly coastal.

Range: S and W Europe, northwards to S Norway, C Finland and N Russia, eastwards to SE Russia.

Ssp. *baltica* Jord. ex Rouy & Fouc. has leaves 1–2-pinnately divided, with segments up to 20 times as long as wide (not up to 5 times). In coastal habitats in the Baltic region. *C. edentula* Hyl. ex P.W. Ball lacks horns to the fruit. In Iceland, the Faeroes, N Norway and N Russia.

---

p.130 **White Ball Mustard**
Calepina irregularis (Asso) Thell.

Description: A *hairless* annual with ascending, branched stems to 60 (80) cm. Basal leaves in a rosette, long-stalked, oblanceolate, pinnately lobed to divided, with rounded end-lobe; stem-leaves alternate, lanceolate, sessile, clasping *stem with 2 pointed auricles*. Flowers 2–4 mm diam., in elongating racemes. Sepals 1–1.5 mm long; *petals unequal, 2–3 mm long*, white (rarely pinkish), clawed, with rounded limb. Fruit an *ovoid, 1-locular, 1-seeded, wrinkled silicule* to 3 mm long, not splitting, with short, conical beak.

Flowering: April–July.

Habitat: Grassland, waste places, scrub, field and wood margins, on moist, oligotrophic, calcareous, sandy, loamy or stony soils; mainly in the lowland.

Range: Native to SW Asia; naturalized (often an archeophyte) in S and C Europe, northwards to the Netherlands.

---

p.205 **Gold-of-pleasure** *Camelina sativa* L.

Description: A hairless annual, with erect, scarcely branched stems to 60 (80) cm. Leaves alternate, lanceolate, entire or slightly dentate; lower ones short-stalked, upper ones sessile and *clasping stem with 2 acute auricles*. Flowers 3–4 mm diam., in elongating terminal racemes. Sepals erect; petals yellow, clawed, with rounded limb. Fruit an *obovoid silicule, 6–9 mm long, 4–5 mm wide, yellow* when ripe, with 2 locules, short style (to 2 mm), hard wall, and numerous seeds.

Flowering: May–July.

Habitat: Arable land and ruderal or waste places, on dry, mesotrophic, often loamy or clayey soils; from sea level to 1,300 m.

Range: Most of Europe except the far north, but often only casual.

A form with both simple and forked hairs, pale-yellow flowers and greyish-green fruits 5–7 mm long, 3–4.5 mm wide, is distinguished as *C. microcarpa* Andrz. ex DC. *C. alyssum* (Miller) Thell., a glabrous or slightly hairy form with strongly dentate leaves and soft-walled, pear-shaped fruits (6) 9–12 mm long, occurs in flaxfields.

These species are connected to Gold-of-pleasure by intermediate forms, and the whole complex can probably be better treated as a single, polymorphic species. Gold-of-pleasure was formerly (as early as Neolithic times) cultivated for its oil. It has seriously declined now.

---

p.132 **Shepherd's Purse** *Capsella bursa-pastoris* L.

Description: A hairy (occasionally glabrous) annual, with erect, branched stems to 40 (60) cm and a basal leaf-rosette. Basal leaves short-stalked, obovate to oblanceolate, pinnately divided to subentire, with stellate hairs (and sometimes simple hairs as well); stem-leaves alternate, lanceolate, dentate to subentire, clasping stem with blunt auricles. Flowers to 2 mm diam., in strongly elongating racemes. Sepals 1–1.5 mm long, green, often hairy; *petals to 3 mm long, unequal, white*, clawed, with rounded limb. Fruit a *compressed, triangular-obcordate, notched silicule* with straight or convex sides, and several seeds.

Flowering: March–October (Winter).

Habitat: Cultivated and wasteland, gardens, roadsides, ruderal places, on dry to moist, eutrophic, often trodden, sandy, clayey or stony soils; a very common weed, from sea level to 2,000 m.

Range: All Europe.

Similar species: *C. rubella* Reuter has short, often pink-edged, petals (1.5–2 mm long) and hardly exceeding the always glabrous, purple-flushed sepals, and silicules with slightly concave sides. In comparable habitats of S Europe, extending northwards to N France and S Britain.

Compare also Teesdalia (see p.602), which has unequal petals.

---

p.130 **Large Bittercress** *Cardamine amara* L.

Description: A (usually) subglabrous perennial to 40 cm, with ascending to erect, branched, *slightly angular, solid stems* (occasionally hairy at base). *Leaves all cauline*, pinnate, with 5–9 ovate, bluntly dentate to crenate, ciliate or glabrous leaflets, those of upper leaves narrower, lanceolate. *Flowers 10–12 mm diam.*, in rather lax terminal racemes. Sepals broadly lanceolate; *petals 7–9 mm long, white* (sometimes pink at top), clawed, much longer than sepals. *Anthers violet (compare C. pratensis, p.576)*. Fruit a linear siliqua to 40 mm long, with *tapering, acute style*.

Flowering: April–July.

Habitat: Damp grassland, flushes, fens, carrs, willow-coppices, stream- and riversides, on wet, mesotrophic to eutrophic, sandy, clayey or peaty soils; from sea level to 2,000 m.

Range: Most of Europe except the far north and the extreme south.

Some varieties are quite hairy. *Compare also* white-flowering *Rorippa* species, which have hollow stems and yellow anthers.

---

p.131 *Cardamine bellidifolia* L.

Description: A *hairless* perennial with erect, rarely branched flowering stems to 15 (25) cm, and *spoon-shaped, slightly fleshy, entire leaves in a basal rosette*; stem-leaves absent or few (stalked). Flowers 7–10 mm diam., 2–5 together in small terminal racemes; flower-stalks to 1.5 mm long. Petals white, 3.5–5 mm long. Fruit a strictly erect, linear, beakless siliqua, 12–25 mm long, to 1.5 mm wide, purplish-brown when ripe.

Flowering: July–August.

Habitat: Meadows, screes, on moist to wet, sandy, peaty or gravelly soils; only in the mountains, to 2,100 m.

Range: In (sub)Arctic N Europe.

The description pertains to ssp. *bellidifolia*. Ssp. *alpina* (Willd.) B.M.G. Jones, which occurs in the Alps (between 1,500 and 3,300 m), has 2–3 entire or 3-lobed, subsessile stem-leaves, 3–8 flowers on stalks 2–3 mm long, and siliquas 10–15 mm long, 1 mm wide.

p.283 **Coralroot Bittercress**
Cardamine bulbifera (L.) Crantz

Description: A hairless perennial with creeping rhizomes
and ascending to erect, scarcely branched
flowering stems to 70 cm. Leaves all
cauline, pinnate, with (3) 5–7 lanceolate,
dentate leaflets; upper leaves undivided,
usually with *brownish, scaly, detachable
bulbils* in axil. Flowers 12–18 mm diam.,
few together in small terminal racemes.
Sepals broadly lanceolate, green; *petals to
15 mm long, pale lilac or purplish*, clawed,
with elliptical, round-tipped limb. Fruit a
linear siliqua, 20–35 mm long, to 2.5 mm
wide, with a tapering beak.

Flowering: May–June.

Habitat: Woods (mostly Beech), along streams, on
moist, oligotrophic to mesotrophic,
calcareous, sandy, loamy or stony soils; from
sea level to 1,600 m.

Range: C Europe, westwards to France and Britain,
and northwards to Belgium, Germany, S
Fennoscandia, and C Russia.

A member of the subgenus *Dentaria*,
characterized by subterranean, scaly
rhizomes and stalked cotyledons. The
axillary bulbils serve as vegetative
propagules. Fruits are seldom formed in
northern regions. Several more species of
the subgenus *Dentaria*, with pinnate or
(doubly) tripartite leaves and white or
yellow flowers can be found in the
mountains of C Europe.

---

p.131 **Hairy Bittercress** *Cardamine hirsuta* L.

Description: A *hairy annual* with *basal leaf-rosette* and
erect, (sub)glabrous, little-branched
flowering stems to 35 cm. Basal leaves
pinnate, with (3) 5–9 (11) suborbicular to
ovate, angular-dentate or 3-lobed leaflets;
stem-leaves 1–4, smaller, usually with
entire leaflets, and without auricles at base
of stalk. Flowers 3–4 mm diam., in
elongating terminal racemes. Petals
2.5–3 mm (occasionally absent), not

exceeding sepals, white. *Stamens 4 (occasionally 5, rarely 6)*. Fruit an erect, *linear siliqua, 18–25 mm long, c. 1 mm wide, in line with stalk*, with short style (to 1 mm); *fruits usually overtop flowers*.

Flowering: (February) March–July (November).

Habitat: Cultivated places, gardens, roadsides, dunes, rocky places, old walls, on dry to moist, oligotrophic to mesotrophic, preferably calcareous, sandy, loamy or stony soils; from sea level to 2,500 m.

Range: All Europe except the high Arctic.

Similar species: **Wavy Bittercress** (*C. flexuosa* With.) is biennial or perennial, with branched, flexuous stems hairy at base, 5–9 stem-leaves with crenate leaflets, and flowers with 6 stamens; fruits 12–20 mm long, up to 0.8 mm wide, making an angle with their stalk and rarely overtopping flowers. In damp deciduous woods, along woodland rides, ditches and streams, often on seasonally inundated places, on wet, mesotrophic to eutrophic, slightly acid, sandy or peaty soils, from sea level to 1,600 m, in most of Europe except Iceland, the high Arctic, and the western parts of Russia.

C. parviflora L. is quite glabrous, and lacks a basal leaf-rosette; stem-leaves have 11–17 lanceolate, entire leaflets. In damp meadows, marshes and along ditches, in S and C Europe, northwards to C France, S Germany, S Sweden, S Finland, and N Russia.

p.131 **Narrow-leaved Bittercress**
Cardamine impatiens L.

Description: A hairless annual or biennial with branched, flexuous stems to 60 cm. Basal leaf-rosette usually withered at anthesis. Stem-leaves numerous, broadly lanceolate, pinnate, with *9–19 lanceolate leaflets* often with *2 large teeth* in the lower half, and with *2 acute, clasping auricles* at base of stalk. Flowers 3–4 mm diam., in elongating terminal racemes. *Petals 2–3 mm long, greenish-white*, scarcely exceeding sepals, and occasionally absent. *Anthers greenish*. Fruit a linear siliqua, 18–30 mm long, to 1.1 mm wide, *erect on widely spreading stalks.*

Flowering: May–August.

Habitat: Damp woods (often Beech or Ash), stream- and riversides, occasionally gardens and parks, also rocky places, screes, old walls, on moist or wet, eutrophic, slightly acid to calcareous, sandy, loamy or stony soils; from sea level to 1,500 m.

Range: Europe northwards to Britain, the Low Countries, Denmark, S Sweden, S Finland, and N Russia.

---

p.283 **Cuckooflower** *Cardamine pratensis* L.

Description: A hairless perennial with erect, scarcely branched stems to 40 cm, and basal leaf-rosette. Basal leaves pinnate, with up to 13 rounded to ovate, subentire, sessile leaflets, the top-leaflet suborbicular to reniform; stem-leaves often less than 5, pinnate, with elliptical to lanceolate, sessile leaflets. Flowers 12–18 mm diam., in terminal racemes. Sepals 3–4.5 mm long, broadly lanceolate, green; petals 6–13 mm long, with short, yellowish claw and broadly obovate, *shallow-notched, pale-lilac or pinkish (rarely white) limb. Anthers yellow (compare C. amara, p.572. Fruit a linear siliqua to 50 mm long, with blunt style.*

Flowering: April–June.

Habitat: Damp meadows, pastures, woods, stream- and riversides, flushes, on wet to moist, mesotrophic to eutrophic, sandy, loamy, clayey or peaty soils; from sea level to 2,600 m.

Range: Most of Europe except Iceland and the high Arctic.

Similar species: *C. nymanii* Gand., in Iceland, the Faeroes, Fennoscandia and N Russia, has thickish leaves, pale-lilac flowers to 15 mm diam., and fruits to 20 mm.

Another name for the Cuckooflower is Lady's Smock. Ssp. *dentata* (Schultes) Čelak. often has more than 5 stem-leaves with short-stalked, ovate leaflets, and dentate, rooting leaflets to the basal leaves; flowers larger, with sepals 4.5–6 mm long, and petals 10–

16 mm, often pale pink or almost white. In the same wide area, but generally in wetter places. The status of this taxon is debatable.

---

p.283 **Tall Rockcress**
Cardaminopsis arenosa (L.) Hayek

Description: A hairy biennial or short-lived perennial (sometimes annual), with erect, branched stems to 50 cm; no stolons. Leaves pinnately lobed to dentate; basal leaves in rosette, stem-leaves alternate. Flowers 7–9 mm diam., in elongating terminal racemes. Sepals broadly lanceolate, the 2 outer ones swollen. Petals 4–9 mm long, lilac (in C Europe) or white (in Fennoscandia), with *2 teeth at claw*, and rounded limb. Fruit a *spreading, strongly compressed, linear siliqua* to 45 mm; *valves with a strong midvein*; seeds in 1 row.

Flowering: April–September.

Habitat: Riverbeds, river-dunes, grassy banks, roadsides, on dry (or seasonally wet), oligotrophic to mesotrophic, calcareous, sandy or gravelly soils; from sea level to 1,400 m.

Range: Much of Europe except Ireland and the far north.

Similar species: **Northern Rockcress** (*C. petraea* (L.) Hiitonen) has stolons, basal leaves ovate to lanceolate, pinnately lobed or dentate, stem-leaves lanceolate, entire-margined, and flowers white or purplish. On stony soils in mountainous areas, in N and C Europe, from Iceland, Fennoscandia and N Russia southwards to Ireland, Britain, Germany, Hungary, and Poland.
C. halleri (L.) Hayek, from C Europe, also has stolons; stem-leaves ovate, flowers always white, and sepals never swollen.

The genus *Cardaminopsis* differs from *Cardamine* in having a strong midvein on the fruit-valves, and branched (not simple) hairs. *Compare also*: *Arabidopsis suecica* (*see* p.561, which has subterete siliquas, and no teeth on petal-claw; and *Sisymbrium supinum* (*see* p.600) which has simple hairs, and rounded siliquas with seeds in 2 rows.

p.134 **Hoary Cress** *Cardaria draba* (L.) Desv.

Description: A greyish-green, glabrous or slightly hairy perennial to 90 cm. Leaves mostly cauline, alternate, ovate to broadly lanceolate, sinuously dentate, sessile, clasping stem with subacute basal lobes. Flowers 5–6 mm diam., very numerous in dense terminal racemes forming large, *umbel-shaped panicle*. Sepals to 2 mm long, ovate; petals to 4 mm long, obovate, white, with rounded tip. Fruit a flattened, 2-locular, 2-seeded, *cordate silicule, 3–4.5 mm long, 3.5–5 mm wide, notched at base*, with short style to 1.5 mm, and *not splitting*.

Flowering: May–July (October).

Habitat: Road verges, waste and ruderal places, field margins, dunes, on dry to moist, eutrophic, neutral or basic (often calcareous) soils; from sea level to 2,000 m.

Range: Native to S Europe and W Asia; naturalized elsewhere in Europe except Iceland, N Fennoscandia and N Russia.

Differs from *Lepidium* in having indehiscent, unwinged silicules.

---

p.139 **Common Scurvy-grass**
Cochlearia officinalis L.

Description: A (sub)glabrous biennial or perennial, with ascending stems to 50 cm. Leaves fleshy; basal ones long-stalked, ovate-cordate to reniform, entire-margined or slightly lobed, cauline ones sessile, ovate, sinuously lobed or bluntly dentate, *clasping stem* with cordate base. Flowers 8–10 mm diam., in terminal racemes. Sepals ovate; petals 4–5.5 mm long, white, obovate, with rounded tip. Fruit a subglobose, 2-locular silicule to 7 mm long, with very short style, and 2–4 (6) seeds in each locule; fruit-stalk longer than fruit.

Flowering: April–August.

Habitat: Brackish reedlands, saltmarshes, sea-walls, cliffs, on wet to moist, saline, sandy, clayey or rocky soils; also inland on mountains (300–2,200 m).

Range: Coasts of NW Europe; also in the mountains of C Europe, westwards to the Pyrenees.

Similar species: **English Scurvy-grass** (*Cochlearia anglica* L., also treated as a subspecies) has ellipsoid, more compressed fruits (8–15 mm long), basal leaves with truncate or cuneate base, and petals 5.5–7 mm long. In saltmarshes, saline meadows, estuaries, and along sea-walls, along Atlantic coasts of NW Europe, from Ireland, Britain and the Netherlands to S Scandinavia; intermediate forms of hybrid character are common.

C. aestuaria (Lloyd) Heywood is also a transitional form, but apparently no immediate hybrid; it has some basal leaves with cuneate base, and obovoid, truncate fruits. Along the coast of W France and N Spain.

Alpine Scurvygrass (*C. pyrenaica* DC.) has (white or pink) petals 3–4 mm long, ellipsoid silicules narrowed at base, with stalks shorter than fruit itself. In the mountains of C Europe, westwards to the Pyrenees, C France, E Belgium; also locally in Britain and Ireland.

Several forms from Arctic N Europe, with small, white flowers (6–9 mm diam.) and small, often 3-lobed, basal leaves (blade less than 20 mm long) are distinguished on the species rank: *C. fenestrata* R. Br. (with narrowly ellipsoid fruits to 8 mm long), *C. arctica* Schlecht. (with broadly ellipsoid fruits), and *C. groenlandica* L. (with subglobose fruits to 5 mm long, and lacking stem-leaves).

Scottish Scurvy-grass (*C. scotica* Druce) is a real dwarf (to 5 cm), with truncate, purplish (occasionally white) petals *c.* 3 mm long, and ovoid fruits to 3 mm long. On sandy and rocky coasts of N Scotland and possibly N and W Ireland.

Danish Scurvy-grass (*C. danica* L.) differs from other species above in being annual, and having stalked, 3–5-lobed stem-leaves, triangular-cordate basal leaves (less than 20 mm diam.), and white or pink petals *c.* 3 mm long; fruit ellipsoid to subglobose, 3–6 mm long. On sandy beaches, in sea-dunes, on rocks and cliffs, along coasts of W Europe, northwards to Norway and the

Baltic region; it is also found along salted motorways inland.

Eutrema edwardsii R. Br. is a subglabrous, rhizomatous perennial, with simple, erect flowering stems to 40 cm, fleshy, mostly long-stalked, basal leaves with ovate or suborbicular, more or less cordate-based, entire blades; stem-leaves few, narrowly ovate to lanceolate, subsessile; flowers in small terminal raceme; petals white, 2–4 mm long. Fruit quite different from *Cochlearia*: an erect, spindle-shaped siliqua, 6–20 mm long, 1.5–3 mm wide, with 1-veined valves and seeds in 1 row. In the Arctic tundra, on moist, oligotrophic, rocky soils, in N Russia and on Spitsbergen.

---

p.206 **Wallflower Cabbage**
Coincya cheiranthos (Vill.) Greuter & Burdet

Description: A bristly-hairy biennial or perennial, with erect, branched stems to 60 cm. Leaves greyish-green, lanceolate, pinnately divided (to almost pinnate); lower ones long-stalked, with 3–5 (7) pairs of ovate to lanceolate segments, upper ones short-stalked, with almost linear segments (rarely undivided). Flowers 20–30 mm diam., in elongating, terminal racemes. Sepals lanceolate, 5–10 mm long; *petals 14–18 mm long, sulphur-yellow with deep-yellow to reddish veins*, clawed, with rounded, obovate limb. Fruit a *linear siliqua, 30–80 mm long, to 2 mm wide*, with *3 veins* and prominent, slightly flattened, attenuate beak (8–22 mm long, housing 1–3 of the many seeds).

Flowering: June–October.

Habitat: Ruderal places, roadsides, field margins, rocky places, on dry to moist, mesotrophic to eutrophic, preferably calcareous, sandy, gravelly or stony soils; from sea level to 2,800 m.

Range: Native to the mountains of SW and C Europe, but naturalized in the lowland, northwards to Britain and the Netherlands; obviously extending its range.

Some endemic forms have been described

from sea-cliffs in Britain: *C. wrightii* (O.E. Schulz) Dandy ex Clapham is perennial with leaves densely grey-hairy at least beneath, and fruits to 65 mm long, 4 mm wide (Lundy Island, Devon); *C. monensis* (L.) Dandy ex Clapham is a (sub)glabrous biennial with yellow, darker-veined flowers, and siliquas 40–90 mm long, 2 mm wide, with a (3–5-seeded) beak 8–18 mm long (W Britain).

---

p.138 **Swinecress**
Coronopus squamatus (Forsk.) Aschers.

Description: A low, spreading, *glabrous annual* to 5 (25) cm, with *prostrate, branched stems*. Leaves alternate, stalked, pinnately divided, with narrow, *anteriorly lobed segments*. Flowers 2–3 mm diam., in *short, crowded, prostrate racemes placed opposite to a leaf*, or in a branch-axil; flower-stalks shorter than flowers. *Petals white*, 1–1.5 mm long, even so *exceeding sepals*. *Fertile stamens 6.* Fruit a 2-locular, 2-seeded, *reniform silicule*, 2–3 mm long, 3.5–4 mm wide, with *knobbly or warty folds*.

Flowering: June–October.

Habitat: Pastures, cultivated ground, pathways, usually in trampled places, on moist, eutrophic, compacted, often heavy soils; from sea level to 1,500 m.

Range: Most of Europe, northwards to C Fennoscandia and the Baltic States.

Similar species: **Lesser Swinecress** (*C. didymus* (L.) Sm.) is more or less hairy, with ascending racemes, and usually 2 fertile stamens; petals cream, to 0.5 mm long, shorter than sepals (or, often, altogether absent); silicules to 2 mm long, 3 mm wide, notched at apex, net-veined, and without knobs. In comparable habitats, also in ruderal places; native to S America, and widely naturalized in Europe except the Arctic.

---

p.130 **Sea Kale** *Crambe maritima* L.

Description: A *hairless, glaucous or purple-flushed* perennial, with *large tufts of basal leaves*, and thick, angular, ascending to erect stems to 80 cm. Basal leaves long-stalked, to 30 cm long, ovate to elliptical, deeply and irregularly *pinnately lobed with wavy lobes and curly margins*; stem-leaves smaller, subsessile; leaves rather fleshy or leathery. Flowers 10–15 mm diam., in *large, often umbel-shaped panicles*. Sepals narrowly ovate, 4–5 mm long, with whitish margin; petals white (rarely pinkish), 6–9 mm long, rounded. *Fruit indehiscent, pear-shaped*, 12–14 mm long, 6–8 mm wide, with small, sterile locule at base, and larger, ovoid to subglobose, 1-seeded locule at the top; fruit-stalk ascending, longer than fruit.

Flowering: May–August.

Habitat: Floodmarks on beaches, dunes, sea-cliffs, sea-walls, on moist, brackish, sandy or gravelly soils; coastal only.

Range: W Europe from Spain northwards to Britain, Ireland and Norway; also found in the Baltic region and around the Black Sea.

The young shoots can be cooked and eaten as a vegetable.

---

p.206 **Flixweed** *Descurainia sophia* (L.) Prantl

Description: A hairy annual, with erect, scarcely branched stems to 90 cm; *hairs stellate with 4 branches*. Leaves alternate, *2–3 times pinnatifid* (or 2–3-pinnate), with *linear segments*. Flowers 3–4 mm diam., in elongating terminal racemes. Sepals lanceolate, *c.* 3 mm long, hairy; petals oblanceolate, *pale yellow, shorter than sepals*. Stamens exserted. Fruit *an ascending, linear siliqua to 45 mm long*, in line with the (shorter) stalk.

Flowering: May–September.

Habitat: Ruderal, often disturbed, places, dunes, roadsides, riversides, on dry, oligotrophic, preferably calcareous, sandy or stony soils; from sea level to 2,000 m.

Range: Throughout most of Europe except the high Arctic.

p.207 **Perennial Wall-rocket**
Diplotaxis tenuifolia (L.) DC.

Description: A *glaucous or greyish-green*, subglabrous perennial, with erect, branched stems to 80 cm, often lignified at base. Leaves alternate, *pinnatifid*, lanceolate, with lanceolate to linear, serrate-dentate to subentire, ciliate segments. Flowers 15–25 mm diam., in elongating terminal racemes; *flower-stalks 3–4 times longer than calyx*. Petals 8–14 mm long, sulphur-yellow, with short claw and rounded limb. Fruit a *linear siliqua to 60 mm, with seeds in 2 rows* (in each locule); valves flattened, with *distinct midvein*.

Flowering: May–September.

Habitat: Ruderal, often disturbed, places, dunes, roadsides, building sites, along railways, also rocks and old walls, on dry, oligotrophic to mesotrophic, preferably calcareous, sandy or stony soils; from sea level to 1,000 m.

Range: Continental Europe, northwards to the Netherlands, Germany and Poland; naturalized in SE England, Denmark, Fennoscandia, and W Russia.

Similar species: **Annual Wall-rocket** (*D. muralis* (L.) DC.) is not always annual: often biennial, or even short-lived perennial, but always herbaceous throughout; most leaves in basal rosette, pinnatifid to pinnately lobed, with broader segments; stem-leaves few; flowers smaller, with petals 4–7.5 mm long; flower-stalks up to twice as long as calyx; siliqua to 45 mm long. In comparable habitats of S and C Europe; naturalized in British Isles, the Netherlands and Scandinavia.
D. viminea (L.) DC. has even smaller flowers, with petals to 5 mm long, and fruits to 35 mm long. In vineyards, gardens, roadsides and on riverbanks, on calcareous, sandy, loamy or stony soils in S Europe, northwards to C France (and naturalized in Germany).
White Wall-rocket (*D. erucoides* (L.) DC.) has lobed or dentate leaves, the cauline ones clasping, and white petals with purplish veins. In S Europe, northwards to SW France.

p.202 **Yellow Whitlowgrass** *Draba aizoides* L.

Description: A *subglabrous, tufted perennial* forming dense cushions, and with erect, leafless flowering stems (scapes) to 15 cm. Leaves all basal, *linear-lanceolate, rigid, bristly-ciliate, with long awn* at tip. Flowers 6–9 mm diam., in small terminal racemes. Sepals more or less erect; *petals yellow*. Fruit a *compressed, ellipsoid silicule, 8–12 mm long*, with numerous seeds.

Flowering: March–May.

Habitat: Cliffs, screes, rock-crevices, on dry or moist, oligotrophic, calcareous, gravelly or rocky soils; mainly in high mountainous regions to 3,600 m.

Range: In the mountains of C Europe, westwards to the Pyrenees, and eastwards to the Carpathians and the Balkan region, with outposts in NE France (Langres), E Belgium (Yvoir), and the Danube delta.

Similar species: **Alpine Whitlowgrass** (*D. alpina* L.) has broader, lanceolate to elliptical leaves, smaller flowers (4–6 mm diam.), and fruits to 8 mm long. In Iceland, Fennoscandia and N Russia (including Spitsbergen), in gravelly or rocky habitats, to 1,650 m.

Several related species occur in the Arctic and the mountains of C Europe, often with a restricted distribution; differences are found in the colour of flowers (yellow, cream or white), and in the indument of leaves and fruits, comprising simple and stellate hairs in various combinations. *See* regional floras for details.

---

p.135 **Hoary Whitlowgrass** *Draba incana* L.

Description: A hairy biennial or perennial, with erect, usually *simple, leafy stems* to 35 cm. Leaves alternate, often numerous and close together, *subsessile*, lanceolate, bluntly dentate, with simple hairs above, branched hairs beneath. Flowers 4–5 mm diam., in terminal raceme. *Petals white, obovate, notched*. Fruit a glabrous, *flattened, elliptical, twisted silicule, 7–9 mm long*; fruit-stalk erect.

Flowering: May–July.
Habitat: On dry, calcareous rocks, cliffs, old walls; mainly in the mountains (to 2,600 m), occasionally in coastal dunes.
Range: In the mountains of C Europe, from the Pyrenees to E Alps; also in (sub)Arctic N Europe, Scotland and adjacent islands.

Northern forms are more often biennial, those from W and C Europe usually perennial. *Compare D. muralis (see below),* which has broader, clasping stem-leaves.

---

p.135 **Wall Whitlowgrass** *Draba muralis* L.

Description: A hairy *annual*, with erect, simple or branched, *leafy stems* to 40 cm. Basal leaves short-stalked, broadly ovate, dentate; stem-leaves alternate, usually rather far apart, *clasping*, (ob)ovate, with cordate base, bluntly dentate, with stellate hairs above, forked hairs beneath. Flowers 2–3 mm diam., in terminal raceme. *Petals white, obovate, rounded.* Fruit a glabrous, *compressed, ellipsoid silicule, 3–6 mm long; fruit-stalk spreading.*
Flowering: April–June.
Habitat: Bare or grassy places, dunes, banks, walls, cliffs, on dry, mesotrophic, calcareous, sandy, gravelly or rocky soils; from sea level to 1,300 m.
Range: Most of Europe, northwards to C Fennoscandia.
Similar species: *D. nemorosa* L., from C Europe, the Pyrenees and Scandinavia, has pale-yellow to cream flowers, and hairy silicules.

---

p.135 **Rock Whitlowgrass** *Draba norvegica* Gunn.

Description: A more or less hairy *perennial*, forming loose cushions or mats, with short, erect, simple, *hairy flowering stems to 50 mm.* Leaves mostly in basal rosettes, obovate to oblanceolate, blunt-tipped, entire or slightly dentate or lobed; *stem-leaves 0–3.* Flowers 4–5 mm diam., in terminal racemes. *Petals white, narrowly obovate, notched*. Fruit a flattened, elliptical silicule, 5–7 mm long, hairy or glabrous; fruit-stalk erect.

Flowering: July–August.

Habitat: Grassland, screes, rocks, often on calcareous, gravelly or rocky soils; mainly in the mountains.

Range: (Sub-)Arctic N Europe (including Iceland and Spitsbergen), also on the Faeroes and in Scotland.

Similar species: **Bald White Whitlowgrass** (*D. fladnizensis* Wulfen) has hairless flowering stems, oblanceolate to elliptical, ciliate basal leaves, and 0 (2) stem-leaves. In Arctic N Europe and in the mountains of C Europe, from the Pyrenees to the Carpathians.

In the high Arctic a number of comparable, white-flowering species can be found; *see* the regional floras.

---

p.136 **Common Whitlowgrass**
Erophila verna (L.) Chevall.

Description: A rather hairy *annual*, with erect, glabrous or hairy, leafless flowering stems to 15 cm. *Leaves all in basal rosette*, obovate to oblanceolate, entire or with some blunt teeth; both *stellate and simple hairs* present. Flowers 3–5 mm diam., in elongating terminal raceme, often with wavy axis. *Petals 2–3 mm long, white, deeply bifid*. Fruit a *compressed, ellipsoid silicule, 4–7 mm long*, with numerous seeds; fruit-stalks long, obliquely rising or ascending.

Flowering: March–June.

Habitat: Bare ground, heaths, cereal fields, gardens, between paving bricks, on walls, cliffs and rocks, on dry to moist, oligotrophic to mesotrophic, preferably calcareous, sandy or stony soils; from sea level to 1,700 m.

Range: Most of Europe except the high Arctic.

Much like a small *Draba*, but differs in being annual (unlike comparable *Draba* species), and in having deeply incised petals.

p.140 **Hairy Rocket**
Erucastrum gallicum (Willd.) O.E. Schulz

Description: A hairy annual, with erect, more or less branched stems to 60 cm; *hairs on stem appressed, simple*. Leaves alternate, *stalked to subsessile*, lanceolate to ovate, pinnately divided, with 5–8 pairs of pinnately lobed segments. Flowers 10–15 mm diam., in elongating *terminal racemes, often with some pinnatifid bracts beneath*. Sepals *erect*, inner ones saccate; petals 7–8 mm long, *pale yellow or cream, with greenish veins*. Fruit a *rounded, linear siliqua to 45 mm long*, with *short, conical beak*; seeds in 1 row.

Flowering: May–October.

Habitat: Ruderal places, wasteland, road verges, along rivers, railways, on moist to dry, mesotrophic to eutrophic, loamy, clayey or stony soils; from sea level to 2,000 m.

Range: Continental SW and WC Europe, northwards to France, Germany and the Netherlands (Rhine valley!); naturalized in Britain and S Scandinavia.

Similar species: *E. nasturtiifolium* (Poiret) O.E. Schulz has bright-yellow flowers to 12 mm diam., and clasping stem-leaves; fruit-beak often contains a seed. In S and C Europe, northwards to N France, S Germany, Hungary; locally naturalized further to the north and east.

---

p.207 **Treacle Mustard** *Erysimum cheiranthoides* L.

Description: A hairy *annual* (rarely biennial), with quadrangular stems to 60 cm. Leaves alternate, elliptical to lanceolate, stalked to subsessile, hairy (with *trifid hairs*); lower ones often deeply dentate, *upper ones weakly dentate to subentire*. Flowers 5–6 mm diam., in elongating terminal racemes; flower-stalks at least as long as calyx. Sepals 2–4 mm long; *petals 3–6 mm long, yellow*, clawed, with rounded limb. Fruit a *linear, quadrangular, curved, ascending siliqua to 30 mm long*, on *short, spreading stalk* to 10 mm; seeds in 1 row.

Flowering: May–September.

Habitat: Arable land, field margins, road verges,
ruderal places, along rivers, on moist
mesotrophic to eutrophic, sandy or clayey
soils; from sea level to 1,700 m.

Range: Europe except Iceland and Spitsbergen.

Similar species: **Wallflower** (*E. cheiri* (L.) Crantz) is a
perennial and well-known ornamental,
with fragrant flowers, yellow or orange to
brown petals 15–25 mm long. Native to
SE Europe, and locally naturalized on cliffs
and old walls in W Europe.

E. odoratum Ehrh. also has fragrant flowers,
but is annual, with flower-stalks shorter than
calyx, and yellow petals 12–16 mm long. In
SE and C Europe, westwards to NE France.

E. hieracifolium L., from C Europe,
westwards to E France and W Germany, is
biennial or perennial, with dentate upper
leaves, yellow petals 8–10 mm long, and
straight, erect siliquas to 90 mm.

Other species occur in C and S Europe.

---

p.202 **Hoary Mustard**
Hirschfeldia incana (L.) Lagrèze-Fossat

Description: A hairy annual to 1 m, with *bristly-hairy
stems*, profusely branched in inflorescence.
Lower leaves stalked, oblanceolate, pinnately
divided with *c.* 5 pairs of rounded segments
and a large end-lobe; *stem-leaves much smaller,
lobed to entire*, narrowed into short stalk.
Flowers 6–8 mm diam., in elongating
racemes forming *large, widely branched panicle*.
Sepals erect, ovate, 3–4 mm long, glabrous
or hairy; petals 5–6 mm long, clawed, the
limb rounded, *pale yellow, often with violet
veins*. Fruit a *linear siliqua 8–17 mm long, erect,
appressed to stem*, with round, *inflated beak
(4–7 mm long) containing 1 or 2 seeds*, and
compressed, 2-locular *lower segment with 3–6
seeds in each locule* (in a single row); fruit-
valves have 1 vein along middle.

Flowering: May–October.

Habitat: Wasteland, road verges, dunes, ruderal
places, docks, on moist, eutrophic, sandy or
stony soils; mainly in the lowlands.

Range: Native to S Europe, northwards to SW France; locally naturalized further north, to Britain, the Low Countries and Denmark; a frequent casual in harbours and near flour-mills.

Compare Erucastrum (*see* p.587), with green-veined petals; *Coincya* (*see* p.580), with deep-yellow or reddish veins in petals, and 3-veined fruit-valves; and *Brassica nigra* (*see* p.567), with stems not bristly at base, and fruits with short beak to 3 mm.

p.137 **Hutchinsia** *Hornungia petraea* (L.) Reichenb.

Description: A subglabrous annual, with ascending to erect, purplish, finely pubescent stems to 15 cm. Leaves alternate (or partly in indistinct rosette), short-stalked to subsessile, pinnate, bright green, glabrous, with wide rhachis and *7–15 elliptical leaflets. Flowers 1–1.5 mm diam.*, in small, elongating terminal racemes. Sepals obovate, blunt-tipped, *often flushed with purple*; petals hardly equalling sepals, *to 1 mm long, obovate, white.* Fruit a *compressed, ellipsoid silicule to 2.5 mm long*, 1 mm wide, with *2 seeds in each locule.*

Flowering: March–May.

Habitat: Bare places, sunny slopes, rocks, on dry, oligotrophic, calcareous, sandy or stony soils; from sea level to 1,500 m.

Range: S and C Europe, extending northwards to Britain, Sweden, the Baltic States, and the Ukraine.

Similar species: *Hymenolobus procumbens* (L.) Nutt. ex Torrey & A. Gray has prostrate stems, stalked leaves with 3–7 leaflets, slightly larger flowers (to 3 mm diam.) with petals distinctly exceeding sepals, and translucent silicules with 4–8 seeds in each locule. On coasts of S Europe, also in Normandy, usually on saline soils, in saltmarshes, sea-dunes; also locally inland in C and E Europe, near saline pools, along roads and ditches, in arable fields, and on walls.

p.136 **Wild Candytuft** *Iberis amara* L.

Description: A subglabrous or hairy annual, with erect, scarcely branched stems to 30 cm. Leaves alternate; lower ones stalked, spatulate or oblanceolate, dentate or lobed, ciliate at base, upper leaves spatulate, *dentate to subentire*, sessile. Flowers 5–8 mm diam., in elongating, *umbel-shaped terminal racemes. Petals very unequal*, outer 2 much enlarged (especially in marginal flowers), white or mauve. Fruit a flattened, *rounded, winged silicule*, with shallow apical notch in wing.

Flowering: May–September.

Habitat: Cereal fields, wasteland, grassland, open woods, often in disturbed places, on dry, mesotrophic, calcareous, sandy, loamy or stony soils; mainly in mountainous or hilly regions.

Range: S and W Europe, northwards to England, Belgium, Germany; naturalized in NC and E Europe. (Extinct in the Netherlands.)

Plants from chalky slopes in Lorraine (NE France), with entire-margined, linear upper leaves, mauve petals, and smaller silicules (5–7 mm long) with a deeply notched wing, have been described as *I. violleti* Soyer-Will. ex Godr., but presumably only deserve subspecific rank.

p.207 **Woad** *Isatis tinctoria* L.

Description: A usually glabrous biennial, with much-branched stems to 1.2 m. Leaves alternate, glaucous or greyish-green, elliptical to lanceolate, *entire-margined*; basal ones stalked, cauline ones sessile, *clasping* stem with 2 subacute basal lobes. Flowers 3–4 mm diam., in elongating terminal *racemes forming large panicle*. Sepals narrow-ovate. Petals 2.5–4 mm long, yellow, oblanceolate. Fruit a *flat, elliptical to oblanceolate, pendulous, 1-seeded silicule*, yellowish-green, *turning dark brown to black* when ripe, not splitting.

Flowering: May–August.

| Habitat: | Wasteland, field margins, ruderal places, riversides, cliffs, on moist, mesotrophic, calcareous, often stony or rocky places; from sea level to 2,000 m. |
| Range: | Native to the steppes of SE Europe and W Asia; naturalized (as an archeophyte) in S, C and W Europe, northwards to England, the Netherlands, S Fennoscandia and N Russia, but rare in the north. |

Formerly cultivated for medical purposes and for the blue dye made from the foliage; Germanic tribes used it to prepare war-paint.

---

p.137 **Field Pepperwort**
Lepidium campestre (L.) R. Br.

Description:	A greyish, hairy annual or biennial, with erect stems, branched only upwards, to 50 cm. Basal leaves stalked, oblanceolate, lobed or dentate, withered at anthesis; stem-leaves alternate, lanceolate, dentate to subentire, sessile, *clasping* stem with 2 acute basal lobes. Flowers *c.* 2 mm diam., in strongly elongating terminal racemes. Sepals *c.* 1.5 mm long, ovate; petals scarcely exceeding sepals, white. *Anthers yellow.* Fruit a *gibbous, 2-locular, 2-seeded silicule*, with *broad, notched wing at top*, and covered with *vesicular hairs; style connate to wing* all along its length.
Flowering:	May–August (September).
Habitat:	Cultivated and waste land, roadsides, banks, ruderal places, along railways, on dry to moist, eutrophic, sandy, clayey or stony soils; from sea level to 2,300 m.
Range:	Most of Europe, except Arctic Russia; only naturalized in Iceland.
Similar species:	**Smith's Cress** (*L. heterophyllum* Bentham) is perennial, with ascending stems, violet anthers, and glabrous silicules; style has free part to 1 mm outside the wing. In comparable habitats of SW Europe, northwards to W France, Britain and Ireland; also in Denmark, Czechia, and (only naturalized) in the Low Countries, Germany and S Scandinavia.

p.137 **Dittander** *Lepidium latifolium* L.

Description: A glabrous *perennial*, with creeping stolons and erect stems to 1 m. Leaves elliptical to ovate; lower ones stalked, *to 30 cm long*, undivided (or occasionally pinnate), serrate, upper ones subsessile, narrowly ovate, *serrate to entire-margined*. Flowers *c.* 3 mm diam., in elongating terminal racemes forming *large panicle*. Sepals 1–1.5 mm long, suborbicular, hairy, with white margins; petals longer than sepals, white. Fruit a compressed, broadly ovoid, 2-locular, 2-seeded, *short-hairy silicule to 2 mm long, unwinged*, rounded or obscurely notched.

Flowering: June–August.

Habitat: Highest parts of saltmarshes, sea-walls, dunes, cliffs, riversides, also near saline pools in the steppe belt, on moist, often brackish, sandy or stony soils; mainly in the lowland.

Range: Most of Europe, northwards to Britain, S Sweden and the Baltic States.

Similar species: **Tall Pepperwort** (*L. graminifolium* L.) has narrower, spatulate to linear, mostly entire-margined upper leaves, long racemes in moderately branched panicles, and glabrous, slightly pointed silicules to 4 mm long. Along rivers, in ruderal places, in S and C Europe, northwards to C France, Germany and the Netherlands (Rhine valley), Hungary and Romania, and eastwards to the Crimea.

---

p.137 **Narrow-leaved Pepperwort** *Lepidium ruderale* L.

Description: A *short-hairy* annual or biennial, with *scarcely branched stems* to 40 cm. Basal leaves 1–2 times pinnately divided, with blunt, linear, entire or dentate segments, withered at anthesis; stem-leaves alternate, shortly stalked to subsessile (*not clasping*), *mostly undivided*, linear-oblanceolate. Flowers *c.* 2 mm diam., in elongating terminal racemes. Sepals narrowly ovate, short-hairy; *petals absent. Stamens 4, with yellow anthers.*

Fruit a compressed, obovoid, 2-locular, 2-seeded, *glabrous silicule to 3 mm long, unwinged*, shorter than stalk.

Flowering: May–September.

Habitat: Ruderal and waste places, roadsides, sea-walls, the highest parts of saltmarshes, also on walls and between paving bricks, on moist, eutrophic, nitrogenous or slightly brackish, sandy or stony soils; from sea level to 1,000 m.

Range: All Europe except Ireland.

Similar species: **Garden Cress** (*L. sativum* L.) is glabrous, and has narrowly winged fruits to 6 mm long, longer than stalk (racemes very narrow); (lower) stem-leaves pinnately divided with lanceolate, lobed or entire segments; petals present, twice as long as sepals, white or pink. In cultivated and waste land, and disturbed places; native to Egypt and W Asia, cultivated as a vegetable and frequently escaped or naturalized in much of Europe.

Several comparable species from N America or S Africa, all with small white petals hardly exceeding sepals, have naturalized in Europe, usually in ruderal places in harbours and urbane environments as has:

Perfoliate Pepperwort (*L. perfoliatum* L.) from SE Europe and W Asia; this species is easily recognized by its pale-yellow flowers to 1 mm, and finely dissected, 2–3 times pinnatifid lower stem-leaves, very dissimilar from the broadly ovate, entire-margined upper leaves fully clasping stem, with 2 overlapping basal lobes.

---

p.335 **Perennial Honesty** *Lunaria rediviva* L.

Description: A more or less hairy perennial, with branched, bristly-hairy stems to 1 (1.5) m. Leaves alternate, stalked, ovate to broadly lanceolate, pointed, dentate, the lower ones with cordate base to blade. Flowers 20–25 mm diam., in elongating terminal racemes. Sepals lanceolate, with sack at base, erect; petals pale blue-violet (rarely white). Fruit a flattened, elliptical silicule to 70 mm long, 20 mm wide, pointed at both ends, with 2 rows of seeds attached to whitish septum that persists after valves have fallen.

Flowering: May–July.

Habitat: Damp, deciduous woods, ravines, on moist, mesotrophic, mostly calcareous, sandy, loamy or stony soils; from 100–1,500 m.

Range: S and C Europe, westwards to Iberia and France, northwards to E Belgium, Germany, Denmark, S Sweden, Poland, and eastwards to C Russia.

Similar species: **Honesty** (*L. annua* l.) is a well-known, usually biennial ornamental, with flat, broadly elliptical, rounded silicules, and violet or white flowers. Native to SE Europe; locally naturalized in W and C Europe.

---

p.284 **Hoary Stock** *Matthiola incana* (L.) R. Br.

Description: A *densely white-tomentose* perennial, with branched, slightly lignified stems to 80 cm. Leaves alternate, *entire or weakly lobed*, stalked to subsessile. Flowers 20–30 (50) mm diam., in terminal racemes. Sepals lanceolate, erect; petals purple, pink or white, clawed, with obovate or obcordate limb. Fruit a short-stalked, *hairy siliqua to 12 (15) cm.*

Flowering: May–August.

Habitat: (Usually calcareous) sea-cliffs.

Range: S and W Europe, along Atlantic coast northwards to W France and S England.

Similar species: **Sea Stock** (*M. sinuata* (L.) R. Br.) has sinuously dentate or lobed, glandular-hairy lower leaves, always pink flowers, and glandular siliquas to 12 cm. In the same general area, on cliffs, dunes, and in sandy, ruderal places along the coast.

---

p.201 **Wild Radish** *Raphanus raphanistrum* L.

Description: A bristly-hairy annual or biennial, with widely branched stems to 1 m. Leaves alternate; lower ones pinnately divided with large, bluntly dentate end-lobe, upper leaves undivided. Flowers 15–30 mm diam., in elongating terminal racemes. Sepals lanceolate, erect, flushed with purple; petals *white, yellow or purplish, usually with dark-purplish veins*, clawed, with obovate to spatulate limb. Fruit a linear siliqua to 90 mm long, 6 mm wide, *constricted between the 3–8 seeds*, with hardening wall and long, tapering beak; fruit not splitting, but *breaking up into 1-seeded segments*.

Flowering: May–September.

Habitat: Cultivated places, wasteland, roadsides, ruderal places, on dry or moist, mesotrophic, sandy, loamy or stony soils; from sea level to 2,000 m.

Range: Most of Europe, but only naturalized in the extreme north.

Similar species: **Sea Radish** (ssp. *maritimus* (Sm.) Thell.) has a more or less thickened taproot, usually yellow flowers, and fruits to 8 mm thick, not easily breaking up. On sea-cliffs and dunes, along Atlantic coast northwards to N France and S Britain.
Garden Radish (*R. sativus* L.) has an edible, fleshy, strongly swollen tuber, and 6–12-seeded siliquas to 15 mm wide, with a spongy wall; frequently cultivated.

Compare Sinapis arvensis (see p.599), which has fruits splitting with 2 valves.

p.201 **Bastard Cabbage** *Rapistrum rugosum* (L.) all.

Description: A bristly-hairy annual to 90 cm, with profusely branched stems. Lower leaves pinnately divided or lobed (often with alternating segments), long-stalked; upper leaves undivided, ovate to lanceolate, *dentate, short-stalked*. Flowers 8–10 mm diam., in elongating terminal racemes forming large panicle. Sepals 2.5–4 mm long, broadly lanceolate, divergent; *petals pale yellow, c. twice as long as sepals, all equal. Fruit pear-shaped*, to 10 mm long, with sterile, smooth lower segment, and wider, ovoid, 1-seeded, warty top segment; style to 4 mm, slightly curved.

Flowering: May–October.

Habitat: Road verges, wasteland, ruderal places, on dry to moist, eutrophic, sandy or rocky soils; from sea level to 800 m.

Range: Native to S Europe; widely naturalized in W and C Europe, northwards to Britain, the Low Countries, Germany, Poland, and eastwards to C Russia.

Similar species: **Perennial Bastard Cabbage** (*Rapistrum perenne* (L.) All.) has subsessile upper leaves, yellow flowers 6–8 mm diam., and fruits with smooth-ribbed, globose top segment and short, conical style. In comparable habitats, in SE and C Europe, westwards to Germany; occasionally naturalized in Poland and W Europe.

Compare also Calepina irregularis (*see* p.570), with white flowers and sessile, clasping upper leaves.

---

p.204 **Great Yellowcress**
Rorippa amphibia (L.) Besser

Description: A glabrous perennial, with creeping stolons and erect, branched flowering stems to 80 (120) cm. Leaves alternate, *short-stalked to subsessile*, lanceolate, *dentate*, occasionally with comb-like margins. Flowers 5–6 mm diam., in elongating terminal racemes. Sepals ovate, to 3 mm long; *petals 4–6 mm long, bright yellow*. Fruit an *ovoid silicule, 3–6 mm long*, 2–3 mm wide, on long, *spreading or deflexed stalk*; style to 3 mm.

Flowering: May–August.

Habitat: Reedlands, marshes, watersides, along ditches, willow-coppices, on wet, mesotrophic to eutrophic, neutral or slightly acid, sandy, clayey or peaty soils; from sea level to 1,200 m.

Range: Most of Europe except Iceland and the high Arctic; rare in the south.

Similar species: **Austrian Yellowcress** (*R. austriaca* (Crantz) Besser) has clasping upper leaves, smaller flowers (petals 3–4 mm long), and subglobose silicules to 3 mm diam. From C and E Europe and SW Asia; naturalized in W Europe, in rather drier habitats, along rivers, road verges, and in ruderal places.

p.136 **Watercress**
Rorippa nasturtium-aquaticum (L.) Hayek

Description: A glabrous, usually aquatic perennial, with creeping or floating rhizomes and thick, ascending, *hollow flowering stems* to 30 (50) cm. *Leaves pinnate*, with short-stalked, blunt-ovate side-leaflets and a markedly larger, suborbicular to elliptical top-leaflet. Flowers 4–6 mm diam., in elongating terminal racemes. Sepals narrowly ovate to broadly lanceolate, *c.* 2 mm long, blunt-tipped; petals *c.* 5 mm long, *white*, with rounded limb. Fruit a linear, 2-locular siliqua, 13–18 mm long, with *2 rows of seeds in each locule*; seeds suborbicular, compressed, with reticulate wall, and 30–50 meshes on each side.

Flowering: May–October.

Habitat: Shallow waters, marshes, flushes, ditch- and streamsides, ponds, on permanently wet, mesotrophic to eutrophic, slightly acid, muddy soils, often with peat in the subsoil; from sea level to 2,000 m.

Range: In Europe northwards to Scotland, S Sweden and C Russia.

Similar species: **Brown Watercress** (*R. microphylla* (Boenn.) Hyl.) has seeds in 1 row, with over 100 meshes on each side. In comparable habitats of W Europe, from N Spain to the British Isles, the Low Countries and S Sweden.

Hybrids, with intermediate characters, are by no means rare, and are also cultivated as a vegetable (as is Watercress itself).

p.204 **Marsh Yellowcress**
Rorippa palustris (L.) Besser

Description: A subglabrous *annual* to 40 (60) cm, with erect, *hollow stems*; no runners or rooting stem-parts. Leaves alternate, pinnately divided; lower ones long-stalked, upper ones short-stalked to subsessile, with relatively *large terminal lobe*. Flowers 3–4 mm diam., in elongating terminal racemes. Sepals 1.6–3 mm long, broadly lanceolate; petals yellow, 1.5–3 mm long. Fruit a *short, slightly curved, cylindrical siliqua*, 4–8 (12) mm long, 1.5–2 (3) mm wide, *less than twice as long as fruit-stalk*; style to 1 mm.

Flowering: June–September.

Habitat: Marshy or seasonally flooded places, pond margins, reedlands, along streams and ditches, on wet, eutrophic, slightly acid to basic, sandy, loamy or peaty soils; from sea level to 2,300 m.

Range: Most of Europe, but less frequent in Mediterranean region.

Plants from the far north (and possibly the mountains of C Europe) with short fruit-stalks (2–4 mm, instead of 4–6 mm, hence siliquas 2–3 times as long as their stalk) belong to **Iceland Yellowcress** (*R. islandica* (Oeder ex Murray) Borbás).

---

p.204 **Creeping Yellowcress**
Rorippa sylvestris (L.) Besser

Description: A glabrous to slightly hairy perennial, with stolons and *prostrate to ascending, solid stems* to 30 (45) cm. Leaves alternate, stalked to subsessile, pinnately divided with oblanceolate, dentate segments and a relatively *small and narrow terminal lobe* (rather like lateral segments). Flowers 3–5 mm diam., in elongating terminal racemes. Sepals narrowly ovate, *c.* 2 mm long; petals 2–3 mm long, yellow. Fruit a *linear, cylindrical siliqua, 9–22 mm long, 1–1.2 mm wide*; style to 1 mm.

Flowering: June–September.

Habitat: Damp grassland, arable land, pathways, pond margins, along ditches, on moist or wet, often seasonally inundated, eutrophic, slightly acid to basic, sandy or loamy soils; from sea level to 2,000 m.

Range: Most of Europe, except the high Arctic; only naturalized in Iceland.

This species forms fertile hybrids with *R. amphibia* (*R.* × *anceps* (Wahlenb.) Reichenb.), which has a large terminal lobe to leaves, partly deflexed fruit-stalks, and short and thick siliquas with a style to 3 mm.

p.201 **Charlock** *Sinapis arvensis* L.

Description: A bristly-hairy annual, with erect, branched stems to 80 cm. Leaves stalked, pinnately divided *only near base*, with very large, elliptical terminal lobe, *dark green*; upper leaves usually undivided, subsessile, ovate to lanceolate, dentate. Flowers 15–20 mm diam., in elongating terminal racemes. Sepals lanceolate, spreading; petals yellow. Fruit a *linear, beaded siliqua, 25–45 mm long*, glabrous or hairy, with *3-veined valves* and *long, rounded beak*; seeds 8–13 in 1 row.

Flowering: April–October.

Habitat: Cultivated and waste land, roadsides, banks, on dry to moist, (very) eutrophic, preferably calcareous, sandy, clayey or stony soils; from sea level to 1,700 m.

Range: Native to Mediterranean region, but naturalized in all of Europe except Spitsbergen and Iceland.

Similar species: **White Mustard** (*S. alba* L.), from the Mediterranean area and the Crimea, has stalked, pinnatifid leaves with 2–3 pairs of side-lobes and a rather small, ovate terminal lobe, slightly larger, yellow flowers, and hairy fruits (20–40 mm long) with 4–8 seeds and strongly compressed beak. Often cultivated for the mustard seed, and naturalized in much of Europe.

Compare Raphanus raphanistrum (*see* p.594), which has non-splitting (but fragmenting) fruits.

p.203 **Tall Rocket** *Sisymbrium altissimum* L.

Description: A bristly-hairy biennial or short-lived perennial, with erect, branched stems to 90 cm (often glabrescent and glaucous above); *branches obliquely rising*. Lower leaves hairy, pinnately divided with *lanceolate, dentate or lobed segments*; upper leaves sessile, with *2–5 pairs of linear segments*. Flowers 10–12 mm diam., in elongating terminal racemes forming large panicle. Sepals lanceolate, *spreading*, outer pair with *short horn* under the top; *petals 5–8 (10) mm long*, pale yellow. Fruit a *linear, ascending siliqua, 5–10 cm long*, in line with the *thick stalk* (5–15 mm long); seeds in 1 row.

Flowering: May–August.

Habitat: Ruderal and waste places, industrial areas, docks, roadsides, along railways, also in coastal dunes, on dry, oligotrophic or mesotrophic, preferably calcareous, sandy or stony soils; mainly in the lowland.

Range: Native to C and E Europe, northwards to Germany, Poland and C Russia; naturalized elsewhere in Europe except Ireland.

Similar species: **Eastern Rocket** (*S. orientale* L.) has short-stalked, undivided, oblanceolate, subentire upper leaves (occasionally with 1 pair of narrow segments near base), and slightly larger flowers; stem and leaves have soft hairs to 1 mm (not bristles to 3 mm), and the (erect) sepals bear no small horns. Native to Mediterranean region, and naturalized in ruderal places of W, N and C Europe, eastwards to W and SE Russia. *S. strictissimum* L. is a hairy perennial with stout, creeping rhizomes, and erect stems to 1.5 m; all leaves undivided, lanceolate, dentate-serrate, pubescent beneath, the upper ones subsessile; flowers 4–6 mm diam., with bright-yellow petals 6–8 mm long; siliquas 30–60 (80) mm long, on thin, spreading stalk, and with 3-veined valves. In road verges, ravines and on cliffs, in the hills and mountains of C Europe (to 1,500 m), westwards to C France, northwards to C Germany and Poland, and eastwards to C Russia; locally naturalized in ruderal places of W Europe. *S. supinum* L. is a hairy annual, with ascending to erect stems to 35 cm; leaves oblanceolate, pinnately divided or lobed, stalked to subsessile. Flowers 3 mm diam., in terminal racemes with some bracts at base. Petals white, 3–4 mm long; siliquas short-stalked, rounded, linear, 10–30 mm long, to 2 mm wide, with seeds in 2 rows (in each locule). On riverbanks and in ruderal places, on calcareous soils in N France, S Sweden (Öland, Gotland), Latvia and Estonia; extinct in Germany and the Low Countries. The only white-flowered

Sisymbrium in the area. *Compare* for this species *Cardaminopsis* (*see* p.577), with branched (instead of simple) hairs, and compressed siliquas with seeds in 1 row.

p.203 **Hedge Mustard**
Sisymbrium officinale (L.) Scop.

Description: A short-hairy annual with erect stems to 80 cm, and *spreading, horizontal branches*. Lower leaves pinnately divided, with 2–3 pairs of dentate side-lobes and a *larger, hastate terminal lobe*; upper leaves usually undivided, short-stalked, hastate, often subentire. Flowers 3–5 mm diam., in strongly elongating terminal racemes, making a wiry impression in fruit. Sepals erect, narrowly elliptical, 1.5–2 mm long, blunt-tipped, usually hairy. Petals 2–4 mm long, spatulate, pale yellow. Fruit a short-hairy or glabrous, *tapering siliqua, 10–20 mm long*, erect, *appressed to stem*, on a short stalk (2–3 mm); valves 3-veined; seeds in 1 row.

Flowering: May–September.

Habitat: A very common species of waste and ruderal places, roadsides, field margins, hedgerows, on dry to moist, eutrophic, sandy, clayey or stony soils; mainly in the lowland.

Range: Most of Europe except the Arctic; only naturalized in Iceland.

p.139 **Awlwort** *Subularia aquatica* L.

Description: A *tiny, aquatic annual* to 12 cm, with simple flowering stalks. Leaves all basal, *30–70 mm long, linear, tapering, entire*, fleshy, often triangular in cross-section. Flowers 2–2.5 mm diam., in lax, few-flowered terminal raceme. Sepals 1–1.5 mm long, ovate; *petals white, up to 2 mm long, often smaller*, occasionally rudimentary or absent. Fruit an *ovoid, 2-locular silicule, 3–5 mm long*, with several seeds.

Flowering: June–September.

Habitat: Shallow base-poor water, pool and lake margins, on muddy, sandy or gravelly

soils; mainly in the mountains
(900–2,200 m), but descending to the
lowland in the north.

Range: From N Europe (including Iceland, but
except Spitsbergen) southwards to the
British Isles, Belgium (not the
Netherlands), the Vosges, Germany,
Denmark, the Baltic States, C Russia, and
the Urals; also in the Pyrenees.

A rare and declining species.

---

p.132 **Shepherd's Cress**
Teesdalia nudicaulis (L.) R. Br.

Description: A usually glabrous annual, with ascending
to erect, simple flowering stems to 20 cm.
Leaves all in basal rosette, stalked,
oblanceolate, *pinnately divided or lobed, with
ovate segments* and blunt terminal lobe.
Flowers *c.* 2 mm diam., in elongating
terminal raceme. Sepals ovate, *c.* 1 mm
long, spreading; *petals white, unequal*, outer
ones 1.5 mm long, inner ones just
equalling sepals. Fruit a *compressed, obovate or
obcordate, 4-seeded silicule, 3–4 mm long*, with
notched wing at top; style very short.

Flowering: April–June (autumn).

Habitat: Bare and grassy places, dunes, heaths, rye-
fields, pathways, on dry, oligotrophic, acid,
sandy or gravelly soils; from sea level to
800 m.

Range: W, N and C Europe, northwards to S
Scandinavia, the Baltic States and C Russia;
rare in Mediterranean area.

Compare Capsella (*see* p.572), which has
equal petals.

---

p.138 **Field Pennycress** *Thlaspi arvense* L.

Description: A glabrous, *yellowish-green annual*, with
scarcely branched, erect, *angular stems* to
50 cm. *Leaves all cauline*, alternate,
lanceolate, sinuously dentate (to
subentire), *clasping stem with 2 acute basal
lobes*. Flowers 4–6 mm diam., in

elongating terminal raceme. Sepals narrowly ovate, more or less erect; petals white, 3–4 mm long. Fruit a *compressed, elliptical silicule, 7–12 (15) mm long, with 10–16 seeds*, and with *broad, deeply notched wing* becoming 2.5–4 mm wide at top; style in notch very short (*c.* 0.2 mm).

Flowering: May–September.

Habitat: Cultivated and waste land, roadsides, along ditches, ruderal and disturbed places, on moist, eutrophic, basic, often loamy or clayey soils; from sea level to 2,000 m.

Range: Most of Europe except the far north.

p.138 **Perfoliate Pennycress** *Thlaspi perfoliatum* L.

Description: A glabrous, *glaucous* (hibernating) *annual* with simple, erect, *rounded flowering stems* to 25 cm. *Leaves in basal rosette* stalked, spatulate, often toothed or shallow-lobed; stem-leaves sessile, cordate, *clasping stem with rounded, appressed basal lobes*, dentate to subentire. Flowers 3–4 mm diam., in strongly elongating terminal raceme. Sepals narrowly obovate, erect; petals 2–3 mm long, white. Anthers yellow. Fruit a *compressed, elliptical silicule, 4–5 mm long, with 6–8 seeds*, and a *narrow, notched wing* becoming *c.* 1 mm wide near top; style in notch very short (*c.* 0.2 mm).

Flowering: March–May.

Habitat: Short grassland, cultivated ground, roadsides, riverbanks, along railways, on dry to moist, oligotrophic, calcareous, loamy or stony soils; from sea level to 1,600 m.

Range: In Europe northwards to England, the Low Countries, C Sweden, and N Russia.

Similar species: **Mountain Pennycress** (*T. montanum* L.) is a green, mat-forming perennial, with many sterile leaf-rosettes; basal leaves long-stalked, ovate, entire-margined, stem-leaves few (1–3) sessile, cordate, entire or denticulate; petals white, 3–5 mm long; silicules broadly winged, 2–4-seeded, to 7 mm long, with style of at least 1 mm. In calcareous grassland and on rocks in the mountains of C

Europe, locally extending westwards to Normandy, northwards to SE Belgium and Czechia, and eastwards to Yugoslavia.

Alpine Pennycress (*T. caerulescens* J. & C. Presl) is a glaucous perennial (also with sterile rosettes), with entire basal leaves, several sessile, cordate stem-leaves, white or purplish petals (5–7 mm long), purple anthers, and narrowly winged, 8–12-seeded silicules to 9 mm, again with style of at least 1 mm. On acid, sandy or stony soils in the mountains of SW and C Europe, often on ore-mine heaps, eastwards to Poland and Yugoslavia. Ssp. *T. c. calaminare* (Lej.) Dvořáková has 2–4-seeded silicules, and grows in grassland on zinc-bearing soils in W Germany, E Belgium and the SE Netherlands.

Several other, local forms have been given specific status; *see* regional floras.

GOURD FAMILY, CUCURBITACEAE

A family of climbing herbs (rarely shrubs), usually with tendrils, with *c.* 700 species in 90 genera, primarily in tropical and warm-temperate regions. Dicots. Leaves alternate, simple or compound, often palmately divided. Flowers regular, mostly unisexual, basically 5-merous (rarely 3-merous or 6-merous). Calyx 5-toothed. Petals 5, often partly connate. Stamens normally 5, the anthers connate (collectively, or in pairs leaving 1 free). Ovary inferior, 3-locular (rarely 1–2-locular). Style 1, often with 3 forked stigmas (rarely 3 separate styles, or no style at all). Fruit a berry or a capsule, often many-seeded, occasionally very large (as in melons, watermelons, pumpkins, gourds, cucumbers, gherkins, all cultivated for the edible fruits).

---

p.118   **White Bryony** *Bryonia cretica* L.

Description: A bristly-hairy perennial with tuberous rhizome, *climbing or straggling stems to 4 m*, and *long, unbranched tendrils* at nodes. Leaves alternate, palmately (3) 5-lobed, the terminal lobe slightly larger than lateral ones. Flowers in small, *stalked, axillary racemes, dioecious*; female flowers 10–14 mm, male flowers 12–18 mm diam. Calyx 5-toothed. Petals 5, connate at base, spreading, obovate, rounded, *white with greenish veins*. Stamens 5, connate in pairs, leaving 1 free. Ovary inferior, *distinctly separated from rest of flower*, globose, 3-locular, with 1 style and 3-lobed stigma. Fruit a rounded berry, 6–10 mm diam., *red when ripe*.

Flowering: May–September.

Habitat: Hedgerows, scrub, wood margins, also in road verges, dunes and ruderal places, on dry, oligotrophic to eutrophic, calcareous soils; from sea level to 1,400 m.

Range: S, SC and W Europe, northwards to S Britain, the Low Countries, Germany, Hungary, and Yugoslavia; naturalized in Ireland, Denmark and Scandinavia. The description above pertains to ssp. *dioica* (Jacq.) Tutin, which occurs almost throughout the range of the species; other subspecies are restricted to Mediterranean area.

Similar species: *B. alba* L. has leaves with large terminal lobe, male and female flowers on same plant (monoecious), and berries 7–8 mm diam., ripening black. In E and C Europe, naturalized in France, Belgium and Germany.

Both species have in the past found medical applications; they are dangerously poisonous!

DIAPENSIA FAMILY, DIAPENSIACEAE

A curious family of herbs or small shrubs, constituting an order on its own, and containing 20 species in 7 genera in cold and temperate regions of the northern hemisphere. Its closest relatives are found in Pyrolaceae and Ericaceae. Dicots. Leaves alternate, simple. Flowers solitary, or in racemes or flowerheads, regular, hermaphrodite, 5-merous. Sepals and petals connate at least at their base. Fertile stamens 5, alternating with corolla lobes, inserted on corolla tube; occasionally, 5 sterile staminodes are present. Ovary superior, 3-locular, with 1 style. Fruit a capsule.

p.104 **Diapensia** *Diapensia lapponica* L.

Description: An *evergreen, cushion-forming dwarf-shrub* to
50 mm. Leaves alternate, *crowded*, to 10 mm
long, elliptical, blunt-tipped, *leathery*,
glabrous, shiny dark green. Flowers
12–16 mm diam., solitary, stalked, scarcely
lifted over leaf-cushion, with *epicalyx* of 2
small, broadly lanceolate bracts at base.
Sepals 5, oblanceolate, with rounded tip,
reddish (at least in fruit); *petals 5, white,
connate at base*, the free part rounded. Stamens
5. Ovary 3-locular, ovoid, with 1 long style
and a 3-lobed stigma. Fruit a many-seeded
capsule, splitting with 3 valves.

Flowering: May–July.

Habitat: Tundra and stony soils in the mountains;
from sea level to 1,600 m.

Range: Iceland, Fennoscandia and N Russia;
1 station in W Scotland.

YAM FAMILY, DIOSCOREACEAE

A family of usually climbing herbs with winding stems and
tuberous rhizomes, and containing *c.* 630 species in 6
genera, mainly in the tropics; several species are cultivated
for the starchy tubers. Monocots. Leaves alternate
(occasionally opposite), mostly cordate or hastate, with
reticulate veins. Flowers in spikes, racemes or panicles,
regular, usually unisexual. Perianth 6-parted, often connate
at base. Stamens 6. Ovary inferior, 3-locular, with 3 styles or
1 style with 3 stigmas; 2 ovules per locule. Fruit a berry or a
3-locular capsule, with 6 seeds.

p.67 **Black Bryony** *Tamus communis* L.

Description: A climbing, glabrous perennial with large
tuber, and winding stems to 3 m. Leaves
alternate, stalked, cordate, (3) 6–10 (16) cm
long, shiny green, with 5–7 strongly arched,
reticulately interconnected main veins.
Flowers 4–5 mm diam., in axillary racemes
(female ones few-flowered). Perianth regular,
with 6 greenish-yellow tepals connate at
base. Stamens 5. Ovary 3-locular, with 1
style and 3 stigmas. Fruit a rounded berry
to 12 mm diam., red when ripe.

Flowering: May–August.

Habitat: Deciduous woods (often Beech), mixed forests, wood margins, hedgerows, fences, on dry to moist, oligotrophic, calcareous, sandy, loamy or stony soils; from sea level to 1,300 m.

Range: Mainly in S Europe, extending northwards to N England, Belgium, S Germany, Hungary, Romania, and the Crimea.

The plant and the berries are highly poisonous.

TEASEL FAMILY, DIPSACACEAE

A family of herbs (rarely half-shrubs), with *c.* 350 species in 11 genera, in the Old World. Dicots. Leaves opposite (rarely whorled), simple or dissected. Flowers normally implanted on a common receptacle, in flowerheads with a common involucre of bracts. Individual flowers usually hermaphrodite, often with a bracteole, and always with a membranous epicalyx at base, apart from the normal calyx which is often reduced to bristles, or a 4–5-lobed to straight, membranous rim; corolla mostly irregular, 2–5-lobed, with long tube. Stamens 2 or 4, inserted on corolla tube. Ovary inferior (in relation to normal calyx and corolla), 1-locular, with 1 ovule; style 1, with 1 stigma. Fruit a small, 1-seeded nut (achene).

p.320 **Wild Teasel** *Dipsacus fullonum* L.

Description: A *prickly biennial*, with erect, symmetrically branched, stems to 2 m. Leaves opposite, *connate around stem*, up to 40 cm long, lanceolate, with prickles on midvein beneath, entire or dentate; large basal rosette present in 1st year. Flowerheads terminal, large (*to 90 mm long*), *ovoid or cylindrical*, with involucre of stiff, *ascending, linear, prickly-dentate bracts*, partly equalling head; flowering starts from the middle. Each individual flower has lanceolate bracteole bearing long, recurving awn. Epicalyx cup-shaped, with 4-lobed rim. Normal calyx short, membranous, not lobed, ciliate. Corolla tube-shaped, 9–12 mm long, with 4 small, unequal, rounded lobes, *pale lilac* (rarely white). Stamens 4. Fruit a quadrangular, ovoid, truncate, appressed-hairy achene to 5 mm long.

Flowering: July–September.

Habitat: Rough grassland, road verges, damp woods, ditch- and riversides, grassy banks, on moist, mesotrophic to eutrophic, calcareous, often clayey or loamy soils; from sea level to 1,000 m.

Range: S, W and C Europe, northwards to the British Isles, the Low Countries, N Germany, Hungary, Romania, and C Russia; naturalized in Denmark.

Similar species: *D. laciniatus* L. has short, spreading, linear-lanceolate involucral bracts, pinnately divided stem-leaves, and pale-pink flowers. In C Europe, westwards to C France, northwards to N Germany, Poland, and W and SE Russia, in meadows, roadsides, waste places, wood margins, along streams, mainly in the lowland.

Fuller's Teasel ssp. *D. f. sativus* (L.) Thellung also has short, spreading involucral bracts; achenes 3–4 mm long. Formerly cultivated for the fruiting heads, which were used for carding wool; naturalized in many parts of Europe.

---

p.171 **Small Teasel** *Dipsacus pilosus* L.

Description: A *bristly-hairy, sparsely prickly biennial*, with symmetrically branched stems to 1.2 m. Basal leaves stalked, ovate, serrate-dentate, withered at anthesis; *stem-leaves short-stalked*, ovate to lanceolate, dentate, upper ones with *pair of narrow side-lobes* at base. Flowerheads terminal, subglobose, to 25 mm long, with ovate, long-pointed bracteoles (10–12 mm long) between flowers; involucral bracts lanceolate, spreading or recurved, much shorter than head and hardly exceeding bracteoles, with white bristle-hairs. Epicalyx cup-shaped, with 4-lobed rim. Normal calyx membranous, ciliate, not lobed. Corolla tubular, with 4 unequal lobes, *pale yellow or white*. Stamens 4. Fruit an angular, ovoid, truncate achene.

Flowering: July–September.

Habitat: Wood margins, damp scrub, along streams, on moist, oligotrophic to mesotrophic, calcareous, loamy or stony soils; from sea level to 1,100 m.

Range: W and C Europe, northwards to S Britain, the Low Countries, Denmark, Poland, and C and SE Russia.

Similar species: *D. strigosus* Willd., from W, C and SE Russia and the Ukraine, grows taller (to 2 m), and has globose flowerheads 25–40 mm long, less hairy involucral bracts, pale-yellow flowers, and interfloral bracteoles 15–20 mm long. Naturalized in Britain, Denmark, S Sweden, Poland, and Slovakia.

---

p.320 **Field Scabious** *Knautia arvensis* L.

Description: A hairy perennial, with symmetrically branched stems to 60 cm; stolons often present, but creeping rhizome absent. Some leaves in basal rosette, long-stalked, elliptical, usually entire-margined; stem-leaves opposite, sessile, *pinnately divided* with narrow, entire segments, the bracts in inflorescence undivided, dentate. Flowerheads terminal, hemispherical, 20–40 mm diam., with common involucre of spreading, (broadly) lanceolate bracts subequalling flowers; *no bracteoles between flowers, but hairs on receptacle*. Epicalyx tetrangular, with 4 short teeth. Normal calyx cup-shaped, with 8 *lanceolate, ciliate teeth*, persistent on fruit. Corolla tubular, with *4 unequal lobes (lobes of marginal flowers much enlarged)*, lilac, occasionally white (rarely yellow). Stamens 4. Fruit a truncate, hairy achene, 5–6 mm long, 2–2.5 mm wide.

Flowering: June–September.

Habitat: Meadows, pasture, road verges, wood margins, grassy banks, on moist, oligotrophic to mesotrophic, preferably calcareous, sandy, loamy or clayey soils; from sea level to 1,900 m.

Range: Most of Europe except parts of the Mediterranean area and the high Arctic; only naturalized in Iceland.

Similar species: **Wood Scabious** (*K. dipsacifolia* Kreutzer) grows taller (to 1.5 m), and has creeping rhizome, no distinct basal rosette, and all leaves undivided, broadly lanceolate, dentate. In open woods, scrub, wood margins, along streams, on moist, oligotrophic, acid, sandy or stony soils, in the mountains of C Europe, westwards to C France, and northwards to the Ardennes, C Germany, Poland and W Russia; 400–2,000 m.

p.320 **Small Scabious** *Scabiosa columbaria* L.

Description: A greyish-green, hairy perennial, with symmetrically branched stems to 90 cm. Basal leaves long-stalked, lanceolate, pinnately divided; stem-leaves few (2–3 pairs), opposite, subsessile, *pinnately divided or pinnate*, with lanceolate segments. Flowerheads terminal, hemispherical, 20–40 mm diam., with common involucre of several lanceolate bracts subequalling flowers; *bracteoles between flowers present*, membranous, *much smaller than flowers*. Epicalyx cup-shaped, *8-ribbed, with widening, membranous rim to 1.5 mm long*. Normal calyx has *5 long-awned teeth*, 3–6 mm long, persistent on fruit (but occasionally absent). Corolla lilac, tubular, with *5 unequal lobes (those of marginal flowers slightly enlarged)*. Fruit a truncate, hairy achene to 3 mm long, with 8 furrows.

Flowering: July–September.

Habitat: Grassland, road verges, on dry to moist, oligotrophic, calcareous, sandy, loamy or stony soils; from sea level to 2,000 m.

Range: In Europe north to S Scotland, S Sweden and Estonia, and east to C and E Russia.

Similar species: *S. pratensis* Jord. is green, with stem-leaves (3–5 pairs) almost doubly pinnatifid, while basal leaves often undivided, lanceolate, crenate-dentate. In W Europe, in dry calcareous grassland; often treated on the subspecies level.

S. canescens Waldst. & Kit. always has un-divided, entire-margined, grey-downy basal leaves, smaller, pale-blue or lilac flowerheads (15–25 mm diam.), with much enlarged marginal flowers (at least twice as long as central ones). In dry calcareous grassland, in C Europe, northwards to S Sweden.

p.240 **Yellow Scabious** *Scabiosa ochroleuca* L.

Description: A hairy *annual or biennial*, with symmetrically branched stems to 60 cm. Basal leaves *pinnately lobed or dentate*; stem-leaves opposite, usually pinnatifid, with narrow segments. Flowerheads terminal, hemispherical, (15) 20–25 mm diam., with common involucre of several lanceolate bracts; *bracteoles present, much smaller than flowers*. Epicalyx cup-shaped, with membranous rim to 1.5 mm long. Normal calyx with 5 long-awned teeth. *Corolla pale yellow*, tubular, with 5 unequal lobes (those of marginal flowers enlarged). Fruit a slightly hairy achene to 3 mm long.

Flowering: July–September.

Habitat: Grassland, roadsides, wasteland, ruderal places, along railways, on dry, oligotrophic, sandy or stony soils; from sea level to 1,000 m.

Range: E and C Europe, extending westwards to S Germany and C France, and northwards to C Russia.

---

p.320 **Devil's-bit Scabious**
Succisa pratensis Moench

Description: A hairy perennial, with *creeping, truncate rhizome*, and symmetrically branched stems to 60 (90) cm. *Leaves all undivided*, elliptical to lanceolate; basal ones long-stalked, subentire, cauline ones narrower, short-stalked to subsessile, often shortly dentate. Flowerheads terminal, hemispherical to subglobose, with common involucre of several lanceolate, hairy bracts; hermaphrodite heads to 30 mm diam., all-female heads smaller; *bracteoles present, at least equalling corolla tube*, lanceolate, acute. Epicalyx tetragonal, with 8 furrows and 4 short, green (herbaceous) teeth. Normal calyx cup-shaped, with 5 (rarely 4) long-awned teeth. Corolla tubular, with 4 (rarely 5) unequal lobes (those of marginal flowers not enlarged). Fruit a hairy achene to 5 mm long.

Flowering: July–September.
Habitat: Meadows, marshes, road verges, wood margins, on moist to wet, oligotrophic, usually acid, sandy, stony or peaty soils; from sea level to 2,400 m.
Range: All Europe except Spitsbergen and many Mediterranean islands.

SUNDEW FAMILY, DROSERACEAE

A cosmopolitan family of herbs (rarely half-shrubs) with 83 species in 4 genera. Dicots. Leaves simple, and capable of catching insects, either by means of stalked, sticky glands (in *Drosera* and *Drosophyllum*), or by leaves closing around victim (in *Dionaea* and *Aldrovanda*, the latter aquatic). In *Drosera* and *Dionaea* leaves are in a basal rosette; in *Drosophyllum* leaves are alternate; in *Aldrovanda* leaves are whorled. Flowers regular, hermaphrodite, basically 5-merous. Sepals and petals 4–8, but usually 5. Stamens 4–20, but usually 5. Ovary superior, 1-locular, with 3–5 styles. Fruit a capsule.

p.141 Round-leaved Sundew
Drosera rotundifolia L.

Description: A small perennial with basal leaf-rosette and erect flowering stems to 30 cm. Basal leaves long-stalked, blade *suborbicular*, to 10 mm diam., with *numerous stalked, sticky glands* on upper face and along margin. Flowers *c.* 5 mm diam., regular, in terminal, recurved (later erect), spike-like raceme. Sepals 5, elliptical, with rounded top. Petals 5, obovate, white. Ovary 1-locular, with 3 (5) bifid styles. Fruit a smooth, ovoid capsule, opening with 3 valves, and with numerous tiny, winged seeds.
Flowering: June–August.
Habitat: Heaths, reedmarshes, bogs, on wet, oligotrophic (to dystrophic), acid, peaty soils, usually covered with *Sphagnum* mosses; from sea level to 2,000 m.
Range: All Europe except Spitsbergen and parts of Mediterranean area.
Similar species: **Great Sundew** (*D. longifolia* L.) has oblanceolate leaf-blades (2–30 mm long, to

5 mm wide), gradually narrowed into stalk. In oligotrophic bogs and slightly richer fens (to 1,900 m), in N and C Europe, westwards to Britain, and eastwards to the Urals. The hybrid with Round-leaved Sundew (*D.* × *obovata* M. & K.) has obovate leaf-blades and is sterile.

Oblong-leaved Sundew (*D. intermedia* Hayne) has ascending flowering stems to 10 cm, elliptical leaf-blades to 10 mm long, 3–4 mm wide, grooved capsules, and unwinged seeds. In wet, oligotrophic heaths and bogs (to 1,900 m) in N, W and C Europe, eastwards to C Russia.

Insects are trapped on the sticky glands, and gradually enveloped by adjacent glands bending towards the prey. Digestion is then accomplished by proteolytic enzymes. This feeding mechanism enables the plant to live in habitats that are extremely poor in nutrients.

WATERWORT FAMILY, ELATINACEAE

A family of more or less aquatic herbs or half-shrubs with *c.* 33 species in 2 genera. Dicots. Leaves opposite (whorled in *Elatine alsinastrum*); stipules present. Flowers hermaphrodite, regular or irregular, solitary in leaf-axils or in small cymes. Sepals 3–5, free or connate only at base. Petals 3–5, free. Stamens twice the number of petals. Ovary superior, 3–5-locular, with 3–5 styles. Fruit a subglobose, many-seeded capsule.

---

p.275 **Eight-stamened Waterwort**
Elatine hydropiper L.

Description: A tiny, glabrous, amphibious *annual*, with branched, *creeping, transparent stems* to 15 cm. Leaves opposite, short-stalked, elliptical to oblanceolate. Flowers *c.* 3 mm diam., solitary, *sessile in leaf-axils*, in submerged plants not opening. *Sepals 4*, ovate, pointed; *petals 4*, ovate, at least equalling sepals, pinkish. *Stamens 8*. Ovary 4-locular, with *4 styles*. Fruit a many-seeded capsule, splitting with 4 valves.

Flowering: June–September.

Habitat: Shallow, stagnant water or bare mud at margins of pools, lakes, streams and rivers, on sandy or clayey soils; mainly in the lowland.

Range: C and N Europe, except Iceland and the high Arctic.

Similar species: **Three-stamened Waterwort** (*E. triandra* Schkuhr) has 3-merous flowers, with 3 sepals, petals, stamens and styles. In comparable habitats, in C, N and E Europe. **Six-stamened Waterwort** (*E. hexandra* (Lapierre) DC.) also has 3-merous flowers, but with 6 stamens; flowers stalked (stalk to 9 mm, but often very short in terrestrial forms), and leaves narrowly obovate. In comparable habitats, in C and W Europe, northwards to S Sweden. **Whorled Waterwort** (*E. alsinastrum* L.) is a glabrous aquatic perennial, with erect, emergent stems to 80 cm, and sessile, whorled leaves; submerged stem-parts with linear leaves to 50 mm, in whorls of 8–10; aerial shoots with ovate leaves to 12 mm, in whorls of 3 (5); flowers (8-stamened), axillary, sessile or short-stalked, *c.* 3 mm diam., greenish-white. In shallow water of pools, marshes and ditches, on sandy or clayey soils in most of Europe, northwards to N France, Germany, Poland, SW Finland, and N Russia, from sea level to 1,600 m; in habit, somewhat reminiscent of *Hippuris*, which is otherwise very different in having apetalous flowers with 1 style and 1 stamen.

All species are declining, due to draining and eutrophication.

CROWBERRY FAMILY, EMPETRACEAE

A family of evergreen shrubs, with 4–6 species in 3 genera, in the northern hemisphere and in the S Andes. Dicots. Leaves alternate to seemingly whorled, small, leathery. Flowers regular, 2–3-merous, with 4–6 free perianth parts in 2 whorls. Stamens 2–4 (usually 3). Ovary superior, 2–9-locular, with 1 ovule per locule; 1 style with as many stigmas as there are locules. Fruit a 2–9-seeded drupe.

p.308 **Crowberry** *Empetrum nigrum* L.

Description: A small, *mat-forming shrub* to 30 (50) cm, with creeping stems and ascending branches. Leaves narrowly elliptical or almost linear, to 7 mm long, the *margins rolled under* and leaving only a narrow opening between them. Flowers to 2 mm diam., solitary in leaf-axils, *dioecious*. Sepals and petals 3, much alike, pink or purple. Stamens 3, long exserted. Ovary 6–9-locular. Fruit a 6–9-seeded drupe, shiny black when ripe.

Flowering: April–June.

Habitat: Heaths, dune-valleys, coniferous woods, bogs, tundra, on moist to dry, oligotrophic, acid, sandy, stony or peaty soils; from sea level to 3,000 m.

Range: N, W and C Europe, but only on mountains in the south.

Similar species: **Mountain Crowberry** (ssp. *hermaphroditum* (Hagerup) Böcher, also treated on the species level) has spreading (not rooting) stems, and hermaphrodite flowers. In bogs in N Europe, and in mountainous areas further south.

JOINT PINE FAMILY, EPHEDRACEAE

A family of shrubs containing only the genus *Ephedra*, with *c.* 35 species in tropical to warm-temperate regions of Eurasia and the Americas. Green branches and opposite, rudimentary, connate, scale-like leaves. Though the seedling has 2 seed-lobes, the group does not belong to the dicots; in fact, it is related to the conifers. Flowers unisexual, and collected in short-stalked cones (male ones with several flowers, female ones with only 1–3), axillary to scale-leaves, or terminal. Male flowers have 2 small bracteoles, and a columnar androphore with 2–8 stamen-like microsporophylls each bearing 2–3 anthers. Female flowers have tubular, perianth-like aril and a naked ovule not enclosed in a carpel. The aril and the scales of the cone become fleshy or hardened in fruit.

p.83 **Joint Pine** *Ephedra distachya* L.

Description: *See also* the family description. A small, densely branched, broom-like shrub to 50 cm, with erect, rigid, often glaucous or greyish-green branches to 2 mm thick;

internodes 30–40 mm long; leaves rudimentary. Flowers small, greenish-yellow, in stalked or subsessile, axillary cones, dioecious; male cones 8–16-flowered, each flower with 6–8 anthers on androphore; female cones 2-flowered. Fruit-cone rounded, 6–7 mm diam., with fleshy, reddish scales and arils, and vaguely reminiscent of a small raspberry.

Flowering: May–June.

Habitat: Sea-dunes, riverbanks, cliffs, walls, on dry, oligotrophic, calcareous, sandy or stony soils; from sea level to 1,100 m.

Range: S and C Europe, westwards to Brittany, northwards to Hungary, and eastwards to C and SE Russia.

HEATHER FAMILY, ERICACEAE

A family of shrubs and small trees with *c.* 3,000 species in 100 genera world-wide. Dicots. Leaves simple, often leathery. Flowers usually regular, hermaphrodite, 4–5-merous (rarely 6–7-merous); sepals and petals usually connate, at least at base. Stamens 6–10, usually twice as numerous as petal-lobes; anthers often with horn-like appendages, and opening with pores. Ovary superior (inferior in *Vaccinium*), 4–10-locular (often 5-locular), with 1 style. Fruit a berry, a drupe or a capsule. A tree-like species, the **Strawberry Tree** (*Arbutus unedo* L.), which has warty, globose, berry-like, edible red fruits, is a Mediterranean-Atlantic species occurring northwards to W France, also in W Ireland, and naturalized in S Britain. **Tree Heather** (*E. arborea* L.) (*see* photograph p.175) from S Europe can attain a height of 6 m, and yields a hard and beautifully grained wood used for pipeheads. *Rhododendron ponticum* L. from SE Europe is the evergreen **Rhododendron** common in parks and gardens, and locally naturalized in open woods of W Europe. A small, mat-forming, also evergreen relative from the tundra and mountain heaths of Fennoscandia is **Lapland Rhododendron** (*R. lapponicum* (L.) Wahlenb.), which has bell-shaped, purplish-violet flowers to 15 mm.

---

p.306 **Bog Rosemary** *Andromeda polifolia* L.

Description: A tiny, evergreen, *glabrous dwarf-shrub*, with thin, woody stems to 30 (50) cm. Leaves narrowly elliptical to oblanceolate, 10–20 (30) mm long, shiny dark green above, *blue-*

green or whitish-pruinose beneath, pointed, the *margins entire and rolled under*. Flowers in short, subumbellate, terminal racemes, long-stalked, nodding; stalks pink. Calyx short, 5-toothed, pink. Corolla ovoid, to 10 mm long, urn-shaped, with 5 short, recurved teeth, pale pink. Stamens 10; anthers with threadlike apical horns. Ovary superior, 5-locular, with 1 style. Fruit an erect, greyish capsule, opening with 5 valves.

Flowering: April–June.

Habitat: *Sphagnum* bogs, marshy heaths, on wet, oligotrophic, acid, peaty soils; from sea level to 2,000 m.

Range: N, W and C Europe, eastwards to the Urals (and to Asia), but only on mountains in the south.

Compare Phyllodoce caerulea (see p.624), which has linear leaves and anthers without horns.

p.305 **Bearberry** *Arctostaphylos uva-ursi* L.

Description: An evergreen dwarf-shrub, with creeping stems to 2 m long, and ascending branches to 60 cm. Leaves alternate, (narrowly) obovate, 20–30 mm long, blunt-tipped, entire-margined, dark green above, slightly paler green and reticulately veined beneath. Flowers in small, subumbellate, terminal racemes, stalked, more or less nodding; stalk whitish. Calyx short, 5-lobed, whitish. Corolla ovoid, 5–6 mm long, pale pink or whitish, with 5 short, suberect, darker pink or greenish teeth. Stamens 10; anthers with 2 thin, dorsal horns. Ovary superior, 4–5-locular, with 1 style. Fruit a rounded drupe, shiny red when ripe, with 5–7 (10) stones.

Flowering: March–July.

Habitat: Heaths, dunes, open woods of Pine or Birch, on moist, oligotrophic, slightly acid to calcareous, sandy or rocky soils; from sea level to 2,400 m.

Range: Most of Europe except Spitsbergen, but only on mountains in the south.

Compare Vaccinium vitis-idaea (see p.627, 627), which has leaf-margins rolled under.

p.308 **Heather** *Calluna vulgaris* (L.) Hull

Description:
A slightly hairy, evergreen, ascending shrub to 1 m (rarely 2 m), with erect branches. Leaves crosswise opposite (in 4 rows), sessile, crowded, 1–3 mm long, appressed and scale-like, lanceolate, with *2 acute spurs* at base, dark green, rigid. Flowers short-stalked, pendulous, 3–4 mm long, axillary to leaves, on short side-branches of terminal shoots, forming *elongate, leafy panicles*; each flower subtended by *epicalyx of 4 small, green or reddish bracts. Calyx 4-parted, large, pink or purplish*. Corolla 4-lobed, slightly shorter than calyx, pink or purplish (rarely white). Stamens 8; anthers with 2 small apical horns. Ovary superior, 4-locular, with 1 style. Fruit a rounded, hairy capsule to 1.5 mm diam., opening with 4 valves, and with numerous minute seeds.

Flowering:
July–October.

Habitat:
Heaths, bogs, dunes, poor grassland, road verges, open woods, on dry to moist, oligotrophic, acid, sandy, loamy, rocky or peaty soils; from sea level to 2,500 m.

Range:
All Europe except Spitsbergen, but rare in the south.

Often dominant in dry heaths. Another name is Ling.

---

p.172 **Matted Cassiope**
Cassiope hypnoides (L.) D. Don

Description:
A mat-forming, evergreen dwarf-shrub to 5 cm, with prostrate, branched stems. *Leaves alternate* (not in distinct rows), crowded, lanceolate, erect to more or less spreading, *needle-like*, dark green. *Flowers solitary, terminal* on ascending branches, long-stalked, nodding. Sepals 5, reddish (like stalk), *c.* 2 mm long. Corolla bell-shaped, 4–5 mm long, with 5 short, broad, blunt, erect teeth, white or pale pink. Stamens 10, with 2 recurved subapical horns. Ovary superior, with 1 style. Fruit an erect, ovoid capsule, *c.* 3 mm long.

Flowering:
June–August.

Habitat: Tundra, snow patches, boggy places on mountains, along streams, on moist to wet, oligotrophic, acid, peaty or stony soils; from sea level to 1,900 m.

Range: In Arctic N Europe, including Iceland and the mountains of Scandinavia.

Similar species: **Cassiope** (*C. tetragona* (L.) D. Don) grows more erect, and has crosswise opposite, appressed, scale-like, oblanceolate leaves (in 4 rows); flowers placed laterally in leaf-axils, often several per branch, corolla cream or pale pink, 6–8 mm long, with 5 triangular teeth. In tundra and heaths, on moist to rather dry, oligotrophic, often calcareous, sandy or stony soils (to 1,650 m), in Arctic N Europe except Iceland.

---

p.174 **Cassandra**
Chamaedaphne calyculata (L.) Moench

Description: An evergreen, erect shrub to 50 cm. Leaves alternate, short-stalked to subsessile, elliptical, with prominent midvein, *finely serrate*, dark green above, with *brownish scales beneath*. Flowers in terminal, leafy racemes, pendulous; each flower with *epicalyx of 2 small bracts*. Normal calyx short, 5-toothed, green. Corolla bell-shaped, white, 5–6 mm long, with 5 long, curved teeth. Stamens 10; *anthers without horns*. Ovary superior, 5-locular, with 1 style. Fruit a pendent, depressed-globose capsule, 2–2.5 mm diam., opening with 5 valves.

Flowering: March–June.

Habitat: Bogs, marshes and damp woods, on wet, oligotrophic, acid, peaty soils; from sea level to 1,000 m.

Range: NE Europe, westwards to NE Sweden, and southwards to N Poland, C Russia and the S Urals.

---

p.308 **Saint Dabeoc's Heath**
Daboecia cantabrica (Hudson) C. Koch

Description: An evergreen shrub with spreading or straggling, glandular-hairy stems to 70 cm. Leaves alternate, elliptical to lanceolate, leathery, long-ciliate, dark green and glandular-hairy above, white-tomentose beneath, the margin rolled under. Flowers short-stalked, 3–9 (12) together in terminal racemes. Calyx small, with *4 lanceolate teeth.* Corolla bell-shaped, *9–14 mm long, with 4 triangular, curved teeth*, purplish-pink, *glandular-hairy on the outside.* Stamens 8; anthers hornless. Ovary superior, 4-locular, with 1 style. Fruit a *warty, leathery capsule*, opening with *4 valves.*

Flowering: June–October.

Habitat: Heaths, open woods, on moist, oligotrophic, acid, sandy or rocky soils; from sea level to 400 m, rarely higher.

Range: SW Europe, from N Portugal to SW France; also in W Ireland.

Compare Phyllodoce caerulea (see p.624), which has linear-lanceolate, inrolled leaves, and 5-merous, terminal, subumbellate flowers; and *Andromeda polifolia (see* p.616), which has 5-merous, subumbellate flowers and horned anthers.

p.307 **Dorset Heath** *Erica ciliaris* L.

Description: An evergreen shrub to 70 cm, with erect, hairy branches. Leaves mostly in *whorls of 3*, sessile, 2–3 mm long, *narrowly ovate, pointed*, with inrolled, *glandular-ciliate margins*, green above, whitish beneath. Flowers short-stalked, spreading, in *elongate, leafless, terminal racemes.* Calyx small, 4-toothed, green, *ciliate. Corolla 8–10 (12) mm long*, urn-shaped, *slightly curved*, purplish-pink (rarely pale pink), with 4 short, blunt teeth. Stamens (6–7) 8; anthers not protruding, subacute, but hornless. Ovary superior, 4-locular, with 1 style. Fruit a glabrous, many-seeded capsule, opening with 4 valves.

Flowering: June–October.

Habitat: Bogs, heaths, scrub, open woods, on moist or wet, oligotrophic, acid, sandy or peaty soils; from sea level to 400 m.

Range: SW Europe, extending northwards to C France, S Britain and W Ireland.

Compare E. tetralix, which has short, subglobose racemes, and ciliate leaves in whorls of 4.

---

p.307 **Bell Heather** *Erica cinerea* L.

Description: A small, glabrescent, evergreen shrub to 60 cm; young twigs often hairy. Leaves in *whorls of 3*, sessile, 2–3 mm long, *narrowly lanceolate to linear*, dark or bronze-green, with inrolled, glabrous or shortly hairy margins, green above, whitish beneath; leaves usually bear *bundles of smaller leaves in their axils*. Flowers short-stalked, spreading to nodding, in *elongate, leafy racemes*. Calyx 2–4 mm long, with 4 green, lanceolate, glabrous or shortly ciliate teeth. *Corolla 5–7 mm long*, urn-shaped, purplish-pink (rarely pale pink or white), with 4 short, triangular, recurved teeth. Stamens 8; anthers not protruding, with *2 basal horns*. Ovary superior, 4-locular, with 1 style. Fruit a glabrous, subglobose, many-seeded capsule.

Flowering: June–September.

Habitat: Heaths, dunes, poor grassland, open woods, on dry to moist, oligotrophic, acid, sandy, loamy or stony soils; from sea level to 1,550 m.

Range: W Europe, from the Iberian peninsula northwards to Ireland, Britain, the Low Countries, W Germany, and Norway, and eastwards to Italy.

---

p.307 **Cross-leaved Heath** *Erica tetralix* L.

Description: A small, evergreen shrub to 40 (60) cm, with erect, hairy branches. Leaves in *whorls of 4*, sessile, 4–5 mm long, *narrowly elliptical to linear-lanceolate*, with inrolled, *glandular-ciliate margins*, green and short-hairy above, whitish beneath. Flowers short-stalked, closely packed in *rounded, leafless, terminal racemes*. Calyx small, 4-toothed, green, short-hairy and *ciliate*. *Corolla 5–8 (9) mm long*, urn-shaped, pink (rarely white), with 4 short, blunt teeth. Stamens 8; anthers not protruding, with *2 basal horns*. Ovary superior, 4-locular, with 1 style. Fruit a 4-locular, 8-angular, truncate, white-hairy, many-seeded capsule.

Flowering: June–October.

Habitat: Heaths, bogs, open woods, on moist to wet, oligotrophic, acid, sandy or peaty soils; from sea level to 2,200 m. Often dominant in wet heaths and bogs; rare on drier soils.

Range: W and N Europe, from Iberia and Ireland northwards to Fennoscandia, and eastwards to Latvia.

Similar species: **Mackay's Heath** (*E. mackaiana* Bab.) has dark-green leaves and smaller, purplish flowers (5–7 mm long). In acid bogs in NW Spain and W Ireland.
E. terminalis Salisb. is a much larger shrub (to 2.5 m), with bright-pink flowers 5–7 mm long in 4–6-flowered, terminal racemes, and hairy capsules. Native to Mediterranean area, and naturalized on sand-dunes in Ireland (Derry).

p.307 **Cornish Heath** *Erica vagans* L.

Description: A hairless, evergreen shrub to 60 cm. Leaves linear, *8–10 mm long*, in whorls of 4–5, with *strongly inrolled margins* (leaving only a narrow opening between them). Flowers shorter than their stalks, in leaf-axils of short side-branches, forming rather dense, leafy racemes; *tip of shoot usually leafy, without flowers*. Calyx short (*c.* 1 mm), with 4 teeth. Corolla bell-shaped, *c.* 3 mm long, lilac, pink or white. Stamens 8; anthers acute, divergent but horn-less, *purplish-brown, exserted*. Ovary superior, 4-locular, with 1 style. Fruit a 4-locular capsule.

Flowering: July–September.

Habitat: Heaths and open woods, on dry, oligotrophic, preferably acid, sandy or stony soils; from sea level to 1,800 m.

Range: W Europe, from C Spain through W and C France to SW Britain and NW Ireland.

Similar species: **Irish Heath** (*E. erigena* R. Ross), to 1–2 m, has leaves in whorls of 4, connate, only slightly protruding anthers, and deep-pink flowers longer than their stalks, all turned to 1 side. In wet heaths and bogs in Iberia, SW France and W Ireland.

E. scoparia L. has leaves in whorls of 3–4, and very small flowers to 2.5 mm long (corolla about doubling calyx), greenish-white (often flushed with red). In heaths, dune-valleys, scrub and open woods (often Pine), on dry to moist, oligotrophic, acid soils, in SW Europe, northwards to W and NC France; naturalized on the Wadden Sea Islands in the Netherlands.

---

p.172 **Labrador Tea** *Ledum palustre* L.

Description: An evergreen shrub to 1.2 m, with spreading to erect branches brown-hairy in youth. Leaves alternate, short-stalked, 20–50 mm long, lanceolate, dark green above, *rusty-hairy below*, with strongly inrolled margins. Flowers 10–15 mm diam., long-stalked, numerous, in *dense, rounded, terminate umbels*. Calyx 5-toothed. *Petals 5, free, 7–9 mm long, elliptical, white*. Stamens 10; anthers hornless. Ovary superior, 5-locular, with 1 style. Fruit a *pendulous, ovoid, many-seeded capsule*.

Flowering: May–July.

Habitat: Bogs, marshy heaths, damp coniferous woods (often Pine), on wet or moist, oligotrophic, acid, usually peaty soils; from sea level to 740 m.

Range: N and NC Europe, westwards to S Germany, and eastwards to C Russia; not in Iceland and Spitsbergen.

Similar species: *L. groenlandicum* Oeder (also treated as a subspecies) has 8 stamens, and the inrolled leaf-margins almost touch, concealing the rusty underside of the leaf. It is the true Labrador Tea used for making an aromatic beverage. In bogs in N America and Greenland, and locally naturalized in Scotland and Germany.

---

p.306 **Mountain Azalea**
Loiseleuria procumbens (L.) Desv.

Description: A hairless, evergreen, *mat-forming shrub or half-shrub only a few cm tall*, with prostrate stems to 30 cm long. *Leaves opposite, elliptical, 5–7 mm long*, the margins rolled under, shiny green on both faces, short-stalked. Flowers terminal, *solitary or 2–5 together in small umbel.* Calyx 5-toothed, reddish. Corolla 4–6 mm long, cup-shaped, with 5 long, divergent to spreading, blunt lobes, pale pink. *Stamens 5*, alternating with corolla lobes. Ovary superior, *2–3-locular*, with 1 style. Fruit a many-seeded capsule, opening with 2–3 valves.

Flowering: May–July.

Habitat: Moors, mountain grassland and bare, humus-rich ground, on dry to moist, oligotrophic, acid, peaty or stony soils; from sea level to 3,000 m, but only on mountains outside the Arctic.

Range: In Iceland, Scandinavia, N and W Russia, southwards to Scotland and the mountains of C Europe, including the Pyrenees.

---

p.306 **Mountain Heath**
Phyllodoce caerulea (L.) Bab.

Description: A *hairy*, evergreen dwarf-shrub to 40 cm, with creeping stems and ascending branches. Leaves alternate, sessile, *crowded, linear to narrowly oblanceolate, to 12 mm long*, blunt-tipped, shiny green above, whitish beneath, with inrolled, *scabrous margins* leaving only a narrow opening between them. Flowers (1) 2–6 together in short, *subumbellate, terminal racemes*, long-stalked, nodding; stalks reddish, hairy. Calyx 3–5 mm long, 5-toothed, reddish, hairy. Corolla ovoid, 7–12 mm long, urn-shaped, with 5 short, recurved teeth, lilac. Stamens 10; *anthers hornless*. Ovary superior, 5-locular, with 1 style. Fruit a many-seeded, *glandular capsule*, opening with 5 valves.

Flowering: June–August.

Habitat: Mountain heaths, rocky moorlands, on moist to dry, oligotrophic, usually acid, sandy, gravelly, rocky or peaty soils; from sea level (in the north) to 2,600 m.

Range: In Iceland, Scotland, Fennoscandia and N Russia; also (very rare) in the Alps and the Pyrenees.

Compare Andromeda polifolia (see p.616), a glabrous plant, with wider leaves, and horns to the anthers.

p.171 **Bilberry** *Vaccinium myrtillus* L.

Description: A small, glabrous, *deciduous* shrub to 50 (150) cm, with *sharply angular, green branches*. Leaves alternate, subsessile, elliptical or ovate, subacute, *hardly leathery, green on both faces*, reticulately veined, *crenate-dentate, with flat margin*. Flowers usually *solitary in leaf-axils*, pendulous or nodding. Calyx short, shallow-lobed. Corolla 4–6 mm long, urn-shaped, *wider than long, greenish-white or flushed with red*, with 5 *very short, greenish-white lobes*. Stamens 8–10; anthers with 2 horns and 2 long, yellow tubules at the top. *Ovary inferior*, 4–5-locular, with 1 style. Fruit a rounded, *black, bluish-pruinose berry*, 6–10 mm diam., crowned by persistent calyx, and with a strongly staining, deep-purple juice.

Flowering: April–June (autumn).

Habitat: Heaths, bogs, open, deciduous or coniferous woods, on moist to rather dry, oligotrophic, acid, sandy or stony soils; from sea level to 2,800 m. Can reach dominance in regions with high annual precipitation.

Range: All Europe except Spitsbergen.

Similar species: **Bog Bilberry** (*V. uliginosum* L.) also has bluish-black berries, but juice colourless, branches rounded, leaves obovate, round-tipped, entire-margined (10–25 mm long, glaucous beneath), and flowers white or pale pink, 1–3 together in terminal clusters. In marshy heaths, dune-valleys, bogs, tundra, open coniferous woods, on wet to moist, oligotrophic, acid, sandy or stony soils, from sea level to 3,000 m, in N and C Europe, southwards in the mountains to Spain (Sierra Nevada) and Italy (N Apennines) and Bulgaria; not in Iceland. Northern forms with small leaves (6–15 mm long) are distinguished as ssp. *microphyllum* Lange. Both species have edible, sweet-tasting berries.

Highbush Blueberry (*V. corymbosum* L.) from N America grows 4 m tall, and has elliptical, acute, usually entire-margined leaves (40–80 mm in length), several white or slightly pinkish flowers in terminal racemes, anthers hornless, and large, bluish-black berries (10–25 mm diam.). Cultivated for fruit, and naturalized in wet heaths, bogs and damp woods on acid soils in the Netherlands.

---

p.305 **Cranberry** *Vaccinium oxycoccus* L.

Description: A tiny, glabrous, evergreen dwarf-shrub, with *threadlike, branching, creeping stems* to 50 cm. Leaves alternate, short-stalked, 4–8 (15) mm long, 3–4 (6) mm wide, ovate to elliptical, acute, dark green above, greyish-white beneath, with margin rolled under. *Flowers solitary or in pairs*, nodding on long, red, finely hairy, erect stalks at end of branches; always a pair of tiny *scale-leaves in middle of stalk*. Calyx small, with 4 pink, rounded lobes. Corolla 6–10 mm long, *deeply divided with 4 lanceolate, recurved, pink lobes*. Stamens 8 (10), long-protruding, each with 2 yellow tubules at the top. *Ovary inferior*, 4-locular, with 1 long style. Fruit a rounded to pear-shaped berry, (4) 8–10 (15) mm diam., *red to brown* (rarely white).

Flowering: May–August.

Habitat: Bogs, marshy heaths, open woods, on wet, oligotrophic, acid, peaty soils; from sea level to 2,000 m.

Range: N and C Europe, except Iceland and the high Arctic, and southwards to C France, N Italy and SE Russia.

Similar species: **Small Cranberry** (*V. microcarpum* (Turcz. ex Rupr.) Schmalh.) has triangular-ovate, acute leaves to 2.5 mm wide, glabrous flower-stalks, and red berries 6–8 mm diam. In bogs, in N and C Europe, from Iceland and N Russia southwards to Scotland, Switzerland, Yugoslavia, and C Russia.
American Cranberry (*V. macrocarpum* (Aiton) Pursh) from N America has blunt, elliptical leaves 6–15 (20) mm long, bluish-green beneath, with an almost flat

margin; flowers in small, 1–5-flowered racemes continuing growth as a leafy shoot (so berries lateral on branches); red berries 10–20 mm diam. Cultivated for the berries, and naturalized in marshes and dune-slacks in N Britain, the Netherlands, Germany, and Switzerland.

---

p.171 **Cowberry** *Vaccinium vitis-idaea* L.

Description: A small, *evergreen* shrub to 40 cm, with creeping or ascending branches. Leaves alternate, short-stalked, 10–20 mm long, elliptical or obovate, round-tipped, *leathery*, dark green above, *pale green and dotted with glands beneath*, margins rolled under (rarely flat and finely denticulate). Flowers nodding on rather short stalks, several together in dense, terminal racemes. Calyx short, 5-lobed, green or flushed with red. Corolla bell-shaped, 5–8 mm long, with 5 *large, rounded lobes*, white or pale pink. Stamens 10; anthers with 2 yellow tubules at the top, but hornless. *Ovary inferior*, 5-locular, with 1 style. Fruit a globose, *acidulous, red berry*.

Flowering: May–July (August).

Habitat: Coniferous woods, heaths, bogs, marshes, tundra, mountain pasture, on wet to dry, oligotrophic, acid, sandy, stony or peaty soils; from sea level to 3,000 m.

Range: N and C Europe except Spitsbergen, southwards to the Pyrenees, N Apennines and Bulgaria, and eastwards to the Urals.

The berries are edible.

PIPEWORT FAMILY, ERIOCAULACEAE

A family of herbs, with *c.* 1,200 species in 13 genera, mainly in warm regions, but some species in N America; only 1 in Europe. Monocots. Leaves grass-like, often basally placed. Flowers usually unisexual, monoecious, in terminal heads with a common involucre. Individual flowers regular or zygomorphic, with a membranous 2–3-merous perianth (occasionally absent) in 1–2 whorls. Stamens 1–6. Ovary superior, 2–3-locular, with 1 style and 2–6 (often 3) stigmas. Fruit a 2–3-locular capsule, with 1 seed per locule.

p.45   **Pipewort** *Eriocaulon aquaticum* (Hill) Druce

Description: *See also* the family description. A glabrous, *aquatic perennial* with creeping rhizomes bearing submerged rosettes of linear, tapering, awl-shaped leaves to 10 cm long, 3–5 mm wide at base. Flowering stems (scapes) simple, erect, angularly ribbed, 7–20 (150) cm, emergent, usually 1 per rosette, with 1 sheathing basal leaf. Flowerheads hemispherical, terminal, 6–11 (20) mm diam., with involucre of greyish bracts to 3 mm long; flowers have perianth of 4 segments to 3 mm long, in 2 whorls, those of (outer) female flowers free, black-tipped, white-ciliate, those of (central) male flowers yellowish-grey, only the 2 inner ones black-tipped and connate. Stamens 4. Ovary 2-lobed, with 2 stigmas. Fruit a 2-seeded capsule.

Flowering: July–September.

Habitat: Shallow water of oligotrophic, acid pools and lakes on peaty soils to 320 m.

Range: W Ireland and on the Scottish islands Skye and Coll.

Also found in N America; the European populations differ from the American ones in chromosome number, but morphological differences are slight.

SPURGE FAMILY, EUPHORBIACEAE

A large family of herbs and shrubs with *c.* 5,000 species in 300 genera, primarily in the tropics (and with many succulent representatives in desert areas). Dicots. Leaves alternate (occasionally opposite or whorled), usually simple; plants often have a poisonous, milky latex. Flowers usually unisexual, regular, but occasionally lacking the perianth. Ovary superior, 2–4-locular (often 3-locular). Fruit a 2–4-lobed capsule, lobes often falling separately (schizocarpous). Of the 2 N European genera, *Euphorbia* is monoecious, latex-bearing, with flowers lacking perianth, but collected in small groups (cyathia) of 1 long-stalked female flower and few to several short-stalked male flowers reduced to 1 stamen, with cup-shaped common involucre bearing 4–5 conspicuous marginal glands; ovary superior, 3-locular, with 3 styles. *Mercurialis* is dioecious, with watery juice, while flowers have greenish, 3-parted perianth; male flowers have 8–15 stamens, female flowers normally have 2-locular ovary with 2 styles.

---

p.76 **Wood Spurge** *Euphorbia amygdaloides* L.

Description: A *hairy perennial* to 1 m, with creeping rhizomes and sterile, hibernating rosettes; flowering stem erect, tough, solid, branched only in inflorescence. Stem-leaves alternate, deep green, the middle ones (in fact, the rosette-leaves of the previous year) short-stalked, crowded, to 70 mm long, narrowly elliptical or oblanceolate, entire-margined, the upper leaves shorter, subsessile, elliptical. Cyathia in dichasial cymes, with opposite, broadly ovate to reniform, *basally connate bracts. Cymes mostly axillary*, distributed over a large part of stem, the whole inflorescence terminated by *5–10-rayed umbel*. Involucre of cyathium with *4 crescent-shaped, yellow marginal glands*. Fruit a 3-lobed, rounded, smooth or finely granular capsule, 3–4 mm diam.

Flowering: March–May.

Habitat: Damp, deciduous forests, on moist, oligotrophic, basic to slightly acid soils; from sea level to 1,300 m.

Range: S, W and C Europe, northwards to the British Isles, the Low Countries, Poland, and W Russia, and eastwards to the Caucasus.

---

p.75 **Cypress Spurge** *Euphorbia cyparissias* L.

Description: A *glabrous perennial* to 50 cm, with short rhizomes and erect flowering stems, branched from base. Leaves alternate, crowded, evenly distributed along stem, sessile, *linear, 10–20 (40) mm long*, 1–2 (3) mm wide, entire-margined, green (*turning yellow or orange* in autumn); leaves of sterile branches often threadlike. Cyathia in dichasial cymes, with opposite, sessile, suborbicular bracts; cymes compose a *terminal, 9–15-rayed umbel*, often with a few axillary cymes below. Involucre of cyathium has 4 crescent-shaped, yellow marginal glands. Fruit a 3-lobed, rounded, finely granular capsule, *c.* 3 mm diam.

Flowering: April–June (September).

Habitat: Road verges, banks, river-dunes, scrub, gardens, on dry, oligotrophic to mesotrophic, preferably calcareous, sandy, loamy or rocky soils; from sea level to 2,650 m.

Range: Most of continental Europe except the extreme north and south, from Spain northwards to the Netherlands, eastwards to Poland and C and SE Russia; naturalized in Britain, Scandinavia and N Russia.

Similar species: **Leafy Spurge** (*Euphorbia esula* L.) is much taller (to 1.2 m), and has linear-oblanceolate leaves to 60 mm long, 4–7 mm wide, staying green after anthesis. A similar distribution, in grassland, damp woods, along rivers, also along railways and in ruderal places, on moist to dry, mesotrophic, calcareous soils, from sea level to 1,000 m.

---

p.74 **Dwarf Spurge** *Euphorbia exigua* L.

Description: A glabrous *annual* to 20 (30) cm, with slender taproot and erect stems often branched from base. Leaves alternate, sessile, 10–25 mm long, 2–3 mm wide, *linear-lanceolate*, tapering, entire-margined. Cyathia in dichasial cymes, with opposite, broadly lanceolate, sessile bracts, the lower ones narrower and often strikingly enlarged; cymes compose a *2–5-rayed umbel*; involucre of cyathium has *4 crescent-shaped, yellow marginal glands with long, slender horns*, alternating with erect, notched lobes. Fruit a 3-lobed, rounded, smooth capsule, *1.6–2 mm diam.*

Flowering: June–October.

Habitat: Cultivated and waste land, open roadsides, disturbed places, on moist, mesotrophic, calcareous, loamy or stony soils; from sea level to 1,000 m.

Range: Most of Europe except Iceland, Finland and the high Arctic.

Similar species: *E. falcata* L. is often glaucous, and has narrowly oblanceolate leaves to 5 mm wide, upper ones pointed; floral bracts ovate; marginal glands have short horns. In S and SC Europe, northwards to C France and S Germany, and eastwards to C Russia, in comparable habitats.

p.75 **Sun Spurge** *Euphorbia helioscopia* L.

Description: A *glabrous or slightly hairy annual* to 30 cm, with slender taproot; stem erect, branched only in inflorescence. Leaves alternate, to 40 mm long, obovate, narrowed into very short stalk, *finely dentate* at least near the (slightly truncate) top. Cyathia in dichasial cymes, with opposite, *obovate, yellowish-green bracts*; cymes compose a *5-rayed umbel*. Involucre of cyathium has *4 reniform, rounded, yellow marginal glands*. Fruit a 3-lobed, rounded, *smooth capsule*, *c.* 3 mm diam.

Flowering: May–August (November).

Habitat: Cultivated and waste land, disturbed roadsides, gardens, on moist, eutrophic, calcareous to slightly acid, sandy, loamy or clayey soils; from sea level to 1,500 m, more frequent in the lowland.

Range: Most of Europe except Iceland and the high Arctic.

Similar species: **Broad-leaved Spurge** (*E. platyphyllos* L.) is often slightly hairy, and has narrowly obovate, slightly clasping leaves finely dentate all round, few to numerous axillary cymes under terminal umbel, broadly ovate-cordate floral bracts, and rounded capsules (3–4 mm diam.) covered with short, blunt warts (except on midveins of valves). In comparable habitats, in S, W and C Europe, northwards to SE England, the Netherlands, Poland, and eastwards to C and SE Russia.

Upright Spurge (*E. stricta* L.) is always glabrous, with narrowly obovate, (sub)sessile, finely dentate leaves, numerous axillary cymes, ovate to cordate floral bracts, and small, bluntly trigonal capsules (to 2 mm diam.) covered with long, slender warts. In moist arable land, under hedges, along ditches, on calcareous soils, from sea level to 1,200 m, in S, W and C Europe, northwards to S Britain (Forest of Dean), the Netherlands, Poland, and eastwards to the Caucasus.

p.76 **Marsh Spurge** *Euphorbia palustris* L.

Description: A *glabrous or slightly hairy perennial* to 1 (1.5) m, with creeping rhizomes and non-flowering shoots; flowering stems erect, brittle, thick and hollow, branched only in inflorescence. Leaves alternate, sessile, greyish-green, to 60 mm long, narrowly elliptical, *finely dentate* to subentire, blunt-tipped, glabrous on both faces. Cymes compose *a terminal umbel with at least 5, often several more, rays*, normally with some axillary cymes below; *rays have triple or quadruple ramifications* and equal number of elliptical, sessile bracts. Involucre of cyathium has *4 reniform, rounded, yellowish marginal glands*. Fruit a 3-lobed, rounded capsule, 5–6 mm diam., covered with short, blunt warts.

Flowering: May–July.

Habitat: Reedlands, marshes, swampy woods, water-sides, ditches, on wet, eutrophic, often basic (occasionally slightly brackish), clayey, muddy or peaty soils; mainly in the lowlands.

Range: Continental Europe except the extreme south, northwards to S Norway and S Finland.

Similar species: **Irish Spurge** (*E. hyberna* L.) grows no taller than 60 cm. Leaves (sub)sessile, blunt, always entire-margined, oblanceolate, to 10 cm, often downy beneath; (paired) floral bracts have cordate, clasping base; terminal umbel has 4–6 rays; involucre of cyathium bears 5 yellow, rounded marginal glands; fruit covered with long, slender warts. In SW Europe, northwards to W and C France, S Britain and SW Ireland, in damp woods and shaded, grassy habitats, from sea level to 2,000 m (in the Pyrenees). **Sweet Spurge** (*E. dulcis* L.) has stems to 50 cm, short-stalked, elliptical leaves to 60 mm long, triangular-ovate, paired floral bracts with truncate base, involucres with 5 rounded marginal glands soon turning purplish, and smaller capsules (3–4 mm diam.) with slender warts. In W and C Europe, northwards to Belgium, S Germany and Poland, in woods on calcareous soils, to 1,800 m.

E. brittingeri Opiz ex Samp. resembles Sweet Spurge in appearance, ecology and range, but has non-creeping rhizome, leaves less than 30 mm in length, and marginal glands turning purple only after anthesis. In dry grassland, road verges and scrub in SW and C Europe, northwards to N France and Germany, eastwards to Hungary and the N Balkan region.

Hairy Spurge (*E. villosa* L.) is much taller, to 1.2 m, with long sterile shoots. Leaves narrowly elliptical, to 10 cm long, 20 mm wide, often dentate near the top, and hairy at least beneath; capsules 3–6 mm diam., finely warted, often hairy as well; 5 rounded marginal glands. In marshes, damp meadows, open woods, willow-coppices, along rivers, in S and C Europe, northwards to NW France and Germany, eastwards to Poland and E Russia. Extinct in Britain.

---

p.76 **Sea Spurge** *Euphorbia paralias* L.

Description: A *glabrous, glaucous perennial* to 60 cm, with creeping rhizomes bearing erect, often reddish flowering stems, branched only in inflorescence, and markedly *lignified below*. Leaves alternate, subsessile, bluish-green (turning pale yellowish when senile), densely crowded, 30–60 mm long, narrowly elliptical or broadly lanceolate, blunt-tipped, entire-margined, *leathery to slightly fleshy*. Cyathia in dichasial cymes, with opposite, broad-ovate to reniform, sessile bracts; cymes compose a *2–9-rayed umbel*, usually with some axillary cymes below. Involucre of cyathium has *4 reniform, 2-horned, yellow marginal glands*. Fruit a 3-lobed, rounded, smooth or finely granular capsule, 3–5 mm diam.

Flowering: (April) May–July (September).

Habitat: Sea-dunes, shingle-beaches, on unstable, dry, brackish, sandy or gravelly soils; exclusively coastal.

Range: Coasts of S and W Europe, northwards to W France, Britain, Ireland, and the Low Countries, and eastwards to Romania.

Similar species: **Portland Spurge** (*E. portlandica* L.) often is biennial, or even annual, and has prostrate or ascending, branched stems to 40 cm, slightly leathery, oblanceolate leaves (to 30 mm long) with prominent midvein beneath, ovate to triangular-ovate floral bracts, involucres with 4 crescent-shaped, greenish marginal glands, and capsules 2.8–3 mm diam. Foliage often turns purplish-red. In comparable, coastal habitats of W Europe, northwards to W France, S Britain and W Ireland.

E. seguieriana Necker grows erect, to 50 cm, and has glaucous, fleshy or leathery, crowded, erect, oblanceolate, sharp-pointed leaves (to 35 mm long) with prominent midvein above, and 2 long side-veins in lower half; terminal umbel has 5–15 rays; floral bracts pale yellow (turning greyish); marginal glands bean-shaped – a crescent with very short, rounded horns. In grassland, road verges, on banks, on dry, oligotrophic to mesotrophic, calcareous, sandy, loamy or stony soils, from sea level to 1,600 m, in continental Europe except the extreme south, and northwards to the Netherlands, Hungary, Romania, and W and SE Russia.

p.75 **Purple Spurge** *Euphorbia peplis* L.

Description: A glabrous *annual*, usually lacking a normal stem, but starting from base with (umbellate) inflorescence, composed of 4 *prostrate, reddish branches* to 40 cm long, forked several times. *Leaves (floral bracts) opposite, glaucous, fleshy,* 8–12 mm long, short-stalked, turned flat to ground, *asymmetric*, with *arched lobe behind stalk*, otherwise elliptical or obovate; stipules present, awl-shaped, to 1.5 mm long. Involucre of cyathium has 5 rounded, purplish marginal glands, alternating with small, erect, acute lobes. Fruit a 3-lobed, rounded, smooth capsule, 3.5–5 mm diam.

Flowering: July–September.

Habitat: Sandy or gravelly beaches, above the floodline, on moist, saline soils; exclusively coastal.

Range: S and W Europe, northwards to W France; probably extinct in SW England.

p.75 **Petty Spurge** *Euphorbia peplus* L.

Description: A glabrous *annual* to 30 cm, with slender
taproot and erect, often reddish stems.
Leaves alternate, short-stalked, 10–25 mm
long, obovate to suborbicular, entire-
margined. Cyathia in dichasial cymes, with
opposite, ovate, sessile bracts; cymes
compose a *3-rayed umbel*. Involucre of
cyathium has *4 crescent-shaped, yellow
marginal glands*. Fruit a 3-lobed, rounded
capsule, 2.8–3 mm diam., with 3 narrow,
double wings on lobes.

Flowering: April–September (late autumn).

Habitat: Cultivated land (often in root-crop fields
and gardens), also in other shaded,
disturbed places, on moist, eutrophic,
calcareous, sandy, loamy or clayey soils;
from sea level to 1,300 m.

Range: Europe northwards to C Fennoscandia and
NC Russia.

---

p.65 **Annual Mercury** *Mercurialis annua* L.

Description: A glabrous or slightly hairy *annual* to
40 cm, with slender taproot, and ascending
to erect, *branched* stems; *no milky latex, no
stolons*. Leaves opposite, short-stalked, ovate
to broadly lanceolate, bluntly dentate, often
pale green. *Flowers unisexual, dioecious*: male
flowers in clusters, composing long-stalked,
erect, axillary spikes; *female flowers subsessile*,
2–3 together in leaf-axils. Perianth
2–4 mm diam., with *3 ovate, greenish tepals*.
Stamens 8–15. Ovary superior, 2-locular,
with 1 style and 2 stigmas. Fruit a *2-lobed
capsule*, 3–4 mm wide, covered with *long,
bristly hairs*.

Flowering: (April) June–October (winter).

Habitat: Cultivated and waste land, gardens,
disturbed roadsides, on moist, mesotrophic
to eutrophic, preferably calcareous, sandy or
loamy soils; from sea level to 700 m.

Range: In Europe northwards to S Britain, the
Netherlands, Denmark, eastwards to C
Russia. An archeophyte from prehistoric
times, more recently naturalized in Ireland
and S Fennoscandia.

Similar species: **Dog's Mercury** (*Mercurialis perennis* L.) is a
hairy perennial (flowering from March to
May), with creeping stolons, erect,
unbranched stems to 40 cm, long-stalked
female flowers, and densely short-hairy
capsules 4–6 mm diam. In deciduous
woods, on moist, oligotrophic, usually
calcareous, sandy, loamy or rocky soils, to
1,800 m, in most of Europe northwards to
C Scandinavia and S Finland, and eastwards
to the Caucasus.

M. ovata Sternb. & Hoppe is similar, but
has purple-based stems, subsessile, broadly
ovate leaves, and yellow hairs on capsule. In
damp woods on stony soils, to 1,900 m, in
C and SE Europe.

GENTIAN FAMILY, GENTIANACEAE

A family of herbs with *c.* 900 species in some 80 genera,
predominantly in temperate regions. Dicots. Leaves
opposite, simple. Flowers often in cymes, usually regular
and hermaphrodite. Calyx 4–5-toothed or 4–5-parted (rarely
12-parted). Corolla connate at least at base, often tube- or
bell-shaped, with 4–5 (12) lobes, usually contort in bud.
Stamens 4–5 (12), occasionally less, inserted on corolla.
Ovary superior (rarely hemi-inferior), usually 1-locular
(occasionally incompletely 2-locular), with 1 style and a
simple or bifid stigma. Fruit a 2-valved capsule or a berry.
Most European species have strongly declined and should be
protected (as they already are in several countries).

p.198   **Yellow-wort**
Blackstonia perfoliata (L.) Hudson

Description: A glabrous, *glaucous annual* to 40 cm, with
simple, erect stems. Leaves opposite;
lowest ones in more or less distinct rosette,
elliptical or spatulate, *cauline ones sessile and
connate around stem*, broadly triangular-
ovate. Flowers 8–15 mm diam., in
dichasial cymes. Calyx incised almost to
base, with 6–8 *linear-lanceolate, tapering,
usually 1-veined teeth*. Corolla broadly
funnel-shaped, *bright yellow, with 6–8 long,
spreading, ovate lobes*. Stamens 6–8, inserted
high in corolla tube. Ovary 1-locular, with

forked style. Fruit an ellipsoid, many-seeded capsule to 10 mm long, opening with 2 valves.

Flowering: June–October.

Habitat: Grassland, dune-valleys, damp woods, streamsides, on moist or wet, oligotrophic, calcareous, sandy, loamy or rocky soils; from sea level to 1,300 m.

Range: S, C and W Europe, northwards to Ireland, Britain, the Low Countries, C Germany, Hungary, and the Crimea.

The description pertains to ssp. *perfoliata*. Ssp. *serotina* (Reichenb.) Vollmann lacks a distinct rosette, and has upper stem-leaves connate for less than full width of leaf; calyx teeth 3-veined, 1.3–1.8 mm wide at base (not less than 1 mm), and often connate to 1 third of their length. In comparable habitats, often inland, in S, C and W Europe, northwards to SW France and S Germany (also in the Netherlands), eastwards to Asia Minor.

---

p.281 **Common Centaury**
Centaurium erythraea Rafin.

Description: A glabrous *biennial* to 50 cm, with 1 to several (sub)erect, simple flowering stems, rising from *distinct leaf-rosette*. Basal leaves elliptical to obovate, *3–7-veined*, 10–20 mm wide; stem-leaves much smaller, opposite, sessile, narrowly ovate, 3-veined. Flowers 9–15 mm diam., in lax dichasial cymes. Calyx narrowly cup-shaped, with 5 lanceolate, keeled teeth *just equalling corolla tube at anthesis* (much shorter than tube in fruit). Corolla pink (rarely white), with 5 narrowly ovate, more or less spreading lobes. Stamens 5, inserted at throat of corolla tube. Ovary superior, with 1 threadlike style; stigma wider than long. Fruit a narrowly ellipsoid capsule, exceeding calyx, and opening with 2 valves.

Flowering: June–September.

Habitat: Grassland, roadsides, pathways, ditch-sides, wood margins, scrub, (non-saline) dune-valleys, grassy slopes, on moist, oligotrophic to mesotrophic, calcareous to slightly acid, sandy, loamy or rocky soils; from sea level to 1,400 m.

Range: In Europe northwards to Britain, S Sweden and N Russia.

Similar species: **Seaside Centaury** (*C. littorale* (Turner) Gilmour) is a halophyte, with linear to spatulate, 1–3-veined leaves to 5 mm wide, slightly larger flowers (11–14 mm diam.), and calyx teeth longer than corolla tube at anthesis (just equalling tube in fruit). In dune-valleys, coastal pasture, and on high, sandy beaches, on wet or moist, oligotrophic, calcareous or brackish, sandy soils, in W and N Europe, from Ireland and NW France northwards to C Fennoscandia, and eastwards to Austria, Hungary, Romania, and C Russia, but mainly coastal. Its subspecies, *uliginosum* (Waldst. & Kit.) Melderis has smaller flowers (5–11 mm diam.) and rough leaf-margins, and grows primarily in saline inland habitats in E and EC Europe, westwards to N Germany.

---

p.216   *Centaurium maritimum* (L.) Fritsch

Description: A delicate, glabrous *annual or biennial* to 20 cm, with solitary stems, branched only in inflorescence; *leaf-rosette present, but withered at anthesis*. Leaves opposite, sessile, narrowly ovate to lanceolate, to 20 mm long, 3–6 mm wide. *Flowers 8–10 mm diam.*, in dichasial cymes. Calyx cylindrical, with 5 lanceolate, tapering teeth. *Corolla yellow*, occasionally with some pink at edges, with 5 broadly lanceolate lobes. Stamens 5, inserted at throat of corolla tube. Ovary superior, with *forked style* and *2 stigmas*. Fruit a 2-valved capsule.

Flowering: April–August.

Habitat: Coastal heaths, scrub and dune-slacks, on dry, oligotrophic, calcareous, sandy soils.

Range: Coasts of S and W Europe, northwards to NW France, and eastwards to Turkey.

The name Yellow Centaury is found in literature, but should be reserved for *Cicendia* (*see* p.640).

p.281 **Lesser Centaury**
Centaurium pulchellum (Swartz) Druce

Description: A delicate, glabrous *annual* to 15 cm, with solitary stems often (widely) branched from below; *no basal leaf-rosette*. Leaves opposite, sessile, narrowly ovate to lanceolate, 4–8 mm wide, 3–7-veined. *Flowers 5–9 mm diam.*, in dichasial cymes. Calyx narrowly cup-shaped, with 5 (rarely 4) lanceolate teeth, just equalling corolla tube at anthesis (shorter tube in fruit). Corolla pale lilac to dark pink, with 5 (rarely 4) broadly lanceolate lobes; corolla tube markedly constricted over ripening fruit. Stamens (4) 5, inserted at throat of corolla tube. Ovary superior, with 1 threadlike style; stigma button-shaped. Fruit a narrowly ellipsoid, 2-valved capsule.

Flowering: June–October.

Habitat: Dune-valleys, high beaches, brackish pastures, also inland on sandy pool banks, loam-pits, even slurried building sites, on wet or moist, oligotrophic to mesotrophic, calcareous or brackish, sandy, loamy or clayey soils; from sea level to 1,000 m.

Range: Most of Europe except Iceland and the high Arctic.

Similar species: **Slender Centaury** (*C. tenuiflorum* (Hoffm. & Link) Fritsch) grows to 30 cm, (erectly) branching only over middle; it has rather crowded, ovate leaves 8–15 mm wide. In comparable habitats, though only coastal, in S and W Europe, northwards to Normandy and S Britain.

p.281 **Perennial Centaury**
Centaurium scilloides (L. f.) Samp.

Description: A glabrous, creeping, *mat-forming perennial* with numerous sterile shoots, and ascending flowering stems to 30 cm. Leaves opposite, (sub)sessile, elliptical (those on creeping stems short-stalked and suborbicular). *Flowers large* (15–20 mm diam.), *solitary or 2–5 together, subsessile in terminal clusters*. Calyx cylindrical, with 5 lanceolate, long-tapering teeth. Corolla bright pink, with a long tube and 5 obovate, rounded lobes. Stamens 5, inserted at throat of corolla tube. Ovary superior, with 1 style; stigma button-shaped. Fruit a 2-valved capsule.

Flowering: July–August.

Habitat: Coastal heaths and grassy sea-cliffs, on dry, oligotrophic, sandy or rocky soils.

Range: Atlantic coasts of Iberia, NW France and SW Britain.

---

p.197 **Yellow Centaury**
Cicendia filiformis (L.) Delarbre

Description: A tiny, glabrous *annual*, 2–15 cm, with threadlike, erect, simple or (irregularly) branched, reddish stems. Some leaves in small, basal rosette, oblanceolate, stalked; stem-leaves opposite, few, sessile, to 6 mm long, lanceolate to linear. Flowers 3–6 mm diam., solitary on long stalks from leaf-axils. Calyx cup-shaped, with *4 triangular teeth. Corolla yellow, with 4 narrowly ovate lobes*, opening only in clear weather. Stamens 4, inserted at throat of corolla tube. Ovary superior, 1-locular, with 1 style; stigma button-shaped. Fruit an ellipsoid, 1-locular capsule, 4–5 mm long, opening with 2 valves.

Flowering: June–October.

Habitat: Dune-valleys, cart-tracks, pathways, poolsides, in heathland or woods, in seasonally wet places drying out in summer, on oligotrophic, slightly acid (or sometimes brackish), sandy, loamy or peaty soils; mainly in the lowland.

Range: S and W Europe, northwards to Ireland, S Britain, the Low Countries, Germany (extinct in Denmark), and eastwards to Turkey.

The basically dichasial structure of the inflorescence is often hard to recognize in this species. *Compare Exaculum pusillum (see* p.647), which has cream or pink flowers, and *Centaurium maritimum (see* p.638), with 5-merous flowers.

p.345 **Cross Gentian** *Gentiana cruciata* L.

Description: A glabrous perennial with stout, ascending
stems to 50 cm. Leaves crosswise opposite,
rather crowded, spreading, 6–10 cm long,
10–20 mm wide, narrowly elliptical to
lanceolate, *3–5-veined; lower ones connate at
base*, forming long sheath, upper ones
subsessile, not sheathing. *Flowers 20–25 mm
long, several together in axillary and terminal
clusters*; upper leaves *longer than flowers*.
Calyx 4-toothed. Corolla broadly trumpet-
shaped, with long, greyish- or purplish-
green tube and *4 blue, spreading, broadly
ovate lobes* with small lobules in between;
throat of corolla tube whitish, with violet
lines. Stamens 4, inserted on corolla tube;
anthers free. Ovary superior, 1-locular, with
1 style and 2 recurved stigmas. Fruit a
many-seeded, 2-valved capsule.

Flowering: June–October.

Habitat: Grassland, wood margins, grassy slopes,
dune-valleys, on dry, oligotrophic,
calcareous, sandy, loamy or stony soils; from
sea level to 2,000 m.

Range: S, C and E Europe, extending westwards to
Spain and France, and northwards to the
Low Countries, Poland and N Russia.

p.333 **Marsh Gentian** *Gentiana pneumonanthe* L.

Description: A glabrous perennial, with slender,
ascending or erect stems to 50 cm. Leaves
crosswise opposite, rather far apart,
spreading to erect, less than 8 mm wide,
lanceolate to linear, *1–3-veined*, blunt-
tipped, all (sub)sessile, not sheathing.
*Flowers 40–50 mm long, solitary or 2–3
together* in upper leaf-axils, terminal; upper
leaves *shorter than flowers*. Calyx 5-toothed.
Corolla trumpet-shaped, *deep blue, with 5
green stripes* on outside, *speckled with green
inside*; corolla lobes 5, erect, broadly ovate,
with small, acute lobules in between.
Stamens 4, inserted on corolla tube, *anthers
connate* around style. Ovary superior, 1-
locular, with 1 style and 2 recurved stigmas.
Fruit a club-shaped, many-seeded capsule.

Flowering: July–October.

Habitat: Marshes, heaths, roadsides, pathways, on wet or moist, oligotrophic, acid, sandy or peaty soils; from sea level to 1,500 m.

Range: Most of Europe (though rare in the south), northwards to Britain, S Scandinavia and N Russia.

---

p.333 **Spring Gentian** *Gentiana verna* L.

Description: A glabrous, often *mat-forming perennial* with short, simple, erect, quadrangular stems to 10 cm. Leaves mostly basal, in concave to spreading rosettes, 15–20 mm long, 5–10 mm wide, elliptical to oblanceolate, usually *3-veined*, blunt-tipped; stem-leaves few (1–3 pairs), even smaller, opposite, sessile, narrowly elliptical, not sheathing. *Flowers 15–20 mm diam., solitary, terminal.* Calyx cylindrical, with 5 narrow wings (1–2 mm wide), and 5 lanceolate teeth. Corolla trumpet-shaped, with long, narrow tube, *deep blue, with 5 green stripes* on outside, *speckled with green inside*; corolla lobes 5, spreading, ovate, with small, notched lobules in between. Stamens 4, inserted on corolla tube. Ovary superior, 1-locular, with 1 style and 2 recurved stigmas. Fruit a sessile, flask-shaped, many-seeded capsule.

Flowering: April–June.

Habitat: Short grassland, heaths, flushes, moraines, on wet or moist, oligotrophic, preferably calcareous, sandy or stony soils; mainly in the mountains, to 2,600 m.

Range: C Europe, extending westwards to the Pyrenees and C France, also in N England (Teesdale) and W Ireland (Galway), northwards to Germany, Poland and N Russia; only on mountains in S Europe.

Similar species: **Snow Gentian** (*G. nivalis* L.) is annual, never mat-forming, with slender, usually branched stem and solitary, blue (rarely violet or white) flowers 8–12 mm diam. (closed under a cloudy sky), with an angular (keeled, not winged) calyx, and acute corolla lobes. In comparable habitats, in the mountains of S and C Europe, the Scottish Highlands, Iceland, Fennoscandia, and N and W Russia. *Compare also Gentianella tenella* (*see* p.646), which has 4-merous flowers and a hairy fringe to corolla throat.

Several closely related species occur in the high mountains of C and S Europe.

p.282 **Felwort** *Gentianella amarella* (L.) Börner

Description: A glabrous *biennial* to 30 cm; stems erect, solitary, with ascending branches from low down; basal leaf-rosette present, but withered at anthesis. Stem-leaves opposite, sessile, narrowly ovate to lanceolate, 3-veined. Flowers 14–22 mm long, short-stalked, in dichasial cymes. Calyx cup-shaped, with 5 *lanceolate, erect, equal teeth*, shorter than corolla tube. Corolla purplish-pink, lilac or violet (rarely cream), with 5 ovate, blunt-tipped or subacute, rather erect lobes; *throat of corolla tube fringed* with white hairs. Stamens 5, inserted on corolla tube. Ovary superior, 1-locular, with very short style and 2 stigmas. Fruit a subsessile capsule.

Flowering: August–October.

Habitat: Heaths, open woods, dune-slacks, on moist, oligotrophic, calcareous, sandy or stony soils; from sea level to 1,700 m.

Range: C and N Europe, eastwards to the Ukraine.

Similar species: **Dune Gentian** (*G. uliginosa* (Willd.) Börner) (also treated as a subspecies) lacks basal rosette, and has 4–5-merous, purplish (rarely cream) flowers 12–18 mm long, opening August–October. In dune-slacks and damp meadows in N Europe (outside the Arctic), southwards to W Britain, France, Germany, Poland, and C Russia. **Early Gentian** (*G. anglica* (Pugsley) E.F. Warburg) is often annual; leaves lanceolate to linear; flowers (April–June), 4–5-merous, dull purplish, with slightly unequal calyx-teeth. In calcareous grassland and dune-slacks in S Britain.

Felwort is also called Autumn Gentian. Some flowers may be 4-merous – often so in ssp. *septentrionalis* (Bruce) Pritchard, from Iceland and Scotland. Several closely related

forms have been described on the
subspecies level, or even as separate species.

p.319 **Field Gentian**
Gentianella campestris (L.) Börner

Description: A glabrous *biennial* to 30 cm; stems erect,
solitary, with ascending branches from low
down; basal leaf-rosette present, with
spatulate leaves, but withered at anthesis.
Stem-leaves opposite, sessile, narrowly
lanceolate to ovate, 3-veined. Flowers (15)
20–30 mm long, short-stalked, in dichasial
cymes. Calyx cup-shaped, with *4 very unequal
teeth*: 1 pair very large, ovate, covering the
other (lanceolate) pair. Corolla violet or lilac
(rarely cream or white), with 4 ovate, blunt-
tipped, rather erect lobes, and *fringe of white
hairs at throat*. Stamens 4, inserted on corolla
tube. Ovary superior, 1-locular, with very
short style and 2 stigmas. Fruit a sessile,
cylindrical capsule opening with 2 valves.
Flowering: June–October.
Habitat: Grassland, heaths, open woods, dune-valleys,
on moist, oligotrophic, calcareous, sandy or
rocky soils; from sea level to 2,750 m.
Range: C and N Europe, extending westwards to
E Spain, southwards to C Italy, and
northwards to the British Isles, Iceland,
Fennoscandia, and N Russia.

Rarely a few of the flowers are 5-merous.
Ssp. *baltica* (Murb.) Tutin is annual, lacks
basal rosette, and has flowers 15–25 mm
long, with calyx subequalling corolla tube
(not markedly shorter). In calcareous
grassland, from NW France and S Sweden
eastwards to Poland.

p.334 **Fringed Gentian**
Gentianella ciliata (L.) Borkh.

Description: A glabrous *perennial* to 30 cm, with erect,
usually simple, angular stems; no basal leaf-
rosette. Stem-leaves opposite, sessile,
spreading to erect; lower ones spatulate,
upper ones narrowly lanceolate, *1-veined*.

Flowers very large, 25–50 mm long, *solitary, terminal*. Calyx cup-shaped, with *4 subequal teeth*. Corolla violet-blue, with 4 large, ovate, subacute, *spreading, long-fringed lobes; throat of corolla tube glabrous*. Stamens 4, inserted on corolla tube. Ovary superior, 1-locular, stalked (inside calyx), club-shaped, with very short style and 2 stigmas. Fruit a long-stalked ellipsoid capsule.

Flowering: August–October.

Habitat: Extensively grazed pasture, open woods, cliff margins, on moist, oligotrophic, calcareous, loamy or rocky soils; from sea level to 2,000 m.

Range: S and C Europe, westwards to C France and the Pyrenees, and northwards to the Low Countries, Poland and N Russia.

Similar species: *G. detonsa* (Rottb.) G. Don f. has short-ciliate corolla lobes, and calyx with very unequal teeth: 1 pair large, broadly lanceolate, partly covering the other (narrowly lanceolate) pair. In dune-slacks and other damp, coastal habitats, in Iceland, Norway and N Russia.

---

p.319 **Chiltern Gentian**
Gentianella germanica (Willd.) Börner

Description: A glabrous *biennial* to 30 cm; stems erect, solitary, with erect branches from base; basal leaf-rosette present, but withered at anthesis. Stem-leaves opposite, sessile, ovate to slightly cordate, *3–5-veined*. Flowers 20–30 (40) mm long, very short-stalked, in cluster-like dichasial cymes. Calyx cup-shaped, with *5 lanceolate, erect, equal teeth*, much shorter than corolla tube. Corolla lilac or violet (rarely cream), with 5 ovate, acute, rather erect lobes; *throat of corolla tube fringed* with white hairs. Stamens 5, inserted on corolla tube. Ovary superior, 1-locular, stalked inside calyx (stalk to 6 mm), with short style and 2 diverging stigmas. Fruit a stalked 2-valved capsule.

Flowering: August–October.

Habitat: Extensively grazed pasture, damp meadows, scrub, on moist, oligotrophic, calcareous, loamy or rocky soils; from sea level to 2,750 m.

Range: W and C Europe, northwards to S England, the Low Countries, Germany, and eastwards to the Carpathians.

Similar species: Closely related species occur in the high mountains of C Europe.
G. aurea (L.) H. Smith has pale-yellow (rarely bluish) flowers to 12 mm diam. In Iceland, Arctic Scandinavia and N Russia, in coastal habitats and at lake margins.
Marsh Felwort (*Swertia perennis* L.) has long-stalked, star-shaped, blue-violet (rarely cream or greenish-white), 4–5-merous flowers, 15–30 mm diam., with very short corolla tube, and lanceolate, spreading corolla lobes (bearing glandular pits at base), in stiffly erect, axillary cymes; capsules ovoid, 10–12 mm long, 2-valved. In grassland, marshes and bogs, in the mountains of C Europe, westwards to C France, and eastwards to Romania and NW Russia.

---

p.334 **Slender Gentian**
Gentianella tenella (Rottb.) Börner

Description: A tiny, glabrous *annual*, 2–10 cm, with small, basal leaf-rosette, and erect, solitary stems. Leaves 5–12 (18) mm long; basal ones spatulate, *stem-leaves few* (1–4 pairs), opposite, sessile, narrowly elliptical to lanceolate. *Flowers small*, to 8 mm long, 4–6 mm diam., *extremely long-stalked* (stalk longer than rest of plant), solitary. Calyx cup-shaped, with *4 lanceolate, erect, equal teeth*, shorter than corolla tube. Corolla sky-blue or violet (rarely cream or white), with 4 ovate, blunt, spreading lobes; *throat of corolla tube fringed* with white hairs. Stamens 5, inserted halfway down on corolla tube. Ovary superior, 1-locular, with very short style and 2 stigmas. Fruit a sessile, 2-valved capsule.

Flowering: July–September.

Habitat: Pasture, gravelly riverbeds, screes, on moist, oligotrophic, acid, often stony or gravelly soils; from sea level to 2,500 m, but only on mountains over 1,500 m in the south.

Range: S and C Europe, westwards to the Pyrenees, eastwards to the Carpathians, again in Arctic N Europe, from Iceland to Fennoscandia and N Russia (including Spitsbergen).

Similar species: **Guernsey Centaury** (*Exaculum pusillum* (Lam.) Caruel) is a tiny, glabrous annual, 3–12 cm (with the port of a *Cicendia*), with a small rosette of subsessile, lanceolate leaves and (usually 3) threadlike, ascending or erect, simple, 1-flowered stems (in fact, the lowest branches of inflorescence); 'cauline' leaves opposite, to 6 mm long, linear-lanceolate; flowers 3–4 mm diam., calyx deeply incised with 4 narrowly lanceolate teeth, corolla cream or pinkish, with 4 ovate lobes; stamens 4, inserted at throat of corolla tube. Ovary superior, (incompletely) 2-locular; capsule narrowly ellipsoid, 5–6 mm long, opening with 2 valves. In short turf and heaths, on pathways, along pools and in fens, on (seasonally) wet to moist, oligotrophic, acid, sandy or peaty soils in SW Europe, northwards to NC and W France and the Channel Islands.

Compare Gentiana nivalis (see p.642), which has 5-merous flowers and a glabrous corolla throat.

CRANE'S-BILL FAMILY, GERANIACEAE

A family of herbs (rarely shrubs) with *c.* 750 species in 11 genera, mostly in subtropical and warm-temperate regions, world-wide. Dicots. Leaves alternate or opposite, palmately or pinnately incised or compound; bracts in inflorescence often opposite. Flowers usually regular and hermaphrodite, 5-merous, in monochasial cymes (with unequally forked branchings, the ultimate ones often equal, hence flowers often in stalked pairs). Stamens usually 10 (occasionally sterile in part). Ovary superior, 5-locular (rarely 3–4-locular), with 5 strongly elongating styles connate around a central column, with (3–4) 5 free stigmas at the top (or 1 undivided stigma). Fruit (in European species) a cluster of (3–4) 5 achenes (mericarps) with a long, hygroscopic beak which detaches itself from the central column (often explosively, hurling away the achene). Of the 2 N European genera, *Erodium* has pinnately divided or pinnate leaves, 5 fertile and 5 sterile, antherless stamens, and spirally coiled beaks to achenes, while *Geranium* has palmately incised to doubly palmate leaves, 10 fertile stamens, and arching beaks. Garden and pot 'geraniums' belong to the large S African genus *Pelargonium*.

---

p.290 **Common Stork's-bill**
Erodium cicutarium (L.) L'Hérit.

Description: A hairy and often slightly glandular annual or biennial, to 40 (60) cm, with basal leaf-rosette and prostrate to erect, branched flowering stems. Basal leaves lanceolate, *pinnate, with pinnately divided leaflets*; stem-leaves smaller. Flowers 12–14 (17) mm diam., 5–7 (9) together in *umbels*. Sepals 5; petals 5, obovate, purplish-pink (occasionally white), the upper pair often slightly larger and with a dark blotch at base. Achenes 5–6 mm long, covered with appressed, brownish bristles, with elliptical pit at the top, and coiled *beak 25–35 mm long*.

Flowering: April–October.

Habitat: Cultivated land, waste places, grassland, roadsides, dunes, on dry, mesotrophic, calcareous to slightly acid, sandy soils; from sea level to 4,000 m.

Range: Most of Europe except the far north.

Similar species: *E. glutinosum* Dumort. is sticky from numerous glandular hairs, and usually has 2–3-flowered umbels, unblotched flowers 6–8 mm diam., and beaks 15–24 mm long. In coastal habitats, in S and W Europe northwards to the Netherlands.
Musk Stork's-bill (*E. moschatum* (L.) L'Hérit.) has musky scent, glandular-hairy, pinnate leaves with ovate, only shortly dentate leaflets, pale-lilac flowers 16–24 mm diam., and beaks 25–40 mm long. In waste or ruderal, sandy places, often near the sea, in S and W Europe, northwards to W France and S Britain.

Coastal forms of Common Stork's-bill, from W Europe, with unblotched flowers 8–14 mm diam., in 3–5-flowered umbels, and with beaks 22–28 mm long, are distinguished as ssp. *dunense* Andreas.

p.104 **Sea Stork's-bill**
Erodium maritimum (L.) L'Hérit.

Description: A *whitish-tomentose annual*, to 10 (30) cm, with prostrate, branched stems. Leaves alternate, stalked, *undivided, ovate with cordate base*, crenate-dentate. Flowers 4–6 mm diam., *solitary or in pairs*. (In solitary flowers, stalk is placed on top of peduncle, the place of junction being marked by 2 small, acute bracteoles, so it could be called a 1-flowered umbel.) Sepals 5; petals 5, obovate, white or pale pinkish, *shorter than sepals* and occasionally absent altogether. Achenes 2.5–3 mm long, with coiled beak to 10 mm long.

Flowering: May–September.

Habitat: Dune-grassland, sea-cliffs, groynes, on dry, oligotrophic, often calcareous, sandy, stony or rocky soils; only coastal.

Range: S Ireland, Britain (northwards to the Solway Firth), the Channel Islands, and NW France (from Brittany to the river Somme).

Similar species: **Mallow-leaved Stork's-bill** (*E. malacoides* (L.) L'Hérit.) also has undivided, cordate leaves, but is a much larger plant, with 3–8-flowered umbels, and beaks to 40 mm long. On coasts as well as inland, mainly in S Europe, northwards to NW France.

Geranium bohemicum L.

Description: A glandular-hairy biennial, with basal leaf-rosette and erect, branched stems to 60 cm. Basal leaves stalked, palmately divided with 5 ovate, acutely lobed and dentate segments; basal pair much smaller, *stem-leaves less deeply incised*, only to middle of blade. Flowers 15–18 mm diam., in pairs; flower-stalks longer than calyx. Sepals 5, spreading; petals 5, with short, *ciliate claw* and obcordate, shallowly notched limb, violet.

Flowering: July–September.

Habitat: Felled or burnt places in coniferous woods, on moist, acid, sandy or stony soils; mainly in the mountains, from 1,200–1,800 m.

Range: C and E Europe, westwards to E France, and northwards to S Scandinavia and S Finland.

Similar species: *G. lanuginosum* has larger flowers on stalks at best equalling calyx, and glabrous, lilac petals; stem-leaves deeply incised, just like basal ones. In woods, scrub and grassy places; mainly Mediterranean, but also in S Sweden.

---

p.273 **Cut-leaved Crane's-bill**
Geranium dissectum L.

Description: A glandular-hairy annual, with straggling or ascending to erect, branched stems to 60 cm; no distinct basal leaf-rosette. Leaves stalked, palmately divided with 5–7 ovate segments, *themselves pinnatifid*, with *narrow, strap-like lobes*. Flowers 8–10 mm diam., in pairs; peduncles shorter than leaves, and flower-stalks about equalling calyx, glandular. Sepals 5, spreading, *glandular, long-awned*; petals 5, with short claw and obcordate, shallowly notched limb, purplish-pink.

Flowering: May–September.

Habitat: Cultivated and waste ground, grassland, roadsides, banks, along ditches, on moist, eutrophic, acid or calcareous, often loamy or clayey soils; from sea level to 1,500 m.

Range: Most of Europe except the extreme north.

Similar species: **Long-stalked Crane's-bill** (*G. columbinum* L.) has peduncles longer than accompanying leaves, flowers 12–18 mm diam., on (glandless) stalks to 6 times longer than (glandless) calyx, and achenes with only 1 line of hairs. In grassland, roadsides, banks, along railways, on moist, mesotrophic, preferably calcareous, sandy, loamy or stony soils to 1,500 m, in most of Europe except the far north.

---

p.272 **Shiny Crane's-bill** *Geranium lucidum* L.

Description: A *glabrous annual*, to 60 cm, with straggling or ascending, branched stems; no distinct basal leaf-rosette. Leaves stalked, palmately divided with *5–7 obovate, often slightly 3-lobed, segments*, bluntly dentate near the top, *shiny fresh green*. Flowers 10–14 mm diam., in pairs; flower-stalks about equalling calyx. Sepals 5, *erect, with prominent keel* and *c.* 4 transverse grooves, pointed and short-awned; petals 5, with *long claw* and narrowly obovate, *round-tipped limb*, purplish-pink. Achenes glabrous.

Flowering: May–August.

Habitat: Roadsides, hedgerows, rocks and walls, on dry to moist, oligotrophic, preferably calcareous, often stony or rocky soils; from sea level to 1,800 m.

Range: S, W and C Europe, northwards to Ireland, Britain, Belgium, Germany, S Scandinavia, S Finland, and C Russia.

In sunny places the whole plant can turn quite red. *Compare also G. robertianum (see* p.653).

p.273 **Dove's-foot Crane's-bill** *Geranium molle* L.

Description: A hairy annual or biennial to 40 cm (often much shorter), with *prostrate or ascending*, branched stems bearing *both long and short hairs*; no distinct basal leaf-rosette. Leaves long-stalked, palmately *lobed to halfway divided* with 5–7 obovate, crenate-dentate segments; *stipules brownish*. Flowers 6–10 (13) mm diam., long-stalked, in pairs. Sepals 5, spreading; petals 5, with short claw and obcordate, shallowly notched limb, purplish-pink (turning violet), rarely white. *Achenes glabrous, transversely grooved*.

Flowering: April–September.

Habitat: Grassland, roadsides, arable fields, waste ground, dunes, banks, on dry to moist, mesotrophic or eutrophic, acid or calcareous, sandy to rocky soils; from sea level to 2,000 m.

Range: Most of Europe except the far north.

Similar species: **Small-flowered Crane's-bill** (*G. pusillum* L.) has stems with very short hairs (to 0.3 mm) and minute glands; flowers only 4–6 mm diam., pale violet; only 5 (not 10) stamens have anthers; achenes hairy, without grooves. In comparable habitats, in most of Europe except the far north.

p.273 **Marsh Crane's-bill** *Geranium palustre* L.

Description: A hairy perennial, to 50 cm, with short, creeping rhizomes and prostrate to erect, branched stems bearing *deflexed bristle-hairs*. Leaves stalked, palmately divided with 5 ovate, dentate, often slightly 3-lobed segments; basal ones much smaller. *Flowers large*, 22–30 mm diam., long-stalked, in pairs. Sepals 5, spreading; petals 5, with short claw and obovate, *round-tipped limb*, purplish or lilac.

Flowering: June–August.

Habitat: Damp meadows, marshes, streamsides, on moist, oligotrophic, sandy or stony soils; from 300 m to 1,500 m, descending lower in the north.

Range: C and E Europe, westwards to the Pyrenees and the Vosges, northwards to S Sweden and S Finland.

---

p.332 **Meadow Crane's-bill** *Geranium pratense* L.

Description: A hairy perennial, to 90 cm, with erect, branched stems bearing *deflexed bristle-hairs beneath*, and often glandular hairs above. Leaves palmately divided with 5–7 lanceolate segments, themselves pinnately lobed to divided; lower leaves stalked, *upper ones sessile. Flowers large*, 25–30 mm diam., short-stalked, in pairs; stalks temporarily deflexed after anthesis. Sepals 5, spreading; petals 5, with short claw and obovate, *round-tipped limb*, pale sky-blue or violet (rarely white), with reddish veins.

Flowering: June–September.

Habitat: Grassland, road verges, hedgebanks, stream- and ditch-sides, on moist, mesotrophic, calcareous, sandy, loamy or stony soils; from sea level to 1,900 m.

Range: C and N Europe, westwards to Ireland.

Similar species: **Wood Crane's-bill** (*G. sylvaticum* L.) has leaf-segments less deeply incised, often only dentate, flowers purplish-pink (and red-veined) 22–26 mm diam., and flower-stalks never deflexed. In grassland, damp woods, hedgebanks, on moist, oligotrophic, acid, sandy to stony soils; from 400 m to

2,500 m, in most of Europe, but mainly on mountains in the south.

---

p.273 **Hedgerow Crane's-bill**
Geranium pyrenaicum Burm. f.

Description: A hairy perennial, to 60 cm, with erect or ascending, branched stems bearing *both hairs and minute glands* (to 0.1 mm, more frequent above). Leaves stalked, palmately divided with 5–7 obovate, apically lobed or dentate segments; *stipules purplish*. Flowers 14–18 mm diam., rather long-stalked, in pairs. Sepals 5, spreading; petals 5, with short claw and *obcordate, shallowly notched limb*, purplish-pink or mauve. Achenes smooth, appressed-hairy.

Flowering: June–August (October).

Habitat: Grassland, cultivated and waste ground, roadsides, hedgerows, banks, on dry to moist, mesotrophic, calcareous or acid, sandy or stony soils; from sea level to 1,900 m.

Range: S and W Europe, northwards to Ireland, Scotland, N France; but naturalized in much larger area further north, to S Fennoscandia and C Russia.

Similar species: **Round-leaved Crane's-bill** (*G. rotundifolium* L.) has a foetid odour, less deeply incised leaves (not quite halfway), and pink flowers 10–12 mm diam., with round-tipped petals; glands on stem longer (0.25–0.4 mm). In roadsides, cultivated ground, on rubble and old walls, on dry, oligotrophic, calcareous, sandy, loamy or stony soils, from sea level to 1,600 m, in most of Europe except the far north.

---

p.272 **Herb Robert** *Geranium robertianum* L.

Description: A glabrous annual or biennial to 60 cm, with ascending to erect, branched stems; no distinct basal leaf-rosette (at least at anthesis). Leaves stalked, palmate with *3–5 ovate, (doubly) pinnately divided leaflets*, deep green, but often flushed with red when growing in full light. Flowers 14–18 mm diam., in pairs; flower-stalks often much longer than calyx.

Sepals 5, erect, glandular-hairy, with 1 or 2 transverse grooves (at most), pointed and awned, not sharply keeled; petals 5, with *long claw* and narrowly obovate, *round-tipped limb* (rarely slightly notched), bright pink (rarely white, then often escaped from gardens).

Flowering: May–September.

Habitat: Woods, scrub, shaded roadsides, hedgebanks, rubble, old walls, along railways, on moist to rather dry, mesotrophic to eutrophic, more or less calcareous soils; from sea level to 2,000 m. *G. r. maritimum* (Bab.) H.G. Baker is small, prostrate, and found on shingle-beaches.

Range: Most of Europe except the far north.

Similar species: **Little Robin** (*G. purpureum* Vill.) has short-stalked, deep purplish-pink flowers only 7–14 mm diam., and yellow (not orange) pollen; plant less inclined to reddening. *Compare also G. lucidum (see p.650)*, which has shiny leaves and keeled sepals.

p.272 **Bloody Crane's-bill** *Geranium sanguineum* L.

Description: A hairy perennial, to 60 cm, with creeping rhizome and erect to spreading, branched stems. Leaves stalked, palmately divided with 5–7 obovate or wedge-shaped, often 3-lobed, segments. *Flowers large,* 25–35 mm diam., very long-stalked, *solitary* (stalk set on top of peduncle, together with 2 small bracteoles). Sepals 5, spreading; petals 5, with short claw and *obovate, round-tipped limb, carmine or red-purplish*.

Flowering: June–August.

Habitat: Grassland, open woods, dunes, on dry, oligotrophic, calcareous, sandy or stony soils; from sea level to 1,900 m.

Range: Most of Europe, northwards to S Fennoscandia and C Russia, and eastwards to the Caucasus and Armenia; absent from many islands, and from the Netherlands.

Similar species: *G. sibiricum* L. also has solitary flowers, but these are very small, bright pink, with notched petals scarcely exceeding calyx. Native to Siberia; naturalized in E Europe.

GLOBULARIA FAMILY, GLOBULARIACEAE

A family of herbs and shrubs, with *c.* 30 species in 2 genera, mainly in S Europe and N Africa. Dicots. Leaves alternate, simple, entire-margined, often partly in basal rosette. Flowers in terminal flowerhead, with common involucre of short bracts; flowers irregular, hermaphrodite, basically 5-merous. Calyx deeply incised, with 3–5 teeth, persistent on fruit. Corolla 2-lipped and 5-lobed, or 1-lipped and 3-lobed. Stamens 4, in 2 unequal pairs, inserted on corolla tube, protruding. Ovary superior, 1-locular, with 1 style and 2 stigmas. Fruit an achene.

---

p.346 **Common Globularia** *Globularia vulgaris* L.

Description: A glabrous, rosette-bearing perennial, to 40 cm, with ascending or erect stems. Leaves leathery; basal ones stalked, ovate or spatulate, finely crenate, with *3–5 arched veins*, and *notched tip* (often with short point in notch), stem-leaves numerous, alternate, sessile, ovate to lanceolate, sharply pointed. Flowers in *rounded flowerhead to 25 mm diam.*, with common involucre of lanceolate bracts. Calyx 2-lipped. Corolla *sky-blue* (rarely lilac or white), 2-lipped, with short, 2-lobed upper lip and long lower lip with 3 narrow, linear lobes. Stamens 4, far protruding.

Flowering: April–July.

Habitat: Grassland, felled woods, grassy slopes, on dry, oligotrophic, calcareous, sandy, loamy or stony soils; from sea level to 1,600 m.

Range: S and C Europe, mainly in mountains; also in S Sweden (Öland and Gotland).

Similar species: *G. punctata* Lapeyr. is smaller, with soft, green, rounded or notched (but rarely 3-toothed), entire-margined, 3-veined basal leaves; calyx regular, and flowerheads to 15 mm diam. In more humid, grassy or wooded habitats, in S and C Europe, northwards to N France, SE Belgium, Germany, and eastwards to the Caucasus. Still smaller forms with glaucous leaves occur in the Pyrenees.

Compare also Jasione montana (see p.391), which is a hairy plant with regular, 5-lobed flowers, and an inferior ovary.

ST JOHN'S-WORT FAMILY, GUTTIFERAE

An important family of trees, shrubs and herbs with *c.* 1,000 species in 40 genera, in tropical and temperate regions. Several species are grown in gardens. Dicots. Leaves opposite (rarely whorled), simple, usually sessile, entire (rarely serrate), often possessing translucent, black or red glands imbedded in leaf-tissue. Flowers basically 5-merous and regular, in dichasial cymes; sepals often slightly unequal. Sepals and petals 4–5, free (or sepals slightly connate at base). Stamens numerous, usually in 3–5 bundles. Ovary superior, (1) 3–5-locular, with 3–5 styles. Fruit a capsule or a berry.

---

p.242   **Tutsan** *Hypericum androsaemum* L.

Description: A *glabrous half-shrub*, to 70 cm, with erect to spreading stems with *2 raised lines*. Leaves opposite, sessile, *at least 40 mm wide*, ovate, blunt-tipped, with rounded to slightly cordate base, entire-margined. Flowers 18–22 mm diam., in small terminal cymes. Sepals 5, *unequal, round-tipped*, persistent and often reddening in fruit. Petals 5, obovate, pale yellow, shorter than calyx. Stamens numerous, *in 5 bundles*. Ovary superior, with 3 styles. Fruit a *shiny, ovoid berry*, 7–10 mm long, *flushed with red or purple*.

Flowering: May–August.

Habitat: Woods, scrub, hedges, on moist, oligotrophic, usually calcareous soils; from sea level to 1,600 m.

Range: S and W Europe, northwards to W and C France, Britain and Ireland.

Similar species: **Rose-of-Sharon** (*H. calycinum* L.), from E Europe and Asia Minor, is patch-forming, with creeping rhizomes, evergreen, leathery, elliptical leaves, solitary, very large flowers (70–80 mm diam.), 5 styles, and large capsule (not berry). Grown in gardens, and locally naturalized in Britain and France.

Tutsan is the only native *Hypericum* with berries; also cultivated for ornament. In regions with a mild climate the plant often stays green in winter.

p.215 **Marsh St John's-wort** *Hypericum elodes* L.

Description: A *densely grey-tomentose, usually aquatic*, perennial to 50 cm, with creeping or floating, ascending, scarcely branched, *rounded stems* without raised lines. The hairs are water-repellent. Leaves opposite, sessile, *crowded, ovate to suborbicular*, to 30 mm long, entire-margined. Flowers 12–15 mm diam., in small terminal cymes. Sepals 5, blunt-tipped, *erect*, with *red glandular hairs* at margin. Petals 5, obovate, rather erect (*not spreading*), yellow. Stamens in 3 bundles, the *filaments connate* for much of their length. Ovary superior, with 3 styles. Fruit a capsule.

Flowering: June–September.

Habitat: Marshes, bogs, shallow pools, ditches, on wet, oligotrophic, acid, sandy, muddy or peaty soils; found from sea level to 1,300 m.

Range: W Europe, northwards to Ireland, Britain, the Low Countries and N Germany.

---

p.214 **Hairy St John's-wort**
Hypericum hirsutum L.

Description: A *hairy perennial*, to 1 m, with creeping rhizomes and erect, *rounded stems* with 2 raised lines. Leaves opposite, sessile, to 50 mm long, ovate to elliptical, blunt-tipped, entire-margined, with translucent dots; no black marginal glands. Flowers 14–20 mm diam., in small cymes composing *long, leafy panicle*. Sepals 5, lanceolate, with *stout, black glandular hairs* at margins. Petals 5, narrowly ovate, yellow, with some *black glands at the top*. Stamens numerous, in 3 bundles, connate only at base. Ovary superior, 3-locular, with 3 styles. Fruit a capsule.

Flowering: July–September.

Habitat: Open, deciduous woods, scrub, rough grassland, shaded road verges, stream- and riversides, on moist, oligotrophic, calcareous, sandy, loamy or stony soils; from sea level to 1,500 m.

Range: Most of Europe except the extreme north.

The only other hairy species in N Europe are *H. montanum* and the usually aquatic *H. elodes*.

---

p.197 **Trailing St John's-wort**
Hypericum humifusum L.

Description: A *glabrous annual, biennial or short-lived perennial*, to 5 (20) cm, with *creeping or ascending, rounded stems* with 2 indistinct raised lines. Leaves opposite, sessile, *turned flat to ground*, to 15 mm long, ovate to elliptical or oblanceolate, blunt-tipped, entire-margined, with few or no translucent dots, and few black marginal glands. Flowers 8–10 mm diam., *axillary, solitary or in small cymes*. Sepals 5, *unequal*, narrowly ovate, blunt (often shortly awned), with *black marginal glands* and often glandular hairs as well. Petals 5, elliptical, yellow, with *black glands at the top*. Stamens in 3 bundles, free. Ovary superior, 3-locular, with 3 styles. Fruit a capsule, not exceeding persistent calyx.

Flowering: June–October.

Habitat: Shaded, often bare ground, pond margins, cart-tracks, pathways, hedges, on moist, oligotrophic, acid, sandy or loamy soils; from sea level to 1,400 m.

Range: W and C Europe, northwards to Ireland, Britain, and S Scandinavia.

Compare also Lysimachia nummularia (see p.919), which has cordate-based leaves and 5-stamened flowers.

---

p.214 **Imperforate St John's-wort**
Hypericum maculatum Crantz

Description: A glabrous perennial, to 50 cm, with erect, *quadrangular stems* with 4 raised lines (but *no wings*); branches erect under sharp angle (*c.* 30°) to main axis. Leaves opposite, sessile, to 30 mm long, ovate to elliptical, blunt-tipped, entire-margined, with few or no translucent dots. Flowers 18–20 mm diam., in small cymes composing *broad, leafy panicle*. Sepals 5, ovate, blunt-tipped, with black marginal glands. Petals 5, narrowly ovate, yellow, with *black glandular dots and stripes* on both faces (not merely marginal). Stamens numerous, in 3 bundles. Ovary superior, 3-locular, with 3 styles. Fruit a capsule.

Flowering: June–August.

Habitat: Grassy heaths, meadows, wood margins, road verges, streamsides, on moist, oligotrophic to mesotrophic, usually acid, sandy, loamy, clayey or stony soils; from sea level to 2,650 m.

Range: Much of continental Europe except the far north; extinct in the Netherlands, and only in W Scotland on the British Isles.

Similar species: **Wavy St John's-wort** (*H. undulatum* Schousboe ex Willd.) has wavy-edged leaves, and petals often flushed with red on outside. In bogs, marshes, stream- and pond-sides, in W Europe, from Iberia to W France and SW Britain.
H. dubium Leers has branches making blunt angle (*c.* 50°) with main axis, sepals finely denticulate at the top, and capsules with long glandular stripes only. Along streams, ditches, wood margins, on wet to moist, oligotrophic, acid, sandy or loamy soils in W and C Europe.
Square-stalked St John's-wort (*H. quadrangulum* Fries) has quadrangular, 4-winged stems, yellow flowers 8–12 mm diam., leaves with many translucent dots (but no black marginal glands), and lanceolate, very acute sepals. In meadows, road verges, wood margins, along streams, in most of Europe except the high Arctic.

p.214 **Mountain St John's-wort**
Hypericum montanum L.

Description: A slightly hairy perennial, to 80 cm, with *rounded, erect stems without raised lines*. Leaves opposite, sessile, to 50 mm long, ovate to elliptical, blunt-tipped, entire-margined, with black marginal glands, and *very short-hairy beneath*; lower leaves rather crowded, lacking translucent dots, upper leaves often widely spaced, much narrower, with cordate base and some translucent dots. Flowers 10–15 mm diam., in *small, rather dense terminal cyme*. Sepals 5, lanceolate, with *stout, black glandular hairs* at margins. Petals 5, narrowly ovate, acute, pale yellow, without black glands. Stamens numerous, in 3 bundles. Ovary superior, 3-locular, with 3 styles. Fruit a capsule.

Flowering: June–September.

Habitat: Open woods, scrub, hedgebanks, rough grassland, on dry, oligotrophic, preferably calcareous, sandy, loamy or stony soils; from sea level to 1,900 m.

Range: Most of Europe except the far north, and eastwards to the Caucasus.

Similar species: **Toadflax-leaved St John's-wort** (*H. linariifolium* Vahl) also has rather small inflorescences on top of long, slender, erect stems, but leaves linear-lanceolate, with margins rolled under; translucent dots always absent. In open woods, scrub, and on grassy slopes, on dry, oligotrophic, acid, stony or rocky soils, in SW Europe, northwards to W and C France, the Channel Islands and SW Britain.

---

p.215 **Perforate St John's-wort**
Hypericum perforatum L.

Description: A glabrous perennial, to 80 cm, with erect, *rounded stems* with 2 raised lines. Leaves opposite, sessile, to 30 (50) mm long, ovate to elliptical (or even linear-oblanceolate in plants from dry habitats), blunt-tipped, entire-margined, with many translucent dots. Flowers 20–35 mm diam., in small cymes composing *broad, leafy panicle*. Sepals 5, lanceolate, acute, with or without black glands. Petals 5, narrowly ovate, yellow, with *few black glandular dots* on both faces (no marginal glands), and with *asymmetrical tip denticulate on 1 side*. Stamens numerous, in 3 bundles. Ovary superior, 3-locular, with 3 styles. Fruit a capsule, with long, vertical, brownish glandular stripes and short, slanting glands.

Flowering: May–September.

Habitat: Grassland, wood margins, scrub, hedgebanks, roadsides, railways, on dry, mesotrophic, neutral or calcareous, sandy, loamy or stony soils; from sea level to 2,000 m.

Range: Most of Europe except the far north.

Compare H. dubium (see p.659), which has comparable habit, but 4 raised lines on stem, and capsules with only long glandular stripes.

p.214 **Slender St John's-wort**
Hypericum pulchrum L.

Description: A glabrous perennial to 60 (90) cm, occasionally much lower (in few-flowered dwarf forms), with slender, erect or ascending, *rounded, reddish stems* without raised lines. Leaves opposite, sessile, to 15 (20) mm long, ovate to elliptical, blunt-tipped, entire-margined, with translucent dots, but *no black glands*; upper leaves have cordate base. Flowers 14–15 mm diam., long-stalked, in small cymes composing small, lax panicle. Sepals 5, elliptical, *round-tipped*, with *short, black glandular hairs* at margins. Petals 5, narrowly ovate, yellow (*often flushed with red* on outside), with *numerous black marginal glands*. Stamens numerous, in 3 bundles. Ovary superior, 3-locular, with 3 styles. Fruit a capsule.

Flowering: June–September.

Habitat: Open woods, scrub, heaths, poor pasture, on dry, oligotrophic, acid, sandy or stony soils; from sea level to 1,000 m.

Range: Most of Europe, northwards to S Scandinavia.

Similar species: **Irish St John's-wort** (*H. canadense* L.) is a delicate annual (rarely perennial) to 25 cm, with threadlike stems bearing flowering branches from base; leaves lanceolate to linear, 1–3-veined, to 20 mm long; flowers small, 6–8 mm diam., with lanceolate petals hardly equalling sepals, which are often red-striped but always without black glands. Native to N America; presumed naturalized only in W Ireland (Mayo, Glengariff) and the Netherlands (Twente).

WATER-MILFOIL FAMILY, HALORAGACEAE

A family of herbs, often aquatics, with *c.* 180 species in 7 genera world-wide. Dicots. Leaves alternate or whorled. Flowers regular, unisexual, monoecious. Sepals 4, or absent; petals 4, rudimentary in female flowers. Stamens 6–8. Ovary inferior, 4-locular, with 4 styles. Fruit a cluster of 4 achenes. All European species are aquatic, with whorled, pinnately dissected leaves, and flowers in emergent spikes with female flowers beneath.

Compare also Ceratophyllum (*see* p.443), which has forked leaves, and *Hottonia* (*see* p.919), which has flat (not threadlike) segments.

p.54   **Spiked Water-milfoil**
Myriophyllum spicatum L.

Description: A hairless, aquatic perennial, with submerged, freely branching stems to 2.5 m. *Leaves pinnately divided*, to 30 mm long, *mostly in whorls of 4–5 (6)*, with *7–11 pairs* of threadlike segments; *upper floral bracts undivided, entire or dentate*, also in whorls of 4, much shorter than flowers. Spike 5–15 cm long, with more than 20 flowers (female flowers beneath, often some hermaphrodite flowers in middle). Petals 2–3 mm long, ovate, greenish or reddish. Fruit a cluster of 4 warty achenes. *See also* family characteristics.

Flowering: June–September.

Habitat: Stagnant or slow-moving, mesotrophic to eutrophic, preferably lime-rich, fresh or brackish waters, to a depth of 6 m; from sea level to 1,500 m.

Range: All Europe except Spitsbergen.

Similar species: **Alternate-flowered Water-milfoil** (*M. alterniflorum* DC.) also has undivided upper floral bracts, but leaves to 25 mm long (with 4–8 pairs of segments) in whorls of 3–4 (5), and short, nodding spikes to 30 mm, with only 4–15 flowers; male flowers mostly solitary (not in whorls), with yellowish, red-striped petals. In oligotrophic, acid or basic, fresh waters to a depth of 3 m, from sea level to 1,000 m, in N, W and C Europe.

p.286 **Whorled Water-milfoil**
Myriophyllum verticillatum L.

Description: A hairless, aquatic perennial, with submerged, freely branching stems to 3 (5) m. *Leaves pinnately divided*, to 50 mm long, *mostly in whorls of (4) 5–6*, with 8–16 *pairs* of threadlike segments; *floral bracts pinnately divided* like leaves, also in whorls of 5, those of female flowers usually smaller. Flower-spike 7–25 cm long. Petals 3–4 mm long, ovate, *serrate, pink*. Fruit a cluster of 4 smooth achenes. *See also* the family characteristics.

Flowering: June–August.

Habitat: Stagnant or slow-moving, mesotrophic, preferably base-rich, fresh waters, to a depth of 3 m; from sea level to 1,000 m.

Range: Most of Europe except the high Arctic.

MARE'S-TAIL FAMILY, HIPPURIDACEAE

A monotypic family of hairless, aquatic perennials, with only 1 species (or 5 species, according to some authors), on all continents but Africa. Closely related to the Haloragaceae. Dicots. Creeping rhizomes and erect, emergent stems with crowded whorls of simple, undivided, linear leaves. Flowers hermaphrodite or unisexual, sessile in leaf-axils. Perianth not obvious, tube-shaped, connate to ovary. Only 1 stamen, inserted on rim of perianth tube. Ovary inferior, 1-locular, with 1 ovule and 1 style. Fruit a smooth, ovoid achene enveloped in fleshy perianth.

---

p.53 **Mare's-tail** *Hippuris vulgaris* L.

Description: Leaves in whorls of 6–12, the submerged ones soft, to 70 mm long, those on emerse stems often shorter, spreading and upcurved, rather stiff. *See* the family description.

Flowering: May–August.

Habitat: Stagnant or slow-moving, mesotrophic to eutrophic, preferably lime-rich, fresh or brackish waters, to a depth of 6 m, and often on clayey soils; from sea level to 1,600 m.

Range: All Europe except Spitsbergen, but rare in the Mediterranean region.

Compare Elatine alsinastrum (see p.614), which has 8-stamened flowers and notable, 4-merous perianth.

FROGBIT FAMILY, HYDROCHARITACEAE

A very polymorphic family of aquatic perennials, with *c.* 106 species in 15 genera, in fresh and saline waters all over the world. Monocots. Leaves simple, often basal or in whorls. Flowers regular, basically 3-merous, usually unisexual, female ones solitary, male ones in clusters; inflorescence enveloped in spatha of 1 or 2 bracts. Sepals and petals 3. Stamens (1) 2–3, or a multiple of 3. Receptacle usually enveloping ovary, and protracted into long tube bearing perianth at the top. Ovary inferior, with 1 or 6 locules, 1 style and (2) 3 or 6 (to 30) stigmas (or 6 free, bifid styles, as in *Stratiotes* and *Hydrocharis*). Fruit a many-seeded capsule, often with a fleshy wall.

p.53 **Nuttall's Water-thyme**
Elodea nuttallii (Planchon) St John

Description: A submerged aquatic perennial, with freely branching, floating, hardly rooting stems to 3 m or more. Leaves in whorls of 3 (4), to 18 mm long, 1–2 mm wide, linear-lanceolate, acute, finely dentate, strongly recurved, turned, often convex and bronze-green. Flowers solitary in leaf-axils, regular, unisexual, dioecious, with 3 ovate, greenish sepals to 2 mm long, and 3 spatulate, white petals (also 2 mm long), placed on top of threadlike perianth-tube (to 10 cm long) reaching for water-surface. Ovary 1-locular, deep down in perianth tube; 1 long style with 3 notched stigmas just protruding from tube.

Flowering: May–August.

Habitat: Stagnant or slow-moving, mesotrophic to eutrophic, preferably basic, fresh waters, to a depth of 3 m; from sea level to 1,600 m.

Range: Native to N America; naturalized in NW and WC Europe since 1939 (starting from Belgium), and still rapidly expanding.

Similar species: **Canadian Pondweed** (*E. canadensis* Michaux), also from N America, has broader (2–5 mm), narrowly elliptical, blunt-tipped, flat or slightly curved, not turned, deep-green leaves. In comparable habitats, more often in mesotrophic waters, in most of Europe except the far north.

Large-flowered Water-thyme (*Egeria densa* Planchon) from Argentina has leaves to 40 mm long, in whorls of 4–6, and showy white petals 9–12 mm long on perianth tube to 70 mm. Cultivated in aquaria, and locally naturalized in NW and C Europe (where all plants from the wild are male, with 9 stamens).

Esthwaite Waterweed (*Hydrilla verticillata* (L. f.) Royle) has stiff, linear, denticulate, acute (almost prickly) leaves to 20 mm long, 1.5 mm wide, in whorls of (2) 3–6 (8), and hermaphrodite flowers to 5 mm diam., with 3 stamens and 3 stigmas. In quiet waters of lakes and ponds in W Ireland, Britain (Lake District), Germany, and Russia.

When Canadian Pondweed started to expand rapidly, following its introduction into Europe *c.* 1835 (Ireland), it was feared that it would develop into a pest. However, the invasion never took serious dimensions, and in many areas it is now being partially replaced by Nutall's Water-thyme, which has a higher tolerance of pollution. Neither species sets fruit in Europe, and male plants have not been observed here in the wild. The plants propagate vegetatively, and hibernate via detached leaf-buds. Any fragment of the stem will quickly resume growth.

---

p.101   **Frogbit** *Hydrocharis morsus-ranae* L.

Description: A glabrous aquatic with long, floating stolons, and long-stalked, *suborbicular, cordate-based, shiny bronze-green leaves* to 30 mm diam., in rosette-like tufts; stipules large, translucent. Flowers emergent, 18–20 mm diam., unisexual, *monoecious* (but never in the same rosette); female ones usually solitary, with sterile anthers, male ones often in 2–4-flowered umbel borne on long peduncle rising from base of rosette.

Sepals 3, ovate, to 5 mm long. Petals 3, rounded, to 10 mm long, *white with yellow base*. Stamens (in male flowers) 12 (only 9 with anthers). Ovary inferior, incompletely 6-locular, with 6 bifid styles. Fruit a rounded, many-seeded, soft-walled capsule, irregularly opening at the top.

Flowering: June–August.

Habitat: Stagnant, mesotrophic to eutrophic, fresh or slightly brackish waters; from sea level to 1,500 m.

Range: Most of Europe northwards to the Baltic region and S Finland, but rare in Mediterranean region.

---

p.101 **Water Soldier** *Stratiotes aloides* L.

Description: A glabrous aquatic, with long, thick, floating stolons, and emergent rosettes of numerous, crowded, sessile, *linear-lanceolate, tapering, rigid, spiny-serrate, erect leaves* to 30 (50) cm long. Flowers emergent, 30–45 mm diam., unisexual, *dioecious*; female ones solitary, with numerous sterile anthers (nectaries), male ones in 2–3-flowered umbel, borne on rather short, stout peduncle rising from base of rosette. Sepals 3, ovate. Petals 3, rounded, *to 25 mm long, white*. Fertile stamens (in male flowers) *c.* 12, surrounded by 15–30 nectaries (staminodes). Ovary inferior, incompletely 6-locular, with 6 bifid styles. Fruit an ovoid, hexagonal capsule with leathery wall, to 35 mm long and half as wide, not splitting, and with 4 (6) brown seeds per locule.

Flowering: May–August.

Habitat: Stagnant, oxygen-poor, mesotrophic to eutrophic, fresh or slightly brackish waters over a thick mud-layer; from sea level to 1,500 m.

Range: Much of Europe but rare in the south and absent from Ireland and the far north.

The plant forms large, often exclusively male or female colonies. Occasionally some apparently fertile stamens are found in female flowers. In autumn the rosettes sink to the bottom, where they decay; the plant hibernates in the form of leaf-buds.

---

p.54 **Tape Grass** *Vallisneria spiralis* L.

Description: A glabrous, submerged aquatic, with long, thin, whitish, creeping stolons, giving off rosette-like tufts of numerous, crowded, sessile, *linear, ribbon-like, soft, finely denticulate leaves* to 60 cm long. Flowers unisexual, *dioecious*; female ones solitary, 4–5 mm diam., with 2-lobed spatha and narrow perianth tube to 40 mm long, *c.* 1 mm thick, on very long, threadlike peduncle rising from base of rosette and reaching for water surface; male ones tiny, extremely reduced, to 0.5 mm diam., numerous, clustered together in rounded, flimsy, 2-lobed spatha borne on short stalk near the bottom. Sepals 3, elliptical, to 2 mm long. Petals 3, elliptical, to 2 mm long, *pinkish*, ciliate. Stamens 2–3 (sterile in female flowers). Ovary inferior, 1-locular, with 1 style and 2–3 notched or bifid stigmas. Fruit a linear, many-seeded capsule with membranous wall, not splitting.

Flowering: June–October.

Habitat: Shallow, moving or stagnant, eutrophic, fresh waters; mainly in the lowland.

Range: S Europe, northwards to NC France and the Ukraine. During the last century the species has expanded along canals and rivers, possibly dispersed by shipping traffic, to Belgium and the Netherlands (Meuse area); locally naturalized in Britain, in waters warmed up by factory effluent.

The male flowers detach themselves from the plant, and drift on the surface; pollination occurs when they bump into a floating female flower. After anthesis the female flowers are pulled under water by their spirally coiling peduncle. Occasionally, juvenile plants of *Sagittaria sagittifolia* (also with ribbon-like leaves, but lacking stolons, *see* p.355) are mistaken for *Vallisneria*.

IRIS FAMILY, IRIDACEAE

A family of perennial herbs with *c.*1,800 species in 70
genera world-wide, especially in warm regions. Monocots
with rhizomes or tuber-like corms. Leaves linear or sword-
shaped, sheathing, all basal or partly cauline (cauline ones
alternate, in 2 rows). Young inflorescence enveloped in
sheath-like bract (spatha). Flowers regular or irregular,
hermaphrodite, basically 3-merous, with 6 showy tepals
often connate into a tube. Stamens 3, opposite to outer
tepals. Ovary inferior, 3-locular (rarely 1-locular), with 3-
branched style, branches occasionally widened into
petaloid structures. Fruit a capsule.

p.335   **Spring Crocus** *Crocus vernus* (L.) Hill

Description: A hairless perennial, with globose
subterranean corm enveloped in fibrous
scales; no aerial stem. *Leaves 2–4*, linear,
4–9 mm wide, dark green, with white stripe
along middle; all leaves basal, protruding
from bundle of sheath-like, whitish scale-
leaves. Flowers solitary, regular, sessile on
corm, to 20 cm long, with membranous
spatha (hidden between leaf-bases), a long
perianth-tube and 6 erect, narrowly
elliptical, *blunt-tipped* tepals, *violet or white*
(or white with violet stripes). *Stamens 3*,
linear, yellow, with long filaments. Ovary
deep down in perianth-tube (subterranean),
with long style and *3 flattened, fringed, deep-
orange stigmas* exceeding stamens. Fruit an
ellipsoid capsule to 20 mm long, with
several globose, reddish-brown seeds.
Flowering: (February) March–April.
Habitat: Grassland and open woods on mountains,
on moist or periodically dry, oligotrophic or
mesotrophic, preferably calcareous, loamy
or stony soils.
Range: Native to the mountains of C and S Europe,
northwards to the French Jura, S Germany
and Czechia; locally naturalized in W
Europe.

Frequently planted in lawns for ornament.
Several other species from the mountains of
S Europe are likewise cultivated, and
occasionally become naturalized: e.g.

C. tommasinianus Herbert (leaves 2–4 mm wide, tepals subacute, spreading, lilac inside, greyish-violet outside); *C. flavus* Weston (deep-yellow tepals, double spatha); and *C. nudiflorus* Sm. (violet-striped tepals, 6 stamens, flowering in autumn when no leaves are present).

p.189 **Yellow Iris** *Iris pseudacorus* L.

Description: A glabrous, perennial halophyte, with thick, creeping rhizomes and tufts of erect, often glaucous, sword-shaped basal leaves to 60 (90) cm long, 30 mm wide. Flowering stems solid, to 1.2 m, with erect, alternate leaves; plant dies down in winter. Flowers 7–10 cm diam., 2–4 (occasionally up to 12) together in terminal raceme, slightly zygomorphic. Tepals 6, *all yellow*; 3 outer ones (falls) large, spatulate, spreading, inner ones (standards) much smaller, oblanceolate, erect. Stamens 3, wrapped in convolute branches of style. Ovary inferior, 3-locular; style 1, with *3 widened, petaloid, yellow branches* (on outside) bearing stigmas at the top. Fruit an ellipsoid to cylindrical, short-beaked, pale-brown capsule to 80 mm long, splitting with 3 valves, and with numerous *disc-shaped, orange-brown, neatly stacked seeds*.

Flowering: May–August.

Habitat: Marshes, reedlands, wet woods and scrub, stream- and ditch-sides, pond margins, on wet, mesotrophic to eutrophic, sandy, clayey or peaty soils; from sea level to 800 m.

Range: Most of Europe except Iceland and the high Arctic.

Another name is Yellow Flag.

p.331 **Siberian Iris** *Iris sibirica* L.

Description: A glabrous perennial, with creeping rhizomes and tufts of erect, linear basal leaves to 60 cm long, *6–10 mm wide, grass-like; flowering stems hollow*, to 1.2 m, with erect, alternate leaves; plant dies down in winter. Flowers 60–80 mm diam., 2–3 together in small, terminal raceme, slightly zygomorphic. Tepals 6, *all violet* and spatulate; 3 outer ones (falls) spreading, with whitish or yellowish, violet-veined base, inner ones (standards) smaller, erect. Stamens 3, wrapped in convolute branches of style. Ovary inferior, 3-locular; style 1, with *3 widened, petaloid, violet branches*. Fruit an ellipsoid, bluntly trigonal, dark-brown capsule to 40 mm long, splitting with 3 valves; seeds flat.

Flowering: June–July.

Habitat: Grassland, heaths and scrub, on moist or (periodically) wet, oligotrophic to mesotrophic, sandy, loamy or peaty soils; from sea level to 1,100 m.

Range: E and C Europe, locally extending westwards to France (Alsace, SW France).

Similar species: **Stinking Iris** (*I. foetidissima* L.) has sword-shaped basal leaves to 70 cm long, (10) 15–25 mm wide, subequalling (solid) flowering stems, and 1–5 dull-violet flowers with cream or yellow centre; seeds rounded, bright orange-red, spongy-walled. In open woods, dunes, roadsides, also on coastal cliffs, on dry, sandy or stony soils; from sea level to 1,200 m, in SW Europe, northwards to N France and England. (Rather inaptly for its unpleasant odour, it is also called Roast Beef Plant.)
Butterfly, or **Blue**, **Iris** (*I. spuria* L.), which also has unpleasant scent when bruised, has narrow, grass-like leaves 8–12 mm wide, and violet or lilac flowers with whitish centre; inner tepals much smaller than outer ones. In wet grassland and marshes, on calcareous, often saline soils, in S and W Europe, with patchy distribution, including W France, England, Denmark, S Sweden, Hungary, and the Ukraine.

Several other species occur in the steppe belt of SE Europe, some of them extending westwards to C Germany. *See* for these species *Flora Europaea* or a good regional flora.

p.95 **Sand Crocus** *Romulea columnae* Seb. & Mauri

Description: A tiny, cormous perennial, to 8 cm, with up
to 6 linear, threadlike, 4-grooved basal leaves
to 1 mm wide (lacking whitish midvein), and
short, leafless flowering stems bearing 1–3 small,
regular, hermaphrodite flowers *7–10 mm
diam.*, partly enveloped by *2 unequal, green
bracts*. Tepals 6, *spreading to recurved*, acute,
pale violet or whitish, violet-veined; perianth
tube short. Ovary inferior, but above ground.
Fruit an obovoid to subglobose, bluntly
trigonal capsule, 5–11 mm long, borne on
fruiting stalk to 50 mm.

Flowering: March–May.

Habitat: Dune-grassland, coastal cliffs, on dry,
oligotrophic, calcareous, sandy or stony
soils; only coastal.

Range: S and W Europe, northwards to W France,
the Channel Islands, and SW England.

---

p.335 **Blue-eyed Grass**
Sisyrinchium bermudianum L.

Description: A small, glabrous perennial, with short
rhizomes and erect, compressed, narrowly
winged flowering stems to 20 cm. *Basal
leaves grass-like*, distichous (in 2 rows), to
15 cm long, 1–5 mm wide, linear, tapering.
Flowers regular, hermaphrodite, 15–20 mm
diam., often in *2 superimposed clusters* each
containing 2–4 flowers, and with a pair of
green bracts at base. Tepals 6, spreading,
sky-blue with yellow base, obovate or
oblanceolate, finely pointed. Stamens have
connate filaments. Ovary inferior, 3-locular.
Fruit a globose, bluntly trigonal, pendulous
capsule to 5 mm long, blackish-purple when
ripe, and opening with 3 valves.

Flowering: (May) July–August.

Habitat: Damp grassland, lake margins, on moist,
oligotrophic, acid soils.

Range: Native only in W and N Ireland; locally
naturalized in France.

More widespread in N America.
Occasionally cultivated in gardens, as are
several other American species.

ARROWGRASS FAMILY, JUNCAGINACEAE

A family of rhizomatous perennial herbs (halophytes, and aquatics), with 3 genera and 14 species in temperate and cool regions of both hemispheres. Monocots. Leaves awl-shaped, basally sheathing; flowering stems simple. Flowers hermaphrodite, regular, in spikes or racemes, lacking bracts. Tepals 6, greenish. Stamens 4 or 6. Carpels 4 or 6, more or less connate to floral axis. Fruit a cluster of follicles, only apically attached to floral axis.

p.66 **Sea Arrowgrass** *Triglochin maritima* L.

Description:
A glabrous perennial, to 60 cm, with stout, oblique rhizome, and tufts of *linear, fleshy, dull-green leaves* to 30 cm long, 2–4 mm wide; all leaves basal. Flowers 3–4 mm diam., crowded, in spike-like racemes. Tepals 6, ovate, green, to 2 mm long. Stamens 6, with very short filament. Ovary 6-locular (composed of 6 carpels), with 6 sessile stigmas; *all carpels fertile.* Fruit a (narrowly) ovoid cluster of 6 *narrowly ellipsoid follicles 4–6 mm long*; fruits more or less spreading, *not appressed to stem.*

Flowering:
May–September.

Habitat:
Saltmarshes, estuaries, coastal grassland, on wet or moist, saline or brackish, clayey or sandy soils; mainly coastal, but also near saline flushes inland.

Range:
Coasts of Europe, except Spitsbergen; locally inland in C and NE France, Hungary, and the steppe belt of SE Europe.

Similar species:
Marsh Arrowgrass (*T. palustris* L.) has thin stolons, narrow, bright-green leaves (1–2 mm wide), smaller flowers (2–3 mm diam.) in lax raceme, and only 3 fertile carpels developing into club-shaped cluster of 3 linear follicles 6–10 mm long; fruits appressed to stem. In marshes, fens, damp meadows, along streams and ditches, also in dune-valleys and the highest parts of saltmarshes, on wet or moist, mesotrophic to eutrophic, occasionally brackish, sandy, clayey or peaty soils, from sea level to 2,000 m, in all of Europe except Spitsbergen and much of the extreme south.

T. bulbosa L. replaces Marsh Arrowgrass in damp, saline habitats of S Europe, northwards to NW France. It has fibre-coated bulb instead of stolons, leaves to 4 mm wide, flowers to 2.5 mm diam., and more patent fruits to 12 mm long (again with 3 fertile carpels).

MINT FAMILY, LABIATAE

A large family of herbs, shrubs and trees, with some 3,000 species in 200 genera world-wide. Dicots. Leaves opposite or alternate, usually simple. Flowers hermaphrodite, irregular, in axillary cymes, often condensed into pseudo-whorls (verticillasters). Calyx usually 5-toothed, often markedly 2-lipped. Corolla mostly tubiform, 2-lipped, often with 3-lobed lower lip and 2-lobed, hooded upper lip, rarely almost regular. Stamens normally 4 (2 long ones, 2 shorter ones), inserted on corolla tube. Ovary 4-locular, composed of 2 carpels, with 1 style descending between locules, and attached to them basally (rarely terminally, e.g. in *Ajuga* and *Teucrium*). Fruit a cluster of 4 achenes, falling apart when ripe. Many species possess glandular hairs secreting volatile, aromatic oils.

p.324 **Basil Thyme** *Acinos arvensis* (Lam.) Dandy

Description: A pubescent, often purple-flushed annual (rarely perennial), to 20 cm, with spreading to ascending, branched, quadrangular stems. Leaves opposite, short-stalked, to 15 mm long, 10 mm wide, *ovate or rhombic, with cuneate base, usually entire*. Flowers axillary, short-stalked, *solitary or in small cymes* (with up to 5 flowers), forming *2–10-flowered verticillasters*. Calyx 13-veined, hairy, *curved, sack-shaped* at base, 2-lipped: 2 lower teeth linear, longer than the 3 upper teeth. *Corolla 7–10 mm long, violet* (rarely white), with straight tube and white, glabrous throat; lower lip 3-lobed (middle lobe larger, notched), about equalling the (flat, erect, glabrous, notched) upper lip. Stamens 4, protruding from corolla tube but not beyond upper lip. Fruit a cluster of 4 ellipsoid, brown or black, smooth achenes to 1.5 mm long.

Flowering: June–September.

Habitat: Arable fields, short turf, dunes, sunny slopes, occasionally railways, on dry, oligotrophic, calcareous, sandy, loamy or stony soils; from sea level to 1,800 m.

Range: Most of Europe except Iceland and the high Arctic.

Compare Stachys arvensis (see p.699), which has crenate-dentate leaves.

---

p.182 **Ground-pine**
Ajuga chamaepitys (L.) Schreber

Description: A *greyish-hairy annual*, with ascending stems to 20 cm; no distinct leaf-rosette. *Leaves 3-partite with linear segments*; lower ones undivided, linear-oblanceolate. *Flowers solitary (rarely paired) in leaf-axils*, much shorter than bracts. Calyx 5-toothed, almost regular. Corolla 7–15 mm long, *yellow*, with red markings near (hairy) throat; upper lip very short, lower lip large, 3-lobed, middle lobe largest, notched, *side-lobes very small*. Stamens 4, upper ones slightly protruding. Fruit a cluster of 4 obovoid achenes, *c.* 3 mm long, strongly net-veined.

Flowering: May–October.

Habitat: Arable fields, wasteland, open, grassy slopes, on dry, oligotrophic to mesotrophic, calcareous, sandy, loamy or stony soils; from sea level to 1,600 m.

Range: S and C Europe, westwards to France and SE Britain, and northwards to C Germany, Poland and C Russia. Very rare in the Low Countries.

The plant has a resinous odour, when crushed.

---

p.324 **Bugle** *Ajuga reptans* L.

Description: A hairy *perennial*, to 40 cm, with long, leafy, creeping stolons, and erect, square stems (often hairy on 2 opposite sides). Leaves ovate, crenate or weakly dentate, 4–70 mm long; lower ones long-stalked, in rosette, upper ones opposite, subsessile.

Inflorescence cylindrical, *rather lax*, with flowers in verticillasters, axillary to large, seldom purple-flushed bracts; *upper bracts shorter than flowers*. Calyx almost regular, hairy, with 5 triangular-lanceolate teeth. *Corolla blue or blue-violet* (rarely pink or white), 14–17 mm long, with *very short, notched upper lip*, and very large, deeply 3-lobed lower lip, middle lobe largest, notched; *corolla tube hairy at throat*. Stamens 4, upper pair protruding, lower pair concealed in corolla tube. Fruit a cluster of 4 obovoid achenes, *c.* 2 mm long.

Flowering: April–June (autumn).

Habitat: Damp, deciduous woods, poor grassland, also dune-valleys, on moist to wet, oligotrophic to mesotrophic, calcareous to slightly acid, sandy, loamy or stony soils; from sea level to 2,000 m.

Range: Most of Europe except Iceland and the high Arctic.

Similar species: **Blue Bugle** (*A. genevensis* L.) lacks stolons, and has stems always hairy on 4 sides; leaves bluntly dentate; basal leaves withered by flowering time. Bracts often strongly flushed with blue or purple; 4 hairy stamens protrude far from bright-blue corolla. In grassland, woodland clearings, ruderal field margins, and along forest-rides, on dry, oligotrophic to mesotrophic, preferably calcareous, sandy, loamy or stony soils, to 1,500 m, in S and C Europe, extending northwards to Belgium, C Germany, Poland, and C Russia. **Pyramidal Bugle** (*A. pyramidalis* L.) also lacks stolons, and has stems to 25 cm, hairy on all sides, and crowded verticillasters in pyramidal inflorescence, with large, blue- or purple-tinged bracts all exceeding the (blue-violet) flowers; stamens glabrous, not protruding. In N and C Europe, mainly in the mountains (to 2,800 m), scattered in the lowland, westwards to the Low Countries, N Britain and W Ireland; also in SE Europe, eastwards to the Caucasus. • Pink or white flowers occasionally seen in all these species.

Bugle is also cultivated for ornament, when it often has purplish-brown foliage.

p.254 **Black Horehound** *Ballota nigra* L.

Description: A (sparsely) hairy perennial, to 60 (90) cm, with erect, quadrangular, rough-hairy stems. Leaves opposite, short-stalked, 30–70 mm long, narrowly ovate, with rounded to slightly cordate base, coarsely dentate-crenate, with awned teeth. Flowers in *short-stalked, axillary verticillasters, often turned to 1 side*; each flower with *2 linear, hairy bracteoles* at its base. Calyx almost regular, 4–6.5 mm long, 10-veined, funnel-shaped, hairy, reddish, with 5 triangular, pointed teeth with apical awn of 1.5–3 mm. Corolla 12–18 mm long, purplish-pink (rarely white), with 3-lobed lower lip (middle lobe larger, notched, with purple marking), and hooded, hairy, notched upper lip; *corolla tube straight, glabrous at throat*. Stamens 4, *straight*, protruding from corolla tube but not beyond upper lip. Fruit a cluster of 4 *glabrous, ellipsoid achenes, rounded above*.

Flowering: June–September.

Habitat: Roadsides, wood margins, along woodland-rides, hedges, in ruderal places, on dry to moist, mesotrophic to eutrophic, sandy or stony soils; from sea level to 1,500 m.

Range: E and C Europe, extending westwards to E France, Germany and S Sweden.

The description above pertains to ssp. *nigra*, which has no particularly unpleasant smell. Ssp. *foetida* Hayek on the other hand gives off a repudiating smell; it also differs in having broadly ovate leaves, and broadly triangular calyx teeth, with short awns to 1 mm. In comparable habitats of W Europe, eastwards to Germany and Italy.

Compare also Nepeta (see p.693), which has 15-veined calyx, greyish-tomentose leaves, and very short hairs at throat of corolla tube, *Lamium (see p.684)*, which has 5-veined calyx, and unawned calyx teeth, and *Stachys (see p.698)*, which has sessile, all-sided verticillasters, and upper stamens curved sideways.

p.311 **Lesser Calamint** *Calamintha nepeta* (L.) Savi

Description: A pubescent, aromatic perennial, with erect, simple or scarcely branched, quadrangular stems to 60 cm. Leaves opposite, short-stalked, *10–20 mm long*, ovate with rounded base, subentire or weakly dentate (with *2–5 shallow teeth on each side*). Flowers short-stalked, in lax, terminal and axillary, spaced, 3–11-flowered, short-stalked axillary cymes; flowers with few bracteoles at their base. Calyx usually 10-veined, *4–6 mm long*, long-hairy, with *straight tube* and 5 subequal, sparsely ciliate teeth (upper ones to 1 mm, lower ones to 2 mm long). *Corolla 9–15 mm long, white or pale lilac* (rarely white), with straight tube and glabrous throat; lower lip 3-lobed (middle lobe larger, notched), slightly larger than the (flat, erect, glabrous, subentire) upper lip. Stamens 4, protruding from corolla tube but not beyond upper lip. Fruit a cluster of 4 achenes.

Flowering: July–October.

Habitat: Scrub, grassy riverbanks, sunny slopes, on dry, oligotrophic, calcareous, sandy or stony soils; from sea level to 1,300 m.

Range: S and W Europe, northwards to E Britain and the Low Countries, locally naturalized in Germany.

Similar species: **Wood Calamint** (*C. sylvatica* Bromf.) in its typical form (ssp. *sylvatica*) has larger, densely ciliate calyx (6–11 mm long, with upper teeth to 2 mm, lower ones to 4 mm long) with inner ring of hairs concealed in tube (instead of slightly protruding); flowers larger (15–22 mm long), leaves larger (25–70 mm long, with 6–10 rather strong teeth on each margin). In open woods, scrub, sunny slopes, on dry, calcareous soils of S and C Europe, westwards to S England and the Low Countries, and eastwards to the Ukraine. Its ssp. *ascendens* (Jord.) P.W. Ball (or **Common Calamint**) has flowers 10–16 mm long, with lower calyx teeth to 3.5 mm, and slightly smaller, subentire or weakly crenate-serrate leaves to 50 mm long. In comparable habitats, in the same general area.

Lesser Calamint description pertains to
C. nepeta ssp. *glandulosa* (Req.) P.W. Ball.
Ssp. *nepeta* has larger leaves (to 35 mm long
with up to 9 teeth on either side), and longer
stalks to axillary cymes (8–22 mm, not 0–5
(10) mm), which have 10–20 flowers. In the
mountains of S and SC Europe.

p.251 **Wild Basil** *Clinopodium vulgare* L.

Description: A pubescent, aromatic perennial, with erect,
simple or scarcely branched stems to 40
(80) cm. Leaves opposite, short-stalked,
20–50 mm long, *ovate, with rounded to cuneate
base, blunt-tipped, weakly crenate or subentire*.
Flowers in dense, terminal and axillary, often
many-flowered, spaced verticillasters; flowers
have several awl-shaped, long-hairy
bracteoles at their base. Calyx 13-veined,
long-hairy, with curved tube and 5 *subequal
teeth. Corolla 12–22 mm long, deep pink* (rarely
white), with straight tube and glabrous
throat; lower lip 3-lobed (middle lobe larger,
notched), slightly larger than the (flat, erect,
glabrous, notched) upper lip. Stamens 4,
protruding from corolla tube but not beyond
upper lip. Fruit a cluster of 4 subglobose,
brown, smooth achenes, *c.* 1 mm long.

Flowering: July–September.

Habitat: Scrub, woodland clearings, grassy slopes,
dunes, on dry, oligotrophic, preferably
calcareous, sandy or stony soils; from sea
level to 2,000 m.

Range: All Europe except Iceland and the high
Arctic.

Compare Stachys officinalis (*see* p.701), which
has cordate, regularly crenate-dentate
leaves, and flowers mostly terminal.

p.325 **Northern Dragonhead**
Dracocephalum ruyschiana L.

Description: An erect or ascending perennial, with
glabrous stems to 40 cm. Leaves lanceolate,
entire, with margins rolled under; lower
ones short-stalked, upper ones subsessile.

Flowers mostly in *terminal cluster*, occasionally a few verticillasters in uppermost leaf-axils. Calyx 15-veined, 2-lipped. Corolla 20–28 mm long, blue or violet (occasionally white), 2-lipped, with hooded, hairy upper lip; middle lobe of lower lip 2-lobed. *Anthers hairy.*

Flowering: June–September.

Habitat: (Mountain) grassland, mixed or coniferous woods (often with *Picea* or *Larix*), on dry, oligotrophic, calcareous or slightly acid, often stony soils; mainly on mountains, from 1,400–2,200 m, but near sea level in the north.

Range: E and C Europe, locally extending westwards to Scandinavia, S Germany and France (Alps, Pyrenees).

Similar species: *D. thymifolium* L., from Siberia, has hairy stems, ovate to broadly lanceolate, bluntly dentate leaves, small, lilac-blue flowers (to 9 mm long), and glabrous anthers; basal leaves broadly ovate, with cordate base, and very long-stalked. Naturalized in E and C Europe.

---

p.256 **Broad-leaved Hemp-nettle**
Galeopsis ladanum L.

Description: A hairy and slightly glandular *annual*, with erect, branched, quadrangular stems to 40 cm; stems *soft-hairy and hardly thickened under nodes*. Leaves opposite, short-stalked to subsessile, to 70 mm long, 30 mm wide, ovate with rounded base, crenate-dentate, more or less hairy. Flowers in dense, terminal and axillary, spaced, 6–10-flowered verticillasters. Calyx 10-veined, 8–10 mm long, *glandular-hairy*, with 5 subequal teeth. Corolla 17–21 mm long, *deep purplish-pink* with *yellow markings* on lower lip, and with straight tube (slightly longer than calyx) and ring of hairs at throat; lower lip 3-lobed, larger than the (hooded, hairy, denticulate) upper lip, with *2 blunt, hollow knobs near base*. Stamens 4, protruding from corolla tube but not beyond upper lip; anthers glabrous. Fruit a cluster of 4 smooth, ellipsoid achenes.

Flowering: June–October.

Habitat: Arable and waste land, also riverside gravel, on moist, oligotrophic to mesotrophic, usually acid, sandy or stony soils; from sea level to 2,000 m.

Range: Most of Europe, northwards to Belgium, Fennoscandia and N Russia. Extinct in Britain and the Netherlands.

Similar species: **Narrow-leaved Hemp-nettle** (*G. angustifolia* Ehrh. ex Hoffm.) has lanceolate to almost linear leaves (less than 10 mm wide), with only a few (up to 4) weak teeth along leaf-margins, and purplish-pink flowers (15–25 mm long) with whitish markings; calyx appressed-hairy (usually not glandular), weakly veined, much shorter than corolla tube. In arable land, on moist, mesotrophic, calcareous, sandy or loamy soils, also along railways, and occasionally on coastal shingle, in S, W and C Europe, northwards to N England, the Low Countries, Poland, and Bulgaria.

Compare also G. pubescens (see p.682), which has some bristle-hairs on nodes (see under G. tetrahit).

---

p.183 **Downy Hemp-nettle**
Galeopsis segetum Necker

Description: A hairy *annual*, with erect, branched, quadrangular stems to 30 cm; stems *soft-hairy and hardly thickened under nodes*. Leaves opposite, short-stalked to subsessile, to 60 mm long, 30 mm wide, ovate to broadly lanceolate, with narrowed base, bluntly serrate-dentate, *densely velvety-hairy at least beneath*. Flowers in dense, terminal and axillary, spaced, 10–30-flowered verticillasters. Calyx 10-veined, 9–10 mm long, *silky-hairy*, with 5 subequal, glandular teeth. Corolla large, 25–30 mm long, *pale yellow* with *deep-yellow markings* on lower lip, and with straight tube and ring of hairs at throat; lower lip 3-lobed, larger than the (hooded, hairy, markedly dentate) upper lip, with *2 blunt, hollow knobs near base*. Stamens 4, protruding from corolla tube but not beyond upper lip; anthers glabrous. Fruit a cluster of 4 smooth, ellipsoid achenes.

Flowering: June–October.

Habitat: Rye-fields, roadsides, gravelly banks, railways, on dry, mesotrophic, acid, sandy or stony soils; from sea level to 2,200 m.

Range: W Europe, from N Spain northwards to Britain (N Wales), the Low Countries and Denmark, and eastwards to Switzerland and N Italy.

---

p.183 **Large-flowered Hemp-nettle**
Galeopsis speciosa Miller

Description: A stout, hairy *annual*, with erect, branched, quadrangular stems to 1.5 m; stems uniformly *bristly-hairy, and thickened under nodes*. Leaves opposite, stalked, to 10 (20) cm long, 50 (80) mm wide, ovate to broadly lanceolate, with rounded or narrowed base, bluntly serrate-dentate, hairy, also glandular beneath. Flowers in dense, terminal, axillary, 10–16-flowered verticillasters. Calyx 10-veined, bristly-hairy, with 5 subequal teeth. Corolla large, 23–34 mm long, *pale yellow* with white-tipped side-lobes and *violet, white-rimmed middle lobe* to lower lip; corolla tube straight, *more than twice as long as calyx*, and with ring of hairs at throat; lower lip larger than the (hooded, hairy, dentate) upper lip, with *2 conical, hollow knobs near base*. Stamens 4, protruding from corolla tube but not beyond upper lip; anthers glabrous. Fruit a cluster of 4 obovoid achenes.

Flowering: June–September.

Habitat: Arable land (often with root-crops), roadsides, wood margins, on moist, mesotrophic, acid, sandy or peaty soils; from sea level to 1,700 m.

Range: Europe northwards to S Britain, S Fennoscandia, and N Russia.

Var. *sulphurea* Reichenb. has uniformly yellow flowers, and glaucous, subglabrous internodes; *compare with G. segetum*, which has soft-hairy, thin (not bristly-hairy, thickened) nodes.

p.256 **Common Hemp-nettle** *Galeopsis tetrahit* L.

Description: A stout, rough-hairy *annual*, with erect, often widely branched, quadrangular stems to 70 cm; stems *bristly-hairy and thickened under nodes*. Leaves opposite, stalked, to 10 cm long, 50 mm wide, ovate to broadly lanceolate, with rounded or narrowed base, bluntly serrate-dentate, hairy. Flowers in dense, terminal, axillary, spaced, 10–16-flowered verticillasters. Calyx 10-veined, 12–14 mm long, bristly-hairy or subglabrous, with 5 subequal teeth. Corolla small, 10–20 (25) mm long, *pink or whitish*, and (if pink) with distally fading, subtruncate middle lobe to lower lip; corolla tube straight, *less than twice as long as calyx*, and with ring of hairs at throat; lower lip larger than the (hooded, hairy, subentire) upper lip, with *2 conical, hollow, yellowish knobs near base*. Stamens 4, protruding from corolla tube but not beyond upper lip; anthers glabrous. Fruit a cluster of 4 obovoid achenes.

Flowering: June–October.

Habitat: Woods, woodland clearings, scrub, hedgebanks, shaded roadsides, ruderal places, watersides, also arable fields, on wet to dry, mesotrophic to eutrophic, acid to neutral, sandy, stony or peaty soils; from sea level to 2,400 m.

Range: Most of Europe, except the high Arctic.

Similar species: **Lesser Hemp-nettle** (*G. bifida* Boenningh.) has flowers always (dark) purplish-pink; middle lobe of lower lip has deflexed side-margins, and a narrow, sharply marked-off white rim at distinctly notched top. In damp woods, woodland clearings, along ditches and canals, generally in moist, ruderal habitats, often on peaty soils, in most of Europe except Iberia, Iceland and Spitsbergen.

Hairy Hemp-nettle (*G. pubescens* Besser) has bright purplish-pink flowers 20–25 mm in length, rather like *G. ladanum* (*see* p.679) but differing in having (at least some) bristle-hairs under (thickened) nodes, which bear soft hairs and short glands as well. Differs further from Common and Lesser hemp-nettles in having appressed hairs on all

4 sides of internodes (instead of on only 2 opposite sides). In wood margins, hedgebanks, roadsides, on dry, oligotrophic, acid, sandy or stony soils, to 1,600 m, in C Europe, westwards to C France, northwards to the Netherlands (only as a casual in Belgium), Poland, and C Russia.

Ground Ivy *Glechoma hederacea* L.

Description: A more or less hairy *perennial*, with long, creeping stems and ascending, square branches to 30 (60) cm. Leaves opposite, stalked, *broadly ovate to suborbicular or reniform*, cordate-based, crenate or bluntly dentate, 10–40 mm long. Flowers axillary, in 2–6-flowered verticillasters, *usually turned to 1 side*; bracteoles under flowers much shorter than calyx, hairy. Calyx *15-veined*, with long, straight, cylindrical tube and 5 short, subequal, triangular teeth. *Corolla blue-violet* (rarely pink or white), 15–20 mm long, with *flat, erect, notched upper lip*, and larger, spreading, 3-lobed lower lip, the middle lobe largest, notched; corolla tube straight, much longer than calyx, hairy at throat. Stamens 4, not protruding. Fruit a cluster of 4 smooth, ellipsoid, yellowish achenes.

Flowering: April–June.

Habitat: Woods, scrub, road verges, grassy banks, hedges, ruderal places, occasionally meadows or cultivated land, on moist to dry, mesotrophic to eutrophic soils; from sea level to 1,600 m.

Range: Most of Europe, except Iceland and Spitsbergen.

Yellow Archangel
Lamiastrum galeobdolon (L.) Ehrend. & Pol.

Description: A hairy, patch-forming perennial, with creeping stolons and erect, simple or scarcely branched, quadrangular stems to 60 cm. Leaves opposite, short-stalked to subsessile, to 80 mm long, ovate, with rounded to subcordate base; doubly crenate, often with small silvery spots (large in the cultivar

'Florentinum', kept in gardens). Flowers in terminal and axillary, rather distant, 2–8-flowered verticillasters; bracteoles under flowers much shorter than calyx. Calyx indistinctly 5-veined, hairy, with short, obliquely truncate tube and 5 subequal teeth. Corolla 17–21 mm long, *yellow* with brown markings on lower lip, and with slightly curved tube, and ring of *hairs at throat*; lower lip 3-lobed (*lobes subequal, acute*), shorter than the (hooded, hairy) upper lip. Stamens 4, protruding from corolla tube but not beyond upper lip; *anthers glabrous*. Fruit a cluster of 4 trigonal, black achenes.

Flowering: April–July.

Habitat: Deciduous woods, coppices, scrub, hedges, on moist, oligotrophic to mesotrophic, calcareous, often loamy or clayey soils; from sea level to 1,900 m.

Range: Continental Europe northwards to the British Isles, the Low Countries, S Sweden, and Estonia, eastwards to the Urals.

The description above pertains to ssp. *galeobdolon*. Ssp. *montanum* (Pers.) Ehrend. & Pol., from S and C Europe, has dense verticillasters with 9–15 flowers, and calyx teeth only half as long as calyx tube (not two-thirds the length).

---

p.87 **White Deadnettle** *Lamium album* L.

Description: A hairy, patch-forming *perennial*, with creeping stolons and erect, simple or scarcely branched, quadrangular stems to 60 cm. Leaves opposite, stalked, to 80 mm long, ovate, pointed, with rounded to subcordate base; dentate-serrate. Flowers in axillary, spaced, 6–16-flowered verticillasters. Calyx 5-veined, hairy, with 5 subequal, linear-lanceolate teeth. Corolla 20–25 mm long, *white or cream* (very rarely with some pink), with curved tube and *oblique ring of hairs* at throat; lower lip 3-lobed with *small, abruptly pointed side-lobes, middle lobe folded, notched*, and with *yellowish markings*; upper lip large, hooded, hairy. Stamens 4, protruding from corolla tube but not beyond upper lip; *anthers hairy, with pale-yellow pollen*. Fruit a cluster of 4 smooth, greenish, trigonal achenes to 3 mm long.

Flowering: April–November.
Habitat: Road verges, ruderal places, heavily fertilized grassland, wood margins, hedges, banks, on moist, eutrophic soils; from sea level to 2,200 m.
Range: Most of Europe except the high Arctic; rare in the extreme south.

A very common weed, and closely associated with human settlement.

---

p.255 **Henbit Deadnettle** *Lamium amplexicaule* L.

Description: A hairy *annual*, with *prostrate to ascending*, scarcely branched, quadrangular, green or reddish stems to 30 cm. Leaves opposite, the lower ones stalked, broadly ovate to suborbicular, 20–60 mm long, with cordate base; blunt-tipped, coarsely crenate-dentate; *bracts in inflorescence clasping, joining with their bases*, reniform, with rounded tip. Flowers in axillary, widely spaced, 2–6-flowered verticillasters. Calyx 5-veined, hairy, with 5 subequal, triangular-lanceolate teeth not spreading after anthesis. Corolla 14–20 mm long, *pink-purple*, with straight tube far exceeding calyx; *no ring of hairs* at throat; lower lip 3-lobed with *small, abruptly pointed side-lobes, middle lobe flat, deeply notched*; upper lip rather short, hooded, hairy. Stamens 4, protruding from corolla tube but not beyond upper lip; *anthers hairy*. Fruit a cluster of 4 ellipsoid, trigonal achenes to 3 mm.

Flowering: April–October (winter).
Habitat: Cultivated and waste land, gardens, open roadsides, ruderal places, building sites, on rather dry to moist, eutrophic, preferably loamy or clayey soils; from sea level to 2,500 m.
Range: Most of Europe, except the high Arctic, but only naturalized in Iceland.

Spring and autumn cleistogamic (non-opening, self-pollinating) flowers are a frequent phenomenon.

p.255 **Spotted Deadnettle** *Lamium maculatum* L.

Description: A hairy, patch-forming *perennial*, with creeping stolons and erect, simple or scarcely branched, quadrangular stems to 60 cm. Leaves opposite, stalked, to 60 mm long, ovate, with rounded to subcordate base; dentate. Flowers in axillary, spaced, 6–10-flowered verticillasters. Calyx 5-veined, hairy, with 5 subequal, triangular-lanceolate teeth. Corolla 25–30 mm long, *purplish-pink* (rarely salmon or white), with curved tube and *transverse ring of hairs* at throat; lower lip 3-lobed with *small, abruptly pointed side-lobes, middle lobe folded, notched*, and with *deep-purple markings*; upper lip large, hooded, hairy. Stamens 4, protruding from corolla tube but not beyond upper lip; *anthers hairy, with orange pollen*. Fruit a cluster of 4 smooth, greenish, trigonal achenes.

Flowering: April–October.

Habitat: Road verges, grassland, wood margins, willow-coppices, hedges, banks, riversides, on moist, mesotrophic, preferably calcareous, sandy, loamy or stony soils; from sea level to 2,000 m.

Range: Continental Europe, northwards to the Low Countries, Germany, Estonia, and NC Russia.

Also grown for ornament, especially in a form with variegated leaves.

---

p.256 **Red Deadnettle** *Lamium purpureum* L.

Description: A hairy *annual*, with ascending to erect, quadrangular, usually *purplish stems* to 30 cm, often branched at base. Leaves opposite, all stalked, (1) 20–50 mm long, (broadly) ovate, with *cordate base*; blunt-tipped, crenate-dentate; *upper leaves often flushed with purple*. Flowers in axillary, 6–10-flowered, often crowded verticillasters. Calyx 5-veined, hairy, with 5 subequal, linear-lanceolate teeth spreading after anthesis. Corolla 10–18 mm long, *pale purplish*, with straight tube hardly exceeding calyx; *throat always with a ring of hairs*; lower lip 3-lobed with *small, abruptly pointed side-lobes, middle lobe flat, deeply notched*; upper lip rather large, hooded, hairy. Stamens 4, protruding from corolla tube but not beyond upper lip; *anthers hairy*. Fruit a cluster of 4 greyish, (almost) smooth, ovoid, trigonal achenes to 2.5 mm long.

Flowering: March–October (winter).

Habitat: Cultivated and waste land, gardens, roadsides, hedges, scrub, also dunes, on rather dry to moist, eutrophic, calcareous to slightly acid soils; from sea level to 2,500 m.

Range: Most of Europe, except the high Arctic; only naturalized in Iceland.

The description above pertains to ssp. *purpureum*, which is very common in the area. Ssp. *incisum* (Willd.) Pers. occasionally lacks the ring of hairs at throat; leaves very coarsely crenate-dentate (incisions to one-fifth of blade), green or bronze-green, and basally truncate then suddenly narrowed into stalk. In comparable habitats, more often on (sandy) clay, in the same general area, but less frequent. What has been described as *L. confertum* Fr. is possibly the hybrid of both subspecies.

p.254 **Motherwort** *Leonurus cardiaca* L.

Description: A slightly hairy to tomentose *perennial*, with erect, simple or branched, often purplish, quadrangular stems to 1 (1.5) m. Leaves opposite, rather long-stalked, paler green beneath, to 80 mm long, *palmately lobed to divided*; lower ones more or less rounded, with cordate base and 5–7 triangular-ovate to lanceolate, dentate segments; upper leaves (bracts) with cuneate base and 3 forward-pointing, remotely dentate or subentire segments. Flowers in axillary, spaced, 6–10-flowered verticillasters. Calyx 5-veined, hairy, with 5 subequal, lanceolate, *awned teeth*, the lower

2 deflexed. Corolla 8–12 mm long, *pink* (occasionally white), with straight tube and *ring of hairs* at throat; lower lip 3-lobed, the lobes small, subequal, soon rolling up; upper lip much larger than lower lip, hooded, *densely long-hairy*. Stamens 4, protruding from corolla tube but not beyond upper lip. Fruit a cluster of 4 obovoid, trigonal achenes.

Flowering: June–September.

Habitat: Roadsides, hedges, wood margins, ruderal places, also dunes and old walls, on disturbed, dry, oligotrophic, calcareous, often sandy soils; from sea level to 1,300 m.

Range: Continental Europe northwards to S Fennoscandia and N Russia.

Similar species: **False Motherwort** (*L. marrubiastrum* L.) has undivided, only dentate leaves; lower ones rounded or ovate, upper ones lanceolate and short-stalked; flowers pale pink, scarcely exceeding (indistinctly 10-veined) calyx, which has all teeth erect; upper lip of corolla short-hairy; no ring of hairs at throat. In C and E Europe, westwards to Germany.

Motherwort is an archeophyte of Asiatic origin; an old medicinal herb.

---

p.87 **Gipsywort** *Lycopus europaeus* L.

Description: A slightly hairy, *perennial halophyte*, with erect, branched, quadrangular stems to 1 m. Leaves opposite, short-stalked to subsessile, to 80 mm long, narrowly ovate to lanceolate, deeply dentate to pinnately lobed, usually *pinnatifid near base* (or altogether pinnatifid, when submerged). Flowers in axillary, spaced, rounded, many-flowered verticillasters. Calyx 13-veined, to 4.5 mm long, short-hairy, with 5 subequal, triangular-lanceolate, *awned teeth*. Corolla 5–7 mm long, white, with purple dots inside; funnel-shaped, *almost regular*, with 4 *subequal lobes*; corolla tube scarcely exceeding calyx. *Fertile stamens 2, far protruding* from corolla; 2 small, sterile staminodia also present. Fruit a cluster of 4 obovate, compressed achenes with thickened rims, to 2 mm long.

Flowering: June–September.

Habitat: Marshes, reedlands, fens, carrs, willow-coppices, ditch-, stream- and canalsides, on wet, mesotrophic soils; from sea level to 1,000 m.

Range: Most of Europe, except Iceland and the high Arctic.

p.86 White Horehound *Marrubium vulgare* L.

Description: A *white-tomentose* perennial, with erect, quadrangular stems to 60 cm, branched at base. Leaves opposite, short-stalked, to 40 mm long, *broadly ovate to suborbicular*, with rounded to slightly cordate base; crenate, wrinkled and grey-hairy above, white-tomentose beneath. Flowers in dense, subglobose, axillary, spaced, many-flowered verticillasters. *Calyx almost regular, c.* 8 mm long, 10-veined, cylindrical, white-tomentose, with *10 (12) long-tapering, recurved or hooked teeth.* Corolla 12–15 mm long, *white*; upper lip erect, bifid; lower lip spreading, much larger than upper lip, 3-lobed (middle lobe larger, notched); corolla tube straight, glabrous at throat. Stamens 4, *enclosed in corolla tube.* Fruit a cluster of 4 smooth, obovoid achenes.

Flowering: June–September.

Habitat: Grassland, ruderal and disturbed places, banks, grazed slopes, on dry, oligotrophic, calcareous, sandy, loamy or stony soils; from sea level to 1,500 m.

Range: Most of Europe, northwards to England, S Sweden and C Russia.

p.251 Bastard Balm *Melittis melissophyllum* L.

Description: A tufted, hairy, *aromatic* perennial, with erect, quadrangular stems to 60 cm. Leaves opposite, stalked, to 80 mm long, ovate, pointed, with rounded to slightly cordate base; crenate. Flowers in 2–6-flowered verticillasters, *turned to 1 side*; no bracteoles under flowers. *Calyx 2-lipped, c.* 12 mm long, widely cup-shaped, irregularly veined, with *3–4 low, arched, ciliate lobes.* Corolla 20–35 mm long, pink or white (or both), dotted with purple on inside; *upper lip erect, scarcely hooded,* ovate; lower lip spreading, much larger than upper lip, 3-lobed (middle lobe much larger, notched, often pink with white margin); corolla tube wide, almost straight, glabrous at throat, much longer than calyx. Stamens 4, protruding from corolla tube but not beyond upper lip. Fruit a cluster of 4 ovoid, trigonous achenes, 4–5 mm long, often hairy on outside.

Flowering: May–July.

Habitat: Open, deciduous woods, coppices, scrub, hedgebanks, ravines, on dry, oligotrophic, calcareous, sandy, loamy or stony soils; from sea level to 1,400 m.

Range: S, W and C Europe, northwards to S Britain, N France, Poland, Estonia, and C Russia.

Also cultivated as a kitchen herb.

---

p.254 **Water Mint** *Mentha aquatica* L.

Description: A hairy or subglabrous, *aromatic* perennial (smelling strongly of peppermint), with erect, symmetrically branched, quadrangular, often reddish stems to 60 (90) cm. Leaves opposite, short-stalked, to 60 mm long, ovate to broadly lanceolate, serrate-dentate to crenate, often flushed with red or red-margined. *Flowers in dense, rounded, terminal head (c. 20 mm diam.),* often with 1–2 axillary, spaced, many-flowered verticillasters beneath. Calyx 10-veined, short-hairy, 4–5 mm long, *almost regular,* with 5 subequal, triangular-lanceolate teeth. Corolla 4–6 mm long, pale lilac or pink (rarely white), *almost regular,* with *4 subequal lobes;* corolla tube shorter than calyx, short-hairy at throat, but without obstructing ring of hairs. Stamens 4, *far protruding* from corolla. Fruit a cluster of 4 finely warty, ovoid, pale-brown achenes to 1 mm long.

Flowering: July–September.

Habitat: Marshes, reedlands, meadows, ditch-sides, also dune-valleys and damp woods, on wet, oligotrophic to mesotrophic, basic or neutral occasionally brackish, sandy, clayey or peaty soils; from sea level to 1,400 m.

Range: Most of Europe except the high Arctic, and only naturalized in Iceland; also in Asia and N Africa, and introduced on other continents.

Similar species: **Corn Mint** (*M. arvensis* L.) is smaller (to 30 cm), and slightly less aromatic, with unpleasant tones in the scent. Foliage green; calyces smaller (2–3 mm long) bearing broadly triangular teeth and sparse hairs inside; corollas smaller (3–4 mm long), pale violet; all flowers in spaced, axillary verticillasters, the upper one small, and overtopped by small tuft of leaves. In cultivated and waste land, but also at watersides, in marshy grassland, and damp woods, on moist to wet, mesotrophic, mineral or peaty soils, to 1,800 m, in most of Europe except the high Arctic.

Both species easily hybridize (*M. ×
verticillata* L., with intermediate characters); in addition, hybrids with several other species are found in the wild. The cultivated **Peppermint** (*M. × piperita* L.) is one such hybrid (of Water Mint, *above*, and *M. spicata*, *see* p.692).

p.311 **Horse Mint** *Mentha longifolia* L.

Description: A hairy, *aromatic* perennial, with *subterranean stolons*, and erect, symmetrically branched, quadrangular stems to 90 cm; *all hairs unbranched*. Leaves opposite, short-stalked to subsessile, to 90 mm long, *lanceolate*, serrate-dentate, green and sparsely hairy above, densely *white-hairy beneath*. *Flowers in a dense, terminal spike* (to 10 cm long, and 15–20 mm diam.), composed of several crowded, many-flowered verticillasters with very short, lanceolate bracts in between (not exceeding flowers); spike elongates in fruit. Calyx

10-veined, hairy, *c.* 3 mm long, almost regular, with 5 subequal, triangular-lanceolate teeth. Corolla 3–5 mm long, pale lilac (rarely white), *almost regular*, with *4 subequal lobes*; corolla tube shorter than calyx, short-hairy at throat, but without obstructing ring of hairs. Stamens 4, *far protruding* from corolla. Fruit a cluster of 4 smooth, ovoid, trigonal achenes.

Flowering: July–October.

Habitat: Marshy meadows, willow-coppices, ditch- and streamsides, ruderal places, on wet, mesotrophic to eutrophic, preferably calcareous, sandy, loamy or stony soils; from sea level to 1,800 m.

Range: Continental Europe, northwards to Belgium, S Sweden, and NC Russia.

Similar species: **Spear Mint** (*M. spicata* L.), probably originated in culture, naturalized in much of Europe, and **Apple Mint** (*Mentha suaveolens* Ehrh.), a wild species from S and W Europe, northwards to Britain and the Low Countries, have comparable spikes, but the former is almost hairless, while the latter has tomentose, ovate to broadly elliptical leaves.

All 3 species form hybrids (with intermediate characters), which are often cultivated in kitchen gardens; locally naturalized in W Europe.

---

p.254 **Pennyroyal** *Mentha pulegium* L.

Description: A hairy or subglabrous, aromatic, mat-forming perennial, with *creeping stolons above ground*, and *ascending, branched flowering stems* to 30 cm. Leaves opposite, short-stalked, *to 20 mm long*, ovate to broadly elliptical, green, entire-margined or with few weak teeth. *Flowers in dense, rounded, axillary, many-flowered verticillasters* (*c.* 20 mm diam.); stem ends with tuft of small leaves. Calyx 10-veined, short-hairy, 3–4 mm long, *slightly 2-lipped*, with 5 unequal, triangular teeth (lower 2 narrower), and with ring of long hairs on inside, closing the entrance over fruit. Corolla 4–6 mm long, pale violet or mauve, *almost regular*, with 4 *subequal lobes*; corolla tube glabrous at throat. Stamens 4, *far protruding* from corolla. Fruit a cluster of 4 brown, ovoid achenes to 0.5 mm long.

Flowering: August–October.

Habitat: Grassland, pool margins, stream- and riverbanks, generally in places flooded in winter, on wet to moist, mesotrophic, sandy or clayey soils; from sea level to 1,800 m.

Range: S, W and C Europe, northwards to Ireland, Britain, Germany, Poland and W Russia.

---

p.86 **Catmint** *Nepeta cataria* L.

Description: A hairy perennial, with erect, quadrangular, greyish-woolly stems to 60 (90) cm. Leaves opposite, short-stalked, 30–50 mm long, ovate with cordate base; coarsely dentate. Flowers numerous in *short-stalked, axillary verticillasters, often turned to 1 side*, and often crowded above; each flower has *2 linear, hairy bracteoles* at its base. Calyx almost regular, 4–7 mm long, *15-veined*, funnel-shaped, hairy, reddish, with 5 subequal, straight, linear-lanceolate, teeth. Corolla 7–12 mm long, *white with purple dots inside*; lower lip 3-lobed (middle lobe larger, notched), upper lip hooded, hairy, notched; *corolla tube straight, minutely papillose-hairy at throat*. Stamens 4, *straight*, protruding from corolla tube but not beyond upper lip. Fruit a cluster of 4 glabrous, brown, ellipsoid achenes to 1.5 mm long.

Flowering: June–September.

Habitat: Pasture, roadsides, scrub margins, ruderal and often disturbed places, on dry, oligotrophic, calcareous, sandy, loamy or stony soils; from sea level to 1,500 m.

Range: Europe northwards to S Britain, the Netherlands, and S Fennoscandia, but presumed only naturalized north of the Alps, the Carpathians and C Russia.

Cats are strangely attracted to this plant. The author once saw a mutilated herbarium specimen with the annotation, 'The cat ate the flowers'.

p.251   **Marjoram** *Origanum vulgare* L.

Description: A hairy, tufted, *aromatic* perennial, with
erect, square, often purplish, symmetrically
branched stems to 60 cm. Leaves opposite,
short-stalked to subsessile, ovate to
elliptical, entire-margined or weakly
crenate-dentate, 10–40 mm long,
glandular-hairy. Flowers in many-flowered
terminal heads, composing *umbel-shaped
panicle*; bracteoles under flowers *ovate, longer
than calyx, purplish*. Calyx short-hairy,
2–3 mm long, *15-veined*, almost regular,
with cup-shaped tube and 5 subequal,
triangular teeth. Corolla pink (rarely white,
then bracteoles often green), 4–7 mm long,
with flat, erect, notched upper lip, and 3-
lobed lower lip (lobes subequal); corolla
tube straight, longer than calyx, glabrous at
throat. Stamens 4, *at least 2 far-protruding*.
Fruit a cluster of 4 smooth, brown,
narrowly ovoid achenes to 1 mm long.

Flowering: July–September.

Habitat: Grassland on sunny slopes, roadsides, banks,
on dry to moist, oligotrophic to mesotrophic,
preferably calcareous, sandy, loamy or stony
soils; from sea level to 2,000 m.

Range: Most of Europe, except Iceland.

p.325   **Selfheal** *Prunella vulgaris* L.

Description: A more or less hairy, patch-forming
perennial, with ascending to erect, square,
symmetrically branched stems to 20
(45) cm. Leaves opposite, short-stalked,
ovate to elliptical, *entire-margined* or weakly
crenate-dentate, 20–40 mm long. Flowers
in *solitary, terminal heads*, subtended by pair
of normal leaves; bracteoles under flowers
equalling calyx, *reniform*. Calyx short-hairy,
purplish-brown, 6–8 mm long, *2-lipped; upper
lip truncate, with 3 short teeth, lower lip deeply
bifid*, with lanceolate teeth. Corolla blue-
violet (rarely pink or white), 10–15 mm
long, with hooded, hairy upper lip, and 3-
lobed lower lip (middle lobe larger); corolla
tube straight, slightly longer than calyx,
and with ring of hairs at throat. Stamens 4,

protruding from corolla tube but not beyond upper lip. Fruit a cluster of 4 smooth, ovoid achenes to 2 mm long, with 3 sharp angles and 1 blunt ridge.

Flowering: May–November.

Habitat: Meadows, pasture, road verges, woodland-rides, dune-valleys, occasionally cultivated land, on moist, mesotrophic, calcareous to slightly acid, sandy, loamy or stony soils; from sea level to 2,400 m.

Range: All Europe except Spitsbergen.

Similar species: **Large Selfheal** (*P. grandiflora* (L.) Scholler) has dentate leaves, much larger flowers (25–30 mm long), and no leaf-like bracts immediately under flowerhead. In dry woods and grassland on calcareous soils, in continental Europe northwards to N France, Denmark, S Sweden, Poland, and C Russia.

Cut-leaved Selfheal (*P. laciniata* (L.) L.) has pinnately divided leaves with narrow segments, and white or cream (rarely pink) flowers with green calyces. In S, W and C Europe, northwards to Belgium and C Poland.

p.325 **Meadow Clary** *Salvia pratensis* L.

Description: A short-hairy, tufted perennial, with erect, quadrangular stems (hairy below, glandular above) to 60 cm. Leaves mostly in *basal rosette*, stalked, ovate to broadly lanceolate, to 17 cm long, with rounded to slightly cordate base; crenate-dentate, short-hairy, *wrinkled*; stem-leaves opposite, few. Flowers in 4–8-flowered verticillasters with very small bracts, forming *long, terminal spike*. *Calyx 2-lipped*, 5–6 mm long, bell-shaped, short-hairy; upper lip with 3 short teeth, lower lip deeply bifid, with lanceolate teeth. Corolla 20–25 mm long, blue-violet (rarely pale blue, pink or white); upper lip arched, hooded, hairy or glandular-hairy; lower lip large, 3-lobed (middle lobe much larger, notched); corolla tube wide, almost straight, *glabrous at throat*, about equalling calyx. *Stamens 2*, bifid (1 anther aborted), protruding from corolla tube but not

beyond upper lip (contrary to *very long style*).
Fruit a cluster of 4 smooth, ovoid, dark-
brown achenes to 2 mm long.

Flowering: May–August.

Habitat: Grassland, grassy banks, road verges, river-
dunes, on moist, oligotrophic to
mesotrophic, preferably calcareous, sandy,
loamy or stony soils; from sea level to
1,500 m.

Range: Europe northwards to S Britain, the Low
Countries, N Germany, Poland, and C
Russia.

Similar species: **Wild Clary** (*S. verbenaca* L.) has coarsely and
irregularly crenate-dentate or even lobed
leaves, and much smaller, purplish-pink
flowers (8–15 mm long, up to twice as long
as calyx) with subglabrous upper lip and
paler, to whitish lower lip; female or
cleistogamic flowers are common. On road
verges, grassy banks, on loamy, calcareous
soils, to 900 m, in S and W Europe,
northwards to NW France, S Britain and S
Ireland.

Whorled Clary (*S. verticillata* L.), from S
and E Europe (westwards to Austria and
Poland), has most leaves cauline, and lilac
or pale-violet flowers 10–15 mm long, in
15–30-flowered verticillasters; corolla
tube has ring of hairs. Locally naturalized
in dry grassland and ruderal places in W
Europe.

---

p.324 **Skullcap** *Scutellaria galericulata* L.

Description: A hairy or subglabrous perennial, with
ascending to erect, occasionally branched,
quadrangular stems to 50 cm. Leaves
opposite, to 30 mm long, narrowly ovate to
lanceolate, weakly crenate-dentate to
subentire, on short stalks (1–5 mm long).
Flowers usually *solitary* in leaf-axils (so 2
per node), *turned to 1 side*; no bracteoles.
Calyx net-veined, glabrous or short-hairy,
2-lipped with *short, blunt, entire lips* (no
teeth), closed after anthesis; *upper lip has
large, hollow knob*. Corolla (10) 15–18 mm
long, violet-blue (rarely pink), 2-lipped;
upper lip rather short, hooded, hairy, with

2 small side-lobes, lower lip entire; corolla tube curved, exceeding calyx, glabrous at throat. Stamens 4, protruding from corolla tube but not beyond upper lip. Fruit a cluster of 4 ovoid, angular, warty, pale-brown achenes to 1 mm long.

Flowering: June–September.

Habitat: Marshes, reedlands, fens and carrs, dune-valleys, stream-, pool- and riversides, lock walls, on wet, mesotrophic, preferably calcareous, sandy, stony or peaty soils; from sea level to 1,000 m.

Range: Most of Europe except Iceland and the high Arctic.

Similar species: **Spear-leaved Skullcap** (*S. hastifolia* L.) has broadly lanceolate leaves with spreading, toothed basal lobes, otherwise entire-margined, and blue-violet flowers 15–20 mm long in 1-sided, terminal racemes, with short bracts to 15 mm long (but no bracteoles); calyx glandular. In comparable habitats, in S and C Europe, westwards to W France, northwards to Denmark, S Sweden, Poland, and the Baltic States.

S. columnae Allioni has ovate, strongly dentate, glandular-hairy leaves with cordate base and stalk 10–50 mm long; flowers 20–30 mm long, purplish-violet, in terminal racemes with short bracts; calyx glandular-hairy. In woods of SE Europe, westwards to Corsica and Sicily, northwards to Hungary and Romania, and locally naturalized in parks and ruderal places in France and the Low Countries.

---

p.257 **Lesser Skullcap** *Scutellaria minor* Hudson

Description: A subglabrous perennial, with ascending to erect, often branched, quadrangular stems to 20 cm. Leaves opposite, to 30 mm long, narrowly ovate to lanceolate, entire or with 1–2 short teeth at base, on short stalks (1–5 mm long). Flowers usually *solitary* in leaf-axils (so 2 per node), *turned to 1 side*; no bracteoles. Calyx weak-veined, with *long hairs on veins, 2-lipped* with *short, blunt, entire lips*, closed after anthesis; *upper lip has large,* hollow knob. Corolla 6–7 mm long, pink, 2-lipped; upper lip rather short, hooded, short-hairy, with 2 small side-lobes, lower lip entire; corolla tube straight, exceeding calyx, glabrous at throat. Stamens 4, protruding from corolla tube but not beyond upper lip. Fruit a cluster of 4 subglobose, warty, pale-brown achenes.

Flowering: June–October.

Habitat: Marshes, meadows, heaths, woodland-rides, damp woods, on wet to moist, oligotrophic, preferably acid, sandy or peaty soils; from sea level to 800 m.

Range: W Europe, northwards to S Sweden, and eastwards to E Germany and W Italy.

---

p.184 **Annual Woundwort** *Stachys annua* (L.) L.

Description: A *hairless annual* to 40 cm, with *spreading or ascending* to erect, quadrangular, branched, often purplish stems. Leaves mostly cauline, opposite, short-stalked to subsessile, ovate or elliptical, 30–50 mm long, crenate-dentate, with narrowed base. Flowers in *sessile, axillary, spaced, all-sided, 4–6-flowered verticillasters*; bracteoles absent or very small. Calyx almost regular, 5–6 mm long, 10-veined, cup-shaped, with long hairs and *minute sessile glands*, and 5 subequal, triangular-lanceolate, short-awned teeth. *Corolla 10–16 mm long*, exceeding calyx, *pale yellow* (rarely white), with 3-lobed, occasionally purple-dotted lower lip (middle lobe larger), and hooded, hairy, rounded upper lip; corolla tube straight, with *horizontal ring of hairs* at throat. Stamens 4, protruding from corolla tube, *2 strongly bent sideways* after anthesis, jutting out from under upper lip. Fruit a cluster of 4 *glabrous, bluntly angular, subglobose, dark-brown achenes* to 2 mm long.

Flowering: June–September.

Habitat: Cultivated and waste land, rubble-heaps, also railways, on dry, oligotrophic to mesotrophic, preferably calcareous, loamy or stony soils; from sea level to 2,000 m.

Range: S and C Europe, northwards to S Scandinavia and the Baltic States, but doubtfully native in the northern parts of its range.

Similar species: **Yellow Woundwort** (*S. recta* L.) is a tufted perennial, with yellowish flowers (15–20 mm long) in spaced, 6–16-flowered verticillasters, composing long, leafy, terminal spikes; calyx (without glands) has triangular-ovate teeth, and corolla tube has oblique ring of hairs. In grassland, open woods, also in wasteland, on dry, oligotrophic, calcareous, often loamy or stony soils; from sea level to 2,100 m, in S and C Europe, northwards to Belgium, Germany, Poland, and C Russia.

p.252 **Field Woundwort** *Stachys arvensis* L.

Description: A hairy *annual*, with *spreading or ascending* to erect, quadrangular, branched, often purplish stems to 30 cm. Leaves mostly cauline, opposite, 10–30 mm long, crenate-dentate; lower ones long-stalked, broadly ovate to suborbicular, blunt-tipped, with rounded to slightly cordate base, upper ones subsessile, narrower. Flowers in *sessile, axillary, spaced, all-sided, 2–6-flowered verticillasters*; bracteoles minute or absent. Calyx almost regular, 5–6 mm long, 10-veined, cup-shaped, with 5 subequal, linear-lanceolate, ciliate, short-awned teeth. Corolla 6–8 mm long, hardly exceeding calyx, pale pink (rarely white), with 3-lobed lower lip (middle lobe larger), and hooded, hairy, rounded upper lip; corolla tube straight, with ring of hairs at throat. Stamens 4, protruding from corolla tube, *2 strongly bent sideways* after anthesis, jutting out from under upper lip. Fruit a cluster of 4 *glabrous, triangular-ovoid, warty, dark-brown achenes*.

Flowering: (April) July–October.

Habitat: Arable land and vegetable gardens, roadsides, ruderal places, on disturbed, moist, mesotrophic to eutrophic, preferably acid, sandy soils; from sea level to 1,000 m.

Range: S, W and C Europe, northwards to the British Isles, S Sweden and Poland.

p.253 **Downy Woundwort** *Stachys germanica* L.

Description: A patch-forming, *greyish- or white-tomentose perennial*, with stout rhizomes and erect, quadrangular, symmetrically branched stems to 80 cm. Leaves mostly cauline, opposite, to 15 cm long, narrowly ovate, *reticulately veined*, crenate-dentate; lower ones stalked, with rounded to subcordate base, upper ones subsessile, with narrowed base. Flowers in *sessile, axillary, spaced, all-sided, 10–20-flowered verticillasters* forming long, interrupted, terminal spike with short bracts in between; bracteoles present, at least equalling calyx tube. Calyx almost regular, 6–8 mm long, 10-veined, cup-shaped, densely tomentose, with 5 erect, subequal, broadly linear-lanceolate, short-awned teeth. Corolla 15–20 mm long, pink or purple, with 3-lobed lower lip (middle lobe larger, notched), and hooded, hairy, rounded upper lip; corolla tube straight, with ring of hairs at throat. Stamens 4, protruding from corolla tube, *2 strongly bent sideways* after anthesis, jutting out from under upper lip. Fruit a cluster of 4 *glabrous, smooth, triangular-ovoid, blackish achenes* to 2.5 mm long.

Flowering: July–September.

Habitat: Grassland, road verges, wasteland, wood margins, hedges, on dry, oligotrophic, calcareous, loamy or stony soils; from sea level to 1,750 m.

Range: S, W and C Europe, northwards to S England, Belgium, Germany, Hungary, C Russia, and eastwards to the Caucasus.

Similar species: **Limestone Woundwort** (*S. alpina* L.) is glandular-hairy (not tomentose), with large bracts under 2–10-flowered verticillasters; bracteoles also present; calyx glandular-hairy, with unequal teeth; corolla 15–22 mm long, dull purple, often with some yellow on lower lip. In wood margins, woodland clearings, ravines, mainly in the mountains (to 1,900 m, descending to 100 m), in the same general area.

Both species are very rare in Britain.

p.253 **Betony** *Stachys officinalis* (L.) Trev.

Description: A soft-hairy perennial, with erect, quadrangular, *unbranched stems* to 60 (90) cm. Leaves mostly in *basal rosette*, to 10 cm long, narrowly ovate with cordate base, regularly crenate-dentate, long-stalked; stem-leaves opposite, in 1–3 pairs, short-stalked. Flowers in *ovoid or rounded terminal head or short spike*, occasionally with 1 or 2 separated verticillasters below; *bracts sessile, small, lanceolate*; bracteoles present, at least equalling calyx tube. Calyx almost regular, 7–8 mm long, 10-veined, cup-shaped, short-hairy, with 5 erect, subequal, triangular-lanceolate, short-awned teeth. Corolla 12–18 mm long, red-purple (rarely pink or white), with 3-lobed lower lip (middle lobe larger, notched), and hooded, hairy, rounded upper lip; corolla tube straight, *glabrous at throat*. Stamens 4, protruding from corolla tube, but not beyond upper lip (*not 2 bent sideways* after anthesis). Fruit a cluster of 4 smooth, ovoid, brown achenes to 2 mm long.

Flowering: June–September.

Habitat: Grassland, wood margins, scrub, heaths, on sunny slopes, on moist, oligotrophic, preferably calcareous soils; from sea level to 1,800 m.

Range: Most of Europe, northwards to Scotland, S Sweden, C and NW Russia.

An old medicinal plant, now strongly declining in many parts of Europe.

---

p.253 **Marsh Woundwort** *Stachys palustris* L.

Description: A (sparsely) stiff-hairy perennial, with creeping, *terminally thickened, subterranean stolons*, and erect, quadrangular, symmetrically branched stems to 1 (2) m. Leaves mostly cauline, to 12 cm long, crenate-dentate, *broadly lanceolate*, with rounded to subcordate base; lower ones short-stalked, upper ones sessile; bracts sessile, small, lanceolate; bracteoles absent or minute. Flowers in 4–10-flowered verticillasters, composing *long, dense, terminal spike, usually interrupted below*; bracteoles under flowers very short, only 1 quarter length of calyx. Calyx almost regular, 5–7 (10) mm long, weak-veined, cup-shaped, *short-hairy* (rarely with glandular hairs as well), with 5 long, erect, subequal, triangular-lanceolate, short-awned teeth. Corolla 12–15 mm long, purplish-pink (rarely white), with 3-lobed lower lip (middle lobe larger, notched, with *whitish markings*), and hooded, hairy upper lip; corolla tube straight, with ring of hairs at throat. Stamens 4, protruding from corolla tube, *2 strongly bent sideways* after anthesis, jutting out from under upper lip. Fruit a cluster of 4 smooth, triangular-ovoid, shiny-brown achenes.

Flowering: June–October.

Habitat: Stream-, ditch- and canalsides, fens and carrs, on wet to moist, eutrophic, preferably calcareous, sandy or peaty soils; from sea level to 1,600 m.

Range: Most of Europe except Iceland, Arctic Fennoscandia and Spitsbergen, but rare in Mediterranean region.

Similar species: **Hedge Woundwort** (*Stachys sylvatica* L.) has long-stalked, ovate, pointed leaves with deeply cordate base, and dark-purplish flowers (13–18 mm long) with whitish markings, mostly in 6-flowered verticillasters; calyx glandular-hairy; subterranean stolons not tuberous at the top. In damp, deciduous woods, wood margins, hedges, shaded ruderal places, to 1,700 m, in the same general area.

---

p.255 **Cut-leaved Germander** *Teucrium botrys* L.

Description: A short-hairy *annual or biennial*, with erect, quadrangular stems to 30 (60) cm, often with basal, ascending branches. Leaves opposite, short-stalked, to 40 mm long, *1–2-times pinnately divided* with oblanceolate to linear segments. Flowers in axillary, 2–6-flowered verticillasters. Calyx cup-shaped, with *ventral, bulging, sac-like knob*, 10-veined, with 5 short, erect, subequal, triangular teeth. Corolla 15–25 mm long, pink (rarely white), with *apparently 5-lobed lower lip* to 8 mm long (middle lobe much larger, often pale pink or whitish); no apparent upper lip (i.e. upper lip largely cut away, reduced to 2 small side-lobes adjoining those of lower lip), so stamens (4) directly protruding from corolla tube. Corolla tube straight, glabrous at throat. Fruit a cluster of 4 grooved, triangular-ovoid achenes to 2 mm long.

Flowering: June–September.
Habitat: Grassland, occasionally cultivated and waste land, on sunny slopes, on dry, oligotrophic, calcareous, sandy, loamy or stony soils; from sea level to 1,500 m.
Range: S, W and C Europe, northwards to S England, the Low Countries, C Germany, S Poland, and Romania.

---

p.255 **Water Germander** *Teucrium scordium* L.

Description: A soft-hairy *perennial, smelling of garlic* when crushed, with creeping stolons and erect, quadrangular stems to 45 cm. Leaves opposite, (sub)sessile, to 50 mm long, ovate to broadly lanceolate, crenate-dentate, with rounded base (or upper ones with narrowed base). Flowers in axillary, 2–6-flowered verticillasters; bracts large, leaf-like. Calyx cup-shaped, with *ventral, bulging, sac-like knob*, 10-veined, with 5 short, erect, subequal, triangular teeth. Corolla 7–10 mm long, purplish-pink, with *apparently 5-lobed lower lip* (middle lobe much larger), and no apparent upper lip (as in the preceding species). Corolla tube straight, glabrous at throat. Stamens 4, directly protruding from corolla tube (the upper lip being largely absent). Fruit a cluster of 4 reticulately grooved achenes to 1 mm long.

Flowering: June–October.
Habitat: Marshy meadows, along rivers, streams and ditches, also in dune-valleys, on wet, oligotrophic, calcareous, sandy or loamy soils; from sea level to 1,000 m.

Range: In C and W Europe, northwards to Ireland,
S Britain, the Low Countries, S Sweden,
Estonia and C Russia.

Similar species: **Wall Germander** (*T. chamaedrys* L.) lacks
stolons (hence grows in dense tufts, with
ascending stems), and has short-stalked,
deeply dentate to subentire, slightly
leathery leaves (often persistent far into
winter) with a cuneate base; flowers
(often turned to 1 side) in long, terminal
spikes, with short bracts in between.
Grassland, open woods, on sunny slopes,
on dry, oligotrophic, calcareous, sandy,
loamy or stony soils, from sea level to
1,800 m, in S and C Europe, northwards
to the Low Countries, C Germany, S
Poland and SC Russia.

---

p.86   **Wood Sage** *Teucrium scorodonia* L.

Description: A short-hairy to subglabrous *perennial* to
60 cm, with a creeping rhizome and erect,
quadrangular, often *basally lignified stems*.
Leaves opposite, rather long-stalked, to
70 mm long, ovate, crenate, with a *cordate*
base, wrinkled (with reticulate, deepened
veins). Flowers mostly in *2-flowered
verticillasters*, composed to *long, slender, 1-
sided spikes with very small bracts* in between.
Calyx cup-shaped, with a *ventral, bulging,
sac-like knob*, 10-veined, *2-lipped*, the upper
lip with 1 large tooth, the lower lip 4-
toothed. Corolla 8–9 mm long, *greenish-
yellow*, with an *apparently 5-lobed lower lip*
(the middle lobe much larger), and no
apparent upper lip (as in *T. botrys*, see
p.702). Corolla tube straight, glabrous at
throat. Stamens 4, directly protruding from
corolla tube (the upper lip being largely
absent). Fruit a cluster of 4 rounded,
smooth achenes to 2 mm long.

Flowering: July–September.

Habitat: Open woods, scrub, wood margins, road
verges, banks, also in the dunes, on dry,
oligotrophic, slightly acid, sandy or stony
soils; from sea level to 1,500 m.

Range: S, W and C Europe, northwards to Ireland,
Scotland, S Scandinavia, and N Poland.

p.252 **Hairy Thyme** *Thymus praecox* Opiz

Description: A more or less hairy, *loosely mat-forming, aromatic* perennial, to 7 (10) cm, with creeping stolons ending with inflorescence, and bluntly quadrangular to almost rounded, ascending to erect flowering branches hairy all round. Leaves opposite, short-stalked to subsessile, 4–8 (11) mm long, obovate to elliptical, narrowed into very short stalk, blunt-tipped, entire-margined, *leathery*, shiny green and (sparsely) *hairy above*, glabrous beneath, with prominent veins beneath joining *thickened marginal vein near top*; lower leaves on flowering branches often smaller, crowded, rosette-like. Flowers in many-flowered *terminal heads*. Calyx hairy, 3–4 mm long, 10-veined, 2-lipped, with cup-shaped tube, 3 narrowly triangular upper teeth (longer than wide), and 2 longer, narrower lower teeth. Corolla purplish-pink (rarely white), 5–7 mm long, with rather flat (not hooded), notched upper lip, and 3-lobed lower lip (lobes subequal); corolla tube straight, shorter than calyx, hairy at throat. Stamens 4, *far protruding*. Fruit a cluster of 4 ellipsoid achenes to 0.7 mm long.

Flowering: June–September.

Habitat: (Short) grassland, heaths, grassy banks, also dunes, on dry, oligotrophic, preferably calcareous, sandy or stony soils; from sea level to 3,000 m.

Range: S, W and C Europe, northwards to Iceland, Norway, Germany, Poland, and Romania.

Similar species: **Breckland Thyme** (*T. serpyllum* L.) has long, creeping stems ending with leaf-rosette, and short, ascending flowering branches (hairy all round); leaves 5–10 mm long, glabrous, elliptical to linear, with prominent, thickened veins beneath but these disappearing, not joining into thickened marginal vein near the top; 3 upper calyx teeth broadly triangular, equally long as wide. In comparable habitats, but usually on acid, sandy or stony soils, in N and NC Europe, from

Fennoscandia southwards to Britain, C France, Austria, and the Ukraine.

Both species have been split into several subspecies. Hairy Thyme description pertains to ssp. *praecox*. Ssp. *arcticus* (Durand) Jálas, also known as **Wild Thyme**, has stems squarish, hairy on 2 opposite faces only, and all leaves subequal, 5–8 mm long, obovate to elliptical, with dense, sessile glands. In comparable habitats, in NW Europe, from C France to Ireland, Britain, the Low Countries, W Norway and Iceland. Other subspecies are often very local in their distribution.

p.252 **Large Thyme** *Thymus pulegioides* L.

Description: A more or less hairy, *tufted, aromatic* perennial, with branched, sharply *quadrangular, ascending to erect stems*, to 30 cm, *hairy only on angles*. Leaves opposite, short-stalked to subsessile, 6–15 mm long, ovate to (narrowly) elliptical, narrowed into very short stalk, blunt-tipped, entire-margined, *scarcely leathery, glabrous*, without strongly thickened veins. Flowers in many-flowered *terminal heads*. Calyx hairy, 4–5 mm long, 10-veined, 2-lipped, with cup-shaped tube, 3 triangular upper teeth (longer than wide), and 2 longer, narrower lower teeth. Corolla purplish-pink (rarely white), 5–9 mm long, with rather flat (not hooded), notched upper lip, and 3-lobed lower lip (lobes subequal); corolla tube straight, shorter than calyx, hairy at throat. Stamens 4, *far protruding*. Fruit a cluster of 4 ellipsoid achenes to 1 mm long.

Flowering: June–September.

Habitat: (Short) grassland, grassy banks, on sunny slopes, on dry, oligotrophic, preferably calcareous, sandy, loamy or stony soils; from sea level to 2,000 m.

Range: Most of Europe, northwards to C Britain, C Scandinavia, S Finland, and eastwards to C Russia.

An extremely variable species. The cultivated **Thyme** (*T. vulgaris* L.) is an erect half-shrub with lignified stems, and elliptical to linear leaves hairy beneath and with inrolled margins. Native to S Europe.

PEA FAMILY, LEGUMINOSAE

A very large family of herbs, shrubs, lianas and trees with *c.* 17,000 species in 700 genera world-wide, especially frequent in warm regions. Leaves compound, basically pinnate, alternate; stipules normally present. Flowers axillary or in terminal racemes, spikes, or flowerheads, irregular (zygomorphic). Sepals usually 5, more or less connate into a cup- or tube-shaped, 5-toothed calyx. Corolla typically 'papilionaceous', usually consisting of a large, dorsal 'standard', 2 lateral 'wings', and a boat-shaped, lower 'keel' made up from 2 ventrally connate petals. Stamens usually 10, connate into a tube (but often 1 dorsal stamen free). Ovary superior, 1-locular, with 1 carpel and 1 terminal style. Fruit a 'pod', usually splitting with 2 valves (or, occasionally, a follicle splitting along 1 seam), with 1–many seeds. The European species are mostly herbs or shrubs, but *Laburnum* reaches arboreal dimensions. Many species are economically important as timber-producers, garden ornamentals, fodder plants, or as a source of food for humans: soy beans, peanuts, peas, lentils, beans, etc. The roots often bear small tubercles housing symbiotic bacteria capable of chemically binding nitrogen from the air, which enables the plant to establish itself on poor soils; some species (e.g., Lupins) are even sown to improve the soil ('green manuring').

p.178 **Kidney Vetch** *Anthyllis vulneraria* L.

Description: A silky-hairy perennial, with ascending to erect stems to 40 cm. Leaves pinnate, with 5–15 entire-margined, elliptical to linear *leaflets gradually increasing* in size, top leaflet largest of all; basal leaves often with fewer (to only 1) leaflets. Flowers in globose, terminal heads, with *common involucre of palmatifid bracts*. Calyx white-tomentose, *c.* 10 mm long, *inflated*, with 5 short, *very unequal teeth*. Corolla papilionaceous, 12–15 mm long, usually yellow, occasionally orange or red. Stamens 10, all connate into a tube. Fruit a short-stalked, stocky, *inflated, 1-seeded pod* to 8 mm long, not splitting.

Flowering: May–September.

Habitat: Grassland, dunes, grassy banks and slopes, cliffs and rock-ledges, also railways, on dry to moist, oligotrophic, calcareous, sandy or rocky soils; from sea level to 3,000 m, but most frequent in coastal habitats.

Range: All Europe except the high Arctic.

Several subspecies are recognized, mainly differing in the number of leaflets, the flower colour and the presence or distribution of hairs and glands. *See Flora Europaea.*

---

p.323 **Purple Milk-vetch** *Astragalus danicus* Retz

Description: A hairy perennial, with spreading to ascending stems to 40 cm. Leaves pinnate, with *13–27 leaflets* narrowly elliptical, blunt-tipped, entire-margined. Flowers in *long-stalked, axillary, globose, headlike racemes*, with very small, lanceolate bracteoles at their bases. Calyx cup-shaped, dark-hairy, with 5 short, subequal teeth. Corolla papilionaceous, 15–18 mm long, deep *purplish-violet* or almost blue, yellowish at base. Stamens 10, all but 1 connate. Fruit a 2-locular, *(sub)sessile*, ovoid, pointed, slightly inflated, white-hairy pod to 8 (15) mm long, 5 mm wide, with 1–2 (6) seeds.

Flowering: May–July.

Habitat: (Short) grassland, dunes, on dry to moist, oligotrophic, calcareous, sandy or stony soils; from sea level to 2,400 m, but mainly on mountains in the south.

Range: W and NC Europe, from the Alps westwards to E France and Ireland, northwards to Denmark, S Sweden, Poland, and N Russia, and eastwards to the Ukraine.

Similar species: **Alpine Milk-vetch** (*A. alpinus* L.) is taller than 10 cm, and has 15–25 glabrescent, elliptical, often pointed leaflets, very pale blue-violet flowers 10–15 mm long, with darker tips to petals (especially keel), and scarcely inflated, dark-hairy pods 10–15 mm long, on distinct stalks inside calyx. In the mountains (700–3,100 m) of

C Europe, also in the Pyrenees, Scotland,
Fennoscandia, and N Russia.
Norwegian Milk-vetch (*A. norvegicus*
Weber) grows taller (to 30 cm), but has up
to only 15 elliptical, often notched leaflets,
pale-violet flowers 10–12 mm long, short,
blunt calyx teeth, and dark-hairy pods to
10 mm long. In the mountains of Arctic
Scandinavia, the Carpathians, the E Alps,
and the Urals. (In Scandinavia, it could be
confused with *A. alpinus* ssp. *arcticus*
Lindman, which also has purplish-violet
flowers: count the leaflets.)
A. arenarius L. has 5–19 linear-lanceolate
leaflets (hairy on both faces), and purple or
lilac (rarely white or yellowish) flowers
13–17 mm long, in small, short-stalked,
3–8-flowered racemes, and hairy pods
12–20 mm long. In poor grassland and on
rocks in Russia, extending westwards to C
Germany and S Sweden.
A. baionensis Loiseleur also has 3–8-flowered
racemes, but pale-blue flowers (12–14 mm
long), 5–13 narrowly elliptical leaflets, and
white-hairy pods to 10 mm long. • Endemic
to the dunes of W France and N Spain.

All *Astragalus* species have blunt-tipped
keel to flowers, while *Oxytropis* has a
pointed ('beaked') keel.

---

p.178 **Wild Liquorice** *Astragalus glycyphyllos* L.

Description: A subglabrous perennial with spreading or
straggling stems up to 1 m. Leaves pinnate,
with *9–13 leaflets* broadly elliptical or ovate,
round-tipped, 20–40 mm long, entire-
margined; stipules free, narrowly ovate.
Flowers in *stalked, axillary, globose, headlike
racemes*, with very small, lanceolate bracteoles
at their bases. Calyx cup-shaped, glabrous,
with 5 short, subequal teeth. Corolla
papilionaceous, 11–15 mm long, *pale
greenish-yellow*. Stamens 10, all but 1
connate. Fruit a 2-locular, (sub)sessile,
cylindrical, pointed, curved, glabrous pod to
30 mm long, 5 mm wide, with several seeds.
Flowering: June–September.

Habitat: Wood margins, scrub, hedges, grassy banks and slopes, railways, on moist to dry, oligotrophic, preferably calcareous, sandy, loamy or stony soils; from sea level to 2,000 m, but mainly on mountains in the south.

Range: Most of Europe, northwards to the British Isles, S Scandinavia, Estonia, and C Russia.

Similar species: **Wild Lentil** (*A. cicer* L.) has 13–25 (31) narrower leaflets, connate stipules, pale-yellow flowers 14–16 mm long, with dark-hairy calyx, and ovoid to almost globose, inflated, hairy pods to 10 (15) mm long. In S and C Europe, northwards to N France, S Germany, Poland, and C Russia.
Yellow Alpine Milk-vetch (*A. frigidus* (L.) A. Gray) grows more erect, and has 7–11 (17) bluish-green leaflets, large, leaflet-like, clasping stipules, cream flowers, and hairy, slightly inflated pods to 25 mm long, 5 mm wide. In meadows and on moraines, on calcareous soils, in Scandinavia, N Russia, and the mountains of C Europe.
Mountain Lentil (*A. penduliflorus* Lam.) grows in comparable habitats (in the Pyrenees, the Alps, the Carpathians, and in C Sweden). It has 15–23 (31) leaflets, small, lanceolate stipules, bright-yellow flowers, and strongly inflated, dark-hairy, later glabrescent pods to 30 mm long, 10 mm wide.

Compare also Vicia pisiformis (see p.748), which has a tendril instead of a top-leaflet.

p.182 **Winged Broom**
Chamaespartium sagittale (L.) P. Gibbs

Description: A mat-forming, slightly hairy half-shrub with creeping stems and ascending, *broadly 2-winged branches* to 30 (50) cm; wings green, interrupted at nodes. Leaves alternate, *simple, elliptical or narrowly ovate*, entire-margined, to 20 mm long, silky-hairy beneath. Flowers in short terminal racemes. *Calyx 2-lipped,* silky-hairy; upper lip with 3 short teeth, lower lip bifid with 2 lanceolate teeth. Corolla papilionaceous,

10–15 mm long, yellow. Stamens 10, all connate into a tube. Fruit a hairy, 2–5-seeded pod to 20 mm long, 5 mm wide.

Flowering: May–September.

Habitat: Grassland, road verges, open woods, grassy banks, on dry, oligotrophic, calcareous, sandy, loamy or stony soils; from sea level to 1,900 m, but mainly on mountains in the south.

Range: S and C Europe, northwards to Belgium, Germany, Hungary, and eastwards to W Russia.

---

p.250 **Crown Vetch** *Coronilla varia* L.

Description: A hairy perennial to 40 cm, with spreading to ascending, ribbed stems. Leaves pinnate, with 15–25 narrowly elliptical to oblanceolate leaflets 6–16 mm long. Flowers in *long-stalked, axillary, 5–20-flowered umbels* without bracts, nodding in bud. Calyx widely cup-shaped, with 5 equal, triangular teeth. Corolla papilionaceous, 10–15 mm long, with pink standard, whitish wings, and pink, purple-tipped, very acute keel (rarely all petals white). Stamens 10, all but 1 connate. Fruit an erect, *linear, tetragonal pod* to 60 mm long, 3–4 mm wide, straight or slightly curved, constricted between (3–7) seeds, *falling apart in oblong, 1-seeded segments* when ripe.

Flowering: June–September.

Habitat: Wasteland, field margins, roadsides, grassy banks and slopes, on moist, oligotrophic to mesotrophic, calcareous, sandy, loamy or stony soils; from sea level to 1,800 m.

Range: S and C Europe, northwards to the Low Countries, Hungary and C Russia.

Similar species: **False Senna** (*C. emerus* L.) is a shrub to 1 m; leaves have (3) 5–9 obovate leaflets to 20 mm long; flowers yellow (often red-tinged), 14–20 mm long, solitary or 2–4 together in axillary umbels; linear pods to 10 cm long, with up to 12 bluntly quadrangular segments. In woodland clearings and along wood margins on calcareous soils in S and C Europe,

westwards to E Spain, northwards to S
Scandinavia, and eastwards to the Crimea;
also grown in gardens, and locally
naturalized in W Europe.

Crown Vetch is also cultivated in gardens,
and occasionally naturalized; it was
formerly grown for fodder.

---

p.181 **Broom** *Cytisus scoparius* (L.) Link

Description: A bushy, slightly hairy shrub to 2 (4) m, with
green, erect, 5-angular, grooved stems and
branches. Leaves alternate, dark green, often
appressed-hairy beneath; *lower ones short-
stalked, ternate*, with elliptical to lanceolate,
entire-margined leaflets, to 20 mm long,
upper leaves simple, sessile, broadly lanceolate.
Flowers short-stalked, *solitary or paired* in
upper leaf-axils, forming leafy racemes. Calyx
glabrous, *2-lipped*, the upper lip with 2 short
teeth, lower lip with 3. Corolla
papilionaceous, 15–20 mm long, yellow.
Stamens 10, all connate into a tube. *Style
coiled*. Fruit a flattened, linear, many-seeded
pod, 25–40 mm long, 5–7 mm wide, hairy
on edges, *black* when ripe, and (explosively)
splitting with 2 valves.

Flowering: April–June (autumn).

Habitat: Heaths, dunes, sunny banks and slopes,
road verges, woodland clearings, on dry,
oligotrophic, acid, sandy or stony soils;
from sea level to 600 m.

Range: S, W and C Europe, northwards to the
British Isles, S Scandinavia, Poland, and the
Baltic States, and eastwards to C Russia and
Romania.

Poisonous to livestock.

---

p.182 **Petty Whin** *Genista anglica* L.

Description: An almost hairless dwarf-shrub to 40 cm
(rarely to 1 m or more), with spreading to
erect, glabrous, *thorny stems* and green
flowering branches; *thorns simple*. Leaves
alternate, bluish-green, *glabrous*, simple,

sessile, to 10 mm long, broadly lanceolate or elliptical, soon falling (leaving stems naked). Flowers in short, terminal racemes, with bracts longer than flower-stalks; often 2 tiny bracteoles (0.5–2 mm long) at top of flower-stalk. Calyx glabrous, *2-lipped*, the upper lip with 2 small teeth, lower lip with 3. Corolla papilionaceous, 6–8 mm long, yellow, *glabrous; standard shorter than keel*. Stamens 10, all connate into a tube. Fruit a slightly compressed, cylindrical, pointed pod, to 20 mm long, 4–5 mm wide, *glabrous*, pale brown when ripe, with 4–10 seeds, and splitting with 2 valves.

Flowering: April–June (August).

Habitat: Heaths, poor grassland, scrub, road verges, on dry to moist, oligotrophic, acid, sandy or stony soils; mainly in the lowland.

Range: W Europe, from Iberia to S Sweden (but not in Ireland), eastwards to NE Germany, C France and SW Italy.

Similar species: **German Greenweed** (*G. germanica* L.) has soft-hairy branches, usually branched thorns, lanceolate, green leaves hairy beneath, bracts shorter than flower-stalks, no bracteoles, and long-hairy pods to 8 mm long. In comparable habitats of C Europe, westwards to C France, and northwards to the Low Countries, S Sweden, the Baltic States, and C Russia.

p.181 **Hairy Greenweed** *Genista pilosa* L.

Description: A hairy dwarf-shrub to 30 cm (rarely to 1 m or more), with spreading (creeping) to ascending stems and green branches; *thorns absent*. Leaves alternate, green above, appressedly *silvery-hairy beneath*, simple, sessile, to 10 mm long, ovate to elliptical, not soon falling. Flowers in short, terminal racemes, with bracts longer than flower-stalks; *no bracteoles*. *Calyx appressedly brown-hairy, 2-lipped*, the upper lip with 2, the lower lip with 3 small teeth. Corolla papilionaceous, 8–10 mm long, yellow; *standard at least equalling keel, both with appressed, brown hairs*. Stamens 10, all connate into a tube. Fruit a slightly compressed,

inflated, shortly linear, pointed pod,
20–25 mm long, 4 mm wide, appressed-
hairy, black when ripe, and splitting with 2
valves.

Flowering: April–July (September).

Habitat: Heaths, poor grassland, open woods, on dry,
oligotrophic, acid, sandy, stony or rocky
soils; from sea level to 1,400 m.

Range: W and C Europe, northwards to Britain
(not in Ireland), the Low Countries, S
Sweden, Poland, and eastwards to
Macedonia.

---

p.181 **Dyer's Greenweed** *Genista tinctoria* L.

Description: A bushy, hairy shrub to 60 cm (occasionally
to 1 m or more), with ascending to erect
stems and green, furrowed branches; *thorns
absent*. Leaves alternate, green, *ciliate at the
margin* (otherwise subglabrous), simple,
sessile, to 10 mm long, *lanceolate* to almost
linear, not soon falling, to 30 mm long.
Flowers in elongate, terminal racemes,
with bracts longer than flower-stalks; top
of flower-stalks with *2 small bracteoles*.
Calyx glabrous, *2-lipped*, the upper lip with
2 small teeth, lower lip with 3. Corolla
papilionaceous, 8–10 mm long, yellow; *all
petals glabrous; standard at least equalling
keel*. Stamens 10, all connate into a tube.
Fruit a slightly compressed, inflated,
shortly linear, curved, round-tipped pod
with a thin style-remnant, 15–25 mm
long, 2–3 (4) mm wide, glabrous, brown
when ripe, with 6–10 seeds, and splitting
with 2 valves.

Flowering: June–August.

Habitat: Dune-valleys, poor grassland, road verges,
heaths, open woods, also sea-cliffs, on dry to
moist, oligotrophic, acid or calcareous, sandy,
loamy, stony or rocky soils; from sea level to
1,800 m.

Range: Much of Europe, northwards to Britain (not
in Ireland), the Low Countries, S Scandinavia,
the Baltic States, and C Russia.

Formerly used as a dye; also cultivated in
gardens.

p.180 **Horseshoe Vetch** *Hippocrepis comosa* L.

Description: A more or less hairy perennial to 30 cm, with spreading to ascending, *rounded, weakly grooved stems*. Leaves alternate, pinnate, with (7) 11–17 narrowly obovate to elliptical or almost linear leaflets 5–15 mm long. Flowers in *long-stalked, axillary, 5–12-flowered umbels* without bracts, nodding in bud. Calyx cup-shaped, with 5 equal, triangular teeth. Corolla papilionaceous, 6–10 mm long, yellow, with very acute keel. Stamens 10, all but 1 connate. Fruit an erect, linear, compressed pod to 30 mm long, 3 mm wide, with articulations between *1-seeded, strongly curved segments*, which are *brown-papillose* on convex side, and break away separately when ripe.

Flowering: April–July.

Habitat: Grassland, grassy banks and slopes, on dry, oligotrophic, calcareous, sandy, loamy or stony soils; from sea level to 2,800 m.

Range: S and C Europe, northwards to N England, Belgium (1 station in the Netherlands), NC Germany, Hungary, and W Russia.

In the mountains of C Europe some similar, yellow-flowered *Coronilla* species occur, with straight fruit-segments.

Peas, *Lathyrus*

This genus is closely related to *Vicia*, but can be distinguished by the following set of characters:

1. In *Lathyrus*, stems are winged, or sharply quadrangular with raised lines; in *Vicia* they are rounded or sharply quadrangular, often even with raised lines on edges, but never with flat wings.
2. Both genera have 10 stamens, of which 9 are connate into a tube, open only dorsally, at the place of the 1 free stamen; the tube-like, connate part is transversely truncate in *Lathyrus*, and obliquely truncate in *Vicia*.
3. In *Lathyrus*, the style is compressed, with hairs on upper side; in *Vicia*, the style is threadlike – rounded or apically compressed, but hairy all round or only on the lower side.

Tendrils, though absent in some species, are common in both genera. They are derived from the top-leaflet, and often

1 or more pairs of adjacent side-leaflets (tendril then branched). For both genera, a series can be formed of species with decreasing numbers of normal side-leaflets. In some *Lathyrus* species, normal side-leaflets are altogether absent, their functions being taken over by the enlarged, leaf-like stipules (as in *L. aphaca*), or by the flattened rhachis (as in *L. nissolia*). All species have alternate leaves.

p.179 **Yellow Vetchling** *Lathyrus aphaca* L.

Description: A glabrous, often glaucous *annual*, with straggling or climbing, quadrangular stems to 60 cm; edges of stem with raised lines, but *not winged*. *Leaves devoid of normal leaflets*, but tendril present, unbranched. *Stipules large*, green, *triangular-ovate*, 10–40 mm long, up to 30 mm wide, with hastate base. Flowers in long-stalked, axillary, usually *1-flowered racemes* (so apparently solitary, but with small bracteole on stalk, at junction of peduncle and pedicel). Calyx weakly 2-lipped, with 2 triangular upper teeth and 3 equally long, but narrower lower teeth. Corolla 6–18 mm long, *yellow*. Fruit a brown, linear pod, 20–35 mm long, glabrous, with several seeds.

Flowering: May–July.

Habitat: Cultivated and waste land, field margins, roadsides, ruderal places, on moist, mesotrophic, calcareous, often loamy soils; from sea level to 1,700 m.

Range: S, W and C Europe, northwards to S Britain, the Low Countries, N Germany, Hungary, and W Russia.

A strongly declining weed of cereal fields; a thermophilous species, germinating in autumn, and often not surviving cold winters in the northern parts of its area.

p.310 **Sea Pea** *Lathyrus japonicus* Willd.

Description: A subglabrous, greyish-green perennial with spreading or straggling, quadrangular, *unwinged stems* to 50 cm. Leaves pinnate; *normal leaflets 4–8* elliptical or ovate, blunt-tipped (often finely pointed or mucronate), 10–40 mm long, up to 30 mm wide, *fleshy, pinnately veined*, with *prominent veins beneath*; tendril absent or present, simple or branched. Stipules large, half the length of a leaflet, triangular-ovate with hastate base. Flowers in rather short-stalked, axillary, 2–7-flowered racemes. Calyx 2-lipped, with 2 triangular upper teeth and 3 much longer, narrower lower teeth. Corolla 18–22 mm long, purple (turning bluish-violet as anthesis proceeds). Fruit a brown, swollen, linear pod, to 50 mm long, glabrous, with several seeds.

Flowering: June–August (September).

Habitat: Shingle-beaches, floodmarks, stone revetments of sea-walls, also coastal dunes, on moist, saline, often gravelly or stony soils; almost exclusively coastal, rarely on shores of large lakes.

Range: NW and N Europe, from England and the Netherlands northwards to the Baltic region, Iceland, Norway, and N and C Russia.

The seeds are dispersed by sea-currents, and remain viable for years in sea-water. Description above pertains to ssp. *japonicus*. Ssp. *maritimus* (L.) P.W. Ball has 5–12-flowered racemes, and flowers 14–18 mm long; in comparable coastal habitats of W Europe, the Baltic region and sub-Arctic Russia.

---

p.249 **Bitter-vetch**
Lathyrus linifolius (Reichard) Bässler

Description: A glabrous perennial with tuberous rhizomes, and erect, quadrangular, *winged stems* to 40 cm. Leaves pinnate; *normal leaflets 4–6 (8)* narrowly elliptical, 2–50 mm long, 5–15 mm wide (those of upper leaves often narrower), with parallel, arched veins; *tendril absent*, rhachis ending in short point (or even, deviantly, in terminal leaflet); leaf-stalk narrowly winged. Stipules large, green, triangular-lanceolate, 10–30 mm long, 3–5 mm wide, with hastate base. Flowers in lax, long-stalked, axillary, 3–6-flowered racemes. Calyx 5.5–7.5 mm long, 2-lipped, with 2 triangular upper teeth and 3 much longer, narrower lower teeth. Corolla 10–15 mm long, *purplish-red, turning blue*. Fruit a brown or blackish, linear pod, 25–45 mm long, glabrous, with several seeds.

Flowering: April–June (August).

Habitat: Grassland, road verges, wood margins, open woods, scrub, heaths, grassy banks, on moist, oligotrophic, acid, sandy, loamy or stony soils; from sea level to 2,200 m.

Range: W and C Europe, northwards to C Scandinavia, S Finland, and eastwards to C Russia.

Similar species: *L. pannonicus* (Jacq.) Garcke has edible tubers and 4–6 linear leaflets (20–60 mm long, 2–4 mm wide) without tendrils, but has unwinged stems (but winged leaf-stalks), cream or pale-yellow, occasionally purplish-tinged flowers (12–20 mm long) in 4–8-flowered racemes, and pale-brown pods. In the steppe belt of SE Europe and SW Asia, locally extending westwards to Germany, W France, Italy and Spain, in damp grassland and open woods.

Bitter-vetch description pertains to var. *montanus* (Bernh.) Bässler. Var. *linifolius* has narrower, linear leaflets, only 2–4 mm wide (even those on lower leaves). The tubers are edible.

---

p.243 **Grass Vetchling** *Lathyrus nissolia* L.

Description: A glabrous or hairy *annual*, with erect or straggling, quadrangular, *unwinged stems* to 90 cm. *Leaves devoid of normal leaflets; rhachis widened to linear, tapering, grasslike 'phyllodium' to 15 cm long, 10 mm wide, assuming the functions of the leaflets; tendril absent.* Stipules minute, lanceolate, semi-hastate (with only 1 basal lobe). Flowers in long-stalked, axillary, *1–2-flowered racemes* (if solitary, then with small bracteole on stalk, at junction of peduncle and pedicel). Calyx 2-lipped, with 2 triangular upper teeth and 3 subequal, but narrower lower teeth. Corolla 8–14 (18) mm long, *crimson or red-purple* (rarely white). Fruit a pale brown, narrowly linear pod, 30–60 mm long, hairy at first, but glabrous when ripe, with up to 20 seeds.

Flowering: May–July.

Habitat: Grassland, road verges, wood margins, grassy banks, also field margins, on moist, mesotrophic, calcareous, often loamy soils; from sea level to 1,700 m.

Range: S, W and C Europe, northwards to Britain, the Low Countries, Germany, Poland, and eastwards to W and SE Russia.

Often overlooked, as the plant is hard to detect in the grass. A declining species.

p.249 **Marsh Pea** *Lathyrus palustris* L.

Description: A slightly hairy perennial, with straggling or climbing, quadrangular, *narrowly winged stems* to 1.2 m long. Leaves pinnate; *normal leaflets 4–10*, narrowly elliptical to almost linear, 25–60 (80) mm long, 3–12 (16) mm wide, with parallel, arched veins; tendril present, branched. Stipules triangular-lanceolate, 10–30 mm long, 3–6 (12) mm wide, with *semi-hastate base* (with 1 basal lobe). Flowers in long-stalked, axillary, 2–8-flowered racemes. Calyx 2-lipped, with 2 triangular, recurved upper teeth and 3 much longer, narrower lower teeth. Corolla 12–20 mm long, *purplish, turning blue-violet*. Fruit a brown, linear pod, 25–50 mm long, glabrous, with 3–12 (20) seeds.

Flowering: May–August.

Habitat: Marshy meadows, reedlands, fens and carrs, dune-valleys, on wet, mesotrophic, preferably calcareous, often peaty soils; mainly in the lowland.

Range: Most of Europe, including Iceland, but absent from the high Arctic and rare in the Mediterranean region.

p.180 **Meadow Vetchling** *Lathyrus pratensis* L.

Description: A glabrous or hairy perennial with creeping rhizomes, and straggling or climbing, quadrangular stems to 1.2 m long; edges of stem have raised lines, but *not winged*. Leaves pinnate, with *only 2 normal leaflets* lanceolate, 20–40 mm long, 5–10 mm wide, with parallel, arched veins; tendril present, branched. Stipules large, green, triangular-lanceolate, 10–30 mm long, 3–6 (12) mm wide, with *hastate base* (usually with *2 basal lobes*). Flowers in long-stalked, axillary, 5–12-flowered racemes. Calyx 2-lipped, with 2 triangular upper teeth and 3 longer, narrower lower teeth. Corolla 10–16 mm long, *yellow*. Fruit a blackish, linear pod, to 33 mm long, 6 mm wide, glabrous or hairy, with 6–12 seeds.

Flowering: May–August.

Habitat: Grassland, road verges, hedgerows, scrub, woodland margins, on moist, mesotrophic, often heavy soils; from sea level to 2,100 m.

Range: All Europe except Spitsbergen.

---

p.249 **Narrow-leaved Everlasting-pea**
Lathyrus sylvestris L.

Description: A glabrous or hairy perennial with creeping rhizomes, and straggling or climbing, quadrangular, *broadly winged stems* to 2 m long. Leaves pinnate, with *only 2 normal leaflets*, these *linear-lanceolate*, 5–10 (15) cm long, 5–20 mm wide, with parallel, arched veins; tendril present, branched; *leaf-stalk with narrow wings* (0.5–1.8 mm wide). Stipules linear-lanceolate, 10–30 mm long, 2–5 mm wide, with *semi-hastate base* (with *1 basal lobe*). Flowers in long-stalked, axillary, 3–12-flowered racemes. Calyx 2-lipped, with 2 triangular-lanceolate upper teeth and 3 longer, narrower lower teeth. Corolla 13–20 mm long; *standard pink (greenish outside), wings purplish, keel greenish-yellow*. Fruit a brown, linear pod, 40–70 mm long, glabrous, often with 3 rough ridges, and with several seeds.

Flowering: June–August.

Habitat: Wood margins, scrub, hedgebanks, road verges, on moist, oligotrophic, calcareous, sandy, loamy or stony soils; from sea level to 1,700 m.

Range: Most of Europe, northwards to Britain (not in Ireland), C Scandinavia, S Finland, and N Russia.

Similar species: **Hairy Vetchling** (*L. hirsutus* L.) is annual, to 1 m, and has small flowers (7–15 mm, rarely 20 mm) with reddish standard, bluish wings and whitish keel, in 1–3-flowered racemes, and rough-hairy, 5–10-seeded pods. In cultivated or waste land, ruderal places and hedgebanks, on moist, calcareous, often loamy or clayey soils, in S and C Europe, northwards to Belgium, Germany, Poland, and eastwards to SE Russia; locally naturalized in Britain and the Netherlands. **Broad-leaved Everlasting-pea** (*L. latifolius* L.) from S and C Europe (northwards to C France, Poland and W Russia), is perennial, and has elliptical to lanceolate leaflets (10–40 mm wide), leaf-stalks with wings 1.5–4 mm wide, larger stipules (30–60 mm long, up to 11 mm wide), and red or red-purplish (rarely white) flowers 15–30 mm long, in 5–15-flowered racemes. Cultivated in gardens, and locally naturalized in roadsides, hedgebanks and along railways in W Europe.

p.243 **Tuberous Pea** *Lathyrus tuberosus* L.

Description: A glabrous perennial with creeping rhizomes bearing edible tubers to 15 mm diam.; stems straggling or climbing, quadrangular, *unwinged*, to 1 m long. Leaves pinnate, with *only 2 normal leaflets broadly elliptical*, 15–45 mm long, (5) 10–15 mm wide, glaucous beneath, with arched, converging veins; tendril present, branched. Stipules linear-lanceolate, 10–20 mm long, 2–4 mm wide, with *semi-hastate base* (with 1 basal lobe). Flowers in long-stalked, axillary, 2–7-flowered racemes. Calyx 2-lipped, with 2 triangular upper teeth and 3 longer, narrower lower teeth. Corolla 12–20 mm long, *bright crimson*. Fruit a brown, linear pod, 20–40 mm long, glabrous, with 3–6 seeds.

Flowering: June–August.

Habitat: Road verges, arable land, vineyards, scrub, hedgebanks, railways, on moist, mesotrophic, calcareous, sandy, loamy or stony soils; from sea level to 1,600 m.

Range: Most of Europe, northwards to the Low Countries, Germany, Poland, the Baltic States and C Russia; also (naturalized) in Britain, Denmark and S Sweden.

p.310 **Spring Vetch** *Lathyrus vernus* (L.) Bernh.

Description: A tufted, (sub)glabrous perennial with erect to spreading, quadrangular, *unwinged stems* to 40 cm. Leaves pinnate, with 4–8 *normal leaflets narrowly elliptical or ovate, long-pointed*, 30–70 mm long, 10–30 mm wide, *with parallel, arched veins; tendril absent*, rhachis ending in short point. Stipules triangular-ovate, 10–30 mm long, 3–8 mm wide, with hastate base. Flowers in lax, long-stalked, axillary, 3–8-flowered racemes. Calyx 2-lipped, with 2 triangular upper teeth and 3 much longer, narrower lower teeth. Corolla 15–20 mm long, *purplish-red, turning blue*. Fruit a brown, linear pod, 40–60 mm long, glabrous, with 8–14 seeds.

Flowering: April–June.

Habitat: Woods, scrub, hedgebanks, on moist, oligotrophic, preferably calcareous, sandy, loamy or stony soils; 400–1,900 m.

Range: Continental Europe, northwards to Fennoscandia and N Russia, but rare in the lowland; also grown for ornament, and naturalized in Belgium.

Similar species: **Black Pea** (*L. niger* (L.) Bernh.) has 6–12, narrowly elliptical, blunt-tipped (and short-pointed), pinnately veined leaflets to 40 mm long, linear stipules to 2 mm wide, smaller flowers (10–15 mm long), and black, 6–10-seeded pods; the whole plant turns black on drying. In comparable habitats, in S and C Europe, northwards to Belgium (extinct in the Netherlands), C Scandinavia, S Finland, and C Russia.

p.177 **Common Bird's-foot Trefoil**
Lotus corniculatus L.

Description: A tufted, hairy or subglabrous perennial to
50 cm, with stout main root and straggling,
(nearly) solid, basally lignified stems. Leaves
alternate, pinnate, with *5 entire-margined
leaflets* 4–18 mm long, the lateral ones
rounded to ovate, usually slightly
asymmetrical, the top-leaflet obovate; *lower
pair of side-leaflets placed close to stem* and
resembling stipules; true stipules minute,
lateral on the node. *Flowers short-stalked, 2–6
together* in long-stalked, axillary and terminal,
head-like umbels, without a common
involucre. Calyx almost regular, bell-shaped,
with 5 triangular-lanceolate, *subequal teeth*
curved over bud. Corolla papilionaceous,
10–16 mm long, *yellow, often red-flushed; keel
abruptly curved upwards*. Stamens 10, all but 1
connate. Fruit a straight, cylindrical pod,
15–30 mm long, with several seeds, and
splitting with 2 valves.

Flowering: June–September.

Habitat: Grassland, road verges, grassy heaths, scrub,
grassy banks, also wasteland, on moist to
dry, mesotrophic to oligotrophic, calcareous
to slightly acid, sandy, loamy, clayey or
stony soils; from sea level to 1,600 m.

Range: All Europe except Spitsbergen, and only
naturalized in Iceland.

Similar species: **Narrow-leaved Bird's-foot Trefoil** (*L.
glaber* Miller) has narrower, lanceolate to
almost linear, shortly pointed leaflets,
yellow flowers 6–12 mm long, 1–4 (6)
together in umbels, and calyx teeth always
shorter than calyx tube. In damp grassland,
swamps, reedlands, saltmarshes and sea-
walls, on wet or moist, calcareous, often
saline, clayey soils, in S, W and C Europe,
northwards to Britain, the Low Countries,
S Sweden, Poland, and W Russia; mainly
coastal, occasionally inland (in the valleys
of major rivers).

Hairy Bird's-foot Trefoil (*L. subbiflorus*
Lag.) is annual, finely hairy all over, with
narrowly elliptical to lanceolate leaflets,
small, yellow flowers (5–10 mm long) in
1–4-flowered umbels, calyx teeth longer

than tube, and pods (6) 10–15 mm long, up to twice as long as calyx. In dunes, and on roadsides and sea-cliffs, on sandy or rocky soils along the coasts of SW Europe, northwards to NW France and S Britain. **Slender Bird's-foot Trefoil** (*L. angustissimus* L.), also annual, is glabrous or hairy, and has small, yellow, occasionally purple-veined flowers; pods 15–30 mm long, 4–6 times as long as calyx (which, again, has teeth longer than tube). In grassy coastal habitats of S and W Europe, northwards to W France and S Britain, and also inland in the steppe region (from Hungary to SE Russia).

---

p.177 **Greater Bird's-foot Trefoil**
Lotus uliginosus L.

Description: A patch-forming, hairy perennial to 60 cm, with creeping rhizome, creeping stolons, and more or less erect, *hollow, compressible flowering stems*. Leaves alternate, pinnate, often bluish-green, with 5 *entire-margined leaflets* 10–30 mm long, the lateral ones rounded to ovate, usually slightly asymmetrical, the top-leaflet obovate, all with distinct side-veins (hardly visible in *L. corniculatus*); *lower pair of side-leaflets placed close to stem* and resembling stipules; true stipules minute, lateral on the node. *Flowers short-stalked, 4–14 together* in long-stalked, axillary and terminal, head-like umbels, without a common involucre. Calyx almost regular, bell-shaped, with 5 triangular-lanceolate, *subequal teeth* spreading before anthesis. Corolla papilionaceous, 10–18 mm long, yellow (but reddish in bud, except in var. *sativus* Chrtková, occasionally sown in roadsides); *keel curved upwards in an almost flowing line*. Stamens 10, all but 1 connate. Fruit a straight, cylindrical pod, 15–30 mm long, with several seeds, and splitting with 2 valves.

Flowering: June–August.

Habitat: Marshes, fens, meadows, ditch- and poolsides, damp road verges, dune-valleys, on wet, mesotrophic, often acid or humus-rich, sandy, loamy or peaty soils; from sea level to 1,500 m.

Range: S, W and C Europe, northwards to S Sweden, and from Ireland to W Russia.

Similar species: **Dragon's-teeth** (*Tetragonolobus maritimus* (L.) Roth) has spreading, square stems, 3-foliolate leaves with large, triangular-ovate stipules resembling leaflets, and large, solitary or paired, long-stalked, axillary yellow flowers (25–30 mm long) with an oblanceolate or 3-foliolate bract at base of calyx; pod square, 30–60 mm long, with 4 raised lines on the angles. In grassland, ditches, saltmarshes, also on wasteland, on moist, mesotrophic to eutrophic, calcareous, often saline soils; from sea level to 1,800 m, in S and C Europe, northwards to Belgium, Germany, Denmark, S Sweden, Poland, and W Russia.

---

p.177 **Spotted Medick**
Medicago arabica (L.) Hudson

Description: A hairy *annual* to 50 cm, with spreading or ascending stems. Leaves alternate, pinnate, with 1 short-stalked top-leaflet and 1 pair of subsessile side-leaflets, these about equal, to 22 mm long, obovate, notched at apex, with *crescent-shaped, brownish blotch* in the middle, sparsely hairy, and with numerous side-veins running straight to *finely serrate-dentate margin*; stipules broadly lanceolate, *dentate*, connate to leaf-stalk. *Flowers short-stalked, solitary or 2–4 (6) together* in stalked, axillary racemes (stalk shorter than subtending leaf). Calyx almost regular, cup-shaped, with 5 triangular-lanceolate, subequal teeth. Corolla papilionaceous, *5–7 mm long, yellow*. Stamens 10, all but 1 connate. Fruit a flattened, strongly coiled pod (3–7 turns), the coils *not closely pressed together*, 5–8 mm diam., with *numerous curved, basally grooved spines* on outer edge; several seeds.

Flowering: April–October.

Habitat: Grassland, road verges, grassy banks, on moist, mesotrophic, calcareous, often clayey soils; mainly in the lowland.

Range: S and W Europe northwards to Britain, the Low Countries, and Germany.

Similar species: **Bur Medick** (*M. minima* (L.) Bartal) has smaller, often densely hairy, unblotched leaflets (to 9 mm long), entire-margined or only basally dentate stipules, and hairy (often also glandular), coiled pods (3–5 mm diam., with 3–5 turns) with numerous hooked spines on outer edge. In short grassland, dunes, cart-tracks, riversides, on dry, oligotrophic, calcareous soils, to 1,600 m, in Europe northwards to England, the Low Countries, S Sweden, and eastwards to W and SE Russia.

Toothed Medick (*M. polymorpha* L.) can be quite glabrous, and has unblotched leaflets, deeply incised (divided) stipules with linear-lanceolate segments, long-stalked racemes (stalk equalling subtending leaf); pods usually have fewer turns to spiral, and are variously spinose; prominent cross-veins on pod are connected by reticulate veinlets (magnifying glass!). From S and C Europe, northwards to W France, S Britain and Germany (and naturalized in the Low Countries), eastwards to the Balkan region and the Crimea.

Compare also Trifolium micranthum (see p.736), which has persistent corolla, and ovoid pods enclosed in calyx.

---

p.177 **Black Medick** *Medicago lupulina* L.

Description: A (usually) hairy *annual or perennial* to 50 cm (but often much lower), with spreading or ascending stems. Leaves alternate, pinnate, with 1 short-stalked top-leaflet and 1 pair of subsessile side-leaflets, all about equal, (3) 5–15 (20) mm long, obovate or slightly rhombic, with small apical notch (and often a tiny awn in notch), unblotched, with numerous side-veins running straight to *finely serrate-dentate margin*; stipules broadly lanceolate, *dentate*, connate to leaf-stalk. *Flowers subsessile*, (1) *10–30 (50) together* in dense, long-stalked, globose, axillary racemes (stalk longer than adjacent leaf); raceme elongated in fruit. Calyx almost regular, cup-shaped, with 5 triangular-lanceolate, subequal teeth.

Corolla papilionaceous, *2–3 mm long, yellow*. Stamens 10, all but 1 connate. Fruit a *black, gibbous, reniform, 1-seeded pod (strongly curved, not coiled)*, 1.5–3 mm wide, without spines.

Flowering: April–October.

Habitat: Grassland, road verges, banks, field margins, on dry to moist, mesotrophic, preferably calcareous, sandy, clayey or stony soils; from sea level to 2,300 m.

Range: All Europe except the high Arctic, and only naturalized in Iceland.

Compare Trifolium dubium (see p.736), which has leaves glabrous (not hairy) beneath, a glabrous (not hairy) calyx tube, a persistent (withering, but not soon falling) corolla, and ovoid pods.

---

p.176 **Coastal Medick** *Medicago marina* L.

Description: A *densely white-hairy perennial*, with spreading stems to 50 cm. Leaves alternate, rather stiff, pinnate, with 1 short-stalked top-leaflet and 1 pair of subsessile side-leaflets, all about equal, 6–12 mm long, obovate, obscurely dentate at apex. *Flowers short-stalked, 2–4 (6) together* in stalked, globose, axillary racemes (stalk shorter than subtending leaf). Calyx almost regular, cup-shaped, with 5 triangular-lanceolate, subequal teeth. Corolla papilionaceous, 6–8 mm long, *yellow*. Stamens 10, all but 1 connate. Fruit a flattened, tightly coiled pod (2–3 turns), 5–7 mm diam., *densely white-tomentose*, with *several curved (ungrooved) spines* on outer edge, and hole through the centre; several seeds.

Flowering: April–June.

Habitat: Sea-dunes, often in places with shifting sand; on dry, oligotrophic, more or less calcareous, sandy soils; coastal only.

Range: S and SW Europe, northwards to Brittany; also round the Black Sea.

Similar species: *M. litoralis* Rohde is a more or less velvety-hairy (but not white-tomentose) plant with deeply incised stipules, glabrous, prominently veined, tightly coiled pods (3–6 turns); coils only 4–5 mm diam., often without spines. In the same area, also on maritime sands.

p.309 **Lucerne** *Medicago sativa* L.

Description: A variable, hairy *perennial*, with *erect or ascending stems* to 80 cm. Leaves alternate, pinnate, with 1 top-leaflet and 1 pair of side-leaflets, all roughly equal, 20–30 mm long, narrowly obovate to oblanceolate or almost linear, dentate in upper half, sparsely hairy; stipules broadly lanceolate, dentate, connate to leaf-stalk. *Flowers short-stalked, 5–40 together* in elongate, stalked, axillary racemes 20–40 mm long. Calyx almost regular, cup-shaped, with 5 triangular-lanceolate, subequal teeth. Corolla papilionaceous, *7–12 mm long, deep purplish-blue or lilac* (rarely white). Stamens 10, all but 1 connate. Fruit a flattened, strongly coiled pod (2–3 turns), the coils not closely pressed together, 4–6 mm diam., leaving hole through middle, and *without spines* on outer edge; several seeds.

Flowering: June–September.

Habitat: Cultivated and wasteland, roadsides, ruderal places, on moist to rather dry, eutrophic, sandy, loamy or clayey soils; from sea level to 1,800 m.

Range: Most of Europe, except Iceland and the high Arctic.

The description pertains to ssp. *sativa*, whose ancestors are possibly SW Asiatic species; it has been cultivated for many centuries in Europe, America (alfalfa) and other temperate regions. Ssp. *falcata* (L.) Arc. (often treated as a separate species) is native to Europe; it has smaller, oblanceolate to linear leaflets (to 10 mm long, 1.5–3 mm wide, rarely wider), yellow flowers 5–8 mm long (with pedicels longer than calyx tube, instead of shorter), and falcate (sickle-shaped) pods not nearly making 1 full turn. In grassland, roadsides, grassy banks, sand-dunes, on moist to dry, oligotrophic to mesotrophic, preferably calcareous soils, to 1,600 m, in Europe northwards to Britain (Brecklands), the Low Countries, S Sweden, C Russia. The hybrid of both subspecies (*M.* × *varia* Martyn) is partially fertile (with short, few-seeded pods), and has flowers in all hues from purplish via greenish to yellow.

p.85 **White Melilot** *Melilotus albus* Medicus

Description: A glabrous, erect *annual or biennial*, with
branched stems to 1.5 m. Leaves alternate,
pinnate, with 1 top-leaflet and 1 pair of
side-leaflets, 10–20 mm long, these
narrowly obovate to oblanceolate, dentate
in upper half; stipules lanceolate, entire,
partly connate to leaf-stalk. Flowers short-
stalked, numerous in stalked, axillary
racemes to 20 cm long. Calyx cup-shaped,
slightly 2-lipped, with 2 short upper teeth
and 3 somewhat longer, triangular-
lanceolate lower teeth. Corolla
papilionaceous, *4–5 mm long, white*. Stamens
10, all but 1 connate. *Fruit an obovoid,
sharply pointed, reticulately veined, greyish-
brown, glabrous, 1–2-seeded pod, 3–5 mm long,*
not splitting.

Flowering: July–September.

Habitat: Cultivated and waste land, ruderal places,
disturbed roadsides, building sites, banks,
along railways, on dry to moist, mesotrophic,
sandy or stony soils; from sea level to
1,800 m.

Range: Most of Europe except Iceland and the high
Arctic; only naturalized in the north.

---

p.178 **Tall Melilot** *Melilotus altissimus* Thuill.

Description: A glabrous, erect *biennial or short-lived
perennial* to 1.5 m, with branched stems.
Leaves alternate, pinnate, with 1 top-leaflet
and 1 pair of side-leaflets, these 20–40 mm
long, oblanceolate to almost linear, dentate in
upper half; stipules lanceolate, entire, partly
connate to leaf-stalk. Flowers short-stalked,
numerous in stalked, axillary racemes to
50 mm long. Calyx cup-shaped, *slightly 2-
lipped*, with 2 short upper teeth and 3
somewhat longer, triangular-lanceolate lower
teeth. Corolla papilionaceous, *5–7 mm long,
bright yellow*, with wings about equalling
keel. Stamens 10, all but 1 connate. *Fruit
an obovoid, long-pointed, reticulately veined,
blackish, finely appressed-hairy, usually 2-seeded
pod, 5–6 mm long*, not splitting.

Flowering: June–October.

Habitat: Roadsides, river- and canalsides, in damp ruderal places, on moist to wet, mesotrophic to eutrophic, slightly acid to neutral, often loamy or clayey soils; from sea level to 1,600 m.

Range: Europe northwards to S Scandinavia (only naturalized in the British Isles), eastwards to C and SE Russia.

Similar species: **Small-flowered Melilot** (*M. dentatus* (Waldst. & Kit.) Pers.) is biennial, and has elliptical, sharply dentate leaflets, stipules dentate at base, flowers only 3–3.5 mm long, with wings surpassing keel, and glabrous, slightly reticulate, blackish-brown pods (4.5–5.5 mm long). In E and C Europe, westwards to S Sweden and Germany, in saline meadows, salt steppes and along rivers.
Ribbed Melilot (*M. officinalis* (L.) Pallas) can reach 2.5 m, even though it is often annual, and has narrowly obovate or elliptical, dentate leaflets, pale-yellow (lemon) flowers 4–7 mm long, with wings surpassing keel, and glabrous, blunt (but bristle-pointed), 3–5 mm long, brown pods. Widely distributed in ruderal places, roadsides, woodland clearings and railway embankments, though probably only naturalized in much of its (now subcosmopolitan) area.
Small Melilot (*M. indicus* (L.) All.), from the Mediterranean area and SW Asia, rarely grows taller than 40 cm, and is always annual, with very small flowers (2–3 mm long), wings equalling keel, and globose, strongly reticulate, glabrous, ivory or greenish pods 1.5–3 mm long. More or less naturalized in C and NW Europe, northwards to S Britain, the Low Countries and Germany.

---

p.250 **Sainfoin** *Onobrychis viciifolia* Scop.

Description: A subglabrous perennial, with erect stems to 40 cm. Leaves pinnate, with 13–29 narrowly elliptical to oblanceolate or even linear leaflets 8–24 mm long; stipules triangular-ovate, papery. Flowers in *long-stalked, axillary, many-flowered, elongate racemes*. Calyx cup-shaped, with 5 equal, triangular-lanceolate teeth, long-hairy. Corolla papilionaceous, 10–14 mm long, *pink with darker veins* (rarely white). Stamens 10, all connate, but 1 only in middle. Fruit an erect, *obovoid pod, 5–8 mm long, 1-seeded*, with hard, pitted, *prickly wall*.

Flowering: May–September.

Habitat: Grassland, roadsides, cultivated and waste land, on moist, mesotrophic, calcareous, sandy, loamy or stony soils; from sea level to 2,500 m.

Range: Probably native in C Europe and SW Asia, and naturalized in Europe northwards to S Britain, S Sweden and C Russia.

Cultivated as a fodder plant ('esparcette') for centuries.

p.250 **Common Restharrow** *Ononis repens* L.

Description: A spreading to ascending *half-shrub* to 60 cm; *stems rounded, hairy all round, usually spineless* (or with some weak, solitary spines). Leaves 3-foliolate, with 3 narrowly elliptical to oblanceolate, *glandular-hairy*, serrate-dentate leaflets 8–18 mm long; stipules triangular-ovate, connate to leaf-stalk, dentate. Flowers erect, short-stalked, *solitary* in leaf-axils. Calyx cup-shaped, with 5 subequal, triangular-lanceolate teeth. Corolla papilionaceous, 15–20 mm long, *pink with darker veins* (rarely white). Stamens 10, all connate. Fruit an erect, smooth, ovoid pod, 5–7 mm long, shorter than calyx, 1–3-seeded, with recurved style, and splitting with 2 valves.

Flowering: June–September.

Habitat: Grassland, roadsides, dunes, riverbanks, on dry, oligotrophic, calcareous, sandy, loamy or clayey soils; from sea level to 1,800 m.

Range: W and C Europe, northwards to Scotland, N Sweden, eastwards to the Baltic States and W Russia.

Similar species: **Spiny Restharrow** (*O. spinosa* L., also treated as a subspecies) has stems with 2 opposite lines of hairs, and stout, often paired spines; leaves hardly glandular. In comparable habitats on rather moist, mesotrophic, calcareous soils, in Europe northwards to England, S Scandinavia and C Russia.

O. arvensis L. is like Spiny Restharrow, but spineless, with flowers often in pairs. In comparable habitats in E Europe, westwards to C Scandinavia and Germany.

Small rest-harrow (*O. reclinata* L.) is a glandular-hairy, spineless annual herb to 25 cm, with thin, spreading stems, obovate leaflets to 8 mm long, and small flowers to 10 mm long, corolla scarcely exceeding calyx. On sea-dunes and coastal rocks in S and W Europe, northwards to W France and S England.

---

p.247 **Bird's-foot** *Ornithopus perpusillus* L.

Description: A hairy annual to 30 cm, with spreading to ascending stems. Leaves pinnate, with 11–27 narrowly elliptical to oblanceolate leaflets 2–7 mm long; upper leaves sessile. Flowers in *long-stalked, axillary, 3–8-flowered, head-like umbels* with pinnate bract just below, about equalling inflorescence. Calyx cylindrical, with 5 very short, subequal, triangular teeth. Corolla papilionaceous, *3–5 mm long, whitish with purple veins*, and *yellowish, blunt keel*. Stamens 10, all but 1 connate. Fruit a *curved, linear, hairy pod*, 10–18 mm long, constricted between (4–9) seeds, *falling apart in oblong, 1-seeded segments* when ripe.

Flowering: May–August.

Habitat: Open grassland, cultivated and waste land, pathways in heaths and woods, on dry, oligotrophic, acid, sandy soils; from sea level to 1,000 m.

Range: W and C Europe, northwards to S Sweden, and eastwards to Poland and Romania; naturalized further east.

Similar species: *O. sativus* L., a SW European species, is taller (to 60 cm) and more erect, and has pink or whitish flowers (6–9 mm long) in long-stalked inflorescences markedly exceeding bracts; calyx teeth equalling calyx tube; pod glabrous, almost straight. Cultivated for fodder ('serradelle'), and naturalized in cultivated places on dry, sandy or clayey soils in W and C Europe, northwards to

Belgium, Germany, Poland, and C Russia.
O. pinnatus (Miller) Druce is subglabrous,
and has all leaves stalked; flowers yellow in
1–5-flowered umbels without adjacent
bracts; pods strongly curved. In cultivated
land or sandy roadsides in S and W Europe,
northwards to W France, the Channel
Islands and the Isles of Scilly.
O. compressus L. also has yellow flowers, but
hairy leaves, bracts under inflorescence, and
hairy, compressed, scarcely constricted,
curved pods with hooked beak. In S
Europe, northwards to W and C France (to
Brittany), on sea-cliffs, and in dunes and
cultivated places.

---

p.179 **Yellow Milk-vetch**
Oxytropis campestris (L.) DC.

Description: A stemless, tufted perennial, to 20 cm,
with basal rosettes of pinnate leaves to
15 cm long, each with *21–31* narrowly
elliptical to linear-lanceolate, entire-
margined, appressed-hairy leaflets. Flowers
in *globose, headlike racemes* on long stalks
directly from rosette. Calyx cup-shaped, hairy,
with 5 short, subequal teeth. Corolla
papilionaceous, 15–20 mm long, *yellow*
(rarely whitish or pale pink). Stamens 10,
all but 1 connate. Fruit an ovoid, pointed,
hairy pod, 14–18 mm long, sessile inside
calyx, incompletely 2 locular, containing
several seeds.

Flowering: June–July.

Habitat: Mountain grassland and cliffs, on
calcareous, stony or rocky soils; mainly in
the mountains.

Range: N and C Russia, Scandinavia, the Scottish
Highlands, and the mountains of C Europe.

Similar species: **Woolly Milk-vetch** (*O. pilosa* (L.) DC.) has
well-developed (though often short), erect-
hairy stems, (alternate) leaves with 19–27
leaflets, pale-yellow flowers 12–14 mm long,
and densely hairy, 1-locular pods 15–20 mm
long, on short stalks inside calyx. In dry
(mountain) grassland, on calcareous, often
rocky, soils, in C and E Europe, northwards
to S Sweden and the Baltic States.

p.323 **Northern Milk-vetch**
Oxytropis lapponica (Wahlenb.) Gay

Description: A tufted perennial, to 10 cm, with short stems and alternate, pinnate leaves with 17–29 lanceolate, entire-margined, hairy leaflets; *stipules connate around stems*. Flowers in *long-stalked, axillary, globose, headlike racemes*. Calyx cup-shaped, hairy, with 5 short, subequal teeth. Corolla papilionaceous, 8–12 mm long, *violet-blue*. Stamens 10, all but 1 connate. Fruit a narrowly ovoid or oblong, pointed, short-hairy, 1-locular pod, 8–15 mm long, *stalked inside calyx*, pendent, containing several seeds.

Flowering: July–August.

Habitat: Meadows, screes, rocks, on dry, oligotrophic, acid, stony or rocky soils; mainly in the mountains, 900–2,800 m.

Range: In Fennoscandia and the mountains of WC Europe, including the Pyrenees.

Similar species: *O. deflexa* (Pallas) DC. has 23–33 leaflets, and whitish flowers in oblong racemes. Endemic in N Norway (Finnmark).
Purple Oxytropis (*O. halleri* Bunge ex Koch) has no visible stem, rosette-leaves with 21–29 leaflets, violet flowers 15–20 mm long, and erect pods 15–20 mm long (sessile inside calyx). At high altitudes in C Europe (Carpathians, Alps, Pyrenees) and in the Scottish Highlands.

Clovers, *Trifolium*

Leaves alternate, stalked, trifoliolate; leaflets usually serrate-dentate, with numerous side-veins running straight to teeth. Stipules always present, connate to leaf-stalk, occasionally also interconnate round stem. Flowers papilionaceous, short-stalked to subsessile, usually numerous, in rounded flowerheads (few-flowered in *T. micranthum*, *T. ornithopodioides*, *T. subterraneum*, and occasionally *T. dubium*). Calyx cup-shaped, with subequal teeth, or more or less 2-lipped. Corolla withering after anthesis but usually persistent on fruit (not so in *T. subterraneum*); petals usually connate to stamens and often interconnate as well; wings longer than keel. Stamens 10, all but 1 connate. Ovary superior, 1-locular, with 1 persistent style. Fruit a small, ovoid to oblong pod with 1–4 (9) seeds, not splitting.

p.247 **Hare's-foot Clover** *Trifolium arvense* L.

Description: An ascending to erect, densely hairy annual to 30 cm, with thin but stiff, solid stems. Leaflets oblanceolate to almost linear; stipules lanceolate, pointed. Flowers numerous, in stalked, densely hairy, ovoid or oblong flowerheads to 25 mm long, 10 mm diam. Calyx (usually) long-hairy, with 5 linear, subequal teeth. Corolla 4 mm long, shorter than calyx, whitish, becoming pink after anthesis. Pod ovoid, 1-seeded. *See also* genus description.

Flowering: June–October.

Habitat: Bare or grassy places, sand-dunes, wasteland, roadsides, on dry, oligotrophic to mesotrophic, preferably acid, sandy, stony or rocky soils; from sea level to 1,600 m.

Range: Most of Europe except Iceland and the high Arctic.

Compare T. striatum and allies (*see* p.742), which have sessile flowerheads.

---

p.176 **Hop Trefoil** *Trifolium campestre* Schreber

Description: An ascending to erect, hairy annual to 30 cm. Leaflets obovate, the top-leaflet with longer stalk; stipules ovate, pointed. Flowers 4–5 mm long, in 20–40-flowered heads 10–15 mm diam. Corolla bright yellow, becoming pale brown after anthesis. Style much shorter than (usually 1-seeded) pod. *See also* genus description.

Flowering: May–October.

Habitat: Cultivated and waste land, sand-dunes, open grassland, road verges, woodland clearings, on dry to moist, oligotrophic to mesotrophic, preferably calcareous, sandy soils; from sea level to 1,400 m.

Range: Most of Europe except Iceland and the high Arctic.

Similar species: **Large Hop Trefoil** (*T. aureum* Pollich) has elliptical or rhombic leaflets, all with equal, very short stalks; stipules lanceolate; flowers 6–7 mm long, in heads to 16 mm diam.; corolla golden yellow, becoming pale brown; style at least equalling (usually 2-seeded) pod. In comparable habitats, on moist, oligotrophic, acid, sandy or clayey soils, from sea level to 1,400 m, in continental Europe northwards to Belgium, S Scandinavia, and N Russia.

Large Brown Clover (*T. spadiceum* L.) has upper leaves almost opposite, with narrowly elliptical to oblanceolate leaflets, and golden-yellow flowers (5–6 mm long) becoming dark brown. In moist grassland on acid, sandy or peaty soils, in N Europe and the mountains of C Europe, including the Pyrenees. On calcareous mountains in C and S Europe.

Brown Clover (*T. badium* Schreber) has opposite upper leaves, golden-yellow flowers (7–9 mm long) becoming chestnut-brown, in heads 15–25 mm diam.

---

p.176 **Lesser Hop Trefoil** *Trifolium dubium* Sibth.

Description: A spreading to ascending, usually hairy annual to 10 (30) cm. Leaflets glabrous beneath, obovate, the top-leaflet with longer stalk; stipules ovate, pointed. Flowers 4–5 mm long, 3–15 (25) in globose heads 6–9 mm diam.; flower-stalks shorter than (glabrous) calyx tube. Corolla bright yellow, becoming yellowish-brown after anthesis. Flowers deflexed after anthesis, making head conical. Pod ovoid, usually 1-seeded. *See also* genus description.

Flowering: May–October.

Habitat: Short grassland, road verges, occasionally arable fields, on moist, mesotrophic to eutrophic, sandy or clayey soils; from sea level to 1,600 m.

Range: Most of Europe except Iceland and the high Arctic.

Similar species: **Slender Trefoil** (*T. micranthum* Viv.) from S and W Europe, northwards to Norway and Hungary, has all leaflets equally short-stalked, orange-yellow flowers (2–3 mm long, becoming almost colourless), only 3–7 (12) in number, in fan-shaped racemes, with flower-stalks longer than calyx tube. *Compare also Medicago lupulina (see* p.726), which has leaves hairy beneath, a hairy calyx tube, a soon falling corolla, and reniform pods.

Lesser Hop Trefoil is also called Suckling Clover.

p.248 **Strawberry Clover** *Trifolium fragiferum* L.

Description: A creeping, subglabrous perennial, to 10 (30) cm. Leaflets obovate to broadly elliptical; stipules lanceolate, membranous. Flowers 6–7 mm long, numerous, in heads 10–15 mm diam., becoming larger in fruit as upper lip of calyx becomes strongly inflated, dry and papery. Calyx 2-lipped, downy. Corolla dull pink or carmine (rarely white), becoming brown after anthesis. Pod 1–2-seeded. *See also* genus description.

Flowering: June–September.

Habitat: Grassland, road verges, river forelands, dune-valleys, highest parts of saltmarshes, on moist to wet, mesotrophic, often brackish, clayey soils; from sea level to 1,300 m.

Range: Most of Europe, northwards to S Scandinavia, S Finland and N Russia.

Similar species: **Reversed Clover** (*T. resupinatum* L.) also has strongly inflated calyces in fruit, but is annual, with drooping flowerheads, and purplish-pink flowers (4–8 mm long) turning upside down during anthesis (ending with the standard below). Native to SW Asia and possibly S Europe; cultivated as a fodder plant or green manure, and locally naturalized in W and C Europe, northwards to Britain, the Low Countries, and Hungary.

p.247 **Clustered Clover** *Trifolium glomeratum* L.

Description: A prostrate, glabrous annual, to 10 (30) cm. Upper leaves short-stalked, opposite; leaflets (narrowly) obovate to obcordate, sharply dentate; stipules broadly lanceolate, membranous. Flowers 4–5 mm long, rather numerous (at least more than 5), in subsessile, axillary, rounded heads 8–12 mm diam. Calyx not inflated in fruit, with triangular-ovate, recurved, subequal teeth. Corolla pink, slightly exceeding calyx. Pod 1–2-seeded. *See also* genus description.

Flowering: June–August.

Habitat: Grassland, roadsides, sand-dunes, also walls and cultivated land, on dry, oligotrophic, sandy soils; mainly coastal.

Range: S and W Europe, northwards to W France, S Britain and SE Ireland.

Similar species: **Suffocated Clover** (*T. suffocatum* L.) forms very low tufts, and has all leaves long-stalked; flowerheads sessile, axillary, clustered close to stem-base; corolla whitish, only 3–4 mm long, shorter than calyx, which has teeth strongly spreading in fruit. In comparable habitats, in S and W Europe, northwards to W France and S Britain.

---

p.248 **Alsike Clover** *Trifolium hybridum* L.

Description: A glabrous perennial to 60 (90) cm; stem ascending to erect, hollow, often solitary, never rooting at nodes. Leaflets obovate to obcordate, plain green; stipules ovate, long-pointed, papery. Flowers 7–10 mm long, numerous, in axillary, long-stalked, rounded heads *c.* 25 mm diam. Calyx glabrous, with 5 lanceolate, subequal teeth and rounded sinuses in between. Corolla white or purplish, turning pink, and withering pale brown. Pod often 4-seeded. *See also* genus description.

Flowering: May–September.

Habitat: Grassland, road verges, on moist, eutrophic, often acid, sandy, clayey or peaty soils; from sea level to 2,100 m.

Range: Probably native to S Europe; more or less naturalized further north, to Fennoscandia and N Russia.

Similar species: *T. michelianum* Savi is annual (lacking sterile shoots), with hollow, erect stems, pale-pink flowers 8–11 mm long (in heads to 30 mm diam.), calyx teeth 3–4 times longer than calyx tube, and usually 2-seeded pods. In marshy habitats and lake margins in S and W Europe, northwards to W France. *Compare also T. repens (see* p.740), which has stipules connate round stem, and flowers always white at first.

Alsike Clover is grown for fodder; its native area is unknown. The ssp. *T. h. elegans* (Savi) Syme from S and W Europe has more prostrate, branched, nearly solid stems (often hairy above), smaller, pink flowers (5–7 mm long) and flowerheads (16–19 mm diam.), leaflets with *c.* 40 side-veins (not *c.* 20), and 2–3-seeded pods.

p.84 **Sulphur Clover**
Trifolium ochroleucon Hudson

Description: An erect, hairy perennial, to 40 cm, with stout rhizomes. Leaflets (narrowly) elliptical, 20–50 mm long, 5–10 mm wide, entire-margined, hairy on both faces; stipules lanceolate, pointed, greenish. Flowers 15–20 mm long, numerous, rather erect, in rounded (later ovoid), short-stalked to subsessile, terminal heads 20–30 mm diam.; no bracteoles under flowers. Calyx 2-lipped, downy, with very unequal teeth and 2 knobs at throat. Corolla whitish-yellow (rarely pink, in S Europe), becoming straw-coloured after anthesis. Pod 1-seeded. *See also* genus description.

Flowering: June–August.

Habitat: Grassland, roadsides, wood margins, on dry, oligotrophic, calcareous, loamy or stony soils; from sea level to 1,800 m.

Range: S, W and C Europe, northwards to E England, Belgium, Germany, Poland, and W Russia.

Compare also T. montanum (see p.741), which has white or cream flowers, bearing bracteoles at their base, and a calyx with 5 subequal teeth and no knobs at throat.

p.249 **Red Clover** *Trifolium pratense* L.

Description: A prostrate to erect, hairy perennial, to 40 cm, with stout rhizomes. Leaflets obovate to elliptical, entire-margined or slightly dentate, often with (pale or darker) blotch in centre, hairy beneath; stipules large, triangular-lanceolate, greenish or brownish; upper ones broad-based and abruptly pointed. Flowers 12–15 mm long, numerous, rather erect, in rounded (later often ovoid), (sub)sessile, terminal heads 20–30 mm diam.; no bracteoles under flowers. Calyx 2-lipped, 10-veined, downy, with unequal teeth. Corolla red-purple or pink (rarely cream or whitish), becoming pale brown after anthesis. Pod 1-seeded. *See also* genus description.

Flowering: May–October.

Habitat: Grassland, road verges, cultivated and waste land, on moist, mesotrophic to eutrophic soils of all sorts; from sea level to 2,400 (3,100) m.

Range: All Europe except the high Arctic; only naturalized in Iceland.

Similar species: **Zig-zag Clover** (*T. medium* L.) has flexuous stems, elliptical, rather stiff leaflets, narrow, gradually tapering stipules, flat-topped flowerheads (flowers spreading), and very large, pink to purplish-red flowers (25–35 mm long) with glabrous calyx tubes (at least in fruit). In comparable habitats (also in scrub) on calcareous soils, in most of Europe except Iceland and the high Arctic.

---

p.84 **White Clover** *Trifolium repens* L.

Description: A creeping, glabrous or slightly hairy perennial to 40 cm; stems rooting at nodes. Leaflets obovate to broadly elliptical, finely serrate-dentate, often with pale, crescent-shaped blotch in centre; stipules large, connate round stem, broadly lanceolate, shortly pointed, membranous, often pierced by nodal roots; leaf-stalks glabrous. Flowers 7–10 mm long, numerous, erect (but strongly deflexed after anthesis), in rounded, axillary heads 15–20 mm diam., on long, glabrous peduncles. Calyx glabrous, with 5 lanceolate, subequal teeth and acute sinuses in between. Corolla white, turning pale pink, and withering pale brown. Pod 3–4-seeded. *See also* genus description.

Flowering: May–October.

Habitat: Grassland, lawns, road verges, field margins, on moist to wet, mesotrophic to eutrophic soils of all sorts (also on brackish ground); from sea level to 2,700 m.

Range: All Europe except the high Arctic.

Similar species: **Western Clover** (*T. repens* var. *biasolettii* (Steud. & Hocht.) Aschers. & Graebn.) has plain bluish-green, thickish leaflets, hairy peduncles and leaf-stalks, often red stipules, and white or pinkish flowers. On sea-cliffs and dunes of S and W Europe, northwards to NW France and SW England.
Mountain Clover (*T. montanum* L.), from the hills and mountains of C and E Europe (northwards to Belgium, Poland and N Russia), has narrowly elliptical leaflets, dense, often paired flowerheads, white or cream (rarely pinkish) flowers, and 1–2-seeded pods. *Compare also T. ochroleucon (see* p.739), which has pale-yellowish flowers, and *T. strictum (see* p.742), which has pink flowers.

---

p.248 **Sea Clover** *Trifolium squamosum* L.

Description: An ascending to erect, rather hairy annual, to 10 (40) cm. Leaflets narrowly elliptical to oblanceolate, subentire, often notched; stipules broadly lanceolate, pointed. Flowerheads terminal, ovoid, to 15 mm long, 10 mm diam., with pair of leaves immediately below. Calyx with widening, slightly hairy tube (with 2 knobs at throat) and 5 triangular-lanceolate teeth (1 tooth longer), these spreading in fruit; calyx long-persisting, even after fruits have fallen (heads then brownish, spiny-looking). Corolla 5–7 mm long, up to twice as long as calyx, pale pink. Pod 1-seeded. *See also* genus description.

Flowering: May–July.

Habitat: Dune-pastures, high saltmarshes, sea-walls, on dry to moist, brackish, sandy or clayey soils; only coastal in the area, but to 800 m in S Europe.

Range: S and W Europe, northwards to W France and England.

---

p.248 **Knotted Clover** *Trifolium striatum* L.

Description: A spreading to ascending, hairy annual to 10 (30) cm. Leaflets obovate, with obscure side-veins; stipules broadly lanceolate, pointed. Flowerheads sessile, axillary, ovoid, to 15 mm long, 10 mm diam. Calyx short-hairy, with 5 short, subequal, soft-tipped teeth; calyx tube slightly inflated in fruit. Corolla 4–5 mm long, at least equalling calyx, pink. Pod ovoid, 1-seeded. *See also* genus description.

Flowering: May–July.

Habitat: Dry grassland, roadsides, dunes, grassy heaths, also cultivated and waste land, on dry, oligotrophic, slightly acid, sandy soils; from sea level to 700 m.

Range: Europe northwards to Scotland, Denmark and S Sweden, eastwards to Poland, Romania and the Crimea.

Similar species: **Rough Clover** (*T. scabrum* L.) has slightly leathery leaflets with prominent, distally thickened side-veins (making margins rough), prickly calyx teeth (spreading in fruit), and whitish corollas shorter than calyx. In comparable habitats, in S and W Europe, northwards to SE Ireland, Scotland, the Low Countries and Germany.
Twin-headed Clover (*T. bocconei* Savi) has flowerheads paired in leaf-axils, and whitish corolla (becoming pink). In S and W Europe, northwards to W France, the Channel Islands and Cornwall.

---

p.247 **Upright Clover** *Trifolium strictum* L.

Description: An erect, branched, glabrous annual, to 30 cm. Leaflets narrowly elliptical, with glandular teeth; stipules large, ovate, connate round stem, pointed. Flowerheads stalked, terminal, rounded, *c.* 10 mm diam.; flowers rather numerous, short-stalked (in dense head). Calyx glabrous,

with 5 triangular-lanceolate, subequal
teeth. Corolla 4–5 mm long, exceeding
calyx, pink. Pod ovoid to subglobose,
1–2-seeded. *See also* genus description.

Flowering: May–July.
Habitat: Short grassland, sand-dunes, roadsides, field
margins, on dry, oligotrophic, acid, sandy
or loamy soils; from sea level to 1,200 m.
Range: S and W Europe, northwards to W and C
France, Jersey and Cornwall.

Compare T. montanum (see p.741) (pink
forms).

---

p.85 **Subterranean Clover**
Trifolium subterraneum L.

Description: A spreading, hairy annual with prostrate
stems to 50 cm long. Leaflets obovate,
subentire, hairy; stipules narrowly ovate,
pointed. Flowerheads *c.* 10 mm diam.,
axillary, on long stalks bending to the
ground after anthesis in an effort to push
ripening pods into soil; flowers few (2–7),
encircling 8–10 empty, sterile calyces,
which become enlarged and reflexed after
anthesis, covering the (equally reflexed)
fertile calyces and preceding these on their
way into the soil. Calyx glabrous, with 5
triangular-lanceolate, subequal teeth.
Corolla 8–12 mm long, much exceeding
calyx, white with pink veins, falling after
anthesis. Pod subglobose, 1-seeded, shorter
than calyx. *See also* genus description.

Flowering: May–June.
Habitat: Short grassland, dune-pastures, margins of
saltmarshes, roadsides, sea-cliffs, grassy
banks, on dry, oligotrophic, acid (occasionally
brackish), sandy soils; mainly coastal.
Range: S and W Europe, northwards to the British
Isles and the Low Countries; also in SE
Europe, northwards to Romania and
Hungary.
Similar species: **Fenugreek** (*T. ornithopodioides* L.) has only
1–4 flowers per head, and no sterile calyces;
leaflets glabrous, markedly dentate; stipules
lanceolate, pointed; corolla 6–8 mm long,
pink (rarely white), persistent after anthesis;

pod 6–8 mm long, 5–9-seeded, exceeding calyx. In comparable habitats, and in the same general area.

---

p.180 **Common Gorse** *Ulex europaeus* L.

Description: A densely branched, thorny shrub to 2 m; twigs hairy in youth; all branches ending in *glabrous, furrowed, straight thorns 12–25 mm long*. Leaves awl-shaped, awned, resembling thorns (hence the true thorns seemingly branched). Flowers solitary in leaf-axils, stalked, with 2 bracteoles 3–5 mm long, 2–3 mm wide under calyx. Calyx 2-parted, with slightly unequal, ovate, hairy parts. Corolla 15–20 mm long, golden yellow; wings longer than keel. Pod 15–20 mm long, ellipsoid, hairy, hardly exceeding calyx.

Flowering: March–May (winter).

Habitat: Heaths, scrub, wood margins, road verges, grassy banks, railways, on dry, oligotrophic, neutral or slightly acid, sandy or stony soils; from sea level to 1,100 m.

Range: W Europe, from Iberia to the British Isles and the Netherlands, naturalized further north to S Scandinavia.

Similar species: **Dwarf Gorse** (*U. minor* Roth) is lower (to 50 cm, rarely 1 m), and has shorter, weakly furrowed or only striped thorns (8–15 mm), smaller, bright-yellow flowers (8–10 mm long, barely exceeding calyx) with wings just equalling keel, very small bracteoles under calyx (only 0.5 mm wide), divergent calyx teeth, and hairy pods 7–8 mm long. **Western Gorse** (*U. gallii* Planchon) has strong thorns (to 25 mm), minute bracteoles (to 0.75 mm wide), small, golden-yellow flowers (10–13 mm long, distinctly exceeding calyx), and convergent calyx teeth.• These 2 species grow in comparable habitats of Iberia, W France and Britain.

Gorse seeds are poisonous. Seedlings have trifoliolate leaves. Common Gorse can be found flowering throughout the year, but often strongly dies back in cold winters in the north of its area.

Vetches, *Vicia*

For the differences between *Vicia* and *Lathyrus* see under latter genus (p.715).

---

p.323 **Tufted Vetch** *Vicia cracca* L.

Description: A hairy or glabrous perennial with straggling or climbing, quadrangular stems to 2 m long. Leaves pinnate, with 12–24 (30) leaflets 5–20 (30) mm long, 3–7 mm wide, narrowly elliptical to linear, subacute, hairy at least beneath; tendril present, branched. Stipules small, semi-hastate. Flowers numerous (15–25), often 1-sided, in long-stalked, axillary racemes; stalk of raceme about equalling subtending leaf. Calyx 2-lipped, lower lip longer. Corolla 8–12 mm long, blue-violet; limb of standard about equalling claw. Fruit a brownish, glabrous, broadly linear pod, 10–25 mm long, to 5 mm wide, with 4–8 seeds.

Flowering: June–September.

Habitat: Grassland, road verges, hedges, scrub, wood margins, ruderal places, also coastal shingle, on moist, mesotrophic, sandy, stony or peaty soils; from sea level to 2,000 m.

Range: All Europe except Spitsbergen.

Similar species: **Fine-leaved Vetch** (*V. tenuifolia* Roth) has 18–22 linear leaflets (2–4 mm wide), rather lax racemes on stalks markedly longer than subtending leaf, pale-violet to purple flowers 12–16 mm in length (limb of standard *c.* twice as long as its claw), and pods 20–35 mm long. In grassland, road verges, field margins, on calcareous soils, in S, C and E Europe, westwards to Belgium (naturalized in the Netherlands and Britain), northwards to S Sweden and N Russia. **Dantzig Vetch** (*V. cassubica* L.) has 10–20 broadly elliptical leaflets (to 12 mm long, 7 mm wide), and 4–15-flowered racemes not exceeding subtending leaf; standard and wings purplish or pink, keel whitish; pod yellowish. In open woods and grassy places of C and E Europe, westwards to C France, and northwards to Germany, S Scandinavia, and N Russia.

p.85 **Hairy Tare** *Vicia hirsuta* (L.) S.F. Gray

Description: A slightly hairy annual with trailing or straggling stems to 70 cm. Leaves pinnate, with 8–20 leaflets 5–20 mm long, 1–3 (5) mm wide, narrowly elliptical to linear, often truncate or notched, glabrous but for rhachis; tendril present, branched. Stipules small, semi-hastate, deeply toothed. Flowers few (1–8), often 1-sided, in long-stalked, axillary racemes; stalk of raceme about equalling subtending leaf, and prolonged beyond top flower by short point. Calyx teeth subequal, at least equalling calyx tube. *Corolla only 2–4 mm long, bluish-white, scarcely exceeding calyx teeth.* Fruit a shortly oblong, dark-brown or blackish, *hairy pod*, 6–11 mm long, to 4 mm wide, with *2 (3) seeds.*

Flowering: May–August.

Habitat: Cultivated and waste land, roadsides, sand-dunes, rough grassland, scrub, wood margins, on dry, mesotrophic, slightly acid or calcareous, sandy, loamy or stony soils; from sea level to 1,800 m.

Range: Most of Europe except the high Arctic; only naturalized in Iceland.

Similar species: **Smooth Tare** (*V. tetrasperma* (L.) Schreber ssp. *tetrasperma*) is almost hairless, and has upper leaves with 6–16 linear, usually acute leaflets, 1–3-flowered racemes on stalks about equalling subtending leaf, and bluish-white or pale-lilac flowers 4–8 mm long (corolla distinctly exceeding calyx teeth, which are shorter than calyx tube); pod glabrous, 9–16 mm long, with 3–5 (often 4) seeds. In cultivated land, roadsides, grassy banks, on moist, mesotrophic, calcareous, loamy or clayey soils, in most of Europe except Iceland and the high Arctic.
Slender Tare (*V. tetrasperma* ssp. *gracilis* (DC.) Aschers. & Graebn., also treated as a separate species) has upper leaves with 4–8 narrowly linear, acute leaflets, 1–5-flowered racemes on stalks distinctly longer than subtending leaf (at least in fruit), flowers 6–9 mm long, and glabrous, brown pods (12–17 mm long) with (4) 5–6 (8) seeds. In cultivated land, scrub, hedgerows, roadsides, and on banks, on moist,

mesotrophic, calcareous, loamy or clayey soils, in S and W Europe, northwards to England and the Low Countries.

---

p.179 **Yellow Vetch** *Vicia lutea* L.

Description: A hairy or glabrous annual with trailing or clambering, quadrangular stems to 80 cm; stem has raised lines on angles. Leaves pinnate, with branched or simple tendril, and 6–20 oblanceolate to narrowly elliptical, subacute leaflets 10–25 mm long, (1) 3–5 mm wide. Stipules small, triangular, with 2–3 triangular-ovate teeth. *Flowers solitary or 2 (3) together* on short stalks in leaf-axils. *Calyx has very unequal teeth*; lower teeth longer than calyx tube. Corolla 20–35 mm long, *pale yellow*, occasionally flushed with pink or purple. Fruit a yellowish-brown to blackish, usually rough-hairy, broadly linear pod, 20–40 mm long, with several seeds.

Flowering: May–July (September).

Habitat: Grassland, roadsides, field margins, cliff-tops, grassy banks, often near the sea, also railways, on moist, mesotrophic, sandy or clayey soils.

Range: S, SC and W Europe, northwards to W France and Britain, and (from the east) to Hungary; locally naturalized in the Netherlands and Germany.

---

p.309 **Wood Bitter-vetch** *Vicia orobus* DC.

Description: A slightly hairy perennial, with *erect, rounded stems* to 60 cm. Leaves pinnate, with 12–30 (narrowly) ovate to elliptical leaflets 20–40 mm long, 10–15 mm wide, with *rounded tip* (often with short awn); *no tendril*, but rhachis ends in short point. Stipules semi-hastate, toothed. Flowers 8–30, slightly 1-sided, in long-stalked, rather short, axillary racemes. Calyx slightly 2-lipped, with triangular teeth, the lower ones longer. Corolla 12–15 mm long, *white with purplish veins*. Fruit a glabrous, broadly linear pod, 2–30 mm long, pale brown, with 4–5 seeds.

Flowering: May–June.

Habitat: Heaths, open woods, grassland, occasionally cliffs, on moist to dry, oligotrophic, slightly acid to calcareous, sandy or stony soils; from near sea level to 1,500 m.

Range: W Europe, from Iberia to S Norway.

Similar species: *V. pisiformis* L. is a glabrous, scrambling perennial with quadrangular stems to 2 m; leaves have branched tendril and 6–10 ovate to broadly elliptical leaflets 20–40 mm long, 10–15 mm wide; flowers (June–August), 8–30 together in slightly 1-sided, stalked, axillary racemes; calyx 2-lipped, with broadly lanceolate teeth, the lower ones longer; corolla 13–20 mm long, pale greenish-yellow; pod glabrous, broadly linear, 25–40 mm long, up to 10 mm wide, pale brown, with 4–7 seeds. In woods, scrub, hedges, on moist, oligotrophic, calcareous, sandy, loamy or stony soils (100–1,000 m), in C and E Europe, westwards to N France, northwards to S Scandinavia, Poland and C Russia. *Compare Astragalus glycyphyllos* (*see* p.709), which has a top-leaflet (not a tendril).

Compare Wood Bitter-vetch with *V. sylvatica* (*see* p.750), which has branched tendrils.

---

p.323 **Common Vetch** *Vicia sativa* L.

Description: A hairy annual with trailing or climbing (occasionally erect), quadrangular stems to 1 m; stem has raised lines on angles. Leaves pinnate, with *unbranched tendril* and 10–16 dark-green, oblanceolate to narrowly elliptical, *notched* leaflets 20–30 mm long, (3) 5–10 (15) mm wide, with small point or awn in notch; lower leaves have only 2–6 (obcordate) leaflets and no tendril. Stipules small, triangular, with 3 triangular-lanceolate teeth. *Flowers solitary or 2 (3) together* on short stalks in leaf-axils. *Calyx has 5 subequal teeth* about equalling calyx tube. Corolla 18–30 mm long; *standard blue-violet,* with dark-violet wings and paler keel. Fruit a *brownish,* linear pod, 25–70 mm long, usually hairy, with 4–12 seeds.

Flowering: May–July (September).

Habitat: Grassland, roadsides, hedges, scrub, cultivated and waste land, on moist, mesotrophic, sandy, loamy or clayey soils; from sea level to 1,600 m.

Range: Native distribution unclear; widely naturalized in most of Europe except the high Arctic.

Similar species: **Bithynian Vetch** (*V. bithynica* (L.) L.) has leaves with only 2–6 large, elliptical to lanceolate, subacute, entire-margined to dentate leaflets, and large, coarsely dentate stipules; tendrils branched; flowers 16–20 mm long, 1–2 (3) together in leaf-axils, each on separate stalk, or clustered at top of short peduncle to form small raceme; standard purple or violet, wings and keel often pink or cream; pod hairy, yellowish, broadly linear (25–50 mm long, 6–10 mm wide), with 4–7 seeds. In grassland, roadsides, scrub, arable fields and ruderal places, also on cliff-tops, often near the sea, in S and W Europe, northwards to W France and S Britain; locally naturalized or as a casual further north.
Spring Vetch (*V. lathyroides* L.) has upper leaves with simple tendril and 6–8 elliptical leaflets, and lower leaves with only 2–4 leaflets and no tendril; flowers small (5–8 mm long), solitary or paired in leaf-axils, violet or white; pod 15–30 mm long, glabrous, with 5–8 seeds. In grassland, heaths, cultivated land, roadsides, on dry, oligotrophic, preferably calcareous, sandy soils, in most of Europe except Iceland and the high Arctic.

Compare also V. sepium (see p.750), which has short-stalked, axillary racemes.

Common Vetch is cultivated for fodder; the description above pertains to ssp. *sativa*. Ssp. *nigra* (L.) Ehrh. has all leaves with a tendril and 8–14 narrow leaflets (less than 3 mm wide), mostly solitary flowers 10–18 mm long (standard purplish-red, wings red), and dark-brown to black pods. In cereal fields, roadsides, sand-dunes, on moist to dry, oligotrophic to mesotrophic, often calcareous, sandy or stony soils in most of Europe, but only naturalized in the north.

p.309 **Bush Vetch** *Vicia sepium* L.

Description: A usually hairy perennial, with stolons
and straggling or climbing, quadrangular
stems to 1 m; stems have raised lines on
angles. Leaves pinnate, with (6) 10–20
bright-green, narrowly ovate to elliptical
leaflets 7–30 mm long, 4–14 mm wide,
with rounded top (often with short awn);
tendril present, branched. Stipules small,
semi-hastate, often with some large teeth.
Flowers (1) 2–6, in short-stalked axillary
racemes. Calyx has *very unequal teeth*, the
upper ones much shorter than calyx tube.
Corolla 12–15 mm long, dull violet with
darker-purple veins (rarely white). Fruit a
glabrescent, broadly linear pod,
18–35 mm long, to 6 mm wide, black
when ripe, with 3–6 seeds.

Flowering: May–August (November).

Habitat: Open woods, wood margins, hedges,
shaded roadsides, on moist, mesotrophic,
slightly acid or calcareous, sandy, loamy or
stony soils; from sea level to 2,100 m.

Range: Most of Europe except the high Arctic.

Compare V. bithynica (see p.749), which has
yellowish, hairy pods.

---

p.310 **Wood Vetch** *Vicia sylvatica* L.

Description: A (sub)glabrous perennial, with *clambering,*
rounded stems to 1 (2) m. Leaves pinnate,
with 10–24 (narrowly) ovate to elliptical
leaflets 15–25 mm long, 5–10 mm wide,
round-tipped (with short awn); tendril
present, branched. Stipules crescent-
shaped, with 7–10 narrow teeth. Flowers
8–15, slightly 1-sided, in long-stalked,
rather lax, axillary racemes. Calyx has
unequal teeth, lower teeth longer. Corolla
12–20 mm long, *white with purple veins*.
Fruit a glabrous, broadly linear pod,
25–30 mm long, *c.* 6 mm wide, *black*, with
4–5 seeds.

Flowering: June–August.

Habitat: Woods (often Beech, or conifer), scrub, on
moist, oligotrophic, slightly acid or

calcareous, sandy, loamy or stony soils; mainly in the mountains (1,000–2,200 m), descending lower in the north.

Range: N, C and E Europe, from the British Isles, S Fennoscandia and N Russia southwards to France, Italy, and Montenegro.

Similar species: *V. dumetorum* L. has 6–10 (broadly) ovate leaflets to 20 mm long, racemes with 3–8 blue or purple flowers, often turning yellowish (*compare V. pisiformis* (*see* p.748), which has clasping lower leaflets), and brown pods 25–60 mm long, *c*. 10 mm wide. In open woods and hedges, in C Europe, northwards to Denmark, S Sweden, and White Russia. *Compare also V. orobus* (*see* p.747), which lacks tendrils.

A dwarfish form of Wood Vetch with few-flowered racemes has been reported from coastal cliffs and shingle-beaches.

---

p.309 **Fodder Vetch** *Vicia villosa* Roth

Description: A hairy annual, with scrambling, quadrangular stems to 1 (2) m. Leaves pinnate, with 8–24 narrowly elliptical to linear, hairy leaflets 10–20 mm long, 3–5 mm wide; tendril present, branched. Stipules semi-hastate. Flowers 12–30, slightly 1-sided, in stalked, rather dense, axillary racemes. Calyx has *bulging knob* at base; calyx teeth very unequal; *lower teeth much longer than calyx tube*, upper teeth convergent. Corolla 10–20 mm long, blue-violet to purplish (rarely white); limb of standard much shorter than its claw. Fruit a glabrous, linear pod, 20–40 mm long, 5–8 mm wide, brown, with 2–8 seeds.

Flowering: May–August (November).

Habitat: Cultivated and waste land, roadsides, railways, in ruderal places, on moist, mesotrophic, preferably calcareous, sandy, loamy or stony soils; from sea level to 1,300 m.

Range: S and C Europe, northwards to N France, Germany, Poland, eastwards to C Russia, and widely naturalized further north.

A variable species, cultivated for fodder and green manure. Forms with 3–12-flowered racemes, and relatively small flowers (12–15 mm long) with paler or cream wings, are distinguished as ssp. *varia* (Host) Corb.

DUCKWEED FAMILY, LEMNACEAE

A family of tiny, floating or submerged aquatic herbs, with *c.* 43 species in 6 genera, on all continents except Antarctica. Plant not differentiated into stems and leaves; plant body ('frond' or 'thallus') disc- or grain-like, with 1–few arched veins (absent in *Wolffia*), and usually propagating vegetatively by budding off young fronds; roots (if present) hair-like, hanging free in the water, ending in thickened root-cap. Flowers buried in small cavities of frond, strongly reduced, without perianth (but often with small, membranous scale or sheath), unisexual, monoecious: female ones with 1 pistil, male ones with 1 or 2 stamens. Ovary 1-locular, with 1 style and 1–7 ovules. Fruit a minute achene or capsule; seeds have fleshy seed-wall. Flowering plants are often rare, or at least hard to find.

p.51 Fat Duckweed *Lemna gibba* L.

Description: Frond floating at the surface, suborbicular, 3–6 mm diam., with slightly narrowed side where young fronds are formed, greyish- or dark green and almost flat above, often strongly convex, spongy (with 7–12 easily visible air-cavities), and greenish-white beneath; veins usually 5 (rarely more), obscure. Root solitary, sublaterally attached near budding spot. Fruit has lateral wing.

Flowering: April–July.

Habitat: Shallow, stagnant or slow-moving, eutrophic or even polluted, fresh or slightly brackish waters; from sea level to 500 m.

Range: Most of Europe, northwards to the British Isles, C Scandinavia, and C Russia.

The veins are more visible in little-thickened fronds, which might otherwise be mistaken for a small *Spirodela* or a large *L. minor*.

p.51 **Common Duckweed** *Lemna minor* L.

Description: Frond floating at the surface, obovate to suborbicular, 2–5 mm long, 1.5–3.5 mm wide, narrower where young fronds are formed, bright green, flat on both faces, not spongy, pale green or whitish beneath; veins usually 3 (rarely 4 or 5). Root solitary, sublaterally attached near budding spot. Fruit unwinged.

Flowering: April–June (autumn).

Habitat: Shallow, stagnant or slow-moving, mesotrophic to eutrophic, fresh or brackish waters; from sea level to 1,500 m.

Range: Most of Europe except Iceland and the high Arctic.

Similar species: **Lesser Duckweed** (*L. minuta* Kunth), native to the Americas, has smaller, elliptical, occasionally slightly curved fronds (1.5–3 mm long, 1–2 mm wide), with faint ridge on upper face, 1 vein, and 1 root attached rather close to centre. Found in Europe since 1968, and now known from England, France, the Low Countries, W Germany, and Switzerland, so it must be rapidly spreading.

p.51 **Ivy-leaved Duckweed** *Lemna trisulca* L.

Description: Frond submerged, floating below the surface, persistently linked together (with opposite branchings at right angles), lanceolate or rhombic, 4–10 mm long, 1–4 mm wide, broadest (and often finely serrate) where young fronds are formed, narrowed into stalk on other side, thin and translucent, dark (watery) green, flat on both faces; veins usually 3. Root solitary, attached near budding spot.

Flowering: May–June.

Habitat: Shallow, stagnant or slow-moving, mesotrophic to eutrophic, fresh or slightly brackish waters; from sea level to 800 m.

Range: Most of Europe except Iceland and the high Arctic.

Flowering fronds are ovate or broadly lanceolate, and float at the surface.

p.52 **Greater Duckweed**
Spirodela polyrhiza (L.) Schleiden

Description: Frond floating at the surface, suborbicular
to broadly obovate, 4–10 mm diam.,
slightly narrowed where the young fronds
are formed, yellowish- to dark green (often
red-tinged in strong light, and turning
yellow when ageing), usually flat on both
faces, scarcely spongy and often reddish
(occasionally whitish) beneath; veins (3)
5–15. Roots few to numerous (at least 2),
attached near the budding spot.
Flowering: May–June.
Habitat: Shallow, stagnant or slow-moving,
eutrophic or even polluted, fresh waters;
from sea level to 800 m.
Range: Most of Europe except Iceland and the high
Arctic.

Flowering plants are rarely found.

p.51 **Rootless Duckweed**
Wolffia arrhiza (L.) Wimmer

Description: Frond floating at the surface, subglobose or
ovoid, convex on both sides (less so above),
0.5–1 (1.5) mm long, budding laterally,
dark or bluish-green; veins and roots absent.
Flowering: Never observed flowering in Europe.
Habitat: Shallow, stagnant or slow-moving,
eutrophic or even polluted, fresh waters;
mainly in the lowland.
Range: W and Central Europe, from Portugal and
England eastwards to Lithuania, C Russia,
and Bulgaria.

These tiniest of all vascular plants are often
hard to detect, but when assembling in
masses they can turn the water smudgy
emerald-green as if someone had spilt green
creosote into it.

BUTTERWORT FAMILY, LENTIBULARIACEAE

A subcosmopolitan family of terrestrial or aquatic
carnivorous herbs, with about 180 species in 4 genera.

Dicots. A 1st group, represented in Europe only by the genus *Pinguicula*, comprises small plants with a basal rosette of simple, entire-margined leaves secreting a transparent, glistening mucus, which traps small insects and is kept from leaking away by the upcurled leaf-margins. A second group of aquatics (in the large genus *Utricularia*) have alternate, finely divided leaves with threadlike segments, and small, urn-shaped bladders trapping small crustaceans or water-insects; they are rootless, but the stems near the bottom can be colourless, half-buried, slightly resembling roots. In both genera, digestion follows through proteolytic enzymes. Flowers are hermaphrodite, borne terminally on leafless scapes, solitary or in small racemes, emergent in aquatic forms. Calyx deeply divided, with 2 segments (in *Utricularia*) or with 5 more or less unequal segments (in *Pinguicula*). Corolla irregular (zygomorphic), 2-lipped, the tube prolonged into a spur. Stamens 2, adnate to base of corolla tube. Ovary superior, 1-locular, with 1 short style, and 8 or more ovules (only 2 ovules in *Utricularia*). Fruit a capsule. *Utricularia* hibernates via detached winter-buds (turions) enveloped in young leaves.

p.88 Alpine Butterwort *Pinguicula alpina* L.

Description: A perennial herb, to 12 cm. Leaves all in basal rosette, (sub)sessile, spreading, elliptical to lanceolate, *yellowish-green*. Flowers solitary on long, erect, glandular-hairy scapes, nodding. *Corolla white or cream*, obliquely trumpet-shaped, 8–10 mm wide; 2-lipped, upper lip 2-lobed, lower lip with 3 larger lobes; throat open, white with *1 or 2 yellow blotches; spur short (2–4 mm), conical, curved downwards, blunt-tipped*, greenish-white or yellow. Capsule obovoid, 7–9 mm long, pointed.

Flowering: June–August.

Habitat: Bogs, flushes, streamsides, meadows, heaths on mountains, on wet, oligotrophic, often peaty soils over calcareous subsoils; from sea level (in the north) to 2,600 m (in the Alps).

Range: Fennoscandia, N and W Russia, and in the mountains of C Europe, to the Pyrenees. Extinct in Britain.

Certain forms from the Alps may have lilac or violet flowers with yellow spur.

p.261 **Pale Butterwort** *Pinguicula lusitanica* L.

Description: A perennial herb, to 12 cm. Leaves all in basal rosette, (sub)sessile, spreading, ovate or elliptical, *pale greyish-green*. Flowers solitary on long, erect, glandular-hairy scapes, nodding. *Corolla pinkish or pale lilac*, obliquely trumpet-shaped, 6–7 mm wide; 2-lipped, upper lip 2-lobed, lower lip with 3 larger lobes; throat open, with yellowish markings; *spur short (2–4 mm), conical, curved downwards*, blunt-tipped. Capsule subglobose.

Flowering: June–October.

Habitat: Damp heaths, bogs, flushes, on wet, oligotrophic, acid, sandy or peaty soils; from sea level to 500 m.

Range: From Portugal and N Spain northwards to W France, S Britain, Ireland and W Scotland; a strictly Atlantic species.

Similar species: **Villous Butterwort** (*P. villosa* L.), which has ovate or rounded, brownish-green leaves, glandular-hairy scapes, pale-violet flowers 7–8 mm wide, with short spur (2–3 mm), and 2 yellow blotches in throat. In *Sphagnum* bogs in S Fennoscandia and NW Russia.

Pale Butterwort is the only *Pinguicula* species with hibernating leaf-rosettes; all others hibernate as buds.

p.325 **Common Butterwort** *Pinguicula vulgaris* L.

Description: A perennial herb, to 15 cm. Leaves all in basal rosette, (sub)sessile, spreading, ovate or elliptical, *yellowish-green*. Flowers solitary on long, erect, glandular scapes, nodding. *Corolla violet*, obliquely trumpet-shaped, 11–13 mm wide; 2-lipped, upper lip 2-lobed, lower lip with 3 larger lobes; throat open, whitish; *spur slender*, awl-shaped, straight or slightly curved, 3–6 mm long (half as long as rest of corolla), tapering into *acute tip*. Capsule obovoid, 5–6 mm long, blunt-tipped, with short style.

Flowering: May–July.

Habitat: Marshy heaths, bogs, fens, flushes, streamsides and paths in damp woods, also wet rocks, on wet, oligotrophic, slightly acid, sandy, stony or peaty soils; from sea level to 1,000 m (or even 2,300 m in the Alps).

Range: Most of Europe except Spitsbergen.

Similar species: **Large-flowered Butterwort** (*P. grandiflora* Lam.) has pale-green leaves, blue-violet flowers 15–20 mm wide, with stout, straight, acute (occasionally notched) spur 10–12 mm long. In comparable habitats, often on calcareous substrates, in the mountains of Iberia and France, and (disjunctly) in SW Ireland; naturalized in Cornwall.

p.184 **Lesser Bladderwort** *Utricularia minor* L.

Description: A submerged aquatic with *stems of 2 kinds*: greenish stems with large leaves and few bladders, and whitish, bottom-near stems with colourless, reduced leaves and numerous bladders *c.* 2 mm diam.; normal leaves 5–20 mm long, rounded, finely *palmately divided*, with threadlike, *untoothed segments*, without bristles. Flowers emergent, 2–6 together in terminal raceme on glabrous scape to 25 cm long, 1 mm thick. Corolla yellow, 6–8 mm long, 2-lipped, with unlobed lips; lower lip broadly obovate, flat or (later) with deflexed sides, with bulging, pale-yellow (often brown-striped) base ('palate') closing throat; *upper lip shorter than palate*. Spur very short, blunt. Capsule globose, 2-seeded, on recurved stalks.

Flowering: June–September.

Habitat: Shallow, stagnant, oligotrophic, acid waters of bogs, fens, heath-pools, often on a peaty substrate; from sea level to 1,800 m.

Range: Most of Europe except the high Arctic, and rare in Mediterranean region.

Similar species: **Intermediate Bladderwort** (*U. intermedia* Hayne) has normal leaves usually devoid of bladders (but numerous bladders on pale stems near bottom), blunt-tipped, weakly toothed leaf-segments with 1 bristle per tooth, 2–4-flowered racemes on scapes to

20 cm, and yellow flowers (8–12 mm long) with purple-striped palate; spur cylindrical, nearly equalling lower lip and parallel to it. In oligotrophic fens and heath-pools of N, W and C Europe.

U. ochroleuca much resembles Intermediate Bladderwort but has rather acute, markedly dentate (and bristle-bearing) leaf-segments, pale-yellow flowers with brown-striped palate and short, divergent spur. In oligotrophic, acid heath-pools and bogs of W, C and N Europe.

U. bremii Heer from C Europe has 2–13-flowered racemes on scapes to 30 (40) cm, pale yellow flowers with suborbicular, flat lower lip 10–12 mm diam., upper lip subequalling palate, and an acute spur. This species is often treated as merely a form or variety of *U. minor*.

---

p.184 **Greater Bladderwort** *Utricularia vulgaris* L.

Description: A submerged aquatic with *only greenish stems* bearing both leaves and numerous bladders *c.* 3 mm diam.; leaves 20–80 mm long, rather oblong, finely *pinnately divided*, with threadlike, toothed segments, with 1–few bristles on each tooth. Flowers emergent, 4–10 together in terminal raceme on glabrous scape to 25 cm long, 2 mm thick; flower-stalks to 15 mm long. Corolla deep yellow, 12–18 mm long, 2-lipped, with unlobed lips; lower lip has strongly recurved sides and bulging, red-striped palate closing throat; *upper lip scarcely equalling palate.* Spur short, conical, subacute. Capsule globose, 2-seeded, on *strongly recurved stalks.*

Flowering: June–August.

Habitat: Shallow, stagnant or slow-moving, mesotrophic, slightly acid or neutral fresh waters; from sea level to 1,000 m.

Range: Most of Europe except Iceland and the high Arctic, and rare in Mediterranean region.

Similar species: *U. australis* R. Br. has thinner scapes, always 1 bristle on each tooth of leaves, straight, erect fruit-stalks, and pale-yellow

flowers with blunt-tipped spur, on stalks to
20 mm (40 mm in fruit); upper lip longer
than palate, and lower lip almost flat, with
wavy margin. In shallow, oligotrophic to
mesotrophic, slightly acid fresh waters, in
most of Europe except Iceland, and only in
the central parts of Russia.

Most *Utricularia* species are declining,
owing to water pollution and peat-digging.

LILY FAMILY, LILIACEAE

A large, cosmopolitan family (*c.* 3,500 species in 250
genera) of usually glabrous, perennial herbs with rhizomes,
corms or bulbs. Monocots. Leaves simple, basically
alternate, often mainly basal, occasionally in whorls, or
reduced to scales (as in *Ruscus* and *Asparagus*); main veins
usually parallel (rarely reticulate, as in *Paris*). Flowers
regular, usually hermaphrodite (unisexual in *Ruscus* and
Asparagus), in racemes, panicles or umbels, placed
terminally on leafy stems or leafless scapes, or axillary (as in
Polygonatum), or placed on leaf-like branches ('cladodes', as
in *Ruscus*); in umbels of *Allium* species the flowers are often
partly replaced by small, onion-shaped, sessile bulbils,
serving as vegetative propagules. Perianth with 6 (rarely 4
or 8–12) subequal tepals in 2 whorls, all showy and petal-
like, free or connate (then perianth tube- or bell-shaped).
Stamens 3 or 6 (rarely 2, 3 or 13), usually free (but connate
into tube in *Ruscus*). Ovary superior, 3-locular (rarely 4–5-
locular, as in *Paris*), with 1 style and simple or 3-lobed
(rarely 4–5-lobed) stigma. Fruit a capsule or a berry. Many
species are grown for ornament, while others are
economically important as vegetables, especially *Asparagus*
and several *Allium* species: onions and shallots (*A. cepa* L.),
Welsh onion (*A. fistulosum* L.), garlic (*A. sativum* L.), leek
(*A. porrum* L.). The family also contains many poisonous
species, of which *Colchicum* is one of the deadliest.

p.293 **Wild Leek** *Allium ampeloprasum* L.

Description: A bulbous perennial to 1 (1.8) m, with
4–10 linear, greyish-green, long-sheathing
leaves in lower half of very stout, solid,
cylindrical flowering stem; blades to 50 cm
long, 40 mm wide, keeled below, with
scabrous margins. Young inflorescence

wrapped in single, whitish, ovate, long-pointed, soon withering bract. Flowers long-stalked, very numerous in globose umbel up to 90 mm diam.; no bulbils. Tepals 6, pink or pale purplish (occasionally whitish), 6–8 mm long, lanceolate. Stamens 6, slightly protruding, with trifid filament, middle tooth bearing anthers. Capsule ovoid, 3-lobed, 3-locular, 4 mm long.

Flowering: July–August.

Habitat: Road verges, hedges, banks, generally in disturbed or ruderal places, on dry to rather moist, mesotrophic, sandy or rocky soils; mainly in the lowland, and often near the sea.

Range: S and W Europe, extending northwards to W France and S Britain.

The plant smells of garlic. The var. *babingtonii* (Borrer) Syme has few-flowered umbels with numerous bulbils 8–15 mm long; only in Cornwall and W Ireland. Var. *bulbiferum* Syme from W France and the Channel Islands has smaller bulbils (6–8 mm long). **Cultivated Leek** (*A. porrum* L.) has been derived from this species through a long process of selection.

p.294 **Field Garlic** *Allium oleraceum* L.

Description: A bulbous perennial, to 80 cm, smelling strongly of garlic. Leaves 3–4, smooth, linear, *channelled*, long-sheathing, *bluish-green*, to 25 cm long, 3–5 mm wide (scabrous and strongly ribbed beneath), in lower half of cylindrical flowering stem. Young inflorescence wrapped in 2 whitish, linear-lanceolate, long-tapering, persistent *bracts to 20 cm long*. Flowers few, long-stalked (often drooping), in lax umbel with several green bulbils. Tepals 6, whitish, often tinged with green or pink, 5–7 mm long, lanceolate. Stamens 6, not protruding, all with simple filament, connate at their base. Style to 3 mm long. Capsule rarely produced.

Flowering: June–August.

Habitat: Grassland, road verges, vineyards, hedges, scrub, open woods, banks, on dry to rather moist, oligotrophic to mesotrophic, preferably calcareous, sandy, loamy or stony soils; from sea level to 1,800 m.

Range: Most of Europe except Ireland and the high Arctic; only naturalized in Iceland.

Similar species: *A. paniculatum* L. is almost scentless, and has green, almost smooth, channelled, much narrower leaves (to 2 mm wide, hollow only near base), 2 unequal, linear-lanceolate bracts to 14 cm, and numerous long-stalked, pink flowers in globose umbel lacking bulbils. On sunny, calcareous slopes in S Europe, northwards to NC France.

Keeled Garlic (*Allium carinatum* L.) has flat leaves to 4 mm wide, few-flowered umbels with numerous bulbils (or no flowers at all), blunt-tipped (not acute), pink or purplish tepals (4–6 mm long), long-protruding, free stamens, and ellipsoid, 3-lobed capsules to 5 mm long. In grassland, heaths and open woods in S and C Europe, northwards to Germany, Denmark, S Fennoscandia, and N Russia; locally naturalized in Britain and the Low Countries.

Compare also *A. vineale* (*see* p.764), which has a single, short bract under umbel.

A form of Field Garlic, with almost flat leaves 7–9 mm wide, and 30–50-flowered umbels without bulbils, has been described as var. *complanatum* Fries.

---

p.294 **Chives** *Allium schoenoprasum* L.

Description: A bulbous, tufted perennial, to 40 cm, with 1–2 greyish-green, smooth, linear, *almost cylindrical, hollow*, sheathing leaves to 35 cm long, 3–5 mm wide at base of cylindrical, hollow flowering stem. Young inflorescence wrapped in 2 whitish, ovate, shortly pointed, withering but persistent bracts to 15 mm long. Flowers 8–30, short-stalked, in dense, subglobose umbel 20–30 (40) mm diam.; no bulbils. Tepals 6, pale violet or purplish-pink (rarely white),

7–15 mm long, lanceolate, *spreading*. Stamens 6, not protruding, all with simple filament. Capsule to 4 mm long.

Flowering: May–August.

Habitat: Grassland, river forelands, river-dunes, streamsides, also naturalized in cultivated or waste land and roadsides, on (seasonally) moist, mesotrophic, preferably calcareous, sandy, loamy, stony or rocky soils; from sea level to 2,600 m.

Range: Most of Europe except Iceland and the high Arctic, and only on mountains in the south.

Often a kitchen-garden escape, and locally naturalized near habitation. *Compare A. vineale (see p.764), which has channelled (but again hollow) leaves.*

---

p.294 **Sand Leek** *Allium scorodoprasum* L.

Description: A bulbous perennial, to 80 cm, with 2–5 linear, greyish-green, long-sheathing leaves in lower half of cylindrical flowering stem; blades flat, solid, to 30 cm long, 5–15 mm wide, with scabrous margins. Young inflorescence wrapped in 2 whitish, ovate, pointed, withering but persistent bracts to 15 mm long. Flowers few, rather unequally (some long-)stalked, in lax, irregular umbel to 30 (50) mm diam., mixed with several purple bulbils (occasionally no flowers at all). Tepals 6, pale lilac or red-purple, 4–6.5 mm long, lanceolate. Stamens 6, not protruding, inner ones with trifid filament, middle tooth bearing anthers. Capsule *c.* 5 mm long.

Flowering: June–August.

Habitat: Cultivated and waste land, grassland, roadsides, scrub, open deciduous woods, banks, on moist to dry, mesotrophic or eutrophic, preferably calcareous, sandy, loamy or stony soils; from sea level to 1,400 m.

Range: NW and C Europe, northwards to Britain, S Fennoscandia and C Russia; only naturalized in Ireland.

Compare A. vineale (see p.764), which has narrower, hollow leaves, and single, soon-falling bract under inflorescence.

p.293 **German Garlic** *Allium senescens* L.

Description: A bulbous perennial, to 30 cm, with 4–9
linear, greyish-green, often twisted,
obscurely veined leaves, all collected at
base; *flowering stem angular* (2-angled at least
above), much shorter than stem; blades flat
above, *rounded beneath*, solid, to 25 cm long,
4–6 mm wide. Young inflorescence
wrapped in short, 2–5-lobed, whitish bract
to 15 mm long. Flowers numerous, rather
long-stalked, in rather dense, globose
umbel to 45 mm diam.; no bulbils. Tepals
6, pale purple, 4–6 mm long, lanceolate.
Stamens 6, distinctly protruding, all with
simple filaments. Capsule to 4 mm long,
with up to 6 seeds.

Flowering: June–August.

Habitat: Grassland, on dry, oligotrophic, sandy or
rocky soils; from sea level to 1,000 m.

Range: S, C and SE Europe, northwards to C France,
Germany, S Sweden, Poland and the Ukraine.

Similar species: *A. angulosum* L. grows taller (to 45 cm), and
has 4–6 keeled, distinctly veined leaves
(also basal, but almost equalling stem),
hemispherical (flat-topped) umbels, and
stamens equalling (not exceeding) tepals. In
marshes, damp meadows, riversides, often
on seasonally flooded places, from sea level
to 1,600 m, in C and E Europe, northwards
to S Germany, Poland, and C Russia.

German Garlic is a xerophyte,
characteristic of the Eurasian steppe belt.
The description pertains to ssp. *montanum*
(Fries) J. Holub; other subspecies occur in
Asia.

p.154 **Ramsons** *Allium ursinum* L.

Description: A bulbous perennial, to 40 cm, with 2–3
bright-green, *narrowly ovate or elliptical,
acute leaves* to 25 cm long, 20–70 mm
wide, narrowed in *distinct leaf-stalk;
flowering stem angular* (2-angled, with flat
and rounded side, or triangular); bulbs
narrow, with only 1 thickened scale.
Young inflorescence wrapped in 2 short,

whitish, ovate bracts (20–30 mm long). Flowers up to 20, long-stalked, in rather lax, often flat-topped umbel; no bulbils. Tepals 6, *white*, 7–12 mm long, lanceolate, *spreading*. Stamens 6, shorter than tepals, the inner ones with trifid filament, the middle tooth bearing the anthers. Capsule 3-lobed, 3–4 mm long.

Flowering: April–June.

Habitat: Damp deciduous woods (usually Beech, Poplar, or Alder), scrub, hedgerows, shaded verges, banks, on moist, oligotrophic to mesotrophic, preferably calcareous, sandy, loamy or stony soils; from sea level to 1,900 m.

Range: Most of Europe, northwards to the British Isles, the Low Countries, S Fennoscandia, and C Russia.

The plant smells strongly of garlic and has useful medicinal properties.

---

p.293 **Crow Garlic** *Allium vineale* L.

Description: A bulbous perennial, to 70 (120) cm, with 2–4 greyish- or brownish-green, smooth, linear, *semicircular*, hollow, long-sheathing leaves to 60 cm long, 3–4 mm wide, scattered along tough, cylindrical, almost solid flowering stem. Young inflorescence wrapped in single whitish or red-flushed, ovate, shortly pointed, soon-falling bract to 15 mm long. Flowers few (wholly absent in var. *compactum* (Thuill.) Syme), rather unequally (some long) stalked, in lax umbel with numerous greenish-red bulbils. Tepals 6, purplish or pink (occasionally greenish-white), 2–4.5 mm long, lanceolate, more or less erect. Stamens 6, protruding, inner ones with trifid filament, the middle tooth bearing anthers. Capsule 3–3.5 mm long, 3-locular, with up to 6 seeds.

Flowering: June–August.

Habitat: Grassland, road verges, sand-dunes, wood margins, grassy banks, also in ruderal places, on dry to moist, mesotrophic to eutrophic, calcareous or slightly acid, sandy,

loamy or stony soils; from sea level to
1,900 m.

Range: Most of Europe except Iceland and N Russia.

Similar species: **Round-headed Leek** (*Allium sphaerocephalon* L.) has hollow leaves markedly channelled above, and dense, rounded umbels (to 30 mm diam.) with numerous short-stalked, deep red-purple (rarely pink) flowers (3.5–5.5 mm long); bulbils usually absent. In grassland, dunes, roadsides, wasteland, on dry, oligotrophic to mesotrophic, calcareous, sandy, loamy or stony soils, in S and C Europe, northwards to W Britain, Belgium, S Germany, Poland, and C Russia.

Compare also *A. oleraceum* (*see* p.760), which has 2 long bracts under umbel.

---

p.128 **St Bernard's Lily** *Anthericum liliago* L.

Description: A rhizomatous perennial, to 60 cm, with terete flowering stems. Leaves all basal, linear, to 40 cm long, 3–7 mm wide, flat or channelled. Flowers in lax raceme, with small, lanceolate bracts to 10 mm. Tepals 6, white, up to 20 mm long, broadly lanceolate, spreading. Stamens 6, shorter than tepals, with glabrous filament. Ovary 3-locular, with 1 threadlike, curved style. Fruit an obovoid, pointed capsule, 8–13 mm long, with several black seeds, and splitting with 3 valves.

Flowering: May–July.

Habitat: Grassland, open woods, deciduous woods (often Oak), grassy banks, on dry, oligotrophic, calcareous, sandy, loamy or rocky soils; from sea level to 1,800 m.

Range: S and C Europe, northwards to Belgium, Denmark, S Sweden, Poland, and Romania.

Similar species: *A. ramosum* L. has leaves 4–5 mm wide, and smaller flowers (with tepals to 10 mm long) in small panicles; style straight; capsule 5–6 mm long. In dry grassland and wood margins on calcareous soils of C Europe, northwards to N France, Germany, S Sweden, Poland, Latvia, and C Russia.

p.95 **Wild Asparagus** *Asparagus officinalis* L.

Description: A rhizomatous perennial to 2 m, with terete, strongly branched, *erect or arching stems*; young basal shoots 5–10 mm thick (in cultivated forms even thicker). *Leaves alternate, minute, scale-like*, pale green, softly awned, with axillary bundles of *3–8 needle-like, soft, green cladodes* (5) 10–25 (30) mm long. Flowers functionally *unisexual*, usually solitary in axils of scale-leaves, pendent on long stalks with *articulation near middle*; male flowers slightly longer. Perianth bell-shaped; tepals 6, greenish-yellow, 4.5–6.5 mm long. Stamens 6, shorter than tepals; anthers equalling their filament, reddish in male flowers, greenish-white and sterile in female flowers. Ovary 3-locular, with *trifid style*. Fruit a *rounded, red berry*, 6–10 mm diam., with several rounded seeds.

Flowering: May–August.

Habitat: Sand-dunes, scrub, road verges, ruderal places, cultivated land, on dry, mesotrophic to eutrophic, preferably calcareous, sandy soils; mainly in the lowland.

Range: Much of Europe, northwards to the British Isles, the Low Countries, Denmark, Poland, and C Russia.

Similar species: *A. tenuifolius* Lam. has young shoots to 4 mm thick, cladodes in bundles of 15–40, flowers 6–8 mm long, on stalks with articulation close to flower, anthers much shorter than their filament, and berries 10–16 mm diam. In grassland, scrub and open woods of S Europe, locally northwards to C and NW France, Austria, and White Russia.

Wild Asparagus is frequently cultivated; the young shoots are eaten as a vegetable. *A. officinalis* ssp. *prostratus* (Dumort.) Corb. has prostrate or ascending stems, short, stiff, thickish, greyish-green cladodes (3) 5–10 (15) mm long, in bundles of 10–25, and flower-stalks 2–6 (8) mm long. Only in coastal sand-dunes of W Europe, from N Spain northwards to the British Isles, the Low Countries and NW Germany.

p.280 **Meadow Saffron** *Colchicum autumnale* L.

Description: A cormous perennial, 10–25 cm, without
normal stem. Leaves 3–4 (6), present only in
spring and early summer, all basal (implanted
on corm), erect, lanceolate, to 30 cm long,
50 mm wide, flat. Flowers solitary or 2–3 (6)
together, with common, whitish sheath,
appearing in autumn after withering of
leaves, and rising directly from ground.
Perianth basally connate to long, narrow,
white tube (10–30 cm long), with 6 free,
pink or pale-lilac (rarely white), lanceolate,
blunt-tipped lobes 4–12 cm long. *Stamens 6.*
Ovary at bottom of perianth tube
(underground during anthesis), 3-locular,
with *3 threadlike styles*; stigmas purplish.
Fruit a large, green, ellipsoid, 3-locular,
many-seeded capsule, 30–60 mm long,
appearing in spring with the leaves, pushed
over ground on stout stalk, dark brown when
ripe, and splitting with 3 valves.

Flowering: August–October.

Habitat: Damp grassland, river-forelands, wood
margins, deciduous woods, on wet or moist,
mesotrophic or eutrophic, neutral or
calcareous, sandy, loamy or clayey soils;
from sea level to 2,000 m.

Range: In Europe northwards to England, the Low
Countries, Germany, Poland, and White
Russia; naturalized in Denmark and S
Sweden.

Another name is Autumn Crocus. Owing
to the presence of colchicine, interfering
with cell division, all parts of the plant are
dangerously poisonous; yet, for the same
reason, the plant has important applications
in medicine and genetics research. The
species is rare and declining in most areas.
Compare Crocus (see p.668), which has only 3
stamens, and linear leaves.

p.128 **Lily-of-the-valley** *Convallaria majalis* L.

Description: A rhizomatous perennial, with erect,
angular flowering stems to 30 cm. Leaves
2–3, directly *implanted on rhizome,*

elliptical, 10–20 cm long, 30–60 mm wide, acute or shortly pointed, deep green, with numerous arched veins; leaf-stalks sheathing (leafless) stem rising from their middle; base of tuft clad in greenish or reddish scales. Flowers in lax, 1-sided raceme, *nodding* on recurved stalks, very fragrant. *Perianth broadly bell-shaped*, 5–9 mm long, pure white (or pinkish, as often in E and C Europe), with 6 *short, triangular-ovate, recurved teeth*. Stamens 6, not protruding, with glabrous filaments. Ovary 3-locular, with 1 style. Fruit a red berry, 8–10 mm diam., with several bluish-white seeds.

Flowering: May–June.

Habitat: Deciduous woods, scrub, hedgebanks, also mountain meadows, on moist to rather dry, oligotrophic, mildly acid, sandy or stony soils; from sea level to 2,300 m.

Range: Most of Europe except Ireland, Iceland and the high Arctic.

Frequently grown in gardens, and often naturalized on estate grounds; also cultivated for the perfume. The plant is considered poisonous. *Compare Maianthemum (see* p.773), which has cordate stem-leaves, and 4-parted perianth.

---

p.279 **Snake's-head Lily** *Fritillaria meleagris* L.

Description: A bulbous perennial to 30 (50) cm, with erect, rounded flowering stems. Leaves 3–7, alternate, sessile, linear, channelled, to 15 cm long, 4–9 mm wide, tapering to fine point. Flowers solitary (rarely 2 or 3 together), terminal, *nodding. Perianth egg-shaped*, 30–45 mm long, *purplish, chequered with pink or whitish spots* (occasionally all white), with 6 *free, narrowly elliptical tepals*. Stamens 6, not protruding, with glabrous filaments. Ovary 3-locular, with 1 style. Fruit an *erect*, obovate or globose, many-seeded capsule, 12–15 mm long.

Flowering: April–May.

Habitat: Damp meadows, marshes, river-forelands, on (seasonally) wet, mesotrophic, neutral or slightly acid, clayey or peaty soils; from sea level to 800 m.

Range: W and C Europe, northwards to England, the Netherlands (extinct in Belgium), Germany, Poland, and C Russia, eastwards to the Caucasus; locally naturalized further north.

A declining species, intolerant of early hay-making and intensive manuring.

---

p.200 **Yellow Star of Bethlehem**
Gagea lutea (L.) Ker-Gawler

Description: A bulbous perennial, with an erect, *glabrous stem* to 15 (25) cm and 1 yellowish-green, narrowly linear, basal leaf to 20 cm long, 7–9 (15) mm wide, flat above, bluntly keeled below, with hooded tip; *1 bulb*. Flowers 15–20 mm diam., long-stalked, 2–7 (10) together in terminal umbel, subtended by *2 subopposite, lanceolate, ciliate, bract-like upper leaves* (3–6 mm wide). Tepals 6, free, greenish-yellow with green stripe on outside, lanceolate, blunt-tipped, *glabrous*, spreading (greenish and strongly recurved after anthesis). Stamens 6. Ovary 3-locular, with 1 style and *1 stigma*. Fruit a small, ellipsoid capsule.

Flowering: March–May.

Habitat: Deciduous woods (often Oak or Beech), scrub, parks, shaded grassland, on moist, oligotrophic, slightly acid to basic, sandy, loamy or stony soils; from sea level to 1,700 m, but more frequent in the lowland.

Range: Most of Europe except Ireland, Iceland and the high Arctic.

Similar species: **Meadow Gagea** (*G. pratensis* (Pers.) Dumort.) has 1 keeled basal leaf 2–5 (7) mm wide, tapering into fine point, 2 subopposite, linear upper leaves (often with small bulbil in axil), 1–4 (6) flowers 20–30 mm diam., with subacute tepals (greyish-blue and erect after anthesis), and 3-lobed stigma. In grassland, road verges, wood margins, parks, also fields, in continental Europe northwards to the Low

Countries and S Sweden, Poland and C
Russia; also in Asia Minor.

Least Gagea (*G. minima* (L.) Ker-Gawler)
has 1 narrowly linear, unkeeled basal leaf
1–2 mm wide, 2 subopposite, lanceolate
upper leaves, and 1–7 yellow flowers
10–15 mm diam., with pointed tepals
(reflexed after anthesis). In meadows and
open woods on calcareous soils in C
Europe, northwards to S Scandinavia, S
Finland and N Russia, and further to W
and C Asia.

---

p.200 **Belgian Gagea**
Gagea spathacea (Hayne) Salisb.

Description: A bulbous perennial to 15 (25) cm, with
erect, *glabrous stem* and 2 (3) greyish-green,
narrowly linear, *tubular basal leaves* to
15 cm long, 2 mm wide; *2 (3) bulbs* in
common pouch, each sending up 1 basal
leaf. Flowers 18–20 mm diam., long-
stalked, 1–3 (5) together in terminal
umbel, subtended by *single, clasping bract-
like upper leaf* (at short distance under
umbel, and 3–6 mm wide). Tepals 6, free,
yellow with brownish stripe on outside,
lanceolate, *glabrous*, spreading. Stamens 6.
Ovary 3-locular, with 1 style. Fruit a small,
ellipsoid capsule.

Flowering: April–May.

Habitat: Damp woods and coppices, wood margins,
woodland clearings, on moist, oligotrophic,
slightly acid, sandy or stony soils; from sea
level to 1,500 m, but more frequent in the
lowland.

Range: Continental Europe, northwards to the Low
Countries, Denmark and S Sweden,
eastwards to C Russia, but local in the
south.

Similar species: *G. villosa* (Pers.) Dumort. has finely hairy
stems, 2 (3) channelled basal leaves, 3–12-
flowered umbels with 2–3 sessile,
subopposite, unequal, broadly linear, hairy
upper leaves (lower one to 10 mm wide,
upper one *c.* 3 mm) directly under umbel,
and often some minute bulbils in upper
leaf-axils; tepals hairy and green-striped on

outside. In shaded grassland, park lawns, road verges, hedges, occasionally in cultivated and waste land, on moist to rather dry, oligotrophic, slightly acid soils, in continental Europe northwards to S Sweden, the Netherlands, and the Ukraine. (Extinct in Belgium.)

Bohemian Gagea (*G. bohemica* (Zauschner) Schultes & Schultes) has stems usually less than 20 mm, 2 threadlike, often wavy or coiled, glabrous basal leaves (to 1 mm diam.), 2–4 alternate, hairy stem-leaves, 1–3 flowers 10–20 mm diam. with oblanceolate, blunt-tipped, hairy tepals (13–17 mm long), and obovoid, notched capsules. In grassland and open woods, on acid, often rocky soils, in S and C Europe, locally extending northwards to W France, Wales, and C Germany, and eastwards to Hungary and Greece, often not flowering in the north. Plants from W France, with basal leaves as well, are attributed to *G. b.* ssp. *gallica* (Rouy) J.B.K. Richardson; plants with stems 4–8 (10) cm, tepals 12–13 mm long, and obovoid, truncate capsules are often distinguished as *G. saxatilis* (Mert. & Koch) Schultes & Schultes. On dry, stony soils in WC Europe, locally westwards to Portugal, northwards to NE Germany, and eastwards to Macedonia.

---

p.243 *Lilium bulbiferum* L.

Description: A bulbous perennial, with erect, leafy flowering stems to 90 cm. Leaves alternate, lanceolate to linear, to 10 cm long, subglabrous, often with small, blackish tubers in axils. *Flowers erect*, 1–3, terminal or axillary to highest leaves. Tepals 6, *erect to spreading*, oblanceolate, to 60 (80) mm long, *deep yellow with dark spots*. Stamens 6, far protruding. Ovary 3-locular, with 1 style and a 3-lobed stigma. Fruit an obovoid, 3-locular, 6-angled, brownish, many-seeded capsule to 40 mm long, splitting with 3 valves.

Flowering: June–July.

Habitat: Woods, scrub, on mountain slopes, on moist, oligotrophic, acid, sandy or rocky soils; mainly in the mountains, 300–2,400 m.

Range: C Europe, westwards to Spain, E France, northwards to S Germany, Poland, and Romania; locally naturalized in the lowland, northwards to S Scandinavia.

Similar species: **Pyrenean Lily** (*L. pyrenaicum* Gouan) from the Pyrenees has ciliate leaves, and nodding flowers with strongly recurved, bright-yellow, brown-streaked tepals; naturalized in woods and grassland of Britain and Ireland.

L. bulbiferum ssp. *croceum* (Chaix) Arc. from the southern Alps lacks axillary tubers, and has orange flowers with blackish dots; formerly a weed in rye-fields in the NE Netherlands and NW Germany, and still found on river-dunes in the Ems valley.

p.280 **Martagon Lily** *Lilium martagon* L.

Description: A bulbous perennial, with erect, leafy flowering stems to 1.5 (1.8) m. Leaves (broadly) lanceolate, to 15 cm long, glabrous or hairy on veins beneath; *lower ones in whorls* of 5–10, upper ones alternate. *Flowers nodding*, 1–8 together in lax, terminal raceme with small, green bracts. Tepals 6, strongly recurved, oblanceolate, round-tipped, 25–35 mm long, *pale to dark purplish with blackish-purple spots*. Stamens 6, far protruding. Ovary 3-locular, with 1 style and 3-lobed stigma. Fruit rounded or ellipsoid, 3-locular, sharply 6-angled, brownish, many-seeded capsule, 23–30 mm long, splitting with 3 valves.

Flowering: June–July.

Habitat: Deciduous woods (often Beech), scrub, mountain meadows, on moist, oligotrophic, preferably calcareous, sandy, loamy or rocky soils; mainly in the mountains, 400–2,800 m.

Range: S and C Europe, northwards to NE France, Poland, Estonia, and C Urals; locally naturalized in Britain, Belgium and S Scandinavia.

p.95 Snowdon Lily
Lloydia serotina (L.) Reichenbach

Description: A bulbous perennial, with terete flowering stems to 15 cm. *Leaves narrowly linear*, to 20 cm long, 1–2 mm wide; usually 2 basal leaves and 2–4 alternate, shorter stem-leaves. *Flowers solitary, terminal, erect to half-nodding.* Perianth bell-shaped; tepals 6, *white with pink to dark-purple veins*, 18–22 mm long, broadly lanceolate, blunt-tipped. Stamens 6, shorter than tepals. Ovary 3-locular, with 1 threadlike, curved style. Fruit globose, 3-ribbed, many-seeded capsule, splitting with 3 valves.

Flowering: May–July.

Habitat: Mountain grassland, tundra, on dry to moist, oligotrophic, acid, stony or rocky soils; from sea level (in the north) to 3,000 m (in the Alps).

Range: The mountains of C Europe, also in Wales, and in Arctic Russia.

---

p.127 May Lily
Maianthemum bifolium (L.) F.W. Schmidt

Description: A rhizomatous perennial, with erect, rounded flowering stems to 20 cm, usually slightly hairy above. Leaves 2 (3), alternate, short-stalked, broadly ovate with cordate base, 30–60 mm long, acute, green, with several strongly arched veins; base of stem has 2 whitish scales. Flowers on short, spreading stalks, in 10–20-flowered raceme. Perianth 4–6 mm diam., pure white, with *4 triangular-lanceolate, spreading to deflexed tepals. Stamens 4*, far protruding, with glabrous filaments. *Ovary 2-locular*, with 1 style. Fruit a red berry, 4–5 mm diam., with up to 4 brown seeds.

Flowering: May–July.

Habitat: Deciduous woods, scrub, hedgebanks, on moist, oligotrophic, on moist to rather dry, oligotrophic, mildly acid, sandy or stony soils; from sea level to 2,100 m.

Range: Most of Europe except Iceland and the high Arctic.

Compare Convallaria (see p.767), which has basally implanted, elliptical leaves, and connate, 6-lobed perianth.

---

p.343 **Tassel Hyacinth** *Muscari comosum* (L.) Miller

Description: A bulbous perennial, with erect, terete flowering stems to 60 (90) cm. Leaves 3–5, all basal, linear, to 40 cm long, 5–10 (15) mm wide, channelled. Flowers in long, terminal raceme; lower (fertile) ones rather short-stalked, spreading to drooping, *purplish-brown* (becoming brownish or olive), *upper ones sterile, violet* (rarely white), and *erect on long stalks*. Perianth 5–9 mm long (much smaller in sterile flowers); tepals connate into pear-shaped tube with 6 short, blunt, whitish teeth. Stamens 6, enclosed. Ovary 3-locular, with 1 short style and 3-lobed stigma. Fruit subglobose, 3-lobed, 6-seeded capsule, 8–9 mm long, splitting with 3 valves; racemes much elongated in fruit, to 40 cm long.

Flowering: May–July.

Habitat: Cereal fields, vineyards, roadsides, grassland, on dry to rather moist, mesotrophic, calcareous, sandy, loamy or stony soils; from sea level to 1,300 m.

Range: S and SC Europe, northwards to N France, S Germany, Poland and W Russia, but doubtfully native in the north.

---

p.343 **(Common) Grape Hyacinth**
Muscari neglectum Guss. ex Ten.

Description: A bulbous perennial, with erect, terete flowering stems to 30 cm. Leaves 3–6, all basal, linear, to 30 cm long, 4 mm wide, channelled, bright green, often red-based. Flowers in short terminal raceme 20–40 (70) mm long, all short-stalked; lower (fertile) ones spreading to nodding, *deep violet-blue, upper ones sterile, pale violet-blue*, spreading to erect, not forming distinct tuft. Perianth 3.5–7 mm long (smaller in sterile flowers); tepals connate into ovoid, urn-shaped tube with 6 short, blunt, white teeth. Stamens 6, enclosed. Ovary 3-locular, with 1 short style and 3-lobed stigma. Fruit subglobose, 3-lobed, 6-seeded capsule, to 8 mm long, splitting with 3 valves.

Flowering: April–May.

Habitat: Grassland, cultivated ground, vineyards, on dry, oligotrophic, preferably calcareous, sandy, loamy or stony soils; from sea level to 1,700 m.

Range: S and C Europe, northwards to England, Belgium, Poland, and C Russia.

Similar species: **Small Grape Hyacinth** (*M. botryoides* (L.) Miller) has 2–3 (4) leaves to 25 cm long, 5–12 mm wide (widest near top), greyish-green above, with hooded tip, and almost globose, pale violet-blue flowers (2) 3.5–5 mm long. In grassland, wasteland, open woods, on dry to rather moist, mesotrophic soils of S and C Europe, eastwards to the Caucasus; locally naturalized in the Low Countries.

Both species are popular garden ornamentals.

p.218 **Bog Asphodel**
Narthecium ossifragum (L.) Hudson

Description: A rhizomatous perennial, with ascending, terete, ribbed flowering stems to 30 cm. Leaves mostly basal, *sword-shaped*, in *2 opposite rows*, to 20 cm long, 3–7 mm wide; stem-leaves few, reduced to sheathing scales. Flowers in lax raceme, with small, linear-lanceolate bracts. Tepals 6, *yellow*, 6–8 mm long, lanceolate, *spreading*. Stamens 6, shorter than tepals, with *densely yellow-hairy filament*. Ovary 3-locular, with 1 short style. Fruit an *ellipsoid, many-seeded capsule*, 10–12 mm long, splitting with 3 valves.

Flowering: June–September.

Habitat: Bogs, marshy heaths and moors, on wet, oligotrophic, acid, peaty soils; from sea level to 1,200 m.

Range: W Europe, from N Portugal northwards to Scotland, the Faeroes and S Scandinavia.

A typically Atlantic species; declining in much of its area, though often forming large colonies at its remaining stations. The whole plant turns orange after anthesis. It is considered poisonous to livestock. *Compare Tofieldia (see p.782)*, which has 3 styles.

p.128 **Star of Bethlehem**
Ornithogalum umbellatum L.

Description:
A bulbous perennial, with subterete flowering stem to 30 (50) cm. Leaves (3) 6–9 (15), all basal, linear, to 30 cm long, 2–8 mm wide, channelled, with *white line along centre*. Flowers 3–20, in lax, *umbel-shaped raceme*, on erect to spreading, unequal stalks 30–60 mm long, with lanceolate, whitish bracts to 30 mm long. Tepals 6, *white, striped green* on outside, 15–20 mm long, elliptical, acute, *spreading*. Stamens 6, much shorter than tepals, with short, glabrous filament, and yellow anthers. Ovary 3-locular, with 1 style. Fruit club-shaped, 6-angled, many-seeded capsule, 8–10 mm long, splitting with 3 valves.

Flowering: May–July.

Habitat: Grassland, road verges, damp deciduous woods (often with Ash), scrub, hedges, also rye-fields, on moist, mesotrophic, preferably calcareous, sandy or loamy soils; from sea level to 1,600 m.

Range: Continental Europe northwards to Britain, the Low Countries, Poland, and W Russia, but doubtfully native in the north; certainly only naturalized in Ireland and Scandinavia.

Similar species: **Drooping Star of Bethlehem** (*O. nutans* L.), from SE Europe and SW Asia, grows taller (to 1 m), and has green, unstriped leaves 3–12 mm wide, 1-sided racemes with 2–12 nodding, bell-shaped flowers (25–30 mm long), on short stalks (to 10 mm) much shorter than their bracts. Locally naturalized in roadsides, scrub and wood margins of W and C Europe.
Bath Asparagus (*O. pyrenaicum* L.) also has unstriped leaves and short flower-stalks, but all-sided racemes with more than 20 small, yellowish-green, starry flowers (14–24 mm diam.), and short bracts (to 7 mm). In damp woods, hedgebanks, grassland, in S, W and SC Europe, northwards to S England, Belgium, Switzerland and Romania.

p.50 Herb Paris *Paris quadrifolia* L.

Description: A glabrous, rhizomatous perennial, with erect, rounded, unbranched flowering stems to 30 cm. Leaves (3) 4 (6), in *single, terminal whorl*, subsessile, broadly elliptical or obovate, to 15 cm long, short-pointed, green, *net-veined* with 3 arched main veins. *Flowers solitary, terminal*, erect, long-stalked, hermaphrodite (occasionally only female). Perianth *c.* 40 mm diam., *yellowish-green*, with 4–6 lanceolate, spreading outer tepals, and usually 4–6 linear, spreading inner tepals. Stamens (6) 8 (10), erect, with glabrous filaments, these prolonged over (yellow) anthers. *Ovary 4–5-locular*, bluish-purple, with 4–5 styles (or single, 4–5-branched style). Fruit a shiny-black, rounded berry, to 10 mm diam., with several red seeds.

Flowering: April–June.

Habitat: Humus-rich, deciduous woods (often Beech), coppices, scrub (often Alder), also wet rocks, on moist, oligotrophic, slightly acid to calcareous, sandy, loamy or stony soils; from sea level to 2,000 m.

Range: All Europe except Ireland and Spitsbergen; rare in Mediterranean region.

The berries are poisonous.

---

p.94 Common Solomon's-seal
Polygonatum multiflorum (L.) All.

Description: A rhizomatous perennial to 60 (100) cm, with erect, *arching*, unbranched, *rounded stems. Leaves numerous, alternate*, in 2 opposite rows, (sub)sessile, (narrowly) ovate to elliptical, to 15 cm long, green, with several strongly arched veins. Flowers drooping, stalked, in small, *2–7-flowered, axillary clusters*. Perianth connate, 10–17 (20) mm long, 2–4 mm wide, cylindrical, *slightly constricted* in middle, *white*, with 6 short, triangular-ovate, *greenish, white-edged teeth*. Stamens 6, not protruding, with *densely hairy filaments*. Ovary 3-locular, with 1 style. Fruit a bluish-black berry, with several seeds.

Flowering: May–June.

Habitat: Deciduous woods, coppices, occasionally coniferous woods, also shaded road verges and ditch-sides, on moist, oligotrophic, slightly acid to calcareous, sandy, loamy or stony soils; from sea level to 2,200 m.

Range: In Europe northwards to Britain, S Fennoscandia, and C Russia.

Similar species: **Angular Solomon's-seal** (*Polygonatum odoratum* (Miller) Druce) has angular stems; flowers solitary or paired (rarely 3–5 together) in leaf-axils, very fragrant; perianth tube straight, not constricted, to 20 mm long, 5–7 mm wide; stamens with glabrous filaments. In scrub, open woods, dunes, on dry, oligotrophic, preferably calcareous, sandy, loamy or rocky soils, from sea level to 2,000 m, in most of Europe, northwards to C Scandinavia and N Russia.

The berries of Solomon's-seal species have emetic properties.

---

p.93 **Whorled Solomon's-seal**
Polygonatum verticillatum (L.) All.

Description: A rhizomatous perennial, with erect, unbranched, angular stems to 80 (100) cm. *Leaves numerous, in whorls of 3–6 (8)*, sessile, lanceolate to linear, to 15 cm long, green, with 1 strong midvein and several parallel side-veins. Flowers stalked, in pendent, *1–3-flowered, axillary clusters*. Perianth connate, 6–8 (10) mm long, 1.5–2 mm wide, cylindrical, *greenish-white*, with 6 short, triangular-ovate teeth. Stamens 6. Ovary 3-locular, with 1 style. Fruit a *red, finally dark-purple berry*, with several seeds.

Flowering: May–June.

Habitat: Damp deciduous woods (usually Oak and Beech), scrub, shaded mountain grassland, on moist, oligotrophic, slightly acid, loamy or stony soils; from sea level to 2,400 m, but rare in the lowland, and only on mountains in the south.

Range: C and N Europe, westwards to N Spain, northwards to England, N Scandinavia, the Baltic States, and W Russia.

p.94 Butcher's Broom *Ruscus aculeatus* L.

Description: A small, bushy, *evergreen shrub*, with erect,
strongly branched stems to 50 (100) cm.
Leaves alternate, minute, scale-like,
membranous, with *ovate, pointed, spine-
tipped, leathery, green, leaf-like cladodes to
40 mm long* in their axil. Flowers 4–5 mm
diam., functionally *unisexual*, usually
dioecious, sessile, *borne solitary or 2 together
on cladodes*. Tepals 6, *greenish*, more or less
spreading. *Stamens 3, with connate filaments.*
Ovary 1-locular (rarely incompletely 3-
locular), with 1 style. Fruit *rounded, red
berry*, 10–12 (15) mm diam., with 1–4
(often 2) rounded, whitish seeds.

Flowering: (Autumn) January–April.

Habitat: Deciduous woods, scrub, hedgebanks,
occasionally sea-cliffs, on dry to rather
moist, oligotrophic, calcareous, loamy,
stony or rocky soils; from sea level to
700 m.

Range: S and W Europe, extending northwards to
W France and C England, and (from the
east) to Romania and Hungary.

---

p.344 Alpine Squill *Scilla bifolia* L.

Description: A bulbous perennial, with erect, rounded
flowering stems to 25 cm. Leaves 2 (3),
basal, broadly linear, to 20 cm long,
12 mm wide, channelled, green, sheathing
at base. Flowers 3–8, in rather lax raceme,
on erect to spreading stalks, *usually without
bracts* (or these very small). Tepals 6, *pale
violet-blue* (rarely pink or white), 6–8 mm
long, narrowly elliptical, *free, spreading from
base*. Stamens 6, inserted on base of tepals,
with violet anthers. Ovary 3-locular, with
1 style. Fruit a 3-lobed, subglobose,
weakly trigonal, slightly pointed, many-
seeded capsule, 7–10 mm long, splitting
with 3 valves.

Flowering: March–April.

Habitat: Deciduous woods (often Oak), scrub,
mountain grassland, on moist,
mesotrophic, preferably calcareous, loamy
or stony soils; from sea level to 1,500 m.

Range: S and C Europe, northwards to Belgium, C Germany, Poland, and C Russia; locally naturalized on estate grounds in the Netherlands.

---

p.344 **Bluebell**
Scilla non-scripta (L.) Hoffmanns & Link

Description: A bulbous perennial, with erect, rounded flowering stems to 50 cm. Leaves 3–6, all basal, broadly linear, to 30 cm long, 15 mm wide, flat, keeled below, green, sheathing at base, and with hooded tip. Flowers up to 16, *nodding* on short, recurved stalks, in lax, 1-sided, arching raceme, with linear-lanceolate, *bifid, violet bracts*. *Tepals connate*; perianth cylindrical, 14–20 mm long, violet-blue (rarely pink or white), with 6 recurved, broadly lanceolate teeth. Stamens 6, halfway connate to perianth-tube, scarcely protruding, with *cream anthers*. Ovary 3-locular, with 1 style. Fruit 3-lobed, ovoid to subglobose, many-seeded capsule, to 10 mm long, splitting with 3 valves.

Flowering: April–June.

Habitat: Damp deciduous woods, scrub, on moist, oligotrophic to mesotrophic, slightly acid, sandy, loamy or stony soils; from sea level to 1,500 m.

Range: W Europe, from Iberia to W France and Scotland; locally naturalized in the Netherlands and Germany.

Frequently planted in gardens, and often escaping; apparently, most northern plants are (fertile) hybrids with **Spanish Bluebell** (*S. hispanica* Miller) from W Iberia, with broadly bell-shaped flowers in an erect raceme.

---

p.344 **Spring Squill** *Scilla verna* Hudson

Description: A bulbous perennial to 30 cm, with erect, rounded flowering stems. Leaves 2–7, all basal, *narrowly linear*, to 20 cm long, 4 mm wide, curly, green. Flowers 2–12, stalked, erect, in short, terminal raceme with linear-lanceolate, *membranous, bluish-purple bracts* exceeding flower-stalks. Tepals 6, *free, spreading from base*, 6–10 mm long, violet-blue (rarely pink or white). Stamens 6, inserted on base of tepals, with violet anthers. Ovary 3-locular, with 1 style. Fruit 3-lobed, subglobose, trigonal, many-seeded capsule, 4–6 (8) mm long, splitting with 3 valves.

Flowering: April–June.

Habitat: Meadows, heaths, dunes, open woods, on dry, oligotrophic, preferably calcareous, sandy or stony soils; from sea level to 2,000 m, but often near the coast.

Range: W Europe, from Portugal northwards to W France, E Ireland, W and N Britain (including the Faeroes) and SW Norway.

Similar species: **Autumnal Squill** (*S. autumnalis* L.) has 5–10 erect, linear, channelled leaves to 2 mm wide, and small, bractless, lilac flowers (August–October, usually before leaves appear) with tepals 4–6 mm long; capsules to 4 mm. In comparable habitats, coastal as well as mountainous (to 2,000 m), in S and W Europe, northwards to W and C France and S England, and (from the east) to Hungary.

Flowers of Spring Squill appear in spring, when the leaves are already present. Several other *Scilla* species are grown in gardens, and may occasionally escape and naturalize.

---

p.128 **Kerry Lily** *Simethis planifolia* (L.) Gren.

Description: A rhizomatous perennial, with erect, flexuous flowering stems to 40 cm. *Leaves narrowly linear*, all basal, to 60 cm long, 7 mm wide, erect, overtopping flowers. Flowers erect, stalked, in lax *panicle*. Tepals 6, *white inside, pink outside*, 10–12 mm long, ovate, blunt-tipped, *spreading*. Stamens 6, shorter than tepals, with *thickened, white-hairy filament* and yellow anthers. Ovary 3-locular, with 1 threadlike style. Fruit subglobose, few-seeded capsule to 5 mm diam., splitting with 3 valves.

Flowering: May–June.

Habitat: Heaths and woods (often Pine), on dry, oligotrophic, acid, sandy or rocky soils; from sea level to 500 m.

Range: S Europe, northwards to W and C France, also in S England (Dorset) and W Ireland (Kerry).

---

p.127 **Scottish Asphodel**
Tofieldia pusilla (Michaux) Pers.

Description: A rhizomatous perennial, with ascending, terete flowering stems to 12 (20) cm. Leaves mostly basal, *sword-shaped*, in *2 opposite rows*, to 80 mm long, 3–4 mm wide, with *3 veins*; stem-leaves few, scale-like. Flowers short-stalked, in short, dense, 5–10-flowered raceme, with *tiny, 3-lobed involucre under perianth*, but no bract at base of stalk. Tepals 6, *white or greenish*, 2–3 mm long, elliptical, *spreading*. Stamens 6, about equalling tepals, with *densely yellow-hairy filament*. Ovary 3-locular, with *3 short styles*. Fruit *rounded, 3-lobed, capsule*, 3–4 mm diam., with several seeds, and splitting with 3 valves.

Flowering: June–August.

Habitat: Marshes, damp meadows, flushes, bogs, tundra, on wet, oligotrophic, calcareous, sandy or peaty soils; mainly in the mountains (solely so in the south), to 2,500 m.

Range: C Europe (the Pyrenees, Alps, Jura, and Carpathians), N Britain, Iceland, Fennoscandia, N and C Russia (including Spitsbergen).

Similar species: **German Asphodel** (*T. calyculata* (L.) Wahlenb.), to 35 cm, has 4–10-veined leaves (to 15 cm), and up to 30 flowers in racemes 1–50 mm long, with lanceolate bracts at base of stalk (and 3-lobed involucre under perianth); tepals yellowish (rarely reddish), 3–4 mm long. In comparable habitats, in the mountains of C Europe (including the Pyrenees), S Sweden (Gotland), Poland, the Baltic States and W and C Russia.

Compare Narthecium (see p.775), which has 1 style.

p.127 **White False Helleborine** *Veratrum album* L.

Description: A rhizomatous perennial, with stout, erect flowering stems to 1.5 m, branched in inflorescence. Leaves alternate, sessile, clasping stem with short sheath, ovate or elliptical with several arched veins, pleated, more or less hairy beneath, crowded towards stem-base, to 25 cm long; upper ones smaller and narrower. Flowers short-stalked, numerous in long, axillary racemes, forming *elongate panicle*. Tepals 6, only connate at base, *whitish inside, greenish outside* (occasionally yellowish inside), 8–15 mm long, obovate, *spreading*. Stamens 6, with threadlike, spreading filaments and subglobose anthers. Ovary 3-locular, with 3 short styles. Fruit an ovoid, 3-lobed, sparsely hairy capsule, 10–15 mm long, containing several winged seeds, and splitting with 3 valves; each locule has a recurved tip.

Flowering: July–August.

Habitat: Damp meadows, woodland clearings, along streams and rivers, on (seasonally) wet or moist, oligotrophic to mesotrophic, sandy, loamy or stony soils; from sea level to 2,400 m.

Range: The mountains of C Europe (northwards to the Vosges and Carpathians), also in Arctic Norway, Finland, and most of Russia.

FLAX FAMILY, LINACEAE

A subcosmopolitan family of herbs or shrubs, with *c.* 300 species in 13 genera, in warm and temperate regions. Dicots. Leaves alternate or opposite, simple. Flowers regular, hermaphrodite in monochasial or dichasial cymes. Sepals 4–5, free or only basally connate. Petals 4–5, usually free and characteristically soon-falling. Stamens 4–5, or twice as many, then every 2nd one sterile; filaments basally connate. Ovary superior, usually 4–5-locular, with 2 ovules per locule (or seemingly 8–10-locular owing to the presence of false septa between the ovules); styles 4–5, free or partly connate. Fruit a capsule. Of the European genera, *Linum* has 5-merous flowers, *Radiola* 4-merous ones.

p.336 **Pale Flax** *Linum bienne* Miller

Description: A glabrous biennial or short-lived perennial, with slender, erect or ascending, usually branched stems to 60 cm, and with sterile shoots. Leaves alternate (or only lowest ones opposite), linear-lanceolate, *0.5–1.5 mm wide, 1–3-veined*, erect. *Flowers 16–24 mm* diam., long-stalked, in lax (monochasial) cymes. Sepals 5, ovate, all pointed, 4–5.5 mm long, only inner ones glandular-ciliate. Petals obovate, short-clawed, *pale blue or lilac*. Stamens 5, with ovoid anthers. Ovary rounded, with 5 divergent styles, each with elongate, *club-shaped stigma*. Capsule subglobose, 5–6 mm diam., 10-seeded, opening with 10 valves; seeds compressed, to 3 mm long.

Flowering: May–September.

Habitat: Grassland, roadsides, woodland clearings, on dry, oligotrophic, calcareous, sandy or stony soils; mainly in the lowland.

Range: S and W Europe, northwards to W and C France, S Britain and SE Ireland.

Similar species: **Flax** (*L. usitatissimum* L.) is annual (without sterile shoots), usually with unbranched stems to 1.2 m, 3-veined leaves (1.5–3 mm wide), and bright-blue (rarely white) flowers (25–35 mm diam.); sepals 6–9 mm long; anthers oblong, 3–4 times as long as wide; capsule 7–9 mm diam., with seeds to 5 mm long. Cultivated for the fibres (linen) and the linseed (oil), and often a casual on roadsides and wasteland in much of Europe.

---

p.143 **Fairy Flax** *Linum catharticum* L.

Description: A glabrous annual, with threadlike, erect, *regularly forked stem* to 20 cm. *Leaves opposite*, elliptical to oblanceolate, 5–10 mm long, 1-veined. *Flowers 4–6 mm* diam., nodding in bud, long-stalked, in lax cymes. Sepals 5, ovate, all glandular-ciliate. Petals obovate, *white with yellow claw*. Stamens 5. Ovary rounded, with 5 free styles. Capsule globose, 2–3 mm diam., opening with 10 valves, and containing 10 compressed seeds.

Flowering: June–September.

Habitat: Short, poor grassland, dune-pastures, heaths, loam-pits, on cliffs, occasionally in fens, on moist, oligotrophic, slightly acid to calcareous, sandy or loamy or stony soils; from sea level to 2,300 m.

Range: All Europe, including Iceland, but except the high Arctic.

Compare Radiola (*see* p.786), which has 4-merous flowers.

p.336 **Perennial Flax** *Linum perenne* L.

Description: A glabrous perennial, with slender, erect, branched stems to 60 cm, and sterile shoots. Leaves alternate (or only lowest ones opposite), linear-lanceolate, to 2.5 mm wide, *1–3-veined*, erect. *Flowers 20–26 mm diam.*, on long, *erect stalks*, numerous, in lax (monochasial) cymes. Sepals 5; outer ones narrowly ovate and pointed, 3.5–5 mm long, inner ones slightly larger and blunt-tipped, glandular-ciliate. Petals obovate, short-clawed, *pale to bright blue*. Stamens 5. Pistils and stamens of different lengths (heterostyly). Ovary rounded, with 5 free styles, each with *globose stigma*. Capsule subglobose, 5–8 mm diam., opening with 10 valves, and containing 10 compressed seeds to 3 mm long; fruit-stalks erect.

Flowering: May–August.

Habitat: Grassland on dry, oligotrophic, calcareous, loamy or stony soils; from sea level to 2,000 m.

Range: C and E Europe, westwards to the Pyrenees and Germany, and S Britain.

Similar species: *L. austriacum* L., from S and C Europe (northwards to Germany, Poland and C Russia), also has pistils and stamens of different lengths, but numerous nodding flowers on deflexed stalks.
L. leonii F.W. Schultz, from France, W Germany and Belgium (Givet), has short stems (to 30 cm), 1–6-flowered cymes, deflexed to suberect flower-stalks, and stamens equalling pistil (homostyly).
L. tenuifolium L., from S and C Europe,

northwards to E Belgium, Germany, Poland, and the Ukraine, is also homostylous, and has pink or whitish flowers (12–18 mm diam.), rough-edged leaves to 1 (2) mm wide, and lanceolate, glandular-ciliate sepals.

The latter 3 species occur in dry, calcareous grassland.

Perennial Flax description pertains to ssp. *perenne*; the British plants (with spreading or ascending stems) belong to ssp. *anglicum* (Miller) Ockendon. Other subspecies occur in the mountains of C Europe.

---

p.143 **Allseed** *Radiola linoides* Roth

Description: A tiny, glabrous annual, with threadlike stem to 8 cm, *regularly forked* almost from base. *Leaves opposite*, elliptical, to 3 mm long, 1-veined. Flowers *c.* 2 mm diam., short-stalked, in elaborately branched (dichasial) cymes. *Sepals 4*, cuneate, *3-toothed. Petals 4*, obovate, white, 1–1.5 mm long, not exceeding sepals. Stamens 4. Ovary rounded, with 4 free styles. Capsule globose, 1–2 mm diam., opening with 8 valves, and containing 8 ovoid seeds.

Flowering: July–August.

Habitat: Bare, seasonally wet places, pathways in heathland or woods, dune-slacks, overgrazed dune-pastures, on moist, oligotrophic, slightly acid, sandy or peaty soils; from sea level to 1,600 m.

Range: In Europe northwards to the British Isles, the Low Countries, S Scandinavia, Poland, and C Russia.

Compare Linum catharticum (see p.784), with 5-merous flowers.

LOOSESTRIFE FAMILY, LYTHRACEAE

A subcosmopolitan family of herbs and shrubs with *c.* 450 species in 22 genera, in warm and temperate regions, often growing in marshes. Dicots. Leaves simple, opposite (rarely whorled or alternate). Flowers regular or slightly irregular, hermaphrodite, 4–6-merous, axillary or in terminal spikes. Sepals 4–6 (8), implanted on tube- or cup-shaped hypanthium (which looks like a calyx tube); epicalyx usually present, often in the form of appendages between sepals. Petals 4–6 (8), also inserted on hypanthium rim, occasionally absent. Stamens 1–16, often twice as numerous as petals, and inserted on hypanthium. Ovary superior, free on bottom of hypanthium, often incompletely 2-locular (rarely 4–6-locular), with 1 style and 1 stigma. Fruit a capsule (opening with 2–6 valves), occasionally a nut.

---

p.279 **Grass-poly** *Lythrum hyssopifolia* L.

Description: A *(sub)glabrous annual*, with erect or ascending stems to 25 (60) cm. *Leaves alternate*, sessile, erect, to 15 mm long, *linear-lanceolate*, entire-margined. Flowers 5 mm diam., solitary or paired in leaf-axils, subsessile, with 2 linear bracteoles at base. Hypanthium ('calyx tube') cylindrical, 4–7 mm long. Epicalyx lobes 6, linear. Sepals 6, triangular, much shorter than epicalyx lobes. Petals 6, obovate, 2–3 mm long, spreading, pink. Stamens 12. Ovary incompletely 2-locular. Capsule cylindrical, splitting with 2 valves, many-seeded, equalling the hypanthium.

Flowering: June–September.

Habitat: Periodically flooded, bare ground, also furrows of arable fields, on wet, mesotrophic, sandy, clayey or gravelly soils; from sea level to 500 m.

Range: S and C Europe, northwards to England, the Low Countries, Germany, Poland, and C Russia.

Similar species: *L. borysthenicum* (Schrank) Litv. has prostrate stems or ascending stems to 15 cm, leaves spreading, obovate, ciliate, flowers solitary in leaf-axils, with minute, purplish petals (often altogether absent), and 6 stamens; epicalyx lobes about equalling sepals. In shallow water or in mud along pools and lakes, in S Europe, northwards to NW France, and eastwards to C Russia.

p.96   **Water Purslane**
Lythrum portula (L.) D.A. Webb

Description: A *glabrous annual* to 5 (25) cm, with
creeping or ascending stems. *Leaves opposite*,
short-stalked, to 15 mm long, *obovate to
spatulate*, entire-margined. Flowers 1–2 mm
diam., solitary in leaf-axils, subsessile.
Hypanthium ('calyx tube') 1–1.5 mm long,
widely cup-shaped. Epicalyx lobes 6, linear.
Sepals (5) 6, triangular-ovate, about
equalling the epicalyx lobes. Petals 6,
obovate, to 1 mm long, slightly shorter than
sepals, purplish-pink or whitish, soon
falling, often absent altogether. Stamens 6.
Ovary ovoid, incompletely 2-locular, with
very short style (or stigma sessile). Capsule
ovoid or subglobose, exceeding hypanthium.

Flowering: June–October.

Habitat: Periodically flooded places, along streams,
ponds and lakes, also shallow water, on wet,
oligotrophic, usually acid, sandy, muddy or
loamy soils; from sea level to 1,500 m.

Range: In Europe northwards to Scotland,
S Fennoscandia, and N Russia (not
Spitsbergen).

Submerged plants do not flower, and
usually have narrower leaves.

---

p.288   **Purple Loosestrife** *Lythrum salicaria* L.

Description: A *more or less hairy perennial* to 1.2 m, with
quadrangular, erect stems. *Leaves opposite*,
sessile, spreading, to 70 mm long,
lanceolate, entire-margined, lower ones often
in whorls of 3. Flowers 10–15 mm diam.,
subsessile, in *whorls forming long, terminal,
leafy spikes*. Hypanthium ('calyx tube')
cylindrical, 4–5 mm long. Epicalyx lobes 6,
linear. Sepals 6, triangular-ovate, much
shorter than epicalyx lobes. Petals 6,
obovate, 5–10 mm long, spreading, red-
purple. Stamens 12, short or long. Ovary
ovoid, with style of variable length: short,
medium or long (heterostyly). Capsule
ovoid, many-seeded, 3–4 mm long.

Flowering: June–September.

Habitat: Marshes, fens, reedlands, damp meadows, dune-slacks, ditches, watersides, on wet, mesotrophic to eutrophic, neutral or calcareous, mineral or peaty soils; from sea level to 1,400 m.

Range: Most of Europe except Iceland and the high Arctic.

The heterostyly serves to prevent self-pollination.

MALLOW FAMILY, MALVACEAE

A subcosmopolitan family of herbs and shrubs with *c.* 1,000 species in 80 genera, in warm and temperate regions. Dicots. Leaves alternate, palmately veined, lobed or divided. Flowers regular, usually hermaphrodite, basically 5-merous, axillary (occasionally in terminal racemes). Epicalyx often present, (2) 3–13-parted. Sepals (4) 5, free or partly connate. Petals 5, free or only basally connate. Stamens numerous; filaments connate into tube round pistil, and inserted on corolla base. Ovary superior, with 5 to several locules and as many styles (these often connate into a central column), mostly with 1 ovule per locule. Fruit a capsule or a ring of achenes (mericarps).

p.275 **Rough Mallow** *Althaea hirsuta* L.

Description: A *rough-hairy annual*, with ascending stems to 60 cm; both simple bristle-hairs (implanted on small tubercles) and stellate hairs present. Leaves alternate, long-stalked; the lower ones *suborbicular*, with 5 crenate lobes and a *cordate base; upper leaves deeply incised* with 3–5 oblanceolate, apically dentate-crenate lobes; stipules rather large, ovate. Flowers axillary, 24–28 mm diam., on stalks exceeding leaves; *epicalyx with 6–9 lanceolate segments*, these basally connate but free from calyx. Sepals 5, almost free, lanceolate, scarcely longer than epicalyx. Petals 5, *lilac or pale bluish-purple*, obovate, truncate or rounded, about equalling calyx. Ovary glabrous, with many styles connate (together with stamens) into a central column. Fruit a ring of several *glabrous*, compressed, dorsally rounded and transversely ridged achenes.

Flowering: July–September.

Habitat: Cultivated and waste land, ruderal places, wood margins, on rather dry, mesotrophic, preferably calcareous, sandy or loamy soils; from sea level to 1,500 m.

Range: S and E Europe, locally northwards to Belgium, C Germany, Slovakia, W and SE Russia.

---

p.275 **Marsh Mallow** *Althaea officinalis* L.

Description: A *softly grey-tomentose perennial*, with erect stems to 1.5 (2) m; only stellate hairs present. Leaves alternate, long-stalked, broadly ovate, with *5 short, dentate-serrate lobes* and *rounded base*; stipules small, lanceolate. Flowers 1–3 together in leaf-axils, 25–40 mm diam., on stalks much shorter than leaves; *epicalyx with 6–9 linear-lanceolate segments*, these basally connate but free from calyx. Sepals 5, almost free, lanceolate, scarcely longer than epicalyx. Petals 5, *white or pink* (rarely crimson), obovate, truncate or slightly notched, *much longer than calyx*. Ovary hairy, with several styles connate (together with stamens) into a central column. Fruit a ring of several dorsally rounded, *hairy achenes*.

Flowering: July–September.

Habitat: Reedlands, dune-slacks, estuaries, also the highest parts of saltmarshes, inland ditch- and riversides, on wet or moist, usually brackish, sandy or clayey soils; often near the sea, but also near saline pools in the steppe belt of SE Europe, and in river valleys.

Range: S and W Europe, northwards to Britain, Denmark, Poland and C Russia.

Formerly an important medicinal herb used in cough syrup.

---

p.274 **Cut-leaved Mallow** *Malva alcea* L.

Description: A *hairy perennial* with erect stems to 80 (120) cm. Leaves alternate, stalked, with *5 long, deeply dentate to divided, blunt-tipped segments*; stipules small, lanceolate. Flowers axillary (lower ones usually solitary), 35–60 mm diam., on *stellate-hairy stalks; epicalyx with 3 broadly lanceolate segments*, connate to base of calyx. Sepals 5, basally connate, triangular-ovate, longer than epicalyx. Petals 5, *pink*, obovate, with truncate or hollowed tip, much longer than calyx. Stamens and styles connate into central column. Fruit a ring of several hairy or glabrous, ribbed achenes.

Flowering: June–September.

Habitat: Rough grassland, roadsides, scrub, wood margins, ruderal places, on moist, mesotrophic, preferably calcareous, sandy, loamy or stony soils; from sea level to 2,000 m.

Range: Continental Europe, northwards to the Low Countries and S Sweden, Poland and C Russia.

Similar species: **Musk Mallow** (*M. moschata* L.) has even more deeply divided leaves, with narrower, subacute leaf-segments, simple hairs on flower-stalks, musk-scented flowers, 3 linear epicalyx segments, and *c.* 15 long-hairy, smooth (not ribbed) achenes. In comparable habitats, often on slightly acid or neutral soils, in S and C Europe, northwards to Britain, the Low Countries, Germany, Poland, and C Russia; only as a casual further north.

Both species are grown in gardens, and easily escape.

---

p.274 **Dwarf Mallow** *Malva neglecta* Wallr.

Description: A *hairy annual* with spreading or straggling, branched stems to 40 cm. Leaves alternate, stalked, suborbicular or reniform, with *5–7 short, crenate-dentate, rounded lobes*; stipules small, lanceolate. Flowers 3–6 together in leaf-axils, 15–25 mm diam., long-stalked; *epicalyx with 3 lanceolate segments*, connate to base of calyx. Sepals 5, basally connate, triangular-ovate, longer than epicalyx. Petals 5, *pale lilac or whitish*, obovate, with ciliate claw and strongly hollowed tip, much longer than calyx. Stamens and styles connate into central column. Fruit a ring of *c.* 15 subglabrous, smooth, dorsally rounded achenes; *fruit-stalks recurved*.

Flowering: May–September.

Habitat: Field margins, roadsides, ruderal places, farmyards, grassy banks, on rather dry to moist, (very) eutrophic, calcareous or slightly acid, sandy, loamy or stony soils; from sea level to 1,800 m.

Range: Most of Europe, except Iceland and the high Arctic.

Similar species: **Small Mallow** (*M. pusilla* Sm.) has pink or whitish flowers only 5–6 mm diam., in axillary clusters of 3–10, with truncate or slightly hollowed petals scarcely exceeding green, hairy, halfway-connate sepals; achenes *c.* 10 per flower, ribbed, with sharp, smooth edges. In comparable habitats of continental Europe, northwards to S Scandinavia, and naturalized in Britain. **Least Mallow** (*M. parviflora* L.) has short-stalked, pale-lilac or mauve flowers 7–9 mm diam., in axillary clusters of 2–4, with truncate or slightly hollowed petals slightly longer than the more than halfway-connate sepals, which become membranous, reddish, and much enlarged in fruit; claw of petals glabrous; achenes *c.* 10 per flower, hairy or glabrous, with sharp, dentate edges. In comparable habitats, in S and W Europe, northwards to France and S Britain; occasionally as a casual further north.

---

p.274 **Common Mallow** *Malva sylvestris* L.

Description: A *hairy biennial or short-lived perennial*, with spreading to erect, branched stems to 1.2 m. Leaves alternate, stalked, suborbicular or reniform, with *(3) 5–7 rather long, crenate-dentate, rounded to triangular-ovate lobes*; stipules small, lanceolate. Flowers 2–6 together in leaf-axils, 30–40 mm diam., stalked; *epicalyx with 3 elliptical segments*, connate to base of calyx. Sepals 5, basally connate, triangular-ovate, longer than epicalyx. Petals 5, *pink or purplish* with darker veins, obovate, with strongly hollowed tip, much longer than calyx. Stamens and styles connate into a central column. Fruit ring of 9–11 (sub)glabrous, sharply ribbed, rough-edged achenes; *fruit-stalks more or less erect.*

Flowering: June–September.

Habitat: Ruderal places, roadsides, grassy banks, on moist, (very) eutrophic, preferably calcareous, sandy, loamy or stony soils; from sea level to 1,500 m.

Range: Most of Europe except Iceland and Spitsbergen, but only naturalized in much of the north.

BOGBEAN FAMILY, MENYANTHACEAE

A family of more or less aquatic, perennial herbs, with some 40 species in 5 genera world-wide, often included in Gentianaceae (*see* p.636), but differing in having alternate, simple or trifoliolate leaves, and petals not overlapping and contort in bud. The flowers are 5-merous, with basally connate petals, often hairy inside. Fruit is a 2-valved capsule.

p.120 **Bogbean** *Menyanthes trifoliata* L.

Description: A subglabrous, usually aquatic perennial to 30 cm, with stout, creeping or floating rhizomes and ascending, emergent flowering stems. Leaves basal (on rhizome), *emergent*, long-stalked, with sheathing base, *trifoliolate*, with subsessile, ovate or slightly rhombic, entire-margined, glabrous, shiny-green leaflets to 80 mm long, 40 mm wide. Flowers 14–18 mm diam., stalked, in rather dense, terminal racemes. Sepals 5, ovate, blunt-tipped. Petals 5, partly connate, with broadly triangular-lanceolate, spreading to recurved lobes, pink and glabrous outside, *white and long-bearded inside.* Stamens 5, with purplish anthers. Ovary superior, 1-locular, with 1 long style. Capsule broadly ovoid, 2-valved, 7–13 mm long, with several ellipsoid or lens-shaped seeds.

Flowering: April–June (October).

Habitat: Shallow water at lake-, pool- and stream margins, fens, bogs and marshes, also dune-slacks, on wet, oligotrophic or mesotrophic, acid, often peaty soils; from sea level to 1,800 m.

Range: Most of Europe except the high Arctic, but only on mountains in the south.

---

p.198   **Fringed Water-lily**
Nymphoides peltata (Gmelin) O. Kuntze

Description: A subglabrous aquatic perennial, with slender, creeping or floating rhizomes to 1.5 m long, and ascending, emergent flowering stems. Leaves basal (on rhizome), *floating at the surface*, long-stalked, suborbicular with cordate base, entire-margined, 5–10 cm diam. Flowers 30–40 mm diam., long-stalked, solitary or few together in cluster, just emergent. Sepals 5, narrowly lanceolate, acute. Petals 5, partly connate, *yellow*, erect to spreading, with flat central zone and *broad, finely fringed side-margins*. Stamens 5, with yellow anthers. Ovary superior, 1-locular, with 1 stout style. Capsule ovoid, pointed, 2-valved, to 25 mm long, with several flat seeds.

Flowering: July–September.

Habitat: Stagnant or slow-moving, mesotrophic to eutrophic waters, lakes, ponds, canals, ditches, often on a clayey or muddy substrate; from sea level to 1,200 m.

Range: In Europe northwards to England, the Low Countries, Germany, Poland, and N Russia. Frequently cultivated in garden ponds, and naturalized in Denmark and S Sweden.

BOG MYRTLE FAMILY, MYRICACEAE

A family of shrubs and trees, with *c.* 35 species in 2 genera world-wide (not in Australia). Dicots. Leaves alternate, simple, often with fragrant, resinous glands. Flowers in spike-like catkins, unisexual, often dioecious; each flower axillary to small bract. Perianth absent, or (as always in female flowers) composed of 2–6 bracteoles. Stamens usually 4 (2–16). Ovary superior, 1-locular, with 1 ovule, 1 short style, and 2 long stigmas. Fruit a small drupe.

p.46 **Bog Myrtle** *Myrica gale* L.

Description: A deciduous, bushy shrub to 1 (2) m, with red-brown branches and yellowish or reddish twigs. Leaves obovate to oblanceolate, with cuneate base, 20–40 (60) mm long, bluntly dentate near top, bluish-green, and with numerous yellow resin-glands beneath. Flowers in brownish catkins, appearing before leaves, unisexual, often dioecious; male catkins 10–15 mm long, ellipsoid, with 4-stamened flowers, each with 1 broadly triangular-ovate bract, but without perianth; female catkins 5–10 mm long, ovoid, each flower with 1 ovate bract and 2–4 minute bracteoles; styles bifid. Fruit a small, flattened, dry, achene-like, 3-lobed drupe, with yellow resin-glands.

Flowering: April–May.

Habitat: Damp heaths, bogs, ditches, wood margins, also dune-slacks, on wet, oligotrophic, acid, sandy or peaty soils; mainly in the lowland.

Range: W and N Europe, from Portugal northwards to Britain, the Low Countries, Scandinavia, then eastwards through Germany and Poland to Finland and N Russia.

Similar species: **Bayberry** (*M. carolinensis* Miller) from eastern N America has downy twigs, persistent leaves, and whitish, waxy, rounded, berry-like drupes. Locally naturalized in wet heaths and woods of S England and the Netherlands.

Bog Myrtle is also called Sweet Gale. The plant is highly aromatic, and can change sex annually.

NAIAD FAMILY, NAJADACEAE

A small family of submerged aquatic herbs, with *c.* 50 species, all in the genus *Najas*, in fresh and brackish waters, in warm and temperate regions world-wide. Monocots. Leaves simple, (sub)opposite or in pseudo-whorls, linear, often remotely dentate. Flowers unisexual, axillary, sessile, solitary or in small cymes; each flower axillary to small bract; male flowers have 2-lipped perianth and thin sheath or spatha round single stamen; female flowers naked or with small, sheath-like, often persistent perianth. Ovary superior, 1-locular, with 1 ovule and 1 style. Fruit a small achene.

---

p.55 **Holly-leaved Naiad** *Najas marina* L.

Description: A slender perennial with branched, basally rooted, submerged stems to 30 (70) cm. Leaves opposite or in whorls of 3, linear, 20–30 mm long, 1.5–4 (6) mm wide, *spiny-dentate* on margins and often also on midrib beneath; sessile with a glabrous, sheathing base. *Flowers dioecious*, solitary in leaf-axils; male flowers have spatha, and *4-celled anther*; female flowers naked. Achene ovoid, 3–4 mm long. *See also* family description.

Flowering: July–September.

Habitat: Lakes, pools, ditches, oxbow-lakes, slow-moving rivers, in mesotrophic, fresh or brackish water; mainly in the lowland.

Range: Most of Europe except Iceland, N Fennoscandia and N Russia.

Similar species: **Slender Naiad** (*N. flexilis* (Willd.) Rostk. & Schmidt) has narrower leaves (1–2.5 mm wide) with 20–36 fine teeth on each side, 1-celled anthers, and achenes 2–3 mm in length. In lakes of Ireland, Britain, Germany, Denmark, Fennoscandia, Poland, C and N Russia.

Lesser Naiad (*N. minor* All.) has even narrower leaves (0.4–0.8 (1) mm wide) with 5–17 minute, soft teeth on each side, a ciliate basal sheath, 1–2-celled anthers, and achenes 2–3 mm long. In brackish (less often fresh) waters to depth of 3 m, in S and C Europe, northwards to Belgium (extinct in the Netherlands), Germany, Poland, and C Russia.

N. tenuissima (A. Braun) Magnus is like *N. minor*, but has bristle-like leaves to 12 mm long, with only 6 teeth on each side. In ponds and lakes in S Finland and NW Russia.

The latter 3 species are monoecious.

WATER-LILY FAMILY, NYMPHAEACEAE

A family of perennial aquatics with creeping rhizomes, with *c.* 90 species in 9 genera world-wide. Dicots, but with some characters otherwise found in only monocots (e.g., in pollen structure). Leaves alternate, long-stalked, floating, ovate to suborbicular, with deeply cordate base; submerged leaves can also be present. Flowers hermaphrodite, emergent, often floating on water surface, solitary on long stalks rising from rhizomes, and with spirally inserted perianth parts and stamens. Sepals 4–5 (6), often petaloid, coloured. Petals 8 to numerous. Stamens numerous, often partly petaloid, then with anthers forming a thickened rim round top. Ovaries superior or hemi-inferior, 8 to numerous, more or less connate, each representing 1 carpel, and containing 1 to several ovules. Styles free or connate, then stigmas fused into a disc. Fruit a capsule, occasionally berry-like.

p.191 **Yellow Water-lily** *Nuphar lutea* L.

Description: A perennial aquatic with stout rhizomes, bearing short-stalked, rounded, irregularly folded, translucent submerged leaves, and long-stalked, leathery floating leaves, shiny green above, palmately veined, *15–40 cm long*, broadly ovate, with rounded tip and deeply cordate base; leaf stalks bluntly triangular; veins 1–3 times forked, not interconnected near leaf-margin. Flowers solitary, long-stalked, emergent, *30–60 mm diam.*, with 5 (6) rounded, *yellow sepals* (to 30 mm long), and several *smaller, yellow petals* (to 15 mm long). Stamens numerous. Ovary superior, many-locular, with styles connate into thick column; *stigmas fused into round, unlobed disc*, with 15–20 stigmatic rays. Fruit broadly flask-shaped or conical, ripening below surface.

Flowering: May–September.

Habitat: Stagnant or slow-moving, mesotrophic to (very) eutrophic, fresh waters, to 3 (5) m deep; from sea level to 1,500 m.

Range: Most of Europe except Iceland and the high Arctic.

Similar species: **Least Water-lily** (*N. pumila* (Timm) DC.) has floating leaves scarcely longer than 10 cm on 2-edged stalks, smaller flowers (15–35 mm diam.) with sepals to 20 mm long, petals not exceeding 5 mm, and a lobed, 8–10-rayed stigmatic disc. In shallower, oligotrophic to mesotrophic, often acid waters, from sea level (in the north) to 1,700 m (in the south), in N and C Europe, southwards to C France, Switzerland, Jugoslavia, and C Russia.

p.97 **White Water-lily** *Nymphaea alba* L.

Description: A perennial aquatic with thick rhizomes, lacking thin submerged leaves; floating leaves leathery, shiny-green above, palmately veined, *10–30 cm long*, broadly ovate to suborbicular, with deeply cordate base, on long, rounded stalks; veins 1–3 times forked, reticulately interconnected near leaf-margin. Flowerbuds round-tipped. Flowers solitary, long-stalked, emergent, *9–20 cm diam.*, with (2) 4 (6) rounded, *greenish sepals* (to 6 cm long), and numerous (at least 20) *white (rarely pink) petals* (to 10 cm long) gradually changing in petaloid stamens; inner stamens have narrow filament. Ovary hemi-inferior, many-locular, with *free styles and greenish-yellow stigmas*. Fruit obovoid, ripening over the surface.

Flowering: May–September.

Habitat: Stagnant or slow-moving, mesotrophic to eutrophic, fresh waters, to 3 m deep; from sea level to 800 m.

Range: Most of Europe except Iceland and the high Arctic.

Similar species: **Northern Water-lily** (*N. candida* C. Presl) has leaves with overlapping basal lobes, slightly smaller, often half-submerged flowers (7–13 cm diam.) with 15–18 petals and reddish stigmas; flowerbuds pointed. In comparable habitats, in N and C Europe, also in N Spain; possibly overlooked in some areas; intermediate forms are common.
N. tetragona Georgi has even smaller flowers (35–60 mm diam.) with only 8–17 petals, and pointed flowerbuds. In comparable habitats of Finland and N and C Russia.

All species are occasionally cultivated in park or garden ponds.

OLIVE FAMILY, OLEACEAE

A family of trees, shrubs and woody climbers, with *c.* 600 species in 29 genera, in warm and temperate regions on most continents, especially in Asia. Dicots. Leaves opposite or whorled (rarely alternate), simple or pinnate. Flowers regular, hermaphrodite (rarely unisexual), basically 4-merous, in cymes or racemes. Sepals cup-shaped, with (3) 4 (8) segments or teeth (or absent). Corolla tube- or trumpet-shaped, with (3) 4 (8) segments or lobes (or absent). Stamens 2 (rarely 4). Ovary superior, 2-locular, with 1 style. Fruit variously organized: capsule, a berry, drupe, or cluster of achenes. European members include **Ash** (*Fraxinus excelsior* L.), **Olive** (*Olea europaea* L.), and **Lilac** (*Syringa vulgaris* L.). The last is a well-known garden tree, native to SE Europe; the genera *Jasminum* and *Forsythia* have yielded several other ornamentals

---

p.172 **Privet** *Ligustrum vulgare* L.

Description: A densely branched shrub to 3 (5) m, with hairy, 2-ribbed twigs. Leaves opposite, 30–60 mm long, narrowly ovate to broadly lanceolate, short-stalked, entire-margined, slightly leathery, glabrous. Flowers 4–6 mm diam., in dense, terminal panicles, sweet-scented. Calyx small, 5-toothed. *Corolla trumpet-shaped, white* (rarely cream), 5-lobed. Stamens 2, inserted on corolla tube. Ovary rounded, with long, straight style. Fruit a rounded, few-seeded, *black* (rarely green or yellow) *berry*, 6–8 mm diam.

Flowering: June–July.

Habitat: Scrub, dune-thickets, open woods, hedgebanks, sunny slopes, on dry, oligotrophic, calcareous, sandy, loamy or stony soils; from sea level to 800 m.

Range: S, W and C Europe, northwards to Britain, S Scandinavia, Poland, and W Russia.

The berries are poisonous. Privet is deciduous, though it does not easily drop its leaves in warm regions (or further north when the winter is very mild). It is occasionally grown in gardens, and naturalizes outside its native area. **Garden Privet** (*L. ovalifolium* Hassk.) from Japan – the species more commonly planted in hedges – is semi-evergreen, shedding its leaves only in very cold winters, and has glabrous twigs, ovate leaves, and berries remaining green.

WILLOWHERB FAMILY, ONAGRACEAE

A family of herbs and shrubs, with *c.* 640 species in 18 genera, in warm and temperate regions. Dicots. Leaves opposite or whorled, simple. Flowers regular or slightly irregular (zygomorphic), hermaphrodite (occasionally unisexual), usually 4-merous (occasionally 2-merous), axillary or in terminal racemes; receptacle often elongated into false 'calyx tube' bearing perianth at its top. Sepals 2 or 4 (rarely 5 or 6). Petals 2–4 (rarely absent). Stamens mostly 2, 4 or 8 (1–12). Ovary inferior, usually 4-locular (1–6-locular), with 1 style. Fruit a capsule, a berry, or nut-like. The family has yielded several ornamentals, including the **Fuchsia** (*Fuchsia magellanica* Lam.), native to S America.

---

p.288 **Rosebay Willowherb**
Chamerion angustifolium (L.) Holub

Description: A subglabrous perennial with creeping stolons and erect, often reddish flowering stems to 1.5 (2.5) m. *Leaves alternate*, sessile, *linear-lanceolate*, entire-margined or weakly dentate, to 15 cm long, 25 mm wide. Flowers 2–30 mm diam., slightly irregular, numerous in *long, terminal racemes*, with *small, linear bracts*; flowerbuds purplish, nodding at first. Sepals 4, narrowly ovate, soon falling. Petals 4, subequal (*upper ones slightly larger*), obovate, often notched, purplish-pink (rarely white). Stamens 8. Ovary 4-locular, with *1 long, deflexed style* and 4-lobed stigma. Fruit linear, 30–80 mm long, opening with 4 linear valves, and containing numerous small seeds bearing tuft of silky, white hairs.

Flowering: June–September.

Habitat: Woodland clearings, open woods, scrub, ruderal places, roadsides, gravelly banks, screes, shell-heaps, railways, on dry to moist, mesotrophic, slightly acid or calcareous, sandy, loamy, stony, rocky or even peaty soils; from sea level to 2,500 m.

Range: Most of Europe except the high Arctic, but rare in the north.

Similar species: **River Beauty** (*C. latifolium* (L.) Holub) has spreading to ascending stems, narrowly elliptical (also alternate) leaves, flowers 35–50 mm diam., with rounded (unnotched) petals, in few-flowered, 1-sided racemes. In rocky or gravelly places, tundra, scrub, often along streams and rivers, in Iceland and NE Russia.

---

p.144 **Alpine Enchanter's Nightshade**
Circaea alpina L.

Description: A subglabrous perennial with short, creeping rhizomes, and erect or ascending flowering stems to 30 cm. Leaves opposite, stalked, ovate with cordate base, markedly dentate, to 60 mm long; *leaf-stalks winged, slightly channelled. Flowers 1–2.5 mm diam.*, short-stalked, *with small bracts*, in narrow, elongating racemes, these terminal or also in axils of highest leaf-pair; open flowers crowded at top of raceme; 'calyx tube' short, strongly constricted over ovary. *Sepals 2*, narrowly ovate. *Petals 2*, deeply cleft (bifid), white or pale pink. *Stamens 2*. Ovary 1-locular, with 1 straight style and club-shaped (not 2-lobed) stigma. *Fruit obovoid or club-shaped*, compressed, opening with 2 valves, *covered with soft hairs*, and containing 1 seed.

Flowering: June–August.

Habitat: Damp woods, shaded, rocky places, streamsides, on wet or moist, oligotrophic, slightly acid, sandy or stony soils; mainly in the mountains, occasionally descending to near sea level.

Range: N and C Europe, but mainly on mountains in the south (to the Pyrenees, the Apennines and Montenegro); extinct in Belgium, and at only 1 station in the Netherlands.

---

p.144 **Enchanter's Nightshade**
Circaea lutetiana L.

Description: A slightly hairy perennial with long, creeping rhizomes, and erect flowering stems to 70 cm. Leaves opposite, stalked, ovate with rounded base, dentate, to 10 cm

long; *leaf-stalks rounded, unwinged. Flowers
4–6 mm diam.*, short-stalked, *without bracts*,
in narrow, elongating racemes, these
terminal or also in axils of highest leaf-pair;
open flowers spaced along axis of raceme;
'calyx tube' short, strongly constricted over
ovary. *Sepals 2*, narrowly ovate. *Petals 2*,
deeply cleft (bifid), white or pale pink.
Stamens 2. Ovary 1–2-locular, with 1
straight style and 2-lobed stigma. *Fruit
obovoid or club-shaped*, compressed, 3–4 mm
long, opening with 2 valves, *covered with
hooked bristles*, and containing 2 seeds.

Flowering: June–September.

Habitat: Damp, deciduous woods along rivers and
streams (often willows, Alder, Ash and
Poplar), also in somewhat drier woods (Oak
and Hornbeam), on (seasonally) wet to moist,
mesotrophic, preferably calcareous, sandy or
loamy soils; from sea level to 1,300 m.

Range: Most of Europe, northwards to the British
Isles, S Scandinavia, Poland and C Russia.

The hybrid of both *Circaea* species (*C. ×
intermedia* Ehrh.) has minute, soon-falling
bracts under flowers, slightly hairy leaves,
and soft-hairy, sterile, precociously falling
fruits to 2 mm; it spreads vegetatively by
its rhizomes, and is found in NW and C
Europe (to C Russia), often together with
C. lutetiana, even in the absence of the
other parent.

Willowherbs, *Epilobium*

A genus of perennial herbs with linear, ascending capsules,
and stalked, solitary flowers in the axils of leaf-like bracts.
Stem-leaves are opposite, but basal leaves may form whorls or
even a rosette, while the bracts in inflorescence are usually
alternate. During anthesis, the receptacle undergoes a strong
elongation into a 'calyx tube' enclosing the (equally
elongating) ovary, and bearing the regular, 4-merous perianth
at its top. In fruit, this 'calyx tube' forms the outer wall of the
capsule, which then contains numerous small seeds bearing a
tuft of silky, white hairs at the top. The capsule splits with 4
curving or even coiling valves. *Chamerion* has the same type of
fruit, but flowers are slightly irregular (zygomorphic), and
even the stem-leaves are alternate. Many *Epilobium* species

easily form hybrids with intermediate characters, which often complicates identification. Important characters are found in the morphology of stems, leaves, buds and stigmatic surfaces, and in the structure of the hibernating organs sent up by the rhizome: long, creeping stolons (often subterranean, and ending in a small leaf-bud), or small, vegetative leaf-rosettes (sessile or at the end of short stolons). These stolons and rosettes are formed in autumn.

---

p.276 **Chickweed Willowherb**
Epilobium alsinifolium Vill.

Description: A subglabrous or slightly hairy perennial with creeping rhizome, threadlike, subterranean stolons and erect, *rounded flowering stems* to 20 cm; stem 2–3 mm thick, with 2 raised lines. Leaves opposite (but alternate in inflorescence), short-stalked to subsessile, ovate, to 30 mm long, 10 mm wide, subacute, weakly dentate, bluish-green. Flowers 8–11 mm diam.; *flowerbuds nodding*. Sepals 4, lanceolate, subacute, reddish. Petals 4, 7–9 mm long, obovate, notched, bright pink, longer than sepals. Stamens 8. Ovary 4-locular, with 1 straight style and a *club-shaped stigma*. *Fruit stiffly erect*, linear, 60–90 mm long, subglabrous.

Flowering: June–August.

Habitat: Flushes, at stream margins, on wet to moist, oligotrophic, preferably base-rich, stony or peaty soils; from sea level to 2,000 m.

Range: N Europe (Iceland, Fennoscandia, N and W Russia), N Britain, Ireland, and in the mountains of C and S Europe.

A boreo-alpine species. *Compare also E. anagallidifolium*, with thinner stems.

---

p.276 **Alpine Willowherb**
Epilobium anagallidifolium Lam.

Description: A subglabrous perennial with a creeping rhizome, threadlike, leafy, aerial stolons, and ascending, *rounded flowering stems* to 10 cm; stem 1–2 mm thick, with 2 raised lines. Leaves opposite (but alternate in inflorescence), short-stalked to subsessile, ovate to elliptical, to 25 mm long, 10 mm wide, blunt-tipped, *subentire*, bright green (those on the stolons smaller, broadly obovate). Flowers 4–5 mm diam.; *flowerbuds drooping*. Sepals 4, lanceolate, blunt-tipped, reddish. Petals 4, 3–5 mm long, obovate, notched, pale purplish, longer than sepals. Stamens 8. Ovary 4-locular, with 1 straight style and a *club-shaped stigma*. *Fruit more or less drooping*, linear, 30–50 mm long, glabrous.

Flowering: June–September.

Habitat: Flushes, tundra, stream margins, mossy slopes, on wet to moist, oligotrophic, acid or base-rich, peaty or stony soils; from sea level to 3,000 m.

Range: N Europe (Iceland, Fennoscandia, N Russia including Spitsbergen), N Britain and the mountains of C and S Europe. A boreo-alpine species.

Similar species: *E. hornemannii* Reichenb., from Arctic and sub-Arctic N Europe, grows taller, and has short, subterranean stolons and slightly larger, pale-violet flowers (petals 4–6 mm long).

E. lactiflorum Hausskn., from the same area, has short aerial stolons, finely serrate-dentate leaves, and smaller, white flowers (petals 2.5–4 mm long). *Compare also E. alsinifolium*, with thicker stems.

p.278 **Great Willowherb**
Epilobium hirsutum L.

Description: A *densely soft-hairy* perennial with creeping stolons, and erect, rounded flowering stems to 1.5 (2) m. Leaves opposite, sessile and often slightly clasping, lanceolate, to 12 cm long, *serrate with sharp, curved teeth; middle leaves shortly decurrent on stem*. Flowers 15–25 mm diam.; *flowerbuds erect*. Sepals 4, lanceolate. Petals 4, obovate, notched, purplish-pink, twice as long as sepals. Stamens 8. Ovary 4-locular, with 1 straight style and a *4-lobed stigma*. Fruit linear, 60–90 mm long, hairy.

Flowering: June–September.

Habitat: Reedlands, watersides, ditches, damp ruderal places, on wet to moist, eutrophic, mineral or peaty soils; from sea level to 1,500 m.

Range: Most of Europe, northwards to Iceland, Norway, S Sweden, Poland and C Russia.

Forms no hibernating rosettes (unlike *E. parviflorum*, which also has much smaller flowers).

---

p.277 **Broad-leaved Willowherb**
Epilobium montanum L.

Description: A slightly hairy perennial with creeping stolons, and erect, rounded flowering stems to 80 cm, with 2 hairy (but not raised) lines. Leaves opposite (but alternate in inflorescence), (sub)sessile, (narrowly) ovate with rounded or slightly cordate base, 40–80 mm long, *dentate even at base.* Flowers 6–12 mm diam.; *flowerbuds arching, pointed.* Sepals 4, lanceolate, acute. Petals 4, obovate, (deeply) notched, 6–9 mm long, pale lilac (rarely white), not much longer than sepals. Stamens 8. Ovary 4-locular, with 1 straight style and *4-lobed stigma.* Fruit linear, 60–90 mm long, downy.

Flowering: June–September.

Habitat: Open woods, hedges, watersides, cultivated and waste land, gardens, also walls, on moist, eutrophic or mesotrophic, preferably slightly acid, sandy, loamy or stony soils; from sea level to 2,600 m.

Range: Most of Europe except Iceland and the high Arctic.

Similar species: *E. collinum* C.C. Gmelin is smaller in all parts, growing to only 40 cm, branching from base; leaves narrowly ovate, round-based, only 1–40 mm long on short stalks to 5 mm, sepals subobtuse, petals 4–6 mm long; plant forms small hibernating rosettes, but has no stolons. In rocky places, road verges and on walls, on acid soils, in S, C and E Europe, northwards to Belgium, S Fennoscandia, and N Russia.
Spear-leaved Willowherb (*E. lanceolatum* Seb. & Mauri) grows to 60 cm; it also has hibernating rosettes, but bluish-green leaves narrowed into stalks 4–7 mm long

(not dentate at base); petals 5–8 mm long, changing from white to pink; only lower stem-leaves are opposite. In open woods, shaded road verges, quarries, also along railways, on walls, old mine-heaps, on moist to rather dry, oligotrophic, preferably acid, often stony or rocky soils, in S, C and W Europe, northwards to S Britain, the Low Countries, Germany, Hungary and Romania, eastwards to the Crimea.

Like *E. hirsutum* and *E. parviflorum*, these 3 species have a 4-lobed stigma; all other *Epilobium* species have a club-shaped stigma.

---

p.277 **Marsh Willowherb** *Epilobium palustre* L.

Description: A subglabrous to slightly hairy perennial with creeping rhizome, threadlike stolons, and ascending to erect, *rounded flowering stems* to 60 cm; (lower) stem occasionally with 2 raised lines or 2–4 hairy lines; stolons ending in an ovoid, bulb-like leaf-bud. Leaves opposite (but alternate in inflorescence), (sub)sessile, *linear-lanceolate* with a narrowed base, 40–70 mm long, 5–10 mm wide, *subentire*, dull green. Flowers 8–12 mm diam.; *flowerbuds arching*. Sepals 4, lanceolate, blunt. Petals 4, obovate, notched, 3–7 mm long, pale pink or whitish, not much longer than sepals. Stamens 8. Ovary 4-locular, with 1 straight style and a *club-shaped stigma*. Fruit linear, 50–70 mm long, hairy on the rims; seeds spindle-shaped.

Flowering: July–August.

Habitat: Marshes, fens, reedlands, flushes, ditch- and streamsides, also dune-slacks, on wet, mesotrophic, preferably acid, sandy or peaty soils; from sea level to 2,200 m.

Range: All Europe except the high Arctic.

Similar species: *E. davuricum* Fischer ex Hornem. has hibernating rosettes, but lacks stolons; leaves linear to narrowly elliptical, remotely dentate, flowers white (rarely pinkish), stems slightly glandular-hairy. In comparable, wet habitats of Fennoscandia and N Russia.

p.278 **Hoary Willowherb**
Epilobium parviflorum Schreber

Description: A more or less densely *soft-hairy* perennial
with erect, rounded flowering stems to
70 cm. Leaves opposite (but alternate in
inflorescence), (sub)sessile (never clasping),
lanceolate, to 90 mm long, *remotely and
weakly dentate; middle leaves not decurrent.*
Flowers 7–12 mm diam.; *flowerbuds erect.*
Sepals 4, lanceolate. Petals 4, obovate,
notched, pink, not much longer than
sepals. Stamens 8. Ovary 4-locular, with 1
straight style and a *4-lobed stigma.* Fruit
linear, 60–90 mm long, hairy.

Flowering: June–September.

Habitat: Marshes, watersides, damp, open woods, on
wet or moist, eutrophic, sandy, clayey or
peaty soils; from sea level to 1,500 m.

Range: Most of Europe except Iceland and the
high Arctic.

Forms hibernating rosettes, but has no
creeping stolons (*compare E. hirsutum*).

p.277 **Pale Willowherb** *Epilobium roseum* Schreber

Description: A subglabrous or slightly hairy perennial
with erect, *rounded, rather brittle flowering
stems* to 90 cm; stem has *4 weak raised lines.*
Leaves opposite (but alternate in
inflorescence), *long-stalked* (stalk 5–20 mm
long), narrowly ovate to lanceolate, with a
narrowed base, 40–70 mm long, sharply
serrate-dentate. Flowers 8–10 mm diam.;
flowerbuds arching. Sepals 4, lanceolate,
acute. Petals 4, obovate, notched, 4–7 mm
long, *white (later on pink-veined),* not much
longer than sepals. Stamens 8. Ovary 4-
locular, with 1 straight style and *club-shaped
stigma.* Fruit linear, 40–60 mm long,
glandular-hairy; seeds ovoid.

Flowering: June–August.

Habitat: Damp woods, ditch-, pool- and streamsides,
also ruderal places, gardens, cultivated land,
on wet to moist, oligotrophic to
mesotrophic, slightly acid, sandy or loamy
soils; from sea level to 2,500 m.

Range: Most of Europe except Iceland and the high Arctic.

Similar species: **American Willowherb** (*E. ciliatum* Rafin.) also has distinct leaf-stalks (though only 2–5 mm long), but differs in having round-based, weakly dentate leaves, erect flowerbuds, slightly smaller, pale-pink flowers, and ellipsoid seeds with a tiny, translucent appendage at the top. Native to N America; naturalized in ruderal places, cultivated land and woodland clearings on moist, acid soils in W Europe, northwards to Scotland and S Fennoscandia.

Both species form hibernating rosettes, but lack stolons.

p.277 **Square-stalked Willowherb**
Epilobium tetragonum L.

Description: A subglabrous perennial to 1 m, with erect, firm, *quadrangular flowering stems*, these with 4 raised lines on the angles. Leaves opposite (but alternate in inflorescence), sessile (and shortly decurrent), narrowly ovate to ellipsoid, with a rounded base, 40–70 mm long, sharply dentate with curved teeth, bright or yellowish-green. Flowers 6–8 mm diam.; *flowerbuds erect, pointed*. Sepals 4, lanceolate, acute. Petals 4, obovate, notched, 4–8 mm long, pink, not much longer than sepals. Stamens 8. Ovary 4-locular, with 1 straight style and a *club-shaped stigma*. Fruit linear, 50–80 mm long, appressedly hairy; seeds ovoid.

Flowering: July–August.

Habitat: Watersides, shaded road verges, ditches, damp woodland, occasionally in cultivated land, on wet or moist, eutrophic, mineral or peaty soils; from sea level to 2,400 m.

Range: Most of Europe except Ireland, Iceland and the high Arctic.

Similar species: **Short-fruited Willowherb** (*E. obscurum* Schreber) has slender, creeping stolons, erect or ascending, more rounded, compressible stems (with 2–4 raised lines), dark-green, weakly dentate leaves, blunt flowerbuds, some glandular hairs on sepals, and fruits

40–60 mm long. In damp woods and scrub, marshes, ditches, streamsides, on wet, mesotrophic to oligotrophic, acid, sandy or peaty soils, in most of Europe except Iceland, the high Arctic and much of Russia.

Square-stalked Willowherb forms hibernating rosettes, but lacks stolons. Plants from SW Russia and Finland, with hairy stems, very short-stalked (not decurrent), lanceolate, weakly dentate, dark or bluish-green, rather hairy leaves and slightly larger flowers, are distinguished as *E. lamyi* F.W. Schultz.

---

p.50 **Hampshire Purslane**
Ludwigia palustris (L.) Elliott

Description: A glabrous perennial with creeping and ascending, *reddish, quadrangular stems* to 30 cm. Leaves opposite, stalked, narrowly (ob)ovate to elliptical or slightly rhombic, to 40 mm long, *entire-margined*, green with *red veins*, often profusely flushed with purple. Flowers solitary in leaf-axils, subsessile, *c.* 3 mm diam., with a pair of *minute bracteoles* at their base; receptacle forming a short, cup-shaped 'calyx tube' round ovary, and bearing sepals at the top. Sepals 4, triangular-ovate, *c.* 4 mm long, greenish, often red-edged, persistent on fruit. *Petals absent. Stamens 4.* Ovary 4-locular, with 1 short style and a 4-lobed stigma. Fruit a *4-angled, ovoid capsule*, to 4 mm long, glabrous, opening with 4 valves, and containing several small seeds.

Flowering: June–September.

Habitat: Shallow water, on mud along streams, pools, fens, on wet, oligotrophic, acid, muddy or peaty soils; mainly in the lowland.

Range: Much of Europe, but local, northwards to England, the Low Countries, Germany, Poland and W Russia.

A strongly declining species. The plant can grow permanently submerged. *Compare Lythrum portula (see p.788)*, with round-tipped leaves and 6-merous flowers.

Evening-primroses, *Oenothera*

A genus of annual, biennial or short-lived perennial herbs with regular, 4-merous, often yellow flowers in long, leafy spikes, and alternate leaves; occasionally, the basal leaves may form a rosette. As flowerbuds develop, receptacle undergoes a strong elongation into a 'calyx tube', which is fused with the ovary and grows out over it as a narrow tube, bearing the perianth at its top; both the perianth and the narrow part of the 'calyx tube' are dropped after anthesis. The fruit is a sessile, cylindrical or club-shaped capsule, opening with 4 valves, and containing numerous glabrous seeds. The genus is native to N America, but after the introduction of some species in Europe, several new forms evolved through hybridization and mutations. Thus arose a complex of several subtly different forms, raised to species rank by botanists interested in their exceptional genetic properties. In this guide only some major, complex species will be described; it should therefore be kept in mind that actual plants may deviate slightly from the description, especially in the colour of stems, fruits and hairs. Intermediate forms are by no means rare, and are interpreted as fertile hybrids. For details on the microspecies (which are often identifiable only on the basis of living material) *see Flora Europaea*, critical regional floras, or other specialized literature.

---

p.213 **Common Evening-primrose**
Oenothera biennis L.

Description: A more or less hairy annual or biennial, with erect, usually unbranched, green stems to 1.2 (1.5) m; all hairs lack red bases. Leaves lanceolate, dentate, alternate (lower ones often in a rosette); older leaves red-veined. Flowers 40–50 mm diam., in long, leafy, terminal *spikes with an erect tip*. Sepals 4, *green*, lanceolate, pointed, the tips convergent in bud. Petals 4, yellow, obovate, shallowly notched, *25–30 mm long*. Stamens 8. Ovary 4-locular, with 1 straight style (to 15 mm long) and 4-lobed stigma. Capsule ellipsoid to almost cylindrical, slightly angular, enveloped by *green* 'calyx tube'.

Flowering: June–September.

Habitat: Ruderal or disturbed places, road verges, sand-dunes, railways, on dry, oligotrophic to mesotrophic, calcareous, sandy or stony soils; from sea level to 1,300 m.

Range: Most of Europe except Iceland and the high Arctic.

The species originated in Europe from an American parent. The *O. biennis* complex comprises some small-flowered forms that could be confused with *O. parviflora*, but they differ from that species in the erect inflorescences.

p.213 **Large-flowered Evening-primrose**
Oenothera erythrosepala Borbás

Description: A hairy biennial, with erect, usually unbranched, green stems to 1.5 m; bristle-hairs placed on red tubercles. Leaves broadly lanceolate, dentate, alternate (lower ones often in rosette), wavy-edged. Flowers 50–80 mm diam., in long, leafy, terminal *spikes with erect tip*. Sepals 4, *red-striped*, eventually flushed with red all over, lanceolate, pointed, the tips convergent in bud. Petals 4, yellow, obovate, shallowly notched, *35–50 mm long*. Stamens 8. Ovary 4-locular, with 1 straight style (20–60 mm long) and 4-lobed stigma. Capsule ellipsoid to almost cylindrical, slightly angular, enveloped by green 'calyx tube' bearing red-based hairs.

Flowering: June–September.

Habitat: Ruderal or disturbed places, road verges, sand-dunes, railways, on dry, oligotrophic to mesotrophic, calcareous, sandy or stony soils; from sea level to 1,300 m.

Range: W and C Europe, from Britain and Portugal to Poland and Romania.

The species originated in Europe from an American parent.

p.213 **Small-flowered Evening-primrose**
Oenothera parviflora L.

Description: A hairy annual or biennial to 1.2 (2) m, with erect, usually unbranched, red-based stems; higher stem parts and fruits with long bristle-hairs. Leaves *linear-lanceolate*, dentate, alternate (lower ones oblanceolate and often in rosette). Flowers 14–18 mm diam., in long, leafy, terminal *spikes with nodding tip*. Sepals 4, green, *becoming red-striped after anthesis*, lanceolate, pointed, the *tips divergent in bud*. Petals 4, yellow, obovate, shallowly notched, *9–11 mm long*. Stamens 8. Ovary 4-locular, with 1 straight style and a 4-lobed stigma. Capsule ellipsoid to almost cylindrical, slightly angular, enveloped by the red-striped 'calyx tube'.

Flowering: June–September.

Habitat: Bare ground, sand-dunes, ruderal places, industrial areas, building sites, railways, on dry, oligotrophic, calcareous, sandy or stony soils; mainly in the lowland.

Range: Native to N America; naturalized in W and C Europe.

The microspecies *O. ammophila* Focke (also treated as a variety) deserves further attention as it has become a characteristic plant of the outer sea-dunes in NW Europe; it has bristle-hairs placed on red tubercles, slightly larger flowers (petals to 16 mm long), and divergent sepal-tips 2–4 mm long (not 1–1.5 mm); this form has been depicted in the photograph on p.213.

ORCHID FAMILY, ORCHIDACEAE

A very large family of perennial herbs with rhizomes or tubers, and usually unbranched flowering stems, with 18,000–25,000 species in 750–800 genera world-wide, primarily in warm regions. Monocots. Leaves simple, alternate or in basal rosette, sessile (often sheathing), entire-margined, with parallel veins; in saprophytic species only sheathing scale-leaves may be present. Flowers irregular (zygomorphic), hermaphrodite, basically 3-merous, in terminal spikes or racemes (occasionally solitary), usually with bracts. Perianth 6-parted, in 2 whorls of 3, comparable to sepals and petals, but all coloured and petaloid; 1 petal ('lip') is usually strongly enlarged and modified, often with honey-bearing spur. Only 1 fertile stamen, connate with style and 3 stigmas into stout column bearing sessile anthers; 2 sterile staminodes may also be present. *Cypripedium* is the only European genus with 2 fertile stamens and 1 staminode. Pollen in anthers glued together, forming 2 lumpy 'pollinia', often equipped with sticky appendage produced by 1 of the stigmas (the 'rostellum'). Ovary inferior, resembling a flower-stalk, 1-locular, built up from 3 connate carpels, and usually rotating through 180° during the development of the buds, bringing the lip down. Fruit a capsule, opening with 3 or 6 longitudinal fissures, and containing numerous minute, wind-dispersed seeds.

Pollination is effected by insects or other small animals carrying the sticky pollinia on their heads or bodies. Often there are close bonds between orchids and certain specialized pollinators. Many orchids are epiphytes growing on trees, but nearly all European species are terrestrial. Most have symbiotic relations with soil fungi; the saprophytic (or more correctly: mycotrophic) species are totally dependent on these fungi, but most others cannot live without them either, especially during germination. As a rule, this makes them unsuitable for cultivation in gardens. Orchids are categorically protected by law in most European countries.

p.47 **Man Orchid**
Aceras anthropophorum (L.) Aiton f.

Description: A tuberous perennial with erect stem to 30 cm. Leaves mostly basal, narrowly elliptical to oblanceolate, glabrous; lower stem often has some large, sheath-like leaves. Flowers numerous, in long, cylindrical spike. Sepals ovate, *greenish* with yellow or reddish margins and veins, forming hood. Upper petals like sepals, but narrower, concealed in hood. *Lip narrowly wedge-shaped*, 12–15 mm long, pendent, with 2 linear side-lobes and *bifid middle lobe, yellowish-green*, often flushed with red; *spur absent. Pollinia fused*. Capsule sessile, subglobose, to 7 mm long.

Flowering: May–June.

Habitat: Grassland, very open woods and scrub, also sea-dunes, on moist to rather dry, oligotrophic, calcareous, sandy, loamy or stony soils; from sea level to 1,500 m.

Range: S and W Europe, northwards to England and the Low Countries.

The lip is vaguely reminiscent of a little man, with the other, hooded perianth parts forming the head.

p.266 **Pyramidal Orchid**
Anacamptis pyramidalis (L.) Rich.

Description: A tuberous perennial with erect stem to
50 cm. Leaves mostly basal, narrowly
lanceolate, glabrous; stem with several
sheath-like leaves all along its length.
Flowers numerous, in *short, dense, pyramidal
to ovoid spike*, becoming cylindrical in fruit.
All perianth parts bright purplish (rarely pale
pink or white). Sepals elliptical or obovate,
spreading. Upper petals like sepals, erect.
Lip 6–8 mm long, held out horizontally,
deeply incised with *2 truncate side-lobes* and
round-tipped middle lobe; spur long, threadlike,
at least equalling ovary. *Pollinia fused*.
Capsule sessile, ellipsoid, 10–15 mm long.

Flowering: June–August.

Habitat: Grassland, fixed dunes, roadsides, grassy
banks, even slightly ruderal places, on dry to
moist, oligotrophic, calcareous, sandy, loamy
or stony soils; from sea level to 1,900 m.

Range: Europe northwards to the British Isles,
Denmark, Gotland, and eastwards to C
Russia.

Often occurs in large populations, but local;
in the north, plants may remain underground
for years, between bursts of flowering.

---

p.261 **Calypso** *Calypso bulbosa* (L.) Oakes

Description: A glabrous perennial with erect flowering
stem to 20 cm, and strongly swollen stem-
base ('pseudobulb'). Only 1 basal leaf, with
long, erect stalk and broadly ovate to
elliptical, strongly veined, deep-green blade
to 50 mm long; stem has few sheath-like,
discoloured scale-leaves near base. *Flowers
solitary, nodding*, up to 50 mm diam., with
small, linear-lanceolate, erect, pinkish bract.
Sepals linear-lanceolate, spreading to erect,
pink with darker veins. Upper petals like
sepals, erect, 10–20 mm long; lip
10–20 mm long, hollow, strongly inflated,
integrated with spur into *dark purplish-striped
sac*, with side-lobes connate into a whitish,
ovate tongue with *pink blotches and yellowish*

beard at base; column widened into petal-like, pink structure, roofing opening of sac; fertile anther solitary. Capsule club-shaped, to 20 mm long.

Flowering: May–June.

Habitat: Damp coniferous woods and bogs, on moist to wet, oligotrophic, acid, peaty or mossy soils; from sea level to 1,000 m.

Range: N Sweden, N Finland, and N and C Russia.

---

p.92 **White Helleborine**
Cephalanthera damasonium (Miller) Druce

Description: A glabrous perennial with creeping rhizomes and erect, angular flowering stems, to 60 cm, with *2–3 brownish sheaths at base*. Normal leaves 4–10, all cauline, sessile, narrowly elliptical or ovate, grading into lanceolate floral bracts. Flowers few to several, erect, in lax spike or raceme. Sepals broadly lanceolate, 15–20 mm long, *creamy white*, erect, *convergent*, rather blunt. Upper petals like sepals, erect. Lip concealed between sepals, 10–15 mm long, cream, with *3–5 deep-yellow ridges* along centre, and 2 rounded side-lobes; spur absent, not counting small 'chin' at base of lip. Ovary mostly shorter than accompanying bract. Capsule sessile or short-stalked, narrowly obovoid, 15–30 mm long, glabrous.

Flowering: May–July.

Habitat: Deciduous woods (often Beech), scrub, occasionally conifer afforestations, on moist to rather dry, oligotrophic, calcareous, sandy, loamy or stony soils; from sea level to 1,300 m.

Range: In Europe northwards to England, the Low Countries, Denmark, Gotland, and eastwards to Poland and SW Russia.

Similar species: **Narrow-leaved Helleborine** (*C. longifolia* (L.) Fritsch) has pure-white, acute, slightly spreading sepals (10–16 mm long), a short lip (5–8 mm long, again with yellow ridges), whitish basal sheaths, lanceolate to linear leaves, most flower-bracts much shorter than ovary, and sessile, spindle-shaped capsules. In comparable habitats, in Europe north to Ireland, Scotland, S Fennoscandia, and NW and C Russia.

p.266 **Red Helleborine**
Cephalanthera rubra (L.) Rich.

Description: A slightly hairy perennial with creeping
rhizomes and erect, weakly angular, often
purplish-green flowering stems, to 60 cm,
with *several brownish sheaths* at base.
Normal leaves 5–8, all cauline, sessile,
narrowly elliptical to lanceolate, grading
into linear-lanceolate floral bracts. Flowers
few to several, erect, in lax spike. Sepals
broadly lanceolate, 17–25 mm long,
purplish-pink, spreading, rather blunt. Upper
petals like sepals, erect. *Lip protruding,
lanceolate*, subacute, 17–22 mm long, with
7–9 yellow ridges along centre, and *2 short,
rounded side-lobes* near base; spur practically
absent. Ovary shorter than accompanying
bract. Capsule sessile, spindle-shaped,
15–30 mm long, hairy.

Flowering: June–July.

Habitat: Deciduous woods (often Beech), scrub,
shaded grassland and verges, on moist to
dry, oligotrophic, usually calcareous,
sandy, loamy or stony soils; from sea level
to 1,800 m.

Range: Europe northwards to England, the Low
Countries, S Scandinavia, S Finland, and
eastwards to NC and SE Russia.

---

p.48 **False Musk Orchid**
Chamorchis alpina (L.) Rich.

Description: A tiny, tuberous perennial with erect
flowering stem to 12 cm. Leaves 4–8, all
basal, *linear, blunt-tipped*, more or less erect,
often equalling stem. Flowers few to several,
in dense spike; *ovary erect, perianth bent
sideways*. Sepals ovate, 3–4 mm long, erect,
convergent, *greenish-yellow*, often red-tinged.
Upper petals like sepals, erect. Lip 3–4 mm
long, pendent, greenish-yellow, often flushed
with purple, elliptical, round-tipped, at most
weakly 3-lobed; spur absent. Pollinia close
together. Ovary shorter than accompanying
bract. Capsule sessile, subglobose or shortly
ellipsoid, to 10 mm long.

Flowering: July–August.

Habitat: Boreal tundra, mountain grassland, on moist, oligotrophic, calcareous, often stony soils; 1,600–2,700 m, descending lower in the north.

Range: The mountains of Fennoscandia; also in the Alps and Carpathians.

A typical boreo-alpine species. *Compare Coeloglossum*, which has broader leaves and distinctly 3-lobed lip.

---

p.48 **Frog Orchid**
Coeloglossum viride (L.) Hartman

Description: A tuberous perennial with erect flowering stem to 12 cm. Leaves 2–5, low on stem, *ovate to lanceolate*, blunt-tipped. Flowers up to 25, in rather dense, cylindrical spike. Sepals ovate, *c.* 3 mm long; upper one erect, lateral ones spreading, *greenish-yellow*, often red-tinged. Upper petals like sepals, erect, forming hood with upper sepal. Lip 4–6 mm long, pendent, *yellowish-brown*, wedge-shaped, with *distinctly 3-lobed tip* (middle lobe shortest); spur short. Pollinia widely separated. Ovary strongly arched, shorter than accompanying bract. Capsule sessile, ovoid to ellipsoid, 8–12 mm long.

Flowering: May–August.

Habitat: Grassland, wood margins, grassy banks and slopes, occasionally sand-dunes or cliff-ledges, on dry to moist, oligotrophic, calcareous to slightly acid, sandy, loamy or stony soils; from sea level to 2,600 m, but mainly in the mountains.

Range: Most of Europe except the high Arctic, but only on mountains in the south.

Compare Chamorchis, which has linear leaves and weakly lobed lip.

---

p.92 **Coralroot Orchid**
Corallorhiza trifida Châtel.

Description: A *greenish-white, saprophytic perennial* with erect flowering stems to 25 cm, often grouped; rhizomes yellowish, fleshy, with numerous short branches. *No normal leaves*; only 2–4 whitish or pale-brown sheaths present, low on stem. Flowers up to 12, short-stalked, in lax, terminal raceme, with very small bracts. Sepals oblanceolate, 6–7 mm long, erect to spreading, *whitish or yellowish*, occasionally purple-tinged. Upper petals like sepals, erect; lip *c.* 5 mm long, pendent, *white with red dots*, 3-lobed, widest near tip; spur short, sac-like. Ovary strongly arched. Capsule to 10 mm long, ellipsoid, nodding or pendent on short, curved stalk.

Flowering: June–July.

Habitat: Coniferous or mixed woods, damp scrub (also in dune-slacks), on moist to wet, oligotrophic, slightly acid, organic substrates; from sea level to 1,900 m, but rare in the lowland.

Range: Most of Europe except Ireland and the high Arctic, but only on mountains in the south.

The plant lives in thick layers of litter and humus in old woods, often of Pine mixed with Birch or Beech, or of Alder and Willow. It is fully dependent on symbiotic fungi; it does not parasitize tree-roots, as was once believed. *Compare also Epipogium (see p.829)*, which has much larger, not turned flowers, and the brownish *Neottia (see p.837)*.

---

p.41 **Lady's-slipper Orchid**
Cypripedium calceolus L.

Description: A rhizomatous perennial with erect, pubescent flowering stems to 50 cm. Leaves 3–4, broadly ovate to elliptical, pointed, strongly veined, sessile with sheathing base. *Flowers solitary* (rarely 2), very large, sessile in axil of large, elliptical bract. *Sepals maroon* (rarely yellow), to 90 mm long; upper one lanceolate, erect, *the other 2 connate* into broadly lanceolate, pendent segment with notched tip. Upper petals maroon (rarely yellow), linear, drooping sideways; lip 30–40 (60) mm long, hollow, strongly inflated, integrated with spur into *yellow shoe-shaped sac*, usually with purplish, hairy stripes inside, and with short, whitish, rounded side-lobes at base; sac opening partly roofed over by yellowish, tongue-shaped staminode. *Fertile stamens 2*; pollen not glued together in pollinia. Stigmas 3, all functional. Capsule stalked, more or less erect, hairy.

Flowering: May–July.

Habitat: Deciduous woods (often Beech), woodland clearings, mountain grassland, on moist, oligotrophic, often calcareous, sandy, loamy or stony soils; from sea level to 2,000 m, but extremely rare in the lowland, and only on mountains in the south.

Range: N, C and E Europe, westwards to England (Yorkshire), NE France (Lorraine), southwards to Pyrenees, SW Alps and Yugoslavia, and eastwards to the Urals.

A rare and highly endangered species.

---

p.262 **Early Marsh-orchid**
Dactylorhiza incarnata (L.) Soó

Description: A glabrous perennial with *palmately lobed tubers* and stout, erect, weakly angular, *compressible, hollow flowering stems* to 70 cm or more, with a few brownish sheaths at base. Normal leaves 4–5, sessile and sheathing, to 20 cm long, 20–40 mm wide, keeled, (narrowly) lanceolate, with hooded tip, *yellowish-green, rarely spotted*, scattered along stem, rather erect, all normally developed (not scale-like, or only the highest 1 or 2 so), reaching beyond base of inflorescence; floral bracts much smaller than highest leaves, but lowest bracts still distinctly longer than flowers. Flowers numerous, in rather dense, ovoid to shortly cylindrical spike. Sepals narrowly elliptical to lanceolate, 5–6 (9) mm long, *deep purplish-pink or flesh-coloured*; lateral ones slanting upwards, upper one nodding to form hood with the almost equally long upper petals. Lip pendent, rhombic, 5–8 mm long, same colour as other tepals but with dark-purple (often U-shaped) lines, and with weakly 3-lobed tip – middle lobe triangular, slightly longer than side-lobes, and often curved forwards; side-lobes strongly bent backwards, causing lip to look folded along middle; spur almost straight, stout, 6–8 mm long, at least 2 mm wide, half as long as (arched) ovary. Capsule sessile, up to 15 mm long, ellipsoid.

Flowering: May–July.

Habitat: Marshes, fens, bogs, dune-slacks, poor meadows, on wet, oligotrophic, slightly acid to calcareous, often peaty soils; from sea level to 2,100 m.

Range: Most of Europe except Iceland and the high Arctic, and rare in Mediterranean region.

Extremely variable, especially in flower colour (from deep crimson to purplish, then to pale pink, whitish and even cream). Several closely related species have been described, often reduced to subspecific rank later; even so, the taxonomic value of many of them needs to be studied. *D. cruenta* (O.F. Mueller) Soó from the Alps, Scotland and Scandinavia is rather better characterized by its short stems (to 25 cm tall), flat-tipped, dark-spotted leaves, and purple flowers. Further, *compare D. lapponica (see p.825 under D. traunsteineri)*, which also has flat-tipped, spotted leaves, but differs in sepals (at least 7 mm long), and longer spur.

p.261   **Heath Spotted-orchid**
Dactylorhiza maculata (L.) Soó

Description: A glabrous perennial with *palmately lobed tubers* and slender, erect, weakly angular, *firm, more or less solid flowering stems* to 60 cm, these with a few brownish sheaths at base. Normal leaves 4–6, sessile and sheathing, to 10 (15) cm long, 20 (25) mm wide, narrowly elliptical to (ob)lanceolate, greyish-green at least beneath, usually *dark-spotted*, scattered along stem, rather erect, the *upper ones appressed and almost scale-like*, resembling the linear-lanceolate floral bracts, which are mostly shorter than flowers. Flowers numerous, in rather dense, ovoid to shortly cylindrical spike. Sepals narrowly elliptical to lanceolate, 7–11 mm long, bright pink (occasionally paler), the lateral ones horizontally spreading, the upper one nodding to form a hood with the pink, almost equally long upper petals. Lip slightly held forward, broadly obovate, rather flat, with a 3-lobed tip (middle lobe triangular, *smaller and shorter than the side-lobes*), 7–11 mm long, *pink with purplish dots and loops*; spur almost straight, rather stout, 6–8 (11) mm long, *at least 1.2 mm wide*, distinctly shorter than ovary. Ovary arched. Capsule sessile, up to 15 mm long, ellipsoid.

Flowering: June–August.

Habitat: Poor grassland, heaths, open woods, on moist, oligotrophic, more or less acid, sandy, stony or peaty soils; from sea level to 2,200 m.

Range: Most of Europe, except the high Arctic and much of the southeast.

The description of Heath Spotted-orchid pertains to ssp. *maculata*. This is the central form in the 'maculata group', which comprises several closely related species, all with spotted leaves, and scale-like upper leaves not quite reaching the inflorescence. For the most part they are better treated on the subspecies level. First there are forms with broader, narrowly obovate, blunt-tipped lower leaves, and several scale-like upper leaves, often distinguished as **Common Spotted-orchid** (*D. fuchsii* (Druce) Vermeulen), having a deeply 3-lobed lip (middle lobe larger and longer than side-lobes), and a large spur (2–3 mm wide, and equalling ovary); this form grows more often in woods, but also in damp grassland, on richer, often calcareous soils. Then there are forms with much narrower, almost linear, long-tapering, acute-tipped lower leaves; these are often found in oligotrophic, acid heaths and bogs, like *D. maculata* ssp. *elodes* (Griseb.) Vermeulen, characterized by a slightly rhombic, backward-folded lip with 3 small, apical lobes, and a short, almost threadlike spur to 5 mm long, 0.5–1 mm wide. Comparable, often dwarfish forms with linear, more spreading or curved lower leaves have been described as ssp. *ericetorum* (Linton) Hunt & Summ., but may represent only an adaptation to drier or dystrophic environments. The members of the group are connected by intermediate forms, which often makes their identification problematical; some botanists prefer to treat the group as 1 polymorphic species. One should study the variability spectrum of a whole population before deciding on any subspecific name. Be also aware of the occurrence of hybridogenic populations whose plants can approach *D. traunsteineri* in general habit.

---

p.262 **Broad-leaved Marsh-orchid**
Dactylorhiza majalis (Rchb.) Hunt & Summ.

Description: A glabrous perennial with *palmately lobed tubers* and short, stout, erect, weakly angular, *compressible, hollow flowering stems* to 30 cm, with a few brownish sheaths at base. Normal leaves 4–8, sessile and sheathing, to 15 cm long, 30–50 mm wide, weakly keeled, (broadly) lanceolate or narrowly elliptical, *bluish-green, usually dark-spotted*, scattered along stem, rather spreading, all normally developed (not scale-like), *reaching beyond base of inflorescence*; floral bracts much smaller than highest leaves, but mostly longer than flowers. Flowers numerous, in rather dense, ovoid to shortly cylindrical spike. Sepals narrowly elliptical to lanceolate, 6–12 mm long, *deep purplish* (rarely white); *lateral ones suberect*, upper one nodding to form a hood with the almost equally long upper petals. Lip pendent, broadly rhombic, 9–10 mm long, same colour as the other tepals but with dark-purple dots, lines and loops, and with 3-lobed tip – middle lobe triangular, longer than side-lobes, these curving backwards during anthesis; spur 7–10 mm long, occasionally almost as long as (arched) ovary. Capsule sessile, up to 15 mm long, ellipsoid.

Flowering: May–July.

Habitat: Marshes, fens, damp meadows, dune-slacks, on wet, oligotrophic to mesotrophic, preferably calcareous, sandy, loamy or stony soils, often with peat in the top soil; from sea level to 2,500 m.

Range: Continental Europe northwards to the Low Countries, S Sweden and N Russia.

The description of Broad-leaved Marsh-orchid pertains to ssp. *majalis*.

Southern Marsh-orchid (*D. m.* ssp. *praetermissa* (Druce) D.M. Moore & Soó), from NW Europe, grows taller (to 60 cm or more), and has narrower, more erect leaves (length:width ratio 4:5, not 3:4), leaves unspotted or with partly ring-shaped spots, and small middle lobe to lip. Both taxa are connected by intermediate forms. Several regional forms have been described as separate species, often on weak grounds: **Western Marsh-orchid** (ssp. *occidentalis* (Pugsley) P.D. Sell), in Britain and Ireland, has violet flowers and purple markings extending to middle lobe of lip; **Northern Marsh-orchid** (ssp. *purpurella* (T. & T.A. Stephenson) D. Moresby Moore & Soó) from NW Europe is rather well defined by short, weakly lobed lips (5–9 mm long), a tapering, subacute spur, and leaves spotted only near tip, or without any spots.

---

p.189 **Elder-flowered Orchid**
Dactylorhiza sambucina (L.) Soó

Description: A glabrous perennial with *palmately lobed tubers* and short flowering stems to 30 cm. Normal leaves 4–8, sessile and sheathing, to 10 cm long, 20 mm wide, narrowly lanceolate or linear-elliptical, *pale green, unspotted*, scattered along stem, rather erect, all normally developed (not scale-like), *not quite reaching base of inflorescence*; floral bracts mostly shorter than flowers. Flowers numerous, in rather dense, ovoid to shortly cylindrical spike. Sepals narrowly elliptical to lanceolate, 7–10 mm long, *pale yellow or purplish-red*; lateral ones slanting upwards, upper one nodding to form hood with the almost equally long upper petals. Lip pendent, very broadly obovate, 7–8 mm long and even wider, yellow or purplish-red (but *always with some yellow near base*) and with purple dots or loops, weakly 3-lobed (middle lobe very small, shorter than side-lobes, these curving backwards during anthesis); spur 8–15 mm long, subequalling arched ovary. Capsule sessile, up to 15 mm long, ellipsoid.

Flowering: April–July.

Habitat: Meadows, open woods, woodland clearings, scrub, on dry to moist, oligotrophic, calcareous, sandy, loamy or stony soils; from sea level to 2,100 m, but only on mountains in the south.

Range: The mountains of S and C Europe, northwards to C and NE France, S Germany, also in S Fennoscandia, and eastwards to C Russia and Balkan region.

The only N European *Dactylorhiza* with at least some yellow in flowers, but *compare D. incarnata (see p.819)*, which occasionally has creamy-white flowers. In purple-flowered forms, floral bracts are purplish, too. Both flower types often occur together in the same population, with all gradations in between.

---

p.264 **Narrow-leaved Marsh-orchid**
Dactylorhiza traunsteineri (Sauter) Soó

Description: A glabrous perennial with *palmately lobed tubers* and flowering stems to 40 cm. Normal leaves few (3–5), sessile and sheathing, to 15 cm long, 10–15 mm wide, *linear-lanceolate*, green, *unspotted or with spots only in upper half*, scattered along stem, *stiffly erect* (often almost appressed), all normally developed (not scale-like), *not quite reaching base of inflorescence*; floral bracts much smaller than highest leaves, and also much smaller than flowers. Flowers not very numerous, in rather lax, ovoid spike. Sepals narrowly elliptical to lanceolate, 7–8 mm long, *pink or pale purplish; lateral ones spreading*, upper one nodding to form hood with the almost equally long upper petals. Lip pendent, broadly obovate, 7–9 mm long, often paler than the other tepals but with dark-purple dots and loops, 3-lobed (middle lobe triangular, shorter than side-lobes, these curving backwards during anthesis); spur 5–8 mm long, about half as long as arched ovary. Capsule sessile, up to 15 mm long, ellipsoid.

Flowering: May–July.

Habitat: Marshes, fens, bogs, on wet, oligotrophic, acid, stony or peaty soils; mainly in mountainous regions, to 2,000 m, but descending to near sea level in the north.

Range: C Europe (Alps, Carpathians), also in British Isles, S Norway, Sweden, Finland, and Baltic region.

Reports from the Low Countries are presumably based on hybridogenic material (*D. maculata × incarnata* or *majalis*) not belonging to this species. *D. lapponica* (Hartman) Rchb. f. (also treated as a subspecies), though approaching *D. incarnata* in some respects, is apparently an independent taxon; it has short stems (to 20 cm), relatively wider, densely spotted leaves, rather lax spikes of small, purplish-red flowers with suberect lateral sepals, a narrow lip (5.5–7 mm long), and a slender spur about 2 thirds the length of ovary; in fens and damp grassland on calcareous soils in Fennoscandia, and also reported from Scotland.

p.316 **Dark-red Helleborine**
Epipactis atrorubens Besser

Description: A rhizomatous perennial to 60 cm, with erect, slightly hairy flowering stems. Leaves up to 10, alternate, *arranged in 2 rows*, sessile, ovate or elliptical to broadly lanceolate. Flowers short-stalked, more or less nodding, up to 20 in long, narrow, more or less 1-sided raceme, with short bracts. Sepals ovate, *dull purplish-red or brown-purplish*, lateral ones slanting downwards. Upper petals ovate, spreading sideways, purplish. Lip 5.5–7.5 mm long, hollow, cup-shaped, greenish on outside, purple inside, with 2 raised side-lobes and pendent, cordate, *flat-rimmed, purplish-red terminal lobe* bearing *2–3 warty knobs* at base. Spur absent. Column yellowish, with pronounced, globose rostellum. Ovary club-shaped, curved (not turned), covered with brownish hairs. Capsule ellipsoid, 7–15 mm long, nodding on curved stalk.

Flowering: June–August.
Habitat: Open woods, wood margins, scrub, on grassy slopes, rock-ledges, also in dunes, on dry, oligotrophic, calcareous, sandy, loamy or stony soils; from sea level to 2,200 m.
Range: Most of Europe except Iceland and the high Arctic, but often local, and rare in the south.

In *Epipactis* it is not the ovaries but the flower-stalks that are turned 180°.

---

p.265 **Broad-leaved Helleborine**
Epipactis helleborine (L.) Crantz

Description: A rhizomatous perennial to 80 cm, with erect flowering stems; stems hairy above, often purplish beneath. Leaves up to 10, green, alternate, *spirally arranged*, sessile, up to 18 cm long, 60 mm wide, ovate or elliptical to broadly lanceolate. Flowers short-stalked, more or less nodding, up to 50 (100) in long, more or less 1-sided raceme, with rather long bracts; flowerbuds pointed. Sepals ovate, *greenish or yellowish*, often tinged or striped with brown or purple; lateral ones slanting downwards. Upper petals ovate, spreading sideways, pink or purplish. Lip 9–10 mm long, hollow, cup-shaped, greenish on outside, purple inside, with *2 erect side-lobes* and pendent, cordate, *flat-rimmed, purplish or pink (rarely whitish) terminal lobe* bearing *2 smooth, purplish knobs at base*. (Flower colour extremely variable: some cream or yellow can often be detected as well.) Spur absent. Column whitish or pink, with pronounced, *globose rostellum*. Ovary club-shaped, curved (not turned). Capsule 7–15 mm long, ellipsoid, smooth or rough, nodding on curved stalk.
Flowering: July–September.
Habitat: Deciduous or coniferous woods, scrub, shaded verges, dune-slacks, on dry, oligotrophic or mesotrophic, preferably calcareous, sandy, loamy or stony soils; from sea level to 1,800 m.

Range: Most of Europe except Iceland and the high Arctic.

Similar species: **Narrow-lipped Helleborine** (*E. leptochila* (Godf.) Godf.) is yellow-green, with leaves arranged in 2 rows, up to 25 greenish flowers (to 15 mm diam.), pointed flowerbuds, and warty capsules; terminal lobe of lip (narrowly) ovate, pointed, narrower than cup, yellowish-green, with 2 smooth, pinkish knobs at base, and flat tip; rostellum rudimentary. In dense woods and scrub, also in coastal Pine plantations, on calcareous soils in NW and C Europe, from Britain, the Low Countries and Denmark eastwards to N Greece.
Mueller's Helleborine (*E. muelleri* Godf.) has rostellum absent; leaves and flowers yellowish-green, but latter smaller (to 10 mm diam.) with broadly cordate terminal lobe to lip, with recurved tip; flowerbuds blunt-tipped. In open woods, scrub, woodland clearings, on calcareous soils from France and the Low Countries eastwards to Hungary.
Dune Helleborine (*E. dunensis* (T. & T.A. Stephenson) Godf.) has leaves scarcely equalling internodes, flowers half-closed, and broadly triangular-ovate terminal lobe to lip, with recurved tip and often a whitish or pink centre. In coastal habitats of Britain
• These 3 species are (primarily) self-pollinating; hence the rostellum could become reduced as it is no longer needed to produce the glue for sticking the pollinia on insects.
Small-leaved Helleborine (*E. microphylla* (Ehrh.) Swartz) is pale or greyish-green, and much smaller (to 40 cm), with only 3–5 small, widely spaced leaves (to 30 mm long, 10 mm wide, distinctly shorter than internodes), and up to 12 small, half-closed, greenish-white flowers in lax raceme; in this species the rostellum is well-developed. In dark woods on calcareous soils of S and C Europe, northwards to Lorraine, the Eifel, Germany and Hungary.

In all these species the cup-shaped part of the lip is purplish inside.

p.89 **Marsh Helleborine**
Epipactis palustris (L.) Crantz

Description: A rhizomatous perennial, to 60 cm, with erect flowering stems; stems hairy above, often purplish beneath. Leaves up to 8, green, alternate, *spirally arranged*, sessile, up to 15 cm long, 30 mm wide, narrowly elliptical to linear-lanceolate. Flowers on rather long stalks (to 15 mm), nodding, up to 14 in lax, 1-sided raceme, with rather long bracts; flowerbuds blunt-tipped. Sepals ovate, *greenish or brownish*, often tinged with purple inside, lateral ones spreading almost sideways. Upper petals ovate, *slanting upwards*, whitish with pink or purplish base or centre. Lip 10–12 mm long, *only slightly hollowed, white*, with 2 *spreading, purple-veined side-lobes* and pendent, bluntly cordate to rounded, *wavy-edged, whitish (rarely cream) terminal lobe* bearing *2–3 smooth, yellow knobs at base*. Spur absent. Column whitish or yellow, with pronounced, *globose rostellum*. Ovary curved (not turned). Capsule 15–22 mm long, narrowly ellipsoid or club-shaped, hairy, pendent on curved stalk.

Flowering: June–August.

Habitat: Marshes, fens, damp meadows, dune-slacks, on wet, oligotrophic, calcareous, sandy, loamy or stony soils; from sea level to 1,800 m.

Range: In Europe northwards to British Isles, S Scandinavia, Estonia, C Russia.

Similar species: **Green-flowered Helleborine** (*E. phyllanthes* G.E. Smith) has 3–6 narrowly ovate to lanceolate leaves (to 70 mm long) in 2 rows; flowers drooping, half-open, with greenish sepals and upper petals, and white, cup-shaped lip (to 8 mm long), with erect side-lobes and greenish-white, cordate terminal lobe. In open woods, scrub, dunes, on dry, oligotrophic, calcareous, sandy or stony soils; locally in NW Europe (Ireland, Britain, France, Denmark, S Sweden).

Marsh Helleborine lip is strongly waisted, leaving the terminal lobe attached only by a narrow strip of tissue; in all other *Epipactis*

species the attachment zone is much wider.
The form *ochroleuca* Barla lacks all red
pigment in flowers and stem.

---

p.42 Violet Helleborine
Epipactis purpurata Smith

Description: A rhizomatous perennial, to 1 m, with
erect, often grouped, purplish flowering
stems, these hairy above. Leaves up to 10,
alternate, spirally arranged, sessile, up to
10 cm long, 25 mm wide, (broadly)
lanceolate, *greyish- or bronze-green above,
purplish below*. Flowers short-stalked, more
or less nodding, up to 50 in long, lax, more
or less 1-sided raceme, with rather long
bracts; flowerbuds pointed. Sepals ovate,
purplish-green, often whitish inside, lateral
ones slanting downwards. Upper petals
ovate, spreading sideways, whitish. Lip
8–10 mm long, hollow, cup-shaped,
yellowish-pink on inside, with *2 erect side-lobes*
and pendent, cordate, *flat-rimmed, white
terminal lobe* bearing *2 smooth, pink knobs* at
base. Spur absent. Column whitish or pink,
with pronounced, *globose rostellum*. Ovary
club-shaped, curved (not turned). Capsule
ellipsoid or club-shaped, up to 15 mm
long, nodding on curved stalk.

Flowering: August–September.

Habitat: Dark deciduous woods (often Beech), on
moist, mesotrophic, calcareous, loamy or
clayey soils; from sea level to 1,400 m.

Range: Locally in NW and C Europe, from Britain,
Belgium and France eastwards to W Russia
and Bulgaria.

---

p.92 Ghost Orchid *Epipogium aphyllum* Swartz

Description: A *whitish perennial* with creeping,
occasionally thickened rhizomes, and
erect, *diaphanous flowering stems* to 30 cm.
No normal leaves; only 1–2 whitish sheaths
present. Flowers 2–5, 15–30 mm diam.,
short-stalked, nodding, in lax, terminal
raceme, with bracts at least twice as long
as flower-stalks. Sepals (and 'upper' petals)

8–10 mm long, linear-lanceolate, *yellowish-white*, often with pink veins, *pendent or slanting downwards*. Lip 10–12 mm long, *erect*, waisted, with 2 spreading side-lobes and cordate, pointed terminal lobe, this longitudinally ridged, *white, with purple dots or lines; spur wide, 6–8 mm long*, blunt, *erect*. Column yellow. Ovary short, ovoid, *not turned*. Capsule drooping on curved stalk.

Flowering: May–August.

Habitat: Old deciduous woods (often Beech), on moist, oligotrophic, humus-rich, sandy or stony soils; from sea level to 1,900 m, but only on mountains in the south.

Range: N and C Europe, southwards to Pyrenees, C Italy and Balkan region, eastwards to Crimea.

One of the orchids in which flowers are not turned 180°; so the lip and the spur point upwards. It lives as a saprophyte, in symbiosis with a fungus, in thick layers of decaying litter, and has lost its green pigment. *Compare also Corallorhiza (see p.817)*, with much smaller, turned flowers.

p.91   **Creeping Lady's-tresses**
Goodyera repens (L.) R. Br.

Description: A rhizomatous perennial with erect, glandular-hairy flowering stems to 25 cm; *stolons also present*, creeping overground. Normal leaves 3–6, all basal, ovate, narrowed into a wide stalk, (sub)acute, with *reticularly interconnected veins*; also some leafless sheaths present, scattered along stem. Flowers up to 20, *spirally arranged* in rather dense, cylindrical raceme, with long bracts. *Perianth whitish, hairy* on the outside; sepals ovate, 3–4 mm long, the lateral ones spreading, the upper one forming a hood with the (slightly narrower) upper petals. Lip 3–4 mm long, *white*, forward-projecting, with a hollowed, sac-like base and a recurved, triangular terminal lobe; side-lobes small, basal; spur absent. Column yellow. Ovary

erect, arched at the top, about equalling
the accompanying bract. Capsule to 6 mm
long, ovoid, short-stalked, more or less
erect.

Flowering: July–August.

Habitat: Woods (often Pine or Birch), scrub, dune-
thickets, on moist, oligotrophic, acid, sandy
or stony soils; from sea level to 2,200 m,
mainly on mountains in the south.

Range: N and C Europe, southwards to Pyrenees,
Alps, and Bulgaria.

This species has expanded into the lowland
during the last 2 centuries, in the wake of
extensive afforestations of Pine. *Compare also
Spiranthes (see p.848), which has tubers, and
non-reticulate veins.*

---

p.262 **Fragrant Orchid**
Gymnadenia conopsea (L.) R. Br.

Description: A tuberous perennial with erect stem to
60 cm; tuber lobed. Normal leaves 2–3,
basal, linear-lanceolate, glabrous, green;
also some small, appressed, scale-like leaves
present, scattered along stem. Flowers
numerous, *c.* 10 mm diam., in rather
dense, cylindrical spike, with short bracts.
All perianth parts bright pink or purplish
(rarely white). Sepals lanceolate or
elliptical, 5–7 mm long, *c.* 1 mm wide;
lateral ones spreading, upper one forming
hood with upper petals. Lip 4.5–7 (8) mm
long, pendent, broadly obovate, shallowly
but distinctly 3-lobed; *spur very long*
(11–18 mm), pendent, slightly curved,
tapering, much longer than ovary. Ovary
arched. Capsule sessile, ellipsoid,
6–10 mm long.

Flowering: June–August.

Habitat: Grassland, fens, marshes, dune-slacks, also
scrub, on wet or moist, oligotrophic,
preferably calcareous, sandy, loamy or stony
soils; from sea level to 2,700 m.

Range: Most of Europe except Iceland and the high
Arctic, and parts of the south.

Similar species: Slender plants from more acid habitats of
England, with linear leaves, smaller flowers

and a narrower, scarcely lobed lip, have been described as *G. borealis* Druce. *G. odoratissima* (L.) Rich. also has relatively narrow lips, and smaller flowers (5–7 mm diam.), but much shorter, apically widened spur (4–5 mm long, just equalling ovary), greyish-green leaves, and stems to 30 cm. In calcareous grassland of C Europe, northwards to Belgium, Germany, S Sweden, Poland, and WC Russia.

All *Gymnadenia* species smell pleasantly of vanilla.

---

p.47 **Bog Orchid**
Hammarbya paludosa (L.) O. Kuntze

Description: A glabrous perennial with erect, *5-angular* flowering stem to 12 (30) cm; stem-base thickened, forming *2 superposed, spaced, ovoid 'pseudobulbs'*, bearing 2–3 (5) sessile, ovate or elliptical leaves, these often with *tiny bulbils along the rounded tip*. Flowers up to 20, erect, sessile, in rather dense, narrow spike (to 60 mm long), with tiny bracts. *Perianth yellowish-green*; sepals (narrowly) ovate, 3–4 mm long; lateral ones erect, *'upper' one pendent.* 'Upper' petals elliptical, 2–3 mm long, sideways spreading, with recurved tip. *Lip 2–2.5 mm long, erect*, narrowly triangular; spur absent. Ovary erect, arched at top, about equalling accompanying bract. Capsule stalked, more or less erect, broadly ellipsoid or subglobose, finely ribbed, 3–5 mm long.
Flowering: July–September.
Habitat: *Sphagnum* bogs, fens, marshes, reedlands, dune-slacks, on wet, oligotrophic, acid, peaty soils; from sea level to 900 m.
Range: N and C Europe except Iceland and the high Arctic.
Similar species: Single-leaved Bog-orchid (*Malaxis monophyllos* (L.) Swartz) has triangular stems, 2 contiguous pseudobulbs, usually only 1 basal leaf; lateral sepals slant upwards, 3rd sepal and (linear) 'upper' petals point down; all perianth parts 2–3 mm long, spur absent again, and

capsule stalked, erect, ellipsoid, to 7 mm long. In marshes, bogs, scrub (often Birch), on wet, oligotrophic, acid, peaty soils; from sea level to 1,600 m, in N, C and E Europe, westwards to Norway, Switzerland and N Italy.

Bog Orchid ovary makes a full turn through 360°, bringing the lip up again, and making the pendent, much-larger median sepal look like a lip. In Single-leaved Bog-orchid, the ovaries are not turned at all, which naturally has the same effect of bringing the lip in an upward position.

---

p.48 **Musk Orchid**
Herminium monorchis (L.) R. Br.

Description: A tuberous perennial with erect stem to 30 cm. Normal leaves 2–3, basal, to 60 mm long, narrowly ovate to lanceolate, glabrous, yellowish-green; also 1 or 2 small, linear, appressed scale-like leaves higher up stem. Flowers 4–5 mm diam., nodding, more or less bell-shaped, numerous in rather lax, cylindrical (occasionally 1-sided) spike, with short bracts. *All perianth parts greenish-yellow.* Sepals 2.5–3 mm long, elliptical or lanceolate. Upper petals *c.* 3.5 mm long. Lip 3.5–4.5 mm long, pendent, *hastate*, with 2 short, narrow, spreading side-lobes and strap-shaped terminal lobe; spur absent. Ovary arched. Capsule sessile, to 10 mm long, shortly ellipsoid, glabrous.

Flowering: June–July.

Habitat: Grassland, dune-slacks, on moist, oligotrophic, calcareous, sandy, loamy or stony soils; from sea level to 1,700 m.

Range: C Europe, from England and the Low Countries eastwards to S Fennoscandia, the Baltic States, C Russia, and southwards to Alps.

The flowers smell of honey. *Compare* the Bog and Fen Orchids (*Malaxis, Liparis* and *Hammarbya*), all with the lip uppermost, and *Pseudorchis, see* p.847), which has 3-toothed lip.

p.41 **Lizard Orchid**
Himantoglossum hircinum (L.) Koch

Description: A tuberous perennial with erect, often
purple-flushed stem to 1 m. Leaves up to 9,
scattered along stem, narrowly elliptical to
linear-lanceolate, glabrous, pale green;
upper ones small, appressed, almost scale-
like. Flowers numerous, short-stalked, in
rather dense, cylindrical raceme, with
bracts at least equalling ovaries. Sepals
ovate, 7–11 mm long, pale green with
brownish veins, all 3 forming hood with
linear, slightly shorter upper petals. *Lip
linear, (15) 30–50 mm long*, 2–3 mm wide,
brownish-pink, pendent, *twisted*, with 2
linear side-lobes (to 10 mm long) near
frilled base, and often with notched or
forked tip; spur short, conical, to 4 (7) mm
long, pointing down. Ovary arched.
Capsule short-stalked, erect, club-shaped.

Flowering: June–July.

Habitat: Grassland, dunes, roadsides, scrub, wood
margins, on rather dry, oligotrophic,
calcareous, sandy or stony soils; from sea
level to 1,800 m.

Range: S and W Europe, northwards to England,
the Low Countries and Germany, also (from
the east) to Hungary, but often ephemeral
in the northern parts of its range.

The flowers give out an unpleasant, musky
scent. The long lip lies coiled in bud.

p.331 **Violet Limodore**
Limodorum abortivum (L.) Swartz

Description: A *violet-tinged, saprophytic perennial* with
creeping, branched rhizomes, and erect
flowering stems to 80 cm. *No normal leaves*;
scale-leaves only few to several, appressed,
scattered along stem. Flowers up to 25, in
lax, terminal raceme, with bracts slightly
shorter than flowers. Sepals 20–25 mm long,
broadly lanceolate, pale violet with darker
veins; lateral ones spreading, upper one
arched over yellowish column. Upper petals
smaller and narrower than sepals, slanting

upwards. Lip 15–18 mm long, triangular-ovate, *whitish with purple-violet stripes*, unlobed, recurved, with raised, finely crenate rims; spur 10–15 mm long, rather stout, pendent. Ovary arched. Capsule short-stalked, erect, 20–35 mm long, spindle-shaped.

Flowering: May–July.

Habitat: Woods (often Oak or Pine), woodland clearings, wood margins, on moist, oligotrophic, calcareous, humus-rich, sandy or loamy soils; from sea level to 1,200 m, but primarily in the mountains.

Range: S and C Europe, northwards to Belgium, Germany, Hungary, and Romania.

Also called Violet Bird's-nest Orchid. Occasionally the plant (and flowers) are whitish.

---

p.48 **Fen Orchid** *Liparis loeselii* (L.) Rich.

Description: A glabrous perennial with erect, *triangular* flowering stem to 20 cm, strongly thickened at base into ovoid 'pseudobulb' surrounded by fibrous remains of old leaf-bases. *Leaves usually 2*, basal, elliptical, *subacute*, yellowish-green, rather erect. Flowers up to 10, erect, short-stalked, in lax, narrow raceme, with tiny bracts. *Perianth greenish-yellow*; sepals linear-lanceolate, 5–8 mm long; lateral ones erect, *'upper' one pendent*. 'Upper' petals linear, 5–7 mm long, sideways spreading or reflexed. *Lip 4–5 mm long, ascending*, narrowly elliptical, unlobed, blunt; spur absent. Ovary ascending, not turned. Capsule 7–12 mm long, ellipsoid, short-stalked, more or less erect.

Flowering: May–July.

Habitat: Bogs, fens, dune-slacks, on wet, oligotrophic, slightly acid to calcareous, sandy or peaty soils; from sea level to 600 m.

Range: C Europe, locally northwards to S Britain, the Low Countries, S Fennoscandia, and C Russia.

One of the orchids in which flowers are not turned 180°; so lip and spur point upwards.

Compare also Malaxis and *Hammarbya* (both with 5-angular stems, *see* p.832), and *Herminium* (*see* p.833), which has turned flowers (lip down).

---

p.47 **Common Twayblade**
Listera ovata (L.) R. Br.

Description: A rhizomatous perennial with erect, rounded flowering stems to 60 cm; stems short-hairy above, with some brownish sheaths at base. *Leaves 2, subopposite*, sessile, in lower half of stem, to 18 cm long, *(broadly) ovate*, spreading, firm. Flowers short-stalked, rather erect, up to 40 in long, narrow, rather lax raceme, with small bracts. Sepals ovate, 4–5 mm long, *greenish-yellow*, all 3 forming hood with much narrower, linear-lanceolate upper petals. Lip 7–15 mm long, greenish-yellow, strap-shaped, pendent, *deeply incised* with 2 linear-lanceolate, slightly divergent end-lobes, but no side-lobes near base. Spur absent. Ovary short. Capsule short-stalked, more or less erect, 5–7 mm long, subglobose.

Flowering: May–July.

Habitat: Deciduous woods, grassland, dune-slacks, road verges, on moist, oligotrophic to mesotrophic, preferably calcareous, sandy, clayey, loamy or stony soils; from sea level to 2,100 m.

Range: All Europe except Spitsbergen, but rare in the extreme south.

Similar species: **Lesser Twayblade** (*L. cordata* (L.) R. Br.) is much smaller (to 20 cm tall, but often much less), with slender stem; leaves 2, sub-opposite, triangular-ovate, cordate-based, to 25 mm long; up to 12 (15) small, pinkish, green-veined flowers in short raceme with tiny bracts; sepals and upper petals 2–2.5 mm long, spreading; lip 3.5–4.5 mm long, strap-shaped, deeply incised with 2 tapering, linear end-lobes, and 2 minute side-lobes at base; capsule 3–4 mm long. In woods (often conifer), also in moors and bogs, on moist, oligotrophic, acid, sandy or peaty soils; from sea level to 2,300 m, but more frequent on mountains, in N and C Europe except Spitsbergen and large areas of the lowland.

p.91 **Dense-flowered Orchid**
Neotinea maculata (Desf.) Stearn

Description: A tuberous perennial with erect stem to
30 cm. Leaves 2–3, mostly basal, narrowly
elliptical to oblanceolate, glabrous, greyish-
green, often with dark-purple, lined-up
spots; also a few small, sheath-like leaves
higher up stem. Flowers numerous, erect,
in long, dense, more or less 1-sided spike.
All perianth parts *whitish or pale pink*; sepals
ovate, converging to form hood concealing
(smaller) upper petals. Lip 3–4 mm long,
projecting forwards, with 2 narrow side-
lobes near base, and larger, *bifid terminal
lobe; spur short* (to 2 mm long). Capsule
sessile, broadly ellipsoid, 8–12 mm long.

Flowering: April–May.

Habitat: Woods, scrub, dunes, grassland, on moist,
oligotrophic, often calcareous, sandy or
rocky soils; mainly at low altitudes.

Range: In Mediterranean region and Portugal, also
in W Ireland and on Isle of Man.

---

p.41 **Bird's-nest Orchid**
Neottia nidus-avis (L.) Rich.

Description: A *pale yellowish-brown, saprophytic perennial*,
to 45 cm, with erect, glabrous flowering
stems; rhizome short, with numerous
tangled, fleshy roots (rather like a bird's
nest). *Normal leaves absent*; up to only 5
pale-brownish sheaths present in lower half
of stem. Flowers short-stalked, half-
nodding to suberect, numerous in long,
narrow, rather dense raceme, with small
bracts; lowest flowers often set apart. *All
perianth parts pale brownish*; sepals ovate,
4–6 mm long, all 3 forming hood with
upper petals. Lip 8–12 mm long, pendent,
ovate, with *2 strongly divergent end-lobes*.
Spur absent. Ovary short, arching. Capsule
short-stalked, more or less erect, ellipsoid,
7–12 mm long.

Flowering: May–July.

Habitat: Deciduous woods (often Beech), on moist,
oligotrophic, calcareous, humus-rich, sandy
or loamy soils; from sea level to 1,700 m.

Range: Most of Europe, northwards to Ireland,
         Scotland, S Fennoscandia, and N Russia.

Compare Corallorhiza – a greenish-white
plant with short-lipped flowers (*see* p.817).

---

p.262   **(Black) Vanilla-orchid**
        Nigritella nigra (L.) Rchb. f.

Description: A tuberous perennial with erect stem to
               60 cm; tuber lobed. Leaves 2–3, basal, linear-
               lanceolate, tapering, channelled, glabrous,
               green, erect, scattered along stem, gradually
               diminishing. Flowers numerous in dense,
               ovoid spike, with short bracts. *All perianth
               parts dark blackish-crimson* (rarely purplish,
               pink or even whitish). Sepals 4–6 mm long,
               narrowly ovate; lateral ones spreading
               sideways, 'upper' one pendent. 'Upper' petals
               lanceolate, slanting downwards. *Lip
               3.5–5 mm long, erect*, ovate, unlobed,
               resembling sepals; *spur short* (to 2 mm),
               directed backwards. Ovary straight. Capsule
               sessile, subglobose, to 7 mm long.

Flowering: June–August.

Habitat: Mountain meadows, on moist, oligotrophic,
           often calcareous, sandy, loamy or stony soils;
           1,000–2,600 m, but descending lower in the
           north.

Range: Mountains of C Europe, westwards to
         Pyrenees and C France; also in Scandinavia.

         One of the orchids in which flowers are not
         turned 180°; so lip and spur point upwards.

---

p.265   **Bee Orchid** *Ophrys apifera* Hudson

Description: A tuberous perennial with erect stem to
               50 cm. Leaves lanceolate, glabrous, partly
               basal and spreading, partly scattered along
               stem and erect, diminishing upwards.
               Flowers up to 11, in lax spike. Sepals
               15–20 mm long, elliptical, *pink or purplish*,
               glabrous; lateral ones spreading, upper one
               arching over column. Upper petals very small
               (3–4 mm long), linear or lanceolate, slanting
               upwards, greenish or pale brownish, short-

hairy. Lip 10–12 mm long, 6–9 mm wide, rounded, pendent, *dark purplish-brown* with 2 yellowish knobs and *round, brick-red blotch* at base and *yellowish markings, strongly convex*, short-hairy, with 2 blunt or truncate, recurved end-lobes, and terminal, glabrous, greenish appendage curved under; side-lobes (near base) bluntly triangular, recurved; spur absent. Column has forward-projecting, sinuous beak. Capsule sessile, 15–25 mm long, spindle-shaped.

Flowering: June–July.

Habitat: Grassland, scrub, roadsides, quarries, grassy banks, sand-dunes, on moist to rather dry, oligotrophic to mesotrophic, calcareous, sandy, loamy or stony soils; from sea level to 1,000 m.

Range: S, W and C Europe, northwards to British Isles, the Low Countries, Germany, Hungary, Romania, and Crimea.

The lip is reminiscent of a bee's abdomen, and indeed bees are observed as pollinators although self-pollination also occurs. In var. *trollii* (Hegelsch.) Rchb., from France and SW England, the lip is protracted into a short, yellow point with brown blotches, and lacking the brick-red, basal blotch.

---

p.265 **Late Spider Orchid**
Ophrys holosericea (Burm. f.) W. Greuter

Description: A tuberous perennial with erect stem to 35 cm. Leaves (ob)lanceolate, glabrous, mostly basal, rather spreading, the few cauline ones abruptly diminishing and erect. Flowers up to 10, in lax spike. Sepals *c.* 10 mm long, ovate, *pink or whitish*, glabrous; lateral ones spreading, upper one arching over column. Upper petals small (4–5 mm long), triangular, often slightly hastate, slanting upwards, pinkish, very short-hairy. Lip 9–12 mm long, 12–15 mm wide, pendent, subquadrate, *red-brown* with 2 blackish knobs and *round, brick-red blotch* at base, and *yellowish markings, flat-rimmed*, with terminal, yellowish appendage curved up; side-lobes weakly developed; spur absent. Column has 2 forward-projecting lobules. Capsule sessile, 15–25 mm long, spindle-shaped.

Flowering: May–July.

Habitat: Grassland, roadsides, field margins, on dry, oligotrophic to mesotrophic, calcareous, sandy, loamy or stony soils; from sea level to 1,300 m.

Range: S, W and SC Europe, northwards to England (Kent), Belgium, S Germany, Moravia, and Romania.

Lip reminiscent of a spider's abdomen, but pollination is effected by certain bees.

---

p.40 **Fly Orchid** *Ophrys insectifera* L.

Description: A tuberous perennial with erect stem to 50 cm. Leaves narrowly lanceolate, glabrous, some basal and rather erect, some cauline and erect, diminishing upwards. Flowers up to 14, in lax spike. Sepals *c.* 6 mm long, ovate, *greenish*, glabrous; lateral ones spreading, upper one erect. Upper petals very small, *threadlike*, 4–5 mm long, slanting upwards, purplish-brown, subglabrous. Lip 9–10 mm long, 6–7 mm wide, pendent, wedge-shaped, *deep purplish-brown* with blackish base and medially constricted, *shiny pale violet-blue blotch* ('speculum') in centre, short-hairy (but for speculum), *flat-rimmed*, with *2 obliquely truncate end-lobes*; side-lobes bluntly triangular, slanting downwards; no terminal appendage. Spur absent. Column without appendages. Capsule sessile, 15–25 mm long, spindle-shaped.

Flowering: May–June.

Habitat: Woods, wood margins, scrub, grassland, fens, on moist, oligotrophic, calcareous, sandy, loamy or stony soils; from sea level to 1,500 m.

Range: C and NW Europe, extending to British Isles, C Scandinavia, S Finland, and N Russia.

Lip mimics a fly; but certain wasps are the actual pollinators.

p.40 **Early Spider Orchid** *Ophrys sphegodes* Miller

Description: A tuberous perennial with erect stem to 35 cm. Leaves broadly lanceolate, glabrous, mostly basal, more or less spreading, the few cauline ones abruptly diminishing, erect. Flowers up to 10, in lax spike. Sepals 10–15 mm long, elliptical, *greenish*, glabrous; lateral ones spreading, upper one erect, truncate. Upper petals 7–9 mm long, slanting upwards, brownish-green, subglabrous. Lip 9–10 mm long, 8–12 mm wide, pendent, rounded, *deep purplish-brown* with blackish base and an (occasionally disjoined) X-shaped, *shiny pale-violet blotch* ('speculum') in centre, short-hairy (but for speculum), *strongly convex*, with *2 recurved end-lobes*; side-lobes bluntly triangular, recurved; spur absent. Column has short, straight, forward-projecting beak. Capsule sessile, 15–25 mm long, spindle-shaped.

Flowering: April–June.

Habitat: Grassland, roadsides, grassy banks, on dry, oligotrophic, calcareous, sandy, loamy or stony soils; from sea level to 800 m.

Range: In Europe northwards to S England, Belgium, S Germany, Hungary, Romania, and Crimea.

Pollination by bees, or self-pollination.

p.264 **Lax-flowered Orchid** *Orchis laxiflora* Lamk.

Description: A glabrous perennial with 2–3 rounded tubers and erect, often purplish flowering stems to 60 cm (1 m). Leaves 3–8, sessile and sheathing, to 16 cm long, 10–20 mm wide, (narrowly) lanceolate, acute, channelled, *unspotted*, scattered along stem, rather erect. Flowers numerous, in rather lax, cylindrical spike; floral bracts shorter than ovary, purplish, with *3–7 reticularly interconnected veins*. All *perianth parts red-purple*; sepals narrowly elliptical to lanceolate, 7–10 mm long; lateral ones erect, upper arching over column; upper petals slanting upwards, often forming hood with upper sepal. Lip pendent, obcordate, 7–9 mm long, red-purple or purple-violet, with paler centre, distinctly 3-lobed, with reflexed side-lobes and *very small middle lobe* (occasionally absent altogether); spur almost straight, slender, *c.* 10 mm long, 1.5 mm wide, about 2 thirds the length of ovary, *widened towards tip.* Ovary erect to spreading, slightly arching. Capsule sessile, narrowly ellipsoid, 15–25 mm long.

Flowering: May–July.

Habitat: Grassland, dune-slacks, on wet to moist, oligotrophic, calcareous, sandy soils; from sea level to 1,200 m, but more frequent at low altitudes.

Range: S and W Europe, northwards to W France, Jersey; probably extinct in Belgium.

The description above pertains to ssp. *laxiflora.* Ssp. *palustris* (Jacq.) Ashrs. & Graebn. has pale-purple flowers, with middle lobe of lip at least as long as side-lobes, and 3–5-veined bracts; spur is narrowed towards tip. In comparable habitats of S and C Europe, northwards to S Sweden. Ssp. *elegans* (Heuffel) Soó, in E Europe, has subentire lip and slightly wider leaves. *Compare O. mascula,* with spotted leaves and 1–3-veined bracts.

---

p.264 **Early Purple Orchid** *Orchis mascula* (L.) L.

Description: A glabrous perennial with 2–3 rounded tubers and erect, often purplish flowering stems to 40 cm. Leaves 3–6, sessile and sheathing, to 10 cm long, 20 mm wide, oblanceolate, round-tipped, *shiny green, often dark-spotted*, gathering in lower half of stem; upper ones erect, smaller but not scale-like. Flowers numerous, in rather dense, cylindrical spike; floral bracts at least equalling ovary, *1–3-veined* (at least upper ones), violet. All *perianth parts purplish* (rarely pink or white); sepals narrowly ovate to lanceolate, 6–8 mm long; lateral ones erect, upper arching over column to form hood with upper petals.

Lip pendent, rounded to rhombic, 8–12 (15) mm long, 3-lobed, middle lobe longer than side-lobes, and truncate, often notched; *spur slanting upwards*, almost straight, about equalling ovary, *widened towards tip*. Ovary erect to spreading, arching. Capsule sessile, narrowly ellipsoid, 15–25 mm long.

Flowering: April–June.

Habitat: Deciduous woods (often Beech or Oak), scrub, grassland, on moist, oligotrophic, calcareous, sandy, loamy or stony soils; from sea level to 2,600 m.

Range: Most of Europe except Iceland and the high Arctic.

Similar species: *O. spitzelii* Sauter ex Koch has dull-green, unspotted leaves, sepals with some green (especially inside), and an equal-lobed, pink lip with numerous purplish dots; spur conical, shorter than ovary. Grassland, woods (often Beech or Pine), 1,100–1,400 m, in S and SC Europe, also on Gotland.

Compare *O. laxiflora*, which has unspotted leaves and 3–7-veined bracts.

p.263 **Green-winged Orchid** *Orchis morio* L.

Description: A glabrous perennial with 2–3 rounded tubers and erect, often purplish flowering stems to 50 cm. Leaves up to 10, mostly basal, sessile and sheathing, to 12 cm long, 30 mm wide, oblanceolate, round-tipped, shiny green, unspotted; upper ones erect, sheath-like. Flowers up to 10, in rather lax, shortly cylindrical spike; floral bracts at most equalling ovary. Sepals ovate to elliptical, *blunt-tipped*, purplish, pink or white with *green veins*, 8–10 mm long, all 3 converging to form hood with (smaller) upper petals. Lip pendent, 7–10 mm long, 9–12 mm wide, *purple, pink or whitish*, often with white, purple-dotted centre, (deeply) 3-lobed, middle lobe notched, longer than (obliquely truncate or rounded) side-lobes; *spur horizontal or slightly curved upwards*, widening towards tip, slightly shorter than erect, arching ovary. Capsule sessile, narrowly ellipsoid, (10) 15–25 mm long.

Flowering: April–June (autumn).

Habitat: Grassland, dune-slacks, scrub, quarries, on wet to moist, oligotrophic, preferably calcareous, sandy, loamy or stony soils; from sea level to 1,800 m.

Range: In Europe northwards to the British Isles, the Low Countries, S Scandinavia, Estonia, and C Russia.

---

p.263 **Lady Orchid** *Orchis purpurea* Hudson

Description: A glabrous perennial with 2–3 rounded tubers and erect, often purplish flowering stems to 80 cm. Leaves up to 8, sessile and sheathing, to 10 cm long, 20 mm wide, elliptical to lanceolate, subacute, shiny green, unspotted, mostly basal; upper ones erect, sheath-like, smaller but not scale-like. Flowers numerous, in dense, cylindrical spike; floral bracts much shorter than ovary. Sepals ovate, 12–14 mm long, *deep pink to brownish-purple*, all 3 convergent to form hood with upper petals. Lip pendent, *white or pink with dots of purple hairs*, more or less rounded, 12–15 mm long, 3-lobed, middle lobe longer and much wider than (narrow, arm-like) side-lobes, and itself deeply notched, with minute lobule in notch; *spur curved downwards*, up to half as long as erect to spreading, arching ovary. Capsule sessile, narrowly ellipsoid, (10) 15–25 mm long.

Flowering: May–June.

Habitat: Woods, scrub, grassland, shaded verges, on moist, oligotrophic, calcareous, sandy, loamy or stony soils; from sea level to 1,500 m.

Range: S and C Europe, northwards to S Britain, the Low Countries, Denmark and S Sweden, Poland, and W Russia.

Lip vaguely reminiscent of a skirted lady. *Compare O. ustulata*, with much darker, blackish-purple sepals.

p.263 **Monkey Orchid** *Orchis simia* Lamk.

Description: A glabrous perennial with 2–3 rounded tubers and erect, often purplish flowering stems to 30 cm. Leaves up to 7, sessile and sheathing, to 80 mm long, 20 mm wide, elliptical to oblanceolate, blunt-tipped, unspotted, mostly basal; upper ones erect, sheath-like, smaller but not scale-like. Flowers numerous, in dense, ovoid spike; floral bracts much shorter than ovary. Sepals ovate, *c.* 10 mm long, *white with purplish veins* (at least inside), all 3 convergent to form hood with upper petals. Lip pendent, *white or pale pink with dots of purple hairs*, slender, 14–16 mm long, 3-lobed, middle lobe longer and much wider than (linear, arm-like, purple, strongly curved) side-lobes, and itself protracted into *2 linear, purple, strongly curved end-lobes*, with minute lobule in between, thus rather suggestive of a monkey in shape; *spur curved downwards*, about half as long as erect, arching ovary. Capsule sessile, narrowly ellipsoid, 10–20 mm long.

Flowering: May–June.

Habitat: Grassland, scrub, wood margins, on moist to rather dry, oligotrophic, calcareous, sandy, loamy or stony soils; from sea level to 1,500 m.

Range: S and W Europe, northwards to England, the Low Countries, C Germany, and (from the east) to Hungary.

Similar species: **Military Orchid** (*O. militaris* L.) has wider, flat end-lobes to lip (*c.* 3 times wider than linear, rather straight side-lobes), and less pronounced contrast between purplish lobes and pale-pink centre of lip. In comparable habitats, more often in open woods, in Europe northwards to England, the Low Countries, Poland, and NW and C Russia.

Monkey Orchid's flowering starts from above, so that at first the lower flowers are closed. The opposite of this is true for Military Orchid.

p.316 **Burnt-tip Orchid** *Orchis ustulata* L.

Description: A glabrous perennial, with 2–3 rounded tubers and erect, often purplish flowering stems to 30 cm. Leaves up to 6, sessile and sheathing, to 80 mm long, 20 mm wide, oblanceolate, rather blunt, unspotted, mostly basal, erect; upper ones sheath-like. Flowers numerous, in dense, ovoid or cylindrical spike; floral bracts at most equalling ovary. Sepals ovate, 3–4 mm long, *deep blackish-purple*, all 3 converging to form hood with upper petals. Lip pendent, *white or pink with purple dots*, 4–8 mm long, 3-lobed, middle lobe much longer than (arm-like) side-lobes (but only slightly wider at base), and itself deeply notched; *spur curved downwards*, only half as long as ascending to erect, arching ovary. Capsule sessile, ellipsoid, to 10 mm long.

Flowering: April–July.

Habitat: Grassland, scrub, on moist, oligotrophic, calcareous, loamy or stony soils; from sea level to 2,000 m.

Range: Much of Europe, northwards to England, Belgium, S Sweden, the Baltic States, and C Russia; extinct in the Netherlands.

The dark sepals make the inflorescence look burnt, especially when flowering is just beginning. *O. purpurea* has the same characteristic but less pronounced.

---

p.90 **Lesser Butterfly-orchid**
Platanthera bifolia (L.) Rich.

Description: A tuberous perennial with erect flowering stem to 50 cm. *Basal leaves 2, elliptical or obovate*, blunt-tipped; also some scale-like stem-leaves. Flowers fragrant (smelling strongly of vanilla), up to 25, in rather lax, cylindrical spike. Sepals ovate, *c.* 10 mm long, narrowly ovate, *greenish-white or cream*; lateral ones spreading, upper one nodding to form hood with lanceolate, more greenish upper petals. Lip 8–12 mm long, pendent, *linear-lanceolate, unlobed*, blunt-tipped, *greenish with white base*; spur 25–30 mm long,

1–1.5 mm wide, curved down, longer than ovary. Pollinia close together, *parallel*. Ovary arched, about equalling accompanying bract. Capsule sessile, ellipsoid, 10–20 mm long.

Flowering: June–July.

Habitat: Poor meadows, reedlands, marshes, dune-slacks, heaths, scrub, also open woods, on wet to moist, oligotrophic, slightly acid to calcareous soils; from sea level to 2,300 m.

Range: Most of Europe except Iceland and the high Arctic.

Similar species: **Greater Butterfly-orchid** (*P. chlorantha* (Custer) Rchb.) has less fragrant, more greenish flowers, pollinia divergent from top, and shorter spurs (18–27 mm long) with slightly widened tip. In comparable habitats, but more strongly bound to calcareous soils, in most of Europe except the far north. Intermediate forms are not rare.
P. hyperborea (L.) Lindley has 4–7 oblanceolate leaves, lower one largest, and greenish flowers with short, broadly lanceolate lip (3–7 mm long) and short spur (3.5–4.5 mm). In meadows and heaths in Iceland.
P. obtusata (Pursh) Lindley has only 1 basal leaf, and a smaller leaf high up on stem; flowers greenish-white, with short, rhombic lip (3–3.5 mm long), and very short spur (2.5–3 mm). In heaths on calcareous soils in mountains of N Scandinavia.

p.90 **Small White Orchid**
Pseudorchis albida (L.) ?. & D. Löve.

Description: A tuberous perennial with erect stem to 35 cm, and a few leafless sheaths at base. Normal leaves 3–5, oblanceolate to almost linear, glabrous, shiny green, erect, scattered along stem, diminishing upwards. Flowers numerous, in rather dense, cylindrical spike. *All perianth parts yellowish- or greenish-white.* Sepals 2–3 mm long, ovate, converge to form hood with (narrower) upper petals. Lip *c.* 3 mm long, pendent, broadly wedge-shaped, with 3-lobed tip; *spur 2–3 mm long*, curved down, *much shorter than ovary*. Ovary erect, arching, about equalling bract. Capsule sessile, (broadly) ellipsoid, 5–9 mm long.

Flowering: May–June.

Habitat: Poor meadows, heaths, on moist, oligotrophic, acid, sandy or stony soils; from sea level to 2,400 m, but mainly on mountains in the south.

Range: N Europe, westwards to Ireland and Iceland, eastwards to N and W Russia, and in mountains of C Europe, northwards to Belgium (extinct in the Netherlands) and Poland.

Compare Herminium (see p.833), which has spreading sepals and hastate lip.

---

p.91 **Summer Lady's-tresses**
Spiranthes aestivalis (Poiret) Rich.

Description: A tuberous perennial with erect, glandular-hairy flowering stem to 40 cm. Leaves 3–7, mostly in lower half of stem, erect, lanceolate; upper ones smaller, linear. Flowers up to 25, *spirally arranged* in rather dense spike to 10 cm long; *bracts nearly equalling flowers*. Perianth *white, glabrous*; sepals lanceolate, 5–6 mm long, erect, forming tube with upper petals. Lip 7–8 mm long, *white*, with hollowed base and recurved, ovate terminal lobe; no side-lobes; spur absent. Column yellow. Ovary erect, arched at top. Capsule sessile, narrowly ellipsoid, to 10 mm long.

Flowering: July–August.

Habitat: Marshy heaths, poor meadows, on wet, oligotrophic, slightly acid, sandy, loamy or peaty soils; from sea level to 1,300 m.

Range: S, W and C Europe, northwards to NW France (apparently extinct in the British Isles and the Low Countries).

Similar species: **Autumn Lady's-tresses** (*S. spiralis* (L.) Chevall.), flowers in autumn (August–September) and then a new rosette of ovate, scarcely stalked leaves develops at base of (ascending) flowering stem, which itself has only 1–3 scale-leaves (last year's basal leaves having withered by flowering time); spike is shorter (to 60 mm), with bracts equalling flowers, and perianth is more yellowish- or greenish-white (especially on outside), with frilled lip; capsule broadly ellipsoid. In short grassland on calcareous, rather drier soils in Europe northwards to the British Isles, the Low Countries, Denmark, Latvia, and W Russia.

Irish Lady's-tresses (*S. romanzoffiana* Cham.) has leaves like Summer Lady's-tresses; flowers creamy- or greenish-white in a triple spiral, more crowded, with strongly upcurved sepals. In drained bogs and damp meadows in W Ireland and the Hebrides; extinct in Cornwall.

Compare also Goodyera (*see* p.830) with creeping rhizomes, stolons, and net-veined leaves.

BROOMRAPE FAMILY, OROBANCHACEAE

A family of parasitic herbs with about 130–180 species in 11–14 genera, mainly in the northern hemisphere. Dicots. Stems erect, often unbranched, with specialized sucking roots (haustoria), and alternate, scale-like leaves; chlorophyll absent. Flowers irregular, hermaphrodite, in terminal spikes; each flower usually has a bract, and often 2 bracteoles as well. Calyx 4–5-toothed or 2-parted (then each part often bifid or trifid). Corolla 2-lipped, with long tube, 2-lobed upper lip (occasionally unlobed, or absent), and 3-lobed lower lip. Stamens 4, in 2 unequal pairs, inserted in lower half of corolla tube, alternating with corolla lobes. Ovary superior, 1-locular, with 1 style and 2 stigmas. Fruit a more or less cylindrical, pointed capsule, splitting with 2 valves, and containing numerous minute seeds. The Orobanchaceae are closely related to the Scrophulariaceae, and the genus *Lathraea* has moved between them now and then. According to recent views, *Orobanche* is the only N European genus to be maintained in the family. The N European species are usually perennial, with a more or less thickened stem-base, but without rhizomes; a few species often behave like annuals, possibly as an adaptation to hosts living in unstable environments. *O. ramosa*, *O. purpurea* and *O. arenaria* have flowers with 1 bract, 2 bracteoles, and a tubular, 4–5-toothed calyx (section **Trionychon**). The other N European species have flowers with 1 bract, no bracteoles, and calyx divided (almost) to base in 2 parts, each of which can be bifid itself (section **Orobanche**). In some of them stamens are inserted near base of corolla tube (less than a quarter its length), as in *O. alba*, *O. caryophyllacea*, *O. gracilis*, *O. rapum-genistae*, and often in *O. reticulata*. In the remaining species stamens are inserted higher up in the tube (usually about 1 third of the tube length); they can be further divided according to the colour of their stigmas during full anthesis: whitish or yellow stigmas (*O. alsatica, O. elatior, O. hederae, O. lutea*); and reddish or purple stigmas (*O. amethystea, O. loricata, O. minor, O. teucrii*, and part of *O. reticulata*). The host plant can often be a clue to the correct name. However, since many species are rare and declining (and often protected), plants should not be dug out just to see what other species they are anchored to.

---

p.260 **Thyme Broomrape**
Orobanche alba Stephan ex Willd.

Description: A glandular-hairy perennial, to 30 cm, with erect, unbranched, *reddish* flowering stems. Scale-leaves lanceolate. Flowers fragrant 3–10 (15) in short spike, each with 1 lanceolate bract; no bracteoles. Calyx at least equalling corolla tube, 2-parted, the parts lanceolate, entire or (rarely) very unequally bifid, well separated. Corolla *yellowish with red or purple veins* (occasionally all red), 15–20 mm long, with dark-purple glandular hairs on outside; upper lip scarcely lobed; lower lip slightly shorter, with 3 rounded lobes (middle one slightly larger). Stamens inserted near base of corolla tube; filaments hairy below. Style glandular-hairy; *stigmas red or purple*. Valves of capsule staying fused at top.

Flowering: (May) June–August.

Habitat: Woods, poor grassland, coastal dunes, on dry, often calcareous soils from sea level to 1,800 m; parasitic on *Thymus* and other Labiatae.

Range: In Europe northwards to Ireland, Cornwall, W Scotland, N France, C Germany, SE Sweden (Öland), S Poland, and C Russia.

---

p.314 *Orobanche amethystea* Thuill.

Description: A glandular-hairy perennial, to 50 cm, with erect, unbranched, *purplish or violet* flowering stems. Scale-leaves linear-lanceolate. Flowers numerous, in long spike, each with 1 narrowly lanceolate bract (12–22 mm long); no bracteoles. Calyx at least equalling corolla tube (and often longer than whole flower), 2-parted, the parts narrowly lanceolate, subequally bifid or entire, well separated. Corolla (often very pale) *lilac with darker veins*, 15–22 mm long, often sparsely glandular-hairy on outside, but with *glabrous margins*; upper lip distinctly 2-lobed, with upturned lobes; lower lip about as long as upper tip, with 3 subequal, rounded lobes. Stamens inserted at about 1 third the length of corolla tube; filaments glabrous, or only slightly hairy below. Style sparsely glandular-hairy; *stigmas very dark violet*. Valves of capsule connate at top.

Flowering: June–August.

Habitat: Arable and wasteland, roadsides, grassy banks, on dry to moist, calcareous soils; from sea level to 2,200 m. Parasitic on various herbs (*Eryngium campestre*, *Ballota*, *Daucus*), also Ivy (*Hedera*).

Range: S and W Europe, northwards to S Britain (Isle of Wight), the Channel Isles, N France, and S Germany.

Compare O. purpurea (1 bract and 2 bracteoles), *O. hederae* (yellow stigmas, and more whitish flowers, especially inside), and *O. loricata* (more yellowish, with densely hairy filaments).

---

p.259 **Bedstraw Broomrape**
Orobanche caryophyllacea Sm.

Description: A glandular-hairy perennial, to 60 cm, with erect, unbranched, *yellowish or purplish* flowering stems. Scale-leaves lanceolate. Flowers up to 15, in lax spike, each with 1 triangular-lanceolate bract (17–25 mm long); no bracteoles. Calyx only half as long as corolla tube, 2-parted, the parts lanceolate, very unequally bifid and often partly connate anteriorly. Corolla *reddish to purplish-brown* (rarely yellowish), *large*, (17) 20–35 mm long, with pale glandular hairs on outside; upper lip scarcely lobed; lower lip slightly longer, with 3 rounded, subequal lobes glandular inside and on margin. Stamens inserted near base of corolla tube; filaments hairy below and densely glandular near top. Style densely glandular-hairy (at least at top); *stigmas reddish or brown-purple* (rarely yellow), well separated. Valves of capsule connate at top.

Flowering: May–July.

Habitat: Grassland, dunes, grassy banks, on dry, calcareous soils; from sea level to 1,600 m. Parasitic on *Galium* species, especially *G. verum* and *G. mollugo*.

Range: Europe northwards to SE Britain (Kent), the Low Countries, S Norway, Poland, and C Russia.

Similar species: **Slender Broomrape** (*O. gracilis* Sm.) is a reddish plant with smaller flowers (corolla 15–25 mm long), often deep red inside, and with yellow, red-edged stigmas. In grassland and woods of S and C Europe, northwards to N France, C Germany and the Carpathians; usually attacks various Leguminosae.

The flowers of both species smell strongly of cloves. *Compare also O. teucrii (see p.859),* which has stamens inserted higher up corolla tube.

---

p.188 **Knapweed Broomrape**
Orobanche elatior Sutton

Description: A glandular-hairy perennial, to 70 cm, with erect, unbranched, *yellowish to purplish-brown* flowering stems. Scale-leaves triangular-lanceolate. Flowers numerous (at least 15, often many more), in long, dense spike, each with 1 lanceolate bract, about equalling flower; no bracteoles. Calyx shorter than corolla tube, 2-parted, the parts usually partly connate anteriorly, lanceolate, entire or (more often) unequally bifid. *Corolla pink* at first, *turning yellowish or orange* during anthesis, 20–32 mm long, glandular-hairy on outside; *upper lip weakly notched*; lower lip slightly shorter, glabrous inside and on margin, with 3 subequal, rounded lobes. Stamens inserted at about 1 third the length of corolla tube; filaments densely hairy below; *stigmas yellow*. Valves of capsule connate at top.

Flowering: June–July.
Habitat: Grassland, on dry, calcareous soils; from sea level to 1,600 m. Parasitic on Compositae, especially *Centaurea scabiosa*, also on *Thalictrum*.
Range: Europe northwards to England, Denmark, Estonia, and C Russia, but local, and absent from large areas.
Similar species: *O. alsatica* Kirschleger has smaller, reddish flowers (to 20 mm long) with purple or violet, ciliate lips, basally connate calyx parts with subequal teeth, and strongly thickened stem-base. In wood margins, in the hills and mountains of C and E Europe, extending to NE France (Lorraine), S Germany, Poland, and C Russia, and further to C Asia; attacks Umbelliferae, especially *Peucedanum cervaria* and *Seseli libanotis*.

---

p.88 **Ivy Broomrape** *Orobanche hederae* Duby

Description: A glandular-hairy perennial, to 60 cm, with erect, unbranched, *yellowish-brown to purple* flowering stems. Scale-leaves lanceolate. Flowers numerous, in long, (initially) dense spike, each with 1 lanceolate bract, about equalling flower; no bracteoles. Calyx shorter than corolla tube, 2-parted, the parts well separated, narrowly ovate to lanceolate, entire or (more often) very unequally bifid. *Corolla white or cream with purplish veins*, usually whitish inside, 12–22 mm long, *scarcely glandular-hairy; upper lip weakly notched*; lower lip slightly shorter, glabrous inside and on margin, with 3 subequal, rounded lobes. Stamens inserted at about 1 third the length of corolla tube; *filaments subglabrous; stigmas yellow* (but *see* below). Valves of capsule connate at top.
Flowering: June–August.
Habitat: Woods, hedgebanks, at foot of old walls, on moist, calcareous soils; from sea level to 500 m. Parasitic on Ivy (*Hedera*).
Range: S, SC and W Europe, northwards to Ireland, S Britain, the Low Countries, and S Germany.

The stigmas often turn violet in older flowers. *Compare O. amethystea, which always has very dark-violet stigmas, and more violet flowers (also inside).*

p.89 **Oxtongue Broomrape**
Orobanche loricata Rchb.

Description: A glandular-hairy perennial or annual, to 70 cm, with erect, unbranched, *yellowish, occasionally purple-tinged* flowering stems. Scale-leaves narrowly lanceolate, densely glandular-hairy. Flowers numerous, in rather dense spike, each with 1 narrowly lanceolate bract 12–20 mm long, usually exceeding flower; no bracteoles. Calyx more than half as long as corolla tube, 2-parted, the parts lanceolate, unequally bifid or entire, touching each other anteriorly. Corolla *white or yellowish with violet veins*, 14–20 mm long, with (pale) glandular hairs on outside; upper lip entire or notched (never distinctly 2-lobed), upturned; lower lip about as long as upper lip, with 3 subequal, rounded lobes and glabrous margin. Stamens inserted at about 1 third the length of corolla tube; *filaments densely hairy below*. Style more or less densely glandular-hairy; *stigmas purple*, 2-lobed, the lobes contiguous. Capsule ovoid, 8–10 mm long; valves connate above.

Flowering: June–September.

Habitat: Grassland, scrub, on moist, calcareous soils; from sea level to 2,200 m. Parasitic on various herbs, such as *Artemisia, Picris, Crepis, Hypochaeris, Daucus.*

Range: S and C Europe, northwards to England, the Low Countries, Denmark, S Poland, and W Russia.

Plants with sparsely hairy styles, and particularly often found parasitizing *Picris,* are frequently treated as a separate species (*O. picridis* F.W. Schultz ex Koch). *Compare O. amethystea* (more violet flowers, subglabrous filaments, and deeply 2-lobed upper lip), *O. hederae* (yellow stigmas) and *O. minor* (straight upper lip).

p.188 *Orobanche lutea* Baumg.

Description: A glandular-hairy perennial, to 50 cm, with erect, unbranched, *yellowish to purplish-brown* flowering stems. Scale-leaves narrowly lanceolate. Flowers rather numerous (at least 15), in rather lax spike, each with 1 lanceolate bract, about equalling flower; no bracteoles. Calyx shorter than corolla tube, 2-parted, the parts free or partly connate anteriorly, unequally bifid. Corolla *yellowish-brown or brownish-red* with paler base, 20–32 mm long, slightly glandular-hairy on outside; upper lip notched or distinctly 2-lobed; lower lip about as long as upper lip, glabrous inside and on margin, with 3 subequal, rounded lobes. Stamens inserted at about 1 third the length of corolla tube; filaments densely hairy below; *stigmas yellow.* Valves of capsule connate at top.

Flowering: May–August.

Habitat: Grassland, grassy banks, river-dunes, on rather dry, oligotrophic, calcareous soils; from sea level to 1,600 m. Parasitic on Leguminosae, especially *Medicago* and *Trifolium.*

Range: S and C Europe, northwards to the Low Countries, Germany, N Poland, and W Russia.

Formerly rather common in cultures of *Medicago sativa* and other Leguminosae.

p.259 **Common Broomrape** *Orobanche minor* Sm.

Description: A more or less glandular-hairy perennial or annual, to 50 cm, with erect, unbranched, *yellowish-brown, often red-tinged* flowering stems. Scale-leaves ovate to lanceolate. Flowers few to numerous, in rather dense spike, each with 1 narrowly lanceolate bract (7–15 mm long) subequalling flower; no bracteoles. Calyx subequalling corolla tube, 2-parted, the parts lanceolate, free, subequally bifid or entire. Corolla *yellowish-white with purplish veins*, often (dorsally) flushed with purple, 10–18 mm long, with at least some (pale) glandular hairs on outside; upper lip notched to distinctly 2-lobed, with forward-protruding lobes; lower lip about as long, with 3 subequal, rounded lobes and a glabrous margin. Stamens inserted at about 1 third the length of corolla tube; filaments glabrous, or only slightly hairy below. Style glabrous or sparsely glandular-hairy; *stigmas red-purple* (rarely yellow), well-separated. Valves of capsule connate at top.

Flowering: June–September.

Habitat: Meadows, pastures, dunes, roadsides, grassy banks, on dry to moist, mesotrophic, sandy, loamy, clayey or stony soils; from sea level to 2,200 m. Parasitic on various herbs, especially *Trifolium* and other Leguminosae.

Range: Europe northwards to Britain, the Low Countries, C Germany, Hungary, and C Russia, and (naturalized) in Ireland, Denmark, S Sweden.

Formerly often numerous in clover fields. Plants with purple stems and unequal lobes to lower lip (occurring in dunes of W France, S Britain and S Spain) are often distinguished as *O. maritima* Pugsley; they parasitize *Daucus*, *Plantago maritima*, and *Ononis repens*.

---

p.331 **Yarrow Broomrape**
Orobanche purpurea Jacq.

Description: A finely glandular-hairy perennial, to 60 cm, with erect, usually unbranched, brownish flowering stems. Flowers each have 1 bract, and *2 bracteoles*, these equalling calyx. *Calyx tubular*, cup-shaped, with 4 triangular-lanceolate teeth (shorter than tube), and often with 5th, small, dorsal tooth in between. Corolla *blue-violet* with darker veins and yellowish base, 18–30 mm long, with subacute lobes. *Stamens (sub)glabrous*. Style densely glandular; *stigmas white or bluish*. Capsule shorter than calyx; *valves free at top*.

Flowering: June–July.

Habitat: Rough grassland, coastal and river sand-dunes, grassy banks, on dry, calcareous soils; from sea level to 1,800 m. Parasitic on *Achillea millefolium*, occasionally on *Artemisia* or *Cirsium*.

Range: Europe northwards to S Britain, the Low Countries, Germany, S Sweden, Poland, and C Russia.

Similar species: *O. arenaria* Borkh. has hairy anthers, yellowish stigmas, and slightly larger flowers (to 35 mm long) with rounded lobes; stems often bluish, with longer glandular hairs. In S and SC Europe, locally northwards to N France, S Germany, Poland and C Russia, on dry, alluvial soils along rivers; parasitic on *Artemisia*, *Anthemis*, and *Eryngium*.

p.331 **Hemp Broomrape** *Orobanche ramosa* L.

Description: A finely glandular-hairy perennial or annual to 30 cm, with erect, *usually branched*, yellowish flowering stems. Flowers each with 1 bract and *2 bracteoles*, these equalling calyx. *Calyx tubular*, cup-shaped, with 4 triangular-ovate teeth (shorter than tube). Corolla *pale blue to violet with darker veins* (occasionally violet-flushed cream), 7–15 (17) mm long, with rounded lobes. *Stamens glabrous* or hairy only at base. Style not exceeding corolla tube, sparsely glandular-hairy, with *funnel-shaped, indistinctly 3–4-lobed, white, cream or bluish stigma*. Capsule ovoid, 6–7 (10) mm long, exceeding calyx; *valves free at top*.

Flowering: June–September.

Habitat: Cultivated fields. Parasitic on *Cannabis*, *Nicotiana* and *Solanum*.

Range: S and SC Europe, northwards to C France, S Germany, Hungary and W Russia; naturalized further north, but extinct again in Britain and the Low Countries.

The only branched *Orobanche* in the area. The species has strongly declined, with the disappearance of the hemp and tobacco cultures from most of Europe. It is now and then seen as a casual in gardens.

p.260 **Greater Broomrape**
Orobanche rapum-genistae Thuill.

Description: A glandular-hairy perennial, to 85 cm,
with erect, unbranched, *pale-yellow*
(occasionally red-tinged) flowering stems.
Scale-leaves ovate to linear-lanceolate.
Flowers numerous (often 30–50), in long
spike, each with 1 linear-lanceolate bract
often exceeding flower; no bracteoles.
Calyx shorter than corolla tube, 2-parted,
the parts lanceolate, unequally bifid,
usually well separated. Corolla wide,
yellowish, strongly suffused with red or purple
(often all salmon or pale reddish-brown),
18–25 mm long, glandular-hairy on
outside; upper lip scarcely lobed, lower lip
slightly shorter, with 3 subequal, rounded
lobes, hairy on margin. Stamens inserted
near base of corolla tube; filaments hairy at
top, but *glabrous below*. Style glandular-
hairy; *stigmas yellow*. Capsule ellipsoid,
long-pointed, with 3 weak knobs at base;
valves connate at top.

Flowering: May–July.

Habitat: Rough grassland, banks, scrub, on dry,
acid, often sandy soils; from sea level to
1,500 m. Parasitic on *Sarothamnus*, *Cytisus*,
Genista, *Ulex*.

Range: SW Europe, northwards to Ireland, Britain
(except most of Scotland), the Low
Countries, and C Germany.

The flowers have an unpleasant smell.

p.89 **Thistle Broomrape**
Orobanche reticulata Wallr.

Description: A glandular-hairy perennial, to 50 (70) cm,
with erect, unbranched, *purplish-brown*
flowering stems. Scale-leaves triangular to
lanceolate (higher up stem). Flowers
numerous (more than 20), in rather long
spike, each with 1 lanceolate bract; no
bracteoles. Calyx mostly shorter than
corolla tube, 2-parted, the parts well
separated, lanceolate, entire or (more often)
very unequally bifid. Corolla *yellowish with*

purplish veins, 20–22 mm long; upper lip has 2 short, rounded lobes, purple-tinged, with *dark-purple glandular hairs* on the back; lower lip about as long as upper lip, with 3 *subequal*, rounded lobes. Stamens inserted near base of corolla tube, or occasionally higher up (at about 1 third the tube length); filaments often slightly hairy below, often glandular at top, like style; *stigmas dark purple* (but *see* below). Valves of capsule connate at top.

Flowering: June–August.

Habitat: Arable fields and rough grassland; from sea level to 2,300 m. Parasitic on *Scabiosa*.

Range: C Europe, northwards to S Germany, S Poland and C Russia.

This description pertains to ssp. *reticulata*. Ssp. *pallidiflora* (Wimm. & Grab.) Hayek has shorter, white or yellowish flowers (corolla 16–18 mm long), with yellow stigmas, and few pale glands on (pale-violet) upper lip. In E France, the Low Countries, Denmark, parasitizing *Cirsium* and *Carduus*; apparently more common in lowland regions. (Ssp. *reticulata* is more frequent in the mountains of C Europe.) *Compare O. lutea* (*see* p.855), which has darker, larger flowers and always yellow stigmas.

---

p.314 **Germander Broomrape**
Orobanche teucrii Holandre

Description: A slender, glandular-hairy perennial, to 30 cm, with erect, unbranched, *purplish or violet* (occasionally yellowish) flowering stems. Scale-leaves narrowly lanceolate. Flowers 8–15, in short, lax spike, each with 1 short, narrowly lanceolate bract (12–20 mm long); no bracteoles. Calyx to 12 mm long, much shorter than corolla tube, 2-parted, the parts bifid with subequal teeth, free or anteriorly connate. Corolla (often very pale) *purple-violet*, 20–30 mm long, with (pale) glandular hairs on outside *and on margins; upper lip unlobed*; lower lip about as long as upper lip, with 3 subequal, rounded lobes. Stamens inserted at about 1 third the length of corolla tube;

filaments hairy below, glandular above. Style glandular-hairy; *stigmas purple*. Valves of capsule connate above.

Flowering: May–July.

Habitat: Grassland, scrub, sunny slopes, on dry, calcareous soils; from sea level to 1,800 m. Parasitic on *Teucrium* (especially *T. chamaedrys* and *T. montanum*).

Range: S and C Europe, northwards to Belgium, S Germany, Hungary and W Russia.

The flowers smell of cloves. *Compare O. caryophyllacea* (*see* p.851), which also has large flowers and purple stigmas, but stamens are inserted near base of corolla tube.

WOOD SORREL FAMILY, OXALIDACEAE

A family of herbs with *c.* 900 species in 3 genera, mainly in subtropical regions. Dicots. Leaves alternate, trifoliolate (occasionally pinnate). Flowers regular, hermaphrodite, 5-merous. Sepals 5, often partly connate. Petals 5, usually free. Stamens mostly 10 (or 5, or 15), usually connate at their bases. Ovary superior, 5-locular, with 5 styles. Fruit a capsule, rarely a berry. Many species in this family have leaves that become folded up during the night, or (in the tropical genus *Biophytum*) after being touched.

---

p.103 **Wood Sorrel** *Oxalis acetosella* L.

Description: A slightly hairy perennial, with scaly, creeping rhizomes and *thin, leafless flowering stems* (scapes) to 10 cm; scape has 2 tiny, opposite bracts around middle. Leaves long-stalked (subequalling scapes), implanted directly on rhizome, trifoliolate, with obcordate leaflets. *Flowers solitary*, 20–25 mm diam., erect to nodding. Sepals 5, obovate, 6–8 mm long, blunt-tipped. Petals 5, narrowly obovate, often slightly notched, 10–15 mm long, *white* (rarely pink or pale violet), with *reddish or purple veins*. Stamens 10. Capsule 5-locular, many-seeded, 3–4 mm long, ovate, angular, nodding.

Flowering: April–June.

Habitat: Shady, deciduous and needle-leaf woods, scrub, hedgebanks, on moist, oligotrophic, slightly acid, sandy, loamy or stony soils; from sea level to 2,000 m.

Range: Most of Europe except the high Arctic.

In strong light, rainy weather, and during the night, the leaflets become deflexed and folded.

---

p.199 **Upright Yellow Sorrel**
Oxalis fontana Bunge

Description: A slightly hairy perennial, with slender, creeping stolons and *erect or ascending, leafy flowering stems* to 30 cm. *Leaves opposite or whorled*, long-stalked, trifoliolate, with broadly obcordate leaflets; stipules absent or minute. Flowers 7–15 mm diam., in long-stalked, *2–5-flowered, axillary cymes*. Sepals 5, broadly lanceolate, 2–4 mm long. Petals 5, narrowly obovate, 4–10 mm long, *yellow*. Stamens 10. Capsule 5-locular, many-seeded, 8–12 mm long, narrowly ellipsoid, long-pointed, sparsely long-hairy, on erect or spreading stalks.

Flowering: June–October.

Habitat: Cultivated land, gardens, shaded roadsides, wood margins, hedges, on moist, eutrophic, sandy, loamy or clayey soils; from sea level to 1,200 m.

Range: Native to N America; naturalized in most of Europe, northwards to the British Isles, S Fennoscandia, and C Russia.

Similar species: **Procumbent Yellow Sorrel** (*O. corniculata* L.) is annual, with spreading or ascending, often creeping stems (but no underground stolons), stipules to 2 mm, alternate leaves, yellow, often notched petals (4–7 mm long), and densely short-hairy capsules on deflexed stalks curving upwards near the top. Native to S Europe, extending northwards to N France, Hungary, and the Ukraine; also grown for ornament (often in a form with purplish foliage), and more or less naturalized in parks and gardens of NW and NC Europe.

POPPY FAMILY, PAPAVERACEAE

A family of herbs with *c.* 650 species in 42 genera, mainly in temperate and subtropical regions of the northern hemisphere. Leaves alternate, simple or compound. Flowers hermaphrodite, regular or irregular – the genera with irregular (zygomorphic) flowers are often placed in a separate family (Fumariaceae). Sepals usually 2. Petals usually 4. Stamens 4 or 12–many, free (occasionally 6, connate into 2 bundles, in Fumariaceae). Ovary superior, 1–2-locular, or incompletely many-locular; style short or absent (in *Papaver*; then stigmas sessile, forming 'rays' on a 'stigmatic disc' at the top of the ovary). Fruit a capsule, opening with 2 valves, or with apical pores (in *Papaver*), or a small nut (in *Fumaria*). **Opium Poppy** (*Papaver somniferum* L.) from E Europe and SW Asia is cultivated for its edible seeds (poppy seed), and of course for opium; it has coarsely lobed leaves, and large, lilac or white (rarely red) flowers to 18 cm diam. Other species are grown in gardens, such as **Oriental Poppy** (*P. orientale* L.), which has equally large, red to pink or white flowers, and deeply pinnately divided, serrate leaves.

p.191 **Greater Celandine** *Chelidonium majus* L.

Description: A bluish-green, subglabrous perennial, with erect, branched stems to 90 cm, and *yellow or orange latex*. Leaves alternate, pinnately divided or pinnate, with 5–7 ovate, coarsely crenate segments or leaflets. Flowers regular, 15–25 mm diam., in long-stalked, 2–6-flowered, *axillary umbels*. Sepals 2. Petals 4, obovate, *yellow*. Stamens numerous. Capsule linear, to 50 mm long, 1-locular, glabrous, splitting with 2 valves.

Flowering: April–October.

Habitat: Open woods, shaded roadsides, hedges, on or beneath old walls, on moist to rather dry, mesotrophic to eutrophic, slightly acid to calcareous, sandy, loamy or stony soils; from sea level to 1,700 m.

Range: Most of Europe except Iceland and the high Arctic.

An old medicinal plant; the biting juice was used against warts.

p.246 **Bulbous Corydalis**
Corydalis cava (L.) Schweigg. & Koerte

Description: A subglabrous, tuberous perennial, with erect flowering stems to 20 cm; *tuber usually hollow*, rounded, to 10 cm diam. Leaves alternate, doubly ternate, with oblanceolate segments; no basal sheath. Flowers irregular, 2-lipped, 18–30 mm long, in dense, 10–20-flowered, *terminal raceme*, with small, *entire, lanceolate bracts*; flower-stalks at least 5 mm long. Sepals 2, minute. Petals 4, *purplish* (occasionally white), the outer (vertical) pair larger, connate at base and prolonged into stout, down-curved spur. Stamens 6, connate into 2 bundles. Capsule linear, to 25 mm long, 2-locular, pendent, glabrous, splitting with 2 valves.

Flowering: March–May.

Habitat: Deciduous woods, hedges, shaded road verges, vineyards, on moist, mesotrophic, preferably calcareous, sandy, loamy or stony soils; from sea level to 2,000 m.

Range: S, C and E Europe, northwards to Belgium, S Sweden, Poland, and C Russia; naturalized in parks and on estate grounds in Britain and the Netherlands.

Similar species: **Solid-tubered Corydalis** (*C. solida* (L.) Clairv.) has solid tubers to 30 mm diam., and stems with scale-like basal sheath; flowers 15–30 mm long, with palmately incised (lower) flower-bracts, and almost straight spurs. In comparable habitats, in most of Europe except Iceland and the high Arctic, both wild and naturalized.
C. intermedia (L.) Mérat has smaller flowers (10–15 mm long), in short, 2–8-flowered racemes, with entire bracts. In woods and pastures on calcareous soils, in C Europe northwards to NE France, S Fennoscandia, and N Russia.
C. pumila (Host) Rchb. also has small flowers in few-flowered racemes, but lobed bracts, and flower-stalks not exceeding 5 mm. In woods and pastures of C Europe northwards to Alsace, S Germany, S Scandinavia, Poland, and Romania.

p.84 **Climbing Corydalis**
Ceratocapnos claviculata (L.) Lidén

Description: A glabrous perennial, with branched, often
reddish, straggling to climbing stems to
1 m long. Leaves alternate, doubly pinnate,
with oblanceolate, pale-green segments;
rhachis ending in branched tendril. Flowers
irregular, 2-lipped, 5–6 (8) mm long, in
small, few-flowered, *axillary racemes*, with
small, lanceolate bracts; flower-stalks
1–2 mm long. Sepals 2, minute. Petals 4,
pale yellow or cream, the outer (vertical) pair
larger, connate at base and prolonged into
short, blunt spur. Stamens 6, connate into 2
bundles. Capsule narrowly ellipsoid, to
10 mm long, 2-locular, pendent, glabrous,
splitting with 2 valves.

Flowering: (March) June–September.

Habitat: Deciduous and needle-leaf woods, scrub,
heath, on moist to rather dry, oligotrophic,
usually acid, sandy, stony or peaty soils;
from sea level to 1,000 m.

Range: W Europe, from Portugal through W and
C France northwards to Scotland and S
Norway, and eastwards to Denmark and
NE Germany.

Similar species: **Yellow Corydalis** (*Pseudofumaria lutea* (L.)
Borckh.) is erect, without tendrils; flowers
golden yellow, 12–20 mm long, in 6–16-
flowered, terminal racemes. On rocks and
screes in S Alps and Balkan peninsula; often
escapes from gardens in W Europe.

p.84 **White Ramping-fumitory**
Fumaria capreolata L.

Description: A subglabrous annual, with branched,
straggling to clambering stems to 1 m
long; no tendrils. Leaves alternate, 2–3
times pinnately divided, with elliptical
segments. Flowers irregular, 2-lipped,
10–14 mm long, in elongating, 12–20-
flowered, long-stalked axillary racemes,
with lanceolate bracts at least equalling
flower-stalks. Sepals 2, ovate, finely serrate-
dentate, about half the length of corolla.
Petals 4, the outer (vertical) pair larger,

cream with dark-purple tip (often all pink after anthesis), connate at base and prolonged into short, blunt spur. Stamens 6, connate into 2 bundles. Fruit nut-like, rounded, to 3 mm diam., with fleshy collar at base, 1-locular, 1-seeded, glabrous, not splitting; *fruit-stalks recurved*.

Flowering: June–September.

Habitat: Cultivated and waste land, gardens, disturbed roadsides, ruderal places, hedges, old walls, on moist to rather dry, mesotrophic to eutrophic, preferably calcareous, sandy, loamy or stony soils; mainly in the lowland.

Range: S, W and C Europe, northwards to the British Isles, the Low Countries, and Poland, and as a casual further north.

Similar species: **Tall Ramping-fumitory** (*F. bastardii* Boreau) has a more erect habit, short-stalked, 15–25-flowered, rather lax racemes, smaller flowers (9–11 mm long, pink with dark-purple tips), and erect fruit-stalks. In S and W Europe, northwards to France, W Britain (Scotland) and Ireland. **Western, or Cornish Fumitory** (*F. occidentalis* Pugsley) can be erect or clambering, and has long-stalked, lax, 12–20-flowered racemes, flowers 12–14 mm long (whitish at first, turning pink, always with dark-purple tips), and erect fruit-stalks. Endemic to SW Cornwall and the Scilly Isles.

All these species have comparatively large flowers (at least 9 mm long), with laterally compressed upper petals.

---

p.246 **Common Ramping-fumitory**
Fumaria muralis Koch

Description: A subglabrous annual, with branched, straggling to clambering stems to 1 m long; no tendrils. Leaves alternate, 2–3 times pinnately divided, with elliptical segments. Flowers irregular, 2-lipped, 9–10 mm long, in elongating, 6–15-flowered, long-stalked axillary racemes, with lanceolate bracts shorter than flower-stalks. Sepals 2, ovate, finely serrate-dentate, about 1 third the length of corolla. Petals 4, the outer (vertical) pair larger, *pink with very dark, purplish-black tip*, connate at base and prolonged into short, blunt spur. Stamens 6, connate into 2 bundles. Fruit nut-like, rounded, to 2.5 mm diam., 1-locular, 1-seeded, glabrous, not splitting; *fruit-stalks straight, erect or spreading.*

Flowering: May–September.

Habitat: Cultivated and waste land, ruderal places, on dry or moist, mesotrophic, preferably calcareous, sandy, loamy or clayey soils; mainly in the lowland.

Range: SW and W Europe, northwards to the British Isles and the Low Countries.

Similar species: **Purple Ramping-fumitory** (*F. purpurea* Pugsley) has long-stalked, 15–25-flowered racemes, purple flowers (10–13 mm long) with a darker tip, and slightly curved fruit-stalks. Endemic to Britain and Ireland. **Martin's Ramping-fumitory** (*F. martinii* Clavaud) has short-stalked, 15–20-flowered racemes, pink (and purple-tipped) flowers 11–13 mm long, and subentire (or only basally dentate) sepals. In SW England, W France and Iberian peninsula.

The description of Common Ramping-fumitory pertains to ssp. *muralis*. In ssp. *boraei* (Jordan) Pugsley the flowers are 10–12 mm long, and the nuts are finely roughened; in ssp. *neglecta* Pugsley sepals are subentire. The taxonomic value of these forms is subject to doubt.

All these species have large flowers (at least 9 mm long) with rounded or rather flat (not laterally compressed) upper petals.

p.246 **Common Fumitory** *Fumaria officinalis* L.

Description: A subglabrous annual, with branched, straggling to clambering stems to 50 cm long; no tendrils. Leaves alternate, 2–3 times pinnately divided, with flat, elliptical segments. Flowers irregular, 2-lipped, 6–8 (9) mm long, in strongly elongating, 20–40-flowered, axillary racemes, with lanceolate bracts shorter than flower-stalks. Sepals 2, ovate, 1–1.5 mm wide, finely serrate-dentate, up to 1 third the length of corolla. Petals 4, the outer (vertical) pair larger, *pink with dark-purple tip*, distinctly *spatulate* with spreading wings near tip, connate at base and prolonged into short, blunt spur. Stamens 6, connate into 2 bundles. Fruit nut-like, rounded or slightly pear-shaped, to 2.5 (3) mm diam., truncate or even notched, 1-locular, 1-seeded, glabrous, slightly rough when dry, not splitting; *fruit-stalks straight, erect or spreading*.

Flowering: May–October.

Habitat: Cultivated and waste land, disturbed roadsides, ruderal places, on rather dry to moist, mesotrophic to eutrophic, slightly acid or calcareous, sandy, loamy or clayey soils; from sea level to 1,800 m.

Range: All Europe except the high Arctic; only as a casual in Iceland.

Similar species: *F. vaillantii* Loisel. has short-stalked, 5–16-flowered racemes, and minute sepals (only 0.5 mm wide, hardly more than 1 tenth the length of corolla). In arable land on calcareous soils in much of Europe, northwards to England, Belgium, Germany, the Baltic States, and C Russia. *F. schleicheri* Soyer-Willemet also has tiny sepals, but 12–20-flowered racemes at least as long as their stalk. In arable land and gardens in S and C Europe, northwards to E France, S Germany, S Poland, and C Russia.

Dense-flowered Fumitory (*F. densiflora* DC.) has linear, channelled leaf-segments, distinctly stalked, 20–25-flowered racemes, subentire sepals at least 1 quarter the length of the (pink, purple-tipped) corolla, and bracts exceeding fruit-stalks. In arable land in S and W Europe, northwards to Ireland, Britain and Belgium.

Fine-leaved Fumitory (*F. parviflora* Lamk.) also has linear, channelled leaf-segments, but almost unstalked, 10–20-flowered racemes, flowers with minute sepals and whitish, purple-tipped petals, and bracts just equalling fruit-stalks. In arable land on calcareous soils in S and C

Europe, northwards to England, N France (extinct in Belgium), Germany, Hungary and W Russia.

Common Fumitory is a variable species. Plants with small flowers (6 mm long) and 10–20-flowered racemes are distinguished as ssp. *wirtgenii* (Koch) Arc. Another form (*F. caroliana* Pugsley) has short-stalked, 10–15-flowered racemes, and shortly pointed nuts; in cultivated land, in the vicinity of Arras in N France only.

All these species have small, spatulate flowers (up to 8 mm in length).

---

p.190 **Yellow Horned-poppy**
Glaucium flavum Crantz

Description: A bluish-green, slightly fleshy annual, biennial or short-lived perennial, with erect, subglabrous, branched stems to 60 cm, and *yellow latex*. Leaves alternate, rough-hairy, pinnately divided with coarsely dentate segments; lower leaves long-stalked; upper ones sessile and clasping. Flowers regular, 60–80 mm diam., solitary, terminal. Sepals 2, falling. Petals 4, rounded, *yellow*. Stamens numerous. Capsule linear, *15–30 cm long*, 2-locular, smooth or warty, hairless, splitting with 2 valves.

Flowering: June–September.

Habitat: Floodmarks, shingle-beaches, sea-cliffs, sea-dunes (often in ruderal places), on moist to dry, brackish, often calcareous, sandy or stony soils; only coastal.

Range: S and W Europe, northwards to the British Isles, the Low Countries and S Norway (Oslo), but ephemerous in the north.

---

p.190 **Welsh Poppy** *Meconopsis cambrica* (L.) Vig.

Description: A slightly hairy perennial, with erect, subglabrous, branched stems to 60 cm, and *yellow latex*. Leaves alternate, pinnately divided with ovate, serrate-dentate segments; lower leaves long-stalked, upper ones subsessile. Flowers regular, 30–40

(80) mm diam., solitary on long stalks in upper leaf-axils. Sepals 2, hairy, soon falling. Petals 4, rounded, *yellow*. Stamens numerous. Style short, with 4–6-lobed stigma. Capsule narrowly ellipsoid, *20–40 mm long*, glabrous, opening apically with 4–6 short valves.

Flowering: June–August.
Habitat: Woods, shaded verges, hedgebanks, stream-sides, also walls, on moist, oligotrophic, sandy or rocky soils; from sea level to 2,000 m, but mainly in the mountains.
Range: SW Europe, from Spain northwards through W and C France to SW Britain and Ireland.

Frequently cultivated in gardens, and locally naturalized in N England.

---

p.244 **Prickly Poppy** *Papaver argemone* L.

Description: A bristly-hairy annual, with erect, branched stems to 45 cm. Leaves alternate, stalked to subsessile, doubly pinnately divided with lanceolate, shortly pointed segments. Flowers regular, (2) 30–60 mm diam., solitary on long stalks in upper leaf-axils. Sepals 2, hairy, soon falling. Petals 4, rounded, *pale scarlet*, often with black base, and barely overlapping at full anthesis. Stamens numerous; *filaments widened* towards top; anthers bluish-grey. Style absent; stigmas connate to dome-shaped disc with 4–6 stigmatic rays. *Capsule club-shaped*, 15–20 mm long, with sparse, *upcurved bristle-hairs*, and opening apically with 4–6 pores under stigmatic disc.

Flowering: May–July.
Habitat: Arable (often cereal) fields, roadsides, disturbed places, also railways, on dry, mesotrophic, sandy or loamy soils; from sea level to 1,500 m.
Range: Most of Europe except Iceland and the high Arctic; an archeotype, originating from S Europe.
Similar species: **Rough Poppy** (*P. hybridum* L.) has deep-crimson, overlapping petals, and strongly bristly-hairy, subglobose capsules to 15 mm long, with 4–8 stigmatic rays. In arable

fields and disturbed places on calcareous soils; native to S Europe, SW Asia and N Africa, naturalized in C and N Europe, northwards to England, S Norway, Poland, and W Russia.

p.244 **Long-headed Poppy** *Papaver dubium* L.

Description: A hairy annual, with erect, branched stems to 60 cm, and white latex. Leaves alternate, stalked to subsessile, pinnately divided with lanceolate, entire to serrate segments. Flowers regular, 30–70 mm diam., solitary on long stalks in upper leaf-axils. Sepals 2, hairy, soon falling. Petals 4, rounded, *pale to deep scarlet* (rarely with black base), and distinctly overlapping at full anthesis. Stamens numerous; filaments threadlike, not widened towards top; anthers purplish-violet. Style absent; stigmas connate to dome-shaped disc with (5) 7–9 *greenish or brown stigmatic rays*. *Capsule club-shaped*, 15–20 mm long, *glabrous*, opening apically with (5) 7–9 pores under stigmatic disc.

Flowering: June–August.

Habitat: Cultivated and waste land, roadsides, ruderal places, on dry or moist, mesotrophic, preferably sandy soils; from sea level to 1,800 m.

Range: Most of Europe except Iceland and the high Arctic.

Similar species: **Yellow-juiced**, or **Babington's**, **Poppy** (*P. lecoqii* Lamotte; also treated as a variety) has brown or yellow anthers, and the latex turns yellow upon contact with air. In arable fields on calcareous soils in England, Belgium and N France, and (very locally) eastwards to Austria and Greece.
Common Poppy (*P. rhoeas* L.) has leaves with distinctly enlarged end-lobe, flowers to 10 cm diam., scarlet (rarely pink or white) petals usually with black base, deep blackish-purple anthers, and (broadly) obovoid capsules with (6) 8–13 stigmatic rays. In cultivated and waste land, roadsides, ruderal places, on dry or moist, mesotrophic to eutrophic, preferably clayey soils, in most of Europe except Iceland and the high Arctic.

p.190 **Arctic Poppy** *Papaver radicatum* Rottb.

Description: A hairy *perennial*, with erect or ascending, unbranched flowering stems to 25 cm, and white or yellow latex; stems covered with *spreading hairs*. Leaves mostly basal, stalked, *pinnately lobed* (not deeply divided) with ovate, *acute lobes*. Flowers regular, 30–50 mm diam., solitary on long, leafless stalks rising from basal leaf-tufts. Sepals 2, hairy, soon falling. Petals 4, rounded, *yellow* (rarely white or pinkish). Stamens numerous; anthers yellow. Style absent; stigmas connate to dome-shaped disc with *5 stigmatic rays*. *Capsule pear-shaped to subglobose*, 10–20 mm long, *densely hairy*, opening apically with 5 pores under stigmatic disc.

Flowering: June–August.

Habitat: Tundra, screes and moraines, on dry to moist, oligotrophic, sandy, gravelly or rocky soils; from sea level to 1,850 m.

Range: Scandinavia, Iceland and the Faeroes.

Similar species: **Lapland Poppy** (*P. lapponicum* (Tolm.) Nordh.) has yellow latex, slightly larger flowers on appressed-hairy stalks, and narrower, blunt-tipped lobes to leaves. In comparable habitats of Arctic Norway and N Russia.

P. dahlianum Nordh., in the same area, has white latex and yellow or white flowers.

Arctic Poppy is an extremely variable species.

PLANTAIN FAMILY, PLANTAGINACEAE

A family of herbs or half-shrubs, with *c.* 265 species in 3 genera, mostly in temperate regions of both hemispheres. Dicots. Leaves simple, alternate or opposite, or all basal. Flowers regular, hermaphrodite or unisexual, often in spikes or heads, basically 4-merous, with 4 (but occasionally 2 or 3) partly connate sepals and 4 connate, membranous petals, the latter occasionally absent in female flowers. Stamens 4 (but sometimes only 1or 2), usually inserted on corolla tube, far-protruding. Ovary superior, (1) 2–4-locular, with 1 style and 1 simple stigma. Fruit a capsule, dehiscing transversely (in *Plantago*), or an indehiscent, 1-seeded achene (in *Littorella*).

p.96 Shoreweed *Littorella uniflora* (L.) Aschers.

Description: A glabrous, usually *aquatic* perennial, with long, creeping stolons. Leaves all basal, *linear, awl-shaped*, semicircular in transverse section, channelled towards base, sheathing, up to 10 cm long, entire-margined. *Flowers unisexual*, monoecious, 4–6 mm long; often a solitary male flower and 2–3 female flowers together in axillary inflorescence. Male flower rises from basal leaf-tuft on *threadlike stalk* (to 8 cm) with a few *minute scale-leaves* along its length), with 3–4 basally connate, lanceolate sepals, a 4-lobed, whitish corolla, and 4 far-protruding, *free stamens*; corolla tube about equalling calyx. *Female flowers sessile* at base of stalk of male flower, with 3–4-parted calyx; *corolla flask-shaped*, whitish, tightly. enveloping (1-locular) ovary; style to 10 mm long. Fruit an *ellipsoid, 1-seeded achene*.

Flowering: June–August.

Habitat: Very shallow, slightly acid to basic water, or mud at margin lake and pond margins, fens, dune-slacks, on oligotrophic, sandy or peaty soils; mainly in the lowland.

Range: W and C Europe, northwards to Iceland and C Fennoscandia, and eastwards to NW Russia and Romania, but local.

The plant can form submerged, non-flowering mats in water depths up to 4 m; flowering occurs only when the mud becomes exposed during summer. A rare and declining species in most parts of its range.

---

p.43 Branched Plantain
Plantago arenaria Waldst. & Kit.

Description: A hairy annual to 50 cm, with ascending to erect, *branched stems. Leaves all cauline, opposite or whorled*, linear, flat (not fleshy), 10–50 mm long, (sub)entire. Flowers hermaphrodite, in stalked, *ovate to subglobose*, headlike, *axillary spikes*; basal flower-bracts in each spike long-pointed, upper ones blunt-tipped. Calyx 4-parted; outer segments obovate, inner ones much smaller, lanceolate. Corolla *c.* 4 mm diam., whitish or straw-coloured, with 4 equal, spreading lobes. Stamens 4, far-protruding. Ovary 2-locular. Fruit an ovoid, pointed, 2-seeded capsule, shedding apical lid.

Flowering: May–September.

Habitat: Arable fields, open grassland, riversides, ruderal or disturbed places, roadsides and railways, on dry to moist, oligotrophic, calcareous, sandy or gravelly soils; mainly in the lowland.

Range: S, C and E Europe, and locally naturalized in W Europe.

Similar species: *P. afra* L. from S Europe has subequal, short-pointed floral bracts, all shorter than flowers; a casual in W Europe.

---

p.42 **Buck's-horn Plantain** *Plantago coronopus* L.

Description: A hairy or subglabrous perennial (rarely annual), with *spreading leaf-rosette* and simple, cylindrical, spreading to ascending flowering stems to 30 cm. Leaves lanceolate, to 20 cm long, (doubly) *pinnately divided* with opposite, lanceolate segments (but occasionally only remotely dentate to subentire, linear), more or less fleshy, with *1 main vein*. Flowers hermaphrodite, in abruptly ascending, cylindrical, terminal spikes to 40 mm long, 6–8 mm wide; floral bracts pointed, spreading. Calyx 4-parted. Corolla straw-coloured, *c.* 3 mm diam., with 4 equal lobes; corolla-tube hairy at base. Stamens 4, far-protruding. Ovary usually 3-locular. Fruit an ovoid capsule containing 3–6 oblong seeds to 1 mm long, and shedding apical lid.

Flowering: May–September.

Habitat: Open grassland, roadsides, coastal cliffs and sea-walls, also shingle-beaches and highest parts of saltmarshes, on dry to moist, mesotrophic, calcareous or saline, usually sandy soils; mainly in the lowland.

Range: S and W Europe, and inland near saline pools in the steppe belt of SE Europe.

Plants with subentire, fleshy, subglabrous leaves are more frequent in coastal habitats. *Compare P. maritima*, which always has linear, fleshy leaves, and larger seeds.

p.43 **Ribwort Plantain** *Plantago lanceolata* L.

Description: A hairy or subglabrous perennial, with a *more or less erect leaf-rosette* and simple, cylindrical, *distinctly grooved, erect flowering stems* to 30 (50) cm. Leaves (narrowly) oblanceolate to almost linear, narrowed into short stalk, to 20 (30) cm long, subentire, with *3–5 parallel main veins*. Flowers hermaphrodite, in short, cylindrical, terminal spikes to 20 mm long, *c.* 7 mm wide. Calyx 3-parted (2 outer segments connate). Corolla whitish or straw-coloured, *c.* 4 mm diam., with 4 equal lobes; corolla-tube glabrous. Stamens 4, far-protruding, *whitish or cream*. Ovary usually 2-locular. Fruit an ovoid, 2-seeded capsule, shedding apical lid.

Flowering: May–October.

Habitat: Grassland, roadsides, banks, on moist to rather dry, mesotrophic, slightly acid to calcareous, sandy, loamy or clayey soils; from sea level to 2,000 m.

Range: Most of Europe, except the high Arctic.

Similar species: **Hoary Plantain** (*P. media* L.) has more spreading, broadly lanceolate to elliptical, 7–9-veined leaves, much shorter than (striped, but not grooved) flowering stems; flowers whitish, *c.* 2 mm diam., in spikes to 6 (10) cm long; stamens pink or lilac; capsules 2-locular, with 2–4 (6) seeds. In comparable, grassy habitats, on calcareous soils, in the same general area. *Compare P. major* ssp. *pleiosperma*, which has long-stalked, dentate leaves.

---

p.43 **Greater Plantain** *Plantago major* L.

Description: A hairy or subglabrous perennial (rarely annual), with *more or less spreading leaf-rosette* and simple, cylindrical, *distinctly grooved, erect flowering stems* to 30 (50) cm. Leaves broadly ovate to suborbicular, abruptly narrowed into rather long stalk, to 20 (30) cm long, subentire, with *(3) 5–9 (11) parallel (arched) main veins*, and numerous reticulate, minor veins in between. Flowers hermaphrodite, in cylindrical, terminal spikes to 15 (30) cm long, *c.* 8 mm wide, usually longer than stem. Calyx 4-parted, cup-shaped, persistent, with membranous margins. Corolla straw-coloured, *c.* 3 mm diam., with 4 equal lobes; corolla-tube glabrous. Stamens 4, far-protruding, *whitish*. Ovary 2-locular. Fruit an ovoid capsule containing 4–15 (on average 8) seeds, shedding apical lid.

Flowering: May–November (winter).

Habitat: Open grassland, roadsides, ruderal places, often on much-trampled places, on dry to moist, mesotrophic to (very) eutrophic, sandy or clayey soils; from sea level to 2,300 m.

Range: All Europe except the high Arctic.

The plant is very tolerant of trampling, and can even be found growing between paving stones of quiet backstreets. The description above pertains to ssp. *major*, which is very common. In ssp. *pleiosperma* Pilger the leaves are narrower (ovate), distinctly and irregularly dentate, more gradually narrowed into long stalk, with 3–5 (7) main veins; spikes rather lax; capsules have 12–26 (on average 16) seeds. In arable fields, open grassland, riversides and dune-slacks, on moist, sandy or clayey, often saline soils in most of Europe, usually in less trampled, more 'natural' habitats. *Compare also P. media* (*see* p.874), which has short-stalked, subentire leaves, pink stamens, and rarely more than 4 seeds per capsule.

---

p.43 **Sea Plantain** *Plantago maritima* L.

Description: A subglabrous perennial (rarely annual), with *spreading leaf-rosette* and simple, cylindrical, ascending flowering stems to 30 (60) cm. *Leaves linear*, to 20 cm long, entire or with few minor teeth, pronouncedly *fleshy*, with *3–5 main veins*. Flowers hermaphrodite, in cylindrical, terminal spikes to 60 mm long, 6–8 mm wide; floral bracts ovate, erect. Calyx 4-parted. Corolla straw-coloured, *c.* 3 mm diam., with 4 equal lobes; corolla-tube hairy at base. Stamens 4, protruding. Ovary 2-locular. Fruit an ovoid capsule containing 2 oblong seeds (these 2–2.5 mm long), shedding apical lid.

Flowering: May–September.
Habitat: Saltmarshes, coastal grassland, brackish reedlands, sea-walls, on wet, saline, sandy or clayey soils; also in saline habitats inland, and along mountain streams, to 2,400 m.
Range: Along the coasts of Europe, northwards to Iceland and the White Sea; locally inland in C Europe.

Compare P. coronopus, which (in forms with linear leaves) has only 1 main vein, and differs further in having pointed, spreading floral bracts, and smaller seeds.

SEA-LAVENDER FAMILY, PLUMBAGINACEAE

A family of herbs or shrubs with *c.* 500 species in 10 genera world-wide, often in deserts or saline habitats. Dicots. Leaves simple, alternate; in N European species, always in basal rosette. Flowers regular, 5-merous, hermaphrodite, in loose panicles (as in *Limonium*) or compact flowerheads (as in *Armeria*). Calyx 5-toothed, usually membranous, persistent in fruit. Corolla 5-lobed. Stamens 5, opposite to corolla lobes, inserted on corolla tube. Ovary superior, 1-locular, with 5 styles (or 1 style with 5 stigmas). Fruit a capsule or achene.

---

p.291 **Thrift** *Armeria maritima* (Miller) Willd.

Description: A hairy perennial, with dense basal leaf-rosettes, forming cushions on branched, more or less woody, vertical rhizome; flowering stems leafless, erect, cylindrical, to 30 cm. *Leaves linear*, to 10 cm long, 2 mm wide, entire-margined, with 1 vein. Flowers in solitary, subglobose (hemispherical), terminal *flowerheads to 25 mm diam.*, with involucre of *blunt-tipped or short-pointed bracts* (scarious, with green midrib), and deflexed, *brownish sheath to 30 mm long* (enveloping stem). Calyx has long tube and 5 narrowly triangular, short-awned teeth, and is hairy at least on ribs. Corolla trumpet-shaped, with 5 short lobes, pink or pale lilac (rarely purple or white). Fruit a blunt, cylindrical or club-shaped achene to 4 mm long, falling with calyx.
Flowering: May–October.

Habitat: Higher parts of saltmarshes (often on levees along tidal gullies), brackish grassland, 'green' beaches, sea-walls, coastal cliffs, on dry to rather wet, saline, sandy, clayey or stony soils; also inland in mountain grassland (to 2,900 m), and on metal-bearing soils.

Range: Most of Europe except the high Arctic.

Similar species: **Jersey Thrift** (*A. alliacea* (Cav.) Hoffm. & Link) has linear-oblanceolate, 3–7-veined leaves (4–8 mm wide), long-pointed involucral bracts, long-awned calyx teeth, and a longer sheath under the flowerhead; it occurs in dry, sandy grassland and dunes of SW Europe, northwards to Jersey, N France and SW Germany.

The description of Thrift pertains to ssp. *maritima*, which represents the common coastal form. Several other subspecies occur in Arctic regions and in the mountains of C Europe (*see* regional floras).

---

p.287 **Matted Sea-lavender**
Limonium bellidifolium (Gouan) Dumort.

Description: A glabrous perennial, with dense basal leaf-rosette, and more or less spreading, much-branched flowering stems to 50 cm. Leaves all basal, spatulate to oblanceolate, to 70 mm long, 20 mm wide, entire-margined, with *3 parallel main veins*, and usually withered by flowering time. Flowers in rather lax, 1-sided spikes (to 20 mm long) composing large panicles with *many non-flowering branches* in lower half; each flower subtended by 3 small, *largely membranous bracts*. Calyx white, with brownish ribs, long tube and 5 triangular teeth. Petals 3–4 mm long, oblanceolate, connate at base, pale lilac. Fruit an achene, irregularly dehiscent.

Flowering: July–August.

Habitat: Coastal saltmarshes, on moist to wet, saline, sandy soils.

Range: SW Europe, northwards to W France (Bay of Biscay) and E Anglia.

Forms from S Europe have shorter, denser spikes (to 10 mm); the northern forms are often treated as a separate species (*L. dubyi* (Gren. & Godron) O. Kuntze).

p.287 **Rock Sea-lavender**
Limonium binervosum (Sm.) Salmon

Description: A glabrous perennial, with dense basal leaf-rosette, and *erect, branched flowering stems* to 40 cm. Leaves all basal, spatulate, 4–12 cm long, 10–30 mm wide, narrowed into flat, broadly winged stalk, often glaucous, entire-margined, with 1–3 parallel main veins. Flowers in 1-sided spikes (to 20 mm long) composing panicles *lacking non-flowering branches* in lower half; each flower subtended by 3 small bracts with narrow membranous margins. Calyx white, with brownish ribs, long tube and 5 blunt, triangular-ovate teeth. Petals 4–7 mm long, connate at base, bluish-violet or lilac. Fruit an oblong, blunt achene.

Flowering: July–September.

Habitat: Sea-cliffs, shingle-beaches, highest parts of saltmarshes, on moist to wet, sandy or stony soils.

Range: SW Europe, northwards to NW France (Cap Gris Nez) and S Britain (to Lincolnshire).

Similar species: *L. paradoxum* Pugsley has short, 1-veined leaves (to 45 mm), and short spikes in narrow panicles. Endemic to Wales (Pembrokeshire) and NW Ireland. Other endemic forms with very compact panicles have been described as *L. recurvum* Salmon (with spatulate, blunt-tipped leaves; Portland, Dorset) and *L. transwallianum* (Pugsley) Pugsley (with oblanceolate, acute leaves; Wales and W Ireland).

Jersey Sea-lavender (*L. auriculae-ursifolium* (Pourret) Druce) is a stouter plant, with 3–7-veined, greyish-green leaves, sticky, channelled leaf-stalks, arching spikes, and red (inner) bracts to flowers. On sea-cliffs in W France and the Channel Islands.

L. ovalifolium (Poiret) O. Kuntze, from the coast of W France, has acute, 3–5-veined leaves, smaller flowers (to 4 mm long) in very short spikes (5–10 mm) composing widely branched panicle.

Rock Sea-lavender is a complex, polymorphic species, often further divided into *L. occidentalis* Lloyd (with narrow, 1-veined leaves) and *L. dodartii* (Girard) O. Kuntze (with wider, 3-veined leaves).

p.287 **Common Sea-lavender** *Limonium vulgare* L.

Description: A glabrous perennial with dense basal leaf-rosette, and *erect, rounded or bluntly angular, branched flowering stems* to 50 cm. Leaves all basal, narrowly elliptical to spatulate, blunt-tipped to subacute (and often short-pointed), 10–15 (20) cm long, 20–30 (60) mm wide, narrowed into broadly winged stalk, erect, often glaucous, entire-margined, with 1 midvein and several minor side-veins (so *pinnately veined*). Flowers in *erect spikelets* to 6 mm long, close together in *1-sided spikes* (to 50 mm long) at end of (arching) branches of inflorescence, which is a dense, umbel-shaped panicle; each spikelet subtended by 3 small, greenish bracts (outer ones rounded). Calyx has long tube, 5 acute, triangular teeth, and *5 minute, accessory teeth in sinuses* in between. Petals 6–8 mm long, connate at base, purplish-red to blue-violet. Fruit a cylindrical achene to 5 mm long.

Flowering: July–October.

Habitat: Coastal saltmarshes, sea-walls, on wet, saline, often clayey soils. The plant can form large colonies, especially on levees of tidal gullies.

Range: W Europe, northwards to Britain and S Sweden, and eastwards to Poland; only coastal.

Similar species: **Lax-flowered Sea-lavender** (*L. humile* Miller) has stiffly erect, solitary or paired spikelets to 10 mm long (with keeled outer floral bracts), well spaced along (erect-arching) branches of inflorescence, which is a loosely branched panicle on relatively short, distinctly angular stem. In saltmarshes of NW Europe, southwards to NW France and England, and W Baltic region.

L. × neumanii Salmon is the hybrid between both species.

JACOB'S-LADDER FAMILY, POLEMONIACEAE

A family of herbs and shrubs with *c.* 300 species in 18 genera in the northern hemisphere and S America. Dicots. Leaves alternate or opposite, simple or compound. Flowers usually regular, hermaphrodite, 5-merous, in panicles or cymes (occasionally condensed into flowerheads). Sepals and petals connate (at least at base). Stamens 5, alternating with corolla lobes, inserted on corolla tube. Ovary superior, usually 3-locular, with a trifid style. Fruit a capsule. Several species are cultivated in gardens, especially members of the American genera *Phlox*, *Gilia*, *Cobaea*, and *Collomia*.

---

p.339 **Jacob's-ladder** *Polemonium caeruleum* L.

Description: An erect perennial, to 90 cm, with hollow, angular, branched stems, glandular-hairy above. Leaves alternate, lanceolate, pinnate, with 13–25 narrowly ovate, entire-margined, glabrous leaflets; lower leaves stalked, to 40 cm long, upper ones (sub)sessile, much smaller. Flowers 20–30 mm diam., in small, dense, long-stalked, terminal panicles. Calyx has 5 broadly lanceolate teeth. Corolla tube short, with 5 spreading, broadly ovate, often slightly pointed lobes, violet-blue (rarely white). Stamens 5, with yellow anthers; filaments hairy at base. Ovary 3-locular, with 1 style and 3 stigmas. Capsule globose, many-seeded, opening with 3 valves.

Flowering: May–August.

Habitat: Grassland, scrub, cliffs and screes, stream-sides, on moist, oligotrophic, often calcareous, sandy or stony soils; from 600–2,000 m.

Range: Sweden, S Finland and N and C Russia, also the Pyrenees and the mountains of C Europe; locally naturalized in W Europe.

Similar species: *P. acutifolium* Willd. has up to 17 leaflets, and smaller, bell-shaped flowers with finely hairy, markedly pointed corolla lobes. In scrub and streamsides in (sub)Arctic Fennoscandia and N Russia.
P. boreale Adams. has all leaves basal (occasionally 1 cauline), with up to 17 hairy leaflets; flowers bell-shaped, to 16 mm

diam., with glabrous, rounded corolla lobes.
In comparable habitats in Arctic Norway
and N Russia, including Spitsbergen.

MILKWORT FAMILY, POLYGALACEAE

A family of herbs, shrubs and trees, with *c.* 1,000 species in
17 genera world-wide, mainly in warm regions. Dicots.
Leaves simple, usually alternate, entire. Flowers irregular
(zygomorphic), usually hermaphrodite, basically 5-merous,
solitary or in racemes (occasionally in panicles or head-like
clusters). Sepals 5; outer 3 small and green, inner, lateral
ones ('wings') much larger, coloured (petaloid). Petals
usually 3; lower one ('keel') much larger and with fringed
appendage at tip, upper ones basally connate to keel (but not
to each other). Stamens usually 8–10, inserted on corolla,
the filaments connate into a dorsally open tube. Ovary
superior, usually 2-locular, with 1 style and 1 stigma. Fruit a
small, 2-locular capsule, with 1 seed in each locule. In
Europe only the genus *Polygala* is represented; in most
species, flower colour is extremely variable.

p.337 Dwarf Milkwort *Polygala amarella* Crantz

Description: A (sub)glabrous, bitter-tasting perennial, to
20 cm (often less), with *basal leaf-rosette at
ground level*, and ascending to erect, more or
less branched, leafy flowering stems. Stem-
leaves alternate, subsessile, to 10 mm long,
(broadly) lanceolate or narrowly elliptical,
subacute, entire-margined. Flowers 3–4
(5) mm long, in 8–25-flowered, terminal
racemes, short-stalked, with tiny, lanceolate
bracts; no tuft of bracts at top of
inflorescence. Wings and petals blue, violet,
pink, greenish or white; keel has white
fringe; *veins of wings have open endings*.
Capsule strongly compressed, obovate, 2-
seeded, 3–4 mm long.

Flowering: May–August.
Habitat: Grassland, on moist to rather dry,
oligotrophic, calcareous, sandy, loamy or
stony soils; from near sea level to 2,600 m.
Range: In Europe northwards to Britain, Belgium,
S Fennoscandia and NC Russia.
Similar species: **Chalk Milkwort** (*P. calcarea* F.W. Schultz)
does not taste bitter, and has obovate basal

leaves in rosette at end of thin stolons (often distinctly raised above ground), and linear-lanceolate stem-leaves; flowers larger (5–6 mm long), with lateral veins of wings running back into midvein; capsules 4–6 mm long. In short grassland on calcareous soils, from sea level to 1,200 m, in SW Europe, northwards to S England, N France and SW Germany.

---

p.337 **Thyme-leaved Milkwort**
Polygala serpyllifolia Hose

Description: A (sub)glabrous perennial to 10 (35) cm, with threadlike, erect flowering stems; no basal leaf-rosette. *Lower stem-leaves opposite*; higher ones alternate, subsessile, to 10 mm long, oblanceolate or elliptical, acute, entire-margined. Flowers 4–6 mm long, *3–6 (10) together in lax, terminal racemes,* short-stalked, with tiny, lanceolate bracts; no tuft of bracts at top of inflorescence. Wings and petals often blue, occasionally violet, pink or white; keel has white fringe; *lateral veins of wings run back into midvein,* but also has branchings ending blind near leaf-margin. Capsule strongly compressed, obovate, 2-seeded, 3–4.5 mm long.

Flowering: May–September.

Habitat: Poor grassland, heaths, on wet to moist, oligotrophic, acid, sandy or peaty soils; from sea level to 1,800 m.

Range: W and C Europe, northwards to the British Isles, W Norway, Denmark, and eastwards to E Germany and N Yugoslavia.

---

p.337 **Common Milkwort** *Polygala vulgaris* L.

Description: A (sub)glabrous perennial, to 20 (35) cm, with branched, lignified rhizome and ascending to erect flowering stems. *Leaves all alternate,* subsessile, to 15 mm long, (broadly) lanceolate or narrowly elliptical, acute, entire-margined. Flowers 6–8 mm long, in 10–40-flowered, terminal racemes, short-stalked, with *tiny, lanceolate bracts* (1–2 mm long, at best equalling flower-stalk); *no tuft of bracts* at top of inflorescence. Wings and petals often blue or violet, occasionally pink or white; keel has white fringe; flowers often turn green after anthesis; lateral *veins of wings run back into midvein*. Capsule strongly compressed, obovate, 2-seeded, equalling persistent sepals.

Flowering: May–July (September).

Habitat: Poor grassland, dunes, heaths, roadsides, on dry to moist, oligotrophic, slightly acid or calcareous, sandy or stony soils; from sea level to 2,200 m.

Range: Most of Europe except Iceland and the high Arctic.

Similar species: **Tufted Milkwort (*P. comosa* Schkuhr)** has smaller, usually pink or lilac flowers (4–6 mm long); flower-bracts to 5 mm long, distinctly exceeding flower-stalks, and sticking out from between buds at top of inflorescence, forming small tuft; veins of wings have open endings. In dry, calcareous grassland, in continental Europe, northwards to the Low Countries, S Sweden, and N Russia.

DOCK FAMILY, POLYGONACEAE

A subcosmopolitan family of herbs and shrubs, with *c.* 750 species in some 30 genera world-wide. Dicots. Stems often knotted. Leaves alternate, simple, stalked; base of leaf-stalk clasping stem with membranous sheath ('ochrea'), derived from (connate) stipules. Flowers regular, unisexual or hermaphrodite, in racemes, panicles, axillary clusters, or solitary, with (2) 3–6 often inconspicuous perianth parts. Stamens 4–12. Ovary superior, 1-locular, with 2–4 free or partly connate styles. Fruit a 1-seeded achene, usually surrounded by persistent perianth.

---

p.121 **Buckwheat** *Fagopyrum esculentum* Moench

Description: A glabrous annual, with erect, branched, hollow, slightly knotted, often reddish stem to 70 cm. Leaves stalked, alternate, *cordate to triangular*, often slightly hastate, (sub)entire, dull green; ochrea short. Flowers hermaphrodite, *4–5 mm diam.*, in leafy panicles. Perianth parts 5, petaloid, *greenish-white or pale pink*. Stamens 8. Styles 3, free. Achene 5–6 mm long, ovoid or ellipsoid, *sharply trigonal, smooth-edged*, much exceeding perianth, which does not develop wings or keels.

Flowering: June–September.

Habitat: Cultivated and waste land, roadsides, ruderal places, on moist to rather dry, oligotrophic to mesotrophic, often acid, sandy or peaty soils; from sea level to 1,200 m.

Range: Probably native to C Asia; more or less naturalized in most of Europe except Ireland, Iceland and the high Arctic.

Similar species: *F. tataricum* (L.) Gaertner, also from C Asia, grows taller, and has green stems, pale-green leaves, and greenish flowers only 2–3 mm diam.; achene toothed on angles. Formerly a weed in buckwheat or potato fields, now more often a casual in ruderal places, occasionally naturalized, especially in E Europe and in the sea-dunes of NW Germany and the Baltic region.

Buckwheat is cultivated for the seeds, though less frequently than in former centuries when large tracts of peatland were sown with it (usually after earthing up with richer topsoil).

---

p.71 **Mountain Sorrel** *Oxyria digyna* (L.) Hill

Description: A glabrous perennial, with erect, branched, almost leafless, often reddish flowering stems to 30 cm, and basal rosette of long-stalked, *suborbicular or reniform*, cordate-based, *subentire leaves*. Flowers hermaphrodite, 2–3 mm diam., clustered in long racemes composing rather dense, *leafless panicle*. Perianth parts 4, greenish. Stamens 6. Styles 2, short. Achene pendent, 4–5 mm long, at least as wide, *strongly compressed*, with *2 broad, red-edged wings*; inner perianth parts applied to fruit, 2 outer ones reflexed, remaining smaller.

Flowering: June–August.

Habitat: Streamsides, rock-ledges, on wet or moist, oligotrophic, acid, often rocky soils; from sea level (in the north) to 3,500 m (in C and S Europe).

Range: Arctic Europe (including Iceland and Spitsbergen), southwards to N Britain, W Ireland, and in high mountains of C and S Europe.

---

p.285 **Amphibious Bistort**
Polygonum amphibium L.

Description: An *aquatic or terrestrial* perennial, with tough, usually branched, reddish, creeping rhizomes. Stems trailing, submerged, to 1.5 m long (aquatic forms), erect or ascending to 50 cm (land forms). Leaves alternate, in aquatic forms long-stalked, *lanceolate with rounded or slightly cordate base*, entire, glabrous, floating at water surface, 6–15 cm long; in land forms rather short-stalked, smaller, narrower, rough-hairy; leaf-stalks departing from upper half of truncate, entire-margined ochrea (which is hairy in land forms). Flowers hermaphrodite, 4 mm long, clustered in ovoid to shortly cylindrical, *terminal spikes* to 50 mm long, 10 mm wide, emergent in aquatic forms. Perianth parts 5, pink. Stamens mostly 5. Styles 2; stigmas button-shaped. Achene triangular, 2–3.5 mm long, blackish.

Flowering: June–October.

Habitat: Shallow pools and lake margins, ditches, canals, road verges, ruderal places, on wet to moist or even rather dry, mesotrophic to (very) eutrophic, acid or basic, sandy, muddy or clayey soils; from sea level to 2,200 m.

Range: All Europe except Spitsbergen.

The land forms are rarely found flowering, especially in drier habitats.

---

p.97 **Knotgrass** *Polygonum aviculare* L.

Description: A (sub)glabrous annual, with tough, branched, ascending stems to 1 (2) m. Leaves alternate, narrowly obovate or elliptical to linear-lanceolate, narrowed into short stalk, entire, glabrous, 10–40 mm long, *those on main stems distinctly larger* than those on flowering side-branches; leaf-stalks partly enveloped by base of ochrea, which is membranous, silvery white, 2–5 mm long, bifid or (in the end) raggedly incised, (often obscurely) 4–6-veined. Flowers hermaphrodite, 2–3 mm long, up to 5 mm diam., sessile, (1) 2–4 (6) together *in axillary clusters* along branches. Perianth parts 5, *greenish with narrow* (to 0.4 mm wide), *whitish or pink margin*. Stamens mostly 5. Styles 2; stigmas button-shaped. Achene ovoid, trigonal, pointed, *2.5–3.5 mm long, dull dark brown or blackish*, just equalling persistent perianth.

Flowering: May–November (winter).

Habitat: Cultivated and waste land, open grassland, roadsides, footpaths and pavements, walls, also shell-heaps and floodmarks, on dry or moist, eutrophic, sandy, loamy or stony soils; from sea level to 2,300 m.

Range: All Europe, but only naturalized in the extreme north.

Knotgrass is a very common, but also very complex species, often split into several microspecies; however, intermediate forms make the separation difficult. In addition to *P. aviculare* s.s. (as described above), the following microspecies can be found in the area. **Equal-leaved Knotgrass** (*P. arenastrum* Boreau) has very prostrate, matted habit, all leaves about equal in size, and rather shiny achenes 1.5–2.5 mm long, with unequal sides. **Cornfield Knotgrass** (*P. rurivagum* Jordan ex Boreau) has linear-lanceolate leaves, reddish-brown ochreas 7–10 mm long, pink flowers, and dull, equal-sided achenes exceeding perianth; often found in cultivated land. **Northern Knotgrass** (*P. boreale* (Lange) Small) has leaf-stalks free from ochrea; it occurs in Iceland, Fennoscandia, the Faeroes and the Shetland Islands, and prefers coastal habitats.

Compare also P. maritimum (see p.890) and allied species, with larger achenes.

p.285 **Bistort** *Polygonum bistorta* L.

Description: A subglabrous perennial, with *fleshy, black, twisted, creeping rhizomes* and erect, unbranched flowering stems to 60 (100) cm. Leaves alternate, with flat, entire margins; lower ones narrowly ovate to lanceolate, 10–20 cm long, *abruptly narrowed into long, winged stalk*; stem-leaves much smaller, mostly sessile, lanceolate, the highest ones almost scale-like; ochrea obliquely truncate, not ciliate. Flowers *c.* 3 mm long, 2–3 mm diam., clustered in cylindrical, *terminal spikes* to 50 mm long, 10–20 mm wide. Perianth parts 5, pink or pale lilac (rarely white). Stamens mostly 8. Styles 3, slightly thickened near top. Achene ovoid, trigonal, pointed, 4–5 mm long, shining, maroon.

Flowering: June–August (autumn).

Habitat: Meadows, scrub, deciduous woods, ditch- and streamsides, on wet or moist, mesotrophic, neutral or acid, humus-rich, sandy, loamy or stony soils; from sea level to 2,400 m.

Range: Most of Europe, but only naturalized in Ireland and Scandinavia.

Similar species: **Alpine Bistort** (*P. viviparum* L.) has lanceolate to almost linear basal leaves (with the margins rolled under) gradually tapering into an unwinged stalk, and spikes to 80 mm long, 5–8 mm wide, with pale pink or whitish flowers; many of the lower flowers are replaced by brownish bulbils, serving as vegetative propagules. In grassland, on screes and wet rocks, in most of Europe except Iceland and much of the lowland.

Bistort is also called Snake-root.

p.120 **Black Bindweed** *Polygonum convolvulus* L.

Description: A finely downy annual with slender, branched, strongly ribbed, *clockwise winding, climbing or trailing stems* to 1.2 m long. Leaves alternate, stalked, *triangular-ovate or arrow-shaped* (occasionally cordate), entire-margined, 20–70 mm long, usually mealy beneath; ochrea short, truncate. Flowers hermaphrodite, 4–6 mm long, clustered in stalked, axillary racemes. Perianth parts 5, greenish-white, the 3 outer ones keeled. Stamens 8. Style 1, with capitate, subsessile stigma. Achene ovoid, trigonal, short-pointed, 4–5 mm long, *dull black* (granular), enveloped by persistent perianth, outer parts of which develop narrow wings; fruit-stalks 1–3 mm long.

Flowering: June–autumn.

Habitat: Fields, field margins, open road verges, ruderal places, also sand-dunes, on moist, eutrophic, preferably calcareous, sandy soils; mainly in the lowland.

Range: All Europe except the Arctic.

Similar species: **Copse Bindweed** (*P. dumetorum* L.) has terete, finely striped stems to 3 m long, broad-winged outer perianth parts (in fruit), shiny-black achenes *c.* 2.5 mm long, and fruit-stalks 5–8 mm long.

On the basis of the winding habit and the winged perianth, these species are often placed in a separate genus (*Fallopia*).

The fruit-stalk consists of the actual stalk, and a stalk-like base of the perianth; between these, a small node can be seen. In Copse Bindweed this stalk-like perianth base is more strongly elongated, bringing the node below the middle.

---

p.120 **Water-pepper** *Polygonum hydropiper* L.

Description: A glabrous annual, with branched, ascending or erect stems to 80 cm. Leaves alternate, (broadly) lanceolate, gradually narrowed into short stalk, entire-margined (often slightly wavy), 5–12 cm long, up to 25 mm wide, rather pale green; ochrea shortly ciliate, otherwise practically glabrous (*hairs connate to surface*). Foliage tastes peppery. Flowers hermaphrodite, 3–5 mm long, sessile, in narrow, arching, terminal spikes (2–5 mm wide) and solitary in upper leaf-axils (these axillary flowers often cleistogamous). *Perianth parts 3–4, green with pink or whitish top, and with numerous sunken glands*. Stamens 6, rarely 8. Styles 2–3, with capitate stigmas. Achene ovoid, compressed, with flat and bluntly keeled side, pointed, *c.* 3 mm long, *dull blackish* (granular).

Flowering: July–September.

Habitat: Damp meadows, ditches and ponds (also partly in water), woodland paths, also arable fields, on wet, (very) eutrophic, acid, sandy, muddy or peaty soils; from sea level to 1,200 m.

Range: Most of Europe, except Iceland and the high Arctic.

Similar species: The following species are not normally peppery, and have more erect spikes, and flat-rimmed, dark-green leaves. **Tasteless Water-pepper** (*P. mite* Schrank) has white or pink tepals, with few or no sunken glands, long-ciliate ochreas with appressed (but free) hairs, shiny-black, trigonal or lenticular achenes 3–4.5 mm long, and a generally more erect habit. In comparable habitats, in Europe northwards to Britain, the Low Countries, Poland and C Russia, eastwards to the Caucasus.

Small Water-pepper (*P. minus* Hudson) is a smaller, ascending plant (to 40 cm), with linear-lanceolate leaves (rather abruptly narrowed into stalk), smaller, purplish-pink or white flowers (with few or no sunken glands), appressed-hairy ochreas, and shiny-black, usually lenticular achenes 1.5–3 mm long. In comparable, but rather mesotrophic habitats, in Europe except Iceland and the high Arctic; forms from Scandinavia, Estonia and NW Russia, with even smaller flowers and achenes (both less than 2 mm), linear leaves and scarcely ciliate ochreas are distinguished as *P. foliosum* H. Lindb.

The foliage of Water-pepper has a hot, burning taste; dried and powdered, it can be used as a seasoning substitute for pepper.

p.97 Sea Knotgrass *Polygonum maritimum* L.

Description: A glabrous, *glaucous perennial* with tough, branched, spreading stems to 50 cm. Leaves alternate, narrowly elliptical or lanceolate, short-stalked, 10–15 mm long, 2–4 (5) mm wide, with entire, inrolled margins; ochrea membranous, silvery white, 4–7 mm long (usually longer than upper internodes), long-fringed, with *6–12 conspicuous veins*. Flowers hermaphrodite, 3–4 mm long, sessile, solitary or 2–4 together in leaf-axils. Perianth parts 5, pink or whitish. Stamens 3–8. Styles 2, with capitate stigmas. Achene ovoid, trigonal, pointed, *3.5–5 mm long, shiny black*, distinctly exceeding persistent perianth.

Flowering: June–October.

Habitat: Floodmarks, beaches, coastal shingle or rocks, on moist to wet, saline, sandy or stony soils; exclusively coastal.

Range: S and W Europe, northwards to the Channel Isles, and eastwards to the Crimea.

Similar species: **Ray's Knotgrass** (*P. oxyspermum* Meyer & Bunge) has larger, flat leaves (to 25 mm long, 10 mm wide), ochreas with *c.* 6 weak veins, and pale-brownish achenes 2.5–5.5 mm long, far exceeding perianth. In comparable, coastal habitats, in W Europe, from S Britain and NW France to Arctic Russia, also in W Mediterranean region. The commonest form (ssp. *raii* (Bab.) Webb) has tepals with white or pink margins; ssp. *oxyspermum* has red margins, large fruits (5–6.5 mm), and is confined to the Baltic region and S Norway.

---

p.285 Redshank *Polygonum persicaria* L.

Description: A subglabrous annual, with branched, ascending or erect, reddish stems to 1 m. Leaves alternate, lanceolate, short-stalked, entire-margined, 6–12 cm long, glabrous, often with *dark, crescent-shaped blotch* in middle; ochrea has *long-ciliate margin*, and is sparsely hairy outside. Flowers hermaphrodite, 2–3 mm long, sessile, in *erect*, terminal spikes (5–10 mm wide). Perianth parts 5, *pink* (rarely whitish). Stamens 5–8. Styles 3, long and drooping, with capitate stigmas. Achene ovoid, usually lenticular, pointed, 2–2.5 mm long, shiny black.

Flowering: June–October.

Habitat: Cultivated and waste land, gardens, roadsides, railway-, canal- and riversides, on moist to wet, (very) eutrophic, neutral or acid, clayey, sandy or stony soils; from sea level to 1,600 m.

Range: All Europe except the high Arctic.

Similar species: **Pale Persicaria** (*P. lapathifolium* L.) has green stems, numerous rounded glands (and often hairs) on lower surface of leaves, shortly ciliate to glabrous-margined ochreas, and greenish-white (occasionally pink) flowers; flower-stalks have some glands. In comparable habitats, and as widely distributed.

Several subspecies are distinguished, but their characteristics are weak, in view of the general plasticity of this highly variable species.

Giant Knotweed
Polygonum sachalinense F. Schmidt

Description: A *tall, erect perennial* to 3 (4) m, with branched, hollow, angular stems. Leaves alternate, stalked, ovate with cordate base, entire-margined, up to 30 cm long, dull green, with *8–12 pairs of side-veins*; ochrea short-hairy, long-pointed. Flowers hermaphrodite, *c.* 6 mm long, sessile, in rather dense spikes composing small, axillary panicles. Perianth parts 5, greenish-yellow. Stamens 8. Styles 3, with fimbriate stigmas. Achene *c.* 5 mm long, enveloped by persistent perianth, the 3 outer parts of which develop large wings.

Flowering: August–October.

Habitat: Gardens, woods, wood margins, shaded roadsides, on moist, eutrophic, preferably acid, sandy or loamy soils; mainly in the lowland.

Range: Native to E Asia; often escaping from gardens, and more or less naturalized in W

Europe, from Ireland and France to Hungary and N Russia.

Similar species: **Japanese Knotweed** (*P. cuspidatum* Siebold & Zucc.) (see photograph p.120) rarely grows taller than 2 m; it has rounded stems, whitish flowers, and smaller, more triangular-ovate leaves (to 12 cm long), with only 4–6 pairs of side-veins. Native to E Asia; naturalized in Europe, in moist, shaded places.

These species are often placed in a separate genus (*Reynoutria*).

---

p.68 **Common Sorrel** *Rumex acetosa* L.

Description: A glabrous or slightly hairy perennial, with erect or ascending stems to 90 cm. Leaves lanceolate or elliptical with *hastate base*, the basal ones long-stalked, the cauline ones short-stalked to sessile, the higher ones clasping stem with 2 (rarely 4) backwards-pointing, rather blunt lobes; ochrea fringed. *Flowers unisexual, dioecious*, clustered in large, lax, often red-flushed panicles; male flowers have 6 stamens, female ones have 3 styles, each with a much-divided stigma. Perianth parts 6, greenish with red edges, the outer 3 much smaller and deflexed. Fruit a triangular-ovoid, shiny-black achene, *c.* 2 mm long, surrounded by 3 inner perianth parts that develop *large, cordate, entire-margined wings* (3.5–5 mm long), *devoid of basal knobs*.

Flowering: May–June.

Habitat: Meadows, pastures, roadsides, on moist to wet, mesotrophic, slightly acid or neutral, sandy, clayey or stony soils; from sea level to 2,100 m.

Range: Almost all of Europe, but rare in the south, and only naturalized in Iceland.

Similar species: A dwarfish form from the sea-dunes of W Ireland and W Scotland is distinguished as *R. hibernicus* Rech. f.; it has stems to 15 cm, and few or no stem-leaves.
R. thyrsiflorus Fingerhut has linear-lanceolate, hastate leaves with (often 4 or more) basal lobes pointing sideways, denser panicles (with ascending branches often in

3s, not solitary), dark-brown achenes, and fruit-wings to 3.5 mm long (rarely longer); it flowers 2–6 weeks later. In grassland, along rivers, also along railways, on moist to rather dry, sandy or stony soils, in E and C Europe, westwards to the Netherlands. *R. arifolius* All. has much wider, triangular-ovate to arrow-shaped, thin, soft leaves, and cordate inner perianth parts (3.5–5 mm long in fruit). In grassland and open woods in the mountains of SE and C Europe (over 500 m), and disjunctly in Iceland and the Faeroes.

Common Sorrel has an acidulous taste, and can be made into a salad; it is rich in vitamin C, and was formerly used against scorbut, but it can be harmful to health when eaten in large quantities.

---

p.69 **Sheep's Sorrel** *Rumex acetosella* L.

Description: A glabrous or hairy perennial to 60 cm, with erect or ascending stems. Leaves lanceolate or elliptical with *hastate base*, alternate, the basal ones long-stalked, the upper cauline ones subsessile (but not clasping), with 2 sideways-pointing, rather acute lobes; ochrea lanceolate, eventually fringed. *Flowers unisexual, dioecious*, clustered in lax, often red-flushed panicles; male flowers have 6 stamens, female ones have 3 styles, each with tasselled stigma. Perianth parts 6, the inner 3 ovate, greenish with red edges, outer ones much smaller, linear, more or less erect. Fruit a triangular-ovoid, shiny-black achene, *c.* 1 mm long, surrounded by 3 inner perianth parts (1–1.5 mm long, not developing wings or knobs).

Flowering: May–August (autumn).

Habitat: Heaths, poor grassland and road verges, dunes, woodland clearings, on dry to moist, oligotrophic to mesotrophic, usually acid, sandy, stony or peaty soils; from sea level to 2,400 m.

Range: All Europe.

A highly variable species. The description above pertains to ssp. *acetosella*; several other subspecies have been described, and these are often difficult to separate. Ssp. *tenuifolius* (Wallr.) O. Schwartz has a more or less prostrate habit, linear leaves with linear basal lobes, and is widely distributed in N and E Europe. Ssp. *angiocarpus* (Murb.) Murb., known from W and C Europe, has inner perianth parts connate to achene. *R. graminifolius* Rudolph ex Lamb., in Arctic Finland and N Russia, has weak, sprawling stems and linear-lanceolate leaves with indistinct basal lobes.

p.70 **Scottish Dock** *Rumex aquaticus* L.

Description: A subglabrous perennial, with erect stems to 1.5 m. Leaves large (to 60 cm long), *broadly triangular-ovate* to elliptical with *cordate base*, flat-edged (or slightly wavy), the basal ones long-stalked, the cauline ones short-stalked to subsessile, narrower; ochrea tubular. Flowers hermaphrodite, clustered in large, dense panicles. Stamens 6. Ovary 1-locular; styles 3, with tasselled stigmas. Perianth parts 6, green; inner 3 ovate, erect, enlarged and often hardened in fruit, outer 3 lanceolate, spreading, remaining small and thin. Fruit a sharply triangular-ovoid, shiny-brown achene, 3–4 mm long, surrounded by 3 inner perianth parts that develop large, *cordate, entire-margined wings* (6–8 mm long), *devoid of basal knobs*; fruiting panicles rusty brown.

Flowering: July–August.

Habitat: Marshes, wet grassland, scrub, on wet, mesotrophic or eutrophic, preferably calcareous, sandy, clayey or peaty soils; from sea level to 1,000 m.

Range: E, N and C Europe, westwards to Germany and E France, extinct in the Low Countries.

Similar species: **Northern Dock** (*R. longifolius* DC.) has broadly lanceolate, distinctly wavy-edged leaves to 80 cm long, and rounded or reniform inner perianth parts without knobs in fruit. In most of Europe, except the Low Countries and the high Arctic, in damp grassland, ditches, along rivers and lakes. *Compare also R. hydrolapathum*, with lanceolate, wavy-edged leaves, and inner perianth parts all with a basal knob in fruit.

Scottish Dock is a helophyte, often growing in shallow water.

---

p.70 **Clustered Dock**
Rumex conglomeratus Murray

Description: A subglabrous perennial, with erect stems to 1 m. Leaves *narrowly elliptical to broadly lanceolate*, with *rounded base*, subentire to crenate, green, the basal ones short-stalked, the cauline ones subsessile, diminishing upwards, present even in inflorescence; ochrea tubular. Flowers hermaphrodite, clustered in large, rather lax, widely branched panicles; individual clusters for a major part with subtending bract. Stamens 6. Ovary 1-locular; styles 3, with tasselled stigmas. Perianth parts 6, greenish-white; inner ones narrowly ovate, erect, outer 3 much smaller, lanceolate, suberect. Fruit a triangular-ovoid, blackish-brown achene, *c.* 1.5 mm long, surrounded by 3 inner perianth parts that scarcely develop wings, but do have *large, reddish basal knob*; fruit-stalk barely equalling perianth.

Flowering: June–October.

Habitat: Marshes, damp meadows, streamsides, pond margins, rivers, ditches, on wet to moist, often seasonally flooded, (very) eutrophic, preferably calcareous, sandy or loamy soils; from sea level to 1,300 m.

Range: In Europe northwards to Scotland, S Sweden and C Russia; locally naturalized further north.

Similar species: **Shore Dock** (*R. rupestris* Le Gall) has narrowly lanceolate, crenate, glaucous leaves, narrower panicles with short, ascending branches and few bracts – only the lower clusters of each branch have them. On maritime rocks, beaches, dune-slacks, in saline habitats of W Europe, northwards to W France and SW Britain.
Wood Dock (*R. sanguineus* L.) also has few bracts in the (rather narrow) inflorescence, but leaves narrowly ovate, slightly cordate-

based, and only 1 of the inner perianth parts bears a well-developed basal knob; fruit-stalk much longer than perianth. In damp, deciduous woods (often Ash or Alder), woodland clearings, paths, shaded verges and ruderal places, on moist, mesotrophic, preferably calcareous, sandy, loamy or clayey soils, from sea level to 1,600 m, in Europe northwards to the British Isles, S Scandinavia, and C Russia. A form with purple stems and veins is cultivated for ornament.

p.70 **Curled Dock** *Rumex crispus* L.

Description: A subglabrous perennial, with erect, flexuous stems to 1.5 m. Leaves large (to 60 cm long), rather rigid, *lanceolate*, not decurrent on stalk, long-pointed, usually *strongly wavy-edged*, often curved or twisted; basal ones stalked, cauline ones subsessile, diminishing upwards, present even in inflorescence; ochrea tubular. Flowers hermaphrodite, clustered in large, dense panicles. Stamens 6. Ovary 1-locular; styles 3, with tasselled stigmas. Perianth parts 6, greenish; inner ones broadly ovate, erect, outer 3 much smaller, lanceolate and spreading. Fruit a triangular-ovoid achene, pointed at both ends, 2.5–3 mm long, surrounded by 3 inner perianth parts that develop large, *broadly ovate to suborbicular, (sub)entire wings* (3.5–6 mm long), often *all with basal knob* (only anterior inner perianth part knobbed: var. *unicallosus* Peterm.).

Flowering: June–October.

Habitat: Grassland, ditches, road verges, cultivated or waste land, ruderal places, also river- and lakesides, occasionally in coastal habitats, on wet or moist, mesotrophic to (very) eutrophic, preferably calcareous, sandy or clayey soils; from sea level to 1,600 m.

Range: Most of Europe, except the high Arctic, and only naturalized in Iceland.

Similar species: *R. stenophyllus* is usually smaller (rarely over 60 cm tall); inner perianth parts finely dentate at base (and all bearing basal knob in fruit); leaves less conspicuously undulate, reminiscent of *R. obtusifolius* in shape, though narrower and not always cordate-based. On saline soils in the steppe belt, from Germany (Harz Mts) through C Europe to E Russia; locally naturalized in coastal saltmarshes and estuaries of Britain, Denmark and Sweden.

p.69 **Water Dock** *Rumex hydrolapathum* Hudson

Description: A subglabrous perennial, with erect stems to 1.5 m. Leaves large (to 1 m long), rather rigid, *lanceolate, gradually narrowed and decurrent on stalk*, long-pointed, usually slightly wavy-edged (but with inrolled margins when young); basal ones short-stalked, cauline ones subsessile, diminishing upwards, present even in inflorescence; ochrea tubular. Flowers hermaphrodite, clustered in large, rather dense panicles. Stamens 6. Ovary 1-locular, with 3 styles and tasselled stigmas. Perianth parts 6, greenish or reddish; inner ones ovate, erect, outer 3 much smaller, lanceolate and spreading. Fruit a triangular-ovoid, shiny-black achene, 4–5 mm long, surrounded by 3 inner perianth parts that develop large, *triangular-ovate, (sub)entire wings* (5–8 mm long), usually *all with whitish basal knob* occupying at least half their length.

Flowering: July–September.

Habitat: Marshes, reedlands, wet grassland, ditches, lake-, stream- and riversides, on wet, mesotrophic to (very) eutrophic, preferably calcareous, sandy, clayey or peaty soils; mainly in the lowland.

Range: Most of Europe, but more frequent in the west.

Compare R. aquaticus. The hybrid of both species (*R. × heterophyllus* C.F. Schultz) can be found where the parents grow together; it has leaf-blades with more or less truncate, asymmetrical base (1 side more clearly decurrent on stalk), and smaller knobs on inner perianth parts (occupying less than half their length). *See also R. crispus*, which has strongly curled leaf-margins.

p.70 **Golden Dock** *Rumex maritimus* L.

Description: A subglabrous *annual or biennial*, with erect stems to 60 (90) cm. Leaves *narrowly elliptical to linear-lanceolate*, narrowed into stalk, subentire; basal ones short-stalked, cauline ones subsessile, diminishing upwards, even numerous in inflorescence; ochrea tubular. Flowers hermaphrodite, clustered in narrow, very dense, almost spike-like panicles. Stamens 6. Ovary 1-locular, with 3 styles and tasselled stigmas. Perianth parts 6, greenish; inner ones erect, narrowly ovate, with *long, linear teeth*, outer 3 much smaller, linear-lanceolate, spreading. Fruit a triangular-ovoid achene, 1.3–1.8 mm long, surrounded by 3 inner perianth parts that develop large, *long-fringed wings* (2–3 mm long), each with *small, yellow basal knob* (shorter than fringe teeth); fruit-stalk thin, longer than perianth.

Flowering: June–September.

Habitat: Marshes, mud flats, watersides, ditches, on wet, periodically flooded, eutrophic, fresh or brackish, sandy, clayey or peaty soils, mainly in the lowland (and most frequent near the coast).

Range: Most of Europe except the extreme south and the Arctic.

Similar species: **Marsh Dock** (*R. palustris* Sm.) also has long-fringed wings to fruit, but larger knobs (longer than fringe teeth), and short, thick fruit-stalks (shorter than perianth). In comparable habitats of S, W and C Europe, northwards to S Sweden, eastwards to Latvia and Bulgaria.

Both species are annual or biennial unlike the other *Rumex* species, which are perennials. In fruit, the whole inflorescence of Golden Dock turns deep golden yellow; that of Marsh Dock becomes rusty orange-brown. In autumn, these species are easily recognizable by their radiant colours, in combination with small, densely clustered fruits and long perianth teeth, which make the infructescence look bristly-hairy.

p.69 **Broad-leaved Dock** *Rumex obtusifolius* L.

Description: A subglabrous perennial, with erect stems
to 1.5 m. Leaves large (to 40 cm long),
rather rigid, (narrowly) ovate with cordate
base, usually *wavy-edged* and blunt-tipped,
shiny green; basal ones long-stalked,
cauline ones narrower and short-stalked,
diminishing upwards, present even in
inflorescence; ochrea tubular. Flowers
hermaphrodite, clustered in large, rather
dense panicles. Stamens 6. Ovary
1-locular, with 3 styles and tasselled
stigmas. Perianth parts 6, greenish; inner
ones broadly ovate, long-toothed, erect,
outer 3 much smaller, lanceolate and
spreading. Fruit a triangular-ovoid achene,
2–2.5 mm long, surrounded by 3 inner
perianth parts that develop large, *ovate,
long-fringed wings* (4–6 mm long), of which
at least 1 bears basal knob.

Flowering: June–October.

Habitat: Grassland, road verges, waste or ruderal
places, on moist, (very) eutrophic, sandy,
clayey or stony soils; from sea level to
1,600 m.

Range: Most of Europe, except Spitsbergen, and
only naturalized in Iceland.

A variable species. Plants with ovate, long-
toothed inner perianth parts, of which
usually only 1 bears a basal knob, are
attributed to ssp. *obtusifolius*, which is
common in W and C Europe. Plants with
narrower, rather short-toothed inner perianth
parts, each with a knob (though 2 knobs
smaller than the 3rd), are distinguished as
ssp. *transiens* (Simonkai) Rech. f.; this form is
apparently common in E and C Europe
(westwards to Belgium), and has a preference
for damp meadows, streamsides, and lake
margins. Ssp. *sylvestris* (Wallr.) Rech. has
subentire inner perianth parts, all with a
knob; it occurs in E Europe, westwards to
Italy and S Sweden.

In autumn, the inflorescence of ssp.
transiens often becomes strikingly yellow;
that of the other subspecies turns greyish-
or reddish-brown.

p.68 Fiddle Dock *Rumex pulcher* L.

Description: A subglabrous, widely branched perennial,
with erect, flexuous stems to 60 m. Leaves
small (to 10 cm long), *rather fleshy*, elliptical
with cordate base, waisted in lower half
(*fiddle-shaped*), subentire or crenate, blunt-
tipped, green above, bluish-green below;
basal ones long-stalked, cauline ones
narrower and short-stalked, diminishing
upwards, present even in inflorescence; ochrea
tubular. Flowers hermaphrodite, clustered in
large, lax panicles. Stamens 6. Ovary 1-
locular, with 3 styles and tasselled stigmas.
Perianth parts 6, greenish; inner ones broadly
ovate, long-toothed, erect, outer 3 much
smaller, lanceolate and spreading. Fruit a
triangular-ovoid achene, up to 2 mm long,
surrounded by 3 inner perianth parts that
develop large, triangular-*ovate, long-fringed
wings* (4–6 mm long), each bearing a reddish
basal knob; fruit-stalks thick.

Flowering: June–August.

Habitat: Short grassland, pasture, common ground,
road verges, waste places, on dry to rather
moist, mesotrophic, calcareous, often sandy
soils; from sea level to 700 m, but more
frequent near coast.

Range: S and W Europe, northwards to W France
and S England, and eastwards to Hungary
and N Romania; also locally naturalized in
Ireland, Denmark and S Sweden.

---

p.68 French Sorrel *Rumex scutatus* L.

Description: A glabrous perennial to 50 (70) cm, with
erect or ascending, branched stems. Leaves
alternate, *glaucous*, 20–50 mm long, all
stalked, *broadly ovate with a hastate base*, the
basal lobes rather blunt, and pointing
obliquely backwards; ochrea fringed. *Flowers
unisexual, dioecious or monoecious*, clustered in
large, lax panicles with erect branches; male
flowers with 6 stamens, the female ones
with 3 styles, each with a much-divided
stigma. Perianth parts 6, greenish with red
edges, the outer 3 much smaller and
deflexed. Fruit a triangular-ovoid, shiny-

black achene, *c.* 3 mm long, surrounded by the 3 inner perianth parts that develop *large, suborbicular, slightly cordate, entire-margined wings* (4.5–6 mm long), *devoid of basal knobs.*

Flowering: May–August.

Habitat: Rocks, screes, mine-refuse heaps, rail and road verges, also old walls and river groynes, on dry to moist, oligotrophic to mesotrophic, calcareous, stony or rocky soils; from sea level to 2,500 m.

Range: S and SC Europe, northwards to Belgium, Germany, Poland, and Romania, and eastwards to the Crimea; also cultivated and locally naturalized in Britain, the Netherlands, and S Sweden.

PURSLANE FAMILY, PORTULACACEAE

A family of herbs with *c.* 500 species in 19 genera, especially frequent in the Americas. Dicots. Leaves simple, mostly opposite. Flowers usually regular, hermaphrodite, with 2 opposite, calyx-like bracteoles, and 4–6 free or only basally connate, petal-like perianth parts (tepals). Stamens 3–many. Ovary superior or hemi-inferior, 1-locular, with 2–6 styles, these occasionally connate. Fruit a capsule, opening with valves or through dehiscence of an apical lid.

p.116 **Springbeauty** *Claytonia perfoliata* Willd.

Description: A glabrous annual to 30 cm, with *rosette of long-stalked, ovate, rather fleshy leaves*; flowering stems usually erect, with *a pair of basally connate bracts* under raceme-like inflorescence. Flowers 4–5 mm diam., with 5 free, *white, rounded or slightly notched tepals. Stamens 5.* Ovary superior, with 3 styles. Fruit a 2–5-seeded, ovoid or globose, few-seeded capsule, shorter than persistent perianth, and splitting with *3 valves.*

Flowering: April–June.

Habitat: Cultivated land, gardens, roadsides, also dunes, usually in slightly shaded places, on dry, oligotrophic to eutrophic, acid or slightly calcareous, sandy or loamy soils; mainly in the lowland.

Range: Native to western N America; formerly cultivated as a vegetable, and naturalized in

NW Europe, from Britain to France, the Low Countries, and Germany.

Similar species: **Pink Purslane** (*C. sibirica* L.), also from N America, has pink (rarely white) flowers to 12 mm diam., and bracts under inflorescence not connate. Locally naturalized in woods of Britain and the Netherlands.

---

p.115 **Blinks** *Montia fontana* L.

Description: A glabrous annual, with creeping and ascending stems to 15 cm. Leaves opposite, *oblanceolate, slightly fleshy*. Flowers minute, *c.* 2 mm diam., 3–5 together at end of stems. Tepals 5, basally connate to short tube (open on 1 side), *the free parts slightly unequal* (2 smaller), *white*, rounded. Stamens 3. Ovary superior, with 3 styles. Fruit a globose, usually 3-seeded capsule, 1.5–2 mm long, splitting with *3 valves*; seeds dull black.

Flowering: April–May.

Habitat: Bare ground, cart-tracks, paths and woodland rides, in cultivated land, gardens, cemeteries, on moist to rather dry, oligotrophic, usually acid, sandy or clayey soils; from sea level to 2,200 m, but more frequent in the lowland.

Range: S, W and C Europe, northwards to S Sweden.

This description pertains to ssp. *chondrosperma* (Fenzl) S.M. Walters, which usually occurs on dry land. Ssp. *fontana* comprises aquatic forms with shiny-black seeds, as can be found in streams, ditches and flushes; they often grow taller (to 40 cm), and flower April–October.

---

p.199 **Purslane** *Portulaca oleracea* L.

Description: A glabrous annual with spreading, branched stems to 50 cm long. Leaves alternate, distinctly fleshy, greyish- or bronze-green, oblanceolate to slightly spatulate, 20–50 mm long; upper leaves crowded and more or less opposite directly below inflorescences. Flowers usually 3 together in terminal clusters, 8–12 mm diam. Tepals 4–6 (usually 5), free, *yellow*, rounded or short-pointed. *Stamens 7–20*. Ovary hemi-inferior, with 3 styles. Fruit an obovoid capsule, up to 9 mm long, containing several seeds, and opening through shedding of whole top-segment.

Flowering: June–September.

Habitat: Cultivated and waste land, gardens, river- and roadsides, even between paving stones, on dry to moist, mesotrophic to (very) eutrophic, sandy, loamy or stony soils.

Range: Native to the E Mediterranean region and SW Asia, naturalized in S and SC Europe, northwards to Britain, the Low Countries, and Denmark.

This description pertains to the wild form (ssp. *oleracea*). Ssp. *sativa* (Haw.) Čelak., which is cultivated as a vegetable, grows more erect, and has larger, obovate leaves.

PONDWEED FAMILY, POTAMOGETONACEAE

A family of submerged or floating aquatic herbs, usually perennials, living in fresh or brackish waters on all continents but Antarctica. Monocots. The larger, broad-leaved species usually have creeping rhizomes; most smaller, linear-leaved species have fibrous roots, and hibernate through winterbuds (consisting of small bundles of leaves) detaching themselves from the plant as it decays in autumn. Leaves alternate (in the 90-odd species of *Potamogeton*) or opposite (in *Groenlandia densa*), stalked or sessile (then occasionally sheathing stem), simple, usually with 2 stipules (these often anteriorly connate and forming a sheath-like 'spatha' around stem, not to be confused with a true leaf-sheath). Flowers regular, hermaphrodite, in axillary or terminal spikes; individual flowers without bracts. Perianth composed of 4 free, greenish or reddish tepals, or altogether absent. Stamens 4, inserted on perianth, with sessile anthers. Ovaries mostly 4, largely free, 1-locular, each with a subsessile stigma. Fruit a cluster of 1–4 greenish or brown achenes (in each individual flower). Important characters are found in the morphology of the leaves, the spikes, and the achenes. The uniform perianth barely gives clue to identification, and is often absent; therefore perianth characters are not mentioned in the descriptions. Hybrids are of common occurrence, even between very different species; identifying them is a job for experts.

p.53 **Opposite-leaved Pondweed**
Groenlandia densa (L.) Fourr.

Description: An entirely submerged aquatic perennial
with creeping rhizome and branched stems
to 50 cm. *Leaves opposite*, crowded, *sessile,
ovate to lanceolate*, 10–30 mm long,
3–15 mm wide, translucent, 3–7-veined,
finely serrate at least near top, often recurved;
stipules adnate to leaf-base, inconspicuous.
Flowers submerged, up to 4 together in
axillary clusters on peduncles to 15 mm
long (and recurved in fruit), with leaf-like
bract (so leaves apparently in whorl of 3 at
that spot). Fruit usually composed of 4
brownish achenes (per flower), these
roughly ellipsoid, compressed, smooth,
with short, oblique beak.

Flowering: May–September.

Habitat: Shallow, still or flowing, eutrophic, often
lime-rich, clear, fresh waters; from sea level
to 900 m.

Range: Most of Europe, northwards to Britain, the
Low Countries, Denmark, eastwards to
Lithuania and Turkey.

Compare Potamogeton crispus (see p.906), which
always has distinctly alternate leaves,
stipules, and often emergent flower-spikes.

p.56 **Sharp-leaved Pondweed**
Potamogeton acutifolius Link

Description: A submerged aquatic perennial, with
branched, compressed (but not winged)
stems to 1 m; hibernates usually through
winterbuds. Leaves alternate, sessile, *linear*,
6–10 (20) cm long, *2–4 (6) mm wide*,
entire-margined, translucent, with *3 strong
veins and several thin parallel fibres* (strong
magnifying glass!), *gradually narrowed
towards top*, barely pointed. Stipules form
open spatha to 20 mm long. Flowers
usually submerged, 4–6 together in axillary
clusters on erect peduncles to 15 mm long,
1 mm thick. Ripe achenes usually solitary
(in each flower), roughly ellipsoid,
compressed, with *distinct knob* on the

(otherwise straight) ventral side, and tiny, blunt warts along (rounded) dorsal side; beak short, curved.

Flowering: June–September.

Habitat: Shallow, stagnant or slow-moving, eutrophic, preferably lime-rich, fresh waters, mainly in the lowland.

Range: In Europe northwards to S Britain, the Low Countries, S Sweden, and NW Russia.

Similar Species: **Grass-wrack Pondweed** (*P. compressus* L.) differs in having strongly compressed, markedly 2-winged stems, distinctly pointed, 5-veined leaves (again with thin fibres in between), spatha 20–40 mm long, 10–15-flowered spikes (to 30 mm long) on peduncles 20–40 mm long, *c.* 2 mm thick, and smooth, straight-beaked achenes (usually 2 per flower). In comparable, stagnant, calcareous or slightly acid, fresh waters, in most of Europe except Ireland, Iceland, and the high Arctic. *Compare P. pusillus* (*see* p.912) and allies, which are usually more delicate plants, lacking thin fibres in leaves.

In Sharp-leaved Pondweed and most other linear-leaved species, the leaves usually bear 2 small, dark glands at base. These glands are absent in Grass-wrack Pondweed.

---

p.57 **Reddish Pondweed**
Potamogeton alpinus Balbis

Description: A partly floating aquatic perennial, with creeping rhizomes, and branched, rounded stems to 1.5 m. Leaves alternate; floating ones *narrowly elliptical to lanceolate* with cuneate base, 60–80 mm long, 20–40 mm wide, *slightly translucent*, green or reddish, with several arched, reticulately connected veins, subacute, with stalks 40–70 mm long; submerged leaves have well-developed, *obovate to spatulate, blunt-tipped blade*, to 15 (25) cm long, 30 mm wide, reticulately veined, often reddish, always entire-margined, subsessile or short-stalked. Stipules 20–60 mm long, free, lanceolate, reddish-brown. Flowers emergent, several together in dense, terminal spikes to 40 mm long, on erect peduncles up to 70 mm long, *c.* 2 mm thick. Ripe achenes 4 per flower, 3–4 mm long, roughly ellipsoid, compressed, smooth, greenish, with short, straight beak.

Flowering: June–August.

Habitat: Shallow, stagnant or flowing, mesotrophic, slightly acid, fresh waters; from sea level to 1,800 m.

Range: Most of Europe except the high Arctic, and rare in the south.

Similar species: **Leafy Pondweed** (*P. epihydrus* Rafin.) has flattened stems, opaque, elliptical floating leaves, and flat, linear submerged leaves to 8 mm wide, with wide bands of air-cells ('lacunae') along the (strong) midrib. In lakes and ponds of the Outer Hebrides, and introduced in N England.

Compare also P. natans and allies, with leathery (not translucent), long-stalked floating leaves.

---

p.57 **Curled Pondweed** *Potamogeton crispus* L.

Description: A submerged aquatic perennial, with creeping rhizomes, and branched, *compressed, bluntly quadrangular stems* to 1 m; axillary winterbuds also present in autumn. Leaves alternate, (sub)sessile, *narrowly elliptical or lanceolate*, blunt-tipped, 20–70 mm long, *5–15 mm wide, rather stiff*, finely *serrate-dentate* (at least near top) and usually *wavy-edged* as well, translucent, with *(3) 5–7 veins*. Stipules *c.* 10 mm long, free. Flowers often emergent, 7–10 together in dense, terminal spikes (up to 20 mm long) on erect peduncles to 50 mm long, 2 mm thick. Ripe achenes 4 per flower, basally connate, 2–3 mm long, roughly ellipsoid, compressed, smooth, with *long, curved beak to 2 mm.*

Flowering: May–September.

Habitat: Stagnant or slow-moving, usually shallow, eutrophic (occasionally slightly polluted), preferably lime-rich waters; from sea level to 1,800 m.

Range: In Europe northwards to the British Isles, S Scandinavia, and C Russia.

Compare Groenlandia (see p.904), with opposite leaves.

p.57 **Various-leaved Pondweed**
Potamogeton gramineus L.

Description: A submerged or (partly) floating aquatic perennial with creeping rhizomes, and branched, rounded stems to 1 m. Leaves alternate, the floating ones *elliptical or ovate*, 20–60 mm long, 10–30 mm wide, *abruptly narrowed into long stalk*, subacute, entire-margined, opaque, slightly leathery, bright green, with several arched veins; *submerged leaves sessile, lanceolate to linear*, 40–80 mm long, up to 10 mm wide, often finely denticulate, more or less translucent, greenish, with 3–7 veins (*compare P. crispus*!). Stipules large (to 50 mm long), free, lanceolate. Flowers emergent, several together in rather dense, terminal spikes (to 30 mm long) on erect, *inflated peduncles* 5–10 cm long, 2–4 mm thick. Ripe achenes up to 4 per flower, 1.5–3.5 mm long, ellipsoid or roughly circular, compressed, smooth, with short, laterally implanted beak.

Flowering: June–August.

Habitat: Stagnant, usually shallow, oligotrophic to mesotrophic, acid or basic, fresh waters; from sea level to 1,000 m.

Range: All Europe except the high Arctic.

A highly variable species; floating leaves are often missing, but can also be the only leaves present. The inflated peduncles are characteristic; *P. lucens* and *P. nodosus* also have thickened peduncles, but are much coarser plants.

p.58 **Shining Pondweed** *Potamogeton lucens* L.

Description: A submerged aquatic perennial with creeping rhizomes, and branched, rounded stems to 3 m. Leaves alternate, *narrowly elliptical or lanceolate*, 10–25 cm long, 20–50 mm wide, *narrowed into short stalk* (*c.* 10 mm long), subacute, subentire to finely dentate (and often wavy-edged), more or less translucent, greenish to bronze- or copper-coloured, with *9–11 (15) interconnected veins*, strong midvein often long protracted beyond leaf-tip; upper leaves often broader and less translucent, but *special floating leaves* absent. Stipules large, free, lanceolate. Flowers emergent, several together in dense, terminal spikes (to 70 mm long) on erect, *inflated peduncles* up to 25 cm long, 5 mm thick, distally widening. Ripe achenes 1–4 per flower, 3.5–4 mm long, broadly ellipsoid to suborbicular, compressed, smooth, with short, oblique beak.

Flowering: June–September.

Habitat: Rather deep, stagnant or slow-moving, mesotrophic to eutrophic, lime-rich waters; from sea level to 1,000 m.

Range: Most of Europe, except Iceland and the high Arctic.

Similar species: *P.* × *zizii* Koch ex Roth is the putative hybrid with *P. gramineus*; it has 2 short-stalked floating leaves at end of stems, just below inflorescence, and back of achenes is distinctly keeled (not rounded). In comparable, often rather oligotrophic waters, in much of Europe.

Long-stalked Pondweed (*P. praelongus* Wulfen) also has all leaves submerged, but blades narrowly lanceolate, entire-margined, 6–15 cm long, 20–40 mm wide, sessile and half-clasping stem with rounded base, and not distinctly net-veined; fruits 4–6 mm long, compressed, smooth, with short, straight, laterally implanted beak, in loose spikes (30–50 mm long) on peduncles to 25 cm, these not inflated; flowering often fails to occur. In rather deep, stagnant or slow-moving, mesotrophic, often mildly acid waters, from sea level to 2,050 m, in N and C Europe, southwards to S France, Yugoslavia and Bulgaria, but only in mountainous areas in the south.

The (lower) leaves of Shining Pondweed may be reduced to a widened stalk.

p.59 Broad-leaved Pondweed
Potamogeton natans L.

Description: A partly floating aquatic perennial, with creeping rhizomes, and branched, rounded stems to 1 m. Leaves alternate; floating ones *elliptical or ovate*, 5–12 cm long, 20–50 mm wide, leathery, opaque, bright green with several arched, translucent veins, often pale green (occasionally purplish) beneath, subacute, with *rounded, slightly folded base*, and making an angle with (long, tough, opaque) stalk, which at the point of junction has *pale, node-like articulation*; submerged leaves mostly reduced to stiff, greenish, linear, channelled stalk, to 50 cm long, up to 3 (5) mm wide. Stipules large (5–12 cm long), free, linear-lanceolate, with 2 dorsal keels. Flowers emergent, several together in dense, terminal spikes (30–80 mm long) on erect peduncles to 10 cm long, 2–3 mm thick. Ripe achenes usually 4 per flower, 4–5 mm long, roughly ellipsoid, compressed, smooth, greenish, with short, laterally implanted beak.

Flowering: June–September.

Habitat: Stagnant or slow-moving, shallow to rather deep, mesotrophic to eutrophic, acid to basic waters; from sea level to 2,200 m. A very common species.

Range: All Europe except the high Arctic.

Similar species: **Bog Pondweed** (*P. polygonifolius* Pourret) lacks node-like articulation to (elliptical to lanceolate, leathery, green or reddish) floating leaves (to 90 mm long, 30 mm wide); submerged leaves have well-developed blades, and persistent stipules 20–60 mm long, without keels; spikes 20–40 mm long; achenes reddish, much smaller (2–2.5 mm long). In shallow, stagnant or flowing, usually oligotrophic, acid, fresh waters, such as bogs and small streams, in Europe northwards to C Norway, and eastwards to SW Finland and Bulgaria.

Fen Pondweed (*P. coloratus* Hornemann) has thin, translucent, reticulately veined, reddish, ovate, short-stalked floating leaves (to 13 cm long, 60 mm wide) lacking an articulation; submerged leaves have well-developed blades; achenes 1.5–2 mm long, greenish, in spikes 20–40 mm long. In shallow, stagnant or flowing, oligotrophic, usually lime-rich, fresh or brackish waters, in most of Europe, northwards to S Sweden. Further *compare P. nodosus*, which has thickened peduncles; and also the unrelated *Polygonum amphibium* (*see* p.885), the aquatic forms of which can be similar in the shape of the floating leaves.

---

p.58　**Loddon Pondweed**
Potamogeton nodosus Poiret

Description:　A submerged or partly floating aquatic perennial, with creeping rhizomes, and branched, rounded stems to 2 (3) m. Leaves alternate; floating ones (if present) *elliptical to broadly lanceolate*, 7–14 cm long, 30–60 mm wide, slightly leathery, opaque, bright green with several arched veins, subacute, more or less in line with (long, tough, opaque, bluntly triangular) stalk; submerged leaves have well-developed, lanceolate blade (to 15 cm long, 50 mm wide), reticulately veined, often minutely dentate, and always long-stalked. Stipules 20–60 mm long, free, lanceolate, soon decaying. Flowers emergent, several together in dense, terminal spikes to 50 mm long, on erect, *thickened peduncles* to 10 cm long, 3–4 mm thick. Ripe achenes usually 4 per flower, 3–4 mm long, roughly ellipsoid, compressed, smooth, greenish, with short, laterally implanted beak.

Flowering:　June–September.

Habitat:　Shallow or rather deep, often flowing, eutrophic, lime-rich to slightly acid, fresh waters; from sea level to 500 m.

Range:　In Europe northwards to S Britain, the Low Countries, Germany, Poland, and Estonia.

In rapidly flowing waters the plant rarely flowers, and the floating leaves may be dragged under water, or never form at all.

p.56 **Fennel Pondweed** *Potamogeton pectinatus* L.

Description: An entirely submerged aquatic perennial with creeping rhizomes, and branched, subterete stems to 2 (3) m. Leaves alternate, sessile, linear, 4–10 (20) cm long, *0.5–2 mm wide*, entire-margined, *thick and opaque*, each half tubular, not visibly veined, *rather stiff*, dark green, the tip gradually narrowed into fine point; *leaf-sheath 10–40 mm long, open* (hence easily pulled off stem), white-margined, slightly inflated (especially lower ones, which usually have reduced leaf-blades). Stipules 10–30 mm long, free to base, *implanted on rim of sheath*. No glands at leaf-base. Flowers submerged, 3–4 (10) together in lax, eventually interrupted, axillary spikes (20–50 mm long) on erect peduncles 40–60 mm long, *c.* 1 mm thick. Ripe achenes usually 4 per flower, 3–5 mm long, ventrally straight, dorsally strongly curved, compressed, smooth; beak minute, laterally implanted.

Flowering: June–September.

Habitat: Shallow to rather deep, still or flowing, (very) eutrophic or even polluted, fresh or brackish waters; from sea level to 1,600 m, but more frequent in the lowland.

Range: All Europe except the high Arctic.

Similar species: **Slender-leaved Pondweed** (*P. filiformis* Pers.) has blunt-tipped, tubular leaves to 1 (1.5) mm wide; leaf-sheaths greenish, closed or at least basally connate around stem. In comparable, often brackish waters, but also in lime-rich waters in the mountains in N and C Europe; absent from the Low Countries. *P. vaginatus* Turcz., from brackish waters of E Sweden and W Finland, has leaves *c.* 1 (2.5) mm wide, with open, slightly inflated, greenish sheaths on leaves with more or less reduced blades, and dense flowerspikes.

p.57 **Perfoliate Pondweed**
Potamogeton perfoliatus L.

Description: A submerged aquatic perennial, with creeping rhizomes, and branched, rounded stems to 2 (6) m. Leaves alternate, *ovate to suborbicular*, 20–60 mm long, 10–40 mm wide, *sessile, fully clasping* stem with *cordate base*, minutely denticulate, more or less translucent, with several veins, dark green, and with flat top; *no special floating leaves*. *Stipules small*, free, lanceolate, soon decaying. Flowers emergent, several together in dense, terminal spikes (20–40 mm long) on erect *peduncles 30–70 mm long*, evenly 2–3 mm thick. Ripe achenes mostly 4 per flower, 3–3.5 mm long, roughly ellipsoid, compressed, smooth, with very short, straight beak.

Flowering: June–September.

Habitat: Deep, stagnant or flowing, eutrophic, lime-rich, fresh or slightly brackish waters; from sea level to 1,800 m.

Range: All Europe except the high Arctic.

Compare also P. praelongus (see p.908), which has narrower, half-clasping, entire leaves and longer peduncles.

---

p.56 **Lesser Pondweed** *Potamogeton pusillus* L.

Description: An entirely submerged aquatic perennial, with branched, subterete stems to 1 m; hibernates through winterbuds. Leaves alternate, sessile, *linear*, 20–40 (60) mm long, *1–2 mm wide*, entire-margined, translucent, with *3 veins*, subacute to round-tipped, often short-pointed; lateral veins re-enter ring midvein well before reaching leaf top. Stipules 10–20 mm long, *largely connate around stem*. Flowers usually submerged, 3–4 (10) together in lax, axillary spikes (to 15 mm long) on erect peduncles *c.* 50 mm long, 0.6 mm thick. Ripe achenes often 4 per flower, *c.* 2 mm long, roughly ellipsoid, compressed, smooth; beak short, oblique, subapically implanted.

Flowering: June–September.

Habitat: Shallow, stagnant, eutrophic, fresh waters; from sea level to 2,000 m.

Range: Most of Europe, except the high Arctic.

Similar species: **Small Pondweed** (*P. berchtoldii* Fieb.) has lateral veins running almost to leaf-top before re-entering, and midvein is usually accompanied by 2 rows of air-cells ('lacunae'), at least near base; also differs in its free stipules, its short, compact spikes, and in having laterally implanted beak to (usually knobbed) fruit. In all of Europe except Iberian peninsula.

Shetland Pondweed (*P. rutilus* Wolfg.) has leaves to 1 mm wide (with 3 conspicuous veins), more gradually narrowed, finely pointed leaf-tips, basally connate stipules, and inconspicuous glands near leaf-base. In N, C and E Europe, except the Arctic.

Flat-stalked Pondweed (*P. mucronatus* Sonder) is a more robust plant, hibernating through winterbuds; stems branched, slightly compressed; leaves 3–7 (10) cm long, 2–3.5 mm wide, entire-margined, acute, often slightly pointed, translucent, with (3) 5 veins; midvein usually accompanied by distinct rows of air-cells ('lacunae'); stipules 10–20 mm long, connate around stem; flowers 3–4 (10) together in lax, axillary spikes on erect peduncles 20–30 mm long, 1 mm thick; ripe achenes 1–3 (usually 2) per flower, 2–3 mm long, roughly ellipsoid, compressed, smooth; beak short, oblique. In shallow, stagnant or slow-moving, eutrophic, fresh waters; from sea level to 1,100 m, in most of Europe except Iceland and the high Arctic.

Blunt-leaved Pondweed (*P. obtusifolius* Mert. & Koch) is still larger, and has obtuse, occasionally subtruncate, extremely short-pointed, rather opaque, bronze-green leaves (to 80 mm long, 2–4 mm wide), and again usually 5-veined; stipules free to base; spikes dense, usually 6–8-flowered on peduncles to 20 mm long, often with 4 well-developed achenes per flower. In comparable, often less eutrophic, fresh waters, in most of Europe except Iceland and the high Arctic. *Compare* for this species *P. acutifolius* (*see* p.904), which has thin fibres between veins.

Generally *compare P. trichoides*, which has much narrower, threadlike leaves; and *P. pectinatus* and allies, which have tubular (not flat) leaves.

p.56 **Hairlike Pondweed**
Potamogeton trichoides Cham. & Schlecht.

Description: An entirely submerged aquatic perennial, with branched, subterete stems to 1 m; hibernates through winterbuds. Leaves alternate, sessile, *almost threadlike*, 20–60 (80) mm long, *0.3–1 mm wide*, entire-margined, rather opaque (but thin), with *1–3 veins*, gradually tapering into hairlike point. Stipules 10–20 mm long, free to base. Flowers usually submerged, 3–4 (10) together in lax, axillary spikes (to 15 mm long) on erect peduncles 20–30 mm long, *c.* 0.6 mm thick. Ripe achenes usually 1–3 per flower, *c.* 2.5 mm long, roughly ellipsoid, compressed, with small knob on ventral side, and often also 1–2 tubercles on (strongly curved) dorsal side; beak short, oblique.

Flowering: June–August.

Habitat: Shallow, stagnant or slow-moving, mesotrophic to eutrophic, fresh waters; from sea level to 500 m.

Range: In Europe northwards to Scotland, the Low Countries, S Sweden, and C Russia.

The lateral veins (if present) re-enter midvein well before reaching leaf-top; they are often difficult to see. The midvein occupies the larger part of the (narrowed) leaf-base (not so in *P. pusillus* and allies). *Compare also P. pectinatus* and allies, with thick, rather stiff leaves, and long, open leaf-sheaths.

PRIMROSE FAMILY, PRIMULACEAE

A family of herbs (rarely half-shrubs) with nearly 1,000 species in 28 genera, mainly in the northern hemisphere. Dicots. Leaves simple, opposite or alternate (occasionally whorled). Flowers regular, hermaphrodite, basically 5-merous. Sepals 4–9 (usually 5), free or partly connate. Petals 4–9 (usually 5), more or less connate. Stamens 5, implanted on corolla, occasionally alternating with sterile staminodia. Ovary superior (rarely hemi-inferior), 1-locular, with 1 style and 1 stigma, and containing 2–many ovules. Fruit a capsule, opening with 5 valves, or through the shedding of an apical lid. In *Primula* and *Hottonia,* styles are of two types ('heterostyly'): short styles, included in corolla tube (then anthers usually close to the rim of the tube), or long and protruding styles (then anthers often lower down in the tube). In this way self-pollination is effectively prevented. Many are grown for ornament, such as **Sowbread** (*Cyclamen*), and diverse *Primula* species (which are notorious for causing allergic reactions in humans).

p.245 **Scarlet Pimpernel** *Anagallis arvensis* L.

Description: A glabrous annual, with quadrangular, more or less erect to spreading (but not rooting) stems to 50 cm long. *Leaves opposite, sessile*, to 20 mm long, *ovate*, entire-margined, bright green, *with dark glandular pits* especially beneath. Flowers regular, 4–7 mm diam., *solitary on long stalks* in leaf-axils. Sepals 5, green, linear-lanceolate, free. Petals 5, obovate, with rounded, often slightly dentate tip, almost free, spreading, barely exceeding sepals, *scarlet or deep orange-red*, occasionally pale purplish, blue, or greenish-white, *densely glandular-ciliate* along margin. Stamens 5, with hairy filaments. Ovary superior, 1-locular. Fruit a many-seeded, subglobose capsule, 4–5 mm long, shedding upper, hemispherical part when ripe (including rather short, persistent style).

Flowering: May–October.

Habitat: Cultivated and waste land, gardens, roadsides, dunes, on dry to moist, mesotrophic to (very) eutrophic, preferably calcareous, sandy, loamy or stony soils; from sea level to 1,800 m.

Range: Most of Europe except Iceland and the high Arctic.

The description pertains to ssp. *arvensis*. Plants with blue flowers are more common in S Europe; they should not be confused with **Blue Pimpernel** (ssp. *coerulea* Hartman) which usually has blue (rarely white) flowers, with narrower, glabrous or remotely glandular-ciliate petals (less than 30 hairs all round), while flower-stalks are shorter, not exceeding (often narrower) leaves. In arable fields on calcareous soils in much of Europe except Ireland, Iceland and the Arctic, but rare and presumably often as an alien in the north.

p.115 **Chaffweed**
Anagallis minima (L.) E.H.L. Krause

Description: A tiny, glabrous annual, with erect, simple or branched stems to 7 cm; branches, if present, ascending. *Leaves alternate* (at least the higher ones), *subsessile*, 3–5 mm long, (broadly) *ovate*, entire-margined, bright green, without dark glands. Flowers regular, *c.* 2 mm diam., *solitary on very short stalks* in leaf-axils. Sepals 5, green, lanceolate, free for 3 quarters of their length. Petals 5, narrowly ovate, pointed, basally connate into short tube, the limbs markedly shorter than sepals, *white or pinkish*. Stamens 5, with glabrous filaments, inserted on rim of corolla tube. Ovary superior, 1-locular. Fruit a many-seeded, subglobose capsule, *c.* 1.5 mm long, shedding upper, hemispherical part when ripe (including rather short, persistent style).

Flowering: June–September.

Habitat: Dune-slacks, short pasture, heaths, common ground, poor arable fields, woodland paths, on (seasonally) wet or moist, oligotrophic, mildly acid, preferably sandy soils; from sea level to 1,200 m.

Range: Most of Europe except Iceland and the Arctic.

---

p.278 **Bog Pimpernel** *Anagallis tenella* (L.) L.

Description: A slender, glabrous annual, with spreading and *creeping, branched, mat-forming, threadlike stems* to 30 cm long. *Leaves normally opposite*, subsessile or short-stalked, 4–9 mm long, *suborbicular to broadly ovate*, entire-margined, bright green, without dark glands. Flowers regular, 6–10 mm diam., *solitary on long, ascending stalks* in leaf-axils. Sepals 5, green, linear-lanceolate, free. Petals 5, oblanceolate to elliptical, blunt-tipped, almost free, rather erect (spreading only in sunny weather), at least twice as long as sepals, *pale pink with darker veins* (occasionally whitish), glabrous. Stamens 5, with hairy filaments. Ovary superior,

1-locular. Fruit a many-seeded, subglobose capsule, 2.5–4 mm long, shedding upper, hemispherical part when ripe (including long, threadlike, persistent style).

Flowering: June–September.

Habitat: Dune-slacks, marshy heaths, bogs, damp pasture, woodland paths, on wet to moist, oligotrophic, acid, sandy or peaty soils; from sea level to 1,800 m.

Range: S and W Europe, northwards to the British Isles, the Faeroes, the Low Countries, and Germany.

Declining in many areas.

---

p.154 **Northern Androsace**
Androsace septentrionalis L.

Description: A finely hairy *annual or biennial*, with *basal leaf-rosette* and leafless, erect, terete flowering stems to 20 cm. Leaves 10–35 mm long, oblanceolate or narrowly elliptical, bluntly dentate, (sub)sessile. Flowers regular, 5–6 mm diam., *5–30 together in terminal umbel*; involucral bracts 2–4 mm long, elliptical or lanceolate; individual flower-stalks (rays) threadlike, stiffly erect, 5–15 mm long, unequal. Calyx widely cup-shaped, glabrous, with *5 large, spreading, triangular teeth*. Corolla *white or pink*, with short tube and 5 rounded, spreading corolla lobes, *these exceeding calyx*. Stamens 5, with very short filaments, implanted on corolla tube. Ovary superior, 1-locular, with a stout, straight style. Fruit a many-seeded, subglobose capsule, 4–5 mm long, opening with 5 valves.

Flowering: May–July.

Habitat: Short grassland, on dry, oligotrophic, sandy or stony soils; from sea level (in the north) to 2,200 m, but mainly on mountains over 1,000 m in the south of its area.

Range: N and C Europe, from C Scandinavia, S Finland and NC Russia southwards to W Alps and S Russia.

Similar species: **Annual Androsace** (*A. maxima* L.) is (apart from being annual) easily recognized by its small, basal rosettes of slightly rhombic, short- and broad-stalked leaves (to 20 mm long); erect, leafless flowering stem to 12 cm; large, flat, ovate involucral bracts (to 10 mm long) under umbel (which has relatively thick, equal rays); and, particularly, by its large calyx forming dish-shaped, green ruff (to 10 mm diam., with 5 ovate, denticulate lobes) below tiny, white or pink flowers (2–3 mm diam.). On rocks, but also in dry, calcareous, loamy arable fields, in mountains of S and C Europe, reaching locally northwards to Lorraine in France and the Eifel in Germany.

Several more or less similar *Androsace* species occur in rocky substrates in the mountains of C Europe (*see* regional floras for more details).

p.278 **Sea Milkwort** *Glaux maritima* L.

Description: A glabrous annual, to 10 (30) cm, with spreading (often partly creeping), mat- or cushion-forming stems, and erect flowering branches. *Leaves crosswise opposite* (at least the lower ones), crowded, *sessile*, 4–6 (12) mm long, *ovate or elliptical*, 1-veined, entire-margined, bright green, rather stiff and *fleshy*. Flowers regular, 3–6 mm diam., *solitary on very short stalks* in leaf-axils. Sepals 5, *pink*, narrowly obovate, almost free, more or less spreading. *Petals absent*. Stamens 5, with long filaments. Ovary superior, 1-locular. Fruit a few-seeded, subglobose, short-pointed capsule, *c.* 3 mm long, and opening with 5 ovate valves.

Flowering: May–September.

Habitat: Highest parts of saltmarshes and beaches, dune-slacks, sea-walls, brackish grassland and reedlands, occasionally inland near saline pools or along salted motorways, on wet, saline or brackish, sandy, gravelly or clayey soils.

Range: Along the coasts of Europe, northwards to the Arctic, and locally inland on saline soils.

p.286 **Water Violet** *Hottonia palustris* L.

Description: A glabrous, perennial, largely submerged
aquatic, with creeping rhizomes and erect
flowering stems to 60 cm. *Leaves whorled* or
partly alternate, all submerged or partly
floating, sessile, to 13 cm long, ovate or
elliptical, (once, occasionally doubly)
pinnately divided with several spreading,
linear segments, *pale green*. Flowers regular,
15–25 mm diam., stalked, in *whorls
composing emergent, leafless, terminal raceme*.
Sepals 5, green, lanceolate, almost free.
Petals 5, *pale lilac or white*, narrowly
obovate, usually notched, basally connate
into very short, wide tube with *yellow
throat*. Stamens 5, with very short
filaments. Ovary superior, 1-locular, with
straight, persistent style (short or long:
heterostyly). Fruit a many-seeded,
subglobose capsule to 6 mm long, opening
with 5 narrowly ovate valves remaining
coherent at apex.

Flowering: May–July.

Habitat: Stagnant or slow-moving, shallow,
mesotrophic to eutrophic, fresh waters,
often on a peaty substrate but occasionally
on clay; mainly in the lowland.

Range: Most of Europe, northwards to E Ireland,
England, the Low Countries, C Sweden, the
Baltic States, and C Russia, but absent from
the extreme south.

Non-flowering plants remotely resemble a
Myriophyllum, but leaf-segments are flat
(not threadlike).

p.197 **Creeping Jenny** *Lysimachia nummularia* L.

Description: A glabrous perennial, with creeping to
ascending, quadrangular stems to 60 cm.
Leaves opposite, short-stalked, usually
turned flat to ground, 10–20 mm long,
ovate to suborbicular, blunt-tipped, with
rounded or slightly cordate base,
subentire, bright green, *with red glandular
pits*. Flowers regular, 15–20 mm diam.,
solitary on long, ascending stalks in leaf-axils;

flower-stalks rather stout, 10–30 mm long, 1 mm thick. Sepals 5, erect, free, 7–10 mm long, *ovate with cordate base*, pointed, with dark glandular pits. Petals 5, obovate, basally connate into short tube, the free parts spreading, *bright yellow with red dots*, and glandular-ciliate along margin. Stamens 5, with long filaments. Ovary superior, 1-locular. Fruit a many-seeded, subglobose capsule, 4–5 mm long, opening with 5 valves.

Flowering: June–August.

Habitat: Marshes, damp meadows, ditch-, lake- and streamsides, in open, deciduous woods, scrub (often willows), shaded roadsides, hedges, on wet to moist, mesotrophic to eutrophic, calcareous to mildly acid, sandy, loamy or peaty soils; from sea level to 1,500 m.

Range: Most of Europe, except Iceland and the Arctic, eastwards to the Caucasus.

Similar species: **Yellow Pimpernel** (*L. nemorum* L.) has a more ascending habit, ovate, rather acute or even short-pointed leaves to 30 mm long (without glandular pits), and smaller flowers (8–15 mm diam.) on long, threadlike stalks (to 35 mm long, *c.* 0.5 mm thick), with linear sepals (3.5–7 mm long). In deciduous woods (usually with Oak and Beech), where it is often in flushes, streamsides or on muddy pathways, on wet or moist, oligotrophic, mildly acid, preferably loamy soils, to 1,800 m; in W and C Europe, northwards to S Sweden, and eastwards to W Russia.

In Creeping Jenny, fruits are not often formed; the plant propagates mainly vegetatively, by means of its creeping rhizomes.

---

p.218 **Tufted Loosestrife** *Lysimachia thyrsiflora* L.

Description: A subglabrous or slightly hairy perennial, with creeping rhizome and erect, quadrangular flowering stems to 60 cm. Leaves opposite, *sessile* (often half-clasping), to 10 cm long, (narrowly) lanceolate, long-pointed, entire-margined, bright green, *with numerous dark glandular pits*. Flowers regular, 4–6 (8) mm diam., several together *in ovate racemes on erect peduncles* in axils of middle stem-leaves. *Sepals 5–7 (often 6), free, linear, acute, with dark glandular pits. Petals 5–7 (often 6), linear, free, bright yellow*, glabrous, but with some red glands near tip. Stamens 5–7 (often 6), long-protruding, with glabrous filaments to 6 mm long; sterile staminodes in the form of small teeth alternating with petals. Ovary superior, 1-locular. Fruit a few-seeded, subglobose capsule, *c.* 3 mm long, opening with 5 valves.

Flowering: May–July.

Habitat: Marshes, bogs, fens, reedlands, canal- and riversides, often in shallow water, on wet, mesotrophic, preferably peaty soils; from sea level to 1,200 m.

Range: W, C and E Europe, from C France to Faeroe Isles, and eastwards to N Russia.

---

p.215 **Yellow Loosestrife** *Lysimachia vulgaris* L.

Description: A soft-hairy perennial, with creeping rhizome and erect, bluntly quadrangular flowering stems to 1.5 m. *Leaves opposite or in whorls of 3–4 (5), sessile* (often half-clasping), to 15 cm long, (broadly) lanceolate, long-pointed, subentire, dull green, *with numerous dark or red glandular pits*. Flowers regular, 15–20 mm diam., in axillary clusters composing *large, pyramidal, leafy, terminal panicle*. Sepals 5, only basally connate, linear-lanceolate, *3–5 mm long*, green with *reddish margin*, and glabrous top (not counting hairs on margins). Petals 5, basally connate, bright yellow with darker or brownish base, with minute glandular hairs on inner face, but with *glabrous margins*. Stamens 5, much shorter than petals, with glandular-hairy filaments to 7 mm long; staminodes absent. Ovary superior, 1-locular. Fruit a many-seeded, subglobose capsule, 4–5 mm long, opening with 5 valves.

Flowering: June–August.

Habitat: Marshes, fens, flushes, ditches, river- and lakesides, damp woods (often with Alder or Willow), on wet, mesotrophic, neutral or calcareous, sandy, muddy or peaty soils; from sea level to 1,200 m.

Range: Most of Europe, except Iceland and the high Arctic.

Similar species: **Dotted Loosestrife** (*L. punctata* L.), from SE Europe and SW Asia, has leaves usually in 3s or 4s (only occasionally opposite), and slightly larger, 5–6-merous, yellow flowers in subsessile, axillary clusters (seemingly whorled), with plain-green sepals (5–10 mm long, glandular-hairy all the way to the top) and glandular-ciliate corolla lobes. Frequently cultivated in gardens, and locally naturalized along ditches, and in damp roadsides and reedlands, in W and C Europe.

---

p.218 Oxlip *Primula elatior* (L.) Hill

Description: A hairy perennial, 10–30 cm tall, with *basal leaf-rosette* and leafless, erect, terete flowering stems. Leaves 5–15 cm long, spatulate, the (crenate, round-tipped) blade *abruptly narrowed* into (about equally long, broad-winged, crenate or dentate) stalk. Flowers regular, not fragrant, 15–25 mm diam., *nodding in 1-sided, terminal umbel*; involucral bracts small, linear; individual flower-stalks (rays) 5–20 mm long. Calyx bell-shaped, with rather narrow, cylindrical, angular tube and *5 triangular-lanceolate, pointed teeth*. Corolla *pale yellow*, the tube about equalling calyx; corolla lobes 5, obovate, notched, *rather flat and spreading*, with *orange markings* near base. Stamens 5, with very short filaments. Ovary superior, 1-locular, heterostylous. Fruit a many-seeded, cylindrical or ovoid capsule, 11–15 mm long, opening with 5 valves.

Flowering: March–May (autumn).

Habitat: Damp, deciduous woods (often with Oak, Ash, or Alder), coppices, streamsides and ditches, meadows, on moist to wet, mesotrophic to oligotrophic, preferably calcareous, loamy or clayey, incidentally peaty soils; from sea level to 2,200 m.

Range: S, W and C Europe, northwards to S Sweden, and eastwards to the Ukraine.

Similar species: **Cowslip** (*P. veris* L.) has more distinctly wrinkled leaves, umbels with up to 30 fragrant, deep-yellow flowers only 8–15 mm diam., with wider, bell-shaped (and angular) calyx tube, blunt or short-pointed, triangular-ovate calyx teeth, and concave, rather erect corolla lobes. In meadows, pasture, scrub, open woods, on moist, oligotrophic to mesotrophic, calcareous, sandy, loamy or stony soils, to 2,000 m, in most of Europe except Iceland and the Arctic; rare in the south.

Cultivars of both species are grown in gardens, in several colours from white and yellow via orange, red, pink and purple to violet; these plants occasionally escape from cultivation. *Compare also P. vulgaris which has sessile umbels.*

---

p.291 **Bird's-eye Primrose** *Primula farinosa* L.

Description: A hairy perennial, 5–25 cm tall, with *basal leaf-rosette* and a (usually) solitary, leafless, erect, terete flowering stem (*mealy white* at least above). Leaves 30–60 mm long, elliptical to spatulate, with broad-winged stalk, *distinctly crenate*, blunt-tipped, *mealy white beneath*. Flowers regular, (8) 10–16 mm diam., *more or less erect, several together in all-sided, terminal umbel*; involucral bracts small, saccate; individual flower-stalks (rays) 5–20 mm long, unequal. Calyx bell-shaped, with round-based, cylindrical, scarcely angular, *mealy-white tube* and 5 *triangular-ovate, blunt, erect, often dark-purplish teeth*. Corolla *pale lilac or purplish-pink* (rarely white); tube barely equalling calyx; corolla lobes 5, obovate, notched, *flat and spreading*, with *yellowish markings* near base. Stamens 5. Ovary superior, 1-locular. Fruit a many-seeded,

cylindrical capsule, 5–9 mm long, opening
with 5 valves.

Flowering: May–August.

Habitat: Damp pasture, fens, mires, on wet or
moist, oligotrophic, often calcareous,
sandy or peaty soils; from sea level (in the
north) to 2,500 m, but mainly on
mountains over 800 m in the south of its
area.

Range: From Scotland, S Sweden and N Russia
southwards to C Spain and Bulgaria.

Similar species: **Scottish Primrose** (*P. scotica* Hooker) has
(sub)entire leaves, dark-purple (rarely
white) flowers (5–8 mm diam.) with
broader petals (not leaving gaps between
them), with yellow ring around throat. In
damp coastal pasture and dunes; endemic to
N Scotland. In Iceland and Scandinavia
some very similar species can be found, all
with violet or lilac (rarely white) flowers (*see*
regional floras for more details).

p.218 **Primrose** *Primula vulgaris* Hudson

Description: A hairy perennial, 5–15 cm tall, with
rosette of oblanceolate, round-tipped,
crenate basal leaves to 15 cm long, these
gradually narrowed to base; leaf-stalk
therefore imperceptible. Flowers regular,
fragrant, 20–35 mm diam., *erect,
apparently solitary* at end of several hairy
flowering stems rising from same rosette
(actually representing rays of a sessile
umbel – the true flowering stem is
strongly reduced in this species). Calyx
bell-shaped, with rather narrow,
cylindrical, angular tube and *5 triangular-
lanceolate, pointed teeth*. Corolla *pale yellow*,
tube about equalling calyx; corolla lobes
5, obovate, notched, *flat and spreading*,
with *darker yellow markings* near base.
Stamens 5, with very short filaments.
Ovary superior, 1-locular, heterostylous.
Fruit a many-seeded, ovoid capsule,
5–9 mm long, opening with 5 valves.

Flowering: March–May.

Habitat: Damp, deciduous woods (often with Ash,
Elm or Oak), coppices, hedgebanks,

streamsides and ditches, also sea-cliffs, on moist, oligotrophic to mesotrophic, weakly acid, humus-rich, sandy or loamy soils; from sea level to 1,500 m.

Range: S and W Europe, northwards to the British Isles, SW Norway, eastwards to Denmark, W Germany, and through SC Europe to the Ukraine.

Hybrids with *P. elatior* or *P. veris* are not rare, and often have intermediate characters (e.g., short peduncles under umbel, but suberect flowers). The description above pertains to ssp. *vulgaris*. Ssp. *sibthorpii* (Hoffmanns.) Smith & Forrest, from E Europe, has pink or purplish flowers and abruptly narrowed leaves.

p.142 **Brookweed** *Samolus valerandi* L.

Description: A glabrous (short-lived) perennial, with creeping rhizomes, and erect, terete flowering stems to 30 (50) cm, often branched in inflorescence. Leaves entire-margined, rather stiff and *slightly fleshy*, obovate to oblanceolate or spatulate, often concave, the lower ones crowded in basal rosette, 20–40 mm long; *stem-leaves alternate*, subsessile, much smaller. Flowers regular, stalked, 2–3 mm diam., several together in *lax, leafless, terminal racemes*; flower-stalks erect, 3–10 mm long, *twisted around middle* (and there with a *tiny bracteole*). Calyx cup-shaped, with short tube and 5 *small, triangular-ovate teeth*. Corolla *white*, with short, wide tube (about equalling calyx), and 5 recurved, broadly obovate, slightly notched lobes. Stamens 5, with short filaments, implanted on corolla tube, with 5 *sterile staminodia in between*, alternating with corolla lobes. *Ovary hemi-inferior, connate to calyx tube*, 1-locular, with straight style. Fruit a many-seeded, subglobose capsule, 2–3 mm long, opening with 5 valves.

Flowering: June–August.

Habitat: Marshy grassland, fens, dune-slacks, pond-, ditch- and streamsides, on wet (often periodically inundated), oligotrophic, calcareous, often brackish, sandy, rocky or peaty soils; from sea level to 1,200 m.

Range: S, W and C Europe, northwards to the British Isles, S Sweden, S Finland, and the Baltic States; often coastal, but locally in basic or brackish environments in C Europe.

The plant can live submerged for prolonged periods. It is often kept as an aquarium plant, or (more successfully) as an ornamental along garden ponds.

p.103 **Chickweed Wintergreen**
Trientalis europaea L.

Description: A glabrous perennial, to 25 cm, with creeping rhizomes, slender, creeping stolons (ending in small tuber), and erect, terete, *unbranched* flowering stems. Normal leaves 6–7, *placed in single whorl* at top of stem, subsessile, 20–50 (80) mm long, oblanceolate or narrowly elliptical, acute, entire-margined, often with a few small, blunt, alternate leaves (to 30 mm long) lower on stem. Flowers regular, long-stalked, 11–19 mm diam., *solitary or 2–4 together* at end of stem, rising from whorl of leaves. *Sepals 5–9 (often 7), linear*, almost free. *Petals white* (occasionally pinkish), 5–9 *(often 7)*, distinctly exceeding calyx, almost free, elliptical to narrowly obovate, spreading. Stamens 5–9, with long, glabrous filaments. Ovary superior, 1-locular, with straight style. Fruit a many-seeded, subglobose, bluish-green capsule, 4 mm long, opening with 5–9 (often 7) valves.

Flowering: May–July.

Habitat: Damp, deciduous woods (often Oak and Birch), also mossy coniferous woods, on moist, oligotrophic, acid, sandy or loamy soils; from sea level to 2,000 m.

Range: Much of Europe, from Iceland and N Russia southwards to Britain, N and E France, the mountains of C and S Europe, and Romania.

WINTERGREEN FAMILY, PYROLACEAE

A family of perennial, often evergreen, rhizomatous herbs or subshrubs, with about 30 species in 5 genera, mainly in cold and temperate regions of the northern hemisphere. Dicots. Leaves alternate (occasionally whorled or opposite), often crowded in basal rosette, simple. Stipules absent. Flowers regular, hermaphrodite, solitary or in terminal racemes. Sepals 4–5, free. Petals 4–5, free or connate. Stamens 8 or 10, free. Ovary superior, 4–5-locular (or incompletely so); style 1, with simple or 4–5-lobed stigma. Fruit a many-seeded capsule, or a berry. Most species are saprophytic or, properly speaking, mycotrophic, i.e., parasitizing fungi that themselves live in symbiosis with tree-roots. The genus *Monotropa*, having lost its chlorophyll, has become completely dependent on these fungi; it is often placed in a separate family (Monotropaceae). Most species show strong affinities to coniferous woods; hence they are rare in W Europe, and usually protected here.

---

p.291 **Umbellate Wintergreen**
Chimaphila umbellata (L.) Barton

Description: A glabrous, *evergreen subshrub*, with erect, angular stems to 30 cm. Leaves 30–50 mm long, oblanceolate, narrowed into short stalk, (remotely) serrate-dentate, shiny dark green, leathery, in a few *whorls of (2) 3–5 leaves*. Flowers 8–12 mm diam., long-stalked, nodding, in *umbel-like racemes* (often with 1-flowered branch below, subtended by solitary, leaf-like bract) on long, rounded peduncle. Sepals 5, small, ovate. Petals 5, rounded, *pale pink*, spreading. Stamens 10. Ovary subglobose, 5-lobed, with subsessile, 5-lobed stigma. Fruit a subglobose, many-seeded capsule, 5–6 mm long, opening with 5 valves.

Flowering: June–July.

Habitat: Coniferous woods (often Pine), occasionally deciduous woods, also damp rocks, on moist, oligotrophic, preferably acid, sandy soils; from sea level to over 1,500 m.

Range: N, C and E Europe, southwards to N Alps and the Crimea.

p.116 **One-flowered Wintergreen**
Moneses uniflora (L.) A. Gray

Description: A glabrous, *evergreen perennial* to 20 cm,
with creeping rhizomes and short, erect
stems. *Leaves (sub)opposite*, close to ground,
1–30 mm long, ovate, crenate; leaf-stalk
shorter than blade. *Flowers solitary*,
terminal, 13–20 mm diam., nodding on
long stalk (to 10 cm). Sepals 5, small,
narrowly ovate. Petals 5, rounded, *white*,
spreading. Stamens 10. Ovary subglobose,
5-lobed, with *long, straight style; stigma disc-shaped*, 5-lobed. Fruit an ovoid, lobed, 5-
locular, many-seeded capsule, 5–8 mm
long, opening with 5 valves.

Flowering: May–August.

Habitat: Deciduous and coniferous woods, on moist,
oligotrophic, mildly acid, sandy, rocky or
peaty soils; from sea level to 2,000 m.

Range: Most of Europe except the Arctic, but only
on mountains in the south.

---

p.144 **Yellow Bird's-nest** *Monotropa hypopitys* L.

Description: A more or less hairy, *cream or pale-brownish,
mycotrophic perennial*, with erect stems (often
in small groups), to 30 cm. *Leaves scale-like,
alternate, c.* 10 mm long, (broadly) elliptical,
entire-margined, translucent, pale
brownish. Flowers 9–12 mm long, 3–5 mm
diam., subsessile, in *nodding*, terminal, *spike-like raceme* (becoming erect in fruit); each
flower has small, cream, lanceolate bract.
Sepals 4, erect, ovate. Corolla narrowly bell-
shaped, *cream*, with 4 obovate petals hairy on
inside. Stamens 10, with hairy filaments.
Ovary narrowly ellipsoid or obovoid, hairy; style
also hairy, 1.5–2 times as long as ovary, with
funnel-shaped stigma. Fruit a (short)
ellipsoid capsule, 6–8 mm long, opening
with 5 valves, and containing thousands of
minute, powdery seeds.

Flowering: (May) June–August.

Habitat: Woods, preferably deciduous, on dry,
oligotrophic to eutrophic, calcareous or
mildly acid, sandy, humus-rich soils; from
sea level to 1,800 m.

Range: Most of Europe, except the far north.

Another name is Dutchman's Pipe. The whole plant turns black on drying. The top flower is usually 5-merous. The description above pertains to ssp. *hypopitys*, also called Dutchman's Pipe. Ssp. *hypophegea* (Wallr.) Holmb., has subglobose, (sub)glabrous ovaries and fruits (5–6 mm long), and (sub)glabrous stamens and petals as well; styles shorter than, or barely equalling ovary. In the same general area, but prefers coniferous woods (often with Pine) on poorer soils; also in coastal scrub. Intermediate forms are frequent.

p.125 **Nodding Wintergreen**
Orthilia secunda (L.) House

Description: A glabrous, *evergreen perennial*, to 20 (30) cm, with long, creeping rhizomes and short, erect or ascending stems. *Leaves alternate*, close to ground, 20–40 mm long, (narrowly) ovate, *subacute, finely serrate-dentate*; leaf-stalk shorter than blade. Flowers 5–6 mm diam., short-stalked, nodding, up to 15 together in erect or arching, *1-sided raceme* on top of long peduncle; each flower has small, whitish, lanceolate bract. Sepals 5, small, narrowly ovate. Petals 5, erect, rounded, *greenish-white*. Stamens 10. Ovary subglobose, 5-lobed, with *long, protruding, straight style*; stigma 5-lobed. Fruit a subglobose, 5-locular, many-seeded capsule, 3–4 mm long, opening with 5 valves.

Flowering: July–August.

Habitat: Coniferous and deciduous woods, also rocks in mountains, and dune-slacks, on moist, oligotrophic, preferably calcareous, sandy, loamy or rocky soils; from sea level to 2,200 m, but only on mountains over 800 m in the south.

Range: Most of Europe except the Low Countries (extinct in the Netherlands), and rare in Mediterranean area.

Another name is Serrated, or Toothed, Wintergreen.

p.125 **Yellow Wintergreen**
Pyrola chlorantha Swartz

Description: A glabrous, *evergreen perennial*, to 18 cm, with
long, creeping rhizomes. Leaves 3–8 together
in basal rosette, 5–20 mm long, obovate to
suborbicular, round-tipped, entire-margined
or weakly crenate, yellowish-green above,
darker beneath; leaf-stalk usually longer than
blade. Flowers widely bell-shaped, 8–12 mm
diam., short-stalked, nodding, 1–13 together
in all-sided raceme on top of long peduncle;
each flower subtended by small, green,
lanceolate bract. Sepals 5, triangular-ovate,
about as wide as long, up to only 1 third the
length of corolla. Petals 5, rounded, *greenish-
white*. Stamens 10. Ovary subglobose, 5-
lobed; *style sinuous, c.* 7 mm long, protruding,
longer than ovary, with disc-shaped, 5-lobed
stigma. Fruit a subglobose, 5-locular, many-
seeded capsule, 4–5 mm long, opening with
5 valves.

Flowering: June–August.

Habitat: Woods (usually coniferous), also rocks, and
meadows in mountains, on moist to rather
dry, oligotrophic, preferably calcareous, sandy,
loamy or stony soils; from sea level to
2,000 m, but only on mountains in the south.

Range: Continental Europe, but rare in the west
(and absent from the Low Countries).

---

p.142 **Common Wintergreen** *Pyrola minor* L.

Description: A glabrous, *evergreen perennial* to 30 cm, with
creeping rhizomes. Leaves 6–12 together in
basal rosette, 20–50 mm long, broadly
elliptical to suborbicular, round-tipped,
crenate, bright green; leaf-stalk usually
shorter than blade. Flowers globose, 5–7 mm
diam., short-stalked, nodding, 4–8 (16)
together in all-sided raceme on top of long
peduncle; each flower subtended by small,
greenish, lanceolate bract. Sepals 5, broadly
triangular-lanceolate, almost as wide as long,
up to 1 third the length of corolla. Petals 5,
rounded, *white or pale pink*. Stamens 10.
Ovary subglobose, 5-lobed; *style straight and
short* (to 2 mm long, shorter than ovary, not

protruding, and lacking disc-shaped expansion below 5-lobed stigma). Fruit a subglobose, 5-locular, many-seeded capsule, 4–5 mm long, opening with 5 valves.

Flowering: June–August.

Habitat: Woods (often with conifers), moors, mountain ledges, occasionally sea-dunes, on moist, oligotrophic, acid, sandy, gravelly or rocky soils; from sea level to 2,700 m, but mainly on mountains in the south.

Range: Most of Europe except Portugal and Spitsbergen.

Similar species: **Intermediate Wintergreen** (*P. media* Swartz) has broader, more often rounded leaves (5–8 mm long), narrower, broadly lanceolate sepals, larger flowers (7–10 mm diam.), straight, protruding styles (4–6 mm long, distinctly longer than ovary), with disc-like, 5-lobed stigma. In mossy coniferous woods (often with Scots Pine), moors, heaths, in most of Europe except the Netherlands, Iceland, and the high Arctic, and only on mountains in the south.

---

p.142 **Round-leaved Wintergreen**
Pyrola rotundifolia L.

Description: A glabrous, *evergreen perennial*, to 40 cm, with creeping rhizomes. Leaves 6–12 together in basal rosette, 30–50 mm long, broadly obovate to suborbicular, round-tipped, weakly crenate-dentate, deep green; leaf-stalk usually longer than blade. Flowers widely bell-shaped, 8–12 mm diam., short-stalked, nodding, 8–15 (30) together in all-sided raceme on top of long, often reddish peduncle, bearing 1–2 lanceolate scales; each flower subtended by small, whitish or reddish, lanceolate bract. Sepals 5, lanceolate, up to 2 thirds the length of corolla. Petals 5, rounded, *pure white* (rarely pinkish). Stamens 10. Ovary subglobose, 5-lobed; *style curved*, up to 10 mm long, protruding, longer than ovary, with disc-shaped, 5-lobed stigma. Fruit a subglobose, 5-locular, many-seeded capsule, 4–6 mm long, opening with 5 valves.

Flowering: June–October.

Habitat: Deciduous and coniferous woods, scrub, dune-slacks, also bogs and fens, short grassland, and mountain ledges, on moist, oligotrophic, weakly acid to calcareous, sandy, loamy, stony or peaty soils; from sea level to 2,000 m.

Range: Most of Europe, except Iceland, eastwards to N Russia and the Caucasus.

Similar species: **Norwegian Wintergreen** (*P. norvegica* Knaben), from dry calcareous slopes in the mountains of Scandinavia, has ovate to elliptical, rather leathery, shiny-green leaves on stalks shorter than blade, and larger, pink or white flowers (10–25 mm diam.); style lacks disc-like expansion below stigmas. *P. grandiflora* Radius, from the tundra of Iceland and Arctic Russia, also has larger flowers (15–20 mm diam.) and shiny, leathery leaves, but flowers can be white, greenish or pink, and leaf-stalks are longer than blade.

The description of Round-leaved Wintergreen pertains to ssp. *rotundifolia*. Small forms, from the dunes of W Europe, with broadly triangular-lanceolate sepals, 2–4 lanceolate scales on peduncle, flower-stalks not exceeding 4 mm (not 4–6 mm), and styles up to 5 mm long, are distinguished as ssp. *maritima* (Kenyon) Warb.

BUTTERCUP FAMILY, RANUNCULACEAE

An important family of herbs (occasionally woody lianas: some *Clematis* species), with about 1,800 species in 50-odd genera, mainly in temperate or cold regions of the northern hemisphere. Dicots. Leaves alternate (opposite in *Clematis*), simple or compound (pinnate or palmate). Flowers regular or irregular, usually hermaphrodite; flower parts often partly spirally placed. Perianth of 2 types: apparently normal sepals and petals, or all petal-like ('tepals'), then often with an inner ring of staminodes (sterile, often petal-like stamens, generally also functioning as nectaries). (Normal) stamens often numerous, free. Ovaries 1–many, free or partly connate. Fruit a cluster of follicles or achenes, occasionally a berry (*Actaea*). Many species are grown for ornament (e.g., *Aconitum, Anemone, Aquilegia, Clematis, Delphinium, Helleborus, Trollius*). The plants are often poisonous, though the seeds of *Nigella sativa* L. can be used as a spice.

p.317 **Monk's-hood** *Aconitum napellus* L.

Description: A more or less hairy perennial, with tuberous rhizomes and simple, erect flowering stems to 1 (1.5) m. *Leaves palmatifid*, with (3) 5–7 deeply lobed segments; lower leaves long-stalked, upper ones smaller, subsessile. Flowers numerous, on erect stalks, in large (often branched) terminal raceme, *very irregular; tepals 5, red- or blue-violet, hairy,* upper one forming *large hood* to 18 mm long and almost as wide; lateral tepals rounded, partly enclosed in hood; lower tepals ovate. Staminodes 10; upper pair much enlarged and spurred, producing nectar, and concealed in hood. Normal stamens numerous. Ovaries few (2–5), developing into cluster of many-seeded follicles.

Flowering: June–September.

Habitat: Marshes, meadows, scrub, damp woods, streamsides, on wet to moist, oligotrophic, calcareous, sandy, loamy or stony soils; from sea level to 2,500 m, but rare in the lowland.

Range: W and C Europe, westwards to N France and S Britain, and eastwards to S Sweden and E Austria.

Similar species: *A. variegatum* L. has glabrous, blue flowers (often streaked with white, occasionally all white) with narrow, broadly conical hood to 15 mm long, distinctly higher than wide. In mountains of C and SE Europe, locally northwards to Poland, and eastwards to W Russia.

Both species are extremely poisonous. They contain aconitin, an alkaloid causing death by paralysis of the respiratory muscles; it is easily taken up by the human skin when these plants are handled. W European forms of Monk's-hood belong to ssp. *neomontanum* (Wulfen) Gáyer; other subspecies, usually with broader leaf-segments, occur in the mountains of C and S Europe. Several are grown in gardens, and may occasionally be found naturalized in W Europe. *Compare A. septentrionale (see p.934)*, which has much narrower, long-tapering hoods.

p.208 **Wolf's-bane** *Aconitum vulparia* Rchb.

Description: Much like *A. napellus*, but *flowers always pale yellow*, and lower leaves have 7–9 segments; hood *c.* 20 mm long, long-tapering, height at least twice the width.

Flowering: June–August.

Habitat: Damp, deciduous woods and scrub, on moist, oligotrophic, calcareous, sandy, loamy or stony, humus-rich soils; from sea level to 2,400 m, but rare in the lowland.

Range: C Europe, westwards to the Pyrenees, E France, E Belgium, and the SE Netherlands.

Similar species: **Northern Wolf's-bane** (*A. septentrionale* Koelle) from Scandinavia and N Russia has dark-violet (rarely yellow) flowers, while the lower leaves have only 4–6 segments.

Both species are extremely poisonous.

---

p.140 **Baneberry** *Actaea spicata* L.

Description: A glabrous, strongly smelling perennial with creeping rhizome and erect, often branched flowering stems to 60 (80) cm. Leaves stalked, alternate, few on a stem, *doubly pinnate or doubly ternate*, with ovate, serrate leaflets. Flowers regular, 6–9 mm diam., few to several together in ovoid or shortly cylindrical, terminal raceme to 80 mm long, regular, with 3–5 (6) narrowly ovate, *white tepals* and *4–10 petal-like, white staminodes*, these with small, obovate limb and linear, stalk-like claw. Normal stamens numerous, white. *Ovary 1*, ellipsoid, with sessile, cushion-shaped stigma. Fruit a *broadly ovoid berry* to 13 mm diam., *shiny black when ripe*.

Flowering: May–August.

Habitat: Damp, deciduous woods (often with Beech or Ash), occasionally in gardens, on moist, oligotrophic, calcareous, sandy, loamy or stony soils; from sea level to 1,900 m.

Range: Most of Europe, northwards to N Scandinavia, but rare in the extreme west (isolated occurrence in N England), and only on mountains in the south.

Similar species: **Red Baneberry** (*A. erythrocarpa* Fischer), from N Sweden, Finland and N and C Russia, more often has bipinnate leaves, and smaller, red berries to 10 mm diam.

Both species are highly poisonous. Perianth of Baneberry (also called Herb Christopher) soon falls.

---

p.244 **Summer Pheasant's-eye** *Adonis aestivalis* L.

Description: A subglabrous annual, to 50 cm, with branched stems, and sessile, 3 times pinnatifid, *finely dissected leaves*. Flowers regular, solitary at top of branches, 15–30 mm diam., with 5–7 glabrous or minutely hairy, obovate, reddish-brown, *erect sepals*, and 5–8 spreading, narrowly obovate, round-tipped, *scarlet petals* with short, *black claw*. Stamens numerous, with *blackish-violet anthers*. Ovaries numerous. Fruit a narrowly ovoid cluster of greenish, 1-seeded, *glabrous achenes*, these 5–6 mm long, with blunt, transverse ridge or shoulder over the middle, and short, straight, sideways-pointing beak.

Flowering: June–July.

Habitat: Arable land, preferably cereal fields, also ruderal places, on dry, oligotrophic to mesotrophic, often calcareous, sandy or stony soils; from sea level to 1,500 m.

Range: S, SC and W Europe, northwards to Belgium, C Germany, Poland, and E Russia; an archeophyte, native to southerly regions, but naturalized in C and W Europe, though here the species is becoming very rare.

Similar species: **Pheasant's-eye** (*A. annua* L.) has stalked lower leaves, flowers 15–25 mm diam., with suberect petals and deflexed sepals, and straight-walled achenes (3.5–5 mm long); flowers May–August. In arable fields on calcareous soils, in the same general area (north to Belgium).

A. flammea Jacq. has long hairs on (erect) sepals, flowers 20–30 mm diam., with spreading petals, and smooth, roughly obovoid (but not ridged) achenes (3.5–5 mm long) with narrow incision between wall and beak. In arable fields on calcareous soils, in the same general area (north to N France).

The last two species are also archeophytes. Plants of all 3 species occasionally occur with yellow flowers; *compare A. vernalis* (below), which is perennial and has more and larger petals.

---

p.191   **Yellow Pheasant's-eye**   *Adonis vernalis* L.

Description: A glabrous perennial, to 30 cm, with branched stems, and sessile, 2–3-times pin-natifid, *finely dissected leaves*. Flowers regular, solitary at top of branches, *40–70 mm diam.*, with 5–8 glabrous, (ob)ovate, brownish, *erect sepals*, and 12–20 spreading, oblanceolate, round-tipped, *yellow petals*. Stamens numerous, with *yellow anthers*. Ovaries numerous. Fruit an ovoid cluster of greenish, 1-seeded, *minutely hairy achenes*, these 5–6 mm long, obovoid, with short, sideways-pointing beak (curving back to fruit).

Flowering: April–May.

Habitat: Grassland, scrub, heaths and rocks, on dry, oligotrophic, calcareous, sandy, loamy or stony soils; from sea level to 1,200 m.

Range: S, C and E Europe, locally extending westwards to C France and S Germany (extinct in the Netherlands); also on Gotland.

The plant is typical of the steppe belt of SE Europe and SW Asia; the sparse populations in the west are often regarded as relics from the glacial periods when steppe-like vegetations dominated large parts of Europe.

---

p.100   **Wood Anemone**   *Anemone nemorosa* L.

Description: A subglabrous perennial, with creeping rhizomes, and erect, unbranched flowering stems to 25 cm. Leaves stalked: partly (1–2) rising directly from rhizome (on long, only slightly hairy stalks), partly (3) cauline, the latter in a terminal *whorl* immediately below flower; leaf-blade palmatifid, with 3–5 lanceolate segments, these often deeply lobed in turn. Flowers solitary, regular, long-stalked, terminal, 20–40 mm diam., with *6–12 elliptical or ovate, white tepals*. Stamens numerous, with yellow anthers. Ovaries numerous. Fruit a rounded cluster of ovoid, pointed, 1-seeded achenes.

Flowering: March–May.

Habitat: Damp, deciduous woods, copses, hedges, shaded grassland and ditch-sides, on moist, oligotrophic to mesotrophic, calcareous to weakly acid, sandy, loamy or stony, humus-rich soils; from sea level to 1,800 m.

Range: Most of Europe, except Iceland.

Similar species: **Snowdrop Windflower** (*A. sylvestris* L.) often has densely pubescent stems and leaf-stalks, 2–6 basal leaves, less incised leaf-segments, and much larger, solitary or paired flowers (40–70 mm diam.) with 5 white, ovate tepals. In woods (often Oak) on calcareous soils in E and C Europe, westwards to N France, C Germany and S Sweden; also grown in gardens.

In Wood Anenome, basal leaves appear after flowering has ended. The flowers can be tinged with pink or blue on the outside; of the cultivars grown in gardens, several have plain-pink or blue-violet flowers.

p.192 **Yellow Anemone** *Anemone ranunculoides* L.

Description: Much like *A. nemorosa*, but hairier, with 0–1 short-stalked basal leaves (on glabrous stalks, for a contrast). Flowers solitary or 2–3 (5) together, 15–20 mm diam., with *5–8 yellow, hairy tepals*.

Flowering: March–May.

Habitat: Damp woods (often with Ash or Oak), copses, occasionally shaded road verges and banks, on moist, oligotrophic to mesotrophic, preferably calcareous, loamy or clayey, humus-rich soils; from sea level to 1,500 m.

Range: Continental Europe, northwards to W and C Scandinavia, S Finland and N Russia; locally naturalized in Britain.

Also often cultivated in gardens.

p.336 **Common Columbine** *Aquilegia vulgaris* L.

Description: A glabrous perennial with erect, branched stems to 60 cm. Leaves stalked, alternate, *doubly ternate*, with obovate, crenate to bluntly lobed leaflets; bracts in inflorescence sessile, much smaller and less divided. Flowers 30–50 mm diam., long-stalked, *nodding*, several together in lax panicle, regular, with 5 recurved, narrowly ovate, *blue-violet tepals* and *5 bluntly ovate, long-spurred, blue-violet, petal-like staminodes*; spurs erect, hooked, containing nectar. Normal stamens numerous, barely protruding, the inner ones sterile. Ovaries 5, largely connate, with 5 threadlike styles. Fruit a *cluster of 5 many-seeded follicles*, to 20 mm long.

Flowering: May–July.

Habitat: Open woods, scrub, woodland clearings, also marshy meadows and shaded banks, on moist to rather wet, oligotrophic, preferably calcareous, sandy, loamy, stony or peaty soils; from sea level to 2,000 m.

Range: S, W and C Europe, northwards to Britain, the Low Countries, Poland, and N Russia; locally naturalized in Fennoscandia, and elsewhere in Russia.

Frequently grown in gardens, in several cultivars and hybrid forms that can occasionally be found naturalized in the wild.

---

p.192 **Marsh Marigold** *Caltha palustris* L.

Description: A glabrous perennial, with creeping rhizomes, and ascending, branched flowering stems to 50 cm; nodes hollow, not distinctly thickened. Leaves alternate, *broadly ovate with cordate base* (to reniform), round-tipped, *crenate*, up to 8 (15) cm diam., shiny dark green; lower ones long-stalked, upper ones smaller and subsessile. Flowers regular, stalked, 20–50 mm diam., erect, in lax, leafy panicles. Tepals 5 (rarely more), *yellow*, often greenish on outside. Stamens numerous, with yellow anthers. Ovaries 5–8 (rarely more), basally connate.

Fruit a star-shaped cluster of ellipsoid, recurved, pointed, glandular-hairy, brownish, many-seeded follicles to 15 mm long.

Flowering: March–May (August).

Habitat: Marshes, fens, reedlands, scrub (often with Willow or Alder), flushes, streamsides and ditches, often partly submerged, on wet to moist, mesotrophic to eutrophic, clayey, muddy or peaty soils; from sea level to 2,500 m.

Range: Most of Europe except Spitsbergen, and rare in Mediterranean region.

A poisonous plant; nevertheless, the petals were once used to colour butter. The description above pertains to ssp. *palustris*. Small-sized plants with thin, creeping stems, often found in oligotrophic ditches and small streams of N Europe, are distinguished as ssp. *minor* (Mill.) Aschrs. & Graebn. Ssp. *araneosa* (Steenis) Meijden, in reedlands and willow coppices along fresh or brackish tidal rivers in the Low Countries and N Germany, is a coarse plant with solid, thickened nodes along flowering stems that develop spider- or nest-like bundles of short, thick roots after flowering; once the softer parts of the plant have decayed in autumn, these root-bearing nodes are dispersed with the tides, and serve as vegetative propagules. *Compare Damasonium (see p.353)*, which also has star-shaped fruits, but differs in having small, white flowers.

p.153 **Traveller's Joy** *Clematis vitalba* L.

Description: A *woody, deciduous* shrub, *climbing* on other shrubs or trees, helped by its *coiling and twisting leaf-stalks*, and thus able to reach treetops 30 m high. *Leaves opposite, pinnate*, with 3–7 (9) stalked, ovate, pointed, lobed to remotely dentate or subentire, yellowish-green leaflets up to 50 (80) mm long. Flowers regular, stalked, 15–20 mm diam., numerous, in axillary and terminal panicles. Tepals 4 (5), *yellowish- or greenish-white, hairy on both faces*. Stamens numerous, with yellow anthers. Ovaries few to several, basally connate. Fruit a small cluster of ovate, hairy, brownish, 1-seeded achenes, 3–4 mm long, with persistent, *feathery style to 40 mm* long (strongly elongating after opening).

Flowering: June–September.

Habitat: Wood margins, scrub, hedges, on moist, mesotrophic to oligotrophic, calcareous, sandy, loamy or clayey soils, but also scrambling over rocks or stones in mountains, on river groynes, and along railways; from sea level to 2,100 m.

Range: S, W and C Europe, northwards to C Britain, the Low Countries, C Germany, Hungary, and Romania, and locally naturalized further north.

Similar species: **Erect Clematis** (*C. recta* L.) is a non-climbing, herbaceous perennial to 1.5 m, with entire-margined leaflets, and ciliate, white tepals. In S, C and E Europe, northwards to NE France, S Germany, Poland and C Russia; often cultivated in gardens.

Traveller's Joy does not parasitize the tree it grows on, but a large specimen can cause some damage to the crown by its weight. The leaves have a burning taste. The flowers were used as a substitute for tea.

---

p.336 **Forking Larkspur**
Consolida regalis S.F. Gray

Description: A slender, hairy annual to 30 (50) cm, with straggling to ascending, diffusely branched stems. Leaves alternate, stalked, rounded, *finely dissected* with threadlike segments; bracts in inflorescence linear, not divided. Flowers long-stalked, 15–25 mm diam., *very irregular*, erect to nodding, in few-flowered, axillary and terminal racemes composing lax panicle. *Tepals 5*, ovate, *blue-violet, glabrous*; upper one bears tapering, backward-pointing *spur to 25 mm long*. *Staminode 1, petal-like*, 2-parted, with 2 rounded side-lobes, and bearing slender, nectar-producing spur enclosed within spur of upper tepal. Normal stamens numerous. *Ovary 1*, developing into solitary, glabrous, ellipsoid, many-seeded follicle, opening from top along 1 seam.

Flowering: June–August.

Habitat: Cereal fields, wasteland, ruderal and disturbed places, on moist, mesotrophic, preferably calcareous, sandy or loamy soils; from sea level to 1,400 m.

Range: Continental Europe except the Arctic; less frequent in the west.

Strongly declining owing to modern agricultural methods.

---

p.100 **Green Hellebore** *Helleborus viridis* L.

Description: A subglabrous perennial, with creeping rhizomes and erect, unbranched flowering stems to 40 cm. Leaves long-stalked, usually *2 together at base of stem, palmately divided* with 7–13 oblanceolate, coarsely serrate, dull bluish-green segments spread out like a fan and *glabrous beneath*. Flowers regular, 30–40 mm diam., long-stalked, often nodding, (1) 2–4 together in terminal umbel, subtended by common involucre of subsessile, palmately divided, leaf-like bracts. Tepals 5, broadly ovate, plain *greenish-yellow*. Staminodes 5, nectar-producing, tubular, funnel-shaped, greenish, much shorter than tepals. Normal stamens numerous, with whitish anthers. Ovaries few, free, sitting close together. Fruit a cluster of *c.* 4 broadly ovoid, pointed, many-seeded follicles, 25–28 mm long, connate at base.

Flowering: January–April.

Habitat: Damp, deciduous woods, scrub, hedges, also shaded, grassy banks, on moist, oligotrophic, calcareous, loamy, clayey or stony, humus-rich soils; from sea level to 1,500 m.

Range: W Europe, from N Spain to England and the Low Countries, locally eastwards to S Poland.

Similar species: **Stinking Hellebore** (*H. foetidus* L.) is an unpleasantly smelling plant with hibernating, leafy stems (all leaves cauline), much reduced, often unlobed floral bracts, numerous nodding flowers (15–20 mm diam.), greenish-yellow, often red-edged tepals, and narrower follicles in clusters of 3. In deciduous woods (often Beech), also in grassland and road verges, on rather drier, calcareous soils, in SW Europe, northwards to England, Belgium, S Germany, and eastwards to Italy.

Both species are highly poisonous but are nevertheless cultivated in gardens. Flowering often starts before the snow has thawed away. The description of Green Hellebore pertains to ssp. *occidentalis* (Reuter) Schiffner; ssp. *viridis*, in C Europe, has finely serrate leaves, pubescent beneath.

---

p.332 **Hepatica** *Hepatica nobilis* (L.) Miller

Description: A glabrous or slightly hairy, tufted perennial, with overwintering, *basal leaf-rosette*, and few to several erect flowering stems to 10 (20) cm. Leaves long-stalked, slightly leathery, rounded or triangular, deeply lobed to divided with *3 broadly ovate, entire-margined segments*, often purplish beneath, dull green and often purple-flushed above; stem-leaves absent, but each flowering stem bears *3 ovate, hairy, sepal-like bracts* directly under solitary, terminal flower, which itself is regular, 15–25 mm diam., with 6–10 broadly elliptical, *bluish-violet* (rarely pink or white) tepals. Stamens numerous, with whitish anthers. Ovaries numerous. Fruit a rounded cluster of ovoid, short-beaked achenes.

Flowering: March–April.

Habitat: Deciduous or mixed woods (often with Oaks or Beech), copses, scrub, also rocks, on moist to rather dry, oligotrophic, preferably calcareous, sandy, loamy or stony soils; from sea level to 2,200 m, but mainly on mountains in the south.

Range: Continental Europe, extending to NE France, Germany, Denmark, Scandinavia, Finland, N Russia.

p.98 **Mousetail** *Myosurus minimus* L.

Description: An inconspicuous, glabrous, tufted annual, 2–10 (20) cm tall, with *basal leaf-rosette*, and few to several erect, leafless flowering stems. *Leaves slightly fleshy, linear*, entire-margined, gradually tapering into long stalk. Flowers regular, solitary, terminal, 4–5 mm diam., with 5–7 narrowly elliptical, *greenish-yellow* tepals, each with *tiny, pendent spur* (to 2 mm long). Staminodes 5–7 (as many as tepals), whitish, linear, tubular. Stamens 5–10, with whitish anthers. Ovaries numerous, implanted on cylindrical receptacle that strongly elongates after anthesis. *Fruit a linear spike* (to 70 mm long, and 2–3 mm wide) covered with numerous tiny, short-beaked achenes.

Flowering: (March) May–June (July).

Habitat: Open, trampled pasture and paths in cultivated and waste land, on wet or moist, mesotrophic to eutrophic, acid, sandy, clayey or peaty soils; from sea level to 1,400 m.

Range: Most of Europe, except the high Arctic; rare in the extreme south.

Easily overlooked, and possibly not as rare as often supposed, though rather local in its occurrence; gates in the wire fencing of pastures are a good place to look for it.

p.332 **Nigella** *Nigella arvensis* L.

Description: A glabrous annual with spreading to erect, widely branched stems to 30 cm. Leaves subsessile, alternate, ovate, *finely dissected*, with threadlike segments. Flowers 20–30 mm diam., long-stalked, *erect*, solitary, terminal, regular. Tepals 5, spreading, with ovate-cordate limb and long claw, *pale blue-violet with green veins*; spurs absent. Staminodes 5, small, placed before tepals. Normal stamens numerous. Ovaries 3–5 (10), only basally connate, with threadlike styles. Fruit a cluster of 3–5 roughly ellipsoid, 3-veined follicles to

15 mm long (25 mm including beak), each with several seeds.

Flowering: June–September.

Habitat: Cereal fields on moist, oligotrophic to mesotrophic, calcareous, sandy or loamy soils; from sea level to 700 m.

Range: Continental Europe, northwards to N France (Lorraine), Germany, Poland, and C Russia; only as a casual further north.

Occasionally grown in gardens, like some related species from S Europe.

---

p.115 **Spring Pasqueflower**
Pulsatilla vernalis (L.) Miller

Description: A *densely long-hairy* perennial, with creeping rhizomes, basal leaf-rosettes, and erect, unbranched flowering stems to 15 cm (35 cm in fruit). Basal leaves stalked, *once pinnatifid*, with (2) 3–5 obovate, dentate segments; stem-leaves 3, sessile, dissected to base in several linear, long-hairy segments forming involucre below solitary, terminal, stalked flower, which is 40–60 mm diam., nodding, with 6 (7) broadly oblanceolate, pointed, *white tepals, flushed with pink* and hairy on outside. Staminodes (nectaries) present (unlike *Anemone*). Stamens numerous, with yellow anthers, much shorter than tepals. Ovaries numerous. Fruit a rounded cluster of *spindle-shaped*, 1-seeded achenes to 8 mm long, bearing *threadlike, feathery beak* to 40 mm.

Flowering: April–June.

Habitat: Meadows and rocks, on dry or moist (often seasonally wet), oligotrophic, calcareous, loamy or stony soils; mainly in the mountains, from 1,300–3,200 m, descending lower in the north.

Range: S Fennoscandia, Denmark, E Germany, Poland, and further south in the mountains of C Europe, westwards to NE and C France.

Other species with white or pink flowers occur in the mountains of C Europe. All species are poisonous.

p.316 **Common Pasqueflower**
Pulsatilla vulgaris Miller

Description: A *densely long-hairy* perennial, with creeping
rhizomes, basal leaf-rosettes, and erect,
unbranched flowering stems to 20 cm
(40 cm in fruit). Basal leaves stalked, *doubly
pinnatifid*, with linear-lanceolate segments;
stem-leaves often simply pinnatifid, 3,
sessile, forming involucre below solitary,
terminal, stalked flower, which is
50–80 mm diam., erect or nodding, with 6
(7) elliptical, *pale- to dark-purple tepals*, hairy
on outside. Staminodes present (unlike
Anemone). Stamens numerous, with yellow
anthers, much shorter than tepals. Ovaries
numerous. Fruit a rounded cluster of
spindle-shaped, 1-seeded achenes to 8 mm
long, bearing threadlike, feathery beak to
50 mm.

Flowering: March–June.

Habitat: Meadows and pastures, grassy river-dunes, on
moist to rather dry, mesotrophic, calcareous,
sandy, loamy or stony soils; from sea level to
1,200 m.

Range: W and C Europe, northwards to England,
Belgium (extinct in the Netherlands),
S Sweden, Poland, eastwards to E Russia.

Similar species: **Small Pasqueflower** (*P. pratensis* (L.) Miller)
has smaller, drooping, bell-shaped, greyish-
violet (occasionally greenish-yellow) flowers
to 40 mm diam., with erect tepals barely
exceeding stamens; stem-leaves 2–3 times
ternate, with linear segments. In comparable
habitats, also in scrub, to 2,100 m, in E and
NC Europe, westwards to Germany and S
Scandinavia, eastwards to E Russia, and
southwards to Yugoslavia and Romania.
Eastern Pasqueflower (*P. patens* (L.) Miller)
has palmately divided basal leaves, with
oblanceolate, dentate segments, but again
finely dissected leaves in a whorl under
flower, which is large (5–8 cm), erect, with
rather spreading, blue-violet tepals. In E
and NC Europe, westwards to Sweden and
Germany, southwards to Hungary and
Romania, and eastwards to E Russia.

All species are poisonous.

Buttercups and Crowfoots, *Ranunculus*

A large genus of terrestrial and aquatic herbs with alternate leaves (often partly basal), yellow or white, normally regular flowers, numerous stamens with yellow anthers, and numerous free ovaries developing into a cluster of 1-seeded achenes. The petals carry a honey-secreting groove or scale ('nectary') at base, and must in fact be homologues of the nectar-producing staminodes found in many other Ranunculaceae. All species are more or less poisonous.

The truly aquatic species ('Water-crowfoots') are placed in a separate subgenus (***Batrachium***). Only the flowers are held above the water-surface; they have white petals (usually with a yellow basal blotch). Most have finely dissected, fan- or tassel-like submerged leaves, and often palmately lobed or divided floating leaves as well: *R. ololeucos*, *R. tripartitus*, *R. aquatilis* var. *aquatilis*, *R. peltatus*, and *R. baudotii*. Often some less finely dissected 'transitional leaves' are present. Floating leaves are always absent in *R. circinatus*, *R. fluitans*, and *R. aquatilis* var. *diffusus*. On the other hand, *R. hederaceus* and *R. omiophyllus* never possess finely dissected submerged leaves; the same is true for land forms of other species, which can be very difficult to identify.

R. ficaria is terrestrial, and has 6–12 petals, and small, club-shaped tubers. For this species a separate subgenus (***Ficaria***) has been established. The (sub)Arctic species *R. lapponicus* and *R. pallasii* also have 6 or more petals, but no tubers. They are usually placed in the 3rd and largest subgenus (***Ranunculus*** s.s., True Crowfoots), but in several respects they seem to represent a transition to Ficaria.

The other True Crowfoots have 5 (rarely fewer) petals. Occasionally these are white, as in *R. platanifolius*, *R. aconitifolius*, and *R. glacialis*, but as a rule they are yellow. Several informal groups can be distinguished:

The Spearwort group (*R. flammula*, *R. reptans*, *R. lingua*, *R. ophioglossifolius*), is characterized by simple, lanceolate, entire or sparsely dentate, glabrous, more or less fleshy leaves with arching, subparallel veins; the basal leaves may be ovate with a cordate base, and pinnately veined. These plants grow in marshy environments, often partly submerged ('helophytes').

All other species in N Europe have palmately veined leaves. Only 1 of them (*R. sceleratus*) is a true helophyte, and can be recognized immediately by its strongly ribbed, hollow stems, its glabrous, slightly fleshy leaves, and its small, pale-yellow flowers (less than 10 mm diam.). Moreover, it is an annual, and obviously forms a group on its own.

Glabrous buttercups with smallish flowers (everything between 5 and 15 mm across), which are otherwise confined to Arctic Europe (including Iceland and the Faeroes). These, however, are perennial, and primarily terrestrial; they constitute the 'Arctic group', which includes *R. nivalis*, *R. pygmaeus*, *R. sulphureus*, and *R. hyperboreus*. The last species is notable for having only 3 petals, a creeping habit, and often a semi-aquatic (amphibious) mode of life.

All remaining terrestrial species are more or less hairy. *R. arvensis* and *R. parviflorus* are annual, often growing in cultivated land; they are further characterized by small flowers (from 3 to 12 mm diam.), and warty or even spiny achenes. They differ considerably in leaf shape, but they are best placed together in a 'Hairy, annual group' group, which can also include *R. sardous* (also annual), with minutely tuberculate achenes, and larger flowers with deflexed sepals.

As a rule, the remaining 'Hairy, perennial group' inhabits grassy or wooded places. Of the species contained in it, only *R. bulbosus* and *R. pedatifidus* have deflexed sepals during anthesis. In the other species sepals are spreading to erect, and appressed against petals. *R. repens* has creeping stolons; the other ones grow more or less erect: *R. acris*, *R. polyanthemos*, *R. lanuginosus*, *R. auricomus* (often scarcely hairy, but always with hairy achenes), and *R. affinis*.

---

p.210 **Meadow Buttercup** *Ranunculus acris* L.

Description: A hairy perennial to 60 (90) cm, with very short, underground rhizomes (to 20 mm) and *erect*, branched stems; no aerial stolons. Basal leaves long-stalked, broadly 5-angular or rounded, palmately divided with 5 (7) obovate, deeply lobed to divided main segments; stem-leaves short-stalked to sessile, with 3–5 narrower to simple and oblanceolate or linear segments. Flowers axillary, 15–25 mm diam., in lax, often many-flowered panicle; receptacle glabrous; *flower-stalks terete, ungrooved.* Sepals 5, ovate, hairy, *erect or spreading.* Petals 5, rounded or shallowly notched, shiny deep yellow. Fruit a cluster of broadly obovoid, smooth achenes, 2–3 mm long, with short, strongly curved beak.

Flowering: April–September (winter).

Habitat: Grassland, road verges, woodland clearings, ditch-sides, on moist, mesotrophic to eutrophic, sandy, loamy or clayey soils; from sea level to 2,500 m.

Range: Practically all of Europe.

Similar species: **Woolly Buttercup** (*R. lanuginosus* L.) has
dense, long, yellow or brownish (not
whitish) hairs, less-divided basal leaves, and
long, coiled beaks to achenes. In mountains
of S and C Europe, westwards to the Jura
Mountains and C Germany, and locally
northwards to Denmark and the Baltic
States. *Compare also R. auricomus*, which has
hairy achenes, and *R. polyanthemos* (*see* p.961),
which has furrowed flower-stalks.

Meadow Buttercup is often conspicuously
present in pasture as its acrid taste
discourages cattle from eating it. The
description above pertains to ssp. *acris*.
Southern forms with longer rhizomes (to
10 cm) bearing basal leaves in 2 rows, with
5 shallowly lobed or only dentate segments,
are distinguished as ssp. *frieseanus* (Jordan)
Rouy & Fouc.; intermediate forms can be
found. Smallish forms (to 20 cm) from N
Britain, Iceland and Scandinavia, having
basal leaves with only 3 main segments,
and often brown-veined petals, are
attributed to ssp. *borealis* (Trautv.) Nyman.

p.98 **Common Water-crowfoot**
Ranunculus aquatilis L.

Description: A glabrous, perennial aquatic, with
trailing, submerged stems to 1.5 (3) m.
Submerged leaves up to 50 mm long, short-
stalked, finely dissected, with spreading,
threadlike, flaccid segments; floating leaves
long-stalked, *rounded, palmately divided with
3–7 obovate, lobed or bluntly dentate segments*.
Flowers solitary in axils of upper (so often
floating) leaves, 12–18 mm diam.; *flower-
stalks less than 50 mm long*, shorter than stalk
of subtending leaf. Sepals 5, ovate. Petals 5,
broadly obovate, 5–10 mm long, much
exceeding sepals, white with yellow basal
blotch; *nectary rounded*. Fruit a rounded or
ovoid, head-like cluster of several (up to
40), *hairy achenes* (2–2.5 mm long) with
short beak, and implanted on *broadly
conical, hairy receptacle*.

Flowering: May–September.

Habitat: Shallow, stagnant or slow-moving, oligotrophic to mesotrophic, fresh water of ponds, ditches, canals, and slow streams; mainly in the lowland.

Range: Most of Europe, except Iceland and the high Arctic.

Similar species: **Pond Water-crowfoot** (*R. peltatus* Schrank), from comparable habitats in most of Europe, has larger flowers with petals 10–20 (30) mm long, oblong or pear-shaped nectaries, and flower-stalks longer than 50 mm; floating leaves have weakly lobed or crenate segments. **Brackish Water-crowfoot** (*R. baudotii* Godron) has rather stiff, yellowish-green submerged leaves, numerous (40–100) winged achenes in more elongate fruiting heads on long and stout, curved or sinuous stalks, and often blue-flushed sepals; again, floating leaves may be absent. In eutrophic, fresh or brackish waters, often close to the sea, along the coasts of Europe, northwards to the Baltic region, but also in brackish inland waters.

The description of Common Water-crowfoot pertains to var. *aquatilis*, in which both submerged and floating leaves are usually present; var. *diffusus* With., often named Thread-leaved Water-crowfoot, never has floating leaves; moreover, petals are narrower, only 3.5–6 mm long, and nectaries are crescent-shaped. Pond Water-crowfoot also has some varieties: var. *peltatus*, which has rather stiff submerged leaves, shorter than accompanying internode, and not collapsing when taken out of the water; achenes always hairy; and var. *heterophyllus* (Cosson & Germ.) Meijden, which has flaccid submerged leaves, longer than internode, floating leaves lacking or, if present, often with narrow, pointed segments, and achenes hairy or glabrous.

The forms without floating leaves are usually found in more rapidly flowing waters. For these, *compare R. fluitans* (see p.954), which has much longer submerged leaves, and a glabrous receptacle. For *R. baudotii*, *compare also R. circinatus* (see p.952), which has flat, fan-shaped submerged leaves.

p.193 **Corn Crowfoot** *Ranunculus arvensis* L.

Description: A slender, tufted, glabrous or slightly hairy *annual*, to 60 cm, with more or less erect, *much-branched stems*. Middle leaves stalked, palmately divided with 3 oblanceolate, main segments often further divided into 3 narrow lobes; upper leaves (sub)sessile, with 3 or more *linear segments*. Flowers axillary, 8–12 mm diam. Sepals 5, ovate, hairy, spreading. Petals 5, rounded, *pale greenish-yellow*. Fruit a cluster of only 3–8 large, roughly ovoid, *spinose, long-beaked achenes* (5–8 mm long).

Flowering: May–July.

Habitat: Cultivated land, often cereal fields, also ruderal places, on moist, mesotrophic, preferably calcareous, loamy or clayey soils; from sea level to 1,700 m.

Range: In Europe northwards to Britain, S Scandinavia and NC Russia.

The first (lowest) leaves of the plant are stalked, with an obovate or elliptical, lobed to divided, rather pinnately veined blade; they are often withered at anthesis.

p.210 **Goldilocks Buttercup**
Ranunculus auricomus L.

Description: A glabrous or slightly hairy perennial, to 50 cm, with *erect*, branched stems; no stolons. Basal leaves long-stalked, reniform or hemi-circular, palmately lobed or divided with 3 (5) crenate-dentate segments; stem-leaves short-stalked to sessile, with 3 narrower to simple and oblanceolate or linear segments. Flowers axillary, 15–25 mm diam., in lax, often many-flowered panicle; receptacle (sub)glabrous; *flower-stalks terete, unfurrowed*. Sepals 5, ovate, hairy, *erect or spreading*. Petals 5 (but *often partly reduced* or even absent), rounded, shiny yellow. Fruit a cluster of broadly obovoid, *downy achenes*, 2–3 mm long, with short, slightly curved beak.

Flowering: April–May.

Habitat: Damp deciduous woods, meadows, hedges, grassy banks, ditch-sides, also rocky places, on moist to wet, oligotrophic to mesotrophic, preferably calcareous, sandy, loamy or stony soils; from sea level to 2,200 m.

Range: Much of Europe except the far north.

Similar species: Other subglabrous species with linear segments to upper leaves are *R. affinis* R. Br. (Iceland and Arctic N Europe), which has glabrous achenes, and 3–5 segmented basal leaves; and *R. pedatifidus* Sm. (Spitsbergen), which has finely downy achenes, 5–9-segmented basal leaves, and deflexed sepals. *Compare also R. acris (see* p.947), which is a much hairier plant with glabrous achenes.

Goldilocks Buttercup may be quite glabrous, but some hairs are often present on the upper stem, and the achenes are always hairy.

---

p.209 **Bulbous Buttercup** *Ranunculus bulbosus* L.

Description: A hairy perennial to 40 (100) cm. Stem erect, branched, *basally thickened* to rounded, tuber-like corm, and with appressed hairs above. Lower leaves stalked, broadly ovate or rounded, palmately divided with 3–5 obovate, lobed to divided main segments; upper leaves subsessile, with 3–5 narrower to simple and oblanceolate segments. Flowers axillary, 20–30 mm diam., in lax, few-flowered panicle; *receptacle hairy; flower-stalks furrowed.* Sepals 5, ovate, hairy, *deflexed.* Petals 5, rounded, shiny deep yellow. Fruit a cluster of broadly ovoid, smooth achenes, 2–3 mm long, with short, curved beak.

Flowering: April–July.

Habitat: Grassland, road verges, grassy banks, dunes, on dry to moist, oligotrophic to mesotrophic, calcareous, sandy, loamy and stony soils; from sea level to 2,500 m.

Range: Most of Europe, except Iceland and the high Arctic.

In ssp. *bulbosus*, top segment of leaf is distinctly stalked, unlike ssp. *bulbifer* (Jordan) Neves, which in addition has nearly smooth (unfurrowed) flower-stalks. *Compare also R. acris (see* p.947), which has unfurrowed flower-stalks and erect sepals.

p.99 Fan-leaved Water-crowfoot
Ranunculus circinatus Sibth.

Description: A glabrous, perennial aquatic, with trailing, submerged stems to 1 m. *Leaves all submerged, up to 30 mm long*, short-stalked to sessile, rounded, finely dissected, with spreading, threadlike segments *in 1 plane, rather rigid* and not collapsing outside the water; *floating leaves absent.* Flowers, 8–18 mm diam., solitary in axils of upper leaves; *flower-stalks much longer than leaves.* Sepals 5, ovate. Petals 5, obovate, 4–9 mm long, longer than sepals, white with yellow basal blotch; *nectary crescent-shaped.* Fruit a rounded or ovoid, head-like cluster of several (up to 40), *(sparsely) hairy achenes* (to 1.5 mm long) with straight beak, and implanted on *hemispherical, hairy receptacle.*

Flowering: June–August.

Habitat: Shallow, stagnant or slow-moving, mesotrophic to eutrophic, fresh water of ponds, lakes, ditches, canals, and slow streams; mainly in the lowland.

Range: Most of Europe except Iceland and the high Arctic, and not known from Iberia.

Compare R. baudotii (see p.949), also with rather stiff submerged leaves, but with segments spreading in all directions (not in 1 plane), and often with floating leaves as well.

p.193 Lesser Celandine *Ranunculus ficaria* L.

Description: A glabrous, tufted perennial to 15 (30) cm, with erect, often branched stems; part of the roots thickened into small, *club-shaped tubers.* Leaves long-stalked, *broadly ovate to reniform*, with cordate base, subentire (rarely coarsely dentate), rather fleshy, shiny dark green (sometimes mottled with purple), partly basal, partly cauline, the latter ones often slightly angular. Flowers solitary, long-stalked, terminal, 20–30 mm diam., with *3 (4) greenish sepals*, and *6–12 narrowly elliptical, shiny-yellow petals*, often streaked with purple on outside. Fruit a rounded cluster of ovoid, blunt-tipped achenes.

Flowering: March–May.

Habitat: Damp woods, scrub, shaded grassland, along ponds, canals, streams and ditches, road verges, parks and gardens, on moist, mesotrophic to eutrophic, calcareous or mildly acid, sandy, clayey or peaty soils; from sea level to 1,600 m.

Range: Most of Europe, except Iceland and the high Arctic; also in W Asia.

Similar species: **Lapland Buttercup** (*R. lapponicus* L.) is glabrous, perennial, with long, creeping stolons, and erect, leafless, unbranched flowering stems to 15 cm. Leaves all basal, long-stalked, palmately divided, reniform, with 3 broadly obovate, weakly 3-lobed segments. Flowers (June–August) solitary, terminal, 8–13 mm diam., with 3 ovate, deflexed sepals, and 6–8 obovate, shiny-yellow petals. Fruit a rounded cluster of narrowly ovoid, slightly waisted achenes (3–4.5 mm long) with long, hooked beak. On tundra, glacial moraines and in stony places in mountains (to 700 m) of Arctic and sub-Arctic Fennoscandia and N Russia (including Spitsbergen). *R. pallasii* Schlecht. has 6–12 purplish or white petals, and obovate to spatulate, shallowly 3-lobed leaves. On stony soils, glacial moraines and in polar deserts of N Russia and Spitsbergen; it often hybridizes with *R. lapponicus*.

The description of Lesser Celandine pertains to ssp. *ficaria*. Ssp. *bulbilifer* Lambinon has narrower petals, and rounded bulbils in axils of lower leaves, serving as vegetative propagules, while achenes are often sterile. The distribution of both subspecies is not yet clear; ssp. *bulbilifer* appears to be widely distributed, while the typical subspecies seems to be restricted to W Europe. A few other subspecies are known from S, C and E Europe; *see* regional floras for more detail.

p.209 **Lesser Spearwort** *Ranunculus flammula* L.

Description: A (sub)glabrous, tufted perennial to 40
(70) cm (often much less), with *prostrate to
ascending, partly creeping stems*; no stolons.
Leaves narrowly elliptical to linear-lanceolate,
narrowed into stalk, subentire or sparsely
dentate, slightly fleshy, shiny yellowish- or
pale green. Flowers axillary, (5) 7–15
(20) mm diam., long-stalked, forming lax,
few-flowered panicle; *flower-stalks furrowed,
slightly hairy*. Sepals 5, ovate. Petals 5,
broadly obovate, shiny yellow. Fruit a
rounded cluster of ovoid, smooth achenes
(1.2–2 mm long) with short beak to
0.3 mm.

Flowering: May–October.

Habitat: Marshes, fens, bogs, damp meadows,
flushes, pool margins, in and along ditches
and streams, periodically inundated paths,
on wet, oligotrophic to mesotrophic,
calcareous to mildly acid, sandy or peaty
soils; from sea level to 2,000 m.

Range: All Europe except Spitsbergen, but mainly
on mountains in the extreme south.

Similar species: **Creeping Spearwort** (*R. reptans* L.) has
threadlike creeping stems (stolons),
giving off small rosettes of long-stalked,
narrowly lanceolate leaves (with blades to
20 mm long) and leafless flowering stems
to 15 cm, with solitary, terminal flower
(5–10 mm diam.). On wet, sandy or
gravelly soils at lake margins in N
Europe (including Iceland), and in
mountains of C and E Europe; freely
hybridizing with *R. flammula*, which
seems to have led to the extinction of the
pure form in N Britain.

---

p.98 **River Water-crowfoot**
Ranunculus fluitans Lamk.

Description: A glabrous, perennial aquatic, with
trailing, submerged stems to 3 (6) m.
Submerged leaves 6–15 (30) cm long, short-
stalked, finely dissected, with long, flaccid
tassels of parallel, threadlike, dark-green

segments; *floating leaves absent*. Flowers, 20–30 mm diam., solitary in leaf-axils; flower-stalks shorter than leaves. Sepals 5, ovate. *Petals (5) 6 (10)*, obovate, 8–15 mm long, much longer than sepals, white with yellow basal blotch; *nectary oblong or pear-shaped*. Fruit a rounded or ovoid, head-like cluster of several (up to 40), *usually glabrous achenes (c. 2 mm long)* with short, curved beak, and implanted on *broadly conical, (sub)glabrous receptacle*.

Flowering: June–August.

Habitat: Usually fast-flowing, shallow or rather deep, mesotrophic to eutrophic water of streams and rivers; often in hilly country.

Range: W and C Europe northwards to Scotland, S Scandinavia, Poland, and Romania.

---

p.100 **Glacier Crowfoot** *Ranunculus glacialis* L.

Description: A (sub)glabrous, tufted perennial to 25 cm (often less), with thickish, *erect, little-branched stems*. Leaves rather fleshy, basal ones stalked, palmately divided or even ternate, with 3 broadly obovate main segments, each further lobed or divided; stem-leaves sessile, with 3 oblanceolate, lobed to entire segments. Flowers terminal, stalked, solitary or 2–3 together, 15–30 mm diam. Sepals 5, broadly ovate, *brown-hairy*. Petals 5, rounded, *white, often tinged with pink*, occasionally all pink or purplish. Fruit a rounded cluster of ovoid achenes (2.5 mm long) with rather straight beak to 1.5 mm.

Flowering: July–October.

Habitat: Bare, rocky places, screes, moraines, often near melting snow or small streams, on moist, oligotrophic, acid, stony soils; only in the mountains, between 1,700 and 4,200 m, but descending lower in the north.

Range: N Europe (including Iceland and Spitsbergen), also in mountains of C Europe, westwards to the Pyrenees and the Sierra Nevada, and eastwards to Romania.

p.99 **Ivy-leaved Water-crowfoot**
Ranunculus hederaceus L.

Description: A glabrous, *annual or perennial* aquatic, with
trailing, submerged stems to 30 cm.
Submerged leaves absent; floating leaves long-
stalked, *reniform, with 3–5 low, entire lobes*.
Flowers 3–6 mm diam., solitary in upper
leaf-axils; *flower-stalks less than 50 mm long*,
shorter than stalk of subtending leaf, and
recurved after anthesis. Sepals 5, ovate.
Petals 5, obovate, *2–4.5 mm long, barely
exceeding sepals*, white with yellow basal
blotch; *nectary crescent-shaped*. Fruit a
rounded or ovoid, head-like cluster of
several (up to 40), *glabrous achenes (c. 2 mm
long)* with very short, eccentric beak, and
implanted on *broadly conical, glabrous
receptacle*.

Flowering: April–September.

Habitat: Very shallow, mesotrophic, usually slightly
acid water of ditches, small streams, ponds,
also on wet mud or peat and in flushes;
mainly in the lowland.

Range: W Europe, northwards to S Sweden, and
eastwards to Germany and E France.

Similar species: **Round-leaved Water-crowfoot**
(*R. omiophyllus* Ten.) has more rounded,
deeply incised floating leaves with 3–5
obovate, often 3-lobed segments, and again
no submerged leaves; flowers larger, with
petals to 7 mm long, much exceeding
sepals. In comparable habitats of SW
Europe, northwards to W France and the
British Isles.
Three-lobed Water-crowfoot
(*R. tripartitus* DC.) (*see* photograph p.99)
also normally has submerged leaves (up to
50 mm long), short-stalked to sessile,
finely dissected, with more or less
spreading, flaccid, threadlike segments
(collapsing out of the water); floating
leaves long-stalked, reniform, palmately
divided with 3 obovate, weakly lobed
segments; flowers (May–July) have small
petals (1.5–5 mm long) barely exceeding
(deflexed, often purple-tinged) sepals;
flower-stalks about as long as subtending
leaf; nectary crescent-shaped; achenes

glabrous, with lateral or subterminal beak, and implanted on subspherical, short-hairy receptacle. In oligotrophic to mesotrophic pools and ditches, mainly in the lowland (often near the coast, but in fresh water), in W Europe, from Portugal northwards to the British Isles and Germany, declining, presumably extinct in the Low Countries; for this species, *compare R. ololeucos*, which has larger, plain-white flowers.

p.192 **Great Spearwort** *Ranunculus lingua* L.

Description: A glabrous, tufted perennial to 1.2 m, with stout, *erect or ascending*, branched, *hollow* stems; *stolons present*. Leaves fleshy, bright green; basal ones long-stalked, ovate with cordate base, dentate, higher ones lanceolate to almost linear, 10–20 cm long, short-stalked to subsessile, (sub)entire. *Flowers large*, 20–50 mm diam., axillary, long-stalked, forming lax, few-flowered panicle; *flower-stalks not furrowed*. Sepals 5, ovate. Petals 5, rounded, shiny yellow, much exceeding sepals. Fruit a rounded cluster of ovoid, *smooth achenes* (*c.* 2.5 mm long) with thick beak to 0.6 mm long.

Flowering: June–September.

Habitat: Marshes, fens, reedlands, in and along ditches, streams and ponds, on wet, mesotrophic, calcareous or mildly acid, often peaty soils; from sea level to 1,200 m.

Range: Most of Europe, except Iceland and the high Arctic, and rare in the deep south.

Similar species: **Adder's-tongue Spearwort** (*R. ophioglossifolius* Vill.) is annual and much smaller (to 40 cm); also has ovate, cordate-based basal leaves, but with broader, elliptical to lanceolate stem-leaves; flowers only 5–9 mm diam., with petals barely exceeding sepals; achenes *c.* 1.2 mm long, minutely papillose; stolons lacking. In marshes, ditches, at pond margins, in S and W Europe, northwards to W France, SW Britain (Gloucestershire), also on Gotland.

p.193 **Snow Buttercup** *Ranunculus nivalis* L.

Description: A tufted perennial to 15 cm, with *erect,
unbranched, glabrous or slightly hairy stems*.
Leaves glabrous (but for stalk), rounded or
reniform, palmately divided with 3 obovate
main segments, lateral ones often 2-lobed
themselves; lower leaves long-stalked,
upper ones sessile, few. Flowers solitary,
terminal, 12–15 (20) mm diam. Sepals 5,
broadly ovate, more or less hairy. Petals 5,
rounded, yellow. Fruit a rounded cluster of
ovoid, smooth, short-beaked achenes (*c.*
2 mm long).

Flowering: June–August.

Habitat: In tundra, on rocks, moraines, often near
melting snow, on moist, oligotrophic,
acid, stony soils; from sea level to
1,550 m.

Range: Arctic Scandinavia and N Russia, including
Spitsbergen.

Similar species: *R. pygmaeus* Wahlenb. rarely grows taller
than 50 mm, and has less deeply incised, 3-
segmented leaves (outer segments often
lobed again), and smaller flowers (5–10 mm
diam.). In stony habitats or in short turf, in
Arctic and sub-Arctic Europe, including
Iceland and the Faeroes; also in the
mountains of C Europe.

R. sulphureus C.J. Phipps has broadly ovate,
cuneate-based, shallowly lobed, not
obviously 3-segmented basal leaves (more
or less pinnately veined, by consequence),
and flowers rather like *R. nivalis*, but for
densely brown-hairy sepals. In tundra and
on glacial moraines in Arctic Scandinavia
and N Russia.

R. hyperboreus Rottb. has creeping, stolon-
like stems, with scattered, long-stalked,
deeply 3–5-lobed, round-based leaves,
with axillary, solitary flowers to 5 mm
diam., on ascending stalks; sepals 3, ovate;
petals 3, rounded, yellow; achenes very
blunt. In wet, often periodically inundated
places on tundra or on stony soils in
mountains, to 2,100 m, in the Arctic and
sub-Arctic parts of Europe (including
Iceland and the Faeroes).

p.99 *Ranunculus ololeucos* Lloyd

Description: A *slightly hairy*, perennial aquatic, with trailing, submerged stems to 60 cm. *Submerged leaves up to 50 mm* long, short-stalked to sessile, finely dissected, with more or less spreading, *flaccid, threadlike segments* (collapsing out of the water); floating leaves long-stalked, reniform to suborbicular, palmately divided with *3 obovate, weakly lobed segments*. Flowers solitary in leaf-axils, 10–20 mm diam.; flower-stalks about as long as subtending leaf. Sepals 5, ovate, deflexed, often flushed with violet. Petals 5, *all white* (without yellow blotch), broadly obovate, 7–15 mm long, at least twice as long as sepals; *nectary crescent-shaped*. Fruit a rounded, head-like cluster of several (up to 40), globose, *slightly pubescent achenes* (*c.* 2.5 mm long, not winged) with lateral or subterminal beak, and implanted on *subspherical, short-hairy receptacle*.

Flowering: May–August.

Habitat: Shallow, stagnant, oligotrophic water of ponds, ditches, fens, often on a peaty bottom; mainly in the lowland.

Range: Continental W Europe, from Portugal northwards to the Low Countries and N Germany.

Compare R. tripartitus (see p.956), which has smaller, yellow-blotched petals.

p.194 **Small-flowered Buttercup**
Ranunculus parviflorus L.

Description: A hairy *annual* to 10 (30) cm, with *prostrate* (not creeping), branched stems. Leaves alternate, stalked, rounded or reniform, palmately divided with 3–5 obovate, lobed main segments; upper leaves (sub)sessile, with 3–5 narrower segments, or simple. Flowers axillary, apparently opposite to their bract, 3–8 mm diam.; receptacle glabrous; *flower-stalks furrowed*. Sepals 5, ovate, hairy, *deflexed*. *Petals up to 5* (often partly or altogether missing), narrowly obovate, pale yellow. Stamens up to 8, roughly proportional to number of petals present. Fruit a cluster of 5–10 ovoid, *finely spinulose achenes, c.* 3 mm long, with stout, recurved beak.

Flowering: May–July.

Habitat: Open, grassy places, roadsides, on banks, also in cultivated land and gardens, on moist, mesotrophic, sandy or stony soils; mainly in the lowland, and often close to the sea.

Range: S and W Europe, northwards to W France, S Britain and SW Ireland.

---

p.140 *Ranunculus platanifolius* L.

Description: A slightly hairy, tufted perennial to 1.3 m, with erect, much-branched stems. Leaves palmately lobed to divided with 5–7 broadly oblanceolate, serrate-dentate segments; lower leaves long-stalked, higher ones subsessile. Flowers 10–20 mm diam., long-stalked, forming lax panicle; *flower-stalks glabrous*. Sepals 5, ovate. Petals 5, rounded, *white*, much exceeding sepals. Fruit a rounded cluster of broadly ovoid, distinctly veined, short-beaked achenes (*c.* 5 mm long).

Flowering: May–August.

Habitat: Woods, scrub, meadows, streamsides, on moist, oligotrophic, often stony soils; from sea level to 1,600 m, but mainly on mountains in the south.

Range: The mountains of S and C Europe (Pyrenees, Alps, Carpathians), northwards to Belgium (Ardennes) and C Germany, also in W Norway and S Sweden, and eastwards to W Russia.

Similar species: **Aconite-leaved Buttercup** (*R. aconitifolius* L.), from the mountains of S and C Europe, has hairy flower-stalks, and more deeply incised leaves with 3–5 narrower segments; top-segment free even to base. In comparable, usually wetter habitats, and generally at higher altitudes (1,000–2,600 m), in the mountains of S and C Europe, northwards to NE France (Vosges), S Germany, and eastwards to W Russia.

p.210 **Multiflowered Buttercup**
Ranunculus polyanthemos L.

Description: A hairy perennial to 60 (90) cm, with short, vertical, underground rhizome and *erect*, branched stems; no aerial stolons. Basal leaves long-stalked, rounded, palmately divided with 3 (5) obovate or diamond-shaped, lobed to divided segments; stem-leaves sessile, with narrower to linear segments. Flowers axillary, 20–35 mm diam., in lax, often many-flowered panicle; *receptacle hairy; flower-stalks furrowed*. Sepals 5, ovate, hairy, *erect or spreading*. Petals 5, rounded or shallowly notched, shiny deep yellow. Fruit a cluster of obovoid, smooth achenes, 2–3 mm long, with strongly curved or even coiled beak *c.* 1.5 mm long.

Flowering: May–July.

Habitat: Deciduous woods, occasionally in shaded grassland, on moist, oligotrophic, acid or calcareous, loamy, clayey or stony soils; from sea level to 2,000 m, but rare in the lowland.

Range: Continental Europe northwards to Denmark, S Sweden (Gotland), the Baltic States and N Russia.

The description above pertains to ssp. *nemorosus* (DC.) Korsh. Ssp. *polyanthemos* has deeply incised, (3) 5-segmented basal leaves with narrow, wedge-shaped lobes, smaller flowers (12–20 mm diam.), and less strongly curved beaks (0.5 mm long) to achenes. In woods and meadows on wet or moist, calcareous soils in the same general area (except France). Both subspecies are also treated as separate species.

p.209 **Creeping Buttercup** *Ranunculus repens* L.

Description: A hairy perennial to 40 cm, with long, creeping, *overground stolons* and short, erect flowering branches. Basal leaves long-stalked, triangular-ovate or rounded, *ternate*, with 3 broadly ovate, deeply lobed or divided, distinctly

stalked leaflets, *top-leaflet long-stalked*;
stem-leaves stalked to subsessile, with
narrower to simple and oblanceolate
segments. Flowers axillary, 20–30 mm
diam., in lax, few-flowered panicle;
receptacle hairy; flower-stalks furrowed.
Sepals 5, ovate, hairy, *spreading to erect.*
Petals 5, rounded, shiny deep yellow.
Fruit a cluster of broadly ovoid or
rounded, smooth achenes, 2–3 mm long,
with straight, apically recurved beak.

Flowering: May–September.

Habitat: Grassland, marshes, fens, road verges,
along ditches, pathways, woodland rides,
on moist to wet, mesotrophic to eutrophic,
calcareous or slightly acid, preferably
clayey or loamy soils; from sea level to
2,500 m.

Range: All Europe. A very common species.

---

p.209 **Hairy Buttercup**
Ranunculus sardous Crantz

Description: A rather hairy *annual* to 40 (100) cm.
Stem erect, branched, with spreading
hairs all along its length. Lower leaves
stalked, broadly ovate, palmately divided
with 3 obovate, lobed to divided main
segments, top-segment much larger,
with an abruptly narrowed, cuneate base;
upper leaves subsessile, with 3 narrower
to simple and oblanceolate segments.
Flowers axillary, 15–25 mm diam., in
lax, few-flowered panicle; receptacle
hairy; *flower-stalks furrowed.* Sepals 5,
ovate, hairy, *deflexed.* Petals 5, obovate,
bright yellow, about twice as long as
sepals. Fruit a cluster of broadly ovoid
achenes, barely 2 mm long, smooth (but
for some *minute, rounded tubercles near
rim*), with very short beak.

Flowering: May–September.

Habitat: Damp grassland, commons, grassy banks,
also in cereal fields, on moist to wet,
eutrophic, calcareous, often brackish, sandy
or loamy soils; from sea level to 1,000 m.

Range: In Europe northwards to Britain, Low
Countries, S Sweden and C Russia.

p.192 **Celery-leaved Crowfoot**
Ranunculus sceleratus L.

Description: A (sub)glabrous annual to 40 (70) cm, with
erect or ascending, strongly ribbed stems. Leaves
rather *fleshy*, shiny pale green, lower ones
stalked, palmately divided with 3 major,
wedge-shaped segments, these often trifid
again, and dentate or lobed near top; upper
leaves subsessile, with 3 oblanceolate,
dentate segments, or undivided at last.
Flowers axillary, 5–10 mm diam., stalked,
forming lax, many-flowered panicle. Sepals
5, ovate, deflexed during anthesis. Petals 5,
rounded, *pale yellow*, barely exceeding
sepals. Fruit a broadly ellipsoid or conical,
head-like cluster of numerous (60–300)
ovoid, smooth achenes (*c.* 1 mm long) with
minute beak (less than 0.1 mm long).

Flowering: May–September.

Habitat: Marshy meadows, reedlands, ditches,
shallow pools, lake, rivers and stream
margins, on wet, eutrophic, calcareous or
mildly acid, fresh or brackish, muddy, clayey
or peaty soils; from sea level to 1,000 m,
especially frequent in coastal regions.

Range: Most of Europe, except Iceland and the
high Arctic.

Submerged plants do not flower, and often
develop large, long-stalked, floating leaves.
The plant is poisonous; the juice can cause
blisters on the skin.

---

p.126 **Greater Meadow-rue**
Thalictrum aquilegifolium L.

Description: A subglabrous perennial with short,
creeping rhizomes and erect, branched
flowering stems to 150 cm. Leaves alternate,
stalked, *2–3 times ternate*, with rounded or
obovate, usually *3-lobed leaflets*; upper leaves
much smaller, subsessile, with narrower
leaflets. Flowers regular, more or less *erect* in
large, *dense panicle*; perianth parts 4, all in 1
row, *purplish or whitish*, ovate, 3–4 mm long;
nectaries absent. Stamens numerous, far
protruding, more or less erect, with lilac or

whitish anthers, filaments distally thickened. Ovaries few, short-stalked; style falling after anthesis. Fruit a small cluster of *stalked, nodding*, ellipsoid, triangular, 1-seeded achenes, each with *3 wide, lateral wings*.

Flowering: June–July.

Habitat: Damp woods, scrub and meadows, on moist or wet, preferably calcareous, stony, sandy or peaty soils; from 500–2,100 m.

Range: C and E Europe, westwards to C France and S Germany, northwards to S Sweden, the Baltic States and N Russia, and locally naturalized further west.

Similar species: **Alpine Meadow-rue** (*Thalictrum alpinum* L.) is rarely taller than 15 cm, and has doubly ternate leaves with very small, rounded leaflets; flowers few, small, nodding or pendent, clustered in single raceme, and with pinkish perianth parts and filaments, but yellowish anthers. In damp mountain grassland and on rocks, often on calcareous soils, in N Russia, Fennoscandia, Iceland, N Britain and NW Ireland; also in mountains of C Europe, southwards to the Pyrenees.

---

p.126 **Common Meadow-rue**
Thalictrum flavum L.

Description: A subglabrous perennial with long, creeping rhizomes and erect, branched flowering stems to 120 cm. Leaves alternate, stalked, *2–3 times pinnate*, with obovate or broadly wedge-shaped, usually *3-lobed leaflets*; upper leaves much smaller, sessile, with narrower (to linear) leaflets. Flowers regular, more or less *erect* in large, rather *dense panicle*; perianth parts 4, all in 1 row, *yellowish or greenish-white*, ovate, 3–4 mm long; nectaries absent. Stamens numerous, far protruding, more or less erect, with threadlike filaments and yellow anthers. Ovaries few; style falling after anthesis. Fruit a small cluster of sessile, erect, ovoid, 1-seeded achenes (1.5–2.5 mm long), each with *6 conspicuous ribs*.

Flowering: June–August.

Habitat: Meadows, streamsides and rivers, in ruderal places and damp woods (often of Willow), on wet or moist, mesotrophic, preferably calcareous, sandy, loamy or stony soils; mainly in the lowland.

Range: Most of Europe, except Iceland and the high Arctic.

Similar species: *T. morisonii* C.C. Gmelin from the mountains of WC Europe grows even taller; it has 8–10-ribbed achenes, and less dense panicles.

Small Meadow-rue (*T. simplex* L.) has nodding flowers in lax, narrow panicle; perianth parts yellowish-green, *c.* 3 mm long; ovaries few or several (3–15); achenes sessile, erect, ellipsoid (occasionally asymmetrical), strongly ribbed, to 5 mm long. In meadows, streamsides and lakes, also on wet rocks, on wet to rather dry, oligotrophic, stony or peaty soils, from sea level (in the north) to 2,000 m, in N Europe, and in the mountains of C Europe; in leaf morphology and the strongly ribbed achenes it resembles *T. flavum* but it flowers more like *T. minus*.

---

p.208 **Lesser Meadow-rue** *Thalictrum minus* L.

Description: A subglabrous perennial with erect, branched flowering stems to 60 (120) cm; creeping rhizomes present or absent. Leaves alternate, stalked, *3–4 times ternate*, with rounded or broadly ovate, usually 3-lobed leaflets; upper leaves much smaller, (sub)sessile, with narrower leaflets. Flowers regular, *nodding or pendent*, in lax panicle; perianth parts 4, all in 1 row, *yellowish-green*, ovate, *c.* 3 mm long; nectaries absent. Stamens numerous, far protruding, with threadlike filaments and yellow anthers. Ovaries few or several (3–15); style falling after anthesis. Fruit a small cluster of sessile, erect, narrowly ovoid (occasionally asymmetrical), 1-seeded, *weakly ribbed achenes* up to 5 mm long, with short beak.

Flowering: June–August.

Habitat: Grassland, dunes, scrub, grassy slopes and rocks, on dry, oligotrophic to mesotrophic, calcareous or weakly acid, sandy, loamy or stony soils; from sea level to 2,400 m.

Range: Most of Europe, except Iceland and the high Arctic.

An extremely variable species, especially in shape and dimensions of leaflets; several subspecies have been described.

MIGNONETTE FAMILY, RESEDACEAE

A family of herbs and half-shrubs with *c.* 75 species in 6 genera, mainly in the Mediterranean region and in warmer parts of N America. Leaves alternate, pinnately veined, simple or compound. Dicots. Flowers in racemes or spikes, usually hermaphrodite and slightly irregular, with 4–6 (8) sepals and often an equal number of deeply incised petals. Stamens numerous (7–25). Ovary superior, composed of 2–7 (often 3 or 4) free or connate carpels, and often placed on stalk- or disc-like 'gynophore', which often also carries stamens (when it is called an 'androgynophore'). Fruit a cluster of 1-seeded, achene-like follicles, or 1-locular, many-seeded capsule, splitting at top.

p.200   **Weld** *Reseda luteola* L.

Description: A glabrous biennial with erect, *hollow stems* to 1 (1.5) m. Leaves alternate (or in basal rosette, in 1st year), oblanceolate to almost linear, *entire or with few small teeth* near base, wavy-edged. Flowers 4–5 mm diam., numerous in strongly elongating, spike-like racemes. Sepals 4, greenish. *Petals 4, greenish-yellow*, unequal, upper one largest and more incised. Fruit an erect, obovoid, 3-lobed capsule, *3–4 mm long*.

Flowering: June–September.
Habitat: Ruderal and disturbed places, along roads and railways, on banks, in old quarries, also in cultivated land and sea-dunes, on dry, oligotrophic, preferably calcareous, sandy, loamy or stony soils; from sea level to 2,000 m.

Range: S, W and C Europe, northwards to the British Isles and S Sweden, eastwards to Romania and the Crimea, but only naturalized in much of the north.

Similar species: **White Mignonette** (*R. lutea* L.) has solid stems, pinnately divided leaves with 2 (4) lanceolate, entire-margined or, again, lobed segments, and long, winged stalk; whitish-yellow flowers have 6 (7) sepals and petals; capsule is oblong, 7–12 mm long. In comparable habitats, northwards to the British Isles, the Low Countries, Poland and Romania; naturalized further north.

Weld is also called Dyer's Rocket; the plant was formerly grown for a yellow dye.

ROSE FAMILY, ROSACEAE

Dicots. A large, subcosmopolitan family of trees, shrubs and herbs with *c.* 3,370 species in 122 genera. Dicots. Leaves alternate, simple or compound. Flowers regular, usually hermaphrodite and basically 5-merous, in cymes, racemes or panicles. Sepals usually 5; an epicalyx can be present. Petals usually 5, occasionally absent. Stamens often numerous, implanted (with petals) on rim of fleshy receptacle, which can be convex, flat or concave (to urn- or tube-shaped, as with 'hips' of roses). Ovaries free or connate, implanted or embedded centrally on receptacle (or enclosed in it), and each carrying single style. Fruit variously organized: a drupe, a berry, a pome, or a cluster of follicles, drupelets or achenes. Often the fruits are edible, and the family has yielded many garden ornamentals.

---

p.211 **Agrimony** *Agrimonia eupatoria* L.

Description: A rosette-bearing perennial, with erect, hairy (but not glandular) flowering stems to 60 (120) cm. Leaves hairy and green above, *white-tomentose beneath*, basal ones oblanceolate, pinnate, with 7–13 ovate or elliptical, dentate main leaflets, and with tiny leaflets in between; stem-leaves few and smaller. Flowers 5–8 mm diam., subsessile, numerous in narrow, terminal raceme; receptacle concave, calyx-like, bearing epicalyx of bristles at top. Sepals triangular-ovate. Petals 5, spreading, yellow, narrowly obovate, with rounded or notched limb and short claw. Stamens 10–20. Ovary 1-locular, enclosed in receptacle, and together with it forming obconical, 1-seeded, *strongly grooved*, achene-like, dry, hairy fruit, crowned with several rows of *spreading to erect, hooked bristles*.

Flowering: June–September.

Habitat: Grassland, road verges, field borders, grassy banks and sunny slopes, also scrub and wood margins, on rather dry to moist, oligotrophic to mesotrophic, preferably calcareous, sandy, loamy or stony soils; from sea level to 1,800 m.

Range: Most of Europe, except the extreme north.

Similar species: *A. pilosa* Ledeb. from NE Europe (westwards to S Finland, NE Poland and C Romania) has leaves green at both faces, narrower main leaflets, and smaller flowers (3–5 mm diam.).

---

p.211 **Fragrant Agrimony**
Agrimonia procera Wallr.

Description: A *glandular-hairy* perennial with erect, leafy flowering stems to 90 (150) cm. Leaves alternate, hairy and green above, glandular-hairy and green beneath, oblanceolate, pinnate, with 7–13 (narrowly) elliptical, dentate main leaflets, and with tiny leaflets in between. Flowers much like *A. eupatoria*, but slightly larger (6–10 mm diam.). Fruit crowned with several rows of *recurved to spreading, hooked bristles*, and *grooves not reaching to base*.

Flowering: June–August.

Habitat: Wood margins, scrub, rough grassland, road verges, on moist, mesotrophic, preferably calcareous, sandy, loamy, clayey or stony soils; from sea level to 1,800 m.

Range: Most of Europe except the extreme north, and eastwards to S Finland and the Ukraine.

Lady's-mantle, *Alchemilla*

A very complex genus of tufted, perennial herbs with long-stalked, palmately veined, radially folded, rounded or reniform leaves (mostly in basal rosette), and small, greenish flowers in rounded or umbel-shaped cymes. The concave, urn-shaped receptacle bears 4 (5) sepals, a 4–5-parted epicalyx, and 4 (5) stamens on its rim; petals absent. Fruit is dry, 1-seeded, achene-like, and incorporates receptacle. Formerly only 1 species was recognized (*A. vulgaris* L. s.l.), but this has been split into numerous microspecies. The plants never produce fertile pollen, so reproduction is achieved via parthenogenesis (forming of seeds without pollination), and also vegetatively (through fragmenting of rhizomes). The many forms are remarkably stable, and can be well delimited, although differences are often subtle. In many cases, their distribution is not yet precisely known. Important characters are found in the way the leaves are incised and toothed, and in indument (hairs) on various organs. Some species, in the mountains of C and N Europe have palmately divided, more or less white-tomentose leaves (*A. alpina* L. and allies); the lowland species usually have less deeply incised, green leaves. Only from the latter group are some widely distributed forms described here; several other microspecies can be found in the area, however. For more details, consult *Flora Europaea*, or a good regional flora.

---

p.73 **Hairy Lady's-mantle**
Alchemilla filicaulis Buser

Description: A dark-green plant to 30 cm, with thin stems (0.5–1.5 mm thick) bearing more or less erect hairs. Leaf-stalks also with erect hairs; leaf-blades rounded, with an open sinus at base, more or less hairy above (at least in the folds). Flowers 3–6 mm diam., in rather lax clusters; flower-stalks hairy, as often also receptacles.

Flowering: June–September.

Habitat: Meadows, road verges, streamsides, at wood margins, on moist to rather dry, mesotrophic, sandy or stony soils; from sea level to 2,200 m, but mainly on mountains in the south.

Range: C and N Europe.

The description above pertains to ssp. *filicaulis*. Ssp. *vestita* (Buser) Bradsh. is slightly more robust, bluish-green, less hairy (especially above), with stems to 2 mm thick; it appears to be more frequent in W Europe.

p.73 Smooth Lady's-mantle
Alchemilla glabra Neygenf.

Description: A dark-green plant to 60 cm (but often much less); stems and leaf-stalks glabrous or appressed-hairy. Leaf-blades rounded, with open sinus at base, glabrous or with sparse hairs only near margin. Flowers *c.* 4 mm diam., in lax clusters; flower-stalks and receptacles glabrous.

Flowering: May–September.

Habitat: Grassland, road verges, open woods, on dry to moist, oligotrophic to mesotrophic, sandy or rocky soils; from sea level to 2,800 m.

Range: C and N Europe, extending southwards to the Pyrenees and the northern Balkan peninsula.

---

p.72 *Alchemilla glaucescens* Wallr.

Description: A blue-green plant to 20 (30) cm; stems and leaf-stalks densely hairy, with erect hairs. Leaf-blades rounded, to 50 mm diam., with closed sinus at base, densely hairy (especially beneath). Flowers *c.* 3 mm diam., in dense clusters; flower-stalks and receptacles densely white-hairy.

Flowering: May–September.

Habitat: Grassland, road verges, woodland clearings, along footpaths, on moist, oligotrophic, often calcareous, sandy, loamy or stony soils; from sea level to 2,500 m.

Range: C and N Europe, locally southwards to C France, N Italy, Bulgaria and the Crimea.

---

p.72 *Alchemilla monticola* Opiz

Description: A green plant to 40 cm; stems and leaf-stalks densely hairy, with erect hairs. Leaf-blades rounded, to 12 cm diam., with closed sinus at base, densely hairy (but not white-tomentose, not even below). Flowers 2–3 mm diam., in dense clusters; flower-stalks and receptacles glabrous.

Flowering: May–August.

Habitat: Meadows, road verges, on moist, oligotrophic

to mesotrophic, often acid, sandy or stony soils; from sea level to 3,100 m.

Range: Most of Europe except the Arctic, and only on mountains in the south.

Similar species: *A. subcrenata* Buser has the hairs on stems and leaf-stalks partly deflexed. In comparable habitats of N and C Europe, often in mountainous regions.

A. glomerulans Buser (*see* photograph p.72) has stems and leaf-stalks densely hairy, with upward-pointing, semi-appressed hairs. The hairy (not white-tomentose) leaf-blades have an open sinus, and unequally-toothed lobes. Flowers *c.* 4 mm diam. In meadows, and at stream- and riversides, on moist or wet, oligotrophic, usually acid, sandy or stony soils, in N Europe (also in N Britain), and in the mountains of C Europe, southwards to the Pyrenees; from sea level to 3,000 m, but less frequent in the lowland.

A. gracilis Opiz is less hairy above; teeth of leaf equal. In moist grassland of C and E Europe, westwards to E England (Northumberland).

---

p.72 *Alchemilla vulgaris* L. s.s.

Description: A robust, green plant to 60 cm; stems and leaf-stalks densely hairy, with erect hairs. Leaf-blades rounded or reniform, to 12 cm diam., with an open sinus at base, sparsely to densely hairy (mainly on the folds and the lobes); lobes almost triangular, with straight, unequal teeth. Flowers 2–3 (4) mm diam., in dense clusters; flower-stalks and receptacles glabrous or with few hairs.

Flowering: May–September.

Habitat: Meadows, road verges, streamsides, on moist, oligotrophic to mesotrophic, sandy or stony soils; from sea level to 2,800 (?) m.

Range: C and N Europe.

Similar species: *A. xanthochlora* Rothm. is yellowish-green, with densely hairy stems and petioles, but leaves glabrous above, with subequal, curved teeth to lobes. In road verges and wood margins, often on calcareous soils, in W and C Europe, northwards to S Sweden, eastwards to W Russia, Bulgaria and C Greece.

Alchemilla vulgaris L. s.s. is also mentioned in literature as *A. acutiloba* Opiz. Many reports of *A. vulgaris* (s.l.) refer to the other species in the complex.

---

p.50 **Parsley-piert** *Aphanes arvensis* L.

Description: A hairy, greyish-green annual to 15 cm, with spreading or ascending stems. Leaves alternate, to 10 mm long, fan-shaped, deeply incised with 3 coarsely dentate to lobed segments; stipules semicircular, connate all along leaf-stalk, with 5–7 *short, bluntly triangular teeth*. Flowers *c.* 1 mm diam., subsessile, few together in leaf-axils, partly hidden by stipules; receptacle concave, calyx-like, bearing 4 erect or divergent, triangular sepals. Petals absent. Stamens 1–2. Ovary 1-locular, enclosed in receptacle. Fruit ovoid, 1-seeded, achene-like, 2–2.5 mm long (including persistent sepals).

Flowering: May–August.

Habitat: Cultivated land, roadsides and other open and disturbed places, on moist, mesotrophic, often calcareous, sandy or loamy soils; from sea level to 1,200 m.

Range: Most of Europe, northwards to S Sweden and C Russia.

Similar species: **Slender Parsley-piert** (*A. inexpectata* Lippert) is fresher green, and has fruits shorter than 2 mm, with convergent sepals; teeth of stipules much longer than wide, exceeding flowers. In comparable habitats, but preferring poor, acid, sandy soils, in S, W and C Europe, northwards to Scotland and S Sweden, eastwards to the Carpathians.

---

p.146 **Goat's-beard Spiraea**
Aruncus dioicus (Walter) Fernald

Description: A glabrous or sparsely hairy, bushy perennial herb with erect flowering stems to 2 m. Leaves large (to 1 m long), alternate, roughly triangular, *doubly pinnate*, with ovate or elliptical, pointed, doubly serrate leaflets (to 15 cm long); *stipules absent*. Flowers *unisexual, dioecious, c.* 5 mm diam., numerous in long, cylindrical, *spike-like racemes*, composing large panicle. Sepals 5, small. Petals 5, obovate, white (in female flowers) or cream (in male flowers). Stamens (in male flowers) 20–30. Ovaries 3–5, superior, free (reduced and abortive in male flowers), developing into (mostly 3) narrowly ellipsoid, pointed, several-seeded follicles, *c.* 3 mm long.

Flowering: May–August.

Habitat: Damp woods, marshes, streamsides and ditches, usually shaded places, on wet or moist, oligotrophic or mesotrophic, preferably acid, sandy or stony soils; 400–1,700 m.

Range: The mountains of C Europe, westwards to the Pyrenees and the Vosges, and northwards to C Germany, S Poland and W Russia. Also cultivated in gardens, and occasionally naturalized elsewhere in Europe.

---

p.301 **Wild Cotoneaster**
Cotoneaster integerrimus Medicus

Description: A deciduous shrub to 1 m, with erect, often twisted stems and branches; twigs downy in youth. Leaves alternate, short-stalked, *broadly obovate to suborbicular*, 15–40 mm long, entire-margined, slightly leathery, shiny green above, greyish-downy beneath. Flowers regular, hermaphrodite, 6–7 mm diam., (1) 2–3 together in short-stalked, axillary clusters, nodding after anthesis. Sepals 5, often flushed with red. Petals 5, obovate, pink. Stamens numerous (20), with red filaments. *Ovary inferior*, with 2–5 carpels (free on ventral side) and 2 (rarely 4 or 5) free styles. Fruit a subglobose, pendulous, fleshy, red, berry-like (compound) drupe, 6–8 mm long, with 2–5 (mostly 3) partly exposed stones.

Flowering: April–June.

Habitat: Scrub, on rocks and screes, on dry or moist, oligotrophic, preferably calcareous, stony soils; from sea level (in the north) to 2,800 m.

Range: Much of Europe except the extreme north and south, eastwards to the Caucasus.

Similar species: **Black Cotoneaster** (*C. niger* Fries) from S
Fennoscandia and E Europe has clusters of
3–8 red-flushed flowers, black fruits, and
twigs turning shiny reddish-brown; leaves
white-tomentose beneath.
C. nebrodensis (Guss.) C. Koch has clusters of
3–12 flowers (pink inside, red outside), red
fruits, and leaves downy on both faces (at
least when young). In the mountains of C
and SE Europe. Some Himalayan species are
cultivated in gardens, from which they
occasionally escape.

---

p.103 **Mountain Avens** *Dryas octopetala* L.

Description: An evergreen *dwarf-shrub* to 10 cm, with
creeping, woody stems and branches. Leaves
alternate, mostly basal, long-stalked, blades
10–20 mm long, elliptical with rounded or
slightly cordate base, blunt-tipped, regularly
crenate-dentate or shallowly lobed, leathery,
green above, *greyish-tomentose beneath*. Flowers
regular, hermaphrodite, 20–40 mm diam.,
solitary, terminal on leafless stalks rising
from plant base. Sepals 8–9, broadly
lanceolate. Petals 8–9, narrowly obovate,
white. Stamens numerous. Ovaries numerous,
free, superior, developing into a cluster of
ellipsoid achenes, 8–10 mm long, crowned
by long tassel of strongly elongated, *white,
feathery styles* (to 30 mm long).

Flowering: May–August.

Habitat: Mountain ledges, cliffs, rocks, tundra, also
sand-dunes, on dry to moist, oligotrophic,
often calcareous, stony soils; from sea level
to 2,500 m, but only on mountains outside
the Arctic.

Range: Arctic Europe (including Iceland), also in
the mountains of Britain and Ireland, and
further in the mountains of C Europe,
westwards to the Pyrenees.

A typical boreo-montane species, once more
widespread and common during the ice
ages; it even gave its name to one of the last
glacial phases (the Dryas phase). It is
increasingly rare, and protected by law in
most countries.

p.146 **Meadowsweet**
Filipendula ulmaria (L.) Maxim.

Description: A more or less hairy perennial with erect,
leafy flowering stems to 1 (1.5) m. Leaves
alternate, to 30 cm long, subglabrous or
white-tomentose beneath, narrowly ovate,
pinnate, with *2–5 pairs* of ovate or elliptical,
pointed, doubly serrate and often irregularly
lobed side-leaflets (to 80 mm long), and
several *tiny leaflets in between*; top-leaflet larger,
often 3-lobed; stipules present, ovate-cordate.
Flowers regular, hermaphrodite, 4–8 mm
diam., very fragrant, numerous in dense,
umbel-shaped, often storied panicles; receptacle
shallowly concave, not enclosing ovaries.
Sepals 5, small. Petals 5 (rarely more),
obovate, *white or cream* (rarely pinkish).
Stamens numerous. Ovaries several, superior,
free but *spirally coiled* into a knot, developing
into strongly curved, elongate, 1-seeded,
glabrous achenes, c. 2 mm long.

Flowering: May–August (autumn).

Habitat: Marshes, meadows, ditch-, stream- and
riversides, occasionally open, damp deciduous
woods, on wet to moist, mesotrophic,
calcareous to mildly acid, sandy, loamy, peaty
or stony soils; from sea level to 1,800 m.

Range: Most of Europe except the high Arctic and
much of the Mediterranean region.

---

p.146 **Dropwort** *Filipendula vulgaris* Moench

Description: A subglabrous or sparsely pubescent
perennial with erect, leafy flowering stems
to 50 (80) cm; roots usually ending in ovoid
tubercles. Leaves alternate, to 20 cm long,
green at both faces, lanceolate, *pinnate*, with
8–24 pairs of (broadly) lanceolate, deeply
dentate or lobed to almost pinnatifid side-
leaflets (to 20 mm long), and *tiny leaflets in
between*; top-leaflet often 3-lobed, not much
enlarged; stipules present, ovate-cordate.
Flowers regular, hermaphrodite, 8–16
(20) mm diam., very fragrant, numerous in
dense, *umbel-shaped panicle*; receptacle
shallowly concave, not enclosing ovaries.
Sepals 5, small. Petals (5) 6 (occasionally

more), obovate, *cream, often flushed with pink on outside*. Stamens numerous. Ovaries several, superior, free (though bundled), *straight*, developing into narrowly ellipsoid, 1-seeded, *hairy achenes*, 3–4 mm long.

Flowering: June–August (September).

Habitat: Meadows, pastures, road verges, wood margins, on moist to rather dry, oligotrophic to mesotrophic, calcareous, sandy, loamy or stony soils; from sea level to 1,500 m.

Range: Most of Europe, except the extreme north.

---

p.114 **Wild Strawberry** *Fragaria vesca* L.

Description: A hairy, rosette-bearing perennial to 15 (30) cm, with long, trailing and rooting stolons and short, erect flowering stems, barely exceeding leaves. Leaves mostly basal, long-stalked, *ternate*, with 3 broadly obovate or rhombic, subsessile, dentate leaflets (each with 15–23 teeth). Flowers regular, hermaphrodite, 12–18 mm diam., few together in lax, terminal cyme; flower-stalks with more or less appressed hairs. Epicalyx parts 5, lanceolate. Sepals 5, ovate, persistent. Petals 5, *white*, rounded, scarcely exceeding sepals. Stamens numerous. Ovaries numerous, free, 1-locular, developing into small, 1-seeded achenes to 1 mm long, implanted on strongly swollen, *fleshy, subglobose receptacle*, which is glabrous but for hairy ring at base, and becomes red and 10–20 mm long when ripe.

Flowering: May–July.

Habitat: Deciduous or mixed woods, woodland clearings, wood margins, scrub, shaded roadsides, also dunes, on moist to dry, oligotrophic, preferably calcareous, sandy, loamy or stony soils; from sea level to 1,900 m.

Range: Most of Europe except Spitsbergen.

Similar species: *F. viridis* Duch. has short (or absent) stolons; (deeply pitted) receptacles hairy all over, rather fibrous and tough, up to 10 mm long, often remaining greenish-white, while leaflets are densely white-hairy even above; flower-stalks with spreading to deflexed hairs; unisexual flowers occasionally present.

Comparable habitats, also widespread in Europe, but rare in the lowland.

Hautbois Strawberry (*F. moschata* Duch.) is larger (to 40 cm), with few or no stolons, flowers 15–25 mm diam., and receptacles to 20 mm long, sparsely hairy all over, and devoid of achenes near base; leaflets usually with 23–27 teeth; flower-stalks with spreading to deflexed hairs; unisexual flowers frequent, and plants can even be dioecious. In deciduous woods of C Europe, from C France to C Russia, more frequent in mountains; cultivated and widely naturalized elsewhere.

Garden Strawberry (*F.* × *ananassa* Duch.) is frequently cultivated, and occasionally naturalizes in woods, road verges, and under hedges; it has long stolons, large flowers (15–30 mm diam.), fruits up to 40 (60) mm long, and distinctly stalked leaflets. • The fruits (receptacles) of all species are edible.

p.245 **Water Avens** *Geum rivale* L.

Description: A tufted, hairy perennial to 50 cm, with erect flowering stems. Basal leaves stalked, pinnate, with 3–6 pairs of small, ovate side-leaflets and large, rounded, dentate top-leaflet; stem-leaves few, subsessile, much smaller, often ternate. Flowers regular, hermaphrodite, 10–20 mm diam., *bell-shaped, nodding on long, arching stalks*, few together in lax, terminal cyme. Epicalyx parts 5, lanceolate, dull purplish. Sepals 5, ovate, dull purplish, persistent, erect on fruit. Petals 5, *pale yellow, flushed with red*, 8–10 mm long, erect, with distinct claw and rounded limb. Stamens numerous. Ovaries numerous (up to 150), free, 1-locular, implanted on *club-shaped, stalked receptacle*. Fruit a dense cluster of hairy, 1-seeded achenes to 4 mm long, each with long, persistent, *hooked, hairy style* (10 mm) bearing feathery tip (8 mm).

Flowering: April–September.

Habitat: Damp deciduous woods, meadows, marshes, shaded places, streamsides and ditches, on moist to wet, mesotrophic, preferably calcareous, humus-rich, sandy, loamy or stony soils; from sea level to 2,000 m.

Range: Most of Europe except Spitsbergen and the deep south.

---

p.211 **Wood Avens** *Geum urbanum* L.

Description: A tufted, hairy perennial, with erect flowering stems, to 60 cm. Basal leaves stalked, pinnate, with 1–5 pairs of smaller, unequal, ovate side-leaflets and large, often deeply 3-lobed to almost ternate, dentate top-leaflet; stem-leaves subsessile, much smaller, often ternate; stipules large (at least 10 mm long). Flowers regular, hermaphrodite, 8–15 mm diam., *erect on long, erect or ascending stalks* (but more or less nodding for some time after anthesis), few together in lax, terminal cyme. Epicalyx parts 5, lanceolate, dull purplish. Sepals 5, ovate, dull purplish. Petals 5, *yellow*, 3–7 mm long, obovate, *spreading*, not clawed. Stamens numerous. Ovaries numerous (*c.* 70), free, 1-locular, implanted on subglobose, *sessile (not stalked) receptacle*. Fruit a dense cluster of finely hairy, 1-seeded achenes to 6 mm long, each with long, persistent, *hooked, glabrous style* (10 mm) with short feathery tip.

Flowering: May–September.

Habitat: Deciduous woods, scrub, hedgebanks, shaded roadsides, ditch-sides, also dunes, on moist, oligotrophic to rather eutrophic, sandy, loamy or stony soils; from sea level to 1,800 m.

Range: Most of Europe, except the far north.

Similar species: *G. hispidum* Fries from SE Sweden is a densely hairy form with small stipules. *G. aleppicum* Jacq. is much larger (to 120 cm tall), with erect, yellow flowers (up to 20 mm diam.) each yielding 200–250 achenes (to 5 mm long). On eutrophic soils, often in ruderal places and near rural buildings, in E Europe, westwards to Czechoslovakia.

Wood Avens is also called Herb Bennet. Hybrids with *G. rivale* (*G.* × *intermedium* Ehrh.) are intermediate between the parents.

Cinquefoils, *Potentilla*

A large, very diverse genus of herbs and shrubs, all with regular, hermaphrodite, basically 5-merous flowers, numerous stamens, and numerous free, 1-locular ovaries, implanted on convex, subsessile receptacle that never becomes swollen and fleshy (unlike strawberries of closely related genus *Fragaria*). Styles short, falling after anthesis. Each ovary develops into a small, 1-seeded achene. Perianth consists of 4 or 5 spreading petals, and equal numbers of sepals and epicalyx parts; epicalyx parts usually smaller and narrower than sepals.

The leaves can be pinnate, but in most species are ternate (with 3 leaflets) or palmate (with 5 or more leaflets), be they basal or cauline. They always have a pair of stipules at the base of the leaf-stalk. With (sub)sessile stem-leaves, stipules often resemble normal leaflets, and a ternate leaf may thus become seemingly palmate; in the following descriptions they are treated as such, but with an asterisk added (*palmate). In stalked, truly palmate leaves, stipules can be found at some distance from normal leaflets, and they are often small and differently shaped.

Of the species from N Europe, only *P. palustris* has large, reddish sepals and reduced, dark brownish-red petals. Normally developed, white flowers are found in *P. rupestris* (with pinnate leaves), and in *P. montana* and *P. sterilis* (both with ternate leaves); in *P. micrantha* (also ternate) they can be pink or white.

All other N European species have yellow flowers. Of these, *P. fruticosa* is a shrub (not treated here, *see* photograph p.241). Some have pinnate (*P. anserina*, *P. supina*) or even doubly pinnate leaves (*P. multifida*). The remaining species have ternate, *palmate or (truly) palmate leaves. *P. erecta* stands alone in having (usually) 4-merous flowers, and *palmate stem-leaves. As to the remaining species, some informal groups can be distinguished, as follows:

A. Plants with thin, trailing or creeping, stolon-like stems, and flowers solitary in leaf-axils: *P. reptans* (stem-leaves palmate with 5–7 leaflets), *P. anglica* (stem-leaves ternate).

B. Plants with short, prostrate to ascending (but not trailing) stems, mainly basal leaves, and few flowers, solitary in leaf-axils or in small terminal cymes. Two are mat-forming: *P. cinerea* (with ternate or palmate basal and stem-leaves), *P. tabernaemontani* (with palmate basal leaves and ternate or palmate stem-leaves). The others are tuft-forming: *P. crantzii* and *P. hyparctica* (both with palmate basal leaves and *palmate stem-leaves with 5–7 leaflets); *P. heptaphylla* is often more erect (basal leaves palmate with 5–7 leaflets, stem-leaves ternate or palmate with 5 leaflets).

C. Plants with ascending to erect stems, often several stem-leaves, and flowers few to numerous in terminal cyme or panicle. Of these, *P. nivea*, *P. chamissonis*, and *P. norvegica* have ternate (occasionally palmate) basal leaves, and always ternate stem-leaves. *P. argentea* and *P. neglecta* have palmate basal and stem-leaves (both with 5 leaflets). *P. collina* also has palmate basal and stem-leaves, but both have 5–7 leaflets (*compare* for this species *P. heptaphylla* (*see* p.985) in group B). Two frequently observed, naturalized species (*P. intermedia* and *P. recta*) also enter this group; they have palmate basal leaves and *palmate stem-leaves (both with 5–7 leaflets).

---

p.195 **Trailing Tormentil** *Potentilla anglica* Laich.

Description: A hairy perennial with thin, trailing or straggling (only occasionally rooting), *stolon-like stems* to 1 m long. Leaves green above, white-hairy beneath, basal ones long-persistent, forming distinct rosette, stalked, usually palmate with 5 narrowly obovate, dentate leaflets (rarely ternate); stem-leaves *distinctly stalked* (stalks 5–20 mm long), *ternate* with 3 narrowly obovate, dentate leaflets; stipules small, lanceolate. Flowers 14–18 mm diam., long-stalked, *solitary* in leaf-axils. *Petals 5 (occasionally 4)*, yellow, 5–8 mm long, much longer than sepals, broadly obovate, shallowly notched.

Flowering: June–September.

Habitat: Meadows, roadsides, on banks, along ditches, at field boundaries, under hedges, in wood margins, on wet or moist, oligotrophic to mesotrophic, weakly acid, sandy, loamy or stony soils; from sea level to 1,500 m.

Range: W and C Europe, northwards to S Scandinavia and SW Finland, eastwards to C Russia.

Compare P. erecta (*see* p.985), which has *palmate stem-leaves, and usually 4-merous flowers. For hybrids with intermediate characters, *see also* under that species.

p.196 **Silverweed** *Potentilla anserina* L.

Description: A hairy perennial, with long, creeping, reddish, stolon-like stems (to 1 m or more, rooting at nodes, and forming leaf-rosettes). Leaves basal, short-stalked, greyish-green above, (densely) silvery-hairy beneath, *pinnate* with 15–25 broadly lanceolate or elliptical, often folded, *sharply serrate leaflets*, and with *tiny leaflets in between*. Flowers 15–20 mm diam., solitary, long-stalked, rising from nodal rosettes. Epicalyx parts usually 3-dentate; sepals ovate, entire. Petals 5, *yellow*, about twice as long as sepals, rounded.

Flowering: May–August.

Habitat: Meadows, pastures, cultivated and waste land, gardens, ruderal places, roadsides, farm-tracks, watersides, also open woods, dunes, and highest reaches of saltmarshes, on wet to rather dry, mesotrophic to (very) eutrophic, preferably calcareous, sandy, clayey or stony soils; from sea level to 2,400 m.

Range: Most of Europe except the high Arctic and parts of the deep south.

A common weed, very tolerant of trampling, even on compacted soils. Ssp. *egedii* (Wormsk.) Hiitonen, in coastal habitats of Sweden and Finland, has only 7–15 leaflets (green at both faces).

p.212 **Hoary Cinquefoil** *Potentilla argentea* L.

Description: A hairy, *tuft-forming* perennial to 50 (70) cm, with spreading to ascending, densely white-tomentose flowering stems. Leaves green above, *white-tomentose beneath*, stalked, palmate – basal and (numerous) stem-leaves both have 5 very coarsely dentate to *almost pinnatifid leaflets*, and ovate stipules. Flowers 10–12 mm diam., long-stalked, few to several in terminal cyme. Sepals ovate, *c.* 5 mm long during anthesis, persistent and enlarged (to 10 mm) on fruit. Petals 5, *yellow*, 4–5 mm long, slightly longer than sepals, broadly obovate, shallowly notched. *Ovaries pale yellow.*

Flowering: June–September.
Habitat: Grassland, road verges, track-sides, waste and ruderal places, also sea-dunes, on dry, oligotrophic, slightly acid, sandy, gravelly or rocky soils; from sea level to 2,000 m.
Range: N Europe (except the high Arctic), and in the mountains of C Europe.
Similar species: *P. neglecta* Baumg. has similar leaves, but greyish-green above, and with 8–11 long teeth instead of only 3–7; the plant grows more erect, and has slightly larger flowers (12–16 mm diam.), with dark-yellow or orange ovaries. Widespread in Europe, but distribution not yet satisfactorily established owing to frequent confusion with the former species.

Norwegian Cinquefoil (*P. norvegica* L.) is an annual or short-lived perennial; leaves green at both faces, basal ones long-stalked, ternate (occasionally palmate) with 3 (5) narrowly elliptical (or obovate, in ssp. *hirsuta* (Michx.) Hyl.), coarsely dentate leaflets (with awned teeth), and lanceolate stipules; stem-leaves numerous, short-stalked, ternate (with rather small, ovate stipules); flowers 10–15 mm diam., long-stalked, in small, terminal cymes; sepals ovate, *c.* 5 mm long during anthesis, persistent and enlarged (to 10 mm) on fruit; petals 5, yellow, at most equalling sepals. In grassland, waste and ruderal places, on moist to dry, mesotrophic, often acid, sandy or stony soils (0–1,000 m), in Fennoscandia and N Russia.

P. intermedia L. from N and C Russia is biennial or perennial, and has palmate basal leaves and *palmate stem-leaves (both with 5–7 leaflets), large inflorescences, and petals 3–6 mm long, barely exceeding sepals, which are strongly enlarged in fruit.

Sulphur Cinquefoil (*P. recta* L.) from S and C Europe is always perennial, with stiffly erect stems, leaves similar to *P. intermedia* (but often greyish-hairy beneath), also large inflorescences, but larger flowers (15–25 mm diam.), with petals (6) 8–12 mm long, much exceeding sepals, which are not much enlarged in fruit. • The last 3 species have naturalized in roadsides, ruderal places and along railways in W and C Europe. *Compare also P. collina (see p.984)*, which has palmate, 5–7-parted leaves.

---

p.196 **Grey Cinquefoil**
Potentilla cinerea Chaix ex Vill.

Description: A *densely grey-hairy, mat-forming* perennial to 20 cm, with *creeping* (rooting), rather *woody stems* and ascending flowering branches, rising from rosettes. Leaves greyish-hairy (with predominantly stellate hairs) at both faces, basal ones stalked, ternate or palmate with 3–5 obovate or elliptical, dentate leaflets; stem-leaves similar, few; stipules lanceolate. Flowers 10–16 mm diam., long-stalked, solitary or 2–6 together in small, terminal cyme. Petals 5, yellow, distinctly longer than sepals, broadly obovate, slightly notched.

Flowering: April–July.

Habitat: Grassland, grassy slopes, scrub and open woods, on dry, oligotrophic, often acid, sandy or stony soils; from sea level to 1,600 m.

Range: The mountains of S and C Europe, northwards to Luxembourg, Denmark, S Sweden and N Russia.

Similar species: **Spring Cinquefoil** (*P. tabernaemontani* Aschrs.) has all leaves palmate, with 5–7 wedge-shaped, only apically toothed leaflets, green above and greyish-hairy beneath (with simple, never stellate hairs), and often larger flowers (8–20 mm diam.). In dry grassland on calcareous, often stony soils, from sea level to 3,000 m (only on mountains in the south), in Europe northwards to Britain and S Scandinavia, eastwards to White Russia and Bulgaria.

Both species easily form hybrids. *P. pusilla* Host appears to descend from such a hybrid, as it is intermediate between both species, with both simple and branched hairs, and all leaves palmate with 5–7 leaflets. In subalpine grassland of C Europe.

p.212 *Potentilla collina* Wibel

Description: A hairy, *tuft-forming* perennial to 30 cm, with ascending to erect flowering stems. Leaves green above, *white-hairy beneath*, both basal and cauline ones *palmate with 5–7 leaflets*, these narrowly elliptical and coarsely dentate; stipules ovate, small. Flowers 8–12 mm diam., long-stalked, numerous in terminal cymes; sepals 5, ovate; petals 5, yellow, barely equalling sepals, broadly obovate, notched. *Style club-shaped*.

Flowering: June–August.

Habitat: Grassy and rocky places in C Europe, northwards to Denmark and S Sweden, eastwards to SE Russia.

Compare *P. heptaphylla* (*see* p.985), and *P. argentea* (p.981), which have ternate or palmate, 5-parted stem-leaves. Several more, comparable species can be found in the mountains of C and S Europe.

p.196 **Alpine Cinquefoil**
Potentilla crantzii (Crantz) G. Beck ex Fritsch

Description: A hairy, *tuft-forming* perennial to 25 cm, with ascending to erect flowering stems. Leaves hairy beneath and on margins, basal ones long-stalked, palmate with 5–7 (broadly) obovate, coarsely dentate leaflets, and with broadly ovate stipules; stem-leaves few, *palmate with 5–7 wedge-shaped, apically toothed leaflets. Flowers 10–25 mm diam., long-stalked, solitary or 2–6 together in small, terminal cyme. Petals 5, *yellow, often with orange base*, distinctly longer than sepals, broadly obovate, notched.

Flowering: June–July.

Habitat: Rock-ledges and cliffs, rock-crevices, also grassy slopes, on dry, oligotrophic, usually calcareous, gravelly or rocky soils; mainly in mountains, 1,000–3,000 m, but descending lower in the north.

Range: The mountains of C Europe, northwards to the Vosges and the Carpathians; also in Wales and N Britain, and in Iceland,

Fennoscandia and N Russia (including Spitsbergen).

Similar species: *P. hyparctica* Malte from Sweden and Spitsbergen has plain yellow flowers, and glandular-hairy leaves.

P. heptaphylla L. has more erect stems (hairy, often also with reddish glands), palmate basal leaves (with 5–7 leaflets and ovate stipules), and ternate or palmate stem-leaves (with 3–5 leaflets). In heaths, grassland and open woods, on more or less acid soils, in the mountains of C and E Europe, westwards to C France, northwards to S Sweden, and eastwards to the Ukraine. *Compare also P. cinerea* (*see* p.983) and allies, which have lanceolate stipules. Several comparable species occur in the high mountains of C Europe.

---

p.195 **Tormentil** *Potentilla erecta* (L.) Räuschel

Description: A hairy perennial with thin, straggling or ascending (but not stolon-like, and never rooting) stems to 1 m long. Leaves green above, white-hairy beneath, basal ones soon withered, stalked, ternate with 3 narrowly obovate, dentate leaflets (rarely palmate with 4 or 5 leaflets); stem-leaves mostly subsessile, *palmate with 5 oblanceolate, dentate leaflets. Flowers 7–12 (15) mm diam., long-stalked, solitary in leaf-axils or composing very lax cyme. *Petals usually 4* (occasionally 5), yellow, 3–6 mm long, barely exceeding sepals, broadly obovate, shallowly notched.

Flowering: May–September.

Habitat: Heaths, moors, poor grassland, common land, woodland rides, also dune-slacks, on wet to moist, oligotrophic, more or less acid, sandy or peaty soils; from sea level to 2,500 m.

Range: Most of Europe, except the high Arctic, and rare in Mediterranean region.

Compare P. anglica (*see* p.980), which has stalked, ternate stem-leaves, and 5-merous flowers. Both species easily form hybrids (as they do with *P. reptans*, p.988); the forms in this hybrid swarm can be hard to identify.

p.212 **Cut-leaved Potentilla** *Potentilla multifida* L.

Description: A hairy perennial to 40 cm, with 2–3 prostrate or ascending stems, not rooting at nodes. Basal leaves long-stalked, green above, white-hairy beneath, *doubly pinnate* with (3) 5 1st-order leaflets, these ovate and themselves compound with (3) 5–9 (11) almost linear, entire segments, margins rolled under; stem-leaves few, smaller, mostly 1-pinnate; stipules lanceolate. Flowers 10–14 mm diam., stalked, few to several together in terminal cyme. Epicalyx parts linear-lanceolate, about equalling narrowly ovate, entire sepals. Petals 5, *yellow*, slightly longer than sepals, notched.

Flowering: July–August.

Habitat: Meadows and rocky places, on moist to rather dry, oligotrophic, often acid, stony soils; mainly in the mountains (1,000–3,000 m), but descending lower in the north.

Range: In the Pyrenees and the Western Alps, further in N Sweden, the Urals and on Spitsbergen; apparently only naturalized in Finland.

---

p.212 **Snowy Cinquefoil** *Potentilla nivea* L.

Description: A hairy, *tuft-forming* perennial to 25 cm, with ascending to erect flowering stems. Leaves greyish-green above, *densely white-tomentose beneath* (and on stalks), basal ones long-stalked, *ternate* (occasionally palmate) with 3 (5) elliptical or obovate, coarsely dentate leaflets (with awned teeth), and with lanceolate stipules; stem-leaves few, subsessile, *ternate*. Flowers 12–18 mm diam., long-stalked, solitary or few together in small, terminal cyme. Petals 5, *yellow*, distinctly longer than sepals, broadly obovate, notched.

Flowering: June–August.

Habitat: Rocky places, cliffs, screes, moraines, on dry, oligotrophic, often calcareous, stony soils; mainly in the mountains (to

3,000 m), but descending lower in the north.

Range: In the Alps and N Apennines (over 1,600 m), also in Fennoscandia, the Urals, and on Spitsbergen.

Similar species: *P. chamissonis* Hultén has straight (not curly) hairs on leaf-stalks, and leaflets with very long teeth. In comparable habitats of Arctic Europe (from Norway to Spitsbergen and N Russia). *Compare P. norvegica (see p.982), which has leaflets green at both faces, and P. argentea (see p.981) and P. collina (p.984), which have palmate stem-leaves.*

---

p.272 **Marsh Cinquefoil**
Potentilla palustris (L.) Scop.

Description: A subglabrous perennial to 50 (90) cm, with creeping rhizomes and erect, reddish stems. Leaves dull greyish-green, often glaucous beneath, stalked, basal ones distinctly *pinnate* with 5–7 narrowly elliptical to oblanceolate, serrate-dentate leaflets (4–10 cm long), lower cauline ones similar, upper ones often (nearly) palmate with 5 leaflets, or even ternate in inflorescence; stipules conspicuous, ovate, more or less papery. Flowers 15–20 (30) mm diam., stalked, few to several together in lax, terminal cyme. Epicalyx small, reddish, the parts lanceolate; *sepals large, purplish or reddish,* ovate, pointed, persistent on fruit. Petals 5, *maroon or dark purplish,* 5–9 mm long, lanceolate, much smaller than sepals.

Flowering: May–July.

Habitat: Bogs, marshes, fens, shallow pools and ditches, also dune-slacks, on wet, oligotrophic to mesotrophic, more or less acid, usually peaty soils; from sea level to 2,100 m.

Range: Most of Europe, except Mediterranean region. A true helophyte; formerly it was often attributed to a separate genus (*Comarum*).

p.195 **Creeping Cinquefoil** *Potentilla reptans* L.

Description: A slightly hairy perennial with thin,
creeping (rooting), reddish, *stolon-like stems* to
1 m long. Leaves glabrous, green at both
faces, basal ones long-persistent, forming
distinct rosette, long-stalked, palmate with
5 (7) narrowly obovate or oblanceolate,
dentate leaflets; stem-leaves similar, also
long-stalked; stipules small, broadly
lanceolate, entire or with some teeth.
Flowers 17–25 mm diam., long-stalked,
solitary in leaf-axils. *Petals 5*, yellow,
7–12 mm long, much longer than sepals,
broadly obovate, shallowly notched.

Flowering: June–September.

Habitat: Grassland, roadsides, dune-slacks, also
cultivated and waste land, and hedges, on
moist to dry, mesotrophic to eutrophic,
calcareous or mildly acid, sandy, clayey or
stony soils; from sea level to 1,700 m.

Range: Most of Europe, except Iceland and the
high Arctic.

Compare P. anglica (see p.980), which has
ternate stem-leaves.

---

p.114 **Rock Cinquefoil** *Potentilla rupestris* L.

Description: A hairy, tufted perennial to 50 cm, with
erect flowering stems; no stolons. Leaves
mostly basal, fresh green, hairy, *pinnate* with
5–9 broadly (ob)ovate, dentate leaflets,
diminishing to base; stem-leaves few, short-
stalked, often ternate. Flowers 15–25 mm
diam., stalked, solitary or few together in
lax, terminal cyme. Epicalyx parts almost
linear; sepals ovate. Petals 5, *white*, much
longer than sepals, rounded.

Flowering: May–June.

Habitat: Rocky habitats, cliffs, ledges, screes, on dry
to moist, oligotrophic, acid or calcareous,
stony soils; mainly in mountains, to
2,200 m.

Range: S and C Europe, northwards to C France
(with isolated stations in Wales and
Scotland), the Ardennes, C Germany, S
Scandinavia, Poland, and W Russia.

p.114 **Barren Strawberry**
Potentilla sterilis (L.) Garcke

Description: A hairy, tufted perennial to 15 cm, with long, creeping (aerial) stolons, and ascending flowering stems. Leaves mostly basal, long-stalked, bluish-green above, greyish-hairy beneath, *ternate* with 3 broadly ovate to suborbicular, bluntly dentate leaflets; stem-leaves similar. Flowers 10–15 mm diam., stalked, solitary or few together in lax, terminal cyme. Epicalyx parts lanceolate; sepals ovate. Petals 5, *white*, shorter to slightly longer than sepals, obovate, notched, distinctly separated. Stamens glabrous.

Flowering: March–May (summer).

Habitat: Deciduous woods (often Oak), scrub, roadsides, grassy slopes, also hedges and old walls, on moist to rather dry, oligotrophic, calcareous, sandy, loamy or stony soils; from sea level to 1,500 m.

Range: W and C Europe, northwards to the British Isles, the Low Countries and S Sweden, eastwards to Poland and the Balkan Peninsula.

Similar species: **Mountain Cinquefoil** (*P. montana* Brot.) has larger flowers (15–25 mm diam.), white, touching petals, and green, elliptical leaflets only toothed towards tip. In woods, scrub, heaths and on banks, on rather dry, oligotrophic, often acid, sandy or rocky soils, in SW Europe, northwards to NW France; an Atlantic species.
Pink Barren Strawberry (*P. micrantha* Ramond ex DC.) lacks stolons, and has smaller, pink or occasionally white flowers (7–9 mm diam.), with hairy stamens; it occurs in mountains of S, SC and SE Europe, where some white-flowering species with palmate leaves can also be found.

Compare also Fragaria vesca (see p.976) and allies, which have similar, more acutely dentate leaves, and swollen, fleshy receptacles in fruit. The fruits of Barren Strawberry remain small, greenish, and dry.

p.196 *Potentilla supina* L.

Description: A hairy annual or short-lived perennial to 40 cm (often much less), with prostrate or ascending stems, not rooting at nodes. Leaves short-stalked, green at both faces, *pinnate* with 5–11 elliptical or (ob)ovate, coarsely crenate-dentate leaflets. Flowers small, 6–8 mm diam., stalked, solitary in leaf-axils. Epicalyx parts lanceolate to ovate, obtuse, longer than ovate, entire sepals. Petals 5, *yellow*, distinctly shorter than sepals, slightly notched.

Flowering: June–September.

Habitat: Meadows, river and lake margins, often seasonally inundated habitats, also ruderal places and roadsides, on wet, eutrophic, often slightly acid, sandy, muddy or clayey soils; from sea level to 600 m.

Range: S and C Europe, northwards to the Low Countries, Poland and W Russia.

Roses, *Rosa*

A large genus of prickly, normally deciduous shrubs, widespread in the northern hemisphere. Leaves pinnate, with 5–11 leaflets; stipules present, connate to leaf-stalk. Flowers solitary or in small terminal cymes, subtended by tongue-shaped, papery bracts often grading into normal leaves lower down. Sepals 5, entire or partly pinnate (then 2 entire, 2 pinnate, 1 unilaterally pinnate). Petals 5, crinkled when appearing from the bud, broadly obovate, overlapping, often shallowly notched at the tip. Stamens numerous, implanted on rim of urn-shaped receptacle (the 'hypanthium'), closed by fleshy 'discus' or disc. Ovaries often numerous, superior, free from each other but enclosed in the hypanthium; styles long, hairy, protruding through circular opening ('orifice') in the disc. Fruit a cluster of hard, bristly-hairy achenes, enclosed in the fleshy, often red hypanthium (the 'hip'). Several species and many hybrids are grown in gardens, often in double-flowered forms. The hips, which are rich in Vitamin C, can be made into a jelly and used as a food supplement.

The Dog Rose and allies (section **Caninae**) have sepals partly pinnate, with several well-developed side-lobes. They constitute a hybridogenic microspecies flock, with an aberrant mode of replication normally involving self-pollination. Members of this section are hereafter marked with an asterisk*. Literally thousands of varieties have been described, although fairly well-recognizable species number but a few dozen. Their identification can be problematical owing to the occurrence of numerous transitional forms, and their distribution is often not well known as yet. The characters of the indument (hairs, glands, prickles) and the disc morphology are important for species delimitation. A marked correlation exists between doubly serrate (biserrate) leaf-margins and the presence of glands at the lower face of the leaflets (at least on the larger veins); uniserrate leaflets lack such glands. Also, a disc with a narrow orifice (less than 1 mm diam., measuring up to 1 fourth of the disc width) is associated with deflexed, soon-falling sepals. The other way round, a disc with a wide orifice (at least 1 mm, measuring at least 1 third of the disc width) is associated with more or less erect, persistent, often thickened sepals. Sepal behaviour is to some extent influenced by the weather, however; the size of the orifice (in relation to the disc width) affords a more reliable test. For accurate identification, always examine plants with ripe hips (from mid-July).

---

p.173 **Field Rose** *Rosa arvensis* Hudson

Description: A low shrub with weak, *trailing or straggling*, often purplish stems to 3 m long. Prickles scattered, hooked, compressed, all about equal. Leaflets 5–7, to 35 mm long (often much less), glabrous, dull green above, pale green or whitish-green beneath, ovate, uniserrate. Flowers solitary or 2–3 together in small cyme, 30–50 mm diam., *always white*, on glandular stalks. Sepals ovate, pointed, entire or weakly pinnate (often some with a few linear side-lobes), deflexed and soon falling after anthesis. Styles glabrous, glued together into long, protruding column, about equalling shortest stamens. Hypanthium glabrous, shiny-red when ripe, only 10–15 mm long.

Flowering: June–August.

Habitat: Open, deciduous woods, scrub, hedgerows, on moist, oligotrophic to mesotrophic, preferably calcareous, loamy or stony soils; from sea level to 2,000 m.

Range: S, W and C Europe, northwards to Ireland, N England, the Low Countries, Poland and W Russia.

Similar species: *R. sempervirens* L. has smaller flowers (20–35 mm diam.) in 3–7-flowered cymes, and entire sepals. Mainly S Europe, northwards to W France.

---

p.303 **Dog Rose** **Rosa canina* L. s.s.

Description: A shrub to 3 (5) m, with terete, arching stems, armed with *hooked, strongly compressed prickles*; no suckers. Young stems greenish, later becoming greyish-brown. Leaflets 5–7, dark green or bluish-green above, slightly paler beneath, ovate, pointed, *uniserrate, completely glabrous*. Flowers mostly 2–5 together in small, terminal cymes, pink (rarely white), to 50 mm diam., on glabrous stalks to 20 mm long. Sepals partly pinnate, *deflexed and soon falling* after anthesis. Styles free, hairy, the *stigmas forming rounded head well above orifice*. Hypanthium subglobose or egg-shaped (rarely flask-shaped), 10–20 (30) mm long, *glabrous*, shiny-red when ripe, with wide, often raised disc, and *narrow orifice*.

Flowering: June–July.

Habitat: Wood margins, woodland clearings, scrub, hedgerows, roadsides, on river banks, on dry, oligotrophic to mesotrophic, preferably calcareous, sandy, loamy or stony soils; from sea level to 2,200 m, but more or less restricted to the lowland in the north.

Range: Most of Europe, except the Arctic.

Similar species: **R. corymbifera* Borkh., equally widespread, though reportedly less frequent in NW Europe, has uniserrate leaflets with appressed hairs beneath, especially on veins. **R. squarrosa* (Rau) Boreau has leaflets biserrate, and is glandular (but not hairy) on veins beneath. In C Europe, westwards to Belgium and S Britain. **R. obtusifolia* Desv. has biserrate leaflets (both hairy and glandular on veins beneath). In whole area except Iceland, Fennoscandia and N Russia.

The 3 following species have glandular bristles on flower-stalks (and occasionally also on hypanthia):

R. andegavensis Bast., in W, C and S
Europe, northwards to the Low Countries
and Poland, and eastwards to W Russia, has
glabrous leaflets;
R. blondaeana Rip. ex Déségl., in Europe
northwards to S Sweden and Poland, and
eastwards to W Russia, has biserrate,
glandular but not hairy leaflets;
R. deseglisei Boreau, in C Europe,
northwards to the Low Countries, Poland,
S Finland and NW Russia, has biserrate,
glandular and hairy leaflets.
  R. jundzillii Besser has slender,
subterete, straight or weakly curved
prickles, often distinctly leathery, ovate,
biserrate leaflets, with some glands on
veins beneath, but usually hairless; flowers
solitary, 30–50 mm diam., pink, with
deflexed, soon falling, glandular sepals;
hypanthium glabrous or with some
glandular bristles; disc wide, flat, with
narrow orifice. In wood margins, scrub
and rough, grassy slopes in the hills and
mountains of C and E Europe, westwards
to C France, northwards to Poland, and
southwards to N Italy and Albania.
Leathery leaves are also found in *R. gallica*,
and occasionally (less pronouncedly) in
R. corymbifera.

Compare Dog Rose especially with *R.
vosagiaca* (*see* p.999) and allies, which have
persistent sepals.

---

p.304 **Red-leaved Rose** *Rosa glauca* Pourret

Description: A shrub with erect, bluish-green (later
brownish) stems up to 3 m, armed with
scattered, hooked and strongly compressed
prickles; *young stems and leaves flushed with
purple*, and often with whitish bloom.
Leaflets 5–9, glabrous. Sepals glabrous,
usually with at least a few linear side-lobes,
soon falling after anthesis. Flowers deep
pink, on glabrous (rarely glandular) stalks.
Hypanthium glabrous, brownish-red when
ripe, with flat disc.
Flowering: June–July.

Habitat: Open woods and scrub, on dry, sandy or
stony soils; mainly in the mountains, to
2,100 m.

Range: C and S Europe, northwards to Germany
and Poland, eastwards to Romania and
Bulgaria, southwards to the Pyrenees,
C Italy and Albania.

Frequently planted in parks, gardens, and
along motorways. *Compare also* *R. vosagiaca*
(*see* p.999), which has persistent sepals.

---

p.302 **Cinnamon Rose** *Rosa majalis* J. Hermann

Description: A shrub with arching, *reddish-brown stems* to
2 m. Prickles slender, subterete, *weakly
curved, often in pairs* directly below nodes.
Leaflets 5–7, to 45 mm long, bluish-green,
ovate, uniserrate, downy beneath. Flowers
solitary, 30–50 mm diam., deep pink, on
glabrous stalks. *Sepals entire*, erect and
persistent after anthesis. Hypanthium
glabrous, shiny-red when ripe.

Flowering: June–July.

Habitat: Wood margins, scrub, hedgerows, on dry or
moist, sandy or stony soils; from near sea
level (in the north) to 2,200 m.

Range: N and C Europe, from E France to E Russia.

Similar species: *R. acicularis* Lindley has straight, solitary
prickles mixed with thin, stiff needles. In
comparable habitats of Fennoscandia and N
Russia.

Alpine Rose (*R. pendulina* L.) has arching
stems without prickles, biserrate leaflets,
and pendent, narrowly ovoid to flask-
shaped, red hips with erect, persistent
sepals. In scrub and rocky places in the
mountains of C Europe (to 2,600 m), and
(descending lower) in Fennoscandia and N
Russia; also planted in gardens.

Provence Rose (*R. gallica* L.), rarely taller
than 80 cm, forms extensive scrub; stems
with straight prickles and glandular
bristles, leaves leathery (*compare* *R.
jundzillii,* p.993), 3–7 dull bluish-green
leaflets (hairy beneath), very large, deep-
pink flowers (60–90 mm diam.), and
subglobose to spindle-shaped hips covered

with glandular bristles. In dry, open places in S and C Europe, northwards to Lorraine and Alsace.

R. rugosa Thunb., from E Asia, has wrinkled, dark-green leaflets (greyish-tomentose and with prominent veins beneath), large, pink or white flowers (40–70 mm diam.), large, carmine hips, and hairy stems with dense armour of straight, terete prickles and needles. Widely cultivated in parks and gardens, and frequently naturalized along roads and railways.

The reddish stems of Cinnamon Rose are reminiscent of cinnamon sticks, hence the name.

p.173 **Burnet Rose** *Rosa pimpinellifolia* L.

Description: A patch-forming shrub, with erect or arching stems to 50 (90) cm, densely clad in *thin, straight, terete prickles* (those on flowering branches much smaller, bristle-like). Leaflets (5) 7–11, often *small*, 6–15 (25) mm long, glabrous, dull green above, paler and (sub)glabrous beneath, ovate, uniserrate. Flowers solitary, 20–40 mm diam., *creamy white*, on glabrous stalks. Sepals ovate, long-pointed, entire, spreading to erect and persistent after anthesis. Styles hairy, scarcely protruding from orifice. Hypanthium glabrous, *purplish-black* when ripe, subglobose, only about 6 mm diam.

Flowering: May–July (autumn).

Habitat: Scrub, often sea-dunes, also inland on riverine dunes, heaths, poor grassland, limestone pavements, mountain ledges, on dry, oligotrophic, calcareous, sandy, loamy or stony soils; from sea level to 2,000 m.

Range: Most of Europe, northwards to Iceland, S Norway, Denmark (extinct in Sweden), Poland, C Russia.

Immediately recognizable by its blackish hips. In dunes, the plant often grows deeply embedded in drifting sand. Hybridizes with *R. rubiginosa*.

p.304 **Sweet Briar** *Rosa rubiginosa* L.

Description: A shrub to 1.5 (3) m, with terete, erect stems, armed with scattered, *curved or hooked, compressed prickles*, and with *straight needles as well* (especially on flowering branches, and there often mixed with glandular bristles). Leaflets 5–7, often yellowish-green, broadly ovate or (as often) suborbicular and round-tipped, biserrate, hairy or almost hairless but *always densely glandular* at least beneath (with dark glands even on smallest veinlets). Flowers solitary or 2–3 together in small, terminal cymes, deep pink, 20–30 mm diam., on glandular-bristly stalks to 20 mm long. Sepals partly pinnate, *spreading to erect* and *persistent after anthesis*. Styles free, hairy, stigmas forming *semiglobose head directly over wide orifice* (almost filling it). Hypanthium subglobose or ovoid to pear-shaped, glabrous or covered with glandular bristles, shiny red when ripe.

Flowering: June–August.

Habitat: Scrub, rough grassland, inland as well as coastal, occasionally hedgerows, on dry, oligotrophic, calcareous, sandy, loamy or stony soils; from sea level to 2,100 m.

Range: Most of Europe except Iceland and the Arctic.

Similar species: The following species, all with biserrate, densely glandular leaflets, are attributed to the 'Rubiginosa-group':
R. elliptica Tausch has stems with slender, curved prickles (but no needles), pink flowers, glabrous flower-stalks, and elliptical leaflets narrowed at both ends.
R. micrantha Borrer ex Sm. has arching stems (with or without needles between the hooked prickles), ovate leaflets with rounded base, white or pale-pink flowers, narrow orifice, and soon-falling sepals (densely glandular on back).
Field Briar (*R. agrestis* Savi) has erect branches (usually without needles), small leaflets with distinctly cuneate base, and again a narrow orifice and soon-falling sepals (glabrous on back). • These species

are less frequent than *R. rubiginosa* itself, and although they are found in comparable habitats, they often appear to prefer warmer sites, like sunny slopes; also, they obviously do not reach as far north. In all species of the Rubiginosa-group the leaves (when rubbed) give out a sweet, apple-like scent. There are many intermediate forms, and part of the specimens will always be difficult to identify.

In exposed, sunny places Sweet Briar often turns quite red. Occasionally hybrids with *R. pimpinellifolia* are found, especially in the sea-dunes; their leaflets less glandular, and usually uniserrate near tip.

Caninae with densely tomentose and also glandular, biserrate leaves, are grouped round **Downy Rose** (*Rosa tomentosa* Sm.). This is a shrub to 1.5 (3) m, with terete, arching stems, armed with scattered, *straight or slightly curved, subterete prickles*. Leaflets 5–7, ovate, 20–40 mm long, biserrate, *densely tomentose at least beneath* (and with glands on veins). Flowers (June–July) pale pink (occasionally white), 30–40 mm diam., usually 2–5 together in small, terminal cymes *on glandular-bristly stalks to 50 mm long*. Sepals partly pinnate, deflexed and soon falling after anthesis. Styles free, hairy, stigmas forming *globose head well over narrow orifice*. Hypanthium subglobose or ovoid to pear-shaped, glabrous or covered with glandular bristles, shiny-red when ripe. At wood margins, in woodland clearings, scrub, hedgerows, on dry, oligotrophic, preferably calcareous, sandy, loamy or stony soils, from sea level to 2,200 m, in Europe northwards to the British Isles, S Scandinavia and C Russia.
    The following species are attributed to the 'Tomentosa group'. *R. scabriuscula* Sm. is quite similar to Downy Rose, but has spreading, persistent sepals and wide orifice. *R. sherardii* Davies has flexuous stems (pruinose when young), bluish-green foliage, pink flowers, soon-falling sepals,

and hyphanthia (with narrow orifice) on shorter, glandular-bristly stalks (to 20 mm). **Apple Rose** (*R. villosa* L.) has very straight prickles, deep purplish-pink flowers, erect, persistent sepals, very short fruit-stalks (*c.* 5 mm, rarely more than 10 mm), and large, subglobose hypanthia (to 30 mm diam., red, usually with glandular bristles); leaflets often large (to 90 mm long) and more elliptical. *R. mollis* Sm. is much like Apple Rose, but with pruinose young stems, small, elliptical or slightly rhombic leaflets (to 30 mm long), and subglabrous hypanthia. • In all species of the Tomentosa group, the leaves give out a resinous scent when rubbed. Apple Rose was formerly cultivated for the fruits, and to that purpose apparently underwent some selection; wild forms with very large hips possibly descend from such garden selections.

Short-styled Field-rose   *Rosa stylosa* Desv.

Description: Much like *R. canina* (see p.992) in habit, but styles subglabrous, *glued into distinct column* far protruding from (narrow) orifice. Flowers white, occasionally pink. Flower-stalks usually with glandular bristles (as, occasionally, hypanthia as well).

Flowering: June–July.

Habitat: Wood margins, hedgerows, on rough, grassy slopes and banks, on dry, oligotrophic or mesotrophic, preferably calcareous, sandy, loamy or stony soils; from near sea level to 2,000 m.

Range: W and C Europe, eastwards to Bulgaria, but local.

Not to be confused with equally white-flowered *R. arvensis* (see p.991), which is a much weaker plant with trailing stems, and leaflets often very pale beneath. The species is thought to descend from a hybrid of *R. arvensis* and some species from the section Caninae.

p.304 **Whitish-stemmed Briar**
*Rosa vosagiaca Fries

Description: A shrub rather like **R. canina*, but with more erect stems, and *suckering* freely. Leaflets glabrous, uniserrate. Styles free, hairy, the stigmas forming *semiglobose head directly over orifice* (almost filling it). Sepals erect or spreading, *persistent on ripe fruit.* Hypanthium has narrow, flat disc and *wide orifice.* Hips like those of **R. canina* — glabrous, shiny-red when ripe.

Flowering: June–August.

Habitat: Wood margins, woodland clearings, scrub, hedgerows, roadsides, on dry, oligotrophic to mesotrophic, preferably calcareous, sandy, loamy or stony soils; from sea level to 1,600 m.

Range: Most of Europe, northwards to Iceland, C Scandinavia, S Finland and NC Russia.

Similar species: A form with spreading, rather soon-falling sepals (but with flat disc and relatively wide orifice) is often distinguished as **R. subcanina* (Christ) Dalla Torre & Sarnth.; its distribution is uncertain, but it is probably less frequent in the west.
*R. caesia Sm. in Sowerby has leaflets (often densely) pubescent beneath. Similar distribution, but does not reach so far north.
*R. subcollina (Christ) Dalla Torre & Sarnth. has young leaves not pruinose, while (biserrate) leaflets hairy and slightly glandular on veins beneath; sepals more or less spreading and relatively soon-falling (after hips ripen), but disc flat, with wide orifice. Similarly distributed, but absent from the far north. *Compare* especially **R. canina* (*see* p.992) and allies.

Whitish-stemmed Briar is obviously less frequent than **R. canina.* Young stems and leaves are often tinged with purple, and carry whitish bloom.

Brambles, *Rubus*

A genus of shrub-like perennial herbs, normally with very prickly stems. Many species yearly produce leafy, non-flowering stems ('turions'), which in their 2nd year will develop (annual) flowering side-branches. Often the turions bend over and root where they touch the ground, giving rise to a new plant. Leaves are alternate, often pinnate with 5–7 leaflets, occasionally ternate or even (as in *R. chamaemorus*) simple and lobed. The many-stamened flowers have 5 sepals and 5 (rarely more) rounded, white or reddish petals. The (few to numerous) free ovaries are accumulated on a conical, fleshy receptacle, and develop into an edible, compound drupe, consisting of several ovoid or rounded, 1-seeded, juicy drupelets, often 'glued' together and coming off simultaneously. Apart from some easily recognizable, sexually reproducing species, several hundred microspecies have been described which reproduce apomictically (without pollination). Their identification is a difficult task even for specialists, and here they are treated collectively as 1 very complex species (*R. fruticosus*).

---

p.271 **Arctic Bramble** *Rubus arcticus* L.

Description: A slightly hairy perennial herb to 40 cm, with *creeping, annual stems*, all flowering; *prickles absent. Leaves ternate* with 3 ovate, coarsely dentate leaflets, lateral ones strikingly asymmetrical. Flowers mostly *solitary*, 15–25 mm diam. Sepals 5, broadly lanceolate. Petals 5–7, obovate, *deep pink*. Fruit rounded, 10–20 mm diam., consisting of several (often numerous) ovoid drupelets, becoming *dark red* when ripe.

Flowering: June–July.

Habitat: Moors, thickets, grassy places, on moist, oligotrophic, acid, sandy, stony or peaty soils; often on mountains, to 1,150 m.

Range: In Fennoscandia and N and C Russia; extinct in Scotland.

---

p.147 **Dewberry** *Rubus caesius* L.

Description: A hairy perennial to 40 cm, with weak, prostrate, subterete, *pruinose* biennial turions; prickles often numerous but weak. *Leaves ternate* with 3 (ob)ovate, serrate-dentate leaflets, lateral ones often with some lobes. Flowers few to several together in raceme at end of (annual) flowering side-branches, 20–25 mm diam. Sepals 5, broadly lanceolate, pointed, pressed to fruit. Petals 5, obovate, *white*. Fruit sour, rounded, 10–20 mm diam., consisting of several rounded drupelets, becoming *blackish* when ripe, but always covered in thick, *bluish or whitish, waxy layer*.

Flowering: May–September.
Habitat: Open woods, scrub, rough grassland, frequently on sea-dunes, on dry to moist, oligotrophic or mesotrophic, preferably calcareous, sandy or stony soils; from sea level to 1,500 m.
Range: Most of Europe, except Iceland and the high Arctic.

The hybrid with *R. fruticosus* (*R.* × *corylifolius* Sm.), which has leaves partly 5-pinnate, often stronger prickles, and badly developed, thinly pruinose fruits, is widespread and rather common, especially in ruderal places.

---

p.102 **Cloudberry** *Rubus chamaemorus* L.

Description: A rather hairy, patch-forming perennial to 20 cm, with *creeping, annual stems*, all flowering; *prickles absent. Leaves simple*, palmately veined, markedly wrinkled, rounded or reniform, 5–7-lobed, dentate, only few per plant. Flowers *solitary*, terminal, 15–25 mm diam., *unisexual, dioecious*. Sepals 5, ovate. Petals 5, obovate, *white*. Fruit edible, rounded, 10–20 mm diam., consisting of few to several (up to 20) rounded drupelets, becoming reddish at first, then *orange* when ripe.
Flowering: June–August.
Habitat: Tundra, moor, bogs, on wet or moist, oligotrophic, acid, peaty, sandy or stony soils; often in mountains, to 1,400 m.
Range: N Europe (except Iceland), from the Arctic southwards to Ireland (Tyrone), W and N Britain, Germany, Poland and C Russia.

Similar species: *R. humulifolius* C.A. Meyer has hermaphrodite flowers, and 3–5-lobed, serrate or biserrate leaves with cordate base; fruit becomes red when ripe, and tastes sour. In similar habitats of N and C Russia; extinct in Finland.

p.148 **Bramble** *Rubus fruticosus* L. s.l.

Description: A (very) prickly plant, to 1.5 (3) m, with tough, 5-angled, erect, arching or scrambling, biennial turions. Leaves pinnate with (3) 5–7 ovate to subcordate, often pointed, variously hairy and/or glandular leaflets. Flowers few to several together in raceme or panicle at end of annual side-branches, white or pink, 15–32 mm diam. Sepals ovate to broadly lanceolate, often pointed, deflexed and persistent on fruit, which is more or less rounded, measuring 1–20 mm diam., and consists of several (usually numerous) drupelets, becoming red at first, and shiny purplish-black when ripe.

Flowering: May–November.

Habitat: Open woods, wood margins, scrub, heaths, roadsides, railways, occasionally hedgerows, field boundaries or waste ground, on dry to moist, oligotrophic to mesotrophic, acid or calcareous, sandy or stony soils; from sea level to 2,000 m.

Range: Most of Europe except the far north, and especially frequent in the west.

Another name is Blackberry. A very complex species, containing several hundred microspecies. Forms with arching, rooting turions often aggregate in dense, impenetrable tangles.

p.147 **Raspberry** *Rubus idaeus* L.

Description: A hairy plant, to 1.5 m, with tough, erect or arching, biennial turions. Leaves ternate or pinnate with 3–7 ovate, pointed, finely serrate-dentate leaflets, densely *white-hairy beneath*. Flowers nodding, few (up to 10) together in raceme at end of annual side-branches, only 9–11 mm diam. Sepals ovate, pointed, spreading to deflexed and persistent on fruit. Petals 5, *white*, (narrowly) elliptical, erect, scarcely equalling sepals. Fruit more or less rounded, 10–20 mm diam., consisting of several (often numerous) rounded, *finely hairy* drupelets, *purplish-red* when ripe, then easily coming off receptacle.

Flowering: May–August.

Habitat: Open woods, woodland clearings, scrub, moors, heaths, occasionally common land or road and rail verges, on moist to wet, oligotrophic to mesotrophic, weakly acid or calcareous, sandy, stony or peaty soils; from sea level to 2,300 m.

Range: Most of Europe, except Iceland and the high Arctic, but mainly on mountains in the south.

Frequently cultivated for the sweet-tasting fruits.

p.147 **Stone Bramble** *Rubus saxatilis* L.

Description: A hairy perennial, with creeping vegetative stems to 3 m long, and erect flowering branches to 30 cm tall, both annual and herbaceous; prickles weak and straight, or altogether absent. *Leaves ternate* with 3 ovate, serrate-dentate leaflets, lateral ones strikingly asymmetrical. Flowers few (2–10) together in terminal racemes, only 8–10 mm diam. Sepals 5, broadly lanceolate, deflexed and persistent on fruit. Petals 5, (narrowly) elliptical, erect, scarcely equalling sepals. Fruit edible but small, up to 10 mm diam., consisting of few (1–6) relatively large, rounded drupelets, becoming *shiny red* when ripe.

Flowering: May–August.

Habitat: Shaded, rocky places, scrub, open woods, on moist, oligotrophic to mesotrophic, preferably calcareous, sandy or stony soils; from sea level to 2,400 m.

Range: All Europe except Spitsbergen, but only on mountains in the south.

p.245 **Salad Burnet** *Sanguisorba minor* Scop.

Description: A tufted, subglabrous or slightly hairy perennial, to 60 cm, with basal leaf-rosette and erect flowering stems. Basal leaves oblanceolate, pinnate, with 9–25 ovate or elliptical, dentate leaflets (5–20 mm long, diminishing towards leaf-base); stem-leaves few and smaller. Flowers tiny (*c.* 3 mm diam.), numerous in subglobose, terminal heads (7–12 mm diam.), upper ones female, with red, protruding styles, lower ones male, with pendent, yellow anthers; receptacle urn-shaped. Perianth parts 4 (in 1 row), ovate, basally connate, greenish (often turning deep red during anthesis). Stamens (10) 20–30. Ovary 1-locular, enclosed in receptacle, and together with it forming narrowly ovoid, 1-seeded, achene-like, dry, wrinkled fruit, *c.* 3 mm long.

Flowering: May–September.

Habitat: Grassland, road verges, also sea-dunes, on dry or moist, oligotrophic, preferably calcareous, sandy, loamy or stony soils; from sea level to 2,200 m.

Range: Most of Europe, northwards to S Sweden and C Russia.

The young leaves can be eaten in salads.

---

p.245 **Great Burnet** *Sanguisorba officinalis* L.

Description: A tufted, glabrous perennial, to 1 m, with basal leaf-rosette and erect flowering stems. Basal leaves narrowly obovate, pinnate, with 7–15 long-stalked, elliptical or ovate, regularly crenate-dentate leaflets (20–70 mm long, diminishing towards leaf-base); stem-leaves few and smaller. Flowers tiny (3–4 mm diam.), hermaphrodite, numerous in ovoid, terminal heads (10–30 mm long, 10–15 mm wide); receptacle urn-shaped. Perianth parts 4 (in 1 row), ovate, basally connate, deep purple. Stamens 4, not far protruding. Ovary 1-locular, enclosed in receptacle, and together with it forming ovoid, 1-seeded, achene-like, dry, wrinkled and distinctly *winged fruit*, *c.* 4 mm long.

Flowering: June–September.

Habitat: Grassland, ditches, road verges, also railways, on moist to wet, mesotrophic, preferably calcareous, sandy, loamy or stony soils; from sea level to 2,300 m.

Range: Most of Europe, except the high Arctic and the deep south.

---

p.219 **Sibbaldia** *Sibbaldia procumbens* L.

Description: A dwarfish, tufted, hairy perennial to 4 (20) cm, with threadlike, spreading or ascending flowering stems. Leaves mostly basal, long-stalked, *ternate*, with 3 obovate to wedge-shaped, apically *3-toothed* leaflets; stem-leaves few and smaller, short-stalked. Flowers *c.* 5 mm diam., hermaphrodite or partly unisexual, few to several together in dense, umbel-shaped, terminal racemes; receptacle subsessile, convex, not swollen in fruit. Sepals 5, ovate, spreading; epicalyx parts 5, lanceolate. Petals 5, oblanceolate, *pale yellow*, shorter than sepals, not unusually rudimentary or even absent. Stamens 4–10 (often 5). Ovaries 4–12, 1-locular; style falling after anthesis. Fruit a cluster of small, 1-seeded achenes.

Flowering: July–August.

Habitat: Short grassland, often by snow patches, on moist, oligotrophic, humus-rich, sandy, gravelly or rocky, rarely calcareous soils; mainly in mountains (400–3,300 m), but descending lower in the north.

Range: Mountains of C Europe (from the Pyrenees to Poland and Yugoslavia), also in N Europe (N Britain, the Faeroe Islands, Iceland, Fennoscandia, the Kola peninsula and Spitsbergen).

BEDSTRAW FAMILY, RUBIACEAE

A family of trees, shrubs and herbs, with *c.* 7,000 species in 500 genera world-wide, predominantly in warm regions. Dicots. Leaves opposite, simple, often seemingly whorled on account of the presence of stipules similar to normal leaves.

Flowers in racemes, cymes, panicles or heads, usually regular, hermaphrodite, and often 4–5-merous. Petals connate. Stamens implanted on corolla tube, alternating with corolla lobes. Ovary inferior, usually 2-locular, with 1 bifid style. Fruit variously built, often a pair of achenes, or a drupe. European species are mostly herbaceous, with whorled leaves, small, 4-merous flowers, and minute, reduced calyces.

---

p.343 **Blue Woodruff** *Asperula arvensis* L.

Description: A slender, subglabrous annual to 30 (50) cm, with thin, erect, quadrangular stems. Leaves in spaced whorls of (4) 6–8, narrowly lanceolate to almost linear, 1-veined, with bristly-ciliate margins. Flowers *c.* 4 mm diam., in terminal, *headlike clusters* surrounded by a ruff of several long, linear, leaf-like bracts. Corolla 4-lobed, *bright blue or pale violet*, with short tube. Fruit a double achene, 2–3 mm long, glabrous, smooth, brown.

Flowering: April–July.

Habitat: Arable fields, waste places, on moist, mesotrophic, calcareous, sandy, loamy or stony soils; from sea level to 1,500 m.

Range: S and C Europe, northwards to N France, S Germany, Hungary, Romania, and W to SE Russia; only as a casual further north.

A strongly declining species.

---

p.282 **Squinancywort** *Asperula cynanchica* L.

Description: A slender, hairless perennial, to 20 (40) cm, with stout, creeping, woody rhizomes and thin, prostrate or ascending, much-branched, quadrangular stems. Leaves usually in whorls of 4, linear, 1-veined, glabrous. Flowers *c.* 3 mm diam., in terminal, umbel-shaped, often paired cymes with linear bracts. Corolla 4-lobed, *pink or purplish* outside, paler or whitish inside, with short tube. Fruit a double achene, 2–3 mm long, glabrous but finely warted, brownish.

Flowering: June–September.

Habitat:	Grassland, dunes, inland and coastal, on dry, oligotrophic, calcareous, sandy, loamy or stony soils; from sea level to 2,100 m.
Range:	S, W and C Europe, northwards to the British Isles, Belgium, Poland and C Russia, and eastwards to the Caucasus.
Similar species:	**Western Woodruff** (*A. occidentalis* Rouy) has orange (not yellowish) rhizomes; it probably does not deserve full specific rank. In coastal habitats, dunes, in W France, SW Britain, and S and W Ireland.

---

p.141 **Dyer's Woodruff** *Asperula tinctoria* L.

Description:	A slender, subglabrous perennial to 80 cm, with stout, creeping, orange rhizomes and rather stout, prostrate or ascending to erect, quadrangular stems. Leaves in spaced whorls of 4–6, narrowly lanceolate to almost linear, 1-veined, with rough margins. Flowers 3–4 mm diam., in rather lax, terminal cymes with lanceolate bracts. Corolla *3-lobed*, *white*, with short tube. Fruit a double achene, 1.5–2 mm long, glabrous but granular, brownish.
Flowering:	June–September.
Habitat:	Grassland, scrub, rocky slopes, on dry, oligotrophic, preferably calcareous, sandy or stony soils; from near sea level to 1,700 m.
Range:	S and C Europe, northwards to the Alsace, N Germany, S Scandinavia, the Baltic States and E Russia.

The plant blackens on drying. The rhizome yields a red dye.

---

p.216 **Crosswort** *Cruciata laevipes* Opiz

Description:	A slender perennial to 60 cm, with creeping rhizomes and rather stout, erect or ascending, little-branched, quadrangular, *hairy stems*. Leaves always in spaced whorls of 4, elliptical or narrowly (ob)ovate, *3-veined*, yellowish-green, hairy. Flowers 2–2.5 mm diam., on hairy stalks, in small, axillary cymes (forming verticillasters), with small bracts (to 8 mm long) below

trifurcations. Corolla 4-lobed, *pale yellow*, with short tube. Fruit a double achene, subglobose, *c.* 2.5 mm long, glabrous and smooth, blackish when ripe.

Flowering: April–June.

Habitat: Wood margins, woodland clearings, scrub, hedgebanks, road verges, on dry or moist, mesotrophic, preferably calcareous, sandy, loamy or stony soils; from sea level to 2,300 m.

Range: In Europe northwards to Britain, the Low Countries, Germany, Poland and SC Russia.

Similar species: *C. glabra* (L.) Ehrend. is more delicate, to 30 cm, usually glabrous but for leaf-margins, and without small bracts in cymes. In grassland, scrub and open woods, on dry, preferably acid soils, in S and SC Europe, northwards to C France, C Poland and SC Russia.

Bedstraws, *Galium*

A major genus of herbs with whorled, (sub)sessile leaves. Stems quadrangular, or cylindrical (but then often with 4 raised lines); they can be smooth, or finely spinose on the angles (then often 'barbed', with downward-pointing bristles). The margins and the midvein of the leaves often carry similar, backwards-pointing 'barbs', but occasionally forward-pointing bristles. The flowers usually have a 4-lobed, starry corolla (normally with very short tube), but 3-merous flowers are typical of *G. trifidum*. Fruits small, of the 'double achene' type. Several species turn black on drying, while giving out a strong, sweet scent of cumarin.

In some species, the flowers are bright or pale yellow (*G. verum*, *G. arenarium*). The others have white (occasionally cream, or slightly pinkish) flowers. First there is a group with cylindrical stems (*G. sylvaticum*, *G. glaucum*). All remaining species possess quadrangular stems. Of these, some have relatively large, broad leaves, be it 3-veined (*G. boreale*, *G. rotundifolium*) or 1-veined (*G. odoratum*, *G. triflorum*).

All others have much smaller, narrow, 1-veined leaves. Some have smooth stems: *G. mollugo*, *G. saxatile*, *G. sterneri* and their respective allies (*see under G. mollugo* for further comparisons). The remaining group, with 'barbed' stems, can be further split into a subgroup of perennials from damp, often marshy places (*G. uliginosum*, *G. palustre* and allies), and a subgroup of annuals from drier, more or less ruderal habitats in the 'agricultural landscape' (*G. aparine*, *G. parisiense* and allies).

p.150 **Cleavers** *Galium aparine* L.

Description: A rather untidy-looking, spreading, straggling or scrambling annual, with brittle, sharply quadrangular, aggressively 'barbed' stems to 2 m long, 2–4 mm wide; nodes hairy. Leaves usually in whorls of 6–9, narrowly oblanceolate, 30–60 mm long, 3–8 mm wide, hairy, with 'barbed' margins and midvein, and awn-tipped. Flowers dull white, *c.* 1.5 mm diam., in stalked, lax, 1–5-flowered, axillary cymes distinctly exceeding leaves. Fruit greenish, becoming purplish- or greyish-brown, 3–5 mm long, clad in dense, hooked bristles; fruit-stalks straight, spreading.

Flowering: June–September.

Habitat: Cultivated and waste land, ruderal places, hedges, scrub, open woods, also maritime shingle, on dry to moist, (very) eutrophic, calcareous or weakly acid, sandy, loamy, clayey or stony soils; from sea level to 2,300 m.

Range: Most of Europe, except Iceland and the high Arctic.

Similar species: **False Cleavers** (*G. spurium* L.) has (sub)glabrous nodes, leaves to 35 mm long, 2–3 mm wide, and smaller fruits (to 2 mm long) with or without hooked bristles. In similar habitats, in Europe northwards to S England, Belgium, S Scandinavia and N Russia.
Corn Cleavers (*G. tricornutum* Dandy) has leaves glabrous above, creamy-white flowers in short-stalked cymes not exceeding leaves, and warted fruits (*c.* 3 mm long) on recurved fruit-stalks, In arable fields, often on heavy, calcareous soils, in Europe northwards to Britain, S Scandinavia and C Russia; only naturalized or merely casual in much of the north. *Compare also G. parisiense*, a delicate plant with forward-pointing bristles at leaf-margins.

Cleavers, also called Goosegrass, is a very common weed. The fruits cling to animal fur or clothing, and are easily dispersed that way.

p.150 **Northern Bedstraw** *Galium boreale* L.

Description: A (sub)glabrous, rather stout perennial, to
60 cm, with creeping stolons and smooth,
quadrangular flowering stems to 4 mm
wide. *Leaves 3-veined*, dark green, slightly
leathery, in whorls of 4, lanceolate or
narrowly elliptical, 20–40 mm long, up to
10 mm wide, gradually tapering into *blunt
tip*, never awned, margins often partly rolled
under. Flowers 4-merous, white or cream,
3–4 mm diam., short-stalked, in rather
small, dense panicle with erect ramifications
and well-developed bracts under the cymes.
Corolla tube relatively long, almost
equalling corolla lobes. Anthers yellow. Fruit
blackish, 1.5–2 mm long, smooth, covered
with thin, hooked hairs, or glabrous.

Flowering: June–August.

Habitat: Damp meadows, wood margins, stream-
and riversides, also mountain grassland and
screes, on wet or moist, oligotrophic to
mesotrophic (occasionally eutrophic),
slightly acid or calcareous, sandy, loamy or
stony soils; from sea level to 2,200 m.

Range: C and N Europe, locally westwards to
France and the Low Countries (also in
Iceland, Ireland and W and N Britain),
northwards to N Scandinavia and S
Finland, and eastwards to E Russia.

Similar species: *G. rotundifolium* L. is shorter, with thin
stems, and much broader, ovate to
suborbicular, thin and translucent leaves,
hairy on margins and on the 3 veins; flowers
long-stalked (making panicle lax); fruits
always hairy (with hooked hairs). In damp
coniferous woods in mountains of C Europe
(to the Pyrenees, C France and S Germany);
also on Gotland.

p.150 **Glaucous Bedstraw** *Galium glaucum* L.

Description: A prostrate, often creeping perennial, with
whitish, smooth, glabrous or hairy,
cylindrical, but 4-ribbed stems to 40 cm
long, 2–3 mm wide, swollen at nodes; no
sterile shoots. Leaves glaucous, in whorls of
(6) 8–10, linear-lanceolate, 20–40 mm long,

1–4 mm wide, pointed, distinctly awned, margins strongly rolled under. Flowers 4-merous, white, 4–6 mm diam., in rather lax, ovoid panicle with spreading ramifications. Corolla tube relatively long, almost equalling corolla lobes. Anthers yellow. Fruit blackish, *c.* 2 mm long, smooth, glabrous; fruit-stalks threadlike, straight.

Flowering: May–July.

Habitat: Grassland, warm, sunny slopes, on dry, oligotrophic, calcareous, sandy or stony soils; from sea level to 900 m.

Range: S and SC Europe, northwards to N France (extinct in the Low Countries), S Germany, Poland, and W Russia.

Plants from W Europe usually have stolons.

---

p.151 **Hedge Bedstraw** *Galium mollugo* L.

Description: A prostrate or ascending, sometimes scrambling perennial, with smooth, glabrous or hairy, quadrangular, solid stems to 2 m long, 1–4 mm wide; most stems flowering, rarely some vegetative shoots near base. Leaves in whorls of 6–8, narrowly elliptical to oblanceolate, 5–25 mm long, 2–5 (8) mm wide, short-pointed, distinctly awned, margins rough with tiny, forwards-pointing bristles. Flowers 4-merous, white or cream, 2–3 mm diam., very numerous in large, rather lax panicle with erect to spreading ramifications. Anthers yellow to red or brownish. Fruit black, 1–2 mm long, smooth or granular, otherwise glabrous; fruit-stalks threadlike, straight.

Flowering: May–September.

Habitat: Grassland, roadsides, hedges, scrub, open woods, banks, also sea-dunes, on moist or rather dry, oligotrophic to mesotrophic, often calcareous, sandy, loamy or stony soils; from sea level to 2,100 m.

Range: In Europe northwards to the British Isles, S Scandinavia and C Russia.

Similar species: **Upright Bedstraw** (*G. album* Mill.; also treated as a subspecies) grows more or less erect, and has larger flowers (3–5 mm diam.) in narrower panicle. Also widely distributed, in comparable habitats, though rare or local in the south and east.

G. lucidum All. has narrower, stiff, almost needle-like leaves, swollen nodes, and shiny, whitish stems. In the mountains of S and C Europe, northwards to C France and S Germany. • *Compare also* mat-forming species *G. saxatile* (with glabrous stems), *G. pumilum* (with hairy stems), and more erect, round-stemmed species *G. glaucum* (bluish-green leaves with margins rolled under), and *G. sylvaticum* (leaves greyish-green, rather wide).

Hedge Bedstraw is a common species. See under *G. verum* for (putative) bastard.

---

p.151 **Sweet Woodruff**
Galium odoratum (L.) Scop.

Description: A subglabrous, loosely mat-forming perennial to 30 (60) cm, with creeping stolons and smooth, quadrangular flowering stems to 3 mm wide, with ring of hairs at each node. Leaves deep green, slightly leathery, in spaced whorls of 6–8 (10), oblanceolate or narrowly elliptical, 1-veined, 20–40 mm long, 5–10 mm wide, pointed and distinctly awned; margins flat, slightly rough with forwards-pointing bristles. Flowers 4-merous, white or cream, 4–6 mm diam., in more or less umbel-shaped, rather dense panicle with erect ramifications and inconspicuous bracts. Corolla tube relatively long, almost equalling corolla lobes. Anthers yellow. Fruit blackish, 2–3 mm long, covered with thin, hooked, black-tipped hairs.

Flowering: May–June.

Habitat: Deciduous woods (often Oak or Beech), on moist, oligotrophic to mesotrophic, preferably calcareous, humus-rich, sandy or loamy soils; from sea level to 1,600 m.

Range: Most of Europe except Iceland and the high Arctic, and rare in Mediterranean region.

Similar species: **Coniferous Bedstraw** (*G. triflorum* Michx.) has smaller, often greenish flowers

(1.5–3 mm diam.), in narrowly pyramidal panicles with few-flowered, long-stalked lateral inflorescences. In coniferous woods, often on stony soils, to 1,200 m, in Fennoscandia, N Russia, and very locally in the Alps.

Sweet Woodruff smells strongly of cumarin, especially when wilting. A common species, also frequently grown in gardens.

---

p.151 **Common Marsh-bedstraw**
Galium palustre L.

Description: A prostrate or scrambling perennial, with quadrangular, 'barbed' stems to 1 m long, 1–3 mm wide; plant otherwise glabrous. Leaves in spaced whorls of 4–6, narrowly elliptical to oblanceolate, 5–20 mm long, 1.5–4 mm wide, *blunt-tipped* (never awned), margins flat with forwards-pointing bristles. Flowers 4-merous (rarely 3-merous), white (often pink in bud), 2–3 mm diam., in lax panicle with spreading ramifications. *Anthers red*. Fruit black, 2–3 mm long, glabrous; fruit-stalks threadlike, straight.

Flowering: June–August.

Habitat: Reed-swamps, marshy meadows, dune-slacks, fens, ditch- and streamsides, also damp, open woods, on wet to moist, oligotrophic to eutrophic, acid to neutral, peaty, sandy or stony soils; from sea level to 2,100 m.

Range: Most of Europe except Spitsbergen.

Similar species: **Great Marsh-bedstraw** (ssp. *elongatum* (C. Presl) Lange) is stouter, to 1 m tall, with leaves 20–35 mm long, and larger flowers (3–4 mm diam.). In reed-swamps and at watersides in all of Europe except Iceland and the high Arctic; intermediate forms are not exceptional.
Slender Marsh-bedstraw (*G. debile* Desv.) is more delicate, with smooth or barely rough stems, linear-lanceolate, short-pointed (but unawned) leaves (5–10 mm long, 0.5–2 mm wide), and long-stalked, dense axillary cymes with erect

ramifications, and flowers *c.* 2.5 mm diam. In comparable habitats of France and S Britain.

G. trifidum L. always has 3-merous flowers (*c.* 1.5 mm diam.), and fruits *c.* 2 mm long. In bogs of Scandinavia and NE Poland, and isolated in the Alps and Pyrenees. *Compare also G. uliginosum*, with distinctly awned leaves.

---

p.150 **Wall Bedstraw** *Galium parisiense* L.

Description: A prostrate or scrambling annual with weak, quadrangular, 'barbed' stems to 40 cm long, *c.* 1 mm wide; nodes glabrous. Leaves in spaced whorls of 5–7, oblanceolate, to 10 mm long, 1.5–3 mm wide, awn-tipped, margins with forwards-pointing bristles; leaves often deflexed, especially after anthesis. Flowers greenish-white, 0.5–1 mm diam., in few-flowered, axillary cymes distinctly exceeding leaves, and composing elongate, lax, terminal panicle. Fruit blackish, *c.* 1 mm long, finely granular; fruit-stalks threadlike, straight, erect to spreading.

Flowering: June–August.

Habitat: Cultivated and waste land, occasionally ruderal places, also old walls, on dry or moist, mesotrophic, preferably calcareous, sandy or stony soils; from sea level to 1,500 m.

Range: S and WC Europe, northwards to E England, N France (Lorraine), and C Germany.

A polymorphic species. Plants from W Europe (e.g. Britain) tend to be stouter, with rather crowded leaf-whorls and short fruit-stalks. Plants from SW Europe, with few-flowered partial inflorescences and large fruits with hooked hairs are often treated as a separate species (*G. decipiens* Jord.).

G. divaricatum Pourret ex Lamk. (also treated as a subspecies) has a wider, ovoid inflorescence with long, spreading ramifications, and glabrous or hairy fruits. In S Europe, northwards to NC France.

p.152 **Limestone Bedstraw**
Galium sterneri Ehrend.

Description: A perennial with prostrate, branched, densely mat-forming vegetative shoots, and ascending or erect flowering stems to 30 cm; all stems smooth, quadrangular, 1–2 mm thick. Leaves oblanceolate, 7–11 mm long, mostly in whorls of 7–8, short-pointed, distinctly awned, with scabrous ('barbed') margins. Flowers creamy-white (occasionally greenish-white), *c.* 3 mm diam., in small, pyramidal panicles. Anthers yellow. Fruit greenish or brownish, 1–1.4 mm long, covered with acute warts (almost spinulose), not hairy.

Flowering: May–July.

Habitat: Grassland, on dry to moist, oligotrophic, calcareous, often rocky soils.

Range: NW Europe (Ireland, W and N Britain, Germany, Denmark, the Faeroes, Norway).

Similar species: **Slender Bedstraw** (*G. pumilum* Murray) has stems 0.5–1 mm thick and hairy at least below; leaves (in spaced whorls of 6–9) often distinctly curved, to sickle-shaped, 10–16 mm long, with smooth or weakly 'barbed' margins; flowers white, 3–4 mm diam., in small, narrow panicles with short, erect to spreading ramifications; fruit 1–2 mm long, smooth or covered with tiny, blunt warts. In grassland, scrub and open woods, on dry to moist, oligotrophic, calcareous, sandy, loamy or stony soils, from sea level to 2,600 m, in W and C Europe, northwards to Britain, the Low Countries, Denmark and W Russia (Kaliningrad), and eastwards to Romania and Yugoslavia. This is a highly variable species; some closely related, endemic forms from NW Europe have been given species rank, e.g. *G. fleurotii* Jord. (NW France and Somerset), *G. normanii* O.C. Dahl (Iceland, W Norway), *G. oelandicum* (Sterner & Hyl.) Ehrend. (Öland), *G. suecicum* (Sterner) Ehrend. (Sweden, NW Germany), and *G. valdepilosum* H. Braun (Denmark, Germany). All are mat-forming, and inhabit dry, calcareous grassland. For more details *see Flora Europaea* or a good regional flora.

p.152 **Heath Bedstraw** *Galium saxatile* L.

Description: A glabrous perennial with several prostrate, branched, mat-forming vegetative shoots (with crowded leaf-whorls, often turned flat to the ground), and ascending flowering stems to 40 cm; all stems smooth, glabrous, quadrangular, 0.5–1.5 mm thick. Leaves in whorls of (4) 6–8, elliptical to broadly oblanceolate, 5–12 mm long, 2–5 mm wide, short-pointed, distinctly awned, margins rough with tiny, forwards-pointing bristles. Flowers white, 2.5–4 mm diam., in small, narrow panicles with short, erect to spreading ramifications. Anthers yellow. Fruit brown or blackish, 1–2 mm long, with acute warts, otherwise glabrous; fruit-stalks threadlike, straight.

Flowering: June–September.

Habitat: Heaths, poor grassland, road verges, scrub, open woods, woodland clearings, on rather dry to moist, oligotrophic, acid, sandy or stony soils; from sea level to 1,500 m.

Range: W and C Europe, northwards to the Faeroe Islands, S Scandinavia and NW Russia.

Compare G. sterneri, also mat-forming, but with 'barbed' leaf-margins, and normally cream flowers; also *G. pumilum*, with hairy stems.

p.152 **Wood Bedstraw** *Galium sylvaticum* L.

Description: An ascending to erect perennial, to 1 m, with thick rhizome and smooth, glabrous, *cylindrical, hollow stems* (often with 4 faint ridges) to 4 mm wide; young stems greyish- or blue-green. Leaves in whorls of 6–8, narrowly elliptical to oblanceolate or even spoon-shaped, 20–40 (60) mm long, 4–10 mm wide, blunt or slightly pointed, distinctly awned, margins rough with tiny, forwards-pointing bristles. Flowers 4-merous, white, 2–3 mm diam., numerous in large, lax panicle with spreading ramifications; buds often nodding. Anthers yellow. Fruit bluish-green (eventually greyish), 1–2 mm long, smooth, glabrous; fruit-stalks threadlike, straight.

Flowering: June–September.

Habitat: Deciduous woods (often Oak or Beech), wood margins, woodland clearings, scrub, on moist, oligotrophic, preferably calcareous, humus-rich, sandy or loamy soils; from near sea level to 1,500 m, more frequent on low mountains.

Range: Continental W and C Europe, northwards to the Low Countries, N Germany and NW Poland, and southwards to SE France, N Italy, and NW Yugoslavia.

---

p.151 **Fen Bedstraw** *Galium uliginosum* L.

Description: A prostrate or ascending perennial, with quadrangular, 'barbed' stems to 80 cm long, 1–2 mm wide; plant otherwise glabrous. Leaves in spaced whorls of 6–8, (narrowly) oblanceolate, 10–20 mm long, 1.5–4 mm wide, acute, distinctly *awned*, margins and midvein 'barbed', with backwards-pointing bristles. Flowers 4-merous, white, 2.5–4 mm diam., in narrow, lax panicle with erect to spreading ramifications. *Anthers yellow*. Fruit dark brown, *c.* 1 mm long, wrinkled, with acute warts, but otherwise glabrous; fruit-stalks threadlike, deflexed.

Flowering: June–August.

Habitat: Damp meadows, marshes, fens, dune-slacks, on wet or moist, oligotrophic to mesotrophic, weakly acid or calcareous, sandy, or peaty soils; from sea level to 2,100 m.

Range: Most of Europe except the high Arctic and the southeast.

Compare G. palustre and allies, all with blunt leaf-tips.

---

p.216 **Lady's Bedstraw** *Galium verum* L.

Description: A perennial with tough, prostrate, creeping, often loosely mat-forming stems, and ascending to erect, (sub)cylindrical, finely 4-ribbed stems to 60 (120) cm long, (1) 2–4 mm wide; no sterile shoots. Leaves in whorls of 8–12, linear-lanceolate, 10–30 mm long, 1–2 (3) mm wide, pointed, distinctly awned, white-papillose beneath, margins strongly rolled under. Flowers 4-merous, *bright yellow*, 2–3.5 mm diam., numerous in rather dense, narrowly pyramidal panicle with more or less erect ramifications; bracts in inflorescence well-developed. Anthers yellow. Fruit black, *c.* 1.5 mm long, smooth, glabrous.

Flowering: June–September.

Habitat: Grassland, road verges, sand-dunes, also scrub or open woods, on dry to rather moist, oligotrophic, preferably calcareous, sandy, loamy or stony soils; from sea level to 2,000 m.

Range: Most of Europe except the high Arctic.

Similar species: **Sand Bedstraw** (*G. arenarium* Loisel.) also has pale-yellow flowers and square stems, but differs in prostrate habit with numerous non-flowering shoots, broadly lanceolate, rather fleshy leaves (with flat margins), and larger, slightly fleshy fruits (to 3 mm long). In coastal habitats, sea-dunes, on dry, oligotrophic, calcareous, sandy soils, in N Spain and W France only.

The putative hybrid between Lady's Bedstraw and *G. mollugo* (*G.* × *pomeranicum* Retz) has pale-yellow flowers, and distinctly quadrangular stems; it is not rare in the whole area. Some Dutch authors think the material may in part represent a pale-yellow form of Lady's Bedstraw, not the hybrid.

p.149 **Wild Madder** *Rubia peregrina* L.

Description: A perennial, with creeping rhizomes and rather stout, trailing or ascending, quadrangular stems to 60 cm, very rough on angles ('barbed' with downwards-pointing bristles, but otherwise glabrous). Leaves in spaced whorls of 4–6, elliptical or narrowly (ob)ovate, 20–60 mm long, 1-veined, *leathery*, deep shiny green, glabrous, but very rough on margins (again 'barbed', with backwards-pointing bristles). Flowers 4–5 mm diam., long-stalked, in axillary cymes forming narrow panicle, with small bracts below trifurcations. Calyx rudimentary. Corolla *yellowish-green*, with short tube and *5 ovate, pointed, awned lobes.* Stamens 5. *Fruit berry-like*, fleshy, globose, 4–6 mm diam., glabrous, blackish when ripe.

Flowering: June–August.

Habitat: Scrub, open woods, road verges, hedges, on dry, oligotrophic to mesotrophic, preferably calcareous, sandy, loamy or stony soils; from sea level to 500 m, but most frequent near the sea-coast.

Range: S and W Europe, northwards to W France, S Britain and Ireland.

Similar species: **Madder** (*R. tinctorum* L.), from S Europe, has bright-yellow, unawned flowers, and softer, lanceolate leaves (with prominent side-veins beneath); it was formerly cultivated for the red dye from the roots, and became locally naturalized in roadsides and hedges in W Europe, northwards to Britain, the Netherlands and S Germany, but it has now largely disappeared from these northern regions.

p.290 **Field Madder** *Sherardia arvensis* L.

Description: A bristly-hairy annual, with prostrate, branched, quadrangular stems to 40 cm long, very rough on angles. Leaves in whorls of 4–6, obovate to lanceolate, pointed, 5–20 mm long, 1-veined, deep shiny green, slightly fleshy, very rough on margins ('barbed', with backwards-pointing bristles). Flowers (3) 4–6 mm diam., subsessile in terminal, head-like cluster, subtended by ruff of several leaf-like, green bracts. *Calyx well-developed*, with (4) 6 triangular teeth, persistent (and even enlarged) on fruit. Corolla *pink or pale lilac* (rarely white), with long *tube* and 4 spreading, ovate-triangular lobes. Stamens 4, protruding. Fruit a 2-lobed 'double achene', roughened by short hairs, *c.* 4 mm long (without calyx).

Flowering: May–September.

Habitat: Cereal fields, roadsides, banks, farmyards, on moist, mesotrophic, calcareous, loamy, clayey or stony (chalk) soils; from sea level to 1,400 m.

Range: Most of Europe except Iceland and the high Arctic; only naturalized (as an archeophyte) in the north.

The species is in the process of extinction from fields, but often perseveres in disturbed roadsides and ruderal places in the agricultural landscape.

TASSELWEED FAMILY, RUPPIACEAE

A small family of perennial aquatic herbs, with only 3 species in 1 genus, living in saline waters in temperate and subtropical regions. Monocots. Closely related to the Potamogetonaceae. Leaves opposite, linear, sessile, and sheathing the threadlike, branched stem; stipules 2. Flowers hermaphrodite, usually in pairs at end of long peduncle. Perianth absent. Stamens 2, subsessile, each with 2 greenish anthers and a minute appendage at base. Ovaries 4–10 (in each flower), free, with 1 sessile stigma. Fruit a cluster of long-stalked, beaked achenes (stalks and beaks developing after anthesis).

---

p.55 **Beaked Tasselweed** *Ruppia maritima* L.

Description: A slender, submerged aquatic with stems to 50 cm, and (sub)opposite, threadlike, often bright-green leaves to 50 mm long, *c.* 0.5 mm wide; leaf-sheaths slightly inflated, 10–20 mm long, greenish-white. Peduncles rarely longer than 50 mm (even in fruit), straight, bringing flowers to surface during anthesis, and recurving afterwards (making up to 1 full turn). Anthers rounded, to 0.7 mm long. Achene asymmetrically flask-shaped, *c.* 3 mm long, with laterally implanted, oblique beak.

Flowering: June–September.

Habitat: Rather calm, shallow, brackish or saline waters; mainly coastal.

Range: Most of Europe except the high Arctic.

Similar species: **Spiral Tasselweed** (*R. cirrhosa* (Petagna) Grande) has dark-green, slightly larger leaves (to 80 mm long, *c.* 1 mm wide, with markedly inflated sheaths), peduncles to 10 cm long (strongly coiled after anthesis), elongate anthers (*c.* 1.5 mm long), and less asymmetrical achenes with subapically implanted beak. In comparable, saline, coastal habitats, often in more agitated water, in most of Europe.

WILLOW FAMILY, SALICACEAE

A family of trees, shrubs and some almost herbaceous dwarf-shrubs, with *c.* 350 species in 4 genera of which *Populus* (Poplars) and *Salix* (Willows) can be found in Europe. Leaves alternate, simple. Flowers unisexual, usually dioecious, in catkins; each flower subtended by scaly bract, but perianth absent or (in female flowers) reduced to 1 or 2 tiny, nectar-producing glands. Male flowers contain 2–8 stamens. Female flowers have 1-locular ovary, with single style. Fruit a small capsule opening with 2–4 valves, and containing several tiny seeds bearing long pappus of hairs, which helps to disperse seeds on the wind. Most species are trees or larger shrubs, and will not be treated here; but in Arctic regions a few dwarfish, more or less herbaceous Willows occur, deserving our attention.

p.83 **Dwarf Willow** *Salix herbacea* L.

Description: A dwarf-shrub with woody, creeping, subterranean stems and herbaceous, ascending or erect aerial branches to 15 cm, often less. Leaves suborbicular or reniform, 10–20 mm long, *dentate*, (sub)glabrous, shiny green above and paler green beneath, with prominent veins at both faces. Catkins terminal, subglabrous, ovoid, 5–15 mm long, male ones pink or reddish, later yellow from ripening, 2-stamened flowers. Fruit a small, 2-valved capsule, containing several white-fluffy seeds.

Flowering: June–July.

Habitat: In tundra, also ledges and rocks in mountains; from sea level to 2,800 m, but only on mountains in the south.

Range: In Iceland, W and N Britain, W and N Fennoscandia, N Russia.

Similar species: **Net-leaved Willow** (*S. reticulata* L.) has creeping (overground) stems, suborbicular to broadly obovate, entire leaves, 20–40 mm long, dark green and wrinkled (with deepened veins) above, white-hairy and with prominent veins beneath; catkins more elongate, 10–25 mm long, and hairy. In comparable habitats of Scotland, W and N Fennoscandia, N Russia; also in the Alps.

Polar Willow (*S. polaris* Wahlenb.) has subterranean stems, broadly elliptical, shiny-green (slightly wrinkled) leaves, up to 15 mm long, 12 mm wide, entire or shallowly sinuous at base, with 3–4 pairs of lateral veins; catkins have dark-purplish, hairy bracts, purple filaments, and long-styled, hairy ovaries. Confined to the Arctic tundra of Scandinavia and N Russia, including Spitsbergen.

S. myrtilloides L. is much taller (to 50 cm), but also has creeping, underground stems; leaves 10–35 mm long, (broadly) elliptical, weakly veined, entire (margins often rolled under), dull green (paler beneath); catkins larger (15–20 mm long). In swamps and bogs of N, C and E Europe.

SANDALWOOD FAMILY, SANTALACEAE

A family of trees, shrubs and herbs, with *c.* 400 species in 35 genera, mainly in the tropics. Dicots. Leaves alternate or opposite, simple. Flowers small, regular, with 3–5 sepals (often petal-like); true petals absent. Stamens 3–5, opposite to sepals. Ovary inferior, 1-locular, with 1 style. Fruit a 1-seeded drupe, nut or achene. The Sandalwood Tree (*Santalum album* L.) is indigenous to the East Indies; its valuable wood is used for furniture, dyeing, and even medicinal purposes. In N Europe only the genus *Thesium* is represented, with some inconspicuous, perennial herbs possessing alternate, narrow, entire-margined leaves, and solitary, axillary flowers, each subtended by 1 or 3 linear bracteoles (or, scientifically more precise, 1 bract and occasionally 2 bracteoles at the same height).

---

p.112 **Bastard Toadflax** *Thesium humifusum* DC.

Description: A glabrous perennial, to 30 cm, with slender, ligneous, underground rhizome and prostrate or ascending flowering stems; *no creeping stolons*. Leaves linear, *1-veined*.

Flowers 2–3 mm diam., with 3 small, unequal, rough-margined bracteoles at base, short-stalked, in narrow panicle with short, scabrous branches. *Perianth bell-shaped*, with 5 ovate, pointed lobes, white inside, greenish on outside. Achene obovoid, *c.* 3 mm long, much longer than persistent perianth, but shorter than longest bracteole.

Flowering: June–August.

Habitat: Grassland, sea-dunes, sunny slopes, on dry, oligotrophic, calcareous, sandy or stony soils, parasitizing *Galium* species; from sea level to 500 m.

Range: W Europe, from Spain northwards to S Britain and the Low Countries.

Similar species: *T. divaricatum* Jan ex M. & K. has thick, ligneous rhizomes with ascending or erect flowering stems (again no stolons); panicles wider, with long, smooth branches; all bracteoles shorter than accompanying fruit (and with smooth margins). In S Europe (to 2,150 m), locally extending to NC France. *T. ebracteatum* Hayne has long, creeping stolons, nuts twice the length of persistent, bell-shaped perianth; lacks bracteoles under flowers, In NE Europe, from Estonia and C Russia westwards to E Denmark and N Germany, to 2,000 m.
• These 2 species have bell-shaped perianths, rolled up after anthesis, and much shorter than fruit. Some related species with linear-lanceolate, mostly 3-veined leaves occur in the mountains of C Europe, northwards to C Germany: *T. bavarum* Schrank (dark green, and lacking stolons), *T. linophyllum* L. (yellowish-green, with creeping stolons).

p.112 *Thesium pyrenaicum* Pourret

Description: A glabrous perennial, to 30 cm, with slender, ligneous, underground rhizome and erect or ascending, sparingly branched, *wavy flowering stems*; no creeping stolons. Leaves linear, *1-veined*. Flowers *c.* 3 mm diam., with 3 small, unequal, linear bracteoles at base, rather long-stalked, in terminal raceme, often with some short side-branches at base. *Perianth tubular*, trumpet-shaped, with 5 ovate lobes, white inside, greenish on outside. Achene obovoid, *c.* 3 mm long, about as long as persistent perianth, but shorter than all bracteoles.

Flowering: June–August.

Habitat: Grassland, on dry, oligotrophic, calcareous, sandy, loamy or stony soils; from near sea level to 2,000 m, but mainly in mountainous regions.

Range: SW and C Europe, northwards to Belgium, Germany and Poland, and eastwards to Yugoslavia; extinct in the Netherlands.

Similar species: *Thesium alpinum* L. has straight stems, and short-stalked, erect, 4-merous flowers in narrow, spike-like, often 1-sided raceme. In dry, calcareous grassland in S and C Europe (mainly in the mountains, to 2,500 m) and locally in Scandinavia.

T. rostratum M. & K. has 5-merous flowers, but lacks bracteoles; in C Europe. • These 2 species have tubular perianths, at least equalling fruit.

SAXIFRAGE FAMILY, SAXIFRAGACEAE

A family of herbs and shrubs with *c.* 1,200 species in some 80 genera, mainly in temperate regions world-wide. Dicots. Leaves simple, alternate (rarely opposite, sometimes all basal). Flowers usually regular, hermaphrodite, (4) 5-merous (always 4-merous in *Chrysosplenium*), often in cymes or panicles (but always in racemes in *Ribes*, and always solitary in *Parnassia*). The (4) 5 sepals can be partly connate. Petals (4) 5, free or basally connate to sepals (together forming short tube, also interpreted as a cup-shaped receptacle); petals absent in *Chrysosplenium*. Stamens usually twice as numerous as sepals (normally 10, but 4 or 8 in *Chrysosplenium*); in *Parnassia* only 5 are fertile, the other 5 are transformed into comb-like staminodes. Ovary is inferior (*Ribes*), hemi-inferior, or superior, 1–5-locular (often 2-locular), with 1–5 (often 2) styles (or styles reduced). Fruit a berry (*Ribes*) or a capsule (the other European genera). The deciduous, shrubby genus *Ribes* is often placed in a separate family (Grossulariaceae). Likewise, the family Parnassiaceae has been erected for *Parnassia* alone.

p.74 Alternate-leaved Golden-saxifrage
Chrysosplenium alternifolium L.

Description: A slightly hairy perennial with creeping stolons and erect, *triangular* flowering stems to 15 cm. Leaves alternate, 10–25 mm wide, reniform, coarsely crenate, lower ones with blades shorter than stalk. *Flowers 4-merous*, *c.* 5 mm diam., in flat, terminal cymes, with *bracts yellowish*, leaf-like but smaller. Sepals 4, *yellowish*. *Petals absent*. Stamens 8. Ovary hemi-inferior, 1-locular, with 2 short, recurved styles. Fruit a rounded capsule, *c.* 3 mm long, opening early with 2 rounded valves, then beaker-shaped and containing several smooth, shiny-brown or blackish seeds.

Flowering: March–May.

Habitat: Damp woods, flushes, marshes, streamsides, on wet, oligotrophic, mildly acid or calcareous, sandy or loamy soils; from sea level to 1,900 m.

Range: Most of Europe except Ireland, Iceland and much of the far north, and only on mountains in the south.

Similar species: *C. tetrandrum* (N. Lund.) T. Fries is glabrous, with greenish flowers and bracts, and only 4 stamens. In similar habitats of N Fennoscandia, N Russia and Spitsbergen. **Opposite-leaved Golden-saxifrage** (*Chrysosplenium oppositifolium* L.) has quadrangular stems, and yellowish-green bracts and flowers (flowers *c.* 3 mm diam., with 8 stamens); leaves opposite, hemicircular, lower ones with blades at least equalling stalk; seeds brown, granular; stolons absent. In similar habitats, mostly on acid soils, in W and C Europe, northwards to Ireland, Britain, Denmark, and W Poland.

p.101 Grass of Parnassus *Parnassia palustris* L.

Description: A glabrous, tufted perennial, with erect, angular flowering stems to 30 cm. Leaves all but 1 basal, long-stalked, 15–40 mm long, *ovate-cordate, entire; single stem-leaf* similar but sessile, clasping. Flowers 5-merous, 15–30 mm diam., solitary, terminal. Sepals 5, broadly lanceolate. Petals 5, broadly ovate, white with greenish-translucent veins. Fertile stamens 5, alternating with 5 greenish, *comb-like staminodes* with golden glands on teeth. Ovary hemi-inferior, 1-locular, with 3–4 sessile stigmas. Fruit an ovoid capsule, 12–16 mm long, apically splitting with 4 valves, and containing numerous smooth, shiny-black seeds.

Flowering: June–September.

Habitat: Moors, fens, meadows, flushes, also dune-slacks, on wet to moist, oligotrophic, mildly acid or calcareous, sandy, stony or peaty soils; from sea level to 2,500 m.

Range: Most of Europe except the extreme north, and only on mountains in the south.

Ssp. *obtusiflora* (Rupr.) D.A. Webb, from Arctic and sub-Arctic Europe, has stem-leaf absent, or short-stalked and placed very low on stem.

---

p.82 **Mountain Currant** *Ribes alpinum* L.

Description: A shrub, with erect stems to 2 m; no thorns. Leaves stalked, 3–60 mm long, palmately veined, triangular-ovate, mostly *3-lobed*, dentate, sparsely glandular above, and with rounded base. Flowers 5-merous, 4–6 mm diam., (functionally) unisexual and *dioecious*; male flowers up to 30, female flowers 2–5 together in axillary racemes, which remain *erect*, even in fruit; each flower with *conspicuous, linear bract* (4–8 mm long). Calyx greenish-yellow, with cup-shaped tube, and 5 spreading, broadly ovate, glabrous lobes. Petals 5, minute, greenish-yellow, erect, implanted on rim of calyx tube. Stamens 5. Ovary inferior, 1-locular, with 2 partly connate styles. Fruit a *translucent, scarlet*, globose, glabrous berry, 6–8 mm diam., with several seeds in insipid, juicy pulp.

Flowering: April–May.

Habitat: Deciduous woods (often Beech), hedges, streamsides, mountain cliffs, on moist, oligotrophic, calcareous, sandy, loamy or stony soils; from sea level to 1,900 m, but mainly on mountains in the south.

Range: In Europe locally northwards to Britain (Wales, N England), NE France, Germany (Eifel), S Fennoscandia and NW Russia, and eastwards to Caucasus.

Frequently cultivated for ornament, and locally naturalized outside the native range.

Blackcurrant *Ribes nigrum* L.

Description: A shrub to 1.5 m, with erect stems; no thorns. Leaves stalked, 4–10 cm long, palmately veined, broadly ovate-cordate, 5-lobed, dentate, with numerous yellowish glands beneath (*smelling aromatically* when rubbed). Flowers 5-merous, 7–8 mm diam., up to 10 together in axillary racemes (drooping after anthesis), with minute bracts to 2 mm long. Calyx has cup-shaped tube, and 5 recurved, ovate, glabrous, red-flushed lobes. Petals 5, minute, whitish, erect, implanted on rim of calyx tube. Stamens 5. Ovary inferior, 1-locular, with 2 partly connate styles. Fruit an *opaque, black*, globose, glabrous berry, 7–12 mm diam., with several seeds in purplish, sweet-tasting, juicy pulp; calyx erect and *persistent* on fruit.

Flowering: April–May.

Habitat: Damp, deciduous woods (often Alder or Willow), fens, stream- and riversides, on wet to moist, mesotrophic, mildly acid or calcareous, sandy, stony or peaty soils; from sea level to 1,500 m.

Range: Most of Europe except Mediterranean region.

Frequently planted for the fruits, and widely naturalized. It is often difficult to establish the status of the wild occurrences; truly indigenous populations may be mainly confined to C and E Europe.

p.81 **Redcurrant** *Ribes rubrum* L.

Description: A shrub to 1.5 m, with erect stems; no thorns. Leaves stalked, 4–10 cm long, palmately veined, broadly ovate-cordate, 5-lobed, dentate, *sparsely hairy beneath* (often on veins only), scarcely glandular (*not aromatic* when bruised), and with narrow sinus between basal lobes. Flowers 5-merous, 5–8 mm diam., up to 20 together in axillary racemes (*drooping* after anthesis), with minute bracts to 2 mm long. Calyx has shallow, saucer-shaped 'tube', and 5 spreading, broadly ovate, glabrous lobes. Petals 5, minute, yellowish-green, erect, implanted on (raised) rim of calyx tube. Stamens 5; anther lobes in each stamen distinctly separated by a strip of tissue. Ovary inferior, 1-locular, with 2 partly connate styles. Fruit a *translucent, red*, globose, glabrous berry, 5–10 mm diam., with several seeds in acidulous, juicy pulp.

Flowering: April–May.

Habitat: Damp, deciduous woods, hedges, streamsides, also in dune-slacks, on wet or moist, oligotrophic to mesotrophic, mildly acid to calcareous, sandy or stony soils; from sea level to 2,100 m.

Range: W Europe, northwards to the Low Countries; presumably only naturalized elsewhere.

Similar species: *R. spicatum* Robson has leaves more or less densely hairy beneath, with wide sinus between basal lobes; calyx tube cup-shaped, with flat rim, in each stamen the anthers almost touch each other. In damp woods and streamsides in N and E Europe, from Britain to Fennoscandia and N Russia. **Rock Redcurrant** (*R. petraeum* Wulfen) has pinkish flowers with ciliate calyx lobes, and dark purplish-red, sour berries, 20–35 to a raceme. In woods and streamsides in the mountains of C Europe, westwards to C France.

Redcurrant is frequently planted for the fruits, also in a form with whitish berries. Many occurrences in the wild may derive from former culture, even in W Europe.

p.81 **Gooseberry** *Ribes uva-crispa* L.

Description: A shrub, with erect, *thorny stems* to 1.2 m;
thorns often in 3s. Leaves stalked, 30–50 mm
long, palmately veined, suborbicular or
reniform, 3–5-lobed, crenate, densely soft-
hairy at least beneath (not aromatic when
bruised), and with wide sinus between basal
lobes. Flowers 5-merous, 8–10 mm diam.,
solitary or 2–3 together on short stalks in
leaf-axils, with minute bracts to 2 mm long.
Calyx has cup-shaped tube and 5 deflexed,
elliptical, hairy, greenish or purplish lobes.
Petals 5, minute, greenish or purplish, erect,
implanted on rim of calyx tube. Stamens 5.
Ovary inferior, 1-locular, with 2 partly
connate styles. Fruit a greenish, often red-
flushed, conspicuously veined, broadly
ellipsoid, *stiff-hairy berry*, 10–20 mm long,
with numerous seeds in acidulous, juicy
pulp; calyx erect and persistent on fruit.

Flowering: March–May.

Habitat: Damp woods (often Ash), ravines,
woodland clearings, scrub, hedgerows,
streamsides, also ruderal and rocky places,
on moist, oligotrophic to mesotrophic,
preferably calcareous, sandy, loamy or stony
soils; from sea level to 1,800 m.

Range: W, C and S Europe, northwards to Britain,
the Low Countries, Germany and Poland,
and eastwards to N Russia.

Frequently planted for the berries, and
occasionally naturalized, even outside its
native range. Cultivars often have larger
fruits.

Saxifrage, *Saxifraga*

A large genus of herbs with over 300 species in Arctic and
north temperate regions, as well as in the Andes mountains;
about 123 species can be found in Europe alone. Leaves
essentially alternate, but often all in basal rosette. Flowers
regular, hermaphrodite, 5-merous, in terminal cymes or
panicles. Sepals 5, green. Petals 5, usually showy, white,
yellow or reddish. Stamens 10. Ovary hemi-inferior or
superior, 2-locular, with 2 divergent styles. Fruit a many-
seeded capsule, opening apically, between 2 styles.

The N European species can be informally grouped, as follows:

A. Flowers greenish, tinged with purple: *S. hieracifolia*.

B. Flowers yellow: *S. aizoides, S. hirculus, S. platysepala*.

C. Flowers pink or purplish: *S. oppositifolia*.

D. Flowers white (occasionally pale pink). Here, for a start, we can distinguish a group having **all (normal) leaves collected in a basal rosette**, though occasionally some smaller, scale-like leaves may be present on stem:

   1. Leaves oblanceolate, finely serrate: *S. cotyledon, S. paniculata*.
   2. Leaves spoon-shaped, crenate-dentate, narrowed into wide stalk: *S. nivalis, S. tenuis, S. stellaris, S. foliolosa, S. spathularis*.
   3. Leaves ovate to reniform, cordate-based, with long, slender stalks: *S. hirsuta*; and *see S. granulata* of group 4.

Then there are the white-flowered species with **at least some normally developed stem-leaves**:

   4. Leaves suborbicular to reniform, the blade not gradually narrowed into stalk: *S. granulata, S. rotundifolia* (leaves coarsely crenate-dentate); *S. cernua, S. rivularis*, and their hybrid *S. × opdalensis* (leaves palmately 3–5-lobed).
   5. Leaves more or less wedge-shaped, deeply incised with 3–5 segments, the blade more or less gradually narrowed into stalk: *S. rosacea, S. cespitosa*, and their intermediate *S. hartii* (all perennials, and densely cushion-forming); *S. hypnoides* (perennial, loosely mat-forming, and with almost linear leaf-segments); and finally the annual or biennial, tufted species *S. adscendens, S. tridactylites*, and their intermediate *S. osloensis*.

Several other species can be found in the mountains of C and S Europe. Only the typically 'boreo-alpine' species are treated here, i.e. the ones that also occur in the (far) north of Europe.

---

p.146 **Biennial Saxifrage** *Saxifraga adscendens* L.

Description: A hairy *annual or biennial* to 20 cm, with erect, little-branched stems; no stolons. Leaves mostly basal, in a rosette, *wedge-*

shaped, gradually narrowed into short, channelled stalk, slightly fleshy, *3-lobed* (rarely 5-lobed) with triangular-ovate, forward-pointing lobes only near tip; stem-leaves few, subsessile, upper ones often narrowly ovate and scarcely lobed; no axillary bulbils. Flowers 6–10 mm diam., few together in *compact*, terminal cyme; flower-stalks at most equalling length of calyx. Petals white or cream.

Flowering: June–August.

Habitat: Mountain pastures, screes and rocks, on moist to rather dry, oligotrophic, preferably calcareous, stony soils; mainly in high mountainous regions, 1,800–3,100 m, but descending lower in the far north.

Range: C Europe (Alps, Carpathians), also in Scandinavia.

Compare *S. tridactylites* (see p.1038).

p.211 **Yellow Saxifrage** *Saxifraga aizoides* L.

Description: A slightly hairy perennial to 20 cm, with ascending to erect flowering stems. Leaves alternate, *sessile*, lanceolate, awned, slightly fleshy, often bluntly dentate and always bristly ciliate along edge. Flowers 5–10 mm diam., in small, terminal cymes. *Petals yellow*, occasionally with red dots.

Flowering: June–September.

Habitat: Rocky places, usually near streams or flushes, on wet or moist, oligotrophic, preferably calcareous, stony (occasionally peaty) soils; mainly in the mountains, to 3,150 m, but descending to sea level in the far north.

Range: Arctic and sub-Arctic Europe, from Fennoscandia and Iceland southwards to N Ireland and N Britain; again in mountainous regions further south (Pyrenees, Alps, Apennines, Carpathians, Balkanic mountains).

Compare *S. hirculus* (see p.1034).

p.113 **Drooping Saxifrage** *Saxifraga cernua* L.

Description: A subglabrous perennial, with erect
flowering stems to 15 cm; no stolons.
Leaves mostly cauline, short-stalked,
slightly fleshy, rounded to reniform,
palmately 3–5-lobed, upper ones often ovate,
scarcely lobed, and bearing small, *dark-
brown bulbils* in their axils; basal leaves few,
with 5–7 lobes. Flowers 12–18 mm diam.,
solitary, terminal, or altogether absent.
Petals white.

Flowering: June–July.

Habitat: Rocky places, on moist, oligotrophic,
preferably calcareous, stony soils; mainly in
the mountains, 900–2,500 m, but
descending lower in the Arctic.

Range: In Iceland, Scandinavia, Scotland, and also
in C Europe (Alps, Carpathians).

Similar species: **Highland Saxifrage** (*S. rivularis* L.) rarely
exceeds 80 mm in height, and never forms
bulbils; it has thin, creeping stolons, 3–5-
lobed leaves (mainly in basal rosette), and
several flowering stems, each with 1–3
white flowers (8–10 mm across). In wet,
rocky places, in Iceland, Scandinavia, and
N Britain. The hybrid (*S.* × *opdalensis*
Blytt), known from S Norway (Updal)
only, is intermediate in character, and has
greenish bulbils.

Drooping Saxifrage often forms no flowers
at all, instead depending wholly on bulbils
for propagation.

p.145 **Pyramidal Saxifrage** *Saxifraga cotyledon* L.

Description: A hairy perennial to 30 cm, with erect,
reddish flowering stems. Leaves all in a
spreading basal rosette, 20–60 mm long,
up to 15 mm wide, oblanceolate or
elliptical, narrowed into short stalk, finely
serrate, with short bristles on teeth; stem-
leaves absent but for tiny bracts in
inflorescence. Flowers 10–18 mm diam.,
numerous in large, pyramidal, often
arching panicle occupying much of stem.
Petals white.

Flowering: June–August.
Habitat: Rock-crevices, moraines, on moist to rather dry, oligotrophic, acid, stony soils; mainly in the mountains (1,500–2,600 m), but descending to sea level in the far north.
Range: Scandinavia and Iceland; also in the Pyrenees and the Southern Alps.
Similar species: **Live-long Saxifrage** (*S. paniculata* Miller) has white or cream flowers (6–12 mm diam.), narrowly oblanceolate basal leaves (to 40 mm long, 8 mm wide) in dense, bowl-shaped rosettes, and few to several small, scale-like, appressed stem-leaves, also below inflorescence, which occupies only upper half of stem. In the mountains of C and S Europe (600–2,700 m), westwards to the Vosges, and again in Iceland and S Norway.

---

p.145 **Meadow Saxifrage** *Saxifraga granulata* L.

Description: A hairy perennial, with erect flowering stems to 60 cm, bearing small, *brownish bulbils* at stem-base (just below surface); no sterile shoots. Leaves mostly basal, in a rosette, long-stalked, rounded to reniform, coarsely crenate-dentate or shallowly lobed; stem-leaves few, short-stalked, with truncate to cuneate base. Flowers 18–30 mm diam., few to several together in lax terminal cymes. Petals white.
Flowering: April–June.
Habitat: Damp meadows, pastures, road verges, streamsides, on moist, oligotrophic to mesotrophic, preferably calcareous, sandy, loamy or stony soils; from sea level to 2,200 m.
Range: Most of Europe, except the far north and the southeast.
Similar species: **Round-leaved Saxifrage** (*S. rotundifolia* L.) lacks bulbils, and has several long-stalked stem-leaves (and basal rosettes as well), white flowers 12–18 mm diam., and petals with yellow dots at base and reddish dots near tip; sterile shoots usually present. In woods and at streamsides in mountains of C and E Europe, also cultivated in gardens and locally naturalized in W Europe.

p.194 **Marsh Saxifrage** *Saxifraga hirculus* L.

Description: A slightly hairy perennial, with ascending to erect flowering stems to 20 cm (with red hairs above). Leaves alternate, *distinctly stalked*, lanceolate with blunt tip, margins always entire, hairy near base, but without stiff bristles. Flowers 20–30 mm diam., solitary or 2–4 together in small, terminal cymes. *Petals yellow*, occasionally with red dots.

Flowering: July–August.

Habitat: Bogs, moors, grassland, on wet, oligotrophic, acid, peaty or stony soils; from sea level to 1,500 m, but only on mountains in the south.

Range: N, E and C Europe, from Iceland, Fennoscandia and N Russia southwards to Ireland, N and W Britain and mountains of C Europe; extinct in the Netherlands and Czechoslovakia, possibly also in France, Switzerland and Austria.

Similar species: *S. platysepala* (Trautv.) Tolm. has sessile, ovate or elliptical, entire, pointed, ciliate leaves, cauline as well as in basal rosettes, and slender, reddish stolons, forming new rosettes at their tip; flowers bright yellow, 10–14 mm diam. Damp, rocky places, on moraines and screes, in N Russia (including Spitsbergen). *Compare also S. aizoides (see p.1031).*

---

p.145 **Kidney Saxifrage** *Saxifraga hirsuta* L.

Description: A hairy perennial, with erect, leafless flowering stems to 20 cm. Leaves all in basal rosette, slightly fleshy, broadly ovate to reniform with slightly cordate base, 10–30 mm long, spoon-shaped, with long, rounded stalk, coarsely crenate-dentate, green at both faces. Flowers 5–8 mm diam., long-stalked, few to several together in lax, terminal panicle, with minute bracts. *Sepals erect or spreading.* Petals blunt-tipped, white or pale pink, with yellow spot at base, and often with red dots on limb.

Flowering: May–July.

Habitat: Shady rocks, streamsides, on wet or moist, oligotrophic, stony soils; mainly in mountains, to 2,500 m.

Range: In the Pyrenees, N Spain and Ireland.

Compare S. nivalis and allies, with spatulate, wide-stalked leaves.

---

p.129 **Mossy Saxifrage** *Saxifraga hypnoides* L.

Description: A hairy, loosely *mat-forming* perennial to 20 cm, with long, prostrate sterile shoots and erect or ascending, little-branched flowering stems. Leaves soft, fresh green, all cauline, appressed to stem, those on sterile shoots crowded near shoot tip, *wedge-shaped*, gradually narrowed into rounded stalk, *deeply 3–5-lobed* with linear-lanceolate, divergent segments, these often trifid again; flowering stems with spaced, subsessile leaves, upper ones often lanceolate, unlobed. Flowers 14–20 mm diam., *nodding in bud*, solitary or up to 5 together in lax, terminal cyme. Petals pure white.

Flowering: May–July.

Habitat: Mountain grassland, streamsides, cliffs, moraines and mountain-ledges, on moist or at least shaded, oligotrophic, preferably calcareous, stony soils; from sea level (in the far north) to 1,200 m.

Range: Norway, Iceland, the Faeroes, Ireland, N and W Britain, NW France, and the Vosges.

During summer, the sterile shoots have tassel-like, leafy 'dormant buds' in leaf-axils, but true bulbils are absent. The French forms have less deeply incised leaves. *Compare* the group of *S. rosacea* especially *S. hartii*, which has ascending, densely foliated sterile shoots (lacking dormant buds), and erect flowerbuds.

---

p.145 **Alpine Saxifrage** *Saxifraga nivalis* L.

Description: A glandular-hairy perennial, with erect, purplish, leafless flowering stems to 20 cm. Leaves all in basal rosette, fleshy, 10–30 mm long, *spoon-shaped*, narrowed into short, wide stalk, coarsely crenate-dentate, purplish beneath or at least purple-edged. Flowers

5–6 mm diam., short-stalked, few together in small, terminal cluster, with minute bracts. *Sepals erect or spreading.* Petals blunt-tipped, white or pale pink, without spots.

Flowering: July–August.

Habitat: Shaded rocks, mountain ledges, screes, moraines, on wet or moist, oligotrophic, acid, soil.

Range: Arctic and sub-Arctic Europe, locally southwards to Ireland, Wales and Poland.

Similar species: *S. tenuis* (Wahlenb.) H. Smith ex Lindm. from comparable habitats in Arctic Europe has long-stalked flowers in lax terminal cyme.

Starry Saxifrage (*S. stellaris* L.) has up to 14 flowers 10–15 mm diam. in lax panicles, white, acute petals with 2 yellow spots at base, and deflexed sepals. On higher ground in Iceland, Scandinavia, Britain and Ireland. Ssp. *alpigena* Temesy, in C Europe (extending northwards to the Vosges), has smaller flowers and subglabrous leaves. *S. foliolosa* R. Br., from Arctic and sub-Arctic Europe, is similar, but has most flowers (except terminal one) replaced by bulbils.

St Patrick's Cabbage (*S. spathularis* Brot.) has glabrous, ascending, rather long-stalked, sharply dentate leaves, flowers 7–9 mm diam. in lax panicles, deflexed sepals, and white petals with 1–3 yellow spots at base, and several red dots on limb. In damp woods and streamsides in Ireland, Spain and Portugal.

Hawkweed Saxifrage (*S. hieracifolia* Waldst. & Kit.) has obovate or oblanceolate, acute, subentire, fleshy, ciliate basal leaves, flowers 3–5 mm diam., subsessile, several together in spaced, dense clusters with ovate bracts in upper half of stem; petals greenish, often edged or flushed with red. On damp rocks, moraines, at streamsides, in tundra, on moist, oligotrophic, calcareous or acid, stony soils, mainly in mountains, to 2,400 m, in Arctic Norway, N Russia and Spitsbergen; also in the Carpathians, Austria (Styria), and France (Auvergne). *Compare also S. hirsuta*, which has more or less rounded leaves on rounded stalks.

p.271 **Purple Saxifrage** *Saxifraga oppositifolia* L.

Description: A slightly hairy, *mat-forming* perennial to
10 cm, with creeping stems and
ascending vegetative and flowering
branches. Leaves all cauline, crowded,
crosswise opposite (in 4 rows), subsessile,
fleshy, keeled, obovate, 2–6 mm long,
entire, bristly-ciliate, with 1–5 *lime-
secreting pores* at recurved tip. Flowers
10–20 mm diam., solitary, terminal.
Anthers bluish. *Petals pink or purple*.

Flowering: March–August.

Habitat: Rocks, moraines, screes, cliffs, mountain-
ledges, on moist, oligotrophic, calcareous,
stony soils; from sea level to 3,800 m, but
only on mountains in the south.

Range: Mountains of C Europe, westwards to the
Pyrenees and the Jura, also in W and N
Britain, N Ireland, the Faeroes, Iceland,
Fennoscandia, and N Russia.

---

p.129 **Irish Saxifrage** *Saxifraga rosacea* Moench

Description: A hairy, densely *cushion-forming, often red-
flushed* perennial to 20 cm, with erect or
ascending sterile shoots and erect, little-
branched flowering stems. Leaves all cauline,
usually ciliate, those on sterile shoots
crowded, *wedge-shaped*, gradually narrowed
into channelled stalk, *deeply 5–7-lobed* with
lanceolate, acute, divergent segments;
flowering stems with few widely spaced,
3–5-lobed leaves, upper ones often lanceolate,
unlobed; no leafy 'dormant buds' in leaf-axils
of sterile shoots. Flowers 12–20 mm diam.,
erect in bud, solitary or up to 8 together in lax,
terminal cyme. Petals pure white.

Flowering: June–August.

Habitat: Cliffs (maritime and inland), mountain
ledges, screes, streamsides, on moist,
oligotrophic, preferably calcareous, stony
soils; from sea level to 2,400 m, but mainly
in the mountains.

Range: The mountains of C Europe, also in Ireland,
Iceland and the Faeroes.

Similar species: **Tufted Saxifrage** (*S. cespitosa* L.) forms
dense, fresh-green, glandular-hairy cushions

to 10 cm, and has deeply 3–5-lobed leaves with lanceolate, blunt lobes and flat stalk; flowers only 7–10 mm diam., dull white, solitary or up to 5 together in small cymes. In comparable habitats of Iceland, Scandinavia, Scotland and Wales.

S. hartii D.A. Webb is more or less intermediate, with dark-green, slightly leathery, ciliate, 3–7-lobed leaves (with acute segments), and pure-white flowers. On moist, calcareous rocks, old walls and slate-heaps in C Europe, northwards to the Vosges and the Ardennes, and also on sea-cliffs in NW Ireland (Donegal); C European forms are often distinguished as ssp. *sponhemica* (C.C. Gmel.) D.A. Webb, and appear closer to *S. cespitosa*.

---

p.129 **Rue-leaved Saxifrage**
Saxifraga tridactylites L.

Description: A hairy, often red-flushed *annual*, with erect, branched stems to 15 cm; no stolons. Leaves partly basal, in a rosette, *wedge-shaped*, gradually narrowed into rather long, flat stalk, fleshy, *deeply 3–5-lobed* with triangular-lanceolate, divergent lobes from near base of blade; stem-leaves rather numerous, subsessile, highest ones (in inflorescence) often scarcely lobed; no axillary bulbils. Flowers 4–6 mm diam., few together in lax, terminal cyme; flower-stalks at least twice as long as calyx. Petals white.

Flowering: April–September.

Habitat: Open grassland, dunes, riversides, also field margins, railways, and walls, on moist to dry, oligotrophic to mesotrophic, calcareous, sandy, loamy or stony soils; from sea level to 1,700 m.

Range: Most of Europe, except Iceland and the high Arctic.

Often ephemeral. *Compare S. adscendens* (*see* p.1030), which has most leaves in a rosette; in *S. tridactylites*, a rosette may be initially present, but it usually withers before anthesis. *S. osloensis* Knaben from S Scandinavia is intermediate between both species, and thought to be of hybrid origin.

RANNOCH-RUSH FAMILY, SCHEUCHZERIACEAE

A monotypic family, containing a single species: *Scheuchzeria palustris*. It is related to Juncaginaceae.

p.66 **Rannoch-rush** *Scheuchzeria palustris* L.

Description: A glabrous, perennial helophyte, with creeping rhizomes and erect flowering stems to 20 cm. Leaves alternate, linear, channelled, erect, up to 40 cm long and often overtopping flowers, with widened, sheathing, papery base and conspicuous apical pore; ligule present. Flowers hermaphrodite, regular, 4–6 mm diam., long-stalked, 3–10 together in terminal raceme. Perianth yellowish-green, with 6 lanceolate parts in 2 rows, persistent. Stamens 6, yellow. Ovaries 3 (rarely 6), superior, 1-locular, connate at base, with sessile stigmas. Fruit a starry cluster of 3 (6) inflated, ovoid, mostly 2-seeded follicles, 5 mm long.

Flowering: May–August.

Habitat: Bogs, fens, moors, on wet, oligotrophic, weakly acid, peaty or muddy soils; from sea level to 2,000 m, but only on mountains in the south.

Range: N Europe, southwards to Scotland, the Netherlands, N Germany and the Baltic States, and again in the mountains of C Europe (over 600 m).

This species prefers wet, mineral soils where peat-building has just begun, hence had its optimum in the period immediately following the ice ages. It is now rare outside the Arctic. In bogs it is restricted to the wettest parts; it often grows in the little gullies between *Sphagnum* humps.

FIGWORT FAMILY, SCROPHULARIACEAE

A large, subcosmopolitan family of herbs, shrubs and some woody climbers, with *c.* 3,000 species in some 220 genera world-wide. Dicots. Leaves alternate or opposite (rarely whorled), often simple but occasionally pinnately composed (as often in *Pedicularis*). Flowers irregular, hermaphrodite, basically 4–5-merous, often with connate sepals and a 2-lipped, tubular corolla. Stamens 2–5 (rarely more), implanted on corolla tube, often 2 long ones and 2 short ones. Ovary superior, 2-locular (occasionally incompletely so), with 1 style. Fruit a capsule (rarely a berry); here lies the main difference with the Mint family (Labiatae), in which fruit is normally composed of 4 achenes. In several genera a hemi-parasitic mode of life is current, as in *Rhinanthus*, *Pedicularis*, *Euphrasia*, *Odontites*, *Bartsia*, *Parentucellia*, and *Melampyrum*; the plants are green then, and can synthesize their own sugars through photosynthesis, but they tap water and dissolved minerals from the roots of other plants. *Lathraea* is an outright parasite, completely lacking chlorophyll; several authors place this genus in the closely related family Orobanchaceae. Many species are cultivated in gardens; some N American *Mimulus* species, which have opposite leaves, and large, yellow flowers, have more or less naturalized in marshes and wet, ruderal places.

p.311	**Small Toadflax** *Chaenorrhinum minus* (L.) Lange
Description:	A glandular-hairy annual, with erect, branched stems to 25 cm. Leaves alternate, short-stalked, oblanceolate or narrowly elliptical, entire-margined. *Flowers solitary* in leaf-axils, on long, threadlike stalks. Calyx 5-toothed. Corolla spurred, 2-lipped, 6–9 mm long, *pale lilac* with darker veins, lower lip deeply 3-lobed, with *2 yellowish bulges* not fully closing throat. Stamens 4 (2 long and 2 short), not protruding. Capsule ovoid, 5–7 mm long, unequally 2-locular, ribbed, finely hairy, with numerous seeds.
Flowering:	May–October.
Habitat:	Cultivated and waste land, gardens, ruderal and disturbed places, also railway lines, on moist, mesotrophic, calcareous, sandy, loamy or stony soils; from sea level to 2,000 m.
Range:	Most of Europe except Iceland and the high Arctic, but often casual in the north.

Compare the lilac-flowered species of *Linaria*, which have flowers in terminal racemes, with fully closed throat.

p.311 **Ivy-leaved Toadflax**
Cymbalaria muralis Gaertner, Meyer & Scherb.

Description: A (sub)glabrous perennial with thin, trailing, branched stems to 60 cm long. Leaves alternate, long-stalked, *reniform, 5–7-lobed*, palmately veined. *Flowers solitary* in leaf-axils, on long, ascending, threadlike stalks. Calyx 5-toothed. Corolla spurred, 2-lipped, 9–15 mm long, *lilac or pale violet*, lower lip deeply 3-lobed, with *2 yellowish bulges* fully closing throat. Stamens 4 (2 long, 2 short), not protruding. Capsule subglobose, *c.* 3 mm long, 2-locular, glabrous; seeds numerous, ovoid, with several irregular crests or flanges.

Flowering: May–October.

Habitat: Shaded rocks, also stone revetments and old brick walls, on moist, oligotrophic to mesotrophic, calcareous, stony soils; from sea level to 2,000 m.

Range: Native to S Europe, but frequently naturalized in W and C Europe, northwards to S Scandinavia.

The recurving fruit-stalks push fruits into fissures of rock or wall, where seeds can successfully develop.

p.187 **Large Yellow Foxglove**
Digitalis grandiflora Miller

Description: Much like *D. purpurea* (*see* below), but rarely taller than 1 m, and less hairy; leaves to 20 cm long, *glabrous* but for margins and veins beneath; calyces glandular-hairy; flowers 30–40 mm long, 12–18 mm wide, *pale yellow* with *brownish, netted markings* inside, hairy on outside, glabrous inside, and with slightly pointed corolla lobes; capsule ovoid.

Flowering: June–August.

Habitat: Open woods, wood margins, woodland
clearings, rocky slopes, on moist or dry,
mesotrophic, sandy, loamy or stony soils;
from sea level to 2,000 m.

Range: E and C Europe, westwards to the Pyrenees,
C France, E Belgium, C Germany, and
northwards to Poland, Estonia and
C Russia.

Similar species: **Small Yellow Foxglove** (*D. lutea* L.) has
smaller, glabrous, pale-yellow or cream
corollas (15–20 mm long, 5–7 mm wide),
usually glabrous, shiny, lanceolate leaves,
and conical capsules. In comparable habitats,
on calcareous soils, in W and WC Europe,
northwards to E Belgium and C Germany.

---

p.259 **Foxglove** *Digitalis purpurea* L.

Description: A densely greyish-tomentose biennial or
short-lived perennial, with erect, unbranched
stems to 1.8 m. Leaves alternate, up to 30 cm
long, 15 cm wide, lower ones stalked, upper
ones subsessile, ovate to lanceolate, crenate,
hairy at both faces. Flowers short-stalked,
nodding in long, terminal raceme, with
lanceolate bracts. Calyx 5-toothed,
tomentose. Corolla narrowly bell-shaped,
with wide tube and 4 short, rounded lobes,
40–50 mm long, 15–20 mm wide, *purplish or
deep pink* (occasionally white or cream), with
open, dark purple-spotted throat, glabrous on
outside, hairy inside; spur absent. Stamens 4
(2 long, 2 short), not protruding. Capsule
conical or ovoid, up to 15 mm long,
2-locular, hairy; seeds numerous.

Flowering: May–October.

Habitat: Open woods, scrub, woodland clearings,
shaded banks and road verges, on moist to
dry, mesotrophic to eutrophic, preferably
acid, sandy or stony soils; from sea level to
1,000 m.

Range: W and WC Europe, northwards to the
British Isles and S Scandinavia, and
eastwards to Czechoslovakia.

Frequently cultivated in gardens; plants from
the wild are often escapes from culture (as
white-flowered plants almost certainly are).

p.312 Common Eyebright
Euphrasia rostkoviana Hayne

Description: A hemi-parasitic annual, with erect, symmetrically branched stems to 40 cm; plant often red-tinged, and with numerous *long glandular hairs* in inflorescence. Leaves opposite, sessile, ovate or broadly elliptical, dentate, shorter than internodes. Flowers solitary in axils of leaf-like bracts, forming lax, leafy spike. Calyx 4-toothed, *glandular*. Corolla 2-lipped, 8–15 mm long (*tube strongly enlarged* during anthesis), white with purplish veins; upper lip often pale lilac, lower lip deeply 3-lobed, with yellow blotch at throat. Stamens 4 (2 long, 2 short). Capsule not exceeding calyx teeth, *c.* 5 mm long, at least half as wide, 2-locular, with several seeds per locule.

Flowering: May–September.

Habitat: Grassland and open woods on moist, oligotrophic, calcareous, sandy, loamy or stony soils; from sea level to 3,000 m.

Range: Most of Europe except Iceland and Spitsbergen, but absent from the deep south.

Forms with fruits exceeding calyx teeth, and 1–3 pairs of branches (not up to 5 pairs) are distinguished as ssp. *montana* (Jordan) Wettst., and occur throughout the range of the species. Some local forms have been given specific rank, especially in the British Isles. Consult a good regional flora for more details.

p.312 Glossy Eyebright
Euphrasia stricta J.F. Lehm.

Description: A hemi-parasitic annual, often strongly flushed with purple, but without long glandular hairs, with erect, symmetrically branched stems to 30 cm. Leaves small, opposite, sessile, ovate to suborbicular, sharply dentate, glabrous and shiny. Flowers solitary in axils of leaf-like bracts (with very long, tapering teeth), forming lax, leafy spike. Calyx 4-toothed. Corolla 2-lipped, 7–11 mm long, not much enlarged during anthesis, white or pale lilac with darker veins, upper lip often purplish, lower lip deeply 3-lobed, with yellow blotch at throat. Stamens 4 (2 long, 2 short). Capsule not exceeding calyx teeth, 4–5.5 (7) mm long, less than half as wide, ciliate (hairy on rims only), 2-locular, with several seeds per locule.

Flowering: June–October.

Habitat: Poor grassland, road verges, grassy heaths, dunes, on rather dry, oligotrophic, mildly acid to calcareous, sandy, loamy, stony or peaty soils; from sea level to 2,600 m.

Range: Most of continental Europe except the extreme north.

Similar species: Forms with flexuous stems and only 1–2 pairs of branches (not 2–6 pairs), found in Birch woods and damp meadows of Fennoscandia and W Russia, are often distinguished as *E. hyperborea* Joerg. *E. confusa* Pugsley, an often profusely branched plant with alternate bracts, white, purple or yellow flowers (5–9 mm long), and capsules exceeding calyx teeth, has been observed in the British Isles, the Faeroes, W Norway and possibly in NW France.

Irish Eyebright (*E. salisburgensis* Funck) (*see* photograph p.326) is often flushed with purple or bronze, and has small, glabrous, lanceolate leaves with only 1–3 acute teeth along each margin; lower bracts often alternate; corolla 5–8 mm long, not enlarged during anthesis, white, upper lip occasionally pale violet, lower lip often with yellow blotch; capsule not exceeding calyx teeth, 4–6.5 mm long, glabrous or with small, curved hairs on rim. In grassland, scrub, on screes, rock-ledges, also in dunes, on dry, oligotrophic, usually calcareous, sandy or stony soils, in mountains of C and S Europe (to 2,600 m), northwards to Fennoscandia and W Russia, also in W Ireland.

Arctic Eyebright (*E. arctica* Lange ex Rostrup) is often pale green, with long glandular hairs, otherwise glabrous; leaves ovate or elliptical, with subacute or pointed teeth; corolla 6.5–11 mm long, not enlarged during anthesis, pale violet or white with darker veins; capsule about equalling calyx teeth, 4–8 mm long, ciliate. In grassland, road verges, grassy heaths, on moist, oligotrophic, often acid, sandy, stony or peaty soils (0–1,600 m), in Ireland, the Orkneys and the Shetland Isles, the Faeroes, Iceland, and Scandinavia; northern forms (ssp. *borealis* (Townsend) Yeo) have smaller capsules (less than 5.5 mm long).

E. tetraquetra (Bréb.) Arrond. from coastal dunes and cliffs of Britain and NW France has fleshy leaves, and corollas 5–7 mm long; it hybridizes with *E. confusa*.

E. frigida Pugsley, from Arctic and sub-Arctic Europe, has blunt-toothed leaves, white, lilac or purplish flowers (corolla 4.5–7 mm long), and capsules at least equalling calyx teeth.

Wind Eyebright (*E. nemorosa* (Pers.) Wallr.) (*see* photograph p.313) is often strongly ramified (with up to 9 pairs of branches) and flushed with purple, but without long glandular hairs; leaves to 12 mm long, ovate or elliptical, sharply dentate (upper ones with up to 6 sharp teeth along each margin), usually hairy, and with prominent veins beneath; corolla 5–8 mm long, not enlarged during anthesis, white or pale lilac with darker veins, upper lip occasionally violet; capsule at most equalling calyx teeth, 4–6 mm long, hairy. In grassland, grassy heaths, open woods, along woodland rides, on rather moist, oligotrophic, often acid, sandy, stony or peaty soils (up to 1,600 m) in W, C and N Europe, from NE Spain extending northwards to the British Isles, S Scandinavia and NC Russia; it forms hybrids with *E. stricta* and *E. confusa*, which obscures delimitations between these species.

E. micrantha Reichenb. has threadlike, little-branched stems, narrowly ovate, glabrous and shiny leaves to 8 mm long, with less obvious veins, and only 2–4 teeth along each margin; bracts erect, flowers very small (4–6 mm long), capsules ciliate. In C and N Europe except Iceland and Spitsbergen.

Several closely related, local forms from NW Europe are treated as separate, endemic species, especially in Britain; some authors from the continent are less inclined to do so, even with the species mentioned here. Consult a good regional flora for more details.

p.257 Gratiole *Gratiola officinalis* L.

Description: A glabrous perennial, with ascending to erect, partly creeping, unbranched, *quadrangular*, hollow stems to 40 cm. Leaves *opposite*, 50 mm long, sessile, lanceolate, weakly dentate or entire, with translucent glandular dots. Flowers stalked, solitary in leaf-axils. Calyx 5-toothed, with 2 linear bracteoles at base. Corolla slightly 2-lipped, with cylindrical tube and 5 rounded lobes, 10–18 mm long, *white or pink*, often with purplish veins, and with yellowish tube; spur absent. *Fertile stamens 2*; also 2 reduced, threadlike, sterile staminodes present. Capsule ovoid, up to 9 mm long, with numerous seeds.

Flowering: June–October.

Habitat: Meadows, pastures, marshes, ditches, streamsides and rivers, at pool margins, often in seasonally flooded places, on wet, mesotrophic, preferably calcareous, sandy, loamy or clayey soils; mainly in the lowland.

Range: Continental Europe northwards to the Netherlands, Poland, Estonia, and C Russia.

Similar species: *Lindernia procumbens* (Krocker) Philcox is a much smaller, delicate, prostrate, often ephemeral annual, to 12 cm tall, with long-stalked, pale-lilac, obliquely trumpet-shaped flowers only 5–6 mm long (not exceeding calyx), with 4 fertile stamens, and lacking the 2 bracteoles. At pool margins and in marshes of SE and C Europe, locally extending to C France and C Germany.
L. dubia (L.) Pennel., from N America, grows more erect, and has flowers with 2 fertile stamens, 2 bifid staminodes, and slightly longer corolla (6–8 mm). Locally naturalized in SW Europe, to NW France.

p.185 **Sharp-leaved Fluellen**
Kickxia elatine (L.) Dumort.

Description: A hairy, often glandular annual, to 45 cm, with trailing or straggling, branched stems. Leaves alternate, short-stalked, *arrow-shaped* (elliptical with hastate base), entire-margined. *Flowers solitary* in leaf-axils, on long, threadlike, *glabrous stalks*. Calyx with 5 lanceolate teeth, not enlarged in fruit. Corolla 2-lipped, 7–10 mm long, *yellow* with *violet upper lip*, lower lip 3-lobed, with *2 yellow bulges* fully closing throat, and with straight spur. Stamens 4 (2 long, 2 short), not pro-truding. Capsule rounded, 4–4.5 mm long, 2-locular, ribbed, glabrous, opening with 2 valves, and containing numerous seeds.

Flowering: June–October.

Habitat: Cultivated and waste land, ruderal places, on moist, mesotrophic, calcareous, sandy, loamy or clayey soils; from sea level to 1,800 m.

Range: Much of Europe, northwards to S Britain, the Low Countries, Poland, C Russia, and naturalized in Ireland, Denmark and S Sweden.

Similar species: **Round-leaved Fluellen** (*K. spuria* (L.) Dumort.) has elliptical, round-based or slightly cordate leaves, flowers 10–15 mm long, with curved spur, and hairy flower-stalks; calyx has wider teeth and becomes enlarged in fruit. In comparable habitats of W and SC Europe, northwards to S Britain, the Low Countries and N Germany.

p.314 **Purple Toothwort** *Lathraea clandestina* L.

Description: A fully parasitic, subglabrous perennial, with yellowish, underground creeping, scaly rhizomes; *no aerial stems*. Leaves alternate or opposite, sessile, scale-like, reniform or broadly ovate-cordate, 4–8 mm long, entire. Flowers long-stalked, rising directly from rhizome, often appearing above ground in dense clusters. Calyx brownish, glabrous, with 4 (5) short, erect, triangular teeth. Corolla 2-lipped, 40–50 mm long, *violet*, upper lip nearly straight with hooded, notched tip, lower lip 3-lobed, purple.

Stamens 4 (2 long, 2 short). Capsule ovoid, 1-locular, glabrous, opening with 2 valves, and containing 4–5 *large seeds*.

Flowering: April–May.

Habitat: Damp woods, coppices, hedgerows, shaded streamsides, on moist, oligotrophic, preferably calcareous, humus-rich, sandy, loamy or stony soils; from sea level to 800 m; parasitic on roots of trees, often Poplars or Willows.

Range: SW Europe, northwards to Belgium, and eastwards to Italy.

Occasionally cultivated in gardens, and naturalized in Britain and at 1 site in the Netherlands.

p.260 **Toothwort** *Lathraea squamaria* L.

Description: A fully parasitic, hairy perennial, with white or cream, underground creeping rhizomes, and *erect aerial stems* to 30 cm. Leaves alternate, sessile, scale-like, rounded or ovate-cordate, 4–8 mm long, entire. Flowers short-stalked, nodding in dense, *1-sided raceme*. Calyx whitish, hairy, with 4 short, erect, equal, triangular teeth. Corolla 2-lipped, 14–17 mm long, *pink or pale lilac*, upper lip nearly straight with truncate tip, lower lip weakly lobed. Stamens 4 (2 long, 2 short), slightly protruding. Capsule ovoid, 1-locular, glabrous, opening with 2 valves, and containing numerous, tiny, *dust-like seeds*.

Flowering: March–May.

Habitat: Damp, deciduous woods, coppices, hedgerows, on moist, oligotrophic, preferably calcareous, sandy, loamy or stony, humus-rich soils, parasitic on roots of woody plants, often Alder, Hornbeam, Beech, or Elm, occasionally Ivy; from sea level to 1,600 m.

Range: In Europe northwards to the British Isles, S Scandinavia and the Baltic States; extinct in the Netherlands.

Occasionally cultivated in gardens. *Compare Monotropa* (*see* p.928), which has regular flowers, and *Orobanche* (*see* p.849), which has 2-lipped calyx.

p.93 **Mudwort** *Limosella aquatica* L.

Description: A delicate, glabrous annual, to 5 cm, with creeping (occasionally floating) stolons, and small rosettes of long-stalked, *spatulate, entire-margined leaves* (2–12 cm long, including stalk), lower ones often almost linear. Flowers long-stalked, solitary, rising directly from rosette. Calyx 5-toothed. *Corolla nearly regular*, bell-shaped, with short tube and 5 rounded lobes, *c.* 3 mm long, *white or pink*; spur absent. Stamens 4, subequal. Capsule ovoid, up to 3 mm long, incompletely 2-locular, with numerous small, ovoid seeds.

Flowering: June–October.

Habitat: Periodically flooded places, pool margins, riversides, dune-slacks, on wet, eutrophic, preferably calcareous, muddy soils; from sea level to 1,800 m.

Range: Most of Europe except Mediterranean region and the high Arctic.

Similar species: **Welsh Mudwort** (*L. australis* R. Br.) has all leaves linear, to 40 mm long, and flowers 3.5–4 mm long, white with orange tube. In comparable habitats, in Wales only (but also in Africa, Australia and eastern N America). *Compare Subularia aquatica* (*see* p.601), with 4-petalled flowers in a raceme.

Mudwort is often ephemeral, and erratic in its appearance; a rare and declining species.

---

p.185 **Sand Toadflax** *Linaria arenaria* (L.) Miller

Description: A *densely glandular-hairy*, sticky, tufted annual, to 15 cm, with ascending or erect, branched stems. Leaves alternate (lower ones often in whorls of 3–4), crowded, erect, subsessile, 10–20 mm long, 2–6 mm wide, (broadly) *lanceolate*, entire-margined, rather fleshy. Flowers short-stalked, in small, terminal racemes, with lanceolate bracts much exceeding flower-stalks and grading into normal leaves below. Calyx 5-toothed. Corolla 2-lipped, 4–7 mm long (including spur), *pale yellow*, lower lip deeply 3-lobed, with *2 deep yellow bulges* fully closing throat; spur conical, almost straight, 2–3 mm long, often violet. Stamens 4 (2 long, 2 short), not protruding. Capsule broadly ovoid, 3–5 mm long, 2-locular; seeds numerous, ovoid, papillose, narrowly winged.

Flowering: May–September.
Habitat: Sand-dunes, maritime cliffs, on dry, oligotrophic, calcareous, sandy or stony soils; only coastal.
Range: Endemic to NW Spain and W France; locally naturalized in SW Britain.

---

p.312 **Pale Toadflax** *Linaria repens* (L.) Miller

Description: A glabrous, tufted perennial, with creeping rhizome and straggling to erect, branched stems to 60 (120) cm. *Leaves mostly in whorls of 3–6* (only upper ones alternate), sessile, linear-lanceolate, entire-margined. Flowers stalked, in *terminal racemes*, with small, linear bracts about equalling flower-stalks. Calyx 5-toothed. Corolla 2-lipped, 9–14 mm long, *pale lilac* or almost white with *violet stripes*, lower lip deeply 3-lobed, with *2 yellowish bulges* fully closing throat; spur conical, almost straight, 3–5 mm long. Stamens 4 (2 long, 2 short), not protruding. Capsule broadly ovoid, 3–4 mm long, 2-locular, glabrous; seeds numerous, trigonal, barely winged.

Flowering: June–September.
Habitat: Cultivated and waste land, roadsides, ruderal places, railway lines, occasionally walls, on dry, mesotrophic, preferably calcareous, sandy or stony soils; from sea level to 2,300 m.
Range: Native to SW Europe, northwards to France, Belgium and S Germany; frequently naturalized further north, to S Scandinavia.
Similar species: **Jersey Toadflax** (*L. pelisseriana* (L.) Miller) is a small annual to 30 cm, with mostly alternate leaves (only lower ones opposite or in whorls of 3); flowers 15–20 mm long, violet with white throat, and with slender spur 7–9 mm long. In comparable habitats of S Europe, northwards to W and C France (including Jersey).
L. arvensis (L.) Desf. is also annual, but has all leaves alternate; flowers small, pale

violet with darker stripes, corolla only 4–7 mm long (including curved spur 1.5–3 mm long); seeds winged, barely papillose; plant stickily glandular-hairy in inflorescence. In cultivated and waste land, on dry, often sandy soils in S Europe, northwards to NC France and SW Germany; becoming rare.

---

p.185 **Common Toadflax** *Linaria vulgaris* Miller

Description: A glabrous or slightly glandular-hairy, tufted perennial, with creeping rhizome and ascending to erect, branched stems to 60 (90) cm. Leaves alternate, crowded, sessile, 30–80 mm long, up to 6 mm wide, linear-lanceolate, entire-margined, often bluish-green. Flowers stalked, in *terminal racemes*, with linear bracts at least equalling flower-stalks and grading into normal leaves below. Calyx 5-toothed. Corolla 2-lipped, 25–35 mm long (including spur), pale or bright *yellow*, lower lip deeply 3-lobed, with *2 orange bulges* fully closing throat; spur conical, almost straight, 10–13 mm long. Stamens 4 (2 long, 2 short), not protruding. Capsule broadly ovoid, 5–11 mm long, 5–7 mm wide, 2-locular, glabrous; seeds numerous, ovoid, papillose, broadly winged.

Flowering: June–October.

Habitat: Cultivated and waste land, grassland, dunes, roadsides, ruderal places, railway lines, on moist to dry, mesotrophic, acid or calcareous, sandy, loamy, clayey or stony soils; from sea level to 1,600 m.

Range: Most of Europe except Iceland and the high Arctic.

Similar species: **Prostrate Toadflax** (*L. supina* (L.) Chaz.) is annual, with ascending stems to 30 cm, leaves 5–25 mm long, 1–2 mm wide, and flowers up to 10 in small racemes; corolla 20–25 mm long (including spur 10–15 mm long); seeds smooth, broadly winged. In comparable habitats of SW Europe, northwards to N France, often as a casual further north and locally naturalized (Cornwall, Belgium, S Sweden). *Compare also L. arenaria.*

p.258 **Field Cow-wheat** *Melampyrum arvense* L.

Description: A hemi-parasitic, finely hairy annual to 50 cm, with erect stems and spreading, opposite branches. Leaves 4–10 cm long, opposite, subsessile, *lanceolate*, entire-margined or upper ones with some teeth at base. Flowers solitary in axils of pinnately divided, *purplish-pink (rarely whitish) bracts*, forming lax to rather dense, cylindrical or conical spike. Calyx-teeth 4, linear, longer than calyx tube, erect. Corolla 2-lipped, 15–25 mm long, *pink or purplish* with 3-lobed, *yellow lower lip* (occasionally all yellow), upper lip concave, with recurved margins. Stamens 4 (2 long, 2 short). Capsule ovoid, compressed, 2-locular, glabrous, and usually containing 1 seed per locule.

Flowering: June–September.

Habitat: Cultivated and waste land, field margins, grassland, road verges, on moist, mesotrophic, calcareous, sandy, loamy or stony soils; from sea level to 1,500 m.

Range: W and C Europe, northwards to England, S Belgium, C Germany, S Sweden and SW Finland, and eastwards to C and SE Russia.

Similar species: *M. nemorosum* L. has wider, more ovate leaves, yellow flowers with purplish lower lip, and violet or white (rarely greenish) bracts. In deciduous and mixed woods of N and C Europe, from Germany and Switzerland eastwards to C Russia, and northwards to S Sweden and S Finland; plants with violet and white bracts often occur in mixed populations.

---

p.258 **Crested Cow-wheat**
Melampyrum cristatum L.

Description: A hemi-parasitic, finely hairy annual to 35 cm, with erect, simple or widely branched stems. Leaves 4–10 cm long, opposite, subsessile, (narrowly) *lanceolate*, entire-margined or upper ones with some teeth at base. Flowers solitary in axils of recurved, (narrowly) lanceolate, (at least basally) long-toothed bracts, upper ones purple, lower ones green with whitish or purplish base, forming dense, distinctly *4-sided spike*. Calyx-teeth 4, triangular, unequal, erect, shorter than calyx tube, which has 2 bands of hairs. Corolla 2-lipped, 12–16 mm long, *yellow* with *purplish upper lip*, lower lip 3-lobed, with a bulge half-closing throat. Stamens 4 (2 long, 2 short). Capsule ovoid, 2-locular, glabrous, splitting along 1 seam, and usually containing 2 seeds per locule.

Flowering: May–September.

Habitat: Wood margins, woodland clearings, grassland, on rather dry, oligotrophic, calcareous, sandy, loamy or stony soils; from sea level to 1,500 m.

Range: Much of Europe, except the extreme north and parts of the extreme west and deep south.

---

p.88 **Common Cow-wheat**
Melampyrum pratense L.

Description: A variable, hemi-parasitic, subglabrous annual, to 50 cm, with erect stems and often some spreading, opposite branches. Leaves 30–80 mm long, opposite, subsessile, *lanceolate*, entire-margined or only upper ones with a few teeth at base. Flowers spaced, solitary in axils of leaf-like, entire-margined or basally dentate, *green bracts*. Calyx-teeth 4, triangular-lanceolate, longer than calyx tube, erect. Corolla 2-lipped, 15–20 mm long, *yellow or cream*, occasionally tinged with red; upper lip concave, with recurved margins, lower lip (shallowly) 3-lobed, with a bulge largely closing throat. Stamens 4 (2 long, 2 short). Capsule ovoid, 2-locular, glabrous, splitting along 1 seam, and usually containing 2 seeds per locule.

Flowering: May–October.

Habitat: Deciduous woods (often oaks or birches), wood margins, clearings, shady road verges, grassland, heaths, on dry, oligotrophic, usually acid, sandy or stony (rarely peaty) soils; from sea level to 2,200 m.

Range: Most of Europe except the extreme north and much of Mediterranean region.

Similar species: **Small Cow-wheat** (*M. sylvaticum* L.) always has entire leaves to 50 mm long, smaller flowers (8–10 mm long) with wide-open throat and, often, red spots on lower lip, calyx teeth shorter than tube, and capsules splitting along 2 seams. In open woods (often Birch or Pine), scrub, heaths and moors of Scandinavia, also (over 400 m) in C Europe.

---

p.257 **Lesser Snapdragon**
Misopates orontium (L.) Rafin.

Description: A glabrous or slightly hairy, tufted annual, to 50 cm, with erect, branched stems, often glandular above. Leaves alternate (lower ones opposite), subsessile, linear-oblanceolate, entire-margined. Flowers subsessile, in lax, *terminal racemes*, with linear bracts exceeding flowers. Calyx 5-toothed, with very unequal teeth. Corolla 2-lipped, not exceeding calyx teeth, 10–15 mm long, *pink* (rarely white) with *purplish lines*, lower lip deeply 3-lobed, with large bulge fully closing throat; corolla tube sac-like, but without distinct spur. Stamens 4 (2 long, 2 short), not protruding. Capsule broadly ovoid, 8–10 mm long, 2-locular, glandular-hairy, opening with 2–3 apical pores; seeds numerous.

Flowering: June–October.

Habitat: Cultivated and waste land, roadsides, ruderal places, railway lines, on moist, mesotrophic, weakly acid, sandy or stony soils; from sea level to 750 m.

Range: S and SC Europe, northwards to S Ireland, S Britain, the Low Countries, Hungary and W Russia; occasionally naturalized further north.

Similar species: **Snapdragon** (*Antirrhinum majus* L.), from the Mediterranean region, is perennial, and has much larger, purple, pink, white or yellow flowers (30–40 mm long). Frequently grown in gardens, and occasionally naturalized in ruderal places.

p.257 **Red Bartsia**
Odontites vernus (Bellardi) Dumortier

Description: A hemi-parasitic, hairy annual, often strongly flushed with purple, with erect stems to 50 cm, generally symmetrically branched (with spreading branches) almost from base. Leaves 10–30 mm long, opposite, sessile, *lanceolate to almost linear*, bluntly serrate-dentate (with 1–5 weak teeth at each margin). Flowers solitary in axils of leaf-like bracts, forming rather dense, *1-sided*, 6–20-flowered, leafy spike. Calyx-teeth 4, triangular-lanceolate, about equalling calyx tube. Corolla 2-lipped, 8–11 mm long, pink or purplish-red (without dark veins), rarely white, *upper lip strongly convex* (helmet-shaped), lower lip deeply 3-lobed. Stamens 4 (2 long, 2 short). Capsule about equalling calyx teeth, 6–8 mm long, narrowly ovoid, compressed, 2-locular, *hairy*, with several seeds per locule.

Flowering: June–October.

Habitat: Meadows, pastures, roadsides, scrub, also dune-slacks, saline coastal grassland, highest parts of saltmarshes, on wet or moist, mesotrophic, preferably calcareous, sandy, loamy or clayey soils; from sea level to 1,800 m.

Range: Most of Europe except the extreme north.

Similar species: **Alpine Bartsia** (*Bartsia alpina* L.) is an unbranched, hairy perennial with short, creeping rhizomes, ovate, bluntly dentate leaves to 20 mm long, large, hairy, dark-purplish flowers (20–30 mm long) in few-flowered, terminal spikes with purple-flushed bracts, and few-seeded capsules. In mountains of C Europe, N Britain, Iceland, Fennoscandia and N Russia.

    Some related, yellow-flowered species occur in C Europe, northwards to N France: **Yellow Odontites** (*O. luteus* (L.) Clairv.), with linear, subentire leaves and protruding stamens; and *O. jaubertianus* (Bor.) Dietr., with linear, entire leaves, and stamens included under upper lip. *Compare also Euphrasia* (*see* p.1043), with dark-veined flowers, and flat upper lip with recurved margin.

The description of Red Bartsia pertains to ssp. *serotinus* (Dumort.) Corb. The typical form (ssp. *vernus*) has erect branches, 6–13-flowered spikes, and slightly longer calyx teeth. In arable fields, but now rare. Ssp. *litoralis* (Fries) Nyman, an erect-branched form with leaves to 20 mm long, 4–6-flowered spikes, and short, triangular-ovate calyx teeth, occurs in saline coastal grassland and saltmarshes of the Baltic region, extending westwards to S Norway and the Netherlands. A dwarf form (ssp. *pumilus* (Nordst.) Pedersen) has been described from coastal grassland in N Scotland.

p.186 **Yellow Bartsia**
Parentucellia viscosa (L.) Caruel

Description: A hemi-parasitic, glandular-hairy (sticky), yellowish-green annual, to 50 cm (often much less), with erect stems. Leaves 15–40 mm long, opposite, sessile, lanceolate or narrowly elliptical, serrate-dentate. Flowers solitary in axils of leaf-like bracts, forming short, rather dense, leafy spike. Calyx-teeth 4, broadly triangular-lanceolate. Corolla 2-lipped, 16–24 mm long, about twice as long as calyx, *deep yellow* (rarely white), hairy, upper lip convex (helmet-shaped), lower lip deeply 3-lobed. Stamens 4 (2 long, 2 short). Capsule about equalling calyx teeth, 7–9 mm long, narrowly ovoid, compressed, 2-locular, *hairy*, with numerous small seeds.

Flowering: June–September.

Habitat: Grassland, fields, sea-cliffs, freshly embanked sand-flats, slurried building sites, on moist or wet, mesotrophic to oligotrophic, calcareous, sandy, loamy or stony soils; mainly coastal.

Range: S and W Europe, northwards to SW Ireland, S Britain and the Low Countries. Yellow Bartsia is apparently extending its range to the north.

Similar species: *P. latifolia* (L.) Caruel has triangular-ovate, strongly dentate leaves, small, purplish (rarely white) flowers 8–10 mm long, and glabrous capsules. In grassland of S Europe, extending northwards to NW France. *Compare also* the yellow-flowered species of *Odontites* (*see* p.1055).

---

p.258 **Marsh Lousewort** *Pedicularis palustris* L.

Description: A hemi-parasitic, subglabrous *annual or biennial* to 50 cm, with single, branched stem. *Leaves alternate*, stalked, broadly lanceolate, *pinnatifid* with crenate or lobed segments. Flowers solitary in axils of leaf-like, *alternate bracts*, forming lax, leafy spike. Calyx bell-shaped, glabrous, *2-lipped*, with 2 large, deeply incised lobes. Corolla 2-lipped, 18–25 mm long, *pale purple*, upper lip almost straight, laterally compressed, with 2 pairs of small teeth in upper half, and hooded tip; lower lip deeply 3-lobed, *ciliate*, slightly forward-pointing. Stamens 4 (2 long, 2 short). Capsule ovoid, obliquely pointed, 12–15 mm long, 2-locular, with numerous seeds.

Flowering: May–September.

Habitat: Marshes, fens, heaths, damp grassland, ditches, dune-slacks, on wet, oligotrophic, slightly acid to calcareous, sandy or peaty soils; from sea level to 1,800 m.

Range: Most of Europe except Iceland and the high Arctic.

Similar species: **Whorled Lousewort** (*P. verticillata* L.), from mountain pastures of C and S Europe (1,500–3,100 m), and also from tundra of N Russia, is very distinctive by its leaves and bracts in whorls of 3–4, flowers to 18 mm long, in dense, leafy spikes, with 5-toothed calyces, and purplish or pink (rarely white) corollas with blunt, untoothed upper lip.

A (sub)Arctic form of Marsh Lousewort, characterized by the possession of less incised, pinnately lobed leaves, and flowers less than 18 mm long, is distinguished as *P. palustris* ssp. *borealis* (J.W. Zett.) Hyl.

p.186 **Moor-king** *Pedicularis sceptrum-carolinum* L.

Description: A hemi-parasitic *perennial* to 80 cm, with single, unbranched, stout, glabrous stem. *Leaves mostly in basal rosette*, stalked, lanceolate, *pinnatifid* with crenate segments, glabrous or slightly hairy beneath; stem-leaves few, much smaller. Flowers solitary in the axils of small, ovate, crenate, *opposite or whorled bracts* not exceeding flowers, forming lax spike with 2–3-flowered storeys. Calyx bell-shaped, glabrous, *5-toothed*, teeth crenate. Corolla 2-lipped, 22–32 mm long, *pale yellow*, with 3-lobed, *red-flushed lower lip*, upper lip curved, laterally compressed, with blunt, hooded tip; flower usually closed by 'wrap-around' lower lip. Stamens 4 (2 long, 2 short). Capsule subglobose, shortly pointed, *c.* 15 mm long, 2-locular, with numerous seeds.

Flowering: June–August.

Habitat: Marshes, fens, bogs, damp woods and scrub, stream- and riversides, on wet, oligotrophic, acid, sandy or peaty soils; mainly in the lowland.

Range: In Fennoscandia, N and C Russia, the Baltic States, and Poland; also in S Germany and C Romania.

Similar species: **Crimson-tipped Lousewort** (*P. oederi* Vahl) rarely exceeds 15 cm, and has dense, cylindrical spikes of pale-yellow, crimson-tipped flowers (12–20 mm long), with hairy calyces and spreading lower lips. Rather local in C Europe and Scandinavia. *P. flammea* L., from Scandinavia, is much like Crimson-tipped Lousewort but has even smaller flowers (10–12 mm long), with glabrous calyces and dark-red upper lips. **Leafy Lousewort** (*P. foliosa* L.) is quite distinct, having large, doubly pinnatifid leaves with lanceolate segments (hairy beneath), and pale-yellow flowers (15–25 mm long) with hairy corollas, in very long, dense, cylindrical, leafy spike (bracts leaf-like, much exceeding flowers). In meadows, scrub and streamsides in mountains (1,500–2,400 m) of C Europe, westwards to C and NE France. *Compare also P. lapponica (see p.1059), which has small heads of uniformly cream flowers.*

p.258 **Lousewort** *Pedicularis sylvatica* L.

Description: A hemi-parasitic *biennial or perennial* to 25 cm (occasionally much less), with erect central stem and few to several *ascending, lateral stems*, all unbranched; stems glabrous or with 2 opposite lines of hairs. *Leaves alternate*, stalked, lanceolate, *doubly pinnatifid*, glabrous or slightly hairy. Flowers solitary in axils of leaf-like, *alternate bracts*, forming lax, leafy spike (starting low). Calyx bell-shaped, glabrous, *5-toothed*, with 1 entire and 4 incised teeth. Corolla 2-lipped, 15–25 mm long, *pink*, upper lip almost straight, laterally compressed, with 1 pair of small teeth near (hooded) tip, lower lip deeply 3-lobed, spreading. Stamens 4 (2 long, 2 short). Capsule ovoid, obliquely pointed, *c.* 12 mm long, 2-locular, with numerous seeds.

Flowering: April–July (September).

Habitat: Poor grassland, grassy heaths, moors, bogs, dune-slacks, along woodland rides, on wet or moist, oligotrophic, acid, sandy or peaty soils; from sea level to 1,800 m.

Range: W and C Europe, northwards to C Sweden, and eastwards to Lithuania and the Ukraine.

Similar species: **Hairy Lousewort** (*P. hirsuta* L.) is perennial, densely woolly above, and has simple stems to 12 cm, once-pinnately divided leaves, flowers 10–15 mm long, in dense, terminal, head-like raceme, with glabrous, bright-pink, untoothed corolla. Along streams, lakes and rivers, and on tundra, on calcareous, often stony soils in Arctic Europe, including Spitsbergen. *P. dasyantha* Hadac, from the stony tundra of Spitsbergen and adjacent N Russia, is much like *P. hirsuta*, but has flowers 17–20 mm long, with purplish-pink, hairy, 2-toothed corolla. **Lapland Lousewort** (*P. lapponica* L.), from Fennoscandia and N Russia, is another perennial with simple stems (to 25 cm) and short, head-like flower-spikes, but with linear, pinnately lobed leaves, and cream or pale-yellow, curved corolla. • All these species have 5-toothed calyces. *Compare also*

P. palustris (*see* p.1057), with branched stems and 2-lipped calyces.

Lousewort plants from Ireland and Norway, with hairy stems and calyces, are attributed to *P. sylvatica* ssp. *hibernica* D.A. Webb.

p.186 **Yellow-rattle** *Rhinanthus minor* L.

Description: A hemi-parasitic, subglabrous annual to 50 cm, with erect, simple or branched, often black-spotted stems; branches opposite, erect or ascending. Leaves opposite, sessile, dark green, to 70 mm long, 15 mm wide, lanceolate, *regularly serrate-dentate*. Flowers solitary on very short stalks in axils of coarsely dentate, greenish, leaf-like bracts, forming rather dense, cylindrical, spike-like raceme. Calyx-teeth 4, triangular, *converging*, much shorter than laterally compressed calyx tube, which has minute hairs on margins only, and becomes *strongly inflated* in fruit. Corolla 2-lipped, 10–15 mm long, *yellow*, upper lip folded lengthways, with pair of white or purplish teeth (to 1 mm long) near tip, lower lip short, 3-lobed; *corolla-tube straight*, with open throat. Stamens 4 (2 long, 2 short). Capsule broadly ovoid, 2-locular, glabrous, containing several seeds per locule.

Flowering: May–September.

Habitat: Meadows, road verges, dune-pastures, fens, on moist to rather dry, oligotrophic, mildly acid or calcareous, sandy or peaty soils; from sea level to 2,000 m.

Range: Most of Europe except Spitsbergen and many Mediterranean islands, eastwards to the Caucasus.

Similar species: *R. groenlandicus* (Ostenf.) Chab. has yellowish-green leaves with long, spreading (not forward-pointing) teeth, and stems with 2 lines of hairs. In grassy places of Scandinavia, Iceland and the Faeroes. **Greater Yellow-rattle** (*R. angustifolius* C.C. Gmel.) often has narrower leaves (to 5 mm wide, but to 15 mm in late-flowering forms), larger flowers (15–25 mm long) with curved corolla-tube, largely closed at throat, and long, purplish teeth (to 2 mm) near tip of upper lip. In meadows, road verges, dune-pastures and watersides, on moist or wet, oligotrophic to mesotrophic soils, in most of Europe but absent from the deep south, the extreme west (Ireland, Iceland) and the high Arctic.

R. alectorolophus (Scop.) Pollich has unspotted stems (hairy all round), lanceolate to ovate, pale-green, hairy leaves, flowers 15–25 mm long, with densely hairy calyx tube, slightly curved corolla-tube, and long, violet teeth (2 mm) near tip of upper lip. In cultivated and waste land, field margins, grassland, on moist, mesotrophic, calcareous, loamy or stony soils, to 2,300 m, in C Europe, extending to W France, the Low Countries, C Germany, S Poland, and WC Russia.

All these species are highly variable, presenting early and late-flowering forms (usually treated as subspecies) differing considerably in leaf shape and mode of ramification; early forms are often unbranched, the late ones more profusely branched, with shorter internodes.

The ripe seeds remain for some time rattling in inflated calyx, until shaken out by the wind; hence the name of these plants.

---

p.40 **Water Figwort** *Scrophularia auriculata* L.

Description: A glabrous perennial, to 1.2 m, with short, creeping rhizomes, and erect, quadrangular, *distinctly winged stems* (wings to 1 mm wide). Leaves *opposite*, 5–15 cm long, stalked, ovate or broadly lanceolate, (regularly) crenate-dentate, blunt-tipped, round-based, lower ones often with 2 small, ovate lobes (*auricles*) at top of (winged) stalk. Flowers in rather dense, axillary cymes, with small, linear bracts. Calyx bell-shaped, deeply 5-lobed, lobes suborbicular, with *wide scarious margins*. Corolla 2-lipped, 7–9 mm long, *purplish-brown*, with cup-shaped, only basally greenish tube, notched upper lip, and shorter, 3-lobed lower lip; spur absent. Fertile stamens 4 (2 long, 2 short); also 1 scale-like, rounded staminode present. Capsule broadly ovoid, mucronate, 4–6 mm long, with numerous seeds.

Flowering: June–September.

Habitat: Marshes, fens, river-, ditch- and streamsides, on wet, mesotrophic, preferably calcareous, sandy, loamy, stony or peaty soils; from sea level to 800 m.

Range: S and W Europe, northwards to Ireland, N England, the Low Countries, and S Germany.

Similar species: **Green Figwort** (*S. umbrosa* Dumort.) has wings on stem 1–3 mm wide, leaves pointed and sharply serrate, without auricles; bracts in inflorescence large and leaf-like; staminode very wide, 2-lobed. In damp woods, springs and flushes, ditch- and streamsides, also in meadows, on wet, mesotrophic, mildly acid or calcareous, sandy, loamy or stony soils; from sea level to 1,200 m, mainly in E and C Europe, locally westwards to E France and the British Isles, and northwards to S Sweden, Lithuania and C Russia.

p.40 **Common Figwort** *Scrophularia nodosa* L.

Description: A glabrous perennial, to 80 cm, with short, creeping rhizomes (with small, nodular tubers), and erect, quadrangular but *unwinged stems*. Leaves *opposite*, 5–15 cm long, stalked, ovate or broadly lanceolate with slightly cordate base and pointed tip, (irregularly) serrate. Flowers in lax, axillary cymes, with small, linear bracts (only lower ones leaf-like). Calyx bell-shaped, deeply 5-lobed, lobes ovate with narrow scarious margins. Corolla 2-lipped, 7–9 mm long, *greenish*, with cup-shaped tube, *purplish-brown*, notched upper lip, and shorter, 3-lobed lower lip; spur absent. Fertile stamens 4 (2 long, 2 short); also 1 scale-like, triangular or reniform staminode present. Capsule broadly ovoid, shortly pointed, *c.* 5 mm long, with numerous seeds.

Flowering: June–September.

Habitat: Wood margins, scrub, shaded roadsides, hedgerows, ditch- and streamsides, on moist, oligotrophic to mesotrophic, mildly acid, sandy, loamy or stony soils; from sea level to 1,800 m.

Range: Most of Europe except the extreme north.

Similar species: **Balm-leaved Figwort** (*S. scorodonia* L.) is densely grey-hairy, and has wrinkled leaves, numerous large, leaf-like bracts in inflorescence, and dull-purple flowers 8–12 mm long; calyx-lobes have wide scarious margins; staminode rounded. In damp, open woods, hedgerows, stream- and riversides, also in dune-slacks and on sea cliffs, in SW Europe, northwards to W France, the Channel Islands and SW Britain. **Yellow Figwort** (*S. vernalis* L.) is densely glandular-hairy, and has greenish-yellow, regular flowers (6–8 mm long), all with leaf-like bracts; staminode absent. In damp mountain woods of C Europe, northwards to NE France and SC Germany, locally naturalized further north, to S Sweden.

All these species have unwinged stems.

---

p.266 **Cornish Moneywort** *Sibthorpia europaea* L.

Description: A delicate, hairy perennial with threadlike, creeping, branched stems to 30 cm long. Leaves alternate, long-stalked, *reniform or suborbicular, shallowly 5–7-lobed*, palmately veined. *Flowers solitary* in leaf-axils, on long, ascending, threadlike stalks. Calyx-parts 4 (5), lanceolate. *Corolla almost regular*, with very short tube and 5 spreading lobes, 3 mm diam., shorter than calyx, 2 *upper lobes yellowish*, 3 *lower lobes pink*. Stamens (3) 4–5, subequal, inserted on corolla tube, slightly protruding. Style straight, about equalling ovary, with simple stigma. Capsule rounded, 1–1.5 mm long, 2-locular, opening with 2 valves, few-seeded.

Flowering: July–October.

Habitat: Shaded banks, roadsides, ditch- and streamsides, on moist, oligotrophic soils; mainly in the mountains, descending lower in the north.

Range: W Europe, from Portugal to the British Isles; also in the mountains of Greece.

Mulleins, *Verbascum*

A genus of stout, hairy biennials or short-lived perennials, forming large rosette of stalked, basal leaves in 1st year, and tall, simple flowering stem with alternate, sessile leaves in 2nd year. Leaf-margins may be crenate-dentate or even shallowly lobed, but teeth are often obscured by a dense cover of hairs; in *V. blattaria*, however, leaves are quite glabrous on both faces. Flowers are nearly regular, hermaphrodite, stalked or subsessile, numerous in long racemes or spikes that often compose a large, narrow panicle. Calyx is 5-parted, with elliptical or lanceolate parts. As a rule, corolla is yellow (but often white in *V. lychnitis*, and violet in *V. phoeniceum*), with short tube and 5 large, subequal, rounded, spreading lobes. The 5 far-protruding stamens can be of 2 types: with transversely attached, reniform anthers ('terminal anthers'), or with laterally attached, pointed anthers ('lateral anthers'). Filaments are often densely woolly (usually white- or yellow-hairy, but with violet hairs in *V. blattaria* and allies, and in *V. nigrum*). Ovary is superior, 2-locular, with a single style; fruit is an ovoid or globose capsule, up to *c.* 10 mm long, opening with 2 bifid valves, and containing numerous wrinkled seeds.

Several species are cultivated in gardens, and therefore often become naturalized far outside their native area, which (as with that of many other plants from ruderal habitats) is often hard to delimit anyway.

---

p.217 **Moth Mullein** *Verbascum blattaria* L.

Description: A plant with angular, usually unbranched stems to 1.5 m, with numerous glandular hairs above (but without stellate hairs). Leaves up to 20 cm long, 10 cm wide, ovate, coarsely crenate-dentate or almost lobed, dark green and glabrous or only sparsely hairy on both faces, basal ones often slightly cordate-based and always long-stalked (on stalks 5–20 cm long), upper ones sessile but not decurrent on stem. Flowers long-stalked (stalk at least twice as long as calyx) in long, lax raceme, each flower solitary in axil of its own bract; inflorescence simple, with glandular hairs but no stellate hairs. Corolla yellow (rarely white), 20–30 mm diam. Stamens 5, 2 lower ones with pointed anthers of 'lateral type', with violet-hairy filaments; 3 upper stamens with reniform anthers of 'terminal type', on violet- or white-hairy filaments.

Flowering: June–October.

Habitat: Rough grassland, waste places, roadsides, stream- and riversides, on moist to dry, mesotrophic, often calcareous, sandy, loamy or stony soils; from sea level to 700 m.

Range: S and C Europe, northwards to Belgium, C Germany, Poland and C Russia; naturalized in S Britain and the Netherlands.

Similar species: **Twiggy Mullein** (*V. virgatum* Stokes) is more glandular-hairy all over (with forked hairs), and has bracts 8–20 mm long (not 7–8 mm), with 1–5 short-stalked flowers (30–50 mm diam.) in their axils. In wasteland, field margins, roadsides, often on sandy soils, in SW Europe, northwards to W and C France and S Britain.

Purple Mullein (*V. phoeniceum* L.) has violet flowers with 5 equal stamens all with reniform anthers of 'terminal type' and violet-hairy filaments. In scrub, rough grassland, on riverbanks, in E and C Europe (westwards to W Germany).

Moth Mullein occasionally behaves like an annual.

p.117 **White Mullein** *Verbascum lychnitis* L.

Description: A plant with angular stems to 1.5 m, stickily hairy above. Leaves up to 30 cm long, 15 cm wide, ovate to lanceolate, crenate or subentire, short-hairy but dark green above, densely greyish-tomentose (with persistent stellate hairs) beneath, lower ones gradually narrowed into short stalk (1–30 mm, occasionally up to 10 cm), upper ones sessile, not decurrent on stem. Flowers rather long-stalked, clustered in dense racemes composing large, pyramidal panicle with stiffly erect branches. Corolla white (occasionally yellow), 10–20 mm diam. Stamens 5, all with reniform anthers of 'terminal type', on densely white-hairy filaments. Stigma button-shaped, wider than long, not decurrent on style.

Flowering: June–October.

Habitat: Scrub, hedgebanks, waste places, grassland, sand-dunes, sunny slopes, railway embankments, on dry or moist, mesotrophic to eutrophic, calcareous, sandy, loamy or stony soils; from sea level to 1,800 m.

Range: Most of Europe, northwards to the British Isles, the Low Countries, Denmark, Poland and C Russia; naturalized in S Fennoscandia.

Similar species: **Hoary Mullein** (*V. pulverulentum* Vill.) has cylindrical stems with divergent branches in inflorescence; leaves densely white-mealy on both faces (with stellate hairs peeling off in floccules), and flowers always yellow (15–20 mm diam.), with club-shaped stigmas (much longer than wide). In comparable habitats of S and W Europe, northwards to SE Britain, Belgium and S Germany.

---

p.217 **Dark Mullein** *Verbascum nigrum* L.

Description: A plant with angular stems to 1.5 m, often branched near base. Leaves up to 20 cm long, 10 cm wide, ovate, crenate-dentate, dark green and only sparsely stellate-hairy above, rather densely hairy and paler green beneath, basal ones often slightly cordate-based and always long-stalked (on stalks 5–20 cm long), upper ones sessile but not decurrent on stem. Flowers clustered (in groups of 5–10 per bract) in long, rather dense raceme; inflorescence simple or only with few branches below, with stellate hairs but no glandular hairs. Flower-stalks about equalling calyx. Corolla yellow with 5 purple blotches at centre, 18–25 mm diam. Stamens 5, all with reniform anthers of 'terminal type', on violet-hairy filaments.

Flowering: June–September.

Habitat: Rough grassland, roadsides, sunny banks and slopes, railway lines, on dry, mesotrophic, preferably calcareous, sandy, loamy or stony soils; from sea level to 1,800 m.

Range: Most of Europe, northwards to England, S Fennoscandia and N Russia, but rare in Mediterranean region.

Compare V. blattaria, which has only 1 flower per bract.

p.217 **Great Mullein** *Verbascum thapsus* L.

Description:
A plant to 2 m. Leaves up to 30 cm long, 15 cm wide, ovate to lanceolate, crenate, densely greyish- or white-tomentose on both faces, and with margins decurrent on stem towards next lower leaf. Flowers subsessile, clustered in dense, long, woolly spike (often little-branched). Corolla yellow, (12) 15–25 (35) mm diam. Stamens 5, the 2 lower ones with pointed anthers of 'lateral type', at most 1 third the length of their filament, which is glabrous or sparsely white-hairy; 3 upper stamens with reniform anthers of 'terminal type', on densely white- or yellowish-hairy filaments. Stigma button-shaped, not decurrent on style.

Flowering: June–October.

Habitat:
Scrub, woodland clearings, sand-dunes, roadsides, waste or ruderal places, also railway lines, on dry, oligotrophic to mesotrophic, preferably calcareous, sandy, loamy or stony soils; from sea level to 1,800 m.

Range:
Most of Europe except the extreme north and much of the Balkan peninsula.

Similar species:
V. densiflorum Bertol. has flowers (20) 30–50 mm diam., lower stamens with 'lateral' anthers at least half as long as their filament, and spatulate stigmas distinctly running down style. In comparable habitats of W and C Europe, northwards to S Sweden, but only naturalized in the British Isles.

Orange Mullein (*V. phlomoides* L.) has (often yellowish-hairy) leaves not or only shortly decurrent on stem (not all the way to next leaf), orange-yellow flowers (20) 30–55 mm diam., in less dense, often interrupted spike, and lower stamens and stigmas as in *V. densiflorum*. In comparable habitats, to 1,400 m, in continental Europe, northwards to Belgium and C Germany, and naturalized further north (and also in C and S Britain).

Great Mullein is also called Aaron's Rod.

Speedwells, *Veronica*

A large genus of herbs with mostly opposite or whorled, simple leaves; bracts in inflorescence often alternate. Flowers basically 4-merous, in axillary, paired (occasionally terminal, solitary) racemes. Sepals 4 (rarely 5), free or only connate at base. Corolla dish-shaped, usually with very short tube (but *see* group D below) and 4 spreading lobes, slightly irregular (with enlarged upper lobe and slightly reduced lower lobe); blue colours prevalent, but purplish, pink or white flowers are found in some species. Stamens 2, implanted on corolla tube, and far protruding from it; staminodes absent. Ovary superior, 2-locular, often with long, curved, descending style. Fruit a more or less compressed, heart-shaped or 2-lobed capsule, opening with 2 valves, and containing few to several seeds.

N European species can be informally grouped as follows:

A. Mostly annual, prostrate species with **flowers solitary** in axils of normal stem-leaves, spread along stem. One of them (*V. filiformisis*) is a mat-forming perennial with reniform, remotely crenate leaves. Of the remaining, annual species, *V. hederifolia* has palmately 3–7-lobed leaves; the others (*V. agrestis, V. opaca, V. polita, V. persica*) have ovate to suborbicular, crenate-dentate leaves.

B. Mostly perennial species with **flowers in axillary racemes** with tiny bracts, whereas main stem continues growth. These can be subdivided into 2 groups. The 1st contains **hairy, terrestrial** species, all with more or less ovate, usually crenate or dentate leaves. Of these, only 2 (*V. austriaca, V. prostrata*) have 5 sepals; the others (*V. officinalis, V. chamaedrys, V. montana*) have 4 sepals. The 2nd contains **subglabrous, aquatic** species: 1 (*V. beccabunga*) has broadly ovate or rounded leaves; the others (*V. anagallis-aquatica, V. anagalloides, V. catenata, V. scutellata*) have lanceolate to almost linear leaves.

C. Annual or perennial species with **flowers in terminal racemes** (rarely umbels, *see V. alpina*), with leaf-like bracts and **very short corolla tubes**. Perennials are *V. serpyllifolia* and the boreo-alpine species *V. fruticans* and *V. alpina*, all with (sub)entire leaves. The annuals are more numerous: of these *V. triphyllos* is quite distinct in having palmately divided leaves, while *V. verna* has pinnately divided leaves; the others (*V. praecox, V. acinifolia, V. arvensis, V. peregrina.*) have undivided leaves.

D. Perennial species with flowers in terminal or axillary, **spike-like racemes**, with inconspicuous bracts and **well-developed corolla tubes**: *V. longifolia, V. spicata*.

p.328 **Green Field-speedwell** *Veronica agrestis* L.

Description: A hairy annual with thin, spreading, simple
or branched stems to 30 cm. Leaves mostly
alternate (only lowest ones opposite), short-
stalked, pale green, broadly ovate to
suborbicular, crenate, 5–20 mm long.
Flowers solitary on long stalks in leaf-axils.
Sepals 4, equal, elliptical, blunt-tipped,
slightly hairy and ciliate. Corolla 5–8 mm
wide, pale blue with dark-blue veins, upper
lobe darker blue or lilac (rarely pink), lower
lobe whitish. Capsule 2-lobed, with
spreading lobes (with glandular hairs only)
and very short style (not protruding from
notch), containing 2–7 seeds per locule;
fruit-stalks recurved, not much longer than
accompanying leaf.

Flowering: April–October (winter).

Habitat: Cultivated land, gardens, churchyards,
hedges, on moist or dry, eutrophic, acid or
calcareous, sandy, loamy or clayey soils; from
sea level to 1,800 m.

Range: Most of Europe except Iceland and the high
Arctic; rare in the deep south.

Similar species: **Grey Field-speedwell** (*V. polita* Fries) has
mostly opposite, dark greyish-green leaves,
uniformly bright-blue flowers (5–8 mm
wide, occasionally with whitish lower lobe,
rarely all white), subacute, broadly ovate
sepals, and glandular-hairy capsules with
(2) 7–9 (15) seeds per locule, and styles to
1.5 mm, distinctly protruding from notch.
In cultivated land, on moist, eutrophic,
calcareous, often heavy soils, in most of
Europe except the Arctic.
V. opaca Fries has mostly opposite, dull-
green leaves, uniformly dark-blue flowers
(3–4, rarely up to 7 mm wide), blunt,
spatulate sepals, and glandular-hairy
capsules with (2) 5–6 (7) seeds per locule,
with short style. In cultivated and waste
land, on moist, eutrophic, calcareous,
heavy soils, in continental Europe,
northwards to S Scandinavia. • These
2 species have become rare. *Compare also
V. persica (see* p.1076), which has larger
flowers and very long fruit-stalks.

p.327 **Blue Water-speedwell**
Veronica anagallis-aquatica L.

Description: A *glabrous* (rarely slightly hairy) perennial, to 60 cm, with erect or ascending, bluntly quadrangular, greenish (occasionally red-flushed), hollow stems. Leaves opposite, (narrowly) *elliptical or lanceolate* (lower ones sometimes ovate), pointed, weakly serrate-dentate, 6–12 cm long, sessile (or only lower ones short-stalked). Flowers short-stalked, in long, dense, *axillary racemes*; flower-bracts minute, linear, not longer than flower-stalks. Sepals 4, ovate to lanceolate, glabrous, erect on fruit. Corolla 5–10 mm wide, pale blue (occasionally lilac or pink) with darker veins. *Capsule ovoid to subglobose* (scarcely compressed, not notched), glabrous; style nearly as long as fruit; fruit-stalks erect.

Flowering: May–September.

Habitat: Shallow water of pools, ditches, streams, rivers, lakes, also marshy meadows, on wet, mesotrophic, sandy, muddy or peaty soils; from sea level to 1,800 m.

Range: Most of Europe except the high Arctic.

Similar species: *V. anagalloides* Guss. has white flowers (3–5 mm wide), occasionally with lilac veins, and ellipsoid capsules. In comparable habitats in S, C and E Europe, northwards to E France, C Germany, Czechoslovakia and C Russia.

Pink Water-speedwell (*V. catenata* Pennell) has often purplish stems, narrowly lanceolate leaves (all sessile), elliptical sepals (divergent on fruit), pale-pink, darker-veined corollas (3–5 mm wide), and lanceolate flower-bracts exceeding flower-stalks that become spreading in fruit. In comparable habitats, in all of Europe except the high Arctic. *Compare also V. scutellata (see* p.1078), which has alternate (not opposite) racemes.

---

p.327 **Wall Speedwell** *Veronica arvensis* L.

Description: A glandular-hairy annual, with erect or prostrate stems to 30 cm, usually branched. Leaves mostly opposite, short-stalked to subsessile, 5–15 mm long, triangular-ovate with cordate base, crenate-dentate. Flowers short-stalked, in dense, *terminal racemes* with alternate, sessile, narrowly ovate or lanceolate, *leaf-like, weakly dentate bracts*. Sepals 4, *very unequal*, lanceolate, glandular-hairy. Corolla 2–3 mm wide, blue. Capsule broadly heart-shaped (about as long as broad), notched, glandular-ciliate on margins; style short (*c.* 1 mm), distinctly exceeding notch.

Flowering: April–August (autumn).

Habitat: Cultivated and waste land, bare places in grassland, sand-dunes, also paving stones and old walls, on dry or moist, oligotrophic to mesotrophic, preferably calcareous, sandy, loamy or stony soils; from sea level to 2,000 m.

Range: Most of Europe except the extreme north.

Similar species: **American Speedwell** (*V. peregrina* L.) is glabrous, with elliptical, weakly dentate leaves narrowed into short, broad stalk, and white flowers. Native to the Americas; locally naturalized in Europe, in cultivated land, damp ruderal places and along streams and ponds.

---

p.326 **Large Speedwell** *Veronica austriaca* L.

Description: A hairy perennial, with erect or ascending stems to 30 (50) cm. Leaves opposite, sessile, ovate or elliptical, deeply crenate-serrate, up to 60 mm long. Flowers in long, dense, *axillary racemes*; flower-bracts small. *Sepals mostly 5*, lanceolate, hairy, 5th one often small. Corolla (8) 10–13 (17) mm wide, violet-blue. Capsule heart-shaped, hairy; style about as long as fruit.

Flowering: May–August.

Habitat: Grassland, riverine sand-dunes, sunny banks and slopes, on dry, oligotrophic, calcareous, sandy, loamy or stony soils; from sea level to 1,800 m.

Range: S and C Europe, locally northwards to N France, the Netherlands, Poland and C Russia.

Similar species: *V. prostrata* L. has prostrate stems, elliptical to almost linear, weakly dentate or subentire leaves, blue flowers (6) 8–11 mm wide, and glabrous calyces and fruits. In comparable habitats of W and C Europe.

The description of Large Speedwell pertains to the widely distributed ssp. *teucrium* (L.) D.A. Webb. Ssp. *austriaca*, which has deeply incised, pinnate leaves, is restricted to mountains of C Europe.

---

p.327 **Brooklime** *Veronica beccabunga* L.

Description: A *glabrous* perennial, with fleshy, creeping and ascending, cylindrical, solid stems to 60 cm. Leaves opposite, *ovate or suborbicular*, round-tipped, shallowly crenate, 30–60 mm long, short-stalked, slightly fleshy. Flowers in long, rather dense, *axillary racemes*; flower-bracts minute. Sepals 4, elliptical, subacute, glabrous. Corolla 6–8 mm wide, pale or bright blue (rarely pink). *Capsule subglobose* (scarcely compressed, nor notched), glabrous; style about half as long as fruit.

Flowering: May–September.

Habitat: Shallow water of pools, ditches, streams, rivers and lakes, also in marshy meadows, flushes, fens, carrs, on wet, mesotrophic to eutrophic, sandy, muddy or peaty soils; from sea level to 2,400 m.

Range: Most of Europe except the high Arctic.

---

p.328 **Germander Speedwell**
Veronica chamaedrys L.

Description: A hairy perennial, with *erect or ascending* stems to 30 (50) cm (hairy on opposite sides). Leaves opposite, ovate or elliptical, crenate-dentate, up to 30 mm long, sessile or short-stalked (stalks to 6 mm). Flowers long-stalked, in rather lax, *axillary racemes*; flower-bracts minute. Sepals 4, oblanceolate, hairy. Corolla (8) 10–14 mm wide, bright blue with darker veins and some white near throat. Capsule heart-shaped, shallowly notched, hairy; style about as long as fruit.

Flowering: April–July.

Habitat: Grassland, road verges, sand-dunes, open woods, hedgerows, grassy banks, on moist to dry, mesotrophic, acid or calcareous, sandy, loamy or stony soils; from sea level to 2,200 m.

Range: Most of Europe except the high Arctic, and only naturalized in Iceland.

Compare *V. officinalis* (creeping stems), and *V. montana* (long-stalked leaves).

---

p.313 **Slender Speedwell** *Veronica filiformis* Sm.

Description: A delicate, hairy, *mat-forming* perennial with numerous *threadlike, creeping* (rooting), branched stems to 30 cm. Leaves alternate (but opposite on non-flowering stems), short-stalked (1–2 mm), pale green, rounded or reniform, remotely crenate, 3–10 mm long. *Flowers solitary* on very long stalks in leaf-axils. Sepals 4, equal, elliptical, blunt-tipped, hairy and ciliate. Corolla 8–12 (15) mm wide, pale lilac with darker veins, lower lobe usually whitish. Capsule (rarely formed) 2-lobed, 4–5 mm wide, ciliate, with subparallel lobes and long style (3 mm) far exceeding sinus; fruit-stalks at least twice the length of accompanying leaf.

Flowering: April–July.

Habitat: Lawns, pastures, road verges, streamsides, occasionally in wasteland, on moist to dry, mesotrophic, sandy or clayey soils; mainly in the lowland.

Range: Native to the Caucasus and Asia Minor; naturalized in much of Europe, northwards to Denmark.

Frequently planted in rock gardens.

---

p.313 **Ivy-leaved Speedwell** *Veronica hederifolia* L.

Description: A hairy annual with spreading, simple or branched stems to 60 cm. Leaves mostly alternate (only lowest ones opposite), long-stalked, dark green and slightly fleshy, 5–15 (25) mm long, reniform or suborbicular, *palmately 3–5-lobed*, middle lobe largest. *Flowers solitary* on long stalks in leaf-axils. Sepals 4, equal, ovate with cordate base, long-ciliate. Corolla 6–9 mm wide, pale bluish-lilac with white centre. *Capsule subglobose*, slightly flattened above but not laterally compressed, *slightly 2–4-lobed*, barely notched, glabrous, with short style (0.7–1.2 mm), containing (1) 2–4 seeds in all; fruit-stalks recurved, longer than accompanying leaf, with a hairy line all way up to flower; *calyx strongly enlarged in fruit*, with sepals pressing against each other.

Flowering: March–August.

Habitat: Cultivated and waste land, open grassland, road verges, ruderal and disturbed places, on dry, mesotrophic to eutrophic, acid or calcareous, sandy or clayey soils; from sea level to 900 m.

Range: Most of Europe except Iceland and the high Arctic.

The description pertains to ssp. *hederifolia* (a very common weed). Ssp. *lucorum* (Richter) Hartl grows more erect, and has thin, pale-green, 5–7-lobed leaves, pale-lilac or whitish corollas (4–6 mm wide), very short styles (0.3–0.7 mm), and fruit-stalks hairy all round (at least under flower). In woods, hedgerows, on shaded banks, often in somewhat ruderal environments, in C, N and NW Europe.

---

p.326 **Long-leaved Speedwell**
Veronica longifolia L.

Description: A stout, glabrous or slightly hairy perennial, with erect stems to 1.2 m. Leaves opposite or in whorls of 3–4, short-stalked, 4–12 cm long, ovate or lanceolate, pointed, sharply serrate. Flowers in long, dense, erect, *terminal, spike-like raceme*, often with 2–3 racemes immediately below; flower-bracts small. Sepals 4, lanceolate, ciliate. Corolla 6–8 mm wide, violet-blue (rarely white), with well-*developed corolla tube* (longer than wide). Capsule heart-shaped, notched, glabrous; style longer than fruit.

Flowering: June–August.

Habitat: River, stream, ditch and pond margins, in damp, ruderal places, also railway lines, on wet, mesotrophic, slightly acid, sandy or loamy soils; from sea level to 1,200 m.

Range: E and C Europe, locally westwards to E France, the Low Countries, S Sweden; naturalized in Britain.

Similar species: **Spiked Speedwell** (*V. spicata* L.) has similar, terminal, spike-like raceme (always borne singly), but is mat-forming, with ascending flowering stems to 30 cm, elliptical to oblanceolate, hairy leaves (lower ones often long-stalked), bright-or violet-blue flowers 4–8 mm wide (also with well-developed tube), and barely notched capsules. In dry, calcareous grassland, often on stony soils, in S, C and E Europe, locally northwards to Britain, C France, S Fennoscandia and NW Russia. Both species are frequently cultivated in gardens.

p.313 **Wood Speedwell** *Veronica montana* L.

Description: A hairy perennial, with *spreading or ascending* stems (hairy all round) to 30 (50) cm. Leaves opposite, ovate or elliptical, crenate-dentate, up to 30 mm long, on stalks (5) 7–15 mm long. Flowers long-stalked, few together in lax, *axillary racemes*; flower-bracts minute. Sepals 4, narrowly obovate, ciliate. Corolla 8–10 mm wide, pale lilac with darker veins. Capsule 2-lobed, notched on both sides, with glandular hairs on margin; style nearly as long as fruit.

Flowering: April–July.

Habitat: Damp, deciduous woods, streamsides, woodland paths, on moist, oligotrophic, weakly acid, humus-rich, sandy, loamy or stony soils; from sea level to 1,500 m.

Range: S and C Europe, northwards to the British Isles, Denmark and Poland, and eastwards to the Caucasus.

Compare V. chamaedrys, which has stems with 2 hairy lines.

p.329 **Heath Speedwell** *Veronica officinalis* L.

Description: A hairy perennial, with *creeping* and ascending stems (hairy all round) to 30 (50) cm. Leaves opposite, (ob)ovate or elliptical, shallowly crenate-serrate, up to 30 mm long, on short stalks to 6 mm. Flowers short-stalked, in long, rather dense, *axillary racemes*; flower-bracts minute. Sepals 4, (ob)lanceolate, hairy. Corolla 6–8 mm wide, pale blue with darker veins (rarely dark blue, lilac, pink or white). Capsule heart-shaped or triangular (scarcely notched), hairy; style about as long as fruit.

Flowering: May–August.

Habitat: Heaths, open woods, woodland clearings, pastures, sand-dunes, road verges, on dry, oligotrophic, mildly acid or calcareous, sandy, loamy or stony soils; from sea level to 2,000 m.

Range: Most of Europe except the high Arctic, eastwards to the Caucasus.

Another name is Common Speedwell. *Compare V. chamaedrys (see* p.1072), which has stems with 2 hairy lines.

---

p.328 **Common Field-speedwell**
Veronica persica Poiret

Description: A hairy annual with thin, spreading (occasionally rooting), simple or branched stems to 60 cm. Leaves mostly alternate (only lowest ones opposite), short-stalked (3–8 mm), pale green, broadly ovate, crenate, 10–30 mm long. *Flowers solitary* on very long stalks in leaf-axils. Sepals 4, equal, narrowly ovate, subacute, ciliate. Corolla 8–12 mm wide, bright blue with darker veins, lower lobe usually whitish. Capsule 2-lobed, reniform, with strongly divergent to almost spreading, hairy, keeled lobes and very long style (far protruding from notch); fruit-stalks recurved, at least twice length of accompanying leaf.

Flowering: April–October (winter).

Habitat: Cultivated and waste land, gardens, manure-heaps, on moist, (very) eutrophic, acid or calcareous, preferably loamy or clayey soils; from sea level to 1,600 m.

Range: Native to SW Asia; naturalized in most of Europe except Iceland and the Arctic.

First observed in W Europe at the start of the 18th century; it soon became very common in the agricultural landscape. *Compare V. agrestis* (*see* p.1069) and allies, which have smaller flowers and shorter fruit-stalks.

---

p.329 **Breckland Speedwell** *Veronica praecox* All.

Description: A tiny, glandular-hairy annual, with erect, branched or simple stems to 25 cm (often much less). Leaves mostly opposite, short-stalked to subsessile, 5–15 mm long, broadly ovate, coarsely crenate-dentate. Flowers rather short-stalked, in long, lax, *terminal racemes* (often occupying much of stem) with alternate, sessile, *leaf-like, dentate or lobed bracts*. Sepals 4, narrowly elliptical, glandular-hairy, slightly shorter than flower-stalk. Corolla (3) 5–7 mm wide, blue. Capsule broadly elliptical or slightly heart-shaped, distinctly notched, glandular-hairy; style rather short, but well exceeding notch.

Flowering: March–June.

Habitat: Cultivated and waste land, short grassland, riverine sand-dunes, sunny banks and slopes, on dry, mesotrophic, preferably acid, sandy or stony soils; from sea level to 500 m.

Range: S, C and W Europe, northwards to England, Belgium (possibly extinct in the Netherlands), S Sweden (Gotland), Poland and W and E Russia.

Similar species: **French Speedwell** (*V. acinifolia* L.) has ovate to lanceolate, entire-margined leaves (lower ones often slightly dentate), flowers only 2–3 mm wide, and broadly heart-shaped capsules (wider than long) with very short style, barely exceeding notch. In comparable habitats, often on heavier soils, in S and SC Europe, north to NC France, S Germany, Czechoslovakia, Romania and the Crimea.

Both species have become very rare in the north.

p.93 **Marsh Speedwell** *Veronica scutellata* L.

Description: A *glabrous* (rarely slightly hairy) perennial,
with creeping and ascending, bluntly
quadrangular, solid stems to 30 cm. Leaves
opposite, *linear-lanceolate*, weakly serrate-
dentate or entire, 20–40 mm long, all sessile.
Flowers long-stalked, in lax, *alternating,
axillary racemes* (only 1 per node); flower-
bracts minute, lanceolate, much shorter than
flower-stalks. Sepals 4, lanceolate, glabrous,
divergent on fruit. Corolla 5–6 mm wide,
white with blue or pink veins. *Capsule strongly
compressed*, 2-lobed, deeply notched, glabrous;
style nearly as long as fruit.

Flowering: May–September.

Habitat: Marshes, bogs, fens, meadows, ditches, dune-
slacks, pond margins, on wet, oligotrophic to
mesotrophic, slightly acid, sandy, muddy or
peaty soils; from sea level to 1,800 m.

Range: Most of Europe except the high Arctic and
the deep south.

*Compare V. anagallis-aquatica (see p.1070)
and allies, which have 2 opposite racemes
per node.*

---

p.326 **Thyme-leaved Speedwell**
Veronica serpyllifolia L.

Description: A *subglabrous* perennial, with creeping and
ascending stems to 25 cm (often less).
Leaves opposite, short-stalked to sessile,
elliptical to suborbicular, *entire-margined*,
10–20 mm long. Flowers in long, *terminal
racemes* with alternate, *leaf-like bracts* much
exceeding flower-stalks. Sepals 4, narrowly
elliptical, glabrous but for some sessile
glands, and shorter than flower-stalk.
Corolla 6–8 mm wide, whitish or pale blue
with dark violet-blue veins. Capsule broadly
heart-shaped, distinctly notched, slightly
glandular; style nearly as long as fruit.

Flowering: March–October.

Habitat: Open pastures, lawns, pathsides, also cultivated and waste land, on moist, mesotrophic,
slightly acid or calcareous, sandy, loamy or
stony soils; from sea level to 2,500 m.

Range: Most of Europe except Spitsbergen.

Similar species: **Rock Speedwell** (*V. fruticans* Jacq.) has stems woody below and hairy above, in dense tufts; leaves and bracts elliptical or narrowly obovate, occasionally weakly dentate, subsessile, *c.* 10 mm long, crowded below; flowers 10–15 mm wide, deep blue with purplish ring round white throat, in lax, few-flowered racemes; capsules ovate, barely notched, with styles nearly as long as fruits. In grassland and rocky places, in mountains of C Europe, and also in Scotland, Iceland and Scandinavia.

Alpine Speedwell (*V. alpina* L.) is similar, but never woody at base; flowers paler blue, 7–8 mm wide, in rather dense, contracted, umbel-shaped racemes; capsules ellipsoid and barely notched with very short style. Distribution similar to Rock Speedwell's.

---

p.327 **Fingered Speedwell** *Veronica triphyllos* L.

Description: A tiny, glandular-hairy annual, with erect or ascending, branched or simple stems to 15 cm (often much less). Leaves mostly opposite, short-stalked to subsessile, 5–15 mm long, broadly ovate, *palmately lobed or divided* with 3–7 obovate or elliptical segments, central lobe largest. Flowers long-stalked, in lax, *terminal racemes* with alternate, sessile, *leaf-like, trifid bracts*; highest bracts often undivided. Sepals 4, lanceolate, glandular-hairy, shorter than flower-stalk. Corolla 6–9 mm wide, blue. Capsule broadly heart-shaped or suborbicular, distinctly notched, glandular-hairy; style short, barely exceeding notch.

Flowering: March–July.

Habitat: Arable fields, bare places in grassland, roadsides, occasionally old walls, on dry or moist, mesotrophic, preferably acid, sandy, clayey or stony soils; from sea level to 1,500 m.

Range: S and C Europe, northwards to England, S Sweden, Latvia and C Russia.

Becoming very rare in the north of its area.

p.329 **Spring Speedwell** *Veronica verna* L.

Description: A tiny, slightly hairy (rarely glandular) annual, with erect stems to 15 cm (often much less), usually branched from base. Leaves mostly opposite, short-stalked to subsessile, 5–15 mm long, ovate, *pinnately lobed or divided* with 3–7 obovate or elliptical segments. Flowers rather short-stalked, in dense, *terminal racemes* with alternate, sessile, *leaf-like, pinnately divided bracts*; highest bracts often undivided. Sepals 4, *unequal*, lanceolate, finely hairy, often slightly longer than flower-stalk. Corolla 2–3 mm wide, blue. Capsule broadly heart-shaped (wider than long), shallowly notched, ciliate on margins; style short (0.5 mm), just exceeding notch.

Flowering: May–July.

Habitat: Short grassland, cultivated and waste land, sand-dunes, sunny banks and slopes, on dry, oligotrophic, slightly acid, sandy, clayey or stony soils; from sea level to 2,000 m.

Range: In Europe northwards to SE England, S Fennoscandia and N Russia.

Becoming very rare in the north.

NIGHTSHADE FAMILY, SOLANACEAE

A family of herbs and some shrubs or small trees with *c.* 2,300 species in 90 genera in warm and temperate regions of the world. Dicots. Leaves usually alternate, simple or pinnate. Flowers mostly regular, hermaphrodite, basically 5-merous, with connate perianth parts. Calyx 5-toothed. Corolla 5-lobed. Stamens 5, implanted on corolla tube, occasionally 1 or 3 reduced to sterile staminodes. Ovary superior, 2–5-locular (often 2-locular), with 1 style. Fruit a berry or a capsule. Many species are poisonous. The genus *Solanum* alone contains *c.* 1,500 species, amongst which the Potato (*S. tuberosum*), Tomato (*S. lycopersicum*) and Egg-plant (*S. melongena*) are economically important as food-plants. Paprika (*Capsicum longum*), Red or Cayenne Pepper (*C. annuum*, *C. frutescens*), Tobacco (*Nicotiana* species), and Cape Gooseberry (*Physalis alkekengi*) also belong to this family.

p.42 **Deadly Nightshade** *Atropa belladonna* L.

Description: A glabrous perennial with erect,
branched stems to 1 (1.5) m. Leaves
short-stalked, alternate, upper ones
opposite (then very *unequal*, 1 leaf much
smaller), up to 20 cm long, ovate or
elliptical, pointed, entire-margined.
Flowers stalked, nodding, solitary in
upper leaf-axils and branch-forkings,
25–30 mm long. Calyx deeply incised,
5-parted, spreading and persistent on
fruit. *Corolla bell-shaped*, with wide tube
and 5 short lobes, *purplish-brown or
greenish*, often yellowish-green inside.
Stamens 5. Fruit a globose, *shiny-black
berry*, 15–20 mm diam.

Flowering: June–September.

Habitat: Open woods, woodland clearings, scrub,
shaded road verges, on moist, oligotrophic,
calcareous, sandy, loamy or stony soils; from
sea level to 1,700 m.

Range: S and C Europe, northwards to England,
the Low Countries, Germany, Poland, and
C Russia.

A highly poisonous plant, containing
several deadly alkaloids, a.o. hyoscyamine
and atropine. From medieval times it was
cultivated for medicinal purposes; many
wild occurrences derive from former
cultivation, especially in the lowland. The
species has become rare in many areas.

p.104 **Thornapple** *Datura stramonium* L.

Description: A (sub)glabrous annual, with erect,
branched stems to 1 (1.5) m. Leaves
stalked, alternate, up to 20 cm long, ovate
or elliptical, coarsely and *irregularly dentate*
or even lobed. Flowers erect, short-stalked
or subsessile, solitary in upper leaf-axils,
5–10 cm long. Calyx tube-shaped, sharply
5-angled, with short, broadly triangular
teeth; only calyx base remains on fruit.
Corolla funnel-shaped, with long, narrow
tube and 5 large, spreading, pointed lobes,
white. Stamens 5. Ovary incompletely

4-locular. Fruit a large, ovoid, brownish capsule, 30–70 mm long, usually covered with numerous stout spines (but occasionally smooth).

Flowering: June–October.

Habitat: Cultivated and waste land, vineyards, ruderal and disturbed places, on dry, oligotrophic to mesotrophic, preferably calcareous, sandy, loamy or stony soils; from sea level to *c.* 1,300 m.

Range: Native to N America; locally naturalized in S and C Europe, but merely casual further north.

The whole plant is highly poisonous. A few related species with spiny stems can be found naturalized in C Europe.

---

p.317 **Henbane** *Hyoscyamus niger* L.

Description: A stickily glandular-hairy annual or biennial, with erect, branched or simple stems to 80 cm. Leaves short-stalked (upper ones sessile and clasping), alternate, up to 20 cm long, ovate or elliptical, pointed, often coarsely dentate or lobed. Flowers subsessile, erect or spreading, solitary in upper leaf-axils, 20–30 mm long, slightly irregular. Calyx urn-shaped, with 5 divergent, triangular teeth, enlarged and persistent on fruit. *Corolla funnel-shaped*, with wide tube and 5 spreading, rounded lobes, *dull yellow with purplish-brown, netted veins*, tube purplish-brown inside. Stamens 5. Fruit a broadly ovoid, brownish capsule, 12–20 mm diam., opening through dehiscence of apical lid.

Flowering: June–October.

Habitat: Ruderal and disturbed places, roadsides, often near farmyards, also sand-dunes and floodmarks at sea, on dry, oligotrophic or mesotrophic, calcareous, sandy or stony soils; from sea level to 1,900 m.

Range: Most of Europe except the extreme north.

The whole plant is highly poisonous, and has a foetid smell, especially when bruised.

p.343 **Bittersweet** *Solanum dulcamara* L.

Description: A more or less hairy perennial, with straggling or climbing, purplish stems to 2 (3) m, often becoming woody at base. Leaves stalked, alternate, dull green, 4–8 cm long, *ovate or hastate* (then with 2 ovate, spreading lobes at base of blade), otherwise entire-margined. Flowers long-stalked, in lax, 10–20-flowered cymes in leaf-axils. Calyx small, with 5 short, blunt lobes, often dark violet. *Corolla star-shaped*, 10–15 mm diam., with very short tube and 5 recurved, lanceolate lobes, *purplish-violet* (rarely white) with 2 small, green spots at base of each corolla lobe. Stamens 5, far-protruding, *anthers connate* into bright-yellow cone, opened at top to let through thin, white style. Fruit an ellipsoid, *scarlet berry*, c. 10 mm long.

Flowering: June–September.

Habitat: Damp, deciduous woods, scrub, hedges, lake- and streamsides, reedlands, occasionally dune-slacks, also pollard-willows, on wet, mesotrophic, acid or calcareous, sandy or muddy soils; from sea level to 1,700 m.

Range: Most of Europe except the extreme north.

Similar species: *S. marinum* (Bab.) Pojark., often treated as a variety, grows prostrate. On floodmarks, on coastal shingle-beeches. Coastal forms are generally more hairy.

---

p.153 **Black Nightshade** *Solanum nigrum* L.

Description: A more or less hairy annual, with erect to spreading, green or dark-violet, usually angular stems to 60 cm. Leaves stalked, alternate, dull green (occasionally tinged with purple, especially beneath), 30–60 mm long, ovate, entire-margined or irregularly dentate to even lobed. Flowers long-stalked, in lax, 5–10-flowered cymes in leaf-axils. Calyx small, 1–3 mm long, with 5 short, blunt lobes. *Corolla star-shaped*, 7–12 mm diam., with very short tube and 5 spreading or recurved, lanceolate lobes, *white*. Stamens 5, far-protruding, *anthers connate* into yellow tube, opened at top to let through stigma. Fruit a globose, *black or green* (rarely yellow) berry, 6–10 mm diam.

Flowering: June–October.

Habitat: Cultivated and waste land, gardens, disturbed roadsides, ruderal places, on moist to rather dry, (very) eutrophic, slightly acid or calcareous soils; from sea level to 1,700 m.

Range: Most of Europe except the extreme north.

Similar species: **Green Nightshade** (*S. nitidibaccatum* Bitter) from S America has locally naturalized along rivers, in cultivated land, and in the industrial landscape of W Europe; it has larger calyces (3–5 mm) becoming strongly enlarged (up to 13 mm long) in fruit, and always shiny green, veined berries.

Hairy Nightshade (*S. luteum* Mill.) is densely glandular-hairy, and has short-stalked flowers in 3–5-flowered cymes, and yellow or red berries. In ruderal places of E, S and C Europe, northwards to N France and S Germany, and locally naturalized further north. *S. triflorum* Nuttall from N America has pinnately divided or lobed leaves, 2–3-flowered cymes, and larger, green berries (10–15 mm) with whitish, netted veins; it has locally naturalized in coastal dunes and other sandy places of W Europe.

The description of Black Nightshade pertains to ssp. *nigrum*, which is a common weed in Europe; plants with green stems and berries appear to be less frequent. The plant is poisonous, although berries are eaten in S Europe, apparently without much damage to health; possibly there are less poisonous races. The ssp. *schultesii* (Opiz) Wessely is generally more hairy, and also has long glandular hairs on upper stem, and regularly dentate leaves. Native to S and E Europe, and locally naturalized in ruderal places in the west.

BUR-REED FAMILY, SPARGANIACEAE

A family of glabrous, usually aquatic, perennial herbs, with creeping rhizomes and erect, emergent flowering stems, with only 1 genus (*Sparganium*) containing *c.* 15 species in cold and temperate regions of the northern hemisphere and Australia. Monocots. Leaves linear, strap-shaped, emergent or floating, all basal, sheathing, in 2 rows. Flowers unisexual, monoecious, in sessile, globose heads forming interrupted terminal or axillary spikes, the latter subtended by leaf-like bract. Each spike bears a few large female heads below and 1 to several small male heads at the top; lower spikes often reduced to single, stalked or even sessile, female head. Perianth small, usually composed of 3 linear or spatulate, free parts (but often 6-parted in female flowers), occasionally absent. Stamens 3–6, far-protruding. Ovary superior, sessile or stalked, 1–2-locular, with 1 stout style. Fruit a small nut or drupe, often with spongy wall, and containing 1–2 seeds; fruiting heads bur-like, rather spiny-looking on account of the prominent styles. For determinations, always study ripe fruits, as can be found from July onwards.

p.44 **Unbranched Bur-reed**
Sparganium emersum Rehmann

Description: An erect, emergent perennial to 60 cm. Leaves erect and emergent or floating, barely overtopping stem, *3–12 mm wide*, triangular in section, or (in floating forms) flat and keeled. Inflorescence apparently *unbranched*, composed of 3–6 single-headed female spikes, only terminal spike with 1–2 female heads (to 15 mm diam.) and (3) 4–10 small male heads. Perianth parts brownish, not dark-tipped. Fruit narrowly ovoid or spindle-shaped, 3–5 mm long, *c.* 2 mm wide, *distinctly stalked* (stalk at least 1 mm long); style straight, 3–4 mm long.

Flowering: June–September.

Habitat: Shallow, stagnant or slow-moving, mesotrophic or eutrophic waters; mainly in the lowland.

Range: Most of Europe except the extreme north and parts of the Mediterranean region.

Similar species: *S. gramineum* Georgi has bent styles, and usually 1–2 stalked spikes below, each with 2–3 clustered, female heads. In comparable habitats of Scandinavia.

Floating Bur-reed (*S. angustifolium* Michx.) has narrower, usually floating leaves (2–6 mm wide, flat above, slightly convex beneath, weakly keeled, and with inflated sheaths), 2–4 single-headed female spikes (with bracts at least 10 cm long, up to 50 cm), and only (1) 2–3 (5) terminal male heads. In oligotrophic waters, often on peaty soils, in all of Europe except Spitsbergen, but is becoming rare owing to eutrophication. *S. glomeratum* Laest. ex Beurl., from Scandinavia, is much like Floating Bur-reed, but has distinctly keeled, flat leaves, and all heads clustered together. *Compare also S. natans.*

---

p.44 **Branched Bur-reed** *Sparganium erectum* L.

Description: An erect, emergent perennial to 1.5 m. Leaves usually erect and emergent, over-topping stem, (6) 10–20 mm wide, strongly keeled, triangular near base. Inflorescence conspicuously *branched*, composed of several long spikes with 1–4 female heads (to 18 mm diam.) and often several small male heads. Perianth parts brownish with dark, rounded tip. Fruit 5–8 mm long, 3–6 mm wide, angled and rimmed (abruptly 'shouldered'), with yellowish-brown, obconical base, and *domed, soot-black apex*; style short, thick, straight, *c.* 2 mm long.

Flowering: June–September.

Habitat: Shallow, mesotrophic or eutrophic, fresh water of lakes, pools and ditches, also in reedlands and marshes, on sandy, muddy or peaty soils; mainly in the lowland.

Range: Most of Europe except the far north.

The description pertains to ssp. *erectum*, which is common throughout the range. Ssp. *neglectum* (Beeby) Schinz & Thell. has narrower, pale-brownish fruits (6–10 mm long), with gently curved rim and high-domed apex gradually narrowed into long, slender style (*c.* 4 mm). In comparable habitats, presumably more frequent in mesotrophic inland waters, especially in stream-valleys.

p.45 **Least Bur-reed** *Sparganium natans* L.

Description:	A floating perennial with trailing, barely emergent stems to 1 m. Leaves always floating, *2–6 mm wide*, flat at both faces, *unkeeled*, translucent. Inflorescence apparently *unbranched*, composed of 2–3 subsessile, single-headed female spikes (to 10 mm diam.), and 1–2 terminal male heads; *all bracts shorter than 80 mm*. Perianth parts brownish, not dark-tipped. Fruit 3–4 mm long, 1.5–2 mm wide, narrowly ovoid or spindle-shaped; style straight, only 0.5–1 mm long.
Flowering:	June–August.
Habitat:	Shallow, oligotrophic or mesotrophic, slightly acid waters, moor pools, fens, flushes, often on peaty substrates; from sea level to 1,000 m.
Range:	Most of Europe except Spitsbergen and much of Mediterranean region.
Similar species:	*S. hyperboreum* Laest. ex Beurl. has slightly thicker, opaque leaves, and clustered female heads. In comparable habitats of Scandinavia. *Compare also S. angustifolium* (see p.1086), which has keeled leaves, inflated leaf-sheaths, and longer bracts.

DAPHNE FAMILY, THYMELAEACEAE

A family of trees and shrubs (rarely herbs) with *c.* 500 species in 45 genera, mainly in warm regions. Dicots. Leaves alternate (occasionally opposite), simple. Flowers regular, usually hermaphrodite and 4-merous, in clusters or short racemes (rarely solitary); receptacle urn- or tube-shaped, resembling a calyx tube. True calyx 4–6-parted, often coloured, implanted on rim of receptacle, together with 4–6-parted corolla (which can be absent). Stamens 2–10 (often 8), implanted high on receptacle. Ovary superior, usually 1-locular, with 1 style. Fruit a 1-seeded drupe or achene.

p.71 **Spurge Laurel** *Daphne laureola* L.

Description:	An erect, *evergreen shrub*, to 1 m, with glabrous, green shoots. Leaves alternate, narrowly obovate or oblanceolate, entire-margined, *leathery*, deep shiny green,

crowded towards shoot tips. Flowers 8–12 mm long, in short, dense, 3–10-flowered, axillary racemes. *Calyx greenish-yellow*, with 4 spreading, petal-like lobes. True corolla absent. Fruit a subglobose, *shiny-black drupe*.

Flowering: (January) March–April.

Habitat: Open, deciduous woods, scrub, on dry, oligotrophic, preferably calcareous, sandy, loamy or stony soils; from sea level to 1,600 m.

Range: S, SC and W Europe, northwards to England, Belgium, S Germany, Hungary, and Romania.

Poisonous!

---

p.282 **Mezereon** *Daphne mezereum* L.

Description: An erect, *deciduous shrub* to 0.8 (1.5) m, with greyish, hairy shoots. Leaves alternate, oblanceolate, entire-margined, thin and soft, often pale or yellowish-green, crowded towards shoot-tips. Flowers appearing just before leaves, fragrant, 7–10 mm long, in mostly 3-flowered clusters (occasionally solitary), axillary to leaf-traces of fallen leaves from previous year. *Calyx purplish-pink*, with 4 spreading, petal-like lobes. True corolla absent. Fruit a globose, *shiny-red drupe*.

Flowering: (December) February–May.

Habitat: Deciduous woods, scrub, on moist, oligo-trophic, preferably calcareous, sandy, loamy or stony soils; from sea level to 2,000 m.

Range: S and C Europe, northwards to England, C Scandinavia, S Finland, and NC Russia.

Occasionally cultivated in gardens, also in a white-flowered variety with yellow fruits. The plant is highly poisonous, especially the berries and the bark.

WATER CHESTNUT FAMILY, TRAPACEAE

A family of floating, aquatic herbs, with only 1 genus (*Trapa*) and 3 species in tropical and warm-temperate parts of the Old World. Dicots. Stem absent. Leaves simple, all in a floating rosette. Flowers regular, hermaphrodite, 4-merous, on long stalks from rosette centre, recurved after anthesis; fruits develop under water surface. Calyx cup-shaped, with 4 triangular teeth, becoming woody and thorn-like in fruit. Petals 4. Stamens 4. Ovary hemi-inferior, 2-locular, with 1 style. Fruit a nut with hard, woody wall, bearing 2–4 stout thorns derived from calyx teeth.

---

p.105 **Water Chestnut** *Trapa natans* L.

Description: An annual aquatic, rooting in mud, with *floating rosette* of *rhombic, dentate leaves* with blades up to 70 mm long; leaf-stalks long, markedly *inflated* at top. Flowers 10–20 mm diam., with 4 obovate, *white petals*. Fruit a blackish, woody nut with *2–4 strong thorns*. *See also* family description.

Flowering: June–July.

Habitat: Shallow, eutrophic, not strongly calcareous waters (lakes, ponds and canals); mainly in lowland.

Range: S Europe, locally northwards to France (Brittany, Lorraine), S Germany, S Poland, and C Russia.

The seeds are edible. The plant needs hot summers; during warm interglacial periods it occurred much farther north. It is occasionally cultivated in garden ponds; in S Europe it may hibernate.

REEDMACE FAMILY, TYPHACEAE

A family of glabrous, usually aquatic, perennial herbs with creeping rhizomes, with some 15 species world-wide in only 1 genus (*Typha*). Flowering stems erect, emergent. Leaves linear, strap-shaped, emergent, all basal, sheathing, in 2 rows. Flowers very small and reduced, unisexual, monoecious, in long, cylindrical, terminal spikes (spadices), male spike placed terminally, female spike close beneath it, both with small, scale-like bract. Perianth absent; male flowers surrounded by long hairs, which may be a rudiment of a perianth. Stamens 1–7 (usually 3, with connate filaments), far-protruding. Ovary superior, 1-locular, on thin, hairy stalk (gynophore); 1 style. Fruit a tiny, 1-seeded achene, borne on fluffy gynophore, which helps in dispersing fruit on the wind.

p.45 **Common Reedmace** *Typha latifolia* L.

Description: A stout aquatic, with single, cylindrical
flowering stem to 2.5 m tall. Leaves all basal,
strap-shaped, erect, slightly overtopping
stem, 10–20 (30) mm wide, bluish-green,
rather thick but practically flat on both faces.
Female spike *velvety dark brown*, up to 20 cm
long, 15–30 mm wide; male spike about
equal in length but narrower, straw-coloured
(yellow at anthesis, from far-protruding
anthers), usually *continuous with female spike*.
See also family description.

Flowering: June–July.

Habitat: Shallow, eutrophic waters, swamps, lake
margins, ponds, canals, ditches, also wet
dune-slacks, on sandy, muddy or peaty
substrates; from sea level to 1,800 m.

Range: Most of Europe except the extreme north.

Similar species: **Lesser Reedmace** (*T. angustifolia* L.) has
dark greyish-green, conspicuously turned
leaves to 3 m long, 3–10 (12) mm wide
(and convex beneath), much overtopping
stem; female spikes pale brown or greenish-
brown, 10–15 (20) mm wide, well
separated from narrower male spike. In
comparable habitats, often in more exposed
places along large lakes, but also in marshes
and ditches, to 1,500 m, in same general
area. The hybrid of both species (*T.* × *glauca*
Godron) is sterile, but often more vigorous
than parents (to 4 m tall).

Least Reedmace (*T. minima* Funck in
Hoppe) rarely grows taller than 70 cm,
and has stiff leaves only 1–3 mm wide;
female spikes narrowly ovoid, to 40 mm
long (distinctly separated from male
spike), each subtended by well-developed,
leaf-like bract. In C Europe, northwards to
NE France (Alsace), C Germany,
Czechoslovakia and Romania.

T. shuttleworthi Koch & Sonder has
glaucous leaves to 1.5 m long, 4–8 mm
wide, and silvery-grey female spikes much
longer than male ones. In more or less acid
waters of C Europe, extending to the E
Pyrenees and Bulgaria.

Common Reedmace is also called Bulrush.

CARROT FAMILY, UMBELLIFERAE

A large family of herbs, with *c.* 3,000 species in some 300 genera world-wide, predominantly in temperate regions. Dicots. Leaves alternate (rarely opposite), usually compound. Flowers usually regular and hermaphrodite, 5-merous, typically in umbels but occasionally congested into heads; umbel can be subtended by *involucre* of *bracts*. Often umbels compound, the rays bearing secondary *umbellules*, often with involucre of *bracteoles* at their base. Calyx small, 5-toothed, often rudimentary or altogether absent. Petals 5, free (rarely absent); outer petals of marginal flowers occasionally enlarged. Stamens 5, alternating with petals. Ovary inferior, typically 2-locular, with 2 divergent styles implanted on cushion-shaped base (stylopodium). Fruit a pair of 1-seeded achenes, usually ribbed, and often with linear oil-glands ('vittae') between ribs. The oil-glands contain essential oils, and can be present in all parts of the plant; therefore, umbellifers are often very aromatic, and many species are valuable food crops: as a vegetable (such as celery, fennel, parsnip and carrots), as a spice (chervil, coriander, cumin, aniseed, fennel seed, parsley, and dill), or as a medicinal herb. On the other hand, several species are highly poisonous.

In the descriptions, the term 'leaflet' generally refers to the smallest stalked sections of the leaf, even in 2–4-times pinnate leaves.

The number of bracteoles is always given as an average for 1 umbellule.

For calyx, examine fruits, on which it often appears as small, 5-toothed rim under styles.

In judging the shape of achenes, look at them from the dorsal side (i.e., the outside). Because the outline of the fruit is considered, we normally describe it in planimetric terms, such as ovate, elliptical, orbicular (rather than in stereometric terms such as ovoid, ellipsoid, globose). Often fruits are dorsoventrally compressed.

In determining these plants, the following, crude key to the genera may be of some use.

Flowers in 1–3 whorls, and leaves orbicular: *Hydrocotyle*

Flowers in simple umbels: *Sanicula, Astrantia, Eryngium,* some *Bupleurum*

Flowers in sessile, compound umbels with only 1–3 rays, and fruits long-beaked: *Scandix*

Flowers in compound umbels; leaves succulent, pinnate: *Crithmum*

Flowers in compound umbels; all leaves simple: *Bupleurum*

Flowers in compound umbels; lower leaves
simply pinnate, with broad (occasionally
deeply incised) leaflets:

    Flowers yellowish: *Pastinaca, Peucedanum carvifolia*
    Flowers white or pink: *Apium, Berula, Heracleum,*
                                 Petroselinum segetum, Pimpinella,
                                 Sison, Sium, Tordylium, and *see*
                                 Peucedanum carvifolia

Flowers in compound umbels, and lower
leaves 2–4-times pinnate (or 2–6 times ternate):

    Flowers red or purplish: *Ligusticum alpinum, see also*
                                 Oenanthe aquatica
    Flowers yellowish: *Angelica archangelica, Foeniculum,*
                                 Meum, Oenanthe pimpinelloides,
                        Pastinaca, Petroselinum crispum, some
                  Peucedanum (P. alsaticum, P. lancifolium,
                and *see P. carvifolia*), *Selinum pyrenaeum,*
                                   Silaum, Smyrnium

    Flowers white or pink:
      Bracts and bracteoles pinnately
      divided with 3–5 segments: *Daucus,* and *see*
                                 Peucedanum cervaria

      Bracts and bracteoles entire
      (occasionally bifid):
        Lower leaves 1–3-ternate: *Aegopodium, Laser,*
                            Ligusticum scoticum, and
                          see *Petroselinum crispum*

        Lower leaves 2–4-pinnate:
        Bracts 0–2 (3):
          Bracteoles 0–2:   *Carum carvi, Conopodium,*
                           Peucedanum carvifolia,
                           Pimpinella, Trinia
          Bracteoles at least 3:   *Aethusa, Angelica,*
                            Anthriscus, Apium
                            inundatum, Caucalis,
                            Chaerophyllum, Cicuta,
                            Conioselinum, Conopodium,
                    Meum, Myrrhis, some *Oenanthe*
                        (O. aquatica, O. fistulosa,
                      O. peucedanifolia, O. silaifolia),
                    Peucedanum ostruthium (see
                      also P. gallicum), Selinum
                      carvifolium, Seseli annuum and
                    S. montanum, Torilis arvensis and
                      T. nodosa, Trinia, and *see*
                            Petroselinum crispum

Bracts 0–2 (4): *Bunium, Carum verticillatum, Cnidium, Conioselinum, Conium, Laserpitium*, some *Oenanthe (O. crocata, O. lachenalii, O. pimpinelloides), Orlaya, Petroselinum segetum*, some *Peucedanum (P. palustre, P. cervaria, P. gallicum, P. oreoselinum), Seseli libanotis, Sium, Torilis japonica*

---

p.157 **Ground Elder** *Aegopodium podagraria* L.

Description: A glabrous perennial, with creeping rhizomes and erect, branched, hollow, ribbed flowering stems to 90 cm. Lower leaves triangular, 10–20 cm long, *doubly ternate* with 7–9 ovate, serrate-dentate leaflets (often 7 leaflets, as 2 can be small or missing); upper leaves simply ternate; leaf-stalk with inflated, sheathing base. Flowers 2–3 mm wide, in domed, 10–20-rayed, compound *umbels to 60 mm* diam., usually without bracts or bracteoles. Petals white (rarely pink), often notched. Achenes scarcely compressed, narrowly ovate, 3–4 mm long, with 5 thin ribs.

Flowering: June–August.

Habitat: Shady, ruderal places, cultivated land, gardens, hedges, ditch- and riversides, on moist, (very) eutrophic, mineral soils; from sea level to 1,800 m. A common weed.

Range: Most of Europe except the high Arctic, and rare in Mediterranean region; only naturalized in Iceland and on the British Isles.

Compare Angelica sylvestris (2–3-pinnate leaves), and *Smyrnium* (yellow flowers) (*see* p.1133).

---

p.157 **Fool's Parsley** *Aethusa cynapium* L.

Description: A glabrous *annual* to 80 cm, with erect, branched, hollow, finely ribbed stems. Leaves shiny dark green, 5–10 cm long, rhombic, *2–3-times pinnate* with ovate, lobed leaflets; highest leaves often simply pinnate. Flowers *c.* 2 mm wide, in flat or domed,

10–20-rayed, compound *umbels to 50 mm* diam.; bracts 0 (1); bracteoles 3–4, linear, *pendent* from outside of ray, and longer than flower-stalks. Petals white. Achenes compressed, broadly ovate, 2.5–3.5 mm long, with thick ribs (2 marginal, 3 dorsal).

Flowering: June–October.

Habitat: Shaded, ruderal places, hedgerows, field margins, on moist, mesotrophic to eutrophic, mineral soils; from sea level to 1,700 m.

Range: Most of Europe except Iceland and the high Arctic.

The whole plant is highly poisonous. The description above pertains to ssp. *cynapium*. Small forms from arable fields, with angular stems, are often attributed to ssp. *agrestis* (Wallr.) Dostál. Ssp. *cynapioides* (Bieb.) Nyman is large (to 2 m), biennial, with whitish-pruinose stems, lanceolate leaflets, and bracteoles at most equalling flower-stalks. In open woods of C Europe.

p.156 **Garden Angelica** *Angelica archangelica* L.

Description: A slightly hairy perennial, to 2.5 m, with erect, little-branched, thick, hollow, grooved stems (green, occasionally red-flushed, and often mottled with purple below). Leaves bright green, *hairy beneath*, very large (to 1 m long), triangular or rhombic, *2–3 (4) times pinnate* with numerous ovate to lanceolate, serrate leaflets, *top-leaflet 3-lobed*; upper leaves 1–2-times pinnate, highest ones with reduced blade; *leaf-stalk cylindrical, tube-like*, hollow, grooved, with strongly inflated, sheathing base. Flowers *c.* 3–4 mm wide, in domed or globose, *20–40-rayed*, compound *umbels to 25 cm* diam., without bracts, but with several bracteoles. Sepals absent. Petals *greenish-white or cream*. Achenes compressed, broadly elliptical, 6–8 mm long, with 2 lateral wings, and 3 dorsal ribs.

Flowering: June–September.

Habitat: Marshes, meadows, river- and lakesides, also damp ruderal places, on wet, (very) eutrophic, mineral or peaty, occasionally brackish soils; from sea level to 1,500 m.

Range: In Iceland, and from Scandinavia and
N Russia southwards to Denmark,
N Germany, Poland, and C Russia;
naturalized in Britain, the Low Countries,
and France.

Formerly cultivated for the seeds (used as a
spice), and for stems, which were candied
and eaten. In the far north, the leaves are
eaten as a vegetable. The plant has
medicinal properties as well.

p.159 **Wild Angelica** *Angelica sylvestris* L.

Description: A subglabrous perennial, with erect, little-
branched, thick, hollow, *purple-striped* stems
to 1.2 (2) m. Leaves dark green, *glabrous* on
both sides, large (to 60 cm long), triangular,
2–3-times pinnate with numerous ovate to
lanceolate, serrate leaflets; upper leaves 1–2-
times pinnate, highest ones with reduced
blade; *leaf-stalk channelled*, grooved, with
strongly inflated, sheathing base. Flowers
c. 2 mm wide, in domed, *15–30-rayed*,
compound *umbels to 15 cm* diam., without
bracts, but with several bracteoles. *Sepals
absent.* Petals white (occasionally pink),
outer ones enlarged. Achenes compressed,
broadly elliptical, 4–5 mm long, with 2
lateral wings, and 3 thick dorsal ribs.
Flowering: July–October.
Habitat: Meadows, fens, watersides, occasionally
damp woods, on wet or moist, mesotrophic,
mineral soils; from sea level to 1,800 m.
Range: Most of Europe except the high Arctic.
Similar species: *A. palustris* (Besser) Hoffm. is shorter, with
small but well-developed, ovate, whitish
sepals on top of fruit, and narrowly winged,
ovate achenes (5–6 mm long). In
comparable wet habitats of E and C Europe,
westwards to C Germany, and northwards
to Estonia.
Conioselinum (*Conioselinum tataricum*
Hoffm.), a glabrous perennial, to 1.5 m,
with ribbed stems, also has inflated leaf-
sheaths; leaves 2–3-times pinnate with
narrowly ovate to lanceolate, acute, serrate-
dentate leaflets; flowers white, *c.* 2–3 mm

wide, in rounded, 15–30-rayed, compound umbels to 80 mm diam., again with few or no bracts but numerous linear, rough-edged bracteoles; calyx teeth absent; achenes broadly elliptical, glabrous, 2.5–3.5 mm long, 5-ribbed, 3 dorsal ribs winged. In woods, scrub, ruderal places, on moist, humus-rich, sandy or stony soils in NE and EC Europe (to 1,600 m), from Arctic Fennoscandia and N Russia southwards to Austria, the Carpathians and SE Russia. *Compare also Aegopodium (see p.1093), which has doubly ternate leaves.*

p.161 **Bur Chervil** *Anthriscus caucalis* Bieb.

Description: A slightly hairy *annual* to 60 cm (often much less), with spreading or ascending, branched, hollow, ribbed stems (glabrous, often purple near base). Leaves yellowish- or fresh green, only 20–40 mm long, lanceolate, usually *doubly pinnate* with ovate, more or less lobed leaflets. Flowers *c.* 2 mm wide, in flat, *(2) 3–6-rayed*, compound *umbels to 40 mm diam.*; rays glabrous; bracts 0–1; bracteoles 4–5, linear-lanceolate, spreading. Petals white. Achenes slightly compressed, narrowly ovate, unribbed, *densely bristly* (with stiff, curved hairs), 4–5 mm long including short *beak* (1–1.5 mm), on short stalks (2–5 mm) bearing some bristles at top.

Flowering: May–June.

Habitat: Scrub, hedgebanks, rough grassland, roadsides, ruderal places, on dry, oligotrophic to mesotrophic, often sandy soils; from sea level to 600 m, mainly coastal in the north.

Range: In Europe northwards to Ireland, Scotland, S Sweden, and W Russia.

p.161 **Cow Parsley** *Anthriscus sylvestris* (L.) Hoffm.

Description: A hairy perennial to 1.5 m, with erect, branched, hollow, ribbed stems (with deflexed hairs near base). Leaves fresh green, 10–40 cm long, triangular-ovate, usually

2–3-times pinnate with broadly lanceolate, acute-lobed leaflets. Flowers 3–4 mm wide, in flat, (4) 8–15-rayed, compound umbels to 70 mm diam.; rays glabrous; bracts 0–1; bracteoles 4–6, broadly lanceolate, spreading. Petals white (rarely pinkish), pointed. Achenes scarcely compressed, lanceolate, unribbed, smooth and glabrous, 7–10 mm long including short beak (1.5–2 mm), longer than their stalks, which bear some bristles at top.

Flowering: April– June.

Habitat: Grassland, road verges, wood margins, on moist, mesotrophic to eutrophic, mineral soils; from sea level to 1,700 m.

Range: Most of Europe except the extreme north, and rare in Mediterranean region.

Similar species: A. nitida (Wahlenb.) Garcke (also treated as a subspecies) has broadly triangular, shiny dark-green leaves, fruits shorter than their stalk (which lacks bristles). In rough grassland and scrub in mountains (400–2,000 m) of C Europe, extending to the Vosges and C Germany.
Garden Chervil (A. cerefolium (L.) Hoffm.) is annual or biennial, with 3–6-rayed umbels, hairy rays, 2–3 linear-lanceolate, deflexed bracteoles, and also linear-lanceolate achenes (7–11 mm with long beak to 4 mm). In rough grassland and ruderal places of E Europe; often cultivated in kitchen gardens, and occasionally naturalized in W and C Europe. Compare also Chaerophyllum (see p.1106), which has notched petals and ribbed, unbeaked achenes.

Cow Parsley is rather poisonous, and children are advised against making flutes from the hollow stems, as is often done.

---

p.156 **Wild Celery** *Apium graveolens* L.

Description: A strongly aromatic, glabrous perennial or biennial, with erect, branched, solid, strongly ribbed stems to 90 cm. Leaves shiny green, to 15 cm long, ovate, pinnate with (broadly) ovate or rhombic, bluntly dentate (occasionally divided) leaflets;

upper leaves ternate. Flowers *c.* 2 mm wide, in flat, short-stalked to sessile, *4–12-rayed*, compound *umbels to 60 mm* diam., opposite to leaves; bracts absent; *bracteoles absent*. Petals whitish. Achenes scarcely compressed, ovate, *c.* 1.5 mm long, with 5 prominent ribs, otherwise smooth and glabrous.

Flowering: June–August (autumn).

Habitat: Marshes, ditches, riversides, damp, ruderal places, on wet, usually brackish, sandy, clayey, or peaty soils; mainly coastal, rarely near saline pools and springs inland (C Germany).

Range: SE, S and W Europe, northwards to the British Isles and Denmark; locally naturalized further north.

Frequently grown as a vegetable, also in a form with tuberous roots (celeriac).

---

p.162 **Lesser Marshwort**
Apium inundatum (L.) Reichenb.

Description: A glabrous, emergent, *aquatic perennial*, with creeping or trailing (floating), branched, solid, weakly ribbed stems to 75 cm. *Submerged leaves 2–3-times pinnate* with threadlike segments, to 10 cm long, ovate or elliptical; upper, emergent leaves *1–2-times pinnate* with wedge-shaped, often narrowly 3-lobed leaflets. Flowers *c.* 2 mm wide, in short-stalked, *2–3-rayed*, compound *umbels to 50 mm* diam., opposite to leaves; bracts absent; *bracteoles 5–6*. Petals white. Achenes scarcely compressed, elliptical, 2.5–3 mm long, with 5 prominent ribs, otherwise smooth and glabrous.

Flowering: June–August.

Habitat: Stagnant or slow-moving, oligotrophic, mildly acid waters, ditches, moor-pools, also dune-slacks, often on temporarily drying, muddy or peaty soils; mainly in the lowland.

Range: SW and W Europe, northwards to Ireland, Scotland, and S Sweden, and eastwards to Poland.

p.163 **Fool's Water-cress**
Apium nodiflorum (L.) Lag.

Description: A glabrous perennial, with ascending, branched, solid, weakly ribbed stems to 1 m, rooting only near base. *All leaves pinnate*, bright green, to 20 cm long, elliptical, with (5) 9–13 ovate or broadly lanceolate, *bluntly dentate* leaflets (15–60 mm long, occasionally more). Flowers *c.* 2 mm wide, in short-stalked, *4–12-rayed*, compound *umbels to 60 mm* diam., axillary to leaves; bracts 0 (1–2); *bracteoles 5–6.* Petals whitish. Achenes scarcely compressed, ovate, 2–2.5 mm long, with 5 thick, prominent ribs, otherwise smooth and glabrous.

Flowering: June–September.

Habitat: Ditches, along and in streams, flushes, swampy woods, on wet, mesotrophic to eutrophic, often calcareous, sandy, clayey or muddy soils; mainly in the lowland.

Range: SW and W Europe, northwards to Britain and the Low Countries, and eastwards to Switzerland and Italy; also in Albania and Bulgaria.

Similar species: **Creeping Marshwort** (*A. repens* (Jacq.) Lag.) is much smaller, creeping, with ovate, serrate-dentate, often weakly 3-lobed leaflets rarely exceeding 10 mm long; umbels 3–6-rayed, long-stalked, with 3–7 bracts and 5–6 bracteoles; petals white; achenes orbicular, *c.* 1 mm long, with thin, weak ribs. In seasonally flooded meadows, ditches, along pools and streams, also in dune-slacks, on wet, oligotrophic, slightly acid, sandy or muddy soils, in Europe northwards to S Britain, the Low Countries, Denmark, and Poland, but less frequent in the west. *Compare also Berula (see* p.1100), which has sharply and irregularly serrate leaflets, and 10–20-rayed umbels.

---

p.155 **Great Masterwort** *Astrantia major* L.

Description: A glabrous perennial, with erect, little-branched stems to 60 cm (1 m). Basal leaves long-stalked, fresh green, 10–15 cm diam., *palmately divided* with 3–7 ovate or lanceolate, serrate segments; stem-leaves few, highest ones sessile. Flowers 2–3 mm wide, polygamous (partly bisexual, partly male, latter ones with degenerate pistils), stalked, numerous, in domed, *head-like, simple umbels 15–30 (50) mm* diam., subtended by conspicuous ruff of several (broadly) lanceolate, *whitish bracts*, often with pink tip and green veins and margins, and slightly exceeding marginal flowers. Calyx teeth well developed, *c.* 1.5 mm long, lanceolate, persistent on fruit. Petals pink, white or greenish. Achenes scarcely compressed, elliptical, 6–8 mm long, glabrous, with 5 very prominent, scaly ribs containing linear oil-glands.

Flowering: May–September.

Habitat: Open woods, woodland clearings, grassland, ravines, streamsides and paths, on moist, oligotrophic, preferably calcareous, usually stony soils; mainly in mountains (600–2,000 m).

Range: The mountains of C Europe, extending to the Pyrenees, C France, C Germany, Czechoslovakia, Poland, C Russia, and further eastwards to the Caucasus; locally naturalized in Britain, Belgium, Denmark, and Finland.

The umbels often compose an umbel-shaped panicle (terminal umbel then larger). The male flowers can occur marginally in the umbels, or be indiscriminately mixed with bisexual ones; often they have longer stalks. *Compare Sanicula (see p.1128)*, which has small bracts and bristly achenes.

---

p.162 **Lesser Water-parsnip**
Berula erecta (Huds.) Coville

Description: A glabrous, often *aquatic perennial*, with spreading stolons and ascending, hollow, finely striped flowering stems to 50 cm. Submerged leaves (formed in spring) 3–4-times pinnate, with linear segments; *emergent leaves simply pinnate*, bright (bluish-)green, to 20 cm long, elliptical, with 15–29 ovate or elliptical, *sharply and irregularly (bi)serrate* leaflets (20–50 mm long), top-leaflet often basally connate to adjacent pair. Flowers *c.* 2 mm wide, in short-stalked, *8–20-rayed*, compound *umbels to 60 mm* diam., lateral to leaf-base; several bracts and bracteoles present, wedge-shaped, often with 3 narrow lobes or teeth. Calyx teeth well developed, but not persistent on fruit. Petals white. Achenes scarcely compressed, broadly ovate or suborbicular, 1.5–2 mm long, with 5 fine ribs, otherwise smooth and glabrous.

Flowering: July–September.

Habitat: Ditches, streams, swamps, lake margins, on wet, mesotrophic to eutrophic, preferably calcareous, mineral or peaty soils; from sea level to 700 m.

Range: Most of Europe, northwards to Scotland, S Scandinavia, Latvia, and C Russia.

Compare *Sium latifolium* (free top-leaflets) (*see* p.1132), and *Apium nodiflorum* (3–6-rayed umbels) (*see* p.1099).

p.160 **Great Pignut** *Bunium bulbocastanum* L.

Description: A slightly hairy perennial, with rounded, blackish tuber to 25 mm diam., and erect, little-branched, solid, ribbed stems to 75 cm; stem-base subterranean, twisted. Leaves 10–20 cm long, triangular, *2–3-times pinnate* with linear-lanceolate leaflets. Flowers 2–3 mm wide, hermaphrodite, in flat or domed, *10–20-rayed*, compound *umbels to 80 mm* diam.; bracts 5–10; bracteoles 5–10, linear, spreading. Petals white. Achenes slightly compressed, bluntly quadrangular, elliptical, with 5 flattened ribs and 2 strongly divergent styles, glabrous, 3–5 mm long.

Flowering: June–July.

Habitat: Grassland, field margins, sand-dunes, ruderal places, on dry or moist, oligotrophic to mesotrophic, calcareous, sandy, loamy or clayey soils; from sea level to 1,500 m.

Range: W Europe, from Iberia northwards to S England, the Low Countries, and Germany, and eastwards to Switzerland, N Italy and NW Yugoslavia.

Similar species: **Pignut** (*Conopodium majus* (Gouan) Loret) also has tubers, but remains smaller; it has finely ribbed, glabrous stems (becoming hollow after anthesis), threadlike leaf-segments, 6–12-rayed umbels with 0 (1–2) bracts and 2–4 bracteoles, mostly unisexual flowers, and triangular-ovate, pointed, distinctly compressed achenes with 5 fine ribs and 2 short, erect styles. In open woods, scrub, rough grassland, commons, grassy heaths, on sandy, often slightly acid soils, to 2,200 m, in W Europe northwards to N France and Britain, also in S Scandinavia.

The tubers of both species are edible.

p.76 **Thorow-wax** *Bupleurum rotundifolium* L.

Description: A glabrous *annual*, with erect, branched, hollow, smooth stems to 50 (75) cm. Leaves greyish-green, often purple-tinged, 20–50 (80) mm long, *undivided, ovate to suborbicular*, entire-margined, blunt-tipped; *upper leaves connate around stem*. Flowers 1.5 mm wide, in flat, stalked, *4–10-rayed*, compound *umbels to 30 mm* diam.; bracts absent; bracteoles 5–6, ovate to lanceolate, pointed, basally connate, forming conspicuous, *yellowish-green ruff* under flowers. Petals *yellowish*, curved inwards. Achenes scarcely compressed, elliptical, finely ribbed, glabrous, 3–3.5 mm long.

Flowering: June–August.

Habitat: Cultivated land, roadsides, ruderal places, on dry, mesotrophic, calcareous or slightly acid, sandy or loamy soils; from sea level to 1,100 m.

Range: S and C Europe, northwards to Belgium, S Germany, Poland, and C Russia; a casual further north (from Britain to the Baltic).

Similar species: **False Thorow-wax** (*B. subovatum* Link) from S Europe (northwards to W and C France) has narrower, subacute leaves, usually 2–3-rayed umbels with rounded, blunt bracteoles, and warted, ovate achenes 3–5 mm long. In comparable habitats. **Long-leaved Hare's-ear** (*B. longifolium* L.) has ovate-cordate upper leaves clasping stem with 2 rounded lobes (but not connate around it), long-stalked, elliptical lower leaves, and 5–12-rayed umbels with 2–4 bracts and 5–8 bracteoles (all ovate); inflorescence is often reddish. In meadows and open woods in mountains of C and E Europe (400–2,000 m), westwards to C and NE France, and northwards to S Germany, Poland, and N Russia.

---

p.76 **Slender Hare's-ear**
Bupleurum tenuissimum L.

Description: A glabrous *annual*, with erect or straggling, much-branched, solid, wiry, smooth and glabrous stems to 60 cm. Leaves often greyish-green, sessile (lower ones short-stalked), 20–50 mm long, *undivided, linear-lanceolate*, 5–7-veined, entire-margined. Flowers *c.* 1.5 mm wide, in stalked, usually *2–3-rayed*, compound *umbels to 30 mm* wide; bracts 3 (5), linear, 3-veined, often rough-margined; bracteoles 5–several, *linear*, less than 1 mm wide, longer than flowers. Petals *yellowish*, curved inwards. Achenes slightly compressed, suborbicular, finely ribbed, *minutely warted*, *c.* 2 mm long.

Flowering: June–September.

Habitat: Coastal grassland, sea-walls, also highest parts of saltmarshes, shingle-beaches, on moist, brackish, clayey soils; mainly coastal, but also near saline pools in the steppe belt.

Range: S, W and C Europe, northwards to Britain and S Sweden (Gotland), and eastwards to SE Russia.

Similar species: *B. gerardii* All. has bright-green, linear-lanceolate leaves 10–20 cm long, 3–15 mm wide, 3–7-rayed umbels, and smooth, elliptical achenes 2–3.5 mm long. In dry grassland, fields, and open woods of S Europe, northwards to W and C France (Channel coast).

Small Hare's-ear (*B. baldense* Turra) is a delicate plant, 5–20 (30) cm tall, with small, linear-lanceolate, 3–5 veined leaves, (1) 2–4-rayed umbels with narrowly ovate, awned bracts and bracteoles (longer than flowers), and ovate achenes *c.* 2 mm long. In grassland, dunes and sea-cliffs, on dry, calcareous, sandy or rocky soils (to 500 m) in SW Europe, northwards to W France and S Britain.

Sickle-leaved Hare's-ear (*B. falcatum* L.) is perennial, with thick rhizome and also non-flowering shoots; leaves elliptical to spatulate or sickle-shaped, 40–80 mm long, umbels 4–15-rayed with 2–5 unequal, lanceolate bracts and 5 linear bracteoles (shorter than flowers) achenes elliptical, smooth, 3–4 mm long. In dry, calcareous grassland and rocky places in S and C Europe, extending to S England, Belgium, C Germany, Poland, and C Russia.

Between grasses Slender Hare's-ear can be easily overlooked.

p.160	**Caraway** *Carum carvi* L.
Description:	A glabrous perennial or biennial, with fleshy, spindle-shaped tuber, and erect, branched, hollow, striped stems to 60 (150) cm. Leaves 10–20 cm long, narrowly ovate, *2–3-times pinnate* with (almost) linear segments. Flowers 2–3 mm wide, in flat, *5–16-rayed*, compound *umbels to 40 mm* diam.; bracts 0–3, bracteoles 0–3, both usually absent. Petals white (rarely pinkish), *notched*. Achenes slightly compressed, elliptical, curved, with 5 low ribs, glabrous, 3–5 mm long.
Flowering:	May–July.
Habitat:	Rough grassland, road verges, banks, on moist, mesotrophic, preferably calcareous, sandy, loamy or clayey soils; from sea level to 2,100 m.
Range:	Most of Europe except Mediterranean region, but frequently only naturalized in the north (presumably so in the British Isles, Iceland and on Spitsbergen).
Similar species:	**Cnidium** (*Cnidium dubium* (Schk.) Thell.) has linear-lanceolate leaf-segments with margins rolled under, and whitish tip; flowers white, in 20–30-rayed umbels, rays distinctly winged; bracts few, bracteoles numerous; achenes suborbicular, 2–3 mm long. In damp woods and ruderal places of C Europe, northwards to Denmark, S Sweden, and N Russia

Caraway is frequently cultivated; the aromatic seeds are used medicinally, and as a spice.

p.163 **Whorled Caraway**
Carum verticillatum (L.) Koch

Description: A glabrous perennial, with fleshy, ellipsoid or club-shaped tuber, and erect, usually unbranched, solid, striped stems to 60 cm. Leaves mostly basal, 10–25 cm long, narrowly lanceolate to linear, *pinnate*, with 10–30 pairs of *palmately divided leaflets* each having 3–5 linear, spreading segments, which are *seemingly arranged in whorls* around rhachis; stem-leaves (0) 1–2, smaller. Flowers 2–3 mm wide, in few (1–3), flat, *6–15-rayed*, compound *umbels to 50 mm* diam.; bracts 6–10, bracteoles 6–10, all linear. Petals white, *notched*. Achenes slightly compressed, elliptical or ovate, with 5 prominent ribs, glabrous, 2.5–3 mm long.

Flowering: July–August.

Habitat: Poor meadows, marshes, fens, (cut) heaths, streamsides, on wet, oligotrophic, mildly acid, sandy or peaty soils; from sea level to 500 m.

Range: W Europe, from Iberia to Ireland, W Britain, the Low Countries, SW Germany; rather local.

Quite distinct by its seemingly whorled, linear leaf-segments, and long, almost leafless stems. The plant is becoming very rare.

p.163 **Small Bur-parsley** *Caucalis platycarpos* L.

Description: A slightly downy annual, with more or less erect, subglabrous, branched, solid, angular stems to 40 cm. Leaves 30–60 mm long, ovate, *2–3-times pinnate*, with lanceolate segments. Flowers *c.* 3 mm wide, in flat, *2–5-rayed*, compound *umbels to 30 mm* diam.; bracts 0–1 (2), bracteoles 3–5, both lanceolate. *Calyx well developed*, with 5 triangular teeth. Petals white, reddish in bud, *c.* 2 mm long, deeply notched, outer ones in marginal flowers *enlarged* (at most 2–3 times longer than others). Achenes slightly compressed, elliptical, 6–10 mm long, with 5 low, scabrous ribs and 4 much larger wings in between, these armed with several reddish, *hooked spines* (1–2 mm long).

Flowering: May-July.

Habitat: Cereal fields, waste places, on dry or moist, mesotrophic, calcareous, loamy or clayey soils; from sea level to 800 m.

Range: S and C Europe, northwards to S Belgium, C Germany, Poland and C Russia.

Similar species: **Greater Bur-parsley** (*C. latifolia* L.) has hollow stems, (once) pinnate leaves with lanceolate, dentate or lobed leaflets, few-rayed umbels (opposite to leaves) with (2) 3–5 whitish, membranous bracts and 3–5 bracteoles, and pink or purplish flowers 4–5 mm wide (again with enlarged petals in marginal flowers); achenes have 18 ribs, 14 of which bear 2–3 rows of straight bristles. In fields and roadsides, on calcareous soils, in S and SC Europe, extending northwards to N France, S Germany, Hungary, and W Russia. **Orlaya** (*Orlaya grandiflora* (L.) Hoffm.) has 2–3-pinnate leaves, 5–12-rayed umbels with 5–8 broadly lanceolate, white-margined bracts, 5–7 whitish bracteoles, white or pink flowers, with outer petals in marginal flowers up to 8 times longer than others; achenes ovate, with several rows of straight bristles. In dry, calcareous grassland, cereal fields (to 1,000 m), in S and C Europe, northwards to S Belgium, S Germany, Hungary, and the Crimea. *Compare also Torilis* (see p.1134, which lacks distinct calyx, and has equal petals, and achenes with scattered spines (not on ribs only).

---

p.160 **Rough Chervil** *Chaerophyllum temulum* L.

Description: A bristly-hairy biennial or short-lived perennial, with slender taproot, and erect, branched, solid, ribbed, richly *purple-spotted stems* to 1 m. Leaves dull green, 5–15 cm long, triangular-ovate, usually *2-times pinnate* with broadly lanceolate, blunt-tipped, bluntly lobed leaflets. Flowers *c.* 2 mm wide, in domed, *5–12-rayed*, compound *umbels to 60 mm* diam. (often nodding in bud); rays hairy; bracts 0–2; bracteoles 5–8, broadly lanceolate, spreading, hairy. Petals white, *notched*. Achenes scarcely compressed, lanceolate, conspicuously 5-ribbed, glabrous, 4–7 mm long, pointed but not beaked.

Flowering: May–July.

Habitat: Open, deciduous woods, wood margins, hedges, shaded road verges, rough grassland, field margins, also old walls and railway lines, on moist to rather dry, mesotrophic to eutrophic, sandy, loamy or stony soils; from sea level to 1,500 m.

Range: In Europe northwards to the British Isles, S Sweden, Lithuania, and N Russia.

Similar species: *C. bulbosum* L. is larger (to 2 m tall), and has fleshy, tuberous root, stems hairy and spotted only beneath, narrower, acute leaflets, and 15–20-rayed, always erect umbels with glabrous rays and bracteoles. In scrub, rough grassland, ruderal places, often along rivers, in E and C Europe, locally extending westwards to Lorraine, the Netherlands and N Germany, and northwards to C Sweden, Finland, and N Russia. Sub-Arctic forms (ssp. *prescottii* (DC.) Nyman) are smaller and have less-divided leaves. Some related species, with achenes 8–20 mm long, can be found in the mountains of C Europe.

All species are highly poisonous.

---

p.159 **Cowbane** *Cicuta virosa* L.

Description: A glabrous perennial, with large, *fleshy, chambered tuber* (to 30 cm long, 70 mm thick), and erect, branched, hollow, ribbed stems to 1.2 (2) m. Leaves shiny green, up to 30 (50) cm long, triangular-ovate, *2–3-times pinnate* with narrowly lanceolate, acute, *sharply serrate* leaflets and long, hollow stalks. Flowers *c.* 3 mm wide, in domed or rounded, *10–30-rayed*, compound *umbels to 13 cm* diam.; bracts absent; bracteoles several (linear, pendent). Calyx small but distinct, 5-toothed. Petals white. Achenes scarcely compressed, suborbicular (wider than long), with 5 broad, flat ribs, glabrous, *c.* 2 mm long.

Flowering: June–August.

Habitat: Marshes, fens, along pools, lakes, streams, often growing in shallow water, on wet, mesotrophic, mildly acid, often peaty soils; from sea level to 1,200 m.

Range: In Europe mainly north of 45°N, but absent from Iceland and the high Arctic.

A dangerously toxic plant.

p.159 **Hemlock** *Conium maculatum* L.

Description: A glabrous biennial or short-lived perennial (rarely annual) to 1.8 (2.5) m, with erect, branched, hollow, smooth and barely ribbed stems, often *brown-spotted* at base. Leaves shiny green, up to 40 cm long, triangular, *2–4-times pinnate* with narrowly ovate to lanceolate, acute, dentate or lobed leaflets. Flowers *c.* 2 mm wide, in flat or domed, *10–20-rayed*, compound *umbels to 50 mm* diam.; bracts 5–6; bracteoles 3–6, linear, 1-sided. Calyx rudimentary, without teeth. Petals white. Achenes scarcely compressed, broadly ovate, with 5 thick, sinuous ribs, glabrous, 2.5–3.5 mm long.

Flowering: June–August.

Habitat: Open woods, scrub, hedgebanks, road verges, rough grassland, dunes, lake- and riversides, banks, sea-walls, occasionally fields, on moist, mesotrophic, preferably calcareous, sandy, loamy or clayey soils; from sea level to 1,500 m.

Range: Most of Europe, northwards to the British Isles, C Scandinavia, S Finland, and NC Russia.

A highly poisonous plant, the juice of which reputedly caused the death of Socrates after his conviction by the Athenian magistrates in 399 BC.

p.164 **Rock Samphire** *Crithmum maritimum* L.

Description: A glabrous, greyish-green perennial to 1.2 (2) m, with erect or ascending, solid, ribbed stems (branched from base). Leaves stalked, *fleshy*, up to 15 cm long, triangular-ovate or rhombic, *doubly pinnate* with linear-oblanceolate, blunt-tipped, *entire-margined* leaflets. Flowers *c.* 2 mm wide, in slightly domed, compound *umbels to 60 mm diam.* with *8–20 (36) thick rays*; bracts and bracteoles 5–10, broadly lanceolate. Calyx teeth rudimentary or absent. Petals *greenish-white or yellowish*. Achenes compressed, ovate to elliptical, with 5 prominent, acute ribs, glabrous, *c.* 5–6 mm long.

Flowering: July–October.

Habitat: Sea-cliffs, quay-walls, stone revetments of sea-walls, shingle-beaches, occasionally sea-dunes, on moist or periodically dry, brackish or saline, usually stony soils; exclusively coastal.

Range: W Europe, northwards to Ireland, W and S Britain, the Netherlands, also in Mediterranean area and around the Black Sea.

The leaves can be eaten (raw or pickled).

---

p.160 **Wild Carrot** *Daucus carota* L.

Description: A stiff-hairy biennial (occasionally perennial) with dark or slightly fleshy, *whitish taproot*, and erect, branched, solid, ribbed stems to 60 (90) cm. Leaves 10–20 cm long, narrowly ovate or lanceolate, *2–3-times pinnate* with lanceolate, pinnatifid leaflets. Flowers 2–3 mm wide, in flat or slightly domed, *20–60-rayed*, compound *umbels to 70 mm* diam., outer rays strongly contracting after anthesis, curving inwards, and making umbel concave, like a bird's nest; *bracts 7–13, pinnatifid* with 3–5 linear segments, spreading or deflexed, equalling rays; bracteoles 7–10, linear and entire or narrowly 3-lobed, equalling flowers. Petals *white or pinkish*, outer ones in marginal flowers slightly enlarged; *central flower* in each umbel very often *dark purple*. Achenes slightly compressed, elliptical, 2–3 mm long, with 5 low, hairy ribs, and 4 large wings in between, these armed with *long, straight, apically hooked spines*.

Flowering: June–September.

Habitat: Grassland, road verges, field margins, banks, also sea-dunes, on moist to rather dry, oligotrophic to mesotrophic, calcareous to slightly acid, sandy, loamy, clayey or stony soils; from sea level to 1,500 m.

Range: Most of Europe except the far north.

The description above pertains to ssp. *carota*, which is common everywhere. The cultivar 'Sativus' is frequently grown for the edible roots, which are orange, and strongly thickened (especially after 2nd season: winter carrots); the cultivated races can be quite glabrous. Ssp. *gummifer* Hook. f. is perennial, with shiny-green, slightly fleshy leaves, and 15–25-rayed umbels, with thickish rays not much contracting after anthesis, and always lacking the solitary purple flower in heart of umbel. On sea-cliffs and in the sea-dunes of W Europe, from N Spain to W France and S Britain. A prostrate form of the last, as found on sea-cliffs of NW France, is occasionally distinguished as ssp. *gadecaei* (Rouy & Camus) Heywood.

---

p.167 **Field Eryngo** *Eryngium campestre* L.

Description: A glabrous, *pale-green* perennial, to 60 cm, with erect, weakly ribbed stems, strongly branched in inflorescence. *Leaves coarsely spiny-dentate*, basal ones stalked, 10–20 cm long, deeply divided with often 3 linear-lanceolate segments, top segment further (pinnately) divided; stem-leaves sessile and clasping, smaller and less incised. Flowers *c.* 3 mm wide, sessile, in *subglobose, stalked heads* to 20 mm diam., subtended by ruff of 5–7 linear-lanceolate, *spiny-tipped bracts*, bearing 1 (2) pair(s) of lateral spines as well, and much exceeding flowers; heads up to 20, composing slightly umbel-shaped panicle. Calyx teeth 5, well developed, to 2.5 mm long, lanceolate, stiff, greenish. Petals *whitish*, shorter than calyx teeth. Stamens whitish. Achenes compressed, 3–4 mm long, broadly elliptical, not ribbed, densely covered with bristle-like papillae.

Flowering: July–August.

Habitat: Rough grassland, riverine and coastal dunes, sunny slopes, on dry or moist, mesotrophic, calcareous, sandy, loamy or stony soils; from sea level to 1,500 m.

Range: S and C Europe, northwards to S England, the Low Countries, N Germany, Poland, and eastwards to C and SE Russia.

Similar species: *E. viviparum* Gay is a small, glaucous biennial, to 20 cm, with linear-lanceolate, crenate-dentate basal leaves in rosette; inflorescence (with up to 50 small, greenish, 5–8-flowered heads 4–6 mm diam.) starts immediately from rosette; each head bears 5 scarcely spiny, lanceolate bracts. Very unlike its relatives, it grows in wet, seasonally flooded, sandy or muddy places in Iberia and W France (Brittany).

p.346 Sea Holly *Eryngium maritimum* L.

Description: A glabrous, *bluish-green* perennial, with erect, smooth stems to 60 cm. *Leaves coarsely spiny-dentate*, blue-green with whitish veins; basal leaves stalked, suborbicular or reniform, 6–12 (20) cm long, shallowly 3–5-lobed, wavy-edged or even irregularly folded; stem-leaves sessile and clasping, smaller. Flowers 4–5 mm wide, sessile, in *subglobose, stalked heads* to 30 mm diam., subtended by ruff of 4–7 *ovate, bluish bracts*, with 1–3 pairs of spiny lateral teeth, and much exceeding flowers; heads 1–4 (9) per stem, on spreading stalks, forming small, umbel-shaped panicle. Calyx teeth 5, well developed, 4–5 mm long, lanceolate, stiff, powder-blue. Petals *white or bluish*, shorter than calyx teeth. Stamens deep blue. Achenes compressed, 5–7 mm long, broadly elliptical, not ribbed, densely covered with bristles or scales.

Flowering: June–September.

Habitat: Sea-dunes, also shingle-beaches, occasionally sea-cliffs, and ruderal places near fishing villages, on dry, brackish, sandy soils, often in drifting sands; exclusively coastal.

Range: W Europe northwards to the British Isles and S Scandinavia, and eastwards to the Baltic States; also in Mediterranean region and around the Black Sea.

---

p.346 *Eryngium planum* L.

Description: An erect perennial, with 1 or few weakly ribbed stems to 1 m. Leaves slightly leathery, *dark green*, basal ones long-stalked, up to 15 cm long, 70 mm wide, elliptical or ovate with cordate *base* and rounde*d tip*, serrate but *not incised*; stem-leaves with progressively shorter stalks, highest ones sessile and more or less palmately incised, with 3 or 5 segments. Inflorescence an umbel-shaped panicle with several heads, often bluish-green; individual flowers *c.* 4 mm wide, sessile, numerous in ovoid heads up to 15 mm long, subtended by ruff of 5–8 narrowly lanceolate (occasionally wider) bracts, these with 1–4 pairs of spiny lateral teeth. Calyx teeth 5, up to 2 mm long, narrowly ovate, persistent on fruit. Petals ovate, *c.* 2 mm long, usually blue, slightly papillose. Achenes compressed, 4–5 mm long, ovate, inconspicuously ribbed, densely scaly.

Flowering: July–September.

Habitat: Dry grassland, ruderal places, field margins, roadsides, sunny slopes, riversides, on dry, mesotrophic, slightly acid to calcareous, sandy, loamy or stony soils; mainly in the lowland and the hills.

Range: E and C Europe, extending westwards to C Germany.

Occasionally cultivated in gardens.

p.162 **Hogweed** *Heracleum sphondylium* L.

Description: A bristly-hairy biennial or short-lived perennial, with erect, branched, hollow, ribbed stems to 1.5 m. Leaves dull green, up to 60 cm long, triangular-ovate, *pinnate* with 5–7 (9) broadly lanceolate, lobed or divided (and serrate-dentate) leaflets, top-leaflet connate to adjacent pair, basal pair stalked. Flowers 5–10 mm wide, in flat or slightly domed, *15–45-rayed*, compound *umbels to 20 cm* diam.; rays glandular-hairy; bracts 0 (2); bracteoles numerous, lanceolate, spreading, hairy. Calyx teeth minute. Petals white (rarely pinkish), *notched*, outer ones in marginal flowers strongly enlarged. Achenes strongly compressed, broadly elliptical, winged, glabrous, 7–10 mm long, with 5 fine ribs and 6 linear oil-glands in upper half (4 dorsal, 2 ventral).

Flowering: May–September.

Habitat: Rough grassland, banks, wood margins, on moist, eutrophic, slightly acid or calcareous, sandy, loamy or clayey soils; from sea level to 1,700 m.

Range: Most of Europe except the extreme north and much of Mediterranean region.

Similar species: **Giant Hogweed** (*H. mantegazzianum* Sommier & Levier), from SW Asia, has red-spotted stems (3 m tall, up to 70 mm diam.), doubly pinnate leaves (to 1 m or more) with coarsely serrate leaflets, very large, 50–150-rayed umbels to 50 cm diam., and often glandular-hairy achenes. Cultivated in gardens, and naturalized in ruderal places, scrub and roadsides of W Europe.

Hogweed is a variable species. In sunlight, the juice can cause severe skin rash.

p.106 **Marsh Pennywort** *Hydrocotyle vulgaris* L.

Description: A subglabrous perennial, with long, thin, creeping, angular stems to 10 (25) cm. Leaves long-stalked, placed singly at nodes, blade 20–50 mm diam., *suborbicular*, crenate, *peltate* (with stalk attached to centre); *stipules present*. Flowers c. 1 mm wide, sessile in 1–2 (3) *few-flowered whorls* to 4 mm diam. (forming sort of storied raceme). Calyx minute or absent. Petals white or reddish, acute. Achenes *laterally compressed*, each pair suborbicular (wider than long) in lateral view, c. 2 mm long, glabrous, faintly 5-ribbed, and lacking oil-glands.

Flowering: June–September.

Habitat: Marshes, fens, damp meadows, ditches, stream-, canal- and pondsides, flushes, also dune-slacks, on wet, oligotrophic to mesotrophic, slightly acid or calcareous, sandy, clayey or peaty soils; from sea level to 700 m.

Range: Most of Europe, northwards to Iceland, S Scandinavia, Lithuania, and C Russia.

A deviant genus, occasionally placed in a separate family (Hydrocotylaceae).

p.164 **Broad-leaved Sermountain**
Laserpitium latifolium L.

Description: A glabrous perennial, with erect, branched, solid, ribbed stems to 1.5 m, with *fibrous leaf-remains* at base. Leaves greyish-green, up to 50 cm long, triangular-ovate, *doubly pinnate* with numerous ovate, serrate leaflets; stalks of upper leaves with strongly inflated sheath. Flowers 2–3 mm wide, in flat, *20–50-rayed*, compound *umbels to 15 cm* diam.; several bracts present, drooping, lanceolate, glabrous; bracteoles few, linear, glabrous. Petals white, pointed, tip curved inwards. Achenes compressed, 5–10 mm long, elliptical, with 5 ribs and *4 broad, wavy wings in between*, glabrous.

Flowering: July–August.

Habitat: Open, deciduous or mixed woods, also rocky places, on moist, oligotrophic, calcareous, sandy, loamy or stony soils; mainly in mountains, 300–2,000 m.

Range: S and C Europe, northwards to C Germany, S Sweden, Estonia, and C Russia.

Similar species: *L. prutenicum* L. has twice-pinnate leaves with deeply incised leaflets, while upper leaf-sheaths are not inflated; umbels 10–20-rayed, with ciliate bracts, white or yellowish flowers, and small achenes (to 5 mm long). In marshes, damp meadows and open, deciduous woods of C Europe, northwards to N Germany, Poland, and C Russia.

L. siler L. has 3-times pinnate, dark bluish-green leaves with ovate, entire-margined leaflets (20–70 mm long), 20–50-rayed umbels with spreading, glabrous bracts, and narrowly winged achenes 6–12 mm long. In mountain woods of C Europe, northwards to C Germany.

Laser (*Laser trilobum* (L.) Borckh.) has fresh-green, 2–3-times pinnate leaves with ovate, crenate or lobed leaflets, 11–20-rayed umbels, and achenes with 5 thick ribs (but no wings in between). In C and E Europe, westwards to France, and northwards to C Germany, Hungary, the Baltic States, and C Russia. • Further compare *Ligusticum*, also with unwinged achenes.

---

p.155 **Scots Lovage** *Ligusticum scoticum* L.

Description: A glabrous perennial to 90 cm, with erect, branched, hollow, ribbed, often purplish stems, without fibrous leaf-remains at base. Leaves fresh-green, up to 20 cm long, triangular, *doubly ternate* with 9 ovate, bluntly dentate leaflets (highest ones often with 3 or 5 leaflets); leaf-stalks with strongly inflated sheath. Flowers *c.* 2 mm wide, in flat, *8–20-rayed*, compound *umbels to 60 mm* diam., on long, erect stalks; bracts 2–3, lanceolate, spreading, glabrous; bracteoles few to several, linear. Calyx teeth 5, persistent. Petals greenish-white, pointed, tip curved inwards. Achenes compressed, 5–8 mm long, ovate, with 5 strong ribs and several linear oil-glands in between, glabrous.

Flowering: July–August.

Habitat: Maritime rocks and cliffs, coastal shingle, on moist, oligotrophic, stony soils.

Range: W Ireland, N Britain, the Faeroes, Iceland, Denmark, Norway, and NW Russia; sporadically in the Baltic region (E Sweden).

Similar species: **Alpine Lovage** (*L. mutellina* (L.) Crantz), from damp woods and meadows in mountains of C and SE Europe (1,500–3,000 m), has leaves 2-times pinnate with lanceolate, pinnately divided leaflets, and stems with fibrous leaf-remains at base; umbels unequally 3–9-rayed, with 0–2 (5) bracts, 3–8 1-sided bracteoles, red or purplish flowers (lacking distinct calyx), and narrowly winged achenes.

---

p.167 **Spignel** *Meum athamanticum* Jacq.

Description: A glabrous, strongly aromatic perennial, with erect, little-branched, *hollow*, striped stems to 60 cm. Leaves fresh-green, mostly basal, 5–15 cm long, lanceolate or ovate, usually *3–4-times pinnate* (finely dissected) with numerous, dense, linear, *seemingly whorled, threadlike segments*. Flowers 2–3 mm wide, in flat or domed, *3–15-rayed*, compound *umbels to 60 mm* diam. (terminal or axillary); bracts 1–2, linear, or absent; bracteoles few, threadlike. Calyx teeth absent. Petals white or cream, occasionally tinged with pink. Achenes slightly compressed, elliptical, conspicuously 5-ribbed, glabrous, 6–10 mm long.

Flowering: June–July.

Habitat: Mountain grassland, on moist, oligotrophic, often acid, stony soils; 400–2,500 m.

Range: W and C Europe, from W and N Britain to Poland, and southwards to the Pyrenees, S Italy and C Bulgaria.

Similar species: **Fennel** (*Foeniculum vulgare* Miller) also has aromatic, 3–4-pinnate, finely dissected leaves with threadlike segments, but grows taller (to 2 m), and has solid stems (at least when young), (4) 12–30-rayed umbels to 80 mm diam., without bracts or bracteoles; flowers always yellow; achenes 4–6 mm long, with 5 thin, blunt ribs. In ruderal places, rough grassland, on cliffs, more frequent near the sea, in S and W Europe, northwards to NW France and S Britain; also cultivated as a vegetable, and locally naturalized further north (e.g., in Belgium and Germany). Compare *Silaum* (*see* p.1132), which also has yellowish flowers, but wider leaflets.

Spignel is also called Baldmoney. The dried root was formerly used as a spice.

---

p.165 **Sweet Cicely** *Myrrhis odorata* (L.) Scop.

Description: A strongly aromatic, hairy perennial, with erect, branched, hollow, ribbed stems to 1.5 m. Leaves fresh green, up to 40 cm long, triangular-ovate, *3-times pinnate* with (broadly) lanceolate, serrate leaflets (becoming pinnatifid near base); leaf-stalks with sheathing base. Flowers 2–4 mm wide, in flat or domed, *4–20-rayed*, compound *umbels to 60 mm* diam.; bracts 0 (1–2); bracteoles 4–6 (often 5), lanceolate, ciliate, spreading. Petals white. Achenes scarcely compressed, *lanceolate, strongly ribbed*, short-hairy, 15–25 mm long (including short beak), longer than their stalks, and becoming dark brown when ripe.

Flowering: May–July.

Habitat: Meadows and rocky places in mountains, also (naturalized) in rough grassland and roadsides, on moist, mesotrophic, preferably calcareous, sandy, loamy or stony soils; from sea level to 2,000 m.

Range: Native to the mountains of C and S Europe, eastwards to the Caucasus; locally naturalized as an archeophyte in W and NC Europe.

Frequently cultivated in kitchen gardens. The leaves are cooked and eaten, e.g., in water gruel. The roots and fruits can be used as a sweetener.

p.167 **Fine-leaved Water-dropwort**
Oenanthe aquatica (L.) Poiret

Description: A glabrous, often aquatic annual, biennial or perennial, to 1.2 m, with erect or ascending, branched, thick, hollow, ribbed stems; root-tubers absent. Submerged leaves (if present) 3–4-times pinnate (finely dissected) with linear segments; aerial leaves shiny yellowish-green, up to 15 cm long, triangular-ovate, *2–3-times pinnate* with ovate, lobed to divided leaflets and *hollow stalks*. Flowers *c.* 2 mm wide, in flat or domed, *5–15-rayed*, compound *umbels to 50 mm* diam., terminal and on short stalks *lateral to leaf-axils*; rays not thickened; bracts usually absent; several linear, threadlike bracteoles present. Calyx well developed, 5-toothed. Petals white (rarely purplish), those of marginal flowers not enlarged. Achenes scarcely compressed, narrowly elliptical, with 5 broad, flat ribs, glabrous, *c.* 4 mm long; styles to 1 mm long.

Flowering: June–September.

Habitat: Ditches, streams, pond margins, carrs, on temporarily drying mud or sand, generally in mesotrophic or slightly eutrophic, shallow, stagnant or slow-moving waters.

Range: Most of Europe except Iceland and the high Arctic.

Similar species: **River Water-dropwort (*O. fluviatilis* (Bab.) Coleman)** has doubly pinnate submerged leaves, 1st-order leaflets (narrowly) wedge-shaped, deeply divided; aerial leaves doubly pinnate with wider, lanceolate segments; umbels always lateral to leaf-axils; achenes 5–6 mm long. In streams and rivers, in neutral or basic, moving (less often stagnant) waters, in Ireland, Wales, England, N France, Belgium, Germany, and Denmark. The plants often grow largely submerged, and rarely flower. *Compare also Peucedanum palustre (see p.1126)*, which has several bracts and winged achenes.

Fine-leaved Water-dropwort often hibernates through creeping stolons. All *Oenanthe* species are poisonous.

p.166 **Hemlock Water-dropwort**
Oenanthe crocata L.

Description: A glabrous, aromatic perennial to 1.5 m,
with a tuberous root and erect, branched,
hollow, ribbed stems. Leaves pale green, up
to 40 cm long, triangular-ovate, basal ones
3–4-times pinnate with ovate to wedge-
shaped, bluntly crenate or lobed to divided
leaflets (often connate at base), and *hollow
stalks*; upper leaves smaller and less incised.
Flowers *c.* 2 mm wide, in flat or domed,
12–40-rayed, compound *umbels to 10 cm*
diam., long-stalked, terminal (never
lateral); rays not thickened; bracts usually
5, lanceolate, occasionally bifid; several
linear, threadlike bracteoles present. Calyx
well developed, 5-toothed. Petals white,
those of marginal flowers not enlarged.
Achenes scarcely compressed, narrowly
elliptical, with 5 narrow, flat ribs,
glabrous, 4–5.5 mm long; styles
2–2.5 mm long.

Flowering: June–August.

Habitat: Damp meadows, stream- and riversides,
often in shaded places, also dune-slacks and
cliffs, on wet, oligotrophic, preferably acid,
occasionally brackish, sandy or stony soils,
often near the sea-coast.

Range: SW Europe, northwards to Ireland, Britain,
and the Low Countries.

A dangerously toxic, exclusively Atlantic
species, known locally as Dead-man's
Fingers on account of its hand-shaped,
fleshy, tuberous root. It is occasionally
mistaken for Garden Parsley, with sad
consequence. The crushed foliage smells
pleasantly of sweet apples; the plant
contains a yellowish juice.

p.166 **Tubular Water-dropwort**
Oenanthe fistulosa L.

Description: A glabrous, often aquatic perennial, with
erect, branched, hollow, inflated, ribbed
stems to 70 cm, often with ovoid or
spindle-shaped root-tubers at stem-bases.

Leaves pale green, lower ones 2–3-times pinnate, upper ones (simply) pinnate, all with lanceolate, lobed or entire leaflets, and with *hollow, markedly inflated stalks* (these longer than blade). Flowers *c.* 3 mm wide, in flat or domed, *2–4-rayed*, compound *umbels to 40 mm* diam., *always terminal*; central flowers in each umbellule usually hermaphrodite, marginal flowers functionally male; rays thickened (2 mm or more); bracts usually absent; several linear, threadlike bracteoles present. Calyx well developed, 5-toothed. Petals white or pinkish, those of marginal (male) flowers enlarged. Achenes scarcely compressed, narrowly elliptical, truncate at both ends (fruit cylindrical), with 5 broad, flat ribs, glabrous, 3–4 mm long; styles 3–5 mm long.

Flowering: June–September.

Habitat: Streams, ditches, marshes, damp meadows, on wet, (very) eutrophic, muddy or peaty soils; mainly in the lowland, to 700 m.

Range: Most of Europe, northwards to the British Isles, S Sweden, and the Baltic States.

Poisonous!

p.165 **Parsley Water-dropwort**
Oenanthe lachenalii C.C. Gmelin

Description: A glabrous perennial, with erect, branched, solid or hollow (but never inflated), ribbed stems to 80 cm; root-tubers narrowly spindle-shaped or cylindrical, to 70 mm long, 3 mm thick, gradually narrowed towards base. Leaves pale green, lower ones doubly pinnate with elliptical or spatulate segments, upper ones simply pinnate with linear segments, and all with solid stalks shorter than blade. Flowers 2–3 mm wide, in flat or domed, *5–15-rayed*, compound *umbels to 50 mm* diam., *always terminal*; rays not thickened; bracts (0) 4–6 (10); several linear, threadlike bracteoles present. Calyx well developed, 5-toothed. Petals white, those of marginal flowers not enlarged. Achenes scarcely compressed, narrowly obovate or elliptical, with 5 broad, flat ribs, glabrous, *c.* 3 mm long; styles *c.* 1 mm long.

Flowering: June–September.

Habitat: Floodmarks in saltmarshes, shingle-beaches, also marshes and dune-slacks, on wet, oligotrophic or mesotrophic, usually brackish, sandy or gravelly soils; mainly coastal.

Range: S and W Europe, northwards to the British Isles and S Sweden.

Similar species: **Narrow-leaved Water-dropwort** (*Oenanthe silaifolia* Bieb.) has hollow stems, abruptly narrowed, cylindrical root-tubers (to 30 mm long, 5 mm thick), all leaf-segments elliptical or spatulate, umbels with 4–8 (10) thickened rays and 0–1 bracts, and achenes 3–3.5 mm long, with styles to 2.5 mm. In wet meadows and marshes along streams and rivers of S and W Europe, northwards to Britain, Belgium and Germany.

O. peucedanifolia Pollich has ovoid root-tubers, 5–15 rays (non-thickened, even in fruit), and styles at most half as long as achene. In wet meadows and marshes on slightly acid, clayey or peaty soils, in S and SW Europe, northwards to W France and Belgium, with a single find in the Netherlands.

Corky-fruited Water-dropwort (*O. pimpinelloides* L.) has solid stems, ovoid root-tubers, lower leaves doubly pinnate with ovate, cuneate-based 1st-order leaflets; upper leaves quite different – doubly pinnate with linear segments; umbels flat, 6–15-rayed, with several threadlike bracts and bracteoles, and cream flowers; achenes to 3 mm, with swollen, corky base and styles to 3 mm long. In damp grassland and along woodland rides, often on clayey soils, in S and W Europe, northwards to W France and S Britain.

All species are poisonous.

p.220 **Wild Parsnip** *Pastinaca sativa* L.

Description: A greyish-woolly biennial, with thin, whitish roots and erect, branched, hollow, angular, ribbed stems to 90 cm; branches rise at steep angle (less than 40°). Leaves up to 20 cm long, ovate, *pinnate* with 5–11 obovate or broadly elliptical, lobed and serrate-dentate, blunt-tipped leaflets (rarely divided, or even pinnate again). Flowers *c.* 1.5 mm wide, in flat or slightly domed, unequally (7) *9–20-rayed*, compound *umbels to 80 mm* diam.; bracts and bracteoles 0–2 (lanceolate, soon falling). *Petals yellow.* Achenes strongly compressed, broadly elliptical, winged, glabrous, 5–7 mm long, with 2 winged lateral ribs, 3 thin dorsal ribs and 6 linear oil-glands running far downwards (4 dorsal, 2 ventral).

Flowering: July–September.

Habitat: Grassland, roadsides, riversides, grassy banks, in wasteland, along railway lines, on moist to rather dry, mesotrophic to eutrophic, preferably calcareous, often loamy or clayey soils; from sea level to 1,600 m.

Range: Most of Europe, except Iceland and the high Arctic.

The description above pertains to ssp. *sativa* var. *sylvestris* Miller (the wild form), which is rather poisonous; less hairy plants with fleshy roots and narrower, acute or pointed leaflets (var. *sativa*) are cultivated for the edible roots, though as a root-crop this plant lost much of its popularity to the potato. Ssp. *urens* (Req. ex Godr.) Čelak., from S and C Europe, has cylindrical, smooth or finely striped stems, more spreading branches (rising at angle of *c.* 60°), ovate, round-tipped leaflets, and 5–7 (9) subequal rays. Naturalized in comparable habitats in much of W Europe. It is definitely poisonous, the juice causing severe skin rash or blisters (in combination with sunlight, as with *Heracleum*).

p.164 **Corn Parsley** *Petroselinum segetum* (L.) Koch

Description: A glabrous, *greyish-green* annual or biennial, with erect, much-branched, solid, finely ribbed stems to 80 cm. Lower leaves up to 30 cm long, *linear-lanceolate, pinnate* with 13–19 ovate, serrate-dentate, acute leaflets to 10 mm long, these often pinnately lobed; upper leaves have reduced blade and 3–5 almost linear leaflets. Flowers *c.* 2 mm wide, in flat, very unequally *3–10-rayed*, compound *umbels to 50 mm* diam.; bracts and bracteoles 3–5, small, linear. Petals white (occasionally pink). Achenes scarcely compressed, ovate or narrowly elliptical, glabrous, 2.5–3 mm long, with 5 prominent ribs.

Flowering: July–October.

Habitat: Cultivated land, road verges, grassland, riverbanks and sea-walls, on moist, mesotrophic, calcareous, often brackish, preferably clayey soils; mainly in the lowland.

Range: SW Europe, northwards to S Britain and the Low Countries.

Similar species: **Garden Parsley** (*P. crispum* (Miller) A.W. Hill) has lower leaves 3-times pinnate or 3-times ternate, triangular, with ovate, often deeply 3–5-lobed (and dentate), cuneate-based, flat or curly, bright-green leaflets, 8–20 subequal rays, 1–3 bracts and 5–8 bracteoles; petals yellowish-green; achenes weakly ribbed. Frequently cultivated, and widely naturalized in cultivated and waste land, grassy and rocky places.

Stone Parsley (*Sison amomum* L.) is dull green, with very lax inflorescences (vaguely reminiscent of *Gypsophila*); lower leaves simply pinnate with 5–9 narrowly ovate, often 3-lobed, serrate leaflets 20–70 mm long; upper leaves often simply ternate, with narrow, cuneate segments; umbels unequally 3–6-rayed, with 1–3 linear bracts, 1–5 threadlike bracteoles; petals white, notched; achenes suborbicular, 2–3 mm long, with 5 thin ribs. In shaded road verges, rough grassland, hedgebanks, scrub, wood margins, on moist, (very) eutrophic, loamy, clayey or stony soils, mainly in the lowland, in S and W Europe, northwards to England, NW France, and W Belgium.

Corn Parsley and Garden Parsley smell pleasantly of parsley. (For safety reasons, compare *Oenanthe crocata*, *see* p.1119.) Stone Parsley has a nauseating, petrol-like odour when crushed.

---

p.220 **Hog's Fennel** *Peucedanum officinale* L.

Description: A glabrous perennial, to 2 m, with stout rhizome, and erect, branched, *solid*, finely striped, cylindrical flowering stems (with fibrous leaf-remains at base). Leaves triangular, *2–6 times ternate* with *linear segments* 30–90 mm long. Flowers *c.* 2 mm wide, in flat, *10–20-rayed*, compound *umbels to 20 cm* diam. (nodding in bud); bracts absent or 1–3 (soon falling); several linear bracteoles present. Calyx teeth 5, ovate, small but distinct. *Petals bright yellow*. Achenes strongly compressed, 5–10 mm long, ovate, with 3 prominent dorsal ribs and 2 winged lateral ribs; fruit-stalks 20–60 mm long.

Flowering: July–September.

Habitat: Rough grassland, fields, wood margins, also sea-cliffs, on moist, oligotrophic to mesotrophic, clayey or stony soils; mainly in the hills.

Range: S and C Europe, northwards to W France, S Britain and S Germany, and eastwards to Hungary and Bulgaria.

Similar species: *P. carvifolia* Vill. has strongly ribbed stems, 1–2-times pinnate leaves with sessile (often seemingly whorled) segments; umbels 6–18-rayed, with slightly hairy, unequal rays, 0–2 bracts, and 0–3 bracteoles; petals yellowish or greenish-white. In meadows, on riverbanks, on wet, mesotrophic, preferably calcareous, clayey soils in S and C Europe, northwards to the Low Countries and Germany.

P. alsaticum L. has hollow, often purplish stems, whorled branches, and 2–3- (4-) times pinnate leaves with lanceolate, lobed leaflets; umbels 6–20-rayed, with short, thick rays to 20 mm long, and several spreading bracts and bracteoles; petals dull yellow. In grassland, road verges, open woods, on sunny slopes, on dry, sandy, loamy or stony soils in C Europe, eastwards through the steppe belt into C Asia.

P. lancifolium Lange has hollow stems lacking fibres at base, linear, unlobed leaf-segments 40–60 mm long, umbels with 5–12 slightly hairy, unequal rays, and several deflexed bracts; petals white or yellowish. In marshes and damp meadows of Iberia and W France (Brittany).

P. oreoselinum (L.) Moench has solid stems, leaves 2–3-times pinnate with narrowly ovate, lobed segments, green on both faces; flowers *c.* 2 mm wide, white, in flat, 15–30-rayed, compound umbels to 10 cm diam., usually with several bracts and bracteoles; achenes 5–10 mm long, suborbicular, with 3 prominent dorsal ribs and 2 winged lateral ribs; fruit-stalks 2–5 mm long. In grassland, scrub, open woods, on sunny slopes, on dry, oligotrophic, preferably acid, sandy or stony soils (to 1,700 m), in C Europe, northwards to Lorraine, Germany, S Sweden (extinct in Denmark), the Baltic States and C Russia, and eastwards to the Caucasus.

P. gallicum Latourr. has 3–4-times pinnate leaves with long-stalked, linear leaflets, (7) 10–20-rayed umbels with (0–2) 3–8 bracts. In woodland clearings on acid soils, in Iberia and W and C France.

p.157 **Masterwort**
Peucedanum ostruthium (L.) Koch

Description: A *hairy* perennial, with erect, branched, usually *hollow*, ribbed, cylindrical flowering stems to 1 m. Leaves triangular, 1–2-times ternate with 3–9 large, ovate, coarsely dentate leaflets to 10 cm long (2nd-order leaflets often basally connate). Flowers *c.* 2 mm wide, in flat or domed, *30–60-rayed*, compound *umbels to 12 cm* diam.; rays glabrous; bracts 0–1 (2); bracteoles few, soon falling. Calyx teeth absent. Petals white or pink. Achenes strongly compressed, 4–5 mm long, suborbicular, with 3 prominent dorsal ribs and 2 very broad lateral wings.

Flowering: June–August.

Habitat: Grassland, scrub, streamsides, on moist, oligotrophic to mesotrophic, acid or calcareous, often stony soils; mainly in mountains, 1,400–2,700 m.

Range: S and C Europe, northwards to S Germany and S Poland, southwards to S Spain and C Italy.

The plant has a pleasant, aromatic smell (reminiscent of celery). In some regions (e.g. Switzerland) it is cultivated for medicinal purposes; formerly, this happened on a wider scale, and plants can still be found naturalized in W and N Europe, down to 400 m. *Compare Aegopodium podagraria (see p.1093)*, which has dark green, normally well-separated leaflets.

---

p.156 **Milk-parsley**
Peucedanum palustre (L.) Moench

Description: A glabrous, pale-green biennial or perennial to 1 (1.5) m, with erect, branched, *hollow*, finely ribbed, angular flowering stems (often purplish beneath, and without fibrous leaf-remains at base). Leaves triangular, 2–4-times pinnate with soft, linear-lanceolate, *white-tipped segments*; often only 1st-order leaflets distinctly stalked. Flowers *c.* 2 mm wide, in flat, *20–40-rayed*, compound *umbels to 80 mm* diam.; rays slightly hairy; bracts and bracteoles 4–10, linear, recurved, often bifid. Calyx teeth 5, ovate, small but distinct. Petals whitish. Achenes strongly compressed, 4–5 mm long, elliptical, with 3 prominent dorsal ribs and 2 winged lateral ribs; fruit-stalks 5–12 mm long.

Flowering:	July–September.
Habitat:	Marshes, damp meadows, ditches, carrs, on wet, oligotrophic to mesotrophic, acid or calcareous, muddy or peaty soils; from sea level to 900 m.
Range:	Most of Europe except the far north, the extreme west and south.
Similar species:	*P. cervaria* (L.) Lapeyr. has stems with fibres at base, rather stiff, ovate, sharply dentate leaflets to 30 mm long, bluish beneath and always stalked; umbels 15–30-rayed, with several white-edged bracts, outer ones often pinnately divided; achenes 5–9 mm long, (broadly) ovate, narrowly winged, on short stalks 2–5 mm long. In rather dry, calcareous places, open woods, grassy slopes, to 1,800 m, in C Europe, northwards to Lorraine and SW Germany, and eastwards to the Caucasus. *Compare also Oenanthe aquatica* (see p.1118), which has unwinged fruits and usually lacks bracts.

Milk-parsley often grows in shallow water, acting as a helophyte. Young plants produce whitish latex when cut.

p.167 **Burnet-saxifrage** *Pimpinella saxifraga* L.

Description:	A more or less hairy perennial, with erect, *solid*, finely striped, cylindrical, usually hairy stems to 60 (100) cm. Lower leaves up to 15 cm long, narrowly ovate, pinnate, with 7–15 subsessile, ovate or elliptical, dentate leaflets 10–30 mm long; upper leaves very different, doubly pinnate, with lanceolate segments; highest leaves often reduced to little more than sheath. Flowers *c.* 2 mm wide, in (6) *10–25-rayed*, compound *umbels to 60 mm* diam.; bracts 0 (1–2); bracteoles always absent. Petals white, notched. Achenes scarcely compressed, ovate, 2–2.5 mm long, with 5 fine ribs, otherwise smooth and glabrous.
Flowering:	June–September.
Habitat:	Grassland, grassy banks and slopes, on dry or moist, oligotrophic to mesotrophic,

preferably calcareous, sandy, loamy or stony soils; from sea level to 2,300 m.

Range: Most of Europe (except the extreme south), northwards to Britain, Denmark, S Sweden, and N Russia.

Similar species: **Greater Burnet-saxifrage** (*Pimpinella major* (L.) Hudson) is taller (to 1.2 m), and has hollow, strongly ribbed, usually glabrous stems (often whitish-pruinose above); lower leaves pinnate, with 5–9 ovate, dentate, mostly short-stalked leaflets to 70 mm long (rarely pinnately divided in var. *bipinnata* (G. Beck) Burnat); upper leaves usually all well developed, doubly pinnate with lanceolate segments; umbels 10–25-rayed; bracts and bracteoles absent; petals white or pink; achenes 2.5–3 mm long, with prominent ribs. In meadows, wood margins, hedgebanks, grassy banks and slopes, dunes, in ruderal places, on moist, oligotrophic, preferably calcareous, often loamy or clayey, but also stony or sandy soils, in most of Europe, northwards to the British Isles, S Scandinavia, the Baltic States, and N Russia, and eastwards to the Caucasus. **Anise** (*P. anisum* L.) from Asia is cultivated in S and E Europe for the (finely hairy) achenes, used as a spice (aniseed).

The description of Burnet-saxifrage pertains to var. *saxifraga*. In var. *seselifolia* Rouy & Camus) all leaves are doubly pinnate, with lanceolate segments; such forms occur throughout the range of the species, and can be more frequent than the type.

---

p.155 **Sanicle** *Sanicula europaea* L.

Description: A glabrous perennial, with erect, little-branched stems to 50 cm. Leaves mostly basal, long-stalked, up to 10 cm diam., shiny green beneath, *palmately divided* with 3–7 (narrowly) obovate, usually 3-lobed and serrate segments; stem-leaves 1–2, subsessile, small, bract-like, with 3

lanceolate, serrate or pinnatifid segments.
Flowers 2–3 mm wide, in globose, *simple,
headlike umbels* 10–20 mm diam., these
usually in 3s, placed on long stalks in axils of
highest stem-leaves; bracts few, 3–5 mm
long, lanceolate to linear, not exceeding
flowers; inner 3–6 flowers hermaphrodite and
sessile, the more numerous outer ones
functionally male and short-stalked. Calyx
teeth well developed, *c.* 1 mm long,
lanceolate, persistent on fruit. Petals whitish
or pink. Achenes scarcely compressed,
broadly elliptical, 4–5 mm long, densely
covered in *hooked bristles*, barely ribbed,
lacking oil-glands.

Flowering: May–July.

Habitat: Deciduous woods, on moist, oligotrophic,
preferably calcareous, sandy, loamy or stony
soils; from sea level to 1,500 m.

Range: Most of Europe, northwards to the British
Isles, S Fennoscandia, the Baltic States, and
C Russia.

Compare Astrantia (see p.1099), which has
large, coloured bracts and glabrous achenes.

---

p.165 **Shepherd's-needle** *Scandix pecten-veneris* L.

Description: A sparsely hairy *annual*, with erect,
ascending or spreading, branched, solid,
ribbed stems to 30 cm. Leaves fresh green,
up to 40 cm long, triangular-ovate, *2–4-
times pinnate* with linear-lanceolate segments.
Flowers 3–5 mm wide, short-stalked, in
1–3-rayed, compound *umbels to 40 mm* diam.
(when 1-rayed, apparently simple); bracts 0
(1–2); bracteoles 4–6 (often 5), lanceolate,
entire or pinnatifid, bristly-ciliate, erect or
spreading. Petals white. Achenes scarcely
compressed, (narrowly) *lanceolate, weakly
ribbed*, hairy only on ribs, 30–80 mm long
including *very long, linear beak* (to 60 mm),
much longer than their stalks, and becoming
pale brown when ripe.

Flowering: May–August.

Habitat: Cultivated and waste land, on moist,
mesotrophic, calcareous, loamy or clayey
soils; from sea level to 1,700 m.

Range: In Europe northwards to the British Isles, S Fennoscandia, C Russia.

Severely declining in N Europe. The plant superficially resembles a fruiting Stork's-bill (*Erodium*), which also has pinnately dissected leaves, umbels, and long-beaked fruits, but quite different, pink flowers.

---

p.164 **Cambridge Milk-parsley**
Selinum carvifolia (L.) L.

Description: A subglabrous perennial, to 90 cm, with erect, branched, *solid*, strongly ribbed, angular stems, *narrowly winged* on angles. Leaves triangular, lower ones 3-times pinnate, upper ones doubly pinnate, leaflets themselves pinnatifid with narrowly elliptical to almost linear, *white-tipped segments*. Flowers *c.* 2 mm wide, in flat, *15–30-rayed*, compound *umbels to 70 mm* diam.; rays papillose on inner side; bracts absent; bracteoles 4–10, linear. Calyx teeth absent. Petals white. Achenes compressed, 3–4 mm long, broadly elliptical, with 3 narrowly winged dorsal ribs and 2 broadly winged lateral ribs.

Flowering: July–September.

Habitat: Damp meadows, fens, open woods (often Beech and Oak), on moist or wet, oligotrophic, mildly acid, sandy or loamy soils; from sea level to 1,400 m.

Range: Most of Europe except Ireland, Iceland and the high Arctic; rare in Mediterranean region.

Similar species: **Pyrenean Angelica** (*S. pyrenaeum* (L.) Gouan) is annual or biennial, and has finely striped stems, umbels with 3–9 unequal rays, and yellowish petals. In moderately manured meadows and marshes in mountains (900–2,300 m) of W Europe, from NW Spain and the Pyrenees to the Vosges. *Compare also Peucedanum palustre* (see p.1126) (also white-flowered and with white-tipped leaf-segments, but with several bracts) and *Silaum silaus* (see p.1132) (yellowish flowers and green-tipped leaf-segments).

p.161 **Moon Carrot** *Seseli libanotis* (L.) Koch

Description: A more or less hairy perennial, with thick taproot and erect, branched, solid, ribbed, angular stems to 1.2 m. Leaves 10–20 cm long, triangular-ovate, (1) *2–3-times pinnate* with narrowly elliptical segments at least 2 mm wide, and often spreading in different planes. Flowers 1–2 mm wide, in domed, (15) *20–40-rayed*, compound *umbels to 60 mm diam.*; rays hairy all round; bracts 8 or more, linear-lanceolate; bracteoles 10–15, linear. Calyx teeth linear, not persistent on fruit. Petals white or pink, *notched, hairy on outside.* Achenes scarcely compressed, elliptical, with 5 low ribs, densely short-hairy (occasionally glabrous), 3–4 mm long, with deflexed styles; fruit-stalk 4–10 mm long.

Flowering: July–September.

Habitat: Rough grassland, scrub, open woods, on dry, oligotrophic, calcareous, sandy, loamy or stony soils; from near sea level to 2,000 m.

Range: Most of Europe, northwards to S Britain, Belgium, Germany, S Scandinavia, S Finland, and NC Russia.

Similar species: *S. montanum* L. has rounded, glabrous stems, linear leaf-segments (to 1 mm wide), and 5–15-rayed umbels with grooved rays (hairy only on inside), 0–1 (3) bracts and several linear, narrowly white-edged bracteoles; calyx teeth pointed, persistent on fruit; fruit-stalks 1–3 mm long. In dry, calcareous grassland of SW Europe, northwards to N France, extinct in Germany.
S. annuum L. is actually perennial, but usually has only 1 rounded, hairy stem, linear leaf-segments (to 1 mm wide), 10–30-rayed umbels with no bracts (rarely 2–4, in the Alps) and several linear, broadly white-edged bracteoles; rays finely hairy on inner side; calyx teeth persistent; fruit-stalks 1–3 mm long. In dry, calcareous grassland of S and C Europe, northwards to NC and NE France and SW Germany.

p.161 **Pepper-saxifrage**
Silaum silaus (L.) Schinz & Thell.

Description: A glabrous perennial, with erect, branched, *solid*, ribbed (but not winged) stems to 1 m. Leaves triangular-ovate, lower ones 3–4-times pinnate, upper ones doubly pinnate, all with lanceolate to linear, finely serrate, often *red-tipped leaflets*. Flowers *c.* 1.5 mm wide, in flat, *4–15-rayed*, compound *umbels to 60 mm* diam; rays finely papillose; bracts 0–3; bracteoles 5–11, linear, with scarious margins. Calyx teeth absent. *Petals pale yellow*, pointed. Achenes compressed, 4–5 mm long, elliptical, with 5 prominent ribs; fruit-stalks 4–7 mm long.

Flowering: June–September.

Habitat: Grassland, road verges, riverbanks, hedgebanks, on wet or moist, mesotrophic, preferably calcareous, loamy, clayey or stony soils; from sea level to 850 m.

Range: In Europe northwards to Britain, the Low Countries, southernmost Sweden, Poland and C Russia.

Compare Selinum carvifolia (see p.1130) and Peucedanum palustre (see p.1126), both of which have white-tipped leaflets.

---

p.162 **Greater Water-parsnip** *Sium latifolium* L.

Description: A glabrous, often *aquatic perennial* to 1.2 m, with creeping stolons and erect, hollow, angular, strongly ribbed flowering stems. Submerged leaves (formed in spring) 2–3-times pinnate, with linear segments; *emergent leaves simply pinnate*, bright green, to 30 cm long, elliptical, with 9–15 (19) narrowly elliptical or broadly lanceolate, *regularly serrate* leaflets (5–10 cm long), top-leaflet free and distinctly stalked. Flowers *c.* 4 mm wide, in long-stalked, *20–35-rayed*, compound *umbels to 10 cm* diam., always terminal; bracts 2–6, lanceolate, often large, (deeply) serrate or lobed; bracteoles 2–6, linear. Calyx teeth well developed. Petals white.

Achenes round in section, (broadly) ovate or elliptical in outline, 3–4 mm long, glabrous, with 5 thick, prominent, rounded ribs.

Flowering: June–September.

Habitat: Marshes, fens, swamps, ditches, carrs, willow-copses, on wet, mesotrophic or eutrophic, mildly acid, muddy or peaty soils; from sea level to 700 m.

Range: Most of Europe, northwards to the British Isles, S Scandinavia, southernmost Finland, C Russia.

Compare Berula erecta (*see* p.1100), a much smaller plant with concrescent top-leaflets.

---

p.220 **Alexanders** *Smyrnium olusatrum* L.

Description: A glabrous biennial, to 1.2 m, with stout, erect, branched, ribbed flowering stems (becoming hollow when older). Lower leaves triangular, to 30 cm long, *2–3-times ternate* with numerous broadly (ob)ovate, crenate or bluntly serrate, often basally connate leaflets; upper leaves simply ternate, yellowish-green; leaf-stalk has inflated, sheathing base. Flowers *c.* 3 mm wide, in domed, *5–15-rayed*, compound *umbels to 80 mm* diam.; bracts 0–2; bracteoles few, minute. *Petals greenish-yellow*. Achenes compressed (hemispherical), broadly ovate to suborbicular, 7–8 mm long, with 5 thin ribs, *black* when ripe.

Flowering: April–June.

Habitat: Wood margins, scrub, hedgebanks, shaded road verges, rough grassland, waste ground, also sea-cliffs, on moist, eutrophic, mildly acid or calcareous, sandy, loamy or stony soils; mainly in the lowland, often near the sea.

Range: S and SW Europe, northwards to C and NW France, and probably naturalized (as an archeophyte) in Ireland, S Britain, and the Netherlands (Texel).

Compare Aegopodium (*see* p.1093), which has creeping rhizomes and white flowers.

p.158 **Hartwort** *Tordylium maximum* L.

Description: A fresh-green *annual or biennial*, with erect, much-branched, hollow, ribbed, appressedly stiff-hairy stems to 1 (1.5) m. Lower leaves up to 20 cm long, ovate or elliptical, *pinnate* with 7–9 ovate or suborbicular, dentate leaflets, top-leaflet often connate to adjacent pair; upper leaves pinnate with 3–7 lanceolate, serrate-dentate leaflets, top-leaflet almost linear, to 40 mm long. Flowers *c.* 3 mm wide, in long-stalked, flat, *5–15-rayed*, compound *umbels to 60 mm* diam.; bracts 1–3, linear-lanceolate; bracteoles 4–8, linear, erect, bristly-hairy. Calyx teeth well developed, linear. Petals white (rarely pinkish), *notched*, outer ones in marginal flowers slightly enlarged. Achenes strongly compressed, broadly elliptical with thick, whitish lateral wings, 5–8 mm long, *bristly-hairy*.

Flowering: June–September.

Habitat: Cultivated and waste land, rough grassland, roadsides, ruderal places, also riversides, on moist, mesotrophic, preferably calcareous, sandy or loamy soils; from sea level to 800 m.

Range: S and SC Europe, northwards to NC and NE France, S Germany, Hungary, Romania, and the Ukraine; naturalized in S Britain (Essex) and probably also in Switzerland and Germany.

Compare Torilis arvensis, which has 2–3-pinnate lower leaves.

p.158 **Upright Hedge-parsley**
Torilis japonica (Houtt.) DC.

Description: A dark-green, hairy *annual or biennial* to 1 m, with erect, branched, solid, ribbed stems (with deflexed bristles). Leaves up to 20 cm long, triangular-ovate, *2–3-times pinnate* with ovate or lanceolate, coarsely dentate leaflets; highest leaves often simply pinnate with 3–5 leaflets, top-leaflet almost linear, pinnatifid, to 30 mm long. Flowers 2–3 mm wide, in long-stalked, terminal, flat or domed, *4–13-rayed*, compound *umbels to 40 mm* diam.; rays hairy; bracts 4–6 (12), linear; bracteoles numerous, awl-shaped, appressed, hairy. Calyx teeth small and inconspicuous, triangular-lanceolate, persistent on fruit. Petals white (occasionally pink), outer ones in marginal flowers slightly enlarged. Achenes scarcely compressed, ovate, 3–3.5 mm long, obscurely ribbed, entirely covered with *small spines* (curved upwards, not hooked); styles glabrous, recurved.

Flowering: June–September.

Habitat: Shaded road verges, wood margins, scrub, hedgebanks, on moist to dry, mesotrophic to eutrophic, mildly acid, sandy or loamy soils; from sea level to 1,500 m.

Range: Most of Europe except Iceland and the Arctic.

Similar species: **Spreading Hedge-parsley** (*T. arvensis* (Hudson) Link) has stems glabrous below, 1–2-pinnate leaves with lanceolate leaflets, 3–5-rayed umbels with 0–1 bracts and numerous subulate, hairy bracteoles; achenes 4–6 mm long, elliptical, slightly compressed, with hairy styles, and entirely covered with hooked bristles. In arable fields, disturbed roadsides, open, grassy banks, ditch-sides, on moist, mesotrophic, calcareous, loamy or clayey soils, in Europe northwards to Britain, the Low Countries, Germany, Poland, and W and E Russia. *Compare also Tordylium* (all leaves simply pinnate), and *Chaerophyllum* (*see* p.1106) (lanceolate, glabrous achenes).

p.158 **Knotted Hedge-parsley**
Torilis nodosa (L.) Gaertner

Description: A greyish-green, stiff-hairy, usually *prostrate annual* to 20 (40) cm, with branched, solid, ribbed stems (with sparse, deflexed bristles). Leaves up to 10 cm long, triangular-ovate, *1–2-times pinnate* with (broadly) lanceolate, pinnately divided leaflets. Flowers 1–1.5 mm wide, few together in *subsessile, axillary, 2–3-rayed*, compound *umbels to 10 mm* diam.; rays very short; bracts absent; bracteoles numerous (*c.* 10), awl-shaped, hairy. Calyx teeth triangular-lanceolate, small and rather inconspicuous, persistent on fruit. Petals white or pinkish. Achenes not compressed, ovate, 2.5–3.5 mm long, obscurely ribbed, outer one in each pair entirely covered with *straight, barbed spines*, inner one only finely warty.

Flowering: April–August.

Habitat: Open grassland, grazed sea-walls, also fields and on brick walls, on moist, mesotrophic, calcareous, occasionally brackish, often loamy or clayey soils; from sea level to 500 m.

Range: S and W Europe, northwards to E Ireland, S Britain, and the Low Countries; probably only naturalized in N Germany, as in C Europe generally.

NETTLE FAMILY, URTICACEAE

A family of herbs and small shrubs with *c.* 1,000 species in 45 genera, in warm and temperate regions world-wide. Dicots. Leaves simple, opposite or alternate, often with stinging hairs. Flowers usually regular, often unisexual (monoecious or dioecious), in cymes (often composing head-like clusters, spikes, or narrow panicles). Perianth (2) 4–5-parted, greenish. Stamens (2) 4–5, opposite to tepals. Ovary superior, 1-locular, with 1 brush-like style. Fruit a 1-seeded achene.

---

p.67 **Pellitory-of-the-wall** *Parietaria judaica* L.

Description: A soft-hairy perennial to 40 (80) cm, with spreading or ascending, branched, reddish, *solid*, rounded stems. Leaves short-stalked, *alternate*, (10) 20–50 mm long, elliptical or ovate, *entire-margined*, pointed; stipules absent. Flowers partly hermaphrodite, partly male, in axillary, 3–8-flowered clusters; each flower subtended by 3 small, ovate, *basally connate bracteoles*. Perianth 3–4-parted, greenish, *c.* 2 mm long, that of hermaphrodite flowers becoming 3–4 mm long in fruit. Stamens 3–4. Achene 1–1.4 mm long, ovoid, blackish.

Flowering: May–October.

Habitat: Rocks, old walls, quays, canal embankments, roadsides, hedgebanks, on moist to dry, oligotrophic, calcareous, often stony soils; mainly in the lowland.

Range: S and W Europe, northwards to the British Isles and the Low Countries, and eastwards to Germany, Switzerland, Yugoslavia, Romania, and the Crimea.

Similar species: *P. officinalis* L. has little-branched, usually erect, hollow stems (to 1.2 m), and larger leaves (5–12 cm long); perianth will not become enlarged in fruit, achenes 1.2–1.9 mm long. In hedgebanks, shaded roadsides, ruderal places, also on old walls, on moist, oligotrophic or mesotrophic, calcareous, often stony soils, in continental S and C Europe, northwards to the Low Countries, Denmark, Poland, and W Russia, but presumably only naturalized in the northern part of its range.

---

p.67 **Stinging Nettle** *Urtica dioica* L.

Description: A dull-green perennial, with creeping rhizomes and erect, unbranched, sharply quadrangular stems to 2 (3) m; whole plant covered in *stinging hairs*; shorter, soft hairs also present. Leaves stalked, *opposite*, to 8 (12) cm long, ovate with cordate base, *serrate-dentate*, pointed; leaf-stalk shorter than blade; stipules present. Flowers normally unisexual, *dioecious*, in narrow, spike-like, pendent, axillary panicles (with shorter side-branches in male plants) exceeding leaf-stalk. Perianth 4-parted, greenish, *c.* 2 mm long. Stamens 4. Achene *c.* 2 mm long, ovoid, glabrous.

Flowering: June–September.

Habitat: Ruderal places, shaded road verges, reedlands, damp, deciduous woods, on moist to wet, (very) eutrophic, mildly acid or calcareous, sandy, loamy or peaty soils; from sea level to 3,100 m.

Range: All of Europe except Spitsbergen.

A very common species. Like many Urticaceae (and also the related Hemp Family, Cannabaceae), it has long stem-fibres, which since prehistoric times have been used for making cloth (muslin).

p.67 **Annual Nettle** *Urtica urens* L.

Description: A pale-green *annual* to 40 (60) cm, with thin taproot, and erect or ascending, branched, quadrangular stems; whole plant covered in *stinging hairs* that may be sparse in some plants; shorter soft hairs absent. Leaves stalked, *opposite*, to 40 (70) mm long, broadly ovate with cordate base, *coarsely dentate*; leaf-stalk longer than blade (at least in lower leaves); stipules present. Flowers normally unisexual, *monoecious*, in narrow, spike-like, spreading or ascending, axillary panicles not exceeding leaf-stalk. Perianth 4-parted, greenish, *c.* 2 mm long. Stamens 4. Achene *c.* 2 mm long, ovoid, glabrous.

Flowering: May–October.

Habitat: Cultivated and waste land, gardens, roadsides, ruderal places, hedges, manure-heaps, on dry or moist, (very) eutrophic, mildly acid or calcareous, sandy or loamy soils; from sea level to 2,700 m.

Range: Most of Europe except the high Arctic.

VALERIAN FAMILY, VALERIANACEAE

A family of herbs or half-shrubs, with *c.* 400 species in 13 genera, mainly in the northern hemisphere and S America. Dicots. Leaves opposite, simple or pinnate. Flowers (slightly) irregular, usually hermaphrodite, in cymes, often composing panicles. Calyx usually reduced, 1–6-toothed, occasionally developing into ring of bristles in fruit. Corolla funnel-shaped, usually 5-lobed, tube often with sac-like spur. Stamens 1–4, implanted on corolla tube. Ovary inferior, 3-locular (but usually only 1 locule fertile), with 1 style. Fruit a 1-seeded achene. Some are edible (Cornsalads, *Valerianella*); some are grown for ornament (*Centranthus*) or for medicinal purposes (*Valeriana*).

---

p.295 **Marsh Valerian** *Valeriana dioica* L.

Description: A slightly hairy perennial to 30 cm, with creeping rhizome, long, creeping stolons and erect flowering stems (hairy at nodes). *Basal leaves simple*, long-stalked, ovate, entire-margined, blunt-tipped, with blades up to 30 mm long; lower stem-leaves pinnately divided with 5–7 (9) narrowly ovate segments (top-segment larger), upper leaves subsessile, with narrower, almost linear segments. Flowers unisexual, normally *dioecious*, in small, terminal, umbel-shaped panicles. Calyx inconspicuous and inrolled at anthesis, but unfurling on fruit, forming ring of *feathery bristles*. Corolla pink or white, 3–4 mm long (those of female flowers smaller, *c.* 2 mm long); corolla tube has small, *sac-like spur*. Stamens 3, protruding. Achene *c.* 2.5 mm long, ovoid, ribbed, glabrous, brownish, crowned by feathery calyx.

Flowering: April–July.

Habitat: Marshes, damp meadows and scrub, dune-slacks, streamsides, on wet, oligotrophic or mesotrophic, weakly acid, sandy, stony or peaty soils; from sea level to 1,800 m.

Range: In Europe northwards to S Scotland, S Scandinavia, Poland, and C Russia.

---

p.295 **Common Valerian** *Valeriana officinalis* L.

Description: A subglabrous perennial, to 1.2 m, with creeping rhizome, and erect flowering stems; stolons absent or short, subterranean. Leaves to 35 cm long, *all pinnate* with 7–13 (17) ovate to lanceolate, acute, remotely dentate, subequal leaflets; basal and lower stem-leaves long-stalked, upper stem-leaves subsessile. Flowers *hermaphrodite*, in large, terminal, domed, umbel-shaped panicles. Calyx inconspicuous and inrolled at anthesis, but unfurling on fruit, forming ring of feathery bristles. Corolla pink, 3–5 mm long; corolla tube with small, *sac-like spur*. Stamens 3, protruding. Achene 4–5 mm long, ovoid, ribbed, glabrous or slightly hairy, brownish, crowned by feathery calyx.

Flowering: June–September.

Habitat: Marshes, damp meadows, ditches, lake- and streamsides, reedlands, woods (often Alder or Willow, also damp Oakwoods), on wet, mesotrophic to eutrophic, mildly acid or calcareous, sandy, loamy or stony soils; from sea level to 2,400 m.

Range: E Europe, extending westwards to S Sweden and the Alps, possibly further west.

1140 *Valerianaceae*

The rhizomes are used medicinally for
their sedative properties. The description
above pertains to ssp. *officinalis*. Ssp.
collina (Wallr.) Nyman, in dry, calcareous
grassland and open woods of W and C
Europe (northwards to the Low Countries
and Denmark, and eastwards to the
Ukraine and SE Russia), has short-stalked
stem-leaves, 13–25 linear, obtuse,
subentire leaflets, and smaller achenes
(2–4 mm long). Forms from wet habitats
of Scandinavia and NC Europe, with
creeping stolons, leaves with only 5–9
lanceolate, strongly dentate leaflets
(terminal one wider), and larger fruits
(4–8 mm long) are attributed to ssp.
sambucifolia (Mikan f.) Čelak. Forms with
hairy stems and 5–17 dentate leaflets
occur in W and WC Europe; they are
occasionally treated as a separate species
(*V. repens* Host) but presumably deserve
subspecific rank at best. • The number of
leaflets is given for middle stem-leaves.

p.295 **Narrow-fruited Cornsalad**
Valerianella dentata (L.) Pollich

Description: A glabrous *annual* to 30 cm, with thin
taproot, and single, erect, forked stem. All
leaves simple, basal ones long-stalked,
spatulate, entire-margined, blunt-tipped, to
50 mm long; stem-leaves subsessile,
lanceolate to almost linear, entire or with
some teeth near base. Flowers
hermaphrodite, in small, terminal, *head-like
clusters*; bracts shorter than flowers, green
with white, scarious margins. *Calyx reduced
but distinct* on fruit, with 1–3 small, unequal,
triangular, finely dentate teeth. Corolla pale
pink or lilac, 1–2 mm diam.; *corolla tube
unspurred*. Stamens 3, protruding. Achene
2–2.5 mm long, narrowly ovoid or conical,
pointed, compressed, ribbed, with 2 thin
ventral ribs representing much-reduced,
sterile locules (see fruit in transverse section).
Flowering: June–August.
Habitat: Arable land, gardens, open roadsides, on
moist, mesotrophic, preferably calcareous,

loamy, clayey or stony soils; from sea level to 1,700 m.

Range: In Europe northwards to England, the Low Countries, S Scandinavia, and W Russia.

Similar species: **Broad-fruited Cornsalad** (*V. rimosa* Bast.) has subglobose, blunt fruits with 2 very large, inflated, sterile locules ventrally to seed. In comparable habitats of S, W and C Europe, northwards to the British Isles, the Low Countries, Denmark, Poland and C Russia.

Common Cornsalad
Valerianella locusta (L.) Laterrade

Description: A glabrous *annual* to 30 cm, with thin taproot, and single, erect, forked stem. All leaves simple, basal ones long-stalked, spatulate to ovate, entire-margined or with some shallow teeth, blunt-tipped, to 70 mm long; stem-leaves subsessile, narrowly elliptical to lanceolate, entire or slightly dentate. Flowers hermaphrodite, in small, terminal, *head-like clusters*; bracts exceeding flowers, green. Calyx reduced and *indistinct* on fruit, with 1–3 minute teeth. Corolla pale pink or bluish-lilac, 1–2 mm diam.; *corolla tube unspurred*. Stamens 3, protruding. Achene *c.* 2 mm long, subglobose, laterally compressed, scarcely angular, with large, corky, dorsal swelling and 2 inflated, ventral, sterile locules (see fruit in transverse section).

Flowering: April–June (August).

Habitat: Dry grassland, dunes, waste places, roadsides, also in gardens and arable land, occasionally old walls, on moist, mesotrophic, mildly acid or calcareous, sandy, loamy or stony soils; from sea level to 1,500 m.

Range: Most of Europe, northwards to the British Isles, S Fennoscandia, and C Russia.

Similar species: **Keeled-fruited Cornsalad** (*V. carinata* Loisel.) lacks corky swelling to fruit, which is oblong and almost quadrangular in transverse section, while sterile, ventral locules are separated by deep furrow, making fruit seem keeled. In comparable habitats (to 1,200 m) of S, W and C Europe, northwards to England, the Low Countries, Poland, and the Ukraine.

Another name is Lamb's Lettuce. The plant originates from S Europe, but is widely grown as a vegetable, and has naturalized (as an archeophyte) elsewhere.

VERVAIN FAMILY, VERBENACEAE

A family of herbs, shrubs and trees with *c.* 3,000 species in 75 genera, mainly in tropical and subtropical regions. Dicots. Leaves opposite, simple (occasionally pinnately divided). Flowers often slightly irregular, hermaphrodite, in racemes or spikes. Calyx 2–5-toothed. Corolla tubular, with 4–5 lobes. Stamens (2) 4, implanted on corolla tube. Ovary superior, 2–4-locular, with 1 apical style. Fruit a drupe or a capsule with 2–8 seeds, often splitting into 4 achenes. **Teak** or **Jati** (*Tectona grandis* L. f.) is an important timber source.

p.288 **Vervain** *Verbena officinalis* L.

Description: A rough-hairy perennial with erect, quadrangular, oppositely branched, tough, wiry stems to 70 cm. Leaves opposite, short-stalked to subsessile, lower ones rhombic, pinnately divided, often with 2 larger basal segments; upper leaves lanceolate, dentate or crenate. Flowers 4–5 mm diam., weakly 2-lipped, in long, leafless, terminal spikes. Calyx 5-toothed. Corolla tube twice as long as calyx; corolla lobes 5, slightly unequal, pink or pale lilac. Stamens 4, of 2 lengths, enclosed in corolla tube. Fruit a cluster of 4 roughly ellipsoid, ribbed nutlets.

Flowering: June–October.

Habitat: Rough grassland, scrub, road verges, grassy banks, in ruderal places, on moist to dry, mesotrophic, calcareous, loamy or stony soils; from sea level to 1,500 m.

Range: Much of Europe, northwards to the British Isles, the Low Countries, Poland, C Russia, and occasionally naturalized further north.

An ancient medicinal herb.

VIOLET FAMILY, VIOLACEAE

A family of herbs or woody plants with *c.* 900 species in 22 genera in warm and temperate regions of the world. Leaves alternate, simple (occasionally in rosette). Flowers irregular, usually hermaphrodite, solitary on long stalks with 2 minute, opposite bracts. Sepals 5, usually with sac-like basal appendage. Petals 5, free, lower one larger and with long, nectar-bearing spur. Stamens 5, with short filaments. Ovary superior, 1-locular, with 1 style. Fruit a many-seeded capsule, splitting with 3 valves. All European species belong to the genus *Viola.* Two groups can be discerned: (1) **violets** (subgenus Viola) with spreading or drooping lateral petals, and style with bent or hooked (sometimes only obliquely truncate) tip; (2) **pansies** (subgenus Melanium) with more or less erect lateral petals and rounded, club-shaped style. Hybrids are frequently formed, and may obscure the species limits to some extent; they are normally sterile. Apart from normal flowers, the true violets often develop cleistogamous (non-opening, self-pollinating) flowers as well. In the following descriptions flower 'length' is measured vertically across corolla.

---

p.87 **Field Pansy** *Viola arvensis* Murray

Description: A slightly hairy *annual* to 40 cm, with ascending to erect, little-branched stems; stolons absent. *Leaves all cauline,* narrowly obovate or oblanceolate with cuneate base, crenate-dentate, blade 10–20 (30) mm long, narrowed into long stalk; *stipules pinnately divided,* with large, leaf-like, oblanceolate end-lobe, exceeding leaf-stalk. Flowers axillary, 8–12 (15) mm long, nodding on long, glabrous stalks with 2 tiny bracts well above middle. Sepals lanceolate, acute, 7–10 mm long, about equalling petals, and with elliptical to circular basal appendages. Petals *creamy white or yellow,* upper pair occasionally (partly) violet, lateral ones more or less erect to almost spreading, lower petal with dark-yellow blotch and some violet lines near base, and with pale-purplish or violet spur 3–6 mm long (about equalling calyx appendages). *Style club-shaped.* Fruit an ovoid, glabrous capsule.

Flowering: April–October.

Habitat: Cultivated land, especially in cereal fields, also in open roadsides and disturbed places, on moist to dry, mesotrophic, neutral or calcareous, sandy or loamy soils; from sea level to 1,800 m.

Range: Most of Europe except Iceland and the Arctic.

Similar species: **Dwarf Pansy** (*V. kitaibeliana* Schultes) is densely greyish-hairy, only up to 10 cm tall, and has very small, cream or yellowish (rarely pale violet) flowers 4–7 mm long, with violet spur; sepals distinctly exceeding petals. In short turf, dune grassland, also in arable fields and disturbed places, on dry, oligotrophic, slightly calcareous, sandy soils, mainly coastal, in S and SC Europe, westwards to W France, the Channel Islands and the Scillies, and northwards to Switzerland, Czechoslovakia, Hungary, and the Ukraine. *Compare also V. tricolor (see* p.1152).

Field Pansy forms intermediate, fertile hybrids with *V. tricolor*.

---

p.188 **Yellow Wood-violet** *Viola biflora* L.

Description: A slightly hairy perennial, with creeping rhizomes, basal leaf-rosettes and ascending, leafy flowering stems to 15 cm. Leaves long-stalked, *reniform*, crenate-dentate, blade 30–40 mm long; stipules small, entire-margined, ciliate. Flowers solitary or in pairs, *c.* 15 mm long, nodding on long, glabrous stalks with 2 tiny bracts well above middle. Sepals narrowly ovate, subacute, much shorter than petals. Petals *bright yellow*, lateral ones more or less erect, lower petal with dark-brown lines near base, and with yellowish spur 2–3 mm long. Style more or less club-shaped, with flattened, 2-lobed stigma. Fruit a narrowly ovoid, glabrous capsule, nodding on erect stalk.

Flowering: May–August.

Habitat: Damp woods, shaded banks, on moist, oligotrophic, preferably acid, sandy, gravelly or stony soils; 700–3,000 m, descending lower in the north.

Range: The mountains of C Europe (westwards to the Pyrenees and the Jura), again in Scandinavia, N Finland, N Russia.

---

p.330 **Heath Dog-violet** *Viola canina* L.

Description: A glabrous or slightly hairy perennial, with creeping rhizomes, and *spreading or ascending stems* to 40 cm; stolons absent. *Leaves all cauline*, (narrowly) triangular-ovate with distinctly cordate to rounded or truncate (rarely cuneate) base, blade 10–20 (30) mm long, crenate; leaf-stalks not or scarcely winged, 20–30 (50) mm long; stipules lanceolate, slightly dentate or entire-margined, much shorter than leaf-stalk. Flowers axillary, 10–18 mm long, nodding on long, glabrous stalks with 2 tiny bracts well above middle. *Sepals acute*. Petals *bluish-violet or pale blue* with violet lines near base (rarely white); lateral petals drooping sideways, lower petal with *whitish or greenish-yellow spur* 4–7 mm long (much exceeding calyx appendages). Style has bent, slightly papillose tip. Fruit an ovoid, glabrous capsule, exceeding calyx.

Flowering: April–July (autumn).

Habitat: Poor grassland, road verges, grassy heaths, open woods, hedgebanks, on moist to dry, oligotrophic, slightly acid, sandy or peaty soils; from sea level to 800 m.

Range: All of Europe except parts of Mediterranean region.

Similar species: **Pale Dog-violet** (*V. lactea* Sm.) usually is glabrous, with ascending stems, (broadly) lanceolate, mostly cuneate-based, often purple-tinged leaves, stipules at least half as long as leaf-stalk, and pale-bluish or greyish-violet flowers (15–20 mm long) with short, yellowish or greenish spur. In heaths of W Europe, from Iberia to W France, S England and Ireland. *Compare also V. persicifolia (see p.1150) and allies, with underground stolons.*

Heath Dog-violet is a variable species. Forms from coastal dunes of W Europe, with distinctly cuneate leaf-bases, are attributed to var. *dunensis* W. Beck. In hills and mountains of C Europe (300–1,800 m) the ssp. *montana* (L.) Hartman can be found, with erect stems, larger, pale-blue flowers (15–22 mm long), and blunt, often asymmetrical, more or less parallel-sided leaves with stipules about half as long as leaf-stalk.

---

p.330 **Hairy Violet** *Viola hirta* L.

Description: A tufted, hairy perennial to 15 cm, with short, vertical rhizome; *stolons and normal stems absent*. Leaves all in basal rosette, long-stalked, (narrowly) ovate-cordate, crenate, hairy (especially beneath), blade to 80 mm long (becoming larger after anthesis); leaf-stalk hairy; stipules triangular or broadly lanceolate, *short-fringed or entire-margined, glandular*. Flowers directly rising from rosettes, 10–15 mm long, not fragrant, nodding on long, normally *hairy stalks* with 2 tiny bracts below middle. *Sepals blunt-tipped.* Petals blue-violet with white claw and dark-blue lines at base, rarely pink or plain white; lateral petals drooping sideways, lower petal with a *dark-violet spur* 4–5 mm long. Style has bent, almost hooked tip. Fruit a globose capsule, 5–7 mm diam., *loosely hairy*.

Flowering: March–June.

Habitat: Open woods, wood margins, coppices, shrubs, shaded grassland, dunes, grassy banks, on rather dry, oligotrophic, preferably calcareous, sandy, loamy or stony soils; from sea level to 2,000 m.

Range: In Europe northwards to the British Isles, S Scandinavia, and N Russia.

Similar species: **Hill Violet** (*V. collina* Besser) has horizontal, creeping rhizome, fragrant, pale bluish-violet flowers with whitish spur to 3 mm long, and leaves to 50 mm long (densely hairy beneath) with linear-lanceolate, long-fringed stipules. In comparable habitats of C and E Europe (500–2,000 m), northwards to

N France, Germany, S Scandinavia, and N Russia.

V. mirabilis L. is much like latter species, but stems have 1 hairy line, leaves are broadly ovate to reniform, shiny green (the basal ones long-stalked, the cauline ones short-stalked) with broadly lanceolate, always entire-margined stipules (ciliate, not fringed); flowers (20–22 mm long) pale-lilac, fragrant with greenish-white spur. In woods and coppices on calcareous soils of C and E Europe, westwards to SC and NE France, and northwards to Denmark, S Fennoscandia, and NC Russia.

---

p.187 **Mountain Pansy** *Viola lutea* Hudson

Description: A glabrous or slightly hairy perennial to 25 cm, with slender, creeping rhizomes, basal leaf-rosettes and ascending, leafy flowering stems; stolons absent. Leaves long-stalked, broadly lanceolate, weakly crenate-dentate, blade 20–30 (40) mm long; stipules *pinnately or palmately divided* with 3–5 segments. Flowers axillary, (15) 20–25 (30) mm long, nodding on long, glabrous stalks with 2 tiny bracts well above middle. Sepals broadly lanceolate, much shorter than petals. Petals *bright yellow or (partly) blue-violet*, lateral ones more or less erect to spreading, lower petal with dark lines near base, and with yellowish or pale-violet spur 3–7 mm long. *Style club-shaped*, with a papillose tip. Fruit a subglobose or broadly ovoid, glabrous capsule, about equalling calyx.

Flowering: May–August.

Habitat: Short grassland, on moist, oligotrophic, neutral or calcareous, sandy or stony soils; mainly in the mountains, 1,000–2,000 m.

Range: W and NC Europe from Ireland and the Pyrenees eastwards to Poland and Austria.

Similar species: **Rouen Pansy** (*V. hispida* Lam.) is similar, but densely stiff-hairy, with ovate, slightly cordate-based leaves, and violet or yellowish flowers 18–20 mm long, with spurs to 4 mm long. Endemic to calcareous cliffs near Rouen in NW France.

V. calaminaria (DC.) Lejeune is a superficially similar but not directly related species (apparently close to *V. tricolor*), adapted to zinc-bearing soils near lead-mines in the hills of W Germany, E Belgium and southernmost tip of the Netherlands; it has creeping, underground stolons, ovate to lanceolate leaves, palmately divided stipules with several subequal segments, (pale) yellow or occasionally (partly) pale-blue or purplish flowers 20–25 mm long, with spurs 5–7 mm long. *Compare also V. tricolor (see* p.1152) and *V. curtisii (see* p.1153).

---

p.330 **Sweet Violet** *Viola odorata* L.

Description: A slightly hairy perennial to 15 cm, with creeping underground rhizomes, creeping (rooting) aerial or underground stolons, and leaves in basal rosettes; *normal stems absent*. Leaves long-stalked, ovate-cordate to reniform, crenate, short-downy or glabrous, blade to 60 mm long (becoming larger after anthesis); leaf-stalk short-hairy; stipules broadly lanceolate, *short-fringed or entire-margined, glandular*. Flowers directly rising from rosettes, 13–15 mm long, fragrant, nodding on long, *glabrous stalks* with 2 tiny bracts in middle. *Sepals blunt-tipped*. Petals violet with white claw and dark-violet lines at base, occasionally pink or plain white; lateral petals drooping sideways, lower petal with *greenish-white* spur 5–7 mm long. Style with hooked tip. Fruit a globose, *densely short-hairy*, bluntly 3–6-angular, subglobose capsule up to 7.5 mm diam., often tinged with violet.

Flowering: March–May (September).

Habitat: Open, deciduous woods, coppices, scrub, hedges, shaded road verges, on moist, mesotrophic, neutral or calcareous, sandy, loamy or stony soils; from sea level to 1,400 m.

Range: Most of Europe, northwards to the British Isles, S Scandinavia, Lithuania, and C Russia.

Similar species: **White Violet** (*V. alba* Besser) always has white flowers on hairy stalks (with bracts in or above middle), non-rooting stolons, stiff-hairy leaves and leaf-stalks, with linear-lanceolate, long-fringed, ciliate (not glandular) stipules, and short spurs (3–4 mm long). In comparable habitats of S and C Europe, westwards to C France, and northwards to Germany and S Sweden (Öland); forms with violet flowers from S Europe are occasionally treated as a separate species (*V. scotophylla* Jord.).

V. suavis Bieb. has short stolons and slightly larger flowers (15–20 mm long, violet with white throat) on long stalks with bracts below middle; stipules lanceolate, fringed and ciliate (not glandular). In S, C and E Europe, northwards to NW France, Switzerland, Czechoslovakia, Poland and C Russia (and, naturalized, in Germany).

p.315 **Marsh Violet** *Viola palustris* L.

Description: A usually *glabrous* perennial, to 15 cm, with long, thin, creeping, whitish rhizomes, and few leaves in basal rosettes; *normal stems absent*. Leaves long-stalked, suborbicular to reniform, crenate, glabrous, blade to 40 mm long (becoming larger after anthesis); leaf-stalks glabrous; stipules entirely free, broadly lanceolate, short-fringed or entire-margined, not glandular. Flowers directly rising from rosettes, 10–13 mm long, not fragrant, nodding on long, glabrous stalks with 2 tiny bracts below middle. *Sepals blunt-tipped.* Petals *pale violet* (rarely white) with dark-violet lines at base; lateral petals slightly drooping sideways, lower petal with blunt, *pale-lilac* spur 3–4 mm long. Style has thickened, obliquely truncate tip. Fruit a bluntly triangular-ovoid, glabrous capsule 9–12 mm long.

Flowering: April–July.

Habitat: Bogs, marshes, reedlands, damp meadows, shrubs (often Alder or Willow), ditch-sides, on wet, oligotrophic, slightly acid, peaty or muddy soils; from sea level to 2,600 m, but mainly on mountains in the south.

Range: Most of Europe, except Spitsbergen, and rare in the south and east.

Similar species: *V. uliginosa* Besser has violet flowers (20–30 mm long) with thick, violet spur, and ovate, short-pointed leaves with stipules partly connate to leaf-stalk. In similar habitats of E and EC Europe, westwards to S Sweden, Denmark and Germany.

V. epipsila Ledebour has (reniform, always paired) leaves slightly hairy beneath, and pale-violet flowers 15–20 mm long. In marshes of Iceland, Scandinavia and N Germany.

Northern Violet (*V. selkirkii* Pursh ex Goldie) has short, vertical rhizome, and pale-violet flowers (13–15 mm long) with a pale-lilac spur 5–7 mm long. In damp coniferous woods and marshes of Fennoscandia and N and C Russia.

---

p.337 **Fen Violet** *Viola persicifolia* Schreber

Description: A usually *glabrous* perennial, with creeping rhizomes, underground stolons, and glabrous, *erect stems* to 30 cm. *Leaves all cauline*, long-stalked, narrowly triangular-ovate with a scarcely cordate, more often truncate or cuneate base, crenate, glabrous, blade 20–45 mm long; leaf-stalks glabrous, distinctly winged near top; stipules lanceolate, dentate or entire-margined, shorter than leaf-stalk. Flowers axillary, 10–15 mm long, nodding on long, glabrous stalks with 2 tiny bracts well above middle. *Sepals acute*. Petals *white or bluish-white* with violet lines near base; lateral petals drooping sideways, lower petal with short, *greenish-white spur* 2–3.5 mm long (slightly exceeding calyx appendages). Style has bent tip. Fruit a narrowly ovoid, pointed, glabrous capsule, exceeding calyx.

Flowering: May–June.

Habitat:	Marshes, fens, damp heaths, on wet, oligotrophic, acid, sandy or peaty soils; from sea level to 500 m.
Range:	Most of Europe, except Mediterranean region and the extreme north.
Similar species:	*V. elatior* Fries grows taller (to 50 cm), and has slightly hairy stems, large, lanceolate, leaf-like stipules exceeding leaf-stalks, and pale-blue flowers 20–25 mm long. In moist, mesotrophic grassland and woods of C and E Europe, westwards to France, and northwards to the Baltic islands and the Baltic States.

Meadow Violet (*V. pumila* Chaix), in the same general area and habitats, has ascending to erect, glabrous stems, lanceolate leaves with cuneate base, large, leaf-like stipules, and pale-blue flowers *c.* 15 mm long, with very short spur (not exceeding calyx appendages). *Compare also V. lactea (see* p.1145*), lacking stolons.*

Fen Violet is a declining species, rather local in its appearance.

---

p.315	**Early Dog-violet**
	Viola reichenbachiana Jord. ex Bor.
Description:	A slightly hairy or glabrous perennial to 25 cm, with a more or less vertical rhizome, a non-flowering, central rosette, and spreading or ascending, leafy, *lateral flowering stems*. Leaves long-stalked, (broadly) ovate with cordate base, crenate, blade 20–40 mm long; leaf-stalks unwinged; stipules linear-lanceolate, long-fringed, much shorter than leaf-stalk. Flowers axillary, (12) 16–20 mm long, nodding on long stalks with 2 tiny bracts in or above middle. *Sepals acute*, with very short basal appendages. Petals narrowly elliptical, not touching, *purplish-violet* with dark-violet lines near base (rarely white); lateral petals drooping sideways, lower petal with straight, gradually *tapering, purplish spur* 3–6 mm long. Style with bent, hairy tip. Fruit an ovoid, pointed, glabrous capsule, 7–15 mm long.

Flowering: April–June (September).

Habitat: Open woods, coppices, hedgebanks, on moist, oligotrophic, preferably calcareous, sandy, loamy or stony soils; from sea level to 1,800 m.

Range: In Europe northwards to the British Isles, S Sweden, the Baltic States, C Russia.

Similar species: **Common Dog-violet** (*V. riviniana* Reichenb.) has broader (to suborbicular) leaves with lanceolate, short-fringed stipules, and slightly larger flowers (20–25 mm long) with wider, neatly overlapping, blue-violet petals and club-shaped, slightly curved, yellowish- or bluish-white spur (truncate and grooved around tip); sepals with well-developed basal appendages. In comparable habitats, also in shaded grassland and on slightly acid soils, in Europe northwards to Iceland, N Scandinavia, S Finland, N Russia, but absent from the southeast.

Teesdale Violet (*V. rupestris* F.W. Schmidt) rarely grows taller than 5 cm, and is densely covered in minute, papillose, greyish hairs; leaves only 10–20 mm long; flowers 10–15 mm long, with pale blue-violet or white petals and short, pale-violet spur (grooved around tip). In grassland, dunes, heaths, on dry, calcareous, sandy, gravelly or stony soils, in C and N Europe, westwards to France, Britain (Teesdale, Cumbria), and northwards to N Fennoscandia and N Russia.

p.315 **Wild Pansy** *Viola tricolor* L.

Description: A glabrous or slightly hairy annual or biennial, to 40 cm (often much lower), with ascending to erect, branched stems; stolons absent. *Leaves all cauline*, rather long-stalked, narrowly obovate or oblanceolate with cordate to cuneate base, crenate-dentate, blade 10–30 (50) mm long; *stipules pinnately divided*, with large, leaf-like, lanceolate end-lobe, exceeding leaf-stalk. Flowers axillary, 15–25 mm long, nodding on long, glabrous stalks with 2 tiny bracts well above middle. Sepals lanceolate, acute, shorter than petals. Upper petals violet or dark blue, lateral ones lilac or pale blue with whitish base (and more or less erect), lower petal creamy white or yellow, and with blunt, pale-purplish spur 3–6 mm long (barely exceeding calyx appendages); rarely all petals yellow. *Style club-shaped.* Fruit an ovoid, glabrous capsule to 10 mm long, barely exceeding calyx.

Flowering: April–October.

Habitat: Grassland, open roadsides, field margins, gardens, waste places, on dry, mesotrophic, sandy soils; from sea level to 1,500 m.

Range: All of Europe except Spitsbergen and Arctic Russia.

Similar species: *V. curtisii* Forster (also treated as a subspecies) is perennial, with vertical rhizome and several ascending flowering stems, often slightly fleshy leaves, flowers (15–20 mm long) in diverse shades of violet, purplish, white and pale yellow, or combinations of these, with a spur distinctly exceeding calyx appendages. In grassland on dry, oligotrophic, slightly acid to calcareous, sandy soils in coastal dunes along the North Sea and the Baltic Sea, southwards to the English Channel. *Compare also V. lutea (see p.1147) and allies.*

Wild Pansy is also called Heartsease. In the cultivar 'Hortensis' all petals may be (deep) violet; this, and many other, often large-flowered cultivars and hybrids are grown in gardens, and occasionally escape.

MISTLETOE FAMILY, VISCACEAE

A family of (hemi-)parasitic shrubs, living on trees, and rooting in tissues of their host, with *c.* 450 species in 11 genera, mainly in the tropics. Dicots. Stems often regularly forked. Leaves opposite or whorled, simple, entire, occasionally scale-like. Flowers regular, unisexual, monoecious or dioecious, usually with 4-parted perianth (occasionally 3–6-parted, or absent). Stamens 3–6 (usually 4). Ovary inferior, 1-locular; 1 style (occasionally absent). Fruit 1-seeded, drupe-like.

p.81 Mistletoe *Viscum album* L.

Description: A glabrous shrub forming rounded clumps (to 1 m diam.) of *repeatedly forked*, yellowish-green stems on branches or boles of trees. Leaves opposite, in terminal pairs at end of branches, 20–80 mm long, narrowly elliptical or oblanceolate to spatulate, round-tipped, gradually narrowed into short, obscure stalk, *yellowish-green, leathery*, persistent during the winter (but falling in next year). Flowers sessile, unisexual, dioecious, 3–5 together in head-like clusters in branch forkings (so in fact terminal, as only side-branches continue growth; whole plant could be interpreted as a dichasial cyme). Perianth small, yellowish-green, (3) 4-parted, with triangular-ovate segments. Stamens connate to perianth parts. Fruit a globose, berry-like drupe, 6–10 mm diam., whitish (occasionally yellow), shiny, slightly translucent, with 1 large seed embedded in sticky, slimy pulp.

Flowering: February–May.

Habitat: Various deciduous trees (often Apple, Poplar, False Acacia, occasionally on oaks).

Range: In Europe northwards to C England, S Scandinavia, Poland, and C Russia.

The fruits often take a full year to ripen, and are present on the plant during winter. They are eaten by birds, which wipe off the sticky seeds on branches, where they can germinate. The plant served Celtic druids for occult purposes. The description above pertains to ssp. *album*, which normally grows on deciduous trees. Ssp. *abietis* (Wiesb.) Abromeit has relatively wide leaves up to 80 mm long, and usually white, pear-shaped drupes; it infests conifers, especially Silver Fir. Ssp. *austriacum* (Wiesb.) Vollmann has smaller, narrow leaves (usually 20–40 mm long), yellow drupes, and lives on Pines and Larches. The last 2 forms are confined to the mountains of C and S Europe.

ZANNICHELLIA FAMILY, ZANNICHELLIACEAE

A small, subcosmopolitan family of perennial aquatic herbs, with 7 or 8 species in 4 genera, living in fresh, brackish or saline waters; closely related to the Potamogetonaceae, and often included in that family. Leaves opposite, linear, sessile and narrowly sheathing the threadlike, branched stem; stipules 2. Flowers unisexual, dioecious, solitary or 2–3 together in leaf-axils, always submerged. Male flowers stalked, with 1–3 stamens, but lacking perianth. Female flowers sessile, with small perianth of 3 (often connate) scales, and 1–9 free, 1-locular ovaries, each with 1 short style and 1 stigma. Fruit an axillary cluster of sessile or short-stalked, long-beaked achenes.

---

p.55 **Horned Pondweed** *Zannichellia palustris* L.

Description: A slender, submerged aquatic with threadlike stems to 50 cm, and opposite, threadlike, often yellowish-green leaves to 80 mm long, 0.5–2 mm wide. Flowers 1–3 together, *sessile in leaf-axils*, male ones naked, with 1–2 stamens; female flowers with inconspicuous, cup-shaped perianth and usually 2–4 free ovaries, each developing into a sessile or short-stalked, asymmetrically flask-shaped achene (1.5–3.5 mm long), with laterally implanted, more or less curved beak (1–2.5 mm long).

Flowering: May–September.

Habitat: Shallow, stagnant or slow-moving, eutrophic, fresh or brackish waters; from sea level to 800 m.

Range: Most of Europe except the high Arctic.

The typical subspecies has (sub)sessile fruits with short styles, and is more often found in fresh water. Forms from brackish environments, with clearly stalked fruits (stalk *c.* 1 mm) and styles about equalling the fruit are attributed to ssp. *pedicellata* (Wahlenb. & Rosén) Hegi. A satisfactory infraspecific classification has not yet resulted, however. *Compare Ruppia* (*see* p.1020), and the linear-leaved species of *Potamogeton*, all with hermaphrodite flowers in stalked inflorescences.

EELGRASS FAMILY, ZOSTERACEAE

A small family of perennial, rhizomatous aquatic herbs, with 18 species in 3 genera, mainly in temperate regions, often completely adapted to a life in shallow coastal seas. Leaves alternate, linear, sessile and sheathing the compressed, more or less branched, often creeping stems. Flowers unisexual, monoecious, in unilateral spikes enveloped by leaf-base during anthesis. Perianth absent or extremely reduced; male flowers consist of 1 stamen with 2 anthers; female flowers contain 1-locular ovary with short style and 2 stigmas. Fruit a small, thin-walled achene.

---

p.55 **Common Eelgrass** *Zostera marina* L.

Description: A submerged, marine aquatic with tough, creeping rhizomes (2–5 mm thick), and linear, strap-shaped, round-tipped, occasionally short-pointed leaves to 50 (150) cm long, 2–6 (12) mm wide; main veins 3–11, reticulately interconnected, outer ones clearly free from leaf-margin. Seeds ribbed. *See also* family description.

Flowering: June–September.

Habitat: Shallow coastal seas, generally below low-tide mark, on sandy, clayey, or gravelly substrates.

Range: Coasts of N Atlantic and N Pacific Oceans, in Europe northwards to Iceland and N Russia; also in Mediterranean region.

Similar species: **Narrow-leaved Eelgrass** (*Z. angustifolia* (Hornem.) Rchb.) has 1–3-veined, often apically notched leaves to 30 cm long, 1–2 (3) mm wide; it may represent only an adaptation to daily exposed stations over low-tide mark.
Dwarf Eelgrass (*Z. noltii* Hornem.) also has narrow, 3-veined, notched leaves (4–20 cm long, 0.5–1.5 mm wide), and is considered to be a truly different species for having lateral veins (nearly) coinciding with leaf-margin, and tiny, hooked bristles around stamens; it also grows over low-tide mark, on daily exposed mud-flats. • Eelgrass used to be very common in the North Sea area until 1933, when a disease broke out from which the populations have never recovered. Earlier it was collected in bulk, to be dried and used as stuffing for pillows and mattresses.

Part III

Appendices

ACKNOWLEDGEMENTS

No modern flora of such a large area as northern Europe can be written unless the author builds on the wealth of information that has been compiled over the centuries since the time of Linnaeus – and even before – by thousands of botanists. A critical revision of any large genus or small family will soon take several years to complete; the revision of a large family may take a lifetime. The distribution patterns and ecology of the many species have been investigated by numerous workers – professionals as well as expert amateurs – during several decades of laborious fieldwork. The author wishes to express his recognition of the work of all his colleagues (both living and deceased) whose efforts have prepared the way for this book.

The bulk of the information in this book has been selected from the following, important literature, which is recommended to the reader for further study. As will be seen, several critical, regional floras are included in the list, and these might be fruitfully consulted whenever this simple guide does not help the reader out. In addition to the works listed, the author has consulted numerous minor, often specialized publications, the references to which cannot be squeezed into this book. Special thanks are extended to the staff of the Rijksherbarium at Leiden, the Netherlands, for granting access to the rich library and collections of that venerable institute.

Bibliography

Europe (General)

BLAMEY, M. & C. GREY-WILSON, 1989. *The Illustrated Flora of Britain and Northern Europe.* London/Sydney/Auckland/Toronto.

ELLENBERG, H., 1978. *Vegetation Mitteleuropas mit den Alpen in ökologischer Sicht*, 2nd edition. Stuttgart.

GIBBONS, B. & P. BROUGH, 1992. *The Hamlyn Photographic Guide to the Wild Flowers of Britain and Northern Europe.* London.

HEGI, G, 1906–1929. *Illustrierte Flora von Mittel-Europa*, vols 1–6. München. (And revised editions forthcoming since 1936.)

HULTÉN, E., 1958. *The Amphi-Atlantic Plants and their Phytogeographical Connections.* Stockholm.

HULTÉN, E., 1962–1971. *The Circumpolar Plants*, vols I & II. Kungl. Svenska Vetenskapsakad. Handl., Band 8 (5) & Band 13 (1). Stockholm.

HULTÉN, E. & M. FRIES, 1986. *Atlas of North European Vascular Plants North of the Tropic of Cancer*, vols 1–3. Königstein FRG.

JALAS, J. & J. SUOMINEN, 1972–. *Atlas Florae Europaeae.* Helsinki. (Still forthcoming, since 1988 also in a revised, bound edition.)

MEUSEL, H., E. JÄGER & E. WEINERT, 1965–1992. *Vergleichende Chorologie der zentraleuropäischen Flora*, vol. 1 (1965), 2 (1978), 3 (1992). Jena (1–2), Stuttgart/New York (3, without E. WEINERT).

TUTIN, T.G., V.H. HEYWOOD, N.A. BURGES, D.M. MOORE, D.H. VALENTINE, S.M. WALTERS & D.A. WEBB (eds), 1964–1980. *Flora Europaea*, vols 1–5. Cambridge. (A revised edition is forthcoming since 1993, partly with other editors.)

WALTER, H, 1960. *Grundlagen der Pflanzenverbreitung, Teil I. Standortslehre. Einführung in die Phytologie 3 (1)*, 2nd and revised edition. Stuttgart.

WALTER, H, & H. STRAKA, 1970.
*Arealkunde. Einführung in die Phytologie 3
(2).* Stuttgart.

British Isles

CLAPHAM, A.R., T.G. TUTIN & E.F.
MOORE, 1987. *Flora of the British Isles*, 3rd
edition. Cambridge.
GODWIN, H., 1975. *The History of the
British Flora*, 2nd edition. Cambridge.
PERRING, G.H. & S.M. WALTERS (eds),
1976. *Atlas of the British Flora.* East
Ardsley, Wakefield.
STACE, C.A., 1997. *New Flora of the British
Isles*, 2nd edition. Cambridge.
STACE, C.A., 1999. *Field Flora of the
British Isles.* Cambridge.

Bulgaria

STOJANOW, N. & V. STEFANOW, 1948.
Flora Balgarija. Sofia.

Czechia and Slovakia

FUTÁK, J. (ed.), 1966–. *Flóra Slovenska.* (5
volumes published up to 1993, still
forthcoming.)
HEJNÝ, S. & B. SLAVÍK, 1988–. *Květena
České Socialistické Republiky.* Prague. (5
volumes published, still forthcoming.)

Denmark

HANSEN, K. (ed.), 1981. *Dansk Feltflora.*
Copenhagen.

France

FOURNIER, P., 1977. *Les Quatres Flores de
la France*, 2nd edition. Vol. 1 (Text); 2
(Atlas). Paris.

GUINOCHET, M. & R. de VILMORIN,
1973–. *Flore de France*. (3 volumes
published up to 1976, later ones not seen
by me.)
RAMEAU, J.C., D. MANSION & G.
DUMÉ, 1989. *Flore Forestière Française.
Guide Écologique Illustré*, vol. 1 (*Plaines &
Collines*). Ministère de l'Agriculture et de la
Forêt. (Only forest plants.)

Germany

BENKERT, D., F. FUKARER & H.
KORSCH (eds), 1996. *Verbreitungsatlas der
Farn- und Blütenpflanzen Ostdeutschlands*.
Jena.
HAEUPLER, H. & P. SCHÖNFELDER,
1988. *Atlas der Farn- und Blütenpflanzen der
Bundesrepublik Deutschland*. Stuttgart.
OBERDORFER, E., 1979.
Pflanzensoziologische Exkursionsflora.
Stuttgart.
ROTHMALER, W., 1976–1988.
*Exkursionsflora für die Gebiete der DDR und
der BRD*, vol. 2 (Gefässpflanzen), 3 (Atlas)
and 4 (kritischer Band). Berlin. (A new
edition started in 1991.)

Hungary

RESZÖ, S. (and others, lately P.
STANISZLÓ), 1964–1985. *A Magyar flóra
és vegetació rendszertani-növényföldrajzi
kézikönyve*, vols 1–7. Budapest.

Iceland

KRISTINSSON, HÖRDUR, 1998. *A
Guide to the Flowering Plants and Ferns of
Iceland*, 2nd edition. Reykjavik.

Low Countries

DE LANGHE, J.-E., L. DELVOSALLE, J.
DUVIGNEAUD, J. LAMBINON & C.

VANDEN BERGHEN, 1978. *Nouvelle Flore de la Belgique, du Grand-Duché de Luxembourg, du Nord de la France et des Régions Voisines*, 2nd edition. Meise.

MEIJDEN, R.M. VAN DER, 1996. *Heukels' Flora van Nederland*, 22nd edition (1st reprint). Groningen.

MEIJDEN, R.M. VAN DER, C.L. PLATE & E.J. WEEDA, 1989. *Atlas van de Nederlandse Flora*, vol. 3. Voorburg/Heerlen.

MENNEMA, J., A.J. QUENÉ-BOTERENBROOD & C.L. PLATE (eds), 1980 & 1985. *Atlas van de Nederlandse Flora*, vols 1–2. Amsterdam (1), Utrecht (2).

ROMPAEY, E. VAN & L. DELVOSALLE, 1972 & 1978. *Atlas van de Belgische en Luxemburgse flora*, vol. 1 (Atlas), 2 (Text). Brussels.

Poland

SZAFER, W. (and others, lately Z. MIREK), 1919–1980. *Flora Polski. Rośliny naczyniowe polski i ziemnościennych*, vols 1–14. Warsaw/Kraków.

Romania

SAVULESCU, T. (ed.), 1952–1976. *Flora Republicii Socialiste România*, vols I–XIII. Bucharest.

Russia and Neighbouring States

FEDOROV, A.A. (ed.), 1999–. *Flora of Russia. The European Part and Bordering Regions.* Rotterdam/Brookfield. (Translation of *Flora Europeiskoi Chasti SSSR*; 2 volumes published, still forthcoming.)

KOMAROV, V.A. (ed.), 1934–1960. *Flora of the USSR*, vols I–XXX. Leningrad. (English translation published from 1968–1977 in Jerusalem. A revised edition, lately edited by B.K. PUSHKIN & E.G. BOBROV, has been published from 1968–1994.)

TOLMACHEV, A.I. (ed.), 1995–. *Flora of the Russian Arctic.* Edmonton. (2 volumes published, still forthcoming.)

Scandinavia and Finland

LID, J., 1963. *Norsk og Svensk Flora.* Oslo.
MALMGREN, U., 1982. *Västmanlands Flora.* Uppsala.
MOSSBERG, B. & L. STENBERG, 1992. *Den Nordiske Flora.* Stockholm.
WEIMARCK, H., 1963. *Skånes Flora.* Lund.

PICTURE CREDITS

All pictures have been researched and supplied via Natural Image.

The positions of the photographs on each page of the colour section is indicated as follows:
t = top; c = centre; b = bottom; l = left; r = right.

Photographs are copyright Bob Gibbons apart from the following:

INDEX

Numbers in **bold** refer to the colour plates. Roman type numbers refer to fully described species, genera and families in the text; when a species is only mentioned under another species, the page number is *italicized*.

INDEX OF ENGLISH NAMES